Windows NT Win32 API SuperBible

Richard J. Simon

WAITE GROUP PRESS™
A Division of
Sams Publishing
Corte Madera, CA

PUBLISHER: Mitchell Waite
ASSOCIATE PUBLISHER: Charles Drucker

ACQUISITIONS MANAGER: Susan Walton

EDITORIAL DIRECTOR: John Crudo
PROJECT EDITORS: Lisa H. Goldstein, Stephanie Wall
DEVELOPMENTAL AND TECHNICAL EDITOR: Richard Wright

PRODUCTION DIRECTOR: Julianne Ososke
PRODUCTION MANAGER: Cecile Kaufman
PRODUCTION EDITOR: Merilee Eggleston/Creative Solutions
COPY EDITORS: Merilee Eggleston, Elizabeth Leahy/Creative Solutions
SENIOR DESIGNER: Sestina Quarequio
DESIGNER: Karen Johnston
COVER DESIGN: Regan Honda
COVER ART:© 1996 Photodisc, Inc.
ILLUSTRATIONS: Casey Price, Marvin VanTiem
PRODUCTION: Mona Brown, C.J. East, Lisa Pletka, Mary Ellen Stephenson, Andrew Stone, Becky Stutzman

Printed in the United States of America
98 99 • 10 9 8 7 6 5 4 3 2

Library of Congress Cataloging-in-Publication Data
Simon, Richard J.
　　Windows NT Win32 API SuperBible / Richard J. Simon.
　　　　p.　　cm.
　　Includes index.
　　ISBN 1-57169-089-1
　　1. Microsoft Windows NT　2. Operating systems (Computers)
3. Microsoft Win32.　I. Title.
QA76.76.063S55873　1997
005.4'469--dc21

97-6052
CIP

Dedication

To Mom and Dad

About the Author

Richard J. Simon is the vice president of development/information systems of a software development company in Irving, Texas. He has been a software developer of business applications for more than twelve years. For the past eight years, Richard has specialized in client/server Windows applications developed in C and C++. He is also the author of the *Windows 95 API Bible* series.

Table of Contents

Contents

Acknowledgments

I would like to thank Lisa Goldstein for her hard work in pulling this book together. No matter how high the hurdle was, she jumped it. I would also like to thank Merilee Eggleston, who spent a great deal of time on this book reformatting the chapters for production and finding things that slipped through the cracks. I would also like to thank all the other people who worked hard on this book, including Richard Wright for his technical editing.

Introduction

The purpose of this book is to save programmers time in developing applications for Windows NT 4 and Windows 95. New standards presented in Windows NT 4, Windows 95, and the Win32 API have changed the way we develop applications. In some respects, this has simplified Windows development; however, the new APIs are complicated and not equally supported across all platforms.

The main focus of this book is to provide a complete reference for the Win32 APIs that are supported in both Microsoft Windows NT 4 and Windows 95, although many new APIs that are only implemented in Windows NT 4 are documented. The compatibility of each API is shown to provide you with the information needed to make your applications compatible on both operating systems. This book focuses on the Win32 APIs supported in both operating systems, not the entire Win32 API, because most applications do not require the Windows NT–specific APIs.

If you are like most Windows programmers trying to convert to the Win32 API, you have been overwhelmed by a mass of documentation that has little organization and very few examples. Trying to figure out how a function is *supposed* to work and what it *really* does quickly becomes an hour-long task. This book contains complete descriptions of each function, detailed parameter descriptions, and examples for each function that are concise and show the functionality.

The same developer-friendly *API Bible* format is maintained in this book. Each chapter covers a group of related functions; for example, Chapter 3, Creating Windows, covers the functions required to create a window. Each chapter starts out with a short overview of the functions covered in the chapter, along with some common background that each function shares. This is followed by a function summary for the chapter and the detailed descriptions of the functions, with examples.

The examples in this book are simple, yet complete, and show all appropriate variable declarations and usage of the function, along with any required supporting functions. The examples are not intended to be tutorials, but to demonstrate one function or at most a few functions in a simple working program. In the interest of keeping the examples short and concise, shortcuts are taken that would not be appropriate in a normal application. This was done to help eliminate the confusion between what is necessary to use the function in the example and the support code that is part of a normal Windows application.

This book was completed using the released copy of Windows NT 4 and Windows 95. Every attempt was made to make sure the references are complete and accurate. The Microsoft Visual C++ 4.2 compiler was used for the examples that are included on the CD-ROM.

The number of APIs that an average Windows application uses has exploded. This book covers the core API for Windows development. The other *API Bible* books in this series—*Common Controls & Messages* and *Multimedia & ODBC*—which are currently on the market, cover other support APIs such as the common controls, ODBC, and the multimedia APIs. *Common Controls & Messages* also contains a complete reference to all messages and macros, which is too large to include in this book.

I hope you enjoy this book, and welcome to the world of Win32!

Richard J. Simon

Installation

The CD-ROM included with this book contains the source code for the example programs featured herein. The code is organized according to chapter; for each chapter of the book, you'll find a corresponding directory on the CD containing the chapter projects. It is in an uncompressed format and can be copied directly from the CD. Be sure to check the README file for updates.

Copying the Source Code with Windows 95

When you are in the Windows 95 desktop, you can copy the source code to your computer's hard disk, using the following steps:

1. Double-click on the My Computer icon to open the My Computer window.
2. Double-click on the icon for your hard drive in the My Computer window.
3. Click on File in the menu bar.
4. Click on New, then on Folder. This will create a new directory on your hard disk into which you can copy the source code.
5. Type in a name for the new directory (such as NT Win32 API SuperBible).
6. Click on My Computer in the chooser bar at the bottom of the Windows 95 desktop to bring up the My Computer dialog box.
7. Double-click on the CD icon to view the CD's contents; you can open any subdirectories by clicking on them. These files can now be moved from the CD to the hard drive.
8. Drag the icon for the files into the new directory you created in step 5. (If you cannot see the new directory, try dragging the My Computer window to a corner of the screen.)
9. Windows 95 will copy the contents of the CD to the new directory, maintaining the same organization as on the CD.

Assistance

If you have difficulty copying the source code from the CD, technical assistance can be obtained from Macmillan Computer Publishing through these channels:

Phone: (317) 581-3833
Email: support@mcp.com

1

WINDOWS 95/NT 4 PROGRAMMING

Microsoft's Windows 95 is a major upgrade for Windows 3.1 that introduces a new object-oriented user interface and most of the capabilities of the Win32 API. Windows NT 4 is the version of Windows NT that includes the user interface introduced with Windows 95 along with many of the other features that were first introduced with Windows 95. Windows 95 and Windows NT 4 present new challenges for developers, such as drag-and-drop functions and object linking and embedding (OLE), to provide smooth and seamless integration between applications. Applications designed for Windows 95 and Windows NT 4 provide more graphical presentation of data, which creates a more intuitive interface for the user (but can be more difficult for the programmer to develop).

New Features

In evolving from a basic and graphical user interface to a more object-oriented interface, Windows has changed from an application-centered interface to a data-centered interface. This means developers must re-think the user interface of their applications, because applications have become tools to deal with objects in the interface.

There are many new features in Windows 95 and Windows NT 4, both visible and behind the scenes, that the developer needs to address when designing an application. Most aspects of the user interface have changed. Note these major enhancements and additions to the user interface:

■ The desktop is now a functional part of the operating system. Applications and documents can be placed on the desktop for later use.

■ A taskbar gives users point-and-click access to applications and lets them switch between currently running applications.

■ Objects can be dragged and dropped to the desktop and between applications.

- Context-sensitive help is available throughout the operating system and within applications.

- Pop-up menus, available with the right mouse button, are context sensitive for the selected object.

- Common controls, such as the TreeView, ListView, Toolbar, and so on, provide the same look and feel to all applications.

- Property sheets provide an easy user interface for changing and viewing the properties of objects.

- Minimized windows have a new look.

- Title bar text is now left-justified, and the system menu is replaced by a small application icon. Also, a new close window is added to the right side of the title bar.

Many behind-the-scenes improvements and additions in Windows 95 make it more stable than earlier versions of Windows and allow it to use the same executable files as Windows NT. Windows 95 also added APIs that Windows NT 3.5x did not include, and therefore the two operating systems were not synchronized. Once Windows NT 4 was released, many of the differences were resolved; the two operating systems now use very similar sets of APIs. These are the major changes and additions introduced in Windows 95:

- Most of the Win32 API is implemented so the same executable works on Windows NT and Windows 95. The main APIs that are not supported deal with Windows NT's security, which Windows 95 does not support.

- Windows 95 is a 32-bit operating system, for the most part, even though key portions remain 16-bit for backward compatibility and a smaller memory footprint. The main portion of the operating system that remains 16-bit is the Graphics Device Interface (GDI).

- The registry is expanded for use as a replacement for initialization (INI) files.

- Preemptive multitasking and multiple threads enable parallel execution of applications. All Win32 applications run as a thread and can have multiple threads of execution within them.

Minimum Requirements

When Windows 95 was introduced, the Designed for Windows 95 logo was also introduced. This logo program insured that software met a minimum set of requirements, of which running on the latest version of Windows NT was one. However, since Windows NT 3.5x did not support the same user interface and other unique Windows 95 features, the logo requirements made some recommendations that were not requirements. The following is the list of requirements for the Designed for Windows 95 logo:

- Must be a Win32 executable, compiled with a 32-bit compiler, such as Microsoft Visual C++ 2.x, that generates an executable of the PE (Portable Executable) format. Or, if the application is not represented in PE format, such as interpreted code, the runtime engine must be a Win32 executable in the PE format. An example of this would be an application developed in Microsoft Access. The application is an MDB file, not an EXE file, but **ACCESS.EXE** would need to be a Win32 PE format executable.

- The product must have a fully automated installation program with a graphical setup program that executes smoothly in Windows 95. The installer must lead the user through the process and not just instruct the user to copy files. Products that ship on CD-ROM must utilize the AutoPlay feature in Windows 95 to begin setup. The installation must also detect which operating system the user is running and set up the version of the product for the operating system. A complete uninstaller must also be included that removes all files and registry entries placed on the system by the installation program. This must be accessible from the Add/Remove Programs option of the control panel.

- Must have UI/Shell support. This means that the application must meet the following minimum requirements:

  1. Must register 16×16– and 32×32–pixel icons for each file type and the application.

  2. Must use the Windows 95 look, described in the Style Guide section later in this chapter. Using the system-supplied dialogs and controls is recommended but not required.

  3. Must call the **GetSystemMetrics** function to determine current sizing of different aspects of the user interface.

  4. Must not use hard-coded shading to gray; instead, call the **GetSysColor** function to determine the current system colors.

  5. Must use the right mouse button for context menus. The right mouse button should not be used for any other function within the application.

  6. Must follow the Windows 95 application setup guidelines to make the application properly visible in the shell. At a minimum, the application should use the registry and provide complete uninstall capability. The application should include an automated installation process for the end user.

  7. Must use OLE 2.x where possible. This is not required but is recommended for Windows 95 applications. OLE is the mechanism Windows 95 applications use to share objects with each other. An application should export all data objects as an OLE server and accept OLE objects as an OLE client. In-place editing of OLE objects is recommended, if at all possible.

  8. Must not add information to the **WIN.INI** or **SYSTEM.INI** files. Some exceptions may apply to this rule when it is unavoidable.

- Must be tested on the latest shipping version of Windows NT , and, if Windows 95–specific APIs are used, the Windows 95–only functionality must degrade gracefully on Windows NT. This also applies conversely for Windows NT–specific APIs. The application must run successfully on both Windows 95 and Windows NT, unless architectural differences between the two operating systems prevent it.

- Must support long file names and use them for displaying all document and data file names in the shell, title bars, dialogs and controls, and with icons. It is also strongly recommended that file extensions not be displayed.

- Plug-and-play event awareness is recommended but not required.

An application does not need to meet all of these requirements to execute under Windows 95, but it must meet each one to be considered for the Designed for Windows 95 logo. This is Microsoft's compatibility logo that is displayed on Windows software that is designed specifically for Windows 95 and meets the minimum requirements. Windows 3.x applications have a similar logo, except the requirements are minimal compared to the requirements for Windows 95. Most Windows 3.x applications will require a significant amount of work, including some redesign of the user interface to make them Windows 95 applications.

When Microsoft released Windows NT 4 with its new user interface to match Windows 95, they also introduced a new logo that indicates that the software runs equally well under Windows NT 4 and Windows 95. Some of the exemptions have been made requirements now that the APIs are more in sync with each other. Other issues deal with Internet awareness and the requirements for distributing software over the Internet. Because this is a very large list of requirements and recommendations, see the document `SOFTREQ.DOC` on the accompanying CD-ROM. You can also get more information on Microsoft's Web site at `http://www.microsoft.com/windows/thirdparty/winlogo/`.

Style Guide

This section covers the basic conventions that developers should use for developing Windows 95/NT 4 applications. Some of these guidelines are flexible, meaning that they are not required for an application to be considered a Windows 95/NT 4 application, and others are required (refer to the previous section for items that are required before an application can use the Designed for Windows NT and Windows 95 logo). However, all guidelines should be followed as closely as possible to produce an application that provides the end user with a common look and feel under Windows 95 and Windows NT 4.

Windows

A user typically interacts with data objects using two different types of windows, a primary window and secondary windows. The primary window is where most of the viewing and editing takes place, whereas secondary windows allow the user to specify options or provide specific details about the objects in the primary window. Secondary windows are usually property sheets or dialog boxes.

Window Components

A typical primary window, shown in Figure 1-1, consists of a frame, client area, and a title bar. If the content of the window exceeds the viewable area, scroll bars are used to give the user the ability to scroll the window. The window can include other components, such as menu bars and status bars.

Every window has a window frame that defines the shape of the window. A sizable window, as shown in Figure 1-1, has a border that provides points for resizing the window, such as the grip and close window button. If the window cannot be resized, the border does not have the extra width of the sizable window.

Title Bar

The title bar or caption extends the width of the window along the top edge inside the border. The title bar identifies what the window shows and lets the user perform many window operations as well. It is the control point for moving the window and the location of the system menu, minimize, maximize, and restore buttons, and the close window button. The user can access the system menu of the application by pressing the left mouse button on the small icon of the application, pressing the ALT-SPACEBAR key combination, or pressing the right mouse button on the title bar.

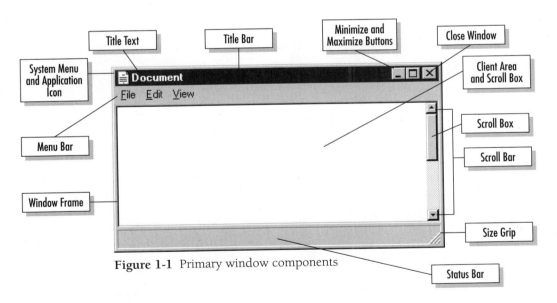

Figure 1-1 Primary window components

The title bar contains a small version of the object's icon on the far-left corner that represents the object currently being viewed in the window. If the application is a "tool" or "utility" (an application that does not view data objects), as shown in Figure 1-2, the icon will be a 16×16-pixel version of the application's icon, and the application name is used as the title bar text. If the application includes a specifier, it should include a dash and the specification text. For example, the Windows Explorer indicates which container it is exploring. If the application does not register a small icon, Windows 95 will shrink the normal 32×32-pixel icon. This can produce unpredictable results (which is why Microsoft made a requirement that Windows 95 applications register a 16×16-pixel icon).

Figure 1-2 Title bar of a "tool" or "utility" application

Applications that use data objects, such as Microsoft WordPad (shown in Figure 1-3), use the icon that represents the data object in the title bar. See the System Integration section later in this chapter for information on how to register icons for an application and data file types. The title bar text is made up of the data object's name and the application's name. If a data object does not currently have a name, create one automatically by using the short name, such as Document. If it is not practical to supply a default name, use the placeholder (Untitled) in the title bar text.

Figure 1-3 Document title bar

A multiple-document interface (MDI) application, such as Microsoft Word, shown in Figure 1-4, uses the application's icon in the parent window's title bar, and the icon that represents the data object in the child window's title bar. The application's name appears as the title bar text on the parent window, and the data object's name is used for the child window's title bar text.

Figure 1-4 Multiple-document interface normal title bar

When the user maximizes the child window in an MDI application, the child window's title bar is hidden, and the title is combined, as shown in Figure 1-5. The icon from the child window's title bar is displayed on the far-left corner of the parent window's menu bar.

Figure 1-5 Multiple-document interface maximized title bar

Command buttons associated with the window appear on the right of the title bar. Table 1-1 shows the primary buttons and the actions they perform.

Table 1-1 Title bar buttons

Command Button	Operation
☒	Closes the window.
▬	Minimizes the window.
☐	Maximizes the window.
⧉	Restores the window.

Window Operations

The basic operations that a user can perform on a window include activation, deactivation, opening, closing, moving, sizing, scrolling, and splitting. All windows perform these operations in the same manner, which allows users to operate windows consistently throughout their applications.

Activating Windows

Even though users can display multiple windows at the same time, most users work with a single window at a time, the active window. The active window is distinguished from other windows by its title bar and window frame color. Inactive windows use the inactive title bar and frame color. (These colors can be set by the user and are dynamic.) An application can retrieve these colors using the `GetSysColor` function described in Chapter 21, System Information. When a window becomes inactive, the application should hide the selection within the window to prevent confusion over which window is receiving keyboard input. An exception to this would be a drag-and-drop operation when the cursor is over the inactive window.

Opening and Closing Windows

When the user opens a primary window, an entry should be created on the taskbar. All open primary windows should have an entry on the taskbar to allow the user to easily switch between open applications. When an application is opened for the first time, use a reasonable default size and position. If the user opens an application that has been opened previously, restore it to its previous size and position. If appropriate, restore the user interface settings, such as selection state, scroll position, and other related view information. If the user attempts to open an application that is already running, follow the recommendations in Table 1-2.

Table 1-2 Actions for already open windows

File Type	Action
Document or data file	Activate the existing window of the object and display it at the top of the window Z order (the order in which the windows are stacked on top of each other).
Application file	Display a message box indicating that an open window of that application already exists and offer the user the option to switch to the open window or to open another window. Either choice activates the selected window and brings it to the top of the window Z order.
Document file that is already open	Activate the existing window of the file. Its MDI parent window comes to the top of the window in an MDI application window Z order, and the file appears at the top of the Z order within its MDI parent window.
Document file that is not already open, but its associated MDI application is already running	Create a new MDI child window for the associated file, place it at the top of the Z order with the MDI parent window, and place the MDI parent window at the top of the Z order.

When the user closes a primary window, close all dependent secondary windows and remove the taskbar entry as well. For most applications, when the user closes the primary window, the application is closed. However, some applications, such as the printer queue, do not terminate when the user closes the primary window. Before closing the primary window, display a message asking the user whether to save or discard any changes or cancel the close operation. This gives the user control over any pending transactions that are not saved. If there are no unsaved transactions, close the window without prompting the user.

Moving Windows

The user can move a window either by dragging the window's title bar to the new location using a pointing device, such as a mouse or pen, or by using the Move command from the window's pop-up menu. Typically, when a window is moved, the outline representation of the window moves as the user moves the window. The window is updated when the move operation is completed. On some systems, the window can be redrawn dynamically while the window is being moved. Applications should not prohibit the redrawing of the window while it is moving. The painting should also be as efficient as possible to provide a smooth appearance while the user is moving the window.

After choosing the Move command, the user can move the window with the keyboard by using the arrow keys and pressing the [ENTER] key to end the move and establish the new window position. Pressing [ESC] aborts the move operation and keeps the window in its previous position. The application should not allow the user to move the window to a location from which it cannot be accessed.

Resizing Windows

All primary windows should be made with resizable frames unless the information displayed is fixed, such as in the Windows Calculator program. Users have several methods to size a window: the sizing frame, the minimize and maximize operations, restore, and the size grip. Application windows that allow sizing should normally implement all of these. At the minimum, windows should implement the minimize and restore operations.

With windows that have sizing borders, the user can size the window by dragging the border with a pointing device. Optionally, the user can use the Size command from the window's pop-up menu. Normally, as the user sizes the window, an outline representation of the window moves with the pointer. On some systems, the window can be redrawn dynamically while the window is being sized. The same rules apply here that apply to moving a window—the drawing should not be prohibited and it should be as efficient as possible. The user can use the keyboard by selecting the Size command and using the arrow keys to size the window. The [ENTER] key accepts the new window size, and the [ESC] key aborts the size operation.

The maximize operation, as its name implies, sizes a window to its maximum size. This size is the display size excluding the space used by the taskbar. For MDI child windows, the maximum size is the size of the parent window's client area. Applications should not use a fixed display size, but should adapt to the shape and size defined by the system. Use a standard system function, such as the `SetWindowPlacement` function, which will automatically place the window correctly. The user can maximize a window by selecting the maximize command button from the title bar of the window or the Maximize command from the window's pop-up menu. When a window is maximized, replace the maximize button with a restore button, disable the Maximize command, and enable the Restore command on the window's pop-up menu.

Windows 95 and Windows NT 4 use a representation of minimized windows that is different from the one Windows 3.x uses. When an application is minimized in Windows 95, the application is represented in the taskbar. For MDI child windows, the window is minimized within the parent window. To minimize a window, the user chooses the minimize command button on the title bar of the window or the Minimize command from the window's pop-up menu. When a window is minimized, the Minimize command is disabled and the Restore command is enabled.

A user can restore a maximized or minimized window by selecting the restore command button (in maximized windows only) or the Restore command from the window's pop-up menu. When a window is restored, disable the Restore command in the window's pop-up menu and enable the Maximize (if appropriate) and Minimize commands. When a maximized window is restored, the restore command button is replaced with the maximize command button on the title bar. The user can restore a window by selecting the application's icon from the taskbar, selecting the Restore command from the window's pop-up menu, selecting the restore command button (in maximized windows only), or using the ALT+TAB and SHIFT+ALT+TAB key combinations.

All sizable windows within an application should include a size grip. A size grip is a special handle, shown in Figure 1-1, for sizing a window in both the horizontal and vertical directions at the same time. To use a size grip, the user drags the grip with the pointing device, and the window resizes in the same manner as when the sizing border is used. The size grip should always be located at the intersection of the horizontal and vertical scroll bars or the lower-right corner of the window. If the window has a status bar, the size grip is located at the right edge of the status bar. A window can have only one size grip at a time.

Scrolling Windows

When a window is too small to completely display a data object, the window should support scrolling. This enables the user to move the view of the window to see other portions of the data object. The application should use a scroll bar (a rectangular control that contains scroll arrows), a scroll box (thumb), and a scroll bar shaft, shown in Figure 1-1.

A window can include a vertical scroll bar, such as the one shown in Figure 1-1, a horizontal scroll bar, or both, depending on the data object that is being viewed. If the data object is too wide, a horizontal scroll bar is appropriate. If it is too high, a vertical one is used. If a scroll bar is not required to view the data object, don't include one. However, if a window that has a scroll bar is sized so that it no longer requires one, continue to display it. Consistently displaying scroll bars will result in a neater appearance.

Arrows appear at each end of a scroll bar and point in the direction the window or view is moved. When the user selects an arrow, the window is moved one scroll unit in the direction of the arrow. The scroll unit is an application-defined unit of measure that is appropriate for the data object the window is displaying. For example, a text file would scroll one line at a time when a scroll arrow is selected, whereas a picture would move a small number of pixels. The scroll unit should remain the same throughout the scrolling range. When a window cannot be scrolled any farther in a direction, disable the scrolling arrow corresponding to that direction.

The scroll box or thumb moves along the scroll bar to indicate the approximate location in the data object the window is currently displaying. For example, if the window is currently displaying the beginning of the data object, the scroll box is at the top of the scroll bar. If it is displaying the middle of the data object, the scroll box is halfway down the scroll bar. The scroll box has changed in Windows 95 from previous versions of Windows. It is now proportionally sized to the amount of the data object viewed in the window and the total size of the data object. For example, if the window can display the entire contents of the data object, the scroll box is sized the entire length of the scroll bar. If the window can display half of the data object, the scroll box will be half the size of the scroll bar. The scroll box also serves another function: The user can drag the scroll box to scroll to approximate locations within the data object.

The scroll bar shaft also serves as part of the scrolling interface. When the user selects the scroll bar shaft with a pointing device, the window is scrolled the equivalent size of the visible area. The direction of the scroll depends on which side of the scroll box the scroll shaft was selected. For example, if the user selects the scroll shaft below the scroll box on a vertical scroll bar, the window will scroll down. When scrolling with the scroll shaft, the application should leave a small portion of the data object visible from the previous screen. For example, if the window is viewing a text file and the user scrolls down, the line that is visible at the bottom of the window becomes the line visible at the top of the window after the scroll is complete.

So far, all the previous scrolling techniques involve the user's explicitly scrolling the window. Sometimes a window should automatically scroll. The following lists common situations in which a window should scroll automatically:

■ When the user drags a selection beyond the edge of the window, the window should scroll in the direction of the drag.

■ When the user drags an object close to the edge of a scrollable area and it is appropriate for the object to be dropped in the window, scroll the window in the appropriate direction.

■ When the user enters text at the edge of a window or places an object into a location at the edge of a window, the window should scroll to allow the user to focus on the area of the object with which the user is working. The amount of the scroll depends upon the application context. For example, when a user generates a new line of text that is being typed in the window, it should scroll one line at a time. When scrolling horizontally, the scroll unit should be greater than the width of a single character to prevent scrolling continuously. Also, when the user transfers a graph object near the edge of the window, the scroll unit is based on the size of the object.

■ If an operation, such as a find, results in the selection or cursor moving, scroll the window to display the new selection or cursor position. Another example is an entry form—the window should scroll to follow the cursor as it moves to fields that are not displayed in the current view of the window.

An application should also use the navigation keys to support scrolling with the keyboard. If the window contains a cursor, such as in a text editor, and the user presses a navigation key next to the edge of the window, the window scrolls in the corresponding direction. Windows that do not contain a cursor, such as a graphic image viewer, should always scroll with the navigation keys. The (PGUP) and (PGDN) keys are comparable to the user's selecting the scroll bar shaft. However, in a window that has a cursor, the cursor is also moved.

Don't crowd scroll bars with adjacent controls. Sometimes it is convenient to place controls, such as a split box, next to a scroll bar. However, too many adjacent controls make it difficult for users to scroll. If a large number of controls are needed, a standard toolbar is a better choice.

Splitting Windows

Some applications benefit from splitting a window into two separate views that can display different information about data objects. An example of this is the Windows Explorer, shown in Figure 1-6. These individual views within a window are referred to as panes.

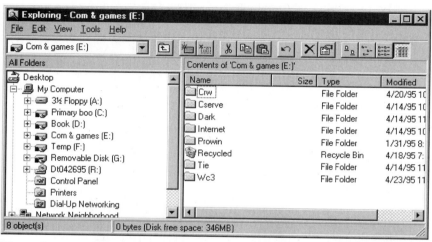

Figure 1-6 Window with a split bar

Although you can split a window to view the contents of multiple data objects at the same time, it is better to use the MDI application architecture to display multiple file types simultaneously. This gives the user a clearer idea of the individual file types.

A window can be set up to be split into panes by default or as a user-configurable option. If a window allows the user to configure a window into panes, it should contain a split box in the appropriate location (at the top of a vertical scroll bar or at the left of a horizontal scroll bar). A split box is a small rectangle (usually the size of the sizing border) placed adjacent to the end of a scroll bar that splits or adjusts the split of a window.

The user splits a window by dragging the split box to the desired position. When the user positions the pointer over the hot spot of the split box or a split bar, the pointer's image should change to provide feedback to the user. While the user drags the split box or split bar, move a representation of the split box and split bar with the pointer, as shown in Figure 1-7. When the drag is finished, display a split bar that extends from one side of the window to the other and defines the panes. The size of the split bar should be, at minimum, the current size of the sizing border.

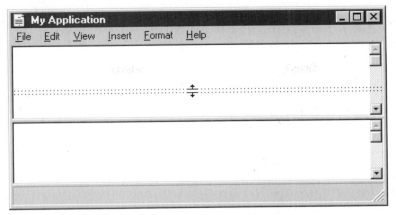

Figure 1-7 Moving a split bar

Provide a keyboard interface for splitting the window and include a Split command for the window or view's menu. When the user selects the Split menu item, split the window in the middle and allow the user to position the split bar using the arrow keys. The ⟨ENTER⟩ key sets the split bar at the current location. The ⟨ESC⟩ key aborts the split mode.

Menus

All applications have some sort of menu to interact with the user. At the very minimum, the primary window's pop-up menu is always available. Other menus depend on the application and which options the user has when working with it. There are several types of menus an application can use, including drop-down, pop-up, and cascading menus. An application can use one or more of these.

One of the most common forms of a menu is the menu bar. The menu bar, shown in Figure 1-8, is a rectangular area across the top of a window just below the title bar. Most applications will include a menu bar on the primary window. It is not good practice to include a menu bar on any other windows within the application, because doing so can confuse the user. All applications that include a menu bar should have, at minimum, the File and Help menu titles.

Even if an application includes a menu bar, it should also include pop-up menus where appropriate, as shown in Figure 1-9. Pop-up menus give the user an efficient way to interact with objects on the screen because they include only those menu items related to the object under the pointer.

Figure 1-8 Menu bar

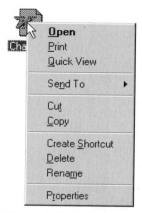

Figure 1-9 Pop-up menu

Applications should use the right mouse button exclusively for displaying pop-up menus within the application. Use the pointer location when the right mouse button is pressed at the upper-left corner of the pop-up menu. Pop-up menus can include any menu items that are appropriate for the object. However, instead of having a menu item for each object property, the menu should include a single Properties menu item, as shown on the menu in Figure 1-9. When the user selects the Properties menu item, a property sheet dialog is displayed with the properties for the object. Avoid making operations accessible only through a pop-up menu. Note that a pop-up menu does not need to be limited to items that appear in a drop-down menu.

Use the following guidelines when ordering items in pop-up menus:

■ Place the object's primary commands first, such as Open, Play, and Print. Then put in the object's transfer commands, other commands supported by the object, and the What's This? command, when supported.

■ The transfer commands should be in the order of Cut, Copy, Paste, and other specialized Paste commands.

■ The Properties command, when appropriate, should be the last item on the menu.

Menu Interface

Users can access menus with a pointer device, such as a mouse or pen, or the keyboard. Menu navigation with a pointer device is straightforward. The user selects the desired menu item by clicking the menu with the pointer device. If the selected menu item is a menu title with a drop-down menu, the drop-down menu is displayed. As the user moves the pointer device over the menu items, they are highlighted, showing the current menu selection. If the user holds down the mouse button used to select the menu, the menu item selected when the mouse button is released is the selected menu item. If the user selects the menu by releasing the mouse button, the next time the mouse button is pressed determines which menu item is selected.

The keyboard interface for drop-down menus uses the (ALT) key to activate the menu bar. Once the menu bar is activated, the user navigates the menu with the arrow keys and selects a menu item by pressing the (ENTER) key. The (ESC) key closes the drop-down menu if one is open; otherwise, it deactivates the menu bar. Pressing an alphanumeric key while holding down the (ALT) key, or after pressing the (ALT) key, displays the drop-down menu associated with the alphanumeric key (the underlined character in the menu item). Subsequently pressing alphanumeric keys brings up the associated menu item. All menu items should have an access character defined. See Chapter 6, Menus, for more information on defining access characters.

Shortcut keys or accelerators can be assigned to menu items in drop-down menus. Commands that are repetitively accessed should have a shortcut key associated with them. When the user presses a shortcut key, the menu command is carried out immediately without the menu ever displaying. Table 1-3 lists the shortcut key and access character that should be used for some common menu items. The access character is the underlined character.

Menu Titles

All drop-down and cascading menus have a menu title. The menu title for a drop-down menu is the entry that appears in the menu bar. The menu title for cascading menus is the name of the parent menu item. Choose menu titles that represent the entire contents of the menu and communicate clearly the purpose of all items in the menu. Do not use spaces in menu titles; Windows interprets a space as the end of one title and the beginning of another and will include two menu titles on the menu bar. Also, uncommon compound words should be avoided.

Menu Items

A menu contains individual choices known as menu items. Menu items can be words, graphics, or a combination of graphics and words. Menu items should provide the user with visual cues about the nature and effect of the menu item. Figure 1-10 shows a menu with the different types of menu items.

Figure 1-10 Menu item types

Group menu items into related sets separated with a menu separator. A standard separator is a single line, as shown in Figure 1-10. Do not use menu items as separators; this isn't standard and will present the user with a confusing user interface. Menu items that are not available, or not appropriate in a particular context, should be disabled or removed. Leaving the menu item enabled and using a message box telling the user the item isn't valid is clumsy and does not provide the user immediate feedback. It is better to disable a menu (as opposed to removing it), because this provides stability to the user interface. However, if the menu item is not applicable and no longer needed, remove it. If all menu items in a menu are disabled, disable the menu title. If the application includes feedback on the status bar, indicate that the command is unavailable and why. When disabling a custom menu item, follow the guidelines outlined later in this chapter under Visual Design.

Menu Item Types

There are different types of menu items to provide the user with visual feedback about the nature of the menu item and the function it performs. If a menu item is a command that requires additional information before it can execute, the menu item should be followed by an ellipsis (…). Such commands, such as the Save As command, usually display a dialog box to gather the missing information. However, not every command that displays a dialog box or other secondary window needs to have an ellipsis in its menu title. For example, after the user completes the Properties command dialog, no further parameters or actions are required to complete the command, so an ellipsis is unnecessary. Commands that result in message boxes don't need an ellipsis either.

Besides carrying out commands, menu items can also switch the state or property of an object or window. An example of this is the View menu, which contains menu items that toggle the view of the toolbar and status bar. These menu items can be mutually exclusive with other menu items or independent. If the state is independent, the menu item is marked with a check, as shown in Figure 1-10, when the state is toggled to the active state. If the state is mutually exclusive with other menu items, the active menu item is identified by an option button mark, as Figure 1-10 shows. An example of a mutually exclusive state is the alignment of a text field. It can be left-justified, centered, or right-justified, but it cannot be more than one of these options at the same time.

A menu can define a default item that also can be selected using a shortcut technique, such as double-clicking or drag-and-drop. For example, if the default command for an icon is Open when the user double-clicks, the Open command would be the default menu item. The system default appearance for designating a default menu item is to display the command as bold text.

Table 1-3 Menu item shortcut keys and access characters

Menu Item	Shortcut Key
New	Ctrl+N
Open	Ctrl+O
Save	Ctrl+S
Save As	
Print	Ctrl+P
Print Preview	
Page Setup	
Send	
Exit	
Undo	Ctrl+Z
Cut	Ctrl+X
Copy	Ctrl+C
Paste	Ctrl+V
Paste Special	
Paste Link	
Clear	Del
Select All	Ctrl+A
Find	Ctrl+F
Find Next	F3
Replace	Ctrl+H
Links	
Object Properties	Alt+Enter
Object	
Help Topics	
About <*Application Name*>	

Menu Item Labels

All menu items should include descriptive text or a graphic label. (Be consistent with whichever you use.) Follow these guidelines for writing menu items:

■ Use unique item names within a menu. Although menu item names can be repeated in different menus to represent similar or different actions, avoid this. It can confuse the user.

■ Use brief one-word descriptions. You can use multiple words if necessary, but verbose menu item names make it harder for the user to scan the menu.

- Define a unique access key for each menu item within a menu. Use the guidelines in Table 1-3 for common menu items. Where possible, define consistent access keys for common commands.

- Follow book title capitalization rules for menu item names. Capitalize the first letter of every word, except for articles, conjunctions, and prepositions that occur other than at the beginning or end of a multiple-word name.

- Avoid formatting individual menu item names with different text properties, even though these properties illustrate a particular text style.

Menu Item Shortcut Keys

Drop-down menu items can also display a keyboard shortcut associated with the command. The shortcuts are typically left-aligned at the first tab position after the longest item in the menu that has a shortcut. Do not use spaces for alignment—a tab '\t' character is placed in the menu item name to space the shortcut properly. Do not include shortcuts in pop-up menus. Pop-up menus are already a shortcut form.

Use CTRL and SHIFT as the key modifiers combined with the actual key with the "+". For example, the Copy command has a common shortcut of CTRL+C. Do not use the ALT key, because it can cause user interface problems.

Common Menus

Some drop-down menus are found in all applications. This does not mean that all applications need to include a drop-down menu. If a common drop-down menu is appropriate for an application, it should follow the guidelines in this section.

File Menu

The File menu is where primary operations that apply to a file should reside. Figure 1-11 shows common commands and where they should be placed. If the application does not support the Exit command because the object remains active when the window is closed, replace the Exit command with a Close command.

Figure 1-11 File menu

Edit Menu

The Edit menu should contain general-purpose editing commands, such as Cut, Copy, Paste, OLE object commands, and commands from Table 1-4, if appropriate. Figure 1-12 shows a typical Edit menu taken from Microsoft WordPad.

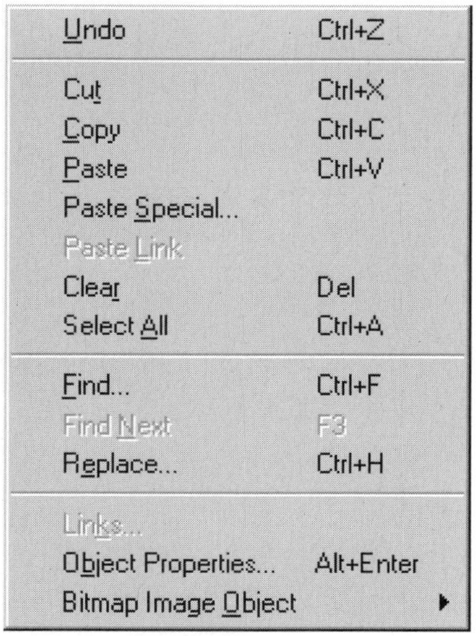

<u>U</u>ndo	Ctrl+Z
Cu<u>t</u>	Ctrl+X
<u>C</u>opy	Ctrl+C
<u>P</u>aste	Ctrl+V
Paste <u>S</u>pecial...	
Paste <u>L</u>ink	
Clea<u>r</u>	Del
Select <u>A</u>ll	Ctrl+A
<u>F</u>ind...	Ctrl+F
Find <u>N</u>ext	F3
<u>R</u>eplace...	Ctrl+H
Lin<u>k</u>s...	
O<u>b</u>ject Properties...	Alt+Enter
Bitmap Image <u>O</u>bject	▶

Figure 1-12 Edit menu

Table 1-4 Optional Edit commands

Command	Function
<u>U</u>ndo	Reverses the last edit action.
<u>R</u>epeat	Repeats the last edit action.
<u>F</u>ind	Searches for text.
<u>R</u>eplace	Searches for and substitutes text.
<u>D</u>elete	Removes the currently selected object.
<u>D</u>uplicate	Creates a copy of the currently selected object.

View Menu

The View menu, shown in Figure 1-13, contains commands that change the user's view of data in the window, such as Zoom or Outline. You can also include commands that control the display of interface elements (such as the toolbar, ruler, and status bar) in the window.

Figure 1-13 View menu

Window Menu

The Window menu, shown in Figure 1-14, is reserved for MDI applications for managing the MDI child windows. The Window menu can contain commands, such as Cascade, Tile, and Close All, that relate to the MDI child windows. The last items in the Window menu are reserved for the current MDI child windows.

Figure 1-14 Window menu

Help Menu

Items in the Help menu, shown in Figure 1-15, assist the user with the application. Include a Help Topics command to provide access to the Help Topics browser for the application's help file. An application can alternatively use a set of menu commands that access specific pages of the Help Topics browser, such as Contents, Index, and Find Topic. Other user assistance commands are also located on this menu.

Figure 1-15 Help menu

To provide access to copyright and version information for an application, include an About *application name* menu command at the bottom of the Help menu. When the user chooses this command, display a window that contains the application's name, copyright information, version number, and any other application properties. Do not use an ellipsis (…) at the end of this menu command, because the resulting window does not accept input from the user.

Window Pop-up Menu

The Window pop-up menu replaces the system menu found on previous versions of Windows. The user accesses this menu by pressing the right mouse button on the title bar of a window. For backward compatibility, the user can also access the Window pop-up menu by selecting the area of the title bar where the small icon is displayed and pressing the left mouse button or the ALT+SPACEBAR key combination.

A common Window pop-up menu, shown in Figure 1-16, includes the Close, Restore, Move, Size, Minimize, and Maximize commands. An application also can include other commands that apply to the window or view, such as the Split command. Secondary windows also contain a Window pop-up menu, but usually include only the Move and Close commands.

Figure 1-16 Window pop-up menu

Icon Pop-up Menus

Pop-up menus displayed for data objects represented as icons include operations for that type of object. The user accesses the pop-up menu for an icon by pressing the right mouse button while the cursor is over the icon.

The application that contains the icon supplies the pop-up menu for the icon. For example, the system provides the pop-up menu for the icons on the desktop. An application that embeds OLE objects into its documents supplies the pop-up menu for the object. The container application stocks an icon's pop-up menu with commands for the object. Figure 1-17 shows a typical pop-up menu for an icon that represents an application. Figure 1-18 shows a pop-up menu for an icon that represents a document.

Input and Controls

Controls are graphic objects that allow the user to interact with and provide input to an application. Some controls only provide feedback to the user or help clarify the user interface. Each type of control has a unique visual appearance and operation. Windows also allows applications to define new controls and variations of existing controls. When designing these, follow the guidelines in the Visual Design section, later in this chapter. This section covers the common types of controls that are used within Windows applications.

Figure 1-17 Application icon pop-up menu

Figure 1-18 Document icon pop-up menu

Buttons

Buttons are controls that, like a menu item, start an action or change properties. Windows applications can use three basic types of buttons—command buttons, option or radio buttons, or a check box.

Command Buttons

Command buttons, also referred to as pushbuttons, are rectangular controls that perform an action when pressed. They normally contain descriptive text and sometimes a graphic. Some common command buttons are the OK, Cancel, and Help buttons normally contained on dialog boxes.

The user selects a command button by placing the pointer over the button and pressing the left mouse button or tapping the pen. If the button has input focus, the spacebar also selects a command button. Once the command button is pressed and released, the command associated with the button is carried out.

The command button text should represent the action the button performs. The button text should follow the same capitalization conventions used for menu items. As with menu items, use an ellipsis (...) as a visual aid for buttons associated with commands that require additional information. If a button is used to enlarge a secondary window to display additional options, include a pair of greater-than characters (>>) at the end of the button's label.

All command buttons in Windows should have the same appearance and follow the same guidelines so that users can identify a command button by its appearance. Table 1-5 shows the different visual states that a command button can have.

Table 1-5 Command button appearance

Visual	Representation
	Normal unpressed button.
	Pressed button.
	Button that represents an option as being set.
	Disabled button.
	Disabled button that represents an option as being set.
	Button that represents a mixed value (see below).
	Button with input focus.

Option Buttons (Radio Buttons)

Option buttons, also known as radio buttons, represent a single choice from a group of possible choices. This means that only one option button in a group of option buttons can be selected at any one time. Because option buttons are only meaningful in a group, they should not be used as a single button.

As with command buttons, the user selects an option button with the left mouse button or by tapping a pen on the button. The user can also tab into a group of option buttons and use the arrow keys to cycle through the options. To arrange this, set a tab stop on the first option button in a group. Also, mark the first option button with the group style. No other option buttons in the group should have a tab stop or be associated with a group style. The control after the last option button in the group, typically a group box, should include the group style. Also, the text of each option button should include an access key to give the user a keyboard shortcut for selecting an option.

Because option buttons are used in groups, a group box is normally used as a marker for the group of option buttons. This visually defines the group of related options for the user. Figure 1-19 shows a typical set of option buttons within a group box.

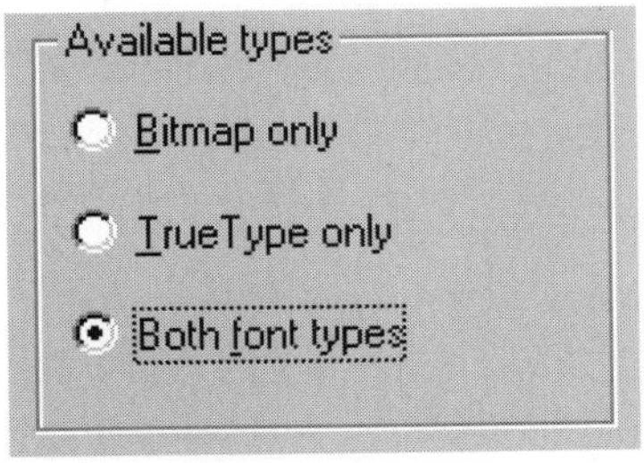

Figure 1-19 Option buttons

Check Boxes

Check boxes are similar to option buttons in that they are either on or off. The difference is that check boxes are nonexclusive and are used to represent individual options. Check boxes are displayed as a small square box with a text label. When the check box is selected, a checkmark is placed in the box.

As with checkmarks on menu items, use a check box only if the two states are clearly opposites and are unambiguous. Otherwise, use option buttons to fully show the two different states.

Group related check box choices together just as you would option buttons. The user can still select individual check boxes, but has a clearer visual indication of the relationship between check box options. If an application requires a large number of related choices or the number of choices varies, use a multiple selection list box or a list box with checkmarks next to the items.

In addition to the standard (TAB) key and arrow key navigation provided in a dialog box, define access keys for the check box labels. If the check box has input focus, the spacebar toggles the state of the check box.

A check box can also display a third state, known as the mixed-value state. This state is normally used when representing a state for multiple items when the state is not the same for all the items. An example of this is in the Windows Explorer's Properties dialog when selecting multiple files. Figure 1-20 shows the Attributes check boxes of the Properties dialog for the Windows Explorer.

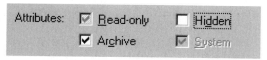

Figure 1-20 Check boxes

List Boxes

Use list boxes to display a list of choices, such as text, color, icons, or other graphics, from which the user can select one or more items. List boxes are best used for a large number of choices or when the number of choices varies. For example, if an option is not valid for the current context, it should not be displayed in the list box.

The entries of a list box should be ordered appropriately to help the user while browsing the list box contents. If there is no logical ordering for the list box content, set it in ascending order (A–Z).

When a list box is disabled, any labels associated with the list box should be disabled as well. The entries in the list box, if possible, should also be disabled to avoid any confusion to the user about the status of the control.

The list box should be wide enough to display the entire content of the items. If this is not possible, use one of the following methods for displaying list box items:

■ Make the list box wide enough so that each of the list box items can be uniquely distinguished and the user can identify the item.

■ Use an ellipsis (…) in the middle of long text entries. For example, long directory names could be reduced in size by only displaying the beginning and ending of the directory: `\Windows\...\example.txt`.

■ Include a horizontal scroll bar. The drawback is that the list box cannot display as many items at the same time in the same screen space. If most of the items do not exceed the width of the list box, do not include a horizontal scroll bar because it is not normally needed.

When including a list box in a window's design, support the edit commands (Cut, Copy, and Paste) and drag-and-drop transfers, if appropriate. List view controls support these operations directly. However, list boxes can have this functionality using the support provided by the system.

Single-Selection List Boxes

Single-selection list boxes allow the user to select one item at a time similar to the mutually exclusive operation in a group of option buttons. The single-selection list box has advantages over a group of option buttons in that it can easily display a large number of options and can change the contents of the list box dynamically during execution of the application.

Make single-selection list boxes large enough to display three to eight items at a time, as shown in Figure 1-21, depending on the design of the window on which the list box is used. Always include a vertical scroll bar. When a list box is scrolled to the beginning or end, disable the scroll arrow for the appropriate direction. If there are not enough items in the list to scroll, disable the scroll bar.

Figure 1-21 Single-selection list box

Extended- and Multiple-Selection List Boxes

Extended- and multiple-selection list boxes are the same as single-selection list boxes, except they allow the user to select more than one item at a time. The difference between extended- and multiple-selection list boxes lies in the user interface and how it is optimized for selection.

Extended-selection list boxes are optimized for selecting a single item or a single range, while still allowing for disjoint (items not necessarily listed together) selections. The user must hold down the [SHIFT] key while selecting a continuous range and the [CTRL] key to make a disjoint selection.

Multiple-selection list boxes are optimized for selecting several disjoint items without using modifier keys. The drawback is that they don't provide an easy method to clear all selections and select a single item as the extended-selection list box does.

Drop-Down List Boxes

The drop-down list box, shown in Figure 1-22, is similar to a single-selection list box in that it allows the user to select one item at a time. The difference is that the list is displayed on demand and only the currently selected item is visible.

The drop-down list should be a few spaces wider than the longest item in the list. The open list box should be sized using the guidelines for a single-selection list box.

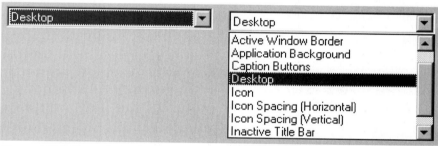

Figure 1-22 Drop-down list box

List View Controls

List view controls are similar to list boxes, except that each item is represented with an icon and a label. The list view control also provides support for alignment, sorting, in-place editing of icon labels, and drag-and-drop operations. List view controls also support four different ways of displaying the items, as given in Table 1-6.

Table 1-6 List view item views

View	Description
Icon	Each item is displayed as a full-size icon with a label below it. This view allows the user to drag the icons to change the arrangement.
Small Icon	Each item is displayed as a small icon with a label to the right of the icon. This view allows the user to drag the icons to change the arrangement.
List	Each item is displayed as a small icon with a label to the right of the icon. The icons are in a sorted columnar layout.
Report	Each item is displayed in a line of a multicolumn layout as a small icon with a label to the right of the icon in the far-left column. Additional columns can be added to provide detail about the item.

Provide a pop-up menu for icons in a list view to provide a consistent paradigm for how the user interacts with icons in Windows. Commands on the pop-up menu should be appropriate for the icon the user selected. Figure 1-23 shows a pop-up menu in a list view control.

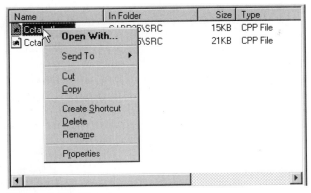

Figure 1-23 List view

Tree View Controls

A tree view control is a special list box that displays a set of objects in a hierarchical view based on the relationship of the objects to each other. A tree view can also contain an optional image for each item in the tree. Different images can be displayed for an item based on the type of object it is. A common use for a tree view is the Windows Explorer, shown in Figure 1-24.

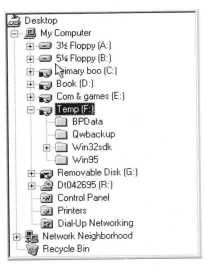

Figure 1-24 Tree view in Windows Explorer

The tree view supports collapsing the hierarchical view to hide part of the tree. It also supports drawing lines that define the hierarchical relationship of the items in the list and buttons for expanding and collapsing in the outline. Even though these are optional items, including them will make it easier for the user to interpret the outline.

Text Fields

Text fields come in a variety of controls that facilitate the display, entry, or editing of a text value. They make up the primary part of the user interface for data entry. Some text entry controls are actually a combination of controls, such as the combo box control.

Text field controls do not include a text label, as the button controls do. However, a static text control (described later in this chapter) can be used as the descriptive text for a text field. All text fields should include some indication, such as static text, as to the nature of the text field. Use sentence capitalization for multiple-word labels. Text labels can also contain access keys to provide quick keyboard access to text-entry fields. Users can also use the [TAB] key to move to the next field in the tab order.

Restricted input text fields should validate as the user types. For example, if the text field only allows numbers, the text field should ignore nonnumeric characters or provide the user with feedback that an invalid character has been entered.

Text Box

Text boxes, also called edit controls, are rectangular controls that allow the user to edit text. Applications can use text boxes for a single line or multiple lines of input. Although the outline border is optional, it is typically turned on for toolbars and secondary windows. A single-line text box, shown in Figure 1-25, can also optionally define horizontal scrolling to accommodate long strings. Horizontal and vertical scroll bars are supported on multiple-line text boxes to allow both horizontal and vertical scrolling.

Figure 1-25 Single-line text box

Text boxes support standard interfaces for navigation and selection. The editing capabilities are limited to basic insertion and deletion of characters with the option of word wrapping. The Cut, Copy, and Paste operations are also part of the standard text box control interface.

Applications can set a limit to the number of characters allowed for input. If a text box has a fixed length, it can also support auto-exit. If a text box has auto-exit, as soon as the maximum number of characters has been reached, the input focus moves to the next control in tab order.

Text boxes can support one font for the entire content of the text box. If more than one font is required, use the rich-text box described next.

Rich-Text Box

A rich-text box, shown in Figure 1-26, picks up where the text box leaves off. It provides support for font properties, such as typeface, size, color, bold, and italic format for each character in a rich-text box. In addition, rich-text boxes allow users to apply paragraph properties, such as alignment, tabs, indents, and numbering. Printing and OLE support is also a part of a rich-text box.

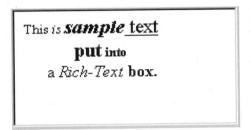

Figure 1-26 Rich-text box

Combo Box

A combo box, shown in Figure 1-27, combines an edit box and a list box. The user has the option of typing a selection or selecting it from the list. The edit box and the list box are dependent upon each other. As the user selects an item from the list, the edit box text is updated with the selected list item text. Also, when the user types text into the edit box, the list box automatically scrolls to the nearest matching item.

Figure 1-27 Combo box

The interface follows the same conventions as the individual components of the combo box, except that the up and down arrow keys only work in the list box portion of the control.

Drop-Down Combo Box

A drop-down combo box, shown in Figure 1-28, is the same as a drop-down list box, with the added functionality of a combo box. It has the same editing characteristics as the combo box, and the list box can be hidden, as with the drop-down list box.

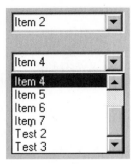

Figure 1-28 Drop-down combo box

Spin Box

Spin boxes are useful for accepting a limited set of ordered values. A spin box is a combination of a text box and an up-down control, as shown in Figure 1-29.

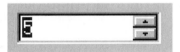

Figure 1-29 Spin box

The user can type a value directly into the text box, or as an alternative, increment or decrement the value by clicking the appropriate arrows of the up-down control. The unit that the value increments or decrements depends on what the control represents. Use a single set of spin box buttons to modify a set of related edit fields, such as the date or time expressed in its components. In this situation, the buttons would only affect the text box that has input focus.

Applications can include a static text field with an access key to provide direct keyboard access to the control. The (TAB) key can also provide access to the control.

Static Text

A static text field, shown in Figure 1-30, is primarily used as descriptive text and to present read-only text information. An application can alter the contents of a static text field at runtime, so it can provide information such as the current directory or status information.

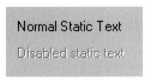

Figure 1-30 Static text

A static text field that is used for a label to another control, such as a text box, can define an access key for text box. Make sure that the access key places input focus on the related control and not the static text field (because the static text field cannot receive input).

Other Controls

The system also provides additional miscellaneous controls designed to organize other controls and provide special user interfaces. All of these controls, with the exception of the group box, are new in Windows 95. Although they may have been used within Windows 3.x applications, they were not standardized and not part of the Windows system. When converting Windows 3.x applications to Windows 95, use the new standard controls in place of custom controls. This will allow the application to easily adopt new standards in future versions of Windows.

Group Box

A group box is a special control used to organize groups of controls, such as option buttons or check boxes. It is a rectangular control, as shown in Figure 1-31, with optional title text that describes the group. The labels within the group box should be relative to the group box's label. For example, with a group box title of Alignment, the option button titles would be Right, Left, and Center. Use sentence capitalization for multiple-word labels.

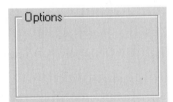

Figure 1-31 Group box

Although group boxes do not process input, they can help users access the items in the group by assigning an access key to the group label.

Column Headings

The column heading control, also called a header control, displays column headings above columns within a list of items. The list view control contains a header control when it is in the report view mode. As shown in Figure 1-32, the control can be divided into two or more parts to provide headings for multiple columns.

Name	Size	Type	Modified	

Figure 1-32 Header control

Each column within the heading control can behave like a command button to support tasks such as sorting the list. Each column can also contain a header label and a graphic image. Use the graphic image to provide feedback to the user about the column, such as the sort order. The header label can be left-, right-, or center-aligned. The user can also drag the column divider to set a new column size.

Property Sheet and Tabs

The property sheet and tab controls are new in Windows 95. Use a property sheet with at least one tab when editing the properties of a data object. A property sheet can contain multiple logical pages identified by multiple tab controls, shown in Figure 1-33.

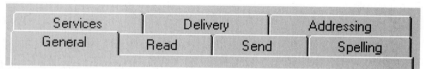

Figure 1-33 Tab controls

When the user selects a tab control, the property page associated with it moves to the foreground, so the user can modify the properties on that page. The user can select a tab with a pointer device or with the arrow keys when the tab has input focus. Optionally, the tab control can contain an access character in the text.

The tab control labels can include text or graphic information, or both. Normally, tabs only include text, but graphics can be used to help the user identify the property page.

Scroll Bars

Scroll bars are horizontal or vertical controls that provide scrolling for scrollable areas other than on a window frame or list box where they are part of the window. Do not use a scroll bar as an interface for setting or adjusting values; instead, use the slider control described next.

When using scroll bars, follow the guidelines for disabling the arrows described earlier in this chapter. Do not allow a scroll bar to receive input focus; rather, define a keyboard interface to scroll the scrollable area. This is more consistent with how list boxes scroll and less confusing to the user.

Slider Controls

Applications should use slider controls, also known as trackbar controls, for setting a value within a continuous range of values, such as the mouse tracking speed or volume control. A slider control, shown in Figure 1-34, consists of a bar that defines the range, and an indicator that shows the current value and provides a user interface for changing the value.

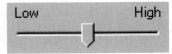

Figure 1-34 Slider control

The user can change the value by using a pointer device, such as a mouse or pen, and dragging the indicator to the new value or selecting the location on the bar that moves the indicator directly to that location. Allow users to move input focus to the slider control using the (TAB) key. For additional keyboard navigation, a static text label can provide an access key. Once the slider control has input focus, the user can change the indicator's position using the arrow keys.

Progress Indicator Controls

A progress indicator or progress control shows a percentage of completion for lengthy operations. The progress indicator, shown in Figure 1-35, is a rectangular control that fills from left to right. When the indicator is half full, the project is 50 percent complete, and when the control is filled, the project is finished.

Figure 1-35 Progress control

A progress indicator can be included in a message box or status bar depending on the mode (modal or background) of the task it represents. The control provides feedback to the user about the status of long operations or background tasks, such as background printing.

Tooltip

A tooltip is a small rectangular pop-up window, shown in Figure 1-36, that includes descriptive text. Applications can use tooltips as a form of help for the user when the pointer is placed over another control, such as a toolbar button.

The tooltip control is most commonly used with toolbars. However, it can be used for other controls on secondary windows. The tooltip is normally displayed at the lower right of the pointer, although this location is automatically adjusted if it does not fit on the screen.

Figure 1-36 Tooltip control

Toolbars and Status Bars

Toolbars and status bars are useful for providing shortcuts to commands and feedback to the user. A toolbar is a panel that contains a set of controls (usually buttons, but other controls can be included). Figure 1-37 shows examples of different types of toolbars. Ribbons, tool boxes, and palettes are also types of toolbars.

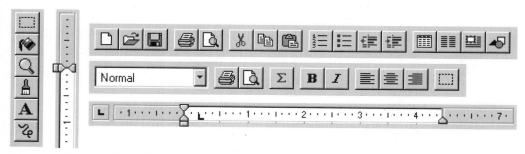

Figure 1-37 Example toolbars

A status bar is a special area within a window, usually at the bottom of the window, that displays information about the current state of what is being viewed in the window or other information, such as menu item help as the user scrolls through the menu. Descriptive text about toolbar items can also be displayed similarly to the way it appears in menu item descriptions. Figure 1-38 shows a variety of status bars.

R1C1		Applications				

Pg 27	Sec1	27/ 36	At 4.7"	Ln8	Col 16	100%

Status Field

Slide 1	New Slide...	Layout...	Template...

Figure 1-38 Status bars

All controls included in toolbars and status bars that do not include label text should include tooltips. Toolbars and status bars should also be designed to provide the user with the option to display or hide toolbars and status bars. Additionally, applications can include the ability to arrange elements in status bars and toolbars.

Applications should include support for the user to change the size of the toolbar buttons to 24×22 and 32×30 pixels through a property sheet accessible from the toolbar pop-up menu. For this support, applications should design graphic images to be 16×16 and 24×24 pixels, respectively. Table 1-7 shows the standard toolbar icons that should be used for common commands.

Table 1-7 Common toolbar buttons

16×16	24×24	Meaning
		New
		Open
		Save
		Print
		Print Preview
		Undo
		Redo
		Cut
		Copy
		Paste
		Delete
		Find
		Replace
		Properties
		Bold
		Italic
		Underline
		What's This? (context-sensitive Help mode)
		Show Help Topics
		Open parent folder
		View as large icons
		View as small icons
		View as list
		View as details
		Region selection tool
		Writing tool (pen)
		Eraser tool (pen)

To avoid confusion and create a common look and feel between applications, use these images only for the function described. When designing new images, follow the conventions supported by the standard system controls.

Visual Design

Users interact with a Windows application via its visual design. The goal of the Windows operating system is to have all applications interact with the user in a similar if not identical manner. If an application follows the design guidelines for a Windows application, its users will be able to focus on the functionality of the application without relearning the user interface for each individual application.

If all applications used the basic controls the system provides in the appropriate manner described earlier in this chapter, this section would not be necessary. However, most applications have some type of user interface feature that is not covered by the basic controls. This is where visual design is important. When designing a unique control or interface for use in an application, these guidelines should be followed so the look and feel of the application will fit within the Windows standard.

It is important to remember when designing custom user interface controls that a graphical user interface needs to be intuitive—the user interface needs to be representative of the operation it performs and not hide functionality that is not standard within Windows.

Border Styles

Almost every window or control has a border that outlines it. There are standards on how these borders appear, based on the type of window or control and its state. Applications can retrieve the colors referenced in this section with the `GetSysColor` function. See Chapter 21, System Information, for more information.

Basic Borders

Windows borders are made up of four basic styles, shown in Figure 1-39 and described in Table 1-8. The Win32 API includes a function that automatically provides these border styles with the correct colors, the `DrawEdge` function. See Chapter 15, Painting and Drawing, for more information.

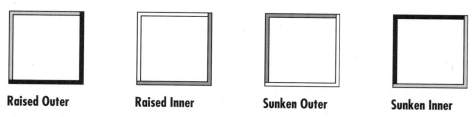

Raised Outer　　　**Raised Inner**　　　**Sunken Outer**　　　**Sunken Inner**

Figure 1-39 Basic border styles

Table 1-8 Basic border style descriptions

Border Style	Description
Raised outer	A single-pixel-width border that uses the button face color for the top and left edges, and the window frame color for the right and bottom edges.
Raised inner	A single-pixel-width border that uses the button highlight color for the top and left edges, and the button shadow color for the right and bottom edges.
Sunken outer	A single-pixel-width border that uses the button shadow color for the top and left edges, and the button highlight color for the right and bottom edges.
Sunken inner	A single-pixel-width border that uses the window frame color for its top and left edges, and the button face color for its right and bottom edges.

Window Borders

All primary and secondary windows, menus, scroll arrow buttons, and other windows where the background color may vary use the window border style. The exception is pop-up windows, such as tooltips and pop-up help windows. The window border style, shown in Figure 1-40, is made up of the raised outer and raised inner basic border styles.

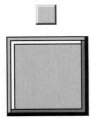

Figure 1-40 Window border style

Button Borders

Button borders differ from window borders in that they have multiple states and the basic border styles do not apply. There are three button borders, shown in Figure 1-41, based on the state of the button.

The Win32 API provides the `DrawFrameControl` function for drawing borders around controls, such as buttons. When a command button is selected, a rectangle is placed around the outer edge of the control and the border remains the same, except it is resized to allow room for the outer rectangle. When the button is pressed, the outer rectangle remains and the border is drawn as pressed and flat. There is no three-dimensional effect when a command button is pressed. For more information on the `DrawFrameControl` function, see Chapter 15, Painting and Drawing.

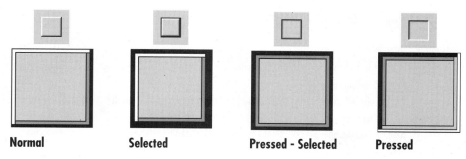

| **Normal** | **Selected** | **Pressed - Selected** | **Pressed** |

Figure 1-41 Button border styles

Field Borders

The field border style, shown in Figure 1-42, is used for editable text boxes, check boxes, drop-down combo boxes, drop-down list boxes, spin boxes, list boxes, wells, and the work area within a window. The field border style is made up of the sunken outer and sunken inner basic border styles. In most cases, except in wells, the interior of the control will use the button highlight color. The interior of a well varies, depending on how the field is used and what is placed in it.

Figure 1-42 Field border style

If the control is showing the status of an item and is noneditable, use the status field border style, shown in Figure 1-43.

Figure 1-43 Status field border style

Grouping Borders

Use group borders for group boxes, menu separators, and other separators. The group border style, shown in Figure 1-44, uses the sunken outer and raised inner basic border styles.

Figure 1-44 Group border style

Visual Control States

When designing the visual aspects of controls, consider the visual appearance of the control in its different states. Standard Windows controls provide specific appearances for these states. For custom controls, use the border style information, covered in the previous section of this chapter, and the information in the following sections to design the controls' appearance.

Pressed State

The pressed appearance of a control tells the user that the button is in the down transition. This occurs when the left mouse button is first pressed and in the down position, a pen touches the screen, or the keyboard key is pressed and is in the down position.

Standard Windows check boxes and option buttons show the pressed state by changing the background color to the button face color. For command buttons, the pressed button border style, shown in Figure 1-41, is used, and the label moves down and right by one pixel. Figure 1-45 shows examples of a check box, option button, and command button in the pressed state.

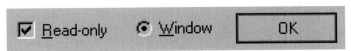

Figure 1-45 Pressed state

Option-Set State

Use the option-set state to indicate that a button's associated value or state is currently set. The state is used on the up transition of the mouse button, pen, or keyboard key and is different from the pressed state appearance. Figure 1-46 shows the option-set appearance for a common check box, option button, and command button.

Figure 1-46 Option-set state

A common use for command buttons that use the option-set appearance is in tool-bars and tool boxes. The command button remains in the pressed appearance, and the face of the button is changed to a checkerboard pattern, using the button face color.

Mixed-Value State

Use the mixed-value state to represent a property or other setting for a set of objects where the value is different across the objects. Leave the field blank for standard controls, except for check boxes and command buttons. Standard check boxes support a special appearance for this state that draws a special mark in the box. For command buttons, use a checkerboard pattern, using the button highlight color. Figure 1-47 shows an example of a check box and command button in the mixed-value state.

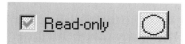

Figure 1-47 Mixed-value state

Unavailable Appearance

Use the unavailable appearance when a control is not available, or disabled, meaning its normal functionality is not available. The disabled appearance is rendered with an engraved appearance, as shown in Figure 1-48.

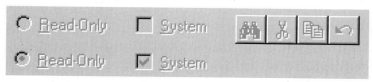

Figure 1-48 Unavailable appearance

If a check box or option button is set, but unavailable, leave the button marked and show the text as unavailable, as Figure 1-48 illustrates.

Input Focus Appearance

To provide a visual indicator of the input focus, use a focus rectangle for controls that do not allow text input. Controls that allow text input show a blinking cursor. A focus rectangle is a dotted outline drawn around the control or control's label, as shown in Figure 1-49. The focus indicator does not change position while the text moves one pixel down and to the right when a command button is pressed.

Figure 1-49 Input focus appearance

The system provides support for drawing the dotted outline input focus indicator, using the `DrawFocusRect` function. See Chapter 15, Painting and Drawing, for more information.

Flat Control Appearance

When a control is included as part of the scrollable area of another control or region, avoid implementing a 3D appearance, because it may not appear correctly against the background. An example of this is a check box in a list box; in order to make the check box appear correctly, the flat check box style, shown in Figure 1-50, is used. The flat appearance is available with the `DrawEdge` and `DrawFrameControl` functions.

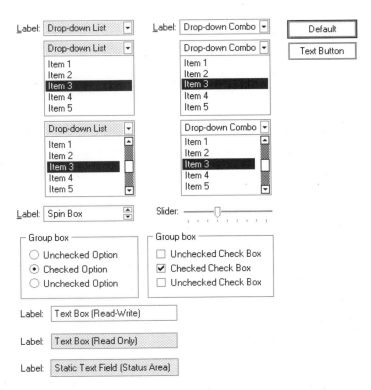

Figure 1-50 Flat appearance controls

System Integration

Windows applications should not only follow the same visual guidelines, but also follow integration guidelines, because users expect Windows applications to integrate and work seamlessly with other applications and the system. This section covers the details about integrating Windows applications with the system to take advantage of the features provided by the system. Some of the conventions and features may not be supported, depending on the version of the operating system that is running. To prevent problems when running on operating systems that do not support all features, the application's functionality should degrade gracefully.

The Registry

Windows uses a central database known as the registry to store application settings and system settings. The registry replaces the INI files found in the Windows 3.x system and is not intended for direct access by the user. However, the user can access the registry with the registry editor, **REGEDIT.EXE** (Windows 95 and Windows NT 4) or **REGEDT32.EXE** (Windows NT 3.5x). This section will cover the types of information and conventions an application should follow when registering information. For more information about the registry and the Win32 API functions that are associated with it, see Chapter 19, The Registry.

State Information

Use the registry to store an application's state information. This is the information that was traditionally stored in INI files in previous versions of Windows. Create subkeys in the **HKEY_LOCAL_MACHINE** and **HKEY_CURRENT_USER** keys that include information about the application. Use the **HKEY_LOCAL_MACHINE** key for settings that apply to the computer or all users of the computer. Use the **HKEY_CURRENT_USER** key for settings that only apply to the current user. Use the following structure in the registry when storing state information. Figures 1-51 and 1-52 show the structure to use for the application. The structure below the version is application dependent.

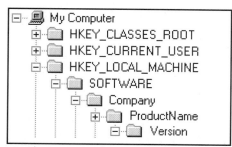

Figure 1-51 Application settings for the computer

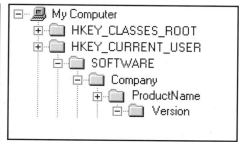

Figure 1-52 Application settings for the user

Save the application's state whenever the user closes the primary window. When the application is restarted, restore the previous window state and location.

If the user shuts down the system, the application can be reopened optionally when the user restarts the system. Do this by adding a **RunOnce** subkey to the registry that contains an entry or entries that will be executed when the system is restarted. The application must support a command line that allows it to restart without user intervention. When the system is restarted, the commands in the **RunOnce** subkey are executed and the subkey is removed. The application can retrieve the state information from the registry to aid in restoring the application to its original state. Figure 1-53 shows an example of the registry structure and a sample entry.

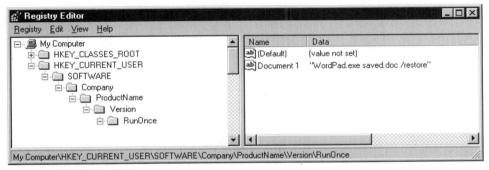

Figure 1-53 **RunOnce** registry entry

If multiple instances need to be reopened, include multiple entries in the **RunOnce** subkey.

A **RunOnce** subkey also can be added under the **HKEY_LOCAL_MACHINE** key. When using this entry, however, the system runs the application before starting up. Use this entry when all users of the computer should be affected. For example, the application may need to start and retrieve the user information to determine how Windows will start.

Path Information

Windows supports per application paths. If an application has a path registered, Windows sets the **PATH** environment to the registered path when it starts your application. To set the application's path, make an entry under the **App Paths** subkey in the **HKEY_LOCAL_MACHINE** key. Create a new key using the name of the application's executable (EXE) file. Under this key, set the **.Default** value to the path of the application's executable file. If other files, such as dynamic link libraries (DLLs), are placed in a separate directory, set a **Path** value to this path. Figure 1-54 shows the registry path entry for the **BACKUP.EXE** application.

These entries are automatically updated by the system if the user moves or renames the application's executable file using the standard system user interface.

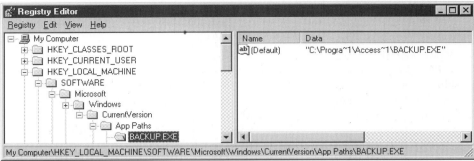

Figure 1-54 Application path information

Any systemwide shared dynamic link libraries should be registered in the subkey **SharedDLL** under the **HKEY_LOCAL_MACHINE** key. If the file already exists, increment the entry's usage count. Figure 1-55 shows the **SharedDLL** section in the registry.

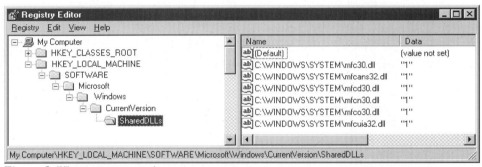

Figure 1-55 **SharedDLL** registry entry

File Extensions

Register the file extensions an application exposes to users for direct use. This allows the user to easily differentiate the different file types by icon and descriptive text. Include at least two entries for every file type registered; a file name–extension key entry and a class-definition key entry. If a file extension is not registered, the default Windows icon is used and the file extension is always displayed.

To register the file name extension, create a subkey under the **HKEY_CLASSES_ROOT** key, using the three-character extension (including the period), and set its value to a unique application identifier. The application identifier should be unique across all extensions registered in the system and is used to match the class-definition key entry. Multiple extensions may have the same application identifier. However, in order to ensure that each file type can be distinguished by the user, define a unique application identifier for each extension.

The class-definition key is the other part to registering a file extension. Create a subkey under the **HKEY_CLASSES_ROOT** key, using the same name used for the application identifier, and assign a type name to the value of the key. The type name is the descriptive name, up to 40 characters, of the file type. Provide, at least, this entry, even if extra information is not registered. This provides a better label with which users can identify the file type.

Additional information can be registered in the class-definition key, such as the OLE class information, for the file type. Applications that support OLE also include a short type name entry in the registry. The short type name is the data type portion of the full type name. For example, Worksheet would be the short name for Microsoft Excel 5.0 Worksheet. Use the short type name in drop-down and pop-up menus and other places where the long name is not reasonable. To register the short type name, create a subkey under the application's registered **CLSID** subkey (under the **CLSID** key). Figure 1-56 shows the entries necessary to register the short name.

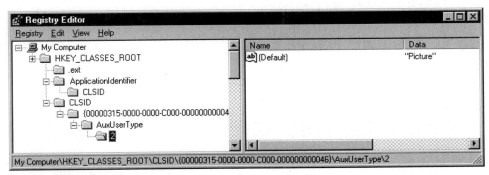

Figure 1-56 Short type name

If a short type name is not available for an object because it is not registered, use the full type name instead. All controls that display the full type name must allocate enough space for 40 characters. By comparison, the short type name requires only 15 characters.

Creation Support

Windows 95 and Windows NT 4 support the creation of new objects in system containers such as folders and the desktop. Register information for each file type that the system should include as a creation object. The registered type will appear on the New command for a folder and the desktop.

Create a **ShellNew** subkey under the extension's subkey in the **HKEY_CLASSES_ROOT** key. Create a value under the **ShellNew** subkey with one of the four methods listed in Table 1-9 for creating a file with the extension.

Table 1-9 Creation values

Value Name	Value	Result
NullFile	""	Creates a new empty file.
Data	Binary data	Creates a new file containing the specified binary data.
FileName	Path	Creates a new file as a copy of the specified file.
Command	Path	Executes the command. Use to run a custom application, such as a wizard, that creates the file.

Registering Icons

The system uses the registry to determine which icon to display for a specific file. An icon can be registered for every data file type that an application supports and the user may need to easily distinguish. When registering icons, provide a 16×16-pixel (16-color) and 32×32-pixel (16-color) image.

Create a **DefaultIcon** subkey under the application identifier of the file type and set the value to the icon file (an EXE, DLL, or ICO file) and icon index. If the icon index is negative, it corresponds to the icon resource identifier. If it is positive or zero, it is the icon position in the file. The icon in position zero should be the application's icon if the icon file is an EXE, so the position will generally be greater than zero. Figure 1-57 shows the **DefaultIcon** entry for a sound file.

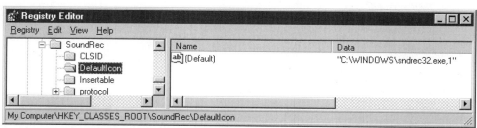

Figure 1-57 **DefaultIcon** registry entry

Registering Commands

Windows 95 and Windows NT 4 allow the user to access commands for icons, including Send To, Cut, Copy, Paste, Create Shortcut, Delete, Rename, and Properties, provided by their container. Additional commands may be added for a specific file type by registering the commands for the file type in the registry. These commands, known as verbs, include Open, Edit, Play, and Print. You can also add other commands that apply specifically to the file type, such as a What's This? command.

To add commands for a file type, create a **Shell** subkey under the
HKEY_CLASSES_ROOT key, a subkey for each verb, and a **Command** subkey for each command name. The following shows the hierarchy for registering commands:

```
HKEY_CLASSES_ROOT
   ApplicationIdentifier
      Shell [ = default verb [,verb2 [,..]] ]
         Verb [ = Menu Name ]
            Command = Path [parameters]
            ddeexec = DDE command string
               Application = DDE Application Name
               Topic = DDE Topic name
```

Windows 95 and Windows NT 4 support a set of common verbs, Open, Print, Find, and Explore, that automatically receive menu names and access key assignments. The menu names are localized for the international version of Windows currently loaded. If a file type has additional verbs registered, supply the appropriate menu names and access keys for the specific version of Windows.

Verbs can support execution by providing the path for the application or a dynamic data exchange (DDE) command string with the appropriate command-line switches. Use the **%1** parameter as the placeholder for the file the user has selected when setting up the command lines. Each verb can have its own command. One application can do the Open command, and another can carry out the Print command, or the verbs can use the same application.

Registering OLE Objects

The registry is the primary storage location of OLE object definitions. To register an OLE object, create a **CLSID** subkey under the **HKEY_CLASSES_ROOT*<ApplicationIdentifier>*** key for the file type. Set the value of this subkey to the OLE object's unique identifier. The second part of registering an OLE object is to create a subkey of the object's class identifier under the **HKEY_CLASSES_ROOT*<CLSID>*** key. Create additional subkeys to define the OLE server and other OLE object information under this subkey.

Installation

When installing applications, these guidelines will help in deciding where to place application files and how to appropriately install shared files. These guidelines are designed to help reduce clutter on the user's disk and shelter the user from irrelevant files when browsing for a file.

Placement of Files

Avoid placing application files in the Windows directory or its system subdirectory. Placing files in these directories can cause name conflict problems and clutter the directories to the point of degrading performance. When installing an application, such as My Application, create a directory, normally the name of the application, in the **Program Files** directory or the directory of the user's choice. Use the **ProgramFilesDir** value in the **HKEY_LOCAL_MACHINE\SOFTWARE\Microsoft\Windows\CurrentVersion** key, because the actual **Program Files** directory may not have the same name on all machines.

Place only the files the user directly works with, such as the executable file, in the primary install directory. Create a **System** subdirectory, in which to place all the application's support files, such as DLLs and help (HLP) files . Hide all the support files and the **System** directory, and register the path in the **App Paths** subkey, as described earlier in this chapter.

If the application uses a shared DLL, such as Microsoft's **VBRUN300.DLL**, place it in the **System** directory for Windows. Follow these steps when installing a shared file:

1. Verify that the file is not already present before copying.

2. If the file exists, check the file version, size, and date to determine whether it is the same version as the one being installed or an older one. If it is the same, increment the usage count for the corresponding registry entry. If the existing file is newer, do not overwrite it but increment the usage count for the corresponding registry entry. If the existing file is older, prompt the user before overwriting. Again, increment the usage count for the corresponding registry entry.

3. If the file does not exist, copy it to the directory and create the appropriate entry in the registry with a usage count of one (**1**).

If a file is shared by a set of applications, but not across the system, create a subdirectory using the application name in the **Common Files** subdirectory of the **Program Files** subdirectory. Use the **CommonFilesDir** value under the **CurrentVersion** subkey under the **HKEY_LOCAL_MACHINE** key as the actual **Common Files** subdirectory. Make sure that shared files are upwardly compatible before installing new versions in the shared directory.

When installing on a shared network drive, use the conventional MS-DOS (8.3) names rather than long file names. This eliminates compatibility problems with networks that do not support long file names.

Do not use the **AUTOEXEC.BAT** or **CONFIG.SYS** files for loading drivers or setting the path to the application. Windows now supports automatic loading of device drivers, and the path entry in the registry replaces the need for the path statement in the **AUTOEXEC.BAT**. Also, do not make entries in the **WIN.INI** file. Instead, use the registry for these settings.

Register all the data types supported by the application in the registry along with the icons for the data types. Also, register additional application information, such as information required to enable printing the data types. See the section The Registry earlier in this chapter for details about the individual registry entries.

Application Accessibility

When installing an application, create a shortcut icon to the main application executable in the Start Menu\Programs folder located in the Windows directory. This adds the entry to the Programs submenu of the Start button. Do not create shortcuts to all files and programs that accompany the application, because this clutters the Start menu. When installing a "suite" of applications, create a subfolder of Programs and place a shortcut to all the main applications in the folder. Avoid creating a subfolder under Programs that contains a single icon.

The Windows 3.x DDE method of communicating with the Program Manager to create groups and add icons is still supported for backward compatibility. However, this is not recommended for applications installed on Windows 95, Windows NT 4, and later releases. If the same installation program is used for both Windows 95 and previous versions of Windows NT, it will have to work using the DDE communications to the Program Manager when running on Windows NT.

Uninstalling

To facilitate the user's removing an application, provide an uninstall process that removes the application, its support files, and settings in the registry. The uninstall program should follow these guidelines:

- Display a window that provides the user with progress feedback during the uninstall process. Optionally, the uninstall program can also have a "silent" mode that does not display any feedback.

- Display messages for any errors the uninstall encounters.

- When uninstalling, decrement the usage count for shared components, such as DLLs. If the usage count is zero, give the user the option to remove the shared component (but equip the application with a warning that other applications may not work afterward).

In Windows 95 and Windows NT 4, register the uninstall program, so it will appear in the Add/Remove Program utility's uninstall list. This feature is not supported on previous versions of Windows NT. Add the following entry in the registry:

```
HKEY_LOCAL_MACHINE
    SOFTWARE
        Microsoft
            Windows
                CurrentVersion
                    Uninstall
                        ApplicationName
                                DisplayName = Application Name
                                UninstallString = path [switches]
```

The `DisplayName` and `UninstallString` keys must be complete in order for the uninstall program to appear in the Add/Remove Program utility.

Supporting Applications on a Network

If the application is a client/server application that multiple users can access, create separate installation programs. One installation program will allow the system administrator to install the server portion of the application. The other installation program is for the clients. Design the client software so that it will self-configure when the user starts it. This allows the application to be deployed over a network.

Do not assume that the installation program can store information in the main Windows directory on the server. Windows itself may be on a server, and the user may not have sufficient privilege to write to the Windows directory. Also, shared application files should not be stored in the "home" directory provided for the user.

The installation program should support Universal Naming Convention (UNC) paths. Also, use UNC paths for shortcut icons installed in the Start Menu.

Auto Play

When the user inserts removable media that supports insertion notification, such as CD-ROM, PCMCIA hard disks, or flash ROM cards, and a file automatically runs, it is known as auto play. This feature is becoming common on CD-ROM software and is easily supported. To support auto play, place a file named `AUTORUN.INF` in the root directory of the removable media.

The `AUTORUN.INF` file is set up similarly to an INI file. To define the statement that executes, use the following form:

```
[autorun]
open = filename
```

If no path is specified for the file name, the system looks for the file in the root of the inserted media. If the file is located in a subdirectory, include the path as part of the file name.

Because the file is executed when the media is inserted, design the specified file to provide visual feedback quickly to confirm that the media was successfully inserted. If the automated process is time-consuming, provide the user with a means to cancel the process. Also, do not rely on this process to execute, because it can be disabled in the system.

The most common usage for this feature is installation programs. However, do not write files to the user's hard disk without first confirming with the user. Minimize the amount of storage required on the user's hard disk by using the inserted media for the bulk of the files.

An icon for the inserted media can be defined by including the following statement in the `AUTORUN.INF` file:

```
icon = filename
```

The file name can be an icon (`.ICO`), a bitmap (`.BMP`), an executable (`.EXE`), or a dynamic link library (`.DLL`). If the file contains more than one icon, specify the icon with a number after the file name just as you do when registering icons in the registry for a file type (described earlier in this chapter). If an absolute path for the icon file is needed, use the following form to define the icon:

```
defaulticon = path
```

The system will automatically provide a pop-up menu with the AutoPlay command as the default. Add additional commands to the pop-up menu using the following form:

```
shell\verb\command = filename
shell\verb = Menu Item Name
```

For example, the following shows how to add a Read Me First item to the menu:

```
shell\readme\command = notepad.exe readme.txt
shell\verb = Read &Me First
```

The default command can be changed from AutoPlay to another command. This changes the command that is executed when the user double-clicks on the icon. Use the following form to change the default command:

```
shell = verb
```

THE WIN32 API

The Win32 API (Application Programming Interface) is the common programming interface for the Microsoft Windows 95 and Windows NT operating systems. The use of a common API allows applications to be developed once and deployed on multiple operating systems. Because Microsoft Windows NT can also be hosted on multiple hardware platforms, Microsoft has released optimizing compilers for each of the hardware platforms that will optimize a Win32 application for the specific target hardware. Microsoft also has ported the Win32 API to the Apple Macintosh and provided a cross-compiler for Visual C++.

Microsoft's commitment to the Win32 API means a lighter work load for a developer providing applications across multiple platforms. Also, new versions of Microsoft's existing operating systems, as well as its new operating systems, such as Windows CE, will be based on the Win32 API, so Win32-based applications should work with minimal or no modification.

This chapter covers the advantages of the Win32 API, besides the obvious, and the issues in converting Windows 3.x applications to Win32.

Advantages of Win32

Windows 3.x applications are, for the most part, 16-bit applications with support for accessing memory using the Windows memory manager. Some Windows 3.x applications are 32-bit, but do not have the advantage of the API's being designed for 32-bit applications. As a result, a 32-bit Windows 3.x application is uncommon and only used by developers requiring truly optimum performance.

When Microsoft released Windows NT, it also released a subset of the Win32 API known as Win32s. Win32s was designed to give developers the ability to create a Win32 application that would run on Windows NT and Windows 3.x. The problem with Win32s is that it cannot make up for the deficiencies in the underlying operating system and does not give the application full access to the Win32 API. As a result, Win32s applications are limited in their support for Win32 features, such as multi-threading. Microsoft has also quit supporting Win32s as an option in its newest compiler, Visual C++ 4.2, and all future versions of this compiler. This indicates that

Microsoft is clearly pushing developers to develop applications that are full Win32 applications.

With the release of Microsoft Windows 95, developers can take advantage of the majority of the Win32 API. The main difference between Windows NT and Windows 95 versions of the Win32 API is that Windows 95 lacks the advanced security that Windows NT provides. This should not be a surprise, because Windows 95 shouldn't have support for APIs that it cannot use. Actually, the Windows 95 version of Win32 does have stubs for the functions it does not support. This allows an application to gracefully run on both Windows 95 and Windows NT without recompiling.

The Win32 API has many advantages, some obvious and others that are not so obvious. The following lists major advantages that applications have when developed with the Win32 API and a 32-bit compiler (such as Microsoft's Visual C++).

■ True multithreaded applications. Win32 applications support true preemptive multitasking when running on Windows 95 and Windows NT.

■ 32-bit linear memory. Applications no longer have limits imposed by segmented memory. All memory pointers are based on the applicationís virtual address and are represented as a 32-bit integer.

■ No memory model. The memory models (small, medium, large, etc.) have no meaning in the 32-bit environment. This means there is no need for near and far pointers, as all pointers can be thought of as far.

■ A well-designed Win32 application is generally faster. Win32 applications execute more efficiently than 16-bit applications.

■ Common API for all platforms. The Win32 API is supported on Windows 95, Windows NT on all supported hardware, Windows CE, and the Apple Macintosh.

Converting 16-Bit Windows Applications

When developing new applications, it is simple to implement and take advantage of the new features of the Win32 API. However, when converting an existing application from Windows 3.x to the Win32 API to run on Windows 95 and Windows NT, several issues need to be addressed. This section covers the main "gotchas" to keep in mind when converting these applications.

Overall, the Win32 API was designed to be as compatible as possible with earlier versions of Windows. However, a few basic changes for Win32 applications will cause problems if not dealt with during the conversion. The following changes need to be addressed in most applications:

■ All pointers are 32 bits wide and are no longer near or far. No assumptions can be made about segmented memory, since it does not apply in the Win32 environment. Some of the items that have changed to 32 bits are pointers, window handles, handles to objects, and graphics coordinates. The graphics coordinates are 32-bit in the API. However, when executing on Windows 95, the graphics coordinates are only meaningful in the first 16 bits.

- Assembly source code is different for Win32 applications and must either be rewritten or replaced with standard source code, such as C or C++.

- Direct hardware calls and MS-DOS calls are not supported.

- Local heaps are obsolete. Because local heaps are near, and near no longer has a meaning, the global and local heaps are the same.

- Several functions are either replaced or not implemented in the Win32 API, as described in Table 2-1.

- The WPARAM is no longer a 16-bit value. As a result, several messages have changed the meaning of the WPARAM and LPARAM parameters. Table 2-2 lists the messages that need to be fixed.

- The window and class data stored with the SetWindowWord and SetClassWord functions has changed. Because the information now requires a 32-bit value, the SetWindowLong and SetClassLong functions now store most of the information.

Obsolete and Deleted Functions

The Win32 API adds several functions to the Windows 3.x API. However, many of the Windows 3.x functions are no longer supported, are replaced with new functions, or are obsolete. Many of the functions that are replaced with newer functions are still available in the Win32 API. However, they are only to help in converting to the Win32 API. You're advised to convert all old function calls to newer ones. Table 2-1 lists the functions that need to be addressed in converting to the Win32 API.

Table 2-1 Function changes in Win32

Function	Change That Occurred
_hread	ReadFile replaces this function, which is included only for compatibility.
_hwrite	WriteFile replaces this function, which is included only for compatibility.
_lclose	CloseHandle replaces this function, which is included only for compatibility.
_lcreat	CreateFile replaces this function, which is included only for compatibility.
_lopen	CreateFile replaces this function, which is included only for compatibility.
_lread	ReadFile replaces this function, which is included only for compatibility.
_lseek	SetFilePointer replaces this function, which is included only for compatibility.
_lwrite	WriteFile replaces this function, which is included only for compatibility.
AccessResource	This function is not implemented. Use the LoadResource, LockResource, and FindResource functions.
AllocDStoCSAlias	This function is obsolete.
AllocResource	This function is not implemented. Use the LoadResource, LockResource, and FindResource functions.
AllocSelector	This function is not implemented. Use the VirtualLock and VirtualUnlock functions.
AnsiLower	This function is obsolete. Use the CharLower function.
AnsiLowerBuff	This function is obsolete. Use the CharLowerBuff function.

continued on next page

continued from previous page

Function	Change That Occurred
AnsiNext	This function is obsolete. Use the `CharNext` function.
AnsiPrev	This function is obsolete. Use the `CharPrev` function.
AnsiToOem	This function is obsolete. Use the `CharToOem` function.
AnsiToOemBuff	This function is obsolete. Use the `CharToOemBuff` function.
AnsiUpper	This function is obsolete. Use the `CharUpper` function.
AnsiUpperBuff	This function is obsolete. Use the `CharUpperBuff` function.
Catch	This function is not implemented. Structured exception handling is built into Win32.
ChangeMenu	This function is replaced by the `AppendMenu`, `InsertMenu`, `ModifyMenu`, and `RemoveMenu` functions.
ChangeSelector	This function is not implemented. Use the `VirtualLock` and `VirtualUnlock` functions.
CloseMetaFile	Use the `CloseEnhMetaFile` function and enhanced metafiles.
CloseSound	This function is not implemented.
CopyLZFile	This function is obsolete. Use the `LZCopy` function.
CopyMetaFile	Use the `CopyEnhMetaFile` function and enhanced metafiles.
CountVoiceNotes	This function is not implemented.
CreateMetaFile	Use the `CreateEnhMetaFile` function and enhanced metafiles.
DefHookProc	This function is obsolete. Use the `CallNextHookEx` function.
DefineHandleTable	This function is obsolete and has no effect.
DeleteMetaFile	Use the `DeleteEnhMetaFile` function and enhanced metafiles.
DlgDirSelect	This function is not implemented. Use the `DlgDirSelectEx` function.
DlgDirSelectComboBox	This function is not implemented. Use the `DlgDirSelectComboBoxEx` function.
DOS3Call	This function is not implemented. Win32 applications cannot access MS-DOS directly.
DragQueryDropFileInfo	This function is obsolete and only included for compatibility.
DragQueryInfo	This function is obsolete and only included for compatibility.
EnumFonts	`EnumFontFamilies` replaces this function, which is only included for compatibility.
EnumMetaFile	Use the `EnumEnhMetaFile` function and enhanced metafiles.
EnumTaskWindows	This function is obsolete. Use the `EnumThreadWindows` function.
ExtDeviceMode	This function is not implemented. Use the `DocumentProperties` function.
FixBrushOrgEx	This function is obsolete and always returns `FALSE`.
FreeModule	This function is obsolete. Use the `FreeLibrary` function.
FreeProcInstance	This function is obsolete and has no meaning.
FreeResource	This function is obsolete. It is not necessary to free loaded resources.
FreeSelector	This function is not implemented. Use the `VirtualLock` and `VirtualUnlock` functions.
GetAspectRatioFilter	This function is not implemented. Use the `GetAspectRatioFilterEx` function.
GetAtomHandle	This function is not implemented. Use the `GetAtomName` function.
GetBitmapBits	`GetDIBits` replaces this function, which is included only for compatibility.
GetBitmapDimension	This function is not implemented. Use the `GetBitmapDimensionEx` function.
GetBrushOrg	This function is not implemented. Use the `GetBrushOrgEx` function.
GetCharWidth	`GetCharWidth32` replaces this function, which is included only for compatibility.
GetCodeHandle	This function is not implemented. Use the `VirtualLock` and `VirtualUnlock` functions.
GetCodeInfo	This function is not implemented.
GetCurrentPDB	This function is not implemented. Use the `GetCommandLine` and `GetEnvironmentStrings` functions.

Function	Change That Occurred
GetCurrentPosition	This function is not implemented. Use the GetCurrentPositionEx function.
GetCurrentTask	This function is not implemented. Use the GetCurrentThread or GetCurrentProcess function.
GetDCOrg	This function is not implemented. Use the GetDCOrg function.
GetDOSEnvironment	This function is not implemented. Use the GetEnvironmentStrings function.
GetFileResource	This function is not implemented.
GetFileResourceSize	This function is not implemented.
GetFreeSpace	This function is obsolete. Use the GlobalMemoryStatus function.
GetFreeSystemResources	This function is obsolete and not implemented.
GetInstanceData	This function is not implemented. Win32 applications have their own address space.
GetKBCodePage	GetOEMCP replaces this function, which is included only for compatibility.
GetMetaFile	Use the GetEnhMetaFile function and enhanced metafiles.
GetMetaFileBits	Use the GetEnhMetaFileBits function and enhanced metafiles.
GetMetaFileBitsEx	Use the GetEnhMetaFileBits function and enhanced metafiles.
GetModuleUsage	This function is not implemented. Win32 applications have their own address space.
GetNumTasks	This function is not implemented.
GetPrivateProfileInt	Provided for compatibility. Use the registry to store information.
GetPrivateProfileSection	Provided for compatibility. Use the registry to store information.
GetPrivateProfileSectionNames	Provided for compatibility. Use the registry to store information.
GetPrivateProfileString	Provided for compatibility. Use the registry to store information.
GetPrivateProfileStruct	Provided for compatibility. Use the registry to store information.
GetProfileInt	Provided for compatibility. Use the registry to store information.
GetProfileSection	Provided for compatibility. Use the registry to store information.
GetProfileString	Provided for compatibility. Use the registry to store information.
GetSysModalWindow	This function is not implemented.
GetTempDrive	This function is not implemented. Use the GetTempPath function.
GetTextExtent	This function is not implemented. Use the GetTextExtentPoint32 function.
GetTextExtentPoint	GetTextExtentPoint32 replaces this function, which is included only for compatibility.
GetThresholdEvent	This function is not implemented.
GetThresholdStatus	This function is not implemented.
GetViewportExt	This function is not implemented. Use the GetViewportExtEx function.
GetViewportOrg	This function is not implemented. Use the GetViewportOrgEx function.
GetWindowExt	This function is not implemented. Use the GetWindowExtEx function.
GetWindowOrg	This function is not implemented. Use the GetWindowOrgEx function.
GetWindowsDir	This function is not implemented. Use the GetWindowsDirectory function.
GetWindowTask	This function is not implemented. Use the GetWindowThreadProcessId function.
GetWinFlags	This function is not implemented. Use the GetSystemInfo function.
GlobalCompact	This function is obsolete and has no meaning.
GlobalDosAlloc	This function is not implemented. Use the VirtualLock and VirtualUnlock functions.
GlobalDosFree	This function is not implemented. Use the VirtualLock and VirtualUnlock functions.
GlobalFix	This function is obsolete and has no meaning.
GlobalRUNewest	This function is obsolete and has no meaning.
GlobalRUOldest	This function is obsolete and has no meaning.

continued on next page

continued from previous page

Function	Change That Occurred
GlobalNotify	This function is not implemented. Use the `GlobalFlags` function.
GlobalPageLock	This function is not implemented. Use the `VirtualLock` and `VirtualUnlock` functions.
GlobalPageUnlock	This function is not implemented. Use the `VirtualLock` and `VirtualUnlock` functions.
GlobalUnfix	This function is obsolete and has no meaning.
GlobalUnWire	This function is obsolete and has no meaning.
GlobalWire	This function is obsolete and has no meaning.
IsBadHugeReadPtr	This function is equivalent to the `IsBadReadPtr` function and is included only for compatibility.
IsBadHugeWritePtr	This function is equivalent to the `IsBadWritePtr` function and is included only for compatibility.
IsTask	This function is not implemented.
LimitEmsPages	This function is obsolete and has no meaning.
LoadModule	`CreateProcess` replaces this function, which is included only for compatibility.
LocalCompact	This function is not implemented.
LocalInit	This function is not implemented.
LocalShrink	This function is not implemented.
LockSegment	This function is not implemented.
LZDone	This function is obsolete. Use the `LZOpenFile` function.
LZStart	This function is obsolete. Use the `LZCopy` function.
MakeProcInstance	This function is obsolete. Win32 functions can be called directly.
MoveTo	This function is not implemented. Use the `MoveToEx` function.
NetConnectionEnum	`WNetEnumResource` replaces this function, which is included only for compatibility.
NetShareEnum	`WNetEnumResource` replaces this function, which is included only for compatibility.
NetUseAdd	`WNetAddConnection2` replaces this function, which is included only for compatibility.
NetUseDel	`WNetCancelConnection2` replaces this function, which is included only for compatibility.
NetUseEnum	`WNetEnumResource` replaces this function, which is included only for compatibility.
NetUseGetInfo	`WNetGetConnection` replaces this function, which is included only for compatibility.
OemToAnsi	This function is obsolete. Use the `OemToChar` function.
OemToAnsiBuff	This function is obsolete. Use the `OemToCharBuff` function.
OffsetViewportOrg	This function is not implemented. Use the `OffsetViewportOrgEx` function.
OffsetWindowOrg	This function is not implemented. Use the `OffsetWindowOrgEx` function.
OpenFile	`CreateFile` replaces this function, which is included only for compatibility.
OpenSound	This function is not implemented.
PlayMetaFile	Use the `PlayEnhMetaFile` function and enhanced metafiles.
PlayMetaFileRecord	Use the `PlayEnhMetaFileRecord` function and enhanced metafiles.
PostAppMessage	`PostThreadMessage` replaces this function, which is included only for compatibility.
ProfClear	This function is not implemented.
ProfFinish	This function is not implemented.
ProfFlush	This function is not implemented.
ProfInsChk	This function is not implemented.
ProfSampRate	This function is not implemented.
ProfSetup	This function is not implemented.
ProfStart	This function is not implemented.
ProfStop	This function is not implemented.
RegCreateKey	`RegCreateKeyEx` replaces this function, which is included only for compatibility.

Function	Change That Occurred
RegEnumKey	RegEnumKeyEx replaces this function, which is included only for compatibility.
RegOpenKey	RegOpenKeyEx replaces this function, which is included only for compatibility.
RegQueryValue	RegQueryValueEx replaces this function, which is included only for compatibility.
RegSetValue	RegSetValueEx replaces this function, which is included only for compatibility.
ScaleViewportExt	This function is not implemented. Use the ScaleViewportExtEx function.
ScaleWindowExt	This function is not implemented. Use the ScaleWindowExtEx function.
ScrollWindow	ScrollWindowEx replaces this function, which is included only for compatibility.
SetBitmapBits	SetDIBits replaces this function, which is included only for compatibility.
SetBitmapDimension	This function is not implemented. Use the SetBitmapDimensionEx function.
SetBrushOrg	This function is not implemented. Use the SetBrushOrgEx function.
SetMessageQueue	This function is obsolete and has no meaning.
SetMetaFileBits	This function is not implemented. If needed, use the SetMetaFileBitsEx function.
SetMetaFileBitsEx	Use the SetEnhMetaFileBits function and enhanced metafiles.
SetResourceHandler	This function is not implemented. Calculated resources are not supported in Win32.
SetScrollPos	SetScrollInfo replaces this function, which is included only for compatibility.
SetScrollRange	SetScrollInfo replaces this function, which is included only for compatibility.
SetSoundNoise	This function is not implemented.
SetSwapAreaSize	This function is obsolete and has no meaning.
SetSysModalWindow	This function is not implemented. System-modal windows are not supported.
SetViewportExt	This function is not implemented. Use the SetViewportExtEx function.
SetViewportOrg	This function is not implemented. Use the SetViewportOrgEx function.
SetVoiceAccent	This function is not implemented.
SetVoiceEnvelope	This function is not implemented.
SetVoiceNote	This function is not implemented.
SetVoiceQueueSize	This function is not implemented.
SetVoiceSound	This function is not implemented.
SetVoiceThreshold	This function is not implemented.
SetWindowExt	This function is not implemented. Use the SetWindowExtEx function.
SetWindowOrg	This function is not implemented. Use the SetWindowOrgEx function.
SetWindowsHook	This function is not implemented. Use the SetWindowsHookEx function.
StartSound	This function is not implemented.
StopSound	This function is not implemented.
SwitchStackBack	This function is not implemented.
SwitchStackTo	This function is not implemented.
SyncAllVoices	This function is not implemented.
Throw	This function is not implemented. Structured exception handling is build into Win32.
UnhookWindowsHook	This function is obsolete. Use the UnhookWindowsHookEx function.
UnlockResource	This function is obsolete. It is not necessary to unlock resources.
UnlockSegment	This function is obsolete and has no meaning.
WaitSoundState	This function is not implemented.
WinExec	CreateProcess replaces this function, which is included only for compatibility.
WritePrivateProfileSection	Provided for compatibility. Use the registry to store information.
WritePrivateProfileString	Provided for compatibility. Use the registry to store information.

continued on next page

continued from previous page

Function	Change That Occurred
WritePrivateProfileStruct	Provided for compatibility. Use the registry to store information.
WriteProfileSection	Provided for compatibility. Use the registry to store information.
WriteProfileString	Provided for compatibility. Use the registry to store information.
Yield	This function is obsolete and has no meaning.

The functions that are no longer implemented are functions that are no longer needed; they either have been replaced with one or more new functions or have been moved to more specialized APIs. For example, all of the sound functions are no longer implemented in the Win32 API; they have been replaced by the Multimedia API.

Other functions are simply obsolete because they only existed to deal with the limitations of Windows 3.x, such as the segmented memory structure or cooperative processing and tasks. With the new memory structure in a Win32 application, there is no need for many of the memory functions that Windows 3.x needed to help manage the segmented memory. Windows 3.x also used cooperative processing between applications, which has been replaced by threads executed in a preemptive multitasking environment.

The profile functions, such as **GetProfileString** and **WriteProfileString**, are listed in Table 2-1. Even though they are still valid, Win32 applications should use the registry in place of initialization (INI) files. The functions are still implemented for compatibility with Windows 3.x applications and the INI files they use.

Changes in Messages

Some messages in the Win32 API have changed the meaning of the **WPARAM** and **LPARAM** parameters to accommodate the larger handle and graphics coordinates. All of the messages listed in Table 2-2 need to be changed to properly use the new parameters when used within a Windows 3.x application. Application-defined messages also should be examined to make sure the parameters are properly used, given the new sizes.

Table 2-2 Message changes

Message	Changes
EM_GETSEL	WPARAM and LPARAM have changed.
EM_LINESCROLL	WPARAM and LPARAM have changed.
EM_SETSEL	WPARAM and LPARAM have changed.
WM_ACTIVATE	WPARAM and LPARAM have changed.
WM_CHANGECBCHAIN	WPARAM and LPARAM have changed.
WM_CHARTOITEM	WPARAM and LPARAM have changed.
WM_COMMAND	WPARAM and LPARAM have changed.
WM_CTLCOLOR	Replaced by WM_CTLCOLOR<type> messages (WM_CTLCOLORBTN, etc.).
WM_DDE_ACK	WPARAM and LPARAM have changed.
WM_DDE_ADVISE	WPARAM and LPARAM have changed.

Message	Changes
WM_DDE_DATA	WPARAM and LPARAM have changed.
WM_DDE_EXECUTE	WPARAM and LPARAM have changed.
WM_DDE_POKE	WPARAM and LPARAM have changed.
WM_HSCROLL	WPARAM and LPARAM have changed.
WM_MDIACTIVATE	WPARAM and LPARAM have changed.
WM_MDISETMENU	WPARAM and LPARAM have changed.
WM_MENUCHAR	WPARAM and LPARAM have changed.
WM_MENUSELECT	WPARAM and LPARAM have changed.
WM_PARENTNOTIFY	WPARAM and LPARAM have changed.
WM_VKEYTOITEM	WPARAM and LPARAM have changed.
WM_VSCROLL	WPARAM and LPARAM have changed.

Segmented to Linear Memory

Win32 applications use 32-bit linear memory blocks. Each application has a virtual address space of 2GB on which application pointers are based. In most circumstances, this does not cause a problem. However, some applications expect segmented memory and use pointer manipulation based on that structure. All direct manipulation of segmented memory must be removed and replaced with simple 32-bit memory allocations.

Sample Program

The program source code shown in Listing 2-1 is a basic Win32 application that is portable to Windows 95 and Windows NT. This is the base application on which all examples listed in this book are built. This application is compatible with Microsoft's Visual C++. However, other 32-bit compilers that can generate a Win32 application should work as well.

Listing 2-1 Example program

GENERIC.H
```
#define IDM_EXIT          100
#define IDM_TEST          200
#define IDM_ABOUT         300


LRESULT CALLBACK WndProc(HWND, UINT, WPARAM, LPARAM);
LRESULT CALLBACK About  (HWND, UINT, WPARAM, LPARAM);
```
GENERIC.RC
```
#include "windows.h"
#include "generic.h"
```

continued on next page

continued from previous page

```
#include "winver.h"

MYAPP                       ICON    DISCARDABLE     "GENERIC.ICO"

MYAPP MENU DISCARDABLE
BEGIN
    POPUP "&File"
    BEGIN
        MENUITEM "E&xit",                   IDM_EXIT
    END
    MENUITEM "&Test!",                      IDM_TEST
    POPUP "&Help"
    BEGIN
        MENUITEM "&About MyApp...",         IDM_ABOUT
    END
END


1 VERSIONINFO
 FILEVERSION 3,3,0,0
 PRODUCTVERSION 3,3,0,0
 FILEFLAGSMASK 0x3fL
#ifdef _DEBUG
 FILEFLAGS 0xbL
#else
 FILEFLAGS 0xaL
#endif
 FILEOS 0X4L
 FILETYPE 0x1L
 FILESUBTYPE 0x0L
BEGIN
    BLOCK "StringFileInfo"
    BEGIN
        BLOCK "040904B0"
        BEGIN
            VALUE "CompanyName", "Your Company\0"
            VALUE "FileDescription", "My Application\0"
            VALUE "FileVersion", "1.0\0"
            VALUE "InternalName", "MyApp\0"
            VALUE "LegalCopyright", "Copyright \251 Your Company. 1995\0"
            VALUE "LegalTrademarks", "Microsoft\256 is a registered trademark of
                                Microsoft Corporation. Windows (TM) is a
                                trademark of Microsoft Corporation\0"
```

```
               VALUE "OriginalFilename", "\0"
               VALUE "ProductName", "MyApp\0"
               VALUE "ProductVersion", "1.0\0"
           END
      END
      BLOCK "VarFileInfo"
      BEGIN
           VALUE "Translation", 0x409, 1200
      END
END
```

GENERIC.C

```c
#include <windows.h>
#include "generic.h"



HINSTANCE hInst;    // current instance

LPCTSTR lpszAppName = "MyApp";
LPCTSTR lpszTitle   = "My Application";



int APIENTRY WinMain( HINSTANCE hInstance, HINSTANCE hPrevInstance,
                      LPTSTR lpCmdLine, int nCmdShow)
{
    MSG         msg;
    HWND        hWnd;
    WNDCLASSEX wc;

    // In Windows 95 or Windows NT the hPrevInstance will always be NULL.
    //.................................................................
    wc.style          = CS_HREDRAW | CS_VREDRAW;
    wc.lpfnWndProc    = (WNDPROC)WndProc;
    wc.cbClsExtra     = 0;
    wc.cbWndExtra     = 0;
    wc.hInstance      = hInstance;
    wc.hIcon          = LoadIcon (hInstance, lpszAppName);
    wc.hCursor        = LoadCursor(NULL, IDC_ARROW);
    wc.hbrBackground  = (HBRUSH)(COLOR_WINDOW+1);
    wc.lpszMenuName   = lpszAppName;
    wc.lpszClassName  = lpszAppName;
    wc.cbSize         = sizeof(WNDCLASSEX);
    wc.hIconSm        = LoadImage(hInstance, lpszAppName,
```

continued on next page

continued from previous page

```
                                  IMAGE_ICON, 16, 16,
                                  LR_DEFAULTCOLOR );


    if ( !RegisterClassEx( &wc ) )
        return( FALSE );



    hInst = hInstance;

    hWnd = CreateWindow( lpszAppName,
                         lpszTitle,
                         WS_OVERLAPPEDWINDOW,
                         CW_USEDEFAULT, 0,
                         CW_USEDEFAULT, 0,
                         NULL,
                         NULL,
                         hInstance,
                         NULL
                       );

    if ( !hWnd )
        return( FALSE );

    ShowWindow( hWnd, nCmdShow );
    UpdateWindow( hWnd );

    while( GetMessage( &msg, NULL, 0, 0) )
    {
        TranslateMessage( &msg );
        DispatchMessage( &msg );
    }

    return( msg.wParam );
}




LRESULT CALLBACK WndProc( HWND hWnd, UINT uMsg, WPARAM wParam, LPARAM lParam )
{
    switch( uMsg )
    {
        case WM_COMMAND :
```

```
                switch( LOWORD( wParam ) )
                {
                    case IDM_TEST :
                            break;

                    case IDM_ABOUT :
                            DialogBox( hInst, "AboutBox", hWnd, (DLGPROC)About );
                            break;

                    case IDM_EXIT :
                            DestroyWindow( hWnd );
                            break;
                }
                break;

        case WM_DESTROY :
                PostQuitMessage(0);
                break;

        default :
                return( DefWindowProc( hWnd, uMsg, wParam, lParam ) );
    }

    return( 0L );
}

LRESULT CALLBACK About( HWND hDlg,
                        UINT message,
                        WPARAM wParam,
                        LPARAM lParam)
{
    switch (message)
    {
        case WM_INITDIALOG:
                return (TRUE);

        case WM_COMMAND:
                if (   LOWORD(wParam) == IDOK
                    || LOWORD(wParam) == IDCANCEL)
                {
                        EndDialog(hDlg, TRUE);
                        return (TRUE);
                }
```

continued on next page

continued from previous page

```
              break;
    }

    return (FALSE);
}
```

3

CREATING WINDOWS

Windows are the most fundamental element of a Microsoft Windows application. All applications have a main "parent" window that can have a menu and icon associated with it. Windows are actually used in almost every aspect of an application's user interface, ranging from the parent window to the individual buttons and edit controls on dialog boxes. Dialog boxes themselves are just another type of window.

There is only one function needed to create windows, the **CreateWindow** function, which is the most complex function in the Windows API. It is also one of the most important functions in the API. There are many types of predefined windows that can easily be created. These include buttons, static controls, list boxes, combo boxes, edit controls, and scroll bars. However, there are no predefined windows available for the first window that an application needs to create, the main window.

Creating the Main Window

An application requires a main window in order to process messages and user input. This window is also the parent for all top-level windows created in the application. **WinMain** is where the main window is created and the message processing loop resides. If it is the first instance of an application to be executed, then a "window class" is first registered with the **RegisterClass** function. Once the new class is registered, the main window can be created. Listing 3-1 shows what a basic **WinMain** function should look like and how the class is registered on the first instance of an application. Figure 3-1 shows the main window that is created and points out the elements of a window.

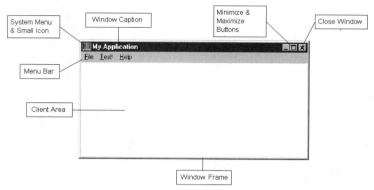

Figure 3-1 Elements of a window

Listing 3-1 *WinMain* function

```
static LPCTSTR lpszAppName = "MyApp";

HINSTANCE hInst;

int APIENTRY WinMain( HINSTANCE hInstance,
                      HINSTANCE hPrevInstance,
                      LPSTR     lpCmdLine,
                      int       nCmdShow )
{
    MSG         msg;
    WNDCLASSEX  wc;
    HWND        hWnd;

    // Fill in window class structure with parameters that describe the
    // main window.
    //...................
    wc.style          = CS_HREDRAW | CS_VREDRAW;
    wc.lpfnWndProc    = (WNDPROC)WndProc;
    wc.cbClsExtra     = 0;
    wc.cbWndExtra     = 0;
    wc.hInstance      = hInstance;
    wc.hIcon          = LoadIcon(hInstance, lpszAppName);
    wc.hCursor        = LoadCursor(NULL, IDC_ARROW);
    wc.hbrBackground  = (HBRUSH)(COLOR_WINDOW+1);
    wc.lpszMenuName   = lpszAppName;
    wc.lpszClassName  = lpszAppName;
    wc.cbSize         = sizeof(WNDCLASSEX);
    wc.hIconSm        = LoadImage(hInstance, lpszAppName,
```

```
                         IMAGE_ICON, 16, 16,
                         LR_DEFAULTCOLOR );


   // Register the window class
   //.........................
   if ( !RegisterClassEx( &wc ) )
      return( FALSE );




   // Save the instance handle for use in
   // the application.
   //................
   hInst = hInstance;


   // Create the main application window
   //..................................
   hWnd = CreateWindow(
                lpszAppName,           // See RegisterClass() call.
                "My Application",      // Text for window title bar.
                WS_OVERLAPPEDWINDOW,   // Window style.
                CW_USEDEFAULT, 0,
                CW_USEDEFAULT, 0,      // Use default positioning
                NULL,                  // Overlapped windows have no parent.
                NULL,                  // Use the window class menu.
                hInstance,             // This instance owns this window.
                NULL  );               // We don't use any data in our WM_CREATE


   if ( hWnd == NULL )
      return( FALSE );


   // Show the window.
   //................
   ShowWindow( hWnd, nCmdShow );


   // Process application messages until the application closes
   //........................................
   while( GetMessage( &msg, NULL, 0, 0) )
   {
      TranslateMessage(&msg);
      DispatchMessage(&msg);
   }

   return( msg.wParam );
}
```

Messages are processed in the message loop in the **WinMain** function until the application ends. Messages are dispatched to the **WndProc** function that was registered when the window class was created. The application will process the message or pass it on to the **DefWindowProc** default processing.

Creating Windows Using Existing Classes

As mentioned earlier, Microsoft Windows has predefined classes such as buttons, list boxes, combo boxes, and edit controls. There are also predefined classes for static text and scroll bars. Dialog boxes use window controls, created with these existing classes, for the majority of their user interface. An application does not have to create the individual controls on a dialog box. Instead, the dialog box manager (internal Windows code that creates and manages dialog boxes) creates the controls using a dialog template for the information needed in the **CreateWindow** function.

An application could create controls as well. They are created as child windows on a one-by-one basis using the **CreateWindow** function from within the body of the application. The existing classes that **CreateWindow** will work with are BUTTON, LISTBOX, COMBOBOX, STATIC, EDIT, MDICLIENT, and SCROLLBAR. Note that MDICLIENT is a special window class used only to create the client area of an MDI application.

Listing 3-2 shows how an application can create a static text, edit control, and button window on the client area of the parent window created in Listing 3-1. Figure 3-2 shows how the static text, edit control, and button appear on the main window's client area once they are created.

Listing 3-2 Creating user controls using existing classes

```
#define IDC_TEXT 101
#define IDC_EDIT 102
#define IDC_BTN  103


LRESULT CALLBACK WndProc( HWND    hWnd,        // window handle
                          UINT    message,     // type of message
                          WPARAM  wParam,      // additional information
                          LPARAM  lParam )     // additional information
{
static HWND hText = NULL;
static HWND hEdit = NULL;
static HWND hBtn  = NULL;

    switch (message)
    {
        case WM_COMMAND :
```

```
switch ( LOWORD( wParam ) )
{
    case IDM_TEST :
            hText = CreateWindow( "STATIC", "Static Text",
                                  WS_CHILD | WS_VISIBLE | SS_LEFT,
                                  10, 10, 100, 15,
                                  hWnd,
                                  (HMENU)IDC_TEXT,
                                  hInst, NULL );

            hEdit = CreateWindow( "EDIT", "",
                                  WS_CHILD | WS_VISIBLE |
                                  ES_LEFT | WS_BORDER,
                                  110, 8, 100, 20,
                                  hWnd,
                                  (HMENU)IDC_EDIT,
                                  hInst, NULL );

            hBtn = CreateWindow( "BUTTON", "Push Button",
                                  WS_CHILD | WS_VISIBLE |
                                  BS_PUSHBUTTON,
                                  50, 50, 100, 32,
                                  hWnd,
                                  (HMENU)IDC_BTN,
                                  hInst, NULL );
            break;
```

.
.
.

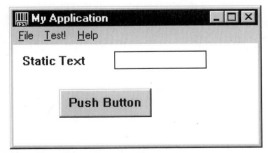

Figure 3-2 Main window with child windows

Messages When Creating Windows

When a window is created, Windows automatically sends messages to the application's WndProc function. Most of these messages are passed to the DefWindowProc. An application's WndProc by default should send messages that are not handled by the application to the DefWindowProc. This allows Windows to do most of the hard work and lets the application deal with only the messages it needs to.

When the CreateWindow function creates the main application window, five messages are sent to the application's WndProc function. The WndProc function normally processes the WM_CREATE message while passing the other four messages to the DefWindowProc. The application uses the WM_CREATE message when initializing the window. The messages are listed in Table 3-1 in the order they are received.

Table 3-1 CreateWindow-generated messages

Message	Meaning
WM_GETMINMAXINFO	Gets the size and position of the window that is being created.
WM_NCCREATE	The nonclient area of the window is about to be created. Memory for the window is allocated and scroll bars are initialized.
WM_NCCALCSIZE	The size and position of the window's client area are calculated.
WM_CREATE	Notification that the window is about to be created. Perform initialization here.
WM_SHOWWINDOW	The window is going to be displayed.

Creating Windows Function Descriptions

Table 3-2 summarizes the functions used in creating windows. The detailed descriptions follow.

Table 3-2 Creating windows function summary

Function	Purpose
CreateWindow	Creates a new window and returns a window handle.
CreateWindowEx	Creates a new window with an extended style.
DestroyWindow	Closes and removes a window.
RegisterClass	Registers a new window class for creating windows.
RegisterClassEx	Registers a new window class for creating windows that need a small icon.
UnregisterClass	Removes a window class that was previously registered.

CreateWindow ■ WINDOWS 95 ■ WINDOWS NT

Description   CreateWindow is used to create a window based on one of the predefined classes or a class that was created with RegisterClass. The size, location, and style of the window are determined by the parameters passed to

`CreateWindow`. `ShowWindow` is used to make the window visible after creation.

The `CreateWindow` function is used to create any type of window. `CreateWindow` is used in the `WinMain` function to create the main application window and within the application for creating child windows and user interface controls.

Syntax

HWND **CreateWindow**(LPCTSTR *lpszClassName,* LPCTSTR *lpszWindowName,* DWORD *dwStyle,* int *x,* int *y,* int *nWidth,* int *nHeight,* HWND *hwndParent,* HMENU *hmenu,* HANDLE *hinst,* LPVOID *lpvParam*)

Parameters

lpszClassName   LPCTSTR: Pointer to a null-terminated case-sensitive string containing a valid class name for the window or an integer atom. The class name can either be one created with `RegisterClass` or one of the predefined classes in Table 3-3. Windows 95 introduced the new common controls (`TreeView`, `ListView`, etc.), which are also defined as window classes; however, they are not defined unless the application initializes the common control DLL. For more information on common controls, refer to Book 2, *Common Controls & Messages*. If *lpszClassName* is an atom, then it must be created with a previous call to `GlobalAddAtom`.

Table 3-3 Predefined window classes

Class	Meaning
BUTTON	A rectangular pushbutton, group box, check box, radio button, or icon window. Buttons can be created with the style BS_OWNERDRAW to give the application control over how the button looks in different states.
COMBOBOX	Combination list box with edit field on top or a drop-down selection list box.
EDIT	A rectangular edit control for user text entry. Can be single line or multiple lines.
LISTBOX	A list box control. A control that has a list of strings that can be selected. The list box can allow multiple selections or limit the selections to one. List boxes can be created with the LBS_OWNERDRAWFIXED or LBS_OWNERDRAW VARIABLE to give the application control over how the strings appear in the control.
MDICLIENT	An MDI (multiple-document interface) client window. This window receives messages that control MDI child windows in an application. An MDI application must create an MDICLIENT window in order to work properly.
SCROLLBAR	A scroll bar control.
STATIC	A static text control. Static text is used to put text or frames on a window.

lpszWindowName   LPCTSTR: Points to a null-terminated string that contains the name of the window. The window name is displayed in the appropriate place for a particular window style.

dwStyle   DWORD: The style of the window that will be created. The style is made up of values that are combined together with a binary **OR** operator. An example of a style would be **WS_CHILD | ES_LEFT**. Styles can be made of the values listed in Table 3-4 (following the example program).

x	**int**: The horizontal position of the upper-left corner of the window or control that will be created. Use **CW_USEDEFAULT** if the position is not important.
	The x and y positions are relative to the upper-left corner of the screen or, for child windows and controls, the parent window. All sizes are measured in pixels, so a 640×480 resolution display would have 640 pixels horizontally and 480 pixels vertically.
y	**int**: The vertical position of the upper-left corner of the window or control. Use **CW_USEDEFAULT** if the position is not important.
nWidth	**int**: The horizontal width of the window or control. If the width is not important, use **CW_USEDEFAULT**.
nHeight	**int**: The vertical height of the window or control. Use **CW_USEDEFAULT** if the height is not important.
hwndParent	**HWND**: A handle to the window or control's parent. Use a **NULL** value if there is no parent window. If no parent window is given, then the window will not be destroyed automatically when the application ends. Use **DestroyWindow** to remove the window before closing the application.
hmenu	**HMENU**: A handle to a window's menu. Use a **NULL** value if the class menu should be used.
	For controls, *hmenu* is set to an integer value that is the ID of the control being created. All **WM_COMMAND** messages reference this ID when an action has occurred with the control.
hinst	**HANDLE**: The instance handle of the application module creating the window or control.
lpvParam	**LPVOID**: A pointer to data that will be passed in as the **LPARAM** of the **WM_CREATE** message. When creating an MDICLIENT, use a pointer to a **CLIENTCREATESTRUCT** structure. For most windows and controls, set *lpvParam* to **NULL**.
Returns	**HWND**: Returns the window handle to the newly created window if the function was successful; **NULL** if the window could not be created.
Include File	winuser.h
See Also	RegisterClass, ShowWindow, DestroyWindow, CreateWindowEx
Related Messages	WM_CREATE, WM_NCCREATE, WM_PARENTNOTIFY
Example	This example shows a simple **WinMain** function and the steps that are needed to create the application's main window.

```
static LPCTSTR lpszAppName = "MyApp";


HWND hwndMain;


int APIENTRY WinMain( HINSTANCE hInst, HINSTANCE hPrevInst, LPSTR lpCmdLine, int nCmdShow )
```

```
{
    WNDCLASSEX  wndclass;
    MSG         msg;
    HWND        hwndMain;

    wndclass.style          = CS_HREDRAW | CS_VREDRAW;
    wndclass.lpfnWndProc    = (WNDPROC)WndProc;
    wndclass.cbClsExtra     = 0;
    wndclass.cbWndExtra     = 0;
    wndclass.hInstance      = hInst;
    wndclass.hIcon          = LoadIcon (hInst, lpszAppName);
    wndclass.hCursor        = LoadCursor (NULL, IDC_ARROW);
    wndclass.hbrBackground  = (HBRUSH)(COLOR_APPWORKSPACE+1);
    wndclass.lpszMenuName   = lpszAppName;
    wndclass.lpszClassName  = lpszAppName;
    wndclass.cbSize         = sizeof( WNDCLASSEX );
    wndclass.hIconSm        = LoadImage( hInstance, lpszAppName,
                                    IMAGE_ICON, 16, 16,
                                    LR_DEFAULTCOLOR );

    if ( RegisterClassEx( &wndclass ) == 0 )
        return( FALSE );

    // Create our main application window using our application
    // class.
    //..............................................................
    hwndMain = CreateWindow( lpszAppName, lpszAppName,
                             WS_OVERLAPPEDWINDOW | WS_CLIPCHILDREN,
                             CW_USEDEFAULT, 0,
                             CW_USEDEFAULT, 0,
                             NULL, NULL, hInst, NULL);

    if (!hwndMain)
        return( FALSE );

    // Display the window we just created.
    //.....................................
    ShowWindow( hwndMain, nCmdShow );

    // Process messages until we exit the application.
    //.......................................
    while( GetMessage(&msg, NULL, 0, 0) )
    {
        TranslateMessage( &msg );
```

continued on next page

continued from previous page

```
        DispatchMessage( &msg );
    }


    return( msg.wParam );
}
```

Table 3-4 Window and control styles

Window Styles	Meaning
WS_BORDER	Creates a window that has a thin-line border.
WS_CAPTION	Creates a window that has a title bar. Includes the WS_BORDER style.
WS_CHILD	Creates a child window or control. WS_POPUP cannot be used if this style is used.
WS_CHILDWINDOW	Same as the WS_CHILD style.
WS_CLIPCHILDREN	Clips around the child windows of a control when painting occurs. This style is used when creating parent windows.
WS_CLIPSIBLINGS	Clips child windows relative to each other when painting occurs. If the style is not specified and a child window receives a WM_PAINT message, the entire area of the window will be included in the update region even if it is overlapped by a sibling window. When the style is used, the area that a sibling window occupies is left out of the update region.
WS_DISABLED	Creates a window that is initially disabled from receiving user input.
WS_DLGFRAME	Creates a window that has a border of a style used with dialog boxes. Windows created with this style cannot have a title bar.
WS_GROUP	Marks the first control in a group of controls. The next control that has the WS_GROUP style ends the group and starts a new group. Radio buttons are commonly grouped together so the arrow keys can be used to select a different option.
WS_HSCROLL	Creates a window with a horizontal scroll bar.
WS_ICONIC	Same as WS_MINIMIZE.
WS_MAXIMIZE	Creates a window that is initially maximized.
WS_MAXIMIZEBOX	Creates a window with a maximize button.
WS_MINIMIZE	Creates a window that is initially minimized.
WS_MINIMIZEBOX	Creates a window with a Minimize button.
WS_OVERLAPPED	Creates a window with a title bar and a border.
WS_OVERLAPPEDWINDOW	Combination of the WS_OVERLAPPED, WS_CAPTION, WS_SYSMENU, WS_THICKFRAME, WS_MINIMIZEBOX, and WS_MAXIMIZEBOX styles.
WS_POPUP	Creates a pop-up window. WS_CHILD cannot be used with this style.
WS_POPUPWINDOW	Combination of the WS_BORDER, WS_POPUP, and WS_SYSMENU styles. WS_CAPTION must be specified to make the System menu visible.
WS_SIZEBOX	Same as WS_THICKFRAME.
WS_SYSMENU	Creates a window that has a System menu box in the title bar.
WS_TABSTOP	Specifies a control that the (TAB) key will stop on.
WS_THICKFRAME	Creates a window with a sizing border.
WS_TILED	Same as WS_OVERLAPPED.
WS_TILED_WINDOW	Same as WS_OVERLAPPEDWINDOW.
WS_VISIBLE	Creates a window that is initially visible.
WS_VSCROLL	Creates a window with a vertical scroll bar.

Button Styles	Meaning
BS_3STATE	Creates a three-selection-state check box. The check box can be unselected, selected, or grayed. The grayed state is normally used to show that the check box value is not determined.
BS_AUTO3STATE	Same as BS_3STATE except the check box will change its state when the user selects it.
BS_AUTOCHECKBOX	Same as BS_CHECKBOX except the check box will change its state when the user selects it.
BS_AUTORADIOBUTTON	Same as BS_RADIOBUTTON except the radio button is selected when the user clicks it, and any other radio buttons in the group are unselected.
BS_BITMAP	Creates a button that will display a bitmap.
BS_BOTTOM	Places the button title at the bottom of the button rectangle.
BS_CENTER	Centers the button title horizontally in the button rectangle.
BS_CHECKBOX	Creates a check box with the title displayed on the right side unless the BS_LEFTTEXT style is used.
BS_DEFPUSHBUTTON	Creates a pushbutton that is pressed if the user presses the ENTER key. The button will have a heavy, black border.
BS_GROUPBOX	Creates a box with the title displayed in the upper-left corner.
BS_ICON	Creates a button that will display an icon.
BS_LEFT	Left-justifies the title in the button rectangle. If the button is a check box or radio button and does not have the BS_RIGHTBUTTON style, the text is left-justified on the right side of the check box or radio button.
BS_LEFTTEXT	Places text on the left side of a radio button or check box.
BS_MONO	Specifies that the button has only one line of text for the title.
BS_MULTILINE	Specifies that the button has multiple lines of text for the title. The title will be wrapped to a second line if it is too long to fit on a single line.
BS_NOTIFY	Sends notification messages to the parent window. This is in addition to the BN_CLICKED and BN_DBLCLK that are sent by default.
BS_OWNERDRAW	Creates an owner-drawn button. The parent window receives a WM_MEASUREITEM message when the button is created and a WM_DRAWITEM message any time the button needs to be painted. This style should not be combined with any other button styles.
BS_PUSHBUTTON	Creates a pushbutton that posts a WM_COMMAND message to the parent window when the button is selected.
BS_PUSHLIKE	Makes a check box or radio button have a pushbutton look and action.
BS_RIGHTBUTTON	Places the radio button or check box selection area on the right side of the button rectangle.
BS_TEXT	Specifies that the button displays text.
BS_TOP	Positions the title at the top of the button rectangle.
BS_VCENTER	Vertically centers the title in the button rectangle.

Combo Box Styles	Meaning
CBS_AUTOHSCROLL	Allows horizontal scrolling in the edit control of the combo box.
CBS_DISABLENOSCROLL	Forces a vertical scroll bar to be visible even when all items in the list are visible. The scroll bar will be disabled unless it is needed to show all the items in the list. Normally, the scroll bar is only visible when needed.
CBS_DROPDOWN	Creates a drop-down combo box. The list is only visible while selecting.
CBS_DROPDOWNLIST	Creates a drop-list combo box. Editing is not allowed; the selected item is display only.
CBS_HASSTRINGS	Used with an owner-drawn combo box to specify strings will be added to the combo box. An application can then use the CB_GETLBTEXT message to retrieve a particular item.
CBS_LOWERCASE	Forces only lowercase characters to be entered into the edit control by converting uppercase characters to lowercase as they are entered.

continued on next page

continued from previous page

Combo Box Styles	Meaning
CBS_NOINTEGRALHEIGHT	Forces the combo box to be exactly the size specified. By default, Windows will size the combo box so no partial items can be displayed.
CBS_OEMCONVERT	Text entered will be converted from the Windows character set to the OEM character set and then back to the Windows set. This will ensure proper conversion when using the AnsiToOem function.
CBS_OWNERDRAWFIXED	Creates an owner-draw combo box. The parent will receive a WM_MEASUREITEM message when the combo box is created and a WM_DRAWITEM message when an item needs to be painted.
CBS_OWNERDRAWVARIABLE	Same as CBS_OWNERDRAWFIXED with the exception that each item in the list can be sized differently. WM_MEASUREITEM is called for an item in the combo box before WM_DRAWITEM is called for that item.
CBS_SIMPLE	Creates a simple combo box where the list of items is always shown and the current selection is in the edit control.
CBS_SORT	Sorts strings added into the list box using the CB_ADDSTRING message.
CBS_UPPERCASE	Forces only uppercase characters to be entered into the edit control by converting lowercase characters to uppercase as they are entered.

Dialog Box Styles	Meaning
DS_3DLOOK	Creates a dialog with 3D controls and borders on applications that are not marked with a version number 4.0 or later.
DS_ABSALIGN	Positions the dialog box relative to the upper-left corner of the screen.
DS_CENTER	Centers the dialog in the working area.
DS_CENTERMOUSE	Centers the mouse cursor in the dialog box.
DS_CONTEXTHELP	Includes a question mark (?) in the title bar of the dialog box for context-sensitive help.
DS_CONTROL	Creates a dialog that works well as a child window of another dialog box, such as a page in a property sheet.
DS_FIXEDSYS	Uses SYSTEM_FIXED_FONT instead of SYSTEM_FONT.
DS_MODALFRAME	Creates a dialog box with a modal dialog-box frame.
DS_NOFAILCREATE	Creates the dialog even if errors occur during the creation.
DS_NOIDLEMSG	Suppresses WM_ENTERIDLE messages to the parent while the dialog box is displayed.
DS_RECURSE	Creates a control-like dialog.
DS_SETFONT	Used to indicate that the dialog box template contains font information. Windows passes the handle of the font to each control in the dialog box with the WM_SETFONT message.
DS_SETFOREGROUND	(Windows NT only) Forces the dialog box to be in the foreground by calling the SetForegroundWindow function.
DS_SYSMODAL	Creates a system-modal dialog box. This is the same as the WS_EX_TOPMOST style.

Edit Control Styles	Meaning
ES_AUTOHSCROLL	Automatically scrolls horizontally if necessary while entering text in the edit control.
ES_AUTOVSCROLL	Automatically scrolls vertically while entering text in a multiline edit control.
ES_CENTER	Centers text in a multiline edit control.
ES_LEFT	Left-aligns text.
ES_LOWERCASE	Forces all characters to be entered in lowercase by converting uppercase characters to lowercase.
ES_MULTILINE	Creates a multiline edit control. In order to use the ENTER key as a carriage return, use the ES_WANTRETURN style.
ES_NOHIDESEL	Causes the selection to always be shown even when the edit control loses focus.
ES_NUMBER	Allows only digits to be entered into the edit control.
ES_OEMCONVERT	Converts the text entered in the edit control from the Windows character set to the OEM character set and then back. This will ensure proper character conversion when the CharToOem function is used.

Edit Control Styles	Meaning
ES_PASSWORD	Displays the password char in place of each character typed. The default password char is an asterisk (*). Use the EM_SETPASSWORDCHAR message to change the password character.
ES_READONLY	Creates an edit control that is read-only and prevents the user from typing or editing text in the control.
ES_RIGHT	Right-aligns text in a multiline edit control.
ES_UPPERCASE	Forces all characters to be entered in uppercase by converting lowercase characters to uppercase.
ES_WANTRETURN	Allows the ENTER key to be used in a multiline edit control as a carriage return. By default the ENTER key selects the default button on a dialog box, and CTRL-ENTER performs a carriage return.

List Box Styles	Meaning
LBS_DISABLENOSCROLL	Forces a vertical scroll bar to be shown on the list box even when the list box does not contain enough items to scroll. The scroll bar will be disabled until there are enough items to scroll. By default the scroll bar is hidden when the list box does not contain enough items.
LBS_EXTENDEDSEL	Allows multiple items to be selected by using the SHIFT key and the mouse or special key combinations.
LBS_HASSTRINGS	Used with an owner-drawn list box to specify that strings will be added to the list box. An application can then use the LB_GETTEXT message to retrieve a particular item.
LBS_MULTICOLUMN	Creates a multicolumn list box that can be scrolled horizontally. Use the LB_SETCOLUMNWIDTH message to set the width of the columns.
LBS_MULTIPLESEL	Allows multiple items to be selected by clicking an item on or off.
LBS_NODATA	Used with an owner-drawn list box to specify there is no data in the list box. Use this style when the total number of items in the list box will exceed 1,000. The LBS_OWNERDRAWFIXED style must be used, and the LBS_SORT or LBS_HASSTRINGS styles cannot be used.
LBS_NOINTEGRALHEIGHT	Forces the list box to be exactly the size specified. By default, Windows will size the list box so no partial items can be displayed.
LBS_NOREDRAW	Specifies that the list box will not receive WM_PAINT messages when changes are made. The WM_SETREDRAW message can be used to change this style.
LBS_NOSEL	Specifies that the list box contains items that can be viewed but not selected.
LBS_NOTIFY	Sends out notifications to the parent window when the user selects or unselects an item in the list box.
LBS_OWNERDRAWFIXED	Creates an owner-draw list box. The parent will receive a WM_MEASUREITEM message when the list box is created and a WM_DRAWITEM message when an item needs to be painted.
LBS_OWNERDRAWVARIABLE	Same as LBS_OWNERDRAWFIXED with the exception that each item in the list can be sized differently. WM_MEASUREITEM is called for an item in the list box before WM_DRAWITEM is called for that item.
LBS_SORT	Automatically sorts strings that are added to the list box with the LB_ADDSTRING message.
LBS_STANDARD	Combines the LBS_SORT, LBS_NOTIFY, and WS_BORDER styles.
LBS_USETABSTOPS	The list box will expand tabs when drawing its strings. Default tab positions are 32 dialog box units. Use the LB_SETTABSTOPS message to set different tab positions.
LBS_WANTKEYBOARDINPUT	The owner of the list box receives WM_VKEYTOITEM messages whenever the user presses a key and the list box has the input focus.

Scroll Bar Styles	Meaning
SBS_BOTTOMALIGN	Aligns the bottom edge of the scroll bar with the bottom edge of the rectangle defined by the CreateWindow parameters. The height is the system default. Use this style with the SBS_HORZ style.
SBS_HORZ	Creates a horizontal scroll bar. If the SBS_BOTTOMALIGN or SBS_TOPALIGN style is not specified, the scroll bar will have the height, width, and position specified by the parameters of CreateWindow.
SBS_LEFTALIGN	Aligns the left edge of the scroll bar with the left edge of the rectangle defined in the CreateWindow parameters. The width is the system default. Use this style with the SBS_VERT style.

continued on next page

continued from previous page

Scroll Bar Styles	Meaning
SBS_RIGHTALIGN	Aligns the right edge of the scroll bar with the right edge of the rectangle defined by the CreateWindow parameters. Use this style with the SBS_VERT style.
SBS_SIZEBOX	Creates a size box. If SBS_SIZEBOXBOTTOMRIGHTALIGN or SBS_SIZEBOXTOPLEFTALIGN are not specified, the size box has the height, width, and position specified by the parameters of CreateWindow.
SBS_SIZEBOXBOTTOMRIGHTALIGN	Aligns the lower-right corner of the size box with the lower-right corner of the rectangle defined by the CreateWindow parameters. The size box has the system default size. Use this style with the SBS_SIZEBOX style.
SBS_SIZEBOXTOPLEFTALIGN	Aligns the upper-left corner of the size box with the upper-left corner of the rectangle defined by the CreateWindow parameters. The size box has the system default size. Use this style with the SBS_SIZEBOX style.
SBS_SIZEGRIP	Same as SBS_SIZEBOX but with a raised edge.
SBS_TOPALIGN	Aligns the top edge of the scroll bar with the top edge of the rectangle defined by the CreateWindow parameters. The height is the system default. Use this style with the SBS_HORZ style.
SBS_VERT	Creates a vertical scroll bar. If the SBS_RIGHTALIGN or SBS_LEFTALIGN style is not specified, the scroll bar will have the height, width, and position specified by the parameters of CreateWindow.
Static Control Styles	**Meaning**
SS_BITMAP	Creates a static control that will display the bitmap specified by the *lpszWindowName* parameter. The *nWidth* and *nHeight* parameters are ignored and will be calculated to accommodate the bitmap.
SS_BLACKFRAME	Creates a box that is drawn in the same color as the window frames. Black is the color in the default Windows color scheme.
SS_BLACKRECT	Creates a filled rectangle in the same color as the window frames.
SS_CENTER	Creates a static text control where the text is centered and word-wrapped if necessary.
SS_CENTERIMAGE	Specifies that the midpoint of the control with the SS_BITMAP or SS_ICON style will remain fixed when the control is resized to accommodate the bitmap or icon.
SS_GRAYFRAME	Creates a box that is drawn in the same color as the screen background (desktop). Gray is the color in the default Windows color scheme.
SS_GRAYRECT	Creates a filled rectangle in the same color as the screen background.
SS_ICON	Creates a static control that will display the icon specified by the *lpszWindowName* parameter. The *nWidth* and *nHeight* parameters are ignored and will be calculated to accommodate the icon.
SS_LEFT	Creates a static text control where the given text is left-aligned and word-wrapped, if necessary.
SS_LEFTNOWORDWRAP	Creates a static text control where the given text is left-aligned. Text is not word-wrapped but tabs are expanded. Text that extends past the end of the line is clipped.
SS_METAPICT	Creates a static control that will display the metafile specified in the *lpszWindowName* parameter. The control's size is fixed and the metafile will be scaled to fit.
SS_NOPREFIX	Turns off the interpretation of the ampersand (&) character as an accelerator.
SS_NOTIFY	Notifies the parent window with STN_CLICKED and STN_DBLCLK notification messages when the user clicks or double-clicks the control.
SS_RIGHT	Creates a static text control where the given text is right-aligned and word-wrapped, if necessary.
SS_RIGHTIMAGE	The bottom-right corner of a static control with the SS_BITMAP or SS_ICON style will remain fixed when the control is resized. Only the top and left sides will be adjusted to accommodate a bitmap or icon.
SS_SIMPLE	Creates a simple static text control with left-aligned text. The parent window or dialog box must not process the WM_CTLCOLORSTATIC message.

Static Control Styles	Meaning
SS_WHITEFRAME	Creates a box that is drawn in the same color as the window background. White is the color in the default Windows color scheme.
SS_WHITERECT	Creates a filled rectangle in the same color as the window background.

CreateWindowEx ■ WINDOWS 95 ■ WINDOWS NT

Description   CreateWindowEx creates an overlapped, pop-up, or child window with an extended style; otherwise, this function is identical to **CreateWindow**.

Syntax   HWND **CreateWindowEx**(DWORD *dwExStyle,* LPCTSTR *lpszClassName,* LPCTSTR *lpszWindowName,* DWORD *dwStyle,* int *x,* int *y,* int *nWidth,* int *nHeight,* HWND *hwndParent,* HMENU *hmenu,* HANDLE *hinst,* LPVOID *lpvParam*)

Parameters

dwExStyle   DWORD: Specifies the extended style that is used to create the window. The extended style can be one of the styles listed in Table 3-5.

Table 3-5 Extended window styles

Style	Meaning
WS_EX_ACCEPTFILES	Creates a window that will accept drag-and-drop files.
WS_EX_APPWINDOW	Forces a top-level window onto the taskbar when the window is minimized.
WS_EX_CLIENTEDGE	The border of the window has a sunken edge.
WS_EX_CONTEXTHELP	Includes a question mark (?) in the title bar of the window. When the user clicks the question mark, the cursor changes to a question mark with a pointer. If the user then clicks a child window, the child receives a WM_HELP message.
WS_EX_CONTROLPARENT	Allows the user to navigate among the child windows of the window by using the TAB key.
WS_EX_DLGMODALFRAME	Creates a window that has a double border. The WS_CAPTION style can be specified in the *dwStyle* parameter to add a title.
WS_EX_LEFT	Creates a window with "left-aligned" properties. This is the default.
WS_EX_LEFTSCROLLBAR	Places the vertical scroll bar (if present) to the left of the client area.
WS_EX_LTRREADING	Creates a window with the text displayed using left to right reading order. This is the default.
WS_EX_MDICHILD	Creates an MDI child window.
WS_EX_NOPARENTNOTIFY	Turns off the WM_PARENTNOTIFY messages.
WS_EX_OVERLAPPEDWINDOW	A combination of the WS_EX_CLIENTEDGE and WS_EX_WINDOWEDGE styles.
WS_EX_PALETTEWINDOW	A combination of the WS_EX_WINDOWEDGE, WS_EX_SMCAPTION, and WS_EX_TOPMOST styles.
WS_EX_RIGHT	Creates a window with "right-aligned" properties.
WS_EX_RIGHTSCROLLBAR	Places the vertical scroll bar (if present) to the right of the client area. This is the default.
WS_EX_RTLREADING	Creates a window with the text displayed using right to left reading order.
WS_EX_STATICEDGE	Creates a window with a three-dimensional border style. This style is intended for items that do not accept user input.
WS_EX_TOOLWINDOW	Creates a tool window. A tool window is intended to be used for floating toolbars.

continued on next page

continued from previous page

Style	Meaning
WS_EX_TOPMOST	Creates a window that will be placed above all nontopmost windows and will stay above them.
WS_EX_TRANSPARENT	Creates a transparent window. Any sibling windows that are covered by this window will receive the WM_PAINT message first, thus creating the appearance of transparency.
WS_EX_WINDOWEDGE	Creates a window that has a border with a raised edge.

lpszClassName	**LPCTSTR**: Pointer to a null-terminated case-sensitive string containing a valid class name for the window or an integer atom. The class name can either be one created with **RegisterClass** or one of the predefined classes in Table 3-3. If *lpszClassName* is an atom, then it must be created with a previous call to **GlobalAddAtom**.
lpszWindowName	**LPCTSTR**: Points to a null-terminated string that contains the name of the window. The window name is displayed in the appropriate place for a particular window style.
dwStyle	**DWORD**: The style of the window that will be created. The style is made up of values that are combined together with a binary **OR** operator. An example of a style would be **WS_CHILD	ES_LEFT**. Styles can be made of the values listed in Table 3-4.
x	**int**: The horizontal position of the upper-left corner of the window or control that will be created. Use **CW_USEDEFAULT** if the position is not important.
	The x and y positions are relative to the upper-left corner of the screen or, for child windows and controls, the parent window. All sizes are measured in pixels, so a 640×480 resolution display would have 640 pixels horizontally and 480 pixels vertically.
y	**int**: The vertical position of the upper-left corner of the window or control. Use **CW_USEDEFAULT** if the position is not important.
nWidth	**int**: The horizontal width of the window or control. Use **CW_USEDEFAULT** if the width is not important.
nHeight	**int**: The vertical height of the window or control. Use **CW_USEDEFAULT** if the height is not important.
hwndParent	**HWND**: A handle to the window or control's parent. A **NULL** value is used if there is no parent window. If no parent window is given, then the window will not be destroyed automatically when the application ends. Use **DestroyWindow** to remove the window before closing the application.
hmenu	**HMENU**: A handle to a window's menu. Use a **NULL** value if the class menu should be used.
	For controls, *hmenu* is set to an integer value that is the ID of the control that is being created. All **WM_COMMAND** messages will reference this ID when an action has occurred with the control.
hinst	**HANDLE**: The instance handle of the application module creating the window or control.

lpvParam	LPVOID: A pointer to data that will be passed in as the **LPARAM** of the **WM_CREATE** message. When creating an MDICLIENT, use a pointer to a **CLIENTCREATESTRUCT** structure. For most windows and controls, set *lpvParam* to **NULL**.
Returns	HWND: Returns the window handle to newly created window if the function was successful; **NULL** if the window could not be created.
Include File	winuser.h
See Also	RegisterClass, ShowWindow, DestroyWindow, CreateWindow
Related Messages	WM_CREATE, WM_NCCREATE, WM_PARENTNOTIFY
Example	This example shows how the **CreateWindowEx** function could be used in the example for **CreateWindow**. The window created would have a small caption such as that used for a "tool box" instead of the normal window caption.

```
hwndMain = CreateWindowEx( WS_EX_SMCAPTION,
                lpszAppName, lpszAppName,
                WS_OVERLAPPEDWINDOW | WS_CLIPCHILDREN,
                CW_USEDEFAULT, O,
                CW_USEDEFAULT, O,
                NULL, NULL, hInst, NULL );
```

DestroyWindow
■ WINDOWS 95   ■ WINDOWS NT

Description	**DestroyWindow** deletes the window identified by *hWnd*. Child windows of *hWnd* are deleted first. The function sends **WM_DESTROY** and **WM_NCDESTROY** messages to the window to deactivate it before deleting it. The window's menu is destroyed, the thread message queue is flushed, and any clipboard ownership is removed.
	Use to remove and delete windows that were created with **CreateWindow**. **DestroyWindow** is also used to end Windows applications by destroying the parent window, and to delete modeless dialogs created with the **CreateDialog** function.
Syntax	BOOL **DestroyWindow**(HWND *hWnd*)
Parameters	
hWnd	HWND: Handle of the window to be destroyed.
Returns	BOOL: **TRUE** if the window was destroyed, **FALSE** if the function failed.
Include File	winuser.h
See Also	UnregisterClass, CreateWindow
Related Messages	WM_DESTROY, WM_NCDESTROY, WM_PARENTNOTIFY
Example	This example shows how to use **DestroyWindow** to end an application. **DestroyWindow** is called when the user selects the Exit menu option.

```
LONG APIENTRY WndProc( HWND hwnd, UINT msg, WPARAM wParam, LPARAM lParam )
{
   switch (msg)
   {
      case WM_COMMAND :
              if ( LOWORD( wParam ) == IDM_EXIT )
                 DestroyWindow(hwnd);
              break;

      default :
              return( DefWindowProc (hwnd, msg, wParam, lParam) );
   }

   return( OL );
}
```

RegisterClass   ■ WINDOWS 95 ■ WINDOWS NT

Description   RegisterClass creates new window classes that can be used to create windows. The same class can be used to create as many windows as your application needs.

Use primarily in WinMain to create a class for the main window of an application. You can also use RegisterClass to create custom control classes and other windows.

Syntax   ATOM **RegisterClass**(CONST WNDCLASS* *lpwc*)

Parameters

lpwc   CONST WNDCLASS*: A pointer to a WNDCLASS data structure. See the definition of the WNDCLASS structure below.

Returns   ATOM: If successful, an atom that uniquely identifies the new class that was registered; otherwise, the return value is 0.

Include File   winuser.h

See Also   RegisterClassEx, CreateWindow, CreateWindowEx, UnregisterClass, GetClassInfo, GetClassName, GetClassLong, GetClassWord, SetClassLong, SetClassWord

WNDCLASS Definition

```
typedef struct tagWNDCLASS
{
    UINT      style;
    WNDPROC   lpfnWndProc;
    int       cbClsExtra;
    int       cbWndExtra;
    HINSTANCE hInstance;
```

```
HICON      hIcon;
HCURSOR    hCursor;
HBRUSH     hbrBackground;
LPCTSTR    lpszMenuName;
LPCTSTR    lpszClassName;
} WNDCLASS;
```

Members

style UINT: The style parameter can be one or more of the styles listed in Table 3-6 combined with the binary OR operator (|).

Table 3-6 Window class styles

Style	Meaning
CS_BYTEALIGNCLIENT	Aligns a window's client area on the byte boundary horizontally to enhance drawing performance. The width of the window and its horizontal position on the display are affected.
CS_BYTEALIGNWINDOW	Aligns a window on a byte boundary horizontally.
CS_CLASSDC	Allocates one device context (DC) to be shared by all windows in the class. If multiple threads in an application attempt to use the DC simultaneously, Windows allows only one thread to finish successfully.
CS_DBLCLKS	Notifies a window when a double-click occurs.
CS_GLOBALCLASS	Creates a class that is available to all applications while the application that created the class is running. A common use would be to create custom controls in a DLL.
CS_HREDRAW	Redraws the entire window if the horizontal size is adjusted.
CS_NOCLOSE	Disables the Close command on the System menu.
CS_OWNDC	Allocates a unique device context for each window that is created with this class.
CS_PARENTDC	Each window created with this class will use the parent window's device context.
CS_SAVEBITS	Saves, as a bitmap, the portion of the screen image obscured by a window. The bitmap is used to recreate the screen image when the window is removed.
CS_VREDRAW	Redraws the entire window if the vertical size is adjusted.

lpfnWndProc WNDPROC: Points to a window callback function for processing messages. (See the description for the WndProc callback function in Chapter 5, Message Processing.)

cbClsExtra int: The number of extra bytes to allocate at the end of the window class structure for storing information. See the SetClassLong function description.

cbWndExtra int: The number of extra bytes to allocate following the window instance. If an application uses the WNDCLASS structure to register a dialog box created by using the CLASS directive in the resource file, it must set this member to DLGWINDOWEXTRA.

hInstance HINSTANCE: The instance handle that the window procedure for this class is in.

hIcon   HICON: A handle to the icon to use for this window class. If set to NULL, then the application must draw the icon whenever the user minimizes the window.

hCursor   HCURSOR: A handle to the cursor to use for this window class. If set to NULL, then the application must set the cursor whenever the mouse cursor moves off the window.

hbrBackground HBRUSH: A handle to a brush used to paint the window background. One of the system colors in Table 3-7 can be used in place of a brush. Add 1 to these values for the class definition.

Table 3-7 System color values

Value	Meaning
COLOR_3DDKSHADOW	Dark shadow color for three-dimensional display elements.
COLOR_3DFACE	Face color for three-dimensional display elements.
COLOR_3DHILIGHT	Highlight color for three-dimensional display elements (for edges facing the light source).
COLOR_3DLIGHT	Light color for three-dimensional display elements (for edges facing the light source).
COLOR_3DSHADOW	Shadow color for three-dimensional display elements (for edges facing away from the light source).
COLOR_ACTIVEBORDER	Active window border.
COLOR_ACTIVECAPTION	Active window caption.
COLOR_APPWORKSPACE	Background color of multiple-document interface (MDI) applications.
COLOR_BACKGROUND	Desktop.
COLOR_BTNFACE	Face shading on pushbuttons.
COLOR_BTNHILIGHT	Highlight color for buttons (same as COLOR_3DHILIGHT).
COLOR_BTNSHADOW	Edge shading on pushbuttons.
COLOR_BTNTEXT	Text on pushbuttons.
COLOR_CAPTIONTEXT	Text in caption, size box, and scroll bar arrow box.
COLOR_GRAYTEXT	Grayed (disabled) text. This color is set to 0 if the current display driver does not support a solid gray color.
COLOR_HIGHLIGHT	Item(s) selected in a control.
COLOR_HIGHLIGHTTEXT	Text of item(s) selected in a control.
COLOR_INACTIVEBORDER	Inactive window border.
COLOR_INACTIVECAPTION	Inactive window caption.
COLOR_INACTIVECAPTIONTEXT	Color of text in an inactive caption.
COLOR_MENU	Menu background.
COLOR_MENUTEXT	Text in menus.
COLOR_MSGBOX	Background color for message boxes and system dialog boxes.
COLOR_MSGBOXTEXT	Color of text in message boxes.
COLOR_SCROLLBAR	Scroll bar gray area.
COLOR_SHADOW	Color of automatic window shadows.
COLOR_WINDOW	Window background.
COLOR_WINDOWFRAME	Window frame.
COLOR_WINDOWTEXT	Text in windows.

lpszMenuName	**LPCTSTR**: Points to a null-terminated string with the default menu name for the class. Set to **NULL** if the class has no default menu.
lpszClassName	**LPCTSTR**: Points to a null-terminated string that contains the class name. This name will be used in the **CreateWindow** function's *lpszClassName* parameter.
Example	See the example for the **UnregisterClass** function.

RegisterClassEx   ■ WINDOWS 95   ■ WINDOWS NT

Description	**RegisterClassEx** is the same as **RegisterClass**, with the exception that it has support for registering a class with a small icon to be used in the title bar of windows created with this class.
Syntax	**ATOM RegisterClassEx(CONST WNDCLASSEX* *lpwc*)**
Parameters	
lpwc	**CONST WNDCLASSEX***: A pointer to a **WNDCLASSEX** data structure. See the definition of the **WNDCLASSEX** structure below.
Returns	**ATOM**: If successful, an atom that uniquely identifies the new class that was registered; otherwise, the return value is **0**.
Include File	winuser.h
See Also	RegisterClass, CreateWindow, CreateWindowEx, UnregisterClass, GetClassInfo, GetClassName, GetClassLong, GetClassWord, SetClassLong, SetClassWord

WNDCLASSEX Definition

```
typedef struct tagWNDCLASSEX
{
    UINT       cbSize;
    UINT       style;
    WNDPROC    lpfnWndProc;
    int        cbClsExtra;
    int        cbWndExtra;
    HINSTANCE  hInstance;
    HICON      hIcon;
    HCURSOR    hCursor;
    HBRUSH     hbrBackground;
    LPCTSTR    lpszMenuName;
    LPCTSTR    lpszClassName;
    HICON      hIconSm;
}WNDCLASSEX;
```

Members	The elements of the **WNDCLASSEX** are the same as the **WNDCLASS** data structure defined in **RegisterClass**, with the exception that *cbSize* and *hIconSm* have been added.

cbSize	**UINT**: The size, in bytes, of this structure. Set this member to `sizeof( WNDCLASSEX )` before using the structure with a function.
hIconSm	**HICON**: A handle to an icon to be used in the title bar of windows created with this class. The icon dimensions should be 16×16. If this member is **NULL**, the system searches the icon resource specified by the *hIcon* member for an icon of the appropriate size to use as the small icon.
Example	In this example, a window class is registered with a small icon. The resource script file includes a 32×32 icon and a 16×16 icon identified as **"SMALL"**. The small icon appears in the upper-left corner of an application's caption.

```
int APIENTRY WinMain( HINSTANCE hInst, HINSTANCE hPrevInst, LPSTR lpCmdLine, int nCmdShow )
{
    WNDCLASS wc;
    MSG      msg;

    wc.style          = CS_HREDRAW | CS_VREDRAW;
    wc.lpfnWndProc    = (WNDPROC)WndProc;
    wc.cbClsExtra     = 0;
    wc.cbWndExtra     = 0;
    wc.hInstance      = hInst;
    wc.hIcon          = LoadIcon (hInst, lpszAppName);
    wc.hCursor        = LoadCursor (NULL, IDC_ARROW);
    wc.hbrBackground  = (HBRUSH)(COLOR_APPWORKSPACE+1);
    wc.lpszMenuName   = lpszAppName;
    wc.lpszClassName  = lpszAppName;
    wc.cbSize         = sizeof( WNDCLASSEX );
    wc.hIconSm        = LoadIcon( hInst, "SMALL" );

    if ( !RegisterClassEx( &wc ) )
        return( FALSE );

            .
            .
            .
```

UnregisterClass   ■ WINDOWS 95   ■ WINDOWS NT

Description	**UnregisterClass** removes a class that was registered with **RegisterClass** or **RegisterClassEx**. All memory that was used by the class is freed.
	Use to remove a class while an application is still executing. Close all windows created with the class before using **UnregisterClass**. An application removes classes registered by the application when it terminates.

Syntax	BOOL **UnregisterClass**(LPCTSTR *lpszClass,* HINSTANCE *hinst*)
Parameters	
lpszClass	LPCTSTR: A pointer to a null-terminated string or an integer atom. If it is a string, the class name is used. If an atom is used, it must be an atom that was previously created with the **GlobalAddAtom** function.
hinst	HINSTANCE: The instance handle of the module that created the class.
Returns	BOOL: **TRUE** if the function was successful. If the class could not be found or windows are still open using the class, then the return value is **FALSE**.
Include File	winuser.h
See Also	RegisterClass, RegisterClassEx
Example	This example shows a **DLLEntryPoint** function and how it uses the **RegisterClass** and **UnregisterClass** in setting up the groundwork for a custom control DLL. There is code included to make sure only one copy of the custom control class is registered and unregistered if the DLL is used by multiple applications simultaneously.

```
static INT        nProcessCount = 0;
static LPCTSTR    szCustCtlClass = "YourClassName";
static HINSTANCE hInstance = NULL;

static WNDCLASS CustCtlClass = {
/* Style         */   CS_HREDRAW | CS_VREDRAW | CS_DBLCLKS | CS_GLOBALCLASS,
/* lpfnWndProc   */   CustCtlFn,
/* cbClsExtra    */   0,
/* cbWndExtra    */   0,
/* hInstance     */   0,               // Will Set to hInstance
/* hIcon         */   NULL,            // No icon
/* hCursor       */   NULL,            // Will Set to IDC_ARROW
/* hbrBackground */   NULL,            // Will Set to COLOR_BTNFACE+1
/* lpszMenuName  */   NULL,            // No menu
/* lpszClassName */   szCustCtlClass
};

BOOL APIENTRY DllMain(HANDLE hInst, DWORD ul_reason_being_called,
                  LPVOID lpReserved)
{
   if ( ul_reason_being_called == DLL_PROCESS_ATTACH )
   {
      // Check to see if this is the first process that has
      // used this DLL and if so register the custom control class.
      //........................
      if ( nProcessCount == 0 )
```

continued on next page

continued from previous page

```
    {
        hInstance = hInst;

        CustCtlClass.hInstance    = hInstance;
        CustCtlClass.hCursor      = LoadCursor(NULL, IDC_ARROW);
        CustCtlClass.hbrBackground = (HANDLE)(COLOR_BTNFACE+1);

        // Register class. If registration fails then return FALSE.
        //......................................
        if ( RegisterClass( &CustCtlClass ) == 0 )
            return( FALSE );
    }


    // Increment our count of processes that are using this DLL.
    //.................
    nProcessCount++;
}
else if( ul_reason_being_called == DLL_PROCESS_DETACH )
{
    // Decrement our count of processes that are using this DLL.
    //.................
    nProcessCount==-;
    // If this is the last process that was using this DLL we can
    // unregister our class now and clean up since the DLL will be
    // unloaded now.
    //.......................
    if ( nProcessCount <= 0 )
    {
        UnregisterClass( szCustCtlClass, hInstance );
        nProcessCount = 0;
        hInstance = NULL;
    }
}


return( TRUE );
}
```

4

WINDOWS SUPPORT FUNCTIONS

The Windows programming interface provides a wide range of functions for dealing with the windows within an application. These functions let you change the size, placement, and display characteristics of a window. An application can determine and change all the characteristics of a window, using the provided functions.

Window Class Data

Window classes are general window types that form the basis of windows. They resemble C++ classes in that all windows created with a particular window class have the same base properties. Each window class stores the base information that applies to all windows created using that class. Any window created within a class automatically takes on the properties of the class, such as the background color or icon. A window class can also store extra data that an application can access and use during operation.

The **WNDCLASSEX** structure is the storage place for class data. The application uses the **WNDCLASSEX** structure when it registers a new window class and when it retrieves class information. Listing 4-1 shows how the **WNDCLASSEX** structure is defined.

Listing 4-1 WNDCLASSEX *structure*

```
typedef struct WNDCLASSEX
{
    UINT      style;
    WNDPROC   lpfnWndProc;
    int       cbClsExtra;
    int       cbWndExtra;
```

continued on next page

continued from previous page

```
    HINSTANCE hInstance;
    HICON     hIcon;
    HCURSOR   hCursor;
    HBRUSH    hbrBackground;
    LPCTSTR   lpszMenuName;
    LPCTSTR   lpszClassName;
    HICON       hIconSm;
} WNDCLASSEX;
```

All of the items shown in the **WNDCLASSEX** structure are 32-bit (long) values that you retrieve using the **GetClassLong** function. Any extra class data will be allocated at the end of the **WNDCLASSEX** structure and can be accessed in either of two ways. If a 32-bit value is required, the **GetClassLong** function can retrieve the value. If the value needed is a 16-bit value, the **GetClassWord** function is used. **GetClassWord** retrieves only one value other than those in the extra class data, the atom value of the class.

When an application changes the value of any class item for a particular class, it affects all windows that were created using the class. An application uses the **SetClassLong** function to change any of the **WNDCLASSEX** structure items along with 32-bit values in the extra class data. To change 16-bit values in the class extra data, use the **SetClassWord** function.

Every window has specific information along with extra window data. As with the window class, there are two sets of functions to determine and change the window-specific information. The **GetWindowLong** and **GetWindowWord** functions retrieve information from the window. An application changes window information using the **SetWindowLong** and **SetWindowWord** functions.

Attaching Data to a Window

A window can keep a list of associated data, called property items. Each property item contains a 32-bit handle for storing data and is uniquely identified by a character string. The window manages the list of properties, and the application can retrieve the data associated with a property item knowing only the window handle and the unique character string. You can use this feature to store virtually any information that relates to a particular window without using global variables. You can associate data with a window by using extra window data and the **SetWindowLong** and **SetWindowWord** functions. (However, in such cases, the data is not structured, and the application has to know the exact offsets for each value that is stored in the extra window data.) To store a large block of data, an application can allocate the memory and store the handle to that memory as the property item.

The **SetProp** function associates a new property with a window. **SetProp** adds the property item to the property list of a window where it can be retrieved later using the **GetProp** function. The **EnumProps** function scans all the properties associated with a window without knowing what the unique identifiers are in advance. **EnumProps** sequentially goes through each property item in the list and sends it to a callback function for the application to interrogate. Property items can be removed from the list, using the `RemoveProp` function.

Changing the Appearance of Windows

The most common attribute of a window that an application changes is the window title. This is the text displayed in a window's caption or the text that appears on a button. An edit control's title is simply the text currently displayed in the edit control. `GetWindowText` and `SetWindowText` retrieve and change the title text of a window or control.

An application can change the size and position of a window during execution. Several functions can change window size and position; the most basic of these is the `MoveWindow` function. With the series of functions `BeginDeferWindowPos`, `DeferWindowPos`, and `EndDeferWindowPos`, you can move and size several windows at a time. These functions also allow you to size a window without knowing the current position of the window and without changing the order of windows.

Windows Support Function Descriptions

Table 4-1 summarizes the windows support functions. The detailed function descriptions follow the table.

Table 4-1 Windows support function summary

Function	Purpose
AdjustWindowRect	Computes the entire window rect to accommodate a given client area size.
AdjustWindowRectEx	Computes the entire window rect for a window with an extended style and a given client area size.
BeginDeferWindowPos	Begins a fast movement of windows on the screen.
BringWindowToTop	Activates a window and brings it to the top if it is behind any other windows.
ChildWindowFromPoint	Determines the child window of a parent window from a given point.
ChildWindowFromPointEx	Determines the child window of a parent window from a given point with the ability to ignore invisible, disabled, or transparent child windows.
CloseWindow	Minimizes a window.
DeferWindowPos	Moves a window using a fast movement process.
EnableWindow	Enables or disables a window from receiving input from the mouse and keyboard.
EndDeferWindowPos	Completes a fast movement of windows on the screen.
EnumChildWindows	Calls an enumeration function for each of the child windows of a parent.
EnumProps	Calls an enumeration function for each property in the property list of a window.
EnumPropsEx	Calls an enumeration function with user data for each property in the property list of a window.
EnumThreadWindows	Calls an enumeration function for each window associated with a thread.
EnumWindows	Calls an enumeration function for each top-level window running in the system.
FindWindow	Finds a top-level window and retrieves the window handle.
FindWindowEx	Finds any window by window name and class name.
FlashWindow	Highlights a window's caption bar or flashes a window's icon if minimized.

continued on next page

continued from previous page

Function	Purpose
GetActiveWindow	Retrieves the window handle to the window that is currently active.
GetClassInfo	Retrieves information about a window class.
GetClassInfoEx	Retrieves extended information about a window class.
GetClassLong	Retrieves a long value from a window class structure.
GetClassName	Retrieves the class name for a given window.
GetClassWord	Retrieves a word value from a window class structure.
GetClientRect	Retrieves a window's client area size.
GetDesktopWindow	Retrieves the desktop's window handle.
GetFocus	Retrieves the window handle for the window that has input focus.
GetForegroundWindow	Retrieves the window handle for the window that the user is currently working with.
GetLastActivePopup	Retrieves the window handle for the last pop-up window that was active.
GetNextWindow	Finds the next parent or child windows.
GetParent	Retrieves the parent window handle of a child window.
GetProp	Retrieves a property data item associated with a window.
GetTopWindow	Finds the child window that is on top of the other child windows.
GetWindow	Retrieves a window's handle.
GetWindowLong	Retrieves a long value from a window's data.
GetWindowPlacement	Retrieves a window's position information.
GetWindowRect	Retrieves the size of the entire window.
GetWindowText	Retrieves the title string of a window.
GetWindowTextLength	Retrieves the length of the title string of a window.
GetWindowThreadProcessId	Retrieves the thread ID that created a window.
GetWindowWord	Retrieves a word value from a window's extra data.
IsChild	Determines if a window is a child of a given parent window.
IsIconic	Checks whether a window is minimized.
IsWindow	Checks whether a handle points to a valid window.
IsWindowEnabled	Checks whether a window is enabled or disabled.
IsWindowUnicode	Checks whether a window is a native Unicode window.
IsWindowVisible	Checks whether a window has been made visible.
IsZoomed	Checks whether a window is maximized.
MapWindowPoints	Maps the coordinates of a window to be relative to another window.
MoveWindow	Moves and resizes a window.
RemoveProp	Removes a property data item associated with a window.
SetActiveWindow	Makes a window active.
SetClassLong	Changes one of the long values of a window class.
SetClassWord	Changes a word value in the window class extra data.
SetFocus	Gives a window input focus.
SetForegroundWindow	Makes a window the foreground window.
SetParent	Changes the parent window of a child window.
SetProp	Associates a property data item with a window.
SetWindowLong	Changes a long value associated with a window.
SetWindowPlacement	Changes the placement of a window.
SetWindowPos	Changes the size, position, and order of a window at one time.

Function	Purpose
SetWindowText	Changes a window's title.
SetWindowWord	Changes a word value associated with a window.
ShowOwnedPopups	Shows or hides all pop-up windows associated with a parent window.
ShowWindow	Displays, hides, or changes the windows show state.
ShowWindowAsync	Displays, hides, or changes the show state of windows created by other threads.
WindowFromPoint	Finds which window is at a given point on the screen.

AdjustWindowRect   ■ WINDOWS 95 ■ WINDOWS NT

Description   AdjustWindowRect adjusts the rect pointed to by *lpRect* from the size of the client area to the size of a bounding rectangle. The bounding rectangle includes the size of the border, caption bar, menu bar, and the client area.

You generally use AdjustWindowRect with CreateWindow to create a window with a known client area size.

Syntax   BOOL **AdjustWindowRect**(LPRECT *lpRect,* DWORD *dwStyle,* BOOL *bMenu*)

Parameters

lpRect   LPRECT: A pointer to a RECT structure containing the coordinates of the client area for the window that will be created. The coordinates will be adjusted to the size of the window.

dwStyle   DWORD: The window styles that will be used to create the window. For a list of available window styles see Table 3-4 in Chapter 3, Creating Windows.

bMenu   BOOL: Set to TRUE if the rect should include space for a menu; otherwise, set to FALSE.

Returns   BOOL: TRUE if the function was successful, and FALSE if the function failed.

Include File   winuser.h

See Also   CreateWindow, AdjustWindowRectEx

Example   This example shows how to create the main window of an application with a specific client area size. The AdjustWindowRect function adjusts the values of the RECT structure to accommodate the title bar, menu, and borders of the window while leaving the client area positioned in the same place.

```
HINSTANCE hInst = NULL;

static LPCTSTR lpszClassName = "My Class";

int APIENTRY WinMain( HINSTANCE hInstance, HINSTANCE hPrevInstance,
                LPSTR lpCmdLine, int nCmdShow )
```

continued on next page

continued from previous page

```
{
    HWND hWnd;
    MSG  msg;
    RECT rect;


    //Register the application class.
    //.................................
    if (  !InitAppInstance( hInstance ) )
        return FALSE;

    hInst = hInstance;

    // Initialize a RECT with the size and position of
    // the client area we want.
    //.................................

    rect.left   = 100; // 100 pixels from the left of the screen.
    rect.top    = 150; // 150 pixels from the top of the screen.
    rect.right  = 200; // The width will be 100 pixels.
    rect.bottom = 200; // The height will be 50 pixels.

    AdjustWindowRect( &rect, WS_OVERLAPPEDWINDOW, TRUE );

    hWnd = CreateWindow( lpszClassName,   // Class name registered.
                    "My Application",     // Title bar text.
                    WS_OVERLAPPEDWINDOW,  // Window style.
                    rect.left,            // Use the rect calculated
                    rect.top,             //   with AdjustWindowRect()
                    rect.right,           //   for the size and
                    rect.bottom,          //   position.
                    NULL,                 // No parent.
                    NULL,                 // Use class menu.
                    hInstance,
                    NULL);

    if ( !hWnd )
       return( FALSE );

    ShowWindow( hWnd, nCmdShow );
    UpdateWindow( hWnd );

    while ( GetMessage( &msg, NULL, 0, 0 ) )
    {
```

```
        TranslateMessage(&msg);
        DispatchMessage(&msg);
    }

    return( TRUE );
}
```

AdjustWindowRectEx   ■ WINDOWS 95   ■ WINDOWS NT

Description	AdjustWindowRectEx performs the same tasks as the AdjustWindowRect function except it has a parameter for an extended window style. You generally use this function with the CreateWindowEx function.
Syntax	BOOL **AdjustWindowRectEx**(LPRECT *lpRect*, DWORD *dwStyle,* BOOL *bMenu,* DWORD *dwExStyle*)
Parameters	
lpRect	LPRECT: A pointer to a RECT structure containing the coordinates of the client area for the window that will be created. The coordinates will be adjusted to the size of the window.
dwStyle	DWORD: The window styles that will be used to create the window. For a list of available window styles see Table 3-4 in Chapter 3, Creating Windows.
bMenu	BOOL: Set to TRUE if the rect should include space for a menu; otherwise, set to FALSE.
dwExStyle	DWORD: The extended style that will be used to create the window. For a list of available extended window styles see Table 3-5 in Chapter 3.
Returns	BOOL: TRUE if the function was successful, and FALSE if the function failed.
Include File	winuser.h
See Also	CreateWindowEx, AdjustWindowRect
Example	The example for the AdjustWindowRect function is modified with the following code segment to create a main window with a small caption.

```
    .
    .
    .

AdjustWindowRectEx( &rect, WS_OVERLAPPEDWINDOW, TRUE, WS_EX_TOOLWINDOW );

hWnd = CreateWindowEx(WS_EX_TOOLWINDOW,  // Create a window with a small caption.
                lpszClassName,       // Class name registered.
                "My Application",     // Title bar text.
                WS_OVERLAPPEDWINDOW,// Window style.
                rect.left,            // Use the rect calculated
                rect.top,             //   with AdjustWindowRect()
```

continued on next page

continued from previous page

```
rect.right,        //   for the size and
rect.bottom,       //   position.
NULL,              // No parent.
NULL,              // Use class menu.
hInstance,
NULL);
```

.
.
.

BeginDeferWindowPos   ■ WINDOWS 95   ■ WINDOWS NT

Description   This is the first function an application calls in the series of functions
BeginDeferWindowPos, DeferWindowPos, and EndDeferWindowPos to move
one or more windows at one time. The screen refreshes once when the
EndDeferWindowPos function is called.

This function lets you move windows quickly with a minimum of time
spent refreshing the appearance of the screen. It's very useful for making
adjustments to multiple windows at the same time.

Syntax   HDWP **BeginDeferWindowPos**(int *nWindows*)

Parameters

nWindows   int: The initial number of windows for which information is allocated in
the position structure. The DeferWindowPos function will increase the size
of the structure if necessary.

Returns   HDWP: If the function succeeds, the return value is a handle to the multiple-
window-position structure used in calls to the DeferWindowPos and
EndDeferWindowPos functions. The return value is NULL if unsuccessful.

Include File   winuser.h

See Also   DeferWindowPos, EndDeferWindowPos, MoveWindow

Related Messages   WM_MOVE, WM_SIZE

Example   See the example for the DeferWindowPos function.

BringWindowToTop   ■ WINDOWS 95   ■ WINDOWS NT

Description   BringWindowToTop brings a window to the top and superimposes it over
other overlapping windows on the screen. The window is activated if it is
a pop-up or top-level window.

You will most commonly use BringWindowToTop to bring pop-up windows
in front of other windows and activate them for user input.

Syntax   BOOL **BringWindowToTop**(HWND *hwnd*)

Parameters

hwnd   HWND: The window handle to be brought to the top.

Returns   BOOL: TRUE if the function was successful, and FALSE if the function failed.

Include File   winuser.h

See Also   SetFocus, IsWindowVisible, SetActiveWindow, SetForegroundWindow,
                          EnableWindow

Related Messages   WM_SETFOCUS, WM_ENABLE

Example   This example shows the WndProc function of an application that creates
                          two overlapping edit controls. When the Test! menu option is selected, the
                          second edit control is moved to the top of the window order.

```
LRESULT CALLBACK WndProc( HWND hWnd, UINT uMsg, WPARAM wParam, LPARAM lParam )
{
static HWND hEdit1 = NULL;
static HWND hEdit2 = NULL;

    switch( uMsg )
    {
        case WM_CREATE :
                // Create two overlapping edit controls.
                //....................................
                hEdit1 = CreateWindow( "EDIT", "Here is Edit 1",
                                    WS_CHILD | WS_BORDER |
                                    WS_VISIBLE |ES_LEFT,
                                    10, 10, 100, 30,
                                    hWnd, (HMENU) 101,
                                    hInst, NULL );

                hEdit2 = CreateWindow( "EDIT", "Here is Edit 2",
                                    WS_CHILD | WS_BORDER |
                                    WS_VISIBLE | ES_LEFT,
                                    15, 20, 100, 30,
                                    hWnd, (HMENU) 102,
                                    hInst, NULL );
                break;

        case WM_COMMAND :
                switch( LOWORD( wParam ) )
                {
                    case IDM_TEST :
                            // Bring hEdit2 to the top of the window order
                            // and refresh the screen.
                            //...........................................
```

continued on next page

continued from previous page

```
                              BringWindowToTop( hEdit2 );
                              InvalidateRect( hWnd, NULL, TRUE );
                              UpdateWindow( hWnd );
                              break;



             .
             .
             .
             .
}
```

ChildWindowFromPoint ■ WINDOWS 95   ■ WINDOWS NT

Description	`ChildWindowFromPoint` returns the handle to the child window that contains the given point relative to the parent window's client area.
	This function is most commonly used to process the **WM_MOUSEMOVE**, **WM_LBUTTONDOWN**, and **WM_RBUTTONDOWN** messages and to determine the window the mouse cursor lies over when the messages occur.
Syntax	HWND **ChildWindowFromPoint**(HWND *hwndParent*, POINT *pt*)
Parameters	
hwndParent	**HWND**: The parent window handle.
pt	**POINT**: A **POINT** structure that contains the client coordinates of the point to be checked.
Returns	**HWND**: If the function succeeds, the handle of the child window that contains the point is returned, even if the child window is hidden or disabled. If the point is outside the parent window's boundaries, the return value is **NULL**. If the point is within the boundaries but not on a child window, the return value is the parent window handle.
Include File	winuser.h
See Also	ChildWindowFromPointEx, WindowFromPoint
Related Messages	WM_MOUSEMOVE, WM_LBUTTONDOWN, WM_RBUTTONDOWN
Example	This example shows a portion of the **WndProc** function of an application that creates a static child control. When the left mouse button is pressed, the application checks to see whether the mouse cursor was over the static control or the client area of the main window.

```
LRESULT CALLBACK WndProc( HWND hWnd, UINT uMsg, WPARAM wParam, LPARAM lParam )
{
static HWND hStatic = NULL;

   switch( uMsg )
   {
      case WM_CREATE :
```

```
            hStatic = CreateWindow( "STATIC", "Here is Static",
                             WS_CHILD | WS_BORDER |
                             WS_VISIBLE | SS_LEFT,
                             10, 10, 100, 30,
                             hWnd, (HMENU) 101,
                             hInst, NULL );
        break;

    case WM_LBUTTONDOWN :
        {
            POINT pt;
            HWND  hwndChild;

            pt.x = LOWORD( lParam );
            pt.y = HIWORD( lParam );

            hwndChild = ChildWindowFromPoint( hWnd, pt );

            if ( hwndChild == hStatic )
                MessageBox( hWnd, "static control!", "Hit", MB_OK );
            else
                MessageBox( hWnd, "client area!", "Hit", MB_OK );
        }
        break;
```

ChildWindowFromPointEx   ■ WINDOWS 95   ■ WINDOWS NT

Description	The same as **ChildWindowFromPoint** except disabled, transparent, and invisible child windows can be skipped when determining the child window.
Syntax	HWND **ChildWindowFromPointEx**(HWND *hwndParent,* POINT *pt,* UINT *uFlags*)
Parameters	
hwndParent	HWND: The parent window handle.
pt	POINT: A **POINT** structure that contains the client coordinates of the point to be checked.
uFlags	UINT: Determines which child windows will be skipped. The parameter can be a combination of the values listed in Table 4-2 combined with the binary OR (|) operator.

Table 4-2 `ChildWindowFromPointEx` flags

Value	Meaning
CWP_ALL	Look at all child windows.
CWP_SKIPDISABLED	Skip disabled child windows.
CWP_SKIPINVISIBLE	Skip invisible child windows.
CWP_SKIPTRANSPARENT	Skip transparent child windows.

Returns   HWND: If the function succeeds, the handle of the child window that contains the point and meets the criteria in *uFlags*. If the point is within the parent boundaries but not within any child window that meets the criteria, the return value is the parent window handle. If the point is outside the boundaries, the return value is NULL.

Include File   winuser.h

See Also   ChildWindowFromPoint, WindowFromPoint

Example   This code segment shows how the example for the ChildWindowFromPoint function can be changed to use the ChildWindowFromPointEx function, so disabled controls will be ignored when testing where the mouse hit.

```
case WM_LBUTTONDOWN :
        {
        POINT pt;
        HWND  hwndChild;

        pt.x = LOWORD( lParam );
        pt.y = HIWORD( lParam );

        hwndChild = ChildWindowFromPointEx( hWnd, pt,
                                            CWP_SKIPDISABLED );

        if ( hwndChild == hStatic )
           MessageBox( hWnd, "static control!", "Hit", MB_OK );
        else
           MessageBox( hWnd, "client area!", "Hit", MB_OK );
        }
        break;
```

CloseWindow   ■ Windows 95   ■ Windows NT

Description   CloseWindow minimizes the specified window and displays the window icon that was registered with the window class. If the window class has no icon, then a blank client area is displayed and the window will receive WM_PAINT messages for painting the icon. The application's main window can be used to minimize the entire application or a child window such as an MDI (multiple-document interface) window.

Syntax	BOOL **CloseWindow**(HWND *hwnd*)
Parameters	
hwnd	HWND: Identifies the window to be minimized.
Returns	BOOL: TRUE if the function was successful, and FALSE if the function failed.
Include File	winuser.h
See Also	IsIconic, IsWindowVisible, IsZoomed
Related Messages	WM_SIZE, WM_PAINT
Example	In this example the **CloseWindow** function minimizes the application when the Test! menu option is selected.

```
LRESULT CALLBACK WndProc( HWND hWnd, UINT uMsg, WPARAM wParam, LPARAM lParam )
{
   switch( uMsg )
   {
      case WM_COMMAND :
              switch( LOWORD( wParam ) )
              {
                  case IDM_TEST :
                          // Minimize the application window.
                          //...............................
                          CloseWindow( hWnd );
                          break;

                          .
                          .
                          .
```

DeferWindowPos   ■ WINDOWS 95   ■ WINDOWS NT

Description	**DeferWindowPos** is the second function in the series **BeginDeferWindowPos**, **DeferWindowPos**, and **EndDeferWindowPos**. The **DeferWindowPos** function sets the new position information for each window that is to be moved.
	DeferWindowPos is useful for moving one or more windows quickly with only one screen update.
Syntax	HDWP **DeferWindowPos**(HDWP *hdwp*, HWND *hwnd*, HWND *hwndInsertAfter*, int *x*, int *y*, int *cx*, int *cy*, UINT *dwFlags*)
Parameters	
hdwp	HDWP: The handle to the multiple-window position structure that was created with the **BeginDeferWindowPos** or returned from a previous call to **DeferWindowPos**.

hwnd	HWND: A handle to the window that will be moved.
hwndInsertAfter	HWND: A handle to the window that will precede the window in *hwnd*. One of the values in Table 4-3 can be used in place of a window handle. This parameter is ignored if the SWP_NOZORDER is set in the *dwFlags* parameter.

Table 4-3 DeferWindowPos *hwndInsertAfter* values

Value	Meaning
HWND_BOTTOM	Moves the window to the bottom position in the stack of child windows.
HWND_NOTOPMOST	Moves the window to the bottom position of all topmost windows. This is above all nontopmost windows.
HWND_TOP	Moves the window to the top position in the stack of child windows.
HWND_TOPMOST	Moves the window to the top position of all topmost windows. When the window is deactivated it will still maintain its topmost position.

x	int: The new x position of the window's upper-left corner.
y	int: The new y position of the window's upper-left corner.
cx	int: The window's new width, in pixels.
cy	int: The window's new height, in pixels.
dwFlags	UINT: Affects how the window is moved and positioned. This parameter is made up of one or more of the values listed in Table 4-4 combined with the binary OR (	) operator.

Table 4-4 DeferWindowPos *dwFlags* values

Value	Meaning
SWP_DRAWFRAME	Draws the frame defined in the window's class around the window.
SWP_FRAMECHANGED	Forces the WM_NCCALCSIZE message to be sent to the window, even if the window's size is not being changed.
SWP_HIDEWINDOW	Hides the window.
SWP_NOACTIVATE	Does not activate the window.
SWP_NOCOPYBITS	Discards the entire contents of the client area. By default, the valid contents of the client area are saved and copied back into the client area after the window is sized or positioned.
SWP_NOMOVE	The *x* and *y* parameters are ignored. The window will only be resized.
SWP_NOOWNERZORDER	Preserves the position in the Z order of the owner window.
SWP_NOREDRAW	Will not cause a repaint after the move takes place. The application must explicitly invalidate or redraw any part that needs to be drawn.
SWP_NOREPOSITION	Same as the SWP_NOOWNERZORDER flag.
SWP_NOSENDCHANGING	Prevents the window from receiving the WM_WINDOWPOSCHANGING message.
SWP_NOSIZE	The *cx* and *cy* parameters are ignored. The window will only be moved.
SWP_NOZORDER	Ignores the *hwndInsertAfter* parameter.
SWP_SHOWWINDOW	Displays the window.

Returns	**HDWP**: The handle to the updated multiple-window position structure. The handle returned could be different from the one passed in and should be used in subsequent calls to **DeferWindowPos** and ultimately **EndDeferWindowPos**. If the function does not succeed, a **NULL** will be returned.
Include File	winuser.h
See Also	BeginDeferWindowPos, EndDeferWindowPos, MoveWindow
Related Messages	WM_MOVE, WM_SIZE
Example	This example (see Figure 4-1) shows a section of the **WndProc** function for an application that creates a static text control and an edit control as child windows of the main window. These controls then are sized using the **BeginDeferWindowPos**, **DeferWindowPos**, and **EndDeferWindowPos** functions when the main window is sized. The width of the static control is kept the same as the main window's width. The width and height of the edit control are changed to match the main window's width and height minus the height of the static control.

```c
LRESULT CALLBACK WndProc(HWND hWnd, UINT uMsg, WPARAM wParam, LPARAM lParam )
{
static HWND hStatic = NULL;
static HWND hEdit   = NULL;

   switch( uMsg )
   {
      case WM_CREATE :
              // Create a static and edit control that will be sized to match
              // the parent window's client area.
              //..........................................................
              hStatic = CreateWindowEx( WS_EX_CLIENTEDGE,
                                   "STATIC", "Here is the Static Control",
                                   WS_CHILD | WS_BORDER |
                                   WS_VISIBLE |
                                   SS_LEFT,
                                   0, 0,
                                   CW_USEDEFAULT,
                                   CW_USEDEFAULT,
                                   hWnd,
                                   (HMENU) 101,   // The control ID.
                                   hInst, NULL );

              hEdit = CreateWindowEx( WS_EX_CLIENTEDGE,
                                   "EDIT", "Here is the Edit Control",
```

continued on next page

continued from previous page

```
                             WS_CHILD | WS_BORDER |
                             WS_VISIBLE |
                             ES_LEFT | ES_MULTILINE,
                             0, 20,          // Set the upper
                                             // left corner
                             CW_USEDEFAULT, // to be under the
                             CW_USEDEFAULT, // static window.
                             hWnd,
                             (HMENU) 102,    // The control ID.
                             hInst, NULL );
        break;


    case WM_SIZE :
        {
            // The parent window was resized. Size the static and edit
            // controls to match the parent window's client area but
            // don't move the controls.
            //........................................................
            HDWP hdwp = BeginDeferWindowPos(2);

            hdwp = DeferWindowPos( hdwp, hStatic, NULL, 0, 0,
                              LOWORD( lParam ), 20,
                              SWP_NOACTIVATE | SWP_NOZORDER |
                              SWP_NOMOVE );

            hdwp = DeferWindowPos( hdwp, hEdit, NULL, 0, 0,
                              LOWORD( lParam ), HIWORD( lParam ),
                              SWP_NOACTIVATE | SWP_NOZORDER |
                              SWP_NOMOVE );

            EndDeferWindowPos( hdwp );
        }
        break;


            .
            .
            .
```

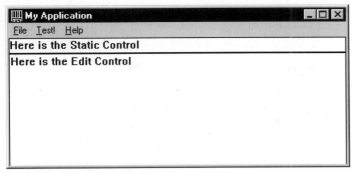

Figure 4-1 `DeferWindowPos` example

EnableWindow   ■ WINDOWS 95   ■ WINDOWS NT

Description   Use `EnableWindow` to enable and disable windows. This function is commonly used to disable edit controls and buttons, so the user cannot input
data or activate the button.

Syntax   `BOOL EnableWindow( HWND ` *hwnd,* ` BOOL ` *bEnable* ` )`

Parameters

hwnd   `HWND`: The handle of the window to be enabled or disabled.

bEnable   `BOOL`: Set to `TRUE` to enable the window, and set to `FALSE` to disable it.

Returns   `BOOL`: If the window was already disabled, the return value is `TRUE`; otherwise, the return value is `FALSE`.

Include File   `winuser.h`

See Also   `SetFocus, GetFocus, SetActiveWindow`

Related Messages `WM_ENABLE`

Example   In this example, the application creates an edit control as a child window
of the main application window. When the Test! menu option is selected,
the edit control is disabled from keyboard input. The edit control could be
enabled by calling the `EnableWindow` function with the *bEnable* parameter
set to `TRUE`.

```
LRESULT CALLBACK WndProc( HWND hWnd, UINT uMsg, WPARAM wParam, LPARAM lParam )
{
static HWND hEdit = NULL;

   switch( uMsg )
   {
      case WM_CREATE :
```

continued on next page

continued from previous page

```
            // Create an edit control.
            //......................
            hEdit = CreateWindow( "EDIT", "Here is Edit",
                                  WS_CHILD | WS_BORDER |
                                  WS_VISIBLE | ES_LEFT,
                                  10, 10, 100, 20,
                                  hWnd, (HMENU) 101,
                                  hInst, NULL );
        break;

    case WM_COMMAND :
        switch( LOWORD( wParam ) )
        {
            case IDM_TEST :
                // Disable the edit control from user input.
                //.........................................
                EnableWindow( hEdit, FALSE );
                break;

            .
            .
            .
```

EndDeferWindowPos

■ WINDOWS 95 ■ WINDOWS NT

Description	EndDeferWindowPos is the third and last function in the series BeginDeferWindowPos, DeferWindowPos, and EndDeferWindowPos. This function simultaneously updates the position and size of one or more windows that have been passed to DeferWindowPos.
	EndDeferWindowPos is useful for moving one or more windows quickly with only one screen update.
Syntax	BOOL **EndDeferWindowPos**(HDWP *hdwp*)
Parameters	
hdwp	HDWP: A handle to the multiple-window position structure that the last call to the DeferWindowPos function returned. The structure that contains size and position information for one or more windows.
Returns	BOOL: TRUE if the function was successful, and FALSE if the function failed.

Include File	winuser.h
See Also	BeginDeferWindowPos, DeferWindowPos, MoveWindow
Related Messages	WM_MOVE, WM_SIZE
Example	See the example for the DeferWindowPos function.

EnumChildWindows   ■ WINDOWS 95   ■ WINDOWS NT

Description	EnumChildWindows sends the handle of each child window belonging to a parent window to a callback function. EnumChildWindows continues until all child windows have been processed or the callback function returns FALSE.
	EnumChildWindows can be used to sequentially process all the child windows when you don't know how many child windows exist.
Syntax	BOOL **EnumChildWindows**(HWND *hwndParent,* WNDENUMPROC *wndenmprc,* LPARAM *lParam*)
Parameters	
hwndParent	HWND: The parent window handle of the child windows that will be enumerated.
wndenmprc	WNDENUMPROC: A pointer to the application-defined callback function.
lParam	LPARAM: A 32-bit value to be sent to the callback function for each child window. See the description of the callback function below.
Returns	BOOL: TRUE if the function was successful, and FALSE if the function failed.
Include File	winuser.h
See Also	EnumProps, EnumPropsEx, EnumThreadWindows, EnumWindows
Callback Syntax	BOOL CALLBACK **EnumChildProc**(HWND *hwnd,* LPARAM *lParam*)
Callback Parameters	
hwnd	HWND: A handle to the child window.
lParam	LPARAM: The 32-bit value that was passed into the *lParam* parameter of the EnumChildWindows function.
Example	This example (see Figure 4-2) uses the EnumChildWindows function to change the text of the edit controls that are created. The string that the edit control text should be set to is passed in as the *lParam* of the EnumChildProc. The class name of each window handle passed to the EnumChildProc is checked to make sure only edit controls are changed.

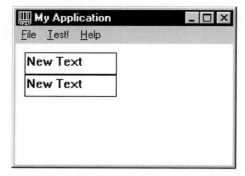

Figure 4-2 EnumChildWindows example

```
BOOL CALLBACK EnumChildProc( HWND hWnd, LPARAM lParam )
{
static char szClass[51];

   GetClassName( hWnd, szClass, 50 );

   if ( stricmp( szClass, "EDIT" ) == 0 )
      SetWindowText( hWnd, (LPCTSTR)lParam );

   return( TRUE );
}


LRESULT CALLBACK WndProc( HWND hWnd, UINT uMsg, WPARAM wParam, LPARAM lParam )
{
static HWND hEdit1 = NULL;
static HWND hEdit2 = NULL;

   switch( uMsg )
   {

      case WM_COMMAND :
            switch( LOWORD( wParam ) )
            {
               case IDM_TEST :
                     // Set the window text for each child window.
                     //.........................................
                     EnumChildWindows( hWnd, (WNDENUMPROC)EnumChildProc,
                                       (LPARAM)(LPCTSTR)"New Text" );
                     break;
```

EnumProps
■ WINDOWS 95 ■ WINDOWS NT

Description   EnumProps passes each property item associated with a window to a callback function. This process continues until the last property item is enumerated or the callback function returns FALSE.

This function is used to find the data associated with a window without the application knowing in advance how many property items exist.

Syntax   int **EnumProps**(HWND *hwnd,* PROPENUMPROC *lpEnumFunc*)

Parameters

hwnd   HWND: A handle to the window with the property list to be enumerated.

lpEnumFunc   PROPENUMPROC: A pointer to the application-defined callback function.

Returns   int: The last value returned by the callback function. The return value is −1 if the window did not have associated property items.

Include File   winuser.h

See Also   EnumPropsEx, EnumChildWindows, SetProp, GetProp, RemoveProp

Callback Syntax   BOOL CALLBACK **EnumPropProc**(HWND *hwnd,* LPCTSTR *lpszString,* HANDLE *hData*)

Callback Parameters

hwnd   HWND: A handle to the window that the property item is associated with.

lpszString   LPCTSTR: A pointer to the null-terminated string or the integer atom that was used with the SetProp function for the property item. If an atom is used, the high-order word should be set to 0, and the low-order word will contain the atom's value.

hData   HANDLE: A handle to the property item's data.

Callback Returns   BOOL: TRUE to continue enumeration. FALSE to stop enumeration.

Example   This example adds three properties to the main application window. The EnumProps function is then used to enumerate the properties and display the name and value of each property in a message box.

```
static LPCTSTR szProp1 = "Value for Property 1";
static LPCTSTR szProp2 = "Value for Property 2";
static LPCTSTR szProp3 = "Value for Property 3";

BOOL CALLBACK EnumPropsProc( HWND hWnd, LPCTSTR lpszString, HANDLE hData )
{
```

continued on next page

continued from previous page
```
    MessageBox( hWnd, (LPCTSTR)hData, lpszString, MB_OK );

    return( TRUE );
}



LRESULT CALLBACK WndProc( HWND hWnd, UINT uMsg, WPARAM wParam, LPARAM lParam )
{

    switch( uMsg )
    {
       case WM_CREATE :
               // Add property items that contain string pointers
               // to the main window
               //..................................................
               SetProp( hWnd, "Property 1", (HANDLE)szProp1 );
               SetProp( hWnd, "Property 2", (HANDLE)szProp2 );
               SetProp( hWnd, "Property 3", (HANDLE)szProp3 );
               break;

       case WM_COMMAND :
               switch( LOWORD( wParam ) )
               {
                  case IDM_TEST :
                          // Enumerate the properties and display in a message
                          // box the property name and value.
                          //.....................................................
                          EnumProps( hWnd, (PROPENUMPROC)EnumPropsProc );
                          break;
         .
         .
         .
```

EnumPropsEx   ■ WINDOWS 95   ■ WINDOWS NT

Description	EnumPropsEx is the same as the **EnumProps** function, except that it has an extra parameter for passing application-defined data to the callback function.
Syntax	int **EnumPropsEx**(HWND *hwnd*, PROPENUMPROCEX *lpEnumFunc*, LPARAM *lParam*)
Parameters	
hwnd	HWND: A handle to the window with the property list to be enumerated.

lpEnumFunc	PROPENUMPROCEX: A pointer to the application-defined callback function.
lParam	LPARAM: A 32-bit application-defined value that will be passed to the callback function for each property item.
Returns	int: The last value returned by the callback function. The return value is −1 if the window did not have associated property items.
Include File	winuser.h
See Also	EnumProps, SetProp, GetProp, RemoveProp
Callback Syntax	BOOL CALLBACK **PropEnumProcEx**(HWND *hwnd,* LPCTSTR *lpszString,* HANDLE *hData,* LPARAM *lParam*)

Callback Parameters

hwnd	HWND: A handle to the window that the property item is associated with.
lpszString	LPCTSTR: A pointer to the null-terminated string or the integer atom that was used with the **SetProp** function for the property item. If an atom is used, the high-order word should be set to **0**, and the low-order word will contain the atom's value.
hData	HANDLE: A handle to the property item's data.
lParam	LPARAM: The 32-bit application-defined value used in the **EnumPropsEx** function call.
Callback Returns	BOOL: Return **TRUE** to continue the property list enumeration. Return **FALSE** to stop the property list enumeration.
Example	Same as the example for **EnumProps**, except that the name of the last property item enumerated is copied to the buffer pointed to by the *lParam* parameter and then displayed in a message box.

```
char szPropName[20];

BOOL CALLBACK EnumPropsProcEx( HWND hWnd, LPCTSTR lpszString, HANDLE hData,
                               LPARAM lParam )
{
    MessageBox( hWnd, (LPCTSTR)hData, lpszString, MB_OK );

    strcpy( (LPTSTR) lParam, lpszString );

    return( TRUE );
}


LRESULT CALLBACK WndProc( HWND hWnd, UINT uMsg, WPARAM wParam, LPARAM lParam )
{
```

continued on next page

continued from previous page

```
    switch( uMsg )
    {
      case WM_CREATE :
                // Add property items that contain string pointers
                // to the main window
                //................................................
                SetProp( hWnd, "Property 1", (HANDLE)szProp1 );
                SetProp( hWnd, "Property 2", (HANDLE)szProp2 );
                SetProp( hWnd, "Property 3", (HANDLE)szProp3 );
                break;

      case WM_COMMAND :
                switch( LOWORD( wParam ) )
                {
                  case IDM_TEST :
                        // Enumerate the properties and display in a message
                        // box the property name and value. Also copy the
                        // property name into the buffer pointed to by
                        // szPropname and display it when finished.
                        //......................................................
                        EnumPropsEx( hWnd, (PROPENUMPROCEX)EnumPropsProcEx,
                                (LPARAM)(LPTSTR)szPropName );

                        MessageBox( hWnd, szPropName, "Last Property Item",
                                MB_OK );
                        break;
```

.
.
.

EnumThreadWindows   ■ WINDOWS 95 ■ WINDOWS NT

Description	EnumThreadWindows sends the window handle of each window belonging to a thread to an application-defined callback function.
	EnumThreadWindows continues until all windows associated with the thread have been processed or the callback function returns FALSE.
Syntax	BOOL **EnumThreadWindows**(DWORD *dwThreadId*, WNDENUMPROC *lpfn*, LPARAM *lParam*)

Parameters

dwThreadId   **DWORD**: The thread identifier for the thread for which windows will be enumerated.

lpfn   **WNDENUMPROC**: A pointer to an application-defined callback function.

lParam   **LPARAM**: A 32-bit application-defined value that will be sent to the callback function for each window in the thread.

Returns   **BOOL**: **TRUE** if the function was successful, and **FALSE** if the function failed.

Include File   `winuser.h`

See Also   `EnumChildWindows, GetWindowThreadProcessId, EnumWindows, GetCurrentThreadId`

Callback Syntax   `BOOL CALLBACK `**`EnumThreadWndProc`**`( HWND `*`hwnd,`*` LPARAM `*`lParam`*` )`

Callback Parameters

hwnd   **HWND**: A handle to a window associated with the thread specified in the `EnumThreadWindows` function.

lParam   **LPARAM**: The 32-bit application-defined value given to the `EnumThreadWindows` function.

Callback Returns   **BOOL**: **TRUE** to continue enumeration. **FALSE** to stop enumeration.

Example   This example shows how to use the `EnumThreadWindows` function to find all the windows associated with the same thread as the main application window. The window title for each window is displayed in a message box. The last window title enumerated is shown in a message box, as seen in Figure 4-3. The example uses the extra data parameter to pass the pointer for the buffer to store the window titles.

Figure 4-3 `EnumThreadWindows` example

```
BOOL CALLBACK EnumThreadProc( HWND hWnd, LPARAM lParam )
{
    GetWindowText( hWnd, (LPTSTR)lParam, 30 );

    MessageBox( hWnd, (LPTSTR)lParam, "Window Name", MB_OK );
    return( TRUE );
}



LRESULT CALLBACK WndProc( HWND hWnd, UINT uMsg, WPARAM wParam, LPARAM lParam )
{
static char szWindowName[31];

    switch( uMsg )
    {
      case WM_COMMAND :
            switch( LOWORD( wParam ) )
            {
               case IDM_TEST :
                  {
                        // Enumerate all the windows associated with the
                        // application's main thread.
                        //...............................................
                        DWORD dwAppThreadID = GetWindowThreadProcessId( hWnd,
                                                                 NULL );

                        EnumThreadWindows( dwAppThreadID,
                                 (WNDENUMPROC)EnumThreadProc,
                                 (LPARAM)(LPTSTR)szWindowName );

                        MessageBox( hWnd, szWindowName, "Last Window Name",
                                 MB_OK );
                        break;
                  }
                 .
                 .
                 .
```

EnumWindows

Description	**EnumWindows** calls an application-defined callback function for all top-level windows on the screen. **EnumWindows** continues until all top-level windows have been passed to the callback function or the callback function returns **FALSE**.
	EnumWindows can be used to determine which other applications are currently running and obtains information about those applications.
Syntax	BOOL **EnumWindows**(WNDENUMPROC *wndenmprc,* LPARAM *lParam*)
Parameters	
wndenmprc	**WNDENUMPROC**: A pointer to an application-defined callback function.
lParam	**LPARAM**: A 32-bit application-defined value that will be passed to the callback function for each window.
Returns	**BOOL**: **TRUE** if the function was successful, and **FALSE** if the function failed.
Include File	winuser.h
See Also	EnumChildWindows, EnumThreadWindows
Callback Syntax	BOOL CALLBACK **EnumWndProc**(HWND *hwnd,* LPARAM *lParam*)
Callback Parameters	
hwnd	**HWND**: A window handle to a top-level window currently running on the system.
lParam	**LPARAM**: The 32-bit application-defined value given to the **EnumWindows** function.
Callback Returns	**BOOL**: **TRUE** to continue enumeration. **FALSE** to stop enumeration.
Example	This example (see Figure 4-4) uses the **EnumWindows** function to list in the list box the names and classes of every top-level window. The handle of the list box control is passed in the *lParam* parameter of the **EnumWindows** function.

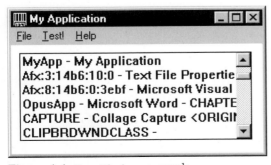

Figure 4-4 EnumWindows example

```
BOOL CALLBACK EnumWndProc( HWND hWnd, LPARAM lParam )
{
static char szWindowName[71];
static char szClassName[31];
static char szAddString[101];

    // Get the window name and class name
    //...................................
    GetWindowText( hWnd, szWindowName, 70 );
    GetClassName( hWnd, szClassName, 30 );

    // Build a string and add it to the list box.
    //...........................................
    wsprintf( szAddString, "%s - %s", szClassName, szWindowName );

    SendMessage( (HWND)lParam, LB_INSERTSTRING, (WPARAM)-1,
                 (LPARAM)(LPTSTR)szAddString );

    return( TRUE );
}



LRESULT CALLBACK WndProc( HWND hWnd, UINT uMsg, WPARAM wParam, LPARAM lParam )
{
static HWND hListBox;

    switch( uMsg )
    {
        case WM_CREATE :
                hListBox = CreateWindow( "LISTBOX", "",
                                         WS_CHILD | WS_BORDER |
                                         WS_VISIBLE | LBS_STANDARD,
                                         10, 10, 250, 100,
                                         hWnd, (HMENU) 101,
                                         hInst, NULL );
                break;

        case WM_COMMAND :
                switch( LOWORD( wParam ) )
                {
                    case IDM_TEST :
                            // Enumerate all top-level windows currently running
                            // and add their class names and window names to the
                            // hListBox.
```

```
//..............................................
EnumWindows((WNDENUMPROC)EnumWndProc,
            (LPARAM)(HANDLE)hListBox );

break;
```

.
.
.

FindWindow   ■ WINDOWS 95 ■ WINDOWS NT

Description	FindWindow finds a top-level window with a given class name and window name. Child windows are not searched.
	FindWindow is used to determine whether a specific application is currently running.
Syntax	HWND **FindWindow**(LPCTSTR *lpszClass,* LPCTSTR *lpszWindow*)
Parameters	
lpszClass	LPCTSTR: A pointer to a null-terminated string that contains the class name or an integer atom that identifies the class. If the parameter is an atom, it must be a global atom. The high-order word should be set to **0**, and the low-order word will contain the atom's value.
lpszWindow	LPCTSTR: A pointer to a null-terminated string that contains the window name. If this parameter is **NULL**, then all window names will match.
Returns	HWND: If a window is found that matches the given class name and window name, the return value will be the window handle of that window; otherwise, it is **NULL**.
Include File	winuser.h
See Also	FindWindowEx, EnumWindows, ChildWindowFromPoint, GetClassName, GetWindowText
Example	This example shows a function that will try to find the Clock program window. If the window is found, then the function returns **TRUE** (presuming the clock program is running).

```
BOOL IsClockRunning()
{
    if ( FindWindow( NULL, "Clock" ) )
        return( TRUE );
    else
        return( FALSE );
}
```

FindWindowEx

Description	FindWindowEx finds any window currently running on the system, including child windows that match the given class name and window name.
	Use FindWindowEx to find a specific type of window with a given name anywhere in the current application or in any application.
Syntax	HWND **FindWindowEx**(HWND *hwndParent*, HWND *hwndChildAfter*, LPCTSTR *lpszClass*, LPCTSTR *lpszWindow*)
Parameters	
hwndParent	HWND: A handle to the parent window whose child windows will be searched. If a NULL is used, all windows will be searched.
hwndChildAfter	HWND: A handle to the child window from which you wish to start the search. The next child window will be the first one searched. If a NULL is used, the search begins with the first child window of the parent.
lpszClass	LPCTSTR: A pointer to a null-terminated string that contains the class name or an integer atom that identifies the class. If the parameter is an atom, it must be a global atom. The high-order word should be set to 0, and the low-order word will contain the atom's value.
lpszWindow	LPCTSTR: A pointer to a null-terminated string that contains the window name. If this parameter is NULL, then all window names will match.
Returns	HWND: If a window is found that matches the given class name and window name, the return value will be the window handle of that window; otherwise, it is NULL.
Include File	winuser.h
See Also	FindWindow, ChildWindowFromPoint, GetClassName, GetWindowText
Example	See the example for the FindWindow function. The only difference is that all windows in the system are searched, not just the top-level ones.

FlashWindow

Description	FlashWindow highlights a window's caption bar or flashes a window's icon if minimized.
	Use FlashWindow to inform the user that a window needs attention when the window does not have input focus.
Syntax	BOOL **FlashWindow**(HWND *hwnd*, BOOL *bInvert*)
Parameters	
hwnd	HWND: The handle of the window that you wish to flash.
bInvert	BOOL: If the window should be toggled from one state to another, set to TRUE. To return the window to its original state, set to FALSE.

Returns	**BOOL**: The window's state before the call to the **FlashWindow** function. If the window was active, it is **TRUE**; otherwise, it is **FALSE**.
Include File	**winuser.h**
See Also	**GetFocus**, **SetFocus**, **SetActiveWindow**
Example	See the example for the **IsIconic** function.

GetActiveWindow ■ WINDOWS 95 ■ WINDOWS NT

Description	**GetActiveWindow** retrieves the handle of the active window associated with the thread that calls the function.
	Use **GetActiveWindow** to find out which window is currently active.
Syntax	HWND **GetActiveWindow**(VOID)
Parameters	This function has no parameters.
Returns	**HWND**: If successful, the return value is the handle of the currently active window associated with the thread that called the function. If the calling thread does not have an active window, the return value is **NULL**.
Include File	**winuser.h**
See Also	**SetActiveWindow, GetFocus, SetFocus**
Example	This example will change the title of the currently active window to Active Window.

```
LRESULT CALLBACK WndProc( HWND hWnd, UINT uMsg, WPARAM wParam, LPARAM lParam )
{

    switch( uMsg )
    {
        case WM_COMMAND :
                switch( LOWORD( wParam ) )
                {
                    case IDM_TEST :
                            // Change the title of the active window.
                            //...........................................
                            SetWindowText( GetActiveWindow(), "Active Window" );
                            break;
            .
            .
            .
```

GetClassInfo ■ WINDOWS 95 ■ WINDOWS NT

Description	`GetClassInfo` retrieves the `WNDCLASS` information for a window class. The information can be used to register a similar window class. This function has been superseded by the `GetClassInfoEx` function. This function still works; however, it will not return information about the class small icon.
Syntax	`BOOL GetClassInfo( HINSTANCE hinst, LPCTSTR lpszClass, LPWNDCLASS lpwc )`
Parameters	
hinst	`HINSTANCE`: The instance handle of the application that created the class. For information about predefined classes such as `BUTTON` and `EDIT`, set to `NULL`.
lpszClass	`LPCTSTR`: A pointer to a null-terminated string or an integer atom. If an atom, it must be a global atom that was created with a call to the `GlobalAddAtom` function. The high-order word should be set to `0`, and the low-order word will contain the atom's value.
lpwc	`LPWNDCLASS`: A pointer to a `WNDCLASS` structure that will receive the information about the class. See the definition of the `WNDCLASS` structure below.
Returns	`BOOL`: If the function succeeds and finds the specified class, the return value is `TRUE`; otherwise, it is `FALSE`.
Include File	`winuser.h`
See Also	`GetClassInfoEx, GetClassWord, GetClassLong, SetClassWord, SetClassLong, RegisterClass, UnregisterClass`
WNDCLASS Definition	

```
typedef struct tagWNDCLASS
{
    UINT     style;
    WNDPROC  lpfnWndProc;
    int      cbClsExtra;
    int      cbWndExtra;
    HANDLE   hInstance;
    HICON    hIcon;
    HCURSOR  hCursor;
    HBRUSH   hbrBackground;
    LPCTSTR  lpszMenuName;
    LPCTSTR  lpszClassName;
} WNDCLASS;
```

Members	For information on the individual members of the `WNDCLASS` structure, see the `RegisterClass` function in Chapter 3, Creating Windows.

Example

This example retrieves the class information for the main window and displays the class menu name in a message box.

```
static LPCTSTR lpszAppClass = "My Class"; // Class name for main window.

LRESULT CALLBACK WndProc( HWND hWnd, UINT uMsg, WPARAM wParam, LPARAM lParam )
{

   switch( uMsg )
   {
      case WM_COMMAND :
            switch( LOWORD( wParam ) )
            {
               case IDM_TEST :
                  {
                     WNDCLASS wc;

                     // Get the class info for the main window.
                     //......................................
                     GetClassInfo( hInst, lpszAppClass, &wc );
                     MessageBox( hWnd, wc.lpszMenuName,"Menu Name", MB_OK );
                  }
                  break;
         .
         .
         .
```

GetClassInfoEx   ■ WINDOWS 95   ■ WINDOWS NT

Description	**GetClassInfoEx** is the same as the **GetClassInfo** function except that it retrieves extended information about a class that was registered with the **RegisterClassEx** function.
Syntax	BOOL **GetClassInfoEx**(HINSTANCE *hinst*, LPCTSTR *lpszClass*, LPWNDCLASSEX *lpwcx*)

Parameters

hinst HINSTANCE: The instance handle of the application that created the class. For information about predefined classes such as **BUTTON** and **EDIT**, set to **NULL**.

lpszClass LPCTSTR: A pointer to a null-terminated string or an integer atom. If an atom, it must be a global atom that was created with a call to the **GlobalAddAtom** function. The high-order word should be set to **0**, and the low-order word will contain the atom's value.

lpwcx	**LPWNDCLASSEX**: A pointer to a **WNDCLASSEX** structure that will receive the information about the class. See the definition of the **WNDCLASSEX** structure below.
Returns	**BOOL**: If the function succeeds and finds the specified class, the return value is **TRUE**; otherwise, it is **FALSE**.
Include File	winuser.h
See Also	GetClassInfo, RegisterClassEx

WNDCLASSEX Definition

```
typedef struct _WNDCLASSEX
{
    UINT     style;
    WNDPROC  lpfnWndProc;
    int      cbClsExtra;
    int      cbWndExtra;
    HANDLE   hInstance;
    HICON    hIcon;
    HCURSOR  hCursor;
    HBRUSH   hbrBackground;
    LPCTSTR  lpszMenuName;
    LPCTSTR  lpszClassName;
    HICON    hIconSm;
} WNDCLASSEX;
```

Members	For information on the individual members of the **WNDCLASSEX** structure, see the **RegisterClass** and **RegisterClassEx** functions in Chapter 3, Creating Windows.
Example	See the example for the **GetClassInfo** function.

GetClassLong   ■ WINDOWS 95 ■ WINDOWS NT

Description	**GetClassLong** retrieves a 32-bit (long) value from the **WNDCLASS** structure associated with the class of a given window.
	Use **GetClassLong** to get 32-bit data defined in the **WNDCLASS** structure or the extra data requested during class registration.
Syntax	DWORD **GetClassLong**(HWND *hwnd,* int *nIndex*)
Parameters	
hwnd	**HWND**: The handle of the window associated with the class from which you wish to retrieve the long value.
nIndex	**int**: One of the values in Table 4-5 or the zero-based offset to the 32-bit value in the extra class data.

Table 4-5 GetClassLong *nIndex* values

Value	Meaning
GCL_CBCLSEXTRA	The size, in bytes, of the extra class data.
GCL_CBWNDEXTRA	The size, in bytes, of the extra window data. Use the GetWindowLong or GetWindowWord functions to access this data.
GCL_HBRBACKGROUND	The class background brush handle.
GCL_HCURSOR	The class cursor handle.
GCL_HICON	The icon handle used with windows created with this class.
GCL_HICONSM	The icon handle of the small icon used with windows created with this class.
GCL_HMODULE	The instance handle of the module that registered the class.
GCL_MENUNAME	A pointer to the menu name string used with this class.
GCL_STYLE	The window-class style.
GCL_WNDPROC	A pointer to the WndProc used for this class.

Returns   DWORD: If successful, the return value is the 32-bit value that was requested; otherwise, it is 0.

Include File   winuser.h

See Also   GetClassInfo, GetClassWord, GetClassName, SetClassLong, GetWindowLong

Example   This example shows a function that will return the background brush for the given window's class.

```
HBRUSH GetClassBackground( HWND hWnd )
{
    return( (HBRUSH)GetClassLong( hWnd, GCL_HBRBACKGROUND ) );
}
```

GetClassName   ■ WINDOWS 95 ■ WINDOWS NT

Description   GetClassName returns the class name that the given window was created with.

Syntax   int **GetClassName**(HWND *hwnd,* LPTSTR *lpClassName,* int *nClassName*)

Parameters

hwnd   HWND: The handle of the window whose class name will be retrieved.

lpClassName   LPTSTR: A pointer to a buffer large enough to receive the class name string.

nClassName   int: The maximum number of characters that can be copied to the buffer pointed to by the *lpClassName* parameter.

Returns   int: If successful, the number of characters copied to the buffer pointed to by *lpClassName*; otherwise, it is 0.

Include File	winuser.h
See Also	GetClassInfo, GetClassLong, GetClassWord
Example	See example for the EnumWindows function.

GetClassWord   ■ WINDOWS 95 ■ WINDOWS NT

Description	GetClassWord retrieves a 16-bit (word) value from the WNDCLASS structure associated with the class of a given window.
	Use GetClassWord to get 16-bit data defined in the WNDCLASS structure or the extra data that was requested when the class was registered.
Syntax	WORD **GetClassWord**(HWND *hwnd,* int *nOffset*)
Parameters	
hwnd	HWND: The handle of the window that is associated with the class from which to retrieve the word value.
nOffset	int: Use GCW_ATOM to retrieve the atom used to uniquely identify the window class when it was registered. To retrieve a 16-bit value from the class extra data, set to the zero-based offset of the value. CGW_HICONSM retrieves the handle of the small icon associated with the window.
Returns	WORD: If successful, the return value is the 16-bit value requested; otherwise, it is 0.
Include File	winuser.h
See Also	GetClassLong, SetClassWord, SetClassLong, GetWindowLong, GetWindowWord
Example	This example registers a new class with extra data and creates a pop-up window using the class. Once the window is created, a word value is set in the extra class data. The **NewWndProc** function is the window procedure for the new class. When the Test! menu option is selected from the new window, a message box is displayed with the word value that was set in the extra class data.

```
LRESULT CALLBACK WndProc( HWND hWnd, UINT uMsg, WPARAM wParam, LPARAM lParam )
{
static HWND hNewWnd = NULL;

   switch( uMsg )
   {
      case WM_CREATE:
              {
                 WNDCLASSEX wc;
```

```
                wc.style          = CS_HREDRAW | CS_VREDRAW | CS_PARENTDC;
                wc.lpfnWndProc    = (WNDPROC)NewWndProc;
                wc.cbClsExtra     = sizeof( WORD );
                wc.cbWndExtra     = 0;
                wc.hInstance      = hInst;
                wc.hIcon          = LoadIcon(hInst, szAppName);
                wc.hCursor        = LoadCursor(NULL, IDC_ARROW);
                wc.hbrBackground  = (HBRUSH)(COLOR_WINDOW + 1);
                wc.lpszMenuName   = szAppName;
                wc.lpszClassName  = "New Class";
                wc.cbSize         = sizeof(WNDCLASSEX);
                wc.hIconSm        = LoadImage(hInst, szAppName,
                                             IMAGE_ICON, 16, 16,
                                             LR_DEFAULTCOLOR );

                if ( RegisterClassEx( &wc ) )
                {
                    hNewWnd = CreateWindow( "New Class",
                                            "Pop-up Window",
                                            WS_POPUP | WS_VISIBLE |
                                            WS_CAPTION,
                                            10, 50, 150, 150,
                                            hWnd,
                                            NULL,
                                            hInst, NULL );
                    if ( hNewWnd )
                        SetClassWord( hNewWnd, 0, 20 );
                }
            }
        .
        .
        .


LRESULT CALLBACK NewWndProc(HWND hWnd, UINT uMsg, WPARAM wParam, LPARAM lParam)
{
   switch( uMsg )
   {
     case WM_COMMAND :
            switch( LOWORD( wParam ) )
            {
                case IDM_TEST :
                    {
```

continued on next page

continued from previous page

```
                                WORD wValue = GetClassWord( hWnd, 0 );
                                char szOut[20];

                                wsprintf( szOut, "Class Value = %d", wValue );

                                MessageBox( hWnd, szOut, szAppName, MB_OK );
                        }
                        break;
```

.
.
.

GetClientRect   ■ WINDOWS 95   ■ WINDOWS NT

Description
GetClientRect retrieves the client rectangle for the given window. The coordinates are relative to the client area of the window, so the upper-left corner will be (0,0).

GetClientRect is useful for determining the client area size of a window.

Syntax
BOOL **GetClientRect**(HWND *hwnd,* LPRECT *lprc*)

Parameters

hwnd
HWND: A handle to the window whose client area rectangle will be retrieved.

lprc
LPRECT: A pointer to a RECT structure that will receive the coordinates of the client area.

Returns
BOOL: TRUE if the function was successful, and FALSE if the function failed.

Include File
winuser.h

See Also
InvalidateRect, GetWindowRect, UpdateWindow

Example
This example will get the rectangle for the client area every time the main window is sized. When the window is painted, the current height and width of the client area are painted in the client area.

```
LRESULT CALLBACK WndProc( HWND hWnd, UINT uMsg, WPARAM wParam, LPARAM lParam )
{
static RECT rect;
static char szOut[31];

    switch( uMsg )
    {
        case WM_SIZE :
                GetClientRect( hWnd, &rect );
                break;
```

```
        case WM_PAINT :
            {
                PAINTSTRUCT ps;
                HDC         dc = BeginPaint( hWnd, &ps );

                wsprintf( szOut, "Height = %d  Width = %d", rect.bottom,
                                                            rect.right );
                TextOut( dc, 10, 10, szOut, lstrlen( szOut ) );
                EndPaint( hWnd, &ps );
            }
            break;
```

GetDesktopWindow ■ WINDOWS 95 ■ WINDOWS NT

Description   Use `GetDesktopWindow` to get a handle to the desktop window. The desktop window covers the entire screen. All icons and other windows are painted on the desktop window. Special-purpose programs, such as screen savers and desktop applications, need to paint on the desktop.

Syntax   `HWND GetDesktopWindow( VOID )`

Parameters   This function has no parameters.

Returns   The return value is the handle of the desktop window.

Include File   `winuser.h`

Example   This example gets the desktop handle and uses it with the `CascadeWindows` function to cascade all the open application windows. This is not something that an application should be doing and is for demonstration purposes only.

```
LRESULT CALLBACK WndProc( HWND hWnd, UINT uMsg, WPARAM wParam, LPARAM lParam )
{

    switch( uMsg )
    {
        case WM_COMMAND :
                switch( LOWORD( wParam ) )
                {
                    case IDM_TEST :
                            CascadeWindows( GetDesktopWindow(),
                                        MDITILE_SKIPDISABLED, NULL, 0, NULL );
```

continued on next page

continued from previous page

```
                         break;
         .
         .
         .
```

GetFocus   ■ WINDOWS 95 ■ WINDOWS NT

Description	GetFocus gets the handle of the window or control that currently has input focus. This is the window to which any keyboard input that the user types is sent.
Syntax	HWND **GetFocus**(VOID)
Parameters	This function has no parameters.
Returns	HWND: If successful, the return value is the handle of the window that has input focus. If the calling thread does not contain a window that has input focus, the return value is NULL.
Include File	winuser.h
See Also	SetFocus
Related Messages	WM_SETFOCUS, WM_KILLFOCUS
Example	This example creates two edit controls as children of the main window. When the Test! menu option is selected, a message box is displayed with the contents of the edit control that currently has input focus.

```
LRESULT CALLBACK WndProc( HWND hWnd, UINT uMsg, WPARAM wParam, LPARAM lParam )
{
static HWND hEdit1 = NULL;
static HWND hEdit2 = NULL;

   switch( uMsg )
   {
      case WM_CREATE :
              // Create two child window edit controls.
              //........................................
              hEdit1 = CreateWindow( "EDIT", "Edit 1",
                                WS_CHILD | WS_BORDER |
                                WS_VISIBLE | ES_LEFT,
                                10, 10, 100, 25,
                                hWnd, (HMENU) 101,
                                hInst, NULL );

              hEdit2 = CreateWindow( "EDIT", "Edit 2",
                                WS_CHILD | WS_BORDER |
                                WS_VISIBLE | ES_LEFT,
```

```
                                10, 35, 100, 25,
                                hWnd, (HMENU) 101,
                                hInst, NULL );
            break;


    case WM_COMMAND :
            switch( LOWORD( wParam ) )
            {
                case IDM_TEST :
                    {
                        HWND hFocus = GetFocus();
                        char szText[31];

                        GetWindowText( hFocus, szText, 30 );
                        MessageBox( hWnd, szText, "Focus", MB_OK );
                    }
                    break;
```

GetForegroundWindow   ■ WINDOWS 95 ■ WINDOWS NT

Description	`GetForegroundWindow` returns the handle of the window the user is currently working with. This is called the foreground window, and the system assigns a slightly higher priority to the thread that the foreground window is in.
Syntax	HWND **GetForegroundWindow**(VOID)
Parameters	This function has no parameters.
Returns	HWND: Returns a handle to the foreground window.
Include File	`winuser.h`
See Also	`SetForegroundWindow`
Example	This example shows the window title of the foreground window in a message box.

```
LRESULT CALLBACK WndProc( HWND hWnd, UINT uMsg, WPARAM wParam, LPARAM lParam )
{

    switch( uMsg )
    {
        case WM_COMMAND :
```

continued on next page

continued from previous page

```
            switch( LOWORD( wParam ) )
            {
                case IDM_TEST :
                    {
                        HWND hForegroundWnd;
                        char szText[41];

                        hForegroundWnd = GetForegroundWindow();
                        GetWindowText( hForegroundWnd, szText, 40 );

                        MessageBox( hWnd, szText, "Foreground Window", MB_OK );
                    }
                    break;
```

.
.
.

GetLastActivePopup   ■ WINDOWS 95 ■ WINDOWS NT

Description	GetLastActivePopup determines which pop-up window owned by the given parent window was the most recently active.
Syntax	HWND **GetLastActivePopup**(HWND *hwndOwner*)
Parameters	
hwndOwner	HWND: A handle to the owner window.
Returns	HWND: A handle to the most recently active pop-up window. The return value is the same as *hwndOwner* if one or more of the following conditions are met:

■ The *hwndOwner* window was most recently active.

■ The *hwndOwner* window does not own any pop-up windows.

■ The *hwndOwner* is not a top-level window.

Include File	winuser.h
See Also	GetActiveWindow, SetActiveWindow
Example	This example will set the title bar of the pop-up window to Last Active when the Test! menu option is selected on the main window.

```
LRESULT CALLBACK WndProc( HWND hWnd, UINT uMsg, WPARAM wParam, LPARAM lParam )
{
static HWND hNewWnd = NULL;
static HWND hLastActive;
```

```
switch( uMsg )
{
   case WM_CREATE:
           {
               WNDCLASSEX wc;

               wc.style         = CS_HREDRAW | CS_VREDRAW | CS_PARENTDC;
               wc.lpfnWndProc   = (WNDPROC)NewWndProc;
               wc.cbClsExtra    = 0;
               wc.cbWndExtra    = 0;
               wc.hInstance     = hInst;
               wc.hIcon         = LoadIcon(hInst, lpszAppName);
               wc.hCursor       = LoadCursor(NULL, IDC_ARROW);
               wc.hbrBackground = (HBRUSH)(COLOR_WINDOW + 1);
               wc.lpszMenuName  = szAppName;
               wc.lpszClassName = "New Class";
               wc.cbSize        = sizeof(WNDCLASSEX);
               wc.hIconSm       = LoadImage( hInst, lpszAppName,
                                            IMAGE_ICON, 16, 16,
                                            LR_DEFAULTCOLOR );

               if ( RegisterClassEx( &wc ) )
               {
                   hNewWnd = CreateWindow( "New Class",
                                           "Pop-up Window",
                                           WS_POPUP | WS_VISIBLE |
                                           WS_CAPTION,
                                           10, 50, 150, 150,
                                           hWnd,
                                           NULL,
                                           hInst, NULL );
               }
           }

   case WM_COMMAND :
          switch( LOWORD( wParam ) )
          {
             case IDM_TEST :
                 {
                      SetFocus( hNewWnd );
                      hLastActive = GetLastActivePopup( hWnd );
                      SetWindowText( hLastActive, "Last Active" );
                 }
                 break;
```

continued on next page

continued from previous page

```
            case IDM_EXIT :
                    DestroyWindow( hWnd );
                    break;
        }
        break;
```

.

.

.

GetNextWindow   ■ WINDOWS 95   ■ WINDOWS NT

Description	**GetNextWindow** retrieves the next or previous window in the order of the windows. If the window is a top-level window, then the next or previous window will be another top-level window. If the given window is a child window, then the next or previous window will be another child window with the same parent window.
	Use **GetNextWindow** in situations where an application has only two or three windows for which to search. The **EnumWindows** and **EnumChildWindows** functions provide better performance when an application has more windows.
Syntax	HWND **GetNextWindow**(HWND *hwnd,* UINT *uDirection*)
Parameters	
hwnd	HWND: A handle to the window where the search will be started.
uDirection	UINT: Set to **GW_HWNDNEXT** to search for the next window or **GW_HWNDPREV** to search for the previous window.
Returns	HWND: If successful, the return value is the handle of the next or previous window, depending on the *uDirection* parameter. If there is no next or previous window handle, the return value is **NULL**.
Include File	winuser.h
See Also	EnumWindows, EnumChildWindows, GetWindow
Example	The following example shows how to walk the window list of top-level windows. Starting from the main window of the application, this example finds the next ten top-level windows and displays the window titles in a message box.

```
LRESULT CALLBACK WndProc( HWND hWnd, UINT uMsg, WPARAM wParam, LPARAM lParam )
{
   switch( uMsg )
   {
     case WM_COMMAND :
```

```
     switch( LOWORD( wParam ) )
     {
        case IDM_TEST :
            {
                HWND hNextWindow;
                char szWndTitle[71];
                int  i;

                hNextWindow = GetNextWindow( hWnd, GW_HWNDNEXT );
                for( i=0; i<10; i++ )
                {
                    GetWindowText( hNextWindow, szWndTitle, 70 );
                    MessageBox( hWnd, szWndTitle, "Next Window",
                             MB_OK );

                    hNextWindow = GetNextWindow( hNextWindow,
                                            GW_HWNDNEXT );
                }
            }
            break;
```

GetParent   ■ WINDOWS 95 ■ WINDOWS NT

Description	`GetParent` retrieves a handle to the window that is the owner of the given window. The relationship of windows can be summed up this way: A parent window has child windows, and a child window can be a parent window for other child windows.
	Use `GetParent` to get a window handle so a child window can communicate with its parent window by sending back messages. `GetParent` can also be used to get information about a window's parent window.
Syntax	HWND **GetParent**(HWND *hwndChild*)
Parameters	
hwndChild	HWND: The window handle whose parent window handle will be retrieved.
Returns	HWND: The handle of the parent window. If the given window does not have a parent, then the return value is **NULL**.
See Also	ChildWindowFromPoint, EnumWindows, GetWindow
Include File	winuser.h

Example   In this example, the application creates a pop-up child window. When the Test! menu option on the pop-up window is selected, the parent window is determined, and the parent window's title is displayed in a message box.

```
LRESULT CALLBACK NewWndProc( HWND hWnd, UINT uMsg, WPARAM wParam, LPARAM lParam )
{
   switch( uMsg )
   {
      case WM_COMMAND :
            switch( LOWORD( wParam ) )
            {
               case IDM_TEST :
                   {
                      HWND hParent;
                      char szWndTitle[71];

                      hParent = GetParent( hWnd );
                      GetWindowText( hParent, szWndTitle, 70 );
                      MessageBox(hWnd, szWndTitle, "Parent window is",
                              MB_OK );
                   }
                   break;
         .
         .
         .
```

GetProp   ■ WINDOWS 95 ■ WINDOWS NT

Description   GetProp retrieves a handle to a property data item associated with a window handle and has the same string identifier specified with the SetProp function.

GetProp allows data to be associated with a window handle and retrieved when needed. This method for storing window-specific data lets it be accessed anywhere in the application without using global variables.

Syntax   HANDLE **GetProp**(HWND *hwnd*, LPCTSTR *lpsz*)

Parameters

hwnd   HWND: The window handle that the property item is associated with.

lpsz   LPCTSTR: A pointer to a null-terminated string or an integer atom that identifies the property item to be retrieved. If an atom is used, the high-order word should be set to 0, and the low-order word will contain the atom's value.

Returns	HANDLE: The handle of the property item if the property list of the window contains the property item identified by the string contained in *lpsz*. If the property item was not found, then the return value is NULL.
Include File	winuser.h
See Also	SetProp, RemoveProp, EnumProps
Example	This example shows how to add a property to a window using SetProp and then retrieve it with the GetProp function. The property value is retrieved and displayed in a message box.

```
LPCTSTR szProp = "Value for Property";

LRESULT CALLBACK WndProc( HWND hWnd, UINT uMsg, WPARAM wParam, LPARAM lParam )
{

   switch( uMsg )
   {
      case WM_CREATE :
            // Add a property item that contains a string
            // pointer to the main window.
            //................................................
            SetProp( hWnd, "Property ID", (HANDLE)szProp );
            break;

      case WM_COMMAND :
            switch( LOWORD( wParam ) )
            {
               case IDM_TEST :
                     // Get the value of the property added to the window
                     // and display it in a message box.
                     //....................................................
                     MessageBox( NULL,
                                 (LPCTSTR)GetProp( hWnd,"Property ID" ),
                                 "Property Value", MB_OK );
                     break;

               case IDM_EXIT :
                     DestroyWindow( hWnd );
                     break;
            }

      case WM_DESTROY :
            // Remove the property item from the window. Since we
            // didn't allocate any memory for the property we don't
```

continued on next page

continued from previous page

```
            // need to free anything.
            //................................
            RemoveProp( hWnd, "Property ID" );
            PostQuitMessage( 0 );
            break;
```

.
.
.

GetTopWindow   ■ WINDOWS 95 ■ WINDOWS NT

Description	Windows maintains the order of the child windows for a parent window. `GetTopWindow` retrieves the first child window for the parent window given in the *hwndParent* parameter.
Syntax	HWND **GetTopWindow**(HWND *hwndParent*)
Parameters	
hwndParent	HWND: The parent window handle. If set to **NULL**, the return value will be the first window.
Returns	HWND: If the window handle *hwndParent* has child windows, the first child window handle based on the internal order will be returned. If the given window has no child windows, **NULL** is returned.
Include File	`winuser.h`
See Also	`ChildWindowFromPoint`, `GetNextWindow`, `GetWindow`
Example	This example (see Figure 4-5) creates two child edit controls that overlap. When the Test! menu option is selected, the text of the edit control that is on top is set to "I'm on Top!" The edit control that is considered to be on top is not the one that is visually on top, but the edit control that was created first.

```
LRESULT CALLBACK WndProc( HWND hWnd, UINT uMsg, WPARAM wParam, LPARAM lParam )
{
static HWND hEdit1 = NULL;
static HWND hEdit2 = NULL;

    switch( uMsg )
    {
       case WM_CREATE :
                // Create two overlapping edit controls
                //......................................
                hEdit1 = CreateWindow( "EDIT", "Here is Edit 1",
```

```
                                WS_CHILD | WS_BORDER |
                                WS_VISIBLE |ES_LEFT,
                                10, 10, 100, 30,
                                hWnd, (HMENU) 101,
                                hInst, NULL );

        hEdit2 = CreateWindow( "EDIT", "Here is Edit 2",
                                WS_CHILD | WS_BORDER |
                                WS_VISIBLE | ES_LEFT,
                                15, 20, 100, 30,
                                hWnd, (HMENU) 102,
                                hInst, NULL );
        break;

case WM_COMMAND :
        switch( LOWORD( wParam ) )
        {
            case IDM_TEST :
                    // Set the text of the edit control that is on
                    // top to "I'm on Top!"
                    //.........................................
                    SetWindowText( GetTopWindow( hWnd ),
                                    "I'm on Top!" );
                    break;
          .
          .
          .
```

Figure 4-5 GetTopWindow example

GetWindow

Description	`GetWindow` searches the window's list of parent and child windows for the window that matches the criteria given in the *uCmd* parameter.
	`GetWindow` gives you a simple alternative to `EnumWindows` and `EnumChildWindows` when there are not many windows that need to be searched.
Syntax	HWND **GetWindow**(HWND *hwnd,* UINT *uCmd*)
Parameters	
hwnd	HWND: The window handle that the search criteria in *uCmd* is based on.
uCmd	UINT: The relationship the window that should be returned has with the window given in the *hwnd* parameter. This can be set to one of the values given in Table 4-6.

Table 4-6 GetWindow *uCmd* values

Value	Meaning
GW_CHILD	Return the window's first child window.
GW_HWNDFIRST	If the given window is a topmost window, return the first topmost window. If the given window is a top-level window, return the first top-level window. If the given window is a child window, return the first sibling child window.
GW_HWNDLAST	If the given window is a topmost window, return the last topmost window. If the given window is a top-level window, return the last top-level window. If the given window is a child window, return the last sibling child window.
GW_HWNDNEXT	Return the next window handle in the window manager's list.
GW_HWNDPREV	Return the previous window handle in the window manager's list.
GW_OWNER	Return the given window's owner or parent window.

Returns	HWND: If successful, the window handle for the window that met the criteria is returned. If no window was found to match the criteria, then NULL is returned.
Include File	winuser.h
See Also	EnumWindows, EnumChildWindows
Example	In this example, the application has an edit control as a child window. When the Test! menu option is selected, the `GetWindow` function is used to find out the handle of the edit control and changes the text to "I'm Found!"

```
LRESULT CALLBACK WndProc( HWND hWnd, UINT uMsg, WPARAM wParam, LPARAM lParam )
{
static HWND hEdit = NULL;

    switch( uMsg )
    {
```

```
case WM_CREATE :
        hEdit = CreateWindow( "EDIT", "Here is Edit",
                              WS_CHILD | WS_BORDER |
                              WS_VISIBLE |ES_LEFT,
                              10, 10, 100, 30,
                              hWnd, (HMENU) 101,
                              hInst, NULL );

        break;

case WM_COMMAND :
        switch( LOWORD( wParam ) )
        {
            case IDM_TEST :
                {
                    HWND hChild = GetWindow( hWnd, GW_CHILD );
                    SetWindowText( hChild, "I'm Found!" );
                }
                break;
```

.
.
.

GetWindowLong   ■ WINDOWS 95 ■ WINDOWS NT

Description   Use **GetWindowLong** to retrieve 32-bit (long) values from the information
stored about the given window. The **GetWindowLong** function also is used
to retrieve information from the extra window memory of the given
window.

Syntax   LONG **GetWindowLong**(HWND *hwnd,* int *nIndex*)

Parameters

hwnd   HWND: The window handle of the window.

nIndex   int: The zero-based offset to the value to retrieve or one of the values
listed in Table 4-7. The DWL_ values only apply if *hwnd* is a handle to a
dialog box.

Table 4-7 GetWindowLong *nIndex* values

Value	Action
GWL_EXSTYLE	The extended window styles.
GWL_HINSTANCE	The instance handle of the application that created the window.
GWL_HWNDPARENT	The window handle of the parent window.

continued on next page

continued from previous page

Value	Action
GWL_ID	The control ID of the window.
GWL_STYLE	The window styles.
GWL_USERDATA	The 32-bit application-defined value associated with the window.
GWL_WNDPROC	The address of the window procedure (WndProc).
DWL_DLGPROC	The address of the dialog box procedure (DlgProc).
DWL_MSGRESULT	The return value of a message processed by the DlgProc.
DWL_USER	Extra information private to the application.

Returns   LONG: If successful, the long value specified is returned; otherwise, 0 is returned.

Include File   winuser.h

See Also   GetWindowWord, SetWindowLong, SetWindowWord, GetClassLong, GetClassWord

Example   In this example, the control ID of an edit control is retrieved using the GetWindowLong function and displayed in the edit control.

```
LRESULT CALLBACK WndProc( HWND hWnd, UINT uMsg, WPARAM wParam, LPARAM lParam )
{
static HWND hEdit = NULL;

    switch( uMsg )
    {
      case WM_CREATE :
              hEdit = CreateWindow( "EDIT", "Here is Edit",
                                    WS_CHILD | WS_BORDER |
                                    WS_VISIBLE |ES_LEFT,
                                    10, 10, 100, 30,
                                    hWnd, (HMENU) 101,
                                    hInst, NULL );

              break;

      case WM_COMMAND :
              switch( LOWORD( wParam ) )
              {
                case IDM_TEST :
                    {
                        char szText[21];
                        UINT nID = GetWindowLong( hEdit, GWL_ID );

                        wsprintf( szText, "My ID is: %d", nID );
```

```
                    SetWindowText( hEdit, szText );
                }
                break;
```

•
•
•

GetWindowPlacement   ■ Windows 95   ■ Windows NT

Description   **GetWindowPlacement** retrieves the state the given window is in (maximized, minimized, or normal). This function also returns the position information for the window when it is in each of the states.

Use **GetWindowPlacement** to find out what the current state of a window is and what position it might occupy if the state is changed. For example, the application can tell what the restored size of a maximized window will be without actually changing the window's state to normal.

Syntax   BOOL **GetWindowPlacement**(HWND *hwnd*, WINDOWPLACEMENT* *lpWndPlc*)

Parameters

hwnd   HWND: A handle to the window.

lpWndPlc   WINDOWPLACEMENT*: A pointer to a **WINDOWPLACEMENT** structure that will receive the placement information. See the definition of the **WINDOWPLACEMENT** structure below.

Returns   BOOL: **TRUE** if the function was successful, and **FALSE** if the function failed.

Include File   winuser.h

See Also   GetWindowRect, SetWindowPlacement, SetWindowPos

WINDOWPLACEMENT Definition

```
            typedef struct tagWINDOWPLACEMENT
            {
                UINT   length;
                UINT   flags;
                UINT   showCmd;
                POINT  ptMinPosition;
                POINT  ptMaxPosition;
                RECT   rcNormalPosition;
            } WINDOWPLACEMENT;
```

Members

length   UINT: The size of the structure. This must be initialized to the size of the structure prior to calling the **GetWindowPlacement** function.

flags   UINT: Can be set to one or both of the values in Table 4-8. The values can be determined by using the binary operator AND (**&**).

Table 4-8 WINDOWPLACEMENT *flags* values

Value	Meaning
WPF_RESTORETOMAXIMIZED	When the window is restored it will be maximized even if the state before it was minimized was normal.
WPF_SETMINPOSITION	The coordinates in *ptMinPosition* are the fixed position of the window when it is minimized.

showCmd   UINT: The current show state of the window. This can be one of the values in Table 4-12 (shown in the **ShowWindow** function).

ptMinPosition   POINT: The upper-left corner of the window when it is minimized.

ptMaxPosition   POINT: The upper-left corner of the window when it is maximized.

rcNormalPosition RECT: The window's coordinates when the window is shown as its normal size.

Example   In this example, the window placement information is retrieved, and the normal position of the window is displayed in a message box.

```
LRESULT CALLBACK WndProc( HWND hWnd, UINT uMsg, WPARAM wParam, LPARAM lParam )
{
   switch( uMsg )
   {
      case WM_COMMAND :
              switch( LOWORD( wParam ) )
              {
                 case IDM_TEST :
                     {
                        WINDOWPLACEMENT wp;

                        wp.length = sizeof( WINDOWPLACEMENT );

                        if ( GetWindowPlacement( hWnd, &wp ) )
                        {
                           char szMsg[100];
                           wsprintf( szMsg,
                                   "Left=%d,top=%d,right=%d,bot=%d",
                                   wp.rcNormalPosition.left,
                                   wp.rcNormalPosition.top,
                                   wp.rcNormalPosition.right,
                                   wp.rcNormalPosition.bottom );
                           MessageBox( hWnd, szMsg, "Window Position",
                                   MB_OK );
                        }
                     }
                     break;
```

GetWindowRect   ■ WINDOWS 95 ■ WINDOWS NT

Description	`GetWindowRect` retrieves the dimensions of a window's bounding rectangle and copies them to the **RECT** pointed to by *lprc*. The coordinates are in pixels and relative to the upper-left corner of the screen.
	Use `GetWindowRect` to determine the current size and position of the window relative to the screen.
Syntax	BOOL **GetWindowRect**(HWND *hwnd,* LPRECT *lprc*)
Parameters	
hwnd	**HWND**: A handle to the window.
lprc	**LPRECT**: A pointer to a **RECT** structure that will receive the bounding rectangle of the window in screen coordinates.
Returns	**BOOL**: **TRUE** if the function was successful, and **FALSE** if the function failed.
Include File	`winuser.h`
See Also	`GetClientRect, GetWindowPlacement`
Example	This example will center the main application window when the Test! menu option is selected. The `GetWindowRect` function is used to determine the current placement of the window and its size, so it can be moved to the center of the screen.

```
LRESULT CALLBACK WndProc( HWND hWnd, UINT uMsg, WPARAM wParam, LPARAM lParam )
{
   switch( uMsg )
   {
      case WM_COMMAND :
            switch( LOWORD( wParam ) )
            {
               case IDM_TEST :
                  {
                     RECT rect;
                     RECT newrect;
                     int  nCX = GetSystemMetrics( SM_CXSCREEN )/2;
                     int  nCY = GetSystemMetrics( SM_CYSCREEN )/2;

                     GetWindowRect( hWnd, &rect );
```

continued on next page

continued from previous page

```
                                newrect.top    = nCY - (rect.bottom - rect.top)/2;
                                newrect.left   = nCX - (rect.right - rect.left)/2;
                                newrect.bottom = (rect.bottom - rect.top);
                                newrect.right  = (rect.right - rect.left);

                                MoveWindow( hWnd, newrect.left,
                                                  newrect.top,
                                                  newrect.right,
                                                  newrect.bottom, TRUE );

                        }
                        break;
                        .
                        .
                        .
```

GetWindowText   ■ WINDOWS 95 ■ WINDOWS NT

Description   Use **GetWindowText** to get the title of parent, pop-up, and child windows
                      or the text from a control such as a button or edit control.

Syntax   int **GetWindowText**(HWND *hwnd,* LPTSTR *lpsz,* int *nChars*)

Parameters

hwnd   HWND: The window or control handle containing the text.

lpsz   LPTSTR: A pointer to a buffer that will receive the text.

nChars   int: The maximum number of characters that can be copied to the buffer.
                      Any characters past this limit will be truncated.

Returns   int: If successful, the return value is the number of characters copied to
                      the buffer pointed to by *lpsz*, not including the null terminator. If unsuc-
                      cessful or there is no title on the window, **0** is returned.

Include File   winuser.h

See Also   SetWindowText, GetWindowTextLength

Related Messages WM_GETTEXT, WM_SETTEXT

Example   This example uses the **GetWindowTextLength** function to determine the
                      length of the window's text and then allocates memory large enough to
                      hold it. The **GetWindowText** function retrieves the window's title and
                      places it into the allocated buffer.

```
LRESULT CALLBACK WndProc( HWND hWnd, UINT uMsg, WPARAM wParam, LPARAM lParam )
{
    switch( uMsg )
    {
```

```
case WM_COMMAND :
        switch( LOWORD( wParam ) )
        {
            case IDM_TEST :
                {
                    int    nLen  = GetWindowTextLength( hWnd );
                    LPTSTR lpText = HeapAlloc( GetProcessHeap(),
                                        HEAP_ZERO_MEMORY, nLen+1 ) ;

                    if ( lpText )
                    {

                        GetWindowText( hWnd, lpText, nLen );
                        MessageBox( hWnd, lpText, "Window Title",
                                MB_OK );


                        HeapFree( GetProcessHeap(), 0, lpText );
                    }
                }
                break;
```

.
.
.

GetWindowTextLength   ■ WINDOWS 95   ■ WINDOWS NT

Description	Use `GetWindowTextLength` to determine the length of a window's title or a control's text prior to calling `GetWindowText`. `GetWindowTextLength` sets up a buffer that will be large enough for the text that will be retrieved.
Syntax	int **GetWindowTextLength**(HWND *hwnd*)
Parameters	
hwnd	HWND: The window or control handle containing the text.
Returns	int: If successful, the length of the text is returned. If unsuccessful or the window has no text, 0 is returned.
Include File	`winuser.h`
See Also	`GetWindowText`
Example	See the example for the `GetWindowText` function.

GetWindowThreadProcessId ■ Windows 95 ■ Windows NT

Description	GetWindowThreadProcessId retrieves the thread and process ID of the thread and process that created a window.
	Use GetWindowThreadProcessId to identify the thread or process that owns a specific window. It can be used with the EnumThreadWindows function.
Syntax	DWORD **GetWindowThreadProcessId**(HWND *hwnd,* LPDWORD *lpdwProcessId*)
Parameters	
hwnd	HWND: The handle of the window.
lpdwProcessId	LPDWORD: A pointer to a 32-bit value that will receive the process identifier. If NULL, the process ID will not be copied.
Returns	DWORD: The thread identifier of the thread that created the window.
Include File	winuser.h
See Also	EnumThreadWindows
Example	See the example for the EnumThreadWindows function.

GetWindowWord ■ Windows 95 ■ Windows NT

Description	Use GetWindowWord to retrieve an application-defined 16-bit (word) value from a given offset in the window's extra window memory.
Syntax	WORD **GetWindowWord**(HWND *hwnd,* int *nIndex*)
Parameters	
hwnd	HWND: The handle to the window.
nIndex	int: The zero-based offset of the value that will be retrieved from the window's extra memory.
Returns	WORD: If successful, the requested 16-bit value is returned; otherwise, 0 is returned.
Include File	winuser.h
See Also	GetWindowLong, SetWindowWord, SetWindowLong
Example	In this example, a new window class is registered and used to create a pop-up window with extra window data. A value of 20 is set into the extra window data with the SetWindowWord function. When the Test! menu option of the pop-up window is selected, the GetWindowWord function retrieves the value that was set and displays it in a message box.

```
LRESULT CALLBACK WndProc( HWND hWnd, UINT uMsg, WPARAM wParam, LPARAM lParam )
{
static HWND hNewWnd = NULL;

   switch( uMsg )
   {
      case WM_CREATE:
            {
                WNDCLASSEX wc;

                wc.style         = CS_HREDRAW | CS_VREDRAW | CS_PARENTDC;
                wc.lpfnWndProc   = (WNDPROC)NewWndProc;
                wc.cbClsExtra    = 0;
                wc.cbWndExtra    = sizeof( WORD );
                wc.hInstance     = hInst;
                wc.hIcon         = LoadIcon(hInst, lpszAppName);
                wc.hCursor       = LoadCursor(NULL, IDC_ARROW);
                wc.hbrBackground = (HBRUSH)(COLOR_WINDOW + 1);
                wc.lpszMenuName  = szAppName;
                wc.lpszClassName = "New Class";
                wc.cbSize        = sizeof( WNDCLASSEX );
                wc.hIconSm       = LoadImage( hInst, lpszAppName,
                                              IMAGE_ICON, 16, 16,
                                              LR_DEFAULTCOLOR );

                if ( RegisterClassEx( &wc ) )
                {
                    hNewWnd = CreateWindow( "New Class",
                                            "Pop-up Window",
                                            WS_POPUP | WS_VISIBLE |
                                            WS_CAPTION,
                                            10, 50, 150, 150,
                                            hWnd,
                                            NULL,
                                            hInst, NULL );
                    if ( hNewWnd )
                        SetWindowWord( hNewWnd, 0, 20 );
                }
            }
                    .
                    .
                    .
```

continued on next page

continued from previous page

```
LRESULT CALLBACK NewWndProc( HWND hWnd, UINT uMsg, WPARAM wParam, LPARAM lParam)
{
   switch( uMsg )
   {
      case WM_COMMAND :
            switch( LOWORD( wParam ) )
            {
               case IDM_TEST :
                  {
                     WORD wValue = GetWindowWord( hWnd, 0 );
                     char szOut[20];

                     wsprintf( szOut, "Window Value = %d", wValue );

                     MessageBox( hWnd, szOut, szAppName, MB_OK );
                  }
                  break;



                  .
                  .
                  .
```

IsChild   ■ WINDOWS 95 ■ WINDOWS NT

Description	**IsChild** checks to see if a window is a direct descendant of the given parent window. A child window is a direct descendant if the parent window handle that was given when **CreateWindow** created the child window is the same as the parent window handle used with the **IsChild** function. For dialog boxes, the dialog controls are direct descendants of the dialog box window.
	Use **IsChild** to determine the relationship of two windows.
Syntax	BOOL **IsChild**(HWND *hwndParent,* HWND *hwnd*)
Parameters	
hwndParent	HWND: A handle to the parent window.
hwnd	HWND: A handle to the child window that will be tested.
Returns	BOOL: TRUE if *hwnd* is the child window of *hwndParent*; otherwise, the return value is FALSE.
Include File	winuser.h
See Also	EnumChildWindows, ChildWindowFromPoint, WindowFromPoint
Example	This example uses the **IsChild** function to check if the edit control is a child of the main window when the user selects the Test! menu item.

```
LRESULT CALLBACK WndProc( HWND hWnd, UINT uMsg, WPARAM wParam, LPARAM lParam )
{
static HWND hEdit = NULL;

   switch( uMsg )
   {
      case WM_CREATE :
              hEdit = CreateWindow( "EDIT", "Here is Edit",
                                    WS_CHILD | WS_BORDER |
                                    WS_VISIBLE |ES_LEFT,
                                    10, 10, 100, 30,
                                    hWnd, (HMENU) 101,
                                    hInst, NULL );

              break;

      case WM_COMMAND :
              switch( LOWORD( wParam ) )
              {
                 case IDM_TEST :
                         if ( IsChild( hWnd, hEdit ) )
                         {
                             char szText[21];
                             GetWindowText( hWnd, szText, 20 );
                             SetWindowText( hEdit, szText );
                         }
                         break;
```
.
.
.

IsIconic   ■ WINDOWS 95 ■ WINDOWS NT

Description	IsIconic checks to see if a window is currently shown in the minimized state. This means that the application is displayed with only its icon on the screen.
	Useful while painting to determine if an icon should be painted or normal painting should occur, IsIconic also can be used anytime to determine the state of an application.
Syntax	BOOL **IsIconic**(HWND *hwnd*)
Parameters	
hwnd	HWND: A handle to the window.

Returns	BOOL: TRUE if the window is currently shown minimized; otherwise, it is FALSE.
Include File	winuser.h
See Also	GetWindowPlacement
Related Messages	WM_SIZE
Example	In this example, when the application is closed, the **IsIconic** function is used to determine if the application is minimized. If it is, a timer is set and the **FlashWindow** function is used to flash the title bar of the window until the user restores the window. At this point, the user is then asked if he or she wants to close the application.

```
UINT uTimer = 0;

LRESULT CALLBACK WndProc( HWND hWnd, UINT uMsg, WPARAM wParam, LPARAM lParam )
{
   switch( uMsg )
   {
      case WM_SIZE :
              if ( uTimer > 0 )
              {
                 KillTimer( hWnd, uTimer );
                 FlashWindow( hWnd, FALSE );
                 PostMessage( hWnd, WM_CLOSE, 0, 0 );
              }
              break;

      case WM_TIMER :
              FlashWindow( hWnd, TRUE );
              break;

      case WM_COMMAND :
              switch( LOWORD( wParam ) )
              {
                 case IDM_EXIT :
                         PostMessage( hWnd, WM_CLOSE, 0, 0 );
                         break;
              }
              break;

      case WM_DESTROY :
              PostQuitMessage(0);
              break;
```

```
        case WM_CLOSE :
                if ( IsIconic( hWnd ) )
                {
                    uTimer = SetTimer( hWnd, 1, 500, NULL );
                    break;
                }
                else if ( MessageBox( hWnd, "Do you want to quit?", lpszAppName, MB_YESNO | ⇐
MB_ICONQUESTION ) == IDNO )
                    break;

                // Fall through..

        default :
                return( DefWindowProc( hWnd, uMsg, wParam, lParam ) );
    }

    return( OL );
}
```

IsWindow   ■ WINDOWS 95 ■ WINDOWS NT

Description	**IsWindow** determines if a window handle points to a valid window. This is useful in cases where a window may have been deleted and the application needs to check if the window is still available.
Syntax	BOOL **IsWindow**(HWND *hwnd*)
Parameters	
hwnd	HWND: The window handle that will be checked.
Returns	BOOL: **TRUE** if the window handle points to an existing window; otherwise, the return value is **FALSE**.
Include File	winuser.h
See Also	IsWindowEnabled, IsWindowVisible, DestroyWindow
Example	This example uses **IsWindow** to determine if the edit control is created.

```
LRESULT CALLBACK WndProc( HWND hWnd, UINT uMsg, WPARAM wParam, LPARAM lParam )
{
static HWND hEdit = NULL;

    switch( uMsg )
    {
        case WM_CREATE :
                hEdit = CreateWindow( "EDIT", "Here is Edit",
                                        WS_CHILD | WS_BORDER |
```

continued on next page

continued from previous page

```
                                     WS_VISIBLE |ES_LEFT,
                                     10, 10, 100, 30,
                                     hWnd, (HMENU) 101,
                                     hInst, NULL );

              break;

      case WM_COMMAND :
              switch( LOWORD( wParam ) )
              {
                  case IDM_TEST :
                          if ( IsWindow( hEdit ) )
                          {
                                  MessageBox( hWnd, "Edit control was created",
                                          szAppName, MB_OK );
                          }
                          break;

          .
          .
          .
```

IsWindowEnabled   ■ Windows 95 ■ Windows NT

Description	IsWindowEnabled checks if a control or window is enabled or disabled for user input.
Syntax	BOOL **IsWindowEnabled**(HWND *hwnd*)
Parameters	
hwnd	HWND: A handle to the window or control that will be checked.
Returns	BOOL: TRUE if the window is enabled; otherwise, the return value is FALSE.
Include File	winuser.h
See Also	IsWindow, EnableWindow, IsWindowVisible
Related Messages	WM_ENABLE
Example	In this example, the edit control is toggled between enabled and disabled when the user selects the Test! menu item.

```
LRESULT CALLBACK WndProc( HWND hWnd, UINT uMsg, WPARAM wParam, LPARAM lParam )
{
static HWND hEdit = NULL;

   switch( uMsg )
   {
```

```
    case WM_CREATE :
            hEdit = CreateWindow( "EDIT", "Here is Edit",
                                    WS_CHILD | WS_BORDER |
                                    WS_VISIBLE |ES_LEFT,
                                    10, 10, 100, 30,
                                    hWnd, (HMENU) 101,
                                    hInst, NULL );

            break;

    case WM_COMMAND :
            switch( LOWORD( wParam ) )
            {
                case IDM_TEST :
                        // Toggle the enabled state of the edit control.
                        //..............................................
                        EnableWindow( hEdit, !IsWindowEnabled( hEdit ) );
                        break;
    .
    .
    .
```

IsWindowUnicode   ■ WINDOWS 95 ■ WINDOWS NT

Description	The `IsWindowUnicode` function determines whether the given window is a native Unicode window.
	`IsWindowUnicode` is normally used by the system to determine if the window procedure for a window expects Unicode parameters. The system automatically checks to see if a window expects Unicode and does the necessary conversion. It is rare that an application would need to use the `IsWindowUnicode` function.
Syntax	BOOL **IsWindowUnicode**(HWND *hwnd*)
Parameters	
hwnd	HWND: A handle to the window that will be checked.
Returns	BOOL: TRUE if the window expects Unicode strings; otherwise, the return value is FALSE.
Include File	`winuser.h`
See Also	`IsWindow`
Example	This example shows how to test a window for Unicode strings. The desktop window under Windows NT will return TRUE and display a message box.

```
LRESULT CALLBACK WndProc( HWND hWnd, UINT uMsg, WPARAM wParam, LPARAM lParam )
{
   switch( uMsg )
   {
      case WM_COMMAND :
              switch( LOWORD( wParam ) )
              {
                 case IDM_TEST :
                         if ( IsWindowUnicode( GetDesktopWindow() ) )
                             MessageBox( hWnd, "The desktop is Unicode",
                                             szAppName, MB_OK );
                         break;

                 .
                 .
                 .
```

IsWindowVisible   ■ WINDOWS 95 ■ WINDOWS NT

Description	**IsWindowVisible** determines whether a window is not currently visible on the screen because it has not been activated with **ShowWindow**. Windows that are obscured by other windows are considered visible.
	Applications can use the **IsWindowVisible** function to determine whether a window or control is visible or hidden. Often control windows are hidden from the user to make the user interface easier to follow.
Syntax	BOOL **IsWindowVisible**(HWND *hwnd*)
Parameters	
hwnd	HWND: A handle to the window that will be checked.
Returns	BOOL: **TRUE** if the window has been made visible by the **ShowWindow** function; otherwise, the return value is **FALSE**.
Include File	winuser.h
See Also	IsWindow, IsZoomed, IsIconic, ShowWindow
Example	This example toggles an edit control between visible and hidden when the user selects the Test! menu item.

```
LRESULT CALLBACK WndProc( HWND hWnd, UINT uMsg, WPARAM wParam, LPARAM lParam )
{
static HWND hEdit = NULL;

   switch( uMsg )
   {
      case WM_CREATE :
```

```
                hEdit = CreateWindow( "EDIT", "Here is Edit",
                                      WS_CHILD | WS_BORDER |
                                      WS_VISIBLE |ES_LEFT,
                                      10, 10, 100, 30,
                                      hWnd, (HMENU) 101,
                                      hInst, NULL );

        break;

   case WM_COMMAND :
           switch( LOWORD( wParam ) )
           {
               case IDM_TEST :
                       // Toggle the edit control from hidden to visible.
                       //..............................................
                       if ( IsWindowVisible( hEdit ) )
                           ShowWindow( hEdit, SW_HIDE );
                       else
                           ShowWindow( hEdit, SW_SHOW );
                       break;
```

.
.
.

IsZoomed   ■ WINDOWS 95 ■ WINDOWS NT

Description	Use **IsZoomed** to determine whether a window is maximized and covering the entire screen.
Syntax	BOOL **IsZoomed**(HWND *hwnd*)
Parameters	
hwnd	HWND: A handle to the window that will be checked.
Returns	BOOL: **TRUE** if the window state is maximized; otherwise, **FALSE** is returned.
Include File	winuser.h
See Also	IsIconic, IsWindowVisible, ShowWindow, CloseWindow
Related Messages	WM_PAINT, WM_SIZE
Example	In this example, the main window is toggled between maximized and restored when the user selects the Test! menu item.

```
LRESULT CALLBACK WndProc( HWND hWnd, UINT uMsg, WPARAM wParam, LPARAM lParam )
{
```

continued on next page

continued from previous page

```
switch( uMsg )
{
   case WM_COMMAND :
            switch( LOWORD( wParam ) )
            {
               case IDM_TEST :
                       // Toggle the window from maximized to normal.
                       //..................................................
                       if ( IsZoomed( hWnd ) )
                          ShowWindow( hWnd, SW_SHOWNORMAL );
                       else
                          ShowWindow( hWnd, SW_SHOWMAXIMIZED );
                       break;

               .
               .
               .
```

MapWindowPoints   ■ WINDOWS 95 ■ WINDOWS NT

Description	MapWindowPoints changes the coordinates for a set of points from being relative to one window to coordinates that are relative to another window. This is useful for converting coordinates of a child window that were retrieved with the **GetWindowRect** function to coordinates that are relative to the parent window.
Syntax	int **MapWindowPoints**(HWND *hwndFrom,* HWND *hwndTo,* LPPOINT *lppt,* UINT *cPoints*)
Parameters	
hwndFrom	HWND: The handle of the window the coordinates are relative to currently. If **NULL** or **HWND_DESKTOP**, the coordinates are relative to the screen.
hwndTo	HWND: The handle of the window the coordinates will be relative to when converted. If **NULL** or **HWND_DESKTOP**, the coordinates will be converted to screen coordinates.
lppt	LPPOINT: A pointer to an array of **POINT** structures or a **RECT** structure that contains the coordinates to be converted.
cPoints	UINT: The number of **POINT** structures pointed to by *lppt*. If *lppt* points to a **RECT** structure, then *cPoints* should be **2**.
Returns	int: If successful, the low-order word is the number of pixels added to the horizontal coordinate of each point, and the high-order word is the number of pixels added to the vertical coordinate of each point.
Include File	winuser.h

See Also   ScreenToClient, ClientToScreen

Example   In this example, the screen coordinates of the edit control are retrieved using the `GetWindowRect` function. The coordinates are then changed to be based on the parent window, using the `MapWindowPoints` function.

```
LRESULT CALLBACK WndProc( HWND hWnd, UINT uMsg, WPARAM wParam, LPARAM lParam )
{
static HWND hEdit = NULL;

    switch( uMsg )
    {
       case WM_CREATE :
               hEdit = CreateWindow( "EDIT", "Here is Edit",
                                      WS_CHILD | WS_BORDER |
                                      WS_VISIBLE |ES_LEFT,
                                      10, 10, 100, 30,
                                      hWnd, (HMENU) 101,
                                      hInst, NULL );

              break;

      case WM_COMMAND :
              switch( LOWORD( wParam ) )
              {
                 case IDM_TEST :
                       {
                            RECT rect;
                            char szMsg[41];

                            GetWindowRect( hEdit, &rect );
                            wsprintf( szMsg,
                                    "left=%d,top=%d,right=%d,bot=%d",
                                    rect.left, rect.top,
                                    rect.right, rect.bottom );
                            MessageBox( hWnd, szMsg, "Before", MB_OK );

                            MapWindowPoints( HWND_DESKTOP, hWnd,
                                            &rect, 2 );
                            wsprintf( szMsg,
                                    "left=%d,top=%d,right=%d,bot=%d",
                                    rect.left, rect.top,
                                    rect.right, rect.bottom );
                            MessageBox( hWnd, szMsg, "After", MB_OK );
```

continued on next page

continued from previous page

```
            }
            break;
```

.
.
.

MoveWindow ■ WINDOWS 95 ■ WINDOWS NT

Description	MoveWindow changes the position and/or size of a window. For a top-level window, the coordinates are relative to the upper-left corner of the screen. For a child window, they are relative to the parent window's client area.
Syntax	BOOL **MoveWindow**(HWND *hwnd,* int *x,* int *y,* int *cx,* int *cy,* BOOL *fRepaint*)
Parameters	
hwnd	HWND: A window handle to the window.
x	int: The new x position of the window's upper-left corner.
y	int: The new y position of the window's upper-left corner.
cx	int: The new width of the window.
cy	int: The new height of the window.
fRepaint	BOOL: TRUE if the window should be repainted to show the new position and size. If set to FALSE, no painting of any kind will occur, and the application will be responsible for updating the window.
Returns	BOOL: TRUE if the function was successful, and FALSE if the function failed.
Include File	winuser.h
See Also	DeferWindowPos, GetClientRect, GetWindowRect, ShowWindow, SetWindowPos
Example	See the example for the GetWindowRect function.

RemoveProp ■ WINDOWS 95 ■ WINDOWS NT

Description   RemoveProp removes a property data item from a window's property list and returns the handle associated with the property item. The application must free the memory associated with the handle once the property item has been removed. Only property items that an application created with the SetProp function should be removed.

Use RemoveProp when a property item is no longer needed or when the application shuts down. Remove all associated properties for a window and free the associated memory before an application shuts down.

Syntax	HANDLE **RemoveProp**(HWND *hwnd,* LPCTSTR *lpsz*)
Parameters	
hwnd	HWND: The window handle that contains the property item to be removed.
lpsz	LPCTSTR: A pointer to a null-terminated character string or an atom. If an atom is used, the high-order word should be set to **0**, and the low-order word will contain the atom's value.
Returns	HANDLE: If successful, the handle that is associated with the property; otherwise, **NULL** is returned.
Include File	winuser.h
See Also	EnumProps, SetProp, GetProp
Example	See the example for the **GetProp** function.

SetActiveWindow   ■ WINDOWS 95 ■ WINDOWS NT

Description	**SetActiveWindow** makes a top-level window associated with the calling thread active. The active window is the top-level window that has input focus.
	Use **SetActiveWindow** to control which top-level window has input focus.
Syntax	HWND **SetActiveWindow**(HWND *hwnd*)
Parameters	
hwnd	HWND: A window handle to be activated.
Returns	HWND: If successful, the window handle of the previous active window.
Include File	winuser.h
See Also	GetActiveWindow, GetLastActivePopup, EnableWindow
Example	In this example, a pop-up child window is created. When the Test! menu option of the pop-up window is selected, the parent window is activated.

```
LRESULT CALLBACK NewWndProc(HWND hWnd, UINT uMsg, WPARAM wParam, LPARAM lParam)
{
   switch( uMsg )
   {
     case WM_COMMAND :
            switch( LOWORD( wParam ) )
            {
               case IDM_TEST :
                    SetActiveWindow( GetParent( hWnd ) );
                    break;
         .
         .
         .
```

SetClassLong

Description	SetClassLong changes a 32-bit (long) value associated with the WNDCLASS structure or the extra class memory for the class of a given window. Items that can be changed include the window procedure for a class, the icon associated with a class, the background color, and other items. If the class has extra data allocated with it, SetClassLong changes the application-defined 32-bit values in this area.
Syntax	DWORD **SetClassLong**(HWND *hwnd,* int *nIndex,* LONG *lNewVal*)
Parameters	
hwnd	HWND: A handle to a window of the class type to be changed.
nIndex	int: The zero-based offset to the extra class data that will be changed or one of the values in Table 4-9.

Table 4-9 SetClassLong *nIndex* values

Value	Meaning
GCL_CBCLSEXTRA	Changes the size, in bytes, of the extra memory associated with the class. This does not change the number of bytes already allocated.
GCL_CBWNDEXTRA	Changes the size, in bytes, of the extra window memory associated with each window that is created with this class. Changing this value will not change the number of bytes already allocated.
GCL_HBRBACKGROUND	Changes the handle of the background brush.
GCL_HCURSOR	Changes the handle of the cursor.
GCL_HICON	Changes the handle of the icon.
GCL_HMODULE	Changes the instance handle of the module that registered the class.
GCL_MENUNAME	Changes the address of the menu resource name.
GCL_STYLE	Changes the window-class style.
GCL_WNDPROC	Changes the address of the window procedure (WndProc) associated with the class.

lNewVal	LONG: The new 32-bit replacement value.
Returns	DWORD: If successful, the previous 32-bit value is returned; otherwise, 0 is returned.
Include File	winuser.h
See Also	SetClassWord, GetClassLong, GetClassWord, RegisterClass
Example	In this example, the background color for the window class of the main application window is changed to light gray. A new pop-up window is created using the new class, and the main application window is repainted to show the color change.

```
LRESULT CALLBACK WndProc( HWND hWnd, UINT uMsg, WPARAM wParam, LPARAM lParam )
{
static HWND hNewWnd;

   switch( uMsg )
   {
      case WM_COMMAND :
              switch( LOWORD( wParam ) )
              {
                 case IDM_TEST :
                        SetClassLong( hWnd, GCL_HBRBACKGROUND,
                                  (LONG)GetStockObject( LTGRAY_BRUSH ) );

                        hNewWnd = CreateWindow( szAppName,
                                       "Pop-up Window",
                                       WS_POPUP | WS_VISIBLE |
                                       WS_CAPTION,
                                       10, 50, 150, 150,
                                       hWnd,
                                       NULL,
                                       hInst, NULL );

                        // Update the parent window also because the
                        // background color will change for it as well.
                        // ...........................................
                        InvalidateRect( hWnd, NULL, TRUE );
                        UpdateWindow( hWnd );
                        break;
```

.
.
.

SetClassWord   ■ WINDOWS 95 ■ WINDOWS NT

Description	An application can associate data with a window class. `SetClassWord` changes a 16-bit (word) value in the window class extra memory for the class of a given window.
Syntax	WORD **SetClassWord**(HWND *hwnd,* int *nIndex,* WORD *wNewWord*)
Parameters	
hwnd	HWND: A handle to a window of the class type to be changed.
nIndex	int: The zero-based offset of the 16-bit value to be changed.
wNewWord	WORD: The new value.

Returns	WORD: If successful, the previous value is returned; otherwise, it is 0.
Include File	winuser.h
See Also	SetClassLong, GetClassWord, GetClassLong, GetWindowWord, SetWindowWord
Example	See the example for the GetClassWord function.

SetFocus   ■ WINDOWS 95   ■ WINDOWS NT

Description	SetFocus gives a window input focus. All keyboard input will be sent to this window, while the previous window will not receive input. Only one window can have input focus at a time.
Syntax	HWND **SetFocus**(HWND *hwnd*)
Parameters	
hwnd	HWND: The handle of the window that will receive input focus. If NULL, keystrokes will be ignored.
Returns	HWND: If successful, the handle of the window that previously had input focus. If input focus was not on a window or the *hwnd* parameter is invalid, the return value is NULL.
Include File	winuser.h
See Also	GetFocus, EnableWindow
Related Messages	WM_SETFOCUS, WM_KILLFOCUS
Example	This example creates two edit controls. When the user selects the Test! menu item, the example uses the GetFocus function to determine which edit control has focus and changes the focus to the other edit control with the SetFocus function.

```
LRESULT CALLBACK WndProc( HWND hWnd, UINT uMsg, WPARAM wParam, LPARAM lParam )
{
static HWND hEdit1 = NULL;
static HWND hEdit2 = NULL;

   switch( uMsg )
   {
      case WM_CREATE :
              // Create two child window edit controls.
              //.....................................
              hEdit1 = CreateWindow( "EDIT", "Edit 1",
                                     WS_CHILD | WS_BORDER |
                                     WS_VISIBLE | ES_LEFT,
                                     10, 10, 100, 25,
```

```
                            hWnd, (HMENU) 101,
                            hInst, NULL );

        hEdit2 = CreateWindow( "EDIT", "Edit 2",
                            WS_CHILD | WS_BORDER |
                            WS_VISIBLE | ES_LEFT,
                            10, 35, 100, 25,
                            hWnd, (HMENU) 101,
                            hInst, NULL );
        break;

case WM_COMMAND :
        switch( LOWORD( wParam ) )
        {
            case IDM_TEST :
                    // Set focus to the other edit control.
                    //..................................
                    if ( GetFocus() == hEdit1 )
                        SetFocus( hEdit2 );
                    else
                        SetFocus( hEdit1 );
                    break;
```

SetForegroundWindow ■ WINDOWS 95 ■ WINDOWS NT

Description	SetForegroundWindow brings the thread that created the given window into the foreground and activates the window, giving it input focus. Keyboard input will now be directed to the given window.
Syntax	BOOL **SetForegroundWindow**(HWND *hwnd*)
Parameters	
hwnd	HWND: A handle to the window that should be activated and brought to the foreground.
Returns	BOOL: If successful, the return value is TRUE; otherwise, it is FALSE.
Include File	winuser.h
See Also	GetForegroundWindow, BringWindowToTop
Example	In this example, a child pop-up window is created. When the Test! menu option is selected on the pop-up window, the parent window is made the foreground window, and the pop-up window loses the foreground status.

```
LRESULT CALLBACK NewWndProc(HWND hWnd, UINT uMsg, WPARAM wParam, LPARAM lParam)
{
   switch( uMsg )
   {
      case WM_COMMAND :
              switch( LOWORD( wParam ) )
              {
                 case IDM_TEST :
                       SetForegroundWindow( GetParent( hWnd ) );
                       break;
                 .
                 .
                 .
```

SetParent   ■ WINDOWS 95 ■ WINDOWS NT

Description	SetParent changes the parent window of the given child window. A child window can be a parent for other child windows.
Syntax	HWND **SetParent**(HWND *hwndChild*, HWND *hwndNewParent*)
Parameters	
hwndChild	HWND: A handle to the child window.
hwndNewParent	HWND: A handle to the new parent window. If set to NULL, the desktop window becomes the new parent window.
Returns	HWND: If successful, the previous parent window handle is returned; otherwise, NULL is returned.
Include File	winuser.h
See Also	GetParent, GetNextWindow, IsWindow
Example	This example creates a pop-up child window and two child edit controls. When the Test! menu option is selected on the main window, the first edit control is moved to the pop-up child window by changing the parent window of the edit control.

```
LRESULT CALLBACK WndProc( HWND hWnd, UINT uMsg, WPARAM wParam, LPARAM lParam )
{
static HWND hNewWnd = NULL;
static HWND hEdit1  = NULL;
static HWND hEdit2  = NULL;

   switch( uMsg )
   {
```

```
case WM_CREATE:
     {
          WNDCLASS wc;

          wc.style          = CS_HREDRAW | CS_VREDRAW | CS_PARENTDC;
          wc.lpfnWndProc    = (WNDPROC)NewWndProc;
          wc.cbClsExtra     = sizeof( WORD );
          wc.cbWndExtra     = 0;
          wc.hInstance      = hInst;
          wc.hIcon          = LoadIcon(hInst, szAppName);
          wc.hCursor        = LoadCursor(NULL, IDC_ARROW);
          wc.hbrBackground  = (HBRUSH)(COLOR_WINDOW + 1);
          wc.lpszMenuName   = szAppName;
          wc.lpszClassName  = "New Class";
          wc.cbSize         = sizeof( WNDCLASSEX );
          wc.hIconSm        = LoadImage( hInst, lpszAppName,
                                         IMAGE_ICON, 16, 16,
                                         LR_DEFAULTCOLOR );

          if ( RegisterClass( &wc ) )
          {
               hNewWnd = CreateWindowEx( "New Class",
                                         "Pop-up Window",
                                         WS_POPUP | WS_VISIBLE |
                                         WS_CAPTION,
                                         10, 50, 150, 150,
                                         hWnd,
                                         NULL,
                                         hInst, NULL );
          }

          // Create two edit controls
          //....................................
          hEdit1 = CreateWindow( "EDIT", "Here is Edit 1",
                                 WS_CHILD | WS_BORDER |
                                 WS_VISIBLE |ES_LEFT,
                                 10, 10, 100, 30,
                                 hWnd, (HMENU) 101,
                                 hInst, NULL );

          hEdit2 = CreateWindow( "EDIT", "Here is Edit 2",
                                 WS_CHILD | WS_BORDER |
                                 WS_VISIBLE | ES_LEFT,
                                 15, 40, 100, 30,
```

continued on next page

continued from previous page

```
                                        hWnd, (HMENU) 102,
                                        hInst, NULL );
            }
            break;

    case WM_COMMAND :
            switch( LOWORD( wParam ) )
            {
                case IDM_TEST :
                        SetParent( hEdit1, hNewWnd );
                        break;

        .
        .
        .
```

SetProp   ■ WINDOWS 95 ■ WINDOWS NT

Description	Each window can have a list of property items that contain an identifier and a data handle. `SetProp` adds a new property item to the property list of a window.
	Property items can be used to store any type of data. The property item contains a handle that can store a handle to allocated memory or any other value. Handles are 32-bit values in Windows 95, so any 32-bit (long) value can be stored with a property item.
Syntax	BOOL **SetProp**(HWND *hwnd,* LPCTSTR *lpsz,* HANDLE *hData*)
Parameters	
hwnd	HWND: A handle to the window where the property item will be added.
lpsz	LPCTSTR: A pointer to a null-terminated string or contains an atom that identifies a string. If this parameter is an atom, it must be a global atom created by a previous call to the `GlobalAddAtom` function. The atom must be placed in the low-order word of *lpsz*; the high-order word must be **0**.
hData	HANDLE: The value to associate with the property item.
Returns	BOOL: If the property item was added to the property list, the return value is **TRUE**; otherwise, it is **FALSE**.
Include File	`winuser.h`
See Also	`GetProp, EnumProps, RemoveProp`
Example	See the example for the `GetProp` function.

SetWindowLong

Description   SetWindowLong changes a 32-bit (long) value that is associated with a window or a 32-bit value that is at a given offset within the extra window data.

Each window has information stored about the style, instance handle, window procedure, and other data. You can use SetWindowLong to change any of the values associated with the window or values that are application specific in the extra window data.

Syntax   LONG **SetWindowLong**(HWND *hwnd,* int *nIndex,* LONG *lNewLong*)

Parameters

hwnd   HWND: A handle to the window whose data will be changed.

nIndex   int: The zero-based offset of the 32-bit value to change within the extra window data or one of the values in Table 4-10. The DWL_ values are only valid for dialog box windows.

Table 4-10 SetWindowLong *nIndex* values

Value	Meaning
GWL_EXSTYLE	Changes the extended window style.
GWL_HINSTANCE	Changes the application instance handle.
GWL_ID	Changes the identifier of the window.
GWL_STYLE	Changes the window style.
GWL_USERDATA	Changes the application-defined 32-bit value associated with the window.
GWL_WNDPROC	Changes the address for the window procedure (WndProc).
DWL_DLGPROC	Changes the address of the dialog box procedure (DlgProc).
DWL_MSGRESULT	Changes the return value of a message processed in the dialog box procedure.
DWL_USER	Changes the extra information that is private to the application, such as handles or pointers.

lNewLong   LONG: The new 32-bit value.

Returns   LONG: If successful, the previous 32-bit value; otherwise, it is 0.

Include File   winuser.h

See Also   GetWindowLong, GetClassLong, GetClassWord GetWindowWord, SetWindowWord

Example   In this example, the control ID of an edit control is changed using the SetWindowLong function.

```
LRESULT CALLBACK WndProc( HWND hWnd, UINT uMsg, WPARAM wParam, LPARAM lParam )
{
static HWND hEdit  = NULL;
```

continued on next page

continued from previous page

```
    switch( uMsg )
    {
      case WM_CREATE:
            hEdit = CreateWindow( "EDIT", "Here is Edit",
                                  WS_CHILD | WS_BORDER |
                                  WS_VISIBLE |ES_LEFT,
                                  10, 10, 100, 30,
                                  hWnd, (HMENU) 101,
                                  hInst, NULL );

            break;

      case WM_COMMAND :
            switch( LOWORD( wParam ) )
            {
              case IDM_TEST :
                    SetWindowLong( hEdit, GWL_ID, (LONG)110 );
                    break;
            .
            .
            .
```

SetWindowPlacement ■ WINDOWS 95 ■ WINDOWS NT

Description	A window can be shown as minimized, normal, or maximized. The way a window is shown is the window's show state. **SetWindowPlacement** allows an application to change the show state and position for each state of a window.
Syntax	BOOL **SetWindowPlacement**(HWND *hwnd,* CONST WINDOWPLACEMENT* *lpwndpl*)
Parameters	
hwnd	HWND: A handle to the window.
lpwndpl	CONST WINDOWPLACEMENT*: A pointer to a **WINDOWPLACEMENT** structure that specifies the new show state and window positions. See the **GetWindowPlacement** function for details on the **WINDOWPLACEMENT** structure.
Returns	BOOL: **TRUE** if successful; otherwise, it is **FALSE**.
Include File	winuser.h
See Also	ShowWindow, GetWindowPlacement, IsIconic, IsZoomed, IsWindowVisible, SetWindowPos
Example	This example uses the **SetWindowPlacement** function to change the show state of the main window to minimized.

```
LRESULT CALLBACK WndProc( HWND hWnd, UINT uMsg, WPARAM wParam, LPARAM lParam )
{
   switch( uMsg )
   {
      case WM_COMMAND :
              switch( LOWORD( wParam ) )
              {
                 case IDM_TEST :
                     {
                         WINDOWPLACEMENT wp;

                         wp.length = sizeof( WINDOWPLACEMENT );
                         if ( GetWindowPlacement( hWnd, &wp ) )
                         {
                             wp.showCmd = SW_MINIMIZE;
                             SetWindowPlacement( hWnd, &wp );
                         }
                     }
                     break;
                 .
                 .
                 .
```

SetWindowPos   ■ WINDOWS 95 ■ WINDOWS NT

Description   **SetWindowPos** changes the size, position, and order of a child, pop-up, or top-level window. This function is similar to **DeferWindowPos** in how it moves a window. The difference is that **DeferWindowPos** moves several windows at once and **SetWindowPos** moves only one window.

The **SetWindowPos** function is a more flexible way to move windows than the **MoveWindow** function. You can resize the window without knowing the current position or reorder it in the window manager's list.

Syntax   BOOL **SetWindowPos**(HWND *hwnd*, HWND *hwndInsertAfter*, int *x*, int *y*, int *cx*, int *cy*, UINT *nFlags*)

Parameters

hwnd   HWND: A handle to the window to be moved.

hwndInsertAfter   HWND: A handle to the window that will precede the window in *hwnd*. One of the values in Table 4-3 (shown in the **DeferWindowPos** function description) can be used in place of a window handle. This parameter is ignored if the **SWP_NOZORDER** is set in the *nFlags* parameter.

x	**int**: The new x position of the window's upper-left corner.
y	**int**: The new y position of the window's upper-left corner.
cx	**int**: The window's new width, in pixels.
cy	**int**: The window's new height, in pixels.
nFlags	**UINT**: Affects how the window is moved and positioned. This parameter is made up of one or more of the values listed in Table 4-11 combined with the binary OR (	) operator.

Table 4-11 SetWindowPos *nFlags* values

Value	Meaning
SWP_DRAWFRAME	Draws the window's class-defined frame around the window.
SWP_FRAMECHANGED	Forces a WM_NCCALCSIZE message to be sent to the window, even if the window's size is not being changed.
SWP_HIDEWINDOW	Hides the window.
SWP_NOACTIVATE	Does not activate the window.
SWP_NOCOPYBITS	Does not restore the contents of the client area.
SWP_NOMOVE	The *x* and *y* parameters are ignored. The window will only be resized.
SWP_NOOWNERZORDER	Does not change the owner window's position in the Z order.
SWP_NOREDRAW	Will not cause a repaint after the move takes place. The application must explicitly invalidate or redraw any part that needs to be drawn.
SWP_NOREPOSITION	Same as the SWP_NOOWNERZORDER flag.
SWP_NOSENDCHANGING	Prevents the window from receiving the WM_WINDOWPOSCHANGING message.
SWP_NOSIZE	The *cx* and *cy* parameters are ignored. The window will only be moved.
SWP_NOZORDER	Ignores the *hwndInsertAfter* parameter.
SWP_SHOWWINDOW	Displays the window.

Returns	**BOOL**: If successful, **TRUE** is returned; otherwise, it is **FALSE**.
Include File	winuser.h
See Also	DeferWindowPos, MoveWindow
Related Messages	WM_SIZE, WM_NCCALCSIZE, WM_MOVE
Example	This example creates an edit control and sizes it to the same size as the client area of the main application window, using the **SetWindowPos** function. The result is a simple editor.

```
LRESULT CALLBACK WndProc( HWND hWnd, UINT uMsg, WPARAM wParam, LPARAM lParam )
{
static HWND hEdit   = NULL;

    switch( uMsg )
    {
        case WM_CREATE :
```

```
          // Create an edit control that will be sized to match
          // the parent window's client area.
          //....................................................
          hEdit = CreateWindow( "EDIT", "Here is the Edit Control",
                                WS_CHILD |
                                WS_VISIBLE |
                                ES_LEFT | ES_MULTILINE,
                                0, 0,          // Set the upper left corner
                                CW_USEDEFAULT, // to be under the static
                                CW_USEDEFAULT, // window.
                                hWnd,
                                (HMENU) 101,   // The control ID.
                                hInst, NULL );
          break;

   case WM_SIZE :
          // The parent window was resized. Size the edit
          // control to match the parent window's client area.
          //....................................................

          SetWindowPos( hEdit, NULL, 0, 0,
                        LOWORD( lParam ), HIWORD( lParam ),
                        SWP_NOACTIVATE | SWP_NOZORDER |
                        SWP_NOMOVE );
          break;
```

.
.
.

SetWindowText   ■ WINDOWS 95 ■ WINDOWS NT

Description	**SetWindowText** changes the text associated with a window. For windows with a title bar, the title is the text that will be changed. For buttons, edit controls, and other window controls, the text the control displays is changed. An application can change the text of button controls to reflect the current action they will perform.
Syntax	BOOL **SetWindowText**(HWND *hwnd*, LPCTSTR *lpsz*)
Parameters	
hwnd	HWND: A handle to the window or control for which text will be changed.
lpsz	LPCTSTR: A pointer to the null-terminated string that contains the new text for the window or control.

Returns	BOOL: TRUE if the function succeeded, and FALSE if the function failed.
Include File	winuser.h
See Also	GetWindowText
Related Messages	WM_GETTEXT, WM_SETTEXT
Example	This example uses SetWindowText to change the main window title to New Title when the user selects the Test! menu item.

```
LRESULT CALLBACK WndProc( HWND hWnd, UINT uMsg, WPARAM wParam, LPARAM lParam )
{
   switch( uMsg )
   {
      case WM_COMMAND :
             switch( LOWORD( wParam ) )
             {
                case IDM_TEST :
                    SetWindowText( hWnd, "New Title" );
                    break;
                        .
                        .
                        .
```

SetWindowWord   ■ WINDOWS 95 ■ WINDOWS NT

Description	SetWindowWord changes a 16-bit (word) value at a given offset in the extra window memory of a window. An application can create a window with associated extra memory for storing application-defined data. SetWindowWord will change a 16-bit value in the extra window data.
Syntax	WORD **SetWindowWord**(HWND *hwnd,* int *nIndex,* WORD *wNewWord*)
Parameters	
hwnd	HWND: A handle to the window for which data will be changed.
nIndex	int: The zero-based offset of the value to be changed.
wNewWord	WORD: The new 16-bit value.
Returns	WORD: If successful, the previous value; otherwise, 0 is returned.
Include File	winuser.h
See Also	GetWindowWord, SetWindowLong, GetWindowLong
Example	See the example for the GetWindowWord function.

ShowOwnedPopups   ■ WINDOWS 95 ■ WINDOWS NT

Description	**ShowOwnedPopups** shows or hides all pop-up windows owned by the given window. This eliminates the need to call the **ShowWindow** function for each individual pop-up window.
Syntax	BOOL **ShowOwnedPopups**(HWND *hwnd,* BOOL *bShow*)
Parameters	
hwnd	**HWND**: A handle to the window that owns the pop-up windows to be shown or hidden.
bShow	**BOOL**: **TRUE** if the pop-up windows should be shown, **FALSE** if all pop-up windows should be hidden.
Returns	**BOOL**: **TRUE** if the function succeeded, and **FALSE** if the function failed.
Include File	winuser.h
See Also	ShowWindow
Related Messages	WM_SHOWWINDOW
Example	This example creates a pop-up window and toggles the show state from visible to hidden using the **ShowOwnedPopups** function.

```
LRESULT CALLBACK WndProc( HWND hWnd, UINT uMsg, WPARAM wParam, LPARAM lParam )
{
static HWND hNewWnd = NULL;

   switch( uMsg )
   {
      case WM_CREATE:
              {
                  WNDCLASSEX wc;

                  wc.style         = CS_HREDRAW | CS_VREDRAW | CS_PARENTDC;
                  wc.lpfnWndProc   = (WNDPROC)NewWndProc;
                  wc.cbClsExtra    = sizeof( WORD );
                  wc.cbWndExtra    = 0;
                  wc.hInstance     = hInst;
                  wc.hIcon         = LoadIcon(hInst, lpszAppName);
                  wc.hCursor       = LoadCursor(NULL, IDC_ARROW);
                  wc.hbrBackground = (HBRUSH)(COLOR_WINDOW + 1);
                  wc.lpszMenuName  = szAppName;
                  wc.lpszClassName = "New Class";
                  wc.cbSize        = sizeof( WNDCLASSEX );
                  wc.hIconSm       = LoadImage( hInst, lpszAppName,
                                          IMAGE_ICON, 16, 16,
                                          LR_DEFAULTCOLOR );
```

continued on next page

continued from previous page

```
                    if ( RegisterClassEx( &wc ) )
                    {
                        hNewWnd = CreateWindow( "New Class",
                                                "Pop-up Window",
                                                WS_POPUP | WS_VISIBLE |
                                                WS_CAPTION,
                                                10, 50, 150, 150,
                                                hWnd,
                                                NULL,
                                                hInst, NULL );
                    }
                }
                break;

        case WM_COMMAND :
                switch( LOWORD( wParam ) )
                {
                    case IDM_TEST :
                            // Toggle the pop-up window from visible to
                            // hidden.
                            // .........................................................
                            if ( IsWindowVisible( hNewWnd ) )
                                ShowOwnedPopups( hNewWnd, FALSE );
                            else
                                ShowOwnedPopups( hNewWnd, TRUE );
                            break;

                            .
                            .
                            .
```

ShowWindow   ■ WINDOWS 95 ■ WINDOWS NT

Description   ShowWindow sets a window's show state. The show state determines how a window is displayed on the screen.

Usually after a window is created, the ShowWindow function is called to make it visible. ShowWindow also can be used to minimize or maximize a window. ShowWindow does not make sure the window is in the foreground. Use the SetWindowPos or SetActiveWindow function to bring a window to the foreground.

Syntax   BOOL **ShowWindow**(HWND *hwnd,* int *nCmdShow*)

Parameters

hwnd	`HWND`: A handle to the window.
nCmdShow	`int`: Determines how the window will be shown. Can be set to one of the values in Table 4-12.

Table 4-12 `ShowWindow` *nCmdShow* values

Value	Meaning
`SW_HIDE`	The window is hidden.
`SW_MAXIMIZE`	The window is maximized.
`SW_MINIMIZE`	The window is minimized and activates the top-level window in the system's list.
`SW_RESTORE`	Activates and displays a window. If the window is minimized or maximized, the window will be restored to its original size and position.
`SW_SHOW`	The window is displayed in its current size and position.
`SW_SHOWDEFAULT`	Used at application startup to set the show state based on the `SW_` flag in the `STARTUPINFO` structure.
`SW_SHOWMAXIMIZED`	The window is maximized.
`SW_SHOWMINIMIZED`	The window is minimized and displayed as an icon.
`SW_SHOWMINNOACTIVE`	The window is minimized and the active window remains active.
`SW_SHOWNA`	The window is displayed in its current state and the active window remains active.
`SW_SHOWNOACTIVATE`	The window is displayed in its most recent size and position and the active window remains active.
`SW_SHOWNORMAL`	The window is shown in its normal size.

Returns	`BOOL`: `TRUE` if the window was previously visible; otherwise, `FALSE` is returned.
Include File	`winuser.h`
See Also	`CreateWindow`, `SetWindowPos`, `SetActiveWindow`, `ShowOwnedPopups`, `ShowWindowAsync`
Related Messages	`WM_SHOWWINDOW`
Example	This example uses **ShowWindow** to maximize the application when the user selects the Test! menu item.

```
LRESULT CALLBACK WndProc( HWND hWnd, UINT uMsg, WPARAM wParam, LPARAM lParam )
{
   switch( uMsg )
   {
      case WM_COMMAND :
              switch( LOWORD( wParam ) )
              {
                 case IDM_TEST :
                        // Maximize the main application window.
                        //.......................................
```

continued on next page

continued from previous page

```
ShowWindow( hWnd, SW_SHOWMAXIMIZED );
break;
```

.
.
.

ShowWindowAsync   ■ WINDOWS 95 ■ WINDOWS NT

Description	**ShowWindowAsync** is the same as the **ShowWindow** function except that it works by posting the show-window event to the window's message queue in a multithreaded application. It then returns without waiting for the event to be processed by the window, which could cause the application to hang waiting for a thread to process the request.
Syntax	BOOL *ShowWindowAsync*(HWND *hwnd*, int *nCmdShow*)
Parameters	
hwnd	**HWND**: A handle to the window.
nCmdShow	**int**: Determines the way the window will be shown. Can be set to one of the values in Table 4-12.
Returns	**BOOL**: **TRUE** if the window was previously visible; otherwise, **FALSE** is returned.
Include File	winuser.h
See Also	ShowWindow
Related Messages	WM_SHOWWINDOW

WindowFromPoint   ■ WINDOWS 95 ■ WINDOWS NT

Description	**WindowFromPoint** finds the window that contains the given point relative to the screen.
Syntax	HWND **WindowFromPoint**(POINT *pt*)
Parameters	
pt	**POINT**: A **POINT** structure that contains the point to be checked.
Returns	**HWND**: If a window is found at the given point, the return value is the handle of the window. The return value is **NULL** if no window was found.
Include File	winuser.h
See Also	ChildWindowFromPoint
Example	This example will capture all mouse actions. When the left button of the mouse is pushed, the **WindowFromPoint** function checks the window the cursor is over. If a window is found, the window title is displayed in a message box.

```
LRESULT CALLBACK WndProc( HWND hWnd, UINT uMsg, WPARAM wParam, LPARAM lParam )
{
    switch( uMsg )
    {
        case WM_CREATE :
                // Capture mouse.
                //...............
                SetCapture( hWnd );
                break;

        case WM_LBUTTONDOWN :
                {
                    POINT pt;
                    HWND  hwnd;
                    char  szTitle[61];

                    pt.x = LOWORD( lParam );
                    pt.y = HIWORD( lParam );

                    hwnd = WindowFromPoint( pt );

                    if ( hwnd != NULL )
                    {
                        GetWindowText( hwnd, szTitle, 60 );
                        MessageBox( hWnd, szTitle, "Hit", MB_OK );
                    }
                }
                break;

        case WM_DESTROY :
                ReleaseCapture();
                PostQuitMessage(0);
                break;
            .
            .
            .
```

5

MESSAGE PROCESSING

Message handling is at the heart of what makes a Windows application work. The system and other applications generate messages for every event that occurs in Windows. Messages allow Windows to run multiple applications at once. Windows 95 and Windows NT expand on the ability of previous versions of Windows by giving each thread or process its own message queue. In previous versions of Windows, all applications shared the message queue. To allow other applications to process messages, an application had to give control back to Windows as often as possible. With Windows 95 and Windows NT, this is no longer an issue.

Message Flow

Windows generates messages for every hardware event, such as when the user presses a key on a keyboard or moves a mouse. It passes these messages to the appropriate thread message queue. Each thread in the system processes the messages in its own message queue. If a message is destined for a specific thread, the message is placed in that thread's message queue. Some messages are systemwide or are destined for multiple threads. These messages are placed in the queues of the appropriate threads. Figure 5-1 shows a simple diagram of how a message is processed by multiple threads.

A message is actually a data structure that is defined as follows:

```
typedef struct tagMSG
{
    HWND       hwnd;      /* window handle */
    UINT       message;   /* message ID    */
    WPARAM     wParam;    /* wParam value  */
    LPARAM     lParam;    /* lParam value  */
    DWORD      time;      /* msec since startup */
    POINT      pt;        /* mouse location, screen coord */
} MSG;
```

The message data contains the window handle (*hwnd*), the coded message type (*message*), the *wParam* and *lParam* data that will be passed to the **WndProc** function, the time the message was sent (in milliseconds after Windows started), and a **POINT** (*pt*) structure containing the x and y coordinates of the mouse cursor when the message was sent.

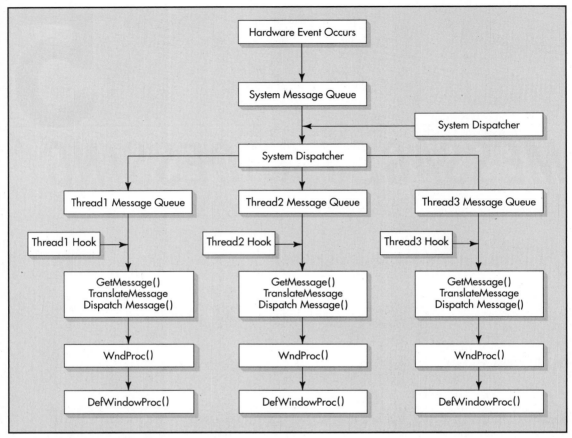

Figure 5-1 Windows message flow diagram

Processing Messages

A thread or process pulls messages off the message queue by using a message loop. The main message loop for an application is at the bottom of the **WinMain** function. Message loops typically have the following form:

```
while( GetMessage( &msg, NULL, 0, 0 ) )
{
    TranslateMessage( &msg );
    DispatchMessage( &msg );
}
```

The `GetMessage` function fetches the message from the message queue. `GetMessage` is followed by `TranslateMessage` and `DispatchMessage`. `DispatchMessage` sends the message data to the `WndProc` function for the window handle contained in the message structure. `DispatchMessage` knows which function should receive the messages, because the `WndProc` function is associated with the window data. The `WndProc` function defaults to the one defined in the window's class definition, but can be changed by subclassing the window.

Subclassing allows an application to change the `WndProc` that is called for a window by the `DispatchMessage` function. The new `WndProc` then calls the default `WndProc` function that is defined in the window's class. This allows an application to modify the behavior of a window by changing the processing of a message before the default message processing takes place.

Sources of Messages

Figure 5-1 shows a simplified flow diagram for a single message through a thread's message logic. Messages can originate in a few more ways. Figure 5-2 examines the message loop in more detail and shows how messages can be placed in the queue.

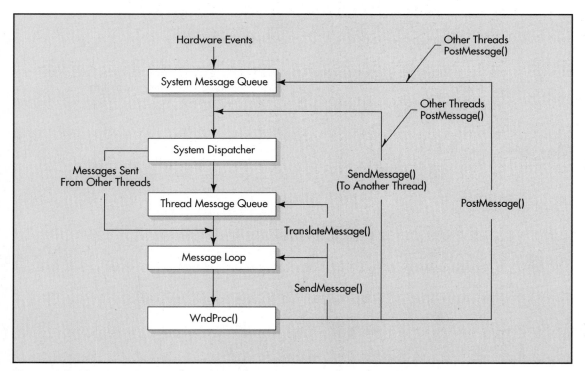

Figure 5-2 Messages entering the message loop

Messages do not all start because of a hardware event. It may be convenient to send a program message from within the body of the program. Threads can pass data back and forth by sending messages. Messages can be placed in the message queue using the **PostMessage** function, or they can be sent directly to the message loop for immediate processing using **SendMessage**. Other applications also can send messages to an application. These are often specialized messages, unique to a set of programs. Windows provides the **RegisterWindowMessage** function to dynamically generate unique message identifiers. The identifiers are sequenced so as to not overlap other message numbers used by unrelated programs. A common way to exchange data between programs is to use dynamic data exchange (DDE). DDE is a series of messages that have been defined to provide a communications standard.

Reentrant Functions

Windows 95 and Windows NT have the capability to run threads in a preemptive multitasking fashion. This means Windows will determine how much CPU time each thread can receive based on priorities and the demand on the system and manage the switching between the threads. The program has to be set up in such a way that the routines used in threads are thread protected. This means the routines are reentrant and don't rely on variables being used only once. A threaded routine could be called several times before Windows gives control back. If static variables are being used, the value that was set when control was taken away may not be the same when control is given back.

WndProc is the most common reentrant function in an application. If, while processing one message, a message is sent to itself using **SendMessage**, **WndProc** will be called again for the new message. This is very similar to recursion, in which a function is called over and over from within itself.

Message Hook Functions

Windows provides a very powerful set of functions that allow you to set message hooks. Hooks let a module (an application or DLL) intercept messages going to other applications. The messages can be acted on, modified, or even stopped. One good way to use a hook function would be to remap the keyboard. Every keyboard message could be intercepted and then modified to reflect a different keyboard layout. More sophisticated uses are to modify the behavior of specific applications.

The **SetWindowsHookEx** function installs the hook procedure. If messages are only to be filtered for an application, the filter functions can reside in the application itself. However, if messages are going to be filtered for all applications, the filter function has to reside in a dynamic link library (DLL). To remove a hook, you use the **UnhookWindowsHookEx** function.

Message-Processing Function Descriptions

Table 5-1 summarizes the Windows message-processing functions. Detailed function descriptions follow the table.

Table 5-1 Message-processing function summary

Function	Purpose
BroadcastSystemMessage	Sends a message to a list of recipients such as applications, drivers, etc.
CallMsgFilter	Activates a message filter (hook) function.
CallNextHookEx	Passes information to the next hook procedure in the current hook chain.
CallWindowProc	Passes message parameters to a message-processing function.
DefWindowProc	Default message-processing function.
DispatchMessage	Sends a Windows message to the application's WndProc function.
ExitWindows	Logs off the current user.
ExitWindowsEx	Logs off the current user, shuts down the computer, or restarts the computer.
GetMessage	Retrieves messages from an application's message queue.
GetMessageExtraInfo	Retrieves extra information about the last message retrieved.
GetMessagePos	Retrieves the position of the cursor when a message was sent.
GetMessageTime	Retrieves the time when a message was sent.
InSendMessage	Determines if a message was sent using the SendMessage function.
PeekMessage	Checks the message queue for a message.
PostMessage	Puts a message in the message queue and returns without waiting.
PostQuitMessage	Shuts down an application.
PostThreadMessage	Puts a message in a thread's message queue and returns without waiting.
RegisterWindowMessage	Creates a new, unique Windows message number.
ReplyMessage	Replies to a message that was sent with SendMessage.
SendMessage	Sends a message directly to a window's message function and waits for a reply.
SendMessageCallback	Sends a message and returns immediately, letting a callback function handle the reply.
SendMessageTimeout	Sends a message and waits for a reply until the time-out has expired.
SendNotifyMessage	Sends a message and returns immediately.
SetWindowsHookEx	Installs a Windows message filter function.
TranslateMessage	Generates WM_CHAR, WM_SYSCHAR, WM_DEADCHAR, and WM_SYSDEADCHAR messages when a virtual-key code is received.
UnhookWindowsHookEx	Removes a message hook function from the system.
WaitMessage	Yields control to other threads while waiting for a message.
WinMain	The entry point for a Windows program and where the main message loop is defined.

BroadcastSystemMessage　■ WINDOWS 95　■ WINDOWS NT

Description　BroadcastSystemMessage sends a message to multiple recipients. The recipients can be applications, installable drivers, Windows-based network drivers, system-level device drivers, or any combination of these system components. Do not send structures with pointers, since these pointers are not translated and are invalid to other applications.

Use **BroadcastSystemMessage** when you need to send a message to all currently running applications or installed drivers.

Syntax   LONG **BroadcastSystemMessage**(DWORD *dwFlags,* LPDWORD *lpdwRecipients,* UINT *uMessage,* WPARAM *wParam,* LPARAM *lParam*)

Parameters

dwFlags   DWORD: A combination of the option flags listed in Table 5-2 that determine the action of this function.

Table 5-2 BroadcastSystemMessage *dwFlags* values

Value	Meaning
BSF_FLUSHDISK	Flush the disk after each recipient processes the message.
BSF_FORCEIFHUNG	Continue to broadcast the message, even if the time-out period elapses or one of the recipients is hung.
BSF_IGNORECURRENTTASK	Do not send the message to windows that belong to the current task. This prevents the sender from receiving its own message.
BSF_NOHANG	Force a hung application to time out. If one of the recipients times out, do not continue broadcasting the message.
BSF_NOTIMEOUTIFNOTHUNG	Wait for a response to the message, as long as the recipient is not hung. Do not time out.
BSF_POSTMESSAGE	Post the message and do not wait for a response. This cannot be used with BSF_QUERY.
BSF_QUERY	Send the message to one recipient at a time, sending to a subsequent recipient only if the current recipient returns TRUE.

lpdwRecipients   LPDWORD: A pointer to a DWORD variable that contains and receives information about the recipients of the message. Use this parameter to determine where the message is sent. The variable can be a combination of the values listed in Table 5-3.

Table 5-3 BroadcastSystemMessage *lpdwRecipients* values

Value	Meaning
BSM_ALLCOMPONENTS	Broadcast message to all system components.
BSM_ALLDESKTOPS	(Windows NT only) Broadcast to all desktops. Requires the SE_TCB_NAME privilege.
BSM_APPLICATIONS	Broadcast to applications.
BSM_INSTALLABLEDRIVERS	Broadcast to installable drivers.
BSM_NETDRIVER	Broadcast to Windows-based network drivers.
BSM_VXDS	Broadcast to all system-level device drivers.

uMessage   UINT: The message identifier of the system message.

wParam   WPARAM: A 32-bit message-specific value.

lParam   LPARAM: A 32-bit message-specific value.

Returns	LONG: If successful, the return value is positive. If the function could not broadcast the message, the return value is –1. If the *dwFlags* parameter contains BSF_QUERY and at least one recipient returned BROADCAST_QUERY_DENY, the return value is 0.
Include File	winuser.h
See Also	SendMessage

CallMsgFilter   ■ WINDOWS 95   ■ WINDOWS NT

Description	CallMsgFilter passes a message and hook code to the hook procedures associated with the WH_SYSMSGFILTER and WH_MSGFILTER hooks. A hook procedure is set up using the SetWindowsHookEx function.
	Use CallMsgFilter to modify the intercepted message or perform an operation when a message is received.
Syntax	BOOL **CallMsgFilter**(LPMSG *lpmsg,* int *nCode*)
Parameters	
lpmsg	LPMSG: A pointer to an MSG structure. This is the message that will be filtered by the filter function.
nCode	int: The application-defined code used by the hook procedure to determine how to process the message. The value cannot be the same as the system-defined hook codes (MSGF_ and HC_). A good way to make sure the code will not conflict is to base the code from WM_USER (WM_USER+1, etc.).
Returns	BOOL: FALSE if the application should process the message further; otherwise, the return value is TRUE.
Include File	winuser.h
See Also	SetWindowsHookEx, UnhookWindowsHookEx
Related Messages	Only messages processed by a WH_MSGFILTER type of filter function will be passed. This includes WM_PAINT messages and messages from menus, dialog boxes, and message boxes. See the SetWindowsHookEx function for details.
Example	In this example, a windows hook is installed to filter the WM_PAINT message when the CallMsgFilter function is called. The CallNextHookEx function is called for all other messages.

```
BOOL  bFilterIt = FALSE;
HHOOK hHook     = NULL;


int APIENTRY WinMain( HINSTANCE hInstance, HINSTANCE hPrevInstance,
                      LPTSTR lpCmdLine, int nCmdShow)
{
    MSG        msg;
    HWND       hWnd;
```

continued on next page

continued from previous page

```
BOOL        bHooked;
WNDCLASSEX wc;

// Register the main application window class.
//............................................
wc.style           = CS_HREDRAW | CS_VREDRAW;
wc.lpfnWndProc     = (WNDPROC)WndProc;
wc.cbClsExtra      = 0;
wc.cbWndExtra      = 0;
wc.hInstance       = hInstance;
wc.hIcon           = LoadIcon( hInstance, lpszAppName );
wc.hCursor         = LoadCursor(NULL, IDC_ARROW);
wc.hbrBackground   = (HBRUSH)(COLOR_WINDOW+1);
wc.lpszMenuName    = lpszAppName;
wc.lpszClassName   = lpszAppName;
wc.cbSize          = sizeof(WNDCLASSEX);
wc.hIconSm         = LoadImage(hInstance, lpszAppName,
                              IMAGE_ICON, 16, 16,
                              LR_DEFAULTCOLOR );

if ( !RegisterClassEx( &wc ) )
   return( FALSE );

hInst = hInstance;

// Create the main application window.
//....................................
hWnd = CreateWindow( lpszAppName,
                     lpszTitle,
                     WS_OVERLAPPEDWINDOW,
                     CW_USEDEFAULT, 0,
                     CW_USEDEFAULT, 0,
                     NULL,
                     NULL,
                     hInstance,
                     NULL
                   );

if ( !hWnd )
   return( FALSE );

if ( hHook = SetWindowsHookEx( WH_MSGFILTER, (HOOKPROC)HookProcedure, NULL,
                              GetWindowThreadProcessId( hWnd, NULL ) ) )
{
   bHooked = TRUE;
}

ShowWindow( hWnd, nCmdShow );
UpdateWindow( hWnd );

while( GetMessage( &msg, NULL, 0, 0) )
{
   // If we are filtering then call the message filter.
   //..................................................
   if ( bHooked && bFilterIt )
      CallMsgFilter( &msg, WM_USER );
```

```
        TranslateMessage( &msg );
        DispatchMessage( &msg );
    }

    UnhookWindowsHookEx( hHook );

    return( msg.wParam );
}


LRESULT CALLBACK HookProcedure( int nCode, WPARAM wParam, LPARAM lParam )
{
    // If this is not our code then pass it on to the next
    // filter proc (if any).
    //.....................................................
    if ( nCode != WM_USER )
        CallNextHookEx( hHook, nCode, wParam, lParam );
    else
    {
        LPMSG msg = (LPMSG)lParam;

        if ( msg->message == WM_PAINT )
        {
            MessageBeep(0);
            return( TRUE );
        }
    }

    return( FALSE );
}


LRESULT CALLBACK WndProc( HWND hWnd, UINT uMsg, WPARAM wParam, LPARAM lParam )
{
    switch( uMsg )
    {
        case WM_COMMAND :
                switch( LOWORD( wParam ) )
                {
                    case IDM_TEST :
                            if ( bFilterIt )
                            {
                                bFilterIt = FALSE;
                                MessageBox( hWnd, "Filtering is OFF", lpszAppName,
                                            MB_OK );
                            }
                            else
                            {
                                bFilterIt = TRUE;
                                MessageBox( hWnd, "Filtering is ON", lpszAppName,
                                            MB_OK );
                            }
                            break;

            .
            .
            .
```

CallNextHookEx
■ Windows 95 ■ Windows NT

Description	`CallNextHookEx` passes information to the next hook procedure in the current hook chain. An application can call this function to pass the hook information on to the next hook in the chain. If an application does not call this function, the hooks that were installed before the application installed its hook will not be called.
Syntax	LRESULT **CallNextHookEx**(HHOOK *hhook,* int *nCode,* WPARAM *wParam,* LPARAM *lParam*)
Parameters	
hhook	HHOOK: The handle of the current hook returned from a previous call to the `SetWindowsHookEx` function.
nCode	int: The *nCode* passed to the current hook procedure.
wParam	WPARAM: The *wParam* value passed to the current hook procedure.
lParam	LPARAM: The *lParam* value passed to the current hook procedure.
Returns	LRESULT: If successful, the return value is the value returned by the next hook procedure in the chain. This value must be returned from the current hook procedure. The meaning of the return value depends on the hook type.
Include File	`winuser.h`
See Also	`SetWindowsHookEx`
Example	See the example for the `CallMsgFilter` function.

CallWindowProc
■ Windows 95 ■ Windows NT

Description	`CallWindowProc` passes the message parameter data (*wParam*, etc.) to the original message procedure for normal processing.
	Applications use `CallWindowProc` while subclassing window controls such as `BUTTON` and `SCROLLBAR`. `CallWindowProc` is used at the end of the new message procedure to pass on the messages for default processing.
Syntax	LRESULT **CallWindowProc**(WNDPROC *wndprcPrev,* HWND *hwnd,* UINT *uMsg,* WPARAM *wParam,* LPARAM *lParam*)
Parameters	
wndprcPrev	WNDPROC: A pointer to the previous window procedure.
hwnd	HWND: The handle of the window receiving the message.
uMsg	UINT: The message (`WM_PAINT`, etc.).
wParam	WPARAM: The *wParam* data of the message. This value depends on the message in *uMsg*.

lParam	LPARAM: The *lParam* data of the message. This value depends on the message in *uMsg*.
Returns	LRESULT: The return value of the message processing. This value should be returned from the subclass function.
Include File	winuser.h
See Also	SetWindowLong, GetWindowLong
Related Messages	All messages potentially pass through this function. An application can act on as many messages as are needed, and call the CallWindowProc function to let the original window message procedure handle the rest.
Example	The default processing of any subclassed window procedure should call the CallWindowProc function with the original WNDPROC obtained when subclassing. This example creates a button control and then subclasses the button, saving the original WNDPROC in *fnOldProc*. The subclass procedure overrides the WM_KEYDOWN and WM_KEYUP messages and then changes the button text to Pressed! and Released!, respectively. All other messages are passed on with the CallWindowProc function.

```
WNDPROC fnOldProc;

LRESULT CALLBACK NewButtonProc( HWND hWnd, UINT uMsg,
                                WPARAM wParam, LPARAM lParam )
{
   switch( uMsg )
   {
      case WM_KEYDOWN :
              SetWindowText( hWnd, "Pressed!" );
              break;

      case WM_KEYUP :
              SetWindowText( hWnd, "Released!" );
              break;
   }

   // Call the button's original window procedure to do default
   // processing.
   //...........................................................
   return( CallWindowProc( fnOldProc, hWnd, uMsg, wParam, lParam ) );
}


LRESULT CALLBACK WndProc( HWND hWnd, UINT uMsg, WPARAM wParam, LPARAM lParam )
{
static HWND hButton = NULL;

   switch( uMsg )
   {
      case WM_CREATE :
              hButton = CreateWindow( "BUTTON", "Button",
                                      WS_CHILD | WS_VISIBLE,
                                      10, 10, 100, 60,
                                      hWnd, NULL, hInst, NULL );
```

continued on next page

continued from previous page

```
        // Subclass the button.
        //....................
        fnOldProc = (WNDPROC)GetWindowLong( hButton, GWL_WNDPROC );
        SetWindowLong( hButton, GWL_WNDPROC, (LONG)NewButtonProc );
        break;
```

.
.
.

DefWindowProc   ■ WINDOWS 95   ■ WINDOWS NT

Description   To ensure that every message is processed, **DefWindowProc** provides default message processing for messages that an application does not process. The default processing function handles the basic operation of a Windows application. The **WndProc** of an application should always have this function as the default message handler.

Syntax   LRESULT **DefWindowProc**(HWND *hwnd,* UINT *uMsg,* WPARAM *wParam,* LPARAM *lParam*)

Parameters

hwnd   HWND: The handle of the window receiving the message.

uMsg   UINT: The message (**WM_PAINT**, etc.). This value, and the following two, will be received by the application's **WndProc** function when a message is sent to the application.

wParam   WPARAM: The *wParam* data passed with the message.

lParam   LPARAM: The *lParam* data passed with the message.

Returns   LRESULT: The value depends on the message being processed. Return this value from the application's **WndProc** function.

Include File   winuser.h

See Also   DefDlgProc, CallWindowProc

Related Messages   All messages can be handled by the default processing function. In most cases, no action is taken.

Example   This example shows how the **DefWindowProc** function is used in the **WndProc** function.

```
LRESULT CALLBACK WndProc( HWND hWnd, UINT uMsg, WPARAM wParam, LPARAM lParam )
{
    switch( uMsg )
    {
        .
        .
        .

        default :
            return( DefWindowProc( hWnd, uMsg, wParam, lParam ) );
    }
```

```
    return( OL );
}
```

DispatchMessage   ■ WINDOWS 95   ■ WINDOWS NT

Description	**DispatchMessage** sends messages from within an application's message loop to the appropriate window procedure for processing.
	You typically use **DispatchMessage** within an application's message loop after completing any necessary translation.
Syntax	LONG **DispatchMessage**(CONST MSG* *lpmsg*)
Parameters	
lpmsg	CONST MSG*: A pointer to an MSG structure that contains the message.
Returns	LONG: The return value for the message being processed. This value is generally ignored.
Include File	winuser.h
See Also	GetMessage, TranslateMessage, TranslateAccelerator
Related Messages	All Windows messages pass through this function for an application.
Example	See the examples for the **GetMessage** and **WinMain** functions.

ExitWindows   ■ WINDOWS 95   ■ WINDOWS NT

Description	**ExitWindows** closes down any user applications in an orderly fashion and logs off the current user. The machine will be left sitting at the login screen. This function is a macro that calls the **ExitWindowsEx** function with the **EWX_LOGOFF** option.
Syntax	BOOL **ExitWindows**(DWORD *dwReserved,* UINT *uReserved*)
Parameters	
dwReserved	DWORD: Reserved; must be 0.
uReserved	UINT: Reserved; must be 0.
Returns	BOOL: TRUE if successful; otherwise, the return value is FALSE.
Include File	winuser.h
See Also	ExitWindowsEx
Related Messages	WM_QUERYENDSESSION, WM_ENDSESSION
Example	See the example for the **ExitWindowsEx** function.

ExitWindowsEx   ■ WINDOWS 95   ■ WINDOWS NT

Description	**ExitWindowsEx** shuts down all applications in an orderly fashion and either logs off, shuts down, or shuts down and restarts the system.

Use **ExitWindowsEx** in applications that need to restart the system, such as installation programs. It can also be used in shell programs to log off or shut down the system.

Syntax   BOOL **ExitWindowsEx**(UINT *uOptions,* DWORD *dwReserved*)

Parameters

uOptions   UINT: The type of shutdown to perform. This can be one of the values shown in Table 5-4.

Table 5-4 ExitWindowsEx *uOptions* values

Value	Meaning
EWX_FORCE	Forces processes that don't respond to terminate.
EWX_LOGOFF	Shuts down all applications for the current user, then logs off the user.
EWX_POWEROFF	Shuts down the system and turns off the power. The system must support the power-off feature. For Windows NT, the application must have the SE_SHUTDOWN_NAME privilege.
EWX_REBOOT	Shuts down the system and then restarts the system. For Windows NT, the application must have the SE_SHUTDOWN_NAME privilege.
EWX_SHUTDOWN	Shuts down the system to where it is safe to turn off the power. For Windows NT, the application must have the SE_SHUTDOWN_NAME privilege.

dwReserved   DWORD: Reserved; this parameter is ignored.

Returns   BOOL: If successful, the return value is **TRUE**; otherwise, it is **FALSE**.

Include File   winuser.h

See Also   ExitWindows

Related Messages   WM_QUERYENDSESSION, WM_ENDSESSION

Example   This example will shut down currently running user applications and then log off the current user. The **WM_QUERYENDSESSION** message is also handled to give the user the option of canceling the close and subsequently the logoff.

```
LRESULT CALLBACK WndProc( HWND hWnd, UINT uMsg, WPARAM wParam, LPARAM lParam )
{
    switch( uMsg )
    {
        case WM_COMMAND:
                switch ( LOWORD( wParam ) )
                {
                    case IDM_TEST:
                            // Start the logoff procedure.
                            //............................
                            if ( ExitWindowsEx( EWX_LOGOFF, 0 ) )
                                DestroyWindow( hWnd );
                            break;
```

```
               case IDM_EXIT:
                       DestroyWindow (hWnd);
                       break;

               default:
                       return ( DefWindowProc( hWnd, uMsg, wParam, lParam ) );
          }
          break;

  case WM_QUERYENDSESSION :
          // Last chance to stop the log off from happening.
          // This is only sent in Windows NT, Windows 95 does
          // not send this to the application that called ExitWindows().
          //.............................................................

          if ( MessageBox( hWnd, "Logoff Windows?", lpszAppName,
                           MB_YESNO | MB_ICONQUESTION ) == IDYES )
          {
              return( TRUE );
          }
          break;

  case WM_DESTROY:
          PostQuitMessage(0);
          break;

  default:
          return ( DefWindowProc( hWnd, uMsg, wParam, lParam ) );
    }
  return (0);
  }
```

GetMessage   ■ Windows 95   ■ Windows NT

Description	**GetMessage** retrieves the next waiting message from the calling thread's message queue into the **MSG** structure pointed to by *lpmsg*. Messages are not retrieved for other threads or applications.
Syntax	BOOL **GetMessage**(LPMSG *lpmsg*, HWND *hwnd*, UINT *uMsgFilterMin*, UINT *uMsgFilterMax*)
Parameters	
lpmsg	LPMSG: A pointer to an **MSG** structure. See the definition of the **MSG** structure below
hwnd	HWND: A handle to the window receiving the messages. Normally set to **NULL** to retrieve messages for any window that belongs to the calling thread, and thread messages posted to the calling thread using the **PostThreadMessage** function.
uMsgFilterMin	UINT: The minimum message value to receive. Normally set to **0**.
uMsgFilterMax	UINT: The maximum message value to receive. If both *uMsgFilterMin* and *uMsgFilterMax* are set to **0**, then all messages will be retrieved. Normally set to **0**.

Returns	BOOL: TRUE until the WM_QUIT message is retrieved, and then FALSE. The message loop should continue until FALSE is returned from GetMessage, which will end the program.
Include File	winuser.h
See Also	PeekMessage, WaitMessage
Related Messages	All Windows messages are processed.

MSG Definition

```
typedef struct tagMSG
{
    HWND      hwnd;       /* window handle */
    UINT      message;    /* message ID      */
    WPARAM    wParam;     /* wParam value   */
    LPARAM    lParam;     /* lParam value   */
    DWORD     time;       /* msec since startup */
    POINT     pt;         /* mouse location, screen coord */
} MSG;
```

Members

hwnd	HWND: The window whose window procedure receives the message.
message	UINT: The message identifier.
wParam	WPARAM: Additional information about the message. The meaning of this member depends on the value of the *message* member.
lParam	LPARAM: Additional information about the message. The meaning of this member depends on the value of the *message* member.
time	DWORD: The time at which the message was posted. The time is in milliseconds since Windows started.
pt	POINT: The cursor position, in screen coordinates, when the message was posted.
Example	This is a typical application message loop, at the end of the WinMain function.

```
while( GetMessage( &msg, NULL, 0, 0 ) )
{
    TranslateMessage( &msg );
    DispatchMessage( &msg );
}
```

GetMessageExtraInfo   ■ WINDOWS 95   ■ WINDOWS NT

Description	GetMessageExtraInfo retrieves extra information about the last message retrieved. The extra information may be added to a message by the driver for a pointing device or keyboard.
Syntax	LONG **GetMessageExtraInfo**(VOID)
Parameters	This function has no parameters.

Returns	LONG: The extra information associated with the message. The meaning of the return value is device specific.
Include File	`winuser.h`
See Also	`GetMessage`, `PeekMessage`
Example	This example shows how to retrieve the extra information (if any) for a mouse message. Extra information may not be provided, and it is up to the device driver for the pointing device to provide it. The meaning of the information depends on the device driver that provided the information.

```
LRESULT CALLBACK WndProc( HWND hWnd, UINT uMsg, WPARAM wParam, LPARAM lParam )
{
    switch( uMsg )
    {
        case WM_LBUTTONDOWN :
            {
                // Check to see if any extra information was attached
                // to this message.
                //.......................................................
                LONG lExtra = GetMessageExtraInfo();
                if ( lExtra != 0 )
                    MessageBox( hWnd, "Extra Information Found!", lpszAppName,
                            MB_OK );
            }
            break;
            .
            .
            .
```

GetMessagePos   ■ WINDOWS 95   ■ WINDOWS NT

Description	`GetMessagePos` returns a long value that gives the cursor position in screen coordinates when the last message retrieved was sent.
	When an application gets behind in message processing, the mouse cursor can move before a message is processed. You use this function to find out the position of the mouse cursor when the message was sent.
Syntax	DWORD **GetMessagePos**(VOID)
Parameters	This function has no parameters.
Returns	DWORD: The return value specifies the x and y coordinates of the cursor position. The x position is in the low-order word, and the y position is in the high-order word.
Include File	`winuser.h`
See Also	`GetMessage`, `PeekMessage`, `GetMessageTime`, `ScreenToClient`, `GetCursorPos`
Related Messages	`WM_MOUSEMOVE`

Example
This example retrieves the screen position when the **WM_MOUSEMOVE** message was placed in the application queue and displays it on the client area of the application window.

```
LRESULT CALLBACK WndProc( HWND hWnd, UINT uMsg, WPARAM wParam, LPARAM lParam )
{
static char   szMsg[31];
static DWORD  dwPos;
static HDC    hDC;

   switch( uMsg )
   {
      case WM_MOUSEMOVE :
            dwPos = GetMessagePos();
            hDC   = GetDC( hWnd );

            wsprintf( szMsg, "X-Pos: %d  Y-Pos: %d",
                  LOWORD( dwPos ), HIWORD( dwPos ) );

            TextOut( hDC, 50, 50, szMsg, strlen( szMsg ) );
            ReleaseDC( hWnd, hDC );
            break;
            .
            .
            .
```

GetMessageTime   ■ WINDOWS 95   ■ WINDOWS NT

Description
GetMessageTime retrieves the time that a message was placed in the message queue. All Windows messages include a time value, which is the number of milliseconds since Windows was started. Compare the value with the value returned from **GetCurrentTime**.

Syntax
LONG **GetMessageTime**(VOID)

Parameters
This function has no parameters.

Returns
LONG: The number of milliseconds since Windows had started when the message was sent.

Include File
winuser.h

See Also
GetCurrentTime

Related Messages
All messages are stamped.

Example
This example calculates how long a **WM_LBUTTONDOWN** message was in the application's message queue by subtracting the message time from the current time. The precision is in milliseconds.

```
LRESULT CALLBACK WndProc( HWND hWnd, UINT uMsg, WPARAM wParam, LPARAM lParam )
{
static char   szMsg[51];
static LONG   lTime;
static HDC    hDC;
```

```
switch( uMsg )
{
    case WM_LBUTTONDOWN :
            lTime = GetCurrentTime() - GetMessageTime();
            hDC   = GetDC( hWnd );

            wsprintf( szMsg, "Message was in queue for %ld milliseconds.",
                    lTime );

            TextOut( hDC, 50, 50, szMsg, strlen( szMsg ) );
            ReleaseDC( hWnd, hDC );
            break;

        .
        .
        .
```

InSendMessage   ■ WINDOWS 95   ■ WINDOWS NT

Description	**InSendMessage** distinguishes between messages that originate from normal Windows delivery messages, and messages sent by another thread using the **SendMessage** function. The **InSendMessage** function will not detect messages sent from within the calling thread. Only messages sent from another thread are detected.
	Use **InSendMessage** when two threads interact to determine if a thread is waiting for the response to a message that was sent.
Syntax	BOOL **InSendMessage**(VOID)
Parameters	This function has no parameters.
Returns	BOOL: If the last message received was sent from another thread with the **SendMessage** function, the return value is **TRUE**; otherwise, the return value is **FALSE**.
Include File	winuser.h
See Also	SendMessage, PostMessage
Related Messages	All messages can be sent with the **SendMessage** function and therefore relate to the **InSendMessage** function.
Example	In this example, a thread is created that sends a message and then posts a message back to the main window of the application. When the message is received by the window, **InSendMessage** determines if the message was sent or posted. The appropriate message box is then displayed.

```
HANDLE hThread = NULL;
DWORD  dwThreadID;

LRESULT CALLBACK WndProc( HWND hWnd, UINT uMsg, WPARAM wParam, LPARAM lParam )
{
    switch( uMsg )
    {
        case WM_USER:
```

continued on next page

continued from previous page

```
                if ( InSendMessage() )
                {
                    MessageBox( hWnd, "Message was sent with SendMessage()",
                                lpszAppName, MB_OK );
                }
                else
                    MessageBox( hWnd, "Message was sent with PostMessage()",
                                lpszAppName, MB_OK );
                break;

        case WM_COMMAND:
                switch ( LOWORD( wParam ) )
                {
                    case IDM_TEST:
                            hThread = CreateThread (NULL, 0,
                                                    NewThreadProc,
                                                    (LPVOID)hWnd, 0,
                                                    &dwThreadID);
                            break;

                    case IDM_EXIT:
                            DestroyWindow (hWnd);
                            break;

                }
                break;

        case WM_DESTROY:
                PostQuitMessage(0);
                break;

        default:
                return ( DefWindowProc( hWnd, uMsg, wParam, lParam ) );
    }
    return (0);
}


DWORD WINAPI NewThreadProc( LPVOID lpData )
{
    HWND hWnd = (HWND)lpData;

    SendMessage( hWnd, WM_USER, 0, 0 );
    PostMessage( hWnd, WM_USER, 0, 0 );

    return( 0 );
}
```

PeekMessage   ■ WINDOWS 95   ■ WINDOWS NT

Description   Similar to the `GetMessage` function. `PeekMessage` does not wait for a mes-
                      sage to be placed in the thread's queue before returning. If a message is in
                      the queue, the message will be put in the `MSG` structure.

Use **PeekMessage** to check if there are any waiting messages while doing long operations. It was used in previous versions of Windows to do background processing; however, threads are more efficient and should be used for such tasks if possible.

Syntax	BOOL **PeekMessage**(LPMSG *lpmsg,* HWND *hwnd,* UINT *uMsgFilterMin,* UINT *uMsgFilterMax,* UINT *uRemoveMsg*)

Parameters

lpmsg LPMSG: A pointer to an **MSG** structure. **PeekMessage** will fill this structure when a message is found.

hwnd HWND: A handle to the window receiving messages. **PeekMessage** will only find messages for this window. If set to **NULL**, all messages will be retrieved for a thread.

uMsgFilterMin UINT: The minimum message value to be retrieved. **WM_MOUSEFIRST** and **WM_KEYFIRST** message numbers are used to specify the lower limit to all client area mouse messages and keystrokes, respectively.

uMsgFilterMax UINT: The maximum message value to be retrieved. **WM_MOUSELAST** and **WM_KEYLAST** message numbers are used to specify the upper limit to all client area mouse messages and keystrokes, respectively. If both *uMsgFilterMin* and *uMsgFilterMax* are set to **0**, all messages are retrieved.

uRemoveMsg UINT: Specifies whether the message should be removed from the queue. This parameter must be one of the values given in Table 5-5.

Table 5-5 PeekMessage *uRemoveMsg* values

Value	Meaning
PM_NOREMOVE	Messages are left in the message queue.
PM_REMOVE	Messages are removed from the message queue. This is commonly used when PeekMessage is used in place of GetMessage for processing messages. WM_PAINT messages are not removed immediately but are removed with BeginPaint and EndPaint when the painting occurs.

Returns	BOOL: **TRUE** if a message is available, otherwise, the return value is **FALSE**.
Include File	winuser.h
See Also	GetMessage, WaitMessage, CreateThread
Related Messages	All messages can be processed by **PeekMessage**.
Example	At the bottom of the listing, a function called **NoMessages** paints randomly colored pages of asterisk (*) characters on the client area. When the user selects the Test! menu option, a loop is entered. The loop is exited when **PeekMessage** finds a client area mouse move. This example has two message loops. The first one is the main message loop in the **WinMain** function,

as shown in the example for the **WinMain** function. The **PeekMessage** loop works independently from the main message loop, allowing a separate process to go on. A preferred way to accomplish this would be to create a thread that would paint the asterisk characters.

```c
LRESULT CALLBACK WndProc( HWND hWnd, UINT uMsg, WPARAM wParam, LPARAM lParam )
{
static MSG msg;

    switch( uMsg )
    {
        case WM_COMMAND:
                switch ( LOWORD( wParam ) )
                {
                    case IDM_TEST:
                            while ( !PeekMessage( &msg, hWnd, WM_MOUSEFIRST,
                                                      WM_MOUSELAST,TRUE ) )
                            {
                                NoMessages( hWnd );
                            }
                            break;

                    case IDM_EXIT:
                            DestroyWindow (hWnd);
                            break;

                }
                break;

        case WM_DESTROY:
                PostQuitMessage(0);
                break;

        default:
                return ( DefWindowProc( hWnd, uMsg, wParam, lParam ) );
    }
    return (0);
}


// Paint random "*" chars in the client area.
//........................................
VOID NoMessages( HWND hWnd )
{
static int nX = 0, nY = 0, nRed = 255, nBlue = 0, nGreen = 0;
    HDC hDC;

    hDC = GetDC( hWnd );
    SetTextColor( hDC, RGB( nRed, nBlue, nGreen ) );
    TextOut( hDC, nX, nY, "*", 1 );

    nX += 10;
    if ( nX > 200 )
    {
        nX = 0;
        nY += 10;
    }
```

```
    if ( nY > 200 )
    {
        nY = 0;
        nRed += 23;
        if ( nRed > 255 )
            nRed = 0;

        nBlue -= 37;
        if ( nBlue < 0 )
            nBlue = 255;
    }

    ReleaseDC( hWnd, hDC );
}
```

PostMessage   ■ WINDOWS 95 ■ WINDOWS NT

Description	**PostMessage** places a message in the message queue associated with the thread that created the given window and returns without waiting for a response. Messages in the queue are retrieved by calls to the **GetMessage** and **PeekMessage** functions.
	You commonly use **PostMessage** to execute another portion of the application after the current message has been processed. **PostMessage** cannot be used to send messages to controls where a return value is expected.
Syntax	BOOL **PostMessage**(HWND *hwnd,* UINT *uMsg,* WPARAM *wParam,* LPARAM *lParam*)
Parameters	
hwnd	HWND: A handle to the window receiving the posted message. If set to HWND_BROADCAST, the message is posted to all top-level windows in the system. If set to NULL, **PostMessage** behaves like the **PostThreadMessage**, with the message going to the current thread.
uMsg	UINT: The message to be posted.
wParam	WPARAM: The *wParam* value to be passed with the message.
lParam	LPARAM: The *lParam* value to be passed with the message.
Returns	BOOL: If successful, the return value is TRUE; otherwise, it is FALSE.
Include File	winuser.h
See Also	SendMessage, PostThreadMessage
Related Messages	All Windows messages can be posted with this function.
Example	When the Test! menu item is selected, the application posts the WM_USER message to the main window's message queue. When the application receives a WM_USER message, it is processed and displays a message box.

```
LRESULT CALLBACK WndProc( HWND hWnd, UINT uMsg, WPARAM wParam, LPARAM lParam )
{
    switch( uMsg )
    {
    case WM_USER:
            MessageBox( hWnd, "Got the posted message!",
                        lpszAppName, MB_OK );
            break;

    case WM_COMMAND:
            switch ( LOWORD( wParam ) )
            {
                case IDM_TEST:
                    PostMessage( hWnd, WM_USER, 0, 0 );
                    break;

                case IDM_EXIT:
                    DestroyWindow (hWnd);
                    break;

            }
            break;

    case WM_DESTROY:
            PostQuitMessage(0);
            break;

    default:
            return ( DefWindowProc( hWnd, uMsg, wParam, lParam ) );
    }
    return (0);
}
```

PostQuitMessage   ■ WINDOWS 95   ■ WINDOWS NT

Description	**PostQuitMessage** posts a **WM_QUIT** message to indicate to Windows that a thread has made a request to terminate.
	You normally use **PostQuitMessage** to process **WM_DESTROY** messages and menu options that force the application to exit. The **DestroyWindow** function should be used elsewhere in the application to start the application shutdown process.
Syntax	VOID **PostQuitMessage**(int *nExitCode*)
Parameters	
nExitCode	int: The application exit code. This value is used as the *wParam* parameter of the **WM_QUIT** message.
Returns	This function does not return a value.
Include File	winuser.h
See Also	PostMessage

Related Messages   WM_QUIT, WM_DESTROY

Example   This code segment shows the proper usage of the **PostQuitMessage** function when the application responds to the **WM_DESTROY** message.

```
LRESULT CALLBACK WndProc( HWND hWnd, UINT uMsg, WPARAM wParam, LPARAM lParam )
{
   switch( uMsg )
   {
      .
      .
      .

      case WM_DESTROY:
              PostQuitMessage(0);
              break;

      default:
              return ( DefWindowProc( hWnd, uMsg, wParam, lParam ) );
   }
   return (0);
}
```

PostThreadMessage   ■ Windows 95   ■ Windows NT

Description   **PostThreadMessage** places a message in the message queue of the given thread without waiting for the message to be processed.

Use **PostThreadMessage** to communicate between two threads. You can send a message to a specific thread without other threads seeing the message. The message is sent with a **NULL** *hwnd* value in the **MSG** structure. The receiving thread should check for **NULL** *hwnd* values and process the messages.

Syntax   BOOL **PostThreadMessage**(DWORD *dwThreadId,* UINT *uMsg,* WPARAM *wParam,* LPARAM *lParam*)

Parameters

dwThreadId   DWORD: The thread identifier for the thread that will receive the message.

uMsg   UINT: The message to be posted.

wParam   WPARAM: The *wParam* value to be passed with the message.

lParam   LPARAM: The *lParam* value to be passed with the message.

Returns   BOOL: If successful, the return value is **TRUE**; otherwise, it is **FALSE**.

Include File   winuser.h

See Also   PostMessage, SendMessage, GetWindowThreadProcessId

Related Messages   All Windows messages can be posted with this function.

Example   In this case, when the user selects the Test! menu item, a **WM_USER** message is sent to the application's message queue. In the main message loop located in the **WinMain** function, the **MSG** structure *hwnd* and message values are checked for the message that was sent with the **PostThreadMessage** function. If the message is detected, a **MessageBeep** is called. This same method can be used to send messages to other threads as well.

```
        .
        .
        .
// Main application message loop from WinMain()
//..................................................
while( GetMessage( &msg, NULL, 0, 0 ) )
{
    if ( msg.hwnd == NULL && msg.message == WM_USER )
        MessageBeep(0);

    TranslateMessage(&msg);
    DispatchMessage(&msg);
}
        .
        .
        .


LRESULT CALLBACK WndProc( HWND hWnd, UINT uMsg, WPARAM wParam, LPARAM lParam )
{
    switch( uMsg )
    {
        case WM_COMMAND:
                switch ( LOWORD( wParam ) )
                {
                    case IDM_TEST:
                            // Post message to my main message loop.
                            //.......................................
                            PostThreadMessage( GetCurrentThreadId(),
                                               WM_USER, 0, 0 );
                            break;
        .
        .
        .
```

RegisterWindowMessage   ■ WINDOWS 95   ■ WINDOWS NT

Description   **RegisterWindowMessage** registers an application-defined message and guarantees that the message number is unique and will not conflict with other messages that have been registered. When two separate applications communicate by sending and receiving messages, it is not safe to use the normal (that is, **WM_USER**, **WM_USER**+1, etc.) message numbers.

Syntax   UINT **RegisterWindowMessage**(LPCTSTR *lpsz*)

Parameters

lpsz	LPCTSTR: A pointer to a null-terminated string value to associate with the message to be registered. If two applications call `RegisterWindowMessage` with the same string value, the same message identifier is returned.

Returns   UINT: If successful, the return value is the message identifier in the range 0xC000 through 0xFFFF; otherwise, it is 0.

Include File   `winuser.h`

See Also   `SendMessage`, `PostMessage`, `FindWindow`

Example   This example shows the **WndProc** functions from two applications. Each application uses the `RegisterWindowMessage` function to obtain a unique message that will be used to communicate with the other application. When the Test! menu option is selected in the first application, the message obtained from `RegisterWindowMessage` is sent to the second application's main window. When the message is received, a message box is displayed.

```
LRESULT CALLBACK WndProc1( HWND hWnd, UINT uMsg, WPARAM wParam, LPARAM lParam )
{
static UINT uNewMsg;

    switch( uMsg )
    {
        case WM_CREATE :
                // Register a common message to use between the two
                // applications. This string has to match in both
                // applications.
                //................................................
                uNewMsg = RegisterWindowMessage( "Common Message" );
                break;

        case WM_COMMAND:
                switch ( LOWORD( wParam ) )
                {
                    case IDM_TEST:
                        {
                            // Post message to other application.
                            //................................
                            HWND hOtherWnd = FindWindow( NULL,
                                                    "Second Application" );

                            if ( hOtherWnd )
                                PostMessage( hOtherWnd, uNewMsg, 0, 0 );
                            break;
                        }

                 .
                 .
                 .

// This is the WndProc() of the second application that will
// receive the message posted by the first application.
```

continued on next page

continued from previous page

```
LRESULT CALLBACK WndProc2( HWND hWnd, UINT uMsg, WPARAM wParam, LPARAM lParam )
{
static UINT uNewMsg;

    if ( uMsg == uNewMsg )
    {
        MessageBox( hWnd, "New Message Received!", lpszAppName, MB_OK );
        return( 0 );
    }

    switch( uMsg )
    {
        case WM_CREATE :
                // Register a common message to use between the two
                // applications. This string has to match in both
                // applications.
                //.................................................
                uNewMsg = RegisterWindowMessage( "Common Message" );
                break;
```

.
.
.

ReplyMessage   ■ WINDOWS 95   ■ WINDOWS NT

Description   ReplyMessage responds to a message sent from another thread calling the
SendMessage function. The value sent with the reply is the return value for
the SendMessage. You don't need to reply to a message that was sent with
the PostMessage function.

Use ReplyMessage to return a value to the thread that sent the message.
ReplyMessage returns control to the thread that sent the message while
continuing to process the message in the receiving thread.

Syntax   BOOL **ReplyMessage**(LRESULT *lResult*)

Parameters

lResult   LRESULT: The return value for the message being processed.

Returns   BOOL: If the calling thread was processing a message sent from another
thread or process, the return value is TRUE; otherwise, it is FALSE.

Include File   winuser.h

See Also   SendMessage, RegisterWindowMessage

Related Messages   User-defined messages, created with RegisterWindowMessage.

Example   This example shows the WndProc of an application that creates a thread
when the Test! menu option is selected. When the thread is created, it
sends a message back to the main window of the application. When the
message is received, the InSendMessage function determines if the message was sent using the SendMessage function. If it was, you use the

ReplyMessage function to return control to the thread immediately. The
thread then displays a message box (see Figure 5-3) showing that control
has returned. The application will also display a message box showing that
the message was received.

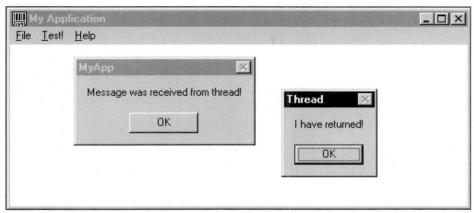

Figure 5-3 **ReplyMessage** example

```
HANDLE hThread = NULL;
DWORD  dwThreadID;

LRESULT CALLBACK WndProc( HWND hWnd, UINT uMsg, WPARAM wParam, LPARAM lParam )
{
    switch( uMsg )
    {
        case WM_USER:
                if ( InSendMessage() )
                    ReplyMessage( OL );

                MessageBox( hWnd, "Message was received from thread!",
                                lpszAppName, MB_OK );
                break;

        case WM_COMMAND:
                switch ( LOWORD( wParam ) )
                {
                    case IDM_TEST:
                            hThread = CreateThread (NULL, O,
                                                    NewThreadProc,
                                                    (LPVOID)hWnd, O,
                                                    &dwThreadID);

                        break;
                .
                .
                .
```

continued on next page

continued from previous page

```
DWORD WINAPI NewThreadProc( LPVOID lpData )
{
    HWND hWnd = (HWND)lpData;

    SendMessage( hWnd, WM_USER, 0, 0 );
    MessageBox( NULL, "I have returned!", "Thread", MB_OK );

    return( 0 );
}
```

SendMessage   ■ WINDOWS 95   ■ WINDOWS NT

Description	**SendMessage** sends a message to another window and waits for a response. The message bypasses the message queue and is acted upon immediately.
	Applications often use **SendMessage** to communicate with control windows, such as buttons and list boxes, in cases where a program has a series of child windows, each of which has separate message-processing functions. The sending window does not restart processing until the message is processed by the receiving window and a result is returned.
Syntax	LRESULT **SendMessage**(HWND *hwnd,* UINT *uMsg,* WPARAM *wParam,* LPARAM *lParam*)
Parameters	
hwnd	**HWND**: The handle of the window to receive the message. If set to **HWND_BROADCAST**, the message is sent to all top-level windows in the system.
uMsg	**UINT**: The message to be sent.
wParam	**WPARAM**: The *wParam* value for the message.
lParam	**LPARAM**: The *lParam* value for the message.
Returns	**LRESULT**: The return value depends on the message sent.
Include File	winuser.h
See Also	SendMessageCallback, SendMessageTimeout, SendNotifyMessage, PostMessage, ReplyMessage, SendDlgItemMessage, RegisterWindowMessage, InSendMessage
Related Messages	All Windows messages can be sent using this function. For application-specific messages, use the base of **WM_USER** to start numbering the messages. **RegisterWindowMessage** generates a unique message identifier that is used to communicate with other applications.
Example	In this example, an edit control is created as a child of the main window. The **SendMessage** function sets the maximum number of characters that the edit control will allow to be entered.

```
LRESULT CALLBACK WndProc( HWND hWnd, UINT uMsg, WPARAM wParam, LPARAM lParam )
{
```

```
static HWND hEdit = NULL;

   switch( uMsg )
   {
     case WM_CREATE :
              // Create two overlapping edit controls
              //.......................................
              hEdit = CreateWindow( "EDIT", "Here I am.",
                                    WS_CHILD | WS_BORDER |
                                    WS_VISIBLE |ES_LEFT,
                                    10, 10, 100, 30,
                                    hWnd, (HMENU) 101,
                                    hInst, NULL );

              // Set the maximum number of characters that
              // can be entered into the edit control to 15.
              //...........................................
              SendMessage( hEdit, EM_SETLIMITTEXT, 15, 0 );
              break;
          .
          .
          .
```

SendMessageCallback   ■ WINDOWS 95   ■ WINDOWS NT

Description

SendMessageCallback is the same as SendMessage, except after sending the message, it returns immediately (like PostMessage). After the message is processed, the system calls the specified callback function with the result of the message processing and an application-defined value.

Useful in multithreaded applications, SendMessageCallback allows one thread to send a message to another thread without waiting for the message to be processed. The return result should not be required to continue processing in the calling thread, since the function will return immediately. The result will be returned to the callback function when the message is processed.

Syntax

BOOL **SendMessageCallback**(HWND *hwnd,* UINT *uMsg,* WPARAM *wParam,* LPARAM *lParam,* SENDASYNCPROC *lpfnResultCallBack,* DWORD *dwData*)

Parameters

hwnd

HWND: The handle of the window to receive the message. If set to HWND_BROADCAST, the message is sent to all top-level windows in the system.

uMsg

UINT: The message to be sent.

wParam

WPARAM: The *wParam* value for the message.

lParam

LPARAM: The *lParam* value for the message.

lpfnResultCallBack

SENDASYNCPROC: A pointer to an application-defined callback function that the system calls after the message is processed.

dwData	**DWORD**: An application-defined value that will be sent to the callback function.
	A description of the callback function follows.
Returns	**BOOL**: If successful, the return value is **TRUE**; otherwise, it is **FALSE**.
Include File	winuser.h
See Also	SendMessage, PostMessage
Related Messages	All Windows messages can be sent using this function.
Callback Syntax	VOID CALLBACK **SendAsyncProc**(HWND *hwnd*, UINT *uMsg*, DWORD *dwData*, LRESULT *lResult*)

Callback Parameters

hwnd	**HWND**: A handle to the window whose window procedure processed the message. If this parameter is **HWND_TOPMOST**, the message was sent to all top-level windows in the system.
uMsg	**UINT**: The message sent.
dwData	**DWORD**: The value specified for the *dwData* parameter of the **SendMessageCallback** function.
lResult	**LRESULT**: The result of the message processing. This value depends on the message that was sent.
Example	In this example, the application creates a thread when the Test! menu option is selected. The thread then sends a message to the main application window for processing using the **SendMessageCallback** function. A pointer to a **BOOL** variable is sent as a flag, which is activated when the message has been processed and the callback has been called. The thread waits until this flag has been set to **TRUE** and then exits.

```
HANDLE hThread = NULL;
DWORD  dwThreadID;

LRESULT CALLBACK WndProc( HWND hWnd, UINT uMsg, WPARAM wParam, LPARAM lParam )
{
   switch( uMsg )
   {
      case WM_USER:
              MessageBox( hWnd, "Message was received from thread!",
                              lpszAppName, MB_OK );

              // Return a value back to the callback.
              //..................................
              return( 20L );

      case WM_COMMAND:
              switch ( LOWORD( wParam ) )
              {
                 case IDM_TEST:
                      hThread = CreateThread (NULL, 0,
                                                 NewThreadProc,
                                                 (LPVOID)hWnd, 0,
```

```
                                          &dwThreadID);
                    break;
        .
        .
        .

DWORD WINAPI NewThreadProc( LPVOID lpData )
{
    HWND hWnd = (HWND)lpData;
    BOOL bMessageProcessed = FALSE;

    SendMessageCallback( hWnd, WM_USER, 0, 0,
                         (SENDASYNCPROC)MessageResult,
                         (DWORD)&bMessageProcessed );

    while( !bMessageProcessed );

    return( 0 );
}

VOID CALLBACK MessageResult( HWND hWnd, UINT uMsg, DWORD dwData,
                             LRESULT lResult )
{
    char szMsg[31];

    wsprintf( szMsg, "Message Result: %ld", lResult );
    MessageBox( hWnd, szMsg, "Message Done", MB_OK );

    *(BOOL*)dwData = TRUE;
}
```

SendMessageTimeout   ■ WINDOWS 95   ■ WINDOWS NT

Description	**SendMessageTimeout** is the same as **SendMessage**, except there is a time-out period. If the message is sent to a window that belongs to a different thread, it does not return until the message is processed or the time-out period expires. If the message is sent to a window that belongs to the same message queue as the current thread, the time-out period is ignored.
	Use **SendMessageTimeout** to send messages to other threads with a maximum amount of time given to process the message. An application can use this function to keep deadlocks from occurring when sending messages to a thread that is "hung."
Syntax	LRESULT **SendMessageTimeout**(HWND *hwnd*, UINT *uMsg*, WPARAM *wParam*, LPARAM *lParam*, UINT *uFlags*, UINT *uTimeout*, LPDWORD *lpdwResult*)
Parameters	
hwnd	HWND: The handle of the window to receive the message. If set to HWND_BROADCAST, the message is sent to all top-level windows in the system.

uMsg	**UINT**: The message to be sent.
wParam	**WPARAM**: The *wParam* value for the message.
lParam	**LPARAM**: The *lParam* value for the message.
uFlags	**UINT**: Determines how the message is sent. This parameter can be a combination of the values given in Table 5-6.

Table 5-6 SendMessageTimeout *uFlags* values

Value	Meaning
SMTO_ABORTIFHUNG	If receiving thread is in the "hung" state, SendMessageTimeout will return without waiting for the time-out period.
SMTO_BLOCK	Prevents the calling thread from processing any other messages until SendMessageTimeout returns.
SMTO_NORMAL	The calling thread is not prevented from processing other messages while waiting for the function to return.

uTimeout	**UINT**: The time-out period in milliseconds.
lpdwResult	**LPDWORD**: A pointer to a **DWORD** that will receive the result of the message processing.
Returns	**LRESULT**: If successful, the return value is **TRUE**; otherwise, it is **FALSE**.
Include File	winuser.h
See Also	SendMessage, PostMessage, SendMessageCallback
Related Messages	All Windows messages can be sent using this function.
Example	This example uses the code example in the **SendMessageCallback** function. This code segment replaces the **NewThreadProc** function code segment. This version uses the **SendMessageTimeout** function to send a message to the main application window and wait for up to ten seconds for a response. If the message does not finish processing within the ten seconds, a message box appears that says, **Message Timed Out!**

```
VOID NewThreadProc( HGLOBAL hData )
{
   DWORD dwResult;
   HWND hWnd = (HWND)hData;

   if ( !SendMessageTimeout( hWnd, WM_USER, 0, 0,
                             SMTO_NORMAL, 10000, &dwResult ) )
   {
      MessageBox( hWnd, "Message Timed Out!", lpszAppName, MB_OK );
   }
   else
      MessageBox( hWnd, "Message Processed!", lpszAppName, MB_OK );
}
```

SendNotifyMessage

Description	**SendNotifyMessage** sends a message to the given window. If the window was created by the calling thread, **SendNotifyMessage** waits for the message to be processed. If the window was created by a different thread, **SendNotifyMessage** returns immediately and does not wait for the message to be processed.
	Use **SendNotifyMessage** to send notification messages when there is no return value and the message does not need to be processed before continuing execution of the calling thread.
Syntax	BOOL **SendNotifyMessage**(HWND *hwnd,* UINT *uMsg,* WPARAM *wParam,* LPARAM *lParam*)
Parameters	
hwnd	HWND: The handle of the window to receive the message. If set to HWND_BROADCAST, the message is sent to all top-level windows in the system.
uMsg	UINT: The message to be sent.
wParam	WPARAM: The *wParam* value for the message.
lParam	LPARAM: The *lParam* value for the message.
Returns	BOOL: If the function is successful, the return value is TRUE; otherwise, it is FALSE.
Include File	winuser.h
See Also	SendMessage, PostMessage, SendMessageCallback, SendMessageTimeout
Related Messages	All Windows messages can be sent with this function.
Example	This example shows a code segment for a thread procedure that notifies the application's parent window that the thread was created.

```
VOID NewThreadProc( HGLOBAL hData )
{
   HWND hWnd = (HWND)hData;

   // Notify the parent that I am up
   //................................
   SendNotifyMessage( hWnd, WM_USER, 0, 0 );


       .
       .
       .


   ExitThread(0);
}
```

SetWindowsHookEx ■ WINDOWS 95 ■ WINDOWS NT

Description	**SetWindowsHookEx** installs a Windows message filter function. There are several different types of filter functions, specified with the *nFilterType* parameter. You can install multiple filters at the same time, forming a chain of message-processing functions. The filtering functions can reside in either a dynamic link library (DLL) or in the application.
	Hook functions can monitor, act on, or change Windows' messages before they are sent to the application programs. Hook functions let you customize Windows' behavior on a systemwide basis. For example, you can remap keyboard messages for all **WM_KEYDOWN** and **WM_KEYUP** messages to specify an alternate keyboard layout when the hook function is set.
Syntax	HHOOK **SetWindowsHookEx**(int *nFilterType,* HOOKPROC *hkprc,* HINSTANCE *hMod,* DWORD *dwThreadID*)
Parameters	
nFilterType	**int**: The type of filtering function and what type of messages will be diverted to the filter before being sent to an application. This should be set to one of the values listed in Table 5-7.

Table 5-7 Hook function types

Value	Meaning
WH_CALLWNDPROC	Monitors messages sent to a window procedure using SendMessage.
WH_CALLWNDPROCRET	Monitors messages after they have been processed by the destination window procedure.
WH_CBT	Receives notifications useful to a computer-based training (CBT) application.
WH_DEBUG	Installs a hook procedure useful for debugging other hook procedures.
WH_GETMESSAGE	Monitors messages immediately after the GetMessage or PeekMessage function is called. All messages are passed to this filter.
WH_JOURNALPLAYBACK	Plays back an event message recorded with WH_JOURNALRECORD when an event is requested by the system. Use it with WH_JOURNALRECORD.
WH_JOURNALRECORD	Installs a hook procedure that records input messages posted to the system message queue. This hook is useful for recording macros. Use the WH_JOURNALPLAYBACK hook to play back the messages.
WH_KEYBOARD	Monitors keystroke message.
WH_MOUSE	Monitors mouse messages.
WH_MSGFILTER	Monitors messages generated as a result of an input event in a dialog box, message box, menu, or scroll bar.
WH_SHELL	Receives notifications useful to shell applications.
WH_SYSMSGFILTER	Monitors messages generated as a result of an input event in a dialog box, message box, menu, or scroll bar. Similar to WH_MSGFILTER, but applies to the entire system.

hkprc	HOOKPROC: A pointer to the hook procedure. If the *dwThreadID* parameter is **0** or specifies the identifier of a thread created by a different process, this parameter must point to a hook procedure in a dynamic link library (DLL). Otherwise, it can point to a hook procedure in the code associated with the current process.
hMod	HINSTANCE: The instance handle of the DLL containing the hook procedure pointed to by the *hkprc* parameter. Must be set to **NULL** if the *dwThreadID* parameter specifies a thread created by the current process and the hook procedure is within the code associated with the current process.
dwThreadID	DWORD: The thread identifier with which the hook procedure is to be associated. If set to **0**, the hook procedure is associated with all existing threads and should be defined in a DLL.
Returns	HHOOK: If successful, the handle of the hook procedure; otherwise, **NULL**.
Include File	winuser.h
See Also	UnhookWindowsHookEx, CallNextHookEx
Related Messages	All messages processed by the hook function.

Hook Function Prototypes

Each type of message hook expects a different kind of filter function. Each of the function types is described below. The filter function can have any name.

The WH_CALLWNDPROC Hook Function Prototype

Description	Monitors messages sent to a window procedure using **SendMessage**.
Syntax	LRESULT CALLBACK **CallWndProc**(int *nCode,* WPARAM *wParam,* LPARAM *lParam*)

Parameters

nCode	int: Specifies whether the hook procedure must process the message. If set to **HC_ACTION**, the hook procedure must process the message. If less than zero, the hook procedure must pass the message to the **CallNextHookEx** function without further processing and should return the value returned by **CallNextHookEx**.
wParam	WPARAM: If the message was sent by the current process, the value is nonzero; otherwise, it is **NULL**.
lParam	LPARAM: A pointer to a **CWPSTRUCT** structure that contains details about the message. See the definition of the **CWPSTRUCT** structure below.
Returns	LRESULT: Must return **0**.

CWPSTRUCT Definition

```
typedef struct tagCWPSTRUCT
{
```

continued on next page

continued from previous page

```
            LPARAM  lParam;
            WPARAM  wParam;
            DWORD   message;
            HWND    hwnd;
        } CWPSTRUCT;
```

Members

lParam   LPARAM: The *lParam* value of the message.

wParam   WPARAM: The *wParam* value of the message.

message   DWORD: The message being sent.

hwnd   HWND: The handle of the window that will receive the message.

The WH_CALLWNDPROCRET Hook Function Prototype

Description   Monitors messages after they have been processed by the destination window procedure.

Syntax   LRESULT CALLBACK **CallWndRetProc**(int *nCode,* WPARAM *wParam,* LPARAM *lParam*)

Parameters

nCode   int: Specifies whether the hook procedure must process the message. If set to **HC_ACTION**, the hook procedure must process the message. If less than zero, the hook procedure must pass the message to the **CallNextHookEx** function without further processing and should return the value returned by **CallNextHookEx**.

wParam   WPARAM: Specifies whether the message is sent by the current process. If the message is sent by the current process, it is nonzero; otherwise, it is **0**.

lParam   LPARAM: A pointer to a **CWPRETSTRUCT** structure that contains details about the message. See the definition of the **CWPRETSTRUCT** structure below.

Returns   LRESULT: Must return **0**.

CWPRETSTRUCT Definition

```
            typedef struct tagCWPRETSTRUCT
            {
                LRESULT lResult;
                LPARAM  lParam;
                WPARAM  wParam;
                DWORD   message;
                HWND    hwnd;
            } CWPRETSTRUCT;
```

Members

lResult   LRESULT: The return value of the window procedure that processed the message in the *message* member.

lParam   LPARAM: Additional information about the message. The exact meaning depends on the *message* member.

wParam	**WPARAM**: Additional information about the message. The exact meaning depends on the *message* member.
message	**DWORD**: The message.
hwnd	**HWND**: The window that processed the message specified by the *message* member.

The WH_CBT Hook Function Prototype

Description   Receives notifications useful to a computer-based training (CBT) application.

Syntax   LRESULT CALLBACK **CBTProc**(int *nCode,* WPARAM *wParam,* LPARAM *lParam*)

Parameters

nCode   **int**: One of the values given in Table 5-8. If less than zero, the hook procedure must pass the message to the **CallNextHookEx** function without further processing and should return the value returned by **CallNextHookEx**.

Table 5-8 WH_CBT *nCode* values

Value	Meaning
HCBT_ACTIVATE	A window is about to be activated.
HCBT_CLICKSKIPPED	The system has removed a mouse message from the system message queue. When this code is received, a CBT application must install a WH_JOURNALPLAYBACK hook procedure in response to the mouse message.
HCBT_CREATEWND	A window is about to be created. A return value of nonzero will cause the CreateWindow to fail. A return value of 0 will allow the window to be created normally.
HCBT_DESTROYWND	A window is about to be destroyed.
HCBT_KEYSKIPPED	The system has removed a keyboard message from the system message queue. When this code is received, a CBT application must install a WH_JOURNALPLAYBACK hook procedure in response to the keyboard message.
HCBT_MINMAX	A window is about to be minimized or maximized.
HCBT_MOVESIZE	A window is about to be moved or sized.
HCBT_QS	The WM_QUEUESYNC message has been retrieved from the system message queue.
HCBT_SETFOCUS	A window is about to receive the keyboard focus.
HCBT_SYSCOMMAND	A system command is about to be carried out. This allows a CBT application to prevent task switching by means of hotkeys.

wParam   **WPARAM**: Depends on the *nCode* value. Table 5-9 lists the meanings.

Table 5-9 WH_CBT *wParam* values

Value	Meaning
HCBT_ACTIVATE	The handle of the window about to be activated.
HCBT_CLICKSKIPPED	The mouse message that was removed from the system message queue.
HCBT_CREATEWND	The handle of the new window.
HCBT_DESTROYWND	The handle of the window about to be destroyed.
HCBT_KEYSKIPPED	The virtual-key code that was removed.
HCBT_MINMAX	The handle of the window being minimized or maximized.
HCBT_MOVESIZE	The handle of the window to be moved or sized.
HCBT_QS	Undefined, must be 0.
HCBT_SETFOCUS	The handle of the window gaining the keyboard focus.
HCBT_SYSCOMMAND	The system-command value (SC_).

lParam LPARAM: Depends on the *nCode* value. Table 5-10 lists the meanings.

Table 5-10 WH_CBT *lParam* values

Value	Meaning
HCBT_ACTIVATE	A pointer to a CBTACTIVATESTRUCT structure containing the handle of the active window. Specifies whether the activation is changing because of a mouse click.
HCBT_CLICKSKIPPED	A pointer to a MOUSEHOOKSTRUCT structure containing the hit-test code and the handle of the window for which the mouse message is intended.
HCBT_CREATEWND	A pointer to a CBT_CREATEWND structure containing initialization parameters for the window.
HCBT_DESTROYWND	Undefined, must be 0.
HCBT_KEYSKIPPED	The repeat count, scan code, key-transition code, previous key state, and context code. See Table 5-13 for more information.
HCBT_MINMAX	The low-order word contains the show-window value (SW_). The high-order word is undefined. See Table 4-11 for a list of values.
HCBT_MOVESIZE	A pointer to a RECT structure containing the coordinates of the window.
HCBT_QS	Undefined, must be 0.
HCBT_SETFOCUS	The handle of the window losing the keyboard focus.
HCBT_SYSCOMMAND	If the *wParam* parameter is SC_HOTKEY, contains the handle of the window that will come to the foreground. Otherwise, undefined.

Returns LRESULT: For operations corresponding to the following CBT hook codes, the return value must be **0** to allow the operation or **1** to prevent it.

HCBT_ACTIVATE

HCBT_CREATEWND

HCBT_DESTROYWND

HCBT_MINMAX

HCBT_MOVESIZE

HCBT_SYSCOMMAND

For operations corresponding to the following CBT hook codes, the return value is ignored.

HCBT_CLICKSKIPPED

HCBT_KEYSKIPPED

HCBT_QS

The WH_DEBUG Hook Function Prototype

Description Installs a hook procedure useful for debugging other hook procedures.

Syntax LRESULT CALLBACK **DebugProc**(int *nCode,* WPARAM *wParam,* LPARAM *lParam*)

Parameters

nCode int: Specifies whether the hook procedure must process the message. If set to HC_ACTION, the hook procedure must process the message. If less than zero, the hook procedure must pass the message to the CallNextHookEx function without further processing and should return the value returned by CallNextHookEx.

wParam WPARAM: The type of hook procedure that is about to be called. One of the values given in Table 5-7.

lParam LPARAM: A pointer to a DEBUGHOOKINFO structure that contains the parameters to be passed to the destination hook procedure. See the definition of the DEBUGHOOKINFO structure below.

Returns LRESULT: To prevent the system from calling the hook, a nonzero value should be returned. Otherwise, the CallNextHookEx function should be called, and the value returned should be the return value from that function call.

DEBUGHOOKINFO Definition

```
typedef struct tagDEBUGHOOKINFO
{
    DWORD  idThread;
    LPARAM reserved;
    LPARAM lParam;
    WPARAM wParam;
    int    code;
} DEBUGHOOKINFO;
```

Members

idThread DWORD: The thread identifier that contains the filter function.

reserved LPARAM: Not used.

lParam LPARAM: The *lParam* value passed to the filter function.

wParam	WPARAM: The *wParam* value passed to the filter function.
code	int: The *nCode* value passed to the filter function.

The WH_GETMESSAGE Hook Function Prototype

Description   Monitors messages immediately after the **GetMessage** or **PeekMessage** function is called. All messages are passed to this filter.

Syntax   LRESULT CALLBACK **GetMsgProc**(int *nCode,* WPARAM *wParam,* LPARAM *lParam*)

Parameters

nCode   int: Specifies whether the hook procedure must process the message. If set to **HC_ACTION**, the hook procedure must process the message. If less than zero, the hook procedure must pass the message to the **CallNextHookEx** function without further processing and should return the value returned by **CallNextHookEx**.

wParam   WPARAM: Specifies whether the message has been removed from the message queue. If the message was not removed, set to **PM_NOREMOVE**. If the message was removed, set to **PM_REMOVE**.

lParam   LPARAM: A pointer to an **MSG** structure containing the message information. See the **GetMessage** function for a definition of the **MSG** structure.

Returns   LRESULT: Should be 0.

The WH_JOURNALPLAYBACK Hook Function Prototype

Description   The filter function plays back an event message recorded with **WH_JOURNALRECORD** when an event is requested by the system.

Syntax   LRESULT CALLBACK **JournalPlaybackProc**(int *nCode,* WPARAM *wParam,* LPARAM *lParam*)

Parameters

nCode   int: Determines how to process the message. Can be one of the values listed in Table 5-11. If less than zero, the hook procedure must pass the message to the **CallNextHookEx** function without further processing and should return the value returned by **CallNextHookEx**.

Table 5-11 WH_JOURNALPLAYBACK *nCode* values

Value	Meaning
HC_GETNEXT	The current mouse or keyboard message should be copied to the EVENTMSG structure pointed to by the *lParam* parameter.
HC_NOREMOVE	An application has called the PeekMessage function with the PM_NOREMOVE flag.
HC_SKIP	Prepare to copy the next mouse or keyboard message to the EVENTMSG structure pointed to by the *lParam* parameter.

Value	Meaning
HC_SYSMODALOFF	A system-modal dialog box has been destroyed. Resume playing back the messages.
HC_SYSMODALON	A system-modal dialog box is being displayed. Until the dialog box is destroyed, stop playing back messages.

wParam	WPARAM: Set to NULL.
lParam	LPARAM: A pointer to an EVENTMSG structure that represents the message being processed. This is only valid when *nCode* is HC_GETNEXT. See the definition of the EVENTMSG structure below.
Returns	LRESULT: If *nCode* is HC_GETNEXT, the return value is the amount of time, in clock ticks, the system should wait. This time can be calculated from the time of the previous message and the current message. If 0 is returned, the message is processed immediately. The return value is ignored if *nCode* is any other value.

EVENTMSG Definition

```
typedef struct tagEVENTMSG
{
    UINT   message;
    UINT   paramL;
    UINT   paramH;
    DWORD  time;
    HWND   hwnd;
} EVENTMSG;
```

Members

message	UINT: The message.
paramL	UINT: Additional message-dependent information about the message.
paramH	UINT: Additional message-dependent information about the message.
time	DWORD: The time that the message was posted.
hwnd	HWND: The handle of the window to which the message was posted.

The WH_JOURNALRECORD Hook Function Prototype

Description	Installs a hook procedure that records input messages posted to the system message queue. This hook is useful for recording macros. Use the WH_JOURNALPLAYBACK hook to play back the messages.
Syntax	LRESULT CALLBACK **JournalRecordProc**(int *nCode,* WPARAM *wParam,* LPARAM *lParam*)
Parameters	
nCode	int: Determines how to process the message. Can be one of the values listed in Table 5-12. If less than zero, the hook procedure must pass the message to the **CallNextHookEx** function without further processing and should return the value returned by **CallNextHookEx**.

Table 5-12 WH_JOURNALRECORD *nCode* values

Value	Meaning
HC_ACTION	Record the contents of the EVENTMSG structure pointed to by the *lParam* parameter by copying them to a buffer or file.
HC_SYSMODALOFF	A system-modal dialog box has been destroyed. Resume recording.
HC_SYSMODALON	A system-modal dialog box is being displayed. Stop recording.

wParam	WPARAM: Set to NULL.
lParam	LPARAM: A pointer to an EVENTMSG structure that represents the message being processed. This is only valid when *nCode* is HC_ACTION.
Returns	LRESULT: The return value is ignored.

The WH_KEYBOARD Hook Function Prototype

Description	Monitors keystroke messages.
Syntax	LRESULT CALLBACK **KeyboardProc**(int *nCode,* WPARAM *wParam,* LPARAM *lParam*)
Parameters	
nCode	int: If HC_ACTION, the *wParam* and *lParam* parameters contain information about a keystroke message. If HC_NOREMOVE, the same as HC_ACTION except the message was not removed from the message queue. If less than zero, the hook procedure must pass the message to the **CallNextHookEx** function without further processing and should return the value returned by **CallNextHookEx**.
wParam	WPARAM: The virtual-key code of the key that generated the message.
lParam	LPARAM: The repeat count, scan code, extended-key flag, context code, previous key-state flag, and transition-state flag. This is made up of the values shown in Table 5-13.

Table 5-13 WH_KEYBOARD *lParam* values

Bit Offsets	Meaning
0–15	The repeat count. The number of times the keystroke is repeated as a result of holding down the key.
16–23	The scan code.
24	Extended key. Set to 1 if the key is an extended key; otherwise, it is 0.
25–28	Reserved.
29	The context code. Set to 1 if the (ALT) key is down; otherwise, it is 0.
30	The previous key state. Set to 1 if the key is down before the message is sent; otherwise, it is 0 if the key is up.
31	The transition state. Set to 0 if the key is being pressed and 1 if it is being released.

Returns	LRESULT: To prevent processing the message, the return value must be nonzero. To allow Windows to pass the message to the target window procedure, bypassing the remaining procedures in the chain, the return value must be 0.

The WH_MOUSE Hook Function Prototype

Description	Monitors mouse messages.
Syntax	LRESULT CALLBACK **MouseProc**(int *nCode,* WPARAM *wParam,* LPARAM *lParam*)

Parameters

nCode	int: If HC_ACTION, the *wParam* and *lParam* parameters contain information about a mouse message. If HC_NOREMOVE, the same as HC_ACTION, except the message was not removed from the message queue. If less than zero, the hook procedure must pass the message to the CallNextHookEx function without further processing and should return the value returned by CallNextHookEx.
wParam	WPARAM: The message identifier.
lParam	LPARAM: A pointer to a MOUSEHOOKSTRUCT structure. See the definition of the MOUSEHOOKSTRUCT structure below.
Returns	LRESULT: Returns 0 to enable the system to process the message; otherwise, returns a nonzero.

MOUSEHOOKSTRUCT Definition

```
typedef struct tagMOUSEHOOKSTRUCT
{
    POINT pt;
    HWND  hwnd;
    UINT  wHitTestCode;
    DWORD dwExtraInfo;
} MOUSEHOOKSTRUCT;
```

Members

pt	POINT: The x and y coordinates of the cursor relative to the screen.
hwnd	HWND: The window handle that will receive the mouse message.
wHitTestCode	UINT: The hit-test code. See the WM_NCHITTEST message for information.
dwExtraInfo	DWORD: Extra information associated with the message.

The WH_MSGFILTER Hook Function Prototype

Description	Monitors messages generated as a result of an input event in a dialog box, message box, menu, or scroll bar.
Syntax	LRESULT CALLBACK **MessageProc**(int *nCode,* WPARAM *wParam,* LPARAM *lParam*)

Parameters

nCode　　　　　　　　`int`: The type of input event that generated the message. Can be one of the values listed in Table 5-14. If less than zero, the hook procedure must pass the message to the `CallNextHookEx` function without further processing and should return the value returned by `CallNextHookEx`.

Table 5-14 `WH_MSGFILTER` *nCode* values

Value	Meaning
MSGF_DDEMGR	The event occurred while the Dynamic Data Exchange Management Library (DDEML) was waiting for a synchronous transaction to finish.
MSGF_DIALOGBOX	The event occurred in a message box or dialog box.
MSGF_MENU	The event occurred in a menu.
MSGF_NEXTWINDOW	The event occurred as a result of pressing the ⎡ALT⎤-⎡TAB⎤ key combination to activate a different window.
MSGF_SCROLLBAR	The event occurred in a scroll bar.

wParam　　　　　　　　`WPARAM`: Set to `NULL`.

lParam　　　　　　　　`LPARAM`: A pointer to an `MSG` structure that contains the message. See the `GetMessage` function for a description of the `MSG` structure.

Returns　　　　　　　　`LRESULT`: If the filter procedure processes the message, the return value must be nonzero; otherwise, it must be `0`.

The `WH_SHELL` Hook Function Prototype

Description　　　　　Receives notifications useful to shell applications.

Syntax　　　　　　　　`LRESULT CALLBACK` **`ShellProc`**`( int `*`nCode,`*` WPARAM `*`wParam,`*` LPARAM `*`lParam`*` )`

Parameters

nCode　　　　　　　　`int`: Can be one of the values in Table 5-15. If less than zero, the hook procedure must pass the message to the `CallNextHookEx` function without further processing and should return the value returned by `CallNextHookEx`.

Table 5-15 `WH_SHELL` *nCode* values

Value	Meaning
HSHELL_ACTIVATESHELLWINDOW	A top-level, unowned window is about to be activated.
HSHELL_GETMINRECT	A window is being minimized or maximized and the system needs the coordinates of the minimized rectangle of the window. The *wParam* parameter contains the handle of the window, and the *lParam* parameter contains the address of a RECT structure that receives the coordinates.
HSHELL_LANGUAGE	The keyboard language was changed or a new keyboard layout was loaded.

Value	Meaning
HSHELL_REDRAW	The title of a window in the taskbar has been redrawn. The *wParam* parameter contains the handle of the window.
HSHELL_TASKMAN	The user has selected the task list. The *wParam* parameter is undefined and should be ignored. A shell application that provides a task list should return TRUE to prevent Windows from starting its task list.
HSHELL_WINDOWACTIVATED	The activation has changed to a different top-level, unowned window. The *wParam* parameter contains the handle of the window.
HSHELL_WINDOWCREATED	A top-level, unowned window has been created.
HSHELL_WINDOWDESTROYED	A top-level, unowned window is about to be destroyed.

wParam	WPARAM: Specifies additional information the shell application may require. If *nCode* is set to HSHELL_WINDOWCREATED or HSHELL_WINDOWDESTROYED, this is the handle of the window being created or destroyed.
lParam	LPARAM: Specifies additional information. The exact value depends on the value of the *nCode* parameter. See Table 5-15 for more information about the usage of this parameter.
Returns	LRESULT: The return value should be 0.

The WH_SYSMSGFILTER Hook Function Prototype

Description	Monitors messages generated as a result of an input event in a dialog box, message box, menu, or scroll bar. Similar to WH_MSGFILTER, but applies systemwide.
Syntax	LRESULT CALLBACK **SysMsgProc**(int *nCode,* WPARAM *wParam,* LPARAM *lParam*)
Parameters	
nCode	int: Can be one of the values in Table 5-14 except for MSGF_DDEMGR. If less than zero, the hook procedure must pass the message to the CallNextHookEx function without further processing and should return the value returned by CallNextHookEx.
wParam	WPARAM: Set to NULL.
lParam	LPARAM: A pointer to an MSG structure that contains the message. See the GetMessage function for a description of the MSG structure.
Returns	LRESULT: If the filter procedure processes the message, the return value must be nonzero; otherwise, it must be 0.
Example	See the example for the CallMsgFilter function.

TranslateMessage WINDOWS 95 ■ WINDOWS NT

Description	The system generates virtual-key messages (VK_TAB, etc.) when a key is pressed. TranslateMessage posts the corresponding WM_CHAR code to the application's message queue when a virtual-key code is received.

Syntax	BOOL **TranslateMessage**(CONST MSG* *lpMsg*)
Parameters	
lpMsg	CONST MSG*: A pointer to the MSG structure that was used with the GetMessage or PeekMessage function to retrieve the message.
Returns	BOOL: TRUE if the message was translated; otherwise, the return value is FALSE.
Include File	winuser.h
See Also	GetMessage, DispatchMessage
Related Messages	The virtual-key codes, WM_CHAR, WM_SYSCHAR, WM_DEADCHAR, and WM_SYSDEADCHAR.
Example	The following code segment shows a typical message loop that would be in the WinMain function and where the TranslateMessage would be called.

```
while( GetMessage( &msg, NULL, 0, 0 ) )
{
    TranslateMessage( &msg );
    DispatchMessage( &msg );
}
```

UnhookWindowsHookEx   ■ WINDOWS 95   ■ WINDOWS NT

Description	There can be any number of hook functions installed of any one type. UnhookWindowsHookEx removes one hook procedure from the chain that was set with the SetWindowsHookEx function.
Syntax	BOOL **UnhookWindowsHookEx**(HHOOK *hhook*)
Parameters	
hhook	HHOOK: The handle to the hook to be removed. This is obtained from the call to the SetWindowsHookEx function that installed the hook.
Returns	BOOL: If successful, the return value is TRUE; otherwise, it is FALSE.
Include File	winuser.h
See Also	SetWindowsHookEx, CallNextHookEx
Example	See the example for the CallMsgFilter function.

WaitMessage   ■ WINDOWS 95   ■ WINDOWS NT

Description	WaitMessage suspends the calling thread until a message is placed in the thread's message queue. While the thread is suspended, other threads are allowed to run.
Syntax	BOOL **WaitMessage**(VOID)

Parameters	This function has no parameters.
Returns	BOOL: If successful, the return value is TRUE; otherwise, it is FALSE.
Include File	winuser.h
See Also	GetMessage, PeekMessage
Related Messages	Any message received will resume message processing.
Example	When the user selects the Test! menu option, **PeekMessage** is used to clear the message queue. The application then waits until a message is placed in the message queue. Once a message is put in the queue, the application continues and displays a message box.

```
LRESULT CALLBACK WndProc( HWND hWnd, UINT uMsg, WPARAM wParam, LPARAM lParam )
{
    switch( uMsg )
    {
        case WM_COMMAND:
                switch ( LOWORD( wParam ) )
                {
                    case IDM_TEST:
                        // Clear the message queue and wait for the next
                        // message to be placed in the message queue.
                        //............................................
                        while( PeekMessage( &msg, hWnd, 0, 0, PM_REMOVE ))
                            ;
                        WaitMessage();
                        MessageBox( hWnd, "Got Message", lpszAppName, MB_OK );
                        break;
            .
            .
            .
```

WinMain   ■ WINDOWS 95   ■ WINDOWS NT

Description	WinMain is the beginning point (entry point) of a Windows program. Comparable to the **main** function in a non-Windows program, the WinMain function is the entry point where program initialization begins.
Syntax	int **WinMain**(HINSTANCE *hInstance*, HINSTANCE *hPrevInstance*, LPTSTR *lpszCmdLine*, int *nCmdShow*)
Parameters	
hInstance	HINSTANCE: The current instance handle for the application.
hPrevInstance	HINSTANCE: The previous instance handle for the application. For a Windows 95 or Windows NT application, this is always NULL.
lpszCmdLine	LPTSTR: A pointer to a null-terminated string containing the command line used to start the application.
nCmdShow	int: The show command, which specifies how the application should be initially displayed. See Table 4-11 for the valid values.

Returns	**int**: The exit code for the application, which should be the value used with the **PostQuitMessage** function.
Include File	`winbase.h`
See Also	`GetMessage`, `TranslateMessage`, `DispatchMessage`, `CreateWindow`, `RegisterClass`
Example	This example shows the **WinMain** function of a typical Windows application. If the program will run on Windows 3.x with Win32s, the *hPrevInstance* should be checked for **NULL** before registering the window class.

```
int APIENTRY WinMain( HINSTANCE hInstance, HINSTANCE hPrevInstance,
                LPTSTR lpCmdLine, int nCmdShow)
{
   MSG         msg;
   HWND        hWnd;
   WNDCLASSEX wc;

   // Register the window class for the application window.
   // In Windows 95 and Windows NT, the hPrevInstance is
   // always NULL so it does not need to be checked. For
   // Windows 3.1 and Win32s the hPrevInstance should be
   // checked before registering another class.
   //......................................................

   wc.style         = CS_HREDRAW | CS_VREDRAW;
   wc.lpfnWndProc   = (WNDPROC)WndProc;
   wc.cbClsExtra    = 0;
   wc.cbWndExtra    = 0;
   wc.hInstance     = hInstance;
   wc.hIcon         = LoadIcon (hInstance, lpszAppName);
   wc.hCursor       = LoadCursor(NULL, IDC_ARROW);
   wc.hbrBackground = (HBRUSH)(COLOR_WINDOW+1);
   wc.lpszMenuName  = lpszAppName;
   wc.lpszClassName = lpszAppName;
   wc.cbSize        = sizeof( WNDCLASSEX );
   wc.hIconSm       = LoadImage(hInstance, lpszAppName,
                             IMAGE_ICON, 16, 16,
                             LR_DEFAULTCOLOR );


   if ( !RegisterClassEx( &wc ) )
      return( FALSE );

   hInst = hInstance;

   // Create the main application window.
   //....................................
   hWnd = CreateWindow( lpszAppName,
                     szTitle,
                     WS_OVERLAPPEDWINDOW,
                     CW_USEDEFAULT, 0,
                     CW_USEDEFAULT, 0,
                     NULL, NULL,
                     hInstance, NULL
                  );
```

```
    if ( !hWnd )
        return( FALSE );

    // Make the window visible.
    //.........................
    ShowWindow( hWnd, nCmdShow );
    UpdateWindow( hWnd );

    // Main message-processing loop. Continue until the application
    // shuts down and the WM_QUIT message is received.
    //.............................................................
    while( GetMessage( &msg, NULL, 0, 0) )
    {
        TranslateMessage(&msg);
        DispatchMessage(&msg);
    }

    return( msg.wParam );
}
```

6

MENUS

Virtually every Windows application that allows the user to select actions uses menus. The Windows Software Development Kit (SDK) and the Win32 API provide a comprehensive set of tools for building menus and dynamically modifying them during execution.

Main Menus and Pop-up Menus

Windows applications use two basic types of menus: top-level menus and pop-up menus. The top-level menu (also called the "main" menu of a program) is a set of commands that is visible in the window's menu bar at all times, assuming the program has a menu. See the style guide in Chapter 1, Windows 95/NT 4 Programming, for a discussion of the basic menu items for an application. For complex programs, it is not practical to put all the menu options that may be needed on the menu bar. This is where pop-up menus (sometimes called "submenus," or "pull down" or "drop down" menus) come in. When selected, the top menu bar items can spawn pop-up menu items with many more options from which to choose.

Building Menus in the Resource File

For most applications, defining a menu is as simple as typing a few lines in the resource (RC) file. The following example produces the menu structure shown in Figure 6-2.

Menu definition in resource file

```
MYAPP MENU DISCARDABLE
BEGIN
    POPUP "&File"
    BEGIN
        MENUITEM "E&xit",                    IDM_EXIT
```

continued on next page

continued from previous page

```
    END
    POPUP "&Test"
    BEGIN
        MENUITEM "Item &1",                IDM_ITEM1
        MENUITEM "Item &2",                IDM_ITEM2
        MENUITEM "Item &3",                IDM_ITEM3
    END
    POPUP "&Help"
    BEGIN
        MENUITEM "&About My Application...",   IDM_ABOUT
    END
END
```

In this case, there are three menu items on the top-level menu bar: File, Test, and Help. The first menu item is for a pop-up that is common to virtually every Windows application. This is where the Exit menu option is located for an application. The next menu item is an application-specific menu item that defines another pop-up with three items: Item 1, Item 2, and Item 3. Applications will normally define other top-level menu items. After the last menu item, there is normally a Help menu item where online help and the application About box are selected. Menu item identifiers can be in the range of 0 through 0x7FFF.

The ampersand (**&**) character lets you create keyboard alternatives to clicking menu items with the mouse. The letter following the ampersand is underlined in the menu. The user can select a menu item by holding down the ALT key while pressing the key for the underlined letter. If the item is a pop-up menu item, this procedure displays the pop-up menu. If the ampersand needs to be displayed in a menu item, use a double ampersand (**&&**).

Adding a Menu to the Application's Window

Defining a menu in the resource (RC) file does not automatically make it viable or make it part of the application's window. Normally, you will attach the application's menu to the window's class definition in the **WinMain** function. Do this by setting the *lpszMenuName* element of the **WNDCLASS** structure to point to the menu name. **RegisterClass** then associates this menu name with any window created from the class.

You also can attach the menu to a window by using the **CreateWindow** and **LoadMenu** functions. Do this by setting the *hmenu* parameter of the **CreateWindow** function equal to the value returned from **LoadMenu**. **LoadMenu** is called using the name of the menu that was given in the resource (RC) file.

The low-level method of adding a menu to the application's window is to use the **SetMenu** and **LoadMenu** functions. **LoadMenu** loads the menu from the resource file, and the **SetMenu** function associates the newly loaded menu with the application's window.

Changing Menus

Complex applications will commonly need to change the menu to reflect changing conditions while the application is executing. The Win32 API provides a rich set of functions to change the menu to reflect the current options within the application. Essentially, every aspect of a menu can be changed. The most common changes alter a menu's character string, check and uncheck menu items, gray and disable them, and delete items. The `SetMenuItemInfo` function allows several of these operations to be carried out in one function call. You can also use more specific functions for single operations, such as `DeleteMenu` to remove an item, `CheckMenuItem` to add and remove checkmarks, and `EnableMenuItem` to enable and disable items. If the top-level menu items are changed, be sure to call `DrawMenuBar` to repaint the menu bar.

Menu Messages

Windows sends the `WM_COMMAND` message every time a menu item is selected. This is normally the only message that an application will process from a menu. When System menu items are selected, the `WM_SYSCOMMAND` message is sent instead. Applications may need to process the `WM_INITMENU` and `WM_INITMENUPOPUP` messages. They are sent right before a main menu or pop-up menu is activated. They provide the application with an opportunity to change the menu before it is displayed. The `WM_MENUCHAR` message is sent if the user attempts to use a keyboard shortcut key that does not match any of the menu characters preceded by an ampersand character (**&**). This allows more than one keyboard shortcut to be programmed per menu item, or it can be used to display an error message. The `WM_MENUSELECT` message is also sent when a menu item is selected. This message is more versatile than the `WM_COMMAND` message, because it is sent even if the menu item is grayed. Normally, this message sets up menu context help that can be displayed on the program status bar.

Menu Support Function Descriptions

Table 6-1 summarizes the menu support functions. The detailed function descriptions follow the table.

Table 6-1 Menu support function summary

Function	Purpose
AppendMenu	Adds a new menu item to the end of a menu.
CheckMenuItem	Checks or unchecks a menu item.
CheckMenuRadioItem	Checks a menu option and clears all other menu checks within a range.
CopyAcceleratorTable	Copies an accelerator table.
CreateAcceleratorTable	Creates an accelerator table.
CreateMenu	Creates a new, empty menu.
CreatePopupMenu	Creates a pop-up menu.
DeleteMenu	Removes an item from a menu.

continued on next page

continued from previous page

Function	Purpose
DestroyAcceleratorTable	Destroys an accelerator table.
DestroyMenu	Removes a menu from memory.
DrawMenuBar	Forces a window's menu bar to be repainted.
EnableMenuItem	Enables, disables, or grays the menu item.
GetMenu	Retrieves the menu handle for a window.
GetMenuCheckMarkDimensions	Retrieves the size and width of the bitmap used to create checkmarks next to menu items.
GetMenuDefaultItem	Retrieves the default menu item.
GetMenuItemCount	Gets the number of menu items in a menu.
GetMenuItemID	Retrieves the ID value associated with a menu item.
GetMenuItemInfo	Retrieves information about a menu item.
GetMenuItemRect	Retrieves the bounding rectangle of a menu item.
GetMenuState	Retrieves the state of a menu item or the number of items in a pop-up menu.
GetMenuString	Retrieves the label displayed in a menu item.
GetSubMenu	Retrieves a handle to a pop-up menu.
GetSystemMenu	Retrieves a handle to the System menu.
HiliteMenuItem	Highlights a top-level menu item.
InsertMenuItem	Adds a new menu item to a menu.
IsMenu	Determines whether a handle is a menu.
LoadAccelerators	Loads an accelerator key table from the resource file.
LoadMenu	Retrieves a handle to a menu defined in the resource file.
LoadMenuIndirect	Retrieves a menu handle for a menu template.
MenuItemFromPoint	Determines the menu item from a point.
RemoveMenu	Removes a menu item from a menu.
SetMenu	Attaches a menu to a window.
SetMenuDefaultItem	Sets the default menu item for a menu.
SetMenuItemBitmaps	Replaces the default menu checkmark bitmap with a custom bitmap.
SetMenuItemInfo	Changes information for a menu item.
TrackPopupMenu	Displays a submenu anywhere on the screen.
TrackPopupMenuEx	Displays a submenu anywhere on the screen except for a given area.
TranslateAccelerator	Translates keystrokes into commands using the accelerator table.

AppendMenu   ■ Windows 95   ■ Windows NT

Description   AppendMenu is similar to InsertMenuItem, except it only adds menu items to the end of the menu. Menus can be dynamically changed while an application executes to reflect changes. An application can use AppendMenu to build new menus at runtime without building them in the resource file.

Syntax	BOOL **AppendMenu**(HMENU *hMenu,* UINT *uFlags,* UINT *idNewItem,* LPCTSTR *lpszNewItem*)

Parameters

hMenu HMENU: Identifies the menu to which the new item is added.

uFlags UINT: The appearance and behavior of the menu item to be added. Can be one or more of the values listed in Table 6-2. The MFT_BITMAP, MFT_SEPARATOR, and MFT_STRING flags cannot be used together.

Table 6-2 AppendMenu *uFlags* values

Value	Meaning
MF_POPUP	Creates a pop-up menu. The *lpszNewItem* parameter contains the handle of the pop-up menu.
MFS_CHECKED	Places a checkmark next to the menu item.
MFS_DEFAULT	Menu item is the default. A menu can contain only one default menu item, which is displayed in bold.
MFS_DISABLED	Menu item cannot be selected. Does not gray the menu item.
MFS_GRAYED	Grays the menu item and disables it so that it cannot be selected.
MFS_HILITE	Highlights the menu item.
MFS_UNCHECKED	The menu item does not have a checkmark.
MFS_UNHILITE	The menu item is not highlighted.
MFT_BITMAP	Displays the menu item using a bitmap. The *lpszNewItem* parameter contains the handle to the bitmap.
MFT_MENUBARBREAK	Places the menu item on a new line if it is in a menu bar, or in a new column if it is in a pop-up menu. A vertical line separates the columns in a pop-up menu.
MFT_MENUBREAK	Same as MFT_MENUBARBREAK except columns are not separated by a vertical line.
MFT_OWNERDRAW	Adds an owner-drawn menu item to the menu. The window receives a WM_MEASUREITEM message before the menu is displayed for the first time, and a WM_DRAWITEM message whenever the appearance of the menu item must be updated. The *lpszNewItem* parameter contains an application-defined 32-bit value.
MFT_RADIOCHECK	Displays checked menu items using a radio button mark instead of a checkmark.
MFT_RIGHTJUSTIFY	Right-justifies the menu item and any subsequent items. This flag is valid only if the menu item is in a menu bar.
MFT_SEPARATOR	Specifies that the menu item is a separator. This flag is only valid if the menu item is in a pop-up menu.
MFT_STRING	Displays the menu item using a text string. The *lpszNewItem* parameter is a pointer to a null-terminated string.

idNewItem UINT: The menu identifier for the new menu item.

lpszNewItem LPCTSTR: The content of the new menu item. The value depends on the value of the *uFlags* parameter.

Returns BOOL: If successful, the return value is TRUE; otherwise, it is FALSE.

Include File winuser.h

See Also InsertMenuItem, CreateMenu, SetMenu, DrawMenuBar

Example In this example (see Figure 6-1), the menu item New Item is added to the end of the menu and on its own line when the Test! menu item is selected.

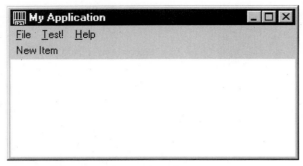

Figure 6-1 AppendMenu example

```
LRESULT CALLBACK WndProc( HWND hWnd, UINT uMsg, WPARAM wParam, LPARAM lParam )
{
   switch( uMsg )
   {
      case WM_COMMAND :
            switch( LOWORD( wParam ) )
            {
               case IDM_TEST :
                     // Add new menu option on a new line.
                     //.................................
                     AppendMenu( GetMenu( hWnd ),
                                 MFT_STRING | MFT_MENUBARBREAK,
                                 120, "&New Item" );
                     DrawMenuBar( hWnd );
                     break;

            .
            .
            .
```

CheckMenuItem   ■ WINDOWS 95   ■ WINDOWS NT

Description	CheckMenuItem checks or unchecks a menu item. Checkmarks generally are used to signify that an option has been turned on or off. For large numbers of options, use a dialog box with radio buttons and check boxes for selections. For radio button appearance in the menu, use the CheckMenuRadioItem function.
Syntax	DWORD **CheckMenuItem**(HMENU *hmenu,* UINT *idCheckItem,* UINT *uFlags*)

Parameters

hMenu   HMENU: A handle to the menu.

idCheckItem   UINT: The menu identifier to be checked or unchecked.

uFlags   UINT: Specifies how the command is to execute. Two of the four possibilities, shown in Table 6-3, are always combined with the binary OR (|) operator to make the *uFlags* parameter. (In other words, either MF_BYCOMMAND or MF_BYPOSITION is always combined with either MFS_CHECKED or MFS_UNCHECKED.)

Table 6-3 CheckMenuItem *uFlags* values

Value	Meaning
MF_BYCOMMAND	The value in *idCheckItem* is the identifier of the menu item.
MF_BYPOSITION	The value in *idCheckItem* is the zero-based relative position of the menu item.
MF_CHECKED	Places a checkmark next to the menu item.
MF_UNCHECKED	The menu item does not have a checkmark.

Returns   DWORD: The previous state of the menu item (MF_CHECKED or MF_UNCHECKED). If the menu item does not exist, the return value is 0xFFFFFFFF.

Include File   winuser.h

See Also   CheckMenuRadioItem, GetMenuItemInfo, EnableMenuItem, SetMenuItemInfo

Related Messages WM_MENUSELECT

Example   In this example, the menu item IDM_ITEM1 toggles between being checked and unchecked each time it is selected. The GetMenuState function is used to determine the menu item status.

```
LRESULT CALLBACK WndProc( HWND hWnd, UINT uMsg, WPARAM wParam, LPARAM lParam )
{
   switch( uMsg )
   {
     case WM_COMMAND :
            switch( LOWORD( wParam ) )
            {
              case IDM_ITEM1 :
                   {
                       HMENU hMenu  = GetMenu( hWnd );
                       UINT  uState = GetMenuState( hMenu, IDM_ITEM1,
                                                    MF_BYCOMMAND );
```

continued on next page

continued from previous page

```
                    if ( uState & MFS_CHECKED )
                        CheckMenuItem( hMenu, IDM_ITEM1,
                                     MF_BYCOMMAND | MFS_UNCHECKED );
                    else
                        CheckMenuItem( hMenu, IDM_ITEM1,
                                     MF_BYCOMMAND | MFS_CHECKED );
                }
                break;
```

CheckMenuRadioItem　　　　　■ WINDOWS 95　■ WINDOWS NT

Description	CheckMenuRadioItem checks the specified menu item with a radio button and unchecks any other menu options within the specified group.
	Use CheckMenuRadioItem to make a group of menu items work the same as a group of radio buttons.
Syntax	BOOL API **CheckMenuRadioItem**(HMENU *hmenu*, UINT *idFirst*, UINT *idLast*, UINT *idCheck*, UINT *uFlags*)
Parameters	
hmenu	HMENU: A handle to the menu that contains the group of menu items.
idFirst	UINT: The first menu item in the group.
idLast	UINT: The last menu item in the group
idCheck	UINT: The menu item to check.
uFlags	UINT: Determines the meaning of the *idFirst*, *idLast*, and *idCheck* parameters. If this parameter is **MF_BYCOMMAND**, the parameters specify menu item identifiers; if it is **MF_BYPOSITION**, the parameters specify the menu item positions.
Returns	BOOL: If successful, the return value is **TRUE**; otherwise, it is **FALSE**.
Include File	winuser.h
See Also	GetMenuItemInfo, SetMenuItemInfo
Example	This example, shown in Figure 6-2, demonstrates how to use a group of menu items as a set of mutually exclusive options. This means that only one menu option in the list can be checked at a time. This functionality is similar to the radio button groups found in dialogs.

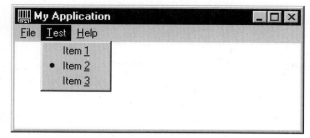

Figure 6-2 `CheckMenuRadioItem` example

The header file *#defines*

```
#define IDM_EXIT    101
#define IDM_ABOUT   102


#define IDM_ITEM1   200
#define IDM_ITEM2   201
#define IDM_ITEM3   202
```

The resource (*.RC*) file

```
MYAPP MENU DISCARDABLE
BEGIN
    POPUP "&File"
    BEGIN
        MENUITEM "E&xit",                    IDM_EXIT
    END
    POPUP "&Test"
    BEGIN
        MENUITEM "Item &1",                  IDM_ITEM1
        MENUITEM "Item &2",                  IDM_ITEM2
        MENUITEM "Item &3",                  IDM_ITEM3
    END
    POPUP "&Help"
    BEGIN
        MENUITEM "&About My Application...",         IDM_ABOUT
    END
END
```

The *WndProc* function

```
LRESULT CALLBACK WndProc( HWND hWnd, UINT uMsg, WPARAM wParam, LPARAM lParam )
{
   switch( uMsg )
   {
     case WM_COMMAND :
             switch( LOWORD( wParam ) )
             {
               case IDM_ITEM1:
               case IDM_ITEM2:
               case IDM_ITEM3:
                     CheckMenuRadioItem( GetMenu( hWnd ),
                                         IDM_ITEM1, IDM_ITEM3,
                                         LOWORD( wParam ), MF_BYCOMMAND );
                     break;
               .
               .
               .
```

CopyAcceleratorTable ■ WINDOWS 95 ■ WINDOWS NT

Description	`CopyAcceleratorTable` copies the given accelerator table into a new location. You can use this function to obtain the accelerator-table data that corresponds to an accelerator-table handle or to determine the size of the accelerator-table data.
	The accelerator-table data can be obtained by copying the data. The number of items in the accelerator table also can be retrieved for use in determining how much memory should be allocated for a subsequent call to obtain the actual data.
Syntax	`int `**`CopyAcceleratorTable`**`( HACCEL `*`hacclOriginal`*`, LPACCEL `*`lpacclCopy`*`, int `*`cAccel`*` )`
Parameters	
hacclOriginal	`HACCEL`: A handle to the accelerator table to copy.
lpacclCopy	`LPACCEL`: A pointer to an array of `ACCEL` structures where the accelerator-table information is to be copied.
cAccel	`int`: The maximum number of accelerator-table entries to copy. See the definition of the `ACCEL` structure below.
Returns	`int`: If *lpacclCopy* is `NULL`, the number of accelerator-table entries is returned. Otherwise, the return value is the number of entries that were copied.

Include File	`winuser.h`
See Also	`CreateAcceleratorTable, DestroyAcceleratorTable,` `LoadAccelerators, TranslateAccelerator`

ACCEL Definition

```
typedef struct tagACCEL
{
    BYTE fVirt;
    WORD key;
    WORD cmd;
}ACCEL;
```

Members

fVirt BYTE: One or more of the values in Table 6-4 combined together using the binary OR (|) operator.

Table 6-4 ACCEL *fVirt* values

Value	Meaning
FALT	The ALT key must be held down when the accelerator key is pressed.
FCONTROL	The CTRL key must be held down when the accelerator key is pressed.
FNOINVERT	No top-level menu item will be highlighted when the accelerator is used.
FSHIFT	The SHIFT key must be held down when the accelerator key is pressed.
FVIRTKEY	The key member specifies a virtual-key code. The default is an ASCII character code.

key WORD: The virtual-key code if the **FVIRTKEY** flag is set; otherwise, the ASCII character code.

cmd WORD: The accelerator identifier that is sent when the accelerator is used.

Example See the example for the **CreateAcceleratorTable** function.

CreateAcceleratorTable ■ WINDOWS 95 ■ WINDOWS NT

Description **CreateAcceleratorTable** creates an accelerator table. An application can create an accelerator table while the application executes without loading it from the resource (RC) file. Accelerator tables can be changed to match menu changes by using both the **CopyAcceleratorTable** and **CreateAcceleratorTable** functions.

Syntax HACCEL **CreateAcceleratorTable**(LPACCEL *lpaccl,* int *nEntries*)

Parameters

lpaccl LPACCEL: A pointer to an array of **ACCEL** structures. See the **CopyAcceleratorTable** function for the definition of the **ACCEL** structure.

nEntries int: The number of **ACCEL** structures pointed to by the *lpaccl* parameter.

Returns	**HACCEL**: If the function succeeds, the return value is the handle of the created accelerator table; otherwise, it is **NULL**.
Include File	`winuser.h`
See Also	`CopyAcceleratorTable`, `DestroyAcceleratorTable`, `LoadAccelerators`, `TranslateAccelerator`
Example	This example demonstrates how an application can dynamically change the menu and accelerator keys. When the Test! menu option is selected, a new menu item is added to the menu (up to four), and a new accelerator key (F1, F2, F3, or F4, respectively) is added for the new menu item. When the new menu items are selected with either the appropriate accelerator key or by selecting it from the menu, a message box is displayed. This same method could be used to give the user a method of adding custom menu items and defining accelerator keys for those items. Figure 6-3 shows the example when New Item2 is selected.

Global variable

```
HACCEL hAccel = NULL;
```

The message loop in `WinMain`

```
while( GetMessage( &msg, NULL, 0, 0) )
{
   if ( !hAccel || !TranslateAccelerator( hWnd, hAccel, &msg ) )
   {
      TranslateMessage( &msg );
      DispatchMessage( &msg );
   }
}
```

Figure 6-3 `CreateAcceleratorTable` example

The *AddNewTestItem* function

```
#define IDM_NEWBASE 300

VOID AddNewTestItem( HWND hWnd )
{
static int nNum = 0;

    char    szMenuItem[20];

    HMENU  hMenu       = GetMenu( hWnd );
    ACCEL* pAccelData = NULL;
    ACCEL* pCurAccel  = NULL;
    HANDLE hAccelData = NULL;
    int    nNumAccel  = 1;

    // Maximum of 4 new items allowed.
    //...............................
    if ( nNum == 4 )
       return;

    // If accelerator table exists, get the number of items.
    //......................................................
    if ( hAccel )
    {
       nNumAccel = CopyAcceleratorTable( hAccel, NULL, 0 ) + 1;
    }

    // Allocate an array of ACCEL structures.
    //.......................................
    hAccelData = GlobalAlloc( GHND, sizeof(ACCEL) * nNumAccel );
    if ( hAccelData )
       pAccelData = (ACCEL*)GlobalLock( hAccelData );

    // If an accelerator table exists, copy the items into
    // the newly allocated array.
    //....................................................
    if ( hAccel && pAccelData )
    {
       CopyAcceleratorTable( hAccel, pAccelData, nNumAccel-1 );

       DestroyAcceleratorTable( hAccel );
       hAccel = NULL;
    }
```

continued on next page

continued from previous page

```
    // Add the new menu option and accelerator key
    //........................................
    if ( pAccelData )
    {
        // Get a pointer to the new accelerator key in
        // the array.
        //........................................
        pCurAccel = (ACCEL*)(pAccelData+nNumAccel-1);

        // Create a new menu option on the menu.
        //........................................
        nNum++;
        wsprintf( szMenuItem, "New Item&%d", nNum );
        AppendMenu( hMenu, MFT_STRING, IDM_NEWBASE+nNum, szMenuItem );
        DrawMenuBar( hWnd );

        // Set up a new accelerator of F1,F2,F3,or F4 for the
        // the new menu option.
        //........................................
        pCurAccel->fVirt = FNOINVERT | FVIRTKEY;
        pCurAccel->cmd   = IDM_NEWBASE+nNum;
        pCurAccel->key   = ( nNum == 1 ? VK_F1 :
                             nNum == 2 ? VK_F2 :
                             nNum == 3 ? VK_F3 :
                             /*default*/ VK_F4 );

        // Create the new accelerator table.
        //........................................
        hAccel = CreateAcceleratorTable( pAccelData, nNumAccel );

        GlobalUnlock( hAccelData );
    }

    if ( hAccelData )
        GlobalFree( hAccelData );
}
```

Part of the *WndProc* function

```
LRESULT CALLBACK WndProc( HWND hWnd, UINT uMsg, WPARAM wParam, LPARAM lParam )
{
    switch( uMsg )
    {
```

```
case WM_COMMAND :
     switch( LOWORD( wParam ) )
     {
       case IDM_TEST :
               AddNewTestItem( hWnd );
               break;

       case IDM_NEWBASE+1 :
               MessageBox( hWnd, "New Item 1 Selected", "Item Selected",
                   MB_OK | MB_ICONINFORMATION );
               break;

       case IDM_NEWBASE+2 :
               MessageBox( hWnd, "New Item 2 Selected", "Item Selected",
                       MB_OK | MB_ICONINFORMATION );
               break;

       case IDM_NEWBASE+3 :
               MessageBox( hWnd, "New Item 3 Selected", "Item Selected",
                       MB_OK | MB_ICONINFORMATION );
               break;

       case IDM_NEWBASE+4 :
               MessageBox( hWnd, "New Item 4 Selected", "Item Selected",
                       MB_OK | MB_ICONINFORMATION );
               break;
       .
       .
       .
```

CreateMenu   ■ WINDOWS 95   ■ WINDOWS NT

Description   CreateMenu is the first step to dynamically creating a menu within an application. The menu is initially empty, but it can be filled with menu items by using the **AppendMenu** and **InsertMenu** functions.

You typically use **CreateMenu** to create menus for child windows or as an alternative to defining all menus in the program's resource (RC) file. Menus created with this function cannot be floating menus. Use **CreatePopupMenu** to create floating menus.

Syntax   HMENU **CreateMenu**(VOID)

Parameters   This function has no parameters.

Returns   HMENU: If successful, the handle of the newly created menu; otherwise, it is NULL.

Include File	`winuser.h`
See Also	`AppendMenu`, `DestroyMenu`, `InsertMenuItem`, `SetMenu`
Example	In this example, the application does not have a menu specified in the resource (RC) file. Instead, the menu is created when the program starts. The menu that is created has only two menu items in it. When the Test! menu option is selected, a message box is displayed.

```
LRESULT CALLBACK WndProc( HWND hWnd, UINT uMsg, WPARAM wParam, LPARAM lParam )
{
   switch( uMsg )
   {
      case WM_CREATE :
            {
               HMENU hMenu = CreateMenu();

               AppendMenu( hMenu, MFT_STRING, IDM_TEST, "Test!" );
               AppendMenu( hMenu, MFT_STRING, IDM_EXIT, "Exit!" );
               SetMenu( hWnd, hMenu );
            }
            break;

      case WM_COMMAND :
            switch( LOWORD( wParam ) )
            {
               case IDM_TEST :
                     MessageBox( hWnd, "The new Test! option was selected",
                                 szAppName, MB_OK | MB_ICONINFORMATION );
                     break;
                  .
                  .
                  .
```

CreatePopupMenu   ■ WINDOWS 95   ■ WINDOWS NT

Description	`CreatePopupMenu` creates an empty pop-up menu. Any menu other than the top menu bar is considered to be a pop-up menu. This function creates an empty pop-up menu, ready to have items added using `AppendMenu` and `InsertMenuItem`.
	Use `CreatePopupMenu` to create menus within the body of the program. This function can be used with `TrackPopupMenu` to create floating pop-up menus (menus not attached to other menus).
Syntax	HMENU **CreatePopupMenu**(VOID)

Parameters	This function has no parameters.
Returns	HMENU: If successful, the handle of the newly created pop-up menu; otherwise, it is NULL.
Include File	winuser.h
See Also	AppendMenu, CreateMenu, InsertMenuItem, SetMenu, TrackPopupMenu
Example	See the example for the TrackPopupMenu function.

DeleteMenu   ■ Windows 95   ■ Windows NT

Description	DeleteMenu removes a single menu item from the given menu. If the menu item is a pop-up menu, the pop-up is destroyed and the memory freed. Use DrawMenuBar afterward to repaint the menu bar.
	Use DeleteMenu to make small changes to menus as a program runs. This function gives you an alternative to having more than one menu and switching between them.
Syntax	BOOL **DeleteMenu**(HMENU *hmenu*, UINT *uItem*, UINT *uFlags*)
Parameters	
hmenu	HMENU: A handle to the menu to be changed. GetMenu can be used to retrieve this handle.
uItem	UINT: The menu item to be deleted. This value depends on the *uFlags* parameter.
uFlags	UINT: Specifies how the *uItem* parameter is interpreted, as shown in Table 6-5.

Table 6-5 DeleteMenu *uFlags* values

Value	Meaning
MF_BYCOMMAND	*uItem* is the menu item ID value. This is the default.
MF_BYPOSITION	*uItem* is the zero-based menu item offset. For submenus (pop-up menus off the menu bar), use the GetSubMenu function to retrieve the menu handle used in the *hmenu* parameter.

Returns	BOOL: TRUE if successful; otherwise, the return value is FALSE.
Include File	winuser.h
See Also	DrawMenuBar, RemoveMenu
Example	In this example, three menu items are added to the menu bar of the application. When one of the new menu items is selected, it is deleted from the menu using the DeleteMenu function.

```
LRESULT CALLBACK WndProc( HWND hWnd, UINT uMsg, WPARAM wParam, LPARAM lParam )
{
    switch( uMsg )
    {
    case WM_CREATE :
            {
                HMENU hMenu = GetMenu( hWnd );

                AppendMenu( hMenu, MFT_STRING, IDM_ITEM1, "Item&1" );
                AppendMenu( hMenu, MFT_STRING, IDM_ITEM2, "Item&2" );
                AppendMenu( hMenu, MFT_STRING, IDM_ITEM3, "Item&3" );
            }
            break;

    case WM_COMMAND :
            switch( LOWORD( wParam ) )
            {
                case IDM_ITEM1 :
                case IDM_ITEM2 :
                case IDM_ITEM3 :
                        {
                                HMENU hMenu = GetMenu( hWnd );

                                DeleteMenu( hMenu, LOWORD(wParam), MF_BYCOMMAND );
                                DrawMenuBar( hWnd );
                        }
                .
                .
                .
```

DestroyAcceleratorTable ■ WINDOWS 95   ■ WINDOWS NT

Description	**DestroyAcceleratorTable** destroys an accelerator table.
	Before an application closes, an application should use this function to destroy any accelerator tables created with the **CreateAcceleratorTable** function. Accelerator tables that were loaded with **LoadAccelerators** should not be destroyed.
Syntax	BOOL **DestroyAcceleratorTable**(HACCEL *haccl*)
Parameters	
haccl	HACCEL: The handle to the accelerator table that was returned from the **CreateAcceleratorTable** function.

Returns	BOOL: TRUE if successful; otherwise, the return value is FALSE.
Include File	winuser.h
See Also	CopyAcceleratorTable, CreateAcceleratorTable, LoadAccelerators, TranslateAccelerator
Related Messages	WM_DESTROY
Example	See the example for the CreateAcceleratorTable function.

DestroyMenu ■ WINDOWS 95 ■ WINDOWS NT

Description	DestroyMenu removes menus created in the resource (RC) file and those created within the body of the program with the CreateMenu or CreatePopupMenu function.
	Use DestroyMenu with applications that have more than one menu. Only the menu attached to the application's window will be deleted when the application terminates. Any other menus will remain in memory. Use DestroyMenu before the application terminates to free the memory consumed by the unattached menus.
Syntax	BOOL **DestroyMenu**(HMENU *hmenu*)
Parameters	
hmenu	HMENU: A handle to the menu to be destroyed.
Returns	BOOL: TRUE if successful; otherwise, the return value is FALSE.
Include File	winuser.h
See Also	CreateMenu, CreatePopupMenu, DeleteMenu, RemoveMenu, GetMenu
Related Messages	WM_DESTROY
Example	See the example for the TrackPopupMenu function.

DrawMenuBar ■ WINDOWS 95 ■ WINDOWS NT

Description	DrawMenuBar forces a window's menu bar to be repainted. The menu bar is not part of the client region of the window and, therefore, is not updated when the UpdateWindow function is called.
	Use DrawMenuBar right after any change to the top-level menu.
Syntax	BOOL **DrawMenuBar**(HWND *hwnd*)
Parameters	
hwnd	HWND: A handle to the window that has the menu.
Returns	BOOL: TRUE if successful; otherwise, the return value is FALSE.
Include File	winuser.h
See Also	AppendMenu, DeleteMenu, InsertMenuItem, RemoveMenu

Related Messages   WM_NCPAINT

Example   The following example adds a new menu item and updates the menu.

```
LRESULT CALLBACK WndProc( HWND hWnd, UINT uMsg, WPARAM wParam, LPARAM lParam )
{
   switch( uMsg )
   {
      case WM_COMMAND :
              switch( LOWORD( wParam ) )
              {
                 case IDM_TEST :
                         // Add new menu option and update the menu.
                         //.........................................
                         AppendMenu( GetMenu( hWnd ),
                                     MFT_STRING,
                                     120, "New Item" );
                         DrawMenuBar( hWnd );
                         break;
          .
          .
          .
```

EnableMenuItem

■ WINDOWS 95   ■ WINDOWS NT

Description	EnableMenuItem enables, disables, or grays the menu item. Menu items are normally enabled, meaning that selecting a menu item causes a WM_COMMAND message to be sent to the window's WndProc function. Menu items can be disabled in such a way that they can't be selected by the user but still appear normal. Menu items can be disabled and made visibly different (gray text with the default Windows colors) from other menu items, so the user can easily see which commands are enabled.
	Some menu actions may not be possible under all situations in a program. For example, it should not be possible to paste data if no data has been cut or copied into the clipboard. In these situations, it is best to disable and gray the menu items that have no function, so that the user intuitively knows that certain actions are not possible.
Syntax	BOOL **EnableMenuItem**(HMENU *hmenu*, UINT *uItem*, UINT *uFlags*)
Parameters	
hmenu	HMENU: A handle to the menu. Use GetMenu to retrieve a window's menu.
uItem	UINT: The menu item to be enabled, disabled, or grayed. This can be an item in the menu bar or in a pop-up menu.
uFlags	UINT: The action to take, and how *uItem* is to be interpreted. The values shown in Table 6-6 can be combined with the binary OR (	) operator.

Table 6-6 EnableMenuItem *uFlags* values

Value	Meaning
MF_BYCOMMAND	The value in *uItem* is the identifier of the menu item.
MF_BYPOSITION	The value in *uItem* is the zero-based relative position of the menu item.
MFS_DISABLED	Disable the menu item without graying the text.
MFS_ENABLED	Enable the menu item and restore the text to the normal menu item color.
MFS_GRAYED	Disable the menu item and gray the text.

Returns	BOOL: The previous state of the menu item (MF_DISABLED, MF_ENABLED, or MF_GRAYED). If the menu item does not exist, the return value is 0xFFFFFFFF.
Include File	winuser.h
See Also	GetMenuItemInfo, CreateMenu, GetMenuItemID, SetMenuItemInfo
Related Messages	WM_COMMAND
Example	In this example, the menu item identified by IDM_ITEM1 is toggled between enabled and disabled when the menu option Test! is selected.

```
LRESULT CALLBACK WndProc( HWND hWnd, UINT uMsg, WPARAM wParam, LPARAM lParam )
{
   switch( uMsg )
   {
     case WM_COMMAND :
            switch( LOWORD( wParam ) )
            {
               case IDM_TEST :
                   {
                       HMENU hMenu  = GetMenu( hWnd );
                       UINT   uState = GetMenuState( hMenu, IDM_ITEM1,
                                             MF_BYCOMMAND );

                       if ( uState & MFS_GRAYED )
                           EnableMenuItem( hMenu, IDM_ITEM1,
                                     MFS_ENABLED | MF_BYCOMMAND );
                       else
                           EnableMenuItem( hMenu, IDM_ITEM1,
                                     MFS_GRAYED | MF_BYCOMMAND );
                   }

               .
               .
               .
```

GetMenu

Description	`GetMenu` retrieves the menu handle for a window. Use `GetMenu` prior to modifying or destroying the menu. This function will not return a valid handle for child windows with menus.
Syntax	`HMENU GetMenu( HWND hwnd )`
Parameters	
hwnd	`HWND`: A handle to the window whose menu will be retrieved.
Returns	`HMENU`: If successful, a handle to the menu of the given window. If the window has no menu, then the return value is `NULL`. If the window is a child window, the return value is undefined.
Include File	`winuser.h`
See Also	`GetSubMenu, SetMenu, AppendMenu, InsertMenuItem, GetMenuItemInfo, SetMenuItemInfo`
Example	See the example for the `EnableMenuItem` function.

GetMenuCheckMarkDimensions

Description	Windows uses a default checkmark bitmap to check menu items. This can be replaced with custom bitmaps using the `SetMenuItemBitmaps` function. `GetMenuCheckMarkDimensions` is used to find the size and width of the bitmap to use for custom checkmarks. This function is obsolete now that the `GetSystemMetrics` function can return this information. New applications should use the `GetSystemMetrics` function.
	Custom checkmarks can dress up an application program, with little penalty in memory consumption. As soon as the new bitmap is assigned to the menu item, the `CheckMenuItem` function will automatically use this bitmap when checking or unchecking an item.
Syntax	`LONG GetMenuCheckMarkDimensions( VOID )`
Parameters	This function has no parameters.
Returns	`LONG`: The high-order word contains the height; the low-order word contains the width.
Include File	`winuser.h`
See Also	`SetMenuItemBitmaps, CheckMenuItem, CheckMenuRadioItem`
Example	In this example, shown in Figure 6-4, a bitmap called **"Checkmark"** is used as the checkmark for the `IDM_CHKITEM` menu item. The application does not know in advance the size of the bitmap or the size of the checkmarks in the menu (this depends on the video resolution). The bitmap is sized to fit the dimensions found when the application starts running.

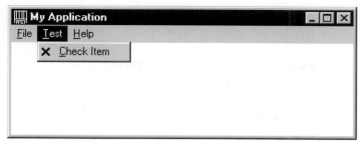

Figure 6-4 GetMenuCheckMarkDimensions example

```
LRESULT CALLBACK WndProc( HWND hWnd, UINT uMsg, WPARAM wParam, LPARAM lParam )
{
static HBITMAP hMemBitmap;

    switch( uMsg )
    {
      case WM_CREATE :
              {
                HDC      hSrcDC, hDstDC;
                BITMAP   bm;
                HBITMAP  hChkBitmap;

                HMENU hMenu      = GetMenu( hWnd );
                LONG  lCheckSize = GetMenuCheckMarkDimensions();
                SHORT nBx        = LOWORD( lCheckSize );
                SHORT nBy        = HIWORD( lCheckSize );
                HDC   hDC        = GetDC( hWnd );

                // Create a memory DC to select the bitmap into.
                //..............................................
                hSrcDC = CreateCompatibleDC( hDC );
                hChkBitmap = LoadBitmap( hInst, "Checkmark" );

                SelectObject( hSrcDC, hChkBitmap );

                GetObject( hChkBitmap, sizeof( BITMAP ), &bm );

                // Create a memory DC to stretch the bitmap into.
                //...............................................
                hDstDC      = CreateCompatibleDC( hDC );
                hMemBitmap = CreateCompatibleBitmap( hDstDC, nBx, nBy );
                SelectObject( hDstDC, hMemBitmap );
```

continued on next page

continued from previous page

```
            StretchBlt( hDstDC, 0, 0, nBx, nBy, hSrcDC, 0, 0,
                        bm.bmWidth, bm.bmHeight, SRCCOPY );

            // Set the bitmap to use for checking to the newly sized
            // bitmap.
            //.......................................................
            SetMenuItemBitmaps( hMenu, IDM_CHKITEM, MF_BYCOMMAND, NULL,
                                hMemBitmap );

            DeleteDC( hSrcDC );
            DeleteDC( hDstDC );
            ReleaseDC( hWnd, hDC );
            DeleteObject( hChkBitmap );
        }
        break;

    case WM_COMMAND :
        switch( LOWORD( wParam ) )
        {
          case IDM_CHKITEM :
                {
                    HMENU hMenu  = GetMenu( hWnd );
                    UINT  uState = GetMenuState( hMenu,
                                                 IDM_CHKITEM,
                                                 MF_BYCOMMAND );

                    if ( uState & MFS_CHECKED )
                        CheckMenuItem( hMenu, IDM_CHKITEM,
                                       MF_BYCOMMAND | MFS_UNCHECKED );
                    else
                        CheckMenuItem( hMenu, IDM_CHKITEM,
                                       MF_BYCOMMAND | MFS_CHECKED );
                }
                break;

          case IDM_EXIT :
                DestroyWindow( hWnd );
                break;

          default :
              return( DefWindowProc( hWnd, uMsg, wParam, lParam ) );
        }
        break;
```

```
    case WM_DESTROY :
          DeleteObject( hMemBitmap );
          PostQuitMessage(0);
          break;

    default :
          return( DefWindowProc( hWnd, uMsg, wParam, lParam ) );
   }

   return( OL );
}
```

GetMenuDefaultItem   ■ WINDOWS 95   ■ WINDOWS NT

Description	GetMenuDefaultItem retrieves the menu identifier of the default menu item for a given menu bar or pop-up menu.
	In the new user interface of Windows NT 4 and Windows 95, each menu bar and pop-up menu can have a default menu item. The default menu item appears visually different from the standard menu items and is selected by double-clicking the mouse on the parent menu item.
Syntax	UINT **GetMenuDefaultItem**(HMENU *hMenu*, UINT *uByPos*, UINT *gmdiFlags*)
Parameters	
hMenu	HMENU: A handle to the menu.
uByPos	UINT: If set to FALSE, the menu item identifier is returned. If set to TRUE, the menu item position is returned.
gmdiFlags	UINT: Specifies how the function searches for the default menu item. This parameter can be set to zero or more of the values listed in Table 6-7.

Table 6-7 GetMenuDefaultItem *gmdiFlags* values

Value	Meaning
GMDI_GOINTOPOPUPS	If the default item is a pop-up item, the function is to search recursively in the corresponding pop-up menu. If the pop-up menu has no default item, the return value identifies the pop-up item. By default, the first default item on the specified menu is returned, regardless of whether it is a pop-up item.
GMDI_USEDISABLED	By default, the function skips disabled or grayed menu items. If this flag is set, these will not be skipped.

Returns	UINT: If successful, the menu identifier or position of the menu item; otherwise, −1 is returned.
Include File	winuser.h

| See Also | SetMenuDefaultItem, GetMenuItemInfo, SetMenuItemInfo |
| Example | See the example for the **SetMenuDefaultItem** function. |

GetMenuItemCount ■ WINDOWS 95 ■ WINDOWS NT

Description	**GetMenuItemCount** determines the number of menu items in a given menu. This includes the top-level heading of any pop-up menus but does not include the pop-up items themselves.
	Use **GetMenuItemCount** to find out how many menu items exist, prior to retrieving data on the menu items, such as their ID numbers, strings, and so on.
Syntax	int **GetMenuItemCount**(HMENU *hmenu*)
Parameters	
hmenu	HMENU: A handle to the menu.
Returns	int: The number of menu items if successful; otherwise, −1 is returned.
Include File	winuser.h
See Also	GetMenu, GetSubMenu
Example	In this example, **GetMenuItemCount** is used to retrieve the number of menu items in the main menu.

```
LRESULT CALLBACK WndProc( HWND hWnd, UINT uMsg, WPARAM wParam, LPARAM lParam )
{
   switch( uMsg )
   {
     case WM_COMMAND :
          switch( LOWORD( wParam ) )
          {
             case IDM_TEST :
                 {
                     HMENU hMenu  = GetMenu( hWnd );
                     char   szMsg[40];

                     wsprintf( szMsg, "There are %d items in the menu.",
                              GetMenuItemCount( hMenu ) );

                     MessageBox( hWnd, szMsg, "Test",
                              MB_OK | MB_ICONINFORMATION );
                 }
                 break;
        .
        .
        .
```

GetMenuItemID

Description	The menu ID values are associated with each item when the menu is defined, either in the resource (RC) file or when the menu items are added during program execution with the **AppendMenu** and **InsertMenuItem** functions. **GetMenuItemID** retrieves the ID for a menu item.
	ID values remain constant, even as other menu items are added and deleted. Retrieving the menu item IDs can be useful in programs that allow the user to add and subtract custom menu items such as macro names.
Syntax	UINT **GetMenuItemID**(HMENU *hmenu,* int *nPos*)
Parameters	
hmenu	HMENU: A handle to the menu bar or pop-up menu that contains the item whose identifier is to be retrieved.
nPos	int: The zero-based relative position of the menu item.
Returns	UINT: The menu item identifier (ID) for the menu item at position *nPos*. If the menu item identifier is **NULL** or if the specified item invokes a pop-up menu, the return value is **0xFFFFFFFF**.
Include File	winuser.h
See Also	GetMenuItemCount, GetMenuString, GetMenuItemInfo, GetMenu, GetSubMenu
Example	In this example, **GetMenuItemID** is used to return the main ID of the second menu item of the main menu.

```
LRESULT CALLBACK WndProc( HWND hWnd, UINT uMsg, WPARAM wParam, LPARAM lParam )
{
   switch( uMsg )
   {
     case WM_COMMAND :
           switch( LOWORD( wParam ) )
           {
             case IDM_TEST :
                  {
                      HMENU hMenu  = GetMenu( hWnd );
                      HMENU hSubMenu = Get SubMenu (hMenu, 0);
                      char  szMsg[40];

                      wsprintf( szMsg, "The menu ID at pos 1 is %d.",
                              GetMenuItemID( hSubMenu, 1 ) );

                      MessageBox( hWnd, szMsg, "Test",
                              MB_OK | MB_ICONINFORMATION );
```

continued on next page

continued from previous page

```
                    }
                break;
```
        .
        .
        .

GetMenuItemInfo   ■ WINDOWS 95   ■ WINDOWS NT

Description	`GetMenuItemInfo` retrieves information about a menu item. Use this function to retrieve all the information about a menu item instead of using the other menu functions to retrieve one attribute at a time.
Syntax	BOOL **GetMenuItemInfo**(HMENU *hMenu,* UINT *uItem,* BOOL *bByPosition,* LPMENUITEMINFO *lpmii*)
Parameters	
hMenu	HMENU: The handle of the menu that contains the menu item.
uItem	UINT: The identifier or position of the menu item to get information about.
bByPosition	BOOL: Set to FALSE if the value in *uItem* is the menu item identifier. Otherwise, *uItem* is the menu item position.
lpmii	LPMENUITEMINFO: A pointer to a MENUITEMINFO structure that receives the information about the specified menu item. See the definition of the MENUITEMINFO structure below.
Returns	BOOL: If successful, the return value is TRUE; otherwise, it is FALSE.
Include File	winuser.h
See Also	SetMenuItemInfo

MENUITEMINFO Definition

```
typedef struct tagMENUITEMINFO
{
    UINT      cbSize;
    UINT      fMask;
    UINT      fType;
    UINT      fState;
    UINT      wID;
    HMENU     hSubMenu;
    HBITMAP   hbmpChecked;
    HBITMAP   hbmpUnchecked;
    DWORD     dwItemData;
    LPTSTR    dwTypeData;
```

```
        UINT    cch;
    } MENUITEMINFO, *LPMENUITEMINFO;
```

Members

cbSize

UINT: The size, in bytes, of the structure. This must be initialized before you use it with a function.

fMask

UINT: One or more of the values listed in Table 6-8, which determine the values in this structure to set or retrieve.

Table 6-8 MENUITEMINFO *fMask* values

Value	Meaning
MIIM_CHECKMARKS	Retrieves or sets the *hbmpChecked* and *hbmpUnchecked* members.
MIIM_DATA	Retrieves or sets the *dwItemData* member.
MIIM_ID	Retrieves or sets the *wID* member.
MIIM_STATE	Retrieves or sets the *fState* member.
MIIM_SUBMENU	Retrieves or sets the *hSubMenu* member.
MIIM_TYPE	Retrieves or sets the *fType* and *dwTypeData* members.

fType

UINT; The menu item type. This can be one or more of the MFT_ values listed in Table 6-2.

fState

UINT: The menu item state. This can be one or more of the MFS_ values listed in Table 6-2.

wID

UINT: The menu item identifier.

hSubMenu

HMENU: A handle to the drop-down menu or submenu associated with the menu item. If the menu item is not an item that opens a drop-down menu or submenu, this member is NULL.

hbmpChecked

HBITMAP: A handle to the bitmap to display next to the item if it is checked. If this member is NULL, a default bitmap is used.

hbmpUnchecked

HBITMAP: A handle to the bitmap to display next to the item if it is not checked. If this member is NULL, no bitmap is used.

dwItemData

DWORD: Application-defined value associated with the menu item.

dwTypeData

LPTSTR: The content of the menu item. The meaning of this member depends on the menu item type.

cch

UINT: The length of the menu item text when information is received about a menu item of the MFT_STRING type. This member is 0 for other menu item types and ignored when this structure is used with the SetMenuItemInfo function.

Example

This example uses the GetMenuItemInfo function to retrieve the menu item text when the Test! menu item is selected. The menu item text is then displayed in a message box.

```
LRESULT CALLBACK WndProc( HWND hWnd, UINT uMsg, WPARAM wParam, LPARAM lParam )
{
    switch( uMsg )
    {
    case WM_COMMAND :
            switch( LOWORD( wParam ) )
            {
                case IDM_TEST :
                    {
                        MENUITEMINFO mii;
                        HMENU        hMenu  = GetMenu( hWnd );
                        char         szText[40];
                        char         szMsg[40];

                        mii.cbSize     = sizeof( MENUITEMINFO );
                        mii.fMask      = MIIM_TYPE;
                        mii.dwTypeData = szText;
                        mii.cch        = sizeof( szText );

                        GetMenuItemInfo( hMenu, LOWORD( wParam ),
                                    FALSE, &mii );

                        wsprintf( szMsg, "The menu text is %s.",
                                szText);

                        MessageBox( hWnd, szMsg, "Test",
                                MB_OK | MB_ICONINFORMATION );
                    }
                    break;
```

.
.
.

GetMenuItemRect   ■ WINDOWS 95   ■ WINDOWS NT

Description	GetMenuItemRect determines the rectangular area that a menu item occupies on the screen.
Syntax	BOOL **GetMenuItemRect**(HWND *hWnd*, HMENU *hMenu*, UINT *uItem*, LPRECT *lprcItem*)
Parameters	
hWnd	HWND: A handle to the window containing the menu bar or pop-up menu.
hMenu	HMENU: A handle to the menu bar or pop-up menu.

uItem	UINT: The zero-based position of the menu item.
lprcItem	LPRECT: A pointer to a RECT structure that receives the bounding rectangle of the specified menu item. If the *hMenu* parameter specifies a menu bar, the function returns window coordinates; otherwise, it returns client coordinates.
Returns	BOOL: If successful, the return value is TRUE; otherwise, it is FALSE.
Include File	winuser.h
See Also	GetMenu, GetSubMenu
Example	In this example, when the user selects the Test! menu item, the rectangle of the Test! menu item is displayed in a message box.

```
LRESULT CALLBACK WndProc( HWND hWnd, UINT uMsg, WPARAM wParam, LPARAM lParam )
{
    switch( uMsg )
    {
        case WM_COMMAND :
            switch( LOWORD( wParam ) )
            {
                case IDM_TEST :
                    {
                        HMENU hMenu  = GetMenu( hWnd );
                        RECT   rect;
                        char   szMsg[40];

                        GetMenuItemRect( hWnd, hMenu, 1, &rect );

                        wsprintf( szMsg,"top=%d, left=%d, bottom=%d, right=%d",
                                rect.top, rect.left,
                                rect.bottom, rect.right );

                        MessageBox( hWnd, szMsg, "The rectangle is:",
                                MB_OK | MB_ICONINFORMATION );
                    }
                    break;
        .
        .
        .
```

GetMenuState   ■ Windows 95   ■ Windows NT

Description	GetMenuState retrieves the state of a menu item or the number of items in a pop-up menu.

You will most often use `GetMenuState` to determine if a menu item is checked, grayed, or disabled.

Syntax   UINT **GetMenuState**(HMENU *hmenu,* UINT *uItem,* UINT *uFlags*)

Parameters

hmenu   HMENU: A handle to the menu.

uItem   UINT: The menu item identifier or position.

uFlags   UINT: Specifies how the *uItem* is to be interpreted, as shown in Table 6-9.

Table 6-9 GetMenuState *uFlags* values

Value	Meaning
MF_BYCOMMAND	The *uItem* value is the menu ID value.
MF_BYPOSITION	The *uItem* value is the zero-based relative position of the menu item.

Returns   UINT: Returns 0xFFFFFFFF on error. If *uItem* identifies a pop-up menu, the high-order byte contains the number of items in the pop-up menu. The low-order byte contains a combination of the flags shown in Table 6-2. The values are combined with the binary OR (|) operator.

Include File   winuser.h

See Also   CheckMenuItem, CheckMenuRadioItem, GetMenuItemInfo

Example   See the example for the `GetMenuCheckMarkDimensions` function.

GetMenuString   ■ WINDOWS 95   ■ WINDOWS NT

Description   `GetMenuString` retrieves the menu item's string, including the ampersand (&) character used to specify the pneumonic character for the menu item, into the given character buffer.

     `GetMenuString` comes in handy in programs that allow the user to add and subtract menu items for user-defined items such as macros.

Syntax   int **GetMenuString**(HMENU *hmenu,* UINT *uItem,* LPTSTR *lpsz,* int *cchMax,* UINT *uFlags*)

Parameters

hmenu   HMENU: A handle to the menu.

uItem   UINT: The menu item identifier or position, as determined by the *uFlags* parameter.

lpsz   LPTSTR: A pointer to a character buffer that will hold the menu item string.

cchMax   int: The maximum number of characters to write to the buffer. Use this parameter to avoid writing beyond the buffer's end.

uFlags	UINT: Specifies how the *uItem* parameter is interpreted. This can be one of the values shown in Table 6-9.
Returns	int: The number of characters retrieved.
Include File	winuser.h
See Also	GetMenuItemID, GetMenuItemCount, GetMenuState, GetMenuItemInfo, GetSubMenu
Example	This example displays the menu item text when the user selects the Test! menu item.

```
LRESULT CALLBACK WndProc( HWND hWnd, UINT uMsg, WPARAM wParam, LPARAM lParam )
{
   switch( uMsg )
   {
     case WM_COMMAND :
          switch( LOWORD( wParam ) )
          {
             case IDM_TEST :
                 {
                     HMENU hMenu  = GetMenu( hWnd );
                     char  szText[41];

                     GetMenuString( hMenu, LOWORD( wParam ), szText, 40,
                              MF_BYCOMMAND );

                     MessageBox( hWnd, szText, "Menu item selected",
                              MB_OK | MB_ICONINFORMATION );
                 }
                 break;
          .
          .
          .
```

GetSubMenu   ■ WINDOWS 95   ■ WINDOWS NT

Description	GetSubMenu retrieves a handle to a pop-up menu. A handle to a pop-up menu can only be found after the handle to the main menu is located, usually with **GetMenu**. When the pop-up menu handle is obtained, all the functions that allow reading and changing menu items can be applied to the pop-up menu.
Syntax	HMENU **GetSubMenu**(HMENU *hmenu,* int *nPos*)
Parameters	
hmenu	HMENU: A handle to the parent menu of the pop-up menu.

nPos	**int**: The zero-based relative position of the menu item in the given menu that activates the pop-up menu.
Returns	**HMENU**: A handle to the pop-up menu. Returns **NULL** if the menu item does not activate a pop-up menu.
Include File	**winuser.h**
See Also	**CreatePopupMenu, GetMenu, GetMenuItemCount, GetMenuItemID, GetMenuState, GetMenuString, AppendMenu, SetMenuItemInfo**
Example	See the example for the **SetMenuDefaultItem** function.

GetSystemMenu ■ WINDOWS 95   ■ WINDOWS NT

Description   **GetSystemMenu** retrieves a handle to the System menu. The System menu is the pop-up menu that is displayed when you click the small icon at the top-left corner of the window. The System menu generates **WM_SYSCOMMAND** messages, not **WM_COMMAND** messages. When a menu item on the System menu is activated, the **WM_SYSCOMMAND** messages have the *wParam* parameter set as shown in Table 6-10.

Table 6-10 WM_SYSCOMMAND *wParam* values

Value	Meaning
SC_ARRANGE	Arranges the minimized window icons.
SC_CLOSE	Closes the window.
SC_CONTEXTHELP	Changes the cursor to a question mark with a pointer. If the user then clicks a control in the dialog box, the control receives a WM_HELP message.
SC_DEFAULT	Selects the default item; the user double-clicked the System menu.
SC_HOTKEY	Activates the window associated with the application-specified hotkey. The low-order word of *lParam* identifies the window to activate.
SC_HSCROLL	Scrolls horizontally.
SC_KEYMENU	Retrieves the System menu as a result of a keystroke.
SC_MAXIMIZE (or SC_ZOOM)	Maximizes the window.
SC_MINIMIZE (or SC_ICON)	Minimizes the window.
SC_MONITORPOWER	Sets the state of the display. This command supports devices that have power-saving features, such as a battery-powered personal computer.
SC_MOUSEMENU	Retrieves the System menu as a result of a mouse click.
SC_MOVE	Moves the window.
SC_NEXTWINDOW	Moves to the next window.
SC_PREVWINDOW	Moves to the previous window.
SC_RESTORE	Restores the window to its normal position and size.
SC_SCREENSAVE	Executes the installed screen saver application.
SC_SEPARATOR	No menu item is selected because the mouse is over a separator.
SC_SIZE	Sizes the window.

SC_TASKLIST	Activates the Windows Task Manager.
SC_VSCROLL	Scrolls vertically.

An application also can modify and add to the System menu using all of the menu modification functions, such as **AppendMenu** and **InsertMenuItem**. If you add menu items, their ID values should be below 0xF000 to avoid overlapping the definitions of the default ID values listed above.

Modifying the System menu is appropriate for small utility programs that may be able to avoid having a menu bar if a few commands are added to the System menu.

Syntax   HMENU **GetSystemMenu**(HWND *hwnd,* BOOL *bRevert*)

Parameters

hwnd   HWND: A handle to the window that contains the System menu.

bRevert   BOOL: If **TRUE**, the function destroys the current System menu and restores the original Windows-defined System menu. If **FALSE**, the function returns a handle to a copy of the current System menu. The copy is initially identical to the System menu, but it can be modified.

Returns   HMENU: If the *bRevert* parameter is **FALSE**, the return value is the handle of a copy of the System menu. If the *bRevert* parameter is **TRUE**, the return value is **NULL**.

Include File winuser.h

See Also   AppendMenu, GetMenu, InsertMenuItem, SetMenuItemInfo

Related Messages WM_SYSCOMMAND, WM_INITMENU

Example   In this example, the menu item Test Item is added to the System menu after the Maximize menu item. A message box is displayed when the new menu item is selected.

```
LRESULT CALLBACK WndProc( HWND hWnd, UINT uMsg, WPARAM wParam, LPARAM lParam )
{
   switch( uMsg )
   {
      case WM_CREATE :
            {
                  MENUITEMINFO   mii;
                  HMENU          hMenu = GetSystemMenu( hWnd, FALSE );

                  mii.cbSize = sizeof( MENUITEMINFO );
                  mii.fMask  = MIIM_ID | MIIM_TYPE;
                  mii.fType  = MFT_STRING;
```

continued on next page

continued from previous page

```
            mii.wID     = IDM_TEST;
            mii.dwTypeData = "&Test Item";

            InsertMenuItem( hMenu, SC_MAXIMIZE, FALSE, &mii );
        }
        break;

    case WM_SYSCOMMAND :
        if ( wParam == IDM_TEST )
        {
            MessageBox( hWnd, "New Item Selected", szAppName,
                        MB_OK | MB_ICONINFORMATION );
            break;
        }

        return( DefWindowProc( hWnd, uMsg, wParam, lParam ) );
    .
    .
    .
```

HiliteMenuItem   ■ WINDOWS 95   ■ WINDOWS NT

Description	Normally, the mouse and default keyboard accelerator key's automatic actions take care of highlighting top-level menu items. If you need to do this directly, you can use **HiliteMenuItem**.
	Use **HiliteMenuItem** to provide additional keyboard alternatives for menu selections.
Syntax	BOOL **HiliteMenuItem**(HWND *hwnd,* HMENU *hmenu,* UINT *uItem,* UINT *uHilite*)
Parameters	
hwnd	HWND: A handle to the window that contains the menu.
hmenu	HMENU: A handle to the menu bar that contains the item to be highlighted.
uItem	UINT: The menu item identifier to highlight. Only top-level menu items can be highlighted.
uHilite	UINT: Controls the interpretation of the *uItem* parameter and indicates whether the menu item is highlighted. Combine two of the values in Table 6-11 with the binary OR (	) operator.

Table 6-11 `HiliteMenuItem` *uHilite* values

Value	Meaning
MF_BYCOMMAND	The value in *uItem* is the identifier of the menu item.
MF_BYPOSITION	The value in *uItem* is the zero-based relative position of the menu item.
MF_HILITE	Highlights the menu item.
MF_UNHILITE	The menu item is not highlighted.

Returns	BOOL: TRUE if successful; otherwise, the return value is FALSE.
Include File	winuser.h
See Also	CheckMenuItem, EnableMenuItem, SetMenuItemInfo
Example	See the example for the MenuItemFromPoint function.

InsertMenuItem   ■ WINDOWS 95   ■ WINDOWS NT

Description	InsertMenuItem adds a new menu item into any location within the given menu. This function is more useful than AppendMenu, which only adds items to the end of the menu.
Syntax	BOOL **InsertMenuItem**(HMENU *hMenu,* UINT *uItem,* BOOL bByPosition, LPMENUITEMINFO lpmii)
Parameters	
hMenu	HMENU: A handle to the menu being changed.
uItem	UINT: The menu item identifier or position in front of which the new item will be inserted. Depending on the value of *bByPosition*, this parameter is either the menu identifier or the menu position.
bByPosition	BOOL: Set to FALSE if *uItem* specifies the menu item identifier; otherwise, set to TRUE to specify the menu item position.
lpmii	LPMENUITEMINFO: A pointer to a MENUITEMINFO structure that contains information about the new menu item. See the definition of the MENUITEM-INFO structure under the GetMenuItemInfo function.
Returns	BOOL: TRUE if the menu item was added; otherwise, the return value is FALSE.
Include File	winuser.h
See Also	GetMenuItemInfo, AppendMenu, SetMenuItemInfo, GetMenu, DrawMenuBar, CreateMenu, DeleteMenu, RemoveMenu
Example	See the example for the GetSystemMenu function.

IsMenu   ■ WINDOWS 95   ■ WINDOWS NT

Description	Use **IsMenu** to check whether a handle is a valid handle for a menu.
Syntax	BOOL **IsMenu**(HMENU *hMenu*)
Parameters	
hMenu	HMENU: The handle to be tested.
Returns	BOOL: TRUE if *hMenu* is a menu handle; otherwise, the return value is FALSE.
Include File	winuser.h
See Also	GetMenu, GetSubMenu, IsWindow
Example	In this example, **IsMenu** is used to determine whether a menu item is really a submenu.

```
LRESULT CALLBACK WndProc( HWND hWnd, UINT uMsg, WPARAM wParam, LPARAM lParam )
{
    switch( uMsg )
    {
        case WM_COMMAND :
            switch( LOWORD( wParam ) )
            {
                case IDM_TEST :
                    {
                        HMENU hMenu    = GetMenu( hWnd );
                        HMENU hSubMenu = GetSubMenu( hMenu, 1 );

                        if ( IsMenu( hSubMenu ) )
                            MessageBox( hWnd, "Item at position 1 is a menu.",
                                        szAppName, MB_OK );
                        else
                            MessageBox( hWnd, "Position 1 is not a menu.",
                                        szAppName, MB_OK );
                    }
                    break;
                    .
                    .
                    .
```

LoadAccelerators   ■ WINDOWS 95   ■ WINDOWS NT

Description	The accelerator key combinations are defined in the resource (RC) file. Before they can be used, the application must use the **LoadAccelerators**

function to retrieve a handle to the accelerator table. This handle is used in the **TranslateAccelerator** function to decode incoming keystrokes that may be in the accelerator table. Like menu items, accelerators generate **WM_COMMAND** messages where the *wParam* value is set to the accelerator ID value. In most cases, this will be the same ID value as a menu item, allowing the accelerator to duplicate the action of a menu command.

Accelerators are used for keystroke shortcuts to common functions that might otherwise require several mouse actions. Accelerators can be used to generate command messages that do not have menu equivalents.

Syntax

HACCEL **LoadAccelerators**(HINSTANCE *hinst,* LPCTSTR *lpTableName*)

Parameters

hinst

HINSTANCE: The instance handle for the module containing the accelerator definitions in the resource data.

lpTableName

LPCTSTR: A pointer to a null-terminated string that names the accelerator table to load. Alternatively, this parameter can specify the resource identifier with the **MAKEINTRESOURCE** macro.

Returns

HACCEL: Returns the handle of the accelerator table if the function was successful; otherwise, the return value is **NULL**. Multiple calls to **LoadAccelerators** continue to return the handle to the accelerator table without reloading the data.

Include File

winuser.h

See Also

TranslateAccelerator, CopyAcceleratorTable, CreateAcceleratorTable, DestroyAcceleratorTable

Related Messages

WM_COMMAND

Example

This code segment shows a typical message loop in the **WinMain** function with accelerators. The **LoadAccelerators** function can be used to load the accelerator table from the application's resource (RC) file.

```
hAccel = LoadAccelerators( hInst, szAppName );

while( GetMessage( &msg, NULL, 0, 0) )
{
    if ( !hAccel || !TranslateAccelerator( hWnd, hAccel, &msg ) )
    {
        TranslateMessage( &msg );
        DispatchMessage( &msg );
    }
}
```

LoadMenu ■ WINDOWS 95 ■ WINDOWS NT

Description	LoadMenu loads a menu from the application's resource file and returns a handle to the menu. Use LoadMenu in the WinMain function to load the program's main menu. Use LoadMenu in the body of a program to load new menus while the program operates.
Syntax	HMENU **LoadMenu**(HINSTANCE *hinst,* LPCTSTR *lpMenuName*)
Parameters	
hinst	HINSTANCE: The instance handle for the module containing the menu definitions in the resource data.
lpMenuName	LPCTSTR: A pointer to a null-terminated string that names the menu to load. Alternatively, this parameter can specify the resource identifier with the MAKEINTRESOURCE macro.
Returns	HMENU: A handle to the menu; NULL if no menu was found.
Include File	winuser.h
See Also	DestroyMenu, LoadMenuIndirect, SetMenu
Example	In this example, the application toggles the main menu between "OLD-MENU" and "NEWMENU". When the New Menu! menu option is selected, the "NEWMENU" is loaded from the resource (RC) file and set as the main menu. When the Old Menu! menu option is selected from the new menu, the original menu is loaded and set back as the main menu.

Menu definition in resource (.RC) file

```
OLDMENU MENU DISCARDABLE
BEGIN
    POPUP "&File"
    BEGIN
        MENUITEM "E&xit",      IDM_EXIT
    END
    MENUITEM "&New Menu!"      IDM_NEW
END


NEWMENU MENU DISCARDABLE
BEGIN
    POPUP "&File"
    BEGIN
        MENUITEM "E&xit",      IDM_EXIT
    END
    MENUITEM "&Old Menu!",     IDM_OLD
END
```

WndProc function

```
LRESULT CALLBACK WndProc( HWND hWnd, UINT uMsg, WPARAM wParam, LPARAM lParam )
{
static HMENU hMenu = NULL;

    switch( uMsg )
    {
        case WM_COMMAND :
            switch( LOWORD( wParam ) )
            {
                case IDM_OLD
                case IDM_NEW :
                    {
                        HMENU hNewMenu;

                        if ( LOWORD( wParam ) == IDM_NEW )
                            hNewMenu = LoadMenu( hInst, "NEWMENU" );
                        else
                            hNewMenu = LoadMenu( hInst, "OLDMENU" );

                        SetMenu( hWnd, hNewMenu );

                        if ( IsMenu( hMenu ) )
                            DestroyMenu( hMenu );

                        hMenu = hNewMenu;
                        DrawMenuBar( hWnd );
                    }
                    break;

            .
            .
            .
```

LoadMenuIndirect   ■ WINDOWS 95   ■ WINDOWS NT

Description   LoadMenuIndirect reads a menu definition in a memory block and
returns a handle to the menu created. The menu then can be attached to a
window with SetMenu. This function is used internally by Windows but
can be called directly.

LoadMenuIndirect provides an alternative to the normal menu creation
and modification functions.

Syntax	HMENU **LoadMenuIndirect**(CONST MENUTEMPLATE* *lpMenuTemplate*)
Parameters	

lpMenuTemplate   CONST MENUTEMPLATE*: A pointer to a memory block containing the menu definition. A menu template consists of a **MENUITEMTEMPLATEHEADER** structure followed by one or more contiguous **MENUITEMTEMPLATE** structures. An extended menu template consists of a **MENUEX_TEMPLATE_HEADER** structure followed by one or more contiguous **MENUEX_TEMPLATE_ITEM** structures. See the definition of the **MENUITEMTEMPLATEHEADER** and **MENU‑ITEMTEMPLATE** structures below.

Returns   HMENU: If successful, the return value is the handle of the menu; otherwise, it is **NULL**.

Include File   `winuser.h`

See Also   LoadMenu, SetMenuItemInfo, AppendMenu, DrawMenuBar

MENUITEMTEMPLATEHEADER Definition

```
typedef struct
{
    WORD versionNumber;
    WORD offset;
}MENUITEMTEMPLATEHEADER;
```

Members

versionNumber   WORD: This should be set to 0.

offset   WORD: The number of bytes from the end of the header to the first **MENU‑ITEMTEMPLATE** data. This is normally 0, assuming that the menu item data follows immediately in memory. Each menu item is defined in a **MENU‑ITEMTEMPLATE** data structure. If the **mtOption** specifies the **MF_POPUP** type, **mtID** is omitted.

MENUITEMTEMPLATE Definition

```
typedef struct
{
    WORD mtOption;
    WORD mtID;
    WCHAR mtString[1];
}MENUITEMTEMPLATE;
```

Members

mtOption   WORD: This is the same as the *uFlags* parameter for the **AppendMenu** function and can be set to the values in Table 6-2 and to **MF_END** (to specify the end of a pop-up or static menu).

mtID	WORD: The menu item identifier.
mtString	WCHAR[1]: The first character of the menu item string. The remaining characters follow immediately after *mtString* with a null-terminator at the end.
Example	This example creates a new menu, as shown in Figure 6-5, when the **WM_CREATE** message is processed. The menu is defined in a global memory block. The **AppendMemory** function at the bottom of the listing is used to simplify dealing with the variable-length fields used to define menus. It adds consecutive chunks of data to the end of a memory block and converts strings into wide-character (Unicode) format.

Header file

```
#define IDM_FIRST   300
#define IDM_SECOND  301

#define MAXMENUNAMES 100

VOID AppendMemory( LPTSTR lpDest, LPTSTR lpSource, int nBytes,
                   BOOL bReset, BOOL bConvert );
```

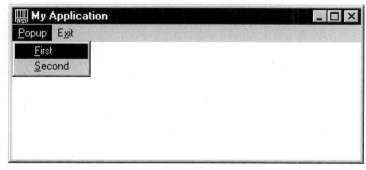

Figure 6-5 LoadMenuIndirect example

WndProc and AppendMemory functions

```
LRESULT CALLBACK WndProc( HWND hWnd, UINT uMsg, WPARAM wParam, LPARAM lParam )
{
   switch( uMsg )
   {
      case WM_CREATE :
               {
                  LPTSTR   lpMem;
                  WORD     wValue;
                  HMENU    hMenu;

                  lpMem = HeapAlloc( GetProcessHeap(), HEAP_ZERO_MEMORY,
                                     sizeof( MENUITEMTEMPLATEHEADER ) +
                                     (6*sizeof( MENUITEMTEMPLATE )) +
                                     MAXMENUNAMES );

                  // Set values for MENUITEMTEMPLATEHEADER structure.
                  //.................................................
                  wValue = 0;
                  AppendMemory( lpMem, (LPTSTR)&wValue, sizeof( WORD ),
                              TRUE, FALSE );
                  wValue = 0;
                  AppendMemory( lpMem, (LPTSTR)&wValue, sizeof( WORD ),
                              FALSE, FALSE );

                  // Add Popup menu and items.
                  //..........................
                  wValue = MF_POPUP;
                  AppendMemory( lpMem, (LPTSTR)&wValue, sizeof( WORD ),
                              FALSE, FALSE );
                  AppendMemory( lpMem, "&Popup", 7, FALSE, TRUE );

                  wValue = 0;
                  AppendMemory( lpMem, (LPTSTR)&wValue, sizeof( WORD ),
                                 FALSE, FALSE );
                  wValue = IDM_FIRST;
                  AppendMemory( lpMem, (LPTSTR)&wValue, sizeof( WORD ),
                                 FALSE, FALSE );
                  AppendMemory( lpMem, "&First", 7, FALSE, TRUE );

                  wValue = MF_END;  // Last Item in Popup menu.
                  AppendMemory( lpMem, (LPTSTR)&wValue, sizeof( WORD ),
                                 FALSE, FALSE );
```

```
                wValue = IDM_SECOND;
                AppendMemory( lpMem, (LPTSTR)&wValue, sizeof( WORD ),
                                    FALSE, FALSE );
                AppendMemory( lpMem, "&Second", 8, FALSE, TRUE );

                // Add last item on menu bar, Exit.
                //................................
                wValue = MF_END;
                AppendMemory( lpMem, (LPTSTR)&wValue, sizeof( WORD ),
                                    FALSE, FALSE );
                wValue = IDM_EXIT;
                AppendMemory( lpMem, (LPTSTR)&wValue, sizeof( WORD ),
                                    FALSE, FALSE );
                AppendMemory( lpMem, "E&xit", 6, FALSE, TRUE );

                // Create the menu and set it as the application's menu.
                //.....................................................
                hMenu = LoadMenuIndirect( lpMem );
                SetMenu( hWnd, hMenu );

                HeapFree( GetProcessHeap(), 0, lpMem );
            }
            break;

    case WM_COMMAND :
            switch( LOWORD( wParam ) )
            {
                case IDM_FIRST :
                        MessageBox( hWnd, "First Menu Item Worked.",
                                    "Message", MB_OK | MB_ICONINFORMATION );
                        break;

                case IDM_SECOND :
                        MessageBox( hWnd, "Second Menu Item Worked.",
                                    "Message", MB_OK | MB_ICONINFORMATION );
                        break;
                .
                .
                .


VOID AppendMemory( LPTSTR lpDest, LPTSTR lpSource, int nBytes, BOOL bReset,
            BOOL bConvert )
{
```

continued on next page

continued from previous page

```
static int    nLastEnd;
static WCHAR wBuf[30];

   LPTSTR lps, lpd;

   lps = lpSource;
   lpd = lpDest;

   if ( bReset )
      nLastEnd = 0;
   else
      lpd += nLastEnd;

   // If this is a character string, we need to convert it to Unicode(TM).
   // This is true for both Windows NT and Windows 95.
   //................................................................
   if ( bConvert )
   {
      MultiByteToWideChar( CP_ACP, MB_PRECOMPOSED, lpSource, -1, &wBuf[0], 30 );

      memcpy( lpd, &wBuf[0], nBytes*sizeof( WCHAR ) );
      nLastEnd += nBytes*sizeof( WCHAR );
   }
   else
   {
      memcpy( lpd, lps, nBytes );
      nLastEnd += nBytes;
   }
}
```

MenuItemFromPoint ■ Windows 95 ■ Windows NT

Description	**MenuItemFromPoint** determines which menu item, if any, is at a given point on the screen. **MenuItemFromPoint** can be useful in custom and pop-up floating menus.
Syntax	UINT **MenuItemFromPoint**(HWND *hWnd,* HMENU *hMenu,* POINT *ptScreen*)
Parameters	
hWnd	HWND: A handle to the window containing the menu bar or pop-up menu.
hMenu	HMENU: A handle to the menu you wish to perform a hit test against.

ptScreen	POINT: The location to test. If the *hMenu* parameter specifies a menu bar, this parameter is in window coordinates; otherwise, it is in client coordinates.
Returns	UINT: The zero-based position of the menu item at the specified location, or −1 if no menu item is at the given location.
Include File	winuser.h
Example	This example shows how you can use the **MenuItemFromPoint** function to find which menu item the mouse cursor lies over. The **HiLiteMenuItem** function is used to show the current item for visual purposes. When the Test! menu option is selected, the mouse is captured and all mouse messages are routed through the application's **WndProc** function. The **WM_MOUSEMOVE** message is handled to find which menu item the mouse is moving over.

```
LRESULT CALLBACK WndProc( HWND hWnd, UINT uMsg, WPARAM wParam, LPARAM lParam )
{
static UINT nLastPos = (UINT)-1;


   switch( uMsg )
   {
      case WM_MOUSEMOVE :
            {
               HMENU hMenu = GetMenu( hWnd );
               POINT pt;
               UINT  nPos;

               // Get the mouse position. This has to be signed
               // because the coordinates are relative to the window
               // client area.
               //.................................................
               pt.x = (SHORT)LOWORD( lParam );
               pt.y = (SHORT)HIWORD( lParam );

               // Convert the coordinates to be relative to the screen.
               //.....................................................
               ClientToScreen( hWnd, &pt );

               // Find out if the mouse is over a menu item.
               //.........................................
               nPos = MenuItemFromPoint( hWnd, hMenu, pt );

               // Check if the position has changed.
               //.................................
```

continued on next page

continued from previous page

```
            if ( nPos != nLastPos )
            {
                // Unhighlight the last item.
                //...........................
                if ( (int)nLastPos > -1 )
                    HiliteMenuItem( hWnd, hMenu, nLastPos,
                                    MF_BYPOSITION | MFS_UNHILITE );

                // Highlight the new item.
                //.......................
                if ( (int)nPos > -1 )
                    HiliteMenuItem( hWnd, hMenu, nPos,
                                    MF_BYPOSITION | MFS_HILITE );

                DrawMenuBar( hWnd );
            }

            nLastPos = nPos;
        }
        return( DefWindowProc( hWnd, uMsg, wParam, lParam ) );

    case WM_COMMAND :
        switch( LOWORD( wParam ) )
        {
          case IDM_TEST :
                SetCapture( hWnd );
                break;

          case IDM_EXIT :
                DestroyWindow( hWnd );
                break;

          default :
              return( DefWindowProc( hWnd, uMsg, wParam, lParam ) );
        }
        break;

    case WM_DESTROY :
        ReleaseCapture();
        PostQuitMessage(0);
        break;
```

```
        default :
                return( DefWindowProc( hWnd, uMsg, wParam, lParam ) );
    }

    return( OL );
}
```

RemoveMenu

Description

RemoveMenu removes a menu item from the given menu. Any pop-up menus are removed but are not destroyed. Pop-ups freed in this way can be reused. Be sure that all menus are either attached to the application's main menu or destroyed with **DestroyMenu** before the application terminates.

Using **RemoveMenu** is considerably simpler in these situations than using **DeleteMenu**, because **RemoveMenu** allows the pop-up menu to be reattached rather than rebuilt from scratch. Call **GetSubMenu** to obtain the pop-up menu handle before using **RemoveMenu**.

Syntax

BOOL **RemoveMenu**(HMENU *hmenu,* UINT *uItem,* UINT *uFlags*)

Parameters

hmenu   HMENU: A handle to the menu to be changed.

uItem   UINT: The menu item identifier or position to be removed.

uFlags   UINT: Specifies how the *uItem* parameter is interpreted. This parameter must be one of the values in Table 6-12.

Table 6-12 RemoveMenu *uFlags* values

Value	Meaning
MF_BYCOMMAND	The *uItem* value is the menu ID value.
MF_BYPOSITION	The *uItem* value is the zero-based relative position of the menu item.

Returns   BOOL: TRUE if successful; otherwise, the return value is FALSE.

Include File   winuser.h

See Also   CreatePopupMenu, DeleteMenu, DrawMenuBar, GetSubMenu, InsertMenuItem, SetMenuItemInfo

Example   The following procedure uses **RemoveMenu** to modify a menu.

```
LRESULT CALLBACK WndProc( HWND hWnd, UINT uMsg, WPARAM wParam, LPARAM lParam )
{
   switch( uMsg )
   {
      case WM_COMMAND :
            switch( LOWORD( wParam ) )
            {
                case IDM_TEST :
                        {
                           HMENU hMenu = GetMenu( hWnd );

                           if ( RemoveMenu( hMenu, IDM_TEST, MF_BYCOMMAND ) )
                           {
                               DrawMenuBar( hWnd );
                               MessageBox( hWnd, "Menu item removed!", szAppName,
                                          MB_OK | MB_ICONINFORMATION );
                           }
                        }
                        break;
```

.
.
.

SetMenu   ■ WINDOWS 95   ■ WINDOWS NT

Description	**SetMenu** attaches a menu to a window. The menu attached can either be defined in a resource (RC) file or created within the application with the **CreateMenu** or **LoadMenuIndirect** function. Any existing menu is removed.
	Use **SetMenu** to change to a new menu, or to remove a menu from the window.
Syntax	BOOL **SetMenu**(HWND *hwnd,* HMENU *hmenu*)
Parameters	
hwnd	HWND: A handle to the window whose menu will be changed.
hmenu	HMENU: A handle to the menu to add. Use **LoadMenu** to retrieve the handle to a menu defined in the resource (RC) file. Set to **NULL** to remove the menu from the window without replacing it.
Returns	BOOL: **TRUE** if the menu has been changed; otherwise, the return value is **FALSE**.
Include File	winuser.h

See Also   CreateMenu, DestroyMenu, DrawMenuBar, GetMenu, LoadMenu, LoadMenuIndirect

Example   See the example for the **LoadMenu** function.

SetMenuDefaultItem   ■ WINDOWS 95   ■ WINDOWS NT

Description   **SetMenuDefaultItem** makes a menu item the default option for the given menu. Each menu bar and pop-up menu can have a default menu option. The default menu option appears different from the other menu options, so the user can visually determine the default option. The default menu item is selected by double-clicking the mouse on the parent menu item.

Syntax   BOOL **SetMenuDefaultItem**(HMENU *hmenu,* UINT *uItem,* UINT *uByPos*)

Parameters

hmenu   HMENU: A handle to the menu containing the menu item.

uItem   UINT: The menu identifier or position of the menu item to set as the default item. Set to **–1** for no default item.

uByPos   UINT: Specifies the meaning of the *uItem* parameter. If this parameter is **FALSE**, *uItem* is a menu item identifier; otherwise, it is a menu item position.

Returns   BOOL: **TRUE** if successful; otherwise, the return value is **FALSE**.

Include File   winuser.h

See Also   GetMenuDefaultItem, GetMenu, GetSubMenu

Example   This example, shown in Figure 6-6, demonstrates how the default menu item can be set and retrieved using the **SetMenuDefaultItem** and **GetMenuDefaultItem** functions. The item in the drop-down menu becomes the default menu item when selected, unless it already was the default, in which case, the default status is turned off.

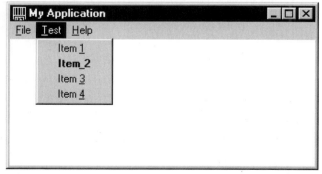

Figure 6-6 SetMenuDefaultItem example

```
LRESULT CALLBACK WndProc( HWND hWnd, UINT uMsg, WPARAM wParam, LPARAM lParam )
{
   switch( uMsg )
   {
     case WM_COMMAND :
          switch( LOWORD( wParam ) )
          {
            case IDM_ITEM1 :
            case IDM_ITEM2 :
            case IDM_ITEM3 :
            case IDM_ITEM4 :
                 {
                     HMENU hMenu  = GetMenu( hWnd );
                     HMENU hSubMenu = GetSubMenu( hMenu, 1 );

                     if ( GetMenuDefaultItem( hSubMenu, FALSE, 0 ) ==
                          LOWORD( wParam ) )
                     {
                        SetMenuDefaultItem( hSubMenu, (UINT)-1, TRUE );
                     }
                     else
                        SetMenuDefaultItem( hSubMenu,LOWORD(wParam),FALSE );
                 }
                 break;
            .
            .
            .
```

SetMenuItemBitmaps   ■ WINDOWS 95   ■ WINDOWS NT

Description

Windows uses a default checkmark bitmap for checking menu items. This can be replaced with custom bitmaps using the **SetMenuItemBitmaps** function. The size of the checkmark bitmaps depends on the video resolution of the system the application is running on. Use the **GetSystemMetrics** function to find this size for scaling the bitmap to fit.

Custom checkmarks can dress up an application program, with little penalty in memory consumption. When the new bitmap is assigned to the menu item, the **CheckMenuItem** function automatically uses this bitmap when checking or unchecking the item.

Syntax

BOOL **SetMenuItemBitmaps**(HMENU *hmenu,* UINT *uItem,* UINT *uFlags,* HBITMAP *hbmUnchecked,* HBITMAP *hbmChecked*)

Parameters

hmenu	HMENU: A handle to the menu.
uItem	UINT: The menu item identifier or position to be removed.
uFlags	UINT: Specifies how the *uItem* parameter is interpreted. This parameter must be one of the values given in Table 6-13.

Table 6-13 SetMenuItemBitmaps *uFlags* values

Value	Meaning
MF_BYCOMMAND	The *uItem* value is the menu ID value.
MF_BYPOSITION	The *uItem* value is the zero-based relative position of the menu item.

hbmUnchecked	HBITMAP: A handle to the bitmap to display when the menu item is not checked. If NULL, the checkmark area is left blank when not checked.
hbmChecked	HBITMAP: A handle to the bitmap to display when the menu item is checked. This can be NULL, but that is not recommended.
Returns	BOOL: If the function succeeds, the return value is TRUE; otherwise, it is FALSE.
Include File	winuser.h
See Also	CheckMenuItem, CheckMenuRadioItem, GetMenu, GetMenuCheckMarkDimensions
Example	See the example for the GetMenuCheckMarkDimensions function.

SetMenuItemInfo
■ Windows 95 ■ Windows NT

Description	SetMenuItemInfo changes information about a menu item. Use this function to change the menu item text or other attributes of a menu item.
Syntax	BOOL **SetMenuItemInfo**(HMENU *hMenu,* UINT *uItem,* BOOL *bByPosition,* LPMENUITEMINFO *lpmii*)

Parameters

hMenu	HMENU: A handle to the menu that contains the item to modify.
uItem	UINT: The menu item identifier or position of the menu item to modify. The meaning of this member depends on the value of the *bByPosition* parameter.
bByPosition	BOOL: Set to FALSE if *uItem* contains a menu item identifier.
lpmii	LPMENUITEMINFO: A pointer to a MENUITEMINFO structure that defines the new information for the identified menu item. See the definition of the MENUITEMINFO structure under the GetMenuItemInfo function.

Returns	BOOL: TRUE if the menu has been changed; otherwise, FALSE.
Include File	winuser.h
See Also	GetMenuItemInfo
Example	This example shows how a menu option can be changed using the SetMenuItemInfo function. The menu item Test! is changed to New Item! when it is selected. The identifier of the menu item is also changed, and when selected, displays a message box.

```
LRESULT CALLBACK WndProc( HWND hWnd, UINT uMsg, WPARAM wParam, LPARAM lParam )
{
    switch( uMsg )
    {
        case WM_COMMAND :
            switch( LOWORD( wParam ) )
            {
                case IDM_TEST :
                    {
                        MENUITEMINFO mii;
                        HMENU        hMenu = GetMenu( hWnd );

                        mii.cbSize = sizeof( MENUITEMINFO );
                        mii.fMask  = MIIM_TYPE | MIIM_ID;
                        mii.wID    = IDM_NEWITEM;
                        mii.fType  = MFT_STRING;
                        mii.dwTypeData = "&New Item!";

                        SetMenuItemInfo( hMenu, IDM_TEST, FALSE, &mii );

                        DrawMenuBar( hWnd );
                    }
                    break;


                case IDM_NEWITEM :
                    MessageBox( hWnd, "New Item Selected!", szAppName,
                                MB_OK | MB_ICONINFORMATION );
                    break;
                    .
                    .
                    .
```

TrackPopupMenu ■ WINDOWS 95 ■ WINDOWS NT

Description TrackPopupMenu displays a submenu anywhere on the screen. The pop-up menu is displayed with its upper-left corner at *x, y* on the screen. Screen coordinates are used, so the menu can be out of the application's client area. Normal Windows menu item selection and WM_COMMAND messages occur for the pop-up menu. The pop-up disappears after a selection is made or after another screen area is clicked. This is a very common feature in Windows 95 applications as well as the operating system when the right mouse button is pressed.

Use TrackPopupMenu to display "context sensitive" menus in an application when the user presses the right mouse button over an application window. The menu can be displayed with the left mouse button, but this is not the Windows 95 standard and should not be done. See the style guide in Chapter 1, Windows 95/NT 4 Programming, for more information.

Syntax BOOL **TrackPopupMenu**(HMENU *hmenu*, UINT *uFlags*, int *x*, int *y*, int *nReserved*, HWND *hwnd*, LPCRECT *lprc*)

Parameters

hmenu HMENU: A handle to the pop-up menu to be displayed. The pop-up menu can be created with the **CreatePopupMenu** function, or by calling **GetSubMenu** to retrieve the handle of a pop-up menu associated with an existing menu item.

uFlags UINT: Specifies positioning and other options for the pop-up menu. This parameter can be zero or more of the values listed in Table 6-14.

Table 6-14 TrackPopupMenu *uFlags* values

Value	Meaning
TPM_BOTTOMALIGN	Aligns the bottom of the menu with the coordinate specified by the *y* parameter.
TPM_CENTERALIGN	Centers the menu horizontally around the coordinate specified by the *x* parameter.
TPM_LEFTALIGN	Aligns the left side of the menu with the coordinate specified by the *x* parameter. This is the default horizontal alignment.
TPM_LEFTBUTTON	Tracks the left mouse button. This is the default tracking option.
TPM_RETURNCMD	Returns the identifier of the selected menu item instead of sending a WM_COMMAND message. The return value is 0 if an error occurs or no menu item is selected; it is −1 if an error occurs in the validation layer. Do not use 0 or −1 as menu item identifiers.
TPM_RIGHTALIGN	Aligns the right side of the menu with the coordinate specified by the *x* parameter.
TPM_RIGHTBUTTON	Tracks the right mouse button.
TPM_TOPALIGN	Aligns the top of the menu with the coordinate specified by the *y* parameter. This is the default vertical alignment.
TPM_VCENTERALIGN	Centers the menu vertically around the coordinate specified by the *y* parameter.

x	**int**: The horizontal location of the pop-up menu, in screen coordinates.
y	**int**: The vertical location of the pop-up menu, in screen coordinates.
nReserved	**int**: Reserved; must be **0**.
hwnd	**HWND**: A handle to the window that owns the pop-up menu. This window receives all messages from the menu. The **WM_COMMAND** message is not sent until the function returns.
lprc	**LPCRECT**: A pointer to a **RECT** structure that specifies the portion of the screen in which the user can select without dismissing the pop-up menu. If **NULL**, the pop-up menu is dismissed if the user clicks outside the pop-up menu.

Returns   **BOOL**: If successful, the return value is **TRUE**; otherwise, it is **FALSE**.

Include File   **winuser.h**

See Also   **AppendMenu**, **CreatePopupMenu**, **GetSubMenu**

Related Messages   **WM_COMMAND**

Example   This example shows how to create a floating pop-up menu using the **CreatePopupMenu** and **TrackPopupMenu** functions. When the right mouse button is pressed over the client area of the application, a pop-up menu is created and then displayed at the coordinates of the mouse cursor. The **ClientToScreen** function converts the coordinates given with the **WM_RBUTTONDOWN** message to screen coordinates. Figure 6-7 shows what the floating pop-up menu looks like.

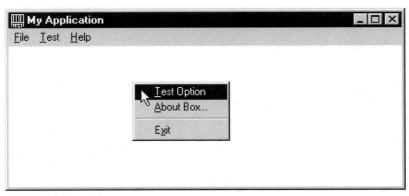

Figure 6-7 **TrackPopupMenu** example

```
LRESULT CALLBACK WndProc( HWND hWnd, UINT uMsg, WPARAM wParam, LPARAM lParam )
{
    switch( uMsg )
    {
    case WM_CONTEXTMENU :
            {
                HMENU hMenu = CreatePopupMenu();

                AppendMenu( hMenu, MFT_STRING, IDM_TEST, "&Test Option" );
                AppendMenu( hMenu, MFT_STRING, IDM_ABOUT, "&About Box..." );
                AppendMenu( hMenu, MFT_SEPARATOR, 0, NULL );
                AppendMenu( hMenu, MFT_STRING, IDM_EXIT, "E&xit" );

                TrackPopupMenu( hMenu, TPM_RIGHTBUTTON |
                                       TPM_TOPALIGN |
                                       TPM_LEFTALIGN,
                                       LOWORD( lParam ),
                                       HIWORD( lParam ), 0, hWnd, NULL );
                DestroyMenu( hMenu );
            }
            break;


    case WM_COMMAND :
            switch( LOWORD( wParam ) )
            {
              case IDM_ABOUT :
                      MessageBox( hWnd, "About Box... Selected",
                                        szAppName, MB_OK );
                      break;

              case IDM_TEST :
                      MessageBox( hWnd, "Test Option selected",
                                        szAppName, MB_OK );
                      break;
              .
              .
              .
```

TrackPopupMenuEx ■ WINDOWS 95 ■ WINDOWS NT

Description	`TrackPopupMenuEx` is similar to `TrackPopupMenu`, except the application can specify a rectangular area of the screen that the menu will not overlap. This function is useful when the application does not want something important to be obscured.
Syntax	BOOL **TrackPopupMenuEx**(HMENU *hmenu,* UINT *uFlags,* int *x,* int *y,* HWND *hwnd,* LPTPMPARAMS *lptpm*)
Parameters	
hmenu	HMENU: A handle to the pop-up menu to be displayed. The pop-up menu can be created with the `CreatePopupMenu` function or by calling `GetSubMenu` to retrieve the handle of a pop-up menu associated with an existing menu item.
uFlags	UINT: Specifies positioning and other options. This parameter can be zero or more of the flags listed in Table 6-14 with the `TrackPopupMenu` function, and may also include one of the values listed in Table 6-15.

Table 6-15 `TrackPopupMenuEx` extended *uFlags* values

Value	Meaning
TPM_HORIZONTAL	If the menu cannot be shown at the specified location without overlapping the excluded rectangle, the requested horizontal alignment is favored over the vertical alignment.
TPM_VERTICAL	If the menu cannot be shown at the specified location without overlapping the excluded rectangle, the requested vertical alignment is favored over the requested horizontal alignment.

x	int: The horizontal location of the pop-up menu, in screen coordinates.
y	int: The vertical location of the pop-up menu, in screen coordinates.
hwnd	HWND: A handle to the window that owns the pop-up menu. This window receives all messages from the menu. The WM_COMMAND message is not sent until the function returns.
lptpm	LPTPMPARAMS: A pointer to a TPMPARAMS structure that specifies an area of the screen that the menu should not overlap. This parameter can be NULL. See the definition of the TPMPARAMS structure below.
Returns	BOOL: If successful, the return value is TRUE; otherwise, it is FALSE.
Include File	winuser.h
See Also	TrackPopupMenu, GetMenu, GetSubMenu, CreatePopupMenu
Related Messages	WM_COMMAND
TPMPARAMS Definition	

```
typedef struct tagTPMPARAMS
{
```

```
                  UINT cbSize;
                  RECT rcExclude;
              } TPMPARAMS, *LPTPMPARAMS;
```

Members

cbSize   UINT: The size, in bytes, of the structure.

rcExclude   RECT: A rectangle to exclude when positioning the window, in screen coor-
                    dinates.

Example   This example is the same as the previous one, except that the pop-up
                    menu won't overlap the child window. The coordinates of the child win-
                    dow are retrieved and passed to the **TrackPopupMenuEx** function.

```
LRESULT CALLBACK WndProc( HWND hWnd, UINT uMsg, WPARAM wParam, LPARAM lParam )
{
static HWND hChildWnd = NULL;

   switch( uMsg )
   {
      case WM_CREATE :
            hChildWnd = CreateWindowEx( WS_EX_CLIENTEDGE,
                                        "STATIC", "",
                                        WS_CHILD | WS_VISIBLE,
                                        10, 10, 200, 200,
                                        hWnd,
                                        (HMENU)101,
                                        hInst,
                                        NULL );
         break;

      case WM_CONTEXTMENU :
            {
               TPMPARAMS tp;
               HMENU     hMenu = CreatePopupMenu();

               AppendMenu( hMenu, MFT_STRING, IDM_TEST, "&Test Option" );
               AppendMenu( hMenu, MFT_STRING, IDM_ABOUT, "&About Box..." );
               AppendMenu( hMenu, MFT_SEPARATOR, 0, NULL );
               AppendMenu( hMenu, MFT_STRING, IDM_EXIT, "E&xit" );

               // Retrieve the window rectangle of the child window.
               //.................................................
               GetWindowRect( hChildWnd, &tp.rcExclude );
               tp.cbSize = sizeof( TPMPARAMS );
```

continued on next page

continued from previous page

```
            TrackPopupMenuEx( hMenu, TPM_RIGHTBUTTON |
                                     TPM_TOPALIGN |
                                     TPM_LEFTALIGN,
                                     LOWORD( lParam ),
                                     HIWORD( lParam ), hWnd, &tp );
        DestroyMenu( hMenu );
    }
    break;
        .
        .
        .
```

TranslateAccelerator ■ WINDOWS 95   ■ WINDOWS NT

Description   Accelerator key combinations are defined in the **ACCELERATOR** portion of
the resource (RC) file. Prior to using the accelerator table, use
LoadAccelerators to retrieve the handle to the table. Use
TranslateAccelerator within the program's message loop to convert from
the keystrokes entered to the command specified in the accelerator table.

Use accelerators to provide keystroke shortcuts for menu commands. They
can also be used to send to the system command messages that do not
have menu equivalents.

If **TranslateAccelerator** returns a nonzero value, it has successfully
translated the keystroke and sent the command to the program's message-
processing function. The application should not allow the normal
TranslateMessage and **DispatchMessage** functions to process the keystrokes again. To avoid this, use the following structure for the program's
message loop in **WinMain**.

```
while( GetMessage( &msg, NULL, 0, 0 ) )
{
    if ( !hAccel || !TranslateAccelerator( hWnd,hAccel,&msg ) )
    {
        TranslateMessage( &msg );
        DispatchMessage( &msg );
    }
}
```

When an accelerator is translated, the message is sent directly to the program's message-processing function, bypassing the message queue. The
accelerator ID value is sent as the *wParam* parameter of either a **WM_COMMAND**
message (normal case) or a **WM_SYSCOMMAND** message (if the ID value is one
of the System menu ID values listed in Table 6-10).

Syntax	int **TranslateAccelerator**(HWND *hwnd,* HACCEL *haccl,* LPMSG *lpmsg*)
Parameters	
hwnd	HWND: The handle of the window with the message-processing function (**WndProc**) that is to receive the translated messages. Normally, this is the main application window.
haccl	HACCEL: The handle to the accelerator table retrieved with **LoadAccelerators** or **CreateAcceleratorTable**.
lpmsg	LPMSG: A pointer to a **MSG** structure. This structure holds the message data received when **GetMessage** was called.
Returns	int: TRUE if a keystroke entry was translated into an accelerator command; otherwise, the return value is FALSE.
Include File	winuser.h
See Also	CreateAcceleratorTable, LoadAccelerators
Related Messages	WM_COMMAND, WM_SYSCOMMAND
Example	See the example for the **LoadAccelerators** function.

7

RESOURCES

Virtually every program uses resources. The RC resource script file defines such things as menus, dialog boxes, icons, bitmaps, and other resource data that an application requires. The resource file lets you avoid having a number of separate files that the application reads when needed. Resources are also efficient because they are usually loaded into memory only when needed.

Resource script files are compiled with a resource compiler (normally named RC.EXE), which produces a RES file. After the executable file (EXE) is linked, the RES file is bound to the end of the executable. All the resources defined in the RC file are now part of the executable file for use during execution.

The Resource Script File

All of the resources used by an application are defined in a resource script file. Listing 7-1 shows a simple resource script file with one single-line resource type, ICON, and one multiple-line resource type, MENU.

Listing 7-1 Simple resource script file

```
#include <windows.h>
#include "myapp.h"

// Single-line resource type
MyApp   ICON   myapp.ico

// Multiple-line resource type
MyApp MENU
BEGIN
    POPUP "&File"
    BEGIN
        MENUITEM "E&xit",   IDM_EXIT
    END
    MENUITEM "&Test!",    IDM_TEST
    POPUP "&Help"
    BEGIN
```

continued on next page

continued from previous page

```
        MENUITEM "&About MyApp...", IDM_ABOUT
    END
END
```

This resource script file includes an icon file used for the application's icon and defines the menu used for the application's main menu.

There are five single-line resource script types: `BITMAP`, `CURSOR`, `ICON`, `FONT`, and `MESSAGETABLE`. Each of these statements loads a data file of the specified type into the resource data. Once included in the resource data, the `LoadBitmap`, `LoadCursor`, and `LoadIcon` functions are provided for direct access to the respective data within a program. `AddFontResource` is normally used to add font data for use by applications. `FormatMessage` is used to load messages from the resource file. There are five multiple-line resource script types: `ACCELERATORS`, `DIALOG`, `MENU`, `RCDATA`, and `STRINGTABLE`. The first three are covered in Chapter 6, Menus, and Chapter 8, Dialog Boxes. The `RCDATA` and `STRINGTABLE` statements are covered later in this chapter. Multiple-line resource script types are easy to identify. They use `BEGIN` and `END` to define blocks of resource data, as shown for the `MENU` type in Listing 7-1.

String Tables

Most applications use a series of character strings in messages and character output. Windows provides string tables as an alternative to the conventional method of placing strings in the static data area of a program. Character strings are defined in the resource script file and are given an ID value. Here is an example:

```
STRINGTABLE
BEGIN
    IDS_STRING1    "Simple string from .RC"
    IDS_STRING2    "This text contains a \ttab,\nand a new line."
    IDS_STRING3    "This text is used with wsprintf() %s %d."
END
```

The string ID values are usually defined in a separate header file that is included in the resource script file as well as the module that will access the strings. When the application needs to use the data, the `LoadString` function copies the character data from the resource file into a memory buffer. Strings in a string table can contain control characters such as tabs and newline characters.

There are a number of advantages to using string tables. The main advantage is the reduction in memory use. The strings are not loaded until they are needed. Windows loads strings in blocks based on the string ID numbers. Strings that are likely to be used together should be numbered sequentially within small groups.

The purpose of using string tables is defeated if the string data is copied into a static memory buffer. The buffer will take up space, even if the character data has not been loaded into it from the string table. Applications should load strings into stack variables (local variables for a block of code) or globally allocated memory.

Another advantage of putting strings in a string table is the support for multiple languages. The Win32 API supports multilingual resources within a single application. The same executable can be distributed in several countries without change.

Custom Resources

Resource files can also be used for other types of static data, which can be anything from metafiles to raw binary data. The `RCDATA` statement in the resource script is used for the raw data. Here is an example:

```
DataID RCDATA
BEGIN
   3
   40
   0x8232
   "String Data (continued)... "
   "More String Data\0"
END
```

Usually, the best place to store custom resource data is in an external file. The file's contents are then added to the resource data when the resource file is compiled. An example of custom resources is shown here:

```
paragraph    TEXT       "paragraph.txt"
picture      METAFILE   "picture.wmf"
```

These two lines define the custom resource types `TEXT` and `METAFILE`. The data for these two resources is in two separate files. The resource compiler reads in the two files and puts the data into the resource file of the executable. `FindResource` and `FindResourceEx` are used to locate custom resource data, and `LoadResource` loads it into a memory block for use in the application.

Resource Function Descriptions

Table 7-1 summarizes the resource functions. Detailed function descriptions follow the table.

Table 7-1 Resource function summary

Function	Purpose
EnumResourceLanguages	Calls a callback function for each resource in a module with the language identifier of the resource.
EnumResourceNames	Calls a callback function for each resource in a module with the resource name.
EnumResourceTypes	Calls a callback function for each type found in the resource file.
FindResource	Locates a resource in the resource file.
FindResourceEx	Locates a resource in the resource file for a given language.
LoadResource	Loads a resource into memory.
LoadString	Loads a string from the resource file string table into a buffer.
LockResource	Locks a global memory block containing a resource.
SizeofResource	Determines the size of a resource.

EnumResourceLanguages   ■ WINDOWS 95   ■ WINDOWS NT

Description   EnumResourceLanguages searches a module for each resource of the given type and name and calls an application-defined callback function, passing the language of each resource it locates. The enumeration continues until all resources have been searched or the callback function returns **FALSE**. An application can use this function to determine which languages are available for a resource.

Syntax   BOOL **EnumResourceLanguages**(HINSTANCE *hModule,* LPCTSTR *lpszType,* LPCTSTR *lpszName,* ENUMRESLANGPROC *lpEnumFunc,* LONG *lParam*)

Parameters

hModule   HINSTANCE: The instance handle of the module to be searched. If this parameter is **NULL**, the module handle of the calling process is used.

lpszType   LPCTSTR: A pointer to a null-terminated string containing the resource type to search. For standard resource types, this parameter can be one of the values in Table 7-2.

Table 7-2 EnumResourceLanguages *lpszType* values

Value	Meaning
RT_ACCELERATOR	Accelerator table
RT_BITMAP	Bitmap resource
RT_CURSOR	Hardware-dependent cursor resource
RT_DIALOG	Dialog box
RT_FONT	Font resource
RT_FONTDIR	Font directory resource
RT_GROUP_CURSOR	Hardware-independent cursor resource
RT_GROUP_ICON	Hardware-independent icon resource
RT_ICON	Hardware-dependent icon resource
RT_MENU	Menu resource
RT_MESSAGETABLE	Message-table entry
RT_RCDATA	Application-defined resource (raw data)
RT_STRING	String-table entry
RT_VERSION	Version resource

lpszName   LPCTSTR: A pointer to a null-terminated string containing the name of the resource whose languages will be enumerated.

lpEnumFunc   ENUMRESLANGPROC: A pointer to an application-defined callback function that will be called for each enumerated resource language. See the description of the callback function below.

lParam	**LONG**: An application-defined 32-bit value passed to the callback function. See the description of the callback function below.
Returns	**BOOL**: **TRUE** if successful; otherwise, the return value is **FALSE**.
Include File	winbase.h
See Also	EnumResourceTypes, EnumResourceNames, LoadResource
Callback Syntax	BOOL CALLBACK **EnumResLangProc**(HANDLE *hModule*, LPCTSTR *lpszType*, LPCTSTR *lpszName*, WORD *wIDLanguage*, LONG *lParam*)

Callback Parameters

hModule	**HANDLE**: The *hModule* parameter used.
lpszType	**LPCTSTR**: The *lpszType* parameter used.
lpszName	**LPCTSTR**: The *lpszName* parameter used.
wIDLanguage	**WORD**: The language identifier for the resource. Use the **PRIMARYLANGID** and **SUBLANGID** macros for extracting the language values. The language values are shown here:

Primary language values:

LANG_BULGARIAN	LANG_JAPANESE
LANG_CHINESE	LANG_KOREAN
LANG_CROATIAN	LANG_NEUTRAL
LANG_CZECH	LANG_NORWEGIAN
LANG_DANISH	LANG_POLISH
LANG_DUTCH	LANG_PORTUGUESE
LANG_ENGLISH	LANG_ROMANIAN
LANG_FINNISH	LANG_RUSSIAN
LANG_FRENCH	LANG_SLOVAK
LANG_GERMAN	LANG_SLOVENIAN
LANG_GREEK	LANG_SPANISH
LANG_HUNGARIAN	LANG_SWEDISH
LANG_ICELANDIC	LANG_TURKISH
LANG_ITALIAN	

The following are also defined as primary languages, but only for Windows 95:

LANG_AFRIKAANS	LANG_HEBREW
LANG_ALBANIAN	LANG_INDONESIAN
LANG_ARABIC	LANG_LATVIAN
LANG_BASQUE	LANG_LITHUANIAN
LANG_BELARUSIAN	LANG_SERBIAN

continued on next page

continued from previous page

LANG_CATALAN	LANG_THAI
LANG_ESTONIAN	LANG_UKRANIAN

Sublanguage values:

SUBLANG_CHINESE_SIMPLIFIED

SUBLANG_CHINESE_TRADITIONAL

SUBLANG_DEFAULT

SUBLANG_DUTCH

SUBLANG_DUTCH_BELGIAN

SUBLANG_ENGLISH_AUS

SUBLANG_ENGLISH_CAN

SUBLANG_ENGLISH_EIRE

SUBLANG_ENGLISH_NZ

SUBLANG_ENGLISH_UK

SUBLANG_ENGLISH_US

SUBLANG_FRENCH

SUBLANG_FRENCH_BELGIAN

SUBLANG_FRENCH_CANADIAN

SUBLANG_FRENCH_SWISS

SUBLANG_GERMAN

SUBLANG_GERMAN_AUSTRIAN

SUBLANG_GERMAN_SWISS

SUBLANG_ITALIAN

SUBLANG_ITALIAN_SWISS

SUBLANG_NEUTRAL

SUBLANG_NORWEGIAN_BOKMAL

SUBLANG_NORWEGIAN_NYNORSK

SUBLANG_PORTUGUESE

SUBLANG_PORTUGUESE_BRAZILIAN

SUBLANG_SERBO_CROATIAN_CYRILLIC

SUBLANG_SERBO_CROATIAN_LATIN

SUBLANG_SPANISH

SUBLANG_SPANISH_MEXICAN

SUBLANG_SPANISH_MODERN

SUBLANG_SYS_DEFAULT

lParam	**LONG**: The *lParam* parameter used.
Example	This example shows how the **EnumResourceLanguages** function could be used to find and load a resource for the given language. The application first starts with the English menu displayed. When the user selects the Test! menu item, the **EnumResourceLanguages** function is used to enumerate the main menus in the resource file. If the given language, in this case, Spanish (Mexican), is found, then the menu is loaded and becomes the new main menu. If the menu for the given language is not found, a message box appears to let the user know.

Menus in resource script file

```
MYAPP MENU DISCARDABLE
LANGUAGE LANG_ENGLISH, SUBLANG_ENGLISH_US
BEGIN
    POPUP "&File"
    BEGIN
        MENUITEM "E&xit",               IDM_EXIT
    END
    MENUITEM "&Test!",                  IDM_TEST
    POPUP "&Help"
    BEGIN
        MENUITEM "&About MyApp...",     IDM_ABOUT
    END
END

MYAPP MENU DISCARDABLE
LANGUAGE LANG_SPANISH, SUBLANG_SPANISH_MEXICAN
BEGIN
    POPUP "&Archivo"
    BEGIN
        MENUITEM "&Salir",              IDM_EXIT
    END
    MENUITEM "&Examinar!",              IDM_TEST
    POPUP "&Ayuda"
    BEGIN
        MENUITEM "&Acerca de MyApp...", IDM_ABOUT
    END
END
```

WndProc and EnumLoadMenu functions

```
LRESULT CALLBACK WndProc( HWND hWnd, UINT uMsg, WPARAM wParam, LPARAM lParam )
{
    switch( uMsg )
    {
      case WM_COMMAND :
            switch( LOWORD( wParam ) )
            {
                case IDM_TEST :
                    {
                        ENUMLANG enumLang;
```

continued on next page

continued from previous page

```
                          enumLang.hWnd = hWnd;
                          enumLang.wLangID = MAKELANGID( LANG_SPANISH,
                                                SUBLANG_SPANISH_MEXICAN );

                          if ( EnumResourceLanguages( hInst, RT_MENU,
                                                szAppName,
                                                EnumLoadMenu,
                                                (LONG)&enumLang ) )
                          {
                              MessageBox( hWnd, "Menu could not be found!",
                                                "EnumLoadMenu",
                                                MB_OK | MB_ICONASTERISK );
                          }
                      }
                      break;

            .
            .
            .


BOOL CALLBACK EnumLoadMenu( HANDLE hModule, LPCTSTR lpszType,
                            LPCTSTR lpszName, WORD wIDLanguage,
                            LONG lParam )
{
    ENUMLANG* pEnumLang = (ENUMLANG*)lParam;

    // Check to see if the language is the right one.
    //.............................................
    if ( pEnumLang->wLangID == wIDLanguage )
    {
        HRSRC res = FindResourceEx( hModule, lpszType, lpszName, wIDLanguage );

        // If we were able to find the resource and it is a menu,
        // then load the menu and set it as the main menu of the application.
        //.................................................................
        if ( res && lpszType == RT_MENU )
        {
            HGLOBAL hmem = NULL;

            hmem = LoadResource( hModule, res );
            if ( hmem )
            {
                LPVOID   lpmenu;
                HMENU    hmenu;

                lpmenu = LockResource( hmem );

                hmenu = LoadMenuIndirect( (CONST MENUTEMPLATE*) lpmenu );
                SetMenu( pEnumLang->hWnd, hmenu );
                DrawMenuBar( pEnumLang->hWnd );

                return( FALSE );
            }
        }
    }

    return( TRUE );
}
```

EnumResourceNames ■ Windows 95 ■ Windows NT

Description	EnumResourceNames searches a module for each resource of the given type, passing the name of each resource located to an application-defined callback function. The enumeration continues until all resources have been searched or the callback function returns FALSE.

Use EnumResourceNames to get the resource names that are available for a given type. You could also use it to find the names of the icon resources available in an application or a dynamic link library (DLL).

Syntax   BOOL **EnumResourceNames**(HINSTANCE **hModule,** LPCTSTR **lpszType,** ENUMRESNAMEPROC **lpEnumFunc,** LONG lParam)

Parameters

hModule   HINSTANCE: The instance handle of the module to be searched. If this parameter is NULL, the module handle of the calling process is used.

lpszType   LPCTSTR: A pointer to a null-terminated string containing the resource type to search. For standard resource types, this parameter can be one of the values in Table 7-2.

lpEnumFunc   ENUMRESNAMEPROC: A pointer to an application-defined callback function that will be called for each enumerated resource of the given type.

lParam   LONG: An application-defined 32-bit value passed to the callback function. See the description of the callback function below.

Returns   BOOL: TRUE if successful; otherwise, the return value is FALSE.

Include File   winbase.h

See Also   EnumResourceTypes, EnumResourceLanguages, LoadResource

Callback Syntax   BOOL CALLBACK **EnumResNameProc**(HANDLE *hModule,* LPCTSTR *lpszType,* LPTSTR *lpszName,* LONG *lParam*)

Callback Parameters

hModule   HANDLE: The *hModule* parameter used.

lpszType   LPCTSTR: The *lpszType* parameter used.

lpszName   LPTSTR: A null-terminated character string containing the resource name of the resource being enumerated.

lParam   LONG: The *lParam* parameter used.

Example   This example shows how the EnumResourceNames function can be used to find the bitmaps in a module's resource (RC) file. The callback function paints each bitmap and name that is found on the application's client area. This could be adapted to become a "thumbnail" viewer for bitmaps within applications. Figure 7-1 shows the results when the Test! menu item is selected.

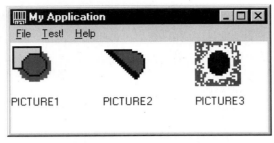

Figure 7-1 EnumResourceNames example

Bitmaps in resource script file

```
Picture1  BITMAP "picture1.bmp"
Picture2  BITMAP "picture2.bmp"
Picture3  BITMAP "picture3.bmp"
```

WndProc and *PaintBitmaps* functions

```
SHORT gnPos = 0;

LRESULT CALLBACK WndProc( HWND hWnd, UINT uMsg, WPARAM wParam, LPARAM lParam )
{
    switch( uMsg )
    {
    case WM_COMMAND :
            switch( LOWORD( wParam ) )
            {
                case IDM_TEST :
                        gnPos = 0;
                        EnumResourceNames( hInst, RT_BITMAP,
                                                PaintBitmaps,
                                                (LONG)hWnd );

                        break;
       .
       .
       .


BOOL CALLBACK PaintBitmaps( HANDLE hModule, LPCTSTR lpszType,
                            LPCTSTR lpszName, LONG lParam )
{
    HBITMAP hBitmap = LoadBitmap( hModule, lpszName );

    if ( hBitmap )
    {
        BITMAP bm;
        HDC    hMemDC;
        HWND   hWnd = (HWND)lParam;
        HDC    hDC  = GetDC( hWnd );
        HFONT  hOldFont;
```

```
    // Get the size of the bitmap.
    // ...........................
    GetObject( hBitmap, sizeof( BITMAP ), &bm );

    // Create a memory DC to select the bitmap into.
    //...............................................
    hMemDC = CreateCompatibleDC( hDC );
    SelectObject( hMemDC, hBitmap );

    // Display the bitmap, stretching it to 50X50 pixels.
    //...................................................
    StretchBlt( hDC, gnPos, 0, 50, 50,
                hMemDC, 0, 0, bm.bmWidth, bm.bmHeight,
                SRCCOPY );

    // Display the bitmap name.
    //.........................
    hOldFont = SelectObject( hDC, GetStockObject( ANSI_VAR_FONT ) );
    TextOut( hDC, gnPos, 60, lpszName, strlen( lpszName ) );
    SelectObject( hDC, hOldFont );

    DeleteDC( hMemDC );
    ReleaseDC( hWnd, hDC );

    DeleteObject( hBitmap );

    gnPos += 100;
  }

  return( TRUE );
}
```

EnumResourceTypes   ■ WINDOWS 95 ■ WINDOWS NT

Description	**EnumResourceTypes** searches a module for resources and passes each resource type found to an application-defined callback function. The enumeration continues until all resources have been searched or the callback function returns **FALSE**. This function can be used to determine the resource types that are available in a given module.
Syntax	BOOL **EnumResourceTypes**(HINSTANCE *hModule,* ENUMRESTYPEPROC *lpEnumFunc,* LONG *lParam*)
Parameters	
hModule	HINSTANCE: The instance handle of the module to be searched. If this parameter is **NULL**, the module handle of the calling process is used.
lpEnumFunc	ENUMRESTYPEPROC: A pointer to an application-defined callback function that will be called for each enumerated resource type.
lParam	LONG: An application-defined 32-bit value passed to the callback function. See the description of the callback function below.
Returns	BOOL: **TRUE** if successful; otherwise, the return value is **FALSE**.

Include File	`winbase.h`
See Also	`EnumResourceNames, EnumResourceLanguages`
Callback Syntax	`BOOL CALLBACK EnumResTypeProc( HANDLE hModule, LPTSTR lpszType, LONG lParam )`

Callback Parameters

hModule   HANDLE: The *hModule* parameter used.

lpszType   LPTSTR: A pointer to a null-terminated string containing the resource type. For standard resource types, this parameter can be one of the values given in Table 7-2.

lParam   LONG: The *lParam* parameter used.

Example   This example, shown in Figure 7-2, uses the **EnumResourceTypes** function to fill a list box with the resource types found in the application's resource file. When the user selects Test! from the menu, the resource types are enumerated and added to the list box.

```
Resource Script File ENUMRTYP.RC
#include "windows.h"
#include "enumrtyp.h"
#include "winver.h"

MYAPP                   ICON    DISCARDABLE      "GENERIC.ICO"

PICTURE1                BITMAP  DISCARDABLE      "PICTURE1.BMP"
PICTURE2                BITMAP  DISCARDABLE      "PICTURE2.BMP"
PICTURE3                BITMAP  DISCARDABLE      "PICTURE3.BMP"

MYAPP MENU DISCARDABLE
BEGIN
    POPUP "&File"
    BEGIN
        MENUITEM "E&xit",                IDM_EXIT
    END
    MENUITEM "&Test!",                   IDM_TEST
    POPUP "&Help"
    BEGIN
        MENUITEM "&About MyApplication...",       IDM_ABOUT
    END
END


ABOUTBOX DIALOG DISCARDABLE  22, 17, 171, 93
STYLE DS_MODALFRAME | WS_CAPTION | WS_SYSMENU
CAPTION "About My Application"
FONT 8, "MS Sans Serif"BEGIN
    DEFPUSHBUTTON   "OK",IDOK,126,71,32,14,WS_GROUP
    ICON            "MyApp",-1,3,2,18,20
    LTEXT           "CompanyName",DLG_VERFIRST,28,2,100,8
    LTEXT           "FileDescription",401,28,10,76,8
    LTEXT           "ProductVersion",402,113,10,53,8
```

```
        LTEXT           "LegalCopyright",403,28,19,137,8
        LTEXT           "LegalTrademarks",DLG_VERLAST,28,34,136,27
        CONTROL         "",501,"Static",SS_BLACKRECT,28,31,138,1
END


1 VERSIONINFO
 FILEVERSION 3,3,0,0
 PRODUCTVERSION 3,3,0,0
 FILEFLAGSMASK 0x3fL
#ifdef _DEBUG
 FILEFLAGS 0xbL
#else
 FILEFLAGS 0xaL
#endif
 FILEOS 0x4L
 FILETYPE 0x1L
 FILESUBTYPE 0x0L
BEGIN
    BLOCK "StringFileInfo"
    BEGIN
        BLOCK "040904B0"
        BEGIN
            VALUE "CompanyName", "Your Company\0"
            VALUE "FileDescription", "My Application\0"
            VALUE "FileVersion", "1.0\0"
            VALUE "InternalName", "MyApp\0"
            VALUE "LegalCopyright", "Copyright \251 Your Company. 1995\0"
            VALUE "LegalTrademarks", "Legal Notice"
            VALUE "OriginalFilename", "\0"
            VALUE "ProductName", "My Application\0"
            VALUE "ProductVersion", "1.0\0"
        END
    END
    BLOCK "VarFileInfo"
    BEGIN
        VALUE "Translation", 0x409, 1200
    END
END
```

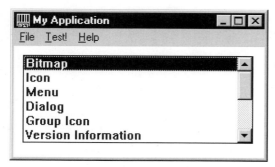

Figure 7-2 EnumResourceTypes example

ListResourceTypes and *WndProc* functions in *ENUMRTYP.C*

```c
BOOL CALLBACK ListResourceTypes( HANDLE hModule, LPTSTR lpszType, LONG lParam )
{
    LPTSTR lpAddString = lpszType;
    HWND   hListBox     = (HWND)lParam;

    // Check to see if the resource type is a pre-defined type. If it is
    // set lpAddString to a descriptive string.
    //..........................................
    switch( LOWORD(lpszType) )
    {
        case RT_ACCELERATOR   : lpAddString = "Accelerator"; break;
        case RT_BITMAP        : lpAddString = "Bitmap"; break;
        case RT_DIALOG        : lpAddString = "Dialog"; break;
        case RT_FONT          : lpAddString = "Font"; break;
        case RT_FONTDIR       : lpAddString = "FontDir"; break;
        case RT_MENU          : lpAddString = "Menu"; break;
        case RT_RCDATA        : lpAddString = "RC Data"; break;
        case RT_STRING        : lpAddString = "String Table"; break;
        case RT_MESSAGETABLE  : lpAddString = "Message Table"; break;
        case RT_CURSOR        : lpAddString = "Cursor"; break;
        case RT_GROUP_CURSOR  : lpAddString = "Group Cursor"; break;
        case RT_ICON          : lpAddString = "Icon"; break;
        case RT_GROUP_ICON    : lpAddString = "Group Icon"; break;
        case RT_VERSION       : lpAddString = "Version Information"; break;
    }

    SendMessage( hListBox, LB_INSERTSTRING, (WPARAM)-1, (LPARAM)lpAddString );

    return( TRUE );
}

LRESULT CALLBACK WndProc( HWND hWnd, UINT uMsg, WPARAM wParam, LPARAM lParam )
{
static HWND hListBox = NULL;

    switch( uMsg )
    {
        case WM_CREATE :
                hListBox = CreateWindow( "LISTBOX", "",
                                         WS_CHILD | WS_BORDER |
                                         WS_VISIBLE | LBS_STANDARD,
                                         10, 10, 250, 100,
                                         hWnd, (HMENU) 101,
                                         hInst, NULL );

            break;

        case WM_COMMAND :
                switch( LOWORD( wParam ) )
                {
                    case IDM_TEST :
                            EnumResourceTypes( hInst, ListResourceTypes,
                                               (LONG)hListBox );
                            break;
        .
        .
        .
```

FindResource

Description	Before a resource can be loaded into memory for use, it must be located. `FindResource` locates a resource with the given name in the given module and returns a handle to the resource. This function is used in conjunction with `LoadResource` to load resources into memory for use.
Syntax	HRSRC **FindResource**(HINSTANCE *hModule*, LPCTSTR *lpszName*, LPCTSTR *lpszType*)

Parameters

hModule	HINSTANCE: The instance handle of the module that contains the resource. This may be the application or a dynamic link library (DLL). Set to NULL for the current application.
lpszName	LPCTSTR: A pointer to a null-terminated character string containing the name of the resource. This is the name specified on the left side of the resource definition line in the resource (RC) file. For integer resource identifiers use the **MAKEINTRESOURCE** macro.
lpszType	LPCTSTR: A pointer to a null-terminated string containing the resource type to be searched. For standard resource types, this parameter can be one of the values given in Table 7-2.
Returns	HRSRC: The handle of the resource in the resource file. NULL if the resource cannot be located. This handle is not the memory handle of the loaded resource. Use **LoadResource** to return a memory handle.
Include File	`winbase.h`
See Also	FindResourceEx, LoadResource
Example	In this example, RCDATA is located using the **FindResource** function and then loaded using the **LoadResource** function. **"TestData"** is the identifier for the RCDATA defined in the application's resource script file. The RESDATA structure is used to access the memory.

Resource data in resource script file

```
TestData RCDATA DISCARDABLE
BEGIN
    0x0001,
    0x0002,
    0x0003
END
```

Data structure in header file

```
typedef struct
{
```

continued on next page

continued from previous page

```
    SHORT Value1;
    SHORT Value2;
    SHORT Value3;
}RESDATA;
```

WndProc function

```
LRESULT CALLBACK WndProc( HWND hWnd, UINT uMsg, WPARAM wParam, LPARAM lParam )
{
    switch( uMsg )
    {
        case WM_COMMAND :
            switch( LOWORD( wParam ) )
            {
                case IDM_TEST :
                {
                    HRSRC hres = FindResource( hInst, "TestData",
                                                RT_RCDATA );

                    if ( hres )
                    {
                        char szMsg[50];
                        DWORD    size = SizeofResource( hInst, hres );
                        HGLOBAL  hmem = LoadResource( hInst, hres );
                        RESDATA* pmem = (RESDATA*)LockResource( hmem );

                        wsprintf( szMsg, "Values loaded: %d, %d, %d\nSize = %d",
                                    pmem->Value1,
                                    pmem->Value2,
                                    pmem->Value3,
                                    size );

                        MessageBox( hWnd, szMsg, szAppName, MB_OK );
                    }
                }
                break;
                .
                .
                .
```

FindResourceEx   ■ WINDOWS 95   ■ WINDOWS NT

Description	Windows supports multilingual resources, allowing an application to be internationalized. **FindResourceEx** is the same as **FindResource**, except that only resources of the given language are searched.
Syntax	HRSRC **FindResourceEx**(HINSTANCE *hModule,* LPCTSTR *lpszType,* LPCTSTR *lpszName,* WORD *wLanguage*)
Parameters	
hModule	**HINSTANCE**: The instance handle of the module that contains the resource. This may be the application or a dynamic link library (DLL). Set to **NULL** for the current application.

lpszType	**LPCTSTR**: A pointer to a null-terminated string containing the resource type to be searched. For standard resource types, this parameter can be one of the values in Table 7-2.
lpszName	**LPCTSTR**: A pointer to a null-terminated character string containing the name of the resource.
wLanguage	**WORD**: Specifies the language of the resource. If the *wLanguage* parameter is **MAKELANGID(LANG_NEUTRAL, SUBLANG_NEUTRAL)**, the current language associated with the calling thread is used. To specify a language other than the current language, use the **MAKELANGID** macro to create this parameter using the values listed in the **EnumResourceLanguages** function description.
Returns	**HRSRC**: The handle of the resource in the resource file. **NULL** if the resource cannot be located.
Include File	winbase.h
See Also	FindResource, LoadResource
Example	See the example for the **EnumResourceLanguages** function.

LoadResource   ■ WINDOWS 95   ■ WINDOWS NT

Description	Resource data must be loaded into memory before it can be used. **LoadResource** loads a resource that has been found using either the **FindResource** or **FindResourceEx** function.
Syntax	HGLOBAL **LoadResource**(HINSTANCE *hModule,* HRSRC *hResInfo*)
Parameters	
hModule	**HINSTANCE**: The instance handle of the module that contains the resource to be loaded. If set to **NULL**, the resource is loaded from the module that was used to create the current process.
hResInfo	**HRSRC**: The handle of the resource to be loaded. This handle must be created using either the **FindResource** or **FindResourceEx** function.
Returns	**HGLOBAL**: The handle to the global memory block that contains the loaded resource. Returns **NULL** if the resource could not be loaded.
Include File	winbase.h
See Also	FindResource, FindResourceEx, LockResource
Example	See the examples for the **FindResource** and **EnumResourceLanguages** functions.

LoadString ■ WINDOWS 95 ■ WINDOWS NT

Description	Strings are added to the program's resource file in a string table. Each string is given an ID value, normally defined in the program's header file. **LoadString** copies the string from the resource file into a buffer, so that it can be manipulated and displayed.

The best place to store string constants is in resource files. This method of storage is memory efficient, and it makes edits or translations of the strings much simpler. |
Syntax	int **LoadString**(HINSTANCE *hinst,* UINT *wID,* LPTSTR *lpBuffer,* int *nBuffer*)
Parameters	
hinst	**HINSTANCE**: The instance handle of the module that contains the string resource.
wID	**UINT**: The ID value for the string in the string table. This is the value to the left of the string in the resource file.
lpBuffer	**LPTSTR**: A pointer to a buffer that will receive the character string. The buffer must be at least *nBuffer* characters long.
nBuffer	**int**: The maximum number of characters to copy to the *lpBuffer* buffer.
Returns	**int**: The number of characters copied to the buffer, not including the null-terminating character. Returns **0** on error.
Include File	winuser.h
See Also	LoadResource
Example	In this example, the string table is used to set up an array of strings that can be accessed using the **LoadString** function. When the Test! menu item is selected, each of the strings in the string table is loaded and displayed in a message box.

Resource data in resource script file

```
STRINGTABLE
BEGIN
    IDS_STRINGBASE+0    "This is String 1"
    IDS_STRINGBASE+1    "This is String 2"
    IDS_STRINGBASE+2    "This is String 3"
END
```

WndProc function

```
LRESULT CALLBACK WndProc( HWND hWnd, UINT uMsg, WPARAM wParam, LPARAM lParam )
{
```

```
switch( uMsg )
{
   case WM_COMMAND :
           switch( LOWORD( wParam ) )
           {
               case IDM_TEST :
                       {
                           char  szString[40];
                           SHORT idx;

                           for ( idx = IDS_STRINGBASE;
                                 idx < IDS_STRINGBASE+2;
                                 idx++ )
                           {
                               LoadString( hInst, idx, szString, 40 );

                               MessageBox( hWnd, szString, "String Loaded",
                                       MB_OK | MB_ICONINFORMATION );
                           }
                       }
                       break;
       .
       .
       .
```

LockResource   ■ WINDOWS 95   ■ WINDOWS NT

Description	**LockResource** locks a resource loaded in memory with the **LoadResource** function and returns a pointer to the memory block's address. It is not necessary for Win32-based applications to unlock resources locked by using the **LockResource** function. Trying to lock a resource by using the handle returned by the **FindResource** or **FindResourceEx** function will not work, and a value that is incorrect and points to random data is returned.
Syntax	LPVOID **LockResource**(HGLOBAL *hglb*)
Parameters	
hglb	HGLOBAL: A handle to the resource to be locked. The **LoadResource** function returns this handle.
Returns	LPVOID: If successful, a pointer to the first byte of the resource; otherwise, it is **NULL**.
Include File	winbase.h
See Also	LoadResource, FindResource
Example	See the examples for the **FindResource** and **EnumResourceLanguages** functions.

SizeofResource   ■ WINDOWS 95   ■ WINDOWS NT

Description	`SizeofResource` returns the size, in bytes, of the given resource. Because the data may be aligned, the size may not be the actual size and should not be relied on. This function was used with the `AllocResource` and `AccessResource` functions, which are obsolete in Win32. It can still be used to estimate the size of a resource that was found using either the `FindResource` or `FindResourceEx` function.
Syntax	`DWORD SizeofResource( HINSTANCE hModule, HRSRC hrsrc )`
Parameters	
hModule	`HINSTANCE`: The instance handle of the module that contains the resource.
hrsrc	`HRSRC`: The handle of the resource that was returned with either the `FindResource` or `FindResourceEx` function.
Returns	`DWORD`: If successful, the number of bytes in the resource; otherwise, `0`.
Include File	`winbase.h`
See Also	`FindResource, FindResourceEx`
Example	See the example for the `FindResource` function.

8

DIALOG BOXES

Dialog boxes are similar to pop-up windows. Both elicit input from the user for some specific task, such as to obtain a file name or a character string for search activity. The main difference between dialog boxes and pop-up windows is that dialog boxes use templates that define the controls created on the dialog box. These templates can be defined in the resource script file using the **DIALOG** resource type. They can also be dynamically created in memory while the application executes.

There are also functional differences between the behavior of a pop-up window and a dialog box. Dialog box functions use a special default message-processing function. This function interprets keystrokes, such as the arrow keys, TAB, and SHIFT-TAB, to allow selection of controls in the dialog box using the keyboard. Any activity that can be performed in a dialog box also can be performed in a child or pop-up window. Dialog boxes are more convenient for simple pop-up windows that make use of normal control items such as buttons and list boxes. Pop-up and child windows are better if extensive painting on the window is required, or the standard behavior of the window is modified.

Types of Dialog Boxes

The most common type of dialog box is a modal dialog box. When a modal dialog box is on the screen, the user cannot switch to another part of the application. By default, it limits access to the other visible windows of the application that called the dialog box. The user can still switch to other applications while the modal dialog box is displayed.

A dialog box is made system modal when you specify the **WS_SYSMODAL** style in the dialog box template. System modal dialog boxes also can be created by calling the **SetSysModalWindow** function. System modal dialog boxes take over the whole screen and are appropriate only if a serious problem exists that the user cannot ignore, such as a system error. Under Windows NT and Windows 95, system modal dialog boxes are always on top, but unlike in previous versions of Windows, the user can switch to another application, but the system modal dialog will cover the other application windows and be in the way.

You create modal dialog boxes and system modal dialog boxes with the `DialogBox` function. With the `DialogBox` function, all of the window's messages are sent to the dialog box function while the dialog box is on the screen.

Less common, but sometimes useful, are modeless dialog boxes, which are basically pop-up windows. Modeless dialog boxes can obtain and lose the input focus. They are frequently used for small windows containing lists of tools called tool boxes. You create modeless dialog boxes with `CreateDialog`. There are several variations of `CreateDialog`, but they all accomplish the same basic task of displaying and initializing a modeless dialog box. Because the modeless dialog box remains on the screen, it must share messages with the message loop. This requires modification to the message loop if the modeless dialog box is to respond to keyboard selections using the TAB and arrow keys. A typical message loop containing a modeless dialog box is as follows:

```
while( GetMessage( &msg, NULL, 0, 0 ) )
{
    if ( hDlgModeless || !IsDialogMessage( hDlgModeless, &msg ) )
    {
        TranslateMessage( &msg );
        DispatchMessage( &msg );
    }
}
```

hDlgModeless is an `HWND` handle for the dialog box. This global variable is set to `NULL` if the modeless dialog box is not displayed, and set to the dialog box handle if the modeless dialog box is currently on the screen.

The `IsDialogMessage` function determines if a message from Windows is meant for the dialog box. If so, the message is sent to the dialog box procedure and should not be processed by the normal `TranslateMessage` and `DispatchMessage` functions.

The Dialog Box Keyboard Interface

The built-in logic Windows provides for dialog boxes includes provisions for a keyboard alternative to selecting items with the mouse. Three sets of keyboard logic can be provided: keyboard hotkeys for selecting items using ALT-letter key combinations; response to the TAB key for big movements; and response to the keyboard arrow keys for smaller movements.

The ALT-letter key selection logic is done the same way for dialog boxes as for menu items. If you precede a letter in the control's text string with an ampersand (&), the letter following the ampersand is underlined. The ampersand characters are not displayed. For example, the following definition for a `DEFPUSHBUTTON` control would use ALT-D for a hotkey to activate the Done button.

```
CONTROL "&Done", IDC_DONE, "BUTTON",
    BS_DEFPUSHBUTTON | WS_TABSTOP | WS_CHILD, 45, 66, 48, 12
```

If you need an ampersand (&) in your text, use a double ampersand (&&), for example `"Revenue && Receipts"` will appear as "Revenue & Receipts".

Using the TAB and arrow keys is sometimes a convenient alternative to using the mouse, and critical for users who don't have a mouse. To take advantage of this logic, set certain elements in the dialog box template with the **WS_TABSTOP** and/or **WS_GROUP** style.

The **WS_TABSTOP** style marks each item that will receive the input focus when the user presses TAB or SHIFT-TAB. The **WS_GROUP** style marks the beginning of a group. All the items up until the next **WS_GROUP** item are part of the same group. The user can use the arrow keys to move between items in a group, but not outside of the group. The ENTER key will select or deselect a pushbutton, check box, or radio button item that has the input focus. This procedure has the same effect as selection with the left mouse button.

Dynamic Dialog Boxes

Some applications require that the dialog box be altered as the program operates. For example, a database application would need to add and subtract fields from a data-entry dialog box to match the structure of the underlying database. For simple changes, the child window controls in the dialog box can be manipulated directly. For example, **MoveWindow** can be called to relocate a control. For complete control over a dialog box during runtime, the application can modify the dialog box definition in memory. This is not a simple matter, as the definition of a dialog box contains three separate data structures, each with variable length fields.

The **CreateDialogIndirect**, **CreateDialogIndirectParam**, **DialogBoxIndirect**, and **DialogBoxIndirectParam** functions read the data in memory in a specified format and create a dialog box. A simple way to create data in the right format is to define the dialog box in the resource script file and load it into memory with **LoadResource** and **LockResource**. The data will be in the format defined below. For a dialog to be truly dynamic, the data format will have to be created from scratch in an allocated memory block.

Figure 8-1 shows the overall structure of a dialog box definition in memory.

The data structures are defined in **WINUSER.H**. Listing 8-1 gives their definitions.

Listing 8-1 Dialog box data structures

```
typedef struct
{
    DWORD style;              // The style of the dialog box.
    DWORD dwExtendedStyle;    // The extended style of the dialog box.
    WORD  cdit;               // The number of items in the dialog box.
    WORD  x;                  // X-pos. of upper left of the dialog box.
    WORD  y;                  // Y-pos. of upper left of the dialog box.
    WORD  cx;                 // The width of the dialog box.
    WORD  cy;                 // The height of the dialog box.
} DLGTEMPLATE;

typedef struct
{
    DWORD style;              // The style of the control.
    DWORD dwExtendedStyle;    // The extended style of the control.
    WORD  x;                  // X-pos. of the upper left of the control.
```

continued on next page

continued from previous page

```
    WORD  y;              // Y-pos. of the upper left of the control.
    WORD  cx;             // The width of the control.
    WORD  cy;             // The height of the control.
    WORD  id;             // The ID of the control.
} DLGITEMTEMPLATE;
```

The size and location of the dialog box and all controls are given in dialog box base units. These are relative to the size of the font in use. Vertical dimensions are in eighths of the font height, and horizontal dimensions are in fourths of the font width. The effect of this system of units is to properly scale the dialog box, regardless of the screen resolution in use. Typically, high-resolution monitors will use more pixels per character, so the character size remains about the same as on a low-resolution monitor. A side effect of this system is that the size of a dialog box is changed by simply picking a different font. The **FONT** statement is provided for this purpose.

All character elements in the dialog box template are variable length arrays of "wide characters," meaning they are 16-bit Unicode characters. The minimum size is one 16-bit value with a value of **0x0000**, which signifies an empty string. If the first element is **0xFFFF**, the next value is a 16-bit integer identifier that is either an atom or a resource identifier. Any other value indicates the array is a null-terminated Unicode string. Table 8-1 lists the class atom values for predefined controls.

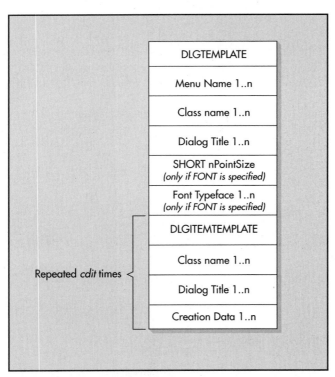

Figure 8-1 Dialog template structure

Table 8-1 Atom values for predefined controls

Value	Meaning
0x0080	Button
0x0081	Edit
0x0082	Static
0x0083	List box
0x0084	Scroll bar
0x0085	Combo box

Dialog Template Statement Descriptions

This section contains a full list of the statements that an application can include in the dialog box template. The following listing is the dialog template for the dialog shown in Figure 8-2.

```
TESTDIALOG DIALOG DISCARDABLE  20, 20, 180, 70
STYLE DS_MODALFRAME | WS_POPUP | WS_VISIBLE | WS_CAPTION | WS_SYSMENU
CAPTION "Test Dialog"
FONT 8, "MS Sans Serif"
BEGIN
    CHECKBOX        "Check box control.",IDC_CHECKBOX,9,7,70,10
    GROUPBOX        "Radio Buttons",-1,7,21,86,39
    RADIOBUTTON     "First", IDC_RADIO1,13,32,37,10,WS_GROUP | WS_TABSTOP
    RADIOBUTTON     "Second",IDC_RADIO2,13,45,39,10
    PUSHBUTTON      "Done",IDCANCEL,116,8,50,14,WS_GROUP
END
```

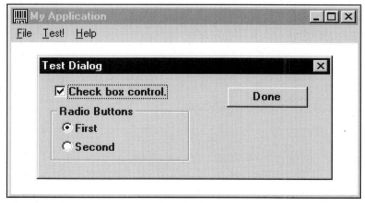

Figure 8-2 Sample dialog box

Dialog

Description   This statement starts the dialog box template definition. All statements from **BEGIN** until the **END** statement is reached are part of the dialog box template.

Syntax   *nameID* **DIALOG** [*load-option*][*mem-option*] *x,y, width, height,* [*option-statements*]

Parameters

nameID   The name of the dialog box. This is the character string or 16-bit unsigned integer that is used with **DialogBox** to specify which dialog box should be loaded and executed.

load-option   Can be either **PRELOAD** or **LOADONCALL**. **PRELOAD** specifies that the dialog box resource data be loaded when the application starts. Doing so takes up memory but makes the dialog box appear quickly. **LOADONCALL** is the normal (default) option, in which the dialog box resource data is not loaded into memory until needed.

mem-option   A combination of **FIXED**, **MOVEABLE**, and **DISCARDABLE**. Normally, both the **MOVEABLE** and **DISCARDABLE** styles are chosen.

x, y, width, height   The position and size of the dialog box. Dialog base units are used for all dimensions. The x,y location is relative to the upper-left corner of the window that called the dialog box.

option-statements   These include **STYLE**, **EXSTYLE**, **CAPTION**, **CHARACTERISTICS**, **MENU**, **CLASS**, **LANGUAGE**, **VERSION**, and **FONT**. All statements after **DIALOG**, up to the **BEGIN** statement in the dialog box definition, are assumed to be option statements.

Example

```
EXMPDLG DIALOG LOADONCALL MOVEABLE DISCARDABLE 10, 18, 145, 80
BEGIN
   (dialog box items defined here)
END
```

DialogEX

Description   This statement is an extension of the **DIALOG** resource. In addition to the functionality offered by **DIALOG**, **DIALOGEX** allows for help IDs on the dialog and controls, use of extended styles on the dialog and controls, font weight and italic settings for the dialog font, control-specific data for controls within the dialog, and use of the **BEDIT**, **IEDIT**, and **HEDIT** predefined system class names.

Controls declared in the body of an extended dialog also have an extended syntax, which is shown under each of the control statements described later in this chapter. Additionally, controls can have associated initialization data. This is done by including a **BEGIN** and **END** block under the control statement, with each data element listed with comma (*,*) separators.

Syntax   *nameID* **DIALOGEX** [*load-option*][*mem-option*] *x,y, width, height,* [*helpID*], [*option-statements*]

Parameters

nameID   The name of the dialog box. This is the character string or 16-bit unsigned integer that is used with **DialogBox** to specify which dialog box should be loaded and executed.

load-option   Can be either **PRELOAD** or **LOADONCALL**. **PRELOAD** specifies that the dialog box resource data be loaded when the application starts. Doing so takes up memory but makes the dialog box appear quickly. **LOADONCALL** is the normal (default) option, in which the dialog box resource data is not loaded into memory until needed.

mem-option   A combination of **FIXED**, **MOVEABLE**, and **DISCARDABLE**. Normally, both the **MOVEABLE** and **DISCARDABLE** styles are chosen.

x, *y*, *width*, *height*   The position and size of the dialog box. Dialog base units are used for all dimensions. The x,y location is relative to the upper-left corner of the window that called the dialog box.

helpID   A numeric expression indicating the ID used to identify the dialog during **WM_HELP** processing.

option-statements   These include **STYLE**, **EXSTYLE**, **CAPTION**, **CHARACTERISTICS**, **MENU**, **CLASS**, **LANGUAGE**, **VERSION**, and **FONT**. All statements after **DIALOG**, up to the **BEGIN** statement in the dialog box definition, are assumed to be option statements.

Example

```
#define HIDEXMPDLG   1001

EXMPDLG DIALOGEX  10, 18, 145, 80,  HIDEXMPDLG
BEGIN
   (dialog box items defined here)
END
```

CAPTION   ■ WINDOWS 95 ■ WINDOWS NT

Description   Used with dialog boxes that have the **WS_CAPTION** style. This is a good idea, as it allows the user to move the dialog box on the screen. The caption is also a visual reminder of what activity is taking place.

Syntax   **CAPTION** *captiontext*

Parameters

captiontext   The character string that is displayed as the dialog caption. The string should be inside quotes (").

Example

```
CAPTION "Dialog Box Title Here"
```

CHARACTERISTICS   ■ WINDOWS 95   ■ WINDOWS NT

Description   Allows the developer to specify information about a resource that can be used by tools that read and write resource-definition files. The value specified does not have significance to Windows.

Syntax   **CHARACTERISTICS** *dword*

Parameters

dword   A user-defined doubleword value. The value appears with the resource in the compiled RES file. However, the value is not stored in the executable.

Example

```
CHARACTERISTICS 388837
```

CLASS   ■ WINDOWS 95   ■ WINDOWS NT

Description   Normally, a dialog box shares the window class of the parent. This statement causes a separate class to be used for the dialog box. Dialog box functions for windows with their own class must specify a separate default message-processing function. See the example under **DefDlgProc** to see how this is done.

Syntax   **CLASS** *classname*

Parameters

classname   The name of the class. The class must be registered in advance with **RegisterClass**. The class must be registered with the *cbWndExtra* element set to **DLGWINDOWEXTRA**. The string should be inside quotes (").

Example

```
CLASS "separate"
```

EXSTYLE   ■ WINDOWS 95   ■ WINDOWS NT

Description   Specifies an extended style used when the dialog box is created.

Syntax   **EXSTYLE** *exstyle*

Parameters

exstyle   All of the extended window styles are described in Chapter 3, Creating Windows, Table 3-5.

Example

```
EXMPDLG DIALOG EXSTYLE=WS_EX_TOOLWINDOW 10, 18, 145, 80
```

-or-

```
EXMPDLG DIALOG 10, 18, 145, 80
EXSTYLE WS_EX_TOOLWINDOW
BEGIN
   (dialog box items defined here)
END
```

FONT   ■ WINDOWS 95   ■ WINDOWS NT

Description   Specifies the font to use inside the dialog box for all controls. As previously mentioned, the font determines not only the typeface, but also the sizing of every control and the dialog box itself. This is because dialog box dimensions use dialog base units, computed as fractions of the font character size. The 8-point MS Sans Serif font is a good choice for most dialog boxes.

Syntax   **FONT** *pointsize, typeface*

Parameters

pointsize   The point size of the font to use.

typeface   The typeface name of the font to use. The string should be inside quotes (").

Example

```
FONT 8,"MS Sans Serif"
```

LANGUAGE   ■ WINDOWS 95   ■ WINDOWS NT

Description   Specifies the language of the dialog. In multilingual applications, the resource script file contains resources for each of the supported languages.

Syntax   **LANGUAGE** *language, sublanguage*

Parameters

language   Language identifier. See Chapter 7, Resources, under the **EnumResourceLanguages** function for valid values.

sublanguage   Sublanguage identifier. See Chapter 7, under the **EnumResourceLanguages** function for valid values.

Example

```
LANGUAGE LANG_SPANISH, SUBLANG_SPANISH_MEXICAN
```

MENU   ■ Windows 95 ■ Windows NT

Description	Used with dialog boxes that have menus. This is unusual, but possible. The menu must be defined elsewhere, such as in the program's RC resource script file.
Syntax	**MENU** *menuname*
Parameters	
menuname	Specifies the menu identifier of the menu to use.

Example

```
MENU testmenu
```

STYLE   ■ Windows 95 ■ Windows NT

Description	Specifies the style used when the dialog is created. If the dialog is a mode-less dialog box, be sure to include the **WS_VISIBLE** style in order to avoid using **ShowWindow** to make the dialog box visible. Dialog boxes cannot use the **WM_MINIMIZEBOX** and **WM_MAXIMIZEBOX** styles.
Syntax	**STYLE** *style*
Parameters	
style	All of the styles described in Chapter 3, Creating Windows, Table 3-4, that start with **WS_** or **DS_** can be used in the dialog box style.

Example

```
STYLE WS_DLGFRAME | WS_VISIBLE | WS_POPUP
```

VERSION   ■ Windows 95 ■ Windows NT

Description	Allows the developer to specify version information about a resource that can be used by tools that read and write resource-definition files. The value specified does not have significance to Windows.
Syntax	**VERSION** *dword*
Parameters	
dword	A user-defined doubleword value. The value appears with the resource in the compiled RES file. However, the value is not stored in the executable.

Example

VERSION 10

Dialog Box Control Statements

Windows provides two equivalent ways to specify a child window control in a dialog box template. One way is to use an explicit statement like **COMBOBOX**. The other way is to use the **CONTROL** statement, which will then include the COMBOBOX style as a parameter. For instance, the following two examples produce the same control.

```
CONTROL "Push Me", IDC_BUTTON1, "button",
    BS_DEFPUSHBUTTON | WS_TABSTOP | WS_CHILD, 45, 66, 48, 12

DEFPUSHBUTTON "Push Me", IDC_BUTTON1, 45, 66, 48, 12, WS_TABSTOP
```

A number of the statements include the position and size of the control. In the descriptions that follow, they will be labeled *x*, *y*, *width*, *height*. Keep in mind that all values are integers, and all use dialog base units.

The ID values for each control are normally defined in a separate header file. For the controls with the optional style parameter, the choices include the **WS_TABSTOP** and/or **WS_GROUP** styles. These control the default keyboard interface, as described earlier. The two styles can be combined with the binary OR operator (|).

Controls of dialogs created as **DIALOGEX** can also contain additional information that defines optional extended styles, the help ID, and control-specific data. The control-specific data is contained in a **BEGIN/END** block under the control declaration. The following shows the format used for all control types. The extended style can be one or more of the **WS_EX_** styles listed in Table 3-5, in Chapter 3, Creating Windows.

```
(Control Type), x, y, cx, cy, [style], [Extended Style], [Help ID]
    [BEGIN
        data element 1,
        data element 2,
        ...
    END]
```

AUTO3STATE   ■ WINDOWS 95   ■ WINDOWS NT

Description   Defines an automatic three-state check box. This control automatically advances between the three states: checked, unchecked, and indeterminate. Check boxes belong to the BUTTON window class. A three-state check box is used when the choice is not a binary on/off choice. The three-state check box also adds the indeterminate state, which is often used when the answer cannot be determined.

Syntax   **AUTO3STATE** *text, id, x, y, width, height,* [*style*], [*extended style*]

Parameters

style   Specifies the styles for the control, which can be a combination of the
BS_AUTO3STATE style and the following styles: WS_TABSTOP, WS_DISABLED,
and WS_GROUP. The default is BS_AUTO3STATE and WS_TABSTOP. For more
information on window styles, see Table 3-4 in Chapter 3, Creating
Windows.

Example

```
AUTO3STATE "File Read Only", IDC_READONLY, 3, 10, 35, 14
```

AUTOCHECKBOX   ■ WINDOWS 95   ■ WINDOWS NT

Description   Defines an automatic check box control. This is the same as the CHECKBOX
control, except that the state is automatically set when the user selects the
control. When the button is chosen, the application is notified with
BN_CLICKED.

Syntax   **AUTOCHECKBOX** *text, id, x, y, width, height, [style], [extended*
style]

Parameters

style   Specifies the styles for the control, which can be a combination of the
BS_AUTOCHECKBOX style and the following styles: WS_TABSTOP,
WS_DISABLED, and WS_GROUP. The default is BS_AUTOCHECKBOX and WS_TAB-
STOP. For more information on window styles, see Table 3-4 in Chapter 3,
Creating Windows.

Example

```
AUTOCHECKBOX "Autosave On/Off", IDC_CHECKBOX, 3, 10, 35, 14
```

AUTORADIOBUTTON   ■ WINDOWS 95   ■ WINDOWS NT

Description   Defines an automatic radio button control. This control is the same as the
RADIOBUTTON control except that it automatically performs mutual exclu-
sion with the other AUTORADIOBUTTON controls within the same group.
When the button is chosen, the application is notified with BN_CLICKED.

Syntax   **AUTORADIOBUTTON** *text, id, x, y, width, height, [style],*
[extended style]

Parameters

style   Specifies the styles for the control, which can be a combination of the
BS_AUTORADIOBUTTON style and the following styles: WS_TABSTOP, WS_DIS-
ABLED, and WS_GROUP. The default is BS_AUTORADIOBUTTON and
WS_TABSTOP. For more information on window styles, see Table 3-4 in
Chapter 3, Creating Windows.

Example

```
AUTORADIOBUTTON "Choice 1", IDC_CHECKBOX, 3, 10, 35, 14
```

CHECKBOX ■ WINDOWS 95 ■ WINDOWS NT

Description	Defines a check box control. Check boxes belong to the BUTTON window class. They are ideal for specifying binary choices, such as whether an autosave feature is on or off.
Syntax	**CHECKBOX** *text, id, x, y, width, height,* [*style*], [*extended style*]
Parameters	
style	Specifies the styles for the control, which can be a combination of the **BS_CHECKBOX** style and the following styles: **WS_TABSTOP**, **WS_DISABLED**, and **WS_GROUP**. The default is **BS_CHECKBOX** and **WS_TABSTOP**. For more information on window styles, see Table 3-4 in Chapter 3, Creating Windows.

Example

```
CHECKBOX "Autosave On/Off", IDC_CHECKBOX, 3, 10, 35, 14
```

COMBOBOX ■ WINDOWS 95 ■ WINDOWS NT

Description	Defines a combo box control. Combo boxes include a static text control or an edit control at the top, combined with a drop-down list box at the bottom for making a selection. The list box can be displayed at all times or pulled down by the user. If the combo box contains a static text control, it always displays the selection (if any) of the list box. If it uses an edit control, the user can type in the desired selection, and the list box highlights the first item that matches what the user has entered in the edit box.
Syntax	**COMBOBOX** *id, x, y, width, height,* [*style*], [*extended style*]
Parameters	
style	Specifies the styles for the control, which can be a combination of the **COMBOBOX** class styles and the following styles: **WS_TABSTOP**, **WS_DISABLED**, **WS_VSCROLL**, and **WS_GROUP**. The default is **CBS_SIMPLE** and **WS_TABSTOP**. For more information on window styles, see Table 3-4 in Chapter 3, Creating Windows.

Example

```
COMBOBOX IDC_COMBO, 40, 10, 60, 90, WS_VSCROLL
```

CONTROL

Description Specifies all forms of child window controls within a dialog box. The text field specifies the character string that will appear in the control. This is not always displayed. For example, list box controls do not display a string until the string is added to the body of the list box using the **LB_ADDTEXT** message.

Syntax **CONTROL** *text, id, class, style, x, y, width, height,* [*extended style*]

Parameters

text Specifies the character string that will appear in the control. Not all controls will display this string.

id Specifies the control identifier.

class Specifies the class of the control. This can be either BUTTON, COMBOBOX, EDIT, LISTBOX, SCROLLBAR, STATIC, or a custom control class defined by the application.

style Specifies the window style. The styles in Chapter 3, Creating Windows, Table 3-4 can be used.

Example

```
CONTROL "Push Me", IDC_BUTTON1, "button",
        BS_DEFPUSHBUTTON | WS_TABSTOP | WS_CHILD,  45, 66, 48, 12
```

CTEXT

Description Defines a centered static text control. The text is centered within the bounds of the rectangle specified by *x, y, width, height*. Normally, static text controls are given an ID value of **-1**, as they are never selected. An exception is when the dialog box function changes the text content as the dialog box operates.

Syntax **CTEXT** *text, id, x, y, width, height,* [*style*], [*extended style*]

Parameters

style Specifies the styles for the control, which can be a combination of the **SS_CENTER**, **WS_TABSTOP**, and **WS_GROUP** styles. The default is **SS_CENTER** and **WS_GROUP**. For more information on window styles, see Table 3-4 in Chapter 3, Creating Windows.

Example

```
CTEXT "Centered Text" -1, 10, 10, 100, 8
```

DEFPUSHBUTTON
■ WINDOWS 95   ■ WINDOWS NT

Description
Defines the default pushbutton for a dialog box. The default pushbutton is the button that will be activated if the user presses (ENTER). There can be only one **DEFPUSHBUTTON** control in a dialog box definition. It will be displayed on the screen with a bold border. The other buttons should have the **PUSHBUTTON** style.

Syntax
DEFPUSHBUTTON *text, id, x, y, width, height, [style], [extended style]*

Parameters

style
Specifies the styles for the control, which can be a combination of the **BS_DEFPUSHBUTTON, WS_TABSTOP, WS_DISABLED**, and **WS_GROUP**. The default is **BS_DEFPUSHBUTTON** and **WS_TABSTOP**. For more information on window styles, see Table 3-4 in Chapter 3, Creating Windows.

Example

```
DEFPUSHBUTTON "Cancel", IDC_CANCEL, 40, 10, 40, 14
```

EDITTEXT
■ WINDOWS 95   ■ WINDOWS NT

Description
Defines an editable text control in a dialog box. Edit controls are the standard method for getting user input for typed text or numbers. Windows includes a lot of built-in logic in edit controls, including selection of groups of characters by clicking and dragging the mouse cursor, deletion and insertion of characters, cursor (arrow) key support, etc. Edit controls can be one line of text or multiple lines, including both horizontal and vertical scrolling of the client area of the edit control.

Syntax
EDITTEXT *id, x, y, width, height, [style], [extended style]*

Parameters

style
Specifies the styles for the control, which can be a combination of the edit class styles and the following styles: **WS_TABSTOP, WS_DISABLED, WS_VSCROLL, WS_HSCROLL, WS_BORDER**, and **WS_GROUP**. The default is **ES_LEFT, WS_TABSTOP**, and **WS_BORDER**. For more information on window styles, see Table 3-4 in Chapter 3, Creating Windows.

Example

```
EDITTEXT IDC_EDIT, 10, 20, 45, 12, WS_HSCROLL
```

GROUPBOX ■ WINDOWS 95 ■ WINDOWS NT

Description   Draws a rectangle with a title at the top left around a group of other controls. Check boxes or radio buttons frequently deal with related options, or choices from a narrow set of possibilities. Surrounding the related options with a group box makes it clear that the controls belong to related functions. The **WS_TABSTOP** and **WS_GROUP** styles can be applied to the group control, but normally it is better to have the first item within the group receive the input focus.

Syntax   **GROUPBOX** *text, id, x, y, width, height,* [*style*], [*extended style*]

Parameters

style   Specifies the styles for the control, which can be a combination of the **BS_GROUPBOX**, **WS_TABSTOP**, **WS_DISABLED**, and **WS_GROUP**. The default is **BS_GROUPBOX**. For more information on window styles, see Table 3-4 in Chapter 3, Creating Windows.

Example

```
GROUPBOX "Filetype Choices", -1, 10, 10, 65, 100
```

ICON ■ WINDOWS 95 ■ WINDOWS NT

Description   Places an icon within a dialog box. Icons belong to the static class of controls.

Syntax   **ICON** *text, id, x, y,* [*style*], [*extended style*]

Parameters

text   The name of the icon, specified elsewhere in the resource script file with an **ICON** statement.

id   The identifier of the icon placeholder in the dialog box.

x, y   The upper-left corner of the icon in dialog base units.

style   The only allowed style is **SS_ICON**.

Example

```
ICON "generic", IDC_ICON, 30, 30
```

LISTBOX ■ WINDOWS 95 ■ WINDOWS NT

Description   Defines a list box control within a dialog box. List box controls are the most common means of allowing users to select an item from a list of possibilities. More than one selection is possible if the list box includes the

LBS_MULTIPLESEL style. The complete list of style possibilities is given in Chapter 3, Creating Windows, Table 3-4.

Syntax	**LISTBOX** `id, x, y, width, height, [style], [extended style]`
Parameters	
`style`	Specifies the control styles, which can be a combination of the list-box class styles and a combination of **WS_BORDER** and **WS_VSCROLL**. For more information on window styles, see Table 3-4 in Chapter 3, Creating Windows.

Example

```
LISTBOX IDC_LIST, 10, 10, 50, 100, LBS_NOTIFY | WS_VSCROLL | WS_BORDER
```

LTEXT   ■ WINDOWS 95   ■ WINDOWS NT

Description	Defines a left-justified static text control. The text is justified to the left border within the bounds of the rectangle specified by *x*, *y*, *width*, and *height*. Normally, static text controls are given an ID value of −1 because they are never selected. An exception is when the dialog box function changes the text content as the dialog box operates.
Syntax	**LTEXT** `text, id, x, y, width, height, [style], [extended style]`
Parameters	
`style`	Specifies the styles for the control, which can be a combination of the **SS_LEFT**, **WS_TABSTOP**, and **WS_GROUP** styles. The default is **SS_LEFT** and **WS_GROUP**. For more information on window styles, see Table 3-4 in Chapter 3, Creating Windows.

Example

```
LTEXT "Left Justified Text", −1, 10, 10, 150, 8
```

PUSHBOX   ■ WINDOWS 95   ■ WINDOWS NT

Description	Defines a push-box control, which is the same as the **PUSHBUTTON**, except that it does not display a button face or frame; only the text is displayed.
Syntax	**PUSHBOX** `text, id, x, y, width, height, [style], [extended style]`
Parameters	
`style`	Specifies the styles for the push-box control, which can be a combination of the **BS_PUSHBOX** style and the following styles: **WS_TABSTOP**, **WS_DIS-ABLED**, and **WS_GROUP** styles. The default is **BS_PUSHBOX** and **WS_TABSTOP**. For more information on window styles, see Table 3-4 in Chapter 3, Creating Windows.

Example

```
PUSHBOX "Press Here", IDC_DONE, 40, 10, 40, 14
```

PUSHBUTTON   ■ WINDOWS 95   ■ WINDOWS NT

Description Defines a pushbutton for a dialog box. Dialog boxes usually have at least one **PUSHBUTTON** (or **DEFPUSHBUTTON**) control to allow the user to exit the dialog box. Dialog boxes also use other buttons to perform actions such as delete, sort, etc.

Syntax **PUSHBUTTON** *text, id, x, y, width, height, [style], [extended style]*

Parameters

style Specifies the styles for the pushbutton control, which can be a combination of the **BS_PUSHBUTTON** style and the following styles: **WS_TABSTOP**, **WS_DISABLED**, and **WS_GROUP** styles. The default is **BS_PUSHBUTTON** and **WS_TABSTOP**. For more information on window styles, see Table 3-4 in Chapter 3, Creating Windows.

Example

```
PUSHBUTTON "Done", IDC_DONE, 40, 10, 40, 14
```

RADIOBUTTON   ■ WINDOWS 95   ■ WINDOWS NT

Description Defines a radio button control in a dialog box. Radio buttons are usually used in groups to specify selection of one out of a limited number of choices. Radio buttons belong to the BUTTON window class. See the **CheckRadioButton** function description later in this chapter for an example.

Syntax **RADIOBUTTON** *text, id, x, y, width, height, [style], [extended style]*

Parameters

style Specifies the styles for the control, which can be a combination of the **BS_RADIOBUTTON** style and the following styles: **WS_TABSTOP**, **WS_DISABLED**, and **WS_GROUP** styles. The default is **BS_RADIOBUTTON** and **WS_TABSTOP**. For more information on window styles, see Table 3-4 in Chapter 3, Creating Windows.

Example

```
RADIOBUTTON "Select Option ON", IDC_RADIO1, 10, 10, 40, 14
```

RTEXT ■ WINDOWS 95 ■ WINDOWS NT

Description   Defines a right-justified static text control. The text is justified to the right border within the bounds of the rectangle specified by *x*, *y*, *width*, and *height*. Normally, static text controls are given an ID value of −1, as they are never selected. An exception is when the dialog box function changes the text content as the dialog box operates.

Syntax   **RTEXT** *text, id, x, y, width, height, [style], [extended style]*

Parameters

style   Specifies the styles for the control, which can be a combination of the SS_RIGHT, WS_TABSTOP, and WS_GROUP styles. The default is SS_RIGHT and WS_GROUP. For more information on window styles, see Table 3-4 in Chapter 3, Creating Windows.

Example

```
RTEXT "Right Justified Text", -1, 10, 10, 150, 8
```

SCROLLBAR ■ WINDOWS 95 ■ WINDOWS NT

Description   Defines a scroll bar control within a dialog box. Scroll bar controls are excellent ways of getting user input for scaleable items, such as integers. Scroll bars can also be used to scroll the client area of a window, but this is unlikely with a dialog box. The most common styles are SBS_VERT for vertical scroll bars, and SBS_HORZ for horizontal ones. See Chapter 3, Creating Windows, Table 3-4 for a full list of scroll bar styles.

Syntax   **SCROLLBAR** *id, x, y, width, height, [style], [extended state]*

Parameters

style   Specifies a combination of the scroll bar–class styles and the following styles: WS_TABSTOP, WS_GROUP, and WS_DISABLED. The default style is SBS_HORZ. For more information on window styles, see Table 3-4 in Chapter 3, Creating Windows.

Example

```
SCROLLBAR DLI_SCROLL, 50, 10, 8, 50, SBS_VERT
```

STATE3 ■ WINDOWS 95 ■ WINDOWS NT

Description   Defines a three-state check box. This control can display three states: checked, unchecked, and indeterminate. Check boxes belong to the BUTTON window class. A three-state check box is used when the choice is not a binary on/off choice. The three-state check box also adds the indeterminate state, which is often used when the answer cannot be determined.

Syntax	STATE3 *text, id, x, y, width, height,* [*style*]*,* [*extended style*]

Parameters

style	Specifies the styles for the control, which can be a combination of the **BS_3STATE** style and the following styles: **WS_TABSTOP**, **WS_DISABLED**, and **WS_GROUP**. The default is **BS_3STATE** and **WS_TABSTOP**. For more information on window styles, see Table 3-4 in Chapter 3, Creating Windows.

Example

```
STATE3 "File Read Only", IDC_READONLY, 3, 10, 35, 14
```

Dialog Box Function Descriptions

Table 8-2 summarizes the dialog box functions. The detailed function descriptions follow the table.

Table 8-2 Dialog box function summary

Function	Purpose
CheckDlgButton	Checks or removes a check from a dialog box control.
CheckRadioButton	Changes the selected item from a group of radio buttons.
CreateDialog	Creates a modeless dialog box.
CreateDialogIndirect	Creates a modeless dialog box.
CreateDialogIndirectParam	Creates a modeless dialog box, and passes a 32-bit value to the dialog box function when it starts processing messages.
CreateDialogParam	Creates a modeless dialog box, and passes a 32-bit value to the dialog box function when it starts processing messages.
DefDlgProc	Provides default message processing logic for dialog boxes created with their own separate window class.
DialogBox	Creates a modal dialog box.
DialogBoxIndirect	Creates a modal dialog box.
DialogBoxIndirectParam	Creates a modal dialog box, and passes a 32-bit data item to the dialog box as it is created.
DialogBoxParam	Creates a modal dialog box, and passes a 32-bit data item to the dialog box as it is created.
DlgDirList	Fills the specified list box with the names of all files matching the specified path or file name.
DlgDirListComboBox	Fills the specified combo box with a directory listing.
DlgDirSelectComboBoxEx	Retrieves the current selection from a combo box filled by using the DlgDirListComboBox function.
DlgDirSelectEx	Retrieves the current selection from a single-selection list box.
EndDialog	Closes a modal dialog box, and returns control to the calling function.
GetDialogBaseUnits	Determines the size of the dialog base units used to create dialog boxes and position controls.
GetDlgCtrlID	Retrieves a dialog box control's ID values given the control's window handle.
GetDlgItem	Retrieves the window handle for a dialog box control, given the control's ID number.
GetDlgItemInt	Retrieves an integer value from a control in a dialog box.
GetDlgItemText	Retrieves a character string from an edit control in a dialog box.

Function	Purpose
GetNextDlgGroupItem	Finds the next (or previous) window handle of the dialog box control that will receive the input focus if the user presses the arrow keys.
GetNextDlgTabItem	Finds the next (or previous) window handle of the dialog box control that will receive the input focus if the user presses the ⊤AB key.
IsDialogMessage	Determines if a message is meant for a dialog box.
IsDlgButtonChecked	Determines if a check box or radio button control is checked.
MapDialogRect	Converts from dialog base units to screen units (pixels).
MessageBeep	Plays a sound to alert the user.
MessageBox	Creates and displays a small window containing a message.
MessageBoxEx	Creates and displays a message box using the specified language.
MessageBoxIndirect	Creates and displays a message box that contains application-defined message text and title, icon, and combination of pushbuttons.
SendDlgItemMessage	Sends a message to a dialog box control.
SetDlgItemInt	Changes the text in a dialog box control to an integer value.
SetDlgItemText	Changes the text in a dialog box control.

CheckDlgButton   ■ WINDOWS 95   ■ WINDOWS NT

Description	**CheckDlgButton** places a checkmark next to (checks) or removes a checkmark from (clears) a button control, or changes the state of a three-state button. Use **CheckDlgButton** with check boxes and three-state buttons to insert and remove the checkmark from the control.
Syntax	BOOL **CheckDlgButton**(HWND *hwndDlg,* int *idButton,* UINT *uCheck*)
Parameters	
hwndDlg	HWND: The handle of the dialog box that contains the button.
idButton	int: The identifier of the button to modify.
uCheck	UINT: The check state of the button. If this parameter is nonzero, **CheckDlgButton** checks the button; if the parameter is **0**, the function clears the button. For a three-state check box, if *uCheck* is **2**, the button is grayed; if *uCheck* is **1**, it is checked; if *uCheck* is **0**, it is cleared.
Returns	BOOL: If successful, the return value is TRUE; otherwise, it is FALSE.
Include File	winuser.h
See Also	CheckRadioButton, CheckMenuItem
Related Messages	BM_SETCHECK
Example	This example, which is illustrated in Figure 8-2, displays a modal dialog box when the user selects the Test! menu item. The dialog box contains a check box and a set of two radio buttons. The **TestDlgProc** at the end of the listing shows typical program logic for handling check boxes and radio buttons that do not have the BS_AUTOXXXX style.

Dialog box definition in CHKDLGBT.RC

```
TESTDIALOG DIALOG DISCARDABLE  20, 20, 180, 70
STYLE DS_MODALFRAME | WS_POPUP | WS_VISIBLE | WS_CAPTION | WS_SYSMENU
CAPTION "Test Dialog"
FONT 8, "MS Sans Serif"
BEGIN
    CHECKBOX        "Check box control.",IDC_CHECKBOX,9,7,70,10
    GROUPBOX        "Radio Buttons",-1,7,21,86,39
    RADIOBUTTON     "First", IDC_RADIO1,13,32,37,10,WS_GROUP | WS_TABSTOP
    RADIOBUTTON     "Second",IDC_RADIO2,13,45,39,10
    PUSHBUTTON      "Done",IDCANCEL,116,8,50,14,WS_GROUP
END
```

Dialog box item defines in CHKDLGBT.H

```
#define IDC_CHECKBOX 101
#define IDC_RADIO1   102
#define IDC_RADIO2   103
```

WndProc *and* TestDlgProc *functions in* CHKDLGBT.C

```
BOOL bChecked = FALSE;
BOOL bRadio1  = TRUE;

LRESULT CALLBACK WndProc( HWND hWnd, UINT uMsg, WPARAM wParam, LPARAM lParam )
{
    switch( uMsg )
    {
        case WM_COMMAND :
                switch( LOWORD( wParam ) )
                {
                    case IDM_TEST :
                            DialogBox( hInst, "TestDialog", hWnd,
                                    (DLGPROC)TestDlgProc );
                            break;

                    case IDM_EXIT :
                            DestroyWindow( hWnd );
                            break;
                }
                break;

        case WM_DESTROY :
                PostQuitMessage(0);
                break;

        default :
                return( DefWindowProc( hWnd, uMsg, wParam, lParam ) );
    }

    return( 0L );
}
```

```
LRESULT CALLBACK TestDlgProc( HWND hDlg, UINT uMsg,
                              WPARAM wParam, LPARAM lParam )
{
   switch( uMsg )
   {
      // Initially set the check box
      // and radio button states.
      //..........................
      case WM_INITDIALOG :
            CheckDlgButton( hDlg, IDC_CHECKBOX, bChecked ? MF_CHECKED :
                                                    MF_UNCHECKED );
            CheckRadioButton( hDlg, IDC_RADIO1, IDC_RADIO2,
                         bRadio1 ? IDC_RADIO1 : IDC_RADIO2 );
            break;

      case WM_COMMAND :
            switch( LOWORD( wParam ) )
            {
               case IDC_CHECKBOX :
                     bChecked = !IsDlgButtonChecked( hDlg, IDC_CHECKBOX );
                     CheckDlgButton( hDlg, IDC_CHECKBOX,
                                 bChecked ? MF_CHECKED : MF_UNCHECKED );
                     break;

               case IDC_RADIO1 :
                     bRadio1 = TRUE;
                     CheckRadioButton( hDlg, IDC_RADIO1, IDC_RADIO2,
                                                    IDC_RADIO1 );
                     break;

               case IDC_RADIO2 :
                     bRadio1 = FALSE;
                     CheckRadioButton( hDlg, IDC_RADIO1, IDC_RADIO2,
                                                    IDC_RADIO2 );
                     break;

               case IDCANCEL :
                     EndDialog( hDlg, IDCANCEL );
                     break;
            }
            break;

      default :
            return( FALSE );
   }

   return( TRUE );
}
```

CheckRadioButton   ■ WINDOWS 95   ■ WINDOWS NT

Description   Radio buttons are used in groups to show a selection from a group of
                        mutually exclusive choices. **CheckRadioButton** adds a checkmark to
                        (checks) a given radio button in a group and removes a checkmark
                        from (clears) all other radio buttons in the group. Use

CheckRadioButton to change a group of radio buttons to reflect a selection.

Syntax	BOOL **CheckRadioButton**(HWND *hwndDlg,* int *idFirstButton,* int *idLastButton,* int *idCheckButton*)
Parameters	
hwndDlg	HWND: The handle of the dialog box that contains the radio button.
idFirstButton	int: The identifier of the first radio button in the group.
idLastButton	int: The identifier of the last radio button in the group.
idCheckButton	int: The identifier of the radio button to select.
Returns	BOOL: If successful, the return value is TRUE; otherwise, it is FALSE.
Include File	winuser.h
See Also	CheckDlgButton, CheckMenuItem
Related Messages	BM_SETCHECK
Example	See the example for the CheckDlgButton function.

CreateDialog ■ WINDOWS 95 ■ WINDOWS NT

Description	CreateDialog creates a modeless dialog box from a dialog box template resource. The dialog box template should contain the WS_VISIBLE style. If not, the ShowWindow function will be needed to make the modeless dialog box visible. Unlike DialogBox, CreateDialog returns immediately, returning the handle of the dialog box window created. Modeless dialog boxes are ended by calling DestroyWindow within the dialog box function. The application's message loop needs to be modified for modeless dialog boxes so keyboard input to the dialog box is properly processed. See the example below.
Syntax	HWND **CreateDialog**(HANDLE *hinst,* LPCTSTR *lpszTemplate,* HWND *hwndOwner,* DLGPROC *dlgprc*)
Parameters	
hinst	HANDLE: The instance handle of the module whose executable file contains the dialog box template.
lpszTemplate	LPCTSTR: A pointer to a character string containing the name of the dialog box template in the resource file. If the parameter specifies a resource identifier, its high-order word must be 0 and its low-order word must contain the identifier. Use the MAKEINTRESOURCE macro to create this value.
hwndOwner	HWND: The parent window's handle. Destroying the parent window will automatically destroy the modeless dialog box.

dlgprc	DLGPROC: A pointer to the dialog box procedure. The dialog box procedure processes messages for the dialog box. See the description of the DlgProc below.
Returns	HWND: If successful, the return value is the handle of the dialog box; otherwise, it is NULL.
Include File	winuser.h
See Also	CreateDialogIndirect, CreateDialogParam, DestroyWindow, IsDialogMessage, SetFocus, DialogBox
Related Messages	WM_INITDIALOG
DlgProc **Syntax**	BOOL APIENTRY **DlgProc**(HWND *hDlg*, UINT *uMsg*, WPARAM *wParam*, LPARAM *lParam*)
DlgProc **Parameters**	
hDlg	HWND: The window handle of the modeless dialog box.
uMsg	UINT: The message being passed to the dialog function. For example, **WM_INITDIALOG** is sent to the dialog function right before the dialog is made visible.
wParam	WPARAM: Message-specific data.
lParam	LPARAM: Message-specific data.
DlgProc **Returns**	BOOL: The dialog box function should return **TRUE** if the function processes the message, and **FALSE** if the message is not acted on. The exception is processing a **WM_INITDIALOG** message. In this case, the function should return **FALSE** if the **SetFocus** function is called; otherwise, **TRUE**. **SetFocus** is used to establish which control will have the input focus when the dialog box is first made visible. If **SetFocus** is not used, the first control in the dialog box definition with the **WS_TABSTOP** style receives the input focus.
Example	This example creates the same dialog box shown in the example under **CheckDlgButton**, except that the dialog box is a modeless dialog box. The dialog box definition is identical to the one for a normal (modal) dialog box. Note that the **DestroyWindow** is used to end the dialog box. Also, the *hDlgModeless* handle is set to **NULL** on the **WM_DESTROY** message to shut down message processing for the dialog.

```
HWND hDlgModeless = NULL;
BOOL bChecked     = FALSE;
BOOL bRadio1      = TRUE;

int APIENTRY WinMain( HINSTANCE hInstance, HINSTANCE hPrevInstance,
                      LPTSTR lpCmdLine, int nCmdShow)
{
    MSG     msg;
    HWND    hWnd;
```

continued on next page

continued from previous page

```
    // Application Initialization.
    //...........................

            .
            .
            .

    while( GetMessage( &msg, NULL, 0, 0) )
    {
        if ( hDlgModeless || !IsDialogMessage( hDlgModeless, &msg ) )
        {
            TranslateMessage( &msg );
            DispatchMessage( &msg );
        }
    }

    return( msg.wParam );
}


LRESULT CALLBACK WndProc( HWND hWnd, UINT uMsg, WPARAM wParam, LPARAM lParam )
{
    switch( uMsg )
    {
    case WM_COMMAND :
            switch( LOWORD( wParam ) )
            {
                case IDM_TEST :
                        if ( !hDlgModeless )
                            hDlgModeless = CreateDialog( hInst, "TestDialog",
                                                  hWnd, (DLGPROC)TestDlgProc );
                        break;

                case IDM_EXIT :
                        DestroyWindow( hWnd );
                        break;
            }
            break;

    case WM_DESTROY :
            PostQuitMessage(0);
            break;

    default :
            return( DefWindowProc( hWnd, uMsg, wParam, lParam ) );
    }

    return( 0L );
}


LRESULT CALLBACK TestDlgProc( HWND hDlg, UINT uMsg,
                              WPARAM wParam, LPARAM lParam )
{
    switch( uMsg )
    {
```

```
    case WM_INITDIALOG :
         CheckDlgButton( hDlg, IDC_CHECKBOX, bChecked ? MF_CHECKED :
                                                         MF_UNCHECKED );
         CheckRadioButton( hDlg, IDC_RADIO1, IDC_RADIO2,
                      bRadio1 ? IDC_RADIO1 : IDC_RADIO2 );
         break;

    case WM_COMMAND :
         switch( LOWORD( wParam ) )
         {
            case IDC_CHECKBOX :
                 bChecked = !IsDlgButtonChecked( hDlg, IDC_CHECKBOX );
                 CheckDlgButton( hDlg, IDC_CHECKBOX,
                            bChecked ? MF_CHECKED : MF_UNCHECKED );
                 break;

            case IDC_RADIO1 :
                 bRadio1 = TRUE;
                 CheckRadioButton( hDlg, IDC_RADIO1, IDC_RADIO2,
                                            IDC_RADIO1 );
                 break;

            case IDC_RADIO2 :
                 bRadio1 = FALSE;
                 CheckRadioButton( hDlg, IDC_RADIO1, IDC_RADIO2,
                                            IDC_RADIO2 );
                 break;

            case IDCANCEL :
                 DestroyWindow( hDlg );
                 break;
         }
         break;

    case WM_DESTROY :
         hDlgModeless = NULL;
         break;

    default :
         return( FALSE );
    }

    return( TRUE );
}
```

CreateDialogIndirect   ■ WINDOWS 95   ■ WINDOWS NT

Description   CreateDialogIndirect is identical to CreateDialog, except that the dialog template is specified with a pointer to memory containing a dialog box template. The dialog box template can be either created from scratch in memory, or loaded into memory with the LoadResource function. The structure of the dialog box definition in memory is discussed at the beginning of this chapter under Dynamic Dialog Boxes.

Use this function to create modeless dialog boxes that can be modified as the program runs (called dynamic dialog boxes). Typical applications are database programs, with which the user can add or subtract fields from the database. Using this function provides greater control over when the program loads and discards the resource data that defines the dialog box. This can be important in applications that use a large number of resources and need to control which ones are preloaded and which are discarded.

Syntax   HWND **CreateDialogIndirect**(HANDLE *hinst,* LPCDLGTEMPLATE *lpTemplate,* HWND *hwndOwner,* DLGPROC *dlgprc*)

Parameters

hinst   HANDLE: The instance handle of the module that creates the dialog box.

lpTemplate   LPCDLGTEMPLATE: A pointer to a global memory object that contains a dialog box template used to create the dialog box. This template is in the form of a **DLGTEMPLATE** structure followed by one or more **DLGITEMTEMPLATE** structures.

hwndOwner   HWND: The parent window's handle. Destroying the parent window will automatically destroy the modeless dialog box.

dlgprc   DLGPROC: A pointer to the dialog box procedure. The dialog box procedure processes messages for the dialog box. See the **CreateDialog** function for a definition of the **DlgProc** function.

Returns   HWND: If successful, the return value is the handle of the dialog box; otherwise, it is **NULL**.

Include File   winuser.h

See Also   CreateDialog, CreateDialogParam, CreateDialogIndirectParam, DestroyWindow, IsDialogMessage, SetFocus, DialogBox

Related Messages   WM_INITDIALOG

Example   This example creates the dialog box definition in memory by loading a dialog box resource. The result is identical to that of the example shown in more detail under **CreateDialog**. The only differences are in the processing of the **IDM_TEST** menu item. Because **CreateDialogIndirect** is used to create the modeless dialog box, some preparation is required. First, load the dialog box information into memory with **LoadResource**. Second, lock the memory block containing the dialog box information in memory using **LockResource**. **LockResource** returns a pointer to the memory area needed to call **CreateDialogIndirect**. Resources do not need to be unlocked and freed in Win32.

```
LRESULT CALLBACK WndProc( HWND hWnd, UINT uMsg, WPARAM wParam, LPARAM lParam )
{
   switch( uMsg )
   {
      case WM_COMMAND :
               switch( LOWORD( wParam ) )
               {
```

```
        case IDM_TEST :
            if ( !hDlgModeless )
            {
                HANDLE hDialog = LoadResource( hInst,
                              FindResource( hInst, "TestDialog",
                                    RT_DIALOG ) );

                LPVOID lpDialog = LockResource( hDialog );

                hDlgModeless = CreateDialogIndirect( hInst,
                            (LPCDLGTEMPLATE)lpDialog, hWnd,
                            (DLGPROC)TestDlgProc );
            }
            break;

        case IDM_EXIT :
            DestroyWindow( hWnd );
            break;
```

CreateDialogIndirectParam   ■ Windows 95   ■ Windows NT

Description   CreateDialogIndirectParam is identical to CreateDialogIndirect,
except it has an added parameter. This added parameter allows a 32-bit
value (usually a handle to memory) to be passed to the dialog box function on startup.

This is the most sophisticated of the modeless dialog box functions. This
function can be used to create dynamic dialog boxes that can be changed
as the program executes. Using a memory pointer for the dialog resource
information, instead of just a dialog box template name, gives more control over when the resource data is loaded and discarded. The 32-bit data
element allows the dialog box to avoid global variables as a means of communication between the dialog box function and the rest of the
application program.

Syntax   HWND **CreateDialogIndirectParam**(HINSTANCE *hinst*, LPCDLGTEMPLATE
lpTemplate, HWND *hwndOwner*, DLGPROC *dlgprc*, LPARAM *lParamInit*)

Parameters

hinst   HINSTANCE: The instance handle of the module that creates the dialog box.

lpTemplate   LPCDLGTEMPLATE: A pointer to a global memory object that contains the
dialog box template used to create the dialog box. This template is in the
form of a **DLGTEMPLATE** structure followed by one or more **DLGITEMTEM-
PLATE** structures.

hwndOwner   HWND: The parent window's handle. Destroying the parent window will
automatically destroy the modeless dialog box.

dlgprc	DLGPROC: A pointer to the dialog box procedure. The dialog box procedure processes messages for the dialog box. See the `CreateDialog` function for a definition of the `DlgProc` function.
lParamInit	LPARAM: The 32-bit value passed to the `DlgProc` in the `WM_INITDIALOG` message. Normally, this value is used to pass a handle to a memory block containing data that the dialog box will use or modify.
Returns	HWND: If successful, the return value is the handle of the dialog box; otherwise, it is NULL.
Include File	`winuser.h`
See Also	`CreateDialog, CreateDialogIndirect, DestroyWindow, IsDialogMessage, SetFocus`
Related Messages	WM_INITDIALOG
Example	This example is identical to the one under `CreateDialogParam`, except for the changes needed for `CreateDialogIndirectParam`. In both cases, the 32-bit value is used to pass the handle to a custom data structure that contains the settings for the dialog box buttons. See the example under `CreateDialogParam` for further details.

```
typedef struct
{
   BOOL bChecked;
   BOOL bRadio1;
} DLGDATA, *LPDLGDATA;

LRESULT CALLBACK WndProc( HWND hWnd, UINT uMsg, WPARAM wParam, LPARAM lParam )
{
static LPDLGDATA lpMem;

   switch( uMsg )
   {
      case WM_CREATE :
            lpMem = (LPDLGDATA)HeapAlloc( GetProcessHeap(), HEAP_ZERO_MEMORY, ⇐
sizeof( DLGDATA );
            lpMem->bChecked = FALSE;
            lpMem->bRadio1  = TRUE;
            break;

      case WM_COMMAND :
            switch( LOWORD( wParam ) )
            {
               case IDM_TEST :
                     if ( !hDlgModeless )
                     {
                        HANDLE hDialog = LoadResource( hInst,
                                        FindResource( hInst, "TestDialog",
                                                      RT_DIALOG ) );

                        LPVOID lpDialog = LockResource( hDialog );

                        hDlgModeless = CreateDialogIndirectParam( hInst,
```

```
                                    (LPCDLGTEMPLATE)lpDialog, hWnd,
                                    (DLGPROC)TestDlgProc,
                                    (LPARAM)lpMem );
                    }
                    break;

            case IDM_EXIT :
                    DestroyWindow( hWnd );
                    break;
        }
        break;
```

CreateDialogParam   ■ WINDOWS 95   ■ WINDOWS NT

Description	CreateDialogParam is identical to CreateDialog, except that there is an added parameter. This added parameter allows a 32-bit value (usually a handle to memory) to be passed to the dialog box function on startup.
Syntax	HWND **CreateDialogParam**(HINSTANCE *hinst,* LPCTSTR *lpszTemplate,* HWND *hwndOwner,* DLGPROC *dlgprc,* LPARAM *lParamInit*)
Parameters	
hinst	HINSTANCE: The instance handle of the module whose executable file contains the dialog box template.
lpszTemplate	LPCTSTR: A pointer to a character string containing the name of the dialog box template in the resource file. If the parameter specifies a resource identifier, its high-order word must be 0 and its low-order word must contain the identifier. Use the MAKEINTRESOURCE macro to create this value.
hwndOwner	HWND: The parent window's handle. Destroying the parent window will automatically destroy the modeless dialog box.
dlgprc	DLGPROC: A pointer to the dialog box procedure. The dialog box procedure processes messages for the dialog box. See the CreateDialog function for a definition of the DlgProc function.
lParamInit	LPARAM: The 32-bit value passed to the DlgProc in the WM_INITDIALOG message as the *lParam* value. Normally, an application uses this value to pass a handle to a memory block containing data that the dialog box will use or modify.
Returns	HWND: If successful, the return value is the handle of the dialog box; otherwise, it is NULL.
Include File	winuser.h
See Also	CreateDialog, CreateDialogIndirect, CreateDialogIndirectParam, DestroyWindow, IsDialogMessage, SetFocus, DialogBox
Related Messages	WM_INITDIALOG

Example

This example is similar to the one under **CreateDialog**, except that **CreateDialogParam** has been used to avoid global variables. A custom structure called **DLGDATA** is defined to hold the status of the buttons needed by the dialog box. A handle to memory containing this data structure is passed to the dialog box function when **CreateDialogIndirect** is called. The handle ends up as the *lParam* value passed to **TestDlgProc** when the **WM_INITDIALOG** message is received.

```c
typedef struct
{
   BOOL bChecked;
   BOOL bRadio1;
} DLGDATA, *LPDLGDATA;

LRESULT CALLBACK WndProc( HWND hWnd, UINT uMsg, WPARAM wParam, LPARAM lParam )
{
static HANDLE     hMem = NULL;
static LPDLGDATA lpMem;

   switch( uMsg )
   {
      case WM_CREATE :
             lpMem = (LPDLGDATA)HeapAlloc( GetProcessHeap(), HEAP_ZERO_MEMORY, ⇐
sizeof( DLGDATA ) );
             lpMem->bChecked = FALSE;
             lpMem->bRadio1  = TRUE;
             break;

      case WM_COMMAND :
             switch( LOWORD( wParam ) )
             {
                case IDM_TEST :
                       if ( !hDlgModeless )
                       {
                           hDlgModeless = CreateDialogParam( hInst,
                                                   "TestDialog",
                                                   hWnd,
                                                   (DLGPROC)TestDlgProc,
                                                   (LPARAM)lpMem );
                       }
                       break;

                case IDM_EXIT :
                       DestroyWindow( hWnd );
                       break;
             }
             break;

      case WM_DESTROY :
             if ( lpMem )
                HeapFree( GetProcessHeap(), 0, lpMem );

             PostQuitMessage(0);
             break;
```

```
        default :
               return( DefWindowProc( hWnd, uMsg, wParam, lParam ) );
    }

    return( OL );
}


LRESULT CALLBACK TestDlgProc( HWND hDlg, UINT uMsg,
                               WPARAM wParam, LPARAM lParam )
{
static LPDLGDATA lpMem;

    switch( uMsg )
    {
      case WM_INITDIALOG :
             lpMem = (LPDLGDATA)lParam;

             CheckDlgButton( hDlg, IDC_CHECKBOX, lpMem->bChecked ? MF_CHECKED :
                                                              MF_UNCHECKED );
             CheckRadioButton( hDlg, IDC_RADIO1, IDC_RADIO2,
                               lpMem->bRadio1 ? IDC_RADIO1 : IDC_RADIO2 );

             break;

      case WM_COMMAND :
             switch( LOWORD( wParam ) )
             {
                case IDC_CHECKBOX :
                       lpMem->bChecked = !IsDlgButtonChecked( hDlg,
                                                        IDC_CHECKBOX );
                       CheckDlgButton( hDlg, IDC_CHECKBOX,
                                       lpMem->bChecked ? MF_CHECKED :
                                                         MF_UNCHECKED );
                       break;

                case IDC_RADIO1 :
                       lpMem->bRadio1 = TRUE;
                       CheckRadioButton( hDlg, IDC_RADIO1, IDC_RADIO2,
                                                           IDC_RADIO1 );
                       break;

                case IDC_RADIO2 :
                       lpMem->bRadio1 = FALSE;
                       CheckRadioButton( hDlg, IDC_RADIO1, IDC_RADIO2,
                                                           IDC_RADIO2 );
                       break;

                case IDCANCEL :
                       DestroyWindow( hDlg );
                       break;
             }
             break;

      case WM_DESTROY :
             hDlgModeless = NULL;
             break;
```

continued on next page

continued from previous page

```
        default :
                return( FALSE );
    }

    return( TRUE );
}
```

DefDlgProc   ■ WINDOWS 95   ■ WINDOWS NT

Description	**DefDlgProc** carries out default message processing for a window procedure belonging to an application-defined dialog box class. This is used for the default message processing instead of the **DefWindowProc** function in the **WndProc** for the class.
	Normally, Windows takes care of processing messages that the dialog box function does not handle. An exception is when a separate window class is used for the dialog box window. To do this, include the **CLASS** statement in the dialog box definition in the application's resource file.
Syntax	LRESULT **DefDlgProc**(HWND *hwndDlg,* UINT *uMsg,* WPARAM *wParam,* LPARAM *lParam*)
Parameters	
hwndDlg	**HWND**: The dialog box window handle.
uMsg	**UINT**: The message identifier.
wParam	**WPARAM**: Additional message-dependent information.
lParam	**LPARAM**: Additional message-dependent information.
Returns	**LRESULT**: The result of the message processing. The value is dependent on the message sent.
Include File	**windowsx.h**
See Also	**RegisterClass**
Related Messages	All Windows messages that are not processed by the dialog box function should be passed to **DefDlgProc** if the dialog box has its own window class.
Example	The dialog box resource definition has had the **CLASS** statement added. In this case, the dialog box will use the **BlueDlg** class for the dialog box. The dialog box is identical to the one shown in Figure 8-2 except the dialog background is blue. Note that the separate class for the dialog box is created in **WndProc** when the **WM_CREATE** message is processed. Dialogs created using this class will have a blue background.

Dialog box definition in DEFDLGP.RC

```
TESTDIALOG DIALOG DISCARDABLE  0, 0, 180, 70
STYLE DS_MODALFRAME | WS_POPUP | WS_VISIBLE | WS_CAPTION | WS_SYSMENU
```

```
CAPTION "Test Dialog"
FONT 8, "MS Sans Serif"
CLASS "BlueDlg"
BEGIN
    CHECKBOX          "Check box control.",IDC_CHECKBOX,9,7,70,10
    GROUPBOX          "Radio Buttons",-1,7,21,86,39
    RADIOBUTTON       "First",IDC_RADIO1,13,32,37,10,WS_GROUP | WS_TABSTOP
    RADIOBUTTON       "Second",IDC_RADIO2,13,45,39,10
    PUSHBUTTON        "Done",IDCANCEL,116,8,50,14,WS_GROUP
END
```

WndProc, BlueDlgProc, *and* TestDlgProc *functions in* DEFDLGP.C

```
BOOL bChecked = FALSE;
BOOL bRadio1  = TRUE;

LRESULT CALLBACK WndProc( HWND hWnd, UINT uMsg, WPARAM wParam, LPARAM lParam )
{
    switch( uMsg )
    {
    case WM_CREATE  :
            {
                WNDCLASS wc;

                wc.style           = CS_HREDRAW | CS_VREDRAW;
                wc.lpfnWndProc     = BlueDlgProc;
                wc.cbClsExtra      = 0;
                wc.cbWndExtra      = DLGWINDOWEXTRA;
                wc.hInstance       = hInst;
                wc.hIcon           = NULL;
                wc.hCursor         = LoadCursor( NULL, IDC_ARROW );
                wc.hbrBackground   = GetStockObject( WHITE_BRUSH );
                wc.lpszMenuName    = NULL;
                wc.lpszClassName   = "BlueDlg";

                RegisterClass( &wc );
            }
            break;

    case WM_COMMAND :
            switch( LOWORD( wParam ) )
            {
            case IDM_TEST :
                    DialogBox( hInst, "TestDialog", hWnd,
                            (DLGPROC)TestDlgProc );
                    break;

            case IDM_EXIT :
                    DestroyWindow( hWnd );
                    break;
            }
            break;

    case WM_DESTROY :
            PostQuitMessage(0);
            break;
```

continued on next page

continued from previous page

```
        default :
                return( DefWindowProc( hWnd, uMsg, wParam, lParam ) );
    }

    return( OL );
}


LRESULT CALLBACK BlueDlgProc( HWND hWnd, UINT uMsg,
                              WPARAM wParam, LPARAM lParam )
{
static HBRUSH hbkgnd = NULL;

    switch( uMsg )
    {
        case WM_CTLCOLORBTN :
        case WM_CTLCOLORSTATIC :
        case WM_CTLCOLORDLG :
                if ( !hbkgnd )
                {
                    LOGBRUSH lb;

                    lb.lbStyle = BS_SOLID;
                    lb.lbColor = RGB( 0, 0, 255 ); // Blue
                    hbkgnd = CreateBrushIndirect( &lb );
                }

                SetBkColor( (HDC)wParam, RGB( 0, 0, 255 ) );
                return( (LRESULT)hbkgnd );

        case WM_DESTROY :
                if ( hbkgnd )
                    DeleteObject( hbkgnd );
                break;
    }

    return( DefDlgProc( hWnd, uMsg, wParam, lParam ) );
}


LRESULT CALLBACK TestDlgProc( HWND hDlg, UINT uMsg,
                              WPARAM wParam, LPARAM lParam )
{
    switch( uMsg )
    {
        case WM_INITDIALOG :
                CheckDlgButton( hDlg, IDC_CHECKBOX, bChecked ? MF_CHECKED :
                                                              MF_UNCHECKED );
                CheckRadioButton( hDlg, IDC_RADIO1, IDC_RADIO2,
                              bRadio1 ? IDC_RADIO1 : IDC_RADIO2 );
                break;

        case WM_COMMAND :
                switch( LOWORD( wParam ) )
                {
                    case IDC_CHECKBOX :
                            bChecked = !IsDlgButtonChecked( hDlg, IDC_CHECKBOX );
                            CheckDlgButton( hDlg, IDC_CHECKBOX,
                                        bChecked ? MF_CHECKED : MF_UNCHECKED );
                            break;
```

```
            case IDC_RADIO1 :
                    bRadio1 = TRUE;
                    CheckRadioButton( hDlg, IDC_RADIO1, IDC_RADIO2,
                                                        IDC_RADIO1 );
                    break;

            case IDC_RADIO2 :
                    bRadio1 = FALSE;
                    CheckRadioButton( hDlg, IDC_RADIO1, IDC_RADIO2,
                                                        IDC_RADIO2 );
                    break;

            case IDCANCEL :
                    EndDialog( hDlg, IDCANCEL );
                    break;
        }
        break;

    default :
            return( FALSE );
    }

    return( TRUE );
}
```

DialogBox
■ WINDOWS 95   ■ WINDOWS NT

Description   DialogBox creates a modal dialog box from a dialog box template resource. Control is not returned until the given callback function terminates the modal dialog box by calling the EndDialog function.

This function is the most common way to create a dialog box. The dialog box template is defined in the application's resource file. A dialog box function must be defined to process messages while the dialog box is in operation.

Syntax   int **DialogBox**(HANDLE *hinst,* LPCTSTR *lpszTemplate,* HWND *hwndOwner,* DLGPROC *dlgprc*)

Parameters

hinst   HANDLE: The instance handle of the module whose executable file contains the dialog box template.

lpszTemplate   LPCTSTR: A pointer to a character string containing the name of the dialog box template in the resource file. If the parameter specifies a resource identifier, its high-order word must be **0** and its low-order word must contain the identifier. Use the **MAKEINTRESOURCE** macro to create this value.

hwndOwner   HWND: The parent window's handle. Destroying the parent window will automatically destroy the modeless dialog box.

dlgprc	**DLGPROC**: A pointer to the dialog box procedure. The dialog box procedure processes messages for the dialog box. See the definition of **DlgProc** under **CreateDialog**.
Returns	**int**: The return value equals the *nResult* parameter passed when **EndDialog** is called. The return value is **−1** if the dialog box could not be created.
Include File	**winuser.h**
See Also	**DialogBoxParam**, **DialogBoxIndirect**, **DialogBoxIndirectParam**, **CreateDialog**
Related Messages	Most Windows messages can be processed by a dialog box. **WM_CREATE** is replaced with **WM_INITDIALOG** for dialog boxes for handling initialization of the dialog box.
Example	This example, shown in Figure 8-3, creates a dialog box for entering an integer value and a character string. Note that the integer and character string values, which can be changed from within the dialog box, are defined as global variables.

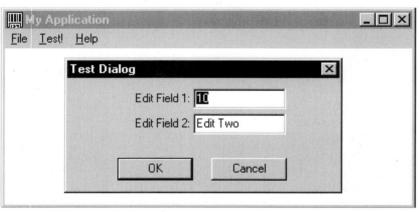

Figure 8-3 **DialogBox** example

Dialog box definition in **DLGBOX.RC**

```
TESTDIALOG DIALOG DISCARDABLE  20, 20, 180, 70
STYLE DS_MODALFRAME | WS_POPUP | WS_VISIBLE | WS_CAPTION | WS_SYSMENU
CAPTION "Test Dialog"
FONT 8, "MS Sans Serif"
BEGIN
    RTEXT           "Edit Field 1:",-1,36,8,45,8
    EDITTEXT        IDC_EDIT1,83,6,61,13,ES_AUTOHSCROLL | WS_BORDER
    RTEXT           "Edit Field 2:",-1,36,24,45,8
    EDITTEXT        IDC_EDIT2,83,22,61,13,ES_AUTOHSCROLL | WS_BORDER
    PUSHBUTTON      "OK",IDOK,33,50,50,14
    PUSHBUTTON      "Cancel",IDCANCEL,95,50,50,14,WS_GROUP
END
```

DLGBOX.C *excerpt*

```
int    nEditOne = 10;
char   szEditTwo[20] = "Edit Two";

LRESULT CALLBACK WndProc( HWND hWnd, UINT uMsg, WPARAM wParam, LPARAM lParam )
{
   switch( uMsg )
   {
      case WM_COMMAND :
              switch( LOWORD( wParam ) )
              {
                 case IDM_TEST :
                         DialogBox( hInst, "TestDialog", hWnd,
                                    (DLGPROC)TestDlgProc );
                         break;

                 case IDM_EXIT :
                         DestroyWindow( hWnd );
                         break;
              }
              break;

      case WM_DESTROY :
              PostQuitMessage(0);
              break;

      default :
              return( DefWindowProc( hWnd, uMsg, wParam, lParam ) );
   }

   return( 0L );
}


LRESULT CALLBACK TestDlgProc( HWND hDlg, UINT uMsg,
                              WPARAM wParam, LPARAM lParam )
{
   switch( uMsg )
   {
      case WM_INITDIALOG :
              SetDlgItemInt ( hDlg, IDC_EDIT1, nEditOne, TRUE );
              SetDlgItemText( hDlg, IDC_EDIT2, szEditTwo );
              break;

      case WM_COMMAND :
              switch( LOWORD( wParam ) )
              {
                 case IDOK :
                         {
                             BOOL bTran;

                             nEditOne = GetDlgItemInt( hDlg, IDC_EDIT1,
                                                 &bTran, TRUE );
                             GetDlgItemText( hDlg, IDC_EDIT2, szEditTwo,
                                             sizeof(szEditTwo)-1 );
```

continued on next page

continued from previous page

```
                        EndDialog( hDlg, IDOK );
                }
                break;

            case IDCANCEL :
                    EndDialog( hDlg, IDCANCEL );
                    break;
        }
        break;

    default :
            return( FALSE );
    }

    return( TRUE );
}
```

DialogBoxIndirect ■ WINDOWS 95 ■ WINDOWS NT

Description	DialogBoxIndirect is identical to DialogBox, except that the dialog box resource data is specified by a memory handle instead of the resource name.
	The dialog box template in memory can be modified to change the dialog box as the application runs (called a "dynamic dialog box"). See the discussion under Dynamic Dialog Boxes at the beginning of the chapter. Specifying the dialog box resource data indirectly allows the program to have more control over when the resource data is loaded and discarded.
Syntax	int **DialogBoxIndirect**(HANDLE *hinst,* LPDLGTEMPLATE *lpTemplate,* HWND *hwndOwner,* DLGPROC *dlgprc*)
Parameters	
hinst	HANDLE: The instance handle of the module that creates the dialog box.
lpTemplate	LPDLGTEMPLATE: A pointer to a global memory object that contains a dialog box template used to create the dialog box. This template is in the form of a **DLGTEMPLATE** structure followed by one or more **DLGITEMTEMPLATE** structures.
hwndOwner	HWND: The handle of the window that owns the dialog box.
dlgprc	DLGPROC: A pointer to the dialog box procedure. The dialog box procedure processes messages for the dialog box. See the **CreateDialog** function for a definition of the **DlgProc** function.
Returns	int: The return value equals the *nResult* parameter passed when **EndDialog** is called. The return value is −1 if the dialog box could not be created.
Include File	winuser.h
See Also	DialogBox, DialogBoxIndirectParam, DialogBoxParam, CreateDialogIndirect

Example   This example is identical to the example under the `DialogBox` function
description, except for the changes needed to use the `DialogBoxIndirect`
function. Note that it is not necessary for a Win32-based application to
unlock or free the loaded dialog box resource.

```
LRESULT CALLBACK WndProc( HWND hWnd, UINT uMsg, WPARAM wParam, LPARAM lParam )
{
   switch( uMsg )
   {
      case WM_COMMAND :
              switch( LOWORD( wParam ) )
              {
                 case IDM_TEST :
                        {
                          HANDLE hDialog = LoadResource( hInst,
                                       FindResource( hInst, "TestDialog",
                                              RT_DIALOG ) );

                          LPVOID lpDialog = LockResource( hDialog );

                          DialogBoxIndirect( hInst, lpDialog, hWnd,
                                  (DLGPROC)TestDlgProc );
                        }
                        break;

                 case IDM_EXIT :
                        DestroyWindow( hWnd );
                        break;
              }
              break;
       .
       .
       .
```

DialogBoxIndirectParam   ■ WINDOWS 95 ■ WINDOWS NT

Description   `DialogBoxIndirectParam` is identical to `DialogBoxIndirect`, except it has
an added parameter. This added parameter allows a 32-bit value (usually a
handle to memory) to be passed as the *lParam* when the dialog procedure
receives the `WM_INITDIALOG` message.

Syntax   int **DialogBoxIndirectParam**(HINSTANCE *hinst,* LPCDLGTEMPLATE
lpTemplate, HWND *hwndOwner,* DLGPROC *dlgprc,* LPARAM *lParamInit*)

Parameters

hinst   HINSTANCE: The instance handle of the module that creates the dialog box.

lpTemplate   LPCDLGTEMPLATE: A pointer to a global memory object that contains a dialog box template used to create the dialog box. This template is in the
form of a **DLGTEMPLATE** structure followed by one or more **DLGITEMTEM-
PLATE** structures.

hwndOwner   HWND: The handle of the window that owns the dialog box.

dlgprc	DLGPROC: A pointer to the dialog box procedure. The dialog box procedure processes messages for the dialog box. See the **CreateDialog** function for a definition of the **DlgProc** function.
lParamInit	LPARAM: The 32-bit value passed to the **DlgProc** in the **WM_INITDIALOG** message. Normally, this value is used to pass a handle to a memory block containing data that the dialog box will use or modify.
Returns	int: The return value equals the *nResult* parameter passed when **EndDialog** is called. The return value is **−1** if the dialog box could not be created.
Include File	winuser.h
See Also	DialogBox, DialogBoxIndirect, DialogBoxParam
Related Messages	WM_INITDIALOG
Example	This example runs the same dialog box shown in the **DialogBox** and **DialogBoxIndirect** function examples. This case uses the more sophisticated **DialogBoxIndirectParam** function, which allows the data for the dialog box to be passed in a custom data structure called **DLGDATA**. Because the function uses "indirect" loading of the dialog box resource, the resource data is specified by a pointer obtained with the function combination of **LoadResource** and **LockResource**.

```
typedef struct
{
   int   nEditOne;
   char  szEditTwo[20];
} DLGDATA, *LPDLGDATA;


LRESULT CALLBACK WndProc( HWND hWnd, UINT uMsg, WPARAM wParam, LPARAM lParam )
{
static LPDLGDATA lpMem;

   switch( uMsg )
   {
      case WM_CREATE :
              lpMem = (LPDLGDATA)HeapAlloc( GetProcessHeap(), HEAP_ZERO_MEMORY, ⇐
sizeof( DLGDATA ) );
              lpMem->nEditOne = 10;
              lstrcpy( lpMem->szEditTwo, "Edit Two" );
              break;

      case WM_COMMAND :
              switch( LOWORD( wParam ) )
              {
                 case IDM_TEST :
                    {
                        HANDLE hDialog = LoadResource( hInst,
                                          FindResource( hInst, "TestDialog",
                                                  RT_DIALOG ) );

                        LPVOID lpDialog = LockResource( hDialog );
```

```
                              DialogBoxIndirectParam( hInst, lpDialog, hWnd,
                                                      (DLGPROC)TestDlgProc,
                                                      (LPARAM)lpMem );
                    }
                    break;

              case IDM_EXIT :
                    DestroyWindow( hWnd );
                    break;
         }
         break;

    case WM_DESTROY :
         if ( lpMem )
            HeapFree( GetProcessHeap(), 0, lpMem );

         PostQuitMessage(0);
         break;

    default :
         return( DefWindowProc( hWnd, uMsg, wParam, lParam ) );
   }

   return( 0L );
}


LRESULT CALLBACK TestDlgProc( HWND hDlg, UINT uMsg,
                              WPARAM wParam, LPARAM lParam )
{
static LPDLGDATA lpMem;

   switch( uMsg )
   {
     case WM_INITDIALOG :
          lpMem = (LPDLGDATA)lParam;
          SetDlgItemInt ( hDlg, IDC_EDIT1, lpMem->nEditOne, TRUE );
          SetDlgItemText( hDlg, IDC_EDIT2, lpMem->szEditTwo );
          break;

     case WM_COMMAND :
          switch( LOWORD( wParam ) )
          {
             case IDOK :
                 {
                     BOOL bTran;


                     lpMem->nEditOne = GetDlgItemInt( hDlg, IDC_EDIT1,
                                                      &bTran, TRUE );
                     GetDlgItemText( hDlg, IDC_EDIT2, lpMem->szEditTwo,
                                     sizeof(szEditTwo)-1 );

                     EndDialog( hDlg, IDOK );
                 }
                 break;
```

continued on next page

continued from previous page

```
            case IDCANCEL :
                    EndDialog( hDlg, IDCANCEL );
                    break;
        }
        break;

    default :
            return( FALSE );
    }

    return( TRUE );
}
```

DialogBoxParam   ■ Windows 95   ■ Windows NT

Description   DialogBoxParam is identical to DialogBox, except it has an added parameter. This added parameter allows a 32-bit value (usually a handle to memory) to be passed as the *lParam* when the dialog procedure receives the WM_INITDIALOG message.

This is probably the best of the DialogBox functions for normal dialog boxes. The 32-bit data item allows data to be exchanged between the program's WndProc function and the dialog box function, without using global variables. DialogBoxParam is more simple to use than DialogBoxIndirectParam in that only the dialog definition name is needed. This function lets you avoid the complexity of separately loading the dialog box resource data, but prohibits you from modifying the dialog box template in memory while the application runs.

Syntax   int **DialogBoxParam**(HINSTANCE *hinst,* LPCTSTR *lpszTemplate,* HWND *hwndOwner,* DLGPROC *dlgprc,* LPARAM *lParamInit*)

Parameters

hinst   HINSTANCE: The instance handle of the module whose executable file contains the dialog box template.

lpszTemplate   LPCTSTR: A pointer to a character string containing the name of the dialog box template in the resource file. If the parameter specifies a resource identifier, its high-order word must be 0 and its low-order word must contain the identifier. Use the MAKEINTRESOURCE macro to create this value.

hwndOwner   HWND: The parent window's handle. Destroying the parent window will automatically destroy the modeless dialog box.

dlgprc   DLGPROC: A pointer to the dialog box procedure. The dialog box procedure processes messages for the dialog box. See the CreateDialog function for a definition of the DlgProc function.

lParamInit   LPARAM: The 32-bit value passed to the DlgProc in the WM_INITDIALOG message.

Returns	**int**: The return value equals the ***nResult*** parameter passed when EndDialog is called. The return value is **–1** if the dialog box could not be created.
Include File	winuser.h
See Also	DialogBox, DialogBoxIndirectParam, DialogBoxIndirect
Related Messages	WM_INITDIALOG
Example	This example runs the same dialog box shown in the **DialogBox** function example. In this case, the more sophisticated **DialogBoxParam** function is used. This example allows the data for the dialog box to be passed in a custom data structure called **DLGDATA**.

```c
typedef struct
{
   int    nEditOne;
   char   szEditTwo[20];
} DLGDATA, *LPDLGDATA;


LRESULT CALLBACK WndProc( HWND hWnd, UINT uMsg, WPARAM wParam, LPARAM lParam )
{

static LPDLGDATA lpMem;

   switch( uMsg )
   {
      case WM_CREATE :
              lpMem = (LPDLGDATA)HeapAlloc( GetProcessHeap(), HEAP_ZERO_MEMORY, ⇐
sizeof( DLGDATA ) );
              lpMem->nEditOne = 10;
              lstrcpy( lpMem->szEditTwo, "Edit Two" );
              break;

      case WM_COMMAND :
              switch( LOWORD( wParam ) )
              {
                 case IDM_TEST :
                         DialogBoxParam( hInst, "TestDialog", hWnd,
                                         (DLGPROC)TestDlgProc,
                                         (LPARAM)lpMem );
                         break;

                 case IDM_EXIT :
                         DestroyWindow( hWnd );
                         break;
              }
              break;

      case WM_DESTROY :
              if ( lpMem )
                 HeapFree( GetProcessHeap(), 0, lpMem );

              PostQuitMessage(0);
              break;
```

continued on next page

continued from previous page

```
        default :
                return( DefWindowProc( hWnd, uMsg, wParam, lParam ) );
    }

    return( 0L );
}


LRESULT CALLBACK TestDlgProc( HWND hDlg, UINT uMsg,
                              WPARAM wParam, LPARAM lParam )
{
static LPDLGDATA lpMem;

    switch( uMsg )
    {
    case WM_INITDIALOG :
            lpMem = (LPDLGDATA)lParam;
            SetDlgItemInt ( hDlg, IDC_EDIT1, lpMem->nEditOne, TRUE );
            SetDlgItemText( hDlg, IDC_EDIT2, lpMem->szEditTwo );
            break;

    case WM_COMMAND :
            switch( LOWORD( wParam ) )
            {
                case IDOK :
                        {
                            BOOL bTran;

                            lpMem->nEditOne = GetDlgItemInt( hDlg, IDC_EDIT1,
                                                      &bTran, TRUE );
                            GetDlgItemText( hDlg, IDC_EDIT2, lpMem->szEditTwo,
                                          sizeof(szEditTwo)-1 );

                            EndDialog( hDlg, IDOK );
                        }
                        break;

                case IDCANCEL :
                        EndDialog( hDlg, IDCANCEL );
                        break;
            }
            break;

    default :
            return( FALSE );
    }

    return( TRUE );
}
```

DlgDirList   ■ WINDOWS 95   ■ WINDOWS NT

Description   DlgDirList fills a list box control in a dialog box with a set of file names
                   that match a file search string.

Syntax   int **DlgDirList**(HWND *hwndDlg*, LPTSTR *lpszPath*, int *nIDListBox*,
                   int *nIDStaticPath*, UINT *uFileType*)

Parameters

hwndDlg	**HWND**: The handle of the dialog box that contains the list box.
lpszPath	**LPTSTR**: A pointer to a character string containing the DOS file search string. For example, "**C:\\DOCUMENTS*.DOC**" would list all files in the **DOCUMENTS** subdirectory with the **.DOC** extension.
nIDListBox	**int**: The identifier of the list box. If this parameter is **0**, **DlgDirList** assumes that no list box exists and does not attempt to fill one.
nIDStaticPath	**int**: The identifier of the static control to use for displaying the current drive and directory. If this parameter is **0**, **DlgDirList** assumes that no such control is present.
uFileType	**UINT**: The attributes of the file names to be displayed. This parameter must be one or more of the values shown in Table 8-3.

Table 8-3 DlgDirList *uFileType* values

Value	Description
DDL_ARCHIVE	Includes archived files.
DDL_DIRECTORY	Includes subdirectories. Subdirectory names are enclosed in square brackets (⌐ ⌐).
DDL_DRIVES	Includes drives. Drives are listed in the form ⌐-*x*-⌐, where *x* is the drive letter.
DDL_EXCLUSIVE	Includes only files with the specified attributes. By default, read-write files are listed even if DDL_READWRITE is not specified.
DDL_HIDDEN	Includes hidden files.
DDL_READONLY	Includes read-only files.
DDL_READWRITE	Includes read-write files with no additional attributes.
DDL_SYSTEM	Includes system files.
DDL_POSTMSGS	Posts messages to the application's message queue. By default, DlgDirList sends messages directly to the dialog box procedure.

Returns	**int**: If a listing is made—even an empty listing—the return value is nonzero. If *lpszPath* does not contain a valid search path, the return value is **0**.
Include File	winuser.h
See Also	DlgDirListComboBox, DlgDirSelectEx
Related Messages	LB_RESETCONTENT, LB_DIR
Example	This example, as shown in Figure 8-4, creates a dialog box when the user selects the Test! menu item. The dialog box contains a list box, showing all the files in the current directory. The dialog box also displays the directory name in a read-only edit control. When the user double-clicks on an item in the list, the file name is displayed in a message box, or the directory is changed if the item selected is a directory or drive.

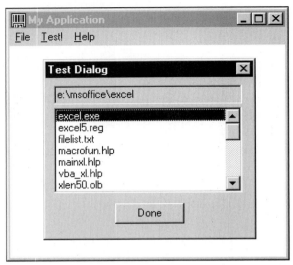

Figure 8-4 `DlgDirList` example

Dialog box definition in `DLGDIRLT.RC`

```
TESTDIALOG DIALOG DISCARDABLE  20, 20, 150, 110
STYLE DS_MODALFRAME | WS_POPUP | WS_VISIBLE | WS_CAPTION | WS_SYSMENU
CAPTION "Test Dialog"
FONT 8, "MS Sans Serif"
BEGIN
    EDITTEXT     IDC_DIRECTORY, 6, 5, 136, 13, ES_AUTOHSCROLL | ES_READONLY | NOT WS_TABSTOP
    LISTBOX      IDC_LIST, 6, 20, 136, 59, LBS_SORT | LBS_NOINTEGRALHEIGHT |
                                          LBS_DISABLENOSCROLL | WS_VSCROLL |
                                          WS_TABSTOP
    PUSHBUTTON   "Done", IDCANCEL, 50, 87, 50, 14, WS_GROUP
END
```

Dialog box control ID numbers in `DLGDIRLT.H`

```
#define IDC_DIRECTORY 101
#define IDC_LIST      102
```

`WndProc` *and* `TestDlgProc` *functions in* `DLGDIRLT.C`

```
LRESULT CALLBACK WndProc( HWND hWnd, UINT uMsg, WPARAM wParam, LPARAM lParam )
{
   switch( uMsg )
   {
      case WM_COMMAND :
              switch( LOWORD( wParam ) )
              {
```

```
                case IDM_TEST :
                        DialogBox( hInst, "TestDialog", hWnd,
                                (DLGPROC)TestDlgProc );
                        break;
        .
        .
        .

LRESULT CALLBACK TestDlgProc( HWND hDlg, UINT uMsg,
                              WPARAM wParam, LPARAM lParam )
{
static char szTmp[255];

    switch( uMsg )
    {
        case WM_INITDIALOG :
                DlgDirList( hDlg, "*.*", IDC_LIST, IDC_DIRECTORY,
                        DDL_DIRECTORY | DDL_DRIVES );
                break;

        case WM_COMMAND :
                switch( LOWORD( wParam ) )
                {
                    case IDC_LIST :
                            if ( HIWORD( wParam ) == LBN_DBLCLK )
                            {
                                if ( DlgDirSelectEx( hDlg, szTmp, sizeof( szTmp ),
                                            IDC_LIST ) )
                                {
                                    strcat( szTmp, "*.*" );
                                    DlgDirList( hDlg, szTmp, IDC_LIST, IDC_DIRECTORY,
                                            DDL_DIRECTORY | DDL_DRIVES );
                                }
                                else
                                    MessageBox( hDlg, szTmp, "File Selected",
                                            MB_OK | MB_ICONINFORMATION );
                            }
                            break;

                    case IDCANCEL :
                            EndDialog( hDlg, IDCANCEL );
                            break;
                }
                break;

        default :
                return( FALSE );
    }

    return( TRUE );
}
```

DlgDirListComboBox   ■ WINDOWS 95   ■ WINDOWS NT

Description   DlgDirListComboBox is the same as DlgDirList, except that instead of
                        working with a list box it works with a combo box.

Syntax	int **DlgDirListComboBox**(HWND *hwndDlg,* LPTSTR *lpszPathSpec,* int *nIDComboBox,* int *nIDStaticPath,* UINT *uFiletype*)

Parameters

hwndDlg
HWND: The handle of the dialog box that contains the combo box.

lpszPathSpec
LPTSTR: A pointer to a character string containing the file search string. For example, "**C:\\DOCUMENTS*.DOC**" would list all files in the **DOCUMENTS** subdirectory with the **.DOC** extension.

nIDComboBox
int: The identifier of the combo box. If this parameter is **0**, **DlgDirListComboBox** assumes that no combo box exists and does not attempt to fill one.

nIDStaticPath
int: The identifier of the static control to use for displaying the current drive and directory. If this parameter is **0**, **DlgDirListComboBox** assumes that no such control is present.

uFileType
UINT: The attributes of the file names to be displayed. This parameter must be one or more of the values listed in Table 8-3.

Returns
int: If a listing is made—even an empty listing—the return value is nonzero. If *lpszPath* does not contain a valid search path, the return value is **0**.

Include File
winuser.h

See Also
DlgDirList, DlgDirSelectEx, DlgDirSelectComboBoxEx

Related Messages
CB_DIR

Example
This example, as shown in Figure 8-5, is identical to the example for **DlgDirList**, except that a combo box is used in place of the list box for showing the list of files.

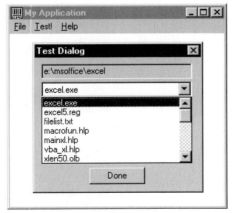

Figure 8-5 DlgDirListComboBox example

Dialog box definition in `DLGDLCB.RC`

```
TESTDIALOG DIALOG DISCARDABLE  20, 20, 150, 114
STYLE DS_MODALFRAME | WS_POPUP | WS_VISIBLE | WS_CAPTION | WS_SYSMENU
CAPTION "Test Dialog"
FONT 8, "MS Sans Serif"
BEGIN
    EDITTEXT        IDC_DIRECTORY, 6, 5, 136, 13, ES_AUTOHSCROLL | ES_READONLY | NOT WS_TABSTOP
    COMBOBOX        IDC_LIST, 6, 20, 136, 61, CBS_DROPDOWNLIST | CBS_SORT |
                                              CBS_DISABLENOSCROLL | WS_VSCROLL |
                                              WS_TABSTOP
    PUSHBUTTON      "Done", IDCANCEL, 49, 94, 50, 14, WS_GROUP
END
```

Dialog box control ID numbers in `DLGDLCB.H`

```
#define IDC_DIRECTORY 101
#define IDC_LIST      102
```

`WndProc` *and* `TestDlgProc` *functions in* `DLGDLCB.C`

```c
LRESULT CALLBACK WndProc( HWND hWnd, UINT uMsg, WPARAM wParam, LPARAM lParam )
{
    switch( uMsg )
    {
    case WM_COMMAND :
            switch( LOWORD( wParam ) )
            {
                case IDM_TEST :
                        DialogBox( hInst, "TestDialog", hWnd,
                                (DLGPROC)TestDlgProc );
                        break;
            .
            .
            .


LRESULT CALLBACK TestDlgProc( HWND hDlg, UINT uMsg,
                            WPARAM wParam, LPARAM lParam )
{
static char szTmp[255];

    switch( uMsg )
    {
    case WM_INITDIALOG :
            DlgDirListComboBox( hDlg, "*.*", IDC_LIST, IDC_DIRECTORY,
                        DDL_DIRECTORY | DDL_DRIVES );
            break;

    case WM_COMMAND :
            switch( LOWORD( wParam ) )
            {
                case IDC_LIST :
                        if ( HIWORD( wParam ) == CBN_SELENDOK )
                        {
```

continued on next page

continued from previous page

```
                        if ( DlgDirSelectComboBoxEx( hDlg, szTmp,
                                                     sizeof( szTmp ),
                                                     IDC_LIST ) )
                        {
                            strcat( szTmp, "*.*" );
                            DlgDirListComboBox( hDlg, szTmp, IDC_LIST,
                                                IDC_DIRECTORY,
                                                DDL_DIRECTORY | DDL_DRIVES );
                        }
                        else
                            MessageBox( hDlg, szTmp, "File Selected",
                                        MB_OK | MB_ICONINFORMATION );
                    }
                    break;

                case IDCANCEL :
                        EndDialog( hDlg, IDCANCEL );
                        break;
            }
            break;

        default :
            return( FALSE );
    }

    return( TRUE );
}
```

DlgDirSelectComboBoxEx   ■ WINDOWS 95   ■ WINDOWS NT

Description	The DlgDirSelectComboBoxEx retrieves the current selection from a combo box filled by using the DlgDirListComboBox function. The selection is interpreted as a drive letter, file, or directory name.
Syntax	BOOL **DlgDirSelectComboBoxEx**(HWND *hwndDlg*, LPTSTR *lpszPath*, int *cchString*, int *nIDComboBox*)
Parameters	
hwndDlg	HWND: The handle of the dialog box that contains the combo box.
lpszPath	LPTSTR: A pointer to the buffer that is to receive the selected path.
cchString	int: The length, in characters, of the buffer pointed to by the *lpszPath* parameter.
nIDComboBox	int: The identifier of the combo box control.
Returns	BOOL: Nonzero if the current selection is a directory name; otherwise, it is 0.
Include File	winuser.h
See Also	DlgDirListComboBox, DlgDirList, DlgDirSelectEx
Example	See the example for the **DlgDirListComboBox** function.

DlgDirSelectEx ■ WINDOWS 95 ■ WINDOWS NT

Description	`DlgDirSelectEx` retrieves the current selection from a single-selection list box. It assumes that the list box has been filled by the `DlgDirList` function and that the selection is a drive letter, file name, or directory name.
Syntax	BOOL **DlgDirSelectEx**(HWND *hwndDlg,* LPTSTR *lpszPath,* int *cchString,* int *nIDListBox*)
Parameters	
hwndDlg	HWND: The handle of the dialog box that contains the list box.
lpszPath	LPTSTR: A pointer to the buffer that is to receive the selected path.
cchString	int: The length, in characters, of the buffer pointed to by the *lpszPath* parameter.
nIDListBox	int: The identifier of the list box control.
Returns	BOOL: Nonzero if the current selection is a directory name; otherwise, it is 0.
Include File	winuser.h
See Also	DlgDirList
Example	See the example for the `DlgDirList` function.

EndDialog ■ WINDOWS 95 ■ WINDOWS NT

Description	`EndDialog` destroys a modal dialog box, causing the system to end any processing for the dialog box. This is the only way to properly exit a modal dialog box and return control to the calling function. If a dialog box is created from within another dialog box function, calling `EndDialog` only deletes the dialog box associated with the active dialog box and dialog box function.
Syntax	BOOL **EndDialog**(HWND *hwndDlg,* int *nResult*)
Parameters	
hwndDlg	HWND: The handle of the dialog box window.
nResult	int: The value returned when `DialogBox` returns.
Returns	BOOL: If successful, the return value is TRUE; otherwise, it is FALSE.
Include File	winuser.h
See Also	DialogBox, DialogBoxIndirect
Example	See the example for the `DialogBox` function.

GetDialogBaseUnits ■ WINDOWS 95 ■ WINDOWS NT

Description	`GetDialogBaseUnits` returns the dialog box base units used by Windows to create dialog boxes. Dialog boxes use measurements based on the size of the font characters, called dialog base units. The x direction is measured in units of one-fourth of the font width. The y direction is measured in units of one-eighth of the font height. The returned value is for the entire bounding rectangle of the font measured in pixels, not one-fourth or one-eighth of the font size.
	`GetDialogBaseUnits` is useful if the application paints on the dialog box window, but the locations of the controls are known only in dialog box units. The location of the controls measured in pixels will change on different displays with different resolutions.
Syntax	`LONG GetDialogBaseUnits( VOID )`
Parameters	This function has no parameters.
Returns	`LONG`: If successful, the low-order word of the return value contains the horizontal dialog box base unit, and the high-order word contains the vertical dialog box base unit.
Include File	`winuser.h`
Related Messages	`WM_PAINT`
Example	This example, as shown in Figure 8-6, creates a dialog box with one large button with the title Press To Create New Button. Pressing this button creates a new button of the same size. Use the `GetDialogBaseUnits` function to retrieve the dialog base units to calculate the size for the `CreateWindow` function.

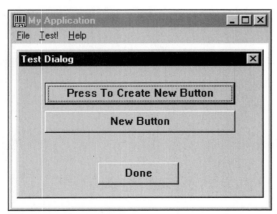

Figure 8-6 `GetDialogBaseUnits` example

Dialog box definition in `GETDLGBU.RC`

```
TESTDIALOG DIALOG DISCARDABLE  20, 20, 150, 82
STYLE DS_MODALFRAME | WS_POPUP | WS_VISIBLE | WS_CAPTION | WS_SYSMENU
CAPTION "Test Dialog"
BEGIN
     PUSHBUTTON        "Press To Create New Button",IDC_CREATE,16,10,118,14
     PUSHBUTTON        "Done",IDCANCEL,49,61,50,14,WS_GROUP
END
```

`TestDlgProc` *function in* `GETDLGBU.C`

```
#define IDC_CREATE 101
#define IDC_NEWBUTTON 102
LRESULT CALLBACK TestDlgProc( HWND hDlg, UINT uMsg,
                             WPARAM wParam, LPARAM lParam )
{
   switch( uMsg )
   {
     case WM_INITDIALOG :
          break;

     case WM_COMMAND :
          switch( LOWORD( wParam ) )
          {
             case IDC_CREATE :
                  {
                     DWORD dwBaseUnits = GetDialogBaseUnits();
                     WORD  wBaseX      = LOWORD( dwBaseUnits );
                     WORD  wBaseY      = HIWORD( dwBaseUnits );

                     HWND hButton = CreateWindow( "BUTTON", "New Button",
                                                 WS_CHILD |
                                                 BS_PUSHBUTTON |
                                                 WS_VISIBLE,
                                                 (wBaseX*16)/4,
                                                 (wBaseY*28)/8,
                                                 (wBaseX*118)/4,
                                                 (wBaseY*14)/8,
                                                 hDlg,
                                                 (HMENU)IDC_NEWBUTTON,
                                                 hInst, NULL );
                     ShowWindow( hButton, SW_SHOW );
                  }
                  break;

             case IDCANCEL :
                  EndDialog( hDlg, IDCANCEL );
                  break;
          }
          break;

     default :
          return( FALSE );
   }
```

continued on next page

continued from previous page

```
    return( TRUE );
}
```

GetDlgCtrlID   ■ WINDOWS 95   ■ WINDOWS NT

Description	GetDlgCtrlID returns the identifier of a control, given the control's window handle.
Syntax	int **GetDlgCtrlID**(HWND *hwndCtl*)
Parameters	
hwndCtl	HWND: The handle of the control.
Returns	int: If successful, the return value is the identifier of the control; otherwise, it is NULL, indicating, for example, that *hwndCtl* is not a valid window handle.
Include File	winuser.h
See Also	GetDlgItem, SendDlgItemMessage
Example	This example, which is shown in Figure 8-7, shows several equivalent ways of sending messages to dialog box controls. When the WM_INITDIALOG message is received, the dialog box control sets the edit control's text to "First Text". The handle to the edit control's window is also retrieved. When the IDC_SECOND button is pressed, the edit text is changed directly by sending the WM_SETTEXT message to the edit control window. This technique is equivalent to using SetDlgItemText. When the IDC_THIRD button is pressed, the dialog box ID value for the edit control is obtained from the edit control's window handle using GetDlgCtrlID. The ID is then used to change the edit control's text, this time using SetDlgItemText.
	This example shows only the dialog box procedure for the program. See the DialogBox function description for a more detailed example.

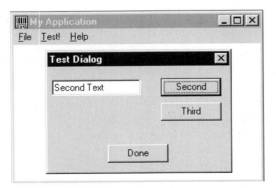

Figure 8-7 GetDlgCtrlID and GetDlgItem example

```
LRESULT CALLBACK TestDlgProc( HWND hDlg, UINT uMsg,
                              WPARAM wParam, LPARAM lParam )
{
static HWND hControl = NULL;

   switch( uMsg )
   {
      case WM_INITDIALOG :
            SetDlgItemText( hDlg, IDC_EDIT, "First Text" );
            hControl = GetDlgItem( hDlg, IDC_EDIT );
            break;

      case WM_COMMAND :
            switch( LOWORD( wParam ) )
            {
               case IDC_SECOND :
                     SendMessage( hControl, WM_SETTEXT, 0,
                                  (LPARAM)(LPCTSTR)"Second Text" );
                     break;

               case IDC_THIRD :
                     {
                         UINT uEditID = GetDlgCtrlID( hControl );
                         SetDlgItemText( hDlg, uEditID, "Third Text" );
                     }
                     break;

               case IDCANCEL :
                     EndDialog( hDlg, IDCANCEL );
                     break;
            }
            break;

      default :
            return( FALSE );
   }

   return( TRUE );
}
```

GetDlgItem   ■ WINDOWS 95   ■ WINDOWS NT

Description	**GetDlgItem** retrieves the handle of a control in the given dialog box. The handle of the dialog box control window can be used to change the behavior of the child window by subclassing. After the window handle is obtained with **GetDlgItem**, the application uses **SetWindowLong** and **CallWindowProc** to subclass the control.
Syntax	HWND **GetDlgItem**(HWND *hwndDlg,* int *idControl*)
Parameters	
hwndDlg	HWND: The dialog box handle that contains the control.
idControl	int: The identifier of the control to be retrieved.

Returns	**HWND**: If successful, the return value is the window handle of the given control; otherwise, it is **NULL**, indicating an invalid dialog box handle or a nonexistent control.
Include File	winuser.h
See Also	CallWindowProc, GetDlgCtrlID, SetWindowLong
Example	See the example for the GetDlgCtrlID function.

GetDlgItemInt   ■ Windows 95   ■ Windows NT

Description	GetDlgItemInt is a shortcut method of retrieving an integer value from a control in a dialog box. The function is equivalent to using the **WM_GETTEXT** message to retrieve the character string from the control, and then using the **atoi** C library function to convert the string to an integer. The text characters in the edit control are converted to an integer value starting with the leftmost character. The first nonnumeric character halts the reading process.
Syntax	UINT **GetDlgItemInt**(HWND *hDlg*, int *nIDDlgItem*, BOOL* *lpTranslated*, BOOL *bSigned*)

Parameters

hDlg	HWND: The dialog box handle.
nIDDlgItem	int: The identifier of the edit control.
lpTranslated	BOOL*: A pointer to a BOOL variable. This is set to TRUE if the edit control contents were properly converted to an integer. It is set to FALSE if an error occurred.
bSigned	BOOL: TRUE if the value to be retrieved is to be a signed integer (int). FALSE if unsigned (UINT).
Returns	UINT: The integer value of the text in the edit control. Because 0 is a valid return value, use the *lpTranslated* parameter to detect errors. If *bSigned* is set to TRUE, the application should cast the return value as a signed integer (int).
Include File	winuser.h
See Also	SetDlgItemInt, GetDlgItemText, SetDlgItemText
Related Messages	WM_GETTEXT
Example	See the example for the DialogBox function.

GetDlgItemText   ■ Windows 95   ■ Windows NT

Description	GetDlgItemText retrieves the title or text associated with a control in a dialog box.

Syntax	UINT **GetDlgItemText**(HWND *hwndDlg,* int *idControl,* LPTSTR *lpsz,* int *cchMax*)
Parameters	
hwndDlg	HWND: The dialog box handle.
idControl	int: The identifier of the control.
lpsz	LPTSTR: A pointer to a buffer to receive the title or text.
cchMax	int: The maximum length, in characters, of the string to be copied to the buffer pointed to by *lpsz*. If the length of the string exceeds the limit, the string is truncated.
Returns	UINT: If successful, the return value specifies the number of characters copied to the buffer, not including the terminating null character; otherwise, it is 0.
Include File	winuser.h
See Also	GetDlgItemInt, SetDlgItemText, SetDlgItemInt
Related Messages	WM_GETTEXT
Example	See the example for the DialogBox function.

GetNextDlgGroupItem   ■ Windows 95   ■ Windows NT

Description	GetNextDlgGroupItem finds the next (or previous) window handle of the dialog box control, within a group of controls, that will receive the input focus if the user presses one of the arrow keys.
Syntax	HWND **GetNextDlgGroupItem**(HWND *hwndDlg,* HWND *hwndCtl,* BOOL *bPrevious*)
Parameters	
hwndDlg	HWND: The handle of the dialog box.
hwndCtl	HWND: The handle of the control to be used as the starting point for the search. If NULL, the function uses the last (or first) control in the dialog box as the starting point for the search.
bPrevious	BOOL: Set to TRUE to find the previous control in the group. This is the item that will have the input focus if the user presses the left or down arrow key. Set to FALSE to find the next control in the group. This is the item that will have the input focus if the user presses the right or up arrow key.
Returns	HWND: The handle of the next or previous dialog box control in the group of controls.
Include File	winuser.h
See Also	GetDlgItem, GetNextDlgTabItem

Example

This example, shown in Figure 8-8, shows a dialog box with four check boxes and a pushbutton. When the dialog box starts, the upper-left check box has the input focus. The dialog box function processes the **WM_INIT-DIALOG** message and changes the names of the controls for the button with the input focus, the next group item, and the next tab item.

Dialog box definition in GETNDGI.RC

```
TESTDIALOG DIALOG DISCARDABLE  20, 20, 156, 68
STYLE DS_MODALFRAME | WS_POPUP | WS_VISIBLE | WS_CAPTION | WS_SYSMENU
CAPTION "Test Dialog"
FONT 8, "MS Sans Serif"
BEGIN
    CONTROL         "",IDC_CHECK1,"Button",BS_AUTOCHECKBOX | WS_GROUP |
                                            WS_TABSTOP,12,8,66,10
    CONTROL         "",IDC_CHECK2,"Button",BS_AUTOCHECKBOX,12,23,67,10
    CONTROL         "",IDC_CHECK3,"Button",BS_AUTOCHECKBOX | WS_GROUP |
                                            WS_TABSTOP,83,8,64,10
    CONTROL         "",IDC_CHECK4,"Button",BS_AUTOCHECKBOX,83,23,66,10
    PUSHBUTTON      "Done",IDCANCEL,52,47,50,14,WS_GROUP
END
```

TestDlgProc *function in* GETNDGI.C

```
LRESULT CALLBACK TestDlgProc( HWND hDlg, UINT uMsg,
                              WPARAM wParam, LPARAM lParam )
{
   switch( uMsg )
   {
      case WM_INITDIALOG :
            {
               HWND hControl, hFirstGroup;

               SetDlgItemText( hDlg, IDC_CHECK1, "1" );
               SetDlgItemText( hDlg, IDC_CHECK2, "2" );
               SetDlgItemText( hDlg, IDC_CHECK3, "3" );
               SetDlgItemText( hDlg, IDC_CHECK4, "4" );

               hFirstGroup = GetDlgItem( hDlg, IDC_CHECK1 );
               SendMessage( hFirstGroup, WM_SETTEXT, 0,
                        (LPARAM)(LPCTSTR)"Focus Here" );

               hControl = GetNextDlgGroupItem( hDlg, hFirstGroup, FALSE );
               SendMessage( hControl, WM_SETTEXT, 0,
                        (LPARAM)(LPCTSTR)"Next Group Item" );

               hControl = GetNextDlgTabItem( hDlg, hFirstGroup, FALSE );
               SendMessage( hControl, WM_SETTEXT, 0,
                        (LPARAM)(LPCTSTR)"Next Tab Stop" );
            }
            break;

      case WM_COMMAND :
            switch( LOWORD( wParam ) )
            {
```

```
        case IDCANCEL :
                EndDialog( hDlg, IDCANCEL );
                break;
        }
        break;

    default :
        return( FALSE );
    }

    return( TRUE );
}
```

GetNextDlgTabItem   ■ WINDOWS 95 ■ WINDOWS NT

Description   GetNextDlgTabItem finds the next (or previous) window handle of the dialog box control that will receive the input focus if the user presses the TAB key. Pressing the TAB key moves input focus to the next item with the **WS_TABSTOP** style. Pressing SHIFT-TAB moves input focus in the opposite direction. GetNextDlgTabItem returns the handle of the control that will receive input focus next if the TAB key is used.

Syntax   HWND **GetNextDlgTabItem**(HWND *hwndDlg*, HWND *hwndCtl*, BOOL *bPrevious*)

Parameters

hwndDlg   HWND: The handle of the dialog box.

hwndCtl   HWND: The handle of the control to be used as the starting point for the search. If **NULL**, the function uses the last (or first) control in the dialog box as the starting point for the search.

Figure 8-8 GetNextDlgGroupItem and GetNextDlgTabItem example

bPrevious	BOOL: Set to TRUE to find the previous control with the WS_TABSTOP style. This is the item that will have the input focus if the user presses SHIFT-TAB. Set to FALSE to find the next WS_TABSTOP control. This is the item that will have the input focus if the user presses TAB.
Returns	HWND: The handle of the next or previous dialog box control that will be selected if the TAB or SHIFT-TAB key is used.
Include File	winuser.h
See Also	GetDlgItem, GetNextDlgGroupItem
Example	See the example for the GetNextDlgGroupItem function.

IsDialogMessage   ■ WINDOWS 95   ■ WINDOWS NT

Description	IsDialogMessage determines whether the specified message is intended for the given dialog box and, if it is, processes the message. During the period a modeless dialog is displayed, the application message loop must determine whether to send the message to the WndProc function or to the dialog box function(s).
Syntax	BOOL IsDialogMessage(HWND hwndDlg, LPMSG lpmsg)
Parameters	
hwndDlg	HWND: The dialog box handle. This value is returned by CreateDialog. The value should be stored in a place that is accessible to the message loop within WinMain.
lpmsg	LPMSG: A pointer to the MSG structure retrieved from Windows by GetMessage or PeekMessage.
Returns	BOOL: TRUE if the message is processed; otherwise, FALSE.
Include File	winuser.h
See Also	GetMessage, CreateDialog
Related Messages	All window messages can be processed.
Example	See the example for the CreateDialog function.

IsDlgButtonChecked   ■ WINDOWS 95   ■ WINDOWS NT

Description	IsDlgButtonChecked determines whether a check box or radio button control has a checkmark next to it or whether a three-state check box control is grayed, checked, or neither.
Syntax	UINT IsDlgButtonChecked(HWND hwndDlg, int nIDButton)
Parameters	
hwndDlg	HWND: The dialog box handle.

nIDButton	int: The integer identifier of the check box or radio button control.
Returns	UINT: The current checked state. Table 8-4 shows the possible values.

Table 8-4 IsDlgButtonChecked **return values**

Value	Meaning
0	Button is unchecked.
1	Button is checked.
2	Button is indeterminate (applies only if the button has the BS_3STATE or BS_AUTO3STATE style).

Include File	winuser.h
See Also	CheckDlgButton, CheckRadioButton
Related Messages	BM_SETCHECK, BM_GETCHECK
Example	See the example for the CheckDlgButton function.

MapDialogRect   ■ WINDOWS 95   ■ WINDOWS NT

Description	MapDialogRect converts (maps) the specified dialog box units to screen units (pixels). The coordinates given in a dialog template are in dialog base units. These are one-fourth of a character width for x coordinates and one-eighth of a character height for y coordinates. This function converts a rectangle from these units to screen units. The resulting coordinates are relative to the upper-left corner of the dialog box window. This means that the upper-left corner of the rectangle will always be (0,0).
Syntax	BOOL **MapDialogRect**(HWND *hwndDlg,* LPRECT *lprc*)
Parameters	
hwndDlg	HWND: The dialog box handle. This function accepts only handles for dialog boxes created by one of the dialog box creation functions; handles for other windows are not valid.
lprc	LPRECT: A pointer to a RECT structure that contains the dialog box coordinates in dialog units to be converted to screen units. After MapDialogRect is called, the RECT data will contain the same rectangle converted to screen units.
Returns	BOOL: If successful, the return value is TRUE; otherwise, it is FALSE.
Include File	winuser.h
See Also	ScreenToClient, ClientToScreen
Related Messages	WM_SIZE

Example

This example, which is shown in Figure 8-9, moves a child window control when either the I Move or Move It pushbutton is pressed. `MapDialogRect` converts the `RECT` data from dialog units to screen units (pixels).

Dialog box definition in `MAPDLGRT.RC`

```
TESTDIALOG DIALOG DISCARDABLE  20, 20, 156, 68
STYLE DS_MODALFRAME | WS_POPUP | WS_VISIBLE | WS_CAPTION | WS_SYSMENU
CAPTION "Test Dialog"
FONT 8, "MS Sans Serif"
BEGIN
    PUSHBUTTON        "Move It",IDC_MOVEIT,4,4,50,14
    PUSHBUTTON        "I Move",IDC_MOVED,4,23,50,14
    PUSHBUTTON        "Done",IDCANCEL,52,47,50,14,WS_GROUP
END
```

TestDlgProc *function in* `MAPDLGRT.C`

```
LRESULT CALLBACK TestDlgProc( HWND hDlg, UINT uMsg,
                              WPARAM wParam, LPARAM lParam )
{
static BOOL bToggle = FALSE;

   switch( uMsg )
   {
    case WM_INITDIALOG :
         break;

    case WM_COMMAND :
          switch( LOWORD( wParam ) )
          {
            case IDC_MOVED :
            case IDC_MOVEIT :
                {
                    RECT rect;
                    HWND hControl;

                    SetRect( &rect, 4, 23, 50+4, 14+23 );
                    MapDialogRect( hDlg, &rect );

                    bToggle = !bToggle;

                    if ( bToggle )
                        OffsetRect( &rect, 35, 0 );

                    hControl = GetDlgItem( hDlg, IDC_MOVED );
                    MoveWindow( hControl, rect.left, rect.top,
                                rect.right-rect.left,
                                rect.bottom-rect.top, TRUE );
                }
                break;

                .
                .
                .
```

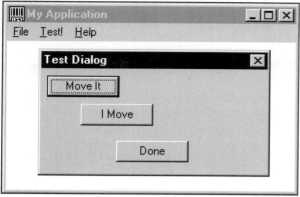

Figure 8-9 `MapDialogRect` example

MessageBeep ■ WINDOWS 95 ■ WINDOWS NT

Description	`MessageBeep` plays a waveform sound if the hardware is capable; otherwise, it plays a sound through the computer speaker. The waveform sound for each sound type is identified by an entry in the `[sounds]` section of the registry. `MessageBeep` is commonly associated with error and warning messages. A good use of this function is to summon the user after a background task, such as a long file transfer, is complete.
Syntax	`BOOL MessageBeep( UINT uType )`
Parameters	
uType	`UINT`: The sound type, as identified by an entry in the `[sounds]` section of the registry. This can be one of the values listed in Table 8-5.

Table 8-5 MessageBeep *uType* values

Value	Sound
0xFFFFFFFF	Standard beep using the computer speaker
MB_ICONASTERISK	SystemAsterisk
MB_ICONEXCLAMATION	SystemExclamation
MB_ICONHAND	SystemHand
MB_ICONQUESTION	SystemQuestion
MB_OK	SystemDefault

Returns	`BOOL`: If successful, the return value is `TRUE`; otherwise, it is `FALSE`.
Include File	`winuser.h`

See Also	MessageBox
Example	See the example for the **MessageBox** function.

MessageBox ■ WINDOWS 95 ■ WINDOWS NT

Description	**MessageBox** creates, displays, and operates a message box. The message box contains an application-defined message and title, plus any combination of predefined icons and pushbuttons.
	Most often used for error and warning messages, **MessageBox** is also useful as a placeholder in program development. You can put message boxes in for menu items that have not yet been developed, etc.
Syntax	int **MessageBox**(HWND *hwndOwner,* LPCTSTR *lpszText,* LPCTSTR *lpszTitle,* UINT *uStyle*)
Parameters	
hwndOwner	HWND: The handle of the parent window. If this parameter is **NULL**, the message box has no owner window.
lpszText	LPCTSTR: A pointer to a null-terminated string containing the message to be displayed.
lpszTitle	LPCTSTR: A pointer to a null-terminated string used for the dialog box title. If this parameter is **NULL**, the default title Error is used.
uStyle	UINT: Specifies the contents and behavior of the dialog box. This parameter can be a combination of the values listed in Table 8-6.

Table 8-6 MessageBox *uStyle* values

Value	Meaning
MB_ABORTRETRYIGNORE	The message box contains three pushbuttons: Abort, Retry, and Ignore.
MB_APPLMODAL	The user must respond to the message box before continuing work in the window identified by the *hwndOwner* parameter. However, the user can move to the windows of other applications and work in those windows.
MB_DEFAULT_DESKTOP_ONLY	The desktop currently receiving input must be a default desktop; otherwise, the function fails. A default desktop is one an application runs on after the user has logged on.
MB_DEFBUTTON1	The first button is the default button. The default button is the one that will be activated if the user presses the ENTER key.
MB_DEFBUTTON2	The second button is the default button.
MB_DEFBUTTON3	The third button is the default button.
MB_DEFBUTTON4	The fourth button is the default button.
MB_HELP	Adds a Help button to the message box. Choosing the Help button or pressing F1 generates a help event.
MB_ICONASTERISK	Same as MB_ICONINFORMATION.
MB_ICONEXCLAMATION	An exclamation-point icon appears in the message box.

Value	Meaning
MB_ICONHAND	Same as MB_ICONSTOP.
MB_ICONINFORMATION	An icon consisting of a lowercase letter *i* in a circle appears in the message box.
MB_ICONQUESTION	A question-mark icon appears in the message box.
MB_ICONSTOP	A stop-sign icon appears in the message box.
MB_OK	The message box contains one pushbutton: OK.
MB_OKCANCEL	The message box contains two pushbuttons: OK and Cancel.
MB_RETRYCANCEL	The message box contains two pushbuttons: Retry and Cancel.
MB_RIGHT	The text is right-justified.
MB_RTLREADING	Displays message and caption text using right-to-left reading order on Hebrew and Arabic systems.
MB_SERVICE_NOTIFICATION	(Windows NT Only) The caller is a service notifying the user of an event. The function displays a message box on the current active desktop, even if there is no user logged onto the computer. If this flag is set, the *hwndOwner* parameter must be NULL so the message box can appear on any desktop.
MB_SETFOREGROUND	The message box becomes the foreground window. Internally, Windows calls the SetForegroundWindow function for the message box.
MB_SYSTEMMODAL	All applications are suspended until the user responds to the message box. Unless the application specifies MB_ICONHAND, the message box does not become modal until after it is created. System modal messages should only be used for serious systemwide messages.
MB_TASKMODAL	Same as MB_APPLMODAL, except that all the top-level windows belonging to the current task are disabled if the *hwndOwner* parameter is NULL. Use this flag when the calling application or library does not have a window handle available but still needs to prevent input to other windows in the current application without suspending other applications.
MB_TOPMOST	The message box is created with the WS_EX_TOPMOST window style.
MB_YESNO	The message box contains two pushbuttons: Yes and No.
MB_YESNOCANCEL	The message box contains three pushbuttons: Yes, No, and Cancel.

Returns   int: The return value is 0 if there is not enough memory to create the message box. Otherwise, it is one of the values listed in Table 8-7.

Table 8-7 MessageBox return values

Value	Meaning
IDABORT	Abort button was selected.
IDCANCEL	Cancel button was selected.
IDIGNORE	Ignore button was selected.
IDNO	No button was selected.
IDOK	OK button was selected.
IDRETRY	Retry button was selected.
IDYES	Yes button was selected.

Include File	winuser.h
See Also	MessageBoxEx, MessageBoxIndirect, MessageBeep, DialogBox
Example	This example displays a message box when the Test! menu item is selected. It also checks to see if the Yes button is pressed on the message box. The sound for an exclamation is played before the message is displayed, using the MessageBeep function.

```
LRESULT CALLBACK WndProc( HWND hWnd, UINT uMsg, WPARAM wParam, LPARAM lParam )
{
   switch( uMsg )
   {
     case WM_COMMAND :
           switch( LOWORD( wParam ) )
           {
              case IDM_TEST :
                  MessageBeep( MB_ICONEXCLAMATION );
                  if ( MessageBox( hWnd, "Hello!", NULL,
                         MB_YESNO | MB_ICONEXCLAMATION ) == IDYES )
                  {
                     // YES was pressed..
                  }
                  break;
```

MessageBoxEx   ■ WINDOWS 95   ■ WINDOWS NT

Description	MessageBoxEx is the same as MessageBox, except that it has an extra parameter that specifies the set of language resources to use for the predefined pushbuttons. Note that each localized release of Windows typically contains resources only for a limited set of languages. Therefore, you can only use a limited set of values based on which locales are installed on the system.
Syntax	int **MessageBoxEx**(HWND *hwndOwner,* LPCTSTR *lpszText,* LPCTSTR *lpszCaption,* UINT *uStyle,* WORD *wLanguageID*)

Parameters

hwndOwner	HWND: The handle of the parent window. If this parameter is NULL, the message box has no owner window.
lpszText	LPCTSTR: A pointer to a null-terminated string containing the message to be displayed.
lpszCaption	LPCTSTR: A pointer to a null-terminated string used for the dialog box title. If this parameter is NULL, the default title Error is used.
uStyle	UINT: Specifies the contents and behavior of the dialog box. This parameter can be a combination of the values listed in Table 8-6.
wLanguageID	WORD: Specifies the language in which to display the text contained in the predefined pushbuttons. This value must be in the form returned by the MAKELANGID macro. Table 8-8 shows valid language values.

Table 8-8 MessageBoxEx `wlanguageId` values

Language	Primary Value	Secondary Value
Default language	LANG_NEUTRAL	SUBLANG_DEFAULT
Albanian	LANG_ALBANIAN	
Arabic	LANG_ARABIC	
Bahasa (Indonesian)	LANG_BAHASA	
Bulgarian	LANG_BULGARIAN	
Catalan	LANG_CATALAN	
Chinese (simplified)	LANG_CHINESE	SUBLANG_CHINESE_SIMPLIFIED
Chinese (traditional)	LANG_CHINESE	SUBLANG_CHINESE_TRADITIONAL
Croatian (Cyrillic)	LANG_SERBO_CROATIAN	SUBLANG_SERBO_CROATIAN_CYRILLIC
Czech	LANG_CZECH	
Danish	LANG_DANISH	
Dutch	LANG_DUTCH	SUBLANG_DUTCH
Dutch (Belgian)	LANG_DUTCH	SUBLANG_DUTCH_BELGIAN
English (Australian)	LANG_ENGLISH	SUBLANG_ENGLISH_AUS
English (UK)	LANG_ENGLISH	SUBLANG_ENGLISH_UK
English (US)	LANG_ENGLISH	SUBLANG_ENGLISH_US
Finnish	LANG_FINNISH	
French	LANG_FRENCH	SUBLANG_FRENCH
French (Belgian)	LANG_FRENCH	SUBLANG_FRENCH_BELGIAN
French (Canadian)	LANG_FRENCH	SUBLANG_FRENCH_CANADIAN
French (Swiss)	LANG_FRENCH	SUBLANG_FRENCH_SWISS
German	LANG_GERMAN	SUBLANG_GERMAN
German (Swiss)	LANG_GERMAN	SUBLANG_GERMAN_SWISS
Greek	LANG_GREEK	
Hebrew	LANG_HEBREW	
Hungarian	LANG_HUNGARIAN	
Icelandic	LANG_ICELANDIC	
Italian	LANG_ITALIAN	SUBLANG_ITALIAN
Italian (Swiss)	LANG_ITALIAN	SUBLANG_ITALIAN_SWISS
Japanese	LANG_JAPANESE	
Korean	LANG_KOREAN	
Norwegian (Bokmål)	LANG_NORWEGIAN	SUBLANG_NORWEGIAN_BOKMAL
Norwegian (Nynorsk)	LANG_NORWEGIAN	SUBLANG_NORWEGIAN_NYNORSK
Polish	LANG_POLISH	
Portuguese	LANG_PORTUGUESE	SUBLANG_PORTUGUESE
Portuguese (Brazilian)	LANG_PORTUGUESE	SUBLANG_PORTUGUESE_BRAZILIAN
Rhaeto-Romanic	LANG_RHAETO_ROMAN	
Romanian	LANG_ROMANIAN	

continued on next page

continued from previous page

Language	Primary Value	Secondary Value
Russian	LANG_RUSSIAN	
Serbian-Croato (Latin)	LANG_SERBO_CROATIAN	SUBLANG_SERBO_CROATIAN_LATIN
Slovak	LANG_SLOVAK	
Spanish	LANG_SPANISH	SUBLANG_SPANISH
Spanish (Mexican)	LANG_SPANISH	SUBLANG_SPANISH_MEXICAN
Swedish	LANG_SWEDISH	
Thai	LANG_THAI	
Turkish	LANG_TURKISH	
Urdu	LANG_URDU	

Returns	`int`: The return value is **0** if there is not enough memory to create the message box. Otherwise, it is one of the values listed in Table 8-7.
Include File	`winuser.h`
See Also	`MessageBox`, `MessageBoxIndirect`
Example	This example is the same as the **MessageBox** example, except the message box is displayed using the Spanish (Mexican) sublanguage.

```
LRESULT CALLBACK WndProc( HWND hWnd, UINT uMsg, WPARAM wParam, LPARAM lParam )
{
   switch( uMsg )
   {
      case WM_COMMAND :
            switch( LOWORD( wParam ) )
            {
               case IDM_TEST :
                     MessageBeep( MB_ICONEXCLAMATION );
                     if ( MessageBoxEx( hWnd, "Hola!", NULL,
                                 MB_YESNO | MB_ICONEXCLAMATION,
                                 MAKELANGID( LANG_SPANISH,
                                 SUBLANG_SPANISH_MEXICAN ) ) == IDYES )
                     {
                        // YES was pressed.
                     }
                     break;
         .
         .
         .
```

MessageBoxIndirect   ■ Windows 95   ■ Windows NT

Description	`MessageBoxIndirect` creates, displays, and operates a message box that is defined by passing a structure as the parameter. This structure allows the application to customize aspects of the message box beyond what is allowed with the **MessageBox** function.
Syntax	`int` **MessageBoxIndirect**(LPMSGBOXPARAMS *lpMsgBoxParams*)

Parameters

lpMsgBoxParams   LPMSGBOXPARAMS: A pointer to a **MSGBOXPARAMS** structure that contains information used to display and operate the message box. See the definition of the **MSGBOXPARAMS** structure below.

Returns

int: The return value is 0 if there is not enough memory to create the message box. Otherwise, it is one of the values listed in Table 8-7.

Include File

winuser.h

See Also

MessageBox, MessageBoxEx

MSGBOXPARAMS Definition

```
typedef struct
{
    UINT            cbSize;
    HWND            hwndOwner;
    HINSTANCE       hInstance;
    LPCSTR          lpszText;
    LPCSTR          lpszCaption;
    DWORD           dwStyle;
    LPCSTR          lpszIcon;
    DWORD           dwContextHelpId;
    MSGBOXCALLBACK  lpfnMsgBoxCallback;
    DWORD           dwLanguageId;
} MSGBOXPARAMS, *LPMSGBOXPARAMS;
```

Members

cbSize   UINT: The size, in bytes, of the structure. This must be initialized before using it with **MessageBoxIndirect**.

hwndOwner   HWND: The owner window of the message box. This can be set to **NULL**.

hInstance   HINSTANCE: The instance containing the icon resource identified by the *lpszIcon* member, and the string resource identified by the *lpszText* and *lpszCaption* members.

lpszText   LPCSTR: A pointer to a null-terminated string, or the identifier of a string resource that contains the message to be displayed.

lpszCaption LPCSTR: A pointer to a null-terminated string, or the identifier of a string resource that contains the message box title. If this member is **NULL**, the default title Error is used.

dwStyle   DWORD: The set of bit flags that determine the contents and behavior of the dialog box. This member can be a combination of flags described in Table 8-6.

lpszIcon   LPCSTR: Identifies an icon resource. This parameter can be either a null-terminated string or an integer resource identifier passed to the **MAKEINTRESOURCE** macro. To use one of the Windows predefined icons, set *hInstance* to **NULL** and set *lpszIcon* to one of the values listed with the **LoadIcon** function.

dwContextHelpId	DWORD: The context help ID to associate with the message box. This value is passed in the **HELPINFO** structure that the message box sends to the owner window or callback function. See the definition of the **HELPINFO** structure in Chapter 28, Interfacing with Help Files.
lpfnMsgBoxCallback	MSGBOXCALLBACK: A pointer to a callback function that processes help events for the message box. See the definition of the callback function below. If this member is set to **NULL**, the message box sends the **WM_HELP** message to the owner window when help events occur.
dwLanguageId	DWORD: Specifies the language in which to display the text contained in the predefined pushbuttons. This value must be in the form returned by the **MAKELANGID** macro. See the **MessageBoxEx** function for more information.

Callback Syntax   VOID CALLBACK **MsgBoxCallback**(LPHELPINFO *lpHelpInfo*)

Callback Parameters

lpHelpInfo	LPHELPINFO: A pointer to a **HELPINFO** structure that contains information about the help event that occurred. See the definition of the **HELPINFO** structure in Chapter 28, Interfacing with Help Files.

Example   This example uses the **MessageBoxIndirect** function to display a message box with a nonstandard icon and context-sensitive help.

```
LRESULT CALLBACK WndProc( HWND hWnd, UINT uMsg, WPARAM wParam, LPARAM lParam )
{
   switch( uMsg )
   {
      case WM_HELP :
              if ( ((LPHELPINFO)lParam)->dwContextId == 100 )
              {
                  // User wants message box help.
              }
              break;

      case WM_COMMAND :
              switch( LOWORD( wParam ) )
              {
                 case IDM_TEST :
                      {
                          MSGBOXPARAMS mbParams;

                          memset( &mbParams, 0, sizeof( MSGBOXPARAMS ) );
                          mbParams.cbSize = sizeof( MSGBOXPARAMS );
                          mbParams.hwndOwner = hWnd;
                          mbParams.hInstance = NULL;
                          mbParams.lpszText = "Custom Message for Message Box";
                          mbParams.lpszCaption = "Custom Messagebox";
                          mbParams.dwStyle = MB_OK | MB_HELP | MB_USERICON;
                          mbParams.lpszIcon = IDI_WINLOGO;
                          mbParams.dwContextHelpId = 100;

                          MessageBoxIndirect( &mbParams );
```

```
        }
        break;
        .
        .
        .
```

SendDlgItemMessage　　　■ WINDOWS 95　■ WINDOWS NT

Description　　SendDlgItemMessage is a shortcut method for sending a message to a dialog box control. It is equivalent to calling GetDlgItem to obtain the control's handle, and then using SendMessage to send the message. Like SendMessage, SendDlgItemMessage sends the message directly to the dialog box function, bypassing the message queue.

Use SendDlgItemMessage to send nonroutine messages to dialog box controls. The normal activities, such as setting the text in a control, are covered by SetDlgItemText. Less common activities, such as adding items to a list box control, are best handled with SendDlgItemMessage.

Syntax　　LONG **SendDlgItemMessage**(HWND *hwndDlg*, int *nIDControl*, UINT *uMsg*, WPARAM *wParam*, LPARAM *lParam*)

Parameters

hwndDlg　　HWND: The dialog box window handle (not the handle of the control).

nIDControl　　int: The integer identifier of the control that will receive the message.

uMsg　　UINT: The message that the control will receive.

wParam　　WPARAM: Additional message-dependent information.

lParam　　LPARAM: Additional message-dependent information.

Returns　　LONG: The value returned after the control processed the message.

Include File　　winuser.h

See Also　　SendMessage, GetDlgItem

Related Messages　　All messages can be sent with this function.

Example　　This example is the same as the example for the GetDlgCtrlID function. The only difference is that SendDlgItemMessage is used to set the text for the IDC_THIRD button. The result of the example is the same.

```
LRESULT CALLBACK TestDlgProc( HWND hDlg, UINT uMsg,
                        WPARAM wParam, LPARAM lParam )
{
static HWND hControl = NULL;

    switch( uMsg )
    {
        case WM_INITDIALOG :
                SetDlgItemText( hDlg, IDC_EDIT, "First Text" );
                hControl = GetDlgItem( hDlg, IDC_EDIT );
                break;
```

continued on next page

continued from previous page

```
    case WM_COMMAND :
        switch( LOWORD( wParam ) )
        {
            case IDC_SECOND :
                    SendMessage( hControl, WM_SETTEXT, 0,
                                 (LPARAM)(LPCTSTR)"Second Text" );
                    break;

            case IDC_THIRD :
                    {
                        UINT uEditID = GetDlgCtrlID( hControl );
                        SendDlgItemMessage( hDlg, uEditID, WM_SETTEXT, 0,
                                     (LPARAM)(LPCTSTR)"Third Text" );
                    }
                    break;

            case IDCANCEL :
                    EndDialog( hDlg, IDCANCEL );
                    break;
        }
        break;

    default :
        return( FALSE );
    }

    return( TRUE );
}
```

SetDlgItemInt ■ Windows 95 ■ Windows NT

Description	SetDlgItemInt sets the text of a given control in a dialog box to the string representation of a given integer.
Syntax	BOOL **SetDlgItemInt**(HWND *hwndDlg,* int *nIDControl,* UINT *uValue,* BOOL *bSigned*)
Parameters	
hwndDlg	HWND: The dialog box handle.
nIDControl	int: The integer identifier of the control to be changed.
uValue	UINT: The integer value to be set as text in the control.
bSigned	BOOL: TRUE if *uValue* parameter is signed (**int**), and FALSE if unsigned.
Returns	BOOL: If successful, the return value is TRUE; otherwise, it is FALSE.
Include File	winuser.h
See Also	GetDlgItemInt, SetDlgItemText, GetDlgItemText
Related Messages	WM_SETTEXT
Example	See the example for the **DialogBox** function.

SetDlgItemText

Description	SetDlgItemText sets the title or text of a control.
Syntax	BOOL **SetDlgItemText**(HWND *hwndDlg,* int *nIDControl,* LPCTSTR *lpsz*)
Parameters	
hwndDlg	HWND: The dialog box handle.
nIDControl	int: The integer identifier of the control to be changed.
lpsz	LPCTSTR: A pointer to a null-terminated string that contains the text to be copied to the control.
Returns	BOOL: If successful, the return value is TRUE; otherwise, it is FALSE.
Include File	winuser.h
See Also	GetDlgItemText, SetDlgItemInt, GetDlgItemInt
Related Messages	WM_SETTEXT
Example	See the example for the DialogBox function.

9

USER INPUT FUNCTIONS

In Windows, an application receives input from the user through either the mouse or the keyboard. Predefined controls built into Windows, such as buttons, edit controls, menus, etc., respond to the keyboard and mouse in the appropriate way by default. Some applications need to change the default keyboard or mouse actions, as in the case of custom controls. The Win32 API provides an extensive set of functions to control the keyboard and mouse.

Mouse Messages

From the programmer's point of view, the mouse interacts with a program by sending a series of messages. Windows generates several messages when the user moves the mouse or presses the mouse buttons. Table 9-1 shows common messages that an application uses.

Table 9-1 Common mouse messages

Message	Meaning
WM_LBUTTONDBLCLK	Left mouse button pressed a second time within the double-click time.
WM_LBUTTONDOWN	Left mouse button pressed.
WM_LBUTTONUP	Left mouse button released.
WM_MOUSEMOVE	Mouse cursor moved.
WM_NCHITTEST	Tests what type of object the cursor is over (border, caption, client area, etc.)
WM_NCMOUSEMOVE	Mouse cursor moved within a nonclient area of a window.
WM_RBUTTONDBLCLK	Right mouse button pressed a second time within the double-click time.
WM_RBUTTONDOWN	Right mouse button pressed.
WM_RBUTTONUP	Right mouse button released.
WM_SETCURSOR	The mouse cursor needs to change.

When an application receives a mouse message, the *lParam* value contains the cursor's x, y position on the screen. The y position is the high-order word, while the x position is in the low-order word. Use the **LOWORD** and **HIWORD** macros to extract the two values. Listing 9-1 shows a typical program fragment that deals with the **WM_MOUSEMOVE** messages in the **WndProc** function.

Listing 9-1 WM_MOUSEMOVE in the WndProc function

```
LRESULT CALLBACK WndProc( HWND hWnd, UINT uMsg, WPARAM wParam, LPARAM lParam )
{
static int nXpos, nYpos;

    switch( uMsg )
    {
        case WM_MOUSEMOVE:
                nXpos = LOWORD( lParam );
                nYpos = HIWORD( lParam );
        .
        .
        .
```

Note that the mouse cursor position is given relative to the upper-left corner of the window's client area. The Win32 API provides two functions for converting back and forth between screen and client coordinates: **ScreenToClient** and **ClientToScreen**. These functions are often used as part of the mouse message-processing logic.

Double-clicking the mouse means that the user presses a mouse button twice within a short period of time set by the system. The user can change this time by using the control panel, or the application can change it using the **SetDoubleClickTime** function. Double-clicks are normally used for selecting an item and doing an action at the same time. For example, if a user double-clicks an item in a list box, the application may automatically continue as if the user had selected the item and then selected the OK button. A window will not automatically receive double-click messages unless the **CS_DBLCLKS** value is added to the window class style.

Keyboard Messages

Windows notifies an application about keypresses by sending messages. Table 9-2 lists the most common messages.

Table 9-2 Common keyboard messages

Message	Meaning
WM_CHAR	The ASCII code for the letter if a character was pressed.
WM_KEYDOWN	Notification that a key has been depressed.
WM_KEYUP	Notification that a key has been released.
WM_SYSCHAR	The ASCII code for the letter pressed while the ⌐ALT⌐ key is pressed.

Message	Meaning
WM_SYSKEYDOWN	Notification that a key has been depressed while the [ALT] key is pressed.
WM_SYSKEYUP	Notification that a key has been released while the [ALT] key was pressed.

The **WM_CHAR** message is generated by the **TranslateMessage** function in the message loop of the thread. This function is discussed in Chapter 5, Message Processing. Generally, an application will use the **WM_KEYDOWN** message to look for function keys, cursor keys, the numeric keypad, and the edit keys, such as [PGUP], [PGDN], etc. These keys make the best use of the virtual-key codes. Use **WM_CHAR** to retrieve ASCII keyboard inputs, such as letters, numbers, and printable symbols. Using the **WM_CHAR** message is the best way to work with letters, because uppercase and lowercase letters have different ASCII values. With **WM_KEYDOWN**, an application would have to check the state of the [SHIFT] key to determine if the key is uppercase or lowercase. If the user presses the [ALT] key while pressing another key, an application receives the message sequence of **WM_SYSKEYDOWN**, **WM_SYSCHAR**, and **WM_SYSKEYUP**. It is unusual to process these messages directly, because they are normally used for keyboard accelerators.

Virtual Keys

Using virtual keys frees the programmer from considering what type of keyboard the user will have, because the virtual-key code for the first function key should always be the same, regardless of the make or model of the keyboard. The **WM_KEYDOWN**, **WM_KEYUP**, **WM_SYSKEYDOWN**, and **WM_SYSKEYUP** messages send the virtual-key codes as the *wParam* of the message.

Table 9-3 lists all of the codes and their meanings as they are defined in the Win32 API. The virtual code for the character and number keys is the same as their ASCII equivalents (in uppercase). Note that numeric keypad numbers are given different codes from the numbers on the top row of the conventional keyboard. Also, note that there is only one virtual-key code for the [SHIFT] keys. Both [SHIFT] keys generate the same **VK_SHIFT**.

Table 9-3 Virtual-key codes

Symbolic Constant Name	Value (hex)	Mouse or Keyboard Equivalent
VK_LBUTTON	01	Left mouse button
VK_RBUTTON	02	Right mouse button
VK_CANCEL	03	Control-break processing
VK_MBUTTON	04	Middle mouse button (three-button mouse) or left and right buttons simultaneously
VK_BACK	08	[BACKSPACE] key
VK_TAB	09	[TAB] key
VK_CLEAR	0C	[CLEAR] key
VK_RETURN	0D	[ENTER] key

continued on next page

continued from previous page

Symbolic Constant Name	Value (hex)	Mouse or Keyboard Equivalent
VK_SHIFT	10	[SHIFT] key
VK_CONTROL	11	[CTRL] key
VK_MENU	12	[ALT] key
VK_PAUSE	13	[PAUSE] key
VK_CAPITAL	14	[CAPSLOCK] key
VK_ESCAPE	1B	[ESC] key
VK_SPACE	20	[SPACEBAR] key
VK_PRIOR	21	[PGUP] key
VK_NEXT	22	[PGDN] key
VK_END	23	[END] key
VK_HOME	24	[HOME] key
VK_LEFT	25	[←] key
VK_UP	26	[↑] key
VK_RIGHT	27	[→] key
VK_DOWN	28	[↓] key
VK_SELECT	29	[SELECT] key
VK_EXECUTE	2B	[EXECUTE] key
VK_SNAPSHOT	2C	[PRINTSCREEN] key
VK_INSERT	2D	[INS] key
VK_DELETE	2E	[DEL] key
VK_HELP	2F	[HELP] key
VK_0–VK_9	30–39	[0]–[9] keys
VK_A–VK_Z	41–5A	[A]–[Z] keys
VK_NUMPAD0	60	Numeric keypad [0] key
VK_NUMPAD1	61	Numeric keypad [1] key
VK_NUMPAD2	62	Numeric keypad [2] key
VK_NUMPAD3	63	Numeric keypad [3] key
VK_NUMPAD4	64	Numeric keypad [4] key
VK_NUMPAD5	65	Numeric keypad [5] key
VK_NUMPAD6	66	Numeric keypad [6] key
VK_NUMPAD7	67	Numeric keypad [7] key
VK_NUMPAD8	68	Numeric keypad [8] key
VK_NUMPAD9	69	Numeric keypad [9] key
VK_MULTIPLY	6A	Multiply key
VK_ADD	6B	Add key
VK_SEPARATOR	6C	Separator key
VK_SUBTRACT	6D	Subtract key
VK_DECIMAL	6E	Decimal key
VK_DIVIDE	6F	Divide key
VK_F1–VK_F24	70–87	[F1]–[F24] keys

Symbolic Constant Name	Value (hex)	Mouse or Keyboard Equivalent
VK_NUMLOCK	90	NUMLOCK key
VK_SCROLL	91	SCROLLLOCK key
VK_LSHIFT	A0	Left SHIFT key. Only GetKeyState and GetAsyncKeyState
VK_RSHIFT	A1	Right SHIFT key. Only GetKeyState and GetAsyncKeyState
VK_LCONTROL	A2	Left CTRL key. Only GetKeyState and GetAsyncKeyState
VK_RCONTROL	A3	Right CTRL key. Only GetKeyState and GetAsyncKeyState
VK_LMENU	A4	Left ALT key. Only GetKeyState and GetAsyncKeyState
VK_RMENU	A5	Right ALT key. Only GetKeyState and GetAsyncKeyState

User Input Function Descriptions

Table 9-4 summarizes the user input functions. The complete function descriptions follow the table.

Table 9-4 User input function summary

Function	Purpose
ActivateKeyboardLayout	Activates a different keyboard layout.
ClientToScreen	Converts a point from client coordinates to screen coordinates.
ClipCursor	Confines the mouse cursor to an area on the screen.
CopyCursor	Copies a cursor.
CreateCaret	Creates a caret shape.
CreateCursor	Creates a cursor shape.
DestroyCaret	Removes a caret from a window.
DestroyCursor	Deletes a cursor created with CreateCursor.
GetAsyncKeyState	Finds out if a key has been pressed.
GetCapture	Retrieves a handle to the window that has captured the mouse.
GetCaretBlinkTime	Finds the current rate at which the caret is flashing.
GetCaretPos	Determines the location of the caret in a window's client area.
GetClipCursor	Determines the rectangle that the mouse was last confined to by ClipCursor.
GetCursor	Retrieves the handle of the current cursor.
GetCursorPos	Retrieves the x, y position of the mouse cursor.
GetDoubleClickTime	Retrieves the double-click time value for the mouse.
GetInputState	Checks the calling thread's message queue for mouse-button or keyboard messages.
GetKeyboardLayout	Retrieves the active keyboard layout for the specified thread.
GetKeyboardLayoutList	Retrieves the keyboard layout handles corresponding to the current set of input locales in the system.
GetKeyboardLayoutName	Retrieves the name of the active keyboard layout.
GetKeyboardState	Finds out the status of all of the keys in one function call.
GetKeyboardType	Retrieves the type of keyboard or the number of function keys.

continued on next page

continued from previous page

Function	Purpose
GetKeyNameText	Retrieves the name of a key.
GetKeyState	Determines if a key is currently down, or if a toggle key is active.
HideCaret	Makes a caret invisible.
LoadCursor	Loads a new cursor shape.
LoadKeyboardLayout	Loads a keyboard layout.
MapVirtualKey	Converts between virtual-key codes, ASCII, and scan codes.
MapVirtualKeyEx	Converts between virtual-key codes, ASCII, and scan codes using a keyboard layout.
OemKeyScan	Converts from ASCII to the keyboard's OEM scan code.
ReleaseCapture	Releases capture of the mouse.
ScreenToClient	Converts from screen coordinates to client window coordinates.
SetCapture	Captures the mouse so that only the program with the mouse captured receives mouse messages.
SetCaretBlinkTime	Sets the rate at which the caret shape flashes on the screen.
SetCaretPos	Sets the position of the caret.
SetCursor	Establishes which cursor shape to display.
SetCursorPos	Moves the mouse cursor to a new location.
SetDoubleClickTime	Changes the mouse button double-click time.
SetKeyboardState	Sets the keyboard status for all 256 virtual keys in one function call.
ShowCaret	Makes the caret visible at its current location.
ShowCursor	Shows or hides the cursor shape.
SwapMouseButton	Reverses the right and left mouse buttons.
UnloadKeyboardLayout	Removes a keyboard layout.
VkKeyScan	Translates an ANSI character to the corresponding virtual-key code.
VkKeyScanEx	Translates an ANSI character to the corresponding virtual-key code using a keyboard layout.

ActivateKeyboardLayout   ■ WINDOWS 95   ■ WINDOWS NT

Description	The **ActivateKeyboardLayout** function activates a different keyboard layout for the current thread. Several keyboard layouts can be loaded at any one time, but only one is active at a time. Loading multiple keyboard layouts makes it possible to rapidly switch between layouts. For multilingual support, this function accepts keyboard layout handles that identify the locale as well as the physical layout.
Syntax	BOOL **ActivateKeyboardLayout**(HKL *hKL,* UINT *uFlags*)
Parameters	
hKL	HKL: The keyboard layout to be activated. The layout must have been loaded by a previous call to the **LoadKeyboardLayout** function. This parameter must be either the handle of a keyboard layout or one of the values listed in Table 9-5.

Table 9-5 ActivateKeyboardLayout *hKL* values

Value	Meaning
HKL_NEXT	Selects the next layout in the circular list of loaded layouts maintained by Windows.
HKL_PREVIOUS	Selects the previous layout in the circular list of loaded layouts maintained by Windows.

uFlags   **UINT**: Specifies how the keyboard layout is to be activated. If less than three keyboard layouts are loaded, this flag is irrelevant. This parameter can be one of the values listed in Table 9-6 combined with the binary OR (|) operator.

Table 9-6 ActivateKeyboardLayout *uFlags* values

Value	Meaning
KLF_REORDER	The system's circular list of loaded keyboard layouts is reordered. For example, if a user had an English layout active as well as having French, German, and Spanish layouts loaded (in that order), then activating the German layout with the KLF_REORDER bit set would produce the following order: German, English, French, Spanish. Activating the German layout without the KLF_REORDER bit set would produce the following order: German, Spanish, English, French.
KLF_UNLOADPREVIOUS	The previously active layout is unloaded.

Returns	**BOOL**: If successful, the return value is **TRUE**; otherwise, it is **FALSE**.
Include File	winuser.h
See Also	LoadKeyboardLayout, GetKeyboardLayoutName, UnloadKeyboardLayout
Example	See the example for the **LoadKeyboardLayout** function.

ClientToScreen   ■ WINDOWS 95   ■ WINDOWS NT

Description	The **ClientToScreen** function converts the coordinates of a point relative to the client area to coordinates that are relative to the upper-left corner of the screen.
Syntax	**BOOL ClientToScreen**(HWND *hwnd,* LPPOINT *lppt*)
Parameters	
hwnd	**HWND**: The handle of the window whose client area is used for the conversion.
lppt	**LPPOINT**: A pointer to a **POINT** structure that contains the client coordinates to be converted. The new screen coordinates are copied into this structure if the function succeeds.

Returns	BOOL: If successful, the return value is TRUE; otherwise, it is FALSE.
Include File	winuser.h
See Also	SetCapture, ScreenToClient
Related Messages	WM_LBUTTONDOWN, WM_RBUTTONDOWN, WM_MOUSEMOVE
Example	This function takes two points in client coordinates (as might be retrieved from the *lParam* data from a WM_LBUTTONDOWN message) and converts them to screen coordinates. The function then draws a rectangle on the screen, outlining an area between the two points.

```
// OutlineBlock() writes a rectangle on the screen given the two corner
// points. The R2_NOT style is used, so drawing twice on the same location
// erases the outline.

VOID OutLine( HWND hWnd, POINT beg, POINT end )
{
    HWND   hDesktopWnd = GetDesktopWindow();
    HDC    hDC = GetDC( hDesktopWnd );

    ClientToScreen( hWnd, &beg );
    ClientToScreen( hWnd, &end );
    SetROP2( hDC, R2_NOT );

    MoveToEx( hDC, beg.x, beg.y, NULL );
    LineTo( hDC, end.x, beg.y );
    LineTo( hDC, end.x, end.y );
    LineTo( hDC, beg.x, end.y );
    LineTo( hDC, beg.x, beg.y );

    ReleaseDC( hDesktopWnd, hDC );
}
```

ClipCursor   ■ WINDOWS 95   ■ WINDOWS NT

Description	The ClipCursor function confines the cursor to a rectangular area on the screen. If a subsequent cursor position (set by the SetCursorPos function or the mouse) lies outside the rectangle, Windows automatically adjusts the position to keep the cursor inside the rectangular area.
	The cursor is a shared resource. If an application confines the cursor, it must release the cursor by using ClipCursor before relinquishing control to another application.
	In Windows NT, the calling process must have the WINSTA_WRITEATTRIBUTES access to the window station.
Syntax	BOOL ClipCursor(CONST RECT* *lprc*)
Parameters	
lprc	CONST RECT*: A pointer to the RECT structure containing the screen coordinates of the upper-left and lower-right corners of the confining rectangle.

If this parameter is NULL, the cursor is free to move anywhere on the screen.

Returns   BOOL: If successful, the return value is TRUE; otherwise, it is FALSE.

Include File   winuser.h

See Also   GetCapture, GetClipCursor

Related Messages   WM_MOUSEMOVE

Example   When the user selects the Test! menu item, the mouse is confined to a region bounded by a rectangle with screen coordinates 10,10 and 200,200. The application frees the mouse when it closes.

```
LRESULT CALLBACK WndProc( HWND hWnd, UINT uMsg, WPARAM wParam, LPARAM lParam )
{
    switch( uMsg )
    {
        case WM_COMMAND :
                switch( LOWORD( wParam ) )
                {
                    case IDM_TEST :
                            {
                                RECT rect;

                                SetRect( &rect, 10, 10, 200, 200 );
                                ClipCursor( &rect );
                            }
                            break;

                    case IDM_EXIT :
                            DestroyWindow( hWnd );
                            break;
                }
                break;

        case WM_DESTROY :
                ClipCursor( NULL );
                PostQuitMessage(0);
                break;

        default :
                return( DefWindowProc( hWnd, uMsg, wParam, lParam ) );
    }

    return( 0L );
}
```

CopyCursor   ■ WINDOWS 95   ■ WINDOWS NT

Description   CopyCursor is a macro that copies a cursor. This macro enables an application or dynamic link library (DLL) to obtain a copy of a cursor shape owned by another module. Then if the other module is freed, the application is still able to use the cursor shape. CopyCursor is defined as a call to the CopyIcon function.

Syntax	HCURSOR **CopyCursor**(HCURSOR *hcur*)
Parameters	
hcur	HCURSOR: The cursor to be copied.
Returns	HCURSOR: If successful, the return value is the handle of the duplicate cursor; otherwise, it is NULL.
Include File	`winuser.h`
See Also	CopyIcon, GetCursor, SetCursor, ShowCursor, LoadCursor
Example	This example loads the DLL named **RESOURCE.DLL** and loads a cursor from that DLL that is similar to the **+** cursor from Excel. Once the cursor is loaded, it is copied with the **CopyCursor** function, and used as the application's cursor. The copied cursor is destroyed when the application exits.

```
LRESULT CALLBACK WndProc( HWND hWnd, UINT uMsg, WPARAM wParam, LPARAM lParam )
{
static HCURSOR hCurCursor = NULL;

   switch( uMsg )
   {
      case WM_SETCURSOR :
              if ( !hCurCursor )
                 SetCursor( LoadCursor( NULL, IDC_ARROW ) );
              else
                 SetCursor( hCurCursor );
              break;

      case WM_COMMAND :
              switch( LOWORD( wParam ) )
              {
                 case IDM_TEST :
                        if ( GetCursor() == LoadCursor( NULL, IDC_ARROW ) )
                        {
                           HINSTANCE hInstRes = LoadLibrary( "RESOURCE.DLL" );

                           if ( hInstRes )
                           {
                              HCURSOR   hCursor;

                              hCursor = LoadCursor( hInstRes, "EXCEL" );

                              if ( hCursor )
                                 hCurCursor = CopyCursor( hCursor );

                              FreeLibrary( hInstRes );
                           }
                           else
                              MessageBox( hWnd, "Resource.DLL could not be loaded", NULL,
                                    MB_OK | MB_ICONSTOP );
                        }
                        break;

                 case IDM_EXIT :
                        DestroyWindow( hWnd );
                        break;
```

```
            }
            break;

    case WM_DESTROY :
            if ( hCurCursor )
                DestroyCursor( hCurCursor );

            PostQuitMessage(0);
            break;

    default :
            return( DefWindowProc( hWnd, uMsg, wParam, lParam ) );
    }

    return( OL );
}
```

CreateCaret   ■ WINDOWS 95   ■ WINDOWS NT

Description	**CreateCaret** creates a new shape for the system caret and assigns ownership of the caret to the given window. The caret shape can be a line, a block, or a bitmap. Only one caret can exist for any given window at a given time. Use **CreateCaret** as the first step in displaying a caret. This function is normally followed by **SetCaretPos** and **ShowCaret**.
Syntax	BOOL **CreateCaret**(HWND *hwnd,* HBITMAP *hBitmap, int nWidth,* int *nHeight*)
Parameters	
hwnd	HWND: A handle to the window that owns the caret.
hBitmap	HBITMAP: A handle to the bitmap that defines the caret shape. If set to NULL, a black caret *nWidth* wide by *nHeight* tall is created. If set to (HBITMAP)1, a gray caret is created. The bitmap handle must have been created by the **CreateBitmap**, **CreateDIBitmap**, or **LoadBitmap** function.
nWidth	int: The width of the caret in logical units. If this parameter is 0, the width is set to the system-defined window border width. If *hBitmap* is a bitmap handle, this parameter is ignored.
nHeight	int: The height of the caret in logical units. If this parameter is 0, the height is set to the system-defined window border height. If *hBitmap* is a bitmap handle, this parameter is ignored.
Returns	BOOL: If successful, the return value is TRUE; otherwise, it is FALSE.
Include File	winuser.h
See Also	DestroyCaret, SetCaretPos, ShowCaret, LoadBitmap
Related Messages	WM_SETFOCUS, WM_KILLFOCUS

Example
This example shows the creation of a caret and how it should be handled when focus changes and painting occurs. The caret is created when the application gains focus and is destroyed when the focus is lost. Note how the caret is hidden before painting (**WM_PAINT** message) and then displayed again.

```
LRESULT CALLBACK WndProc( HWND hWnd, UINT uMsg, WPARAM wParam, LPARAM lParam )
{
static PAINTSTRUCT ps;

   switch( uMsg )
   {
      case WM_SETFOCUS :
              CreateCaret( hWnd, NULL, 3, 20 );
              SetCaretPos( 10, 10 );
              ShowCaret( hWnd );
              break;

      case WM_KILLFOCUS :
              DestroyCaret();
              break;

      case WM_PAINT :
              HideCaret( hWnd );
              BeginPaint( hWnd, &ps );
              TextOut( ps.hdc, 10, 10, "Text Output.", 12 );
              EndPaint( hWnd, &ps );
              ShowCaret( hWnd );
              break;

      case WM_COMMAND :
              switch( LOWORD( wParam ) )
              {
                  case IDM_EXIT :
                          DestroyWindow( hWnd );
                          break;
              }
              break;

      case WM_DESTROY :
              PostQuitMessage(0);
              break;

      default :
              return( DefWindowProc( hWnd, uMsg, wParam, lParam ) );
   }

   return( 0L );
}
```

CreateCursor   ■ WINDOWS 95   ■ WINDOWS NT

Description
CreateCursor creates a mouse cursor having the specified size, bit patterns, and hot spot. The cursor shape is controlled by two memory areas

that contain masks for the cursor. The bits in these memory blocks are compared to the screen pixels using a logical AND and logical exclusive OR operations. Table 9-7 shows the results. The cursor can be made to change depending on where it is on the screen, or what action is occurring.

Table 9-7 Cursor Boolean masks

AND Bit Mask Value	XOR Bit Mask Value	Result on Screen
0	0	Black
0	1	White
1	0	Transparent
1	1	Inverted color

Syntax	HCURSOR **CreateCursor**(HINSTANCE *hinst,* int *xHotSpot,* int *yHotSpot,* int *nWidth,* int *nHeight,* CONST VOID* *pvANDplane,* CONST VOID* *pvXORplane*)
Parameters	
hinst	HINSTANCE: The instance handle of the application creating the cursor.
xHotSpot	int: The horizontal position, in pixels, of the cursor's hot spot.
yHotSpot	int: The vertical position, in pixels, of the cursor's hot spot.
nWidth	int: The width, in pixels, of the cursor.
nHeight	int: The height, in pixels, of the cursor.
pvANDplane	CONST VOID*: A pointer to an array of bytes that contains the bit values for the AND bit mask of the cursor, as in a device-dependent monochrome bitmap.
pvXORplane	CONST VOID*: A pointer to an array of bytes that contains the bit values for the XOR bit mask of the cursor, as in a device-dependent monochrome bitmap.
Returns	HCURSOR: If successful, the return value identifies the cursor; otherwise, it is NULL.
Include File	winuser.h
See Also	LoadCursor, DestroyCursor
Related Messages	WM_MOUSEMOVE, WM_SETCURSOR
Example	This example uses **CreateCursor** to build a rectangular cursor shape filled with a gray pattern. When the user selects the Test! menu item, the cursor shape is modified by drawing an X on the gray background. The cursor shape is only active in the window's client area.

```
HCURSOR   hCursor = NULL;
int       nCursX, nCursY, nByteArea;
```

continued on next page

CHAPTER 9

continued from previous page

```
HBITMAP   hBM;
HDC       hDCBitmap;
LPTSTR    lpAND, lpXOR;

LRESULT CALLBACK WndProc( HWND hWnd, UINT uMsg, WPARAM wParam, LPARAM lParam )
{
    switch( uMsg )
    {
        case WM_CREATE:
            {
                HDC     hDC;

                // Get the cursor size.
                //.....................
                nCursX = GetSystemMetrics( SM_CXCURSOR );
                nCursY = GetSystemMetrics( SM_CYCURSOR );

                // Create a memory DC and select a bitmap into it.
                //................................................
                hBM = CreateBitmap( nCursX, nCursY, 1, 1, NULL );
                hDC = GetDC( hWnd );
                hDCBitmap = CreateCompatibleDC( hDC );
                SelectObject( hDCBitmap, hBM );
                ReleaseDC( hWnd, hDC );

                // Allocate memory for cursor masks.
                //..................................
                nByteArea = (nCursX/8) * nCursY;
                lpAND = HeapAlloc( GetProcessHeap(), HEAP_ZERO_MEMORY, (DWORD)nByteArea );
                lpXOR = HeapAlloc( GetProcessHeap(), HEAP_ZERO_MEMORY, (DWORD)nByteArea );

                // Create a gray rectangle cursor.
                //...............................
                SelectObject( hDCBitmap, GetStockObject( LTGRAY_BRUSH ) );
                PatBlt( hDCBitmap, 0, 0, nCursX, nCursY, PATCOPY );
                GetBitmapBits( hBM, (DWORD)nByteArea, lpAND );

                // Set XOR memory to all 0's.
                //..........................
                memset( lpXOR, 0, nByteArea );

                hCursor = CreateCursor( hInst, 0, 0, nCursX,
                                        nCursY, lpAND, lpXOR );
            }
            break;

        case WM_SETCURSOR :
            if ( hCursor )
                SetCursor( hCursor );
            break;

        case WM_COMMAND :
            switch( LOWORD( wParam ) )
            {
                case IDM_TEST :
                    {
                        // Clear current cursor and delete it.
                        //...................................
```

```
                              SetCursor( NULL );
                              DestroyCursor( hCursor );

                              // Add an X to the cursor bitmap.
                              //.............................
                              SelectObject( hDCBitmap,
                                          GetStockObject( BLACK_PEN ) );
                              MoveToEx( hDCBitmap, 0, 0, NULL );
                              LineTo( hDCBitmap, nCursX, nCursY );
                              MoveToEx( hDCBitmap, 0, nCursY, NULL );
                              LineTo( hDCBitmap, nCursX, 0 );
                              GetBitmapBits( hBM, (DWORD)nByteArea, lpAND );

                              hCursor = CreateCursor( hInst, 0, 0, nCursX,
                                                 nCursY, lpAND, lpXOR );

                              SetCursor( hCursor );
                         }
                         break;

                 case IDM_EXIT :
                         DestroyWindow( hWnd );
                         break;
             }
             break;

     case WM_DESTROY :
             DestroyCursor( hCursor );
             DeleteObject( hBM );
             DeleteDC( hDCBitmap );

             HeapFree( GetProcessHeap(), 0, lpAND );
             HeapFree( GetProcessHeap(), 0, lpXOR );

             PostQuitMessage(0);
             break;

     default :
             return( DefWindowProc( hWnd, uMsg, wParam, lParam ) );
   }

   return( 0L );
}
```

DestroyCaret

Description	**DestroyCaret** destroys the caret's current shape, frees the caret from the window, and removes the caret from the screen. If the caret shape is based on a bitmap, **DestroyCaret** does not free the bitmap. Use **HideCaret** and **ShowCaret** for temporary hiding and displaying of the caret.
Syntax	BOOL **DestroyCaret**(VOID)
Parameters	This function has no parameters.
Returns	BOOL: If successful, the return value is TRUE; otherwise, it is FALSE.

Include File	`winuser.h`
See Also	`ShowCaret, HideCaret, CreateCaret, DeleteObject`
Related Messages	`WM_SETFOCUS, WM_KILLFOCUS`
Example	See the example for the `CreateCaret` function.

DestroyCursor ■ Windows 95   ■ Windows NT

Description	`DestroyCursor` destroys a cursor created by the `CreateCursor` function and frees any memory the cursor occupied. Do not use this function to destroy a cursor that was not created with the `CreateCursor` function.
Syntax	`BOOL DestroyCursor( HCURSOR hcur )`
Parameters	
hcur	`HCURSOR`: The cursor to be destroyed. The cursor must not be in use.
Returns	`BOOL`: `TRUE` if the cursor was destroyed; otherwise, the return value is `FALSE`.
Include File	`winuser.h`
See Also	`CreateCursor, DeleteObject`
Example	See the example for the `CreateCursor` function.

GetAsyncKeyState ■ Windows 95   ■ Windows NT

Description	`GetAsyncKeyState` will determine if a key is currently pressed, or if it has been pressed after the last call to `GetAsyncKeyState`.
	This function is particularly useful for applications that use shifted keys or function keys to change an operation. For example, `GetAsyncKeyState` can determine if the user pressed a function key prior to selecting an item with the mouse.
Syntax	`SHORT GetAsyncKeyState( int nVirtKey )`
Parameters	
nVirtKey	`int`: The virtual-key code for the key. See Table 9-3 for a complete list of codes.
Returns	`SHORT`: The high-order byte is `1` if the key is currently down, `0` if not. The low-order byte is `1` if the key was pressed since the last call to `GetAsyncKeyState`, `0` if not. Use the `LOBYTE` and `HIBYTE` macros to retrieve these values.
Include File	`winuser.h`
See Also	`GetKeyboardState, GetKeyState`
Related Messages	`WM_KEYDOWN, WM_KEYUP`

Example   This example displays the current status of the [SHIFT] keys when the Test!
menu item is selected.

```
LRESULT CALLBACK WndProc( HWND hWnd, UINT uMsg, WPARAM wParam, LPARAM lParam )
{
   switch( uMsg )
   {
      case WM_COMMAND :
              switch( LOWORD( wParam ) )
              {
                  case IDM_TEST :
                       {
                           char  szMsg[30];
                           SHORT nState = GetAsyncKeyState( VK_SHIFT );

                           if ( HIBYTE( nState ) )
                               lstrcpy( szMsg, "Shift is Pressed.\n" );
                           else
                               lstrcpy( szMsg, "Shift is not Pressed.\n" );

                           MessageBox( hWnd, szMsg, "Shift Key State",
                                   MB_OK | MB_ICONINFORMATION );
                       }
                       break;
```
.
.
.

GetCapture   ■ WINDOWS 95   ■ WINDOWS NT

Description   **GetCapture** retrieves the handle of the window (if any) that has captured
the mouse. Only one window at any given time can capture the mouse;
this window receives mouse input whether or not the cursor is within its
borders.

Only applications that use the mouse to outline or store images off of the
screen normally capture the mouse. Use **GetCapture** to locate the window
that has the mouse captive, so that you can send that window a message to
release the mouse.

Syntax   HWND **GetCapture**(VOID)

Parameters   This function has no parameters.

Returns   HWND: The handle of the capture window associated with the current
thread. If no window in the thread has captured the mouse, the return
value is NULL.

Include File   winuser.h

See Also   SetCapture, ReleaseCapture

Related Messages   WM_MOUSEMOVE

Example   This example prints the name of the window with the mouse captured on the window's client area every time the window receives a **WM_MOUSEMOVE** message. When the user selects the Test! menu item, the program captures the mouse itself. Clicking the left mouse button releases the mouse.

```
LRESULT CALLBACK WndProc( HWND hWnd, UINT uMsg, WPARAM wParam, LPARAM lParam )
{
   switch( uMsg )
   {
      case WM_COMMAND :
              switch( LOWORD( wParam ) )
              {
                 case IDM_TEST :
                         SetCapture( hWnd );
                         break;

                 case IDM_EXIT :
                         DestroyWindow( hWnd );
                         break;
              }
              break;

      case WM_MOUSEMOVE :
              {
                 HWND hWndCap = GetCapture();
                 HDC  hDC     = GetDC( hWnd );

                 TextOut( hDC, 10, 10,
                          "The window with the mouse captured is:", 38 );

                 if ( !hWndCap )
                    TextOut( hDC, 10, 40, "<None>", 6 );
                 else
                 {
                    char szBuf[31];

                    GetWindowText( hWndCap, szBuf, 30 );
                    TextOut( hDC, 10, 40, szBuf, lstrlen( szBuf ) );
                 }

                 ReleaseDC( hWnd, hDC );
              }
              break;

      case WM_LBUTTONDOWN :
              ReleaseCapture();
              break;
              .
              .
              .
```

GetCaretBlinkTime   ■ WINDOWS 95   ■ WINDOWS NT

Description   GetCaretBlinkTime returns the elapsed time, in milliseconds, between flashes of the caret. The time is returned even if the caret is not visible.

Syntax	UINT **GetCaretBlinkTime**(VOID)
Parameters	This function has no parameters.
Returns	UINT: The blink time in milliseconds.
Include File	winuser.h
See Also	SetCaretBlinkTime, CreateCaret
Example	In this example, the blink rate of the caret is slowed down by 0.1 seconds every time the user selects the Test! menu item. The blink rate is restored to 0.5 (500 milliseconds) when the application is closed. Starting a second copy steals the caret from the first program's client area. Selecting the Test! menu item in either instance of the application slows the blink rate in the window that displays it. The changed blinking rate remains in effect in any application that gains the caret. This example visually demonstrates that the caret is a shared resource between applications and instances.

```
LRESULT CALLBACK WndProc( HWND hWnd, UINT uMsg, WPARAM wParam, LPARAM lParam )
{
    switch( uMsg )
    {
        case WM_SETFOCUS :
                CreateCaret( hWnd, NULL, 3, 20 );
                SetCaretPos( 10, 10 );
                ShowCaret( hWnd );
                break;

        case WM_KILLFOCUS :
                DestroyCaret();
                break;

        case WM_COMMAND :
                switch( LOWORD( wParam ) )
                {
                    case IDM_TEST :
                        {
                            UINT uTime = GetCaretBlinkTime();

                            uTime += 100;
                            SetCaretBlinkTime( uTime );
                        }
                        break;

                    case IDM_EXIT :
                        DestroyWindow( hWnd );
                        break;
                }
                break;

        case WM_DESTROY :
                SetCaretBlinkTime( 500 );
                PostQuitMessage(0);
                break;
```

continued on next page

continued from previous page

```
        default :
                return( DefWindowProc( hWnd, uMsg, wParam, lParam ) );
    }

    return( 0L );
}
```

GetCaretPos   ■ Windows 95 ■ Windows NT

Description   GetCaretPos copies the caret's position, in client coordinates, to the **POINT** structure pointed to by *lpPoint*. The application should use ShowCaret before using GetCaretPos. The caret position is always given in the client coordinates of the window that contains the caret.

Syntax   BOOL **GetCaretPos**(LPPOINT *lpPoint*)

Parameters

lpPoint   LPPOINT: A pointer to a **POINT** structure that will receive the client coordinates of the caret.

Returns   BOOL: If successful, the return value is **TRUE**; otherwise, it is **FALSE**.

Include File   winuser.h

See Also   SetCaretPos, CreateCaret

Example   In this example, the caret is moved 10 units to the right every time the user selects the Test! menu item.

```
LRESULT CALLBACK WndProc( HWND hWnd, UINT uMsg, WPARAM wParam, LPARAM lParam )
{
    switch( uMsg )
    {
        case WM_SETFOCUS :
                CreateCaret( hWnd, NULL, 3, 20 );
                SetCaretPos( 10, 10 );
                ShowCaret( hWnd );
                break;

        case WM_KILLFOCUS :
                DestroyCaret();
                break;

        case WM_COMMAND :
                switch( LOWORD( wParam ) )
                {
                    case IDM_TEST :
                        {
                            POINT ptCaretPos;

                            GetCaretPos( &ptCaretPos );
                            SetCaretPos( ptCaretPos.x+10, ptCaretPos.y );
                        }
                        break;
```

```
            case IDM_EXIT :
                    DestroyWindow( hWnd );
                    break;
            }
            break;

    case WM_DESTROY :
            PostQuitMessage(0);
            break;

    default :
            return( DefWindowProc( hWnd, uMsg, wParam, lParam ) );
    }

    return( 0L );
}
```

GetClipCursor   ■ WINDOWS 95   ■ WINDOWS NT

Description	GetClipCursor retrieves the screen coordinates of the rectangular area to which the cursor is confined. The cursor is a shared resource between all applications running on the system. Limiting the cursor to an area on the screen with the ClipCursor function violates the Windows design principle of allowing programs to behave independently and should be avoided.
Syntax	BOOL **GetClipCursor**(LPRECT *lpRect*)
Parameters	
lpRect	LPRECT: A pointer to a RECT structure that receives the screen coordinates of the confining rectangle. The dimensions of the screen are retrieved if the cursor is not confined to a rectangle.
Returns	BOOL: If successful, the return value is TRUE; otherwise, it is FALSE.
Include File	winuser.h
See Also	ClipCursor, GetWindowRect
Related Messages	WM_MOUSEMOVE
Example	This example, shown in Figure 9-1, confines the mouse cursor to the limits of the application's window. The rectangle is recalculated when either a WM_MOVE or WM_SIZE message is received. The coordinates of the clipping rectangle are displayed in the client area. Selecting the Test! menu item temporarily removes the mouse limits.

```
LRESULT CALLBACK WndProc( HWND hWnd, UINT uMsg, WPARAM wParam, LPARAM lParam )
{
static RECT        rcCage;
static PAINTSTRUCT ps;
static char        szMsg[128];

    switch( uMsg )
    {
```

continued on next page

continued from previous page

```
    case WM_MOVE :
    case WM_SIZE :
            GetWindowRect( hWnd, &rcCage );
            ClipCursor( &rcCage );
            InvalidateRect( hWnd, NULL, TRUE );
            break;

    case WM_PAINT :
            BeginPaint( hWnd, &ps );
            GetClipCursor( &rcCage );

            wsprintf( szMsg, "Mouse cage = [%d, %d, %d, %d]",
                             rcCage.left,
                             rcCage.top,
                             rcCage.right,
                             rcCage.bottom );

            TextOut( ps.hdc, 0, 0, szMsg, lstrlen( szMsg ) );
            EndPaint( hWnd, &ps );
            break;

    case WM_COMMAND :
            switch( LOWORD( wParam ) )
            {
                case IDM_TEST :
                        ClipCursor( NULL );
                        break;

                case IDM_EXIT :
                        DestroyWindow( hWnd );
                        break;
            }
            break;

    case WM_DESTROY :
            ClipCursor( NULL );
            PostQuitMessage(0);
            break;

    default :
            return( DefWindowProc( hWnd, uMsg, wParam, lParam ) );
    }

    return( 0L );
}
```

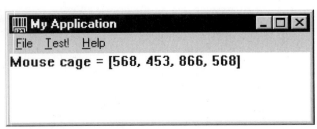

Figure 9-1 GetClipCursor example

GetCursor   ■ WINDOWS 95   ■ WINDOWS NT

Description	`GetCursor` retrieves the handle of the current mouse cursor.
Syntax	HCURSOR **GetCursor**(VOID)
Parameters	This function has no parameters.
Returns	HCURSOR: The handle of the current cursor. If there is no cursor, the return value is NULL.
Include File	winuser.h
See Also	SetCursor, GetCursorPos
Related Messages	WM_SETCURSOR
Example	See the example for the `CopyCursor` function.

GetCursorPos   ■ WINDOWS 95   ■ WINDOWS NT

Description	`GetCursorPos` retrieves the cursor's position, in screen coordinates. An application uses this function to determine the location of the mouse cursor.
Syntax	BOOL **GetCursorPos**(LPPOINT *lpPoint*)
Parameters	
lpPoint	LPPOINT: A pointer to a POINT structure that will receive the screen coordinates of the cursor.
Returns	BOOL: If successful, the return value is TRUE; otherwise, it is FALSE.
Include File	winuser.h
See Also	SetCursorPos, ScreenToClient, SetCapture, ReleaseCapture
Related Messages	WM_MOUSEMOVE
Example	In this example, shown in Figure 9-2, the mouse position is shown as the mouse moves over the client area of the window.

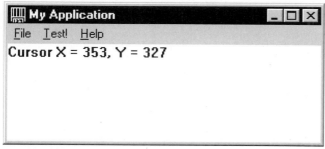

Figure 9-2 GetCursorPos example

```
LRESULT CALLBACK WndProc( HWND hWnd, UINT uMsg, WPARAM wParam, LPARAM lParam )
{
static POINT  ptCursor;
static HDC    hDC;
static char   szMsg[128];

   switch( uMsg )
   {
      case WM_MOUSEMOVE :
              GetCursorPos( &ptCursor );
              hDC = GetDC( hWnd );
              SetBkMode( hDC, OPAQUE );

              wsprintf( szMsg, "Cursor X = %d, Y = %d",
                          ptCursor.x, ptCursor.y );

              TextOut( hDC, 0, 0, szMsg, lstrlen( szMsg ) );
              ReleaseDC( hWnd, hDC );
              break;
       .
       .
       .
```

GetDoubleClickTime   ■ WINDOWS 95   ■ WINDOWS NT

Description	GetDoubleClickTime retrieves the current double-click time for the mouse. A double-click is a series of two clicks of the mouse button, the second occurring within a specified time after the first. The double-click time is the maximum number of milliseconds that may occur between the first and second click of a double-click.
	Use before activating the SetDoubleClickTime function to find the current double-click time value, prior to changing it.
Syntax	UINT **GetDoubleClickTime**(VOID)
Parameters	This function has no parameters.
Returns	UINT: The current double-click time, in milliseconds.
Include File	winuser.h
See Also	SetDoubleClickTime
Related Messages	WM_LBUTTONDBLCLK, WM_MBUTTONDBLCLK, WM_RBUTTONDBLCLK
Example	This example detects the left mouse button double-clicks and displays a message box when one is received. When the user selects the Test! menu item, the double-click time is increased by 0.1 second. Receiving double-clicks requires that the **CS_DBLCLKS** style be added to the window's class definition in the **WinMain** function. Note that the double-click time is reset to the original timing when the application exits.

```
LRESULT CALLBACK WndProc( HWND hWnd, UINT uMsg, WPARAM wParam, LPARAM lParam )
{
static UINT   uOldDblTime;
```

```
switch( uMsg )
{
    case WM_CREATE :
            uOldDblTime = GetDoubleClickTime();
            break;

    case WM_LBUTTONDBLCLK :
            MessageBox( hWnd, "Double click received.", "Message",
                            MB_OK | MB_ICONINFORMATION );
            break;

    case WM_COMMAND :
            switch( LOWORD( wParam ) )
            {
                case IDM_TEST :
                    {
                        UINT uTime = GetDoubleClickTime();

                        uTime += 100;
                        SetDoubleClickTime( uTime );
                    }
                    break;

                case IDM_EXIT :
                    DestroyWindow( hWnd );
                    break;
            }
            break;

    case WM_DESTROY :
            SetDoubleClickTime( uOldDblTime );
            PostQuitMessage(0);
            break;

    default :
            return( DefWindowProc( hWnd, uMsg, wParam, lParam ) );
    }

    return( 0L );
}
```

GetInputState   ■ WINDOWS 95   ■ WINDOWS NT

Description	`GetInputState` determines whether there are mouse-button or keyboard messages in the calling thread's message queue.
	Use `GetInputState` in lengthy operations to check whether the user has pressed a key or the mouse button. This may indicate that the user wants to abort the procedure. Because `GetInputState` does not pull the messages off the input queue, they are still there to be processed by the thread.
Syntax	`BOOL GetInputState( VOID )`
Parameters	This function has no parameters.
Returns	`BOOL`: If the queue contains one or more new mouse-button or keyboard messages, the return value is `TRUE`; otherwise, it is `FALSE`.

Include File	winuser.h
See Also	GetQueueStatus
Related Messages	WM_KEYDOWN, WM_KEYUP, WM_TIMER, WM_LBUTTONDOWN, WM_RBUTTONDOWN
Example	This example sets a one-second timer. Every time a WM_TIMER message is sent, the GetInputState function checks for mouse-button or keyboard input pending in the application's message queue.

```
LRESULT CALLBACK WndProc( HWND hWnd, UINT uMsg, WPARAM wParam, LPARAM lParam )
{
static HDC hDC;

    switch( uMsg )
    {
        case WM_CREATE :
                SetTimer( hWnd, 1, 1000, NULL );
                break;

        case WM_TIMER :
                InvalidateRect( hWnd, NULL, TRUE );
                UpdateWindow( hWnd );

                hDC = GetDC( hWnd );
                if ( GetInputState() )
                   TextOut( hDC, 10, 10,
                           "Keyboard or mouse messages ARE in the queue.", 44 );
                else
                   TextOut( hDC, 10, 10,
                           "NO Keyboard or mouse messages in the queue.", 43 );

                ReleaseDC( hWnd, hDC );
                break;

        case WM_COMMAND :
                switch( LOWORD( wParam ) )
                {
                    case IDM_EXIT :
                            DestroyWindow( hWnd );
                            break;
                }
                break;

        case WM_DESTROY :
                KillTimer( hWnd, 1 );
                PostQuitMessage(0);
                break;

        default :
                return( DefWindowProc( hWnd, uMsg, wParam, lParam ) );
    }

    return( 0L );
}
```

GetKeyboardLayout   ■ WINDOWS 95   ■ WINDOWS NT

Description	GetKeyboardLayout retrieves the active layout for the specified thread. If the thread parameter is NULL, the layout for the active thread is returned.
Syntax	HKL **GetKeyboardLayout**(HANDLE *hThread*)
Parameters	
hThread	HANDLE: The handle of the thread to query, or NULL for the current thread.
Returns	HKL: The keyboard layout handle of the input locale for the thread.
Include File	winuser.h
See Also	GetKeyboardLayoutList, GetKeyboardLayoutName, LoadKeyboardLayout
Example	See the example for the LoadKeyboardLayout function.

GetKeyboardLayoutList   ■ WINDOWS 95   ■ WINDOWS NT

Description	GetKeyboardLayoutList retrieves the keyboard layout handles of the keyboard layouts currently loaded in the system. The function copies the handles to the buffer pointed to by *lpBuff*.
Syntax	UINT **GetKeyboardLayoutList**(UINT *nItems,* HKL* *lpBuff*)
Parameters	
nItems	UINT: The maximum number of handles that the buffer pointed to by *lpBuff* can hold.
lpBuff	HKL*: A pointer to an array that receives the keyboard layout handles.
Returns	UINT: The number of layout handles copied to the buffer or, if *nItems* is 0, the number of array elements needed to receive all currently held layout handles is returned.
Include File	winuser.h
See Also	GetKeyboardLayoutName, GetKeyboardLayout, LoadKeyboardLayout
Example	This example retrieves the keyboard layout list and activates the last keyboard layout when the user selects the Test! menu item.

```
LRESULT CALLBACK WndProc( HWND hWnd, UINT uMsg, WPARAM wParam, LPARAM lParam )
{
    switch( uMsg )
    {
      case WM_COMMAND :
            switch( LOWORD( wParam ) )
            {
                case IDM_TEST :
                    {
```

continued on next page

continued from previous page

```
                    UINT nNumLayouts = GetKeyboardLayoutList( 0, NULL );
                    HKL* pmem        = (HKL*)HeapAlloc( GetProcessHeap(),
                                          HEAP_ZERO_MEMORY,
                                          sizeof( HKL ) * nNumLayouts );

                    GetKeyboardLayoutList( nNumLayouts, pmem );

                    ActivateKeyboardLayout( *(pmem+(nNumLayouts-1)), 0);

                    HeapFree( GetProcessHeap(), 0, pmem );
                }
                break;
```

GetKeyboardLayoutName   ■ WINDOWS 95   ■ WINDOWS NT

Description   GetKeyboardLayoutName retrieves the name of the current keyboard layout of the calling thread. To support multilingual applications, the system maintains a current layout for each thread rather than for the system as a whole.

Syntax   BOOL **GetKeyboardLayoutName**(LPTSTR *lpszName*)

Parameters

lpszName   LPTSTR: A pointer to a buffer that receives the name of the keyboard layout, including the terminating null character. The buffer should be at least **KL_NAMELENGTH** characters in length.

Returns   BOOL: **TRUE** if successful; otherwise, the return value is **FALSE**.

Include File   winuser.h

See Also   ActivateKeyboardLayout, UnloadKeyboardLayout

Example   This example retrieves the active keyboard layout name for the application and displays it in a message box when the user selects the Test! menu item.

```
LRESULT CALLBACK WndProc( HWND hWnd, UINT uMsg, WPARAM wParam, LPARAM lParam )
{
    switch( uMsg )
    {
        case WM_COMMAND :
                switch( LOWORD( wParam ) )
                {
                    case IDM_TEST :
                        {
                            char szKBName[ KL_NAMELENGTH ];

                            GetKeyboardLayoutName( szKBName );
                            MessageBox( hWnd, szKBName, "Active Keyboard",
                                    MB_OK | MB_ICONINFORMATION );
```

```
              }
          break;
```

.
.
.

GetKeyboardState   ■ WINDOWS 95   ■ WINDOWS NT

Description   GetKeyboardState copies the status of all 256 virtual keys to a given
                   buffer. Use this function to read more than one key's status, for example,
                   SHIFT-ALT key combinations.

Syntax   BOOL **GetKeyboardState**(PBYTE *pbKeyState*)

Parameters

pbKeyState   PBYTE: A pointer to a 256-byte array that will receive the status data for
                   each virtual-key. Use the virtual-key codes listed in Table 9-3 as indices
                   into the array of key states. A given key's byte will have the high bit set to
                   1 if the key is down, or to 0 if the key is up. The low bit is set to 1 if the
                   key has been pressed an odd number of times; otherwise, it is 0.

Returns   BOOL: If successful, the return value is TRUE; otherwise, it is FALSE.

Include File   winuser.h

See Also   GetInputState, SetKeyboardState

Related Messages WM_KEYDOWN

Example   This example retrieves the keyboard state when the user selects the Test!
                   menu item. The status of the SHIFT and ALT keys is checked to see if they
                   are currently pressed. A message box appears to indicate the status of the
                   keys.

```
LRESULT CALLBACK WndProc( HWND hWnd, UINT uMsg, WPARAM wParam, LPARAM lParam )
{
   switch( uMsg )
   {
     case WM_COMMAND :
             switch( LOWORD( wParam ) )
             {
               case IDM_TEST :
                    {
                        BYTE cBuf[256];

                        GetKeyboardState( cBuf );

                        if ( cBuf[ VK_SHIFT ] & 0x80  &&
                             cBuf[ VK_MENU ] & 0x80 )
                        {
                           MessageBox( hWnd,
                                   "The Shift-Alt keys are pressed.",
                                   "Message",
                                   MB_OK | MB_ICONINFORMATION );
```

continued on next page

continued from previous page

```
                    }
                    else
                        MessageBox( hWnd,
                                "The Shift-Alt keys are NOT pressed.",
                                "Message",
                                MB_OK | MB_ICONINFORMATION );
                    }
                    break;
```

.
.
.

GetKeyboardType ■ Windows 95 ■ Windows NT

Description   `GetKeyboardType` retrieves information about the current keyboard. Depending on the value of the *nKeybInfo*, this function will retrieve either a code for the type of keyboard in use, or the number of function keys on the keyboard.

Syntax   int **GetKeyboardType**(int *nKeybInfo*)

Parameters

nKeybInfo   `int`: The type of keyboard information to retrieve. This can be one of the values listed in Table 9-8.

Table 9-8 `GetKeyboardType` *nKeybInfo* values

Value	Meaning
0	Keyboard type
1	Keyboard subtype
2	Number of function keys on the keyboard

Returns   `int`: Specifies the requested information. Otherwise, it is **0**. If *nKeybInfo* is 0, the return value has the meanings shown in Table 9-9. If *nKeybInfo* is 1, the return value is hardware dependent. If *nKeybInfo* is **2**, the return value is the number of function keys on the keyboard.

Table 9-9 `GetKeyboardType` keyboard types

Value	Meaning
1	IBM PC/XT or compatible (83-key) keyboard.
2	Olivetti "ICO" (102-key) keyboard.
3	IBM PC/AT (84-key) or similar keyboard.

Value	Meaning
4	IBM enhanced (101- or 102-key) keyboard.
5	Nokia 1050 and similar keyboards.
6	Nokia 9140 and similar keyboards.
7	Japanese keyboard.

Include File   winuser.h

Example   This example displays the type of keyboard and the number of function keys when the user selects the Test! menu item.

```
static LPCTSTR lpszKBTypes[] =
{
    "IBM PC/XT or compatible (83-key) keyboard.",
    "Olivetti \"ICO\" (102-key) keyboard.",
    "IBM PC/AT (84-key) or similar keyboard.",
    "IBM enhanced (101- or 102-key) keyboard.",
    "Nokia 1050 and similar keyboards.",
    "Nokia 9140 and similar keyboards.",
    "Japanese keyboard.",
};


LRESULT CALLBACK WndProc( HWND hWnd, UINT uMsg, WPARAM wParam, LPARAM lParam )
{
    switch( uMsg )
    {
        case WM_KEYDOWN :
                break;

        case WM_COMMAND :
                switch( LOWORD( wParam ) )
                {
                    case IDM_TEST :
                        {
                            char szMsg[128];
                            char szNum[10];
                            int  nType    = GetKeyboardType( 0 );
                            int  nNumFKeys = GetKeyboardType( 2 );

                            lstrcpy( szMsg, lpszKBTypes[ nType-1 ] );
                            lstrcat( szMsg, "\n" );
                            lstrcat( szMsg, "Number of Function Keys: " );
                            lstrcat( szMsg, itoa( nNumFKeys, szNum, 10 ) );

                            MessageBox( hWnd, szMsg, "Keyboard Type",
                                    MB_OK | MB_ICONINFORMATION );

                        }
                        break;
                        .
                        .
                        .
```

GetKeyNameText ■ WINDOWS 95 ■ WINDOWS NT

Description	GetKeyNameText retrieves a string that represents the name of a key. This function is used in processing the WM_KEYDOWN and WM_KEYUP messages. The *lParam* parameter is passed to GetKeyNameText, at which point the function puts the key description into a character buffer pointed to by *lpBuffer*.
Syntax	int **GetKeyNameText**(LONG *lParam,* LPTSTR *lpszBuffer,* int *cchMaxKey*)
Parameters	
lParam	LONG: The second parameter of the keyboard message (such as WM_KEYDOWN) to be processed. The function interprets *lpParam* as shown in Table 9-10.

Table 9-10 GetKeyNameText *lParam* values

Bits	Meaning
16–23	Scan code.
24	Extended-key flag. Distinguishes some keys on an enhanced keyboard.
25	"Don't care" bit. Set this bit to indicate that the function should not distinguish between left and right CTRL and SHIFT keys.

lpszBuffer	LPTSTR: A pointer to a buffer that receives the key name.
cchMaxKey	int: The maximum length, in characters, of the key name, not including the terminating null character.
Returns	int: If successful, a null-terminated string is copied into the buffer pointed to by *lpszBuffer*, and the return value is the length of the string, in characters, not including the terminating null character.
Include File	winuser.h
See Also	GetInputState
Related Messages	WM_KEYDOWN, WM_KEYUP
Example	This program excerpt shows the key name anytime a key is pressed. Figure 9-3 shows what is displayed when the right SHIFT key is pressed.

```
LRESULT CALLBACK WndProc( HWND hWnd, UINT uMsg, WPARAM wParam, LPARAM lParam )
{
    switch( uMsg )
    {
        case WM_KEYDOWN :
            {
                char szName[31];
                HDC  hDC;
```

```
            InvalidateRect( hWnd, NULL, TRUE );
            UpdateWindow( hWnd );

            hDC = GetDC( hWnd );

            GetKeyNameText( lParam, szName, 30 );
            TextOut( hDC, 10, 10, szName, lstrlen( szName ) );

            ReleaseDC( hWnd, hDC );
          }
        break;
          .
          .
          .
```

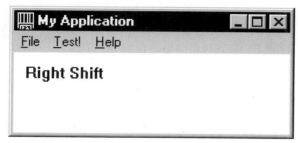

Figure 9-3 `GetKeyNameText` example

GetKeyState ■ WINDOWS 95 ■ WINDOWS NT

Description	`GetKeyState` retrieves the status of the specified virtual key. The status specifies whether the key is up, down, or toggled. You normally use `GetKeyState` to check the status of the toggled keys: CAPSLOCK, SCROLLLOCK, and NUMLOCK.
Syntax	`SHORT GetKeyState( int nVirtKey )`
Parameters	
nVirtKey	**int**: The virtual-key code. See Table 9-3 for the complete list. If the desired virtual key is a letter or digit (A through Z, a through z, or 0 through 9), *nVirtKey* must be set to the ASCII value of that character.
	If a non-English keyboard layout is used, virtual keys with values in the range ASCII A through Z and 0 through 9 are used to specify most of the character keys. For example, for the German keyboard layout, the virtual key of value ASCII O (**0x4F**) refers to the "o" key, whereas **VK_OEM_1** refers to the "o with umlaut" (ö) key.
Returns	**SHORT**: The status of the key is encoded in two bits. If the high-order bit is **1**, the key is down; otherwise, it is up. If the low-order bit is **1**, the key is toggled. A key, such as the CAPSLOCK key, is toggled if it is turned on.

Include File	`winuser.h`
See Also	`GetInputState, GetAsyncKeyState`
Related Messages	`WM_KEYDOWN, WM_KEYUP`
Example	This example is the same as the example for the **GetKeyNameText** function, except the CAPSLOCK key is checked. If the key is toggled on, the key name is uppercased; otherwise, it is lowercased.

```c
LRESULT CALLBACK WndProc( HWND hWnd, UINT uMsg, WPARAM wParam, LPARAM lParam )
{
   switch( uMsg )
   {
      case WM_KEYDOWN :
           {
               char szName[31];
               HDC  hDC;

               InvalidateRect( hWnd, NULL, TRUE );
               UpdateWindow( hWnd );

               hDC = GetDC( hWnd );

               GetKeyNameText( lParam, szName, 30 );

               // Check to see if the caps lock key is on.
               // .........................................
               if ( 0x0001 & GetKeyState( VK_CAPITAL ) )
                  strupr( szName );
               else
                  strlwr( szName );

               TextOut( hDC, 10, 10, szName, lstrlen( szName ) );

               ReleaseDC( hWnd, hDC );
           }
           break;
           .
           .
           .
```

HideCaret   ■ WINDOWS 95   ■ WINDOWS NT

Description	**HideCaret** removes the caret from the screen. Hiding the caret does not destroy its current shape or invalidate the insertion point. Hiding the caret aids the user while doing operations that take the focus of activities away from the client area (menu selections, etc.), or during **WM_PAINT** processing. As soon as the activity is done, the caret can be made visible again with **ShowCaret**. The caret is shared by all applications. If a caret is displayed on one program's window, a caret in another running program's window will disappear automatically.

Syntax	BOOL **HideCaret**(HWND *hwnd*)
Parameters	
hwnd	HWND: A handle to the window that owns the caret. If NULL, **HideCaret** searches the current task for the window that owns the caret.
Returns	BOOL: If successful, the return value is TRUE; otherwise, it is FALSE.
Include File	winuser.h
See Also	ShowCaret, CreateCaret, DestroyCaret, SetCaretBlinkTime
Related Messages	WM_PAINT
Example	See example for the **CreateCaret** function.

LoadCursor   ■ WINDOWS 95   ■ WINDOWS NT

Description	The **LoadCursor** function loads the specified cursor resource from the executable (EXE) file or dynamic link library (DLL) associated with the given instance handle. If the cursor is loaded as part of the window's class definition, the mouse cursor will change to the loaded cursor shape anytime the mouse is within the window's client area. If the goal is to have different cursor shapes within the same window's client area at different times, then the window class cursor shape should be set to NULL, and the cursor specified by calling **SetCursor** every time a WM_SETCURSOR message is received.
Syntax	HCURSOR **LoadCursor**(HINSTANCE *hinst,* LPCTSTR *lpszCursor*)
Parameters	
hinst	HINSTANCE: The instance handle of the module whose executable file contains the cursor to be loaded. Set to NULL if a predefined cursor shape is to be loaded.
lpszCursor	LPCTSTR: A pointer to a null-terminated string that contains the name of the cursor resource to be loaded. Alternatively, this parameter can be a resource identifier created with the MAKEINTRESOURCE macro.
	To use one of the Win32 predefined cursors, the application must set the *hinst* parameter to NULL and the *lpszCursor* parameter to one of the values listed in Table 9-11.

Table 9-11 Predefined cursor identifiers

Value	Description
IDC_APPSTARTING	Standard arrow and small hourglass.
IDC_ARROW	Standard arrow.
IDC_CROSS	Cross hair.
IDC_IBEAM	Text I-beam.

continued on next page

continued from previous page

Value	Description
IDC_ICON	Empty icon.
IDC_NO	Slashed circle.
IDC_SIZE	Four-pointed arrow.
IDC_SIZEALL	Same as IDC_SIZE.
IDC_SIZENESW	Double-pointed arrow pointing northeast and southwest.
IDC_SIZENS	Double-pointed arrow pointing north and south.
IDC_SIZENWSE	Double-pointed arrow pointing northwest and southeast.
IDC_SIZEWE	Double-pointed arrow pointing west and east.
IDC_UPARROW	Vertical arrow.
IDC_WAIT	Hourglass.

Returns   HCURSOR: The handle of the newly loaded cursor. NULL is returned if the cursor could not be loaded.

Include File   winuser.h

See Also   SetCursor, CreateCursor

Related Messages WM_MOUSEMOVE, WM_SETCURSOR

Example   This example shows the most common usage of the LoadCursor function in an application. When an application starts and registers the main window class, LoadCursor is normally used to set the *hCursor* item of the WNDCLASS structure.

```
int APIENTRY WinMain( HINSTANCE hInstance, HINSTANCE hPrevInstance,
                      LPTSTR lpCmdLine, int nCmdShow)
{
   MSG         msg;
   HWND        hWnd;
   WNDCLASSEX wc;

   // In Windows 95 and Windows NT, hPrevInstance is always NULL.
   //...........................................................
   if ( !hPrevInstance )
   {
      wc.style          = CS_HREDRAW | CS_VREDRAW;
      wc.lpfnWndProc    = (WNDPROC)WndProc;
      wc.cbClsExtra     = 0;
      wc.cbWndExtra     = 0;
      wc.hInstance      = hInstance;
      wc.hIcon          = LoadIcon (hInstance, lpszAppName);
      wc.hCursor        = LoadCursor(NULL, IDC_ARROW);
      wc.hbrBackground  = (HBRUSH)(COLOR_WINDOW+1);
      wc.lpszMenuName   = lpszAppName;
      wc.lpszClassName  = lpszAppName;
      wc.cbSize         = sizeof( WNDCLASSEX );
      wc.hIconSm        = LoadImage( hInstance, lpszAppName,
                                     IMAGE_ICON, 16, 16,
                                     LR_DEFAULTCOLOR );
```

```
    if ( !RegisterClassEx( &wc ) )
        return( FALSE );
}
```

.
.
.

LoadKeyboardLayout   ■ WINDOWS 95 ■ WINDOWS NT

Description	LoadKeyboardLayout loads a new keyboard layout into the system. To support multilingual applications, this function supports a language/layout menu and visual indication of the currently active one.
Syntax	HKL **LoadKeyboardLayout**(LPTSTR *lpszKLName,* UINT *uFlags*)
Parameters	
lpszKLName	LPTSTR: Points to the buffer that specifies the name of the keyboard layout. The name should be derived from the hexadecimal value of the language identifier corresponding to the layout. For example, U.S. English has a language identifier of **0x0409**, so the primary U.S. English layout is named **"00000409"**. Variants of the U.S. English layout, such as the Dvorak layout, are named **"00010409"**, **"00020409"**, and so on. The **MAKELANGID** macro can be used to get the language identifier.
uFlags	UINT: Specifies how the keyboard layout is loaded. This parameter can be one or more of the values listed in Table 9-12 combined using the binary OR (	) operator.

Table 9-12 LoadKeyboardLayout *uFlags* values

Value	Meaning
KLF_ACTIVATE	The layout is loaded (if it is not already loaded) and activated.
KLF_NOTELLSHELL	(Windows 95) Prevents a ShellProc hook procedure from receiving an HSHELL_LANGUAGE hook code when the new layout is loaded.
KLF_REORDER	If KLF_ACTIVATE is set and the layout is already loaded, the specified layout is removed from its position in the system's circular list of loaded layouts and placed at the head as the active layout.
KLF_REPLACELANG	(Windows 95) If the new layout has the same language identifier as a current layout, the new layout replaces the current one as the layout for that language.
KLF_SUBSTITUTE_OK	A substitution for the layout is looked up in the user's profile (in the registry under the key HKEY_CURRENT_USER\Keyboard Layout\Substitutes). For example, if there was a value in this section of name "00000409" equal to "00010409", loading the U.S. English layout ("00000409") with the KLF_SUBSTITUTE_OK flag set would cause the Dvorak U.S. English layout ("00010409") to be loaded.
KLF_UNLOADPREVIOUS	(Windows NT) The previously active layout is unloaded.

Returns	HKL: The handle of the keyboard layout. NULL is returned if the keyboard layout could not be loaded.
Include File	winuser.h
See Also	ActivateKeyboardLayout
Example	In this example, the Spanish-Mexican keyboard layout is loaded and activated when the user selects the Test! menu item. If the Spanish-Mexican keyboard layout is already active, then the next keyboard layout is activated when the Test! menu item is selected. If only the English-US keyboard layout is loaded, Figure 9-4 shows how the keyboard layouts appear in the control panel after the Spanish-Mexican keyboard layout is loaded. When the example ends, the keyboard layout is unloaded.

```
HKL    hKbLayout = NULL;

LRESULT CALLBACK WndProc( HWND hWnd, UINT uMsg, WPARAM wParam, LPARAM lParam )
{
   switch( uMsg )
   {
      case WM_COMMAND :
              switch( LOWORD( wParam ) )
              {
                 case IDM_TEST :
                         // If the keyboard layout has not been
                         // loaded, load it.
                         //....................................
                         if ( !hKbLayout )
                         {
                            char szName[9];
                            DWORD dwLangID = MAKELANGID( LANG_SPANISH,
                                             SUBLANG_SPANISH_MEXICAN );

                            wsprintf( szName, "%8.8X", dwLangID );
                            hKbLayout = LoadKeyboardLayout( szName,
                                                 KLF_REPLACELANG );
                         }

                         if ( hKbLayout != GetKeyboardLayout( NULL ) )
                            ActivateKeyboardLayout( hKbLayout, 0 );
                         else
                            ActivateKeyboardLayout( HLF_NEXT, 0 );

                         break;

                 case IDM_EXIT :
                         DestroyWindow( hWnd );
                         break;
              }
              break;

      case WM_DESTROY :
              if ( hKbLayout )
              {
                 ActivateKeyboardLayout( (HKL)HKL_NEXT, 0 );
                 UnloadKeyboardLayout( hKbLayout );
              }
```

```
            PostQuitMessage(0);
            break;

    default :
            return( DefWindowProc( hWnd, uMsg, wParam, lParam ) );
    }

    return( 0L );
}
```

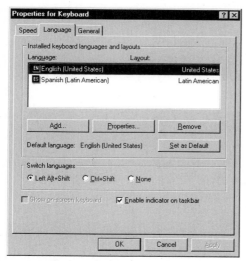

Figure 9-4 Keyboard layouts in Control
Panel

MapVirtualKey   ■ WINDOWS 95   ■ WINDOWS NT

Description   **MapVirtualKey** performs three separate operations, depending on the
value set for **_uMapType_**. One is the conversion of a virtual-key code used in
Windows messages to the computer's OEM scan code. The second mode
does the reverse; it converts from OEM scan code to the virtual-key code
used by Windows. The third mode converts virtual-key codes to ASCII
values.

The most common use is to convert the virtual-key code used in Windows
messages to ASCII values that can be printed on the screen. You may find
yourself dealing with the OEM scan color codes in rare cases, such as distinguishing between the left and right SHIFT keys (both generate the same
virtual-key code).

Syntax   UINT **MapVirtualKey**(UINT *uCode,* UINT *uMapType*)

Parameters

uCode   **UINT**: The virtual-key code or scan code of the key. How this value is inter-
                      preted depends on the value of the *uMapType* parameter.

uMapType   **UINT**: The translation to perform. Use the values listed in Table 9-13.

Table 9-13 MapVirtualKey *uMapType* values

Value	Meaning
0	*uCode* is a virtual-key code. A scan code is returned. If the virtual-key code does not distinguish between left- and right-hand keys, the left-hand scan code is returned.
1	*uCode* is a scan code. A virtual-key code is returned that does not distinguish between left- and right-hand keys.
2	*uCode* is a virtual-key code. An unshifted ASCII character value is returned in the low-order word. Indicate dead keys (diacritics) by setting the top bit of the return value.
3	*uCode* is a scan code. A virtual-key code that distinguishes between left- and right-hand keys is returned.

Returns   **UINT**: Either a scan code, a virtual-key code, or a character value, depend-
                      ing on the value of *uCode* and *uMapType*. If there is no translation, the
                      return value is 0.

Include File   winuser.h

See Also   OemKeyScan, MapVirtualKeyEx

Related Messages   WM_KEYDOWN, WM_KEYUP, WM_CHAR

Example   This code fragment shows two uses of the **MapVirtualKey** function. The
                      virtual-key code is encoded in the *wParam* parameter when the **WM_KEY-
                      DOWN** message is received. **MapVirtualKey** converts the virtual-key code to
                      the OEM scan code and the ASCII value.

```
LRESULT CALLBACK WndProc( HWND hWnd, UINT uMsg, WPARAM wParam, LPARAM lParam )
{
    switch( uMsg )
    {
        case WM_KEYDOWN :
                {
                    HDC   hDC;
                    UINT  uCode
                    char  szBuf[10];

                    InvalidateRect( hWnd, NULL, TRUE );
                    UpdateWindow( hWnd );

                    hDC = GetDC( hWnd );
                    uCode = MapVirtualKey( wParam, 0 );
                    itoa( uCode, szBuf, 10 );

                    TextOut( hDC, 10, 10, szBuf, strlen( szBuf ) );
                    TextOut( hDC, 50, 10, "= scan code.", 12 );
```

```
          uCode = MapVirtualKey( wParam, 2 );
          itoa( uCode, szBuf, 10 );

          TextOut( hDC, 10, 30, szBuf, strlen( szBuf ) );
          TextOut( hDC, 50, 30, "= ASCII.", 8 );

          ReleaseDC( hWnd, hDC );
       }
       break;
       .
       .
       .
```

MapVirtualKeyEx   ■ Windows 95 ■ Windows NT

Description	**MapVirtualKeyEx** translates a virtual-key code into a scan code or character value, or translates a scan code into a virtual-key code. The function translates the codes using the input language and physical keyboard layout identified by the given keyboard layout handle.
Syntax	UINT **MapVirtualKeyEx**(UINT *uCode,* UINT *uMapType,* HKL *dwhkl*)
Parameters	
uCode	UINT: The virtual-key code or scan code of the key. How this value is interpreted depends on the value of the *uMapType* parameter.
uMapType	UINT: The translation to perform. Use the values listed in Table 9-13.
dwhkl	HKL: The keyboard layout to use for translating the given code. This parameter can be any keyboard layout handle previously returned by the **LoadKeyboardLayout** function.
Returns	UINT: Either a scan code, a virtual-key code, or a character value, depending on the value of *uCode* and *uMapType*. If there is no translation, the return value is **0**.
Include File	winuser.h
See Also	MapVirtualKey
Related Messages	WM_KEYDOWN, WM_KEYUP, WM_CHAR

OemKeyScan   ■ Windows 95 ■ Windows NT

Description	The **OemKeyScan** function maps OEM ASCII codes **0** through **0xFF** into the OEM scan codes and shift states. The OEM scan code is part of the *lParam* parameter accompanying every **WM_KEYDOWN** and **WM_KEYUP** message.
	OemKeyScan is used in sending other Windows messages that simulate key-presses. This can be an efficient way to pass information between windows that already have message-processing logic to handle keyboard input.

Syntax	DWORD **OemKeyScan**(WORD *wOemChar*)
Parameters	
wOemChar	WORD: The ASCII value of the OEM character.
Returns	DWORD: The low-order word contains the scan code of the given OEM character, and the high-order word contains the shift state, which can be a combination of the bit flags shown in Table 9-14. If the character cannot be produced by a single keystroke using the current keyboard layout, 0xFFFFFFFF is returned.

Table 9-14 OemKeyScan return value bit flags

Bit	Meaning
1	Either SHIFT key is pressed.
2	Either CTRL key is pressed.
4	Either ALT key is pressed.

Include File	winuser.h
See Also	VkKeyScan, MapVirtualKey
Related Messages	WM_KEYDOWN, WM_KEYUP
Example	This example shows how the **VkKeyScan** and the **OemKeyScan** functions are used to send **WM_KEYDOWN** messages. When the user selects the Test! menu item, a **WM_KEYDOWN** message is sent to the application's main window simulating the Ⓐ key being pressed. When the **WM_KEYDOWN** message is received, a message box appears showing the character that was pressed.

```
LRESULT CALLBACK WndProc( HWND hWnd, UINT uMsg, WPARAM wParam, LPARAM lParam )
{
   switch( uMsg )
   {
      case WM_KEYDOWN :
            {
                char szChar[2];

                szChar[0] = (char)MapVirtualKey( wParam, 2 );
                szChar[1] = 0;

                MessageBox( hWnd, szChar, "Key Received",
                            MB_OK | MB_ICONINFORMATION );
            }
            break;

      case WM_COMMAND :
            switch( LOWORD( wParam ) )
            {
                case IDM_TEST :
                    {
```

```
        SHORT nVirtKey = VkKeyScan( 'A' );
        DWORD dwOemKey = ((OemKeyScan( (WORD)'A' ) & 0x00FF)
                    << 16) | 1;

        SendMessage( hWnd, WM_KEYDOWN, (WPARAM)nVirtKey,
                dwOemKey );
    }
    break;
```
.
.
.

ReleaseCapture   ■ WINDOWS 95   ■ WINDOWS NT

Description	`ReleaseCapture` releases the mouse capture from a window in the current thread and restores normal mouse input processing. A window that has captured the mouse receives all mouse input, regardless of the position of the cursor, except when a mouse button is clicked while the cursor hot spot is in the window of another thread.
Syntax	BOOL **ReleaseCapture**(VOID)
Parameters	This function has no parameters.
Returns	BOOL: TRUE if successful; otherwise, the return value is FALSE.
Include File	`winuser.h`
See Also	`SetCapture`, `GetCapture`
Related Messages	WM_MOUSEMOVE
Example	See the example for the `GetCapture` function.

ScreenToClient   ■ WINDOWS 95   ■ WINDOWS NT

Description	`ScreenToClient` converts the screen coordinates contained in a POINT structure pointed to by *lpPoint* to client coordinates. This function is frequently used in conjunction with `GetCursorPos` to convert the mouse cursor's location to an x, y location in the window's client area. This is typically done when processing WM_MOUSEMOVE messages while drawing lines or positioning text in the client area.
Syntax	BOOL **ScreenToClient**(HWND *hwnd,* LPPOINT *lpPoint*)
Parameters	
hwnd	HWND: The handle of the window whose client area will be used for the conversion.
lpPoint	LPPOINT: A pointer to a POINT structure that contains the screen coordinates to be converted.
Returns	BOOL: TRUE if successful; otherwise, the return value is FALSE.

Include File	winuser.h
See Also	GetCursorPos, ClientToScreen
Related Messages	WM_MOUSEMOVE, WM_LBUTTONDOWN, WM_NCMOUSEMOVE
Example	This example shows the cursor's location in client coordinates when the cursor passes over the nonclient area of the window. This includes the borders, caption, and menu bars. The **WM_NCMOUSEMOVE** message passes the screen coordinates of the cursor location as the *lParam* value.

```
LRESULT CALLBACK WndProc( HWND hWnd, UINT uMsg, WPARAM wParam, LPARAM lParam )
{
static POINT    ptCursor;
static HDC      hDC;
static char     szMsg[128];

   switch( uMsg )
   {
      case WM_NCMOUSEMOVE :
              ptCursor.x = LOWORD( lParam );
              ptCursor.y = HIWORD( lParam );
              ScreenToClient( hWnd, &ptCursor );

              hDC = GetDC( hWnd );
              SetBkMode( hDC, OPAQUE );

              wsprintf( szMsg, "Cursor X = %d, Y = %d",
                          ptCursor.x, ptCursor.y );

              TextOut( hDC, 0, 0, szMsg, lstrlen( szMsg ) );
              ReleaseDC( hWnd, hDC );
              break;
              .
              .
              .
```

SetCapture   ■ WINDOWS 95   ■ WINDOWS NT

Description	SetCapture sets the mouse capture to the given window belonging to the current thread. Once a window has captured the mouse, all mouse input is directed to that window, regardless of whether the cursor is within the borders of that window. Only one window at a time can capture the mouse. If the mouse cursor is over a window created by another thread, the system will direct mouse input to the window only if a mouse button is pressed down.
Syntax	HWND **SetCapture**(HWND *hwnd*)
Parameters	
hwnd	HWND: A handle to the window in the current thread that will capture the mouse.
Returns	HWND: The handle of the window that had previously captured the mouse. If no such window exists, the return value is **NULL**.

Include File	`winuser.h`
See Also	`ReleaseCapture`, `GetCapture`
Related Messages	`WM_MOUSEMOVE`, `WM_SETFOCUS`
Example	See the example for the `GetCapture` function.

SetCaretBlinkTime
■ WINDOWS 95 ■ WINDOWS NT

Description	`SetCaretBlinkTime` sets the time, in milliseconds, between cursor flashes. Because the caret is a shared resource between all applications, changing the blink time in one application affects the blink time in all other programs running at that time.
Syntax	`BOOL SetCaretBlinkTime( UINT wMSeconds )`
Parameters	
wMSeconds	`UINT`: The new blink time, in milliseconds.
Returns	`BOOL`: `TRUE` if successful; otherwise, the return value is `FALSE`.
Include File	`winuser.h`
See Also	`GetCaretBlinkTime`
Example	See the example for the `GetCaretBlinkTime` function.

SetCaretPos
■ WINDOWS 95 ■ WINDOWS NT

Description	`SetCaretPos` moves the caret to the specified coordinates. If the window that owns the caret was created with the `CS_OWNDC` class style, then the specified coordinates are subject to the mapping mode associated with that window.
	This is the basic function for moving a caret on the window's client area. A window can own a maximum of one caret at any one time. Use `CreateCaret` to load or build a caret.
Syntax	`BOOL SetCaretPos( int nX, int nY )`
Parameters	
nX	`int`: The new x coordinate of the caret.
nY	`int`: The new y coordinate of the caret.
Returns	`BOOL`: `TRUE` if successful; otherwise, the return value is `FALSE`.
Include File	`winuser.h`
See Also	`CreateCaret`, `HideCaret`, `ShowCaret`, `DPtoLP`
Example	See the example for the `CreateCaret` function.

SetCursor

Description	`SetCursor` changes the shape of the cursor. Normally used when processing `WM_SETCURSOR` or `WM_MOUSEMOVE` messages, `SetCursor` is fast if the cursor has already been used once, so it can be called repeatedly to change a cursor shape without noticeably slowing the program. Cursor shapes must first be loaded with `LoadCursor`. Using `SetCursor` within the bounds of a window that has a cursor definition causes the cursor shape to flicker. This is because Windows is switching back and forth between the class cursor and the cursor loaded with `SetCursor` every time a `WM_MOUSEMOVE` message is sent. Set the class cursor to `NULL` to avoid this problem.
Syntax	HCURSOR **SetCursor**(HCURSOR *hCursor*)
Parameters	
hCursor	HCURSOR: A handle to the cursor you want to show. Use `LoadCursor` to obtain the handle.
Returns	HCURSOR: A handle to the previous cursor shape. If there was no previous cursor, the return value is `NULL`.
Include File	`winuser.h`
See Also	`LoadCursor`
Related Messages	`WM_SETCURSOR`, `WM_MOUSEMOVE`
Example	See the example for the `CreateCursor` function.

SetCursorPos

Description	`SetCursorPos` moves the cursor to the specified screen coordinates. If the coordinates are not within the rectangle set by the most recent `ClipCursor` call, Windows adjusts the coordinates so that the cursor stays within the rectangle. `SetCursorPos` could be used to provide keyboard support for mouse movements. For example, the arrow keys might move the mouse cursor.
Syntax	BOOL **SetCursorPos**(int *nX,* int *nY*)
Parameters	
nX	int: The new x coordinate, in screen coordinates, of the cursor.
nY	int: The new y coordinate, in screen coordinates, of the cursor.
Returns	BOOL: `TRUE` if successful; otherwise, the return value is `FALSE`.
Include File	`winuser.h`
See Also	`GetCursorPos`, `ClientToScreen`
Related Messages	`WM_MOUSEMOVE`

Example   When the user selects the Test! menu option, the mouse cursor is moved to the upper-left corner of the window's client area.

```
LRESULT CALLBACK WndProc( HWND hWnd, UINT uMsg, WPARAM wParam, LPARAM lParam )
{
   switch( uMsg )
   {
      case WM_COMMAND :
            switch( LOWORD( wParam ) )
            {
               case IDM_TEST :
                  {
                     POINT ptCursPoint;

                     ptCursPoint.x = 0;
                     ptCursPoint.y = 0;
                     ClientToScreen( hWnd, &ptCursPoint );
                     SetCursorPos( ptCursPoint.x, ptCursPoint.y );
                  }
                  break;
         .
         .
         .
```

SetDoubleClickTime   ■ WINDOWS 95   ■ WINDOWS NT

Description	SetDoubleClickTime sets the double-click time for the mouse. The double-click time is the maximum number of milliseconds that may occur between the first and second clicks of a double-click. The double-click time is only changed for the duration of the Windows session.
Syntax	BOOL **SetDoubleClickTime**(UINT *uInterval*)
Parameters	
uInterval	UINT: The number of milliseconds that can occur between the first and second clicks of a double-click. If set to **0**, Windows uses the default double-click time of 500 milliseconds.
Returns	BOOL: TRUE if successful; otherwise, the return value is FALSE.
Include File	winuser.h
See Also	GetDoubleClickTime
Related Messages	WM_LBUTTONDBLCLK, WM_MBUTTONDBLCLK, WM_RBUTTONDBLCLK
Example	See the example for the GetDoubleClickTime function.

SetKeyboardState   ■ WINDOWS 95   ■ WINDOWS NT

Description	SetKeyboardState copies a 256-byte array of keyboard key states into the calling thread's keyboard-input state table. The state table can be accessed by the GetKeyboardState and GetKeyState functions. Changes made to this table do not affect keyboard input to any other thread.

To set one of these toggle keys to the on state, use a value of **0x81** in the 256-byte array. To set a nontoggle (normal) key to on, use a value of **0x80**. The virtual key is the index to the item in the array.

Syntax	BOOL **SetKeyboardState**(LPBYTE *lpbKeyState*)
Parameters	
lpbKeyState	LPBYTE: A pointer to a 256-byte array that contains keyboard key states.
Returns	BOOL: If successful, the return value is TRUE; otherwise, it is FALSE.
Include File	winuser.h
See Also	GetKeyboardState
Related Messages	WM_KEYDOWN, WM_KEYUP, WM_CHAR
Example	This example sets the state of the CTRL key to be pressed when the user selects the Test! menu item. The state of the CTRL key remains pressed until the user physically presses the CTRL key.

```
LRESULT CALLBACK WndProc( HWND hWnd, UINT uMsg, WPARAM wParam, LPARAM lParam )
{
   switch( uMsg )
   {
      case WM_COMMAND :
            switch( LOWORD( wParam ) )
            {
               case IDM_TEST :
                  {
                     BYTE cBuf[256];

                     GetKeyboardState( cBuf );

                     // Set the CONTROL key state to pressed.
                     //.....................
                     cBuf[ VK_CONTROL ] |= 0x80;

                     SetKeyboardState( cBuf );
                  }
                  break;
         .
         .
         .
```

ShowCaret

■ WINDOWS 95   ■ WINDOWS NT

Description	**ShowCaret** makes the caret visible on the screen at the caret's current position. When the caret becomes visible, it begins flashing automatically. It helps the user if the caret is hidden while processing **WM_PAINT** messages or while doing operations that take the focus of activities away from the client area (menu selections, etc.). When the user returns to the work area, the caret can be made visible again with **ShowCaret**. The caret is shared by all applications. If a caret is displayed on one program's window, a caret in another program's window will disappear.

Syntax	BOOL **ShowCaret**(HWND *hwnd*)
Parameters	
hwnd	**HWND**: A handle to the window that owns the caret. If this parameter is **NULL**, **ShowCaret** searches the current task for the window that last displayed the caret.
Returns	**BOOL**: **TRUE** if successful; otherwise, it is **FALSE**.
Include File	winuser.h
See Also	HideCaret, CreateCaret, DestroyCaret, SetCaretBlinkTime
Related Messages	WM_PAINT
Example	See the example for the **CreateCaret** function.

ShowCursor   ■ WINDOWS 95 ■ WINDOWS NT

Description	**ShowCursor** displays or hides the mouse cursor depending on the value given in the *bShow* parameter.
Syntax	int **ShowCursor**(BOOL *bShow*)
Parameters	
bShow	**BOOL**: If **TRUE**, the display count of the cursor is incremented by one. If **FALSE**, the display count is decremented by one. The cursor is displayed if the count is greater than or equal to zero.
Returns	**int**: The new display counter.
Include File	winuser.h
See Also	ClipCursor, GetCursorPos, SetCursor, SetCursorPos
Example	This example shows how an application could hide an inactive mouse until it is moved or a button is pressed. A timer is set for two seconds. Every time a mouse action occurs, the timer is reset. If the timer expires, the mouse is hidden until a mouse action occurs again.

```
LRESULT CALLBACK WndProc( HWND hWnd, UINT uMsg, WPARAM wParam, LPARAM lParam )
{
static BOOL bCursorState = TRUE;

   switch( uMsg )
   {
      case WM_CREATE :
               SetTimer( hWnd, 1, 2000, NULL );
               break;

      case WM_NCMOUSEMOVE :
      case WM_MOUSEMOVE :
      case WM_LBUTTONDOWN :
      case WM_RBUTTONDOWN :
               {
               KillTimer( hWnd, 1 );
               SetTimer( hWnd, 1, 2000, NULL );
```

continued on next page

continued from previous page

```
            if ( !bCursorState )
            {
                ShowCursor( TRUE );
                bCursorState = TRUE;
            }
        }
        break;

    case WM_TIMER :
            if ( bCursorState )
            {
                ShowCursor( FALSE );
                bCursorState = FALSE;
            }
            break;

    case WM_COMMAND :
            switch( LOWORD( wParam ) )
            {

                case IDM_EXIT :
                        DestroyWindow( hWnd );
                        break;
            }
            break;

    case WM_DESTROY :
            KillTimer( hWnd, 1 );
            if ( !bCursorState )
                ShowCursor( TRUE );

            PostQuitMessage(0);
            break;

    default :
            return( DefWindowProc( hWnd, uMsg, wParam, lParam ) );
    }

    return( OL );
}
```

SwapMouseButton   ■ WINDOWS 95   ■ WINDOWS NT

Description	**SwapMouseButton** reverses or restores the meaning of the left and right mouse buttons. Calling this function only changes the mouse button orientation for the duration of the Windows session.
Syntax	BOOL **SwapMouseButton**(BOOL *bSwap*)
Parameters	
bSwap	BOOL: If set to TRUE, the left button generates right-button messages and the right button generates left-button messages. If set to FALSE, the buttons are restored to their original meanings.

Returns	BOOL: If the mouse buttons were previously reversed, before the function was called, the return value is TRUE; otherwise, it is FALSE.
Include File	winuser.h
See Also	SetDoubleClickTime
Related Messages	WM_LBUTTONDOWN, WM_RBUTTONDOWN
Example	In this example, the left mouse button is swapped with the right mouse button each time the user selects the Test! menu item. The mouse is restored to normal when the application exits.

```
LRESULT CALLBACK WndProc( HWND hWnd, UINT uMsg, WPARAM wParam, LPARAM lParam )
{
static BOOL bMouseState = TRUE;

   switch( uMsg )
   {
      case WM_COMMAND :
             switch( LOWORD( wParam ) )
             {
                 case IDM_TEST :
                      bMouseState = !bMouseState;
                      SwapMouseButton( bMouseState );
                      break;

                 case IDM_EXIT :
                      DestroyWindow( hWnd );
                      break;
             }
             break;

      case WM_DESTROY :
             if ( !bMouseState )
                SwapMouseButton( FALSE );
             PostQuitMessage(0);
             break;

      default :
             return( DefWindowProc( hWnd, uMsg, wParam, lParam ) );
   }

   return( 0L );
}
```

UnloadKeyboardLayout ■ WINDOWS 95 ■ WINDOWS NT

Description	UnloadKeyboardLayout removes the given keyboard layout. This ensures that the user always has one layout available that is capable of typing in the character set of the shell and file system.
Syntax	BOOL **UnloadKeyboardLayout**(HKL *hkl*)
Parameters	
hkl	HKL: The handle of the keyboard layout to unload.

Returns	BOOL: TRUE if successful; otherwise, it is FALSE.
Include File	winuser.h
See Also	ActivateKeyboardLayout, GetKeyboardLayoutName, LoadKeyboardLayout
Example	See the example for the LoadKeyboardLayout function.

VkKeyScan　　　　　　　　　　■ WINDOWS 95　■ WINDOWS NT

Description	VkKeyScan translates a character to the corresponding virtual-key code and shift state for the current keyboard.
	Use VkKeyScan to send WM_KEYDOWN and WM_KEYUP messages to other windows. This can be an efficient way to pass information between windows if the receiving window already has keyboard input logic in its WndProc function.
Syntax	SHORT VkKeyScan(TCHAR ch)
Parameters	
ch	TCHAR: The character to be translated into a virtual-key code.
Returns	SHORT: If the function succeeds, the low-order byte of the return value contains the virtual-key code, and the high-order byte contains the shift state, which can be a combination of the bit flags shown in Table 9-14. If the function finds no key that translates to the passed character code, both the low-order and high-order bytes contain –1.
Include File	winuser.h
See Also	VkKeyScanEx, OemKeyScan, MapVirtualKey
Related Messages	WM_KEYDOWN, WM_KEYUP
Example	See the example for the OemKeyScan function.

VkKeyScanEx　　　　　　　　　　■ WINDOWS 95　■ WINDOWS NT

Description	VkKeyScanEx is the same as the VkKeyScan function, except VkKeyScanEx translates the character using the input language and physical keyboard layout identified by the given keyboard layout handle.
Syntax	SHORT VkKeyScanEx(UINT uChar, HKL hkl)
Parameters	
uChar	UINT: The character to be translated into a virtual-key code.
hkl	HKL: The keyboard layout to use to translate the character. This parameter can be any keyboard layout handle previously returned by the LoadKeyboardLayout function.
Returns	SHORT: If the function succeeds, the low-order byte of the return value contains the virtual-key code, and the high-order byte contains the shift

state, which can be a combination of the bit flags shown in Table 9-14. If the function finds no key that translates to the passed character code, both the low-order and high-order bytes contain **-1**.

Include File   `winuser.h`

See Also   `VkKeyScan, OemKeyScan, MapVirtualKey`

Related Messages   `WM_KEYDOWN, WM_KEYUP`

Example   This example is the same as the example for the `OemKeyScan` function, except the `VkKeyScanEx` function is used to get the virtual-key value using the active keyboard layout.

```
LRESULT CALLBACK WndProc( HWND hWnd, UINT uMsg, WPARAM wParam, LPARAM lParam )
{
   switch( uMsg )
   {
      case WM_KEYDOWN :
            {
                char szChar[2];

                szChar[0] = (char)MapVirtualKey( wParam, 2 );
                szChar[1] = 0;

                MessageBox( hWnd, szChar, "Key Received",
                          MB_OK | MB_ICONINFORMATION );
            }
            break;

      case WM_COMMAND :
            switch( LOWORD( wParam ) )
            {
               case IDM_TEST :
                     {
                         SHORT nVirtKey;
                         DWORD dwOemKey;
                         HKL   hKL = GetKeyboardLayout( 0 );

                         nVirtKey = VkKeyScanEx( ';', hKL );
                         dwOemKey = ((OemKeyScan( (WORD)';' ) & 0x00FF)
                                      << 16) | 1;

                         SendMessage( hWnd, WM_KEYDOWN, (WPARAM)nVirtKey,
                                    dwOemKey );
                     }
                     break;

               case IDM_EXIT :
                     DestroyWindow( hWnd );
                     break;
            }
            break;

      case WM_DESTROY :
            PostQuitMessage(0);
            break;
```

continued on next page

continued from previous page

```
     default :
           return( DefWindowProc( hWnd, uMsg, wParam, lParam ) );
  }

  return( 0L );
}
```

10

SCROLL BARS

A window in an application can display a data object, such as a document or a graphic image, that is larger than the window's client area. When the window has a scroll bar, the user can scroll the data object within the client area to view the entire document or graphic image. An application should include a scroll bar on a window when the client area's contents extend beyond the size of the window's client area.

Scroll Bar Basics

Scroll bar controls are child windows. You initially create scroll bars using the `CreateWindow` function discussed in Chapter 3, Creating Windows. Once created, scroll bars can either be placed on the program's client area or added as part of the window's border for scrolling the client area. Scroll bars placed on the client area are referred to as slider or trackbar controls. Trackbar controls provide a simple way for the user to give approximate input or for the application to give approximate feedback. In previous versions of Windows, a simple scroll bar was used as a trackbar. Windows NT 4 and Windows 95 provide a new common control appropriately called a Track Bar control. Common controls are covered in the second book of the Windows 95 API Bible series, *Common Controls & Messages*. Figure 10-1 illustrates the different types of scroll bars and a trackbar. This figure points out the different parts of a scroll bar.

Scroll bars are attached to the window's border when the scroll bar control is made visible. You use `ShowScrollBar` for scroll bars the same way you use `ShowWindow` for other types of windows. The difference is that `ShowScrollBar` will attach scroll bars to the window's border if the `SB_HORZ` or `SB_VERT` style is specified. Windows automatically subtracts the width of the scroll bar from the client area, so that painting on the client area does not run over the scroll bars. The other way to attach a scroll bar to a window's frame is to create the window with one or both of the `WS_HSCROLL` and `WS_VSCROLL` styles.

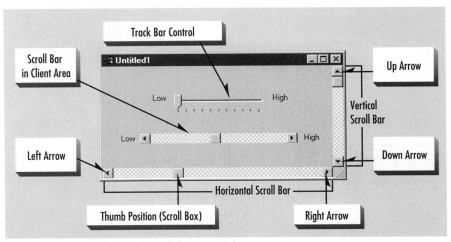

Figure 10-1 Examples of scroll bar controls

Scroll bars are attached automatically to list boxes and combo boxes when the list of items exceeds the size of the list window. Edit controls also can have scroll bars attached. Single-line edit controls can only take advantage of the horizontal scroll bar, but multiline edit controls can use both vertical and horizontal scroll bars. Edit controls are nothing more than small windows, so add the WS_HSCROLL and/or WS_VSCROLL styles when creating the edit control.

Scroll Bar Position and Range

When you create a scroll bar, the range of values represented by the two ends of the control are 0 to 100. In most cases, an application will change the range to reflect the size of the document or graphic image. The thumb position (scroll box) is the value within the range where the scroll box is located. For example, if the range is 0 to 100 and the thumb position is 50, the scroll box will be located halfway between the two ends of the control. Windows 95 (this is not exclusive to Windows 95) introduces another feature of the scroll bar, the ability to set a page size for the scroll bar. The page size is the number of increments within the scroll range that can be displayed at one time. If the range is 0 to 100 and the page size is set to 50, the scroll box will be half the size of the scroll bar. Figure 10-2 shows how this would appear. You use the SetScrollInfo and GetScrollInfo functions to set and retrieve the range, thumb position, and page size of a scroll bar.

Figure 10-2 Windows 95 scroll bar

Scroll Bar Messages

When the user clicks part of a scroll bar, Windows sends either a **WM_HSCROLL** or **WM_VSCROLL** message, depending on the orientation of the scroll bar. The low-order word of the *wParam* tells where on the scroll bar the mouse was located when the user clicked the mouse button. Figure 10-3 shows the values for each part of the scroll bar. When the mouse button is released after an action on the scroll bar, Windows sends an **SB_ENDSCROLL** message. The exception to this is if the user was moving the scroll box. In this case, releasing the mouse generates the **SB_THUMBPOSITION** message.

Scroll Bar Function Descriptions

Table 10-1 summarizes the scroll bar support functions. The detailed function descriptions follow the table.

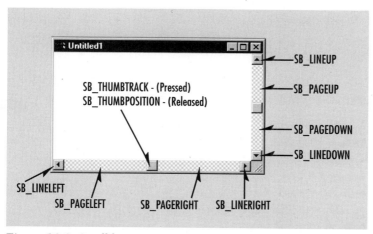

Figure 10-3 Scroll bar messages

Table 10-1 Scroll bar function summary

Function	Purpose
EnableScrollBar	Enables or disables a scroll bar control.
GetScrollInfo	Retrieves the parameters of a scroll bar.
GetScrollPos	Retrieves the current position of the scroll bar's thumb.
GetScrollRange	Retrieves the minimum and maximum value range of a scroll bar.
ScrollDC	Scrolls a region in a device context and computes the update areas.
ScrollWindowEx	Scrolls the content of a window's client area.
SetScrollInfo	Sets the parameters of a scroll bar.
SetScrollPos	Sets the position of the scroll bar thumb.
SetScrollRange	Sets the minimum and maximum values of a scroll bar.
ShowScrollBar	Displays the scroll bar, optionally attaching it to the window's border.

EnableScrollBar ■ WINDOWS 95 ■ WINDOWS NT

Description	EnableScrollBar enables or disables one or both scroll bar arrows. When a scroll bar is disabled, no action or messages occur if the user attempts to use the scroll bar.
Syntax	BOOL **EnableScrollBar**(HWND *hwnd,* UINT *uSBFlags,* UINT *uArrowFlags*)
Parameters	
hwnd	HWND: A handle to a window or a scroll bar control, depending on the value of the *uSBFlags* parameter.
uSBFlags	UINT: The scroll bar type to enable or disable. This parameter can be one of the values listed in Table 10-2.

Table 10-2 EnableScrollBar *uSBFlags* values

Value	Meaning
SB_BOTH	Enables or disables the horizontal and vertical scroll bars associated with a window. The *hwnd* parameter must be the handle of the window.
SB_CTL	The *hwnd* parameter is the handle of a scroll bar control.
SB_HORZ	Enables or disables the horizontal scroll bar associated with a window. The *hwnd* parameter must be the handle of the window.
SB_VERT	Enables or disables the vertical scroll bar associated with a window. The *hwnd* parameter must be the handle of the window.

uArrowFlags	UINT: Determines whether the scroll bar arrows are enabled or disabled and indicates which arrows are enabled or disabled. This parameter can be one of the values listed in Table 10-3.

Table 10-3 EnableScrollBar *uArrowFlags* values

Value	Meaning
ESB_DISABLE_BOTH	Disables both arrows on a scroll bar.
ESB_DISABLE_DOWN	Disables the down arrow on a vertical scroll bar.
ESB_DISABLE_LEFT	Disables the left arrow on a horizontal scroll bar.
ESB_DISABLE_LTUP	Disables the left arrow on a horizontal scroll bar or the up arrow on a vertical scroll bar.
ESB_DISABLE_RIGHT	Disables the right arrow on a horizontal scroll bar.
ESB_DISABLE_RTDN	Disables the right arrow on a horizontal scroll bar or the down arrow on a vertical scroll bar.
ESB_DISABLE_UP	Disables the up arrow on a vertical scroll bar.
ESB_ENABLE_BOTH	Enables both arrows on a scroll bar.

Returns	BOOL: TRUE if the arrows are enabled or disabled as specified. FALSE if the arrows are already in the requested state or an error occurs.
Include File	winuser.h
See Also	ShowScrollBar
Example	This example demonstrates how you use EnableScrollBar to disable a scroll bar until it is needed. Each time the user selects the Test! menu option, a counter is incremented to add a new line of text to the window. When the number of lines can't fit on the window's client area, the scroll bar is enabled. If the window is sized so that it can accommodate the number of lines added, the scroll bar is disabled again. Figure 10-4 shows the application after nine items are added.

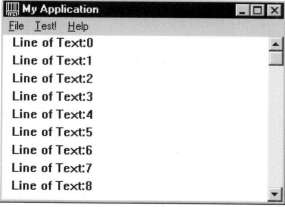

Figure 10-4 EnableScrollBar() Example

```
int APIENTRY WinMain( HINSTANCE hInstance, HINSTANCE hPrevInstance,
                      LPTSTR lpCmdLine, int nCmdShow)
{
        .
        .
        .

hWnd = CreateWindow( lpszAppName,
                        lpszTitle,
                        WS_OVERLAPPEDWINDOW | WS_VSCROLL,
                        CW_USEDEFAULT, 0,
                        CW_USEDEFAULT, 0,
                        NULL,
                        NULL,
                        hInstance,
                        NULL
                     );
        .
        .
        .

}

LRESULT CALLBACK WndProc( HWND hWnd, UINT uMsg, WPARAM wParam, LPARAM lParam )
{
static int  nDspLines;
static int  nNumItems = 0;
static int  nCurPos   = 0;
static char szBuf[10];

    switch( uMsg )
    {
        case WM_CREATE :
                ShowScrollBar( hWnd, SB_VERT, TRUE );
                break;

            // Every time the window is sized, recalculate the number of lines
            // the client area can display and set the scroll bar accordingly.
            //.............................................................
        case WM_SIZE :
                {
                    RECT rect;
                    GetClientRect( hWnd, &rect );

                    nDspLines = rect.bottom / 20;

                    if ( nDspLines < nNumItems )
                    {
                        EnableScrollBar( hWnd, SB_VERT, ESB_ENABLE_BOTH );
                        SetScrollRange( hWnd, SB_VERT, 0,
                                        nNumItems-nDspLines, FALSE );
                        SetScrollPos( hWnd, SB_VERT, nCurPos, FALSE );
                    }
                    else
                        EnableScrollBar( hWnd, SB_VERT, ESB_DISABLE_BOTH );
                }
                break;

        case WM_PAINT :
                {
```

```
            PAINTSTRUCT ps;
            int         i,j;
            int         nNumPaint;

            nNumPaint = min( nCurPos+nDspLines, nNumItems );

            BeginPaint( hWnd, &ps );

            for ( j=0,i=nCurPos; i<nNumPaint; i++,j++ )
            {
                itoa( i, szBuf, 10 );
                TextOut( ps.hdc, 10, j*20, "Line of Text:", 13 );
                TextOut( ps.hdc, 90, j*20, szBuf, strlen( szBuf ) );
            }

            EndPaint( hWnd, &ps );
        }
        break;

case WM_COMMAND :
        switch( LOWORD( wParam ) )
        {
        case IDM_TEST :
                if ( nDspLines == nNumItems )
                    EnableScrollBar( hWnd, SB_VERT, ESB_ENABLE_BOTH );

                nNumItems++;
                if ( nDspLines < nNumItems )
                    SetScrollRange( hWnd, SB_VERT, 0,
                                    nNumItems-nDspLines, TRUE );

                InvalidateRect( hWnd, NULL, FALSE );
                break;
    .
    .
    .
```

GetScrollInfo   ■ WINDOWS 95 ■ WINDOWS NT

Description	GetScrollInfo retrieves the parameters of a scroll bar, including the minimum and maximum scrolling positions, the page size, and the thumb position.
Syntax	BOOL **GetScrollInfo**(HWND *hwnd,* int *nBar,* LPSCROLLINFO *lpsi*)
Parameters	
hwnd	HWND: A handle to a window with a standard scroll bar or a scroll bar control, depending on the value of the *nBar* parameter.
nBar	int: The type of scroll bar for which to retrieve parameters. This parameter can be one of the values listed in Table 10-4.

Table 10-4 GetScrollInfo *nBar* values

Value	Meaning
SB_CTL	Retrieves the parameters for a scroll bar control. The *hwnd* parameter must be the handle of the scroll bar control.
SB_HORZ	Retrieves the parameters of a window's standard horizontal scroll bar.
SB_VERT	Retrieves the parameters of a window's standard vertical scroll bar.

lpsi	LPSCROLLINFO: A pointer to a SCROLLINFO structure that receives information about the scroll bar. Before calling GetScrollInfo, the application is required to initialize the *fMask* member item, and *cbsize*. See the definition of the SCROLLINFO structure below.
Returns	BOOL: If the function retrieved any values, the return value is TRUE; otherwise, it is FALSE.
Include File	winuser.h
See Also	SetScrollInfo, GetScrollPos, GetScrollRange

SCROLLINFO Definition

```
typedef struct tagSCROLLINFO
{
    UINT cbSize;
    UINT fMask;
    int  nMin;
    int  nMax;
    UINT nPage;
    int  nPos;
} SCROLLINFO, *LPSCROLLINFO;
```

Members

cbSize	UINT: The size, in bytes, of this structure.
fMask	UINT: The scroll bar parameters to retrieve. This can be a combination of the values in Table 10-5.

Table 10-5 SCROLLINFO *fMask* values

Value	Meaning
SIF_PAGE	Retrieve the *nPage* value of the scroll bar.
SIF_POS	Retrieve the *nPos* value of the scroll bar.
SIF_RANGE	Retrieve the *nMin* and *nMax* values of the scroll bar.

nMin	int: The minimum scrolling position.
nMax	int: The maximum scrolling position.
nPage	UINT: The page size. A scroll bar uses this value to determine the appropriate size of the proportional thumb.

nPos	`int`: The position of the thumb.
Example	See the example for the `ScrollWindowEx` function.

GetScrollPos ■ WINDOWS 95 ■ WINDOWS NT

Description	`GetScrollPos` retrieves the current thumb position in a given scroll bar. The current position is a relative value that depends on the current scrolling range. For example, if the scrolling range is 0 through 100 and the scroll box is in the middle of the bar, the current position is 50.
	This function exists for compatibility with Windows NT 3.5 and earlier versions of Windows. With Windows NT 4 and Windows 95, use the `GetScrollInfo` function.
Syntax	`int GetScrollPos( HWND hwnd, int nBar )`
Parameters	
hwnd	`HWND`: A handle to a scroll bar control or a window with a standard scroll bar, depending on the value of the *nBar* parameter.
nBar	`int`: The scroll bar to be examined. This parameter can be one of the values listed in Table 10-6.

Table 10-6 `GetScrollPos` *nBar* values

Value	Meaning
SB_CTL	Retrieves the thumb position of a scroll bar control. The *hwnd* parameter must be the handle of the scroll bar control.
SB_HORZ	Retrieves the thumb position of the window's standard horizontal scroll bar.
SB_VERT	Retrieves the thumb position of the window's standard vertical scroll bar.

Returns	`int`: If successful, the return value is the current position of the scroll box; otherwise, it is `0`.
Include File	`winuser.h`
See Also	`SetScrollPos, SetScrollRange, GetScrollRange, GetScrollInfo`
Related Messages	`WM_HSCROLL, WM_VSCROLL`
Example	See the example for the `ScrollDC` function.

GetScrollRange ■ WINDOWS 95 ■ WINDOWS NT

Description	`GetScrollRange` retrieves the current minimum and maximum thumb positions for a given scroll bar.

This function exists for compatibility with Windows NT 3.5 and earlier versions of Windows. With Windows NT 4 and Windows 95, use the GetScrollInfo function.

Syntax	BOOL **GetScrollRange**(HWND *hwnd,* int *nBar,* LPINT *lpMinPos,* LPINT *lpMaxPos*)
Parameters	
hwnd	HWND: A handle to a scroll bar control or a window with a standard scroll bar, depending on the value of the *nBar* parameter.
nBar	int: The scroll bar to be examined. This parameter can be one of the values listed in Table 10-7.

Table 10-7 GetScrollRange *nBar* values

Value	Meaning
SB_CTL	Retrieves the positions of a scroll bar control. The *hwnd* parameter must be the handle of the scroll bar control.
SB_HORZ	Retrieves the positions of the window's standard horizontal scroll bar.
SB_VERT	Retrieves the positions of the window's standard vertical scroll bar.

lpMinPos	LPINT: A pointer to an integer variable that receives the minimum position.
lpMaxPos	LPINT: A pointer to an integer variable that receives the maximum position.
Returns	BOOL: If successful, the return value is TRUE; otherwise, it is FALSE.
Include File	winuser.h
See Also	GetScrollPos, SetScrollRange, SetScrollPos, GetScrollInfo
Related Messages	WM_HSCROLL, WM_VSCROLL
Example	See the example for the ScrollDC function.

ScrollDC   ■ WINDOWS 95 ■ WINDOWS NT

Description	ScrollDC scrolls a rectangle on the given device context (DC) horizontally and vertically.
	Use ScrollDC to scroll a window's client area, or to scroll all or part of a bitmap in a memory device context.
Syntax	BOOL **ScrollDC**(HDC *hdc,* int *dx,* int *dy,* CONST RECT* *lprcScroll,* CONST RECT* *lprcClip,* HRGN *hrgnUpdate,* LPRECT *lprcUpdate*)
Parameters	
hdc	HDC: The device context to be scrolled.

dx	**int**: The amount, in device units (pixels), of horizontal scrolling. This parameter must be a negative value to scroll to the left.
dy	**int**: The amount, in device units (pixels), of vertical scrolling. This parameter must be a negative value to scroll up.
lprcScroll	**CONST RECT***: A pointer to a **RECT** structure that contains the scrolling rectangle.
lprcClip	**CONST RECT***: A pointer to a **RECT** structure that contains the coordinates of the clipping rectangle. Only the area within the clipping rectangle is scrolled.
hrgnUpdate	**HRGN**: The region uncovered by the scrolling process. **ScrollDC** defines this region; it is not necessarily a rectangle. This parameter may be set to **NULL**.
lprcUpdate	**LPRECT**: A pointer to a **RECT** structure that receives the coordinates of the rectangle bounding the scrolling update region. This is the largest rectangular area, in client coordinates, that requires repainting. This parameter may be set to **NULL**.

Returns	**BOOL**: If successful, the return value is **TRUE**; otherwise, it is **FALSE**.
Include File	**winuser.h**
See Also	**ScrollWindowEx, InvalidateRgn, GetDC**
Related Messages	**WM_HSCROLL, WM_VSCROLL, WM_PAINT**
Example	This example uses **ScrollDC** to scroll the center part of the window's client area, based on the window's horizontal scroll bar position. The clipping region is set smaller than the client area by 20 units, so that the outermost 20 units are not scrolled. After the user selects the Test! menu item (drawing the lines) and selects the right scroll bar arrow once, the window looks like Figure 10-5.

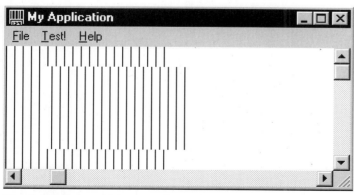

Figure 10-5 ScrollDC example

```
VOID Scroll( HWND hWnd, int* pnCurPos, WORD wScroll )
{
    int nMin, nMax;
    int nPos;

    // Retrieve the scroll information of the scroll bar.
    //.................................................
    GetScrollRange( hWnd, SB_HORZ, &nMin, &nMax );
    nPos = GetScrollPos( hWnd, SB_HORZ );

    switch( wScroll )
    {
        // Scroll to the right.
        //....................
        case SB_LINERIGHT :
                if ( *pnCurPos < nMax )
                  *pnCurPos += 1;
                break;

        // Scroll to the left.
        //...................
        case SB_LINELEFT :
                if ( *pnCurPos > 0 )
                  *pnCurPos -= 1;
                break;
    }

    // If the position has changed,
    // actually scroll the window.
    //............................
    if ( nPos != *pnCurPos )
    {
        RECT cltRect;
        HDC  hDC  = GetDC( hWnd );

        GetClientRect( hWnd, &cltRect );
        cltRect.left    += 20;
        cltRect.right   -= 20;
        cltRect.top     += 20;
        cltRect.bottom  -= 20;

        ScrollDC( hDC, (*pnCurPos-nPos)*20, 0, NULL, &cltRect,
                  NULL, NULL );

        SetScrollPos( hWnd, SB_HORZ, *pnCurPos, TRUE );
    }
}


LRESULT CALLBACK WndProc( HWND hWnd, UINT uMsg, WPARAM wParam, LPARAM lParam )
{
static int   nCurPos   = 0;

    switch( uMsg )
    {
        case WM_CREATE :
                ShowScrollBar( hWnd, SB_HORZ, FALSE );
                SetScrollRange( hWnd, SB_HORZ, 0, 10, FALSE );
```

```
                    SetScrollPos( hWnd, SB_HORZ, 0, TRUE );
                    break;

          case WM_HSCROLL :
                    Scroll( hWnd, &nCurPos, LOWORD( wParam ) );
                    break;

          case WM_COMMAND :
                    switch( LOWORD( wParam ) )
                    {
                       case IDM_TEST :
                               {
                                 HDC  hDC  = GetDC( hWnd );
                                 RECT rect;
                                 int  i;

                                 // Paint vertical lines in client area.
                                 //......................................
                                 GetClientRect( hWnd, &rect );

                                 for( i=0; i<20; i++ )
                                 {
                                    MoveToEx( hDC, i*8, 0, NULL );
                                    LineTo( hDC, i*8, rect.bottom );
                                 }

                                 ReleaseDC( hWnd, hDC );
                               }
                               break;
```

ScrollWindowEx   ■ WINDOWS 95   ■ WINDOWS NT

Description   ScrollWindowEx scrolls the contents of the given window's client area.
This is similar to the ScrollDC function, except ScrollWindowEx works
with a window handle and ScrollDC works with a device context (DC).

Syntax   int **ScrollWindowEx**(HWND *hwnd,* int *dx,* int *dy,* CONST RECT*
lprcScroll, CONST RECT* *lprcClip,* HRGN *hrgnUpdate,* LPRECT
lprcUpdate, UINT *uScroll*)

Parameters

hwnd   HWND: A handle to the window where the client area is to be scrolled.

dx   int: The amount, in device units, of horizontal scrolling. This parameter
must be a negative value to scroll to the left.

dy   int: The amount, in device units, of vertical scrolling. This parameter
must be a negative value to scroll up.

lprcScroll   CONST RECT*: A pointer to a RECT structure specifying the portion of the
client area to be scrolled. If this parameter is NULL, the entire client area is
scrolled.

lprcClip	CONST RECT*: A pointer to a RECT structure that contains the coordinates of the clipping rectangle. Only the area within the clipping rectangle is scrolled.
hrgnUpdate	HRGN: The region uncovered by the scrolling process. ScrollDC defines this region; it is not necessarily a rectangle. This parameter may be set to NULL.
lprcUpdate	LPRECT: A pointer to a RECT structure that receives the coordinates of the rectangle bounding the scrolling update region. This is the largest rectangular area, in client coordinates, that requires repainting. This parameter may be set to NULL.
uScroll	UINT: Flags that control scrolling. This parameter can be one or more of the values given in Table 10-8 combined with the binary OR (	) operator.

Table 10-8 ScrollWindowEx *uScroll* values

Value	Meaning
SW_ERASE	Erase the newly invalidated region when combined with the SW_INVALIDATE flag.
SW_INVALIDATE	Invalidates the region revealed after scrolling.
SW_SCROLLCHILDREN	Scrolls all child windows that intersect the rectangle pointed to by the *lprcScroll* parameter. The child windows are scrolled by the number of pixels specified by the *dx* and *dy* parameters. Windows sends a WM_MOVE message to all child windows that intersect the *lprcScroll* rectangle, even if they do not move.

Returns	int: SIMPLEREGION (rectangular invalidated region), COMPLEXREGION (non-rectangular invalidated region; overlapping rectangles), or NULLREGION (no invalidated region). Otherwise, the return value is ERROR.
Include File	winuser.h
See Also	ScrollDC, DeferWindowPos
Related Messages	WM_VSCROLL, WM_HSCROLL, WM_MOVE, WM_PAINT
Example	This example is the same as the example shown for the SetScrollInfo function, with the scrolling logic added. When the user selects the Test! menu item, a line is added to the list. The scroll bar will scroll one line at a time when the user selects either the up or down arrow of the scroll bar. Figure 10-6 shows a list of ten items scrolled to the last item.

```
VOID Scroll( HWND hWnd, int* pnCurPos, WORD wScroll )
{
    SCROLLINFO si;

    // Use GetScrollInfo() to get information
    // about the scroll bar.
    //..........................................
    si.cbSize = sizeof( SCROLLINFO );
    si.fMask  = SIF_PAGE | SIF_RANGE | SIF_POS;
    GetScrollInfo( hWnd, SB_VERT, &si );
```

```
    switch( wScroll )
    {
        case SB_LINEDOWN :
                if ( *pnCurPos <= (int)(si.nMax - si.nPage) )
                    *pnCurPos += 1;
                break;

        case SB_LINEUP :
                if ( *pnCurPos > 0 )
                    *pnCurPos -= 1;
                break;
    }

    if ( si.nPos != *pnCurPos )
    {
        RECT cltRect;

        GetClientRect( hWnd, &cltRect );

        ScrollWindowEx( hWnd, 0, (si.nPos-*pnCurPos)*20, NULL,
                        &cltRect, NULL, NULL, SW_INVALIDATE );

        si.fMask = SIF_POS;
        si.nPos  = *pnCurPos;
        SetScrollInfo( hWnd, SB_VERT, &si, TRUE );
    }
}

LRESULT CALLBACK WndProc( HWND hWnd, UINT uMsg, WPARAM wParam, LPARAM lParam )
{
static int  nDspLines;
static int  nNumItems = 0;
static int  nCurPos   = 0;
static char szBuf[10];

    switch( uMsg )
    {
        case WM_VSCROLL :
                Scroll( hWnd, &nCurPos, LOWORD( wParam ) );
                break;
                .
                .
                .
```

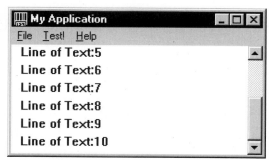

Figure 10-6 `ScrollWindowEx` example

SetScrollInfo
■ WINDOWS 95   ■ WINDOWS NT

Description	The **SetScrollInfo** function sets the parameters of a scroll bar, including the minimum and maximum scrolling positions, the page size, and the thumb position. The function also redraws the scroll bar, if requested.
Syntax	int **SetScrollInfo**(HWND *hwnd,* int *nBar,* LPSCROLLINFO *lpsi,* BOOL *bRedraw*)
Parameters	
hwnd	HWND: A handle to a window with a standard scroll bar or a scroll bar control, depending on the value of the *nBar* parameter.
nBar	int: The type of scroll bar for which to set parameters. This parameter can be one of the values listed in Table 10-9.

Table 10-9 SetScrollInfo *nBar* values

Value	Meaning
SB_CTL	Sets the parameters of a scroll bar control. The *hwnd* parameter must be the handle of the scroll bar control.
SB_HORZ	Sets the parameters of a window's standard horizontal scroll bar.
SB_VERT	Sets the parameters of a window's standard vertical scroll bar.

lpsi	LPSCROLLINFO: A pointer to a **SCROLLINFO** structure that contains the new scroll bar parameters. Before calling **SetScrollInfo**, the application is required to initialize the *fMask* member item, and *cbsize*. See the definition of the **SCROLLINFO** structure below.
bRedraw	BOOL: Determines whether the scroll bar is redrawn to reflect the changes to the scroll bar. If this parameter is TRUE, the scroll bar is redrawn; otherwise, it is not redrawn.
Returns	int: The current thumb position.
Include File	winuser.h
See Also	GetScrollInfo, SetScrollPos, SetScrollRange
SCROLLINFO Definition	

```
typedef struct tagSCROLLINFO
{
    UINT cbSize;
    UINT fMask;
    int  nMin;
    int  nMax;
    UINT nPage;
    int  nPos;
} SCROLLINFO, *LPSCROLLINFO;
```

Members

cbSize	UINT: The size, in bytes, of this structure.
fMask	UINT: The scroll bar parameters to retrieve. This can be a combination of the values given in Table 10-10.

Table 10-10 SCROLLINFO *fMask* values

Value	Meaning
SIF_DISABLENOSCROLL	Disables the scroll bar instead of removing it, if the scroll bar's new parameters make the scroll bar unnecessary.
SIF_PAGE	Sets the scroll page to the value specified in *nPage*.
SIF_POS	Sets the scroll position to the value specified in *nPos*.
SIF_RANGE	Sets the scroll range to the value specified in *nMin* and *nMax*.

nMin	int: The minimum scrolling position.
nMax	int: The maximum scrolling position.
nPage	UINT: The page size. A scroll bar uses this value to determine the appropriate size of the proportional thumb.
nPos	int: The position of the thumb.
Example	This example, shown in Figure 10-7, is the same as the example for EnableScrollBar, except that SetScrollInfo is used to set the scroll bar range and page size. Notice that the scroll box is now proportional.

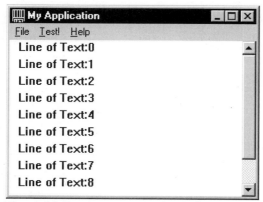

Figure 10-7 SetScrollInfo example

```
LRESULT CALLBACK WndProc( HWND hWnd, UINT uMsg, WPARAM wParam, LPARAM lParam )
{
static int   nDspLines;
static int   nNumItems = 0;
static int   nCurPos   = 0;
static char  szBuf[10];

    switch( uMsg )
    {
        case WM_CREATE :
                ShowScrollBar( hWnd, SB_VERT, TRUE );
                break;

            // Every time the window is sized, recalculate the number of lines
            // the client area can display and set the scroll bar accordingly.
            //..............................................................
        case WM_SIZE :
                {
                    RECT rect;
                    GetClientRect( hWnd, &rect );

                    nDspLines = rect.bottom / 20;

                    if ( nDspLines < nNumItems )
                    {
                        SCROLLINFO si;

                        si.cbSize = sizeof( SCROLLINFO );
                        si.fMask  = SIF_POS | SIF_RANGE | SIF_PAGE;
                        si.nMin   = 0;
                        si.nMax   = nNumItems-1;
                        si.nPage  = nDspLines;
                        si.nPos   = nCurPos;

                        EnableScrollBar( hWnd, SB_VERT, ESB_ENABLE_BOTH );
                        SetScrollInfo( hWnd, SB_VERT, &si, TRUE );
                    }
                    else
                        EnableScrollBar( hWnd, SB_VERT, ESB_DISABLE_BOTH );
                }
                break;

        case WM_PAINT :
                {
                    PAINTSTRUCT ps;
                    int         i,j;
                    int         nNumPaint;

                    nNumPaint = min( nCurPos+nDspLines, nNumItems );

                    BeginPaint( hWnd, &ps );

                    for ( j=0,i=nCurPos; i<nNumPaint; i++,j++ )
                    {
                        itoa( i, szBuf, 10 );
                        TextOut( ps.hdc, 10, j*20, "Line of Text:", 13 );
                        TextOut( ps.hdc, 90, j*20, szBuf, strlen( szBuf ) );
                    }
```

```
                EndPaint( hWnd, &ps );
        }
        break;

case WM_COMMAND :
        switch( LOWORD( wParam ) )
        {
            case IDM_TEST :
                if ( nDspLines == nNumItems )
                    EnableScrollBar( hWnd, SB_VERT, ESB_ENABLE_BOTH );

                nNumItems++;
                if ( nDspLines < nNumItems )
                {
                    SCROLLINFO si;

                    si.cbSize = sizeof( SCROLLINFO );
                    si.fMask  = SIF_RANGE | SIF_PAGE;
                    si.nMin   = 0;
                    si.nMax   = nNumItems-1;
                    si.nPage  = nDspLines;

                    SetScrollInfo( hWnd, SB_VERT, &si, TRUE );
                }

                InvalidateRect( hWnd, NULL, FALSE );
                break;
        .
        .
        .
```

SetScrollPos   ■ WINDOWS 95   ■ WINDOWS NT

Description   SetScrollPos sets the thumb position of the given scroll bar and, if requested, redraws the scroll bar to reflect the new position of the scroll box.

You generally use **SetScrollPos** when the scroll bar is first created or shown, to make the thumb position match the value represented. It can also be used for building keyboard interface functionality.

This function exists for compatibility with Windows NT 3.5 and earlier versions of Windows. With Windows NT 4 and Windows 95, use the **SetScrollInfo** function.

Syntax   int **SetScrollPos**(HWND *hwnd,* int *nBar,* int *nPos,* BOOL *bRedraw*)

Parameters

hwnd   HWND: A handle to a scroll bar control or a window with a standard scroll bar, depending on the value of the *nBar* parameter.

nBar   int: The scroll bar to be set. This parameter can be one of the values listed in Table 10-11.

Table 10-11 SetScrollPos *nBar* values

Value	Meaning
SB_CTL	Sets the thumb position of a scroll bar control. The *hwnd* parameter must be the handle of the scroll bar control.
SB_HORZ	Sets the thumb position of a window's standard horizontal scroll bar.
SB_VERT	Sets the thumb position of a window's standard vertical scroll bar.

nPos	int: The new thumb position. The position must be within the scrolling range set by the **SetScrollRange** function.
bRedraw	BOOL: Determines whether the scroll bar is redrawn to reflect the changes to the scroll bar. If this parameter is **TRUE**, the scroll bar is redrawn; otherwise, it is not redrawn.
Returns	int: If successful, the return value is the previous thumb position; otherwise, it is **0**.
Include File	winuser.h
See Also	SetScrollInfo, SetScrollRange, GetScrollPos, GetScrollRange
Related Messages	WM_HSCROLL, WM_VSCROLL
Example	See the example for the **EnableScrollBar** function.

SetScrollRange   ■ WINDOWS 95 ■ WINDOWS NT

Description	**SetScrollRange** sets the minimum and maximum position values for the given scroll bar. You can also use it to hide or show a standard scroll bar.
	Use **SetScrollRange** when the scroll bar is created to establish the upper and lower limits of the scroll bar range. Set both *nMinPos* and *nMaxPos* to **0** to hide the scroll bar.
	This function exists for compatibility with Windows NT 3.5 and earlier versions of Windows. With Windows NT 4 and Windows 95, use the **SetScrollInfo** function.
Syntax	BOOL **SetScrollRange**(HWND *hwnd,* int *nBar,* int *nMinPos,* int *nMaxPos,* BOOL *bRedraw*)
Parameters	
hwnd	HWND: A handle to a scroll bar control or a window with a standard scroll bar, depending on the value of the *nBar* parameter.
nBar	int: The scroll bar to be set. This parameter can be one of the values listed in Table 10-12.

Table 10-12 SetScrollRange *nBar* values

Value	Meaning
SB_CTL	Sets the range of a scroll bar control. The *hwnd* parameter must be the handle of the scroll bar control.
SB_HORZ	Sets the range of a window's standard horizontal scroll bar.
SB_VERT	Sets the range of a window's standard vertical scroll bar.

nMinPos	int: The minimum scrolling position.
nMaxPos	int: The maximum scrolling position.
bRedraw	BOOL: Determines whether the scroll bar is redrawn to reflect the changes to the scroll bar. If this parameter is TRUE, the scroll bar is redrawn; otherwise, it is not redrawn.
Returns	BOOL: If successful, the return value is TRUE; otherwise, it is FALSE.
Include File	winuser.h
See Also	SetScrollPos, GetScrollRange, GetScrollPos
Related Messages	WM_HSCROLL, WM_VSCROLL
Example	See the example for the EnableScrollBar function.

ShowScrollBar　　　　　　■ WINDOWS 95　■ WINDOWS NT

Description	ShowScrollBar shows or hides a scroll bar. Use this function during the initial creation of a scroll bar, or later to hide or redisplay the scroll bar. Do not call the function while processing a scroll bar message.
Syntax	BOOL **ShowScrollBar**(HWND *hwnd,* int *nBar,* BOOL *bShow*)
Parameters	
hwnd	HWND: A handle to a scroll bar control or a window with a standard scroll bar, depending on the value of the *nBar* parameter.
nBar	int: The scroll bar(s) to be shown or hidden. This parameter can be one of the values listed in Table 10-13.

Table 10-13 ShowScrollBar *nBar* values

Value	Meaning
SB_BOTH	Shows or hides a window's standard horizontal and vertical scroll bars.
SB_CTL	Shows or hides a scroll bar control. The *hwnd* parameter must be the handle of the scroll bar control.
SB_HORZ	Shows or hides a window's standard horizontal scroll bar.
SB_VERT	Shows or hides a window's standard vertical scroll bar.

bShow	BOOL: Determines whether the scroll bar is shown or hidden. If this parameter is TRUE, the scroll bar is shown; otherwise, it is hidden.
Returns	BOOL: If successful, the return value is TRUE; otherwise, it is FALSE.
Include File	winuser.h
See Also	ShowWindow
Example	See the example for the EnableScrollBar function.

11

MEMORY MANAGEMENT

Windows 3.x applications dealt with such issues as memory models and segments, which were limiting and made programming difficult. The Win32 environment, used by both Windows 95 and Windows NT, greatly simplifies memory management. Memory models and segments do not exist in Win32 applications. Without memory models, there is no distinguishing between near and far memory. Without segments, the program and its data reside in the same linear memory, which makes handling very large programs and data blocks much easier.

Memory Architecture

In the Win32 environment, each process has its own 32-bit virtual address space of up to 4 gigabytes (GB). The 2GB in low memory (0x00000000 to 0x7FFFFFFF) are available to the user, and the 2GB in high memory (0x80000000 to 0xFFFFFFFF) are reserved for the kernel. The addresses used by a process do not represent the actual physical location in memory. The kernel maintains a page map for each process used to translate virtual addresses into corresponding physical addresses. A process cannot write outside its own address space (to protect processes from each other).

GlobalAlloc and LocalAlloc functions are available in the Win32 API. The memory allocated by these functions won't reside in segments as it did in Windows 3.x. Instead, both types of memory are identical, allocated in the address space for the process, and are accessible using 32-bit pointers. The GlobalAlloc and LocalAlloc functions are provided for completeness and compatibility with 16-bit versions of Windows.

Two new types of memory, virtual memory and a local heap manager, are introduced in the Win32 environment. The virtual memory manager API is similar to the global memory manager API, except that memory can be reserved in large blocks and later actually allocated. The new heap manager allows the creation of multiple separate heaps, giving you an efficient way to allocate small portions of memory.

Global and Local Memory

As just mentioned, in the linear 32-bit environment of Win32, the local heap and global heap are not distinguished. As a result, the memory objects allocated by GlobalAlloc and LocalAlloc are the same. Because the global and local functions are the same and there is no longer a local heap, the LocalAlloc and other local heap functions are not covered in this book, although they are supported for compatibility with 16-bit Windows applications. The memory is allocated in private, committed pages with read-write access. Private memory cannot be accessed by other processes.

Using GlobalAlloc with the GMEM_DDESHARE flag is not shared globally as it is in Windows 3.x. The flag is provided for compatibility and can be used by some applications to enhance the performance of dynamic data exchange (DDE) operations. Applications that require shared memory for other purposes must use file-mapping objects. For information on file mapping, see Chapter 17, I/O with Files.

GlobalAlloc can allocate a block of memory of any size that can be represented by 32 bits and can fit within the available memory (including storage in the paging file). The memory objects allocated can be fixed or moveable. Moveable objects also can be marked as discardable. In Windows 3.x, moveable memory objects were important for memory management. By using virtual memory in Win32, the system can manage memory without affecting the virtual addresses of the memory. When the system moves a page of memory, the process's virtual page is simply mapped to the new location. Moveable memory is still used for allocating discardable memory, which is used infrequently and which an application can regenerate easily.

Virtual Memory

The virtual address space for each process is much larger than the total physical memory available to all processes. To increase the size of memory, the system uses the disk for additional storage. The total amount of memory available to all processes is the sum of physical memory and the free space on disk available to the paging file, a disk file used to increase memory. The virtual memory space is organized into pages, or units of memory. The size of a page depends on the host computer and is determined by using the GetSystemInfo function. On x86 computers the page size is 4 kilobytes (KB).

Many applications are able to satisfy their memory needs by using GlobalAlloc. However, virtual memory functions provide some functionality not available with GlobalAlloc. They can perform the following operations:

- Reserve a range of a process's virtual address space. Reserving address space does not physically allocate any storage, but it prevents the address space from being used by other allocation operations.

- Commit a range of reserved pages in a process's virtual address space so that it is accessible only to the allocating process.

- Specify read-write, read-only, or no access for a range of committed pages. Memory allocated with `GlobalAlloc` is always read-write.

- Free a range of reserved pages.

- Decommit a range of committed pages, releasing their physical storage.

- Lock one or more pages of committed memory into physical memory (RAM).

- Query information about a range of virtual memory pages.

- Change the access protection of a range of committed virtual memory pages.

Because virtual memory is allocated in pages, it is not efficient for use in storing small memory objects. The Win32 environment provides a better method of allocating small amounts of memory, the `HeapAlloc` function.

Heaps

The heap functions allow a process to create a private heap, a block of one or more pages in the address space of the process. The `HeapCreate` function creates a heap of a given size, and the `HeapAlloc` and `HeapFree` functions allocate and free memory in the heap. There is no difference between memory allocated from a private heap and that allocated using `GlobalAlloc`.

Heap objects can grow dynamically within the range given to `HeapCreate`. The maximum size of the heap determines the number of reserved pages of memory. The initial size determines the number of committed, read-write pages initially allocated for the heap. Additional pages are automatically committed from the reserved space if requests by `HeapAlloc` exceed the current size of committed pages. Once pages are committed, they are not decommitted until the process is terminated or the heap is destroyed with the `HeapDestroy` function. Because memory allocated in the heap with `HeapAlloc` is fixed and the system cannot compact the heap, an application should be written so that it minimizes fragmentation of the heap.

The memory of a private heap is accessible only to the process that created it. If a dynamic link library (DLL) creates a private heap, it is created in the address space of, and available only to, the process that called the DLL.

Memory Management Function Descriptions

Table 11-1 summarizes the memory management functions. The detailed function descriptions follow the table.

Table 11-1 Memory management function summary

Function	Purpose
GlobalAlloc	Allocates a block of memory in the global heap.
GlobalDiscard	Discards a memory block from the global heap.

continued on next page

continued from previous page

Function	Purpose
GlobalFlags	Determines if a memory block in the global heap is locked, discarded, or potentially discardable.
GlobalFree	Frees a block of memory allocated in the global heap.
GlobalHandle	Returns the handle of a global memory block, given its address.
GlobalLock	Locks an allocated memory block in the global heap.
GlobalMemoryStatus	Retrieves information about the available physical and virtual memory.
GlobalReAlloc	Changes the size and/or attributes of a global memory block.
GlobalSize	Determines the size of a memory block allocated in the global block.
GlobalUnlock	Unlocks a loaded memory block in the global heap.
HeapAlloc	Allocates a block of memory from a heap.
HeapCompact	Attempts to compact a given heap.
HeapCreate	Creates a private heap object for the calling process.
HeapDestroy	Destroys a heap object.
HeapFree	Frees a memory block allocated from a heap.
HeapReAlloc	Reallocates a block of memory from a heap.
HeapSize	Returns the size, in bytes, of a memory block allocated from a heap.
IsBadCodePtr	Verifies that the calling process has read access to a memory address.
IsBadReadPtr	Verifies that the calling process has read access to a range of memory.
IsBadStringPtr	Verifies that the calling process has read access to a range of memory pointed to by a string pointer.
IsBadWritePtr	Verifies that the calling process has write access to a range of memory.
MulDiv	Computes the result of $(a \times b) \div c$, where a, b, and c are short integers.
VirtualAlloc	Allocates a region of pages in the virtual address space.
VirtualAllocEx	Allocates a region of pages in the virtual address space of a specified process.
VirtualFree	Frees a region of pages within the virtual address space.
VirtualFreeEx	Frees a region of pages within the virtual address space of a specified process.
VirtualLock	Locks a region of the virtual address space into memory.
VirtualProtect	Changes the access protection on a region of committed pages in the virtual address space.
VirtualProtectEx	Changes the access protection on a region of committed pages in the virtual address space of a specified process.
VirtualQuery	Provides information about a range of pages in the virtual address space.
VirtualQueryEx	Provides information about a range of pages in the virtual address space of a specified process.
VirtualUnlock	Unlocks a range of pages in the virtual address space.

GlobalAlloc ■ WINDOWS 95 ■ WINDOWS NT

Description	GlobalAlloc allocates a block of memory from the heap. In the linear memory of the Win32 environment, there is no difference between the local heap and the global heap.
Syntax	HGLOBAL **GlobalAlloc**(UINT *uFlags,* DWORD *dwBytes*)

Parameters

uFlags UINT: Determines how to allocate the memory. If **0** is specified, the default is **GMEM_FIXED**. Except for the incompatible combinations that are specifically noted, you can use any combination of the flags listed in Table 11-2.

Table 11-2 GlobalAlloc flags

Value	Description
GHND	Combination of the GMEM_MOVEABLE and GMEM_ZEROINIT flags.
GMEM_DDESHARE	Allocates memory to be used by the dynamic data exchange (DDE) functions for a DDE conversation. In Windows version 3.x, this memory is shared globally. In Win32, the memory is not shared globally. However, this flag is available for compatibility purposes. It may be used by some applications to enhance the performance of DDE operations and should, therefore, be specified if the memory is to be used for DDE. Only processes that use DDE or the clipboard for interprocess communications should specify this flag.
GMEM_DISCARDABLE	Allocates discardable memory. Cannot be combined with the GMEM_FIXED flag. Some Win32-based applications may ignore this flag.
GMEM_FIXED	Allocates fixed memory. Cannot be combined with the GMEM_MOVEABLE or GMEM_DISCARDABLE flag. The return value is a pointer to the memory block. To access the memory, cast the return value to a pointer.
GMEM_MOVEABLE	Allocates movable memory. Cannot be combined with the GMEM_FIXED flag. The return value is the handle of the memory object. The handle is a 32-bit value that is private to the calling process. To translate the handle into a pointer, use the GlobalLock function.
GMEM_NOCOMPACT	Does not compact or discard memory to satisfy the allocation request.
GMEM_NODISCARD	Does not discard memory to satisfy the allocation request.
GMEM_SHARE	Same as the GMEM_DDESHARE flag.
GMEM_ZEROINIT	Initializes memory contents to 0.
GPTR	Combination of the GMEM_FIXED and GMEM_ZEROINIT flags.

dwBytes DWORD: The number of bytes to allocate.

Returns HGLOBAL: If successful, the handle to the allocated memory object; otherwise, NULL.

Include File winbase.h

See Also GlobalLock, GlobalReAlloc, GlobalFree

Example This example shows the allocation of memory to store a string using the **GlobalAlloc** and **GlobalReAlloc** functions. When the application first starts (**WM_CREATE** received), a 27-character buffer is allocated (26 characters and a null terminator). **GlobalAlloc** actually allocates 28 bytes in Windows 95. A string is stored in the memory block. This string, along with the allocated size and memory status, is displayed on the window's client area. When the user selects the Test! menu item, the memory block is reallocated to make room for another 26 characters. The additional characters are written to the buffer and are displayed. Figure 11-1 shows the window's appearance after the Test! menu item was selected. Note that the handle of the memory is not unlocked and only the pointer to the memory is maintained. `GlobalHandle` is used when the memory handle is needed. This practice has no adverse effects, because Windows NT and Windows 95 run in protected mode and locked memory can move if necessary without changing the memory pointer.

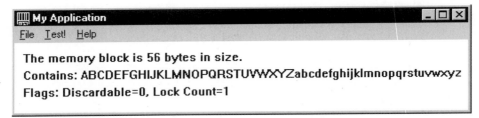

Figure 11-1 GlobalAlloc example

```
LRESULT CALLBACK WndProc( HWND hWnd, UINT uMsg, WPARAM wParam, LPARAM lParam )
{
static PAINTSTRUCT ps;
static char        szBuf[128];
static LPTSTR      pMem = NULL;

    switch( uMsg )
    {
        case WM_CREATE :
                {
                    // Allocate initial block of memory and
                    // initialize it with the alphabet in uppercase.
                    //.............................................
                    HGLOBAL hMem = GlobalAlloc( GHND, 27 );
                    LPTSTR  pCur;

                    if ( hMem && (pMem = (LPTSTR)GlobalLock( hMem )) != NULL )
                    {
                        int i;

                        pCur = pMem;
                        for( i=0; i<26; i++ )
                            *pCur++ = 'A'+i;

                        *pCur = 0;
                    }
                    else
                    {
                        MessageBox( hWnd, "Could not allocate memory",
                                    "Memory Error",
                                    MB_OK | MB_ICONSTOP );

                        DestroyWindow( hWnd );
                    }
```

```
        }
        break;

case WM_PAINT :
        // Paint the status of the memory.
        //...............................
        BeginPaint( hWnd, &ps );
        if( pMem )
        {
            // Retrieve the handle for
            // the memory and memory status.
            //..............................
            HGLOBAL hMem  = GlobalHandle( pMem );
            DWORD   dwSize = GlobalSize( hMem );
            UINT    uFlags = GlobalFlags( hMem );

            TextOut( ps.hdc, 10, 10, szBuf, wsprintf( szBuf,
                    "The memory block is %ld bytes in size.", dwSize ) );
            TextOut( ps.hdc, 10, 30, szBuf, wsprintf( szBuf,
                    "Contains: %s", pMem ) );
            TextOut( ps.hdc, 10, 50, szBuf, wsprintf( szBuf,
                    "Flags: Discardable=%d, Lock Count=%d",
                    uFlags & GMEM_DISCARDABLE,
                    uFlags & GMEM_LOCKCOUNT ) );
        }
        EndPaint( hWnd, &ps );
        break;

case WM_COMMAND :
        switch( LOWORD( wParam ) )
        {
        case IDM_TEST :
                // Reallocate memory and add the
                // lowercase alphabet to the memory.
                //..................................
                if ( pMem )
                {
                    HGLOBAL hMem = GlobalHandle( pMem );

                    GlobalUnlock( hMem );
                    pMem = NULL;

                    hMem = GlobalReAlloc( hMem, (26*2)+1,
                                          GMEM_MOVEABLE );
                    if ( hMem )
                    {
                        LPTSTR pCur;
                        int    i;

                        pMem = (LPTSTR)GlobalLock( hMem );

                        // Skip the old values.
                        //.....................
                        pCur = pMem+26;

                        // Set the new values.
                        //....................
                        for( i=0; i<26; i++ )
                            *pCur++ = 'a'+i;
```

continued on next page

continued from previous page

```
                                *pCur = 0;
                        }
                        else
                            MessageBox( hWnd, "Could not allocate memory",
                                        "Memory Error",
                                        MB_OK | MB_ICONSTOP );

                        InvalidateRect( hWnd, NULL, TRUE );
                    }
                    break;

                case IDM_EXIT :
                        DestroyWindow( hWnd );
                        break;
            }
            break;

        case WM_DESTROY :
            if ( pMem )
            {
                HGLOBAL hMem = GlobalHandle( pMem );

                GlobalUnlock( hMem );
                GlobalFree( hMem );
            }

            PostQuitMessage(0);
            break;

        default :
            return( DefWindowProc( hWnd, uMsg, wParam, lParam ) );
    }

    return( 0L );
}
```

GlobalDiscard   ■ WINDOWS 95   ■ WINDOWS NT

Description   GlobalDiscard discards a global memory block that was allocated with
the GMEM_DISCARDABLE and GMEM_MOVEABLE flags set. The memory block
must be unlocked, meaning the lock count of the memory object must be
zero. The *hMem* handle remains usable after the block is discarded,
although it does not point to active memory. *hMem* can be reused by using
GlobalReAlloc to allocate another block of memory.

Use GlobalDiscard to discard memory and make room for other blocks.
Note that GlobalFree both removes the memory block and invalidates the
memory handle. GlobalDiscard only discards the memory block, but the
hMem handle remains valid.

Syntax   HGLOBAL **GlobalDiscard**(HGLOBAL *hMem*)

Parameters

hMem
  HGLOBAL: The handle of the global memory object returned by either the GlobalAlloc or GlobalReAlloc function.

Returns
  HGLOBAL: If successful, the handle of the memory object; otherwise, NULL.

Include File
  winbase.h

See Also
  GlobalFree, GlobalAlloc, GlobalReAlloc, GlobalUnlock

Example
  This example uses GlobalDiscard to release allocated memory but retain a valid handle. When the user selects the Test! menu item, *hMem* is checked to see if GlobalAlloc has already been called. If it has, GlobalReAlloc is used to reallocate memory. The memory is used and then discarded.

```c
LRESULT CALLBACK WndProc( HWND hWnd, UINT uMsg, WPARAM wParam, LPARAM lParam )
{
static HGLOBAL hMem = NULL;

   switch( uMsg )
   {
      case WM_COMMAND :
            switch( LOWORD( wParam ) )
            {
               case IDM_TEST :
                  if ( hMem )
                     hMem = GlobalReAlloc( hMem, 50, GMEM_MOVEABLE );
                  else
                     hMem = GlobalAlloc( 50, GHND );

                  // Use the memory.
                  //...............
                  if ( hMem )
                  {
                     int    i;
                     LPTSTR pMem = (LPTSTR)GlobalLock( hMem );

                     for( i=0; i<26; i++ )
                        *(pMem+i) = 'a'+i;

                     *(pMem+i) = 0;

                     MessageBox( hWnd, pMem, "Memory Contents",
                              MB_OK | MB_ICONINFORMATION );

                     // Get rid of memory allocated
                     // but keep handle valid.
                     //.......................
                     GlobalDiscard( hMem );
                  }
                  else
                     MessageBox( hWnd, "Could not allocate memory",
                              "Memory Error",
                              MB_OK | MB_ICONSTOP );

                  break;
```

continued on next page

continued from previous page

```
                    case IDM_EXIT :
                            DestroyWindow( hWnd );
                            break;
                }
                break;

        case WM_DESTROY :
                PostQuitMessage(0);
                break;

        default :
                return( DefWindowProc( hWnd, uMsg, wParam, lParam ) );
    }

    return( 0L );
}
```

GlobalFlags   ■ WINDOWS 95   ■ WINDOWS NT

Description	GlobalFlags returns the status and lock count of a memory block allocated in the global heap. In the linear memory of the Win32 environment, there is no difference between the local heap and the global heap.
	Use GlobalFlags to check the validity of a memory handle or to check if a memory block has been locked more than once.
Syntax	UINT GlobalFlags(HGLOBAL *hMem*)
Parameters	
hMem	HGLOBAL: The handle of the global memory object returned by either the GlobalAlloc or GlobalReAlloc function.
Returns	UINT: A 32-bit value specifying the allocation flags and the lock count for the memory object; otherwise, the GMEM_INVALID_HANDLE flag is returned if *hMem* is not a valid global memory handle. The low-order byte of the low-order word contains the lock count. Use the GMEM_LOCKCOUNT flag with the bitwise AND (&) operator to retrieve the lock count. The high-order byte of the low-order word indicates the allocation flags of the memory object. This can be 0 or any combination of the flags listed in Table 11-3.

Table 11-3 GlobalFlags return flags

Flag	Description
GMEM_DDESHARE	The memory was allocated for use with the dynamic data exchange (DDE) functions for a DDE conversation.
GMEM_DISCARDABLE	The memory can be discarded.
GMEM_DISCARDED	The memory has been discarded.

Include File	winbase.h
See Also	GlobalAlloc, GlobalSize, GlobalLock
Example	See the example for the GlobalAlloc function.

GlobalFree
■ WINDOWS 95   ■ WINDOWS NT

Description	GlobalFree frees a global memory object and invalidates its handle. Freeing a memory block returns the memory to the system for reuse. All memory blocks allocated within an application should be freed before the application exits to return the memory to Windows. There should be a call to GlobalFree for every call to GlobalAlloc in a program.
Syntax	HGLOBAL **GlobalFree**(HGLOBAL *hMem*)
Parameters	
hMem	HGLOBAL: The handle of the global memory object returned by either the GlobalAlloc or GlobalReAlloc function.
Returns	HGLOBAL: If successful, the return value is NULL; otherwise, it is equal to the handle of the global memory object.
Include File	winbase.h
See Also	GlobalAlloc, GlobalDiscard, GlobalReAlloc
Example	See the example for the GlobalAlloc function.

GlobalHandle
■ WINDOWS 95   ■ WINDOWS NT

Description	GlobalHandle retrieves the handle associated with a given pointer to a global memory block. When GlobalAlloc allocates memory with the GMEM_MOVEABLE flag set, it returns a handle to the memory object. GlobalLock converts this handle into a pointer to the memory block, and GlobalHandle converts the pointer back into a handle.
	With locked memory blocks, the address does not change, so storing only the block's address and not the handle is more efficient. Use GlobalHandle to retrieve the handle if necessary to free the block.
Syntax	HGLOBAL **GlobalHandle**(LPCVOID *lpvMem*)
Parameters	
lpvMem	LPCVOID: A pointer to the first byte of the global memory block. This pointer is returned by the GlobalLock function.
Returns	HGLOBAL: The handle of the global memory block. NULL is returned if the function is not successful.
Include File	winbase.h
See Also	GlobalFlags, GlobalLock, GlobalAlloc
Example	See the example for the GlobalAlloc function.

GlobalLock   ■ WINDOWS 95   ■ WINDOWS NT

Description   GlobalLock locks a global memory object and returns a pointer to the first byte of the object's memory block. The locked memory block cannot be moved or discarded. This function increments the lock count associated with the memory object for memory objects allocated with the GMEM_MOVEABLE flag.

Use GlobalLock to obtain a pointer to a global memory object allocated with the GlobalAlloc or GlobalReAlloc function with the GMEM_MOVEABLE flag. The pointer will remain valid until the block is unlocked with GlobalUnlock.

Syntax   LPVOID **GlobalLock**(HGLOBAL *hglbMem*)

Parameters

hglbMem   HGLOBAL: The handle of the global memory object returned by either the GlobalAlloc or GlobalReAlloc function.

Returns   LPVOID: If successful, a pointer to the first byte of the memory block; otherwise, NULL.

Include File   winbase.h

See Also   GlobalUnlock, GlobalAlloc

Example   See the example for the GlobalAlloc function.

GlobalMemoryStatus   ■ WINDOWS 95   ■ WINDOWS NT

Description   GlobalMemoryStatus retrieves information about current available memory. The function returns information about both physical and virtual memory.

Use GlobalMemoryStatus to determine how much memory an application can allocate without causing a major impact on applications. The information changes from one call to another.

Syntax   VOID **GlobalMemoryStatus**(LPMEMORYSTATUS *lpmstMemStat*)

Parameters

lpmstMemStat   LPMEMORYSTATUS: A pointer to a MEMORYSTATUS structure in which information about current memory availability is returned. The *dwLength* member item should be set before calling this function. See the definition of the MEMORYSTATUS structure below.

Include File   winbase.h

See Also   GlobalAlloc, VirtualAlloc

MEMORYSTATUS Definition

```
typedef struct _MEMORYSTATUS
{
    DWORD dwLength;        // sizeof(MEMORYSTATUS)
    DWORD dwMemoryLoad;    // percent of memory in use
    DWORD dwTotalPhys;     // bytes of physical memory
    DWORD dwAvailPhys;     // free physical memory bytes
    DWORD dwTotalPageFile; // bytes of paging file
    DWORD dwAvailPageFile; // free bytes of paging file
    DWORD dwTotalVirtual;  // user bytes of address space
    DWORD dwAvailVirtual;  // free user bytes
} MEMORYSTATUS, *LPMEMORYSTATUS;
```

Members

dwLength   DWORD: The size of the structure. The calling process should set this member prior to calling `GlobalMemoryStatus`.

dwMemoryLoad   DWORD: The current memory utilization. This is a number between 0 and 100, in which **0** represents no memory load and **100** represents full memory load.

dwTotalPhys   DWORD: The total number of bytes of physical memory.

dwAvailPhys   DWORD: The number of bytes of physical memory available.

dwTotalPageFile   DWORD: The total number of bytes that can be stored in the paging file. This does not represent the actual size of the paging file on the disk.

dwAvailPageFile   DWORD: The number of bytes available in the paging file.

dwTotalVirtual   DWORD: The total number of bytes of virtual memory available to the calling process.

dwAvailVirtual   DWORD: The number of unreserved and uncommitted bytes of virtual memory.

Example   In this example, shown in Figure 11-2, the memory status is retrieved and displayed when the user selects the Test! menu option.

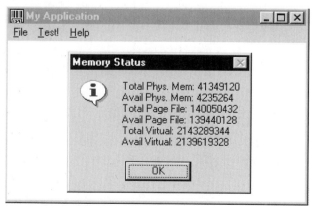

Figure 11-2 `GlobalMemoryStatus` example

```
LRESULT CALLBACK WndProc( HWND hWnd, UINT uMsg, WPARAM wParam, LPARAM lParam )
{
    switch( uMsg )
    {
        case WM_COMMAND :
                switch( LOWORD( wParam ) )
                {
                    case IDM_TEST :
                        {
                            MEMORYSTATUS ms;
                            char         szMsg[256];

                            ms.dwLength = sizeof( MEMORYSTATUS );
                            GlobalMemoryStatus( &ms );

                            wsprintf( szMsg, "Total Phys. Mem: %ld\n"\
                                             "Avail Phys. Mem: %ld\n"\
                                             "Total Page File: %ld\n"\
                                             "Avail Page File: %ld\n"\
                                             "Total Virtual: %ld\n"\
                                             "Avail Virtual: %ld",
                                      ms.dwTotalPhys,
                                      ms.dwAvailPhys,
                                      ms.dwTotalPageFile,
                                      ms.dwAvailPageFile,
                                      ms.dwTotalVirtual,
                                      ms.dwAvailVirtual );

                            MessageBox( hWnd, szMsg, "Memory Status",
                                     MB_OK | MB_ICONINFORMATION );
                        }
                        break;
```

.
.
.

GlobalReAlloc   ■ WINDOWS 95   ■ WINDOWS NT

Description	GlobalReAlloc changes the size or attributes of a global memory object. The size of the object can increase or decrease to fit the changing needs of an application.
Syntax	HGLOBAL **GlobalReAlloc**(HGLOBAL *hMem,* DWORD *dwBytes,* UINT *uFlags*)
Parameters	
hMem	HGLOBAL: The handle of the global memory object to be reallocated returned by either the GlobalAlloc or GlobalReAlloc function.
dwBytes	DWORD: The new size, in bytes, of the memory block. If this parameter is 0 and the *uFlags* parameter specifies the GMEM_MOVEABLE flag, the handle of a memory object that is marked as discarded is returned. If *uFlags* specifies the GMEM_MODIFY flag, this parameter is ignored.

uFlags   UINT: Determines how to reallocate the global memory object. The
                  GMEM_MODIFY flag can be combined with the flags listed in Table 11-4.

Table 11-4 GlobalReAlloc GMEM_MODIFY *uFlags* values

Flag	Description
GMEM_DDESHARE	Takes ownership of the memory object.
GMEM_DISCARDABLE	Allocates discardable memory. This flag is ignored, unless the object was previously allocated as moveable or the GMEM_MOVEABLE flag is also specified.
GMEM_MOVEABLE	Changes a fixed memory object to moveable memory.

If this parameter does not specify GMEM_MODIFY, it can be any combination
of the flags listed in Table 11-5.

Table 11-5 GlobalReAlloc *uFlags* values

Flag	Description
GMEM_MOVEABLE	Allocates moveable memory. If *dwBytes* is 0, this discards a previously moveable and discardable memory block. If the lock count of the object is not zero or if the block is not moveable and discardable, the function fails. If *dwBytes* is nonzero, the system is allowed to move the reallocated block to a new location without changing the moveable or fixed attribute of the memory object. If the memory is fixed, the handle returned may be different from the handle specified by the *hMem* parameter. If memory is moveable, the block can be moved without invalidating the handle, even if the memory is currently locked by a previous call to the GlobalLock function. To get the new address of the memory block, use GlobalLock.
GMEM_NOCOMPACT	Does not compact or discard memory to make room for the allocation.
GMEM_ZEROINIT	Initializes new memory to zero if the memory object is growing.

Returns   HGLOBAL: If successful, the handle of the reallocated memory object; other-
                 wise, NULL.

Include File   winbase.h

See Also   GlobalAlloc, GlobalDiscard, GlobalFree

Example   See the example for the GlobalAlloc function.

GlobalSize   ■ WINDOWS 95   ■ WINDOWS NT

Description   GlobalSize determines the actual number of bytes allocated for a global
                 memory object. The size of the memory block may be larger than the
                 requested size when the memory object was allocated.

Syntax   DWORD **GlobalSize**(HGLOBAL *hMem*)

Parameters

hMem   HGLOBAL: The handle of the global memory object returned by either the `GlobalAlloc`, `GlobalReAlloc`, or `GlobalHandle` function.

Returns   DWORD: The size, in bytes, of the global memory block. If *hMem* is not a valid handle or if the object has been discarded, the return value is 0.

Include File   `winbase.h`

See Also   `GlobalFlags`, `GlobalAlloc`, `GlobalHandle`, `GlobalReAlloc`

Example   See the example for the `GlobalAlloc` function.

GlobalUnlock   ■ WINDOWS 95   ■ WINDOWS NT

Description   `GlobalUnlock` unlocks a global memory object. Every time an application calls the `GlobalLock` function for a memory object, the lock count is incremented. `GlobalUnlock` decrements the lock count of the memory object that was allocated with the **GMEM_MOVEABLE** flag. `GlobalUnlock` has no effect on memory objects allocated with the **GMEM_FIXED** flag. `GlobalUnlock` has to be called the same number of times as `GlobalLock` before the memory can be moved or discarded by Windows.

Syntax   BOOL **GlobalUnlock**(HGLOBAL *hMem*)

Parameters

hMem   HGLOBAL: The handle of the global memory object returned by either the `GlobalAlloc` or `GlobalReAlloc` function.

Returns   BOOL: If the memory object is still locked after decrementing the lock count, the return value is **TRUE**; otherwise, it is **FALSE**.

Include File   `winbase.h`

See Also   `GlobalLock`, `GlobalAlloc`, `GlobalReAlloc`, `GlobalFree`

Example   See the example for the `GlobalAlloc` function.

HeapAlloc   ■ WINDOWS 95   ■ WINDOWS NT

Description   `HeapAlloc` allocates a block of memory from a heap. The allocated memory is not moveable.

Syntax   LPVOID **HeapAlloc**(HANDLE *hHeap,* DWORD *dwFlags,* DWORD *dwBytes*)

Parameters

hHeap   HANDLE: The handle of the heap within which the memory shall be allocated. This is the handle returned by the `HeapCreate` or `GetProcessHeap` function.

dwFlags   DWORD: Determines how the memory is allocated. These flags will override the corresponding flag specified when the heap was created with `HeapCreate`. One or more of the flags listed in Table 11-6 can be specified.

Table 11-6 HeapAlloc *dwFlags* values

Flag	Description
HEAP_GENERATE_EXCEPTIONS	Raises an exception to indicate errors instead of returning NULL.
HEAP_NO_SERIALIZE	Mutual exclusion will not be used while this function is accessing the heap. If specified, only one thread should access the heap at a time. If multiple threads are sharing the same heap, this flag should not be set.
HEAP_ZERO_MEMORY	Initializes the allocated memory to 0.

dwBytes	DWORD: The number of bytes to be allocated. If the heap specified by the *hHeap* parameter has a fixed maximum size, *dwBytes* must be less than 0x0007FFF8.
Returns	LPVOID: If successful, the return value is a pointer to the allocated memory block. NULL is returned if the allocation attempt failed because of a lack of available memory or heap corruption. If the function fails and HEAP_GENERATE_EXCEPTIONS has been specified, the exception values listed in Table 11-7 can be generated.

Table 11-7 HeapAlloc exception errors

Value	Meaning
STATUS_ACCESS_VIOLATION	An access violation occurred during the allocation attempt.
STATUS_NO_MEMORY	The allocation attempt failed due to lack of available memory.

Include File	winbase.h
See Also	GetProcessHeap, HeapCreate, HeapDestroy, HeapFree, HeapReAlloc, HeapSize, HeapCompact
Example	In this example, a heap is created using the **HeapCreate** function when the application starts. Memory is then allocated and used as a dynamic array of strings. When the user selects the Allocate! menu item, memory is allocated from the heap to store a new string and the pointer to the memory added to the array. If there is no room left in the array, **HeapReAlloc** is used to expand the array. When the user selects the Free! menu item, the last string allocated is freed. When enough strings are freed to leave a significant amount of unused space, the array is reallocated to shrink the array. Each time the array is reallocated, the heap is compacted with the **HeapCompact** function.

```
#define BLOCKSIZE 32

LRESULT CALLBACK WndProc( HWND hWnd, UINT uMsg, WPARAM wParam, LPARAM lParam )
{
static LPTSTR* lpStrList;
static int     nBlocks;
```

continued on next page

continued from previous page

```
static int     nStrings;
static HANDLE  hHeap      = NULL;

    switch( uMsg )
    {
        case WM_CREATE  :
                hHeap     = HeapCreate( 0, 1024, 0 );
                lpStrList = HeapAlloc( hHeap, HEAP_ZERO_MEMORY,
                                     sizeof( LPTSTR )*BLOCKSIZE );

                nBlocks  = 1;
                nStrings = 0;
                break;

        case WM_COMMAND :
                switch( LOWORD( wParam ) )
                {
                    case IDM_ALLOCATE :
                        {
                            // If there is no room in the array then allocate
                            // more space to store the new item in.
                            //.....................................
                            if ( nStrings == nBlocks*BLOCKSIZE )
                            {
                                nBlocks++;
                                lpStrList = HeapReAlloc( hHeap, HEAP_ZERO_MEMORY,
                                                       lpStrList,
                                                       sizeof( LPTSTR )
                                                       *BLOCKSIZE*nBlocks );

                                // Compact out any dead spots in memory.
                                //.....................................
                                HeapCompact( hHeap, 0 );
                            }

                            *(lpStrList+nStrings) = HeapAlloc( hHeap,
                                                   HEAP_ZERO_MEMORY, 12 );
                            strcpy( *(lpStrList+nStrings), "Test String" );
                            nStrings++;

                        }
                        break;

                    case IDM_FREE :
                        if ( nStrings > 0 )
                        {
                            nStrings--;
                            HeapFree( hHeap, 0, *(lpStrList+nStrings) );

                            if ( nStrings < (nBlocks-1)*BLOCKSIZE )
                            {
                                nBlocks--;
                                lpStrList = HeapReAlloc( hHeap, 0,
                                                       lpStrList,
                                                       sizeof( LPTSTR )
                                                       *BLOCKSIZE*nBlocks );
                            }
                        }
                        break;
```

```
            case IDM_EXIT :
                    DestroyWindow( hWnd );
                    break;
            }
            break;

    case WM_DESTROY :
            HeapDestroy( hHeap );
            PostQuitMessage(0);
            break;

    default :
            return( DefWindowProc( hWnd, uMsg, wParam, lParam ) );
    }

    return( 0L );
}
```

HeapCompact   ■ WINDOWS 95   ■ WINDOWS NT

Description	**HeapCompact** attempts to compact the given heap. It compacts the heap by coalescing adjacent free blocks of memory and decommitting large free blocks of memory. There is no guarantee that an application can successfully allocate a memory block of the size returned by **HeapCompact**. Other threads or the commit threshold might prevent such an allocation.
Syntax	UINT **HeapCompact**(HANDLE *hHeap*, DWORD *dwFlags*)
Parameters	
hHeap	HANDLE: The handle to the heap that the function will attempt to compact.
dwFlags	DWORD: Set to **HEAP_NO_SERIALIZE** to not serialize heap access while the function accesses the heap. If set to **0**, heap access is serialized while the heap is being compacted. This is the safe and simple default condition.
Returns	UINT: If successful, the size, in bytes, of the largest committed free block in the heap is returned; otherwise, **0** is returned. Use the **GetLastError** function to retrieve extended error information.
Include File	winbase.h
See Also	HeapCreate
Example	See the example for the **HeapAlloc** function.

HeapCreate   ■ WINDOWS 95   ■ WINDOWS NT

Description	**HeapCreate** creates a heap object that is private to the calling process. The function reserves a contiguous block of memory in the virtual address space of the process and allocates physical storage for the initial portion of this block.

Use **HeapCreate** to create a private heap for a thread where it can efficiently allocate memory instead of using the global heap.

Syntax

HANDLE **HeapCreate**(DWORD *dwOptions,* DWORD *dwInitialSize,* DWORD *dwMaximumSize*)

Parameters

dwOptions

DWORD: Optional attributes for the new heap. These options will affect subsequent access to the new heap through calls to the heap functions (**HeapAlloc**, **HeapFree**, **HeapReAlloc**, and **HeapSize**). One or more of the flags listed in Table 11-8 can be specified.

Table 11-8 HeapCreate *dwOptions* values

Flag	Description
HEAP_GENERATE_EXCEPTIONS	Raises an exception on errors instead of returning NULL.
HEAP_NO_SERIALIZE	Mutual exclusion will not be used when the heap functions allocate and free memory from this heap. When not specified, access to the heap is serialized. Serialization of heap access allows two or more threads to simultaneously allocate and free memory from the same heap.

dwInitialSize

DWORD: The initial size, in bytes, of the heap. This determines the initial amount of physical storage that is allocated for the heap, rounded to the next page boundary. Use **GetSystemInfo** to determine the size of a page on the host computer.

dwMaximumSize

DWORD: The maximum size, in bytes, of the heap. If set to **0**, the maximum size is limited only by available memory. If *dwMaximumSize* is nonzero, the size is fixed at the number of bytes given by *dwMaximumSize*, rounded up to the next page boundary. A block of this size is reserved in the process's virtual address space.

If a heap has a fixed maximum, individual allocation requests made using the **HeapAlloc** or **HeapReAlloc** functions must be less than 0x7FFF8 bytes; requests for larger blocks fail, even if the maximum size of the heap is large enough to contain the block.

If allocation requests exceed the initial amount of physical storage specified by *dwInitialSize*, the system allocates additional pages of physical storage for the heap, up to the heap's maximum size.

Returns

HANDLE: The handle of the newly created heap. If an error occurs, **NULL** is returned.

Include File

winbase.h

See Also

HeapFree, HeapAlloc, HeapReAlloc, HeapDestroy

Example

See the example for the **HeapAlloc** function.

HeapDestroy

Description	**HeapDestroy** destroys a heap object. This function decommits and releases all the pages of a private heap object, and invalidates the handle. It is not necessary to call **HeapFree** before calling **HeapDestroy**.
Syntax	BOOL **HeapDestroy**(HANDLE *hHeap*)
Parameters	
hHeap	HANDLE: The handle of the heap to be destroyed. This should be a handle returned by the **HeapCreate** function. Handles returned by the **GetProcessHeap** function should not be used.
Returns	BOOL: TRUE if successful; otherwise, it is FALSE.
Include File	winbase.h
See Also	HeapFree, HeapCreate
Example	See the example for the **HeapAlloc** function.

HeapFree

Description	**HeapFree** frees a memory block allocated from a heap by the **HeapAlloc** or **HeapReAlloc** function.
Syntax	BOOL **HeapFree**(HANDLE *hHeap,* DWORD *dwFlags,* LPVOID *lpMem*)
Parameters	
hHeap	HANDLE: The handle of the heap returned by the **HeapCreate** or **GetProcessHeap** function.
dwFlags	DWORD: If set to **HEAP_NO_SERIALIZE**, the heap access is not serialized, meaning exclusive access is not guaranteed and should not be used if the heap is shared between threads. Specifying this flag will override the options set when the heap was created using the **HeapCreate** function.
lpMem	LPVOID: A pointer, returned by **HeapAlloc** or **HeapReAlloc**, to the memory block to free.
Returns	BOOL: TRUE if successful; otherwise, it is FALSE.
Include File	winbase.h
See Also	HeapCreate, HeapAlloc, HeapReAlloc, HeapDestroy
Example	See the example for the **HeapAlloc** function.

HeapReAlloc

Description	The **HeapReAlloc** function reallocates a block of memory from a heap. The resulting memory block is not moveable.

Syntax	LPVOID **HeapReAlloc**(HANDLE *hHeap,* DWORD *dwFlags,* LPVOID *lpMem,* DWORD *dwBytes*)
Parameters	
hHeap	HANDLE: The handle of the heap returned by the **HeapCreate** or **GetProcessHeap** function.
dwFlags	DWORD: Determines how the memory is reallocated. These flags will override the corresponding flag specified when the heap was created with **HeapCreate**. One or more of the flags shown in Table 11-9 can be specified.

Table 11-9 HeapReAlloc flags

Flag	Description
HEAP_GENERATE_EXCEPTIONS	Raises exceptions on errors instead of returning NULL.
HEAP_NO_SERIALIZE	Mutual exclusion will not be used while this function is accessing the heap. If specified, only one thread should access the heap at a time. If multiple threads are sharing the same heap, this flag should not be set.
HEAP_REALLOC_IN_PLACE_ONLY	There can be no movement when reallocating a memory block to a larger size. If not specified and the reallocation request is for a larger size, the function may move the block to a new location. If specified and the block cannot be enlarged without moving, the function will fail.
HEAP_ZERO_MEMORY	Initializes the new memory, if the block is being enlarged, to 0.

lpMem	LPVOID: A pointer, returned by an earlier call to the **HeapAlloc** or **HeapReAlloc** function, to the block of memory the function reallocates.
dwBytes	DWORD: The number of bytes to be allocated. If the heap specified by the *hHeap* parameter has a fixed maximum size, *dwBytes* must be less than 0x7FFF8.
Returns	LPVOID: If successful, the return value is a pointer to the reallocated memory block. **NULL** is returned if the allocation attempt failed because of a lack of available memory or heap corruption.
	If the function fails and **HEAP_GENERATE_EXCEPTIONS** has been specified, the exception values listed in Table 11-10 can be generated.

Table 11-10 HeapReAlloc exception errors

Value	Meaning
STATUS_ACCESS_VIOLATION	An access violation occurred during the reallocation attempt.
STATUS_NO_MEMORY	The reallocation attempt failed for lack of available memory.

Include File	`winbase.h`
See Also	`HeapCreate`, `HeapAlloc`, `GetProcessHeap`
Example	See the example for the `HeapAlloc` function.

HeapSize

Description	`HeapSize` returns the size, in bytes, of a memory block allocated from a heap by the `HeapAlloc` or `HeapReAlloc` function.
Syntax	DWORD **HeapSize**(HANDLE *hHeap,* DWORD *dwFlags,* LPCVOID *lpMem*)
Parameters	
hHeap	HANDLE: The handle of the heap where the memory block resides. This handle is returned by the `HeapCreate` or `GetProcessHeap` function.
dwFlags	DWORD: If set to `HEAP_NO_SERIALIZE`, the heap access is not serialized, meaning exclusive access is not guaranteed and should not be used if the heap is shared between threads. Specifying this flag will override the options set when the heap was created using the `HeapCreate` function.
lpMem	LPCVOID: A pointer to the memory block whose size will be determined. This is a pointer returned by the `HeapAlloc` or `HeapReAlloc` function.
Returns	DWORD: The size, in bytes, of the allocated memory block.
Include File	`winbase.h`
See Also	`HeapCreate`, `GetProcessHeap`, `HeapAlloc`, `HeapReAlloc`
Example	When the user selects the Test! menu item, this example creates a heap and allocates a block of memory. The actual size of the memory block is then displayed in a message box.

```
LRESULT CALLBACK WndProc( HWND hWnd, UINT uMsg, WPARAM wParam, LPARAM lParam )
{
    switch( uMsg )
    {
        case WM_COMMAND :
                switch( LOWORD( wParam ) )
                {
                    case IDM_TEST :
                        {
                            HANDLE hHeap = HeapCreate( 0, 1024, 2048 );
                            LPTSTR lpMem = HeapAlloc( hHeap,
                                                HEAP_ZERO_MEMORY, 20 );

                            wsprintf( lpMem, "Memory Size = %d",
                                    HeapSize( hHeap, 0, lpMem ) );

                            HeapDestroy( hHeap );
                        }
                        break;
        .
        .
        .
```

IsBadCodePtr

Description	IsBadCodePtr determines whether the calling process has read access to the memory at the specified address. This function does not guarantee read access to a range of memory.
	In a preemptive multitasking environment, other threads can change the process's access to the tested memory. Even when the function indicates the process has read access, an application should use structured exception handling when attempting to access the memory.
Syntax	BOOL **IsBadCodePtr**(FARPROC *lpfnProc*)
Parameters	
lpfnProc	FARPROC: A pointer to an address in memory.
Returns	BOOL: FALSE if the calling process has read access to the specified memory; otherwise, it is TRUE.
Include File	winbase.h
See Also	IsBadReadPtr, IsBadStringPtr, IsBadWritePtr
Example	This example shows how an application can call a function with minimized risk of generating a protection fault.

```
BOOL CallFunction( FARPROC lpfnProc, LPTSTR lpString,
                   LPVOID lpReadMem, LPVOID lpWriteMem )
{
   // Check all pointers to make sure they are
   // valid and the proper access is set.
   //.......................................
   if ( IsBadCodePtr( lpfnProc ) ||
        IsBadReadPtr( lpReadMem ) ||
        IsBadWritePtr( lpWriteMem ) ||
        IsBadStringPtr( lpString ) )
   {
      return( FALSE );
   }

   // Call the function.
   //...................
   return( (*lpfnProc)( lpString, lpReadMem, lpWriteMem ) );
}
```

IsBadReadPtr

Description	IsBadReadPtr verifies that the calling process has read access to the specified range of memory. If the calling process has read access to some, but not all, of the memory in the range, the return value indicates no read access.

In a preemptive multitasking environment, other threads can change the process's access to the tested memory. Even when the function indicates the process has read access, an application should use structured exception handling when attempting to access the memory.

Syntax	BOOL **IsBadReadPtr**(CONST VOID* *lpvPtr,* UINT *cbBytes*)
Parameters	
lpvPtr	CONST VOID*: A pointer to the first byte of the memory block.
cbBytes	UINT: The size, in bytes, of the memory block.
Returns	BOOL: FALSE if the calling process has read access to all bytes in the specified memory range; otherwise, it is TRUE.
Include File	winbase.h
See Also	IsBadCodePtr, IsBadStringPtr, IsBadWritePtr
Example	See the example for the IsBadCodePtr function.

IsBadStringPtr ■ WINDOWS 95 ■ WINDOWS NT

Description	IsBadStringPtr verifies that the calling process has read access to a range of memory pointed to by a string pointer. If the calling process has read access to some, but not all, of the memory in the range, the return value indicates no read access.
	In a preemptive multitasking environment, other threads can change the process's access to the tested memory. Even when the function indicates the process has read access, an application should use structured exception handling when attempting to access the memory.
Syntax	BOOL **IsBadStringPtr**(LPCTSTR *lpszStr,* UINT *cchMax*)
Parameters	
lpszStr	LPCTSTR: A pointer to a null-terminated string, either Unicode or ASCII.
cchMax	UINT: The maximum size, in characters, of the string.
Returns	BOOL: FALSE if the calling process has read access to all bytes up to the string's terminating null character or up to the number of bytes specified by *cchMax*; otherwise, it is TRUE.
Include File	winbase.h
See Also	IsBadCodePtr, IsBadReadPtr, IsBadWritePtr
Example	See the example for the IsBadCodePtr function.

IsBadWritePtr ■ WINDOWS 95 ■ WINDOWS NT

Description	IsBadWritePtr verifies that the calling process has write access to a range of memory. If the calling process has write access to some, but not all, of the memory in the range, the return value indicates no write access.

In a preemptive multitasking environment, other threads can change the process's access to the tested memory. Even when the function indicates the process has write access, an application should use structured exception handling when attempting to access the memory.

Syntax	BOOL **IsBadWritePtr**(LPVOID *lpvPtr,* UINT *cbBytes*)
Parameters	
lpvPtr	LPVOID: A pointer to the first byte of the memory block.
cbBytes	UINT: The size, in bytes, of the memory block.
Returns	BOOL: FALSE if the calling process has write access to all bytes in the specified memory range; otherwise, it is TRUE.
Include File	winbase.h
See Also	IsBadCodePtr, IsBadReadPtr, IsBadStringPtr
Example	See the example for the IsBadCodePtr function.

MulDiv   ■ WINDOWS 95   ■ WINDOWS NT

Description	MulDiv multiplies two 32-bit values (*nMultiplicand* × *nMultiplier*) and then divides the 64-bit result by a third 32-bit value (*nDivisor*). The return value is rounded up or down to the nearest integer.
	Use MulDiv for calculations where the result of multiplying will overflow the 32-bit precision.
Syntax	int **MulDiv**(int *nMultiplicand,* int *nMultiplier,* int *nDivisor*)
Parameters	
nMultiplicand	int: The multiplicand.
nMultiplier	int: The multiplier.
nDivisor	int: The number by which the result of the multiplication (*nMultiplicand* × *nMultiplier*) is to be divided.
Returns	int: The result of the multiplication and division. If either an overflow occurred or *nDivisor* was 0, the return value is −1.
Include File	winbase.h
Example	This example, shown in Figure 11-3, shows the calculation (200000 × 300000) ÷ 100000. Done with pure integer math, the values overflow the 32-bit limit. Using MulDiv provides the correct result.

```
LRESULT CALLBACK WndProc( HWND hWnd, UINT uMsg, WPARAM wParam, LPARAM lParam )
{
    switch( uMsg )
    {
        case WM_COMMAND :
                switch( LOWORD( wParam ) )
                {
```

```
case IDM_TEST :
    {
        char szMsg[128];

        int n1   = 200000;
        int n2   = 300000;
        int n3   = 100000;
        int nAns = (n1 * n2)/n3;

        wsprintf( szMsg, "Answer done wrong: %d\n" \
                         "Answer done right: %d",
                         nAns, MulDiv( n1, n2, n3 ) );

        MessageBox( hWnd, szMsg, "Answers",
                    MB_OK | MB_ICONINFORMATION );
    }
    break;
```

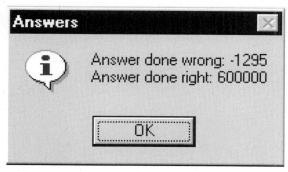

Figure 11-3 MulDiv example

VirtualAlloc   ■ WINDOWS 95   ■ WINDOWS NT

Description   **VirtualAlloc** reserves or commits a region of pages in the virtual address space of the calling process. Memory allocated by this function is automatically initialized to **0**.

Use **VirtualAlloc** initially to reserve a block of pages, and then make additional calls to **VirtualAlloc** to commit individual pages from the reserved block. This enables a process to reserve a range of its virtual address space without consuming physical storage until it is needed.

Syntax   LPVOID **VirtualAlloc**(LPVOID *lpvAddress,* DWORD *dwSize,* DWORD *dwAllocationType,* DWORD *dwProtect*)

Parameters

lpvAddress	**LPVOID**: A pointer to the desired starting address of the region. When memory is being reserved, the address is rounded down to the next 64KB boundary. If the memory is being committed, the address is rounded down to the next page boundary. Use **GetSystemInfo** to determine the size of a page on the host computer. If set to **NULL**, the system determines where to allocate the region.
dwSize	**DWORD**: The size, in bytes, of the region. If the *lpvAddress* parameter is **NULL**, this value is rounded up to the next page boundary. Otherwise, the allocated pages include all pages containing one or more bytes in the range from *lpvAddress* to (*lpvAddress* + *dwSize*).
dwAllocationType	**DWORD**: The type of allocation to perform. An application can specify any combination of the flags listed in Table 11-11.

Table 11-11 VirtualAlloc *dwAllocationType* values

Flag	Description
MEM_COMMIT	Commits a region of pages. This allocates physical storage in memory or in the paging file on disk to accommodate the request.
MEM_RESERVE	Reserves a range of the process's virtual address space without allocating any physical storage.
MEM_TOP_DOWN	Allocates memory at the highest possible address.

dwProtect	**DWORD**: The type of access protection for the committed pages. **PAGE_GUARD** and **PAGE_NOCACHE** modifiers can be combined with any one of the flags listed in Table 11-12.

Table 11-12 VirtualAlloc *dwProtect* values

Flag	Description
PAGE_EXECUTE	Allows execute access to the committed region of pages. Any attempt to read or write to the committed region causes an access violation.
PAGE_EXECUTE_READ	Allows execute and read access to the committed region of pages. Any attempt to write to the committed region causes an access violation.
PAGE_EXECUTE_READWRITE	Allows execute, read, and write access to the committed region of pages.
PAGE_EXECUTE_WRITECOPY	Allows execute, read, and write access to the committed region of pages. The pages are shared read-on-write and copy-on-write.
PAGE_GUARD	Pages in the region become guard pages. Any attempt to read from or write to a guard page causes the system to raise a STATUS_GUARD_PAGE exception and turn off the guard page status. This flag cannot be used with PAGE_NOACCESS.

Flag	Description
PAGE_NOACCESS	Disables all access to the committed region of pages. Any attempt to access the committed region causes a general protection (GP) fault.
PAGE_NOCACHE	Allows no caching of the committed regions of pages. This is not recommended for general usage. This flag cannot be used with PAGE_NOACCESS.
PAGE_READONLY	Allows read access to the committed region of pages. Any attempt to write to the committed region causes an access violation. If the system differentiates between read-only and execute access, attempts to execute code in the committed region will cause an access violation.
PAGE_READWRITE	Allows read and write access to the committed region of pages.
PAGE_WRITECOPY	Allows copy-on-write access to the committed region of pages.

Returns   LPVOID: If successful, the base address of the allocated region of pages; otherwise, the return value is NULL.

Include File   winbase.h

See Also   VirtualFree, VirtualLock, VirtualAllocEx

Example   This example reserves 1MB of virtual memory when started. When the user selects the Test! menu item, 70KB of virtual memory are committed and used. Values are placed in every 1KB block of the memory. The access of the entire committed block of memory is changed to read-only. A value in the memory block is accessed and displayed in a message box. A value is then set into the memory, which causes a protection fault. This example uses **try-except** to catch the protection faults. This form of exception handling works with Microsoft's Visual C++. Figure 11-4 shows the message box displayed when the application attempts to set a value into the read-only memory.

Figure 11-4 VirtualAlloc example

```
LRESULT CALLBACK WndProc( HWND hWnd, UINT uMsg, WPARAM wParam, LPARAM lParam )
{
static LPVOID lpMem = NULL;

    switch( uMsg )
    {
        case WM_CREATE  :
                // Reserve 1MB of virtual memory.
                //...............................
                lpMem = VirtualAlloc( NULL, 1048576, MEM_RESERVE, 0 );
                break;

        case WM_COMMAND :
                switch( LOWORD( wParam ) )
                {
                    case IDM_TEST :
                        {
                            // Commit a 70KB block of memory from virtual
                            // memory and then use it.
                            //...........................................
                            DWORD   dwoldAccess;
                            LPTSTR lpBuf = VirtualAlloc( lpMem, 71680,
                                                MEM_COMMIT, PAGE_READWRITE );

                            // Set each 1KB block of memory to a number.
                            //.........................................
                            if ( lpBuf )
                            {
                                int i;
                                for( i = 0; i < 70; i++ )
                                {
                                    if ( VirtualLock( (lpBuf+(i*1024)), 1024 ) )
                                    {
                                        memset( (lpBuf+(i*1024)), i, 1024 );
                                        VirtualUnlock( (lpBuf+(i*1024)), 1024 );
                                    }
                                }
                            }

                            // Protect the memory with Read-Only access.
                            //.........................................
                            VirtualProtect( lpBuf, 71680, PAGE_READONLY,
                                            &dwoldAccess );

                            try // To read from the memory.
                            {
                                char szMsg[20];

                                wsprintf( szMsg, "Memory Value = %d",
                                        *(lpBuf+2048) );
                                MessageBox( hWnd, szMsg, "Read",
                                            MB_OK | MB_ICONINFORMATION );
                            }
                            except( 1 )
                            {
                                MessageBox( hWnd, "Error accessing memory",
                                            "Read",
                                            MB_OK | MB_ICONEXCLAMATION );
                            }
```

```
                    try   // To write to the memory.
                    {
                        *lpBuf = 10;
                    }
                    except( 1 )
                    {
                        MessageBox( hWnd, "Error accessing memory",
                                    "Write",
                                    MB_OK | MB_ICONEXCLAMATION );
                    }
                }
                break;

            case IDM_EXIT :
                    DestroyWindow( hWnd );
                    break;
        }
        break;

    case WM_DESTROY :
            // Free virtual memory.
            //....................
            VirtualFree( lpMem, 0, MEM_RELEASE );
            PostQuitMessage(0);
            break;

    default :
            return( DefWindowProc( hWnd, uMsg, wParam, lParam ) );
    }

    return( 0L );
```

VirtualAllocEx   ■ WINDOWS 95 ■ WINDOWS NT

Description	VirtualAllocEx is the same as the **VirtualAlloc** function, except that **VirtualAlloc** allocates memory within the address space of the calling process, while **VirtualAllocEx** can allocate memory for a specified process.
Syntax	LPVOID **VirtualAllocEx**(HANDLE *hProcess,* LPVOID *lpvAddress,* DWORD *dwSize,* DWORD *dwAllocationType,* DWORD *dwProtect*)
Parameters.	
hProcess	HANDLE: The handle to the process for which to allocate memory. The handle must have **PROCESS_VM_OPERATION** access.
lpvAddress	LPVOID: A pointer to the desired starting address of the region. When memory is being reserved, the address is rounded down to the next 64KB boundary. If the memory is being committed, the address is rounded down to the next page boundary. Use **GetSystemInfo** to determine the size of a page on the host computer. If set to **NULL**, the system determines where to allocate the region.

dwSize	DWORD: The size, in bytes, of the region. If the *lpvAddress* parameter is NULL, this value is rounded up to the next page boundary. Otherwise, the allocated pages include all pages containing one or more bytes in the range from *lpvAddress* to (*lpvAddress* + *dwSize*).
dwAllocationType	DWORD: The type of allocation to perform. An application can specify any combination of the flags listed in Table 11-11.
dwProtect	DWORD: The type of access protection for the committed pages. PAGE_GUARD and PAGE_NOCACHE modifiers can be combined with any one of the flags listed in Table 11-12.
Returns	LPVOID: If successful, the base address of the allocated region of pages; otherwise, the return value is NULL.
Include File	winbase.h
See Also	VirtualAlloc, VirtualFreeEx

VirtualFree   ■ WINDOWS 95   ■ WINDOWS NT

Description	VirtualFree releases or decommits (or both) a region of pages within the virtual address space of the calling process. To release a region of pages, the entire range of pages must be in the same state (all reserved or all committed), and the entire region originally reserved by the VirtualAlloc function must be released at the same time. If only some of the pages in the original reserved region are committed, an application must first call VirtualFree to decommit the committed pages and then call VirtualFree again to release the entire block.
Syntax	BOOL **VirtualFree**(LPVOID *lpvAddress,* DWORD *dwSize,* DWORD *dwFreeType*)
Parameters	
lpvAddress	LPVOID: A pointer to the base address of the region of pages to be freed. If the *dwFreeType* parameter includes the MEM_RELEASE flag, this parameter must be the base address returned by the VirtualAlloc function when the region of pages was reserved.
dwSize	DWORD: The size, in bytes, of the region to be freed. If the *dwFreeType* parameter includes the MEM_RELEASE flag, this parameter must be 0.
dwFreeType	DWORD: The type of free operation. One of the flags listed in Table 11-13 can be specified.

Table 11-13 VirtualFree flags

Flag	Description
MEM_DECOMMIT	Decommits the specified region of committed pages.
MEM_RELEASE	Releases the specified region of reserved pages.

Returns	BOOL: If successful, the return value is TRUE; otherwise, it is FALSE.
Include File	winbase.h
See Also	VirtualAlloc
Example	See the example for the VirtualAlloc function.

VirtualFreeEx
■ Windows 95 ■ Windows NT

Description VirtualFreeEx is the same as the VirtualFree function, except that VirtualFree frees memory within the address space of the calling process, while VirtualFreeEx can free memory for a specified process.

Syntax BOOL **VirtualFreeEx**(HANDLE *hProcess,* LPVOID *lpvAddress,* DWORD *dwSize,* DWORD *dwFreeType*)

Parameters

hProcess HANDLE: The handle to the process for which to free memory. The handle must have **PROCESS_VM_OPERATION** access.

lpvAddress LPVOID: A pointer to the base address of the region of pages to be freed. If the *dwFreeType* parameter includes the **MEM_RELEASE** flag, this parameter must be the base address returned by the **VirtualAllocEx** function when the region of pages was reserved.

dwSize DWORD: The size, in bytes, of the region to be freed. If the *dwFreeType* parameter includes the **MEM_RELEASE** flag, this parameter must be 0.

dwFreeType DWORD: The type of free operation. One of the flags listed in Table 11-13 can be specified.

Returns BOOL: If successful, the return value is TRUE; otherwise, it is FALSE.

Include File winbase.h

See Also VirtualAllocEx

VirtualLock
■ Windows 95 ■ Windows NT

Description VirtualLock locks the specified region of the process's virtual address space into memory, ensuring that subsequent access to the region will not incur a page fault. The limit on the number of pages that can be locked is 30 pages. This limit is intentionally imposed to avoid severe performance degradation.

Locking pages into memory may degrade the performance of the system by reducing the available RAM and forcing the system to swap out other critical pages to the paging file.

Syntax BOOL **VirtualLock**(LPVOID *lpvAddress,* DWORD *dwSize*)

Parameters

lpvAddress	LPVOID: A pointer to the base address of the region of pages to be locked.
dwSize	DWORD: The size, in bytes, of the region to be locked.
Returns	BOOL: TRUE if successful; otherwise, the return value is FALSE.
Include File	winbase.h
See Also	VirtualUnlock, VirtualAlloc
Example	See the example for the VirtualAlloc function.

VirtualProtect ■ WINDOWS 95 ■ WINDOWS NT

Description	VirtualProtect changes the access protection on a region of committed pages in the virtual address space of the calling process.
Syntax	BOOL **VirtualProtect**(LPVOID *lpvAddress,* DWORD *dwSize,* DWORD *dwNewProtect,* PDWORD *pdwOldProtect*)

Parameters

lpvAddress	LPVOID: A pointer to the base address of the region of pages whose access-protection attributes are to be changed.
dwSize	DWORD: The size, in bytes, of the region whose access-protection attributes are to be changed.
dwNewProtect	DWORD: The new type of access protection. PAGE_GUARD and PAGE_NOCACHE modifiers can be combined with any one of the flags listed in Table 11-12.
pdwOldProtect	PDWORD: A pointer to a variable that receives the previous access protection of the first page in the specified region of pages.
Returns	BOOL: If successful, the return value is TRUE; otherwise, it is FALSE.
Include File	winbase.h
See Also	VirtualAlloc
Example	See the example for the VirtualAlloc function.

VirtualProtectEx ■ WINDOWS 95 ■ WINDOWS NT

Description	VirtualProtectEx is the same as the VirtualProtect function, except that it can act on virtual memory of other processes while the VirtualProtect function acts on the calling process.
Syntax	BOOL **VirtualProtectEx**(HANDLE *hProcess,* LPVOID *lpvAddress,* DWORD *dwSize,* DWORD *dwNewProtect,* PDWORD *pdwOldProtect*)

Parameters

hProcess   HANDLE: The handle to the process for which to change the memory protection. The handle must have **PROCESS_VM_OPERATION** access.

lpvAddress   LPVOID: A pointer to the base address of the region of pages whose access-protection attributes are to be changed.

dwSize   DWORD: The size, in bytes, of the region whose access-protection attributes are to be changed.

dwNewProtect   DWORD: The new type of access protection. **PAGE_GUARD** and **PAGE_NOCACHE** modifiers can be combined with any one of the flags listed in Table 11-12.

pdwOldProtect   PDWORD: A pointer to a variable that receives the previous access protection of the first page in the specified region of pages.

Returns   BOOL: If successful, the return value is **TRUE**; otherwise, it is **FALSE**.

Include File   winbase.h

See Also   VirtualAlloc

VirtualQuery   ■ WINDOWS 95 ■ WINDOWS NT

Description   VirtualQuery provides information about a range of pages in the virtual address space of the calling process.

Syntax   DWORD **VirtualQuery**(LPCVOID *lpvAddress,*
PMEMORY_BASIC_INFORMATION *pmbiBuffer,* DWORD *dwLength*)

Parameters

lpvAddress   LPCVOID: A pointer to the base address of the region of pages to be queried.

pmbiBuffer   PMEMORY_BASIC_INFORMATION: A pointer to a MEMORY_BASIC_INFORMATION structure in which information about the specified page range is returned. See the definition of the **MEMORY_BASIC_INFORMATION** structure below.

dwLength   DWORD: The size, in bytes, of the buffer pointed to by the *pmbiBuffer* parameter.

Returns   DWORD: The actual number of bytes returned in the information buffer.

Include File   winbase.h

MEMORY_BASIC_INFORMATION Definition

```
typedef struct _MEMORY_BASIC_INFORMATION
{
    PVOID BaseAddress;        // base address of region
    PVOID AllocationBase;     // allocation base address
    DWORD AllocationProtect;  // initial access protection
    DWORD RegionSize;         // size, in bytes, of region
    DWORD State;              // committed, reserved, free
    DWORD Protect;            // current access protection
    DWORD Type;               // type of pages
} MEMORY_BASIC_INFORMATION, *PMEMORY_BASIC_INFORMATION;
```

Members

BaseAddress	PVOID: A pointer to the base address of the region of pages.
AllocationBase	PVOID: A pointer to the base address of a range of pages allocated by the **VirtualAlloc** function.
AllocationProtect	DWORD: The access protection given when the region was initially allocated. **PAGE_GUARD** and **PAGE_NOCACHE** modifiers can be combined with any one of the flags in Table 11-12.
RegionSize	DWORD: The size, in bytes, of the region beginning at the base address in which all pages have identical attributes.
State	DWORD: The state of the pages in the region. This is one of the values listed in Table 11-14.

Table 11-14 MEMORY_BASIC_INFORMATION *State* values

State	Description
MEM_COMMIT	The pages are committed.
MEM_FREE	The pages are not accessible to the calling process and available to be allocated.
MEM_RESERVE	The pages are reserved.

Protect	DWORD: The access protection of the pages in the region. One of the flags listed for the *AllocationProtect* member is specified.
Type	DWORD: The type of pages in the region. Table 11-15 lists valid types.

Table 11-15 MEMORY_BASIC_INFORMATION *Type* values

Type	Description
MEM_IMAGE	The memory pages are mapped into the view of an image section.
MEM_MAPPED	The memory pages are mapped into the view of a section.
MEM_PRIVATE	The memory pages are private.

Example   In this example, shown in Figure 11-5, a 70KB block of virtual memory is committed. **VirtualQuery** returns the region size the memory actually occupies. Note the region size is divisible by 4096 (4KB), which is the page size of x86 computers.

```
LRESULT CALLBACK WndProc( HWND hWnd, UINT uMsg, WPARAM wParam, LPARAM lParam )
{
static LPVOID lpMem = NULL;

   switch( uMsg )
   {
      case WM_CREATE  :
              lpMem = VirtualAlloc( NULL, 1048576, MEM_RESERVE, 0 );
              break;

      case WM_COMMAND :
              switch( LOWORD( wParam ) )
              {
                 case IDM_TEST :
                       {
                          MEMORY_BASIC_INFORMATION meminfo;
                          char    szMsg[30];
                          LPTSTR lpBuf = VirtualAlloc( lpMem, 71680,
                                       MEM_COMMIT, PAGE_READWRITE );

                          VirtualQuery( lpBuf, &meminfo,
                                      sizeof( MEMORY_BASIC_INFORMATION ) );

                          wsprintf( szMsg, "Region Size = %ld",
                                   meminfo.RegionSize );

                          MessageBox( hWnd, szMsg, "Virtual Memory",
                                   MB_OK | MB_ICONINFORMATION );
                       }
                       break;

                 .
                 .
                 .
```

Figure 11-5 VirtualQuery example

VirtualQueryEx   ■ WINDOWS 95   ■ WINDOWS NT

Description	VirtualQueryEx is the same as the VirtualQuery function, except that it can provide information about a range of pages in the virtual address space of the specified process.
Syntax	DWORD **VirtualQueryEx**(HANDLE *hProcess*, LPCVOID *lpvAddress*, PMEMORY_BASIC_INFORMATION *pmbiBuffer*, DWORD *dwLength*)
Parameters	
hProcess	HANDLE: The handle to the process for which to query information. The handle must have PROCESS_QUERY_INFORMATION access.
lpvAddress	LPCVOID: A pointer to the base address of the region of pages to be queried.
pmbiBuffer	PMEMORY_BASIC_INFORMATION: A pointer to a MEMORY_BASIC_INFORMATION structure in which information about the specified page range is returned. See the definition of the MEMORY_BASIC_INFORMATION structure under the VirtualQuery function.
dwLength	DWORD: The size, in bytes, of the buffer pointed to by the *pmbiBuffer* parameter.
Returns	DWORD: The actual number of bytes returned in the information buffer.
Include File	winbase.h
See Also	VirtualQuery, VirtualProtectEx

VirtualUnlock   ■ WINDOWS 95   ■ WINDOWS NT

Description	VirtualUnlock unlocks a specified range of pages in the virtual address space of a process, enabling the system to swap the pages out to the paging file if necessary.
	Pages locked with the VirtualLock function should be unlocked as soon as possible to prevent the system performance from degrading. VirtualUnlock does not need to be called for each call to VirtualLock, as is the case with the GlobalLock and GlobalUnlock functions.
Syntax	BOOL **VirtualUnlock**(LPVOID *lpvAddress*, DWORD *dwSize*)
Parameters	
lpvAddress	LPVOID: A pointer to the base address of the region of pages to be unlocked.
dwSize	DWORD: The size, in bytes, of the region being unlocked.
Returns	BOOL: If successful, the return value is TRUE; otherwise, it is FALSE.
Include File	winbase.h
See Also	VirtualLock
Example	See example for the VirtualAlloc function.

12

THE GRAPHICS DEVICE INTERFACE

The Graphics Device Interface (GDI) provides Windows applications with a device-independent interface to the screen and printers. The GDI is a layer between the application and the different types of hardware. This architecture frees the programmer from having to deal with each type of device directly by letting the GDI resolve differences in hardware instead. A well-designed Windows application will function the same on all types of current hardware and any new hardware introduced in the future.

All GDI functions in Win32 use 32-bit values for GDI coordinates; however, in Windows 95, the high-order word is ignored, resulting in a 16-bit value for coordinates. Only in Windows NT can an application use the full 32-bit values. This is because in Windows 95, the GDI along with other key portions of the operating system are implemented as 16-bit for maximum backward compatibility with Windows 3.x.

The Device Context

The basic tool that Windows uses to provide device independence for an application is called a device context, or DC. The DC is an internal structure that Windows uses to maintain information about an output device. Instead of sending output directly to the hardware, an application sends it to the DC, and then Windows sends it to the hardware. The following example shows the steps necessary to output a string to the client area of a window.

```
HDC hDC;                   // A handle to the device context.

hDC = GetDC( hWnd );       // Get a handle to the window's client area DC.

// Output a text string to the client area.
```

continued on next page

continued from previous page

```
//.........................................
TextOut( hDC, 0, 0, "Text output to client area.", 27 );

ReleaseDC( hWnd, hDC ); // Release the DC.
```

This example takes advantage of what the GDI provides by default. Notice the lack of information about the text color or font. All of these parameters were based on the default values stored in the device context. To expand on the example, change the font and color of the text by adding calls to the **SelectObject** and **SetTextColor** functions, as shown here:

```
HDC hDC;

hDC = GetDC( hWnd );

// Set the text attributes.
//.........................
SelectObject( hDC, GetStockObject( ANSI_VAR_FONT ) );
SetTextColor( hDC, RGB( 255, 0, 0 ) );

TextOut( hDC, 0, 0, "Text output to client area.", 27 );

ReleaseDC( hWnd, hDC );
```

SelectObject selects a new font into the device context. In this case, a stock font is loaded, and the **SetTextColor** function changes the text color to red. The result of these changes is that this time **TextOut** writes the output with red letters, using the **ANSI_VAR_FONT** character font. An application can also make a wide range of other changes to the device context with the functions provided by the Win32 API.

Selecting Objects into a Device Context

A device context always contains one pen to draw lines, one brush to fill areas, one font to output characters, and a series of other values to control how the device context behaves. If the application requires a different font, the font is selected into the device context prior to displaying the text. Selecting a new font does not change existing text on the window's client area.

When using a shared device context, have the application restore the settings of the device context before calling **ReleaseDC**. Objects, such as pens and brushes, created and selected into the DC should be deleted after calling **ReleaseDC**. Do not attempt to delete objects retrieved with the **GetStockObject** function. See Chapter 15, Painting and Drawing, for more information about stock objects.

Private Device Contexts

Normally, applications share and retrieve device contexts right before use and release them right after use. This works best for applications that do not frequently require a DC for painting.

An application that requires a DC on an ongoing basis can create a window with its own private DC by specifying the `CS_OWNDC` class style in the class definition for the window. With this class style, the device context exists for the life of the window. The application still uses `GetDC` to retrieve a handle to the device context but doesn't need to call `ReleaseDC` after using the device context. Using a private device context with programs that alter the device context settings means changes—such as new text colors, pens, and brushes—remain in effect until the application alters them again.

Origins and Extents

A device context has two special mapping modes, `MM_ISOTROPIC` and `MM_ANISOTROPIC`, which are not constrained by a fixed size. These mapping modes use two rectangular regions to derive a scaling factor and an orientation: the window and the viewport. The window is in logical coordinates, and the viewport is in physical coordinates. Together they determine how logical units are mapped to physical units. Both the window and the viewport contain an origin, an x extent, and a y extent. The origin is a point that describes any one of the four corners. The viewport origin is an offset from the window origin. The x extent is the horizontal distance from the origin to its opposing corner. The y extent is the vertical distance from the origin to its opposing corner. See the example under the `GetViewportOrgEx` function for an example of origins.

Windows defines a horizontal scaling factor by dividing the viewport's x extent by the window's x extent and a vertical scaling factor by dividing the viewport's y extent by the window's y extent. These scaling factors determine the number of logical units that Windows maps to a number of pixels. In addition to determining scaling factors, the window and viewport determine the orientation of an object. See the example under the `SetMapMode` function to see how scaling works with the window and viewport.

GDI Function Descriptions

Table 12-1 summarizes the Graphics Device Interface functions. Detailed function descriptions follow the table.

Table 12-1 Graphics Device Interface function summary

Function	Purpose
AddFontResource	Loads a font resource from a file into the system.
CancelDC	Cancels any pending operation on a device context.
ChangeDisplaySettings	Changes the display settings.
CreateCompatibleDC	Creates a memory device context compatible with a given device.
CreateDC	Creates a device context to a physical device, such as a printer.
CreateFont	Creates a logical font, ready to be used in text output.
CreateFontIndirect	Creates a logical font from a LOGFONT structure.
CreateIC	Retrieves a device context for a physical device, but only for informational purposes.

continued on next page

continued from previous page

Function	Purpose
CreateScalableFontResource	Creates a font resource file for a scaleable font.
DeleteDC	Deletes a device context created with CreateDC or CreateIC.
DPtoLP	Converts from device points to logical points.
EnumDisplaySettings	Retrieves information about a display device's graphics modes.
EnumFontFamilies	Enumerates the fonts in a specific font family available on a given device.
EnumFontFamiliesEx	Enumerates all the fonts that match the font characteristics specified in a LOGFONT structure.
GetDC	Retrieves a handle to the device context for the client area of a window.
GetDCEx	Retrieves a handle to the device context for a window.
GetDCOrgEx	Determines the screen coordinates for the logical origin of a device context.
GetDeviceCaps	Determines the capabilities of a device.
GetFontData	Retrieves the font metric data for a TrueType font.
GetFontLanguageInfo	Returns language characteristics about the currently selected font for a display context.
GetGraphicsMode	Returns the current graphics mode for a device.
GetMapMode	Determines the mapping mode in use by a device context.
GetSystemMetrics	Retrieves the dimensions of different window items on the video display.
GetViewportExtEx	Retrieves the x and y extents of the current viewport for a device context.
GetViewportOrgEx	Retrieves the x and y coordinates of the viewport origin for a device context.
GetWindowDC	Retrieves the device context for the entire window.
GetWindowExtEx	Retrieves the x and y extents of the window for a device context.
GetWindowOrgEx	Retrieves the x and y coordinates of the window origin for a device context.
LPtoDP	Converts a point from logical coordinates to device coordinates.
OffsetViewportOrgEx	Modifies the viewport origin of a device context using horizontal and vertical offsets.
OffsetWindowOrgEx	Modifies the window origin of a device context using horizontal and vertical offsets.
PtVisible	Determines if a point is within the current clipping region.
RectVisible	Determines if a rectangle has points within the current clipping region.
ReleaseDC	Frees the device context.
RemoveFontResource	Removes a font from the system and frees all memory associated with the font.
RestoreDC	Restores an old device context saved with SaveDC.
SaveDC	Saves a device context for future use.
ScaleViewportExtEx	Scales the viewport of a device context.
ScaleWindowExtEx	Scales the window extents of a device context.
SelectObject	Selects an object into a device context.
SetGraphicsMode	Sets the graphics mode for a device context.
SetMapMode	Changes the mapping mode of a device context.
SetMapperFlags	Adjusts how CreateFont and CreateFontIndirect adjust for font dimensions outside of those specified in the font data.
SetViewportExtEx	Sets the x and y extents of the viewport for a device context.
SetViewportOrgEx	Sets the viewport origin of a device context.

Function	Purpose
SetWindowExtEx	Sets the x and y extents of the window for a device context.
SetWindowOrgEx	Sets the window origin of a device context.
WindowFromDC	Returns the handle of the window associated with a display device context.

AddFontResource ■ WINDOWS 95 ■ WINDOWS NT

Description   AddFontResource adds a font resource from a file to the Windows font table. The font table is the table of fonts that are available to Windows applications.

Syntax   int **AddFontResource**(LPCTSTR *lpszFilename*)

Parameters

lpszFilename   LPCTSTR: A pointer to a null-terminated character string that contains a valid font file name. The file name may specify either a .FON font resource file, a .FNT raw bitmap font file, a .TTF raw TrueType file, or a .FOT TrueType resource file.

Returns   int: If successful, the number of fonts added; otherwise, the return value is 0.

Include File   wingdi.h

See Also   RemoveFontResource, FindResource

Related Messages   WM_FONTCHANGE should be sent to all top-level windows to notify all programs running of a change in the available fonts.

Example   This example shows how to add a TrueType font to the system when the application starts and remove it when finished. Use **SendMessage** to notify all other top-level programs of the font's presence.

```
LRESULT CALLBACK WndProc( HWND hWnd, UINT uMsg, WPARAM wParam, LPARAM lParam )
{
static int nFontLoad = 0;

   switch( uMsg )
   {
      case WM_CREATE :
              if ( CreateScalableFontResource( 0, "NEWFONT.FOT",
                                                "NEWFONT.TTF", NULL ) )
              {
                  nFontLoad = AddFontResource( "NEWFONT.FOT" );

                  if ( !nFontLoad )
                     MessageBox( hWnd, "Could not load font!", "Warning",
                                 MB_OK | MB_ICONASTERISK );
                  else
                     SendMessage( HWND_BROADCAST, WM_FONTCHANGE, 0, 0 );
              }
              break;
```

continued on next page

509

continued from previous page

```
            .
            .
            .

    case WM_DESTROY :
            if ( nFontLoad )
            {
                RemoveFontResource( "NEWFONT.FOT" );
                SendMessage( HWND_BROADCAST, WM_FONTCHANGE, 0, 0 );
            }
            PostQuitMessage(0);
            break;

    default :
            return( DefWindowProc( hWnd, uMsg, wParam, lParam ) );
    }

    return( 0L );
}
```

CancelDC   ■ WINDOWS 95   ■ WINDOWS NT

Description	CancelDC cancels any pending operation on the specified device context (DC). Use this function with multithreaded applications to cancel lengthy drawing operations. If one thread initiates a lengthy drawing operation, another thread may cancel that operation by calling this function. If an operation is canceled, the affected thread returns an error and the result of its drawing operation is undefined.
Syntax	BOOL **CancelDC**(HDC *hDC*)
Parameters	
hDC	HDC: The device context (DC) on which to cancel the pending operations.
Returns	BOOL: If successful, TRUE is returned; otherwise, the return value is FALSE.
Include File	wingdi.h
See Also	CreateThread

ChangeDisplaySettings   ■ WINDOWS 95   ■ WINDOWS NT

Description	ChangeDisplaySettings changes the display settings to the specified graphics mode. Using the DEVMODE structure filled with the EnumDisplaySettings function ensures that the DEVMODE structure contains only values supported by the display driver. When the display mode is changed dynamically, the WM_DISPLAYCHANGE message is sent to all running applications.
Syntax	LONG **ChangeDisplaySettings**(LPDEVMODE *lpDevMode,* DWORD *dwFlags*)

Parameters

lpDevMode   LPDEVMODE: A pointer to a DEVMODE structure that describes the graphics mode to switch to. The *dmSize* member must be initialized to the size, in bytes, of the DEVMODE structure. The *dmBitsPerPel*, *dmPelsWidth*, *dmPelsHeight*, *dmDisplayFlags*, and *dmDisplayFrequency* members are used. See the definition of the DEVMODE structure under the CreateDC function later in this chapter. If this parameter is set to NULL, the settings stored in the registry are used. This is the easiest way to return to the default mode after dynamic mode change.

dwFlags   DWORD: Indicates how the graphics mode should be changed. If set to 0, the graphics mode for the current screen will be changed. If the CDS_UPDATEREGISTRY flag is specified, the graphics mode for the current screen is changed and the registry is updated with the new values. If the CDS_TEST flag is specified, the new graphics mode is tested.

Returns   LONG: One of the values listed in Table 12-2 is returned.

Table 12-2 ChangeDisplaySettings return values

Value	Meaning
DISP_CHANGE_BADFLAGS	An invalid set of flags was passed in.
DISP_CHANGE_BADMODE	The graphics mode is not supported.
DISP_CHANGE_FAILED	The display driver failed the specified graphics mode.
DISP_CHANGE_NOTUPDATED	(Windows NT only) The application was unable to write the new settings to the registry.
DISP_CHANGE_RESTART	The computer must be restarted in order for the graphics mode to work.
DISP_CHANGE_SUCCESSFUL	The settings change was successful.

Include File	winuser.h
See Also	EnumDisplaySettings, CreateDC
Related Message	WM_DISPLAYCHANGE
Example	See the example under the EnumDisplaySettings function.

CreateCompatibleDC   ■ WINDOWS 95 ■ WINDOWS NT

Description   CreateCompatibleDC creates a memory device context (DC) compatible with a given device. Before a memory DC can be used for drawing operations, the application must select and place a bitmap of the correct width and height into the DC. Once a bitmap has been selected, the DC can prepare images that will be copied to the screen or printed. When a memory DC is no longer needed, the application must use DeleteDC to delete it.

CreateCompatibleDC can be used only with devices that support raster operations. An application can determine whether a device supports these operations by using the GetDeviceCaps function.

Syntax   HDC **CreateCompatibleDC**(HDC *hdc*)

Parameters

hdc   HDC: The DC of the device for which to create a memory DC. If **NULL**, the function creates a memory DC compatible with the application's current screen.

Returns   HDC: If successful, the return value is the handle of a memory DC; otherwise, it is **NULL**.

Include File   wingdi.h

See Also   DeleteDC

Example   This example shows how to paint a bitmap on the client area of a window. A memory device context is created using the **CreateCompatibleDC** function. The bitmap is loaded into the memory DC and then displayed using the **BitBlt** function.

```
LRESULT CALLBACK WndProc( HWND hWnd, UINT uMsg, WPARAM wParam, LPARAM lParam )
{
   switch( uMsg )
   {
      case WM_COMMAND :
              switch( LOWORD( wParam ) )
              {
                case IDM_TEST :
                      {
                         HDC      hDC;
                         HDC      hMemDC;
                         HBITMAP  hBmp;
                         BITMAP   bm;

                         // Load bitmap and retrieve
                         // information about the bitmap.
                         //.........................
                         hBmp = LoadBitmap( hInst, "BITMAP1" );
                         GetObject( hBmp, sizeof( BITMAP ), &bm );

                         // Retrieve a DC for the window and
                         // create a compatible DC.
                         hDC    = GetDC( hWnd );
                         hMemDC = CreateCompatibleDC( hDC );

                         // Select bitmap into the memory DC and
                         // display it on the client area of the window.
                         //.............................................
                         SelectObject( hMemDC, hBmp );

                         BitBlt( hDC, 0, 0, bm.bmWidth, bm.bmHeight,
                                 hMemDC, 0, 0, SRCCOPY );

                         ReleaseDC( hWnd, hDC );
```

```
        DeleteDC( hMemDC );
        DeleteObject( hBmp );
    }
    break;
```

CreateDC ■ WINDOWS 95 ■ WINDOWS NT

Description	`CreateDC` creates a device context for the specified device by using the given name. Commonly used to create a device context for a printer, `CreateDC` is also used to get the device context of the screen (the hardware screen, not a window's client area). Use this function carefully, because it allows an application to draw anywhere on the screen, not just within the window's boundaries. Use **GetDC** or **BeginPaint** to get a device context to a window on the screen.
Syntax	HDC **CreateDC**(LPCTSTR *lpszDriver,* LPCTSTR *lpszDevice,* LPCTSTR *lpszOutput,* CONST DEVMODE* *lpInitData*)
Parameters	
lpszDriver	LPCTSTR: A pointer to a null-terminated character string that specifies the file name (without extension) of the device driver. For example, **"DISPLAY"** can refer to a display driver, or **"WINSPOOL"** to a printer driver. Note that **WINSPOOL** is only valid for Windows NT.
lpszDevice	LPCTSTR: A pointer to a null-terminated character string that specifies the name of the specific output device being used, as shown by the Print Manager (for example, **"HP LaserJet"**).
lpszOutput	LPCTSTR: Ignored; set to **NULL**. See the **StartDoc** function for information on how to send output to a file.
lpInitData	CONST DEVMODE*: A pointer to a **DEVMODE** structure containing device-specific initialization data for the device driver. Set to **NULL** to use default initialization (if any) specified by the user. See the definition of the **DEVMODE** structure below.
Returns	HDC: If successful, the handle of a DC for the specified device; otherwise, the return value is **NULL**.
Include File	wingdi.h
See Also	DeleteDC, DocumentProperties, GetDC, BeginPaint, DeviceCapabilities
DEVMODE Definition	

```
typedef struct _devicemode
{
    TCHAR  dmDeviceName[CCHDEVICENAME];
    WORD   dmSpecVersion;
```

continued on next page

continued from previous page

```
WORD    dmDriverVersion;
WORD    dmSize;
WORD    dmDriverExtra;
DWORD   dmFields;
short   dmOrientation;
short   dmPaperSize;
short   dmPaperLength;
short   dmPaperWidth;
short   dmScale;
short   dmCopies;
short   dmDefaultSource;
short   dmPrintQuality;
short   dmColor;
short   dmDuplex;
short   dmYResolution;
short   dmTTOption;
short   dmCollate;
TCHAR   dmFormName[CCHFORMNAME];
WORD    dmLogPixels;
USHORT  dmBitsPerPel;
DWORD   dmPelsWidth;
DWORD   dmPelsHeight;
DWORD   dmDisplayFlags;
DWORD   dmDisplayFrequency;
WORD    dmICMMethod;
WORD    dmICMIntent;
WORD    dmMediaType;
WORD    dmDitherType;
DWORD   dmReserved1;
DWORD   dmReserved2;
} DEVMODE;
```

Members

dmDeviceName   TCHAR[CCHDEVICENAME]: The name of the device that the driver supports (for example, **"PCL/HP LaserJet"** in the case of PCL/HP LaserJet). This name is unique among device drivers.

dmSpecVersion   **WORD**: The version number of the initialization data specification on which the structure is based. The current version, defined as **DM_SPECVERSION**, is 0x0400.

dmDriverVersion   **WORD**: The printer driver version number assigned by the printer driver developer.

dmSize   **WORD**: The size, in bytes, of the **DEVMODE** structure except any device-specific data that might follow the public members of the **DEVMODE** structure. If an application manipulates only the driver-independent portion of the data, it can use this member to determine the length of the structure without having to account for different versions.

dmDriverExtra   **WORD**: The size, in bytes, of the private driver data that follows this structure. If a device driver does not use device-specific information, this member should be **0**.

dmFields   DWORD: A combination of the flags listed in Table 12-3 that determine whether the printer driver uses or ignores the remaining members in the **DEVMODE** structure. Use the binary OR (|) operator to combine the flags.

Table 12-3 DEVMODE *dmFields* values

Value	Meaning
DM_ORIENTATION	Use the *dmOrientation* member.
DM_PAPERSIZE	Use the *dmPaperSize* member. If *dmPaperSize* is set to DMPAPER_USER, an application must also include the DM_PAPERWIDTH and DM_PAPERLENGTH flags.
DM_PAPERLENGTH	Use the *dmPaperLength* member. Include this flag only if *dmPaperSize* is set to DMPAPER_USER.
DM_PAPERWIDTH	Use the *dmPaperWidth* member. Include this flag only if *dmPaperSize* is set to DMPAPER_USER.
DM_SCALE	Use the *dmScale* member.
DM_COPIES	Use the *dmCopies* member.
DM_DEFAULTSOURCE	Use the *dmDefaultSource* member.
DM_PRINTQUALITY	Use the *dmPrintQuality* member.
DM_COLOR	Use the *dmColor* member.
DM_DUPLEX	Use the *dmDuplex* member.
DM_YRESOLUTION	Use the *dmYResolution* member.
DM_TTOPTION	Use the *dmTTOption* member.
DM_COLLATE	Use the *dmCollate* member.
DM_FORMNAME	Use the *dmFormName* member.
DM_BITSPERPEL	Use the *dmBitsPerPel* member.
DM_PELSWIDTH	Use the *dmPelsWidth* member.
DM_PELSHEIGHT	Use the *dmPelsHeight* member.
DM_DISPLAYFLAGS	Use the *dmDisplayFlags* member.
DM_DISPLAYFREQUENCY	Use the *dmDisplayFrequency* member.
DM_ICMMETHOD	Use the *dmICMMethod* member.
DM_ICMINTENT	Use the *dmICMIntent* member.
DM_MEDIATYPE	Use the *dmMediaType* member.
DM_DITHERTYPE	Use the *dmDitherType* member.
DM_RESERVED1	Use the *dmReserved1* member.
DM_RESERVED2	Use the *dmReserved2* member.

dmOrientation   short: The orientation of the paper. This member can be either the **DMORIENT_PORTRAIT** or **DMORIENT_LANDSCAPE** value.

dmPaperSize   short: The size of the paper to print on. This member can be one of the values in Table 12-4.

Table 12-4 DEVMODE *dmPaperSize* values

Value	Meaning
DMPAPER_10X14	10×14-inch sheet.
DMPAPER_11X17	11×17-inch sheet.
DMPAPER_A3	A3 sheet, 297×420 millimeters.
DMPAPER_A4	A4 sheet, 210×297 millimeters.
DMPAPER_A4SMALL	A4 small sheet, 210×297 millimeters.
DMPAPER_A5	A5 sheet, 148×210 millimeters.
DMPAPER_B4	B4 sheet, 250×354 millimeters.
DMPAPER_B5	B5 sheet, 182×257 millimeter paper.
DMPAPER_CSHEET	C sheet, 17×22 inches.
DMPAPER_DSHEET	D sheet, 22×34 inches.
DMPAPER_ENV_9	#9 envelope, 3 7/8×8 7/8 inches.
DMPAPER_ENV_10	#10 envelope, 4 1/8×9 1/2 inches.
DMPAPER_ENV_11	#11 envelope, 4 1/2×10 3/8 inches.
DMPAPER_ENV_12	#12 envelope, 4 3/4×11 inches.
DMPAPER_ENV_14	#14 envelope, 5×11 1/2 inches.
DMPAPER_ENV_B4	B4 envelope, 250×353 millimeters.
DMPAPER_ENV_B5	B5 envelope, 176×250 millimeters.
DMPAPER_ENV_B6	B6 envelope, 176×125 millimeters.
DMPAPER_ENV_C3	C3 envelope, 324×458 millimeters.
DMPAPER_ENV_C4	C4 envelope, 229×324 millimeters.
DMPAPER_ENV_C5	C5 envelope, 162×229 millimeters.
DMPAPER_ENV_C6	C6 envelope, 114×162 millimeters.
DMPAPER_ENV_C65	C65 envelope, 114×229 millimeters.
DMPAPER_ENV_DL	DL envelope, 110×220 millimeters.
DMPAPER_ENV_ITALY	Italy envelope, 110×230 millimeters.
DMPAPER_ENV_MONARCH	Monarch envelope, 3 7/8×7 1/2 inches.
DMPAPER_ENV_PERSONAL	6 3/4 envelope, 3 5/8×6 1/2 inches.
DMPAPER_ESHEET	E sheet, 34×44 inches.
DMPAPER_EXECUTIVE	Executive, 7 1/4×10 1/2 inches.
DMPAPER_FANFOLD_LGL_GERMAN	German legal fanfold, 8 1/2×13 inches.
DMPAPER_FANFOLD_STD_GERMAN	German standard fanfold, 8 1/2×12 inches.
DMPAPER_FANFOLD_US	U.S. standard fanfold, 14 7/8×11 inches.
DMPAPER_FOLIO	Folio, 8 1/2×13 inch paper.
DMPAPER_LEDGER	Ledger, 17×11 inches.
DMPAPER_LEGAL	Legal, 8 1/2×14 inches.
DMPAPER_LETTER	Letter, 8 1/2×11 inches.
DMPAPER_LETTERSMALL	Letter small, 8 1/2×11 inches.
DMPAPER_NOTE	Note, 8 1/2×11 inches.

Value	Meaning
DMPAPER_QUARTO	Quarto, 215×275 millimeter paper.
DMPAPER_STATEMENT	Statement, 5 1/2×8 1/2 inches.
DMPAPER_TABLOID	Tabloid, 11×17 inches.
DMPAPER_USER	User-defined paper size. The *dmPaperLength* and *dmPaperWidth* members must specify the size.

dmPaperLength   **short**: The length, in tenths of a millimeter, of the paper, in portrait mode. The *dmPaperSize* member must specify the **DMPAPER_USER** value; otherwise, this member is ignored.

dmPaperWidth   **short**: The width, in tenths of a millimeter, of the paper, in portrait mode. The *dmPaperSize* member must specify the **DMPAPER_USER** value; otherwise, this member is ignored.

dmScale   **short**: The factor by which the printed output is to be scaled. The apparent page size is scaled from the physical page size by a factor of *dmScale*÷100.

dmCopies   **short**: The number of copies printed if the device supports multiple-page copies.

dmDefaultSource   **short**: The default paper bin from which the paper is fed. The member can be one of the predefined values in Table 12-5 or a driver-defined value greater than the value of **DMBIN_USER**.

Table 12-5 DEVMODE *dmDefaultSource* values

Value	Meaning
DMBIN_AUTO	Automatic paper bin selection
DMBIN_CASSETTE	Paper cassette
DMBIN_ENVELOPE	Envelope feeder
DMBIN_ENVMANUAL	Manual envelope feeder
DMBIN_LARGECAPACITY	Large capacity paper bin
DMBIN_LARGEFMT	Large paper source
DMBIN_LOWER	Lower paper bin
DMBIN_MANUAL	Manual paper feeder
DMBIN_MIDDLE	Middle paper bin
DMBIN_ONLYONE	Only one paper source
DMBIN_SMALLFMT	Small paper source
DMBIN_TRACTOR	Tractor feeder
DMBIN_UPPER	Upper paper bin

dmPrintQuality   `short`: The printer resolution. There are four predefined device-independent values in Table 12-6. If a positive value is given, it specifies the number of dots per inch (DPI) and is, therefore, device-dependent. This member controls the graphics resolution only. Text is not affected by this setting, unless the text is printed as graphics.

Table 12-6 DEVMODE *dmPrintQuality* values

Value	Meaning
DMRES_HIGH	High resolution
DMRES_MEDIUM	Medium resolution
DMRES_LOW	Low resolution
DMRES_DRAFT	Draft print resolution

dmColor   `short`: Determines whether to use color or monochrome on color printers. Possible values are `DMCOLOR_COLOR` or `DMCOLOR_MONOCHROME`.

dmDuplex   `short`: Set to one of the values in Table 12-7 to specify which type of duplex or double-sided printer to use for printers capable of duplex printing.

Table 12-7 DEVMODE *dmDuplex* values

Value	Meaning
DMDUP_SIMPLEX	No duplexing
DMDUP_HORIZONTAL	Horizontal (long edge) duplexing
DMDUP_VERTICAL	Vertical (short edge) duplexing

dmYResolution   `short`: The y resolution, in dots per inch, of the printer. If the printer initializes this member, the *dmPrintQuality* member specifies the x resolution, in dots per inch, of the printer.

dmTTOption   `short`: Specifies how TrueType fonts should be printed. Set to one of the values in Table 12-8.

Table 12-8 DEVMODE *dmTTOption* values

Value	Meaning
DMTT_BITMAP	Prints TrueType fonts as graphics. This value is the default action for dot-matrix printers.
DMTT_DOWNLOAD	Downloads TrueType fonts as soft fonts. This value is the default action for Hewlett-Packard printers that use Printer Control Language (PCL).

Value	Meaning
DMTT_DOWNLOAD_OUTLINE	Downloads TrueType fonts as outline soft fonts.
DMTT_SUBDEV	Substitutes device fonts for TrueType fonts. This value is the default action for PostScript printers.

dmCollate	short: Set to DMCOLLATE_TRUE to use collation when printing multiple copies. Use the DMCOLLATE_FALSE if collation is not desired. Using DMCOLLATE_FALSE provides faster, more efficient output on printers that support multiple copies, since the data is sent to a page printer just once, no matter how many copies are required. The printer is simply told to print the page again.
dmFormName	TCHAR[CCHFORMNAME]: The name of the form to use (for example, "Letter" or "Legal"). This member is not supported in Windows 95.
dmLogPixels	WORD: The number of pixels per logical inch.
dmBitsPerPel	USHORT: The color resolution, in bits per pixel, of the display device (for example, 4 bits for 16 colors, 8 bits for 256 colors, or 16 bits for 65,536 colors). This member is not supported in Windows 95.
dmPelsWidth	DWORD: The width, in pixels, of the visible device surface. This member is not supported in Windows 95.
dmPelsHeight	DWORD: The height, in pixels, of the visible device surface. This member is not supported in Windows 95.
dmDisplayFlags	DWORD: The device's display mode. This can be one of the values in Table 12-9. This member is not supported in Windows 95.

Table 12-9 DEVMODE *dmDisplayFlags* values

Value	Meaning
DM_GRAYSCALE	Display is a noncolor device. If this value is not specified, color is assumed.
DM_INTERLACED	Display mode is interlaced. If this value is not specified, noninterlaced is assumed.

dmDisplayFrequency	DWORD: The frequency, in hertz (cycles per second), of the display device in a particular mode. This member is not supported in Windows 95.
dmICMMethod	WORD: For a non-ICM application, this member determines if ICM is enabled or disabled. For ICM applications, Windows examines this member to determine how to handle ICM support. This member can be one of the predefined values in Table 12-10, or a driver-defined value greater than the value of DMICMMETHOD_USER. The printer driver must provide a user interface for setting this member. Most printer drivers support only the DCMICMMETHOD_SYSTEM or DCMICMMETHOD_NONE value. Drivers for PostScript printers support all values.

Table 12-10 DEVMODE *dmICMMethod* values

Value	Meaning
DMICMMETHOD_DEVICE	ICM handled by the destination device.
DMICMMETHOD_DRIVER	ICM is handled by the device driver.
DMICMMETHOD_NONE	ICM is disabled.
DMICMMETHOD_SYSTEM	ICM is handled by Windows.

dmICMIntent   WORD: Specifies which of the three possible color-matching methods, or intents, should be used by default. This member is primarily for non-ICM applications. ICM applications can establish intents by using the ICM functions. This member can be one of the predefined values in Table 12-11, or a driver-defined value greater than the value of DMICM_USER. This member is ignored for Windows NT.

Table 12-11 DEVMODE *dmICMIntent* values

Value	Meaning
DMICM_COLORMETRIC	Color matching should optimize to match the exact color requested. This value is most appropriate for use with business logos or other images when an exact color match is desired.
DMICM_CONTRAST	Color matching should optimize for color contrast. This value is the most appropriate choice for scanned or photographic images when dithering is desired.
DMICM_SATURATE	Color matching should optimize for color saturation. This value is the most appropriate choice for business graphs when dithering is not desired.

dmMediaType   WORD: The type of media being printed on. The member can be one of the predefined values in Table 12-12, or a driver-defined value greater than the value of DMMEDIA_USER.

Table 12-12 DEVMODE *dmMediaType* values

Value	Meaning
DMMEDIA_STANDARD	Plain paper
DMMEDIA_GLOSSY	Glossy paper
DMMEDIA_TRANSPARENCY	Transparent film

dmDitherType   WORD: Specifies how dithering is to be done. The member can be one of the predefined values in Table 12-13, or a driver-defined value greater than the value of DMDITHER_USER.

The Graphics Device Interface

Table 12-13 DEVMODE *dmDitherType* values

Value	Meaning
DMDITHER_NONE	No dithering.
DMDITHER_COARSE	Dithering with a coarse brush.
DMDITHER_FINE	Dithering with a fine brush.
DMDITHER_LINEART	Line art dithering; a special dithering method that produces well-defined borders between black, white, and grayscalings. It is not suitable for images that include continuous graduations in intensity and hue, such as scanned photographs.
DMDITHER_GRAYSCALE	Device does grayscaling.

dmReserved1	DWORD: Not used; must be 0.
dmReserved2	DWORD: Not used; must be 0.
Example	This example writes a single line of text to the printer when the user selects the Test! menu item. **CreateDC** creates the device context for the printer. The printer name is "HP DeskJet 550C".

```
LRESULT CALLBACK WndProc( HWND hWnd, UINT uMsg, WPARAM wParam, LPARAM lParam )
{
    switch( uMsg )
    {
        case WM_COMMAND :
                switch( LOWORD( wParam ) )
                {
                    case IDM_TEST :
                        {
                            HDC     hDC;
                            DOCINFO di;

                            // Create a DC for the printer.
                            //............................
                            hDC = CreateDC( "WINSPOOL", "HP DeskJet 550C",
                                        NULL, NULL );

                            memset( &di, 0, sizeof( DOCINFO ) );
                            di.cbSize      = sizeof( DOCINFO );
                            di.lpszDocName = "Sample Document";

                            // Print a string to the printer.
                            //..............................
                            if ( StartDoc( hDC, &di ) > 0 )
                            {
                                StartPage( hDC );
                                TextOut( hDC, 10, 10,
                                        "This output is to the printer.", 30 );
                                EndPage( hDC );
                                EndDoc( hDC );
                            }

                            DeleteDC( hDC );
                        }
                        break;
```

continued on next page

continued from previous page

.
.
.

CreateFont ■ WINDOWS 95 ■ WINDOWS NT

Description

`CreateFont` creates a logical font with specific characteristics. An application can use this font by selecting it as the font for any device. You generally use `CreateFont` when an application has only one font to create. In many cases, the `CreateFontIndirect` function is easier to use because the font data is supplied in a `LOGFONT` structure.

Syntax

HFONT **CreateFont**(int *nHeight,* int *nWidth,* int *nEscapement,* int *nOrientation,* int *nWeight,* DWORD *dwItalic,* DWORD *dwUnderline,* DWORD *dwStrikeOut,* DWORD *dwCharSet,* DWORD *dwOutputPrecision,* DWORD *dwClipPrecision,* DWORD *dwQuality,* DWORD *dwPitchAndFamily,* LPCTSTR *lpszFace*)

Parameters

nHeight

`int`: The desired height, in logical units, of the requested font's character cell or character. If *nHeight* is greater than zero, it specifies the character cell height. If *nHeight* is less than zero, the absolute value specifies the character height. If set to `0`, the default height is used. To specify a height in points, use the following formula:

nHeight = MulDiv(PointSize, GetDeviceCaps(hDC, LOGPIXELSY), 72)

nWidth

`int`: The average width, in logical units, of characters in the requested font. If set to `0`, the font mapper chooses a closest match value. The closest match value is determined by comparing the absolute values of the difference between the current device's aspect ratio and the digitized aspect ratio of available fonts.

nEscapement

`int`: The angle, in tenths of degrees, between the escapement vector and the x-axis of the device. The escapement vector is parallel to the baseline of a row of text.

nOrientation

`int`: The angle, in tenths of degrees, between each character's baseline and the x-axis of the device. *nEscapement* and *nOrientation* must be the same for Windows 95; they can be different for Windows NT when the graphics mode is set to `GM_ADVANCED`.

nWeight

`int`: The desired weight of the font. If set to `0`, a default weight is used. This parameter can be one of the values shown in Table 12-14.

Table 12-14 CreateFont *nWeight* values

Value	Weight
FW_DONTCARE	0
FW_THIN	100
FW_EXTRALIGHT	200
FW_LIGHT	300
FW_NORMAL	400
FW_MEDIUM	500
FW_SEMIBOLD	600
FW_BOLD	700
FW_EXTRABOLD	800
FW_HEAVY	900

dwItalic   DWORD: Set to **TRUE** for italics.

dwUnderline   DWORD: Set to **TRUE** for underline.

dwStrikeOut   DWORD: Set to **TRUE** for strikeout.

dwCharSet   DWORD: The desired character set. The OEM character set is operating-system dependent. This parameter is important in the font mapping process. To ensure consistent results, specify a specific character set. If a typeface name in the *lpszFace* parameter is specified, make sure that the *dwCharSet* value matches the character set of the typeface specified. The following values are predefined:

ANSI_CHARSET

DEFAULT_CHARSET

SYMBOL_CHARSET

SHIFTJIS_CHARSET

HANGEUL_CHARSET

GB2312_CHARSET

CHINESEBIG5_CHARSET

JOHAB_CHARSET

GREEK_CHARSET

TURKISH_CHARSET

HEBREW_CHARSET

ARABIC_CHARSET

BALTIC_CHARSET

RUSSIAN_CHARSET

THAI_CHARSET

	`EASTEUROPE_CHARSET`
	`OEM_CHARSET`
	`MAC_CHARSET`
dwOutputPrecision	**DWORD**: The desired output precision. The output precision defines how closely the output must match the requested font's height, width, character orientation, escapement, and pitch. Applications can use the **OUT_DEVICE_PRECIS**, **OUT_RASTER_PRECIS**, and **OUT_TT_PRECIS** values to control which font to use when the system contains more than one font with a given name. *dwOutputPrecision* can be one of the following values:

`OUT_DEFAULT_PRECIS`

`OUT_STRING_PRECIS`

`OUT_CHARACTER_PRECIS`

`OUT_STROKE_PRECIS`

`OUT_TT_PRECIS`

`OUT_DEVICE_PRECIS`

`OUT_RASTER_PRECIS`

`OUT_TT_ONLY_PRECIS`

`OUT_OUTLINE_PRECIS`

dwClipPrecision	**DWORD**: The desired clipping precision. The clipping precision defines how to clip characters that are partially outside the clipping region. To use an embedded read-only font, applications must specify **CLIP_EMBEDDED**. *dwClipPrecision* can be one or more of the following values:

`CLIP_DEFAULT_PRECIS`

`CLIP_CHARACTER_PRECIS`

`CLIP_STROKE_PRECIS`

`CLIP_MASK`

`CLIP_LH_ANGLES`

`CLIP_TT_ALWAYS`

`CLIP_EMBEDDED`

dwQuality	**DWORD**: The desired output quality. The output quality determines how closely the GDI attempts to match the logical-font attributes. *dwQuality* can be one of the values shown in Table 12-15.

Table 12-15 CreateFont *dwQuality* values

Value	Meaning
DEFAULT_QUALITY	Appearance of the font does not matter.
DRAFT_QUALITY	Appearance of the font is less important than when the PROOF_QUALITY value is used. For GDI raster fonts, scaling is enabled.
PROOF_QUALITY	Character quality of the font is more important than exact matching of the logical-font attributes. For GDI raster fonts, scaling is disabled and the font closest in size is chosen.

dwPitchAndFamily DWORD: The pitch and family of the font. Use one of the following values to specify the pitch of the font:

DEFAULT_PITCH

FIXED_PITCH

VARIABLE_PITCH

Combine with one of the values in Table 12-16 using the binary OR (|) operator to specify the font family.

Table 12-16 CreateFont *dwPitchAndFamily* values

Value	Meaning
FF_DECORATIVE	Decorative fonts. Old English is an example.
FF_DONTCARE	Don't care or don't know.
FF_MODERN	Fonts with constant stroke width, with or without serifs. Pica, Elite, and Courier New are examples.
FF_ROMAN	Fonts with variable stroke width and with serifs. MS Serif is an example.
FF_SCRIPT	Fonts designed to look like handwriting. Script and Cursive are examples.
FF_SWISS	Fonts with variable stroke width and without serifs. MS Sans Serif is an example.

lpszFace LPCTSTR: A pointer to a null-terminated string, up to 32 characters, that specifies the typeface name of the font. If *lpszFace* is NULL, the GDI uses a default typeface.

Returns HFONT: If successful, the handle of a logical font; otherwise, the return value is NULL.

Include File wingdi.h

See Also CreateFontIndirect, SelectObject, TextOut, AddFontResource, EnumFontFamilies

Example This example, shown in Figure 12-1, creates a Times New Roman font 24 by 16 units in size and uses it to bring some text onto the window's client area when the user selects the Test! menu item.

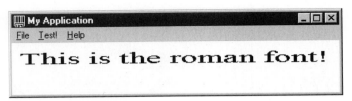

Figure 12-1 CreateFont example

```
LRESULT CALLBACK WndProc( HWND hWnd, UINT uMsg, WPARAM wParam, LPARAM lParam )
{
    switch( uMsg )
    {
        case WM_COMMAND :
                switch( LOWORD( wParam ) )
                {
                    case IDM_TEST :
                        {
                            HDC    hDC;
                            HFONT  hFont;
                            HFONT  hOldFont

                            // Create a Times New Roman font.
                            //..............................
                            hFont = CreateFont( 24, 16, 0, 0, FW_NORMAL,
                                                0, 0, 0, ANSI_CHARSET,
                                                OUT_DEFAULT_PRECIS,
                                                CLIP_DEFAULT_PRECIS,
                                                DEFAULT_QUALITY,
                                                DEFAULT_PITCH | FF_ROMAN,
                                                "Times New Roman" );

                            hDC   = GetDC( hWnd );

                            // Force exact font matching and select
                            // the font into the device context.
                            //.....................................
                            SetMapperFlags( hDC, 1 );
                            hOldFont = SelectObject( hDC, hFont );

                            TextOut( hDC, 10, 10,
                                     "This is the roman font!", 23 );

                            ReleaseDC( hWnd, hDC );
                            SelectObject( hDC, hOldFont );
                            DeleteObject( hFont );
                        }
                        break;
                    case IDM_EXIT :
                        DestroyWindow( hWnd );
                        break;
                }
                break;

        case WM_DESTROY :
                PostQuitMessage(0);
                break;
```

```
       default :
            return( DefWindowProc( hWnd, uMsg, wParam, lParam ) );
    }

    return( OL );
}
```

CreateFontIndirect   ■ WINDOWS 95 ■ WINDOWS NT

Description   CreateFontIndirect creates a logical font that has the characteristics specified in a given **LOGFONT** structure. An application can use this font by selecting it as the font for any device.

Syntax   HFONT **CreateFontIndirect(CONST LOGFONT*** *lplf* **)**

Parameters

lplf   CONST LOGFONT*: A pointer to a **LOGFONT** structure that defines the characteristics of the logical font. The definition of the **LOGFONT** structure is given below.

Returns   HFONT: If successful, the handle of a logical font; otherwise, the return value is **NULL**.

Include File   wingdi.h

See Also   CreateFont, SelectObject, TextOut, AddFontResource, EnumFontFamilies

LOGFONT Definition   The members of this structure correspond directly to the parameters in the **CreateFont** function.

```
typedef struct tagLOGFONT
{
    LONG lfHeight;
    LONG lfWidth;
    LONG lfEscapement;
    LONG lfOrientation;
    LONG lfWeight;
    BYTE lfItalic;
    BYTE lfUnderline;
    BYTE lfStrikeOut;
    BYTE lfCharSet;
    BYTE lfOutPrecision;
    BYTE lfClipPrecision;
    BYTE lfQuality;
    BYTE lfPitchAndFamily;
    CHAR lfFaceName[LF_FACESIZE];
} LOGFONT;
```

Members

lfHeight   LONG: Same as the *nHeight*.

lfWidth   LONG: Same as the *nWidth*.

lfEscapement   LONG: Same as the *nEscapement*.

lfOrientation	LONG: Same as the *nOrientation*.
lfWeight	LONG: Same as the *nWeight*.
lfItalic	BYTE: Same as the *dwItalic*.
lfUnderline	BYTE: Same as the *dwUnderline*.
lfStrikeOut	BYTE: Same as the *dwStrikeOut*.
lfCharSet	BYTE: Same as *dwCharSet*.
lfOutPrecision	BYTE: Same as *dwOutputPrecision*.
lfClipPrecision	BYTE: Same as *dwClipPrecision*.
lfQuality	BYTE: Same as *dwQuality*.
lfPitchAndFamily	BYTE: Same as *dwPitchAndFamily*.
lfFaceName	CHAR[LF_FACESIZE]: Same as *lpszFace*.
Example	See the example for the **EnumFontFamilies** function.

CreateIC ■ WINDOWS 95 ■ WINDOWS NT

Description   **CreateIC** creates an information context for a device to provide a fast way to get information about the device without creating a device context. **CreateIC** is commonly used with **GetDeviceCaps** to retrieve information about a printer or screen device.

Syntax   HDC **CreateIC**(LPCTSTR *lpszDriver,* LPCTSTR *lpszDevice,* LPCTSTR *lpszOutput,* CONST DEVMODE* *lpdvmInit*)

Parameters

lpszDriver   LPCTSTR: A pointer to a null-terminated character string containing the name of the device driver (for example, **"Epson"**, or **"DISPLAY"** for the screen).

lpszDevice   LPCTSTR: A pointer to a null-terminated character string containing the name of the output device, as shown by the Print Manager (for example, **"Epson FX-80"**). It is not the printer model name. This parameter must be used for printers and set to **NULL** for the screen.

lpszOutput   LPCTSTR: This parameter is ignored; it is present to keep the function prototype identical with Windows 3.x.

lpdvmInit   CONST DEVMODE*: A pointer to a **DEVMODE** structure containing device-specific initialization data for the device driver. The **DocumentProperties** function can be used to retrieve this structure filled in for a given device. Set to **NULL** to use default initialization (if any) specified by the user. See the **CreateDC** function for the definition of the **DEVMODE** structure.

Returns   HDC: If successful, the handle of an information context; otherwise, the return value is **NULL**.

Include File

`wingdi.h`

See Also

`DeleteDC, CreateDC, GetDeviceCaps, CreateCompatibleDC`

Example

This example uses **CreateIC** to get an information context for the screen. Using the context, the application finds the number of bits per pixel and the number of color planes for the display. For an SVGA screen, this will show 8 bits and 1 color plane.

```
LRESULT CALLBACK WndProc( HWND hWnd, UINT uMsg, WPARAM wParam, LPARAM lParam )
{
    switch( uMsg )
    {
    case WM_COMMAND :
            switch( LOWORD( wParam ) )
            {
            case IDM_TEST :
                {
                    HDC    hIC;
                    char   szMsg[40];

                    // Retrieve information and display context.
                    //.........................................
                    hIC = CreateIC( "DISPLAY", NULL, NULL, NULL );

                    // Display bits per pixel.
                    //.......................
                    wsprintf( szMsg, "Bits per pixel = %d",
                            GetDeviceCaps( hIC, BITSPIXEL ) );
                    MessageBox ( hWnd, szMsg, "Message", MB-OK );

                    // Display color planes.
                    //.....................
                    wsprintf( szMsg, "Color planes = %d",
                            GetDeviceCaps( hIC, PLANES ) );
                    MessageBox ( hWnd, szMsg, "Message", MB-OK );

                    DeleteDC( hIC );
                }
                break;
            .
            .
            .
```

CreateScalableFontResource ■ WINDOWS 95 ■ WINDOWS NT

Description

Used by applications that install TrueType fonts, **CreateScalableFontResource** creates a font resource file for a scaleable font. Currently only TrueType fonts are supported. An application uses the **CreateScalableFontResource** function to create a font resource file (typically with a `.FOT` file name extension) and then uses the **AddFontResource** function to install the font.

Syntax	BOOL **CreateScalableFontResource**(DWORD *dwHidden,* LPCTSTR *lpszFontRes,* LPCTSTR *lpszFontFile,* LPCTSTR *lpszCurrentPath*)

Parameters

dwHidden   DWORD: If the font has read-only permission and should be hidden from other applications in the system, set to **1**. Otherwise, set to **0**.

lpszFontRes   LPCTSTR: A pointer to a null-terminated string containing the name of the font resource file that this function creates.

lpszFontFile   LPCTSTR: A pointer to a null-terminated string containing the name of the scaleable font file from which to create the font resource file. If this parameter contains the full path, *lpszCurrentPath* should be **NULL** or point to a **NULL** string. If the path is not specified, the TTF file is expected to be in the **SYSTEM** directory of Windows before **AddFontResource** can be used.

lpszCurrentPath   LPCTSTR: A pointer to a null-terminated string containing the path to the scaleable font file.

Returns   BOOL: **TRUE** if successful; otherwise, the return value is **FALSE**.

Include File   wingdi.h

See Also   AddFontResource

Example   See the example for the **AddFontResource** function.

DeleteDC   ■ WINDOWS 95   ■ WINDOWS NT

Description   DeleteDC deletes the given device context (DC). An application must not delete a DC that was retrieved with **GetDC**. Instead, it must use the **ReleaseDC** function.

Syntax   BOOL **DeleteDC**(HDC *hdc*)

Parameters

hdc   HDC: The DC handle to delete.

Returns   BOOL: **TRUE** if successful; otherwise, the return value is **FALSE**.

Include File   wingdi.h

See Also   CreateDC, CreateCompatibleDC, CreateIC, ReleaseDC

Example   See the example for the **CreateCompatibleDC** function.

DPtoLP   ■ WINDOWS 95   ■ WINDOWS NT

Description   DPtoLP converts device coordinates into logical coordinates. The conversion depends on the mapping mode of the device context (DC), the settings of the origins and extents for the window and viewport, and the world transformation.

Syntax   BOOL **DPtoLP**(HDC *hdc,* LPPOINT *lpPoints,* int *nCount*)

Parameters

hdc	**HDC**: The DC handle.
lpPoints	**LPPOINT**: A pointer to an array of **POINT** structures. The x and y coordinates contained in each **POINT** structure will be converted.
nCount	**int**: The number of points in the array.
Returns	**BOOL**: **TRUE** if successful; otherwise, the return value is **FALSE**.
Include File	**wingdi.h**
See Also	**SetMapMode, LPtoDP**
Example	See the example for the **SetMapMode** function.

EnumDisplaySettings ■ WINDOWS 95 ■ WINDOWS NT

Description	**EnumDisplaySettings** obtains information about one of the display device's graphics modes. Use this function successively to obtain information for all of a display device's graphics modes. To obtain information for all of a display device's graphics modes, set *iModeNum* to **0** for the first call, and increment *iModeNum* by one for each subsequent call. Continue calling the function until the return value is **FALSE**.
	When you call **EnumDisplaySettings** with *iModeNum* set to **0**, the operating system initializes and caches information about the display device. When you call **EnumDisplaySettings** with *iModeNum* set to a nonzero value, the function returns the information that was cached with the last function call.
Syntax	**BOOL EnumDisplaySettings(** LPCTSTR *lpszDeviceName,* DWORD *iModeNum,* LPDEVMODE *lpDevMode* **)**

Parameters

lpszDeviceName	**LPCTSTR**: A pointer to a null-terminated string that specifies the display device whose graphics mode the function will obtain information about. This parameter can be **NULL**, which specifies the current display device on the computer the calling thread is running. The string must be in the form "\\.\DisplayX", where *X* can have the values **1**, **2**, or **3**. On Windows 95 this parameter must be **NULL**.
iModeNum	**DWORD**: The index value that specifies the graphics mode for which information is obtained. Graphics mode indexes start at zero.
lpDevMode	**LPDEVMODE**: A pointer to a **DEVMODE** structure into which the function stores information about the specified graphics mode. For more information on which members of the **DEVMODE** structure that are filled, see the **ChangeDisplaySettings** function. See the definition of the **DEVMODE** structure under the **CreateDC** function earlier in this chapter.
Returns	**BOOL**: If the function is successful, the return value is **TRUE**; otherwise, **FALSE** is returned.

Include File	winuser.h
See Also	ChangeDisplaySettings
Example	This example uses the **EnumDisplaySettings** function to determine which display settings are supported by the current hardware. It adds each of these settings to a list box for the user to view. If the user selects one of the settings and chooses the Test! menu item, the display settings are changed for a duration of five seconds and the original setting is then restored.

```
LRESULT CALLBACK WndProc( HWND hWnd, UINT uMsg, WPARAM wParam, LPARAM lParam )
{
static HWND hList;

    switch( uMsg )
    {
        case WM_CREATE  :
                {
                    DEVMODE dm;
                    DWORD   dwMode = 0;
                    char    szSetting[100];

                    // Create a list box and fill it with the
                    // available display modes.
                    //.....................................
                    hList = CreateWindow( "LISTBOX", "",
                                    WS_CHILD | WS_VISIBLE | LBS_STANDARD |
                                    LBS_NOINTEGRALHEIGHT ,
                                    0, 0, 200, 200, hWnd, (HMENU)101, hInst,
                                    NULL );

                    while( EnumDisplaySettings( NULL, dwMode, &dm ) )
                    {
                        if ( dm.dmDisplayFrequency == 0 || dm.dmDisplayFrequency == 1 )
                            wsprintf( szSetting, "%d-Bit Color, %d x %d, Default Refresh Rate",
                                    dm.dmBitsPerPel, dm.dmPelsWidth, dm.dmPelsHeight );
                        else
                            wsprintf( szSetting, "%d-Bit Color, %d x %d, %dHz",
                                    dm.dmBitsPerPel, dm.dmPelsWidth, dm.dmPelsHeight,
                                    dm.dmDisplayFrequency );

                        SendMessage( hList, LB_INSERTSTRING,
                                    (WPARAM)dwMode, (LPARAM)szSetting );
                        dwMode++;

                    }
                    SendMessage( hList, LB_SETCURSEL, 0, 0 );
                }
                break;

        case WM_COMMAND :
                switch( LOWORD( wParam ) )
                {
                    case IDM_TEST :
                        {
                            DEVMODE dm;
                            int     nIdx;
```

```
                    nIdx = SendMessage( hList, LB_GETCURSEL, 0, 0 );

                    if ( nIdx > LB_ERR )
                    {
                        EnumDisplaySettings( NULL, nIdx, &dm );
                        MessageBox( hWnd, "This setting will be in effect for 5 ⇐
seconds.",
                                    "Display Settings", MB_OK | MB_ICONINFORMATION );
                        ChangeDisplaySettings( &dm, 0 );
                        Sleep( 5000 );
                        ChangeDisplaySettings( NULL, 0 );
                    }
                }
                break;
```

.
.
.

EnumFontFamilies   ■ WINDOWS 95 ■ WINDOWS NT

Description	**EnumFontFamilies** enumerates the fonts in a font family or one font from each font family available for a device context. It is recommended to use the **EnumFontFamiliesEx** function rather than this function.
Syntax	int **EnumFontFamilies**(HDC *hdc*, LPCTSTR *lpszFamily*, FONTENUMPROC *lpEnumFontFamProc*, LPARAM *lParam*)
Parameters	
hdc	HDC: The handle of the device context.
lpszFamily	LPCTSTR: A pointer to a null-terminated string containing the family name of the desired fonts. If set to **NULL**, **EnumFontFamilies** randomly selects and enumerates one font of each available type family.
lpEnumFontFamProc	FONTENUMPROC: The address of the application-defined callback function. The format of the callback function is defined below.
lParam	LPARAM: A 32-bit application-defined value to be passed to the callback function along with the font information.
Returns	**int**: The last value returned by the callback function.
Include File	wingdi.h
See Also	EnumFontFamiliesEx
Callback Syntax	int CALLBACK **EnumFontFamProc**(ENUMLOGFONT* *lpelf*, NEWTEXTMETRIC* *lpntm*, int *nFontType*, LPARAM *lParam*)
Callback Parameters	
lpelf	ENUMLOGFONT*: A pointer to an **ENUMLOGFONT** structure that contains information about the logical attributes of the font. This structure is defined below.

lpntm	**NEWTEXTMETRIC***: If the font is a TrueType font, a pointer to a **NEWTEXT-METRIC** structure that contains information about the physical attributes of the font; otherwise, a pointer to a **TEXTMETRIC** structure. These structures are defined below.
nFontType	**int**: The type of the font. This parameter can be a combination of **DEVICE_FONTTYPE**, **RASTER_FONTTYPE**, and **TRUETYPE_FONTTYPE**. Use the binary AND (**&**) operator to determine which types are set.
lParam	**LPARAM**: The application-defined data passed as the *lParam* of the **EnumFontFamilies** function.

ENUMLOGFONT Definition

```
typedef struct tagENUMLOGFONT
{
    LOGFONT elfLogFont;
    BCHAR   elfFullName[LF_FULLFACESIZE];
    BCHAR   elfStyle[LF_FACESIZE];
} ENUMLOGFONT;
```

Members

elfLogFont	**LOGFONT**: See the **CreateFontIndirect** function for information.
elfFullName	**BCHAR**: A null-terminated string containing the full font name.
elfStyle	**BCHAR**: A null-terminated string containing the font style. For example "Bold", "Italic", etc.

TEXTMETRIC Definition

```
typedef struct tagTEXTMETRIC
{
    LONG tmHeight;
    LONG tmAscent;
    LONG tmDescent;
    LONG tmInternalLeading;
    LONG tmExternalLeading;
    LONG tmAveCharWidth;
    LONG tmMaxCharWidth;
    LONG tmWeight;
    LONG tmOverhang;
    LONG tmDigitizedAspectX;
    LONG tmDigitizedAspectY;
    BYTE tmFirstChar;
    BYTE tmLastChar;
    BYTE tmDefaultChar;
    BYTE tmBreakChar;
    BYTE tmItalic;
    BYTE tmUnderlined;
    BYTE tmStruckOut;
    BYTE tmPitchAndFamily;
    BYTE tmCharSet;
} TEXTMETRIC;
```

Members

tmHeight	LONG: The height (ascent + descent) of characters.
tmAscent	LONG: The ascent (units above the baseline) of characters.
tmDescent	LONG: The descent (units below the baseline) of characters.
tmInternalLeading	LONG: The amount of leading (space between lines) inside the bounds set by the *tmHeight* member. The designer may set this member to 0.
tmExternalLeading	LONG: The amount of extra leading (space between lines) that the application adds between rows. This area contains no marks and is not altered by text output calls in either OPAQUE or TRANSPARENT mode. The designer may set this member to 0.
tmAveCharWidth	LONG: The average width of characters in the font not including overhang required for bold or italic characters (usually defined as the width of the letter x).
tmMaxCharWidth	LONG: The width of the widest character in the font.
tmWeight	LONG: The weight of the font.
tmOverhang	LONG: The extra width per string that may be added to some synthesized fonts. When synthesizing some attributes, such as bold or italic, the GDI or a device may have to add width to a string on both a per-character and per-string basis. The *tmOverhang* member allows the application to determine how much of the character width is the actual character width and how much is per-string extra width.
tmDigitizedAspectX	LONG: The horizontal aspect of the device for which the font was designed.
tmDigitizedAspectY	LONG: The vertical aspect of the device for which the font was designed.
tmFirstChar	BYTE: The value of the first character defined in the font.
tmLastChar	BYTE: The value of the last character defined in the font.
tmDefaultChar	BYTE: The value of the character to be substituted for characters not in the font.
tmBreakChar	BYTE: The value of the character that will be used to define word breaks for text justification.
tmItalic	BYTE: Set to nonzero if an italic font.
tmUnderlined	BYTE: Set to nonzero if an underlined font.
tmStruckOut	BYTE: Set to nonzero if a strikeout font.

tmPitchAndFamily	**BYTE**: Information about the pitch, the technology, and the family of a physical font. The four low-order bits of this member specify information about the pitch and the technology of the font. Table 12-17 defines the values for each bit. The four high-order bits of *tmPitchAndFamily* designate the font's family. An application can use 0xF0 and the binary AND (**&**) operator to obtain the font family. Font families are defined in Table 12-16.

Table 12-17 TEXTMETRIC *tmPitchAndFamily* values

Value	Meaning
TMPF_DEVICE	If set, the font is a device font.
TMPF_FIXED_PITCH	If this bit is set, the font is a variable pitch font; otherwise, it is a fixed-pitch font. Note the meanings are the opposite of what the name implies.
TMPF_TRUETYPE	If set, the font is a TrueType font.
TMPF_VECTOR	If set, the font is a vector font.

tmCharSet	**BYTE**: The character set of the font. The following character sets are predefined:

ANSI_CHARSET

DEFAULT_CHARSET

SYMBOL_CHARSET

SHIFTJIS_CHARSET

HANGEUL_CHARSET

GB2312_CHARSET

CHINESEBIG5_CHARSET

JOHAB_CHARSET

GREEK_CHARSET

TURKISH_CHARSET

HEBREW_CHARSET

ARABIC_CHARSET

BALTIC_CHARSET

RUSSIAN_CHARSET

THAI_CHARSET

EASTEUROPE_CHARSET

OEM_CHARSET

MAC_CHARSET

NEWTEXTMETRIC **Definition**

```
typedef struct tagNEWTEXTMETRIC
{
    // Same as TEXTMETRIC structure
        .
        .
        .
    DWORD ntmFlags;
    UINT  ntmSizeEM;
    UINT  ntmCellHeight;
    UINT  ntmAvgWidth;
} NEWTEXTMETRIC;
```

Members

ntmFlags   DWORD: A bit mask indicating whether the font is italic, underscored, out-lined, bold, etc. Table 12-18 shows the meanings for each bit.

Table 12-18 NEWTEXTMETRIC *ntmFlags* values

Bit	Meaning
0	Italic
1	Underscore
2	Negative
3	Outline
4	Strikeout
5	Bold

ntmSizeEM   UINT: The size of the em square for the font in notional units (the units for which the font was designed).

ntmCellHeight   UINT: The height, in notional units, of the font to be compared with the value of the *ntmSizeEM* member.

ntmAvgWidth   UINT: The average width of characters in the font, in notional units to be compared with the value of the *ntmSizeEM* member.

Example   This example, shown in Figure 12-2, uses **EnumFontFamilies** to fill a list box with the available TrueType font names. When the user selects the Test! menu item, the application uses **EnumFontFamilies** to retrieve a **LOGFONT** structure for the font. It then creates the font using the **CreateFontIndirect** function and displays sample output in the new font.

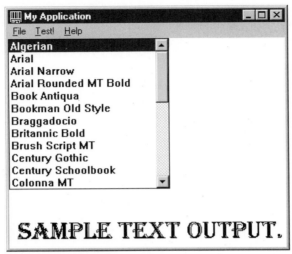

Figure 12-2 EnumFontFamilies example

```
LRESULT CALLBACK WndProc( HWND hWnd, UINT uMsg, WPARAM wParam, LPARAM lParam )
{
static HWND hList;

    switch( uMsg )
    {
    case WM_CREATE  :
            {
                HDC hDC;

                // Create a list box and fill it with the
                // available TrueType font names.
                //.........................................
                hList = CreateWindow( "LISTBOX", "",
                                WS_CHILD | WS_VISIBLE | LBS_STANDARD,
                                0, 0, 200, 200, hWnd, (HMENU)101, hInst,
                                NULL );

                hDC = GetDC( hWnd );
                EnumFontFamilies( hDC, NULL, EnumFontProc,(LPARAM)hList );
                ReleaseDC( hWnd, hDC );

                SendMessage( hList, LB_SETCURSEL, 0, 0 );
            }
            break;


    case WM_COMMAND :
            switch( LOWORD( wParam ) )
            {
                case IDM_TEST :
                        {
                            HDC      hDC;
                            LOGFONT  lf;
```

```
                    HFONT    hFont;
                    char     szFaceName[128];
                    int      nSel;
                    HFONT hOldFont;

                    // Retrieve the currently selected font name.
                    //...........................................
                    nSel = SendMessage( hList, LB_GETCURSEL, 0, 0 );
                    SendMessage( hList, LB_GETTEXT, nSel,
                                 (LPARAM)szFaceName );

                    // Repaint the client area of the window.
                    //.......................................
                    InvalidateRect( hWnd, NULL, TRUE );
                    UpdateWindow( hWnd );

                    // Find the selected font and retrieve the
                    // LOGFONT structure for the font.
                    //.........................................
                    hDC = GetDC( hWnd );
                    EnumFontFamilies( hDC, szFaceName,
                                      FindFontProc,(LPARAM) &lf );

                    // Create the font and output a sample text string.
                    //.................................................
                    hFont = CreateFontIndirect( &lf );
                    hOldFont = SelectObject( hDC, hFont );

                    TextOut( hDC, 10, 230, "Sample Text Output.", 19 );
                    SelectObject ( hDC, hOldFont );
                    ReleaseDC( hWnd, hDC );
                    DeleteObject( hFont );
                }
                break;
              .
              .
              .


int CALLBACK EnumFontProc( ENUMLOGFONT* lpelf, NEWTEXTMETRIC* lpntm,
                           int nFontType, LPARAM lParam )
{

    // Load only TrueType fonts into the list box.
    //...........................................
    if ( nFontType & TRUETYPE_FONTTYPE )
    {
        if ( IsWindow( (HWND)lParam ) )
        {
            SendMessage( (HWND)lParam, LB_ADDSTRING, 0,
                         (LPARAM)lpelf->elfLogFont.lfFaceName );
        }
    }

    return( TRUE );
}


int CALLBACK FindFontProc( ENUMLOGFONT* lpelf, NEWTEXTMETRIC* lpntm,
```

continued on next page

continued from previous page

```
                              int nFontType, LPARAM lParam )
{
   // Find the regular font.
   //......................
   if ( strcmp( lpelf->elfStyle, "Regular" ) == 0 )
      memcpy( (LOGFONT*)lParam, &lpelf->elfLogFont, sizeof( LOGFONT ) );

   return( TRUE );
}
```

EnumFontFamiliesEx   ■ WINDOWS 95 ■ WINDOWS NT

Description	`EnumFontFamiliesEx` enumerates all fonts in the system that match the font characteristics specified by a given **LOGFONT** structure. This function enumerates fonts based on typeface name, character set, or both. This function, rather than **EnumFontFamilies**, is recommended for Win32-based applications.
Syntax	int **EnumFontFamiliesEx**(HDC *hDC*, LPLOGFONT *lpLogFont*, FONTENUMPROC *lpEnumFontFamExProc*, LPARAM *lParam*, DWORD *dwFlags*)
Parameters	
hDC	**HDC**: The device context for which to enumerate available fonts.
lpLogFont	**LPLOGFONT**: A pointer to a **LOGFONT** structure that contains information about the fonts to enumerate. The members listed in Table 12-19 are used to match fonts. See the definition of the **LOGFONT** structure under the **CreateFontIndirect** function earlier in this chapter.

Table 12-19 LOGFONT members to use with EnumFontFamiliesEx

Member	Description
lfCharSet	If set to DEFAULT_CHARSET, the function enumerates all fonts in all character sets. If set to a valid character set value, the function enumerates only fonts in the specified character set.
lfFaceName	If set to an empty string, the function enumerates one font in each available typeface name. If set to a valid typeface name, the function enumerates all fonts with the specified name.
lfPitchAndFamily	Must be set to 0 for all language versions of the operating system except Hebrew and Arabic. For these languages, set this member to MONO_FONT to enumerate only fonts that provide all code-page characters within the font.

lpEnumFontFamExProc	**FONTENUMPROC**: A pointer to the application-defined callback function. See the definition of the callback function below.
lParam	**LPARAM**: Specifies a 32-bit application-defined value that is passed to the callback function during font enumeration.
dwFlags	**DWORD**: Reserved; must be **0**.

Returns	int: If the function is successful, the return value is the last value returned by the callback function.

Include File   `wingdi.h`

See Also   `EnumFontFamilies`

Callback Syntax   `int CALLBACK EnumFontFamExProc( ENUMLOGFONTEX* lpelfe, NEWTEXTMETRICEX* lpntme, int FontType, LPARAM lParam )`

Callback Parameters

lpelfe   `ENUMLOGFONTEX*`: A pointer to an `ENUMLOGFONTEX` structure that contains information about the logical attributes of the font. See the definition of the `ENUMLOGFONTEX` structure below.

lpntme   `NEWTEXTMETRICEX*`: A pointer to a `NEWTEXTMETRICEX` structure that contains information about the physical attributes of a font. In Windows 95, the `NEWTEXTMETRICEX` structure is not implemented; use `NEWTEXTMETRIC` instead. See the definition of the `NEWTEXTMETRICEX` structure below. See the definition of the `NEWTEXTMETRIC` structure under the `EnumFontFamilies` function earlier in this chapter.

FontType   `int`: The type of the font. This parameter can be a combination of `DEVICE_FONTTYPE`, `RASTER_FONTTYPE`, and `TRUETYPE_FONTTYPE`. Use the binary AND (&) operator to determine which types are set.

lParam   `LPARAM`: The application-defined data passed to the `EnumFontFamiliesEx` function.

Callback Returns   `int`: The return value must be a nonzero value to continue enumeration; to stop enumeration, the value must be `0`.

ENUMLOGFONTEX Definition

```
typedef struct tagENUMLOGFONTEX
{
    LOGFONT  elfLogFont;
    BCHAR    elfFullName[LF_FULLFACESIZE];
    BCHAR    elfStyle[LF_FACESIZE];
    BCHAR    elfScript[LF_FACESIZE];
} ENUMLOGFONTEX;
```

Members

elfLogFont   `LOGFONT`: See the `CreateFontIndirect` function for information.

elfFullName   `BCHAR`: A null-terminated string containing the full font name.

elfStyle   `BCHAR`: A null-terminated string containing the font style. For example "Bold", "Italic", etc.

elfScript   `BCHAR`: A null-terminated string containing the script of the font. For example, "Cyrillic".

NEWTEXTMETRICEX Definition

```
typedef struct tagNEWTEXTMETRICEX
{
    NEWTEXTMETRIC  ntmentm;
```

continued on next page

continued from previous page

```
                    FONTSIGNATURE  ntmeFontSignature;
               } NEWTEXTMETRICEX;
```

Members

ntmentm 　　　**NEWTEXTMETRIC**: See the definition under the **EnumFontFamilies** function.

ntmeFontSignature 　**FONTSIGNATURE**: See the definition below.

FONTSIGNATURE Definition

```
typedef struct tagFONTSIGNATURE
{
    DWORD fsUsb[4];
    DWORD fsCsb[2];
}
```

Members

fsUsb 　　**DWORD[4]**: A 128-bit Unicode subset bitfield (USB) identifying up to 126 Unicode subranges. Each bit, except the two most significant bits, represents a single subrange. The most significant bit is always **1** and identifies the bitfield as a font signature; the second most significant bit is reserved and must be **0**. Unicode subranges are numbered in accordance with the ISO 10646 standard.

fsCsb 　　**DWORD[2]**: A 64-bit, code-page bitfield (CPB) that identifies a specific character set or code-page. Windows code-pages are in the lower 32-bits of this bitfield. The high 32-bits are used for non-Windows code-pages.

Example

This example is the same as the one for the **EnumFontFamilies** function, except that the **EnumFontFamiliesEx** function is used to enumerate the available fonts. Only the initialization code is shown in this example to show how to initialize the **LOGFONT** structure and use it with the function.

```
LRESULT CALLBACK WndProc( HWND hWnd, UINT uMsg, WPARAM wParam, LPARAM lParam )
{
static HWND hList;

    switch( uMsg )
    {
        case WM_CREATE  :
                {
                    HDC     hDC;
                    LOGFONT lf;

                    // Create a list box and fill it with the
                    // available TrueType font names.
                    //.....................................
                    hList = CreateWindow( "LISTBOX", "",
                                WS_CHILD | WS_VISIBLE | LBS_STANDARD,
                                0, 0, 200, 200, hWnd, (HMENU)101, hInst,
                                NULL );
```

```
        hDC = GetDC( hWnd );
        lf.lfCharSet = DEFAULT_CHARSET;
        lf.lfFaceName[0] = '\0';
        lf.lfPitchAndFamily = 0;
        EnumFontFamiliesEx( hDC, &lf, EnumFontProcEx,(LPARAM)hList, 0 );
        ReleaseDC( hWnd, hDC );

        SendMessage( hList, LB_SETCURSEL, 0, 0 );
    }
    break;
```

GetDC ■ Windows 95 ■ Windows NT

Description	GetDC retrieves the handle of a display device context (DC) for the client area of a window. You can use the display DC in subsequent GDI functions to draw in the client area of the window. Depending on the class style of the window, GetDC retrieves a common, class, or private DC. Default attributes are assigned to common DCs each time they are retrieved. Attributes for class and private DCs are left unchanged. When the application finishes using the DC, use ReleaseDC to free the device context. This is not necessary for class or private device contexts.
Syntax	HDC GetDC(HWND *hwnd*)
Parameters	
hwnd	HWND: The window whose DC is to be retrieved.
Returns	HDC: If successful, the DC for the given window's client area; otherwise, the return value is NULL.
Include File	wingdi.h
See Also	BeginPaint, ReleaseDC, RegisterClass
Example	See the example for the EnumFontFamilies function.

GetDCEx ■ Windows 95 ■ Windows NT

Description	GetDCEx is the same as the GetDC function, except the application has more control over how and whether clipping occurs in the client area.
Syntax	HDC GetDCEx(HWND *hwnd*, HRGN *hrgnClip*, DWORD *flags*)
Parameters	
hwnd	HWND: The window whose DC is to be retrieved.
hrgnClip	HRGN: A clipping region that may be combined with the visible region of the client window.
flags	DWORD: Determines how the DC is created. This parameter can be some combination of the values listed in Table 12-20.

Table 12-20 `GetDCEx` *flags* values

Value	Meaning
DCX_CACHE	Override the `CS_OWNDC` and `CS_CLASSDC` by returning a DC from the cache.
DCX_CLIPCHILDREN	Exclude the visible regions of all child windows below the window identified by *hwnd*.
DCX_CLIPSIBLINGS	Exclude the visible regions of all sibling windows above the window identified by *hwnd*.
DCX_DEFAULTCLIP	Return a DC using the default clipping flags specified by `WS_CLIPCHILDREN`, `WS_CLIPSIBLINGS`, and `CS_PARENTDC`.
DCX_EXCLUDERGN	Exclude the clipping region identified by *hrgnClip* from the visible region of the returned DC.
DCX_EXCLUDEUPDATE	Exclude the update region from the visible region of the returned DC.
DCX_INTERSECTRGN	The clipping region identified by *hrgnClip* is intersected with the visible region of the returned DC.
DCX_INTERSECTUPDATE	The update region is intersected with the visible region of the returned DC.
DCX_LOCKWINDOWUPDATE	Allow drawing even if there is a `LockWindowUpdate` call in effect that would otherwise exclude this window. Used for drawing during tracking.
DCX_NORECOMPUTE	If an exact match in the cache is not found, return `NULL` rather than creating a new DC. When used with `DCX_NORESETATTRS`, applications can determine whether they must reselect any special attributes.
DCX_NORESETATTRS	Do not reset the attributes of this DC to the default attributes when this DC is released.
DCX_PARENTCLIP	Use the visible region of the parent window. The DC origin is set to the upper-left corner of the window identified by *hwnd*.
DCX_USESTYLE	The function computes the value of the *flags* parameter based on the class styles of the window identified by *hwnd*.
DCX_VALIDATE	When used with `DCX_INTERSECTUPDATE`, the DC is completely validated.
DCX_WINDOW	Return a DC corresponding to the window rectangle rather than the client rectangle.

Returns   `HDC`: If successful, the handle of the DC for the given window; otherwise, `NULL` is returned, indicating the *hwnd* parameter is invalid.

Include File   `wingdi.h`

See Also   `GetDC`, `ReleaseDC`

Example   In this example, shown in Figure 12-3, when the user selects the Test! menu item, the application uses the **GetDCEx** function to get a device context for the client area of the window, excluding a region. A gray rectangle is then painted on the client area, showing the excluded region.

Figure 12-3 GetDCEx example

```
LRESULT CALLBACK WndProc( HWND hWnd, UINT uMsg, WPARAM wParam, LPARAM lParam )
{
    switch( uMsg )
    {
    case WM_COMMAND :
            switch( LOWORD( wParam ) )
            {
                case IDM_TEST :
                    {
                        HDC   hDC;
                        RECT  rect;
                        POINT pt;
                        HRGN  hrgn;

                        // Find the screen
                        // coordinates of the DC origin.
                        //...............................
                        hDC = GetDC( hWnd );
                        GetDCOrgEx( hDC, &pt );
                        ReleaseDC( hWnd, hDC );

                        // Create a region on the client area
                        // to exclude from painting.
                        //....................................
                        hrgn = CreateRectRgn( pt.x+20,  pt.y+20,
                                              pt.x+200, pt.y+200 );

                        // Get a DC for the window
                        // excluding the region.
                        //........................
                        hDC = GetDCEx( hWnd, hrgn,
                                       DCX_EXCLUDERGN | DCX_CACHE );

                        // Fill a rectangle on
                        // the client area.
```

continued on next page

continued from previous page

```
//...................
rect.top    = 0;
rect.left   = 0;
rect.right  = 220;
rect.bottom = 220;

FillRect( hDC, &rect,
          GetStockObject( GRAY_BRUSH ) );

ReleaseDC( hWnd, hDC );
}
break;
```

.
.
.

GetDCOrgEx   ■ WINDOWS 95 ■ WINDOWS NT

Description	GetDCOrgEx obtains the final translation origin for a given device context (DC). The final translation origin is the offset that Windows uses to translate device coordinates into client coordinates.
Syntax	BOOL **GetDCOrgEx**(HDC *hdc,* LPPOINT *lpPoint*)
Parameters	
hdc	HDC: The DC for which to retrieve the final translation origin.
lpPoint	LPPOINT: A pointer to a **POINT** structure that will receive the final translation origin, in device coordinates.
Returns	BOOL: **TRUE** if successful; otherwise, the return value is **FALSE**.
Include File	wingdi.h
See Also	CreateIC
Example	See the example for the **GetDCEx** function.

GetDeviceCaps   ■ WINDOWS 95 ■ WINDOWS NT

Description	GetDeviceCaps retrieves device-specific information about a given device, such as if a printer can display graphics, the resolution of the screen, etc.
Syntax	int **GetDeviceCaps**(HDC *hdc,* int *nIndex*)
Parameters	
hdc	HDC: The handle of the device context (DC).
nIndex	int: The information to return. This parameter can be one of the values shown in Table 12-21.

Table 12-21 GetDeviceCaps *nIndex* values

Index	Meaning
ASPECTX	Relative width of a device pixel used for line drawing.
ASPECTXY	Diagonal width of the device pixel used for line drawing.
ASPECTY	Relative height of a device pixel used for line drawing.
BITSPIXEL	Number of adjacent color bits for each pixel.
BLTALIGNMENT	(Windows NT only) Preferred horizontal drawing alignment, expressed as a multiple of pixels. For best drawing performance, windows should be horizontally aligned to a multiple of this value. A value of 0 indicates that the device is accelerated, and any alignment may be used.
CLIPCAPS	Flag that indicates the clipping capabilities of the device. The following return values are valid:

Capability	Meaning
CP_NONE	Device cannot clip output.
CP_RECTANGLE	Device can clip output to a rectangle.
CP_REGION32	Device can clip output to a region.

Index	Meaning
COLORRES	Actual color resolution of the device, in bits per pixel. This is valid only if the device driver sets the RC_PALETTE bit in the RASTERCAPS index.
CURVECAPS	The curve capabilities of the device. The return value can be a combination of the following flags:

Value	Meaning
CC_CHORD	Device can draw chord arcs.
CC_CIRCLES	Device can draw circles.
CC_ELLIPSES	Device can draw ellipses.
CC_INTERIORS	Device can draw interiors.
CC_NONE	Device does not support curves.
CC_PIE	Device can draw pie wedges.
CC_ROUNDRECT	Device can draw rounded rectangles.
CC_STYLED	Device can draw styled borders.
CC_WIDE	Device can draw wide borders.
CC_WIDESTYLED	Device can draw borders that are wide and styled.

Index	Meaning
DESKTOPHORZRES	(Windows NT only) Width, in pixels, of the virtual desktop. This value may be larger than HORZRES if the device supports a virtual desktop or multiple displays.
DESKTOPVERTRES	(Windows NT only) Height, in pixels, of the virtual desktop.
DRIVERVERSION	The device driver version.
HORZRES	Width, in pixels, of the screen.
HORZSIZE	Width, in millimeters, of the physical screen.
LINECAPS	The line capabilities of the device. The return value can be a combination of the following flags:

Value	Meaning
LC_INTERIORS	Device can draw interiors.
LC_MARKER	Device can draw a marker.
LC_NONE	Device does not support lines.

continued on next page

continued from previous page

Index	Meaning	
	Value	**Meaning**
	LC_POLYLINE	Device can draw a polyline.
	LC_POLYMARKER	Device can draw multiple markers.
	LC_STYLED	Device can draw styled lines.
	LC_WIDE	Device can draw wide lines.
	LC_WIDESTYLED	Device can draw lines that are wide and styled.
LOGPIXELSX	Number of pixels per logical inch along the screen width.	
LOGPIXELSY	Number of pixels per logical inch along the screen height.	
NUMBRUSHES	Number of device-specific brushes.	
NUMCOLORS	Number of entries in the device's color table.	
NUMFONTS	Number of device-specific fonts.	
NUMPENS	Number of device-specific pens.	
NUMRESERVED	Number of reserved entries in the system palette; this is valid only if the device driver sets the RC_PALETTE bit in the RASTERCAPS index.	
PDEVICESIZE	Reserved.	
PHYSICALHEIGHT	Height, in pixels, of the physical page.	
PHYSICALOFFSETX	Offset in the x direction, in pixels, from the upper-left corner of the physical page where the actual printing or drawing begins.	
PHYSICALOFFSETY	Offset in the y direction, in pixels, from the upper-left corner of the physical page where the actual printing or drawing begins.	
PHYSICALWIDTH	Width, in pixels, of the physical page.	
PLANES	Number of color planes.	
POLYGONALCAPS	The polygon capabilities of the device. The return value can be a combination of the following values:	
	Value	**Meaning**
	PC_INTERIORS	Device can draw interiors.
	PC_NONE	Device does not support polygons.
	PC_POLYGON	Device can draw alternate-fill polygons.
	PC_RECTANGLE	Device can draw rectangles.
	PC_SCANLINE	Device can draw a single scan line.
	PC_STYLED	Device can draw styled borders.
	PC_TRAPEZOID	Device can draw trapezoids.
	PC_WIDE	Device can draw wide borders.
	PC_WIDESTYLED	Device can draw borders that are wide and styled.
	PC_WINDPOLYGON	Device can draw winding-fill polygons.
RASTERCAPS	The raster capabilities of the device. The return value can be a combination of the following flags:	
	Capability	**Meaning**
	RC_BANDING	Requires banding support.
	RC_BITBLT	Capable of transferring bitmaps.
	RC_BITMAP64	Capable of supporting bitmaps larger than 64K.

Capability	Meaning
RC_DI_BITMAP	Capable of supporting the SetDIBits and GetDIBits functions.
RC_DIBTODEV	Capable of supporting the SetDIBitsToDevice function.
RC_DEVBITS	Capable of supporting device-dependent bitmaps.
RC_FLOODFILL	Capable of performing flood fills.
RC_NEWDIB	Capable of supporting device-independent bitmap formats other than 1, 4, 8, and 24 bits per pixel.
RC_NONE	Device has no raster capabilities.
RC_OP_DX_OUTPUT	Capable of background opaquing at the same time character glyphs are drawn. Supports the *Dx* array of the ExtTextOut function.
RC_PALETTE	Specifies a palette-based device.
RC_SAVEBITMAP	Capable of saving a single bitmap from the display or restoring a single, previously stored bitmap to the display.
RC_SCALING	Capable of scaling.
RC_STRETCHBLT	Capable of performing the StretchBlt function.
RC_STRETCHDIB	Capable of performing the StretchDIBits function.

SCALINGFACTORX	Scaling factor for the x-axis of a printer.
SCALINGFACTORY	Scaling factor for the y-axis of a printer.
SIZEPALETTE	Number of entries in the system palette; this is valid only if the device driver sets the RC_PALETTE bit in the RASTERCAPS index.
TECHNOLOGY	Device technology. If the *hdc* parameter identifies the DC of an enhanced metafile, the device technology is that of the referenced device given to the CreateEnhMetaFile function. Use the GetObjectType function to determine whether it is an enhanced metafile DC. The following return values are valid:

Value	Meaning
DT_CHARSTREAM	Character stream.
DT_DISPFILE	Display file.
DT_METAFILE	Metafile.
DT_PLOTTER	Vector plotter.
DT_RASCAMERA	Raster camera.
DT_RASDISPLAY	Raster display.
DT_RASPRINTER	Raster printer.

TEXTCAPS	The text capabilities of the device. The return value can be a combination of the following values:

Bit	Meaning
TC_CP_STROKE	Device is capable of stroke clip precision.
TC_CR_90	Device is capable of 90-degree character rotation.
TC_CR_ANY	Device is capable of any character rotation.
TC_EA_DOUBLE	Device can draw double-weight characters.
TC_IA_ABLE	Device can italicize.
TC_OP_CHARACTER	Device is capable of character output precision.
TC_OP_STROKE	Device is capable of stroke output precision.

continued on next page

549

continued from previous page

Index	Meaning	
	Bit	**Meaning**
	TC_RA_ABLE	Device can draw raster fonts.
	TC_RESERVED	Reserved; must be 0.
	TC_SA_CONTIN	Device uses any multiples for exact character scaling.
	TC_SA_DOUBLE	Device is capable of doubled character for scaling.
	TC_SA_INTEGER	Device uses integer multiples only for character scaling.
	TC_SCROLLBLT	Device cannot scroll using bit-block transfer.
	TC_SF_X_YINDEP	Device can scale independently in the x and y directions
	TC_SO_ABLE	Device can draw strikeouts.
	TC_UA_ABLE	Device can underline.
	TC_VA_ABLE	Device can draw vector fonts.
VERTRES	Height, in raster lines, of the screen.	
VERTSIZE	Height, in millimeters, of the physical screen.	
VREFRESH	(Windows NT only) For display devices, the current vertical refresh rate of the device in hertz. A vertical refresh rate value of 0 or 1 represents the display hardware's default refresh rate.	

Returns	`int`: The value of the desired item.
Include File	`wingdi.h`
See Also	`CreateIC`, `CreateDC`, `GetDC`
Example	See the example for the `CreateIC` function.

GetFontData   ■ WINDOWS 95 ■ WINDOWS NT

Description	`GetFontData` retrieves font metric data for a TrueType font. The application can retrieve the entire font file by specifying **0** for the *dwTable*, *dwOffset*, and *cbData* parameters.
Syntax	DWORD **GetFontData**(HDC *hdc,* DWORD *dwTable,* DWORD *dwOffset,* LPVOID *lpvBuffer,* DWORD *cbData*)
Parameters	
hdc	HDC: The handle of the device context.
dwTable	DWORD: The name of a font metric table from which the font data is to be retrieved. If this parameter is **0**, the information is retrieved starting at the beginning of the font file.
dwOffset	DWORD: The offset from the beginning of the font metric table to the location where the function should begin retrieving information. If this parameter is **0**, the information is retrieved starting at the beginning of the table.

lpvBuffer	LPVOID: A pointer to a buffer to receive the font information. If set to NULL, the size of the buffer required for the font data is returned.
cbData	DWORD: The length, in bytes, of the information to be retrieved. If set to 0, the size of the data specified in the *dwTable* parameter is returned.
Returns	DWORD: The number of bytes returned. If an error occurred, GDI_ERROR is returned.
Include File	wingdi.h
See Also	GetTextMetrics, GetOutlineTextMetrics
Example	This example shows how you can use the GetFontData function to retrieve font data that can be embedded into a document.

```
LRESULT CALLBACK WndProc( HWND hWnd, UINT uMsg, WPARAM wParam, LPARAM lParam )
{
    switch( uMsg )
    {
        case WM_COMMAND :
                switch( LOWORD( wParam ) )
                {
                    case IDM_TEST :
                        {
                            HDC     hDC;
                            HGLOBAL hBuf;
                            LPTSTR  lpBuf;
                            int     nSize;
                            HFONT   hFont, hOldFont;
                            OUTLINETEXTMETRIC ot;

                            // Create a Times New Roman font.
                            //.................................
                            hFont = CreateFont( 24, 16, 0, 0, FW_NORMAL,
                                                0, 0, 0, ANSI_CHARSET,
                                                OUT_DEFAULT_PRECIS,
                                                CLIP_DEFAULT_PRECIS,
                                                DEFAULT_QUALITY,
                                                DEFAULT_PITCH | FF_DONTCARE,
                                                "Times New Roman" );

                            // Get a DC for the window and
                            // select the font for it.
                            //..............................
                            hDC = GetDC( hWnd );
                            hOldFont = SelectObject( hDC, hFont );

                            // Get the outline text metrics for
                            // the font to find out if it can
                            // be embedded.
                            //...............................
                            GetOutlineTextMetrics( hDC,
                                                   sizeof(OUTLINETEXTMETRIC),
                                                   &ot );

                            // Can the font be embedded?
                            //..........................
```

continued on next page

continued from previous page

```
                        if ( !(ot.otmfsType & 0x00000001) )
                        {
                            // Find out the size of the font data.
                            //....................................
                            nSize = GetFontData( hDC, 0, 0, NULL, 0 );

                            // Allocate a buffer and retrieve the
                            // font data. It can then be embedded.
                            //....................................
                            if ( nSize > 0 )
                            {
                                hBuf  = GlobalAlloc( GHND, nSize );
                                lpBuf = (LPTSTR) GlobalLock( hBuf );

                                GetFontData( hDC, 0, 0, lpBuf, nSize );

                                // We have the font data.. now it could
                                // be saved in a document for embedding

                                GlobalUnlock( hBuf );
                                GlobalFree( hBuf );
                            }
                        }
                        else
                            MessageBox( hWnd,
                                "Embedding is not allowed for this font.",
                                NULL, MB_OK | MB_ICONASTERISK );

                    SelectObject( hWnd, hOldFont );
                    ReleaseDC( hWnd, hDC );
                    DeleteObject( hFont );
                }
                break;
                .
                .
                .
```

GetFontLanguageInfo ■ Windows 95 ■ Windows NT

Description	GetFontLanguageInfo returns language information about the currently selected font for a display context. An application can use this information and the GetCharacterPlacement function to prepare a character string for display.
Syntax	DWORD **GetFontLanguageInfo**(HDC *hdc*)
Parameters	
hdc	HDC: The handle of the display context.
Returns	DWORD: The characteristics of the currently selected font. If the font is "normalized" and can be treated as a simple Latin font, 0 is returned. If an error occurs, GCP_ERROR is returned. Otherwise, the function returns a combination of the values listed in Table 12-22 that when masked with FLI_MASK can be passed directly to the GetCharacterPlacement function.

Table 12-22 GetFontLanguageInfo return values

Value	Meaning
GCP_DBCS	The character set is a double-byte character set (DBCS).
GCP_DIACRITIC	The font contains diacritic glyphs.
GCP_GLYPHSHAPE	The font contains multiple glyphs per code point or per code point combination (supports shaping and/or ligation), and the font contains advanced glyph tables to provide extra glyphs for the extra shapes. If this value is given, the lpGlyphs array should be used with the GetCharacterPlacement function and the ETO_GLYPHINDEX value needs to be passed to the ExtTextOut function when the string is drawn.
GCP_KASHIDA	The font permits Kashidas.
GCP_LIGATE	The font contains ligation glyphs that can be substituted for specific character combinations.
GCP_REORDER	The font covers characters that require reordering for display, for example Hebrew or Arabic.
GCP_USEKERNING	The font contains a kerning table that can be used to provide better spacing between the characters and glyphs.

Include File	wingdi.h
See Also	GetCharacterPlacement
Example	This example shows how an application can use the GetFontLanguageInfo function to determine if the double-byte character set is supported by the font selected into a device context.

```
LRESULT CALLBACK WndProc( HWND hWnd, UINT uMsg, WPARAM wParam, LPARAM lParam )
{
   switch( uMsg )
   {
      case WM_COMMAND :
              switch( LOWORD( wParam ) )
              {
                 case IDM_TEST :
                     {
                        HDC    hDC;
                        BOOL   bDBCS;

                        hDC   = GetDC( hWnd );
                        bDBCS = (GCP_DBCS & GetFontLanguageInfo( hDC ));
                        ReleaseDC( hWnd, hDC );

                        if ( bDBCS )
                           MessageBox( hWnd,
                                   "Double-byte character set is supported.",
                                   "DBCS", MB_OK | MB_ICONINFORMATION );
                        else
                           MessageBox( hWnd,
                                  "Double-byte character set is not supported.",
                                  "DBCS", MB_OK | MB_ICONINFORMATION );

                     }
                     break;
                        .
                        .
                        .
```

GetGraphicsMode ■ Windows 95 ■ Windows NT

Description	GetGraphicsMode retrieves the current graphics mode for the specified device context.
Syntax	int **GetGraphicsMode**(HDC *hDC*)
Parameters	
hDC	HDC: Identifies the device context.
Returns	int: If the function succeeds, the return value is the current graphics mode. GM_COMPATIBLE is returned if the current graphics mode is the compatible graphics mode, which is a mode that is compatible with Windows 3.x. In this graphics mode, an application cannot set or modify world transformation for the specified device context. This is the only mode supported by Windows 95. Windows NT can be GM_ADVANCED, which indicates the current mode is the advanced graphics mode. In this graphics mode, an application can set or modify the world transformation for the specified device context.
Include File	wingdi.h
See Also	SetGraphicsMode

GetMapMode ■ Windows 95 ■ Windows NT

Description	GetMapMode retrieves the current mapping mode. An application normally uses this with windows that include the CS_OWNDC style. This allows the window to keep track of changes to the device context in its own private storage area for the DC.
Syntax	int **GetMapMode**(HDC *hdc*)
Parameters	
hdc	HDC: The handle of the device context.
Returns	int: If successful, the mapping mode; otherwise, the return value is 0. See the SetMapMode function for the meaning of the different mapping modes.
Include File	wingdi.h
See Also	SetMapMode
Example	See the example for the SetMapMode function.

GetSystemMetrics ■ Windows 95 ■ Windows NT

Description	GetSystemMetrics retrieves the metrics of a Windows display element or a system configuration setting. All dimensions are in pixels.
Syntax	int **GetSystemMetrics**(int *nIndex*)

Parameters

nIndex

    `int`: The system metric or configuration setting to retrieve. This parameter must be one of the values listed in Table 12-23.

Table 12-23 `GetSystemMetrics` *nIndex* values

Value	Meaning
SM_ARRANGE	Flags specifying how the system arranges minimized windows. The return value consists of a starting position and direction. The starting position can be one of these values:

Value	Meaning
ARW_BOTTOMLEFT	Start at lower-left corner of screen (default position).
ARW_BOTTOMRIGHT	Start at lower-right corner of screen.
ARW_HIDE	Hide minimized windows by moving them off of the visible area of the screen.
ARW_STARTRIGHT	Same as ARW_BOTTOMRIGHT.
ARW_STARTTOP	Start at upper-left corner of screen.
ARW_TOPLEFT	Same as ARW_STARTTOP.
ARW_TOPRIGHT	Start at upper-right corner of screen. Equivalent to ARW_STARTTOP | ARW_STARTRIGHT.

The direction in which to arrange can be one of these values:

Value	Meaning
ARW_DOWN	Arrange vertically, top to bottom.
ARW_LEFT	Arrange horizontally, left to right.
ARW_RIGHT	Arrange horizontally, right to left.
ARW_UP	Arrange vertically, bottom to top.

Value	Meaning
SM_CLEANBOOT	Value that specifies how the system was started:

Value	Meaning
0	Normal boot.
1	Fail-safe boot.
2	Fail-safe with network boot.

Value	Meaning
SM_CMETRICS	Number of system metrics and flags.
SM_CMOUSEBUTTONS	Number of buttons on mouse, or 0 if no mouse is installed.
SM_CXBORDER	Width of a single border, in pixels.
SM_CYBORDER	Height of a single border, in pixels.
SM_CXCURSOR	Width of standard cursor bitmaps, in pixels.
SM_CYCURSOR	Height of standard cursor bitmaps, in pixels.
SM_CXDLGFRAME	Obsolete in Windows 95 and later; use SM_CXFIXEDFRAME instead.
SM_CYDLGFRAME	Obsolete in Windows 95 and later; use SM_CYFIXEDFRAME instead.
SM_CXDOUBLECLK	Width, in pixels, of the rectangle within which two successive mouse clicks must fall to generate a double-click.
SM_CYDOUBLECLK	Height, in pixels, of the rectangle within which two successive mouse clicks must fall to generate a double-click.

continued on next page

continued from previous page

Value	Meaning
SM_CXDRAG	Width, in pixels, of the rectangle used to detect the start of a drag operation.
SM_CYDRAG	Height, in pixels, of the rectangle used to detect the start of a drag operation.
SM_CXEDGE	Width of an edge (a double border), in pixels.
SM_CYEDGE	Height of an edge (a double border), in pixels.
SM_CXFIXEDFRAME	Width, in pixels, of the window frame for a window that has the WS_DLGFRAME style.
SM_CYFIXEDFRAME	Height, in pixels, of the window frame for a window that has the WS_DLGFRAME style.
SM_CXFRAME	Obsolete in Windows 95 and later; use SM_CXSIZEFRAME instead.
SM_CYFRAME	Obsolete in Windows 95 and later; use SM_CYSIZEFRAME instead.
SM_CXFULLSCREEN	Default width of a maximized top-level window's client area, in pixels.
SM_CYFULLSCREEN	Default height of a maximized top-level window's client area, in pixels.
SM_CXICON	Width of a large icon, in pixels.
SM_CYICON	Height of a large icon, in pixels.
SM_CXICONSPACING	Width of a grid cell for items in large icon view, in pixels. This value is always greater than or equal to SM_CXICON.
SM_CYICONSPACING	Height of a grid cell for items in large icon view, in pixels. This value is always greater than or equal to SM_CYICON.
SM_CXMAXIMIZED	Default width of a maximized top-level window, in pixels.
SM_CYMAXIMIZED	Default height of a maximized top-level window, in pixels.
SM_CXMAXTRACK	Default maximum width of a window that has a caption and sizing borders.
SM_CYMAXTRACK	Default maximum height of a window that has a caption and sizing borders.
SM_CXMENUCHECK	Width of the default menu checkmark bitmap, in pixels.
SM_CYMENUCHECK	Height of the default menu checkmark bitmap, in pixels.
SM_CXMENUSIZE	Width of menu bar buttons, in pixels.
SM_CYMENUSIZE	Height of menu bar buttons, in pixels.
SM_CXMIN	Obsolete. Same as SM_CXMINTRACK.
SM_CYMIN	Obsolete. Same as SM_CYMINTRACK.
SM_CXMINIMIZED	Width of a normal minimized window, in pixels.
SM_CYMINIMIZED	Height of a normal minimized window, in pixels.
SM_CXMINSPACING	Width of a grid cell for minimized windows, in pixels. This value is always greater than or equal to SM_CXMINIMIZED.
SM_CYMINSPACING	Height of a grid cell for minimized windows, in pixels. This value is always greater than or equal to SM_CYMINIMIZED.
SM_CXMINTRACK	Default minimum width of a window that has a caption and sizing borders.
SM_CYMINTRACK	Default minimum height of a window that has a caption and sizing borders.
SM_CXSCREEN	Width of the screen, in pixels.
SM_CYSCREEN	Height of the screen, in pixels.
SM_CXSIZE	Width of caption buttons, in pixels.
SM_CYSIZE	Height of caption buttons, in pixels.
SM_CXSIZEFRAME	Width, in pixels, of the window frame for a window that has the WS_THICKFRAME style.
SM_CYSIZEFRAME	Height, in pixels, of the window frame for a window that has the WS_THICKFRAME style.
SM_CXSMICON	Recommended width of a small icon, in pixels.

Value	Meaning
SM_CYSMICON	Recommended height of a small icon, in pixels.
SM_CXSMSIZE	Width of small caption buttons, in pixels.
SM_CYSMSIZE	Height of small caption buttons, in pixels.
SM_CXVSCROLL	Width of a vertical scroll bar, in pixels.
SM_CYVSCROLL	Height of the arrow bitmap on a vertical scroll bar, in pixels.
SM_CXHSCROLL	Width of the arrow bitmap on a horizontal scroll bar, in pixels.
SM_CYHSCROLL	Height of the horizontal scroll bar, in pixels.
SM_CXHTHUMB	Default width of thumb on a horizontal scroll bar, in pixels.
SM_CYVTHUMB	Default height of thumb on a vertical scroll bar, in pixels.
SM_CYCAPTION	Height of normal caption area, in pixels.
SM_CYKANJIWINDOW	For double-byte character set (DBCS) versions of Windows, height of the Kanji window at the bottom of the screen.
SM_CYMENU	Height of single-line menu bar, in pixels.
SM_CYSMCAPTION	Height of a small caption, in pixels.
SM_DBCSENABLED	TRUE if the double-byte character set (DBCS) version of USER.EXE is installed; otherwise, FALSE.
SM_DEBUG	TRUE if the debugging version of USER.EXE is installed; otherwise, FALSE.
SM_HIGHCONTRAST	TRUE if the user needs visual information to be displayed with high contrast between foreground and background; otherwise, FALSE.
SM_KEYBOARDPREF	TRUE if the user relies on the keyboard instead of the mouse, and wants applications to display keyboard interfaces that would otherwise be hidden; otherwise, FALSE.
SM_MENUDROPALIGNMENT	TRUE if pop-up menus are right-aligned relative to the corresponding menu-bar item; FALSE if they are left-aligned.
SM_MOUSEPRESENT	TRUE if a mouse is installed; otherwise, FALSE.
SM_NETWORK	If a network is present, the least significant bit is set; otherwise, it is cleared. The other bits are reserved for future use.
SM_PENWINDOWS	TRUE if the Microsoft Windows for Pen computing extensions are installed; otherwise, FALSE.
SM_SCREENREADER	TRUE if a screen review utility is running, otherwise FALSE. A screen review utility directs textual information to an output device, such as a speech synthesizer or Braille display. If this flag is set, an application should provide textual information in situations where it would otherwise present the information graphically.
SM_SECURE	TRUE if security is present; otherwise, FALSE.
SM_SHOWSOUNDS	TRUE if the user requires an application to present information visually in situations where it would otherwise present the information only in audible form; otherwise, FALSE.
SM_SLOWMACHINE	TRUE if the computer has a low-end processor; otherwise, FALSE.
SM_SWAPBUTTON	TRUE if the meanings of the left and right mouse buttons are swapped; otherwise, FALSE.

Returns	`int`: The requested system metric or configuration flag.
Include File	`winuser.h`
See Also	`GetDeviceCaps`
Example	See the example for the `GetWindowDC` function.

GetViewportExtEx   ■ WINDOWS 95 ■ WINDOWS NT

Description	GetViewportExtEx retrieves the x and y extents of the current viewport for a device context (DC). The MM_ISOTROPIC and MM_ANISOTROPIC mapping modes allow the logical coordinate system of a device context to be any arbitrary scaled ratio to the physical device. Use GetViewportExtEx and GetWindowExtEx together to determine the current scaling. The scaling factor is the ratio of the viewport extent divided by the window extent.
Syntax	BOOL **GetViewportExtEx**(HDC *hdc,* LPSIZE *lpSize*)
Parameters	
hdc	HDC: The handle of the DC.
lpSize	LPSIZE: A pointer to a SIZE structure. The x and y extents, in device units, are placed in this structure.
Returns	BOOL: TRUE if successful; otherwise, the return value is FALSE.
Include File	wingdi.h
See Also	GetWindowExtEx, GetViewportOrgEx
Example	See the example for the SetMapMode function.

GetViewportOrgEx   ■ WINDOWS 95 ■ WINDOWS NT

Description	GetViewportOrgEx retrieves the x and y coordinates of the viewport origin for a device context (DC). Windows allows two offsets to be applied to the origin (0,0 location) of the logical coordinate system. SetWindowOrgEx sets up the first offset, called the "window origin." SetViewportOrgEx sets up the second offset, called the "viewport origin." The viewport origin is relative to the window origin, so the viewport origin could be thought of as an offset from another offset.
Syntax	BOOL **GetViewportOrgEx**(HDC *hdc,* LPPOINT *lpPoint*)
Parameters	
hdc	HDC: The handle of the DC.
lpPoint	LPPOINT: A pointer to a POINT structure that receives the origin coordinates.
Returns	BOOL: TRUE if successful; otherwise, the return value is FALSE.
Include File	wingdi.h
See Also	GetWindowOrgEx, GetViewportExtEx
Example	This example, shown in Figure 12-4, creates a window with its own private device context (the window class has the CS_OWNDC style specified). Every time a WM_SIZE message is received, the program resets the logical device scaling and origins in the MM_ISOTROPIC mapping mode. The viewport origin is set equal to the lower-left corner of the window and the

window origin is offset by 10 units. Because the window origin is always offset by 10 units in both the horizontal and vertical directions using **SetWindowOrgEx**, the viewport origin appears at a location 10 units above and to the right of the lower-left corner. The text will always be painted above the bottom border of the window, even when it is sized.

```
LRESULT CALLBACK WndProc( HWND hWnd, UINT uMsg, WPARAM wParam, LPARAM lParam )
{
    switch( uMsg )
    {
    case WM_SIZE  :
            {
            HDC hDC = GetDC( hWnd );

            // Set the mapping mode and set the
            // scaling of the DC.
            //................................
            SetMapMode( hDC, MM_ISOTROPIC );
            SetWindowExtEx( hDC, 1, 1, NULL );
            SetViewportExtEx( hDC, 2, -2, NULL );

            // Set the origin of the device context.
            //......................................
            SetWindowOrgEx( hDC, -10, -10, NULL );
            SetViewportOrgEx( hDC, 0, HIWORD(lParam), NULL );
            }
            break;

    case WM_COMMAND :
            switch( LOWORD( wParam ) )
            {
            case IDM_TEST :
                    {
                    HDC    hDC;
                    POINT  ptWOrg;
                    POINT  ptVOrg;
                    char   szMsg[40];

                    hDC = GetDC( hWnd );

                    // Display the origin of the
                    // device context.
                    //.........................
                    GetWindowOrgEx( hDC, &ptWOrg );
                    GetViewportOrgEx( hDC, &ptVOrg );

                    wsprintf( szMsg, "Viewport Org = %d, %d",
                                        ptVOrg.x, ptVOrg.y );
                    TextOut( hDC, 0, 0, szMsg, strlen( szMsg ) );

                    wsprintf( szMsg, "Window Org = %d, %d",
                                        ptWOrg.x, ptWOrg.y );
                    TextOut( hDC, 0, 10, szMsg, strlen( szMsg ) );
                    }
                    break;
```

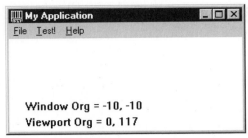

Figure 12-4 `GetViewportOrgEx` example

GetWindowDC ■ WINDOWS 95 ■ WINDOWS NT

Description	`GetWindowDC` retrieves the device context (DC) for the entire window, including title bar, menus, and scroll bars. The origin of the DC is the upper-left corner of the window instead of the client area.
Syntax	HDC **GetWindowDC(HWND** *hwnd* **)**
Parameters	
hwnd	HWND: The handle of the window for which to retrieve a DC.
Returns	HDC: If successful, the handle of a DC for the given window; otherwise, the return value is **NULL**.
Include File	`wingdi.h`
See Also	`GetDC`, `BeginPaint`
Related Messages	`WM_NCPAINT`, `WM_PAINT`, `WM_NCACTIVATE`
Example	This example, shown in Figure 12-5, paints a pattern in the caption of the application when the user selects the Test! menu item. Use the `GetWindowDC` function to retrieve a device context for the entire window. Use `GetSystemMetrics` to determine the sizes of the borders and caption so the pattern can be properly placed in the caption.

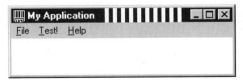

Figure 12-5 `GetWindowDC` example

```
LRESULT CALLBACK WndProc( HWND hWnd, UINT uMsg, WPARAM wParam, LPARAM lParam )
{
    switch( uMsg )
    {
        case WM_COMMAND :
                switch( LOWORD( wParam ) )
                {
                    case IDM_TEST :
                        {
                            HDC    hDC;
                            RECT   rect;
                            int    i;

                            // Figure out the position and size of the first
                            // block in the pattern.
                            //.............................................
                            rect.top      = GetSystemMetrics( SM_CYSIZEFRAME );
                            rect.left     = GetSystemMetrics( SM_CXSIZEFRAME );
                            rect.left    += GetSystemMetrics( SM_CXSMICON )+100;
                            rect.bottom   = rect.top +
                                            GetSystemMetrics( SM_CYCAPTION )-1;
                            rect.right    = rect.left+5;

                            hDC = GetWindowDC( hWnd );

                            // Paint 10 blocks in the caption of the window.
                            //.............................................
                            for ( i = 0; i < 10; i++ )
                            {
                                FillRect( hDC, &rect,
                                        GetStockObject( WHITE_BRUSH ) );
                                rect.left  += 10;
                                rect.right += 10;
                            }

                            ReleaseDC( hWnd, hDC );
                        }
                        break;
                    .
                    .
                    .
```

GetWindowExtEx   ■ WINDOWS 95 ■ WINDOWS NT

Description	GetWindowExtEx retrieves the x and y extents of the window for the given device context (DC). The MM_ISOTROPIC and MM_ANISOTROPIC mapping modes allow the logical coordinate system of a device context to be any arbitrary scaled ratio to the physical device. You use GetViewportExtEx and GetWindowExtEx together to determine the current scaling. The scaling factor is the ratio of the viewport extent divided by the window extent.
Syntax	BOOL **GetWindowExtEx**(HDC *hdc,* LPSIZE *lpSize*)

Parameters

hdc   HDC: The handle of the DC for the window.

lpSize   LPSIZE: A pointer to a SIZE structure that receives the extents, in page-space units, of the window.

Returns   BOOL: TRUE if successful; otherwise, the return value is FALSE.

Include File   wingdi.h

See Also   GetWindowOrgEx, GetViewportExtEx

Example   See the example for the SetMapMode function.

GetWindowOrgEx   ■ Windows 95 ■ Windows NT

Description   GetWindowOrgEx retrieves the x and y coordinates of the window origin for the given device context (DC). Windows allows two offsets to be applied to the origin (0,0 location) of the logical coordinate system. SetWindowOrgEx sets up the first offset, called the "window origin." SetViewportOrgEx sets up the second offset, called the "viewport origin." The viewport origin is relative to the window origin, so the viewport origin could be thought of as an offset from another offset.

Syntax   BOOL **GetWindowOrgEx**(HDC *hdc,* LPPOINT *lpPoint*)

Parameters

hdc   HDC: The handle of the DC for the window.

lpPoint   LPPOINT: A pointer to a POINT structure that receives the coordinates, in page units, of the window origin.

Returns   BOOL: TRUE if successful; otherwise, the return value is FALSE.

Include File   wingdi.h

See Also   GetWindowExtEx, GetViewportOrgEx

Example   See the example for the GetViewportOrgEx function.

LPtoDP   ■ Windows 95 ■ Windows NT

Description   LPtoDP converts logical coordinates into device coordinates. The conversion depends on the current mapping mode, origins and extents for the window and viewport, and the world transformation.

Syntax   BOOL **LPtoDP**(HDC *hdc,* LPPOINT *lpPoints,* int *nCount*)

Parameters

hdc   HDC: The handle of the DC.

lpPoints   LPPOINT: A pointer to an array of POINT structures containing the x and y coordinates to be transformed.

nCount	int: The number of POINT structures in the array pointed to by *lpPoints*.
Returns	BOOL: TRUE if successful; otherwise, the return value is FALSE.
Include File	wingdi.h
See Also	DPtoLP, SetMapMode
Example	See the example for the SetMapMode function.

OffsetViewportOrgEx   ■ WINDOWS 95 ■ WINDOWS NT

Description	OffsetViewportOrgEx modifies the viewport origin for the given device context (DC) using the given horizontal and vertical offsets.
Syntax	BOOL **OffsetViewportOrgEx**(HDC *hdc,* int *nXOffset,* int *nYOffset,* LPPOINT *lpPoint*)
Parameters	
hdc	HDC: The handle of the DC.
nXOffset	int: The horizontal offset, in device units.
nYOffset	int: The vertical offset, in device units.
lpPoint	LPPOINT: A pointer to a POINT structure that receives the previous viewport origin in device units. If *lpPoint* is NULL, the previous viewport origin is not returned.
Returns	BOOL: TRUE if successful; otherwise, the return value is FALSE.
Include File	wingdi.h
See Also	GetViewportOrgEx, SetViewportOrgEx
Example	This example creates a window with its own private device context (the window class has the CS_OWNDC style specified). Every time a WM_SIZE message is received, the program resets the logical device scaling and origins. The MM_ISOTROPIC mapping mode is used. The viewport origin is set equal to the lower-left corner of the window. Because the window origin is always offset by 10 units in both the horizontal and vertical directions using SetWindowOrgEx, the viewport origin appears at a location 10 units above and to the right of the lower-left corner.
	When the user selects the Test! menu item, the window horizontal offset is eliminated (10 added to the old offset of -10). The viewport origin is also offset by 5 in both the horizontal and vertical directions. The combined effect of these two offsets shifts the origin to the right 15 pixels and down 5. Figure 12-4 shows what the example looks like.

```
LRESULT CALLBACK WndProc( HWND hWnd, UINT uMsg, WPARAM wParam, LPARAM lParam )
{
   switch( uMsg )
   {
      case WM_SIZE :
```

continued on next page

continued from previous page

```
            {
                HDC hDC = GetDC( hWnd );

                // Set the mapping mode and set the
                // scaling of the DC.
                //..............................
                SetMapMode( hDC, MM_ISOTROPIC );
                SetWindowExtEx( hDC, 1, 1, NULL );
                SetViewportExtEx( hDC, 2, -2, NULL );

                // Set the origin of the device context.
                //.........................................
                SetWindowOrgEx( hDC, -10, -10, NULL );
                SetViewportOrgEx( hDC, 0, HIWORD(lParam), NULL );
            }
            break;

    case WM_COMMAND :
            switch( LOWORD( wParam ) )
            {
                case IDM_TEST :
                    {
                        HDC    hDC;
                        POINT ptWOrg;
                        POINT ptVOrg;
                        char  szMsg[40];

                        hDC = GetDC( hWnd );

                        // Change the origin by an offset.
                        //................................
                        OffsetWindowOrgEx( hDC, 10, 0, NULL );
                        OffsetViewportOrgEx( hDC, 5, 5, NULL );

                        // Display the origin of the
                        // device context.
                        //...........................
                        GetWindowOrgEx( hDC, &ptWOrg );
                        GetViewportOrgEx( hDC, &ptVOrg );

                        wsprintf( szMsg, "Viewport Org = %d, %d",
                                        ptVOrg.x, ptVOrg.y );
                        TextOut( hDC, 0, 0, szMsg, strlen( szMsg ) );

                        wsprintf( szMsg, "Window Org = %d, %d",
                                        ptWOrg.x, ptWOrg.y );
                        TextOut( hDC, 0, 10, szMsg, strlen( szMsg ) );
                    }
                    break;
                .
                .
                .
```

OffsetWindowOrgEx   ■ WINDOWS 95 ■ WINDOWS NT

Description   OffsetViewportOrgEx modifies the window origin for the given device
                         context (DC) using the given horizontal and vertical offsets.

Syntax	BOOL **OffsetWindowOrgEx**(HDC *hdc,* int *nXOffset,* int *nYOffset,* LPPOINT *lpPoint*)

Parameters

hdc	HDC: The handle of the DC.
nXOffset	int: The horizontal offset, in logical units.
nYOffset	int: The vertical offset, in logical units.
lpPoint	LPPOINT: A pointer to a **POINT** structure that receives the previous window origin. If *lpPoint* is NULL, the previous origin is not returned.
Returns	BOOL: TRUE if successful; otherwise, the return value is FALSE.
Include File	wingdi.h
See Also	GetWindowOrgEx, SetWindowOrgEx, OffsetViewportOrgEx
Example	See the example for the OffsetViewportOrgEx function.

PtVisible

■ WINDOWS 95 ■ WINDOWS NT

| Description | PtVisible determines whether a given point is within the clipping region of a device context (DC). |
| Syntax | BOOL **PtVisible**(HDC *hdc,* int *X,* int *Y*) |

Parameters

hdc	HDC: The handle of the DC.
X	int: The logical x coordinate of the point.
Y	int: The logical y coordinate of the point.
Returns	BOOL: TRUE if the given point is within the clipping region of the device context; otherwise, the return value is FALSE.
Include File	wingdi.h
See Also	RectVisible, PtInRegion, PtInRect, SelectClipRgn
Example	This example displays text indicating whether or not the mouse cursor is within the clipping region when the user selects the Test! menu item. Figure 12-6 shows the example when the Test! menu item is selected with the mouse cursor within the clipping region. Note that the black rectangle is only displayed if a portion of the rectangle will show within the clipping region.

```
LRESULT CALLBACK WndProc( HWND hWnd, UINT uMsg, WPARAM wParam, LPARAM lParam )
{
   switch( uMsg )
   {
     case WM_COMMAND :
             switch( LOWORD( wParam ) )
             {
               case IDM_TEST :
```

continued on next page

continued from previous page

```
{
    HDC    hDC;
    HRGN   hRgn;
    RECT   rect;
    POINT  pt;

    // Clear the client area of the window.
    //.......................................
    InvalidateRect( hWnd, NULL, TRUE );
    UpdateWindow( hWnd );

    // Create a region and set it as the
    // clipping region of the DC.
    //...................................
    hRgn = CreateRectRgn( 10, 10, 300, 100 );
    hDC  = GetDC( hWnd );

    SelectClipRgn( hDC, hRgn );

    // Retrieve the mouse cursor
    // position and convert it to
    // client coordinates.
    //............................
    GetCursorPos( &pt );
    ScreenToClient( hWnd, &pt );

    // Check to see if the mouse
    // cursor is within the clipping region.
    //.......................................
    if ( PtVisible( hDC, pt.x, pt.y ) )
        TextOut( hDC, 10, 10,
                "Cursor is within the clipping rgn.",
                34 );
    else
        TextOut( hDC, 10, 10,
                "Cursor is not within the clipping rgn.",
                38 );

    // Create a rect based on the
    // position of the cursor.
    //............................
    rect.top    = pt.y;
    rect.left   = pt.x;
    rect.right  = rect.left + 20;
    rect.bottom = rect.top  + 20;

    // Determine if the rect is visible and
    // if it is, paint it.
    //.......................................
    if ( RectVisible( hDC, &rect ) )
        FillRect( hDC, &rect,
                    GetStockObject( BLACK_BRUSH ) );

    ReleaseDC( hWnd, hDC );
}
break;
```

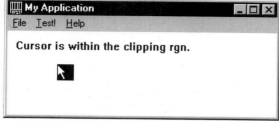

Figure 12-6 `PtVisible` example

RectVisible
■ WINDOWS 95 ■ WINDOWS NT

Description	`RectVisible` determines whether any part of the specified rectangle lies within the clipping region of a device context (DC). Use this function to determine if there is any reason to draw the contents of a rectangle that may fall outside of the clipping region.
Syntax	`BOOL RectVisible( HDC hdc, CONST RECT* lprc )`
Parameters	
hdc	`HDC`: The handle of the DC.
lprc	`CONST RECT*`: A pointer to a `RECT` structure that contains the logical coordinates of the rectangle to check.
Returns	`BOOL`: `TRUE` if any portion of the rectangle lies within the clipping region; otherwise, the return value is `FALSE`.
Include File	`wingdi.h`
See Also	`PtVisible, RectInRegion, SelectClipRgn, CreateRectRgn`
Example	See the example for the `PtVisible` function.

ReleaseDC
■ WINDOWS 95 ■ WINDOWS NT

Description	`ReleaseDC` releases a device context (DC), making it available for use by other applications. `ReleaseDC` frees only common and window DCs; it has no effect on class or private DCs. It is good practice to use `ReleaseDC` immediately after output is completed. Use `EndPaint` to release the device context retrieved by `BeginPaint` in processing a `WM_PAINT` message.
Syntax	`int ReleaseDC( HWND hwnd, HDC hdc )`
Parameters	
hwnd	`HWND`: The handle of the window whose DC is to be released.
hdc	`HDC`: The handle of the DC to release.
Returns	`int`: `TRUE` if the DC is released; otherwise, the return value is `FALSE`.

Include File	wingdi.h
See Also	GetDC, GetWindowDC, EndPaint, DeleteDC
Example	See the example for the GetWindowDC function.

RemoveFontResource ■ WINDOWS 95 ■ WINDOWS NT

Description	RemoveFontResource removes the fonts in the specified file from the Windows font table. An application that adds or removes fonts from the Windows public font table should notify other windows of the change by sending a WM_FONTCHANGE message to all top-level windows in the system.
	You usually use RemoveFontResource when processing the WM_DESTROY message to remove added font resources. Do not remove the normal Windows system fonts, or any other font that was not loaded by the application.
Syntax	BOOL **RemoveFontResource**(LPCTSTR *lpFileName*)
Parameters	
lpFileName	LPCTSTR: A pointer to a null-terminated string that contains the font resource file name.
Returns	BOOL: TRUE if successful; otherwise, the return value is FALSE.
Include File	wingdi.h
See Also	AddFontResource, FindResource
Related Messages	WM_FONTCHANGE, WM_DESTROY
Example	See the example for the AddFontResource function.

RestoreDC ■ WINDOWS 95 ■ WINDOWS NT

Description	RestoreDC restores a device context (DC) to a saved state. The DC is restored to a state saved earlier by the SaveDC function. The DC states are stored in a stack. If the application restores a state that is not at the top of the stack, RestoreDC deletes all state information between the top of the stack and the specified instance.
Syntax	BOOL **RestoreDC**(HDC *hdc*, int *nSavedDC*)
Parameters	
hdc	HDC: The handle of the DC to restore.
nSavedDC	int: The instance of the DC to restore. If the instance is positive, *nSavedDC* represents a specific instance of the DC to be restored. If the instance is negative, *nSavedDC* represents an instance relative to the current DC. For example, −1 restores the most recently saved state.
Returns	BOOL: TRUE if successful; otherwise, the return value is FALSE.

Include File	`wingdi.h`
See Also	`SaveDC, GetDC, BeginPaint`
Related Messages	`WM_PAINT`
Example	See the example for the `SetMapMode` function.

SaveDC ■ WINDOWS 95 ■ WINDOWS NT

Description	`SaveDC` saves the current state of a device context (DC) by copying data describing selected objects and graphic modes (such as the bitmap, brush, palette, font, pen, region, drawing mode, and mapping mode) to a context stack.
Syntax	`int SaveDC( HDC hdc )`
Parameters	
hdc	HDC: The handle of the DC to save.
Returns	`int`: If successful, the saved instance of the device context; otherwise, the return value is `0`.
Include File	`wingdi.h`
See Also	`RestoreDC, ReleaseDC, EndPaint`
Related Messages	`WM_PAINT`
Example	See the example for the `SetMapMode` function.

ScaleViewportExtEx ■ WINDOWS 95 ■ WINDOWS NT

Description	`ScaleViewportExtEx` modifies the viewport for a device context (DC) by using the ratios formed by the given multiplicands and divisors.

The viewport extents are modified as follows:

New Viewport Extent X = (Old Viewport Extent X × Xnum) ÷ Xdenom

New Viewport Extent Y = (Old Viewport Extent Y × Ynum) ÷ Ydenom

Syntax	`BOOL ScaleViewportExtEx( HDC hdc, int Xnum, int Xdenom, int Ynum, int Ydenom, LPSIZE lpSize )`
Parameters	
hdc	HDC: The handle of the DC to scale.
Xnum	`int`: The amount by which to multiply the current horizontal extent.
Xdenom	`int`: The amount by which to divide the current horizontal extent.
Ynum	`int`: The amount by which to multiply the current vertical extent.
Ydenom	`int`: The amount by which to divide the current vertical extent.

lpSize	LPSIZE: A pointer to a SIZE structure that receives the previous viewport extents in device units. If *lpSize* is NULL, the previous viewport extent is not returned.
Returns	BOOL: TRUE if successful; otherwise, the return value is FALSE.
Include File	wingdi.h
See Also	ScaleWindowExtEx, SetViewportExtEx, GetViewportExtEx
Example	When this example starts, it initializes the window and viewport extents. Every time the user selects the Test! menu item, the window and viewport extents are scaled. The effect is that the same line gets larger as it moves down the screen. The window class has the CS_OWNDC style specifying a private device context. This means that the class style CS_OWNDC is specified in the WinMain function.

```
wndclass.style = CS_HREDRAW | CS_VREDRAW | CS_OWNDC;

LRESULT CALLBACK WndProc( HWND hWnd, UINT uMsg, WPARAM wParam, LPARAM lParam )
{
    switch( uMsg )
    {
    case WM_CREATE  :
            {
                HDC hDC = GetDC( hWnd );

                // Initialize the device context.
                //................................
                SetMapMode( hDC, MM_ISOTROPIC );
                SetWindowExtEx( hDC, 1, 1, NULL );
                SetViewportExtEx( hDC, 2, 2, NULL );
            }
            break;

    case WM_COMMAND :
            switch( LOWORD( wParam ) )
            {
            case IDM_TEST :
                    {
                        HDC    hDC;

                        InvalidateRect( hWnd, NULL, TRUE );
                        UpdateWindow( hWnd );

                        hDC = GetDC( hWnd );

                        // Increase the Viewport extents by 1.5.
                        //.....................................
                        ScaleViewportExtEx( hDC, 3, 2, 3, 2, NULL );

                        // Increase the Window extents by 1.25.
                        //....................................
                        ScaleWindowExtEx( hDC, 5, 4, 5, 4, NULL );

                        MoveToEx( hDC, 0, 2, NULL );
                        LineTo( hDC, 3, 2 );
```

```
        }
        break;
```

.
.
.

ScaleWindowExtEx ■ WINDOWS 95 ■ WINDOWS NT

Description	`ScaleWindowExtEx` modifies the window extent for a device context (DC) using the ratios formed by the given multiplicands and divisors.

The window extents are modified as follows:

New Window Extent X = (Old Window Extent X × **Xnum** *) ÷* **Xdenom**

New Window Extent Y = (Old Window Extent Y × **Ynum** *) ÷* **Ydenom**

Syntax

`BOOL` **`ScaleWindowExtEx`**`( HDC` *hdc,* `int` *Xnum,* `int` *Xdenom,* `int` *Ynum,* `int` *Ydenom,* `LPSIZE` *lpSize* `)`

Parameters

hdc	`HDC`: The handle of the DC to scale.
Xnum	`int`: The amount by which to multiply the current horizontal extent.
Xdenom	`int`: The amount by which to divide the current horizontal extent.
Ynum	`int`: The amount by which to multiply the current vertical extent.
Ydenom	`int`: The amount by which to divide the current vertical extent.
lpSize	`LPSIZE`: A pointer to a `SIZE` structure that receives the previous window extents in logical units. If *lpSize* is `NULL`, the previous window extents are not returned.
Returns	`BOOL`: `TRUE` if successful; otherwise, the return value is `FALSE`.
Include File	`wingdi.h`
See Also	`ScaleViewportExtEx, GetWindowExtEx, SetWindowExtEx`
Example	See the example for the `ScaleViewportExtEx` function.

SelectObject ■ WINDOWS 95 ■ WINDOWS NT

Description	`SelectObject` selects an object into the specified device context. The new object replaces the previous object of the same type within the device context. `SelectObject` returns the previously selected object. The application should always restore the original object once it is done with the device context.

Syntax

`HGDIOBJ` **`SelectObject`**`( HDC` *hDC,* `HGDIOBJ` *hGDIObj* `)`

Parameters

hDC	`HDC`: The device context into which the object is selected.

hGDIObj	**HGDIOBJ**: The object to be selected. The specified object must have been created with a GDI function from the See Also section of this function or a stock system object retrieved with the **GetStockObject** function.
Returns	**HGDIOBJ**: If the selected object is not a region and the function succeeds, the return value is the handle of the object being replaced. If the selected object is a region and the function succeeds, the return value is either **SIMPLEREGION** if the region consists of a single rectangle, **COMPLEXREGION** if the region consists of more than one rectangle, or **NULLREGION** if the region is empty.
	If an error occurs and the selected object is not a region, **NULL** is returned; otherwise, **GDI_ERROR** is returned.
Include File	wingdi.h
See Also	CombineRgn, CreateBitmap, CreateBitmapIndirect, CreateBrushIndirect, CreateCompatibleBitmap, CreateDIBitmap, CreateDIBPatternBrush, CreateEllipticRgn, CreateEllipticRgnIndirect, CreateFont, CreateFontIndirect, CreateHatchBrush, CreatePatternBrush, CreatePen, CreatePenIndirect, CreatePolygonRgn, CreateRectRgn, CreateRectRgnIndirect, CreateSolidBrush
Example	See the example for the **CreateFont** function.

SetGraphicsMode ■ Windows 95 ■ Windows NT

Description	**SetGraphicsMode** sets the graphics mode for the specified device context. In Windows 95, only the compatible graphics mode is supported. The advanced graphics mode is only supported under Windows NT. This graphics mode supports world-to-device transformation. Since Windows 95 does not support this mode, it does its best to ensure that enhanced metafiles look the same as they do on Windows NT. To accomplish this, Windows 95 may simulate the advanced graphics mode when playing specific enhanced metafile records.

The following lists the three areas in which graphics output differs according to the graphics mode.

■ Text output: When in compatible mode, TrueType (or vector font) text output behaves much the same way as raster font text output with respect to the world-to-device transform in the DC. The TrueType text is always written from left to right and right side up, even if the rest of the graphics will be flipped in the x- or y-axis. Only the height of the TrueType text is scaled appropriately. The only way to write nonhorizontal text in compatible mode is to specify a nonzero escapement or orientation for the logical font selected in the device context. In advanced graphics mode, TrueType text output fully conforms to the world-to-device transform in the device context.

■ Rectangle exclusion: If the compatible graphics mode is set, the system excludes bottom and rightmost edges when it draws rectangles. In the advanced graphics mode, these edges are included.

■ Arc drawing: If the compatible graphics mode is set, GDI draws arcs using the current arc direction in the device space. With this convention, arcs do not respect page-to-device transforms that require a flip along the x- or y-axis. In the advanced graphics mode, GDI always draws arcs in the counterclockwise direction in logical space.

Syntax	int **SetGraphicsMode**(HDC *hDC,* int *iMode*)
Parameters	
hDC	HDC: The device context of the device for which to set the graphics mode.
iMode	int: Set to **GM_COMPATIBLE** for the compatible graphics mode; otherwise, set to **GM_ADVANCED** for the advanced graphics mode.
Returns	int: If the function succeeds, the return value is the old graphics mode; otherwise, the return value is **0**.
Include File	wingdi.h
See Also	GetGraphicsMode

SetMapMode

Description	SetMapMode sets the mapping mode of a device context (DC). The mapping mode defines the unit of measure used to transform page-space units into device-space units. The mapping mode also defines the orientation of the device's x- and y-axes.
Syntax	int **SetMapMode**(HDC *hdc,* int *nMapMode*)
Parameters	
hdc	HDC: The handle of the DC.
nMapMode	int: The new mapping mode. It can be one of the values listed in Table 12-24.

Table 12-24 SetMapMode *nMapMode* values

Value	Meaning
MM_ANISOTROPIC	Logical units are mapped to arbitrary units with arbitrarily scaled axes. Use the SetWindowExtEx and SetViewportExtEx functions to specify the units, orientation, and scaling.
MM_HIENGLISH	Each logical unit is mapped to 0.001 inch. Positive x is to the right; positive y is up.
MM_HIMETRIC	Each logical unit is mapped to 0.01 millimeter. Positive x is to the right; positive y is up.
MM_ISOTROPIC	Logical units are mapped to arbitrary units with equally scaled axes. Use the SetWindowExtEx and SetViewportExtEx functions to specify the units and the orientation of the axes that you want. Adjustments are made as necessary to ensure the x and y units remain the same size.

continued on next page

continued from previous page

Value	Meaning
MM_LOENGLISH	Each logical unit is mapped to 0.01 inch. Positive x is to the right; positive y is up.
MM_LOMETRIC	Each logical unit is mapped to 0.1 millimeter. Positive x is to the right; positive y is up.
MM_TEXT	Each logical unit is mapped to one device pixel. Positive x is to the right; positive y is down.
MM_TWIPS	Each logical unit is mapped to one-twentieth of a printer's point (1/1440 inch, also called a "twip"). Positive x is to the right; positive y is up.

Returns   **int**: If successful, the previous mapping mode; otherwise, the return value is **0**.

Include File   wingdi.h

See Also   SetWindowExtEx, SetViewportExtEx, GetMapMode

Example   This example, shown in Figure 12-7, creates a window with its own private device context.

The application sets up the **MM_ISOTROPIC** mapping mode during startup (when the **WM_CREATE** message is received). The scaling is fixed at two logical units to one device unit (200 percent) by the **SetWindowExtEx** and **SetViewportExtEx** function calls. When the user selects the Test! menu item, two lines are displayed. One line is in the **MM_ISOTROPIC** mapping mode and the other is in **MM_TEXT**. Note the **MM_ISOTROPIC** line is twice as long. This is because of the scaling factor set at the beginning of the application.

```
LRESULT CALLBACK WndProc( HWND hWnd, UINT uMsg, WPARAM wParam, LPARAM lParam )
{
static int nSave;

    switch( uMsg )
    {
        case WM_CREATE  :
                {
                    HDC hDC = GetDC( hWnd );

                    // Initialize the device context.
                    //................................
                    SetMapMode( hDC, MM_ISOTROPIC );
                    SetWindowExtEx( hDC, 1, 1, NULL );
                    SetViewportExtEx( hDC, 2, 2, NULL );
                }
                break;

        case WM_COMMAND :
                switch( LOWORD( wParam ) )
                {
                    case IDM_TEST :
                            {
                                HDC   hDC;
                                SIZE  sizeWExt;
```

```
    SIZE  sizeVExt;
    POINT pt;
    char  szMsg[40];

    hDC = GetDC( hWnd );

    // Check to see if the mapping mode has
    // changed. If it has, restore it.
    //...........................
    if ( GetMapMode( hDC ) != MM_ISOTROPIC )
       RestoreDC( hDC, nSave );

    // Get the mapping mode ratio.
    //.........................
    GetWindowExtEx( hDC, &sizeWExt );
    GetViewportExtEx( hDC, &sizeVExt );

    wsprintf( szMsg, "MM_ISOTROPIC - %d%%",
            MulDiv( sizeVExt.cx, 100, sizeWExt.cx ));

    // Determine where to place the text
    // for the MM_TEXT line.
    //..............................
    pt.x = 110;
    DPtoLP( hDC, &pt, 1 );

    // Draw the labels for the lines.
    //..............................
    TextOut( hDC, pt.x, 37, "MM_TEXT - 100%", 14 );
    TextOut( hDC, 105, 17, szMsg, strlen( szMsg ) );

    // Draw the MM_ISOTROPIC line.
    //.........................
    MoveToEx( hDC, 0, 20, NULL );
    LineTo( hDC, 100, 20 );

    // Determine placement for the
    // MM_TEXT line.
    //.........................
    pt.y = 40;
    LPtoDP( hDC, &pt, 1 );

    // Save the device context
    // before changing it.
    //.....................
    nSave = SaveDC( hDC );

    // Draw the MM_TEXT line.
    //....................
    SetMapMode( hDC, MM_TEXT );
    MoveToEx( hDC, 0, pt.y, NULL );
    LineTo( hDC, 100, pt.y );
}
break;
```

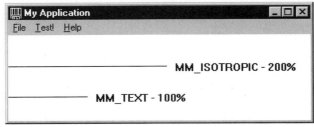

Figure 12-7 `SetMapMode` example

SetMapperFlags ■ WINDOWS 95 ■ WINDOWS NT

Description	`SetMapperFlags` sets the algorithm the font mapper uses when it maps logical fonts to physical fonts. `CreateFont` and `CreateFontIndirect` will normally interpolate to achieve specified font sizes and aspect ratios not described in the font data. Use `SetMapperFlags` to force the use of the nearest matching font or to allow interpolation.
Syntax	`DWORD SetMapperFlags( HDC hdc, DWORD dwFlag )`
Parameters	
hdc	`HDC`: The handle of the device context that contains the font-mapper flag.
dwFlag	`DWORD`: If bit `0` is set, the mapper selects only matching fonts; otherwise, interpolation is allowed.
Returns	`DWORD`: If successful, the return value is the previous value of the font-mapper flag; otherwise, `GDI_ERROR` is returned.
Include File	`wingdi.h`
See Also	`CreateFont`, `CreateFontIndirect`, `GetAspectRatioFilterEx`
Example	See the example for the `CreateFont` function.

SetViewportExtEx ■ WINDOWS 95 ■ WINDOWS NT

Description	`SetViewportExtEx` sets the horizontal and vertical extents of the viewport for a device context (DC).
Syntax	`BOOL SetViewportExtEx( HDC hdc, int nXExtent, int nYExtent, LPSIZE lpSize )`
Parameters	
hdc	`HDC`: The handle of the DC.
nXExtent	`int`: The horizontal extent, in device units, of the viewport.
nYExtent	`int`: The vertical extent, in device units, of the viewport.

lpSize	LPSIZE: A pointer to a SIZE structure that receives the previous viewport extents in device units. If *lpSize* is NULL, the previous viewport extents are not returned.
Returns	BOOL: TRUE if successful; otherwise, the return value is FALSE.
Include File	wingdi.h
See Also	GetViewportExtEx, ScaleViewportExtEx, SetViewportOrgEx
Example	See the example for the SetMapMode function.

SetViewportOrgEx ■ Windows 95 ■ Windows NT

Description	SetViewportOrgEx sets the viewport origin of a device context (DC).
Syntax	BOOL **SetViewportOrgEx**(HDC *hdc,* int *X,* int *Y,* LPPOINT *lpPoint*)
Parameters	
hdc	HDC: The handle of the DC.
X	int: The x coordinate, in device units, of the new viewport origin.
Y	int: The y coordinate, in device units, of the new viewport origin.
lpPoint	LPPOINT: A pointer to a POINT structure that receives the previous viewport origin in device coordinates. If *lpPoint* is NULL, the previous viewport origin is not returned.
Returns	BOOL: TRUE if successful; otherwise, the return value is FALSE.
Include File	wingdi.h
See Also	GetViewportOrgEx
Example	See the example for the GetViewportOrgEx function.

SetWindowExtEx ■ Windows 95 ■ Windows NT

Description	SetWindowExtEx sets the horizontal and vertical extents of the window for a device context (DC).
Syntax	BOOL **SetWindowExtEx**(HDC *hdc,* int *nXExtent,* int *nYExtent,* LPSIZE *lpSize*)
Parameters	
hdc	HDC: The handle of the DC.
nXExtent	int: The horizontal extent in logical units.
nYExtent	int: The vertical extent in logical units.
lpSize	LPSIZE: A pointer to a SIZE structure that receives the previous window extents in logical units. If *lpSize* is NULL, the previous window extents are not returned.

Returns	BOOL: TRUE if successful; otherwise, the return value is FALSE.
Include File	wingdi.h
See Also	SetWindowOrgEx, SetViewportExtEx, GetWindowOrgEx
Example	See the example for the SetMapMode function.

SetWindowOrgEx ■ WINDOWS 95 ■ WINDOWS NT

Description	SetWindowOrgEx sets the window origin of a device context (DC).
Syntax	BOOL **SetWindowOrgEx**(HDC *hdc,* int *X,* int *Y,* LPPOINT *lpPoint*)
Parameters	
hdc	HDC: The handle of the DC.
X	int: The logical x coordinate of the new window origin.
Y	int: The logical y coordinate of the new window origin.
lpPoint	LPPOINT: A pointer to a POINT structure that receives the previous origin of the window. If *lpPoint* is NULL, the previous origin is not returned.
Returns	BOOL: TRUE if successful; otherwise, the return value is FALSE.
Include File	wingdi.h
See Also	GetWindowOrgEx, SetWindowExtEx
Example	See the example for the GetViewportOrgEx example.

WindowFromDC ■ WINDOWS 95 ■ WINDOWS NT

Description	WindowFromDC returns the handle of the window associated with a display device context (DC).
Syntax	HWND **WindowFromDC**(HDC *hdc*)
Parameters	
hdc	HDC: The handle of the DC from which the handle of the associated window is retrieved.
Returns	HWND: If successful, the handle of the window associated with the display DC; otherwise, the return value is NULL.
Include File	winuser.h
See Also	GetDC
Example	This example shows how you can use the WindowFromDC function to retrieve the window handle the DC belongs to.

```
VOID PaintImage( HDC hDC )
{
   HWND hWnd = WindowFromDC( hDC );
```

```
    // Clear the client area
    // before painting.
    //....................
    InvalidateRect( hWnd, NULL, TRUE );
    UpdateWindow( hWnd );

    // Do painting...

        .
        .
        .
}
```

13

BITMAPS, ICONS, AND METAFILES

Windows provides three different picture types that an application can use: bitmaps, icons, and metafiles. Each type of picture has a different use within an application. You typically use *bitmaps* for pictures that will not be scaled or contain text. *Icons* are small versions of bitmaps that you usually use as graphic identifiers for windows. You use *metafiles* in place of bitmaps where bitmaps fall short of your needs. A metafile can contain text and be scaled without losing picture or text quality.

Bitmaps

Bitmaps are blocks of pixel data that can be output directly to a device, such as a video display. They can be thought of as a way to store the pixel data directly from the screen into a memory buffer. Painting bitmaps onto the screen is much faster than using GDI functions like `Rectangle` and `LineTo`. The drawbacks to bitmaps are that they take up a lot of memory and disk space, and they do not scale well, especially if they contain text. When you scale a bitmap it loses quality and distorts the text.

Windows provides two types of bitmaps: the device-dependent bitmap (DDB) and the device-independent bitmap (DIB). The device-dependent bitmap is an older format that is, as its name implies, less flexible than the device-independent bitmap. All Win32 applications should use device-independent bitmaps, because most of the functions that deal with DDBs are provided in Win32 only for compatibility with the Win16 API. These functions may not be available in future versions of the Win32 API.

Using DDB Bitmaps

You normally create bitmaps with a paint program such as the SDKPaint or the bitmap editor built into Visual C++. These bitmaps are stored as disk files with the extension

.BMP. The bitmap is actually saved as a DIB and converted automatically to the DDB format when **LoadBitmap** is called. You add bitmap files to an application's resource script file (RC) with the **BITMAP** statement. Listing 13-1 shows how to load a device-dependent bitmap and display it on the screen.

Listing 13-1 DDB example

Resource script file

```
pen      BITMAP     pen.bmp
```

Sample code

```
HBITMAP hBitmap;
HDC     hDC;
HDC     hMemDC;

// Load the bitmap into memory.
//.............................
hBitmap = LoadBitmap( hInst, "pen" );

// Paint the bitmap on the screen.
//...............................
hDC = GetDC( hWnd );
hMemDC = CreateCompatibleDC( hDC );

SelectObject( hMemDC, hBitmap );
BitBlt( hDC, 10, 10, 60, 60, hMemDC, 0, 0, SRCCOPY );

DeleteDC( hMemDC );
ReleaseDC( hWnd, hDC );
DeleteObject( hBitmap );
```

This example loads a file called **PEN.BMP** and gives the bitmap resource the name "**pen**". With the bitmap loaded as part of the application's resources, the application uses **LoadBitmap** to bring the bitmap into memory. Painting the bitmap on the screen is somewhat more involved. The application loads the bitmap into a memory device context, and then paints the memory device context onto the screen with the **BitBlt** function.

The DDB format works well for copying parts of the screen into memory and pasting them back onto other locations of the screen. Problems occur when the application needs to save bitmap data in disk files, and then display it on another type of device. The DDB header does not have a place to store the colors used in creating the bitmap. The assumption is that the bitmap will be displayed on the same type of device, with the same colors. If the bitmap is displayed on another device, the colors may end up completely different. This is where the device-independent bitmaps work well.

Using DIB Bitmaps

The device-independent bitmap, called a DIB, fixes the shortcomings of the DDB. The big difference between DIBs and DDBs is that DIBs include a table of the colors the bitmap will use. The header of the bitmap is also more complex. Unlike a DDB, a DIB is not a graphics object; it is a data format. An application cannot select a DIB into a device context.

The DIB format consists of three sections, as shown in Figure 13-1. The first section is the **BITMAPINFOHEADER** structure shown below. For more information on this structure, see the **CreateDIBitmap** function later in this chapter.

```
typedef struct tagBITMAPINFOHEADER
{
    DWORD   biSize;              // size of BITMAPINFOHEADER
    LONG    biWidth;            // width in pixels
    LONG    biHeight;           // height in pixels
    WORD    biPlanes;           // always 1
    WORD    biBitCount;         // color bits per pixel
    DWORD   biCompression;      // BI_RGB, BI_RLE8, or BI_RLE4
    DWORD   biSizeImage;        // total bytes in image
    LONG    biXPelsPerMeter;    // 0, or opt. horz. res.
    LONG    biYPelsPerMeter;    // 0, or opt. vert. res.
    DWORD   biClrUsed;          // normally 0, can be lower than biBitCount
    DWORD   biClrImportant;     // normally 0
} BITMAPINFOHEADER, *LPBITMAPINFOHEADER;
```

After the **BITMAPINFOHEADER** structure, a DIB will contain the color table. This is a set of **RGBQUAD** data structures, holding the RGB color for each of the colors used in the bitmap. There will be as many **RGBQUAD** entries as there are color choices in the bitmap. The **RGBQUAD** structure is shown here:

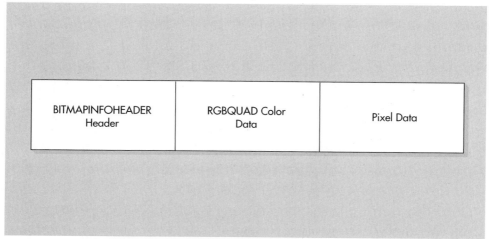

Figure 13-1 Device-independent bitmap (DIB) format

```
typedef struct tagRGBQUAD
{
    BYTE rgbBlue;
    BYTE rgbGreen;
    BYTE rgbRed;
    BYTE rgbReserved;
} RGBQUAD;
```

Windows provides an alternative to specifying the bitmap colors using RGB color values. The color table can be an array of 16-bit unsigned integers, each of which is an index into the currently realized logical palette. Using palette index values allows bitmap colors to change as the palette is changed. Several of the DIB functions include a *uUsage* parameter that can be set to **DIB_PAL_COLORS** if the color table contains palette entries. RGB colors should be used if the bitmap is to be saved to disk, potentially for use by some other type of device that may have a different color resolution.

Listing 13-2 shows an example of loading the color data from a DIB, and then displaying the bitmap. The example assumes that the **PEN.BMP** DIB bitmap was made part of the resource script file as in Listing 13-1. The color data from the DIB is read and converted to a logical palette when the **WM_CREATE** message is processed. This procedure is complex, because the program has to calculate how many color values are stored with the bitmap. Note that although the logical palette is created while processing the **WM_CREATE** message, it is not realized until the **WM_PAINT** message is processed.

You use the **SetDIBitsToDevice** function to display the bitmap. This function requires a pointer to both the **BITMAPINFO** data and the DIB bitmap data. The latter is calculated as an offset from the start of the **BITMAPINFO** data, because the resource data loads the bitmap bits right after the end of the color data.

Listing 13-2 Example of loading a DIB bitmap

```
LRESULT CALLBACK WndProc( HWND hWnd, UINT uMsg, WPARAM wParam, LPARAM lParam )
{
static HPALETTE hPalette;
static int      nColorData;

    switch( uMsg )
    {
        case WM_CREATE  :
                {
                    HANDLE        hRes;
                    LPBITMAPINFO  lpBi;
                    LPLOGPALETTE  lpPal;
                    int           i;

                    // Load the bitmap.
                    //.................
                    hRes = LoadResource( hInst,
                            FindResource( hInst, "pen", RT_BITMAP ) );

                    lpBi = (LPBITMAPINFO)LockResource( hRes );

                    // Find out how many colors we need.
                    //..................................
                    if ( lpBi->bmiHeader.biClrUsed != 0 )
```

```
                nColorData = lpBi->bmiHeader.biClrUsed;
            else
                switch( lpBi->bmiHeader.biBitCount )
                {
                    case 1  : nColorData = 2;    break; // Monochrome
                    case 4  : nColorData = 16;   break; // VGA
                    case 8  : nColorData = 256;  break; // SVGA
                    case 24 : nColorData = 0;    break; // True Color
                }

            // Allocate memory for color palette.
            //....................................
            lpPal = (LPLOGPALETTE)HeapAlloc( GetProcessHeap(), HEAP_ZERO_MEMORY,
                                        sizeof(LOGPALETTE)+(nColorData * ⇐
sizeof(PALETTEENTRY)) );

            lpPal->palVersion    = 0x300;
            lpPal->palNumEntries = nColorData;

            // Load each color into the palette.
            //....................................
            for ( i = 0; i < nColorData; i++ )
            {
                lpPal->palPalEntry[i].peRed   = lpBi->bmiColors[i].rgbRed;
                lpPal->palPalEntry[i].peGreen = lpBi->bmiColors[i].rgbGreen;
                lpPal->palPalEntry[i].peBlue  = lpBi->bmiColors[i].rgbBlue;
            }

            // Create the palette.
            //.....................
            hPalette = CreatePalette( lpPal );
            HeapFree( GetProcessHeap(), 0, lpPal );
        }
        break;

    case WM_PAINT :
        {
            PAINTSTRUCT  ps;
            LPBITMAPINFO lpBi;
            HANDLE       hRes;
            LPTSTR       lpBits;

            BeginPaint( hWnd, &ps );

            // Select palette and realize it.
            //................................
            SelectPalette( ps.hdc, hPalette, FALSE );
            RealizePalette( ps.hdc );

            // Load the bitmap.
            //..................
            hRes = LoadResource( hInst,
                        FindResource( hInst, "pen", RT_BITMAP ) );

            lpBi = (LPBITMAPINFO)LockResource( hRes );

            // Locate the bitmap data.
            //.........................
```

continued on next page

continued from previous page

```
        lpBits =  (LPSTR) lpBi;
        lpBits +=  lpBi->bmiHeader.biSize +
                 ( nColorData*sizeof(RGBQUAD) );

        // Paint the bitmap.
        //.................
        SetDIBitsToDevice( ps.hdc, 10, 10,
                                 lpBi->bmiHeader.biWidth,
                                 lpBi->bmiHeader.biHeight,
                                 0, 0,
                                 0, lpBi->bmiHeader.biHeight,
                                 lpBits, lpBi, DIB_RGB_COLORS );

        EndPaint( hWnd, &ps );
     }
     break;

  case WM_COMMAND :
        switch( LOWORD( wParam ) )
        {
            case IDM_EXIT :
                 DestroyWindow( hWnd );
                 break;
        }
        break;

  case WM_DESTROY :
        DeleteObject( hPalette );
        PostQuitMessage(0);
        break;

  default :
        return( DefWindowProc( hWnd, uMsg, wParam, lParam ) );
  }

  return( 0L );
}
```

Icons

Icons are small bitmaps that Windows uses as visual representations of objects such as applications, files, and directories. In Windows NT 4 and Windows 95, you'll see icons in every aspect of the user interface. In earlier versions of Windows and Windows NT 3.5, you'll see icons in such places as the Program Manager and when an application is minimized.

Using Icons

Windows NT 4 and Windows 95 applications should have at least one icon with three different icon sizes supported, a 256-color (48×48) icon, 16-color (32×32) icon, and a smaller 16-color (16×16) icon. The small icon is displayed when the application is minimized and in the upper-left corner of the application window. The large is used for the desktop icon and in large icon views. Additional icons should be created for each data type that an application supports.

As with bitmaps, you normally create icons using the Win32 SDK Image Editor or with another editor such as the Visual C++ icon editor. You then add these icons to the application's resource script file using the `ICON` statement. A typical example of the use of icons is the registration of the main window class. Listing 13-3 shows how to register a window class with a large and small icon.

Listing 13-3 Icon usage in window class registration

```
int APIENTRY WinMain( HINSTANCE hInstance, HINSTANCE hPrevInstance,
                      LPTSTR lpCmdLine, int nCmdShow)
{
    WNDCLASSEX wc;

    wc.style         = CS_HREDRAW | CS_VREDRAW;
    wc.lpfnWndProc   = (WNDPROC)WndProc;
    wc.cbClsExtra    = 0;
    wc.cbWndExtra    = 0;
    wc.hInstance     = hInstance;
    wc.hIcon         = LoadIcon (hInstance, "APPICON" );      // Set large icon.
    wc.hCursor       = LoadCursor(NULL, IDC_ARROW);
    wc.hbrBackground = (HBRUSH)(COLOR_WINDOW+1);
    wc.lpszMenuName  = lpszAppName;
    wc.lpszClassName = lpszAppName;
    wc.cbSize        = sizeof(WNDCLASSEX);
    wc.hIconSm       = LoadImage(hInstance, "APPICON",
                                 IMAGE_ICON, 16, 16,
                                 LR_DEFAULTCOLOR );            // Set small icon.

    if ( !RegisterClassEx( &wc ) )
        return( FALSE );
        .
        .
        .
```

Creating Icons at Runtime

Windows allows icons to be created and modified while the program is running. The `CreateIcon` function is similar to `CreateCursor`. Both functions create an image by combining two bitmaps. `CreateIcon` lets you create icons from a binary array, bitmap data, and device-independent bitmaps. The `DestroyIcon` function lets you delete an icon created with `CreateIcon`, freeing memory consumed by the icon's data. Don't modify icons at runtime, because users expect icons to remain unchanged.

Metafiles

Metafiles are coded GDI (Graphics Device Interface) function calls. When a metafile is played, the result is the same as if the GDI functions had been used directly. The difference is that metafiles can be stored in memory or as disk files, reloaded, and played any number of times by different applications. Metafiles are also more device-independent than bitmaps, because the GDI functions are interpreted at runtime, based on the output device context.

The Windows 3.x metafile is supported under Windows NT 4 and Windows 95; however, it is recommended that Win32 applications use a new enhanced metafile. The main difference between the Windows 3.x metafile and the enhanced metafile is that enhanced metafiles are truly device independent and work with the new GDI calls available in the Win32 API. For every function that deals with Windows 3.x metafiles, there is a matching enhanced metafile function in the Win32 API. For example, the `PlayMetaFile` function has a matching enhanced metafile function named `PlayEnhMetaFile`. Because the functions that work with Windows 3.x metafiles are only provided for compatibility and not recommended for Win32 applications, this chapter covers only the enhanced metafile functions.

Creating and Playing a Metafile

You create metafiles by using GDI functions on a metafile device context. You use the reference device context as the basis for the metafile to maintain picture dimensions across output devices. This reference device is the device on which the picture first appeared. Listing 13-4 shows how to create an enhanced metafile that draws a rectangle filled with a hatched brush pattern. Note that the size of the client area is calculated in 0.01-millimeter units and passed to the `CreateEnhMetaFile` function.

Listing 13-4 Creating an enhanced metafile

```
static HENHMETAFILE hMetaFile;

HDC   hMetaDC;
HDC   hRefDC;
RECT  rect;
int   iWidthMM, iHeightMM, iWidthPels, iHeightPels;
int   iMMPerPelX, iMMPerPelY;

hRefDC = GetDC( hWnd );

// Compute the size of the client area in 0.01 mm.
//...............................................
iWidthMM    = GetDeviceCaps(hRefDC, HORZSIZE);
iHeightMM   = GetDeviceCaps(hRefDC, VERTSIZE);
iWidthPels  = GetDeviceCaps(hRefDC, HORZRES);
iHeightPels = GetDeviceCaps(hRefDC, VERTRES);

iMMPerPelX = (iWidthMM * 100)/iWidthPels;
iMMPerPelY = (iHeightMM * 100)/iHeightPels;

GetClientRect(hWnd, &rect);

rect.right = rect.right * iMMPerPelX;
rect.bottom = rect.bottom * iMMPerPelY;

// Create an enhanced metafile.
//.............................
hMetaDC = CreateEnhMetaFile( hRefDC, NULL, &rect, "Test Metafile" );
if ( hMetaDC )
{
```

```
    HBRUSH hBrush;

    hBrush = CreateHatchBrush( HS_DIAGCROSS, RGB(0, 0, 255) );

    SelectObject( hMetaDC, hBrush );
    Rectangle( hMetaDC, 10, 10, 100, 100 );

    hMetaFile = CloseEnhMetaFile( hMetaDC );
    DeleteObject( hBrush );
}

ReleaseDC( hWnd, hRefDC );
```

Metafiles in a Disk File

An application can record a metafile to a disk file just as easily as in a memory block. The advantage of using a disk file is that the metafile can be saved and played later without the time required to recreate all of the GDI function calls. Here is the `CreateEnhMetaFile` function used in Listing 13-4, but now a disk file is created.

```
hMetaDC = CreateEnhMetaFile( hRefDC, "mymeta.emf", &rect, "Test Metafile" );
```

The metafile is now stored in the file name passed to the `CreateEnhMetaFile` function. Later, the application can use the `GetEnhMetaFile` function to load the disk metafile into memory so that it can be played using `PlayEnhMetaFile`.

There are two common uses for disk metafiles. One is as a compact method of storing graphics data for use in an application. The metafiles are generated as the application is developed. The final application is distributed with the metafiles on the distribution disks. The second use of disk metafiles is as a means of storing graphics data for a painting or design application. Metafiles are ideal if the application uses objects like lines, rectangles, and ellipses for drawing. Metafiles are not useful if the application is pixel based.

Bitmap, Icon, and Metafile Function Descriptions

Table 13-1 summarizes the bitmap, icon, and metafile functions. Detailed function descriptions follow the table.

Table 13-1 Bitmap, icon, and metafile function summary

Function	Purpose
BitBlt	Copies a bitmap from a memory device context to another device context.
CloseEnhMetaFile	Closes an enhanced metafile device context (DC) and returns a handle that identifies the metafile.
CopyEnhMetaFile	Copies an enhanced metafile to a file or memory.
CopyIcon	Copies an icon from another module to the current module.
CopyImage	Creates a new image (icon, cursor, or bitmap) and copies the attributes of an image to the new one.
CreateBitmap	Creates a bitmap based on an array of color bit values.

continued on next page

continued from previous page

Function	Purpose
CreateBitmapIndirect	Creates a bitmap based on data in a BITMAP data structure.
CreateCompatibleBitmap	Creates a memory bitmap compatible with a device.
CreateDIBitmap	Creates a memory bitmap based on device-independent bitmap (DIB) data.
CreateDIBSection	Creates a device-independent bitmap (DIB) to which both GDI and applications can directly write.
CreateEnhMetaFile	Creates a device context (DC) for an enhanced metafile.
CreateIcon	Creates an icon based on two memory blocks containing bit data.
CreateIconFromResource	Creates an icon or cursor from resource bits describing the icon.
CreateIconFromResourceEx	Creates an icon or cursor of a desired size from resource bits describing the icon.
CreateIconIndirect	Creates an icon or cursor from an ICONINFO structure.
DeleteEnhMetaFile	Deletes an enhanced metafile.
DestroyIcon	Destroys an icon previously created with the CreateIcon function.
DrawIcon	Draws an icon on a device.
DrawIconEx	Draws an icon of a specified size on a device, using raster operations.
EnumEnhMetaFile	Enumerates the records within an enhanced metafile by retrieving each record and passing it to an application-defined callback function.
GdiComment	Places a comment in an enhanced metafile.
GetBitmapDimensionEx	Retrieves the dimensions of a bitmap previously set by the SetBitmapDimensionEx function.
GetDIBits	Retrieves the bits of a bitmap and copies them into a buffer using a specified format.
GetEnhMetaFile	Creates a handle that identifies the enhanced metafile stored in a file.
GetEnhMetaFileBits	Retrieves the contents of an enhanced metafile.
GetEnhMetaFileDescription	Retrieves an optional text description from an enhanced metafile.
GetEnhMetaFileHeader	Retrieves the record containing the header of an enhanced metafile.
GetEnhMetaFilePaletteEntries	Retrieves optional palette entries from an enhanced metafile.
GetIconInfo	Retrieves information about an icon or cursor.
GetMetaRgn	Retrieves the current meta-region for a device context.
GetStretchBltMode	Determines the current bitmap stretching mode of a device context.
GetWinMetaFileBits	Converts an enhanced metafile into a Windows 3.x metafile.
LoadBitmap	Loads a bitmap resource into memory.
LoadIcon	Retrieves a handle to an icon listed in the program's resource file.
LoadImage	Retrieves a handle to an image (icon, cursor, or bitmap) listed in the program's resource file.
LookupIconIdFromDirectory	Finds an icon or cursor within the icon or cursor data that best fits the current display device.
LookupIconIdFromDirectoryEx	Finds an icon or cursor within the icon or cursor data that best fits the current display device returning an icon or cursor of a specified size.
PatBlt	Outputs a pattern brush to a device.
PlayEnhMetaFile	Outputs an enhanced metafile to a device context.
PlayEnhMetaFileRecord	Plays an enhanced metafile record by executing the Graphics Device Interface (GDI) functions identified by the record.
SetBitmapDimensionEx	Assigns preferred dimensions to a bitmap.
SetDIBits	Sets device-independent bitmap (DIB) pixel data to the data in a memory buffer.

Function	Purpose
SetDIBitsToDevice	Paints from a device-independent bitmap (DIB) directly on a device context.
SetEnhMetaFileBits	Creates an enhanced metafile in memory from supplied data.
SetMetaRgn	Intersects the current clipping region of a device context with the current meta-region and saves the combined region as the new meta-region for the device context.
SetStretchBltMode	Sets the bitmap stretching mode for the StretchBlt function.
SetWinMetaFileBits	Converts a Windows 3.x metafile to an enhanced metafile.
StretchBlt	Copies a bitmap from one device context to another, stretching or compressing the image to fit the destination rectangle.
StretchDIBits	Paints from a DIB directly on a device context, stretching and/or compressing the image as it is painted.

BitBlt

■ Windows 95   ■ Windows NT

Description   BitBlt is the standard function for displaying a bitmap. This function copies a bitmap from a memory device context to another device context, such as the device context of a window. The bitmap first must be selected into a memory device context, created with the CreateCompatibleDC function. The bitmap can be combined with the existing background using any of the raster-operation codes. Not all devices support BitBlt. Check the RASTERCAPS value returned from the GetDeviceCaps function to determine if BitBlt operations are supported.

Syntax   BOOL **BitBlt**(HDC *hdcDest,* int *nXDest,* int *nYDest,* int *nWidth,* int *nHeight,* HDC *hdcSrc,* int *nXSrc,* int *nYSrc,* DWORD *dwRop*)

Parameters

hdcDest   HDC: The device context handle to receive the bitmap.

nXDest   int: The logical x coordinate of the upper-left corner of the destination rectangle.

nYDest   int: The logical y coordinate of the upper-left corner of the destination rectangle.

nWidth   int: The width, in logical units, of the source and destination rectangles.

nHeight   int: The height, in logical units, of the source and destination rectangles.

hdcSrc   HDC: The device context from which the bitmap will be copied. This is normally a memory device context created with CreateCompatibleDC.

nXSrc   int: The logical x coordinate of the upper-left corner of the source rectangle.

nYSrc   int: The logical y coordinate of the upper-left corner of the source rectangle.

dwRop	DWORD: The raster-operation code. These codes define how the color data for the source rectangle is to be combined with the color data for the destination rectangle to achieve the final color. Table 13-2 shows some common raster-operation codes.

Table 13-2 Raster-operation codes

Value	Description
BLACKNESS	Sets all output to the color associated with index 0 in the physical palette (black for the default physical palette).
DSTINVERT	Inverts the destination rectangle.
MERGECOPY	The source and destination bitmaps are combined with the Boolean AND operator.
MERGEPAINT	The source and destination bitmaps are combined with the Boolean OR operator.
NOTSRCCOPY	Inverts the source bitmap, then copies it to the destination.
NOTSRCERASE	Inverts the result of combining the source and destination bitmaps using the Boolean OR operator.
PATCOPY	Copies a pattern to the destination.
PATINVERT	Combines the destination bitmap with the pattern using Boolean XOR operator.
PATPAINT	Combines the colors of the pattern with the colors of the inverted source rectangle using the Boolean OR operator. The result is combined with the colors of the destination bitmap using the Boolean OR operator.
SRCAND	Combines the source and destination bitmaps with the Boolean AND operator.
SRCCOPY	Copies the source directly to the destination.
SRCERASE	Combines the inverted colors of the destination bitmap with the colors of the source bitmap using the Boolean AND operator.
SRCINVERT	Combines the source and destination bitmaps using the Boolean XOR operator.
SRCPAINT	Combines the source and destination bitmaps using the Boolean OR operator.
WHITENESS	Sets all output to the color associated with index 1 in the physical palette (white for the default physical palette).

Returns	BOOL: TRUE if successful; otherwise, the return value is FALSE.
Include File	wingdi.h
See Also	PatBlt, CreateCompatibleDC, DeleteObject, LoadBitmap, SelectObject, GetDeviceCaps
Example	In this example, shown in Figure 13-2, when the user selects the Test! menu item, the bitmap "SmileBMP" is loaded from the resource file (RC) and tiled on the client area of the window. The GetObject function is used to retrieve the bitmap size.

```
LRESULT CALLBACK WndProc( HWND hWnd, UINT uMsg, WPARAM wParam, LPARAM lParam )
{
    switch( uMsg )
    {
      case WM_COMMAND :
            switch( LOWORD( wParam ) )
               {
                 case IDM_TEST :
                     {
                          HBITMAP hBitmap;
                          BITMAP  bm;
```

```
HDC      hDC;
HDC      hMemDC;
RECT     rect;
int      x,y;

// Load the bitmap into memory.
//............................
hBitmap = LoadBitmap( hInst, "SmileBMP" );

// Get the bitmap information.
//............................
GetObject( hBitmap, sizeof( BITMAP ), &bm );

// Paint the bitmap on the screen.
//............................
hDC = GetDC( hWnd );
hMemDC = CreateCompatibleDC( hDC );

SelectObject( hMemDC, hBitmap );

GetClientRect( hWnd, &rect );

for ( y=0; y < rect.bottom; y += bm.bmHeight )
   for ( x=0; x < rect.right; x += bm.bmWidth )
   {
       BitBlt( hDC, x, y,
                  bm.bmWidth,
                  bm.bmHeight,
                  hMemDC, 0, 0, SRCCOPY );
   }

DeleteDC( hMemDC );
ReleaseDC( hWnd, hDC );
DeleteObject( hBitmap );
}
break;
```

.
.
.

Figure 13-2 `BitBlt` example

CloseEnhMetaFile   ■ WINDOWS 95   ■ WINDOWS NT

Description	CloseEnhMetaFile closes an enhanced metafile device context (DC) and returns a handle that can be used to play the metafile. After painting operations to a metafile device context opened with CreateEnhMetaFile are complete, the metafile must be closed before it can be used.
Syntax	HENHMETAFILE **CloseEnhMetaFile**(HDC *hdc*)
Parameters	
hdc	HDC: The enhanced metafile DC created with the CreateEnhMetaFile function.
Returns	HENMETAFILE: The handle of an enhanced metafile. NULL is returned on an error.
Include File	wingdi.h
See Also	CreateEnhMetaFile
Example	See the example for the CreateEnhMetaFile function.

CopyEnhMetaFile   ■ WINDOWS 95   ■ WINDOWS NT

Description	CopyEnhMetaFile copies the contents of an enhanced metafile to a file. Alternatively, if the *lpszFileName* parameter is set to NULL, the source metafile is copied to a memory metafile.
Syntax	HENHMETAFILE **CopyEnhMetaFile**(HENHMETAFILE *hemSrc,* LPCTSTR *lpszFileName*)
Parameters	
hemSrc	HENHMETAFILE: The handle of the source enhanced metafile.
lpszFileName	LPCTSTR: A pointer to a null-terminated string containing the name of the destination file. If set to NULL, the source enhanced metafile is copied to memory.
Returns	HENHMETAFILE: The handle of the copy of the enhanced metafile. If an error occurs, NULL is returned.
Include File	wingdi.h
See Also	DeleteEnhMetaFile
Example	This example creates a metafile when the application starts up by processing the WM_CREATE message. When the user selects the Test! menu item, the metafile is saved to the file SAVE.EMF using the CopyEnhMetaFile function.

```
LRESULT CALLBACK WndProc( HWND hWnd, UINT uMsg, WPARAM wParam, LPARAM lParam )
{
static HENHMETAFILE hMetaFile = NULL;
```

```
switch( uMsg )
{
    case WM_CREATE   :
            {
                HDC   hMetaDC;
                HDC   hRefDC;
                RECT  rect;
                int   iWidthMM, iHeightMM, iWidthPels, iHeightPels;
                int   iMMPerPelX, iMMPerPelY;

                hRefDC = GetDC( hWnd );

                // Compute the size of the client area in 0.01 mm.
                //...............................................
                iWidthMM    = GetDeviceCaps(hRefDC, HORZSIZE);
                iHeightMM   = GetDeviceCaps(hRefDC, VERTSIZE);
                iWidthPels  = GetDeviceCaps(hRefDC, HORZRES);
                iHeightPels = GetDeviceCaps(hRefDC, VERTRES);

                iMMPerPelX = (iWidthMM * 100)/iWidthPels;
                iMMPerPelY = (iHeightMM * 100)/iHeightPels;

                GetClientRect(hWnd, &rect);

                rect.right = rect.right * iMMPerPelX;
                rect.bottom = rect.bottom * iMMPerPelY;

                // Create an enhanced metafile.
                //............................
                hMetaDC = CreateEnhMetaFile( hRefDC, NULL, &rect,
                                             "Test Metafile" );
                if ( hMetaDC )
                {
                    HBRUSH hBrush;

                    hBrush = CreateHatchBrush( HS_DIAGCROSS, RGB(0, 0, 255) );

                    SelectObject( hMetaDC, hBrush );
                    Rectangle( hMetaDC, 10, 10, 200, 200 );

                    hMetaFile = CloseEnhMetaFile( hMetaDC );
                    DeleteObject( hBrush );
                }

                ReleaseDC( hWnd, hRefDC );
            }
            break;

    case WM_PAINT    :
            {
                PAINTSTRUCT ps;
                RECT        rect;

                BeginPaint( hWnd, &ps );

                GetClientRect( hWnd, &rect );
                PlayEnhMetaFile( ps.hdc, hMetaFile, &rect );
```

continued on next page

continued from previous page

```
                    EndPaint( hWnd, &ps );
            }
            break;

    case WM_COMMAND :
            switch( LOWORD( wParam ) )
            {
                case IDM_TEST :
                        if ( CopyEnhMetaFile( hMetaFile, "save.emf" ) )
                            MessageBox( hWnd, "Meta file saved.", "Save",
                                        MB_OK | MB_ICONINFORMATION );
                        else
                            MessageBox( hWnd, "Meta file NOT saved.", "Error",
                                        MB_OK | MB_ICONINFORMATION );
                        break;

                case IDM_EXIT :
                        DestroyWindow( hWnd );
                        break;
            }
            break;

    case WM_DESTROY :
            DeleteEnhMetaFile( hMetaFile );
            PostQuitMessage(0);
            break;

    default :
            return( DefWindowProc( hWnd, uMsg, wParam, lParam ) );
    }

    return( 0L );
}
```

CopyIcon   ■ Windows 95   ■ Windows NT

Description	CopyIcon copies an icon from another module to the current module. Used to acquire a copy of an icon from a dynamic link library (DLL) or an application that will remain valid even if that module is closed.
Syntax	HICON **CopyIcon**(HICON *hicon*)
Parameters	
hicon	HICON: The handle of the icon to be copied.
Returns	HICON: The handle of the duplicate icon. If an error occurs, **NULL** is returned.
Include File	winuser.h
See Also	CopyCursor, CopyImage
Example	This example, shown in Figure 13-3, loads and copies an icon from a dynamic link library (DLL) when the user selects the Test! menu item. The icon is displayed on the client area using the **DrawIcon** function.

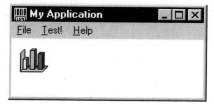

Figure 13-3 CopyIcon example

```c
LRESULT CALLBACK WndProc( HWND hWnd, UINT uMsg, WPARAM wParam, LPARAM lParam )
{
static HICON hIcon = NULL;

    switch( uMsg )
    {
        case WM_PAINT   :
                {
                    PAINTSTRUCT ps;

                    BeginPaint( hWnd, &ps );

                    // Paint the icon if we have one.
                    //...............................
                    if ( hIcon )
                        DrawIcon( ps.hdc, 10, 10, hIcon );

                    EndPaint( hWnd, &ps );
                }
                break;

        case WM_COMMAND :
                switch( LOWORD( wParam ) )
                {
                    case IDM_TEST :
                        {
                            HINSTANCE hInstRes = LoadLibrary( "RESOURCE.DLL" );

                            if ( hInstRes )
                            {
                                HICON   hExIcon;

                                hExIcon = LoadIcon( hInstRes, "EXCEL" );

                                if ( hExIcon )
                                    hIcon = CopyIcon( hExIcon );

                                FreeLibrary( hInstRes );
                                InvalidateRect( hWnd, NULL, TRUE );
                            }
                            else
                                MessageBox( hWnd, "Resource.DLL could not be loaded", NULL,
                                            MB_OK | MB_ICONSTOP );
                        }
                        break;
                .
                .
                .
```

CopyImage
■ WINDOWS 95　■ WINDOWS NT

Description	CopyImage creates a new image (icon, cursor, or bitmap) with the attributes of another image. If necessary, the function stretches the bits to fit the desired size of the new image.
Syntax	HANDLE **CopyImage**(HANDLE *hImage,* UINT *uType,* int *cxDesired,* int *cyDesired,* UINT *uFlags*)
Parameters	
hImage	HANDLE: The handle of the image to be copied.
uType	UINT: The type of image to be copied. This parameter can be one of the values listed in Table 13-3.

Table 13-3 CopyImage *uType* values

Value	Meaning
IMAGE_BITMAP	Copies a bitmap.
IMAGE_CURSOR	Copies a cursor.
IMAGE_ENHMETAFILE	Copies an enhanced metafile.
IMAGE_ICON	Copies an icon.

cxDesired	int: The desired width, in pixels, of the new image.
cyDesired	int: The desired height, in pixels, of the new image.
uFlags	UINT: Determines how the image is copied. This parameter can be a combination of the values listed in Table 13-4 combined with the binary OR (	) operator.

Table 13-4 CopyImage *uFlags* values

Value	Meaning
LR_COPYDELETEORG	Deletes the original image after creating the copy.
LR_COPYRETURNORG	Creates an exact copy of the image, ignoring the *cxDesired* and *cyDesired* parameters.
LR_MONOCHROME	Creates a new monochrome image.

Returns	HANDLE: The handle of the newly created image. If an error occurs, **NULL** is returned.
Include File	winuser.h
See Also	LoadImage, CopyIcon, CopyCursor
Example	This example is exactly the same as the example for the **CopyIcon** function, except that the **CopyImage** function is used to copy the icon and make a monochrome icon.

```
LRESULT CALLBACK WndProc( HWND hWnd, UINT uMsg, WPARAM wParam, LPARAM lParam )
{
static HICON hIcon = NULL;

   switch( uMsg )
   {
      case WM_COMMAND :
              switch( LOWORD( wParam ) )
              {
                 case IDM_TEST :
                    {
                       HINSTANCE hInstRes = LoadLibrary( "RESOURCE.DLL" );

                       if ( hInstRes )
                       {
                          HICON    hExIcon;

                          hExIcon = LoadIcon( hInstRes, "EXCEL" );

                          // Copy the icon, creating
                          // a monochrome icon.
                          //........................
                          if ( hExIcon )
                              hIcon = CopyImage( hExIcon, IMAGE_ICON,
                                             32, 32, LR_MONOCHROME );

                          FreeLibrary( hInstRes );

                          InvalidateRect( hWnd, NULL, TRUE );
                       }
                       else
                          MessageBox( hWnd, "Resource.DLL could not be loaded", NULL,
                                   MB_OK | MB_ICONSTOP );
                    }
                    break;
              .
              .
              .
```

CreateBitmap   ■ WINDOWS 95   ■ WINDOWS NT

Description	CreateBitmap creates a bitmap based on an array of color bit values with the given width, height, and color format (color planes and bits per pixel).
Syntax	HBITMAP **CreateBitmap**(int *nWidth*, int *nHeight*, UINT *uPlanes*, UINT *uBitsPerPel*, CONST VOID* *lpvBits*)

Parameters

nWidth	int: The bitmap width, in pixels.
nHeight	int: The bitmap height, in pixels.
uPlanes	UINT: The number of color planes in the bitmap.
uBitsPerPel	UINT: The number of bits required to identify the color of a single pixel.

lpvBits	**CONST VOID***: A pointer to an array of byte values containing the pixel data. Each scan line in the rectangle must be word aligned (scan lines that are not word aligned must be padded with zeros). If set to **NULL**, the new bitmap is undefined.
Returns	**HBITMAP**: The handle of the new bitmap. If an error occurs, **NULL** is returned.
Include File	wingdi.h
See Also	CreateBitmapIndirect, BitBlt, SelectObject, DeleteObject
Example	This example uses the **CreateBitmap** function to create a monochrome bitmap when the user selects the Test! menu item. The bitmap is selected into a memory device context, and a rectangle and ellipse are drawn on the bitmap. The resulting bitmap, shown in Figure 13-4, is then displayed.

```
LRESULT CALLBACK WndProc( HWND hWnd, UINT uMsg, WPARAM wParam, LPARAM lParam )
{
   switch( uMsg )
   {
      case WM_COMMAND :
              switch( LOWORD( wParam ) )
              {
                case IDM_TEST :
                      {
                         HBITMAP hBitmap;
                         HDC     hDC, hMemDC;

                         // Create a blank bitmap.
                         //.......................
                         hBitmap = CreateBitmap( 64, 64, 1, 1, NULL );

                         // Get the DC and create a
                         // compatible DC.
                         //.......................
                         hDC    = GetDC( hWnd );
                         hMemDC = CreateCompatibleDC( hDC );

                         // Select the bitmap into the
                         // compatible DC and draw on it.
                         //..............................
                         SelectObject( hMemDC, hBitmap );
                         Rectangle( hMemDC, 0, 0, 64, 64 );

                         SelectObject( hMemDC, GetStockObject(GRAY_BRUSH) );
                         Ellipse( hMemDC, 0, 0, 64, 64 );

                         // Display the bitmap on the window.
                         //.................................
                         BitBlt( hDC, 40, 40, 64, 64,
                                 hMemDC, 0, 0, SRCCOPY );

                         ReleaseDC( hWnd, hDC );
                         DeleteDC( hMemDC );
                         DeleteObject( hBitmap );
                      }
                      break;
```

.
.
.

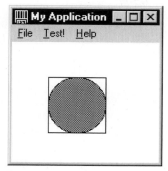

Figure 13-4 `CreateBitmap`
example

CreateBitmapIndirect ■ WINDOWS 95 ■ WINDOWS NT

Description	`CreateBitmapIndirect` creates a bitmap from a `BITMAP` structure. The `BITMAP` structure describes the width, height, color format (color planes and bits per pixel), and actual bitmap bits of a bitmap.
Syntax	HBITMAP **CreateBitmapIndirect**(CONST BITMAP* *lpbm*)
Parameters	
lpbm	CONST BITMAP*: A pointer to a `BITMAP` structure that contains information about the bitmap. If an application sets the *bmWidth* or *bmHeight* members to 0, `CreateBitmapIndirect` returns the handle of a 1×1 pixel, monochrome bitmap. See the definition of the `BITMAP` structure below.
Returns	HBITMAP: If successful, a handle to the new bitmap; otherwise, the return value is NULL.
Include File	`wingdi.h`
See Also	`CreateBitmap, SelectObject, DeleteObject`
BITMAP Definition	

```
typedef struct tagBITMAP
{
    LONG    bmType;
    LONG    bmWidth;
    LONG    bmHeight;
    LONG    bmWidthBytes;
    WORD    bmPlanes;
    WORD    bmBitsPixel;
    LPVOID  bmBits;
} BITMAP;
```

Members

bmType	**LONG**: The bitmap type. This member must be **0**.
bmWidth	**LONG**: The width, in pixels, of the bitmap.
bmHeight	**LONG**: The height, in pixels, of the bitmap.
bmWidthBytes	**LONG**: The number of bytes in each scan line. This value must be divisible by two, because Windows assumes that the bit values of a bitmap form a word-aligned array.
bmPlanes	**WORD**: The number of color planes.
bmBitsPixel	**WORD**: The number of bits required to indicate the color of a pixel.
bmBits	**LPVOID**: A pointer to the location of the bit values for the bitmap. The *bmBits* member must be a pointer to an array of character (1-byte) values.

Example This example creates a bitmap using the **CreateBitmapIndirect** function when the user selects the Test! menu item. The bitmap is an X displayed on the client area of the window.

```
BYTE bBitmap[32] =
{
   0x80, 0x01,  0x40, 0x02,
   0x20, 0x04,  0x10, 0x08,
   0x08, 0x10,  0x04, 0x20,
   0x02, 0x40,  0x01, 0x80,
   0x01, 0x80,  0x02, 0x40,
   0x04, 0x20,  0x08, 0x10,
   0x10, 0x08,  0x20, 0x04,
   0x40, 0x02,  0x80, 0x01
};


LRESULT CALLBACK WndProc( HWND hWnd, UINT uMsg, WPARAM wParam, LPARAM lParam )
{
    switch( uMsg )
    {
      case WM_COMMAND :
              switch( LOWORD( wParam ) )
              {
                case IDM_TEST :
                         {
                              BITMAP  bm;
                              HBITMAP hBitmap;
                              HDC     hDC, hMemDC;

                              // Fill the BITMAP structure.
                              //.........................
                              bm.bmType       = 0;
                              bm.bmWidth      = 16;
                              bm.bmHeight     = 16;
                              bm.bmWidthBytes = 2;
                              bm.bmPlanes     = 1;
                              bm.bmBitsPixel  = 1;
                              bm.bmBits       = bBitmap;
```

```
        // Create the bitmap.
        //..................
        hBitmap = CreateBitmapIndirect( &bm );

        // Display the bitmap.
        //..................
        hDC    = GetDC( hWnd );
        hMemDC = CreateCompatibleDC( hDC );

        SelectObject( hMemDC, hBitmap );

        BitBlt( hDC, 10, 10, 16, 16,
                hMemDC, 0, 0, SRCCOPY );

        ReleaseDC( hWnd, hDC );
        DeleteDC( hMemDC );
        DeleteObject( hBitmap );
    }
    break;
```

.
.
.

CreateCompatibleBitmap ■ Windows 95 ■ Windows NT

Description	`CreateCompatibleBitmap` creates a bitmap compatible with the device that is associated with a given device context (DC). The resulting memory bitmap has the same number of color planes and the same number of color bits per pixel as the device. The bitmap then can be selected into a memory device context for drawing.
Syntax	HBITMAP **CreateCompatibleBitmap**(HDC *hdc,* int *nWidth,* int *nHeight*)
Parameters	
hdc	`HDC`: The device context handle for the physical device with which the bitmap is to be compatible.
nWidth	`int`: The bitmap width, in pixels.
nHeight	`int`: The bitmap height, in pixels.
Returns	`HBITMAP`: If successful, the handle of the new bitmap; otherwise, the return value is `NULL`.
Include File	`wingdi.h`
See Also	`CreateCompatibleDC`
Example	This example is the same as the example for the `CreateBitmap` function, except this example guarantees that the bitmap will be compatible with the display device by using the `CreateCompatibleBitmap` function.

```
LRESULT CALLBACK WndProc( HWND hWnd, UINT uMsg, WPARAM wParam, LPARAM lParam )
{
    switch( uMsg )
    {
        case WM_COMMAND :
                switch( LOWORD( wParam ) )
                {
                    case IDM_TEST :
                        {
                            HBITMAP hBitmap;
                            HDC     hDC, hMemDC;

                            hDC = GetDC( hWnd );

                            // Create a compatible bitmap.
                            //.........................
                            hBitmap = CreateCompatibleBitmap( hDC, 64, 64 );

                            // Create a compatible DC.
                            //.......................
                            hMemDC = CreateCompatibleDC( hDC );

                            // Select the bitmap into the
                            // compatible DC and draw on it.
                            //.............................
                            SelectObject( hMemDC, hBitmap );
                            Rectangle( hMemDC, 0, 0, 64, 64 );

                            SelectObject( hMemDC, GetStockObject(GRAY_BRUSH) );
                            Ellipse( hMemDC, 0, 0, 64, 64 );

                            // Display the bitmap on the window.
                            //.................................
                            BitBlt( hDC, 40, 40, 64, 64,
                                    hMemDC, 0, 0, SRCCOPY );

                            ReleaseDC( hWnd, hDC );
                            DeleteDC( hMemDC );
                            DeleteObject( hBitmap );
                        }
                        break;
                            .
                            .
                            .
```

CreateDIBitmap   ■ WINDOWS 95   ■ WINDOWS NT

Description	`CreateDIBitmap` creates a device-dependent bitmap (DDB) from a device-independent bitmap (DIB) and, optionally, sets the bitmap bits.
Syntax	HBITMAP **CreateDIBitmap**(HDC *hdc*, CONST BITMAPINFOHEADER* *lpbmih*, DWORD *dwInit*, CONST VOID* *lpbInit*, CONST BITMAPINFO* *lpbmi*, UINT *uUsage*)

Parameters

hdc HDC: The device context of the physical device to which the bitmap will be mapped.

lpbmih CONST BITMAPINFOHEADER*: A pointer to a BITMAPINFOHEADER structure. If *dwInit* is CBM_INIT, the function uses the BITMAPINFOHEADER structure to obtain the desired width and height of the bitmap as well as other information. See the definition of the BITMAPINFOHEADER structure below.

dwInit DWORD: Determines if the created bitmap is initialized or uninitialized. If set to 0, the bitmap is not initialized. If set to CBM_INIT, the data pointed to by the *lpbInit* and *lpbmi* parameters is used to initialize the bitmap.

lpbInit CONST VOID*: A pointer to an array of bytes containing the initial bitmap data. The format of the data depends on the *biBitCount* member of the BITMAPINFOHEADER structure contained in the BITMAPINFO structure pointed to by the *lpbmi* parameter.

lpbmi CONST BITMAPINFO*: A pointer to a BITMAPINFO structure that describes the dimensions and color format of the array pointed to by the *lpbInit* parameter. See the definition of the BITMAPINFO structure below.

uUsage UINT: Specifies whether the *bmiColors* member of the BITMAPINFO structure was initialized and, if so, whether *bmiColors* contains explicit RGB values or palette indices. DIB_PAL_COLORS specifies palette entries. DIB_RGB_COLORS specifies explicit colors.

Returns HBITMAP: If successful, the handle of the new bitmap; otherwise, the return value is NULL.

Include File wingdi.h

See Also GetDIBits, CreateBitmap

BITMAPINFOHEADER Definition

```
typedef struct tagBITMAPINFOHEADER
{
    DWORD   biSize;
    LONG    biWidth;
    LONG    biHeight;
    WORD    biPlanes;
    WORD    biBitCount;
    DWORD   biCompression;
    DWORD   biSizeImage;
    LONG    biXPelsPerMeter;
    LONG    biYPelsPerMeter;
    DWORD   biClrUsed;
    DWORD   biClrImportant;
} BITMAPINFOHEADER, *LPBITMAPINFOHEADER;
```

Members

biSize DWORD: The number of bytes required by the structure.

biWidth LONG: The width of the bitmap, in pixels.

biHeight	**LONG**: The height of the bitmap, in pixels. If *biHeight* is positive, the bitmap is a bottom-up DIB and its origin is the lower-left corner. If *biHeight* is negative, the bitmap is a top-down DIB and its origin is the upper-left corner.
biPlanes	**WORD**: The number of planes for the target device. This value must be set to **1**.
biBitCount	**WORD**: The number of bits per pixel. This value must be **1**, **4**, **8**, **16**, **24**, or **32**.
biCompression	**DWORD**: The type of compression for a compressed bottom-up bitmap (top-down DIBs cannot be compressed). Use one of the values listed in Table 13-5.

Table 13-5 BITMAPINFOHEADER *biCompression* values

Value	Description
BI_RGB	An uncompressed format.
BI_RLE8	A run-length encoded (RLE) format for bitmaps with 8 bits per pixel. The compression format is a 2-byte format consisting of a count byte followed by a byte containing a color index.
BI_RLE4	An RLE format for bitmaps with 4 bits per pixel. The compression format is a 2-byte format consisting of a count byte followed by two word-length color indices.
BI_BITFIELDS	Specifies that the bitmap is not compressed and that the color table consists of three doubleword color masks that specify the red, green, and blue components, respectively, of each pixel. This is valid when used with 16- and 32-bits-per-pixel bitmaps.

biSizeImage	**DWORD**: The size, in bytes, of the image.
biXPelsPerMeter	**LONG**: The horizontal resolution, in pixels per meter, of the target device for the bitmap.
biYPelsPerMeter	**LONG**: The vertical resolution, in pixels per meter, of the target device for the bitmap.
biClrUsed	**DWORD**: The number of color indices in the color table that are actually used by the bitmap. If this value is **0**, the bitmap uses the maximum number of colors corresponding to the value of the *biBitCount* member for the compression mode specified by *biCompression*.
biClrImportant	**DWORD**: The number of color indices that are considered important for displaying the bitmap. If this value is **0**, all colors are important.

BITMAPINFO Definition

```
typedef struct tagBITMAPINFO
{
    BITMAPINFOHEADER bmiHeader;
    RGBQUAD          bmiColors[1];
} BITMAPINFO, *LPBITMAPINFO;
```

Members

bmiHeader   BITMAPINFOHEADER: A BITMAPINFOHEADER structure that contains informa-
                   tion about the dimensions and color format of a DIB.

bmiColors   RGBQUAD[]: An array of RGBQUAD or doubleword data types that define the
                   colors in the bitmap.

Example   This example paints a small globe image on the window's client area when
                  the user selects the Test! menu item. The image shown in Figure 13-5 is
                  created by painting on a memory device context containing a 50×50 pixel
                  device-independent bitmap.

```
LRESULT CALLBACK WndProc( HWND hWnd, UINT uMsg, WPARAM wParam, LPARAM lParam )
{
    switch( uMsg )
    {
    case WM_COMMAND :
            switch( LOWORD( wParam ) )
            {
                case IDM_TEST :
                    {
                        BITMAPINFOHEADER   bi;
                        BITMAPINFOHEADER*  lpbi;
                        HBITMAP            hBitmap;
                        HDC                hDC, hMemDC;


                        // Initialize the BITMAPINFOHEADER structure.
                        //...........................................
                        bi.biSize      = sizeof( BITMAPINFOHEADER );
                        bi.biWidth     = 50;
                        bi.biHeight    = 50;
                        bi.biPlanes    = 1;
                        bi.biBitCount  = 4;
                        bi.biCompression   = BI_RGB;
                        bi.biSizeImage     = 0;
                        bi.biXPelsPerMeter = 0;
                        bi.biYPelsPerMeter = 0;
                        bi.biClrUsed       = 0;
                        bi.biClrImportant  = 0;

                        hDC = GetDC( hWnd );

                        // Create DIB.
                        //............
                        hBitmap = CreateDIBitmap( hDC, &bi, OL, NULL,
                                                  NULL, 0 );

                        // Allocate memory for BITMAPINFO structure.
                        //..........................................
                        lpbi = (BITMAPINFOHEADER*)HeapAlloc( GetProcessHeap(),⇐
HEAP_ZERO_MEMORY,
                                                  sizeof(BITMAPINFOHEADER) + ⇐
16*sizeof(RGBQUAD) );
```

continued on next page

continued from previous page

```
                            // Copy bi to top of BITMAPINFO structure.
                            //........................................
                            *lpbi = bi;

                            // Use GetDIBits() to init bi struct data.
                            //........................................
                            GetDIBits( hDC, hBitmap, 0, 50, NULL,
                                       (LPBITMAPINFO)lpbi, DIB_RGB_COLORS );

                            // Create a memory device context
                            // and select the DIB into it.
                            //..............................
                            hMemDC = CreateCompatibleDC( hDC );
                            SelectObject( hMemDC, hBitmap );

                            // Paint on memory device context.
                            //................................
                            SelectObject( hMemDC, GetStockObject(BLACK_BRUSH));
                            Rectangle( hMemDC, 0, 0, 50, 50 );

                            SelectObject( hMemDC, GetStockObject(WHITE_BRUSH));
                            Ellipse( hMemDC, 0, 0, 50, 50 );
                            Ellipse( hMemDC, 10, 0, 40, 50 );
                            Ellipse( hMemDC, 20, 0, 30, 50 );

                            // Paint the bitmap on the display.
                            //................................
                            BitBlt( hDC, 0, 0, 50, 50,
                                    hMemDC, 0, 0, SRCCOPY );

                            DeleteDC( hMemDC );

                            HeapFree( GetProcessHeap(), 0, lpbi );
                            ReleaseDC( hWnd, hDC );
                        }
                        break;
                            .
                            .
                            .
```

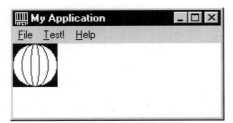

Figure 13-5 CreateDIBitmap example

CreateDIBSection
■ WINDOWS 95　■ WINDOWS NT

Description	`CreateDIBSection` creates a device-independent bitmap (DIB) to which both GDI and applications can directly write. The application must close memory mapped objects after calling `DeleteObject` to delete the bitmap.
Syntax	HBITMAP `CreateDIBSection`(HDC *hdc,* CONST BITMAPINFO* *pbmi,* UINT *uUsage,* VOID** *ppvBits,* HANDLE *hSection,* DWORD *dwOffset*)
Parameters	
hdc	HDC: The handle of the device context (DC).
pbmi	CONST BITMAPINFO*: A pointer to a BITMAPINFO structure that describes the format of the bitmap to create. See the definition of the BITMAPINFO structure under the `CreateDIBitmap` function.
uUsage	UINT: Specifies whether the *bmiColors* member of the BITMAPINFO structure contains RGB values or palette indices. DIB_PAL_COLORS specifies palette entries. DIB_RGB_COLORS specifies explicit colors.
ppvBits	VOID**: A pointer to a buffer that receives the address of the bitmap bits.
hSection	HANDLE: The handle of a memory mapped object from which the bitmap should be created. The object must have been allocated by a previous call to the `CreateFileMapping` function. Handles created by other means cause the `CreateDIBSection` function to fail. If set to NULL, GDI allocates memory for the bitmap bits and ignores the *dwOffset* parameter. Also, the object and the handle cannot be queried later by using the `GetObject` function.
dwOffset	DWORD: The offset from the beginning of the section to the beginning of the bitmap bits. This parameter must be a multiple of 32 (32-bit aligned).
Returns	HBITMAP: If successful, the handle of the bitmap; otherwise, the return value is NULL.
Include File	`wingdi.h`
See Also	`CreateFileMapping, CreateDIBitmap`
Example	This example shows how the `CreateDIBSection` function is used to create a device-independent bitmap and return a pointer, *lpBits*, to the bitmap data. This is useful if the application needs to directly modify the bitmap contents.

```
LRESULT CALLBACK WndProc( HWND hWnd, UINT uMsg, WPARAM wParam, LPARAM lParam )
{
static HBITMAP hBitmap = NULL;
static LPTSTR  lpBits = NULL;
```

continued on next page

continued from previous page

```
    switch( uMsg )
    {
      case WM_CREATE :
                {
                    BITMAPINFOHEADER  bi;
                    BITMAPINFOHEADER* lpbi;
                    RGBQUAD*          lpQuad;
                    HBITMAP           hBitmap;
                    HDC               hDC;

                    int               i;

                    // Initialize the BITMAPINFOHEADER structure.
                    //.........................................
                    bi.biSize      = sizeof( BITMAPINFOHEADER );
                    bi.biWidth     = 50;
                    bi.biHeight    = 50;
                    bi.biPlanes    = 1;
                    bi.biBitCount = 4;
                    bi.biCompression    = BI_RGB;
                    bi.biSizeImage      = 25 * 50; //(width / pixels per byte)
                                                   // * height

                    bi.biXPelsPerMeter = 0;
                    bi.biYPelsPerMeter = 0;
                    bi.biClrUsed       = 0;
                    bi.biClrImportant  = 0;

                    lpbi = (BITMAPINFOHEADER*)HeapAlloc( GetProcessHeap(), HEAP_ZERO_MEMORY,
                                       sizeof( BITMAPINFOHEADER ) + 16*sizeof( RGBQUAD )⇐
);

                    *lpbi = bi;
                    lpQuad = &((LPBITMAPINFO)lpbi)->bmiColors[0];

                    for ( i = 0; i < 16; i++ )
                    {
                        lpQuad->rgbBlue  = i*16;
                        lpQuad->rgbRed   = 0;
                        lpQuad->rgbGreen = 0;

                        lpQuad++;
                    }

                    hDC = GetDC( hWnd );

                    // Create DIB.
                    //............
                    hBitmap = CreateDIBSection( hDC, (LPBITMAPINFO)lpbi,
                                     DIB_RGB_COLORS, &lpBits, NULL, 0 );

                    ReleaseDC( hWnd, hDC );
                    HeapFree( GetProcessHeap(), 0, lpbi );
                }
            break;
              .
              .
              .
```

CreateEnhMetaFile ■ WINDOWS 95 ■ WINDOWS NT

Description CreateEnhMetaFile creates a device context (DC) for an enhanced metafile. The resulting DC is used with GDI functions and the CloseEnhMetaFile function to create an enhanced metafile.

Syntax HDC **CreateEnhMetaFile**(HDC *hdcRef,* LPCTSTR *lpFilename,* CONST RECT* *lpRect,* LPCTSTR *lpDescription*)

Parameters

hdcRef HDC: A reference device context for the enhanced metafile. If set to NULL, the metafile uses the current display device for reference.

lpFilename LPCTSTR: A pointer to a null-terminated character string containing the file name for the enhanced metafile to be created. If set to NULL, the enhanced metafile is memory based.

lpRect CONST RECT*: A pointer to a RECT structure that specifies the dimensions (in .01-millimeter units) of the picture to be stored in the enhanced metafile. If set to NULL, GDI computes the smallest rectangle that surrounds the picture.

lpDescription LPCTSTR: A pointer to a string that contains the name of the application that created the picture, as well as the picture's title. The string must contain a null character between the application name and the picture name and must terminate with two null characters. If set to NULL, there is no corresponding entry in the enhanced metafile.

Returns HDC: If successful, the handle of the DC for the enhanced metafile; otherwise, the return value is NULL.

Include File wingdi.h

See Also CloseEnhMetaFile, DeleteEnhMetaFile

Example This example creates an enhanced metafile at startup by processing the WM_CREATE message. The metafile contains a rectangle that is filled with a crosshatched brush (see Figure 13-6). The metafile is played on the WM_PAINT message. The metafile is scaled based on the size of the client area.

```
LRESULT CALLBACK WndProc( HWND hWnd, UINT uMsg, WPARAM wParam, LPARAM lParam )
{
static HENHMETAFILE hMetaFile = NULL;

   switch( uMsg )
   {
      case WM_CREATE :
              {
                 HDC   hMetaDC;
                 HDC   hRefDC;
                 RECT  rect;
                 int   iWidthMM, iHeightMM, iWidthPels, iHeightPels;
                 int   iMMPerPelX, iMMPerPelY;
```

continued on next page

continued from previous page

```
            hRefDC = GetDC( hWnd );

            // Compute the size of the client area in 0.01 mm.
            //...............................................
            iWidthMM    = GetDeviceCaps(hRefDC, HORZSIZE);
            iHeightMM   = GetDeviceCaps(hRefDC, VERTSIZE);
            iWidthPels  = GetDeviceCaps(hRefDC, HORZRES);
            iHeightPels = GetDeviceCaps(hRefDC, VERTRES);

            iMMPerPelX = (iWidthMM * 100)/iWidthPels;
            iMMPerPelY = (iHeightMM * 100)/iHeightPels;

            GetClientRect(hWnd, &rect);

            rect.right = rect.right * iMMPerPelX;
            rect.bottom = rect.bottom * iMMPerPelY;

            // Create an enhanced metafile.
            //............................
            hMetaDC = CreateEnhMetaFile( hRefDC, NULL, &rect,
                                         "Test Metafile" );

            // Draw on the metafile.
            //......................
            if ( hMetaDC )
            {
                HBRUSH hBrush;

                GdiComment( hMetaDC, 23, "This is for an example." );
                hBrush = CreateHatchBrush( HS_DIAGCROSS, RGB(0, 0, 255) );

                SelectObject( hMetaDC, hBrush );
                Rectangle( hMetaDC, 10, 10, 200, 200 );

                hMetaFile = CloseEnhMetaFile( hMetaDC );
                DeleteObject( hBrush );
            }

            ReleaseDC( hWnd, hRefDC );
        }
        break;

    case WM_PAINT   :
        {
            PAINTSTRUCT ps;
            RECT        rect;

            BeginPaint( hWnd, &ps );

            GetClientRect( hWnd, &rect );
            PlayEnhMetaFile( ps.hdc, hMetaFile, &rect );

            EndPaint( hWnd, &ps );
        }
        break;
```

```
    case WM_COMMAND :
         switch( LOWORD( wParam ) )
         {
            case IDM_EXIT :
                    DestroyWindow( hWnd );
                    break;
         }
         break;

    case WM_DESTROY :
         DeleteEnhMetaFile( hMetaFile );
         PostQuitMessage(0);
         break;

    default :
         return( DefWindowProc( hWnd, uMsg, wParam, lParam ) );
    }

    return( 0L );
}
```

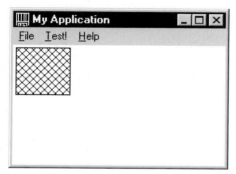

Figure 13-6 `CreateEnhMetaFile` example

CreateIcon

■ WINDOWS 95 ■ WINDOWS NT

Description   `CreateIcon` creates an icon that has a specified size, colors, and bit patterns. This function provides an alternative to loading icons from the resource file, creating icon images dynamically as the application operates. The icon can be created from binary data, a bitmap, or a device-independent bitmap (DIB). The icon is created by combining two bitmaps, the AND mask and the XOR mask. The AND mask is always a monochrome bitmap, with one bit per pixel. Table 13-6 shows how the two bitmaps are combined.

Table 13-6 Monochrome icon bit masks

AND Bit Mask Value	XOR Bit Mask Value	Result Onscreen
0	0	Black
0	1	White
1	1	Transparent
1	1	Inverted color

Syntax	HICON **CreateIcon**(HINSTANCE *hinst,* int *nWidth,* int *nHeight,* BYTE *cPlanes,* BYTE *cBitsPixel,* CONST BYTE* *lpbANDbits,* CONST BYTE* *lpbXORbits*)
Parameters	
hinst	HINSTANCE: The instance handle of the module creating the icon.
nWidth	int: The width, in pixels, of the icon.
nHeight	int: The height, in pixels, of the icon.
cPlanes	BYTE: The number of color planes in the XOR bit mask of the icon.
cBitsPixel	BYTE: The number of bits per pixel in the XOR bit mask of the icon.
lpbANDbits	CONST BYTE*: A pointer to an array of monochrome bits, specifying the AND mask for the icon.
lpbXORbits	CONST BYTE*: A pointer to an array of bits specifying the XOR mask for the icon. Alternatively, the pointer can point to a memory block containing a monochrome bitmap or device-dependent color bitmap.
Returns	HICON: The handle of the new icon. If an error occurs, NULL is returned.
Include File	winuser.h
See Also	DestroyIcon, CreateIconFromResource, CreateIconFromResourceEx, CreateIconIndirect, GetSystemMetrics
Example	This example creates a monochrome icon, shown in Figure 13-7, by directly specifying the bit values of both the AND mask and the XOR mask of the icon. The icon is created when the WM_CREATE message is processed, and painted to the client area when a WM_PAINT message is received.

Figure 13-7 CreateIcon example

```
#define EVENBYTE( i )  ((i+7)/8*8)

LRESULT CALLBACK WndProc( HWND hWnd, UINT uMsg, WPARAM wParam, LPARAM lParam )
{
static HICON hIcon;

    switch( uMsg )
    {
        case WM_CREATE :
                {
                    LPBYTE lpA, lpX;
                    LPBYTE lpAND, lpXOR;
                    int    i,j;
                    int    nWidth     = GetSystemMetrics( SM_CXICON );
                    int    nHeight    = GetSystemMetrics( SM_CYICON );
                    int    nIconBytes = (EVENBYTE(nWidth)/8)*nHeight;

                    // Allocate memory for the bit masks.
                    //.....................................
                    lpA = lpAND = (LPBYTE)HeapAlloc( GetProcessHeap(), HEAP_ZERO_MEMORY, ⇐
nIconBytes );

                    lpX = lpXOR = (LPBYTE)HeapAlloc( GetProcessHeap(), HEAP_ZERO_MEMORY, ⇐
nIconBytes );

                    // Fill masks with icon image.
                    //............................
                    for( i=0; i < EVENBYTE( nWidth ) / 8; i++ )
                    {
                        for( j=0; j < nHeight; j++ )
                        {
                            *lpA++ = 0xFF;
                            if ( i > j )
                                *lpX++ = 0xFF;
                            else
                                *lpX++ = 0x11;
                        }
                    }

                    // Create icon.
                    //.............
                    hIcon = CreateIcon( hInst, nWidth, nHeight, 1, 1,
                                        lpAND, lpXOR );

                    HeapFree( GetProcessHeap(), 0, lpAND );
                    HeapFree( GetProcessHeap(), 0, lpXOR );
                }
                break;

        case WM_PAINT   :
                {
                    PAINTSTRUCT ps;

                    BeginPaint( hWnd, &ps );
                    DrawIcon( ps.hdc, 10, 10, hIcon );
                    EndPaint( hWnd, &ps );
                }
                break;
```

continued on next page

continued from previous page

```
        case WM_COMMAND :
                switch( LOWORD( wParam ) )
                {
                    case IDM_EXIT :
                            DestroyWindow( hWnd );
                            break;
                }
                break;

        case WM_DESTROY :
                DestroyIcon( hIcon );
                PostQuitMessage(0);
                break;

        default :
                return( DefWindowProc( hWnd, uMsg, wParam, lParam ) );
    }

    return( 0L );
}
```

CreateIconFromResource   ■ WINDOWS 95 ■ WINDOWS NT

Description	CreateIconFromResource creates an icon or cursor from resource bits describing the icon. These bits are typically loaded using the LookupIconIdFromDirectoryEx and LoadResource functions.
Syntax	HICON **CreateIconFromResource**(PBYTE *pbIconBits,* DWORD *cbIconBits,* BOOL *bIcon,* DWORD *dwVersion*)
Parameters	
pbIconBits	PBYTE: A pointer to a buffer containing the icon or cursor resource bits.
cbIconBits	DWORD: The size, in bytes, of the buffer pointed to by the *pbIconBits* parameter.
bIcon	BOOL: Set to TRUE to create an icon. Set to FALSE to create a cursor.
dwVersion	DWORD: The version number of the icon or cursor format for the resource bits pointed to by the *pbIconBits* parameter. This parameter can be one of the values in Table 13-7. All Win32-based applications use the Windows 3.x format for icons and cursors.

Table 13-7 CreateIconFromResource *dwVersion* values

Format	dwVersion
Windows 2.x	0x00020000
Windows 3.x	0x00030000

Returns   HICON: The handle of the icon or cursor. If an error occurs, NULL is returned.

Include File   winuser.h

See Also   DestroyIcon, CreateIcon, CreateIconFromResourceEx, CreateIconIndirect, GetSystemMetrics

Example   When the user selects the Test! menu item, this example uses the LookupIconIdFromDirectory function to find the appropriate icon in the icon directory "MYAPP". CreateIconFromResource is used to create an icon from the resource bits loaded with the FindResource function.

```
LRESULT CALLBACK WndProc( HWND hWnd, UINT uMsg, WPARAM wParam, LPARAM lParam )
{
   switch( uMsg )
   {
     case WM_COMMAND :
             switch( LOWORD( wParam ) )
             {
               case IDM_TEST :
                    {
                       HICON hIcon;
                       HRSRC hResource;
                       HRSRC hMem;
                       BYTE *lpResource;
                       int   nID;
                       HDC   hDC;

                       // Find the icon directory
                       // whose identifier is MYAPP.
                       //.........................
                       hResource = FindResource(hInst, "MYAPP",
                                           RT_GROUP_ICON);

                       // Load and lock the icon directory.
                       //..................................
                       hMem = LoadResource(hInst, hResource);
                       lpResource = LockResource(hMem);

                       // Get the identifier of the icon that is most
                       // appropriate for the video display.
                       //............................................
                       nID = LookupIconIdFromDirectory((PBYTE)lpResource,
                                              TRUE);

                       // Find the bits for the nID icon.
                       //................................
                       hResource = FindResource( hInst,
                                       MAKEINTRESOURCE(nID),
                                       MAKEINTRESOURCE(RT_ICON));

                       // Load and lock the icon.
                       //........................
                       hMem = LoadResource(hInst, hResource);
                       lpResource = LockResource(hMem);
```

continued on next page

continued from previous page

```
                    // Create a handle to the icon.
                    //............................
                    hIcon = CreateIconFromResource((PBYTE)lPResource,
                                SizeofResource(hInst, hResource),
                                TRUE,
                                0x00030000);

                    // Draw the icon in the client area.
                    //.................................
                    hDC = GetDC( hWnd );
                    DrawIcon(hDC, 10, 20, hIcon);
                    ReleaseDC( hWnd, hDC );

                    DestroyIcon( hIcon );
                }
                break;
```

CreateIconFromResourceEx   ■ WINDOWS 95   ■ WINDOWS NT

Description	`CreateIconFromResourceEx` is exactly the same as `CreateIconFromResource`, except a size can be specified.
Syntax	HICON **CreateIconFromResourceEx**(PBYTE *pbIconBits*, DWORD *cbIconBits*, BOOL *bIcon*, DWORD *dwVersion*, int *cxDesired*, int *cyDesired*, UINT *uFlags*)
Parameters	
pbIconBits	PBYTE: A pointer to a buffer containing the icon or cursor resource bits.
cbIconBits	DWORD: The size, in bytes, of the buffer pointed to by the *pbIconBits* parameter.
bIcon	BOOL: Set to TRUE to create an icon. Set to FALSE to create a cursor.
dwVersion	DWORD: The version number of the icon or cursor format for the resource bits pointed to by the *pbIconBits* parameter. This parameter can be one of the values in Table 13-7. All Win32-based applications use the Windows 3.x format for icons and cursors.
cxDesired	int: The desired width, in pixels, of the icon or cursor. If set to 0 and *uFlags* does not include LR_LOADREALSIZE, the SM_CXICON or SM_CXCURSOR system metric value is used.
cyDesired	int: The desired height, in pixels, of the icon or cursor. If set to 0 and *uFlags* does not include LR_LOADREALSIZE, the SM_CYICON or SM_CYCURSOR system metric value is used.
uFlags	UINT: A combination of the values in Table 13-8 combined with the binary OR (	) operator.

Table 13-8 `CreateIconFromResourceEx` *uFlags* values

Value	Meaning
LR_DEFAULTCOLOR	Use the default color format.
LR_LOADREALSIZE	Set the width and height as specified by the *biWidth* and *biHeight* members of the BITMAPINFOHEADER structure that defines the icon or cursor. The *cxDesired* and *cyDesired* parameters are ignored.
LR_MONOCHROME	Create a monochrome icon or cursor.

Returns	HICON: The handle of the icon or cursor. If an error occurs, NULL is returned.
Include File	`winuser.h`
See Also	`DestroyIcon`, `CreateIcon`, `CreateIconFromResource`, `CreateIconIndirect`, `GetSystemMetrics`
Example	This example is the same as the example for the `CreateIconFromResource` function, except that the `LookupIconIdFromDirectoryEx` function is used to find a 16×16 icon in the icon directory and the `CreateIconFromResourceEx` function is used to create an icon from the found resource.

```
LRESULT CALLBACK WndProc( HWND hWnd, UINT uMsg, WPARAM wParam, LPARAM lParam )
{
    switch( uMsg )
    {
        case WM_COMMAND :
                switch( LOWORD( wParam ) )
                {
                    case IDM_TEST :
                        {
                            HICON   hIcon;
                            HRSRC   hResource;
                            HRSRC   hMem;
                            BYTE    *lpResource;
                            int     nID;
                            HDC     hDC;

                            // Find the icon directory
                            // whose identifier is MYAPP.
                            //..........................
                            hResource = FindResource(hInst, "MYAPP",
                                                RT_GROUP_ICON);

                            // Load and lock the icon directory.
                            //..................................
                            hMem = LoadResource(hInst, hResource);
                            lpResource = LockResource(hMem);

                            // Get the identifier of the icon that
                            // is 16x16 in size and appropriate
                            // for the video display.
                            //....................................
```

continued on next page

continued from previous page

```
                          nID = LookupIconIdFromDirectoryEx(
                                              (PBYTE) lpResource, TRUE,
                                              16, 16, LR_DEFAULTCOLOR );

                          // Find the bits for the nID icon.
                          //................................
                          hResource = FindResource( hInst,
                                              MAKEINTRESOURCE(nID),
                                              MAKEINTRESOURCE(RT_ICON));

                          // Load and lock the icon.
                          //........................
                          hMem = LoadResource(hInst, hResource);
                          lpResource = LockResource(hMem);

                          // Create a handle to the icon.
                          //.............................
                          hIcon = CreateIconFromResourceEx((PBYTE)lpResource,
                                      SizeofResource(hInst, hResource),
                                      TRUE,
                                      0x00030000,
                                      16, 16, LR_DEFAULTCOLOR );

                          // Draw the icon in the client area.
                          //..................................
                          hDC = GetDC( hWnd );
                          DrawIconEx(hDC, 10, 20, hIcon, 16, 16,
                                  0, 0, NULL, DI_NORMAL );
                          ReleaseDC( hWnd, hDC );

                          DestroyIcon( hIcon );
                      }
                      break;

                  .
                  .
                  .
```

CreateIconIndirect   ■ WINDOWS 95   ■ WINDOWS NT

Description	CreateIconIndirect creates an icon or cursor from an **ICONINFO** structure.
Syntax	HICON **CreateIconIndirect**(PICONINFO *pici*)
Parameters	
pici	**PICONINFO**: A pointer to an **ICONINFO** structure the function uses to create the icon or cursor. See the definition of the **ICONINFO** structure below.
Returns	**HICON**: The handle of the icon or cursor that is created. If an error occurs, **NULL** is returned.
Include File	winuser.h

See Also   DestroyIcon, CreateIcon, CreateIconFromResource,
CreateIconFromResourceEx, GetSystemMetrics

ICONINFO Definition

```
typedef struct _ICONINFO
{
    BOOL     fIcon;
    DWORD    xHotspot;
    DWORD    yHotspot;
    HBITMAP  hbmMask;
    HBITMAP  hbmColor;
} ICONINFO, *PICONINFO;
```

Members

fIcon   **BOOL**: Set to **TRUE** to create an icon. Set to **FALSE** to create a cursor.

xHotspot   **DWORD**: The x coordinate of a cursor's hot spot. This is ignored for an icon.

yHotspot   **DWORD**: The y coordinate of the cursor's hot spot. This is ignored for an icon.

hbmMask   **HBITMAP**: The icon bit mask bitmap. If this structure defines a black-and-white icon, this bit mask is formatted so that the upper half is the icon AND bit mask and the lower half is the icon XOR bit mask. If this structure defines a color icon, this mask only defines the AND bit mask of the icon.

hbmColor   **HBITMAP**: The icon color bitmap. Optional if this structure defines a black-and-white icon. The AND bit mask of *hbmMask* is applied with the **SRCAND** flag to the destination; subsequently, the color bitmap is applied (using XOR) to the destination by using the **SRCINVERT** flag.

Example   This example uses the **CreateIconIndirect** function to create an icon from two bitmaps when the user selects the Test! menu item. The bitmaps and the resulting icon are displayed in the client area of the window as shown in Figure 13-8.

Figure 13-8 CreateIconIndirect
example

```
LRESULT CALLBACK WndProc( HWND hWnd, UINT uMsg, WPARAM wParam, LPARAM lParam )
{
    switch( uMsg )
    {
      case WM_COMMAND :
              switch( LOWORD( wParam ) )
              {
                case IDM_TEST :
                        {
                        HICON     hIcon;
                        HDC       hDC, hMemDC;
                        HBITMAP   hMask;
                        HBITMAP   hColor;
                        ICONINFO  icInfo;

                        // Load the mask and color bitmaps.
                        //...............................
                        hMask  = LoadBitmap( hInst, "ICONA" );
                        hColor = LoadBitmap( hInst, "ICONB" );

                        icInfo.fIcon    = TRUE;
                        icInfo.xHotspot = 0;
                        icInfo.yHotspot = 0;
                        icInfo.hbmMask  = hMask;
                        icInfo.hbmColor = hColor;

                        // Create a handle to the icon.
                        //............................
                        hIcon = CreateIconIndirect( &icInfo );

                        // Draw the bitmaps and icon
                        // in the client area.
                        //........................
                        hDC = GetDC( hWnd );
                        hMemDC = CreateCompatibleDC( hDC );

                        SelectObject( hMemDC, hMask );
                        BitBlt( hDC, 10, 20, 32, 32, hMemDC, 0, 0,SRCCOPY);

                        SelectObject( hMemDC, hColor );
                        BitBlt( hDC, 40, 20, 32, 32, hMemDC, 0, 0,SRCCOPY);

                        TextOut( hDC, 78, 26, "=", 1 );

                        DrawIcon(hDC, 90, 20, hIcon );

                        ReleaseDC( hWnd, hDC );
                        DeleteDC( hMemDC );
                        DestroyIcon( hIcon );
                        DeleteObject( hMask );
                        DeleteObject( hColor );
                        }
                        break;
                        .
                        .
                        .
```

DeleteEnhMetaFile ■ WINDOWS 95 ■ WINDOWS NT

Description	`DeleteEnhMetaFile` deletes an enhanced metafile from memory. If the enhanced metafile is stored in memory, this function deletes the metafile. If the metafile is stored on a disk, the function deletes the metafile handle but does not destroy the actual metafile.
Syntax	BOOL **DeleteEnhMetaFile**(HENHMETAFILE *hemf*)
Parameters	
hemf	HENHMETAFILE: A handle to the enhanced metafile.
Returns	BOOL: TRUE if successful; otherwise, the return value is FALSE.
Include File	`wingdi.h`
See Also	`CreateEnhMetaFile`, `CloseEnhMetaFile`, `GetEnhMetaFile`
Example	See the example for the `CreateEnhMetaFile` function.

DestroyIcon ■ WINDOWS 95 ■ WINDOWS NT

Description	`DestroyIcon` destroys an icon created by the `CreateIcon` function and frees any memory the icon occupied. Do not use `DestroyIcon` to destroy an icon that was not created by the `CreateIcon` function.
Syntax	BOOL **DestroyIcon**(HICON *hicon*)
Parameters	
hicon	HICON: The handle of the icon to be destroyed. The icon must not be in use.
Returns	BOOL: TRUE if successful; otherwise, the return value is FALSE.
Include File	`winuser.h`
See Also	`CreateIcon`, `CreateIconFromResource`, `CreateIconFromResourceEx`, `CreateIconIndirect`
Example	See the example for the `CreateIcon` function.

DrawIcon ■ WINDOWS 95 ■ WINDOWS NT

Description	`DrawIcon` draws an icon in the client area of the window that belongs to the given device context (DC). The icon is normally loaded from the resource data using **LoadIcon** or **LoadImage**. It also can be created using **CreateIcon**. The device context must be in the **MM_TEXT** mapping mode for this function to operate properly.
Syntax	BOOL **DrawIcon**(HDC *hdc,* int *X,* int *Y,* HICON *hicon*)

Parameters

hdc	HDC: The handle of the DC for the window in which to draw the icon.
X	int: The logical x coordinate of the upper-left corner of the icon.
Y	int: The logical y coordinate of the upper-left corner of the icon.
hicon	HICON: The handle of the icon to be drawn.
Returns	BOOL: TRUE if successful; otherwise, the return value is FALSE.
Include File	winuser.h
See Also	LoadIcon, LoadImage, CreateIcon
Example	See the example for the CopyIcon function.

DrawIconEx ■ WINDOWS 95 ■ WINDOWS NT

Description	DrawIconEx draws an icon or cursor in the client area of the window that belongs to the given device context (DC), while performing the specified raster operations, and stretching or compressing the icon or cursor as specified.
Syntax	BOOL **DrawIconEx**(HDC *hdc,* int *X,* int *Y,* HICON *hicon,* int *cx,* int *cy,* DWORD *ropMask,* DWORD *ropImage,* HBRUSH *hbrSrc,* UINT *uFlags*)

Parameters

hdc	HDC: The handle of the DC for the window in which to draw the icon.
X	int: The logical x coordinate of the upper-left corner of the icon or cursor.
Y	int: The logical y coordinate of the upper-left corner of the icon or cursor.
hicon	HICON: The handle of the icon to be drawn.
cx	int: The logical width of the icon or cursor.
cy	int: The logical height of the icon or cursor.
ropMask	DWORD: The raster operation used to combine the icon or cursor bit mask bitmap with the screen colors. This parameter is ignored if *uFlags* is not set to the DI_MASK flag. If *uFlags* is set to DI_MASK and *ropMask* is 0, the raster operation defaults to the SRCAND flag.
ropImage	DWORD: Indicates the raster operation used to combine the icon color bitmap with the screen colors. This parameter is ignored if *uFlags* does not include the DI_IMAGE flag. If *uFlags* includes DI_IMAGE and *ropMask* is 0, the raster operation defaults to the SRCINVERT flag.
hbrSrc	HBRUSH: The handle of a brush to be selected into the DC identified by the *hdc* parameter. If the raster operation specified by *ropMask* or *ropImage* requires a brush, this is the brush that is used.
uFlags	UINT: The drawing flags. This parameter can be one of the values listed in Table 13-9.

Table 13-9 DrawIconEx *uFlags* values

Value	Meaning
DI_COMPAT	Draws the icon or cursor using the system default image.
DI_DEFAULTSIZE	Draws the icon or cursor in its default width, ignoring the *cx* and *cy* parameters.
DI_IMAGE	Performs the raster operation specified by *ropImage*.
DI_MASK	Performs the raster operation specified by *ropMask*.
DI_NORMAL	Combination of DI_IMAGE and DI_MASK.

Returns	BOOL: TRUE if successful; otherwise, the return value is FALSE.
Include File	winuser.h
See Also	LoadImage, CopyImage
Example	See the example for the **CreateIconFromResourceEx** function.

EnumEnhMetaFile ■ WINDOWS 95 ■ WINDOWS NT

Description   EnumEnhMetaFile enumerates the records within an enhanced metafile by retrieving each record and passing it to an application-defined callback function. The enumeration continues until the last record is processed or when the callback function returns 0.

Syntax   BOOL **EnumEnhMetaFile**(HDC *hdc*, HENHMETAFILE *hemf*, ENHMFENUMPROC *lpEnhMetaFunc*, LPVOID *lpData*, CONST RECT* *lpRect*)

Parameters

hdc   HDC: A handle to a device context (DC) to be passed to the callback function.

hemf   HENHMETAFILE: The handle of the enhanced metafile to enumerate.

lpEnhMetaFunc   ENHMFENUMPROC: A pointer to the application-defined callback function. See the description of the callback syntax below.

lpData   LPVOID: A pointer to optional application-defined data to be passed to the callback function for each record.

lpRect   CONST RECT*: A pointer to a RECT structure that specifies the coordinates of the picture's upper-left and lower-right corners. The dimensions of this rectangle are specified in logical units.

Returns   BOOL: If the callback function successfully enumerates all the records in the enhanced metafile, the return value is TRUE; otherwise, it is FALSE.

Include File   wingdi.h

See Also   CloseEnhMetaFile, GetEnhMetaFile

Callback Syntax   int CALLBACK **EnhMetaFileProc**(HDC *hDC*, HANDLETABLE* *lpHTable*, ENHMETARECORD* *lpEMFR*, int *nObj*, LPVOID *lpData*)

Callback Parameters

hDC	**HDC**: The handle of an enhanced metafile device context (DC).
lpHTable	**HANDLETABLE***: A pointer to an array of **HGDIOBJECT** handles associated with the graphics objects (pens, brushes, and so on) in the metafile. The first entry contains the enhanced metafile handle.
lpEMFR	**ENHMETARECORD***: A pointer to one of the records in the metafile. This record should not be modified.
nObj	**int**: The number of objects with associated handles in the handle table pointed to by *lpHTable*.
lpData	**LPVOID**: The application-defined data passed in the *lpData* parameter of the **EnumEnhMetaFile** function.

Callback Returns **int**: Nonzero to continue enumeration; to stop enumeration, return **0**.

Example This example loads an enhanced metafile and displays it on the client area of the window as shown in Figure 13-9. When the user selects the Test! menu item, the metafile is played using the **EnumEnhMetaFile** function. The callback function intercepts the **EMR_CREATEBRUSHINDIRECT** metafile record and replaces it with a light gray brush. Figure 13-10 shows the results.

```
LRESULT CALLBACK WndProc( HWND hWnd, UINT uMsg, WPARAM wParam, LPARAM lParam )
{
static HENHMETAFILE hMetaFile;

    switch( uMsg )
    {
        case WM_CREATE  :
                // Load the metafile.
                //....................
                hMetaFile = GetEnhMetaFile( "sample.emf" );
                break;

        case WM_PAINT :
                {
                    PAINTSTRUCT ps;
                    RECT        rect;

                    GetClientRect( hWnd, &rect );

                    BeginPaint( hWnd, &ps );
                    PlayEnhMetaFile( ps.hdc, hMetaFile, &rect );
                    EndPaint( hWnd, &ps );
                }
                break;

        case WM_COMMAND :
                switch( LOWORD( wParam ) )
                {
                    case IDM_TEST :
                            {
                                HDC  hDC;
                                RECT rect;
```

```
                            GetClientRect( hWnd, &rect );
                            hDC = GetDC( hWnd );

                            // Play the metafile using the Enum proc.
                            //.........................................
                            EnumEnhMetaFile( hDC, hMetaFile,
                                             (ENHMFENUMPROC)PaintMetaFile,
                                             NULL, &rect );

                            ReleaseDC( hWnd, hDC );
                        }
                        break;

                    case IDM_EXIT :
                            DestroyWindow( hWnd );
                            break;
                }
                break;

        case WM_DESTROY :
                DeleteEnhMetaFile( hMetaFile );
                PostQuitMessage(0);
                break;

        default :
                return( DefWindowProc( hWnd, uMsg, wParam, lParam ) );
    }

    return( 0L );
}


int CALLBACK PaintMetaFile( HDC hDC, HANDLETABLE* lpHTable,
                            ENHMETARECORD* lpEMFR, int nObj, LPVOID lpData )
{
    // If this statement is the brush, change the brush to light gray.
    //...............................................................
    if ( lpEMFR->iType == EMR_CREATEBRUSHINDIRECT )
        SelectObject( hDC, GetStockObject( LTGRAY_BRUSH ) );
    else
        PlayEnhMetaFileRecord( hDC, lpHTable, lpEMFR, nObj );

    return( 1 );
}
```

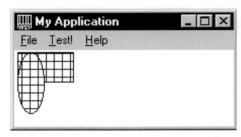

Figure 13-9 EnumEnhMetaFile example

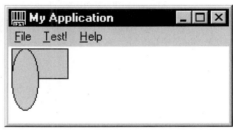

Figure 13-10 The light gray results

GdiComment ■ WINDOWS 95 ■ WINDOWS NT

Description	GdiComment places a comment into an enhanced metafile.
Syntax	BOOL **GdiComment**(HDC *hdc,* UINT *cbSize,* CONST BYTE* *lpData*)
Parameters	
hdc	HDC: The handle of the device context (DC) for the enhanced metafile.
cbSize	UINT: The length of the comment buffer, in bytes.
lpData	CONST BYTE*: A pointer to the buffer that contains the comment.
Returns	BOOL: TRUE if successful; otherwise, the return value is FALSE.
Include File	wingdi.h
See Also	CreateEnhMetaFile
Example	See the example for the **CreateEnhMetaFile** function.

GetBitmapDimensionEx ■ WINDOWS 95 ■ WINDOWS NT

Description	GetBitmapDimensionEx retrieves the dimensions of a bitmap set by a previous call to the SetBitmapDimensionEx function.
Syntax	BOOL **GetBitmapDimensionEx**(HBITMAP *hBitmap,* LPSIZE *lpDimension*)
Parameters	
hBitmap	HBITMAP: The handle of the bitmap.
lpDimension	LPSIZE: A pointer to a SIZE structure to receive the bitmap dimensions.
Returns	BOOL: TRUE if successful; otherwise, the return value is FALSE.
Include File	wingdi.h
See Also	SetBitmapDimensionEx
Example	See the example for the **SetBitmapDimensionEx** function.

GetDIBits ■ WINDOWS 95 ■ WINDOWS NT

Description	GetDIBits retrieves the bits of the specified bitmap into an application-supplied buffer using the specified format.
Syntax	int **GetDIBits**(HDC *hdc,* HBITMAP *hbmp,* UINT *uStartScan,* UINT *cScanLines,* LPVOID *lpvBits,* LPBITMAPINFO *lpbi,* UINT *uUsage*)
Parameters	
hdc	HDC: The device context.
hbmp	HBITMAP: The handle of the bitmap.
uStartScan	UINT: The first scan line to retrieve.

cScanLines	UINT: The number of scan lines to retrieve.
lpvBits	LPVOID: A pointer to a buffer to receive the bitmap data. If set to NULL, the function passes the dimensions and format of the bitmap to the BITMAPIN-FO structure pointed to by the *lpbi* parameter.
lpbi	LPBITMAPINFO: A pointer to a BITMAPINFO structure that specifies the desired format for the device-independent bitmap (DIB) data. See the definition of the BITMAPINFO structure under the CreateDIBitmap function.
uUsage	UINT: Specifies whether the *bmiColors* member of the BITMAPINFO structure contains RGB values or palette indices. DIB_PAL_COLORS specifies palette entries. DIB_RGB_COLORS specifies explicit colors.
Returns	int: The number of scan lines copied from the bitmap. If an error occurs, 0 is returned.
Include File	wingdi.h
See Also	SetDIBits, SetDIBitsToDevice, StretchDIBits, CreateDIBitmap
Example	See the example for the CreateDIBitmap function.

GetEnhMetaFile
■ WINDOWS 95 ■ WINDOWS NT

Description	GetEnhMetaFile creates a handle for an enhanced metafile stored in a file.
Syntax	HENHMETAFILE **GetEnhMetaFile**(LPCTSTR *lpszMetaFile*)
Parameters	
lpszMetaFile	LPCTSTR: A pointer to a null-terminated string that contains the name of the enhanced metafile.
Returns	HENHMETAFILE: The handle of the enhanced metafile. If an error occurs, NULL is returned.
Include File	wingdi.h
See Also	DeleteEnhMetaFile
Example	See the example for the EnumEnhMetaFile function.

GetEnhMetaFileBits
■ WINDOWS 95 ■ WINDOWS NT

Description	GetEnhMetaFileBits retrieves the content of an enhanced metafile.
Syntax	UINT **GetEnhMetaFileBits**(HENHMETAFILE *hemf,* UINT *cbBuffer,* LPBYTE *lpbBuffer*)
Parameters	
hemf	HENHMETAFILE: The handle of the enhanced metafile.
cbBuffer	UINT: The size, in bytes, of the buffer to receive the data.

lpBuffer	**LPBYTE**: A pointer to the buffer large enough to contain the metafile data. If *lpBuffer* is **NULL**, the function returns the size necessary to hold the data.
Returns	**UINT**: If *lpBuffer* is **NULL**, the return value is the size of the enhanced metafile; otherwise, it is the number of bytes copied to the buffer. If an error occurs, **0** is returned.
Include File	`wingdi.h`
See Also	`SetEnhMetaFileBits`
Example	This example shows how to retrieve the data for an enhanced metafile allowing the application to use the raw data of the metafile. `SetEnhMetaFileBits` is used to get an enhanced metafile handle for the raw data.

```
LRESULT CALLBACK WndProc( HWND hWnd, UINT uMsg, WPARAM wParam, LPARAM lParam )
{
static HENHMETAFILE hMetaFile;

    switch( uMsg )
    {
        case WM_COMMAND :
                switch( LOWORD( wParam ) )
                {
                    case IDM_TEST :
                            {
                                LPBYTE   lpMem;
                                int      nSize;

                                // Retrieve the size of the metafile.
                                //.....................................
                                nSize = GetEnhMetaFileBits( hMetaFile, 0, NULL );
                                lpMem = (LPBYTE)HeapAlloc( GetProcessHeap(), HEAP_ZERO_MEMORY, ⇐
nSize );

                                // Retrieve the metafile contents.
                                //................................
                                GetEnhMetaFileBits( hMetaFile, nSize, lpMem );

                                // Use the metafile data.
                                //......................
                                    .
                                    .
                                    .

                                // Get a metafile handle for the metafile data.
                                //.............................................
                                hMetaFile = SetEnhMetaFileBits( nSize, lpMem );
                                HeapFree( GetProcessHeap(), 0, lpMem );

                                InvalidateRect( hWnd, NULL, TRUE );
                                UpdateWindow( hWnd );
                            }
                            break;
```

GetEnhMetaFileDescription

Description	GetEnhMetaFileDescription retrieves the optional text description from an enhanced metafile.
Syntax	UINT **GetEnhMetaFileDescription**(HENHMETAFILE *hemf,* UINT *cchBuffer,* LPTSTR *lpszDescription*)
Parameters	
hemf	HENMETAFILE: The handle of the enhanced metafile.
cchBuffer	UINT: The size, in characters, of the buffer to receive the data.
lpszDescription	LPTSTR: A pointer to the buffer to receive the text description. If set to NULL, the length of the text string, in characters, is returned.
Returns	UINT: If *lpszDescription* is NULL, the length of the text string, in characters; otherwise, the number of characters copied into the buffer. If an error occurs, GDI_ERROR is returned. If the optional text description does not exist, 0 is returned.
Include File	wingdi.h
See Also	CreateEnhMetaFile
Example	In this example, shown in Figure 13-11, a metafile is loaded and displayed on the client area of the window when the WM_PAINT message is processed. When the user selects the Test! menu item, the example retrieves and displays the description of the metafile.

```
LRESULT CALLBACK WndProc( HWND hWnd, UINT uMsg, WPARAM wParam, LPARAM lParam )
{
static HENHMETAFILE hMetaFile;

    switch( uMsg )
    {
        case WM_CREATE  :
                // Load the metafile.
                //.................
                hMetaFile = GetEnhMetaFile( "sample.emf" );
                break;

        case WM_PAINT :
                {
                    PAINTSTRUCT ps;
                    RECT        rect;

                    GetClientRect( hWnd, &rect );

                    BeginPaint( hWnd, &ps );
                    PlayEnhMetaFile( ps.hdc, hMetaFile, &rect );
                    EndPaint( hWnd, &ps );
                }
                break;
```

continued on next page

continued from previous page

```
case WM_COMMAND :
        switch( LOWORD( wParam ) )
        {
            case IDM_TEST :
                    {
                        char szDescription[128];
                        HDC  hDC;

                        GetEnhMetaFileDescription( hMetaFile, 128,
                                                   szDescription );

                        hDC = GetDC( hWnd );
                        TextOut( hDC, 20, 100, szDescription,
                                 strlen( szDescription ) );
                        ReleaseDC( hWnd, hDC );
                    }
                    break;
        .
        .
        .
```

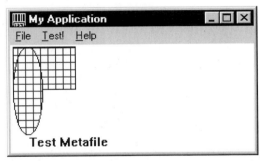

Figure 13-11 `GetEnhMetaFileDescription` example

GetEnhMetaFileHeader ■ WINDOWS 95 ■ WINDOWS NT

Description	`GetEnhMetaFileHeader` retrieves the record containing the header from an enhanced metafile.
Syntax	UINT **GetEnhMetaFileHeader**(HENHMETAFILE *hemf,* UINT *cbBuffer,* LPENHMETAHEADER *lpemh*)
Parameters	
hemf	HENHMETAFILE: The handle of the enhanced metafile.
cbBuffer	UINT: The size, in bytes, of the buffer to receive the data.
lpemh	LPENHMETAHEADER: A pointer to an **ENHMETAHEADER** structure to receive the header record. If set to **NULL**, the size of the header record is returned. See the definition of the **ENHMETAHEADER** structure below.

Returns	UINT: If *lpemh* is NULL, the size of the record that contains the header; otherwise, the number of bytes copied. If an error occurs, **0** is returned.
Include File	`wingdi.h`
See Also	`PlayEnhMetaFile, CreateEnhMetaFile`

ENHMETAHEADER Definition

```
typedef struct tagENHMETAHEADER
{
    DWORD iType;
    DWORD nSize;
    RECTL rclBounds;
    RECTL rclFrame;
    DWORD dSignature;
    DWORD nVersion;
    DWORD nBytes;
    DWORD nRecords;
    WORD  nHandles;
    WORD  sReserved;
    DWORD nDescription;
    DWORD offDescription;
    DWORD nPalEntries;
    SIZEL szlDevice;
    SIZEL szlMillimeters;
} ENHMETAHEADER;
```

Members

iType	DWORD: The record type (**EMR_HEADER**).
nSize	DWORD: The size, in bytes, of the structure.
rclBounds	RECTL: The dimensions, in device units, of the smallest rectangle that can be drawn around the picture stored in the metafile.
rclFrame	RECTL: The dimensions, in .01-millimeter units, of the application-supplied rectangle that surrounds the picture stored in the metafile.
dSignature	DWORD: The doubleword signature (**ENHMETA_SIGNATURE**).
nVersion	DWORD: The metafile version (for this release, **0x00010000**).
nBytes	DWORD: The size, in bytes, of the enhanced metafile.
nRecords	DWORD: The number of records in the enhanced metafile.
nHandles	WORD: The number of handles in the enhanced metafile handle table. Index **0** is used for the handle of the metafile.
sReserved	WORD: Reserved; must be **0**.
nDescription	DWORD: The number of characters in the array that contains the description of the enhanced metafile's content. Set to **0** if the description does not exist.
offDescription	DWORD: The offset from the beginning of the **ENHMETAHEADER** structure to the array that contains the description of the enhanced metafile's content. Set to **0** if the description does not exist.

nPalEntries	DWORD: The number of entries in the enhanced metafile's palette.
szlDevice	SIZEL: The resolution, in pixels, of the reference device.
szlMillimeters	SIZEL: The resolution, in millimeters, of the reference device.
Example	See the example for the GetEnhMetaFilePaletteEntries function.

GetEnhMetaFilePaletteEntries ■ WINDOWS 95 ■ WINDOWS NT

Description	GetEnhMetaFilePaletteEntries retrieves optional palette entries from an enhanced metafile. An application can store an optional palette in an enhanced metafile by calling the CreatePalette and SetPaletteEntries functions before creating the picture and storing it in the metafile. This achieves consistent colors when the picture is displayed on a variety of devices.
Syntax	UINT **GetEnhMetaFilePaletteEntries**(HENHMETAFILE *hemf,* UINT *uEntries,* LPPALETTEENTRY *lppe*)
Parameters	
hemf	HENHMETAFILE: The handle of the enhanced metafile.
uEntries	UINT: The number of entries to be retrieved from the palette.
lppe	LPPALETTEENTRY: A pointer to an array of **PALETTEENTRY** structures to receive the palette colors. If set to **NULL**, the number of entries in the palette is returned. See the description of the **PALETTEENTRY** structure below.
Returns	UINT: If *lppe* is NULL and the enhanced metafile contains an optional palette, the number of entries in the enhanced metafile's palette; otherwise, the number of entries copied is returned. If the metafile does not contain a palette, 0 is returned. If an error occurs, **GDI_ERROR** is returned.
Include File	wingdi.h
See Also	CreatePalette, SetPaletteEntries

PALETTEENTRY Definition

```
typedef struct tagPALETTEENTRY
{
    BYTE peRed;
    BYTE peGreen;
    BYTE peBlue;
    BYTE peFlags;
} PALETTEENTRY;
```

Members

peRed	BYTE: The red intensity value.
peGreen	BYTE: The green intensity value.
peBlue	BYTE: The blue intensity value.

peFlags   BYTE: Determines how the palette entry is to be used. This may be set to **NULL** or one of the values listed in Table 13-10.

Table 13-10 PALETTEENTRY *peFlags* values

Value	Meaning
PC_EXPLICIT	The low-order word of the logical palette entry designates a hardware palette index.
PC_NOCOLLAPSE	Specifies that the color be placed in an unused entry in the system palette instead of being matched to an existing color in the system palette. If there are no unused entries in the system palette, the color is matched normally.
PC_RESERVED	Specifies that the logical palette entry be used for palette animation; this flag prevents other windows from matching colors to the palette entry, because the color frequently changes. If an unused system palette entry is available, the color is placed in that entry.

Example   This example shows how to check for a palette in an enhanced metafile, and if one exists, how to load and create the palette. When the user selects the Test! menu item, the enhanced metafile **SAMPLE.EMF** is loaded. The header information for the metafile is retrieved with the **GetEnhMetaFileHeader** function, and the number of palette entries is checked. Any palette entries are retrieved with the **GetEnhMetaFilePaletteEntries** function, and the palette is created and selected into the device context. The application then plays the metafile on the device context.

```
LRESULT CALLBACK WndProc( HWND hWnd, UINT uMsg, WPARAM wParam, LPARAM lParam )
{
    switch( uMsg )
    {
    case WM_COMMAND :
            switch( LOWORD( wParam ) )
            {
                case IDM_TEST :
                    {
                        HENHMETAFILE   hMetaFile;

                        // Load enhanced metafile.
                        //......................
                        hMetaFile = GetEnhMetaFile( "sample.emf" );

                        if ( hMetaFile )
                        {
                            ENHMETAHEADER mh;
                            HDC          hDC;
                            RECT         rect;

                            GetClientRect( hWnd, &rect );
                            hDC = GetDC( hWnd );

                            // Retrieve enhanced metafile header.
                            //................................
                            GetEnhMetaFileHeader( hMetaFile, sizeof( mh ), &mh );
```

continued on next page

continued from previous page

```
                    // Check for palette entries and create
                    // the palette if one exists.
                    //.........................
                    if ( mh.nPalEntries > 0 )
                    {
                        PALETTEENTRY* lpEntries;
                        LOGPALETTE*   lp;
                        HPALETTE      hPalette;

                        // Allocate memory for the palette.
                        //...............................
                        lp = (LOGPALETTE*)HeapAlloc( GetProcessHeap(), HEAP_ZERO_MEMORY,
                                        sizeof( LOGPALETTE ) +
                                        (mh.nPalEntries*sizeof( PALETTEENTRY )) );

                        lpEntries = &lp->palPalEntry[0];

                        // Retrieve the palette entries.
                        //..............................
                        GetEnhMetaFilePaletteEntries( hMetaFile,
                                                      mh.nPalEntries,
                                                      lpEntries );

                        lp->palVersion    = 0x300;
                        lp->palNumEntries = (WORD)mh.nPalEntries;

                        // Create the palette, and select and realize
                        // the palette for the device context.
                        //.......................................
                        hPalette = CreatePalette( lp );

                        SelectPalette( hDC, hPalette, FALSE );
                        RealizePalette( hDC );
                        HeapFree( GetProcessHeap(), 0, lp );
                    }

                    // Play the enhanced metafile.
                    //...........................
                    PlayEnhMetaFile( hDC, hMetaFile, &rect );

                    ReleaseDC( hWnd, hDC );
                    DeleteEnhMetaFile( hMetaFile );
                }
            }
            break;

            .
            .
            .
```

GetIconInfo   ■ WINDOWS 95   ■ WINDOWS NT

Description	GetIconInfo retrieves information about an icon or cursor.
Syntax	BOOL **GetIconInfo**(HICON *hicon*, PICONINFO *piconinfo*)

Parameters

hicon

HICON: The handle of the icon or cursor. To retrieve information about a standard system icon or cursor, specify one of the values listed in Table 13-11.

Table 13-11 Standard system icons and cursors

Value	Description
IDC_APPSTARTING	Application-starting cursor (arrow and hourglass)
IDC_ARROW	Arrow cursor
IDC_CROSS	Crosshair cursor
IDC_HELP	Help cursor (arrow and question mark)
IDC_IBEAM	I-beam cursor
IDC_NO	"No" cursor
IDC_SIZEALL	Sizing cursor, points north, south, east, and west
IDC_SIZENESW	Sizing cursor, points northeast and southwest
IDC_SIZENS	Sizing cursor, points north and south
IDC_SIZENWSE	Sizing cursor, points northwest and southeast
IDC_SIZEWE	Sizing cursor, points west and east
IDC_UPARROW	Up-arrow cursor
IDC_WAIT	Hourglass cursor
IDI_APPLICATION	Application icon
IDI_ASTERISK	Asterisk icon (letter *i* in a circle)
IDI_EXCLAMATION	Exclamation-point icon
IDI_HAND	Stop-sign icon
IDI_QUESTION	Question-mark icon
IDI_WINLOGO	Windows logo icon

piconinfo

PICONINFO: Points to an ICONINFO structure that receives the icon information. See the description of the ICONINFO structure under the CreateIconIndirect function.

Returns

BOOL: TRUE if successful; otherwise, the return value is FALSE.

Include File

winuser.h

See Also

CreateIcon, CreateIconIndirect

Example

This example loads the application's icon when the user selects the Test! menu item. The icon information is retrieved using the GetIconInfo function. The bitmaps that make up the icon are displayed as shown in Figure 13-12.

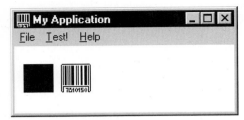

Figure 13-12 `GetIconInfo` example

```
LRESULT CALLBACK WndProc( HWND hWnd, UINT uMsg, WPARAM wParam, LPARAM lParam )
{
    switch( uMsg )
    {
        case WM_COMMAND :
                switch( LOWORD( wParam ) )
                {
                    case IDM_TEST :
                            {
                                HICON    hIcon;
                                HDC      hDC, hMemDC;
                                ICONINFO icInfo;

                                hIcon = LoadIcon( hInst, "MYAPP" );

                                // Retrieve the icon information for the
                                // application's icon.
                                //........................................
                                GetIconInfo( hIcon, &icInfo );

                                // Draw the bitmaps that make
                                // up the icon in the client area.
                                //................................
                                hDC = GetDC( hWnd );
                                hMemDC = CreateCompatibleDC( hDC );

                                SelectObject( hMemDC, icInfo.hbmMask );
                                BitBlt( hDC, 10, 20, 32, 32, hMemDC, 0, 0,SRCCOPY);

                                SelectObject( hMemDC, icInfo.hbmColor );
                                BitBlt( hDC, 50, 20, 32, 32, hMemDC, 0, 0,SRCCOPY);

                                ReleaseDC( hWnd, hDC );
                                DeleteDC( hMemDC );
                            }
                            break;
                    .
                    .
                    .
```

GetMetaRgn ■ WINDOWS 95 ■ WINDOWS NT

Description	`GetMetaRgn` retrieves the current meta-region for a device context. The current clipping region of a device context is defined by the intersection of its clipping region and its meta-region.
Syntax	`int` **`GetMetaRgn`**`( HDC` *`hdc,`* `HRGN` *`hrgn`* `)`
Parameters	
hdc	`HDC`: The device context.
hrgn	`HRGN`: A handle to an existing region. After the function returns, this parameter identifies a copy of the current meta-region.
Returns	`int`: `TRUE` if successful; otherwise, the return value is `FALSE`.
Include File	`wingdi.h`
See Also	`SetMetaRgn`
Example	See the example for the `SetMetaRgn` function.

GetStretchBltMode ■ WINDOWS 95 ■ WINDOWS NT

Description	`GetStretchBltMode` retrieves the current stretching mode. This defines how color data is added to or removed from bitmaps that are stretched or compressed with the `StretchBlt` function.
Syntax	`int` **`GetStretchBltMode`**`( HDC` *`hdc`* `)`
Parameters	
hdc	`HDC`: The device context.
Returns	`int`: The current stretching mode. If an error occurs, `0` is returned. Table 13-21 gives the possible stretching modes.
Include File	`wingdi.h`
See Also	`SetStretchBltMode, StretchBlt`
Example	See the example for the `StretchBlt` function.

GetWinMetaFileBits ■ WINDOWS 95 ■ WINDOWS NT

Description	`GetWinMetaFileBits` converts an enhanced metafile into a Windows 3.x metafile and stores the converted records in the given buffer. Windows 95 and Windows NT applications use the enhanced metafile format. When an enhanced metafile needs to be exported to Win32s or Windows 3.x applications, it first must be converted to the older format.
Syntax	`UINT` **`GetWinMetaFileBits`**`( HENHMETAFILE` *`hemf,`* `UINT` *`cbBuffer,`* `LPBYTE` *`lpbBuffer,`* `INT` *`fnMapMode,`* `HDC` *`hdcRef`* `)`

Parameters

hemf   HENHMETAFILE: The handle of the enhanced metafile.

cbBuffer   UINT: The size, in bytes, of the buffer into which the converted records are to be copied.

lpbBuffer   LPBYTE: A pointer to the buffer into which the converted records are to be copied. If set to NULL, the number of bytes required to store the converted metafile records is returned.

fnMapMode   INT: The mapping mode to use in the converted metafile. See Table 12-24 in Chapter 12, The Graphics Device Interface, for possible values.

hdcRef   HDC: The reference device context (DC).

Returns   UINT: If *lpbBuffer* is set to NULL, the number of bytes required to store the converted records is returned; otherwise, the size of the metafile data in bytes is returned. If an error occurs, 0 is returned.

Include File   wingdi.h

See Also   DeleteEnhMetaFile

Example   This example converts the enhanced metafile SAMPLE.ENF to a Windows 3.x format metafile using the GetWinMetaFileBits function when the user selects the Test! menu item. The Windows 3.x metafile is saved to the file SAMPLE.WMF with the CopyMetaFile function.

```
LRESULT CALLBACK WndProc( HWND hWnd, UINT uMsg, WPARAM wParam, LPARAM lParam )
{
   switch( uMsg )
   {
   case WM_COMMAND :
           switch( LOWORD( wParam ) )
              {
              case IDM_TEST :
                     {
                         HDC            hDC;
                         HENHMETAFILE   hMetaFile;
                         HMETAFILE      hOldMetaFile;
                         UINT           uBufSize;
                         LPBYTE         lpMeta;

                         hDC = GetDC( hWnd );

                         // Load the enhanced metafile.
                         //..............................
                         hMetaFile = GetEnhMetaFile( "sample.emf" );

                         // Find out how much memory we need.
                         //...................................
                         uBufSize = GetWinMetaFileBits( hMetaFile, 0, NULL,
                                                        MM_TEXT, hDC );

                         // Allocate memory and convert the enhanced
                         // metafile to a Windows 3.x metafile.
                         //...........................................
```

```
        lpMeta = HeapAlloc( GetProcessHeap(), HEAP_ZERO_MEMORY, uBufSize );
        GetWinMetaFileBits( hMetaFile, uBufSize, lpMeta,
                            MM_TEXT, hDC );

        // Get a Windows 3.x metafile handle to the
        // converted metafile.
        //........................................
        hOldMetaFile = SetMetaFileBitsEx( uBufSize,
                                          lpMeta );

        // Play the Windows 3.x metafile.
        //..............................
        PlayMetaFile( hDC, hOldMetaFile );

        // Save the metafile to a file.
        //.............................
        CopyMetaFile( hOldMetaFile, "sample.wmf" );

        HeapFree( GetProcessHeap(), 0, lpMeta );
        DeleteMetaFile( hOldMetaFile );
        DeleteEnhMetaFile( hMetaFile );
        ReleaseDC( hWnd, hDC );
    }
    break;
```

LoadBitmap ■ Windows 95 ■ Windows NT

Description	**LoadBitmap** loads a bitmap resource from a module's resource file. The application must list the bitmap in the resource script file (RC), using the **BITMAP** statement. When finished using the bitmap, the application should call **DeleteObject** to free the bitmap from memory. This function will load either device-dependent bitmaps (DDBs) or device-independent bitmaps (DIBs). If a DIB is loaded, it will be converted to a DDB and lose color information.
Syntax	HBITMAP **LoadBitmap**(HINSTANCE *hinst,* LPCTSTR *lpszBitmap*)
Parameters	
hinst	**HINSTANCE**: The instance handle of the module whose executable file contains the bitmap to be loaded.
lpszBitmap	**LPCTSTR**: A pointer to a null-terminated string that contains the name of the bitmap resource to be loaded. Use the **MAKEINTRESOURCE** macro to specify a bitmap by a resource identifier.
Returns	**HBITMAP**: The handle of the loaded bitmap. If an error occurs, **NULL** is returned.
Include File	winuser.h
See Also	DeleteObject, CreateBitmap
Example	See the example for the **CreateIconIndirect** function.

LoadIcon
■ WINDOWS 95 ■ WINDOWS NT

Description	**LoadIcon** loads an icon from the resource script file (RC) associated with an application. Icons are defined in the RC file using the **ICON** resource statement. This function also can retrieve system-defined icons. To load system icons, the *hinst* parameter must be set to **NULL**.
Syntax	HICON **LoadIcon**(HINSTANCE *hinst,* LPCTSTR *lpszIcon*)
Parameters	
hinst	**HINSTANCE**: The instance handle of the module whose executable file contains the icon to be loaded. This parameter must be **NULL** when a standard icon is being loaded.
lpszIcon	**LPCTSTR**: A pointer to a null-terminated string that contains the name of the icon resource to be loaded. Use the **MAKEINTRESOURCE** macro to load an icon using a resource identifier. To load one of the system icons, set the *hinst* parameter to **NULL** and the *lpszIcon* parameter to one of the values listed in Table 13-12.

Table 13-12 System icons

Value	Description
IDI_APPLICATION	Default application icon
IDI_ASTERISK	Asterisk (used in informative messages)
IDI_EXCLAMATION	Exclamation point (used in warning messages)
IDI_HAND	Hand-shaped icon (used in serious warning messages)
IDI_QUESTION	Question mark (used in prompting messages)
IDI_WINLOGO	Windows logo

Returns	**HICON**: The handle of the newly loaded icon. If an error occurs, **NULL** is returned.
Include File	winuser.h
See Also	DrawIcon, LoadImage
Example	See the example for the **GetIconInfo** function.

LoadImage
■ WINDOWS 95 ■ WINDOWS NT

Description	The **LoadImage** function loads an icon, cursor, or bitmap from a file or the resource script file (RC) associated with an application.

Syntax	HANDLE **LoadImage**(HINSTANCE *hinst,* LPCTSTR *lpszName,* UINT *uType,* int *cxDesired,* int *cyDesired,* UINT *uLoad*)

Parameters

hinst   HINSTANCE: The instance handle of the module that contains the image to be loaded. To load an OEM image, set this parameter to **0**.

lpszName   LPCTSTR: A pointer to a null-terminated string that contains the name of the image to load. If the *uLoad* parameter includes the **LR_LOADFROMFILE** value, this parameter must be the name of the file that contains the image. If the *hinst* parameter is **0**, the low-order word of this parameter must be the identifier of the OEM image to load. The OEM image identifiers are defined in **WINUSER.H** and have the prefixes given in Table 13-13.

Table 13-13 OEM image prefixes

Prefix	Meaning
OBM_	OEM bitmaps
OCR_	OEM cursors
OIC_	OEM icons

uType   UINT: The type of image to be loaded. This parameter can be one of the values listed in Table 13-14.

Table 13-14 LoadImage *uType* values

Value	Meaning
IMAGE_BITMAP	Loads a bitmap.
IMAGE_CURSOR	Loads a cursor.
IMAGE_ENHMETAFILE	Loads an enhanced metafile.
IMAGE_ICON	Loads an icon.

cxDesired   int: The desired width, in pixels, of the icon or cursor. If this parameter is **0**, the function uses the **SM_CXICON** or **SM_CXCURSOR** system metric value.

cyDesired   int: The desired height, in pixels, of the icon or cursor. If this parameter is **0**, the function uses the **SM_CYICON** or **SM_CYCURSOR** system metric value.

uLoad   UINT: Determines how the image is loaded. This parameter can be a combination of the values listed in Table 13-15.

Table 13-15 LoadImage *uLoad* values

Value	Meaning
LR_DEFAULTCOLOR	Uses the color format of the display.
LR_LOADDEFAULTSIZE	Uses the width or height specified by the system metric values for cursors and icons, if the *cxDesired* or *cyDesired* values are set to 0.
LR_LOADFROMFILE	Loads the image from the file specified by the *lpszName* parameter. Supported only on Windows NT 4 and Windows 95.
LR_LOADMAP3DCOLORS	Replaces the following shades of gray in the image with the corresponding 3D color:

Color	Replaced With
Dk Gray, RGB(128,128,128)	COLOR_3DSHADOW
Gray, RGB(192,192,192)	COLOR_3DFACE
Lt Gray, RGB(223,223,223)	COLOR_3DLIGHT

Value	Meaning
LR_LOADTRANSPARENT	Replaces the color table entry for the color of the first pixel in the image with the default window color (COLOR_WINDOW). All pixels in the image that use that entry become the default window color. This value applies only to images that have corresponding color tables.
LR_MONOCHROME	Loads the image in black and white.
LR_SHARED	Shares the image handle if the image is loaded multiple times. Do not use this value for images that have nontraditional sizes, that may change after loading, or that are loaded from a file.

Returns   HANDLE: The handle of the newly loaded image. If an error occurs, NULL is returned.

Include File   winuser.h

See Also   CopyImage, LoadIcon, LoadBitmap

Example   This example loads the application's icon using the **LoadImage** function when the user selects the Test! menu item. The icon is displayed on the client area of the application's window.

```
LRESULT CALLBACK WndProc( HWND hWnd, UINT uMsg, WPARAM wParam, LPARAM lParam )
{
    switch( uMsg )
    {
    case WM_COMMAND :
            switch( LOWORD( wParam ) )
            {
            case IDM_TEST :
                {
                    HDC     hDC;
                    HICON   hIcon;

                    // Load application's icon.
                    //........................
                    hIcon = (HICON)LoadImage( hInst, "MYAPP",
                                              IMAGE_ICON,
                                              0, 0,
                                              LR_DEFAULTCOLOR );
```

```
        // Draw the icon.
        //...............
        hDC = GetDC( hWnd );
        DrawIcon( hDC, 10, 10, hIcon );
        ReleaseDC( hWnd, hDC );
    }
    break;
```

.
.
.

LookupIconIdFromDirectory   ■ Windows 95   ■ Windows NT

Description	LookupIconIdFromDirectory searches through icon or cursor data for the icon or cursor that best fits the current display device. A resource file of type **RT_GROUP_ICON** or **RT_GROUP_CURSOR** contains icon or cursor data in several device-dependent and device-independent formats. This function searches the resource file for the icon or cursor that best fits the current display device and returns its integer identifier. Use the **FindResource** and **FindResourceEx** functions with the **MAKEINTRESOURCE** macro and this identifier to locate the resource in the module.
Syntax	int **LookupIconIdFromDirectory**(PBYTE *presbits,* BOOL *bIcon*)
Parameters	
presbits	PBYTE: A pointer to the icon or cursor directory data. This function does not validate the resource data and will cause a general protection (GP) fault or return an undefined value if this parameter is pointing to invalid resource data.
bIcon	BOOL: **TRUE** if the function is searching for an icon; **FALSE** if searching for a cursor.
Returns	int: An integer resource identifier for the icon or cursor that best fits the current display device.
Include File	winuser.h
See Also	LookupIconIdFromDirectoryEx, FindResource, FindResourceEx, LoadIcon, LoadCursor
Example	See example for the **CreateIconFromResource** function.

LookupIconIdFromDirectoryEx   ■ Windows 95   ■ Windows NT

Description	LookupIconIdFromDirectoryEx is exactly the same as the LookupIconIdFromDirectory function, except that a desired size for the icon or cursor can be specified.
Syntax	int **LookupIconIdFromDirectoryEx**(PBYTE *presbits,* BOOL *bIcon,* int *cxDesired,* int *cyDesired,* UINT *uFlags*)

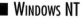

Parameters

presbits   **PBYTE**: A pointer to the icon or cursor directory data. This function does not validate the resource data and will cause a general protection (GP) fault or return an undefined value if this parameter is pointing to invalid resource data.

bIcon   **BOOL**: **TRUE** if the function is searching for an icon; **FALSE** if searching for a cursor.

cxDesired   **int**: The desired width, in pixels, of the icon or cursor. If this parameter is 0 and *uFlags* does not include **LR_LOADREALSIZE**, the function uses the **SM_CXICON** or **SM_CXCURSOR** system metric value.

cyDesired   **int**: The desired height, in pixels, of the icon or cursor. If this parameter is 0 and *uFlags* does not include **LR_LOADREALSIZE**, the function uses the **SM_CYICON** or **SM_CYCURSOR** system metric value.

uFlags   **UINT**: Specifies a combination of the values given in Table 13-16.

Table 13-16 LookupIdFromDirectoryEx *uFlags* values

Value	Meaning
LR_DEFAULTCOLOR	Uses the default color format.
LR_LOADREALSIZE	Sets the width and height as specified by the *biWidth* and *biHeight* members of the BITMAPINFOHEADER struc-ture that defines the icon or cursor. The *cxDesired* and *cyDesired* parameters are ignored.
LR_MONOCHROME	Creates a monochrome icon or cursor.

Returns   **int**: An integer resource identifier for the icon or cursor that best fits the current display device.

Include File   winuser.h

See Also   LookupIconIdFromDirectory, FindResource, FindResourceEx, LoadIcon, LoadCursor

Example   See the example for the **CreateIconFromResourceEx** function.

PatBlt   ■ WINDOWS 95   ■ WINDOWS NT

Description   **PatBlt** fills a rectangle with a pattern. The currently selected brush is output to the device referenced by *hdc*. You use the brush to fill the rectangle defined by the *nXLeft*, *nYLeft*, *nWidth*, and *nHeight* parameters. The brush is combined with the background colors in different ways, depending on the raster-operation code specified in *dwRop*.

Used to fill regions with a pattern.

Syntax   BOOL **PatBlt**(HDC *hdc*, int *nXLeft,* int *nYLeft,* int *nWidth,* int *nHeight,* DWORD *dwRop*)

Parameters

hdc	HDC: The device context.
nXLeft	int: The x coordinate, in logical units, of the upper-left corner of the rectangle to fill.
nYLeft	int: The y coordinate, in logical units, of the upper-left corner of the rectangle to fill.
nWidth	int: The width, in logical units, of the rectangle.
nHeight	int: The height, in logical units, of the rectangle.
dwRop	DWORD: The raster-operation code. This code may be one of the values listed in Table 13-17.

Table 13-17 PatBlt *dwRop* values

Value	Meaning
BLACKNESS	Fills the destination rectangle using the color associated with index 0 in the physical palette. (This color is black for the default physical palette.)
DSTINVERT	Inverts the destination rectangle.
PATCOPY	Copies the pattern into the destination bitmap.
PATINVERT	Combines the colors of the pattern with the colors of the destination rectangle by using the Boolean OR operator.
WHITENESS	Fills the destination rectangle using the color associated with index 1 in the physical palette. (This color is white for the default physical palette.)

Returns	BOOL: TRUE if successful; otherwise, the return value is FALSE.
Include File	wingdi.h
See Also	BitBlt, CreatePatternBrush, LoadBitmap
Example	This example, shown in Figure 13-13, paints a gray box with a 3D border using the PatBlt function when the user selects the Test! menu item.

Figure 13-13 PatBlt example

```
LRESULT CALLBACK WndProc( HWND hWnd, UINT uMsg, WPARAM wParam, LPARAM lParam )
{
    switch( uMsg )
    {
        case WM_COMMAND :
                switch( LOWORD( wParam ) )
                {
                    case IDM_TEST :
                        {
                            HDC      hDC;
                            HBRUSH   hOldBrush;
                            RECT     rect;

                            GetClientRect( hWnd, &rect );

                            hDC = GetDC( hWnd );

                            // Paint gray box.
                            //................
                            hOldBrush = SelectObject( hDC,
                                          GetStockObject( LTGRAY_BRUSH ) );
                            PatBlt( hDC, 5, 5, 60, 40, PATCOPY );

                            // Paint 3D border.
                            //.................
                            SelectObject( hDC, GetStockObject( GRAY_BRUSH ) );
                            PatBlt( hDC, 10, 40, 52, 2, PATCOPY );
                            PatBlt( hDC, 60,  8, 2, 32, PATCOPY );

                            SelectObject( hDC, GetStockObject( WHITE_BRUSH ) );
                            PatBlt( hDC, 8,  8, 52, 2, PATCOPY );
                            PatBlt( hDC, 8, 10,  2, 32, PATCOPY );

                            SelectObject( hDC, hOldBrush );
                            ReleaseDC( hWnd, hDC );
                        }
                        break;
```

.
.
.

PlayEnhMetaFile ■ WINDOWS 95 ■ WINDOWS NT

Description	**PlayEnhMetaFile** displays the picture stored in an enhanced metafile on a given device context (DC). If the metafile was recorded on Windows NT with coordinates outside the range of −32768 to 32767, it will not play back correctly under Windows 95.
Syntax	BOOL **PlayEnhMetaFile**(HDC *hdc,* HENHMETAFILE *hemf,* CONST RECT* *lpRect*)
Parameters	
hdc	HDC: The DC on which the picture will appear.
hemf	HENHMETAFILE: The handle of the enhanced metafile.

lpRect	CONST RECT*: A pointer to a RECT structure that contains the coordinates, in logical units, of the bounding rectangle used to display the picture.
Returns	BOOL: TRUE if successful; otherwise, the return value is FALSE.
Include File	wingdi.h
See Also	GetEnhMetaFile, CreateEnhMetaFile, CloseEnhMetaFile
Example	See example for the CreateEnhMetaFile function.

PlayEnhMetaFileRecord ■ WINDOWS 95 ■ WINDOWS NT

Description	PlayEnhMetaFileRecord plays an enhanced metafile record by executing the Graphics Device Interface (GDI) functions identified by the record. This function is used in conjunction with the EnumEnhMetaFile function within the callback function.
Syntax	BOOL **PlayEnhMetaFileRecord**(HDC *hdc,* LPHANDLETABLE *lpHandletable,* CONST ENHMETARECORD* *lpEnhMetaRecord,* UINT *nHandles*)
Parameters	
hdc	HDC: The device context (DC) passed to the EnumEnhMetaFile function.
lpHandletable	LPHANDLETABLE: A pointer to a table of handles identifying GDI objects used when playing the metafile. The first entry in this table contains the enhanced-metafile handle.
lpEnhMetaRecord	CONST ENHMETARECORD*: A pointer to the enhanced metafile record to be played.
nHandles	UINT: The number of handles in the handle table pointed to by *lpHandletable*.
Returns	BOOL: TRUE if successful; otherwise, the return value is FALSE.
Include File	wingdi.h
See Also	EnumEnhMetaFile
Example	See the example for the EnumEnhMetaFile function.

SetBitmapDimensionEx ■ WINDOWS 95 ■ WINDOWS NT

Description	SetBitmapDimensionEx assigns preferred dimensions to a bitmap. These dimensions are only useful to applications because they have no meaning to Windows. The application can retrieve the dimensions from the bitmap with the GetBitmapDimensionEx function.
Syntax	BOOL **SetBitmapDimensionEx**(HBITMAP *hBitmap,* int *nWidth,* int *nHeight,* LPSIZE *lpSize*)

Parameters

hBitmap	HBITMAP: The handle of the bitmap. This cannot be a DIB section bitmap.
nWidth	int: The width of the bitmap.
nHeight	int: The height of the bitmap.
lpSize	LPSIZE: A pointer to a SIZE structure that receives the previous dimensions of the bitmap. If set to NULL, the previous dimensions are not returned.
Returns	BOOL: TRUE if successful; otherwise, the return value is FALSE.
Include File	wingdi.h
See Also	GetBitmapDimensionEx
Example	In this example, the "smileBMP" bitmap is loaded in the WM_CREATE message and the dimensions are set in the bitmap using the SetBitmapDimensionEx function. When the application processes the WM_PAINT message, the dimensions are retrieved from the bitmap using the GetBitmapDimensionEx function, and the bitmap is painted.

```
LRESULT CALLBACK WndProc( HWND hWnd, UINT uMsg, WPARAM wParam, LPARAM lParam )
{
static HBITMAP hBitmap;

    switch( uMsg )
    {
        case WM_CREATE :
                {
                    BITMAP bm;

                    // Load bitmap and retrieve the size.
                    //...................................
                    hBitmap = LoadBitmap( hInst, "smileBMP" );
                    GetObject( hBitmap, sizeof( BITMAP ), &bm );

                    // Set the bitmap dimensions into the bitmap.
                    //..........................................
                    SetBitmapDimensionEx( hBitmap, bm.bmWidth, bm.bmHeight,
                                    NULL );
                }
                break;

        case WM_PAINT :
                {
                    PAINTSTRUCT ps;
                    SIZE        size;
                    HDC         hMemDC;
                    HBITMAP     hOldBitmap;

                    BeginPaint( hWnd, &ps );

                    // Retrieve the dimensions from the bitmap.
                    //........................................
                    GetBitmapDimensionEx( hBitmap, &size );
                    hMemDC = CreateCompatibleDC( ps.hdc );
```

```
        hOldBitmap = SelectObject( hMemDC, hBitmap );

        // Paint the bitmap.
        //.................
        BitBlt( ps.hdc, 10, 10, size.cx, size.cy,
                hMemDC, 0, 0, SRCCOPY );
        SelectObject( hMemDC, hOldBitmap );
        DeleteDC( hMemDC );

        EndPaint( hWnd, &ps );
    }
    break;
        .
        .
        .
```

SetDIBits   ■ WINDOWS 95   ■ WINDOWS NT

Description	**SetDIBits** sets the pixels in a bitmap using the color data found in the given device-independent bitmap (DIB). The bitmap must not be selected into a device context at the time **SetDIBits** is called. For large bitmaps, the image can be changed in horizontal segments to minimize memory use. Specify a series of *uStartScan* and *uScanLines* values to process bands of the bitmap data.
	You use **SetDIBits** when the application modifies the pixel data for the DIB bitmap prior to displaying it. One possible use is to change the colors of a button to show selection status.
Syntax	int **SetDIBits**(HDC *hdc*, HBITMAP *hbmp*, UINT *uStartScan*, UINT *uScanLines*, CONST VOID* *lpvBits*, CONST BITMAPINFO* *lpbmi*, UINT *uColorUse*)
Parameters	
hdc	HDC: The device context.
hbmp	HBITMAP: The bitmap that is to be altered using the color data from the given DIB.
uStartScan	UINT: The starting scan line for the device-independent color data in the array pointed to by the *lpvBits* parameter.
uScanLines	UINT: The number of scan lines found in the array pointed to by the *lpvBits* parameter.
lpvBits	CONST VOID*: A pointer to the DIB color data, stored as an array of bytes. The format of the bitmap values depends on the *biBitCount* member of the **BITMAPINFOHEADER** structure contained in the **BITMAPINFO** structure pointed to by the *lpbmi* parameter.
lpbmi	CONST BITMAPINFO*: A pointer to a **BITMAPINFO** data structure that contains information about the DIB. See the **CreateDIBitmap** function for a definition of the **BITMAPINFO** structure.

uColorUse	UINT: Specifies whether the *bmiColors* member of the **BITMAPINFO** structure contains explicit red, green, blue (RGB) values or palette indices. The *uColorUse* parameter must be one of the values listed in Table 13-18.

Table 13-18 SetDIBits *uColorUse* values

Value	Meaning
DIB_PAL_COLORS	The color table consists of an array of 16-bit indices into the logical palette of the device context identified by the *hdc* parameter.
DIB_RGB_COLORS	The color table is provided and contains literal RGB values.

Returns	int: The number of scan lines copied. If an error occurs, 0 is returned.
Include File	wingdi.h
See Also	CreateDIBitmap, GetDIBits, GetSystemPaletteEntries
Example	This example paints a device-independent bitmap on the window's client area as shown in Figure 13-14. Initially, the bitmap is colored black and white. When the user selects the Test! menu item, the bitmap data is altered so that any two black pixels next to each other (0 value for a byte within a 16-color bitmap) are changed to a blue-black pixel combination.

```
#define ALIGNLONG(i) ((i+3)/4*4)
#define WIDTH        50
#define HEIGHT       50
#define COLORBITS    4

LRESULT CALLBACK WndProc( HWND hWnd, UINT uMsg, WPARAM wParam, LPARAM lParam )
{
static HBITMAP            hBitmap;
static LPBITMAPINFOHEADER lpbi;
static BITMAPINFOHEADER   bi;

    switch( uMsg )
    {
        case WM_CREATE :
                {
                    HDC     hDC, hMemDC;
                    LPTSTR  lpstBitmap;

                    hDC = GetDC (hWnd) ;

                    // Intialize BITMAPINFOHEADER data.
                    //..............................
                    bi.biSize      = sizeof (BITMAPINFOHEADER) ;
                    bi.biWidth     = WIDTH;
                    bi.biHeight    = HEIGHT;
                    bi.biPlanes    = 1;
                    bi.biBitCount  = COLORBITS;
                    bi.biCompression = BI_RGB;
                    bi.biSizeImage = ( ALIGNLONG( (WIDTH * COLORBITS)/8 )
                                            * HEIGHT);
```

```
            bi.biXPelsPerMeter = O;
            bi.biYPelsPerMeter = O;
            bi.biClrUsed       = O;
            bi.biClrImportant  = O;

            // Create uninitialized DIB bitmap.
            //...............................
            hBitmap = CreateDIBitmap( hDC, &bi, OL, NULL,
                                    NULL, O);

            // Allocate memory for BITMAPINFO structure.
            //.........................................
            lpbi = (BITMAPINFOHEADER*)HeapAlloc( GetProcessHeap(), HEAP_ZERO_MEMORY,
                                    sizeof(BITMAPINFOHEADER) +
                                    16 * sizeof (RGBQUAD) +
                                    (ALIGNLONG((WIDTH * COLORBITS)/8)
                                    * HEIGHT) );
            // Copy BITMAPINFOHEADER information.
            //.................................
            *lpbi = bi;

            // Initialize structure data with GetDIBits().
            //...........................................
            GetDIBits( hDC, hBitmap, O, 50, NULL,
                    (LPBITMAPINFO) lpbi, DIB_RGB_COLORS);

            // Create memory device context and select bitmap.
            //...............................................
            hMemDC = CreateCompatibleDC( hDC );

            SelectObject( hMemDC, hBitmap );

            // Paint on memory device context.
            //...............................
            SelectObject( hMemDC, GetStockObject(BLACK_BRUSH) );
            Rectangle (hMemDC, O, O, WIDTH, HEIGHT);

            SelectObject( hMemDC, GetStockObject(WHITE_BRUSH) ) ;
            Ellipse( hMemDC, O, O, WIDTH, HEIGHT );
            MoveToEx( hMemDC, O, O, NULL );
            LineTo( hMemDC, WIDTH / 2, HEIGHT / 2 );
            LineTo( hMemDC, WIDTH, O );

            // Set pointer to bitmap's bit data.
            //.................................
            lpstBitmap = (LPSTR)lpbi + (WORD)sizeof(BITMAPINFOHEADER) +
                                    (16 * sizeof(RGBQUAD));

            GetDIBits( hDC, hBitmap, O, HEIGHT, lpstBitmap,
                    (LPBITMAPINFO) lpbi, DIB_RGB_COLORS);

            DeleteDC( hMemDC );
            ReleaseDC( hWnd, hDC);
        }
        break;

case WM_PAINT :
        {
```

continued on next page

continued from previous page

```
                PAINTSTRUCT ps;
                HDC         hMemDC;

                BeginPaint( hWnd, &ps );
                hMemDC = CreateCompatibleDC( ps.hdc );

                SelectObject( hMemDC, hBitmap );
                BitBlt( ps.hdc, 10, 10, WIDTH, HEIGHT,
                        hMemDC, 0, 0, SRCCOPY );

                DeleteDC( hMemDC );
                EndPaint( hWnd, &ps );
            }
            break;

    case WM_COMMAND :
            switch( LOWORD( wParam ) )
            {
                case IDM_TEST :
                    {
                        HDC     hDC;
                        int     nBytes, i;
                        LPTSTR  lpstBitmap, lpstTemp;

                        hDC = GetDC( hWnd );

                        lpstBitmap = (LPSTR)lpbi +
                                    (WORD) sizeof(BITMAPINFOHEADER) +
                                    (16 * sizeof (RGBQUAD));

                        nBytes = ALIGNLONG((WIDTH * COLORBITS)/8)
                                    * HEIGHT;

                        lpstTemp = lpstBitmap;

                        // Change 0 bytes to 0x2C in bitmap data.
                        //........................................
                        for( i = 0; i < nBytes; i++ )
                        {
                            if ( 0 == *lpstTemp )
                                *lpstTemp = 0x2C;

                            lpstTemp++;
                        }

                        // Make the changes to the bitmap.
                        //................................
                        SetDIBits( hDC, hBitmap, 0, HEIGHT, lpstBitmap,
                                    (LPBITMAPINFO) lpbi, DIB_RGB_COLORS );

                        ReleaseDC( hWnd, hDC );

                        InvalidateRect( hWnd, NULL, TRUE );
                        UpdateWindow( hWnd );
                    }
                    break;

                case IDM_EXIT :
                        DestroyWindow( hWnd );
```

```
                    break;
            }
            break;

    case WM_DESTROY :
            HeapFree( GetProcessHeap(), 0, lpbi );
            PostQuitMessage(0);
            break;

    default :
            return( DefWindowProc( hWnd, uMsg, wParam, lParam ) );
    }

    return( 0L );
}
```

Figure 13-14 `SetDIBits` example

SetDIBitsToDevice   ■ WINDOWS 95   ■ WINDOWS NT

Description   `SetDIBitsToDevice` draws a device-independent bitmap on the device
associated with the destination device context. Unless the **BITMAPINFO**
color data is separately processed to realize a logical palette, the color data
will be lost when the DIB is output to the device context. For example, a
256-color bitmap will be mapped to the 20 default system colors when
output to a VGA device.

Memory demands for painting the DIB can be reduced by successively
painting horizontal bands out of a DIB bitmap, rather than painting all of
the image at once.

Normally, the **BITMAPINFO** data pointed to by *lpbmi* will be right in front
of the bitmap pixel data (pointed to by *lpvBits*), all in the same memory
block.

Note that the origin for the DIB pixel data is the bottom-left corner. The
data is upside down relative to the default **MM_TEXT** mapping mode.

Syntax   int **SetDIBitsToDevice**(HDC *hdc*, int *XDest*, int *YDest*, DWORD
dwWidth, DWORD *dwHeight*, int *XSrc*, int *YSrc*, UINT *uStartScan*,
UINT *uScanLines*, CONST VOID* *lpvBits*, CONST BITMAPINFO* *lpbmi*,
UINT *uColorUse*)

Parameters

hdc	HDC: The device context.
XDest	int: The x coordinate, in logical units, of the upper-left corner of the destination rectangle.
YDest	int: The y coordinate, in logical units, of the upper-left corner of the destination rectangle.
dwWidth	DWORD: The width, in logical units, of the DIB.
dwHeight	DWORD: The height, in logical units, of the DIB.
XSrc	int: The x coordinate, in logical units, of the lower-left corner of the DIB.
YSrc	int: The y coordinate, in logical units, of the lower-left corner of the DIB.
uStartScan	UINT: The starting scan line in the DIB.
uScanLines	UINT: The number of DIB scan lines contained in the array pointed to by the *lpvBits* parameter.
lpvBits	CONST VOID*: A pointer to DIB color data stored as an array of bytes.
lpbmi	CONST BITMAPINFO*: A pointer to a BITMAPINFO structure that contains information about the DIB.
uColorUse	UINT: Specifies whether the *bmiColors* member of the BITMAPINFO structure contains explicit red, green, blue (RGB) values or palette indices. The *uColorUse* parameter must be one of the values listed in Table 13-19.

Table 13-19 SetDIBitsToDevice *uColorUse* values

Value	Meaning
DIB_PAL_COLORS	The color table consists of an array of 16-bit indices into the logical palette of the device context identified by the *hdc* parameter.
DIB_RGB_COLORS	The color table contains literal RGB values.

Returns	int: The number of scan lines set. If an error occurs, 0 is returned.
Include File	wingdi.h
See Also	CreateDIBitmap, GetDIBits, SetDIBits, StretchDIBits
Example	In this example, shown in Figure 13-15, a DIB and palette entries are loaded in the WM_CREATE message. On the WM_PAINT message, the DIB is painted normal size with the SetDIBitsToDevice function and painted 200 percent of normal size using the StretchDIBits function.

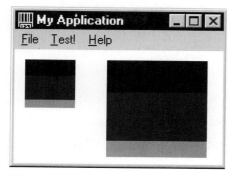

Figure 13-15 `SetDIBitsToDevice` example

```
LRESULT CALLBACK WndProc( HWND hWnd, UINT uMsg, WPARAM wParam, LPARAM lParam )
{
static HPALETTE hPalette;
static int      nColorData;

    switch( uMsg )
    {
        case WM_CREATE :
                {
                    HANDLE          hRes;
                    LPBITMAPINFO    lpBi;
                    LPLOGPALETTE    lpPal;
                    int             i;

                    // Load the bitmap.
                    //................
                    hRes = LoadResource( hInst,
                                FindResource( hInst, "testdib", RT_BITMAP ) );

                    lpBi = (LPBITMAPINFO)LockResource( hRes );

                    // Find out how many colors we need.
                    //..................................
                    if ( lpBi->bmiHeader.biClrUsed != 0 )
                        nColorData = lpBi->bmiHeader.biClrUsed;
                    else
                        switch( lpBi->bmiHeader.biBitCount )
                        {
                            case 1  : nColorData = 2;   break; // Monochrome
                            case 4  : nColorData = 16;  break; // VGA
                            case 8  : nColorData = 256; break; // SVGA
                            case 24 : nColorData = 0;   break; // True Color
                        }

                    // Allocate memory for color palette.
                    //..................................
                    lpPal = (LPLOGPALETTE)HeapAlloc( GetProcessHeap(), HEAP_ZERO_MEMORY,
                                    sizeof(LOGPALETTE)+(nColorData*sizeof(PALETTEENTRY))⇐
);
```

continued on next page

657

continued from previous page

```
                lpPal->palVersion     = 0x300;
                lpPal->palNumEntries = nColorData;

                // Load each color into the palette.
                //..................................
                for ( i = 0; i < nColorData; i++ )
                {
                    lpPal->palPalEntry[i].peRed    = lpBi->bmiColors[i].rgbRed;
                    lpPal->palPalEntry[i].peGreen =
                                                lpBi->bmiColors[i].rgbGreen;

                    lpPal->palPalEntry[i].peBlue   =
                                                lpBi->bmiColors[i].rgbBlue;

                }

                // Create the palette.
                //....................
                hPalette = CreatePalette( lpPal );

                HeapFree( GetProcessHeap(), 0, lpPal );
            }
            break;

        case WM_PAINT :
            {
                PAINTSTRUCT   ps;
                LPBITMAPINFO lpBi;
                HANDLE        hRes;
                LPTSTR        lpBits;

                BeginPaint( hWnd, &ps );

                // Select palette and realize it.
                //...............................
                SelectPalette( ps.hdc, hPalette, FALSE );
                RealizePalette( ps.hdc );

                // Load the bitmap.
                //.................
                hRes = LoadResource( hInst,
                        FindResource( hInst, "testdib", RT_BITMAP ) );

                lpBi = (LPBITMAPINFO)LockResource( hRes );

                // Locate the bitmap data.
                //........................
                lpBits =  (LPSTR) lpBi;
                lpBits +=  lpBi->bmiHeader.biSize +
                        ( nColorData*sizeof(RGBQUAD) );

                // Paint the bitmap normal size.
                //..............................
                SetDIBitsToDevice( ps.hdc, 10, 10,
                                        lpBi->bmiHeader.biWidth,
                                        lpBi->bmiHeader.biHeight,
                                        0, 0,
                                        0, lpBi->bmiHeader.biHeight,
                                        lpBits, lpBi, DIB_RGB_COLORS );
```

```
                      // Paint the bitmap 200% size.
                      //.........................
                      StretchDIBits( ps.hdc, 40+lpBi->bmiHeader.biWidth, 10,
                                        lpBi->bmiHeader.biWidth*2,
                                        lpBi->bmiHeader.biHeight*2,
                                        0, 0,
                                        lpBi->bmiHeader.biWidth,
                                        lpBi->bmiHeader.biHeight,
                                        lpBits, lpBi, DIB_RGB_COLORS,
                                        SRCCOPY );

                      EndPaint( hWnd, &ps );
                  }
                  break;

        case WM_COMMAND :
                  switch( LOWORD( wParam ) )
                  {
                      case IDM_EXIT :
                              DestroyWindow( hWnd );
                              break;
                  }
                  break;

        case WM_DESTROY :
                  DeleteObject( hPalette );
                  PostQuitMessage(0);
                  break;

        default :
                  return( DefWindowProc( hWnd, uMsg, wParam, lParam ) );
    }

    return( 0L );
}
```

SetEnhMetaFileBits

■ WINDOWS 95   ■ WINDOWS NT

Description SetEnhMetaFileBits creates a memory-based enhanced metafile from the supplied data. When the application no longer needs the enhanced metafile handle, it should delete the handle by calling the DeleteEnhMetaFile function. This function does not accept metafile data in the Windows 3.x format. Use the SetWinMetaFileBits function for these metafiles.

Syntax HENHMETAFILE **SetEnhMetaFileBits**(UINT *cbBuffer,* CONST BYTE* *lpData*)

Parameters

cbBuffer UINT: The size, in bytes, of the data pointed to by *lpData.*

lpData CONST BYTE*: A pointer to a buffer that contains enhanced metafile data. The data should be in the format as received from the GetEnhMetaFileBits function.

Returns	HENHMETAFILE: The handle of the memory-based enhanced metafile. If an error occurs, NULL is returned.
Include File	wingdi.h
See Also	GetEnhMetaFileBits, DeleteEnhMetaFile
Example	See the example for the GetEnhMetaFileBits function.

SetMetaRgn   ■ WINDOWS 95   ■ WINDOWS NT

Description	SetMetaRgn intersects the current clipping region of a device context (defined by the intersection of its clipping region and its meta-region) with the current meta-region and saves the combined region as the new meta-region for the device context. The clipping region is reset to a null region. An application should save the device context with the SaveDC function prior to calling this function.
Syntax	int **SetMetaRgn**(HDC *hdc*)
Parameters	
hdc	HDC: The device context for which to set the meta-region.
Returns	int: If successful, the new clipping region's complexity. This can be any one of the values listed in Table 13-20.

Table 13-20 SetMetaRgn return values

Value	Description
COMPLEXREGION	Region is more than one rectangle.
ERROR	An error occurred (the previous clipping region is unaffected).
NULLREGION	Region is empty.
SIMPLEREGION	Region is a single rectangle.

Include File	wingdi.h
See Also	GetMetaRgn, SelectClipRgn
Example	This example uses the GetMetaRgn and SetMetaRgn functions to change the meta-region during painting of a metafile. When the user selects the Test! menu item, the decrement size is increased by 10 units in the horizontal and vertical directions. The effect is that the metafile is scaled down by 10 units each time the user selects the Test! menu item.

```
LRESULT CALLBACK WndProc( HWND hWnd, UINT uMsg, WPARAM wParam, LPARAM lParam )
{
static HENHMETAFILE hMetaFile;
static int          size = 0;
```

```
switch( uMsg )
{
    case WM_CREATE  :
            // Load the metafile.
            //....................
            hMetaFile = GetEnhMetaFile( "sample.emf" );
            break;

    case WM_PAINT :
            {
                PAINTSTRUCT ps;
                RECT        rect;
                HRGN        hgn;

                BeginPaint( hWnd, &ps );

                // Retrieve the current meta-region.
                //..................................
                GetMetaRgn( ps.hdc, hgn );
                GetRgnBox( hgn, &rect );

                // If size has a value then decrease
                // the meta-region in size.
                //..................................
                if ( size > 0 )
                {
                    rect.right -= size;
                    rect.bottom -= size;

                    hgn = CreateRectRgn( rect.left, rect.top,
                                         rect.right, rect.bottom );

                    SelectClipRgn( ps.hdc, hgn );
                    SetMetaRgn( ps.hdc );
                }

                PlayEnhMetaFile( ps.hdc, hMetaFile, &rect );

                EndPaint( hWnd, &ps );
            }
            break;

    case WM_COMMAND :
            switch( LOWORD( wParam ) )
            {
                case IDM_TEST :
                        size += 10;
                        InvalidateRect( hWnd, NULL, TRUE );
                        UpdateWindow( hWnd );
                        break;
        .
        .
        .
```

SetStretchBltMode ■ WINDOWS 95 ■ WINDOWS NT

Description	SetStretchBltMode sets the bitmap stretching mode for a device context. The stretching mode determines how pixels are eliminated if a bitmap image is reduced in size. Bitmaps that are increased in size simply add more matching pixels between existing ones. The stretching mode becomes a property of the device context, and remains in effect until the device context is deleted or a new stretching mode is set.
	The most desirable stretching mode will depend on the bitmap being reduced. Images with a few thin lines will be processed most effectively by STRETCH_ANDSCANS. Images with a few fat lines will be processed more effectively by STRETCH_ORSCANS. General color images can use STRETCH_DELETESCANS.
Syntax	int **SetStretchBltMode**(HDC *hdc,* int *nStretchMode*)
Parameters	
hdc	HDC: Identifies the device context.
nStretchMode	int: The new stretching mode. This can be one of the values listed in Table 13-21.

Table 13-21 SetStretchBltMode *nStretchMode* values

Value	Meaning
STRETCH_ANDSCANS	Performs a Boolean AND operation using the color values for the eliminated and existing pixels. If the bitmap is a monochrome bitmap, this mode preserves black pixels at the expense of white pixels. This value is also defined as BLACKONWHITE.
STRETCH_DELETESCANS	Deletes the pixels. This mode deletes all eliminated lines of pixels without trying to preserve their information. This value is also defined as COLORONCOLOR.
STRETCH_HALFTONE	Maps pixels from the source rectangle into blocks of pixels in the destination rectangle. The average color over the destination block of pixels approximates the color of the source pixels. This value is also defined as HALFTONE. After setting the STRETCH_HALFTONE stretching mode, an application must call the SetBrushOrgEx function to set the brush origin; otherwise brush misalignment occurs.
STRETCH_ORSCANS	Performs a Boolean OR operation using the color values for the eliminated and existing pixels. If the bitmap is a monochrome bitmap, this mode preserves white pixels at the expense of black pixels. This value is also defined as WHITEONBLACK.

Returns	int: If successful, the previous stretching mode; otherwise, the return value is 0.
Include File	wingdi.h
See Also	GetStretchBltMode, StretchBlt
Example	See the example for the **StretchBlt** function.

SetWinMetaFileBits

Description	SetWinMetaFileBits converts a metafile from the older Windows 3.x format to the new enhanced format. When the application no longer needs the enhanced-metafile handle, it should delete it by calling the DeleteEnhMetaFile function. If the reference device context is not the same one in which the metafile was originally created, some GDI functions that use device units may not draw the picture correctly.
Syntax	HENHMETAFILE **SetWinMetaFileBits**(UINT *cBuffer*, CONST BYTE* *lpbBuffer*, HDC *hdcRef*, CONST METAFILEPICT* *lpmfp*)
Parameters	
cBuffer	UINT: The size, in bytes, of the buffer that contains the Windows 3.x metafile.
lpbBuffer	CONST BYTE*: A pointer to a buffer that contains the Windows 3.x metafile data. This data should be in the format retrieved from the GetWinMetaFileBits function.
hdcRef	HDC: The reference device context.
lpmfp	CONST METAFILEPICT*: A pointer to a **METAFILEPICT** structure that contains the suggested size of the metafile picture and the mapping mode that was used when the picture was created. See the definition of the **METAFILEPICT** structure below.
Returns	HENHMETAFILE: If the function succeeds, the return value is a handle of a memory-based enhanced metafile; otherwise, it is **NULL**.
Include File	wingdi.h
See Also	GetWinMetaFileBits, DeleteEnhMetaFile

METAFILEPICT Definition

```
typedef struct tagMETAFILEPICT
{
    LONG     mm;
    LONG     xExt;
    LONG     yExt;
    HMETAFILE hMF;
} METAFILEPICT;
```

Members

mm	LONG: The mapping mode in which the picture is drawn. See Table 12-24 in Chapter 12, The Graphics Device Interface, for valid mapping modes.
xExt	LONG: The width of the metafile picture for all modes except the **MM_ISOTROPIC** and **MM_ANISOTROPIC** modes. For these modes, *xExt* contains the suggested size.
yExt	LONG: The height of the metafile picture for all modes except the **MM_ISOTROPIC** and **MM_ANISOTROPIC** modes. For these modes, *yExt* contains the suggested size.

hMF	**HMETAFILE**: The memory metafile.
Example	This example converts the Windows 3.x metafile **SAMPLE.WMF** to an enhanced format metafile using the **SetWinMetaFileBits** function when the user selects the Test! menu item. The Windows 3.x metafile was saved to the file **SAMPLE.WMF** with a previous call to the **CopyMetaFile** function.

```
LRESULT CALLBACK WndProc( HWND hWnd, UINT uMsg, WPARAM wParam, LPARAM lParam )
{
   switch( uMsg )
   {
     case WM_COMMAND :
            switch( LOWORD( wParam ) )
            {
               case IDM_TEST :
                   {
                      HDC            hDC;
                      HENHMETAFILE   hMetaFile;
                      HMETAFILE      hOldMetaFile;
                      UINT           uBufSize;
                      LPBYTE         lpMeta;
                      RECT           rect;

                      hDC = GetDC( hWnd );

                      // Load the Windows 3.x metafile.
                      //...............................
                      hOldMetaFile = GetMetaFile( "sample.wmf" );

                      // Find out how much memory we need.
                      //..................................
                      uBufSize = GetMetaFileBitsEx( hOldMetaFile, 0,
                                             NULL );

                      // Allocate memory to retrieve the
                      // Windows 3.x metafile.
                      //..................................
                      lpMeta = HeapAlloc( GetProcessHeap(), HEAP_ZERO_MEMORY, uBufSize );
                      GetMetaFileBitsEx( hOldMetaFile, uBufSize,
                                         lpMeta );

                      // Get an enhanced metafile handle to the
                      // Windows 3.x metafile.
                      //........................................
                      hMetaFile = SetWinMetaFileBits( uBufSize, lpMeta,
                                              hDC, NULL );

                      // Play the enhanced metafile.
                      //............................
                      GetClientRect( hWnd, &rect );
                      PlayEnhMetaFile( hDC, hMetaFile, &rect );

                      HeapFree( GetProcessHeap(), 0, lpMeta );
                      DeleteMetaFile( hOldMetaFile );
                      DeleteEnhMetaFile( hMetaFile );
                      ReleaseDC( hWnd, hDC );
```

```
        }
        break;
```

.
.
.

StretchBlt

Description	StretchBlt copies a bitmap from a source rectangle into a destination rectangle, if necessary stretching or compressing the bitmap according to the stretching mode to fit the dimensions of the destination rectangle. The image can be reversed or inverted by using unmatched signs (one positive, one negative) for the source and destination width or height parameters.

This function is convenient for windows that are sizeable, but you may need to enlarge or contract bitmap images depending on the size of the window. Large expansions of bitmaps will result in jagged edges. Consider using a metafile for large images.

Syntax   BOOL **StretchBlt**(HDC *hdcDest,* int *nXOriginDest,* int *nYOriginDest,* int *nWidthDest,* int *nHeightDest,* HDC *hdcSrc,* int *nXOriginSrc,* int *nYOriginSrc,* int *nWidthSrc,* int *nHeightSrc,* DWORD *dwRop*)

Parameters

hdcDest   HDC: The destination device context.

nXOriginDest   int: The x coordinate, in logical units, of the upper-left corner of the destination rectangle.

nYOriginDest   int: The y coordinate, in logical units, of the upper-left corner of the destination rectangle.

nWidthDest   int: The width, in logical units, of the destination rectangle.

nHeightDest   int: The height, in logical units, of the destination rectangle.

hdcSrc   HDC: The source device context.

nXOriginSrc   int: The x coordinate, in logical units, of the upper-left corner of the source rectangle.

nYOriginSrc   int: The y coordinate, in logical units, of the upper-left corner of the source rectangle.

nWidthSrc   int: The width, in logical units, of the source rectangle.

nHeightSrc   int: The height, in logical units, of the source rectangle.

dwRop   DWORD: The raster operation to be performed. Table 13-2 lists raster-operation codes.

Returns   BOOL: TRUE if successful; otherwise, the return value is FALSE.

Include File wingdi.h

Example   This example, shown in Figure 13-16, stretches a bitmap to the size of the client area using the **StretchBlt** function when the user selects the Test! menu item.

```c
LRESULT CALLBACK WndProc( HWND hWnd, UINT uMsg, WPARAM wParam, LPARAM lParam )
{
   switch( uMsg )
   {
      case WM_COMMAND :
              switch( LOWORD( wParam ) )
              {
                 case IDM_TEST :
                       {
                          HBITMAP hBitmap;
                          BITMAP  bm;
                          HDC     hDC;
                          HDC     hMemDC;
                          RECT    rect;

                          // Load the bitmap into memory.
                          //............................
                          hBitmap = LoadBitmap( hInst, "SmileBMP" );

                          // Get the bitmap information.
                          //...........................
                          GetObject( hBitmap, sizeof( BITMAP ), &bm );

                          // Paint the bitmap on the screen.
                          //...............................
                          hDC = GetDC( hWnd );
                          hMemDC = CreateCompatibleDC( hDC );

                          SelectObject( hMemDC, hBitmap );

                          GetClientRect( hWnd, &rect );

                          // Check the StretchBlt mode and set if necessary.
                          //...............................................
                          if (GetStretchBltMode(hDC) != STRETCH_DELETESCANS)
                             SetStretchBltMode( hDC, STRETCH_DELETESCANS );

                          // Paint the bitmap the size of the client area.
                          //.............................................
                          StretchBlt( hDC, 0, 0, rect.right, rect.bottom,
                                      hMemDC, 0, 0, bm.bmWidth, bm.bmHeight,
                                      SRCCOPY );

                          DeleteDC( hMemDC );
                          ReleaseDC( hWnd, hDC );
                          DeleteObject( hBitmap );
                       }
                       break;
```

```
        case IDM_EXIT :
                DestroyWindow( hWnd );
                break;
        }
        break;

    case WM_DESTROY :
        PostQuitMessage(0);
        break;

    default :
        return( DefWindowProc( hWnd, uMsg, wParam, lParam ) );
    }

    return( 0L );
}
```

Figure 13-16 `StretchBlt` example

StretchDIBits   ■ Windows 95   ■ Windows NT

Description   `StretchDIBits` copies the color data for a rectangle of pixels in a device-independent bitmap (DIB) to the given destination rectangle. This function is similar to `SetDIBitsToDevice`. The bitmap can be stretched and/or compressed as it is painted to the device context. No provision is given for banding the output (painting the bitmap in sections to conserve memory), so the entire bitmap must be output in one call to `StretchDIBits`. The image can be reversed or inverted by using unmatched signs (one positive, one negative) for the source and destination width or height parameters.

Like `SetDIBitsToDevice`, `StretchDIBits` will not preserve the color data in the DIB header but will map the colors in the DIB to the existing color palette. To preserve the color information, the DIB color data must be used to realize a logical palette.

Syntax	int **StretchDIBits**(HDC *hdc,* int *XDest,* int *YDest,* int *nDestWidth,* int *nDestHeight,* int *nXSrc,* int *nYSrc,* int *nSrcWidth,* int *nSrcHeight,* CONST VOID* *lpBits,* CONST BITMAPINFO* *lpBitsInfo,* UINT *uColorUse,* DWORD *dwRop*)
Parameters	
hdc	HDC: The destination device context.
XDest	int: The x coordinate, in logical units, of the upper-left corner of the destination rectangle.
YDest	int: The y coordinate, in logical units, of the upper-left corner of the destination rectangle.
nDestWidth	int: The width, in logical units, of the destination rectangle.
nDestHeight	int: The height, in logical units, of the destination rectangle.
nXSrc	int: The x coordinate, in pixels, of the source rectangle in the DIB.
nYSrc	int: The y coordinate, in pixels, of the source rectangle in the DIB.
nSrcWidth	int: The width, in pixels, of the source rectangle in the DIB.
nSrcHeight	int: The height, in pixels, of the source rectangle in the DIB.
lpBits	CONST VOID*: A pointer to the DIB bits, which are stored as an array of bytes.
lpBitsInfo	CONST BITMAPINFO*: A pointer to a BITMAPINFO structure that contains information about the DIB. See the CreateDIBitmap function for a description of the BITMAPINFO structure.
uColorUse	UINT: Specifies whether the *bmiColors* member of the BITMAPINFO structure contains explicit red, green, blue (RGB) values or palette indices. The *uColorUse* parameter must be one of the values listed in Table 13-22.

Table 13-22 StretchDIBits *uColorUse* values

Value	Meaning
DIB_PAL_COLORS	The color table consists of an array of 16-bit indices into the logical palette of the device context identified by the *hdc* parameter.
DIB_RGB_COLORS	The color table contains literal RGB values.

dwRop	DWORD: The raster operation to be performed. Table 13-2 lists raster-operation codes.
Returns	int: The number of scan lines copied. If an error occurs, GDI_ERROR is returned.
Include File	wingdi.h
See Also	CreateDIBitmap, GetDIBits, SetDIBitsToDevice
Example	See the example for the SetDIBitsToDevice function.

14

PRINTING AND TEXT OUTPUT

Sending output to a printer in a Windows program is almost the same as sending output to the screen. The same functions that work with screen output also work with printer output, except that the application uses a device context for the printer instead of the screen. See Chapter 12, The Graphics Device Interface, for more information about device contexts.

Printer Support

Previous versions of Windows used printer driver messages called escapes and the `Escape` function to communicate with the printer. For the most part, in the Win32 API, the `Escape` function is obsolete and has been replaced with more specific functions, such as `StartDoc`, `EndDoc`, `StartPage`, `EndPage`, etc.

An application must create a device context for a printer using the `CreateDC` function before it can print. Once the application has a device context for a printer, it can start the printing process by calling the `StartDoc` function. The `StartDoc` function requires a `DOCINFO` structure that describes the document that is about to be printed (see the detailed definition of the `DOCINFO` structure under the `StartDoc` function later in this chapter). Each page is started by calling the `StartPage` function and ended with the `EndPage` function. A page can be thought of as a drawing screen. All the drawing for a page is done before the next page can be drawn. When printing finishes, the `EndDoc` function is called. Listing 14-1 shows a minimal program fragment for sending a text string on two pages to the printer identified by `"HP Laser Printer"`.

Listing 14-1 Minimal printing

```
HDC     hDC;
DOCINFO di;
```

continued on next page

continued from previous page

```
// Create a device context for the
// printer to which text will be output.
//....................................
hDC = CreateDC( "WINSPOOL", "HP Laser Printer", NULL, NULL );

// Set up the DOCINFO structure.
//..............................
memset( &di, 0, sizeof( DOCINFO ) );
di.cbSize      = sizeof( DOCINFO );
di.lpszDocName = "Test Document";

// Start the printing.
//....................
if ( StartDoc( hDC, &di ) != SP_ERROR )
{
    // Print page 1.
    //..............
    StartPage( hDC );
    TextOut( hDC, 10, 10, "This is on Page 1.",18);
    EndPage( hDC );

    // Print page 2.
    //..............
    StartPage( hDC );
    TextOut( hDC, 10, 10, "This is on Page 2.",18);
    EndPage( hDC );

    // End printing.
    //..............
    EndDoc( hDC );
}

DeleteDC( hDC );
```

The simple example shown in Listing 14-1 is suitable only for small print jobs. For larger jobs, an application should provide a way for the user to stop a print job that is in progress. You can have a dialog box with a Cancel button appear to show that printing is going on and give users a way to halt it. An application also could use threads to provide background printing on large print jobs, so that users can continue working without waiting for the printing process. See Chapter 25, Processes, Threads, and Fibers, for more information on creating and using threads.

If an application does not use threads, Windows can use an abort procedure, which is an application-defined function that processes messages while the application is printing. This function is set using the **SetAbortProc** function prior to printing. Windows periodically sends messages to the abort procedure during printing. This gives the application a chance to stop printing when one of these messages is being processed. The example under the **AbortDoc** function later in this chapter shows how this is done.

Printer Information

Although Windows shields the application from direct dealings with the printer hardware, a few situations require it to retrieve hardware-specific information. For example, an application may need to determine the size of the paper, the number of paper bins, the graphics capabilities, and so on.

Windows has two functions, `DeviceCapabilities` and `GetDeviceCaps`, that provide the information that an application needs about a printer. The `GetDeviceCaps` function is a general function that provides information about displays, printers, plotters, etc. It retrieves information that is common among all types of devices, such as graphics capability, resolution, number of colors, and so on. The `DeviceCapabilities` function retrieves information that is specific to printers, such as information about paper bins, duplexing capabilities, paper size, etc. In previous versions of Windows, this function was not directly supported by the API, it was part of the printer driver. The Win32 API supports this function.

Text Characteristics

When an application outputs text, it can control several characteristics with the functions provided in the Win32 API: placement of the text, the distance between characters, the color of the text and the background text color, etc.

Each font has different sizing characteristics that can be determined with the `GetTextMetrics` function. TrueType fonts also contain more information about characteristics such as kerning pairs. Kerning pairs are pairs of characters that, when placed together in a string, have the spacing between them adjusted to get the best appearance. These combinations of characters can be retrieved using the `GetKerningPairs` function. TrueType fonts also have other characteristics that are not applicable to other fonts. These characteristics can be retrieved with the `GetOutlineTextMetrics` function.

When using and scaling fonts in an application, it is important to understand the system of measurements used to describe a character. Figure 14-1 shows the names of each measurement.

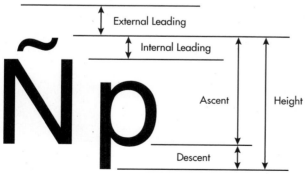

Figure 14-1 Text dimensions (metrics)

Printing and Text Output Function Descriptions

Table 14-1 summarizes the printing and text output functions. Detailed function descriptions follow the table.

Table 14-1 Printing and text output function summary

Function	Purpose
AbortDoc	Aborts the current print job.
DeviceCapabilities	Retrieves information about a printer.
EndDoc	Ends a print job.
EndPage	Ends drawing of a page.
Escape	Sends special information to a device, such as a printer, not directly available through GDI.
ExtEscape	Sends driver-defined information to a device, such as a printer, not directly available through GDI.
ExtTextOut	Output of text within a rectangular area, with separate control over the spacing between each character.
GetCharABCWidths	Retrieves the widths, in logical units, of consecutive characters from a TrueType font.
GetCharacterPlacement	Retrieves placement information about a character string.
GetCharWidth32	Determines the width of one or more characters in a font.
GetCharWidthFloat	Determines the fractional width of one or more characters in a font.
GetGlyphOutline	Retrieves the outline or bitmap for a character in a TrueType font.
GetKerningPairs	Retrieves the character-kerning pairs for a font.
GetOutlineTextMetrics	Retrieves text metrics for TrueType fonts.
GetRasterizerCaps	Determines if TrueType fonts are installed in the system.
GetTabbedTextExtent	Determines the logical dimensions of a string containing tab characters.
GetTextAlign	Determines the text alignment settings of a device context.
GetTextCharacterExtra	Determines the amount of extra character spacing defined for a device context.
GetTextColor	Retrieves the text color setting for a device context.
GetTextExtentExPoint	Determines the number of characters in a string that will fit within a given space.
GetTextExtentPoint32	Determines the width and height of a string when output to a device context.
GetTextFace	Retrieves the name of the current typeface.
GetTextMetrics	Retrieves basic data about the font currently selected for a device context.
ResetDC	Updates a printer device context.
SetAbortProc	Sets the AbortProc function that allows a print job to be canceled during spooling.
SetTextAlign	Changes the text alignment for a device context.
SetTextCharacterExtra	Adds additional space between characters of a device context.
SetTextColor	Changes the text color for a device context.
SetTextJustification	Justifies a string prior to using TextOut for output.
StartDoc	Starts a print job.
StartPage	Prepares the printer driver to accept data for a page.
TabbedTextOut	Outputs a text string, expanding at tab characters.
TextOut	Outputs a character string at a location on the selected device context.

AbortDoc

Description	**AbortDoc** stops the current print job and removes it from the print queue. Applications typically use **AbortDoc** in response to the user canceling a print job. This function replaces the **ABORTDOC** printer escape.
Syntax	int **AbortDoc**(HDC *hdc*)
Parameters	
hdc	HDC: The device context for the print job.
Returns	int: If successful, a value greater than zero; otherwise, **SP_ERROR** is returned.
Include File	wingdi.h
See Also	StartDoc, EndDoc, SetAbortProc
Example	This example shows how to set up an abort dialog and an abort procedure using the **SetAbortProc** function. If the user presses the Cancel button on the abort dialog while printing, the document is aborted using the **AbortDoc** function.

Abort dialog in resource script file

```
ABORTDLG DIALOG 20, 20, 90, 64
STYLE DS_MODALFRAME | WS_CAPTION | WS_SYSMENU
CAPTION "Printing"
BEGIN
   DEFPUSHBUTTON "Cancel", IDCANCEL,    29, 44, 32, 14, WS_GROUP
   CTEXT         "Sending",             -1,           0,  8, 90,  8
   CTEXT         "",                    IDC_FILENAME, 0, 18, 90,  8
   CTEXT         "to print spooler.",  -1,           0, 28, 90,  8
END
```

WndProc, AbortDlg, *and* Abort *in source file*

```
BOOL bAbort     = FALSE;
HWND hAbortDlg = NULL;

LRESULT CALLBACK WndProc( HWND hWnd, UINT uMsg, WPARAM wParam, LPARAM lParam )
{
   switch( uMsg )
   {
      case WM_COMMAND :
              switch( LOWORD( wParam ) )
              {
                 case IDM_TEST :
                      {
                         HDC      hDC;

                         bAbort = FALSE;
```

continued on next page

continued from previous page

```
                        // Create a device context for the printer
                        // to which we are going to print.
                        //......................................
                        hDC = CreateDC( "WINSPOOL", "My Printer",
                                        NULL, NULL );

                        // Create the abort dialog.
                        //.........................
                        hAbortDlg = CreateDialog( hInst, "ABORTDLG",
                                                  hWnd, (DLGPROC)AbortDlg );

                        // Disable the main application window.
                        //.....................................
                        EnableWindow( hWnd, FALSE );

                        // Set the abort procedure to handle
                        // messages for the abort dialog.
                        //..................................
                        SetAbortProc( hDC, (ABORTPROC)Abort );


                        .
                        .
                        .
                        Send output to the printer...
                        .
                        .
                        .

                        // If the user aborts the print job,
                        // abort the document; otherwise
                        // destroy the abort dialog.
                        //..................................
                        if ( bAbort )
                            AbortDoc( hDC );
                        else
                            DestroyWindow( hAbortDlg );

                        EnableWindow( hWnd, TRUE );
                        SetFocus( hWnd );
                        DeleteDC( hDC );
                    }
                    break;

                case IDM_EXIT :
                        DestroyWindow( hWnd );
                        break;
            }
            break;

    case WM_DESTROY :
            PostQuitMessage(0);
            break;

    default :
            return( DefWindowProc( hWnd, uMsg, wParam, lParam ) );
    }

    return( 0L );
}
```

```
LRESULT CALLBACK AbortDlg( HWND hWnd, UINT message,
                           WPARAM wParam, LPARAM lParam )
{
    switch( message )
    {
      case WM_INITDIALOG :
                ShowWindow( hWnd, SW_NORMAL );
                SetFocus( hWnd );
                UpdateWindow( hWnd );
                return( TRUE );

      case WM_COMMAND    :
                // The cancel button was pressed,
                // abort the document.
                //..............................
                if ( LOWORD(wParam) == IDCANCEL )
                {
                    bAbort = TRUE;
                    DestroyWindow( hWnd );
                    return( TRUE );
                }
                break;
    }

    return( FALSE );
}


int CALLBACK Abort( HDC hdcPrinter, int Code )
{
    MSG msg;

    while ( !bAbort && PeekMessage( &msg, NULL, 0, 0, PM_REMOVE) )
    {
        if ( !IsDialogMessage( hAbortDlg, &msg ) )
        {
            TranslateMessage( &msg );
            DispatchMessage( &msg );
        }
    }

    // The bAbort argument is TRUE (return is FALSE)
    // if the user has canceled the print operation.
    //..............................................

    return (!bAbort);
}
```

DeviceCapabilities   ■ WINDOWS 95   ■ WINDOWS NT

Description   `DeviceCapabilities` retrieves the capabilities of a printer device driver.

Syntax   DWORD **DeviceCapabilities**(LPCTSTR *pDevice*, LPCTSTR *pPort*, WORD
fwCapability, LPTSTR *pOutput*, CONST DEVMODE* *pDevMode*)

Parameters

pDevice	LPCTSTR: A pointer to a null-terminated string that contains the name of a printer device (for example, **"PCL/HP LaserJet"**).
pPort	LPCTSTR: A pointer to a null-terminated string that contains the name of the port to which the device is connected (for example, **"LPT1"**).
fwCapability	WORD: The capabilities to retrieve. This parameter can be one of the values listed in Table 14-2.

Table 14-2 DeviceCapabilities *fwCapability* values

Value	Meaning
DC_BINADJUST	Retrieves the abilities of the driver to adjust the paper bins. The return value can be one or more of the following values: DCBA_FACEUPNONE DCBA_FACEUPCENTER DCBA_FACEUPLEFT DCBA_FACEUPRIGHT DCBA_FACEDOWNNONE DCBA_FACEDOWNCENTER DCBA_FACEDOWNLEFT DCBA_FACEDOWNRIGHT
DC_BINNAMES	Copies an array containing a list of the names of the paper bins. This array is in the form char PaperNames[cBinMax][cchBinName] where cchBinName is 24. If the *pOutput* parameter is NULL, the return value is the number of bin entries required. Otherwise, the return value is the number of bins copied.
DC_BINS	Retrieves a list of available bins. The function copies the list to *pOutput* as a WORD array. If *pOutput* is NULL, the function returns the number of supported bins to allow the application the opportunity to allocate a buffer with the correct size. For more information about these bins, see the description of the *dmDefaultSource* member of the DEVMODE structure.
DC_COPIES	Returns the number of copies the device can print.
DC_DRIVER	Returns the version number of the printer driver.
DC_DUPLEX	Returns the level of duplex support. If the printer is capable of duplex printing, the return value is 1; otherwise, it is 0.
DC_ENUMRESOLUTIONS	Returns a list of available resolutions. If *pOutput* is NULL, the function returns the number of available resolution configurations. Resolutions are represented by pairs of LONG integers representing the horizontal and vertical resolutions (specified in dots per inch).
DC_EXTRA	Returns the number of bytes required for the device-specific portion of the DEVMODE structure for the printer driver.
DC_FIELDS	Returns the *dmFields* member of the printer driver's DEVMODE structure. The *dmFields* member indicates which members in the device-independent portion of the structure are supported by the printer driver.
DC_FILEDEPENDENCIES	Returns a list of files that also need to be loaded when a driver is installed. If *pOutput* is NULL, the function returns the number of files. Otherwise, *pOutput* points to an array of file names in the form char[chFileName, 64]. Each file name is a null-terminated string.

Value	Meaning
DC_MAXEXTENT	Returns a POINT structure containing the maximum paper size that the *dmPaperLength* and *dmPaperWidth* members of the printer driver's DEVMODE structure can specify.
DC_MINEXTENT	Returns a POINT structure containing the minimum paper size that the *dmPaperLength* and *dmPaperWidth* members of the printer driver's DEVMODE structure can specify.
DC_ORIENTATION	Returns the relationship between portrait and landscape orientations for a device (that is, the number of degrees that portrait orientation is rotated counterclockwise to produce landscape orientation). The return value can be one of the following values:

Value	Meaning
0	No landscape orientation.
90	Portrait is rotated 90 degrees to produce landscape.
270	Portrait is rotated 270 degrees to produce landscape.

Value	Meaning
DC_PAPERNAMES	Retrieves a list of supported paper names (for example, "Letter" or "Legal"). If *pOutput* is NULL, the function returns the number of paper sizes available. Otherwise, *pOutput* points to an array of paper names in the form char[cPaperNames, 64]. Each paper name is a null-terminated string.
DC_PAPERS	Retrieves a list of supported paper sizes. The function copies the list to *pOutput* as a WORD array and returns the number of entries in the array. If *pOutput* is NULL, the function returns the number of supported paper sizes to allow the application the opportunity to allocate a buffer with the correct size. For more information on paper sizes, see the description of the *dmPaperSize* member of the DEVMODE structure.
DC_PAPERSIZE	Copies the dimensions of all supported paper sizes, in tenths of a millimeter, to an array of POINT structures pointed to by the *pOutput* parameter. The width (x dimension) and length (y dimension) of a paper size are returned as if the paper were in the DMORIENT_PORTRAIT orientation.
DC_SIZE	Returns the *dmSize* member of the printer driver's DEVMODE structure.
DC_TRUETYPE	Retrieves the abilities of the driver to use TrueType fonts. For DC_TRUETYPE, *pOutput* should be NULL. The return value can be one or more of the following values:

Value	Meaning
DCTT_BITMAP	Device can print TrueType fonts as graphics.
DCTT_DOWNLOAD	Device can download TrueType fonts.
DCTT_SUBDEV	Device can substitute device fonts for TrueType fonts.
DCTT_DOWNLOAD_OUTLINE	Device can download outline TrueType fonts.

Value	Meaning
DC_VERSION	Returns the specification version to which the printer driver conforms.

pOutput	LPTSTR: A pointer to an array of bytes. The format of the array depends on the value specified by *fwCapability*. If set to NULL, the function returns the number of bytes required for the output data.
pDevMode	CONST DEVMODE*: A pointer to a DEVMODE structure. If set to NULL, the function retrieves the current default initialization values for the printer driver. Otherwise, the function retrieves the values contained in the DEVMODE structure. See the definition of the DEVMODE structure below.
Returns	DWORD: If successful, the value varies depending on the value specified by the *fwCapability* parameter; otherwise, it is −1.

Include File	wingdi.h
See Also	GetDeviceCaps

DEVMODE Definition

```
typedef struct _devicemode
{
    TCHAR   dmDeviceName[CCHDEVICENAME];
    WORD    dmSpecVersion;
    WORD    dmDriverVersion;
    WORD    dmSize;
    WORD    dmDriverExtra;
    DWORD   dmFields;
    short   dmOrientation;
    short   dmPaperSize;
    short   dmPaperLength;
    short   dmPaperWidth;
    short   dmScale;
    short   dmCopies;
    short   dmDefaultSource;
    short   dmPrintQuality;
    short   dmColor;
    short   dmDuplex;
    short   dmYResolution;
    short   dmTTOption;
    short   dmCollate;
    TCHAR   dmFormName[CCHFORMNAME];
    WORD    dmLogPixels;
    USHORT  dmBitsPerPel;
    DWORD   dmPelsWidth;
    DWORD   dmPelsHeight;
    DWORD   dmDisplayFlags;
    DWORD   dmDisplayFrequency;
    WORD    dmICMMethod;
    WORD    dmICMIntent;
    WORD    dmMediaType;
    WORD    dmDitherType;
    DWORD   dmReserved1;
    DWORD   dmReserved2;
} DEVMODE;
```

Members

dmDeviceName TCHAR[CCHDEVICENAME]: The name of the device that the driver supports (for example, "PCL/HP LaserJet" in the case of PCL/HP LaserJet). This name is unique among device drivers.

dmSpecVersion WORD: The version number of the initialization data specification on which the structure is based. The current version, defined as DM_SPECVERSION, is 0x0400.

dmDriverVersion WORD: The printer driver version number assigned by the printer driver developer.

dmSize WORD: The size, in bytes, of the DEVMODE structure, except the *dmDriverData* (device-specific) member. If an application manipulates only the driver-independent portion of the data, it can use this member to determine the length of the structure without having to account for different versions.

dmDriverExtra	WORD: The size, in bytes, of the private driver data that follows this structure. If a device driver does not use device-specific information, this member should be 0.
dmFields	DWORD: A combination of the flags listed in Table 14-3 that determines whether the printer driver uses or ignores the remaining members in the DEVMODE structure. Use the binary OR (	) operator to combine the flags.

Table 14-3 DEVMODE *dmFields* values

Value	Meaning
DM_ORIENTATION	Use the *dmOrientation* member.
DM_PAPERSIZE	Use the *dmPaperSize* member. If *dmPaperSize* is set to DMPAPER_USER, an application must also include the DM_PAPERWIDTH and DM_PAPERLENGTH flags.
DM_PAPERLENGTH	Use the *dmPaperLength* member. Include this flag only if *dmPaperSize* is set to DMPAPER_USER.
DM_PAPERWIDTH	Use the *dmPaperWidth* member. Include this flag only if *dmPaperSize* is set to DMPAPER_USER.
DM_SCALE	Use the *dmScale* member.
DM_COPIES	Use the *dmCopies* member.
DM_DEFAULTSOURCE	Use the *dmDefaultSource* member.
DM_PRINTQUALITY	Use the *dmPrintQuality* member.
DM_COLOR	Use the *dmColor* member.
DM_DUPLEX	Use the *dmDuplex* member.
DM_YRESOLUTION	Use the *dmYResolution* member.
DM_TTOPTION	Use the *dmTTOption* member.
DM_COLLATE	Use the *dmCollate* member.
DM_FORMNAME	Use the *dmFormatName* member.
DM_BITSPERPEL	Use the *dmBitsPerPel* member.
DM_PELSWIDTH	Use the *dmPelsWidth* member.
DM_PELSHEIGHT	Use the *dmPelsHeight* member.
DM_DISPLAYFLAGS	Use the *dmDisplayFlags* member.
DM_DISPLAYFREQUENCY	Use the *dmDisplayFrequency* member.
DM_ICMMETHOD	Use the *dmICMMethod* member.
DM_ICMINTENT	Use the *dmICMIntent* member.
DM_MEDIATYPE	Use the *dmMediaType* member.
DM_DITHERTYPE	Use the *dmDitherType* member.
DM_RESERVED1	Use the *dmReserved1* member.
DM_RESERVED2	Use the *dmReserved2* member.

dmOrientation	short: The orientation of the paper. This member can be either the DMORIENT_PORTRAIT or DMORIENT_LANDSCAPE value.
dmPaperSize	short: The size of the paper to print on. This member can be one of the values in Table 14-4.

Table 14-4 DEVMODE *dmPaperSize* values

Value	Meaning
DMPAPER_10X14	10×14 inches.
DMPAPER_11X17	11×17 inches.
DMPAPER_A3	A3 sheet, 297×420 millimeters.
DMPAPER_A4	A4 sheet, 210×297 millimeters.
DMPAPER_A4SMALL	A4 small sheet, 210×297 millimeters.
DMPAPER_A5	A5 sheet, 148×210 millimeters.
DMPAPER_B4	B4 sheet, 250×354 millimeters.
DMPAPER_B5	B5 sheet, 182×257 millimeters.
DMPAPER_CSHEET	C sheet, 17×22 inches.
DMPAPER_DSHEET	D sheet, 22×34 inches.
DMPAPER_ENV_9	#9 envelope, 3 7/8×8 7/8 inches.
DMPAPER_ENV_10	#10 envelope, 4 1/8×9 1/2 inches.
DMPAPER_ENV_11	#11 envelope, 4 1/2×10 3/8 inches.
DMPAPER_ENV_12	#12 envelope, 4 3/4×11 inches.
DMPAPER_ENV_14	#14 envelope, 5×11 1/2 inches.
DMPAPER_ENV_B4	B4 envelope, 250×353 millimeters.
DMPAPER_ENV_B5	B5 envelope, 176×250 millimeters.
DMPAPER_ENV_B6	B6 envelope, 176×125 millimeters.
DMPAPER_ENV_C3	C3 envelope, 324×458 millimeters.
DMPAPER_ENV_C4	C4 envelope, 229×324 millimeters.
DMPAPER_ENV_C5	C5 envelope, 162×229 millimeters.
DMPAPER_ENV_C6	C6 envelope, 114×162 millimeters.
DMPAPER_ENV_C65	C65 envelope, 114×229 millimeters.
DMPAPER_ENV_DL	DL envelope, 110×220 millimeters.
DMPAPER_ENV_ITALY	Italy envelope, 110×230 millimeters.
DMPAPER_ENV_MONARCH	Monarch envelope, 3 7/8×7 1/2 inches.
DMPAPER_ENV_PERSONAL	6 3/4 envelope, 3 5/8×6 1/2 inches.
DMPAPER_ESHEET	E sheet, 34×44 inches.
DMPAPER_EXECUTIVE	Executive, 7 1/4×10 1/2 inches.
DMPAPER_FANFOLD_LGL_GERMAN	German legal fanfold, 8 1/2×13 inches.
DMPAPER_FANFOLD_STD_GERMAN	German standard fanfold, 8 1/2×12 inches.
DMPAPER_FANFOLD_US	U.S. standard fanfold, 14 7/8×11 inches.
DMPAPER_FOLIO	Folio, 8 1/2×13 inches.
DMPAPER_LEDGER	Ledger, 17×11 inches.
DMPAPER_LEGAL	Legal, 8 1/2×14 inches.
DMPAPER_LETTER	Letter, 8 1/2×11 inches.
DMPAPER_LETTERSMALL	Letter small, 8 1/2×11 inches.

Value	Meaning
DMPAPER_NOTE	Note, 8 1/2×11 inches.
DMPAPER_QUARTO	Quarto, 215×275 millimeters.
DMPAPER_STATEMENT	Statement, 5 1/2×8 1/2 inches.
DMPAPER_TABLOID	Tabloid, 11×17 inches.
DMPAPER_USER	User-defined paper size. The *dmPaperLength* and *dmPaperWidth* members must specify the size.

dmPaperLength	**short**: The length, in tenths of a millimeter, of the paper in portrait mode. The *dmPaperSize* member must specify the **DMPAPER_USER** value; otherwise, this member is ignored.
dmPaperWidth	**short**: The width, in tenths of a millimeter, of the paper in portrait mode. The *dmPaperSize* member must specify the **DMPAPER_USER** value; otherwise, this member is ignored.
dmScale	**short**: The factor by which the printed output is to be scaled. The apparent page size is scaled from the physical page size by a factor of *dmScale*÷100.
dmCopies	**short**: The number of copies printed if the device supports multiple-page copies.
dmDefaultSource	**short**: The default paper bin from which the paper is fed. The member can be one of the predefined values given in Table 14-5, or a driver-defined value greater than the value of **DMBIN_USER**.

Table 14-5 DEVMODE *dmDefaultSource* values

Value	Meaning
DMBIN_AUTO	Automatic paper bin selection
DMBIN_CASSETTE	Paper cassette
DMBIN_ENVELOPE	Envelope feeder
DMBIN_ENVMANUAL	Manual envelope feeder
DMBIN_LARGECAPACITY	Large capacity paper bin
DMBIN_LARGEFMT	Large paper source
DMBIN_LOWER	Lower paper bin
DMBIN_MANUAL	Manual paper feeder
DMBIN_MIDDLE	Middle paper bin
DMBIN_ONLYONE	Only one paper source
DMBIN_SMALLFMT	Small paper source
DMBIN_TRACTOR	Tractor feeder
DMBIN_UPPER	Upper paper bin

dmPrintQuality **short**: The printer resolution. Table 14-6 lists four predefined device-independent values. If a positive value is given, it specifies the number of dots per inch (DPI) and is, therefore, device dependent. This member controls the graphics resolution only. Text is not affected by this setting, unless the text is printed as graphics.

Table 14-6 DEVMODE *dmPrintQuality* values

Value	Meaning
DMRES_HIGH	High resolution
DMRES_MEDIUM	Medium resolution
DMRES_LOW	Low resolution
DMRES_DRAFT	Draft print resolution

dmColor **short**: Determines whether to use color or monochrome on color printers. Possible values are **DMCOLOR_COLOR** or **DMCOLOR_MONOCHROME**.

dmDuplex **short**: Set to one of the values in Table 14-7 to specify which type of duplex or double-sided printer to use for printers capable of duplex printing.

Table 14-7 DEVMODE *dmDuplex* values

Value	Meaning
DMDUP_SIMPLEX	No duplexing
DMDUP_HORIZONTAL	Horizontal (long edge) duplexing
DMDUP_VERTICAL	Vertical (short edge) duplexing

dmYResolution **short**: The y resolution, in dots per inch, of the printer. If the printer initializes this member, the *dmPrintQuality* member specifies the x resolution, in dots per inch, of the printer.

dmTTOption **short**: Specifies how TrueType fonts should be printed. Set to one of the values in Table 14-8.

Table 14-8 DEVMODE *dmTTOption* values

Value	Meaning
DMTT_BITMAP	Prints TrueType fonts as graphics. This value is the default action for dot-matrix printers.
DMTT_DOWNLOAD	Downloads TrueType fonts as soft fonts. This value is the default action for Hewlett-Packard printers that use Printer Control Language (PCL).

Value	Meaning
DMTT_DOWNLOAD_OUTLINE	Downloads TrueType fonts as outline soft fonts.
DMTT_SUBDEV	Substitutes device fonts for TrueType fonts. This value is the default action for PostScript printers.

dmCollate	**short**: Set to **DMCOLLATE_TRUE** to use collation when printing multiple copies. Use the **DMCOLLATE_FALSE** if collation is not desired. Using **DMCOL-LATE_FALSE** provides faster, more efficient output on printers that support multiple copies, since the data is sent to a page printer just once, no matter how many copies are required. The printer is simply told to print the page again.
dmFormName	**TCHAR[CCHFORMNAME]**: The name of the form to use (for example, **"Letter"** or **"Legal"**). This member is not supported in Windows 95.
dmLogPixels	**WORD**: The number of pixels per logical inch.
dmBitsPerPel	**USHORT**: The color resolution, in bits per pixel, of the display device (for example, 4 bits for 16 colors, 8 bits for 256 colors, or 16 bits for 65,536 colors). This member is not supported in Windows 95.
dmPelsWidth	**DWORD**: The width, in pixels, of the visible device surface. This member is not supported in Windows 95.
dmPelsHeight	**DWORD**: The height, in pixels, of the visible device surface. This member is not supported in Windows 95.
dmDisplayFlags	**DWORD**: The device's display mode. This can be one of the values given in Table 14-9. This member is not supported in Windows 95.

Table 14-9 DEVMODE *dmDisplayFlags* values

Value	Meaning
DM_GRAYSCALE	Display is a noncolor device. If this value is not specified, color is assumed.
DM_INTERLACED	Display mode is interlaced. If this value is not specified, noninterlaced is assumed.

dmDisplayFrequency	**DWORD**: The frequency, in hertz (cycles per second), of the display device in a particular mode. This member is not supported in Windows 95.
dmICMMethod	**WORD**: For a non-ICM application, this member determines if ICM is enabled or disabled. For ICM applications, Windows examines this member to determine how to handle ICM support. This member can be one of the predefined values listed in Table 14-10, or a driver-defined value greater than the value of **DMICMMETHOD_USER**. The printer driver must provide a user interface for setting this member. Most printer drivers support only the **DMICMMETHOD_SYSTEM** or **DMICM-METHOD_NONE** value. Drivers for PostScript printers support all values.

Table 14-10 DEVMODE *dmICMMethod* values

Value	Meaning
DMICMMETHOD_DEVICE	ICM handled by the destination device.
DMICMMETHOD_DRIVER	ICM is handled by the device driver.
DMICMMETHOD_NONE	ICM is disabled.
DMICMMETHOD_SYSTEM	ICM is handled by Windows.

dmICMIntent   WORD: Specifies which of the three possible color-matching methods, or intents, should be used by default. This member is primarily for non-ICM applications. ICM applications can establish intents by using the ICM functions. This member can be one of the predefined values shown in Table 14-11, or a driver-defined value greater than the value of DMICM_USER.

Table 14-11 DEVMODE *dmICMIntent* values

Value	Meaning
DMICM_COLORMETRIC	Color matching should optimize to match the exact color requested. This value is most appropriate for use with business logos or other images when an exact color match is desired.
DMICM_CONTRAST	Color matching should optimize for color contrast. This value is the most appropriate choice for scanned or photographic images when dithering is desired.
DMICM_SATURATE	Color matching should optimize for color saturation. This value is the most appropriate choice for business graphs when dithering is not desired.

dmMediaType   WORD: The type of media being printed on. The member can be one of the predefined values given in Table 14-12, or a driver-defined value greater than the value of DMMEDIA_USER.

Table 14-12 DEVMODE *dmMediaType* values

Value	Meaning
DMMEDIA_STANDARD	Plain paper
DMMEDIA_GLOSSY	Glossy paper
DMMEDIA_TRANSPARENCY	Transparent film

dmDitherType   WORD: Specifies how dithering is to be done. The member can be one of the predefined values listed in Table 14-13, or a driver-defined value greater than the value of DMDITHER_USER.

Table 14-13 DEVMODE *dmMediaType* values

Value	Meaning
DMDITHER_NONE	No dithering.
DMDITHER_COARSE	Dithering with a coarse brush.
DMDITHER_FINE	Dithering with a fine brush.
DMDITHER_LINEART	Line art dithering: a special dithering method that produces well-defined borders between black, white, and grayscaling. It is not suitable for images that include continuous graduations in intensity and hue, such as scanned photographs.
DMDITHER_GRAYSCALE	Device does grayscaling.

dmReserved1	Not used; must be **0**.
dmReserved2	Not used; must be **0**.
Example	This example shows how the **DeviceCapabilities** function is used to determine if a printer supports font substitution. This is a feature that many PostScript printers support.

```
LRESULT CALLBACK WndProc( HWND hWnd, UINT uMsg, WPARAM wParam, LPARAM lParam )
{
    switch( uMsg )
    {
        case WM_COMMAND:
            switch( LOWORD( wParam ) )
            {
                case IDM_TEST :
                    {
                        DWORD dwResult;

                        dwResult = DeviceCapabilities( "HP Laserjet",
                                                       NULL,
                                                       DC_TRUETYPE,
                                                       NULL, NULL );

                        if ( dwResult & DCTT_SUBDEV )
                        {
                            MessageBox( hWnd,
                                "Printer supports font substitution.",
                                "Message", MB_OK | MB_ICONINFORMATION );
                        }
                    }
                    break;
            .
            .
            .
```

EndDoc ■ Windows 95 ■ Windows NT

Description   **EndDoc** ends a print job previously started with the **StartDoc** function. The print queue will typically start printing the document after **EndDoc** is called. This function replaces the **ENDDOC** printer escape.

Syntax	`int EndDoc( HDC hdc )`
Parameters	
hdc	`HDC`: The device context for the print job.
Returns	`int`: If successful, a value greater than zero; otherwise, `SP_ERROR` is returned.
Include File	`wingdi.h`
See Also	`StartDoc`, `AbortDoc`
Example	See the example for the `EndPage` function.

EndPage   ■ WINDOWS 95 ■ WINDOWS NT

Description	`EndPage` informs the device that the application is done writing a page. This function is typically used in conjunction with the `StartPage` function to advance to a new page. This function replaces the `NEWFRAME` printer escape. For each new page, the application should set up the DC with the appropriate settings. This is because the settings are not preserved between pages on Windows 95.
Syntax	`int EndPage( HDC hdc )`
Parameters	
hdc	`HDC`: The device context for the print job.
Returns	`int`: If successful, a value greater than zero; otherwise, `SP_ERROR` is returned.
Include File	`wingdi.h`
See Also	`StartPage`, `EndDoc`
Example	This example prints two pages to a printer named `"HP Laser Printer"` when the user selects the Test! menu item. Note that the beginning of each page starts with a call to the `StartPage` function and the end of the page is finished when the `EndPage` function is called.

```
LRESULT CALLBACK WndProc( HWND hWnd, UINT uMsg, WPARAM wParam, LPARAM lParam )
{
   switch( uMsg )
   {
      case WM_COMMAND :
             switch( LOWORD( wParam ) )
             {
                case IDM_TEST :
                       {
                           HDC     hDC;
                           DOCINFO di;

                           // Create a device context for the
                           // printer to which text will be output.
```

```
//.............................................
hDC = CreateDC( "WINSPOOL", "HP Laser Printer",
                NULL, NULL );

// Set up the DOCINFO structure.
//..............................
memset( &di, 0, sizeof( DOCINFO ) );
di.cbSize      = sizeof( DOCINFO );
di.lpszDocName = "Test Document";

// Start printing.
//.....................
if ( StartDoc( hDC, &di ) != SP_ERROR )
{
    // Print page 1.
    //...............
    StartPage( hDC );
    TextOut( hDC, 10, 10, "This is on Page 1.",18);
    EndPage( hDC );

    // Print page 2.
    //...............
    StartPage( hDC );
    TextOut( hDC, 10, 10, "This is on Page 2.",18);
    EndPage( hDC );

    // End printing.
    //...............
    EndDoc( hDC );
}

DeleteDC( hDC );
}
break;
```

Escape
■ WINDOWS 95   ■ WINDOWS NT

Description

Escape allows applications to access capabilities of a device not directly available through GDI functions. Escape calls made by an application are translated and sent directly to the driver. The Win32 API defines GDI functions that replace most of the printer escapes found in the Windows 3.x API. These new functions must be used instead of the printer escapes.

Syntax

int **Escape**(HDC *hdc,* int *nEscape,* int *cbInput,* LPCTSTR *lpvInData,*
LPVOID *lpvOutData*)

Parameters

hdc

HDC: The device context for the device to receive the escape.

nEscape	**int**: The escape function to be performed. A Win32-based application can only use the two escapes shown in Table 14-14. If an application defines a private escape value, it should use the **ExtEscape** function. See the description of the escapes below.

Table 14-14 Escape *nEscape* values

Escape	Description
PASSTHROUGH	Allows the application to send data directly to a printer.
QUERYESCSUPPORT	Determines whether a particular escape is implemented by the device driver.

cbInput	**int**: The number of bytes of data pointed to by *lpvInData*.
lpvInData	**LPCTSTR**: A pointer to the data buffer containing the information to send to the device.
lpvOutData	**LPVOID**: A pointer to the data structure to receive data returned by the **Escape** function call. Set to **NULL** if no data is returned.
Returns	**int**: If the function succeeds, see the escape definitions below for the return value. Otherwise, a value of less than zero indicates an error. Table 14-15 shows the possible error codes.

Table 14-15 Escape error codes

Value	Meaning
SP_ERROR	General error.
SP_OUTOFDISK	Not enough disk space is currently available for spooling, and no more space will become available.
SP_OUTOFMEMORY	Not enough memory is available for spooling.
SP_USERABORT	The user terminated the job through Windows Print Manager.

Include File	wingdi.h
See Also	AbortDoc, EndDoc, EndPage, SetAbortProc, StartDoc, StartPage, GetDeviceCaps, DeviceCapabilities, ResetDC, ExtEscape

PASSTHROUGH Escape Definition

Description	The **PASSTHROUGH** printer escape allows the application to send data directly to the printer, bypassing the standard print-driver code. To use this escape, an application must have complete information about how the particular printer operates. It is strongly recommended that applications not perform actions that consume printer memory, such as downloading a font or a macro. To avoid corruption of the data stream when issuing consecutive **PASSTHROUGH** escapes, an application should not access the printer in any other way during the sequence.

Syntax	int **Escape**(HDC *hdc,* PASSTHROUGH, NULL, LPCSTR *lpInData,* NULL)

Parameters

hdc	HDC: Identifies the device context.
lpInData	LPCSTR: A pointer to a structure whose first word (16 bits) contains the number of bytes of input data. The remaining bytes of the structure contain the data itself.
Returns	int: The number of bytes transferred to the printer. The return value is less than zero or 0 if the function is not successful.

QUERYESCSUPPORT Escape Definition

Description	The QUERYESCSUPPORT printer escape allows the application to determine if a particular escape is supported by the device driver.
Syntax	int **Escape**(HDC *hdc,* QUERYESCSUPPORT, sizeof(int), LPINT *lpEscNum,* NULL)

Parameters

hdc	HDC: Identifies the device context.
lpEscNum	LPINT: Points to an integer that specifies the escape function to be checked.
Returns	int: Nonzero if the escape is supported; otherwise, 0.
Example	This example shows how the PASSTHROUGH escape is used to send a printer a specific printer code. When the user selects the Test! menu item, three copies of a two-page printout are sent to the printer. The number of copies is set with the PASSTHROUGH escape. Note that this example is very dependent on the specific printer model. This example shows how the Escape function works, but is not the best way of setting the number of copies to print. Instead, use the DEVMODE structure with the CreateDC function to specify the number of copies to print.

```
typedef struct
{
  WORD wSize;
  char szEsc[5];
} NUMCOPIES;


LRESULT CALLBACK WndProc( HWND hWnd, UINT uMsg, WPARAM wParam, LPARAM lParam )
{
   switch( uMsg )
   {
      case WM_COMMAND :
            switch( LOWORD( wParam ) )
            {
               case IDM_TEST :
                  {
                     HDC       hDC;
                     DOCINFO   di;
                     NUMCOPIES nc;
```

continued on next page

continued from previous page

```
                    // Fill the structure and set up
                    // an escape of "Esc&l3X" which
                    // prints 3 copies on a HP 4M Laser printer.
                    //.........................................
                    nc.wSize    = sizeof( NUMCOPIES );
                    nc.szEsc[0] = 27;
                    nc.szEsc[1] = '&';
                    nc.szEsc[2] = 'l';
                    nc.szEsc[3] = '3';
                    nc.szEsc[4] = 'X';

                    hDC = CreateDC( "WINSPOOL", "HP Laserjet 4M",
                                    NULL, NULL );

                    memset( &di, 0, sizeof( DOCINFO ) );
                    di.cbSize      = sizeof( DOCINFO );
                    di.lpszDocName = "Test Document";

                    if ( StartDoc( hDC, &di ) != SP_ERROR )
                    {
                        Escape( hDC, PASSTHROUGH, 0,(LPCSTR)&nc, NULL);

                        StartPage( hDC );
                        TextOut( hDC, 10, 10, "This is on Page 1.",18);
                        EndPage( hDC );

                        StartPage( hDC );
                        TextOut( hDC, 10, 10, "This is on Page 2.",18);
                        EndPage( hDC );

                        EndDoc( hDC );
                    }

                    DeleteDC( hDC );
                }
                break;
```

.
.
.

ExtEscape   ■ WINDOWS 95   ■ WINDOWS NT

Description	ExtEscape allows applications to access capabilities of a device that are not available through GDI functions or the Windows-defined escapes.
Syntax	int **ExtEscape**(HDC *hdc*, int *nEscape*, int *cbInput*, LPCSTR *lpszInData*, int *cbOutput*, LPSTR *lpszOutData*)
Parameters	
hdc	HDC: The device context for the device to receive the escape.
nEscape	int: The escape function to be performed.
cbInput	int: The number of bytes of data pointed to by *lpszInData*.
lpszInData	LPCSTR: A pointer to the input structure required for the specified escape.

cbOutput	`int`: The number of bytes of data pointed to by *lpszOutData*.
lpszOutData	`LPSTR`: A pointer to the structure that receives output from the escape. If the escape is a query, this parameter must not be `NULL`. If no data is to be returned in this structure, *cbOutput* should be `0`.
Returns	`int`: The outcome of the function. If the function succeeds, it is greater than or equal to zero. Otherwise, a return value of less than zero indicates an error.
Include File	`wingdi.h`
See Also	`Escape`
Example	See the example for the `Escape` function. Even though the `ExtEscape` function is not used in the example, it is similar in usage to the `Escape` function. `ExtEscape` usage depends on the particular hardware that the application is using.

ExtTextOut   ■ WINDOWS 95   ■ WINDOWS NT

Description	`ExtTextOut` draws a character string using the currently selected font. An optional rectangle may be provided, to be used for clipping, opaquing, or both. If used with the `SetTextAlign` function with *uMode* set to `TA_UPDATECP`, the *X* and *Y* parameters will be ignored on subsequent calls to `ExtTextOut`. Instead, Windows will keep track of the current position.
Syntax	`BOOL` **ExtTextOut**(`HDC` *hdc,* `int` *X,* `int` *Y,* `UINT` *uOptions,* `CONST RECT*` *lprc,* `LPCTSTR` *lpszString,* `UINT` *cbCount,* `CONST INT*` *lpDx*)
Parameters	
hdc	`HDC`: The output device context.
X	`int`: The logical x coordinate of the reference point used to position the string.
Y	`int`: The logical y coordinate of the reference point used to position the string.
uOptions	`UINT`: Determines how `ExtTextOut` uses the application-defined rectangle. This parameter can be a combination of the values listed in Table 14-16.

Table 14-16 `ExtTextOut` *uOptions* values

Value	Meaning
ETO_CLIPPED	The text will be clipped to the rectangle.
ETO_GLYPH_INDEX	The *lpszString* parameter points to an array returned from `GetCharacterPlacement` and should be parsed directly by GDI. Glyph indexing only applies to TrueType fonts, but this flag is used to bypass language processing with bitmap and vector fonts. Note that all glyph indices are 16-bit values even though the string is assumed to be an array of 8-bit values. (Windows 95 only)

continued on next page

continued from previous page

Value	Meaning
ETO_OPAQUE	The rectangle will be filled with the current background color.
ETO_RTLREADING	Right-to-left reading order will be used if the current font is Hebrew or Arabic. The ETO_GLYPH_INDEX and ETO_RTLREADING values cannot be used together. (Windows 95 only)

lprc	CONST RECT*: Points to an optional RECT structure that specifies the dimensions of a rectangle used for clipping, opaquing, or both.
lpszString	LPCTSTR: A pointer to the character string to be drawn. The string does not need to be null-terminated, since *cbCount* specifies the length of the string.
cbCount	UINT: The number of characters in the string.
lpDx	CONST INT*: A pointer to an optional array of values that indicates the distance between origins of adjacent character cells.
Returns	BOOL: TRUE if the string is drawn; otherwise, the return value is FALSE.
Include File	wingdi.h
See Also	TextOut, DrawText, SetTextAlign, GetTextAlign
Example	This example, as shown in Figure 14-2, shows the use of **ExtTextOut** to print a character string confined by a rectangle. This is a simplistic example of how an edit control is painted by Windows.

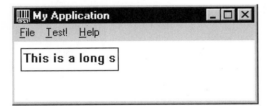

Figure 14-2 ExtTextOut example

```
LRESULT CALLBACK WndProc( HWND hWnd, UINT uMsg, WPARAM wParam, LPARAM lParam )
{
   switch( uMsg )
   {
      case WM_COMMAND :
            switch( LOWORD( wParam ) )
            {
               case IDM_TEST :
                     {
                        HDC   hDC;
                        RECT  rect;

                        // Define a clipping rectangle.
```

```
//.............................
SetRect( &rect, 10, 10, 110, 30 );
hDC = GetDC( hWnd );

// Draw a rectangle around
// the clipping rectangle.
//.......................
Rectangle( hDC, rect.left-3, rect.top-3,
           rect.right+3, rect.bottom+3 );

// Draw the text.
//..............
ExtTextOut( hDC, 10, 10, ETO_CLIPPED, &rect,
            "This is a long string", 21, NULL );

ReleaseDC( hWnd, hDC );
}
break;
```

．
．
．

GetCharABCWidths ■ WINDOWS 95 ■ WINDOWS NT

Description	GetCharABCWidths retrieves the widths, in logical units, of a range of characters from the current TrueType font. This function only works with TrueType fonts.
Syntax	BOOL **GetCharABCWidths**(HDC *hdc,* UINT *uFirstChar,* UINT *uLastChar,* LPABC *lpabc*)
Parameters	
hdc	HDC: The device context that has the TrueType font.
uFirstChar	UINT: The first character in the range of characters from the current font.
uLastChar	UINT: The last character in the range of characters from the current font.
lpabc	LPABC: A pointer to an array of **ABC** structures that receives the character widths when the function returns. See the definition of the **ABC** structure below.
Returns	BOOL: **TRUE** if successful; otherwise, the return value is **FALSE**.
Include File	wingdi.h
See Also	GetCharWidth32
ABC Definition	

```
typedef struct _ABC
{
    int    abcA;
    UINT   abcB;
    int    abcC;
} ABC;
```

Members

abcA   `int`: The **A** spacing of the character. This is the distance to add to the current position before drawing the character glyph.

abcB   `UINT`: The **B** spacing of the character. This is the width of the drawn portion of the character glyph.

abcC   `int`: The **C** spacing of the character. This is the distance to add to the current position to provide white space to the right of the character glyph.

Example   This example, shown in Figure 14-3, displays the widths of the **W** and **X** characters when the user selects the Test! menu item. The character widths are retrieved from the **"Times New Roman"** font, which is created and selected into the device context of the main window.

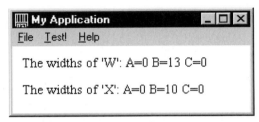

Figure 14-3 `GetCharABCWidths` example

```
LRESULT CALLBACK WndProc( HWND hWnd, UINT uMsg, WPARAM wParam, LPARAM lParam )
{
    switch( uMsg )
    {
      case WM_COMMAND :
            switch( LOWORD( wParam ) )
            {
              case IDM_TEST :
                    {
                        HDC    hDC;
                        HFONT  hFont, hOldFont;
                        ABC    abc[2];
                        char   szMsg[40];

                        // Create a Times New Roman font.
                        //............................
                        hFont = CreateFont( 16, 0, 0, 0, FW_NORMAL,
                                            FALSE, FALSE, FALSE,
                                            ANSI_CHARSET,
                                            OUT_DEFAULT_PRECIS,
                                            CLIP_DEFAULT_PRECIS,
                                            PROOF_QUALITY,
                                            DEFAULT_PITCH | FF_DONTCARE,
                                            "Times New Roman" );
```

```
                    // Retrieve the device context and
                    // select the font into it.
                    //...............................
                    hDC = GetDC( hWnd );
                    hOldFont = SelectObject( hDC, hFont );

                    // Retrieve the widths of the 'W' and 'X'
                    // characters in the selected font.
                    //......................................
                    GetCharABCWidths( hDC, 'W','X', abc );

                    // Output the widths to the window.
                    //.................................
                    wsprintf( szMsg,
                            "The widths of 'W': A=%d B=%d C=%d",
                            abc[0].abcA, abc[0].abcB, abc[0].abcC );
                    TextOut( hDC, 10, 10, szMsg, strlen( szMsg ) );

                    wsprintf( szMsg,
                            "The widths of 'X': A=%d B=%d C=%d",
                            abc[1].abcA, abc[1].abcB, abc[1].abcC );
                    TextOut( hDC, 10, 40, szMsg, strlen( szMsg ) );

                    SelectObject( hDC, hOldFont );
                    ReleaseDC( hWnd, hDC );
                    DeleteObject( hFont );
                }
                break;
```

GetCharacterPlacement ■ WINDOWS 95 ■ WINDOWS NT

Description   GetCharacterPlacement retrieves information about how a character string is displayed on a device context, such as character widths, caret positioning, ordering within the string, and glyph rendering. This function ensures that an application can correctly process text regardless of the international setting and type of fonts available.

Use this function prior to using the ExtTextOut function and in place of the GetTextExtentPoint32 function. For non-Latin fonts, applications can improve the speed at which the ExtTextOut function renders text by using GetCharacterPlacement before calling ExtTextOut when rendering the same text repeatedly or when using intercharacter spacing to position the caret.

Syntax   DWORD **GetCharacterPlacement**(HDC *hdc,* LPCSTR *lpString,* UINT *uCount,* int *nMaxExtent,* GCP_RESULTS *lpResults,* DWORD *dwFlags*)

Parameters

hdc	HDC: The device context on which the text will be rendered.
lpString	LPCSTR: A pointer to the character string to process.
uCount	UINT: The number of characters in the string pointed to by *lpString*.
nMaxExtent	int: The maximum extent (width) of the output string. This parameter is used only if the GCP_MAXEXTENT or GCP_JUSTIFY value is given in the *dwFlags* parameter.
lpResults	GCP_RESULTS: A pointer to a GCP_RESULTS structure that receives the result of the function. See the definition of the GCP_RESULTS structure below.
dwFlags	DWORD: Specifies how to process the string into the required arrays. This parameter can be one of the values listed in Table 14-17.

Table 14-17 GetCharacterPlacement *dwFlags* values

Value	Meaning
GCP_CLASSIN	The *lpClass* array contains partial character classifications on input. All valid nonzero values remain unchanged and GetCharacterPlacement sets others to appropriate classification values.
GCP_GLYPHSHAPE	Display characters using nonstandard shapes.
GCP_JUSTIFY	Pad the extents in the *lpDx* array so that the string length is equal to the value given by *nMaxExtent*. This flag must be used in conjunction with the GCP_MAXEXTENT flag.
GCP_JUSTIFYIN	The *lpDx* array contains justification weights on input. Justification weights for non-Arabic fonts can be either 0 or 1, where 1 indicates that the width of the character can be padded for justification. For Arabic fonts, a justification weight can be in the range 0 to 8.
GCP_KASHIDA	Use Kashidas instead of padding to modify the length of the string so that it is equal to the value in *nMaxExtent*. A Kashida is indicated by a negative justification index in the *lpDx* array. This flag must be used in conjunction with the GCP_JUSTIFY flag and only if the font (and language) support Kashidas.
GCP_LIGATE	Use ligations for characters that ligate. If the GCP_REORDER flag is required for the character set but is not set, the output will be meaningless.
GCP_MAXEXTENT	Truncate the resulting output string (if necessary) so that the resulting extent, in logical units, does not exceed the value given by the *nMaxExtent* parameter.
GCP_NODIACRITICS	Ignore any diacritics in the string. This also removes the diacritics from the resulting output string.
GCP_REORDER	Reorder the string. Typically used for fonts that are neither SBCS nor left-to-right reading order. If this flag is not set, the string is assumed to be in display order.
GCP_USEKERNING	Use kerning pairs in the font.

Returns	DWORD: If successful, a nonzero value; otherwise, 0.
Include File	wingdi.h
See Also	ExtTextOut, GetTextExtentPoint32

GCP_RESULTS Definition

```
typedef struct tagGCP_RESULTS
{
    DWORD    lStructSize;
    LPTSTR   lpOutString;
    UINT*    lpOrder;
    INT*     lpDx;
    INT*     lpCaretPos;
    LPTSTR   lpClass;
    UINT*    lpGlyphs;
    UINT     nGlyphs;
    UINT     nMaxFit;
} GCP_RESULTS;
```

Members

lStructSize DWORD: The size in bytes of the structure.

lpOutString LPTSTR: Address of the buffer that receives the output string. Set to **NULL** if the output string is not needed.

lpOrder UINT*: Address of the array that receives the ordering indices for the characters in the output string. Set to **NULL** if ordering indices are not needed. The original string needs reordering if the **GetFontLanguageInfo** function returns the **GCP_REORDER** value.

lpDx INT*: Address of the array that receives the distances between adjacent character cells. Set to **NULL** if these distances are not needed. If glyph rendering is done, the distances are for the glyphs, not the characters, so the resulting array can be used with the **ExtTextOut** function. On input, this member must contain justification weight values if the **GCP_JUSTIFYIN** flag is set.

The distances in this array are in display order. To find the distance for the *i*th character in the original string, use the *lpOrder* array as follows:

width = *lpDx*[*lpOrder*[*i*]]

lpCaretPos INT*: Address of the array that receives the caret position values. Set to **NULL** if caret positions are not needed. This array matches the original string and not the output string, which means that some adjacent values may be the same.

lpClass LPTSTR: Address of the array that contains and/or receives character classifications. The classification values, most useful in non-Latin systems, depend on the language and character set of the font selected into the device context. Each element of the array can be set to **0** or one of the values shown in Table 14-18.

Table 14-18 GCP_RESULTS *lpClass* values

Value	Meaning
GCPCLASS_ARABIC	Arabic character.
GCPCLASS_HEBREW	Hebrew character.
GCPCLASS_LATIN	Character from a Latin or other single-byte character set for left-to-right language.
GCPCLASS_LATINNUMBER	Digit from a Latin or other single-byte character set for left-to-right language.
GCPCLASS_LOCALNUMBER	Digit from the character set associated with the current font.
GCPCLASS_LATINNUMERICSEPARATOR	(Input only) Character used to separate Latin digits, such as a comma or decimal point.
GCPCLASS_LATINNUMERICTERMINATOR	(Input only) Character used to terminate Latin digits, such as a plus or minus sign.
GCPCLASS_NEUTRAL	(Input only) Character has no specific classification.
GCPCLASS_NUMERICSEPARATOR	(Input only) Character used to separate digits, such as a comma or decimal point.

lpGlyphs   UINT*: Address of the array that receives the values identifying the glyphs used for rendering the string. Set to NULL if glyph rendering is not needed. There may be fewer glyphs in the array than the number of characters in the original string if the array contains ligated glyphs. The glyphs may not be sequential if reordering is required. The array can be used with the ExtTextOut function.

nGlyphs   UINT: The number of values in the *lpGlyph* and *lpDx* arrays. On input, this member must be set to the size of the arrays pointed to by the *lpGlyph* and *lpDx* members.

nMaxFit   UINT: The number of characters that fit within the extents specified by the *nMaxExtent* parameter of the GetCharacterPlacement function. This is also the number of elements in the *lpOutString*, *lpOrder*, *lpCaretPos*, and *lpClass* arrays.

Example   This example, shown in Figure 14-4, uses the GetCharacterPlacement function to justify the output text when the user selects the Test! menu item. The normal text is output below the justified text to show the difference.

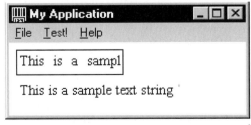

Figure 14-4 GetCharacterPlacement example

```
LPCSTR lpszText = "This is a sample text string";
char    szNewText[29];
int     anDX[29];
USHORT  auGlyphs[29];

LRESULT CALLBACK WndProc( HWND hWnd, UINT uMsg, WPARAM wParam, LPARAM lParam )
{
    switch( uMsg )
    {
        case WM_COMMAND :
                switch( LOWORD( wParam ) )
                {
                    case IDM_TEST :
                        {
                            HDC         hDC;
                            HFONT       hFont, hOldFont;
                            RECT        rect;
                            GCP_RESULTS results;

                            // Create font to use.
                            //....................
                            hFont = CreateFont( 16, 0, 0, 0, FW_NORMAL,
                                                FALSE, FALSE, FALSE,
                                                ANSI_CHARSET,
                                                OUT_DEFAULT_PRECIS,
                                                CLIP_DEFAULT_PRECIS,
                                                PROOF_QUALITY,
                                                DEFAULT_PITCH | FF_DONTCARE,
                                                "Times New Roman" );

                            SetRect( &rect, 10, 10, 110, 30 );

                            // Retrieve device context and
                            // select the font into it.
                            //...........................
                            hDC = GetDC( hWnd );
                            hOldFont = SelectObject( hDC, hFont );

                            Rectangle( hDC, rect.left-3, rect.top-3,
                                            rect.right+3, rect.bottom+3 );

                            // Set up the structure for calling
                            // the GetCharacterPlacement() function.
                            //......................................
                            results.lStructSize = sizeof( results );
                            results.lpOutString = &szNewText[0];
                            results.lpOrder     = NULL;
                            results.lpDx        = &anDX[0];
                            results.lpCaretPos  = NULL;
                            results.lpClass     = NULL;
                            results.lpGlyphs    = &auGlyphs[0];
                            results.nGlyphs     = 15;
                            results.nMaxFit     = 0;

                            // Justify the text to fit within the
                            // maximum extent defined by the rect.
                            //....................................
                            GetCharacterPlacement( hDC, lpszText, 15,
```

continued on next page

continued from previous page

```
                                    rect.right-rect.left,
                                    &results,
                                    GCP_JUSTIFY|GCP_MAXEXTENT );

            // Output the justified text.
            //...........................
            ExtTextOut( hDC, rect.left, rect.top, 0,
                        NULL, szNewText,
                        strlen( szNewText ), anDX );

            // Output the normal text.
            //........................
            ExtTextOut( hDC, 10, 40, 0, NULL,
                        lpszText, strlen( lpszText ), NULL );

            SelectObject( hDC, hOldFont );
            ReleaseDC( hWnd, hDC );
            DeleteObject( hFont );
        }
        break;
```

GetCharWidth32 ■ WINDOWS 95 ■ WINDOWS NT

Description	**GetCharWidth32** retrieves the widths, in logical units, for a range of characters in the current font. If a character does not exist in the current font, it is assigned the width of the default character.
Syntax	BOOL **GetCharWidth32**(HDC *hdc*, UINT *uFirstChar*, UINT *uLastChar*, LPINT *lpBuffer*)
Parameters	
hdc	HDC: The device context in which the font is selected.
uFirstChar	UINT: The first character in the range of characters.
uLastChar	UINT: The last character in the range of characters.
lpBuffer	LPINT: A pointer to a buffer large enough to receive the character widths.
Returns	BOOL: TRUE if successful; otherwise, the return value is FALSE.
Include File	wingdi.h
See Also	GetCharABCWidths, GetCharWidthFloat
Example	In this example, you use the **GetCharWidth32** function to retrieve the widths of the '**W**' and '**X**' characters in the default font of the window when the user selects the Test! menu item. The widths are displayed onscreen as seen in Figure 14-5.

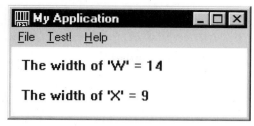

Figure 14-5 `GetCharWidth32` example

```
LRESULT CALLBACK WndProc( HWND hWnd, UINT uMsg, WPARAM wParam, LPARAM lParam )
{
   switch( uMsg )
   {
   case WM_COMMAND :
          switch( LOWORD( wParam ) )
          {
             case IDM_TEST :
                {
                   HDC    hDC;
                   int    nWidths[2];
                   char   szMsg[40];

                   hDC = GetDC( hWnd );

                   // Retrieve the widths of the
                   // 'W' and 'X' characters.
                   //............................
                   GetCharWidth32( hDC, 'W','X', nWidths );

                   // Output the widths to the window.
                   //.................................
                   sprintf( szMsg, "The width of 'W' = %d",
                                    nWidths[0] );
                   TextOut( hDC, 10, 10, szMsg, strlen( szMsg ) );

                   sprintf( szMsg, "The width of 'X' = %d",
                                    nWidths[1] );
                   TextOut( hDC, 10, 40, szMsg, strlen( szMsg ) );

                   ReleaseDC( hWnd, hDC );
                }
                break;
          .
          .
          .
```

GetCharWidthFloat   ■ WINDOWS 95 ■ WINDOWS NT

Description   `GetCharWidthFloat` retrieves the fractional widths for a range of characters in the current font. If a character does not exist in the current font, it is assigned the width of the default character.

Syntax	BOOL **GetCharWidthFloat**(HDC *hdc,* UINT *uFirstChar,* UINT *uLastChar,* PFLOAT *lpBuffer*)
Parameters	
hdc	HDC: The device context in which the font is selected.
uFirstChar	UINT: The first character in the range of characters.
uLastChar	UINT: The last character in the range of characters.
lpBuffer	PFLOAT: A pointer to a buffer large enough to receive the character widths.
Returns	BOOL: TRUE if successful; otherwise, the return value is FALSE.
Include File	wingdi.h
See Also	GetCharABCWidths, GetCharWidth32

GetGlyphOutline   ■ WINDOWS 95   ■ WINDOWS NT

Description	GetGlyphOutline retrieves the outline or bitmap for a character in the current font. This function only works with TrueType fonts. The glyph outline returned is a grid-fitted glyph, in which the bitmapped image conforms as closely as possible to the original design of the glyph. An application can also request an unmodified glyph for a character.
Syntax	DWORD **GetGlyphOutline**(HDC *hdc,* UINT *uChar,* UINT *uFormat,* LPGLYPH-METRICS *lpgm,* DWORD *cbBuffer,* LPVOID *lpvBuffer,* CONST MAT2* *lpmat2*)
Parameters	
hdc	HDC: The device context in which the font is selected.
uChar	UINT: The character for which data is to be returned.
uFormat	UINT: The format in which the function returns the data. This can be one of the values shown in Table 14-19.

Table 14-19 GetGlyphOutline *uFormat* values

Value	Meaning
GGO_BITMAP	Returns the glyph bitmap.
GGO_GRAY2_BITMAP	Returns a glyph bitmap that contains 4 levels of gray.
GGO_GRAY4_BITMAP	Returns a glyph bitmap that contains 16 levels of gray.
GGO_GRAY8_BITMAP	Returns a glyph bitmap that contains 255 levels of gray.
GGO_METRICS	Returns only the GLYPHMETRICS structure specified by *lpgm.* The other buffers are ignored.
GGO_NATIVE	Returns the curve data points in the rasterizer's native format and uses the font's design units. Any transformation specified in the *lpmat2* parameter is ignored.

lpgm	**LPGLYPHMETRICS**: A pointer to the **GLYPHMETRICS** structure that receives the placement of the glyph in the character cell. See the definition of the **GLYPHMETRICS** structure below.
cbBuffer	**DWORD**: The size of the buffer where the function is to copy information about the outline character. If set to **0**, the required size of the buffer is returned.
lpvBuffer	**LPVOID**: A pointer to the buffer where the information about the outline character is copied. If set to **NULL**, the required size of the buffer is returned.
lpmat2	**CONST MAT2***: A pointer to a **MAT2** structure specifying a transformation matrix for the character. For an object that is identical to the source object, the identity matrix value of *eM11* is **1**, the value of *eM12* is **0**, the value of *eM21* is **0**, and the value of *eM22* is **1**. See the definition of the **MAT2** structure below.
Returns	**DWORD**: If *uFormat* specifies **GGO_BITMAP**, **GGO_GRAY2_BITMAP**, **GGO_GRAY4_BITMAP**, **GGO_GRAY8_BITMAP**, or **GGO_NATIVE**, and the function is successful, the return value is greater than zero; otherwise, the return value is **GDI_ERROR**.
	If **GGO_METRICS** is specified, and the function is successful, the return value is **0**; otherwise the return value is **GDI_ERROR**.
Include File	**wingdi.h**
See Also	**GetOutlineTextMetrics**

GLYPHMETRICS Definition

```
typedef struct _GLYPHMETRICS
{
    UINT  gmBlackBoxX;
    UINT  gmBlackBoxY;
    POINT gmptGlyphOrigin;
    short gmCellIncX;
    short gmCellIncY;
} GLYPHMETRICS;
```

Members

gmBlackBoxX	**UINT**: The width of the smallest rectangle, or black box, that completely encloses the glyph.
gmBlackBoxY	**UINT**: The height of the smallest rectangle, or black box, that completely encloses the glyph.
gmptGlyphOrigin	**POINT**: The x and y coordinates of the upper-left corner of the black box.
gmCellIncX	**short**: The horizontal distance from the origin of the current character cell to the origin of the next character cell.
gmCellIncY	**short**: The vertical distance from the origin of the current character cell to the origin of the next character cell.

MAT2 **Definition**

```
typedef struct _MAT2
{
    FIXED eM11;
    FIXED eM12;
    FIXED eM21;
    FIXED eM22;
} MAT2;
```

Members

eM11   **FIXED**: A fixed-point value for the **M11** component of a 3×3 transformation matrix.

eM12   **FIXED**: A fixed-point value for the **M12** component of a 3×3 transformation matrix.

eM21   **FIXED**: A fixed-point value for the **M21** component of a 3×3 transformation matrix.

eM22   **FIXED**: A fixed-point value for the **M22** component of a 3×3 transformation matrix.

FIXED **Definition**

```
typedef struct _FIXED
{
    WORD  fract;
    short value;
} FIXED;
```

Members

fract   **WORD**: The fractional part of the number.

value   **short**: The integer part of the number.

Example   This example demonstrates how an application uses the **GetGlyphOutline** function to retrieve a bitmap of a font character that has been rotated 45 degrees. When the user selects the Test! menu item, a **"Times New Roman"** font is created and selected into a device context. The glyph outline for the letter **'A'** is then retrieved using the **GetGlyphOutline** function, and a bitmap is created and displayed, as shown in Figure 14-6, from the outline data.

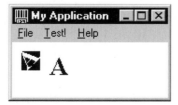

Figure 14-6 **GetGlyphOutline** example

```
// Convert degrees to radians.
//.............................
#define RAD(x) ((x) * 3.1415927 / 180)

LRESULT CALLBACK WndProc( HWND hWnd, UINT uMsg, WPARAM wParam, LPARAM lParam )
{
    switch( uMsg )
    {
        case WM_COMMAND :
                switch( LOWORD( wParam ) )
                {
                    case IDM_TEST :
                            {
                                HDC           hDC, hMemDC;
                                HFONT         hFont, hOldFont;
                                GLYPHMETRICS  gm;
                                MAT2          m2;
                                DWORD         dwRet;
                                LPBYTE        lpBuf;
                                HBITMAP       hBitmap, hOldBmp;

                                // Create a Times New Roman font.
                                //................................
                                hFont = CreateFont( 32, 0, 0, 0, FW_BOLD,
                                                    FALSE, FALSE, FALSE,
                                                    ANSI_CHARSET,
                                                    OUT_DEFAULT_PRECIS,
                                                    CLIP_DEFAULT_PRECIS,
                                                    PROOF_QUALITY,
                                                    DEFAULT_PITCH | FF_DONTCARE,
                                                    "Times New Roman" );

                                // Retrieve the device context,
                                // select the font into it,
                                // and create a compatible device context.
                                //.........................................
                                hDC     = GetDC( hWnd );
                                hMemDC = CreateCompatibleDC( hDC );
                                hOldFont = SelectObject( hDC, hFont );

                                // Set up the translation matrix to
                                // rotate the font 45 degrees.
                                //................................
                                m2.eM11 = FixedFromDouble(cos(RAD(45)));
                                m2.eM12 = FixedFromDouble(sin(RAD(45)));
                                m2.eM21 = FixedFromDouble(-sin(RAD(45)));
                                m2.eM22 = FixedFromDouble(cos(RAD(45)));

                                // Retrieve the size of the bitmap
                                // and allocate memory to hold it.
                                //................................
                                dwRet = GetGlyphOutline( hDC, 'A', GGO_BITMAP,
                                                    &gm, 0, NULL, &m2 );

                                lpBuf = HeapAlloc( GetProcessHeap(), HEAP_ZERO_MEMORY, dwRet );
```

continued on next page

continued from previous page

```
                        // Retrieve the bitmap for the letter 'A'.
                        //.........................................
                        GetGlyphOutline( hDC, 'A', GGO_BITMAP,
                                         &gm, dwRet, lpBuf, &m2 );

                        // Create a HBITMAP and display it.
                        //................................
                        hBitmap = BitmapFromBits( lpBuf,
                                                  (WORD)gm.gmBlackBoxX,
                                                  (WORD)gm.gmBlackBoxY );

                        hOldBmp = SelectObject( hMemDC, hBitmap );

                        BitBlt( hDC, 10,
                                     10,
                                     gm.gmBlackBoxX,
                                     gm.gmBlackBoxY,
                                     hMemDC, 0, 0, SRCCOPY);

                        // Output a normal 'A' character.
                        //..............................
                        TextOut( hDC, 40, 10, "A", 1 );

                        // Clean up.
                        //..........
                        SelectObject( hMemDC, hOldBmp );
                        DeleteObject( hBitmap );
                        HeapFree( GetProcessHeap(), 0, lpBuf );
                        SelectObject( hDC, hOldFont );
                        ReleaseDC( hWnd, hDC );
                        DeleteObject( hFont );
                    }
                    break;
        .
        .
        .

HBITMAP BitmapFromBits( void * lpBits, WORD width, WORD height )
{
    BITMAP bm;

    bm.bmType       = 0;
    bm.bmWidth      = width;
    bm.bmHeight     = height;
    bm.bmWidthBytes = ((width + 31) >> 5) << 2;
    bm.bmPlanes     = 1;
    bm.bmBitsPixel  = 1;
    bm.bmBits       = lpBits;

    return ( CreateBitmapIndirect( &bm ) );
}

FIXED FixedFromDouble( double d )
{
    long l;

    l = (long) (d * 65536L);
    return *(FIXED *)&l;
}
```

GetKerningPairs

Description	GetKerningPairs retrieves the character-kerning pairs for the currently selected font of a device context (DC). Kerning pairs are pairs of characters that, when placed together in a string, have the spacing between them adjusted to get the best appearance.
Syntax	DWORD **GetKerningPairs**(HDC *hdc,* DWORD *nNumPairs,* LPKERNINGPAIR *lpkrnpair*)
Parameters	
hdc	HDC: The device context in which the font is selected.
nNumPairs	DWORD: The number of pairs that fit in the *lpkrnpair* array. If the font has more than *nNumPairs* kerning pairs, an error is returned.
lpkrnpair	LPKERNINGPAIR: A pointer to an array of **KERNINGPAIR** structures to receive the kerning pairs. The array must contain at least as many structures as specified by the *nNumPairs* parameter. If set to **NULL**, the function returns the total number of kerning pairs for the font. See the definition of the **KERNINGPAIR** structure below.
Returns	DWORD: If successful, the number of kerning pairs returned; otherwise, **0**.
Include File	wingdi.h

KERNINGPAIR Definition

```
typedef struct tagKERNINGPAIR
{
    WORD wFirst;
    WORD wSecond;
    int  iKernAmount;
} KERNINGPAIR;
```

Members	
wFirst	WORD: The character code for the first character in the kerning pair.
wSecond	WORD: The character code for the second character in the kerning pair.
iKernAmount	int: The amount, in logical units, this pair will be kerned if they appear side by side in the same font and size. This value is typically negative, because pair kerning usually results in two characters being set more tightly than normal.
Example	This example retrieves the kerning pairs for the **"Times New Roman"** font using the **GetKerningPairs** function and displays them when the user selects the Test! menu item. Use the **TabbedTextOut** function to keep the information in aligned columns as shown in Figure 14-7. Note that not all the kerning pairs fit within the window and are clipped to the size of the client area.

Figure 14-7 GetKerningPairs example

```
LRESULT CALLBACK WndProc( HWND hWnd, UINT uMsg, WPARAM wParam, LPARAM lParam )
{
   switch( uMsg )
   {
      case WM_COMMAND :
            switch( LOWORD( wParam ) )
            {
               case IDM_TEST :
                  {
                     HDC           hDC;
                     HFONT         hFont, hOldFont;
                     KERNINGPAIR*  lpKp;
                     DWORD         dwRet;
                     int           i;
                     int           nTabs[2];
                     char          szMsg[50];

                     // Create a Times New Roman font.
                     //................................
                     hFont = CreateFont( 16, 0, 0, 0, FW_NORMAL,
                                         FALSE, FALSE, FALSE,
                                         ANSI_CHARSET,
                                         OUT_DEFAULT_PRECIS,
                                         CLIP_DEFAULT_PRECIS,
                                         PROOF_QUALITY,
                                         DEFAULT_PITCH | FF_DONTCARE,
                                         "Times New Roman" );


                     // Retrieve the device context and
                     // select the font into it.
                     //................................
                     hDC     = GetDC( hWnd );
                     hOldFont = SelectObject( hDC, hFont );

                     // Retrieve the number of kerning pairs
                     // and allocate memory to hold them.
                     //................................
                     dwRet = GetKerningPairs( hDC, 0, NULL );
                     lpKp = HeapAlloc( GetProcessHeap(), HEAP_ZERO_MEMORY,
                                       dwRet * sizeof( KERNINGPAIR ) );
```

```
        // Retrieve the actual kerning pairs.
        //...............................
        GetKerningPairs( hDC, dwRet, lpKp );

        nTabs[0] = 50;
        nTabs[1] = 100;

        // Display all the kerning pairs.
        //..............................
        for( i = 0; i < (int)dwRet; i++ )
        {
            wsprintf( szMsg,
                    "First: %c\tSecond: %c\tKerning: %d",
                    (lpKp+i)->wFirst,
                    (lpKp+i)->wSecond,
                    (lpKp+i)->iKernAmount );

            TabbedTextOut( hDC, 10, i*16, szMsg,
                        strlen( szMsg ),
                        2, nTabs, 10 );
        }

        HeapFree( GetProcessHeap(), 0, lpKp );
        SelectObject( hDC, hOldFont );
        ReleaseDC( hWnd, hDC );
        DeleteObject( hFont );
    }
    break;
```

GetOutlineTextMetrics ■ WINDOWS 95 ■ WINDOWS NT

Description	GetOutlineTextMetrics retrieves text metrics for TrueType fonts.
Syntax	UINT **GetOutlineTextMetrics**(HDC *hdc,* UINT *cbData,* LPOUTLINETEXTMETRIC *lpOTM*)
Parameters	
hdc	HDC: The device context in which the font is selected.
cbData	UINT: The size, in bytes, of the array in which the text metrics are to be returned.
lpOTM	LPOUTLINETEXTMETRIC: A pointer to an array of OUTLINETEXTMETRIC structures. If set to NULL, the function returns the size of the buffer required for the retrieved metric data.
Returns	UINT: If successful, TRUE or the size of the required buffer; otherwise, the return value is FALSE.
Include File	wingdi.h
See Also	GetTextMetrics

OUTLINETEXTMETRIC Definition

```
typedef struct _OUTLINETEXTMETRIC
{
    UINT        otmSize;
    TEXTMETRIC  otmTextMetrics;
    BYTE        otmFiller;
    PANOSE      otmPanoseNumber;
    UINT        otmfsSelection;
    UINT        otmfsType;
    int         otmsCharSlopeRise;
    int         otmsCharSlopeRun;
    int         otmItalicAngle;
    UINT        otmEMSquare;
    int         otmAscent;
    int         otmDescent;
    UINT        otmLineGap;
    UINT        otmsCapEmHeight;
    UINT        otmsXHeight;
    RECT        otmrcFontBox;
    int         otmMacAscent;
    int         otmMacDescent;
    UINT        otmMacLineGap;
    UINT        otmusMinimumPPEM;
    POINT       otmptSubscriptSize;
    POINT       otmptSubscriptOffset;
    POINT       otmptSuperscriptSize;
    POINT       otmptSuperscriptOffset;
    UINT        otmsStrikeoutSize;
    int         otmsStrikeoutPosition;
    int         otmsUnderscoreSize;
    int         otmsUnderscorePosition;
    PSTR        otmpFamilyName;
    PSTR        otmpFaceName;
    PSTR        otmpStyleName;
    PSTR        otmpFullName;
} OUTLINETEXTMETRIC;
```

Members

otmSize	UINT: The size, in bytes, of the **OUTLINETEXTMETRIC** structure.
otmTextMetrics	TEXTMETRIC: More information about the font. See the definition of the **TEXTMETRIC** structure under the **GetTextMetrics** function.
otmFiller	BYTE: Filler for byte alignment.
otmPanoseNumber	PANOSE: The **PANOSE** number for this font. See the definition of the **PANOSE** structure below.
otmfsSelection	UINT: The nature of the font pattern. Table 14-20 shows the meanings of this member's bits.

Table 14-20 OUTLINETEXTMETRIC *otmfsSelection* bits

Bit	Meaning
0	Italic
1	Underscore

Bit	Meaning
2	Negative
3	Outline
4	Strikeout
5	Bold

otmfsType   UINT: Specifies whether the font is licensed. Licensed fonts must not be modified or exchanged. If bit **1** is set, the font may not be embedded in a document. If bit **1** is clear, the font can be embedded. If bit **2** is set, the embedding is read-only.

otmsCharSlopeRise   int: The slope of the cursor. This value is **1** if the slope is vertical. Use this value and the value of the *otmsCharSlopeRun* member to create an italic cursor that has the same slope as the main italic angle.

otmsCharSlopeRun   int: The slope of the cursor. This value is **0** if the slope is vertical. Use this value and the value of the *otmsCharSlopeRise* member to create an italic cursor that has the same slope as the main italic angle.

otmItalicAngle   int: The main italic angle of the font, in counterclockwise degrees from vertical.

otmEMSquare   UINT: The number of logical units defining the x and y dimension of the em square for the font.

otmAscent   int: The maximum distance characters in the font can extend above the baseline.

otmDescent   int: The maximum distance characters in the font can extend below the baseline.

otmLineGap   UINT: The typographic line spacing.

otmsCapEmHeight   UINT: Not supported.

otmsXHeight   UINT: Not supported.

otmrcFontBox   RECT: The bounding box for the font.

otmMacAscent   int: The maximum distance characters in the font can extend above the baseline for the Macintosh computer.

otmMacDescent   int: The maximum distance characters in the font can extend below the baseline for the Macintosh computer.

otmMacLineGap   UINT: The line-spacing information for the Macintosh computer.

otmusMinimumPPEM   UINT: The smallest recommended size for the font, in pixels per em-square.

otmptSubscriptSize   POINT: The recommended horizontal and vertical size for subscripts.

otmptSubscriptOffset	**POINT**: The recommended horizontal and vertical offset for subscripts. This is measured from the character origin to the origin of the subscript character. (Refer to Figure 14-1.)
otmptSuperscriptSize	**POINT**: The recommended horizontal and vertical size for superscripts.
otmptSuperscriptOffset	**POINT**: The recommended horizontal and vertical offset for superscripts. This is measured from the character baseline to the baseline of the superscript character.
otmsStrikeoutSize	**UINT**: The width of the strikeout stroke for the font.
otmsStrikeoutPosition	**int**: The position of the strikeout stroke relative to the baseline for the font.
otmsUnderscoreSize	**int**: The thickness of the underscore character for the font.
otmsUnderscorePosition	**int**: The position of the underscore character for the font.
otmpFamilyName	**PSTR**: The offset from the beginning of the structure to a string specifying the font family name.
otmpFaceName	**PSTR**: The offset from the beginning of the structure to a string specifying the font typeface.
otmpStyleName	**PSTR**: The offset from the beginning of the structure to a string specifying the font style name.
otmpFullName	**PSTR**: The offset from the beginning of the structure to a string specifying the full name of the font.

PANOSE Definition   This definition shows values that are valid for Latin fonts.

```
typedef struct tagPANOSE
{
    BYTE bFamilyType;
    BYTE bSerifStyle;
    BYTE bWeight;
    BYTE bProportion;
    BYTE bContrast;
    BYTE bStrokeVariation;
    BYTE bArmStyle;
    BYTE bLetterform;
    BYTE bMidline;
    BYTE bXHeight;
} PANOSE;
```

Members

bFamilyType	**BYTE**: The font family type. This can be one of the values listed in Table 14-21.

Table 14-21 PANOSE *bFamilyType* values

Value	Meaning
PAN_ANY	Any
PAN_FAMILY_DECORATIVE	Decorative

Value	Meaning
PAN_FAMILY_PICTORIAL	Pictorial
PAN_FAMILY_SCRIPT	Script
PAN_FAMILY_TEXT_DISPLAY	Text and display
PAN_NO_FIT	No fit

bSerifStyle	BYTE: The serif style. This can be one of the values listed in Table 14-22.

Table 14-22 PANOSE *bSerifStyle* values

Value	Meaning
PAN_ANY	Any
PAN_NO_FIT	No fit
PAN_SERIF_BONE	Bone
PAN_SERIF_COVE	Cove
PAN_SERIF_EXAGGERATED	Exaggerated
PAN_SERIF_FLARED	Flared
PAN_SERIF_NORMAL_SANS	Normal sans serif
PAN_SERIF_OBTUSE_COVE	Obtuse cove
PAN_SERIF_OBTUSE_SANS	Obtuse sans serif
PAN_SERIF_OBTUSE_SQUARE_COVE	Obtuse square cove
PAN_SERIF_PERP_SANS	Perp sans serif
PAN_SERIF_ROUNDED	Rounded
PAN_SERIF_SQUARE	Square
PAN_SERIF_SQUARE_COVE	Square cove
PAN_SERIF_THIN	Thin
PAN_SERIF_TRIANGLE	Triangle

bWeight	BYTE: The font weight. This can be one of the values listed in Table 14-23.

Table 14-23 PANOSE *bWeight* values

Value	Meaning
PAN_ANY	Any
PAN_NO_FIT	No fit
PAN_WEIGHT_VERY_LIGHT	Very light
PAN_WEIGHT_LIGHT	Light

continued on next page

continued from previous page

Value	Meaning
PAN_WEIGHT_THIN	Thin
PAN_WEIGHT_BOOK	Book
PAN_WEIGHT_MEDIUM	Medium
PAN_WEIGHT_DEMI	Demibold
PAN_WEIGHT_BOLD	Bold
PAN_WEIGHT_HEAVY	Heavy
PAN_WEIGHT_BLACK	Black
PAN_WEIGHT_NORD	Nord

bProportion   BYTE: The font proportion. This can be one of the values listed in Table 14-24.

Table 14-24 PANOSE *bProportion* values

Value	Meaning
PAN_ANY	Any
PAN_NO_FIT	No fit
PAN_PROP_CONDENSED	Condensed
PAN_PROP_EVEN_WIDTH	Even width
PAN_PROP_EXPANDED	Expanded
PAN_PROP_MODERN	Modern
PAN_PROP_MONOSPACED	Monospaced
PAN_PROP_OLD_STYLE	Old style
PAN_PROP_VERY_CONDENSED	Very condensed
PAN_PROP_VERY_EXPANDED	Very expanded

bContrast   BYTE: The font contrast. This can be one of the values listed in Table 14-25.

Table 14-25 PANOSE *bContrast* values

Value	Meaning
PAN_ANY	Any
PAN_CONTRAST_HIGH	High
PAN_CONTRAST_LOW	Low
PAN_CONTRAST_MEDIUM	Medium
PAN_CONTRAST_MEDIUM_HIGH	Medium high
PAN_CONTRAST_MEDIUM_LOW	Medium low

Value	Meaning
PAN_CONTRAST_NONE	None
PAN_CONTRAST_VERY_HIGH	Very high
PAN_CONTRAST_VERY_LOW	Very low
PAN_NO_FIT	No fit

bStrokeVariation   BYTE: The font stroke variation. This can be one of the values listed in Table 14-26.

Table 14-26 PANOSE *bStrokeVariation* values

Value	Meaning
PAN_ANY	Any
PAN_NO_FIT	No fit
PAN_STROKE_GRADUAL_DIAG	Gradual/diagonal
PAN_STROKE_GRADUAL_HORZ	Gradual/horizontal
PAN_STROKE_GRADUAL_TRAN	Gradual/transitional
PAN_STROKE_GRADUAL_VERT	Gradual/vertical
PAN_STROKE_INSTANT_VERT	Instant/vertical
PAN_STROKE_RAPID_HORZ	Rapid/horizontal
PAN_STROKE_RAPID_VERT	Rapid/vertical

bArmStyle   BYTE: The font arm style. This can be one of the values listed in Table 14-27.

Table 14-27 PANOSE *bArmStyle* values

Value	Meaning
PAN_ANY	Any
PAN_BENT_ARMS_DOUBLE_SERIF	Nonstraight arms/double-serif
PAN_BENT_ARMS_HORZ	Nonstraight arms/horizontal
PAN_BENT_ARMS_SINGLE_SERIF	Nonstraight arms/single-serif
PAN_BENT_ARMS_VERT	Nonstraight arms/vertical
PAN_BENT_ARMS_WEDGE	Nonstraight arms/wedge
PAN_NO_FIT	No fit
PAN_STRAIGHT_ARMS_DOUBLE_SERIF	Straight arms/double-serif
PAN_STRAIGHT_ARMS_HORZ	Straight arms/horizontal
PAN_STRAIGHT_ARMS_SINGLE_SERIF	Straight arms/single-serif
PAN_STRAIGHT_ARMS_VERT	Straight arms/vertical
PAN_STRAIGHT_ARMS_WEDGE	Straight arms/wedge

bLetterform	**BYTE**: The font letter form. This can be one of the values listed in Table 14-28.

Table 14-28 PANOSE *bLetterform* values

Value	Meaning
PAN_ANY	Any
PAN_LETT_NORMAL_BOXED	Normal/boxed
PAN_LETT_NORMAL_CONTACT	Normal/contact
PAN_LETT_NORMAL_FLATTENED	Normal/flattened
PAN_LETT_NORMAL_OFF_CENTER	Normal/off center
PAN_LETT_NORMAL_ROUNDED	Normal/rounded
PAN_LETT_NORMAL_SQUARE	Normal/square
PAN_LETT_NORMAL_WEIGHTED	Normal/weighted
PAN_LETT_OBLIQUE_BOXED	Oblique/boxed
PAN_LETT_OBLIQUE_CONTACT	Oblique/contact
PAN_LETT_OBLIQUE_FLATTENED	Oblique/flattened
PAN_LETT_OBLIQUE_OFF_CENTER	Oblique/off center
PAN_LETT_OBLIQUE_ROUNDED	Oblique/rounded
PAN_LETT_OBLIQUE_SQUARE	Oblique/square
PAN_LETT_OBLIQUE_WEIGHTED	Oblique/weighted
PAN_NO_FIT	No fit

bMidline	**BYTE**: The font midline. This can be one of the values listed in Table 14-29.

Table 14-29 PANOSE *bMidline* values

Value	Meaning
PAN_ANY	Any
PAN_MIDLINE_CONSTANT_POINTED	Constant/pointed
PAN_MIDLINE_CONSTANT_SERIFED	Constant/with serif
PAN_MIDLINE_CONSTANT_TRIMMED	Constant/trimmed
PAN_MIDLINE_HIGH_POINTED	High/pointed
PAN_MIDLINE_HIGH_SERIFED	High/with serif
PAN_MIDLINE_HIGH_TRIMMED	High/trimmed
PAN_MIDLINE_LOW_POINTED	Low/pointed
PAN_MIDLINE_LOW_SERIFED	Low/with serif
PAN_MIDLINE_LOW_TRIMMED	Low/trimmed
PAN_MIDLINE_STANDARD_POINTED	Standard/pointed

Value	Meaning
PAN_MIDLINE_STANDARD_SERIFED	Standard/with serif
PAN_MIDLINE_STANDARD_TRIMMED	Standard/trimmed
PAN_NO_FIT	No fit

bXHeight **BYTE**: This can be one of the values listed in Table 14-30.

Table 14-30 PANOSE *bXHeight* values

Value	Meaning
PAN_ANY	Any
PAN_NO_FIT	No fit
PAN_XHEIGHT_CONSTANT_LARGE	Constant/large
PAN_XHEIGHT_CONSTANT_SMALL	Constant/small
PAN_XHEIGHT_CONSTANT_STD	Constant/standard
PAN_XHEIGHT_DUCKING_LARGE	Ducking/large
PAN_XHEIGHT_DUCKING_SMALL	Ducking/small
PAN_XHEIGHT_DUCKING_STD	Ducking/standard

Example This example shows how the `GetOutlineTextMetrics` function can be used to determine if a font can be embedded into a document.

```
LRESULT CALLBACK WndProc( HWND hWnd, UINT uMsg, WPARAM wParam, LPARAM lParam )
{
   switch( uMsg )
   {
   case WM_COMMAND :
           switch( LOWORD( wParam ) )
           {
              case IDM_TEST :
                 {
                    HDC     hDC;
                    HGLOBAL hBuf;
                    LPTSTR  lpBuf;
                    int     nSize;
                    HFONT   hFont;
                    OUTLINETEXTMETRIC ot;

                    // Create a Times New Roman font.
                    //..............................
                    hFont = CreateFont( 24, 16, 0, 0, FW_NORMAL,
                                        0, 0, 0, ANSI_CHARSET,
                                        OUT_DEFAULT_PRECIS,
                                        CLIP_DEFAULT_PRECIS,
                                        DEFAULT_QUALITY,
                                        DEFAULT_PITCH | FF_DONTCARE,
                                        "Times New Roman" );
```

continued on next page

continued from previous page

```
                    // Get a DC for the window and
                    // select the font into it.
                    //...........................
                    hDC = GetDC( hWnd );
                    SelectObject( hDC, hFont );

                    // Get the outline text metrics for
                    // the font to find out if it can
                    // be embedded.
                    //...................................
                    GetOutlineTextMetrics( hDC,
                                       sizeof(OUTLINETEXTMETRIC),
                                       &ot );

                    // Can the font be embedded?
                    //..........................
                    if ( !(ot.otmfsType & 0x00000001) )
                    {
                        // It is okay to embed the font.
                    }
                    else
                        MessageBox( hWnd,
                            "Embedding is not allowed for this font.",
                            NULL, MB_OK | MB_ICONASTERISK );

                    ReleaseDC( hWnd, hDC );
                    DeleteObject( hFont );
                }
                break;
```

.
.
.

GetRasterizerCaps   ■ WINDOWS 95   ■ WINDOWS NT

Description	GetRasterizerCaps returns flags indicating whether TrueType fonts are installed on the system and if they are enabled.
Syntax	BOOL **GetRasterizerCaps**(LPRASTERIZER_STATUS *lprs,* UINT *cb*)
Parameters	
lprs	LPRASTERIZER_STATUS: A pointer to a **RASTERIZER_STATUS** structure to receive information about the font rasterizer. See the definition of the **RASTERIZER_STATUS** structure below.
cb	UINT: The size of the buffer pointed to by the *lprs* parameter.
Returns	BOOL: TRUE if successful; otherwise, the return value is FALSE.
Include File	wingdi.h
See Also	GetOutlineTextMetrics

RASTERIZER_STATUS Definition

```
                typedef struct _RASTERIZER_STATUS
                {
```

```
                short nSize;
                short wFlags;
                short nLanguageID;
        } RASTERIZER_STATUS;
```

Members

nSize   short: The size, in bytes, of the **RASTERIZER_STATUS** structure.

wFlags   short: A combination of the flags in Table 14-31. Use the binary AND (**&**) operator to determine which flags are set.

Table 14-31 RASTERIZER_STATUS *wFlags* values

Flag	Meaning
TT_AVAILABLE	At least one TrueType font is installed on the system.
TT_ENABLED	TrueType fonts are enabled on the system.

nLanguageID short: The current system language. See the description of the language ID under the **EnumResourceLanguages** function in Chapter 7, Resources.

Example   This example shows how to use **GetRasterizerCaps** to determine if TrueType fonts are installed and enabled.

```
LRESULT CALLBACK WndProc( HWND hWnd, UINT uMsg, WPARAM wParam, LPARAM lParam )
{
    switch( uMsg )
    {
        case WM_COMMAND :
                switch( LOWORD( wParam ) )
                {
                    case IDM_TEST :
                        {
                            HDC   hDC;
                            RASTERIZER_STATUS rs;

                            hDC = GetDC( hWnd );
                            GetRasterizerCaps( &rs, sizeof( rs ) );

                            if ( rs.wFlags & TT_AVAILABLE )
                                TextOut( hDC, 10, 10,
                                        "TrueType installed.", 19 );

                            if ( rs.wFlags & TT_ENABLED )
                                TextOut( hDC, 10, 40,
                                        "TrueType enabled.", 17 );

                            ReleaseDC( hWnd, hDC );
                        }
                        break;
        .
        .
        .
```

GetTabbedTextExtent

Description	GetTabbedTextExtent computes the width and height of a character string based on the currently selected font. If the string contains one or more tab characters, the width of the string is based on the given tab stops. Use this function in conjunction with the TabbedTextOut function. Some devices perform kerning to optimize character spacing and do not put characters in regular-sized character cells; GetTabbedTextExtent will not return the correct text extent on these devices.
Syntax	DWORD **GetTabbedTextExtent**(HDC *hdc,* LPCTSTR *lpszStr,* int *cchString,* int *nTabPos,* LPINT *lpnTabStopPos*)

Parameters

hdc	HDC: The device context.
lpszStr	LPCTSTR: A pointer to a character string.
cchString	int: The number of characters in the string pointed to by the *lpszStr* parameter.
nTabPos	int: The number of tab-stop positions in the array pointed to by the *lpnTabStopPos* parameter. If set to 0 and the *lpnTabStopPos* is NULL, tabs are expanded to an even eight average character widths.
lpnTabStopPos	LPINT: A pointer to an array containing the tab-stop positions, in device units (pixels) and in ascending order.
Returns	DWORD: If successful, the dimensions of the string; otherwise, the return value is 0. The high-order word contains the height and the low-order word contains the width.
Include File	winuser.h
See Also	TabbedTextOut
Example	This example displays a character string using the **TabbedTextOut** function when the user selects the Test! menu item. The length of the resulting display string is calculated with the **GetTabbedTextExtent** function to display an underline as shown in Figure 14-8.

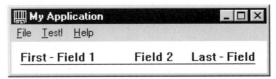

Figure 14-8 TabbedTextOut and
GetTabbedTextExtent example

```
int      nTabs[] = { 30, 45 };
LPCTSTR lpText  = "First - Field 1\tField 2\tLast - Field";

LRESULT CALLBACK WndProc( HWND hWnd, UINT uMsg, WPARAM wParam, LPARAM lParam )
{
   switch( uMsg )
   {
      case WM_COMMAND :
              switch( LOWORD( wParam ) )
              {
                 case IDM_TEST :
                       {
                          HDC    hDC;
                          DWORD dwExtent;

                          hDC = GetDC( hWnd );

                          // Calculate the length of the tabbed text
                          // string as it will be displayed.
                          //........................................
                          dwExtent = GetTabbedTextExtent( hDC, lpText,
                                                    strlen( lpText ),
                                                    2, nTabs );

                          // Display the string and underline it.
                          //....................................
                          TabbedTextOut( hDC, 10, 10, lpText,
                                          strlen( lpText ), 2, nTabs, 10 );

                          MoveToEx( hDC, 10, 10+HIWORD( dwExtent ), NULL );
                          LineTo( hDC, 10+LOWORD( dwExtent ),
                                       10+HIWORD( dwExtent ) );

                          ReleaseDC( hWnd, hDC );
                       }
                       break;
                       .
                       .
                       .
```

GetTextAlign ■ Windows 95   ■ Windows NT

Description	**GetTextAlign** retrieves the text-alignment settings of a device context (DC). The text-alignment settings are set with the **SetTextAlign** function. These settings determine how the *X*, *Y* parameters passed with **TextOut** and **ExtTextOut** are interpreted.
Syntax	UINT **GetTextAlign**(HDC *hdc*)
Parameters	
hdc	HDC: The device context.
Returns	UINT: If successful, one or more of the text-alignment flags shown in Table 14-32; otherwise, the return value is **GDI_ERROR**.

Table 14-32 GetTextAlign return flags

Value	Meaning
TA_BASELINE	The reference point is on the baseline of the text.
TA_BOTTOM	The reference point is on the bottom edge of the bounding rectangle.
TA_CENTER	The reference point is aligned horizontally with the center of the bounding rectangle.
TA_LEFT	The reference point is on the left edge of the bounding rectangle.
TA_NOUPDATECP	The current position is not updated after each text output call.
TA_RIGHT	The reference point is on the right edge of the bounding rectangle.
TA_RTLREADING	The text is laid out in right-to-left reading order, as opposed to the default left-to-right order. This only applies when the font selected into the device context is either Hebrew or Arabic.
TA_TOP	The reference point is on the top edge of the bounding rectangle.
TA_UPDATECP	The current position is updated after each text output call.

Note   The default values for a device context are **TA_LEFT**, **TA_TOP**, and **TA_NOUP-DATECP**. The **TA_** flags are not defined as unique binary values. You must break the three types of flags into groups, and then compare each group with the flag values. The example shows how this is done.

Include File   wingdi.h

See Also   SetTextAlign, TextOut, ExtTextOut

Example   This example shows how to process the returned value from **GetTextAlign**. This function is useful only when a window is created with its own private device context. This means that the class definition will include the **CS_OWNDC** style. This code segment shows how the text alignment is set when the application first starts. When the user selects the Test! menu item, the text-alignment values are determined via a series of switch statements and output to the device context, as shown in Figure 14-9.

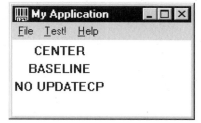

Figure 14-9 SetTextAlign and GetTextAlign example

```
LRESULT CALLBACK WndProc( HWND hWnd, UINT uMsg, WPARAM wParam, LPARAM lParam )
{
static HDC   hDC ;
static WORD wAlign ;

    switch( uMsg )
    {
        case WM_CREATE:
                hDC = GetDC( hWnd );
                SetTextAlign( hDC, TA_BOTTOM | TA_CENTER );
                break;

        case WM_COMMAND:
                switch( LOWORD( wParam ) )
                {
                    case IDM_TEST :
                            wAlign = GetTextAlign( hDC );

                            // Display the appropriate line for
                            // left, center, or right justification.
                            //......................................
                            switch(wAlign & (TA_LEFT | TA_CENTER | TA_RIGHT))
                            {
                                case TA_LEFT:
                                        TextOut(hDC, 50,20, "LEFT", 4); break;

                                case TA_CENTER:
                                        TextOut(hDC, 50,20, "CENTER", 6); break;

                                default:
                                        TextOut(hDC, 50,20, "RIGHT", 5); break;
                            }

                            // Display the appropriate line for
                            // how the text is aligned vertically.
                            //......................................
                            switch(wAlign & (TA_TOP | TA_BOTTOM | TA_BASELINE))
                            {
                                case TA_TOP:
                                        TextOut(hDC, 50,40, "TOP", 3); break;

                                case TA_CENTER:
                                        TextOut(hDC, 50,40, "BOTTOM", 6); break;

                                default:
                                        TextOut(hDC, 50,40, "BASELINE", 8); break;
                            }

                            // Determine if the update character position
                            // is turned on and display the status.
                            //..........................................
                            switch( wAlign & TA_UPDATECP )
                            {
                                case TA_UPDATECP:
                                        TextOut(hDC, 50,60, "UPDATECP", 8); break;
```

continued on next page

continued from previous page

```
        default:
            TextOut(hDC, 50,60, "NO UPDATECP", 11);
            break;
    }

    break;
```

.
.
.

GetTextCharacterExtra   ■ WINDOWS 95   ■ WINDOWS NT

Description	GetTextCharacterExtra retrieves the current intercharacter spacing of a device context. The SetTextCharacterExtra function is used to add extra space between letters output by TextOut and ExtTextOut.
Syntax	int **GetTextCharacterExtra**(HDC *hdc*)
Parameters	
hdc	HDC: The device context.
Returns	int: If successful, the current intercharacter spacing; otherwise, the return value is 0x80000000.
Include File	wingdi.h
See Also	SetTextCharacterExtra, TextOut, ExtTextOut, GetMapMode
Example	In this example the CS_OWNDC style is set as part of the window's class definition in the WinMain function. This example sets 10 extra units of space between characters when the application starts. When the user selects the Test! menu item, the application checks whether the extra space is still defined. Because this application has its own private device context, the response will always be "Extra spacing." as shown in Figure 14-10.

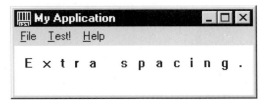

Figure 14-10 SetTextCharacterExtra and GetTextCharacterExtra example

```
LRESULT CALLBACK WndProc( HWND hWnd, UINT uMsg, WPARAM wParam, LPARAM lParam )
{
static HDC   hDC ;

   switch( uMsg )
   {
      case WM_CREATE:
            hDC = GetDC( hWnd );
            SetTextCharacterExtra( hDC, 10 );
            break;

      case WM_COMMAND:
            switch( LOWORD( wParam ) )
            {
               case IDM_TEST :
                    {
                        int nExSpace;

                        hDC = GetDC( hWnd );
                        nExSpace = GetTextCharacterExtra( hDC );

                        if ( nExSpace == 0 )
                           TextOut( hDC, 10, 10, "Normal spacing.", 15 );
                        else
                           TextOut( hDC, 10, 10, "Extra spacing.", 14 );
                    }
                    break;
```

.
.
.

GetTextColor   ■ WINDOWS 95   ■ WINDOWS NT

Description	GetTextColor retrieves the current text color for a device context (DC). The default text color for a device context is black. An application can change the text color using the **SetTextColor** function. GetTextColor allows the application to determine the current text color and is typically used with windows that have their own private device context.
Syntax	COLORREF **GetTextColor**(HDC *hdc*)
Parameters	
hdc	HDC: The device context.
Returns	COLORREF: If successful, the current text color as a **COLORREF** value; otherwise, the return value is **CLR_INVALID**.
Include File	wingdi.h
See Also	SetTextColor, SetBkColor, SetBkMode, GetRValue, GetGValue, GetBValue

Example　　　　This example, shown in Figure 14-11, has a window with a private device context. When the application starts, the text color is set to blue. When the user selects the Test! menu item, the current color value is output as RGB values.

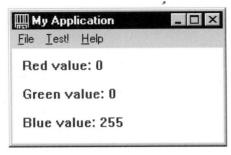

Figure 14-11 `SetTextColor` and `GetTextColor` example

```
LRESULT CALLBACK WndProc( HWND hWnd, UINT uMsg, WPARAM wParam, LPARAM lParam )
{
static HDC   hDC ;

   switch( uMsg )
   {
      case WM_CREATE:
            hDC = GetDC( hWnd );

            // Set the text color to blue.
            //..........................
            SetTextColor( hDC, RGB( 0, 0, 255 ) );
            break;

      case WM_COMMAND:
            switch( LOWORD( wParam ) )
            {
               case IDM_TEST :
                        {
                           COLORREF crColor;
                           char     szMsg[40];

                           crColor = GetTextColor( hDC );

                           wsprintf( szMsg, "Red value: %d",
                                        GetRValue( crColor ) );
                           TextOut( hDC, 10, 10, szMsg, strlen( szMsg ) );

                           wsprintf( szMsg, "Green value: %d",
                                        GetGValue( crColor ) );
                           TextOut( hDC, 10, 40, szMsg, strlen( szMsg ) );

                           wsprintf( szMsg, "Blue value: %d",
```

```
                          GetBValue( crColor ) );
              TextOut( hDC, 10, 70, szMsg, strlen( szMsg ) );
          }
          break;
```

.
.
.

GetTextExtentExPoint   ■ WINDOWS 95   ■ WINDOWS NT

Description	GetTextExtentExPoint calculates how many characters in a given string will fit within a given space. This function also fills an array with the text extent for each of the characters that fit within the given space. This function is useful in word-wrapping calculations.
Syntax	BOOL **GetTextExtentExPoint**(HDC *hdc,* LPCTSTR *lpszStr,* int *cchString,* int *nMaxExtent,* LPINT *lpnFit,* LPINT *alpDx,* LPSIZE *lpSize*)
Parameters	
hdc	HDC: The device context.
lpszStr	LPCTSTR: A pointer to the null-terminated string for which extents are to be retrieved.
cchString	int: The number of bytes in the string pointed to by the *lpszStr* parameter.
nMaxExtent	int: The maximum allowable width, in logical units, of the formatted string.
lpnFit	LPINT: A pointer to an integer that receives the maximum number of characters that will fit in the space specified by the *nMaxExtent* parameter. If set to NULL, the *nMaxExtent* parameter is ignored.
alpDx	LPINT: A pointer to an array of integers that receives partial string text extents. Each element in the array gives the distance, in logical units, between the beginning of the string and the corresponding character in the string that fits in the given space. This array should have at least as many elements as characters specified by the *cchString* parameter; however, the function fills the array with extents only for the characters that fit within the given space. If set to NULL, the function does not compute partial string text extents.
lpSize	LPSIZE: A pointer to a SIZE structure that receives the dimensions of the string, in logical units. This value cannot be NULL.
Returns	BOOL: TRUE if successful; otherwise, the return value is FALSE.
Include File	wingdi.h
See Also	GetTextExtentPoint32

Example

This example shows how to use the `GetTextExtentExPoint` function to determine how many characters can fit within a rectangle. When the user selects the Test! menu item, a rectangle is drawn and the string **"This is a long string."** is displayed within the rectangle, which clips any characters that do not fit.

```
LPCTSTR lpText = "This is a long string.";

LRESULT CALLBACK WndProc( HWND hWnd, UINT uMsg, WPARAM wParam, LPARAM lParam )
{
    switch( uMsg )
    {
        case WM_COMMAND:
            switch( LOWORD( wParam ) )
            {
                case IDM_TEST :
                    {
                        HDC      hDC;
                        SIZE     size;
                        int      nFit;

                        hDC = GetDC( hWnd );

                        // Draw a rectangle.
                        //.................
                        Rectangle( hDC, 10, 10, 120, 50 );

                        // Find out how many characters will
                        // fit within the rectangle.
                        //.................................
                        GetTextExtentExPoint( hDC, lpText,
                                            strlen( lpText ),
                                            100, &nFit, NULL, &size );

                        // Output the number of characters
                        // returned from GetTextExtentExPoint().
                        //.....................................
                        TextOut( hDC, 15, 20, lpText, nFit );

                        ReleaseDC( hWnd, hDC );
                    }
                    break;
            .
            .
            .
```

GetTextExtentPoint32   ■ WINDOWS 95 ■ WINDOWS NT

Description

`GetTextExtentPoint32` computes the width and height, in logical units, of a given character string. This function uses the currently selected font to compute the dimensions of the string. Because some devices kern characters, the sum of the extents of the characters in a string may not equal the extent of the string. `GetTextExtentPoint32` takes into account interchar-acter spacing set by the `SetTextCharacterExtra` function when computing the extent of the string.

Syntax	BOOL **GetTextExtentPoint32**(HDC *hdc*, LPCTSTR *lpsz,* int *cbString,* LPSIZE *lpSize*)
Parameters	
hdc	HDC: The device context.
lpsz	LPCTSTR: A pointer to a character string. A null-terminator is not required, because the *cbString* parameter determines the length of the string.
cbString	int: The number of characters in the string.
lpSize	LPSIZE: A pointer to a SIZE structure that receives the dimensions of the string.
Returns	BOOL: TRUE if successful; otherwise, the return value is FALSE.
Include File	wingdi.h
See Also	GetTextExtentExPoint
Example	See the example for the `SetTextJustification` function.

GetTextFace   ■ Windows 95   ■ Windows NT

Description	`GetTextFace` retrieves the typeface name of the font that is currently selected into a device context. The default typeface for a device context is the system font. If another font is selected, `GetTextFace` will retrieve its name as a null-terminated string.
Syntax	int **GetTextFace**(HDC *hdc*, int *nCount*, LPSTR *lpFaceName*)
Parameters	
hdc	HDC: The device context.
nCount	int: The maximum number of characters to copy to the buffer pointed to by the *lpFaceName* parameter.
lpFaceName	LPSTR: A pointer to the buffer that is to receive the typeface name. If set to NULL, the function returns the number of characters in the name, including the null-terminator.
Returns	int: If successful, the number of characters copied to the buffer; other-wise, the return value is 0.
Include File	wingdi.h
See Also	EnumFontFamilies, CreateFont, CreateFontIndirect, GetTextAlign
Example	This example outputs the name of the current typeface to the window's client area when the user selects the Test! menu item.

```
LRESULT CALLBACK WndProc( HWND hWnd, UINT uMsg, WPARAM wParam, LPARAM lParam )
{
    switch( uMsg )
    {
        case WM_COMMAND:
                switch( LOWORD( wParam ) )
                {
                    case IDM_TEST :
                        {
                            HDC   hDC;
                            char szFaceName[40];

                            hDC = GetDC( hWnd );

                            GetTextFace( hDC, 39, szFaceName );
                            TextOut( hDC, 10, 10, szFaceName,
                                        strlen( szFaceName ) );

                            ReleaseDC( hWnd, hDC );
                        }
                        break;

        .
        .
        .
```

GetTextMetrics ■ WINDOWS 95 ■ WINDOWS NT

Description	GetTextMetrics retrieves data from the currently selected font by filling a **TEXTMETRIC** data structure.
Syntax	BOOL **GetTextMetrics**(HDC *hdc*, LPTEXTMETRIC *lptm*)
Parameters	
hdc	HDC: The device context.
lptm	LPTEXTMETRIC: A pointer to a **TEXTMETRIC** structure that receives the text metrics. See the definition of the **TEXTMETRIC** structure below. Figure 14-1 illustrates the various text measurements.
Returns	BOOL: **TRUE** if successful; otherwise, the return value is **FALSE**.
Include File	wingdi.h
See Also	GetTextAlign, GetTextExtentPoint32

TEXTMETRIC Definition

```
typedef struct tagTEXTMETRIC
{
    LONG tmHeight;
    LONG tmAscent;
    LONG tmDescent;
    LONG tmInternalLeading;
    LONG tmExternalLeading;
    LONG tmAveCharWidth;
    LONG tmMaxCharWidth;
    LONG tmWeight;
    LONG tmOverhang;
```

```
              LONG  tmDigitizedAspectX;
              LONG  tmDigitizedAspectY;
              BYTE  tmFirstChar;
              BYTE  tmLastChar;
              BYTE  tmDefaultChar;
              BYTE  tmBreakChar;
              BYTE  tmItalic;
              BYTE  tmUnderlined;
              BYTE  tmStruckOut;
              BYTE  tmPitchAndFamily;
              BYTE  tmCharSet;
          } TEXTMETRIC;
```

Members

tmHeight	LONG: The height (ascent + descent) of characters.
tmAscent	LONG: The ascent, units above the baseline, of characters.
tmDescent	LONG: The descent, units below the baseline, of characters.
tmInternalLeading	LONG: The amount of leading, space, inside the bounds set by the *tmHeight* member. The font designer may set this member to 0.
tmExternalLeading	LONG: The amount of extra leading that the application adds between rows. The font designer may set this member to 0.
tmAveCharWidth	LONG: The average width of characters in the font. This value does not include overhang required for bold or italic characters.
tmMaxCharWidth	LONG: The width of the widest character in the font.
tmWeight	LONG: The weight of the font.
tmOverhang	LONG: The extra width per string that may be added to some synthesized fonts. When synthesizing some attributes, such as bold or italic, the Graphics Device Interface (GDI) or a device may have to add width to a string on both a per-character and per-string basis. This member enables the application to determine how much of the character width returned by a **GetTextExtentPoint32** function call on a single character is the actual character width and how much is the per-string extra width. The actual width is the extent minus the overhang.
tmDigitizedAspectX	LONG: The horizontal aspect of the device for which the font was designed.
tmDigitizedAspectY	LONG: The vertical aspect of the device for which the font was designed.
tmFirstChar	BYTE: The value of the first character defined in the font.
tmLastChar	BYTE: The value of the last character defined in the font.
tmDefaultChar	BYTE: The value of the character to be substituted for characters not in the font.
tmBreakChar	BYTE: The value of the character to be used to define word breaks for text justification.
tmItalic	BYTE: Set to nonzero for an italic font.

tmUnderlined	**BYTE**: Set to nonzero for an underlined font.
tmStruckOut	**BYTE**: Set to nonzero for a strikeout font.
tmPitchAndFamily	**BYTE**: Specifies information about the pitch, the technology, and the family of a physical font. The four low-order bits specify the pitch and technology. Table 14-33 gives the defined values for each of the four bits.

Table 14-33 Font pitch and technology

Constant	Meaning
TMPF_DEVICE	If this bit is set, the font is a device font.
TMPF_FIXED_PITCH	If this bit is set, the font is a variable-pitch font. If this bit is clear, the font is a fixed-pitch font. Note very carefully that those meanings are the opposite of what the constant name implies.
TMPF_TRUETYPE	If this bit is set, the font is a TrueType font.
TMPF_VECTOR	If this bit is set, the font is a vector font.

The four high-order bits designate the font family. Use the value **0xF0** and the bitwise AND (**&**) operator to mask out the four low-order bits of *tmPitchAndFamily*, thus obtaining a value that can be directly compared with font family names to find an identical match. Table 14-34 lists the defined font families.

Table 14-34 Font family

Value	Description
FF_DECORATIVE	Novelty fonts. Old English is an example.
FF_DONTCARE	Don't care or don't know.
FF_MODERN	Fonts with constant stroke width, with or without serifs. Pica, Elite, and Courier New are examples.
FF_ROMAN	Fonts with variable stroke width and with serifs. MS Serif is an example.
FF_SCRIPT	Fonts designed to look like handwriting. Script and Cursive are examples.
FF_SWISS	Fonts with variable stroke width and without serifs. MS Sans Serif is an example.

tmCharSet	**BYTE**: The character set of the font.
Example	This example shows the most common use of **GetTextMetrics**. The *tmHeight* and *tmExternalLeading* elements total the height of the font. The font height is used to set the line spacing.

```
LRESULT CALLBACK WndProc( HWND hWnd, UINT uMsg, WPARAM wParam, LPARAM lParam )
{
    switch( uMsg )
    {
```

```
case WM_COMMAND:
    switch( LOWORD( wParam ) )
    {
        case IDM_TEST :
            {
                HDC        hDC;
                TEXTMETRIC tm;
                int        nLineSpace;

                hDC = GetDC( hWnd );

                GetTextMetrics( hDC, &tm );
                nLineSpace = tm.tmHeight +
                             tm.tmExternalLeading;

                TextOut( hDC, 10, nLineSpace,
                             "These three", 11 );
                TextOut( hDC, 10, 2*nLineSpace,
                             "Lines are", 9 );
                TextOut( hDC, 10, 3*nLineSpace,
                             "evenly spaced.", 14 );

                ReleaseDC( hWnd, hDC );
            }
            break;
```

.
.
.

ResetDC　　　　　　　　　　■ WINDOWS 95　　■ WINDOWS NT

Description	**ResetDC** updates the given printer or plotter device context (DC), based on the information in a **DEVMODE** structure. An application will typically use this function when it receives a **WM_DEVMODECHANGE** message. You may also use **ResetDC** to change the paper orientation or paper bins while printing a document. You cannot use **ResetDC** to change the driver name, device name, or the output port. If an information device context is passed to the **ResetDC** function, a printer device context will always be returned.
Syntax	HDC **ResetDC**(HDC *hdc,* CONST DEVMODE* *lpInitData*)
Parameters	
hdc	HDC: The device context to be updated.
lpInitData	CONST DEVMODE*: A pointer to a **DEVMODE** structure that contains the new device context information.
Returns	HDC: If successful, the handle of the original device context; otherwise, the return value is **NULL**.
Include File	wingdi.h
See Also	DeviceCapabilities

Example   This example demonstrates how to use the **ResetDC** function to change the paper orientation from portrait to landscape while printing. When the user selects the Test! menu item, the first page is printed in portrait and the second is printed in landscape. Note that the call to **ResetDC** before printing the portrait page just ensures that the printer will print portrait in the case the printer is set up to print landscape by default.

```c
LRESULT CALLBACK WndProc( HWND hWnd, UINT uMsg, WPARAM wParam, LPARAM lParam )
{
    switch( uMsg )
    {
        case WM_COMMAND :
                switch( LOWORD( wParam ) )
                {
                    case IDM_TEST :
                            {
                                HDC     hDC;
                                DOCINFO di;
                                DEVMODE dm;

                                // Create a device context for the
                                // printer to which text will be output.
                                //......................................
                                hDC = CreateDC( "WINSPOOL", "HP Laserjet 4M",
                                                NULL, NULL );

                                // Set up the DEVMODE structure.
                                //........................
                                memset( &dm, 0, sizeof( dm ) );
                                dm.dmSpecVersion = DM_SPECVERSION;
                                dm.dmSize        = sizeof( DEVMODE );
                                dm.dmFields      = DM_ORIENTATION;

                                // Set up the DOCINFO structure.
                                //............................
                                memset( &di, 0, sizeof( DOCINFO ) );
                                di.cbSize      = sizeof( DOCINFO );
                                di.lpszDocName = "Test Document";

                                // Start printing.
                                //..................
                                if ( StartDoc( hDC, &di ) != SP_ERROR )
                                {
                                    // Print page 1 portrait.
                                    //......................
                                    dm.dmOrientation = DMORIENT_PORTRAIT;
                                    hDC = ResetDC( hDC, &dm );

                                    StartPage( hDC );
                                    TextOut( hDC, 10, 10,
                                                "This is print portrait.",23);
                                    EndPage( hDC );


                                    // Print page 2 landscape.
                                    //......................
                                    dm.dmOrientation = DMORIENT_LANDSCAPE;
                                    hDC = ResetDC( hDC, &dm );
```

```
            StartPage( hDC );
            TextOut( hDC, 10, 10,
                        "This is print landscape.",24);
            EndPage( hDC );

            // End printing.
            //.............
            EndDoc( hDC );
        }

        DeleteDC( hDC );
    }
    break;
```

.
.
.

SetAbortProc   ■ WINDOWS 95   ■ WINDOWS NT

Description	`SetAbortProc` sets the `AbortProc` function that allows a print job to be canceled during spooling.
Syntax	int **SetAbortProc**(HDC *hdc*, ABORTPROC *lpAbortProc*)
Parameters	
hdc	`HDC`: The device context for the print job.
lpAbortProc	`ABORTPROC`: A pointer to the application-defined abort function. For more information about the callback function, see the description of `AbortProc` below.
Returns	`int`: If successful, a value greater than zero; otherwise, it returns the `SP_ERROR` value.
Include File	`wingdi.h`
See Also	`AbortDoc`
Callback Syntax	BOOL CALLBACK **AbortProc**(HDC *hdc*, int *nError*)
Callback Parameters	
hdc	`HDC`: The device context for the print job.
nError	`int`: If no error has occurred, this parameter is `0`; otherwise, it is one of the error values listed in Table 14-35.

Table 14-35 `AbortProc` error codes

Value	Meaning
SP_ERROR	General error.
SP_OUTOFDISK	Not enough disk space is currently available for spooling, and no more space will become available.
SP_OUTOFMEMORY	Not enough memory is available for spooling.
SP_USERABORT	The user terminated the job through Windows Print Manager.

Callback Returns	BOOL: The callback should return TRUE to continue printing or FALSE to abort the print job.
Example	See the example for the AbortDoc function.

SetTextAlign ■ WINDOWS 95 ■ WINDOWS NT

Description	SetTextAlign sets the text-alignment flags for a device context. The TextOut and ExtTextOut functions specify where the output string should start based on a logical x,y position. By default, the device context uses the upper-left corner of the first character as the x,y location. This function allows an application to change this alignment location to other locations on the first character.
	A special flag, labeled TA_UPDATECP, keeps track of where the end of the last output string landed on the device context. This allows subsequent calls to the output functions, with each successive string ending up at the end of the last one.
Syntax	UINT SetTextAlign(HDC *hdc,* UINT *uMode*)
Parameters	
hdc	HDC: The device context.
uMode	UINT: The text alignment to set for the device context. This parameter value is made by using a mask of the values listed in Table 14-36. Only one flag can be chosen from those that affect horizontal and vertical alignment. In addition, only one of the two flags that alter the current position can be enabled at once.

Table 14-36 SetTextAlign *uMode* values

Value	Meaning
TA_BASELINE	The reference point is on the baseline of the text.
TA_BOTTOM	The reference point is on the bottom edge of the bounding rectangle.
TA_CENTER	The reference point is aligned horizontally with the center of the bounding rectangle.
TA_LEFT	The reference point is on the left edge of the bounding rectangle.
TA_NOUPDATECP	The current position is not updated after each text output call.
TA_RIGHT	The reference point is on the right edge of the bounding rectangle.
TA_RTLREADING	The text is laid out in right-to-left reading order, as opposed to the default left-to-right order. This only applies when the font selected into the device context is either Hebrew or Arabic.
TA_TOP	The reference point is on the top edge of the bounding rectangle.
TA_UPDATECP	The current position is updated after each text output call.

Returns	UINT: If successful, the previous text-alignment setting; otherwise, the return value is GDI_ERROR.

Include File	`wingdi.h`
See Also	`GetTextALign, ExtTextOut`
Example	See the example for the `GetTextALign` function.

SetTextCharacterExtra   ■ Windows 95   ■ Windows NT

Description	`SetTextCharacterExtra` sets the intercharacter spacing for the currently selected font of a device context. Intercharacter spacing is added to each character, including break characters, when a line of text is drawn on the device context. This spaces out the string and makes the characters look better.
Syntax	`int` **`SetTextCharacterExtra`**`( HDC hdc, int nCharExtra )`
Parameters	
hdc	`HDC`: The device context.
nCharExtra	`int`: The amount of extra space, in logical units, to be added to each character. If the current mapping mode is not `MM_TEXT`, the *nCharExtra* parameter is transformed and rounded to the nearest device unit.
Returns	`int`: If successful, the previous intercharacter spacing; otherwise, `0x80000000` is returned.
Include File	`wingdi.h`
See Also	`GetTextCharacterExtra, ExtTextOut, TextOut, DrawText`
Example	See the example for the `GetTextCharacterExtra` function.

SetTextColor   ■ Windows 95   ■ Windows NT

Description	`SetTextColor` sets the text color for a device context to a specified color. The default text color for a device context is black. This function allows any RGB color to be set for text output. The color stays in effect until the device context is released, or another text color is set.
Syntax	`COLORREF` **`SetTextColor`**`( HDC hdc, COLORREF crColor )`
Parameters	
hdc	`HDC`: The device context.
crColor	`COLORREF`: The color of the text. The `RGB` macro returns a `COLORREF` value.
Returns	`COLORREF`: If successful, the color reference for the previous text color; otherwise, the return value is `CLR_INVALID`.
Include File	`wingdi.h`
See Also	`GetTextColor, ExtTextOut, TextOut, SetBkColor`
Example	See the example for the `GetTextColor` function.

SetTextJustification ■ WINDOWS 95 ■ WINDOWS NT

Description	`SetTextJustification` specifies the amount of space Windows should add to the break characters in a string of text. The space is added when an application calls the `TextOut` or `ExtTextOut` functions to make the string fit within a specific space.
	An application should retrieve the extent of the character string by calling the `GetTextExtentPoint32` function and then calculate the amount of justification space required to make the string fit within the space. The justification space is set with the `SetTextJustification` function prior to calling the `TextOut` or `ExtTextOut` function. For strings with multiple fonts, justify and output each group of characters, one font type at a time. `SetTextJustification` accumulates the round-off errors on each call in order to average the errors over the length of the line. Call `SetTextJustification` with *nBreakExtra* set to **0** to clear the round-off error at the start of each new line.
Syntax	`BOOL SetTextJustification( HDC hdc, int nBreakExtra, int nBreakCount )`
Parameters	
hdc	`HDC`: The device context.
nBreakExtra	`int`: The total extra space, in logical units, to be added to the line of text. If the current mapping mode is not **MM_TEXT**, the value identified by this parameter is transformed and rounded to the nearest device unit.
nBreakCount	`int`: The number of break characters in the line.
Returns	`BOOL`: **TRUE** if successful; otherwise, the return value is **FALSE**.
Include File	`wingdi.h`
See Also	`GetTextExtentPoint32`, `ExtTextOut`, `TextOut`
Example	This example justifies a three-word string to fit exactly within the bounds of a rectangle as shown in Figure 14-12. `GetTextExtentPoint32` is used to calculate the size of the string prior to justification. `SetTextJustification` then adds enough space to expand the string to the full size of the rectangle. The next call to `TextOut` uses the justification during output to space the words.

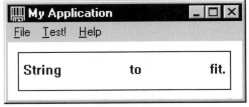

Figure 14-12 `SetTextJustification` example

```
LPCTSTR lpText = "String to fit.";

LRESULT CALLBACK WndProc( HWND hWnd, UINT uMsg, WPARAM wParam, LPARAM lParam )
{
    switch( uMsg )
    {
        case WM_COMMAND:
                switch( LOWORD( wParam ) )
                {
                    case IDM_TEST :
                        {
                            HDC        hDC;
                            SIZE       size;

                            hDC = GetDC( hWnd );

                            // Draw a rectangle.
                            //..................
                            Rectangle( hDC, 10, 10, 220, 50 );

                            // Find out the size of the string.
                            //.................................
                            GetTextExtentPoint32( hDC, lpText,
                                                  strlen( lpText ),
                                                  &size );

                            // Set the justification space.
                            //.............................
                            SetTextJustification( hDC, 200 - size.cx, 2 );

                            // Output the text.
                            //.................
                            TextOut( hDC, 15, 20, lpText, strlen( lpText ) );

                            ReleaseDC( hWnd, hDC );
                        }
                        break;
```

.
.
.

StartDoc   ■ WINDOWS 95   ■ WINDOWS NT

Description	StartDoc starts a print job on a given printer device.
Syntax	int **StartDoc**(HDC *hdc*, CONST DOCINFO* *lpdi*)
Parameters	
hdc	HDC: The device context for the print job.
lpdi	CONST DOCINFO*: A pointer to a DOCINFO structure that contains the name of the document file and the name of the output file. See the definition of the DOCINFO structure below.
Returns	int: If successful, a value greater than zero, which is the print job identifier for the document; otherwise, the return value is SP_ERROR.

Include File	`wingdi.h`
See Also	`EndDoc, AbortDoc, StartPage`

DOCINFO Definition

```
typedef struct
{
    int     cbSize;
    LPTSTR  lpszDocName;
    LPTSTR  lpszOutput;
    LPTSTR  lpszDatatype;
    DWORD   fwType;
} DOCINFO;
```

Members

`cbSize`	`int`: The size, in bytes, of the structure.
`lpszDocName`	`LPTSTR`: A pointer to a null-terminated string that specifies the name of the document.
`lpszOutput`	`LPTSTR`: A pointer to a null-terminated string that specifies the name of an output file. If set to `NULL`, the output is sent to the device identified by the *hdc* parameter passed to the `StartDoc` function.
`lpszDatatype`	`LPTSTR`: A pointer to a null-terminated string that specifies the type of data used to record the print job.
`fwType`	`DWORD`: Additional information about the print job. Can be `0` or `DI_APP-BANDING` if the application will use banding. For optimal performance during printing, banding applications should specify `DI_APPBANDING`.
Example	See the example for the `ResetDC` function.

StartPage ■ WINDOWS 95 ■ WINDOWS NT

Description	`StartPage` informs the printer driver to start accepting data for a new page. An application should call this function after the `EndPage` function each time a page break occurs during printing.
Syntax	`int StartPage( HDC hDC )`
Parameters	
hDC	`HDC`: The device context for the print job.
Returns	`int`: If successful, a value greater than zero; otherwise, the return value is `SP_ERROR`.
Include File	`wingdi.h`
See Also	`EndPage`
Example	See the example for the `EndPage` function.

TabbedTextOut

Description	`TabbedTextOut` draws a character string at a specified location on a device context, expanding tabs to the values specified in an array of tab-stop positions. Text is drawn in the currently selected font.

Syntax	`LONG` **`TabbedTextOut`**`( HDC `*`hdc`*`, int `*`x`*`, int `*`y`*`, LPCTSTR `*`lpString`*`,`
	`int `*`nCount`*`, int `*`nTabPositions`*`, LPINT `*`lpnTabStopPositions`*`,`
	`int `*`nTabOrigin`*` )`

Parameters

hdc	`HDC`: The device context.
x	`int`: The x coordinate of the starting point of the string, in logical units.
y	`int`: The y coordinate of the starting point of the string, in logical units.
lpString	`LPCTSTR`: A pointer to the character string to draw.
nCount	`int`: The number of characters in the string pointed to by the *lpString* parameter.
nTabPositions	`int`: The number of values in the array of tab-stop positions pointed to by the *lpnTabStopPositions* parameter. If set to **0**, tabs will be expanded to eight times the average character width. If set to **1**, tabs will be expanded to the distance specified by the first tab stop pointed to by *lpnTabStopPositions*.
lpnTabStopPositions	`LPINT`: A pointer to an array containing the tab-stop positions in ascending order, in logical units. Under Windows 95, specify negative values for right alignment.
nTabOrigin	`int`: The x coordinate of the starting position from which tabs are expanded, in logical units.
Returns	`LONG`: If successful, the dimensions, in logical units, of the string. The height is in the high-order word and the width is in the low-order word.
Include File	`winuser.h`
See Also	`DrawText, TextOut, ExtTextOut, SetTextAlign`
Example	See the example for the `GetTabbedTextExtent` function.

TextOut

Description	The `TextOut` function writes a character string at the specified location, using the currently selected font. The interpretation of the location depends on the current text-alignment mode. An application can retrieve this mode by calling the `GetTextAlign` function and modify it by calling the `SetTextAlign` function.

Syntax	`BOOL` **`TextOut`**`( HDC` *`hdc,`* `int` *`nXStart,`* `int` *`nYStart,`* `LPCTSTR` *`lpszString,`* `int` *`cbString`* `)`
Parameters	
hdc	`HDC`: The device context.
nXStart	`int`: The logical x coordinate of the reference point used to align the string.
nYStart	`int`: The logical y coordinate of the reference point used to align the string.
lpszString	`LPCTSTR`: A pointer to the string to be drawn.
cbString	`int`: The number of characters in the string.
Returns	`BOOL`: `TRUE` if successful; otherwise, the return value is `FALSE`.
Include File	`wingdi.h`
See Also	`ExtTextOut, SetTextAlign, DrawText`
Example	See the example for the `SetTextJustification` and `ResetDC` functions.

15

PAINTING AND DRAWING

Windows interacts with the user through a graphical user interface (GUI). There are many aspects involved in implementing a GUI, but the most obvious to the user is that information is presented graphically, in charts, pictures, and drawings. The Win32 API provides more than 120 functions to assist applications in presenting graphics to the user. In addition, Windows provides a device-independent analogy that hides the details of the presentation device from the application.

You have already been exposed to the concept of a device context. The device context is the basis for all graphics in the Windows environment—it is used by Windows to describe the physical aspects of a graphics device. By using a device context, the application can create graphics presentations in a device-independent manner. Windows uses the device context to convert the graphics into the commands and data required by the specific device.

Because Windows 95 implements the Graphics Device Interface (GDI) as a 16-bit component, all functions that are implemented by the GDI have 16-bit coordinate limitations, while the same functions under Windows NT use 32-bit coordinates. Even though a GDI function takes 32-bit coordinates under Windows 95 and Windows NT, Windows 95 ignores the high-order word of the value.

Pens, Brushes, and Other Logical Tools

Drawing on a device requires that the application specify information such as the width of lines, the colors of lines, the color and pattern of the background, etc. All of these things must be specified in a device-independent manner, and Windows converts the information into data that is specific to the device. One way of implementing this would be to require the application to specify the information every time it wished to draw to a device. This would require Windows to perform the conversion during every graphics request. A more practical approach, and a more efficient one, is to allow the application to specify common information, and to apply that common information to all subsequent graphics. This is the approach that Windows uses.

A device context contains the common information that Windows uses to draw to the device. Windows separates this information into functional groups and has each functional group represented by a tool. Windows provides functions that an application can use to create a new tool from one of the functional groups. The tool is considered a logical tool because it is not specific to any device or device context. To use the tool, the application must select the tool into a device context. It is at this point that Windows converts the device-independent information represented by the tool into the information required by the specific device. Refer to Table 15-1 for a list of the available tools and their use.

Table 15-1 Windows drawing tools

Tool Type	Description
Brush	The brush tool defines the pattern and color that Windows uses to fill the interiors of drawn figures.
Font	The font tool identifies the font that Windows will use when drawing text.
Palette	The palette tool specifies the colors that Windows can use to draw on a given device. Windows applications can specify up to 16,777,216 different colors. Since most devices cannot represent this many different colors, Windows allows an application to specify a subset of these colors for use when drawing.
Pen	The pen tool defines the width, color, and style of lines that Windows uses to outline drawn figures.
Region	A region defines an area on a device. Regions can be used to create complex figures and to control clipping.

Specifying an Area for Drawing

There are many ways to specify where you wish to draw on a device. At times you will specify specific points, such as when drawing a straight line. Other times you will specify that a figure is to be drawn within a bounding rectangle. In this case, you will typically specify either the x and y points of the upper-left and lower-right corners of the rectangle, or you will create a RECT structure that contains these coordinates.

Often, more complex drawing areas must be defined. In these cases, Windows provides regions and paths. You can create a region based on a rectangle, ellipse, or polygon, and you can combine multiple regions to create new regions. You create a path using the BeginPath function, after which you may specify various drawing functions that will be used in creating the path. Once the path is complete, use the EndPath function to close the path. Paths let you create very complex areas.

Invalidation, Clipping, and the WM_PAINT Message

When you draw into a device context that is associated with a window on the user's screen, there is the possibility that a portion of the window will be obscured by other windows. Windows handles this situation by clipping the drawing that your application does. Windows creates a clipping region that defines the portion of the window that is visible to the user. Windows does not draw to any area of the window that is not currently visible. Your application may draw anywhere it wants, but those areas that are not visible will not appear. Windows handles this using a technique called clipping. A device context includes a clipping region. Drawing that is done outside of the clipping region is not drawn. There are many functions that you can use that affect the clipping region.

What happens when a portion of your window that has been obscured becomes uncovered? In this case, that portion of the window that is no longer obscured needs to be redrawn. Windows handles this by using an invalidation region, and the **WM_PAINT** message. Windows maintains an invalidation region for every window that defines the portion of the window that is not currently valid. This can be because a portion of the window was previously obscured and has been made visible because your application has used one of the functions that affects the invalidation region, such as **InvalidateRect**, or for other reasons. Anytime the invalidation region for any window is not empty, Windows will send a **WM_PAINT** message to your application. When your application receives a **WM_PAINT** message, it must redraw that portion of the window that is invalid. You must use the **BeginPaint** and **EndPaint** functions to coordinate the handling of the invalidation region. When you use **BeginPaint**, Windows will fill in a **PAINTSTRUCT** structure that defines the current invalidation region. In addition, Windows will not allow your application to draw to any area that is not within the invalidation region. You may attempt to draw to the entire window, but Windows will clip your drawing to the invalidation region. After using the **BeginPaint** function, Windows assumes that the invalidation region will be redrawn. Refer to the description of the **BeginPaint** function for an example.

Painting and Drawing Function Descriptions

Table 15-2 summarizes the functions used in painting and drawing. A detailed description of each function follows the table.

Table 15-2 Painting and drawing function summary

Function	Purpose
AbortPath	Closes and discards the current path.
AngleArc	Draws a line segment and an arc.
Arc	Draws an arc.
ArcTo	Draws an arc. The current position is moved to the end of the arc.
BeginPaint	Prepares for painting by allocating a device context and returning painting information.
BeginPath	Starts a path bracket.
Chord	Draws a chord.
CloseFigure	Closes an open figure in a path.
CombineRgn	Combines two regions, creating a third region.
CopyRect	Copies one rectangle to another.
CreateBrushIndirect	Creates a brush given a LOGBRUSH structure.
CreateDIBPatternBrushPt	Creates a brush given a device-independent bitmap.
CreateEllipticRgn	Creates an elliptical region.

continued on next page

continued from previous page

Function	Purpose
CreateEllipticRgnIndirect	Creates an elliptical region given a RECT structure.
CreateHatchBrush	Creates a hatched brush.
CreatePatternBrush	Creates a brush given a handle to a bitmap.
CreatePen	Creates a logical pen.
CreatePenIndirect	Creates a logical pen given a LOGPEN structure.
CreatePolygonRgn	Creates a polygonal region.
CreatePolyPolygonRgn	Creates a region based on multiple polygons.
CreateRectRgn	Creates a rectangular region.
CreateRectRgnIndirect	Creates a rectangular region given a RECT structure.
CreateRoundRectRgn	Creates a rectangular region with rounded corners.
CreateSolidBrush	Creates a logical brush.
DeleteObject	Deletes a GDI object (pen, brush, font, region, bitmap, or palette).
DrawAnimatedRects	Animates the opening or closing of a rectangle.
DrawCaption	Draws a window caption.
DrawEdge	Draws edges of a rectangle using a 3D style.
DrawFocusRect	Draws a rectangle in the "focus" style.
DrawFrameControl	Draws a frame control, such as a button, menu, or scroll bar.
DrawIcon	Draws an icon.
DrawIconEx	Draws an icon or cursor, stretching and applying a given raster operation.
DrawState	Draws the given object, such as an icon or bitmap, using normal, disabled, or other effects.
DrawText	Draws text within the specified rectangle.
DrawTextEx	Draws text within the specified rectangle.
Ellipse	Draws an ellipse.
EndPaint	Indicates the end of the painting process.
EndPath	Closes the current path and selects it into the device context.
EnumObjects	Enumerates the available brushes or pens.
EqualRect	Determines if two rectangles are equal.
EqualRgn	Determines if two regions are equal.
ExcludeClipRect	Excludes the given rectangle from the current clipping area.
ExcludeUpdateRgn	Prevents drawing within invalid regions by removing the update region from the clipping region.
ExtCreatePen	Creates a logical cosmetic or geometric pen.
ExtCreateRegion	Creates a region, applying the given transformation.
ExtFloodFill	Fills an area of the window with the current brush.
ExtSelectClipRgn	Adds the given region to the current clipping region.
FillPath	Fills the current paths, interior.
FillRect	Fills the specified rectangle.
FillRgn	Fills the specified region.
FlattenPath	Converts curves within the current path into a sequence of straight lines.
FrameRect	Draws a border around the given rectangle.
FrameRgn	Draws a border around the given region.

Function	Purpose
GetArcDirection	Returns the current arc direction, used by arc and rectangle functions.
GetAspectRatioFilterEx	Returns the current aspect ratio filter, which is based on the width and height of pixels on the given device.
GetBkColor	Returns the current background color.
GetBkMode	Returns the current background color mode.
GetBoundsRect	Returns the current bounding rectangle of a device context.
GetBrushOrgEx	Returns the current brush origin.
GetClipBox	Returns the dimensions of the smallest rectangle that encloses the visible area of a device context.
GetClipRgn	Returns a handle to the current clip region.
GetCurrentPositionEx	Returns the current position in logical coordinates.
GetMiterLimit	Returns the miter limit for the device context.
GetObject	Returns information about a GDI object.
GetObjectType	Returns the type of an object.
GetPath	Returns the endpoints, control points, and vertex information for the current path.
GetPixel	Returns the RGB value of the specified pixel in the device context.
GetPolyFillMode	Returns the current polygon fill mode.
GetRegionData	Returns information about the specified region.
GetRgnBox	Returns the bounding rectangle of the given region.
GetROP2	Returns the current foreground raster operation code.
GetStockObject	Returns a handle to one of various predefined objects.
GetUpdateRect	Returns the smallest rectangle that surrounds the current update region.
GetUpdateRgn	Returns the current update region.
InflateRect	Enlarges or shrinks the given rectangle.
IntersectClipRect	Creates a new clipping region that is the intersection of the current clipping region and the given rectangle.
IntersectRect	Returns the intersection of two rectangles.
InvalidateRect	Adds the given rectangle to the current update region.
InvalidateRgn	Adds the given region to the current update region.
InvertRect	Inverts all pixels within the given rectangle.
InvertRgn	Inverts all pixels within the given region.
IsRectEmpty	Determines whether a rectangle is empty or not.
LineDDA	Computes the points within the line, and calls a user function with each point.
LineTo	Draws a line from the current location to the given location.
LockWindowUpdate	Disables or enables drawing within a window.
MoveToEx	Moves the current location within the device context.
OffsetClipRgn	Moves the clipping region by the given amount.
OffsetRect	Moves the specified rectangle by the given amount.
OffsetRgn	Moves the specified region by the given amount.
PaintRgn	Paints the given region.
PathToRegion	Creates a region from the current path.
Pie	Draws a pie-shaped wedge.

continued on next page

continued from previous page

Function	Purpose
PolyBezier	Draws one or more bezier curves.
PolyBezierTo	Draws one or more bezier curves, moving the current position.
Polygon	Draws one or more lines.
Polyline	Draws one or more lines.
PolylineTo	Draws one or more lines, moving the current position.
PolyPolygon	Draws one or more closed polygons.
PolyPolyline	Draws one or more line series.
PolyTextOut	Draws one or more text strings.
PtInRect	Determines if the given point is within the given rectangle.
PtInRegion	Determines if the given point is within the given region.
Rectangle	Draws a filled rectangle.
RectInRegion	Determines if any part of the given rectangle is within the given region.
RedrawWindow	Redraws the specified portion of the window.
RoundRect	Draws a filled rectangle with rounded corners.
SelectClipPath	Selects the current path as the clipping region.
SelectClipRgn	Selects the given region as the clipping region.
SetArcDirection	Selects the drawing direction for arcs and rectangles.
SetBkColor	Sets the current background color.
SetBkMode	Sets the current background color mode.
SetBoundsRect	Sets the mode that Windows uses to accumulate bounding rectangles.
SetBrushOrgEx	Sets the origin for the next brush selected into the device context.
SetMiterLimit	Sets the limit for the length of miter joints.
SetPixel	Sets the color of the given pixel and returns the old pixel color.
SetPixelV	Sets the color of the given pixel.
SetPolyFillMode	Sets the mode Windows uses to fill polygons.
SetRect	Sets the specified rectangle coordinates.
SetRectEmpty	Sets the rectangle to an empty rectangle.
SetRectRgn	Converts the given region into a rectangular region.
SetROP2	Sets the foreground mix raster operation mode.
StrokeAndFillPath	Draws the outline of the current path and fills its interior.
StrokePath	Draws the outline of the current path.
SubtractRect	Returns the rectangle obtained by subtracting two given rectangles.
UnionRect	Returns the rectangle that is the union of the two given rectangles.
UnrealizeObject	Unrealizes the logical palette, so that the next RealizePalette will remap the palette.
UpdateWindow	Sends a WM_PAINT message to the given window if there is an update region.
ValidateRect	Removes the given rectangle from the update region.
ValidateRgn	Removes the given region from the update region.
WidenPath	Widens the current path based on the current pen.

AbortPath ■ WINDOWS 95 ■ WINDOWS NT

Description	AbortPath discards the current path for the specified device context. If a path is currently being defined, it is closed.
Syntax	BOOL **AbortPath**(HDC *hDC*)
Parameters	
hDC	HDC: Specifies the target device context.
Returns	BOOL: Returns TRUE if successful; otherwise, returns FALSE.
Include File	wingdi.h
See Also	BeginPath, EndPath
Example	This example creates a path on the client area of the window when the user selects the Test! menu item. If the window size is too small for the path, the path is aborted with the AbortPath function.

```
LRESULT CALLBACK WndProc( HWND hWnd, UINT uMsg, WPARAM wParam, LPARAM lParam )
{
   switch( uMsg )
   {
      case WM_COMMAND :
            switch( LOWORD( wParam ) )
            {
               case IDM_TEST :
                  {
                     RECT rect;
                     HDC  hDC = GetDC( hWnd );

                     GetClientRect( hWnd, &rect );

                     if( BeginPath( hDC ) )
                     {
                        try
                        {
                           MoveToEx( hDC, 10, 10, NULL );

                           // Check if the coordinates
                           // are within the rect.
                           //........................
                           if ( rect.right < 200 )
                              RaiseException( 1, 0, 0, NULL );

                           LineTo( hDC, 200, 10 );

                           if ( rect.bottom < 200 )
                              RaiseException( 1, 0, 0, NULL );

                           LineTo( hDC, 200, 200 );

                           // close final figure
                           // and end the path.
                           //..................
                           CloseFigure( hDC );
                           EndPath( hDC );
```

continued on next page

continued from previous page

```
                        // Outline the path so it is visible.
                        //...................................
                        StrokePath( hDC );
                    }
                    except( EXCEPTION_EXECUTE_HANDLER )
                    {
                        AbortPath( hDC );
                    }
                }

                ReleaseDC( hWnd, hDC );
            }
            break;
```

.
.
.

AngleArc   ■ WINDOWS 95   ■ WINDOWS NT

Description   AngleArc draws a line segment and an arc. The line segment is drawn from the current position to the beginning of the arc. The arc is drawn along the perimeter of a circle with the given radius and center. The length of the arc is defined by the given start and sweep angles.

Syntax   BOOL **AngleArc**(HDC *hDC,* int *x,* int *y,* DWORD *dwRadius,* FLOAT *fStartAngle,* FLOAT *fSweepAngle*)

Parameters

hDC   HDC: The device context.

x   int: The logical x coordinate of the center of the circle.

y   int: The logical y coordinate of the center of the circle.

dwRadius   DWORD: The radius, in logical units, of the circle. This value must be positive.

fStartAngle   FLOAT: The start angle, in degrees, relative to the x-axis.

fSweepAngle   FLOAT: The sweep angle, in degrees, relative to the starting angles.

Returns   BOOL: If successful, TRUE is returned; otherwise, FALSE is returned.

Include File   wingdi.h

See Also   Arc, ArcTo, MoveToEx

Example   This example uses the **AngleArc** function to draw two-thirds of a pie segment. The **LineTo** function finishes the pie segment.

```
LRESULT CALLBACK WndProc( HWND hWnd, UINT uMsg, WPARAM wParam, LPARAM lParam )
{
    switch( uMsg )
    {
        case WM_COMMAND :
                switch( LOWORD( wParam ) )
                {
```

```
case IDM_TEST :
    {
        HDC  hDC = GetDC( hWnd );

        MoveToEx( hDC, 50, 100, NULL );
        AngleArc( hDC, 150, 150, 100, 10.5F, 40.75F );
        LineTo( hDC, 50, 100 );
        ReleaseDC( hWnd, hDC );
    }
    break;
```

.
.
.

Arc

Description	Arc draws an elliptical arc contained within the given rectangle, starting and ending at the given points. On Windows NT the arc is drawn in the current arc direction set with **SetArcDirection** using the current pen, but is not filled. On Windows 95, the arc is always drawn in the counterclockwise direction. The start and end points do not have to lie on the arc. Windows calculates a line from the specified point to the center of the bounding rectangle and uses the arc's intersection with this line. The sum of the bounding rectangle coordinates cannot exceed 32,767 on Windows 95.
Syntax	BOOL **Arc**(HDC *hDC,* int *nLeft,* int *nTop,* int *nRight,* int *nBottom,* int *nStartX,* int *nStartY,* int *nEndX,* int *nEndY*);
Parameters	
hDC	HDC: Specifies the device context that the arc is to be drawn in.
nLeft	int: Specifies the x coordinate of the upper-left corner of the bounding rectangle.
nTop	int: Specifies the y coordinate of the upper-left corner of the bounding rectangle.
nRight	int: Specifies the x coordinate of the lower-right corner of the bounding rectangle.
nBottom	int: Specifies the y coordinate of the lower-right corner of the bounding rectangle.
nStartX	int: Specifies the x coordinate of the starting point for the arc.
nStartY	int: Specifies the y coordinate of the starting point for the arc.
nEndX	int: Specifies the x coordinate of the ending point for the arc.
nEndY	int: Specifies the y coordinate of the ending point for the arc.
Returns	BOOL: Returns TRUE if successful; otherwise, FALSE is returned.
Include File	wingdi.h

See Also AngleArc, ArcTo, Chord, Ellipse, SetArcDirection

Example The following example draws the upper quarter of a circle, as shown in Figure 15-1, defined by the specified rectangle when the user selects the Test! menu item.

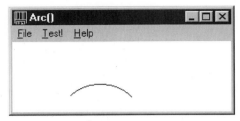

Figure 15-1 Arc example

```
LRESULT CALLBACK WndProc( HWND hWnd, UINT uMsg, WPARAM wParam, LPARAM lParam )
{
   switch( uMsg )
   {
   case WM_COMMAND :
         switch( LOWORD( wParam ) )
         {
            case IDM_TEST :
                {
                   HDC   hDC = GetDC( hWnd );

                   Arc( hDC, 50, 50, 150, 150, 150, 50, 50, 50 );
                   ReleaseDC( hWnd, hDC );
                }
                break;
             .
             .
             .
```

ArcTo   ■ WINDOWS 95   ■ WINDOWS NT

Description ArcTo draws an elliptical arc contained within the given rectangle, starting and ending at the given points. The arc is drawn in the current arc direction set with SetArcDirection using the current pen, but is not filled. On Windows 95, the arc is always drawn in the counterclockwise direction. The start and end points do not have to lie on the arc. Windows calculates a line from the specified point to the center of the bounding rectangle and uses the arc's intersection with this line. The current position is moved to the end of the arc.

Syntax BOOL **ArcTo**(HDC *hDC*, int *nLeft*, int *nTop*, int *nRight*, int *nBottom*, int *nStartX*, int *nStartY*, int *nEndX*, int *nEndY*)

Parameters

hDC	HDC: Specifies the device context that the arc is to be drawn in.
nLeft	int: Specifies the x coordinate of the upper-left corner of the bounding rectangle.
nTop	int: Specifies the y coordinate of the upper-left corner of the bounding rectangle.
nRight	int: Specifies the x coordinate of the lower-right corner of the bounding rectangle.
nBottom	int: Specifies the y coordinate of the lower-right corner of the bounding rectangle.
nStartX	int: Specifies the x coordinate of the starting point for the arc.
nStartY	int: Specifies the y coordinate of the starting point for the arc.
nEndX	int: Specifies the x coordinate of the ending point for the arc.
nEndY	int: Specifies the y coordinate of the ending point for the arc.
Returns	BOOL: Returns TRUE if successful; otherwise, FALSE is returned.
Include File	wingdi.h
See Also	AngleArc, Arc, SetArcDirection
Example	This function is identical to the Arc function, except that when ArcTo is used in place of the Arc function, the current position is moved to the end of the arc. See the example for the Arc function.

BeginPaint   ■ WINDOWS 95   ■ WINDOWS NT

Description	BeginPaint initiates the window painting process by allocating a device context and returning information about the update region. This function is used in response to the WM_PAINT message. When BeginPaint is called, Windows assumes that the update region has been repainted and sets the update region to an empty region.
Syntax	HDC **BeginPaint**(HWND *hWnd,* LPPAINTSTRUCT *lpPaintStruct*)

Parameters

hWnd	HWND: Window handle of the window to be painted.
lpPaintStruct	LPPAINTSTRUCT: A pointer to a PAINTSTRUCT structure. Windows will fill in this structure with information about the update region of the specified window. See the definition of the PAINTSTRUCT structure below.
Returns	HDC: If successful, a handle to a device context that should be used in painting the window is returned; otherwise, NULL is returned.
Include File	winuser.h

See Also   EndPaint

Related Messages   WM_PAINT

PAINTSTRUCT Definition

```
typedef struct tagPAINTSTRUCT
{
    HDC   hdc;
    BOOL  fErase;
    RECT  rcPaint;
    BOOL  fRestore;
    BOOL  fIncUpdate;
    BYTE  rgbReserved[32];
} PAINTSTRUCT;
```

Members

hdc   HDC: The device context to use for painting.

fErase   BOOL: A nonzero value if the background must be erased. The application
                    is responsible for erasing the background if the window was created with-
                    out a background brush.

rcPaint   RECT: The bounding rectangle of the area that is requested to be updated.

fRestore   BOOL: Reserved.

fIndUpdate   BOOL: Reserved.

rgbReserved   BYTE[32]: Reserved.

Example   The following example demonstrates the use of the **BeginPaint** and
                    EndPaint functions by painting a rectangle on the client area of the win-
                    dow when the **WM_PAINT** message is received.

```
LRESULT CALLBACK WndProc( HWND hWnd, UINT uMsg, WPARAM wParam, LPARAM lParam )
{
    switch( uMsg )
    {
        case WM_PAINT :
            {
                PAINTSTRUCT ps;

                // Begin Painting.
                //................
                BeginPaint( hWnd, &ps );

                // Paint the client area.
                //......................
                Rectangle( ps.hdc, 10, 10, 100, 100 );

                // End Painting.
                //.............
                EndPaint( hWnd, &ps );
            }
            break;

            .
            .
            .
```

BeginPath

Description	BeginPath begins a path definition. The path is terminated by calling either **EndPath** or **AbortPath**. Once a path definition has been started, the GDI functions listed in the See Also below are considered part of the path.
Syntax	BOOL **BeginPath**(HDC *hDC*)
Parameters	
hDC	HDC: Specifies the device context that the path is to be used in.
Returns	BOOL: Returns **TRUE** if successful; otherwise, **FALSE** is returned.
Include File	wingdi.h
See Also	AngleArc, Arc, ArcTo, Chord, CloseFigure, Ellipse, EndPath, ExtTextOut, LineTo, MoveToEx, Pie, PolyBezier, PolyBezierTo, Polygon, Polyline, PolylineTo, PolyPolygon, PolyPolyline, Rectangle, RoundRect, TextOut
Example	See **AbortPath** for an example of this function.

Chord

Description	Chord draws a chord, using the current pen. The chord is filled in with the current brush. A chord is the region bounded by an ellipse and a line segment. The ellipse is specified by using a rectangle.
Syntax	BOOL **Chord**(HDC *hDC,* int *nLeft,* int *nTop,* int *nRight,* int *nBottom,* int *nXRadial1,* int *nYRadial1,* int *nXRadial2,* int *nYRadial2*)
Parameters	
hDC	HDC: Specifies the device context that the chord is to be drawn in.
nLeft	int: Specifies the x coordinate of the upper-left corner of the bounding rectangle.
nTop	int: Specifies the y coordinate of the upper-left corner of the bounding rectangle.
nRight	int: Specifies the x coordinate of the lower-right corner of the bounding rectangle.
nBottom	int: Specifies the y coordinate of the lower-right corner of the bounding rectangle.
nXRadial1	int: Specifies the x coordinate of the first radial's endpoint.
nYRadial1	int: Specifies the y coordinate of the first radial's endpoint.
nXRadial2	int: Specifies the x coordinate of the second radial's endpoint.
nYRadial2	int: Specifies the y coordinate of the second radial's endpoint.

Returns   BOOL: Returns TRUE if successful; otherwise, FALSE is returned.

Include File   wingdi.h

See Also   AngleArc, Arc, ArcTo, Pie

Example   The following example draws the bottom half of a circle, as shown in Figure 15-2, with the Chord function when the user selects the Test! menu item.

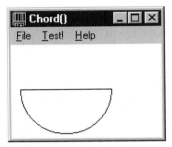

Figure 15-2 Chord example

```
LRESULT CALLBACK WndProc( HWND hWnd, UINT uMsg, WPARAM wParam, LPARAM lParam )
{
    switch( uMsg )
    {
    case WM_COMMAND :
            switch( LOWORD( wParam ) )
            {
            case IDM_TEST :
                {
                    HDC  hDC = GetDC( hWnd );

                    Chord( hDC, 10, 0, 110, 100, // The bounding rectangle.
                               10, 50,          // The endpoint of the start of the
arc
                               110, 50 );       // The endpoint of the end of the arc

                    ReleaseDC( hWnd, hDC );
                }
                break;
            .
            .
            .
```

CloseFigure   ■ WINDOWS 95   ■ WINDOWS NT

Description   The CloseFigure function closes the figure in the currently open path by drawing a line from the current position to the first point of the figure. The end of the line is joined to the figure using the current line-join style.

Syntax	BOOL **CloseFigure**(HDC *hDC*)
Parameters	
hDC	HDC: Specifies the device context of the figure that is to be closed.
Returns	BOOL: Returns TRUE if successful; otherwise, FALSE is returned.
Include File	wingdi.h
See Also	AbortPath, BeginPath, EndPath
Example	See AbortPath for an example of this function.

CombineRgn   ■ WINDOWS 95   ■ WINDOWS NT

Description	The CombineRgn function combines two existing regions to produce a third region. The handle of the resulting region must already have been created, and the region it represents is replaced by the new region.
Syntax	int **CombineRgn**(HRGN *hDest,* HRGN *hSource1,* HRGN *hSource2,* int *nMode*)
Parameters	
hDest	HRGN: A handle to a region. If this function is successful, this region will be set to the combined regions of *hSource1* and *hSource2*.
hSource1	HRGN: A handle to a region. This region is combined with *hSource2* to create *hDest*.
hSource2	HRGN: A handle to a region. This region is combined with *hSource1* to create *hDest*.
nMode	int: Specifies the combine mode, which can be one of the values listed in Table 15-3.

Table 15-3 Mode values for CombineRgn

Mode	Description
RGN_AND	The destination region is the intersection of the two regions.
RGN_COPY	The destination region is a copy of region *hSource1*.
RGN_DIFF	The destination region is that part of *hSource1* that is not also part of *hSource2*.
RGN_OR	The destination region is the union of the two regions.
RGN_XOR	The destination region is the union of the two regions, excluding any portion where the two regions overlap.

Returns	int: The return value can be one of the values specified in Table 15-4.

Table 15-4 Return values for CombineRgn

Return Value	Description
NULLREGION	The region is empty.
SIMPLEREGION	The region is a simple rectangle.
COMPLEXREGION	The region is more than a simple rectangle.
ERROR	No region was created.

Include File	wingdi.h
See Also	CreateEllipticRgn, CreateEllipticRgnIndirect, CreatePolygonRgn, CreatePolyPolygonRgn, CreateRectRgn, CreateRectRgnIndirect, CreateRoundRectRgn, ExtCreateRegion, SetRectRgn
Example	The following example creates three regions. The first region is rectangular, the second is elliptic, and the third is a polygon. The rectangular and elliptic regions are combined to create a new region. The polygon region is then combined with the results to form a region that contains all three regions. Finally, the resulting region is filled with a hatched brush, and all objects are deleted. The resulting figure is shown in Figure 15-3.

```
LRESULT CALLBACK WndProc( HWND hWnd, UINT uMsg, WPARAM wParam, LPARAM lParam )
{
   switch( uMsg )
   {
      case WM_COMMAND :
             switch( LOWORD( wParam ) )
                {
                 case IDM_TEST :
                    {
                        POINT     ptArray[3];
                        HRGN      Rgn1, Rgn2, Rgn3, Rgn4;
                        LOGBRUSH  lb;
                        HBRUSH    hBrush;
                        HDC       hDC = GetDC( hWnd );

                        // Create a rectangular region.
                        //............................
                        Rgn1 = CreateRectRgn( 10, 10, 110, 110 );

                        // Create an elliptic region.
                        //...........................
                        Rgn2 = CreateEllipticRgn( 60, 60, 160, 160 );

                        // Create a polygonal region consisting of three points.
                        //......................................................
                        ptArray[0].x = 10;  ptArray[0].y = 160;
                        ptArray[1].x = 60;  ptArray[1].y = 60;
                        ptArray[2].x = 110; ptArray[2].y = 160;
                        Rgn3 = CreatePolygonRgn( ptArray,
                                          sizeof(ptArray)/sizeof(POINT), ALTERNATE⇐
);
```

```
                // Create a dummy region to combine into.
                //....................................
                Rgn4 = CreateRectRgn( 0, 0, 10, 10 );

                // Combine the elliptic and rectangular regions.
                //.............................................
                CombineRgn( Rgn4, Rgn2, Rgn1, RGN_OR );

                // Combine the results with the polygon region.
                //............................................
                CombineRgn( Rgn4, Rgn4, Rgn3, RGN_OR );

                // Now create a hatched brush and draw the resulting region.
                //..........................................................
                lb.lbStyle = BS_HATCHED;
                lb.lbColor = RGB(0, 0, 0);
                lb.lbHatch = HS_DIAGCROSS;
                hBrush = CreateBrushIndirect( &lb );

                FillRgn( hDC, Rgn4, hBrush );

                //  Finally, delete all created GDI objects.
                //.........................................
                DeleteObject( hBrush );
                DeleteObject( Rgn1 );
                DeleteObject( Rgn2 );
                DeleteObject( Rgn3 );
                DeleteObject( Rgn4 );

                ReleaseDC( hWnd, hDC );
        }
        break;
            .
            .
            .
```

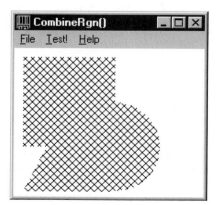

Figure 15-3 CombineRgn example

CopyRect

Description   CopyRect copies the coordinates of a source rectangle to a destination rectangle.

Syntax   BOOL **CopyRect**(LPRECT *lpDest,* LPRECT *lpSource*)

Parameters

lpDest   LPRECT: A pointer to a RECT structure that will receive the coordinates of the source rectangle.

lpSource   LPRECT: A pointer to a RECT structure that will provide the coordinates for the destination rectangle.

Returns   BOOL: Returns TRUE if successful; otherwise FALSE is returned.

Include File   winuser.h

See Also   InflateRect, InvertRect, SetRect, SetRectEmpty, SubtractRect, UnionRect

Example   The following example creates a rectangle, and then copies that rectangle. The copy of the rectangle is then expanded and offset to a new location with the InflateRect and OffsetRect functions.

```
LRESULT CALLBACK WndProc( HWND hWnd, UINT uMsg, WPARAM wParam, LPARAM lParam )
{
    switch( uMsg )
    {
        case WM_COMMAND :
            switch( LOWORD( wParam ) )
            {
                case IDM_TEST :
                    {
                        RECT Rect1, Rect2;
                        HDC  hDC = GetDC( hWnd );

                        // Create first rectangle.
                        //.......................
                        SetRect( &Rect1, 10, 10, 110, 110 );

                        // Create second rectangle.
                        //.........................
                        CopyRect( &Rect2, &Rect1 );
                        InflateRect( &Rect2, 10, -10 );
                        OffsetRect( &Rect2, 20, 10 );

                        FillRect( hDC, &Rect1, GetStockObject( LTGRAY_BRUSH ) );
                        FillRect( hDC, &Rect2, GetStockObject( DKGRAY_BRUSH ) );

                        ReleaseDC( hWnd, hDC );
                    }
                    break;
```

CreateBrushIndirect ■ WINDOWS 95 ■ WINDOWS NT

Description	CreateBrushIndirect creates a logical brush, given a **LOGBRUSH** structure that specifies the style, color, etc.
Syntax	HBRUSH **CreateBrushIndirect**(LOGBRUSH* *lpLogBrush*)
Parameters	
lpLogBrush	LOGBRUSH*: A pointer to a **LOGBRUSH** structure. See the definition of the **LOGBRUSH** structure below.
Returns	HBRUSH: Returns the handle of the created brush if successful; otherwise, **NULL** is returned.
Include File	wingdi.h
See Also	CreateDIBPatternBrushPt, CreateHatchBrush, CreatePatternBrush, CreateSolidBrush, GetStockObject

LOGBRUSH Definition

```
typedef struct tagLOGBRUSH
{
        UINT     lbStyle;
        COLORREF lbColor;
        LONG     lbHatch;
} LOGBRUSH;
```

Members

lbStyle　　　　　　　　UINT: The brush style. This must be one of the values listed in Table 15-5.

Table 15-5 LOGBRUSH *lbStyle* values

Value	Description
BS_DIBPATTERN	A pattern brush defined by a device-independent bitmap (DIB) specification. If *lbStyle* is BS_DIBPATTERN, the *lbHatch* member contains a handle to a DIB. Windows 95 does not support creating brushes from bitmaps larger than 8×8 pixels.
BS_DIBPATTERN8X8	Same as BS_DIBPATTERN.
BS_DIBPATTERNPT	A pattern brush defined by a device-independent bitmap (DIB) specification. The *lbHatch* member contains a pointer to a DIB.
BS_HATCHED	Hatched brush.
BS_HOLLOW	Hollow brush.
BS_NULL	Same as BS_HOLLOW.
BS_PATTERN	Pattern brush defined by a memory bitmap.
BS_PATTERN8X8	Same as BS_PATTERN.
BS_SOLID	Solid brush.

lbColor	COLORREF: The color of the brush. If *lbStyle* is set to BS_HOLLOW or BS_PATTERN, this parameter is ignored. If *lbStyle* is set to BS_DIBPATTERN or BS_DIBPATTERNPT, the low-order word of *lbColor* is set to DIB_PAL_COLORS or DIB_RGB_COLORS. DIB_PAL_COLORS indicates that the DIB contains an array of 16-bit indices into the currently realized logical palette. DIB_RGB_COLORS indicates the DIB contains literal RGB color values.
lbHatch	LONG: The hatch style of the brush. If *lbStyle* is set to BS_DIBPATTERN, this member is set to the handle to the DIB. If *lbStyle* is set to BS_DIBPATTERNPT, this member is set to the pointer of the DIB. If *lbStyle* is set to BS_PATTERN, this member is set to the handle of the pattern bitmap. If the *lbStyle* is set to BS_HATCHED, this member can be one of the values listed in Table 15-6.
Example	See CombineRgn for an example of this function.

CreateDIBPatternBrushPt ■ WINDOWS 95 ■ WINDOWS NT

Description	CreateDIBPatternBrushPt creates a logical brush that is built from the given device-independent bitmap.
Syntax	HBRUSH **CreateDIBPatternBrushPt**(LPVOID *lpDIBData,* UINT *uColorSpec*)
Parameters	
lpDIBData	LPVOID: A pointer to a memory block. This memory block should contain a BITMAPINFO structure, immediately followed by the pixel color data. See the definition of the BITMAPINFO structure under the CreateDIBitmap function in Chapter 13, Bitmaps, Icons, and Metafiles.
uColorSpec	UINT: Contains either DIB_PAL_COLORS or DIB_RGB_COLORS. DIB_PAL_COLORS specifies that the pixel color data in the *bmiColors* table contains indexes into the currently selected palette. DIB_RGB_COLORS specifies that the pixel color data in the *bmiColors* table contains RGB color information.
Returns	HBRUSH: If successful, the handle of the new brush is returned; otherwise, NULL is returned.
Include File	wingdi.h
See Also	CreateBrushIndirect, CreateHatchBrush, CreatePatternBrush, CreateSolidBrush, GetStockObject
Example	The following example illustrates the use of the CreateDIBPatternBrushPt function. When the user selects the Test! menu item, a DIB is loaded and used with the CreateDIBPatternBrushPt function to create a brush. The client area of the window is then filled with the new brush.

```
LRESULT CALLBACK WndProc( HWND hWnd, UINT uMsg, WPARAM wParam, LPARAM lParam )
{
    switch( uMsg )
    {
        case WM_COMMAND :
                switch( LOWORD( wParam ) )
                {
                    case IDM_TEST :
                        {
                            HDC      hDC;
                            HRSRC    hRes;
                            HGLOBAL  hgRes;
                            LPVOID   lpRes;
                            HBRUSH   hBrush;
                            RECT     rect;

                            hDC     = GetDC( hWnd );

                            // Find, Load, and Lock the DIB.
                            //.............................
                            hRes    = FindResource( hInst, "BRUSH", RT_BITMAP );
                            hgRes   = LoadResource( hInst, hRes );
                            lpRes   = LockResource( hgRes );

                            // Create a brush from the DIB.
                            //.............................
                            hBrush = CreateDIBPatternBrushPt( lpRes, DIB_RGB_COLORS );

                            // Fill the client area with the new brush.
                            //.........................................
                            GetClientRect( hWnd, &rect );
                            FillRect( hDC, &rect, hBrush );

                            DeleteObject( hBrush );
                            ReleaseDC( hWnd, hDC );
                        }
                        break;
```

CreateEllipticRgn   ■ Windows 95   ■ Windows NT

Description   CreateEllipticRgn creates a region based on an ellipse defined by the given rectangle.

Syntax   HRGN **CreateEllipticRgn**(int *nLeft,* int *nRight,* int *nTop,* int *nBottom*)

Parameters

nLeft   int: Specifies the x coordinate of the upper-left corner of the bounding rectangle.

nRight   int: Specifies the x coordinate of the lower-right corner of the bounding rectangle.

nTop	**int**: Specifies the y coordinate of the upper-left corner of the bounding rectangle.
nBottom	**int**: Specifies the y coordinate of the lower-right corner of the bounding rectangle.
Returns	**HRGN**: If successful, the handle of the created region is returned; otherwise, **NULL** is returned.
Include File	wingdi.h
See Also	CombineRgn, CreateEllipticRgnIndirect, CreatePolygonRgn, CreatePolyPolygonRgn, CreateRectRgn, CreateRectRgnIndirect, CreateRoundRectRgn, ExtCreateRegion, SetRectRgn
Example	See **CombineRgn** for an example of this function.

CreateEllipticRgnIndirect ■ WINDOWS 95 ■ WINDOWS NT

Description	**CreateEllipticRgnIndirect** creates a region based on the ellipse defined by the given rectangle.
Syntax	HRGN **CreateEllipticRgnIndirect**(LPRECT *lpRect*)
Parameters	
lpRect	**LPRECT**: A pointer to a **RECT** structure that defines the bounding rectangle.
Returns	**HRGN**: If successful, the handle of the created region is returned; otherwise, **NULL** is returned.
Include File	wingdi.h
See Also	CombineRgn, CreateEllipticRgn, CreatePolygonRgn, CreatePolyPolygonRgn, CreateRectRgn, CreateRectRgnIndirect, CreateRoundRectRgn, ExtCreateRegion, SetRectRgn
Example	The following example creates a rectangle, using the **SetRect** function, then creates an elliptic and rectangular region based on this rectangle, and fills the regions when the user selects the Test! menu item.

```
LRESULT CALLBACK WndProc( HWND hWnd, UINT uMsg, WPARAM wParam, LPARAM lParam )
{
    switch( uMsg )
    {
      case WM_COMMAND :
            switch( LOWORD( wParam ) )
              {
                case IDM_TEST :
                      {
                          HDC  hDC;
                          RECT rect;
                          HRGN hElRgn, hRectRgn;

                          hDC = GetDC( hWnd );
```

```
        // Create a regions from a RECT structure.
        //.........................................
        SetRect( &rect, 10, 10, 110, 110 );
        hElRgn   = CreateEllipticRgnIndirect( &rect );
        hRectRgn = CreateRectRgnIndirect( &rect );

        FillRgn( hDC, hRectRgn, GetStockObject( BLACK_BRUSH ) );
        FillRgn( hDC, hElRgn, GetStockObject( GRAY_BRUSH ) );

        DeleteObject( hElRgn );
        DeleteObject( hRectRgn );
        ReleaseDC( hWnd, hDC );
    }
    break;
```

.
.
.

CreateHatchBrush ■ WINDOWS 95 ■ WINDOWS NT

Description	CreateHatchBrush creates a logical brush using the given color and hatch pattern specifications.
Syntax	HBRUSH **CreateHatchBrush**(int *nHatchPattern,* COLORREF *crColor*)
Parameters	
nHatchPattern	int: Specifies the hatch pattern. This value can be one of the pattern specification values listed in Table 15-6.
crColor	COLORREF: Defines the color of the resulting brush.

Table 15-6 Pattern specification values for CreateHatchBrush

Pattern	Description
HS_BDIAGONAL	Specifies a hatch pattern running from the upper-left to the lower-right at a 45-degree angle.
HS_CROSS	Specifies a hatch pattern consisting of both horizontal and vertical lines.
HS_DIAGCROSS	Specifies a hatch pattern similar to HS_CROSS but rotated 45 degrees.
HS_FDIAGONAL	Specifies a hatch pattern running from the lower-left to the upper-right at a 45-degree angle.
HS_HORIZONTAL	Specifies a hatch pattern consisting of horizontal lines.
HS_VERTICAL	Specifies a hatch pattern consisting of vertical lines.

Returns	HBRUSH: If successful, the handle of the new brush is returned. Otherwise, NULL is returned.
Include File	wingdi.h
See Also	CreateBrushIndirect, CreateDIBPatternBrushPt, CreatePatternBrush, CreateSolidBrush, GetStockObject

Example   The following example creates a hatched brush with the
`CreateHatchBrush` function that is identical to the brush created in the
example shown in Figure 15-3. A rectangle is filled with the new brush.

```
LRESULT CALLBACK WndProc( HWND hWnd, UINT uMsg, WPARAM wParam, LPARAM lParam )
{
   switch( uMsg )
   {
      case WM_COMMAND :
              switch( LOWORD( wParam ) )
              {
                 case IDM_TEST :
                     {
                         HDC     hDC;
                         HBRUSH  hBrush;
                         RECT    rect;

                         hDC = GetDC( hWnd );

                         hBrush = CreateHatchBrush( HS_DIAGCROSS, RGB( 0, 0, 0 ) );
                         SetRect( &rect, 10, 10, 110, 110 );
                         FillRect( hDC, &rect, hBrush );

                         DeleteObject( hBrush );
                         ReleaseDC( hWnd, hDC );
                     }
                     break;
```

.
.
.

CreatePatternBrush   ■ WINDOWS 95   ■ WINDOWS NT

Description	CreatePatternBrush creates a logical brush based on the given bitmap. The bitmap may not have been created using `CreateDIBSection`.
Syntax	HBRUSH **CreatePatternBrush**(HBITMAP *hBitmap*)
Parameters	
hBitmap	HBITMAP: The handle of a bitmap that specifies the pattern to be used in creating the logical brush.
Returns	HBRUSH: If successful, the handle of the new brush is returned; otherwise, NULL is returned.
Include File	wingdi.h
See Also	CreateBrushIndirect, CreateDIBPatternBrushPt, CreateHatchBrush, CreateSolidBrush, GetStockObject
Example	The following example creates a brush based on the bitmap identified by the handle *hBitmap*. A red dashed pen is created, and the pen and brush are selected into a device context and used to draw a rectangle.

```
LRESULT CALLBACK WndProc( HWND hWnd, UINT uMsg, WPARAM wParam, LPARAM lParam )
{
    switch( uMsg )
    {
    case WM_COMMAND :
            switch( LOWORD( wParam ) )
            {
                case IDM_TEST :
                    {
                        HDC     hDC;
                        HBRUSH  hBrush;
                        HBITMAP hBitmap, hOldBrush;
                        HPEN    hPen, hOldPen;

                        hDC    = GetDC( hWnd );

                        // Create the brush and pen.
                        //.........................
                        hBitmap = LoadBitmap( hInst, "BRUSH" );
                        hBrush  = CreatePatternBrush( hBitmap );
                        hPen    = CreatePen( PS_DASH, 1, RGB( 255, 0, 0 ) );

                        // Paint a rectangle with the new brush and pen.
                        //..............................................
                        hOldBrush = SelectObject( hDC, hBrush );
                        hOldPen   = SelectObject( hDC, hPen );

                        Rectangle( hDC, 10, 10, 110, 110 );

                        SelectObject( hDC, hOldBrush );
                        SelectObject( hDC, hOldPen );

                        DeleteObject( hBrush );
                        DeleteObject( hPen );
                        DeleteObject( hBitmap );
                        ReleaseDC( hWnd, hDC );
                    }
                    break;
                .
                .
                .
```

CreatePen   ■ WINDOWS 95 ■ WINDOWS NT

Description	The **CreatePen** function creates a logical pen using the specified width, style, and color. The pen can be used when drawing lines and curves.
Syntax	HPEN **CreatePen**(int *nStyle*, int *nWidth*, COLORREF *crColor*)
Parameters	
nStyle	**int**: Specifies a pen style. Use one of the values listed in Table 15-7.
nWidth	**int**: Specifies the width of the resulting pen, in logical units.
crColor	**COLORREF**: Specifies the color of the resulting pen.

Table 15-7 Pen styles for CreatePen

Pen Style	Description
PS_DASH	The line or curve drawn with this pen will be a dashed line. You must specify a pen width that is one or less device units when using this style.
PS_DASHDOT	The line or curve drawn with this pen will consist of alternating dashes and dots. You must specify a pen width that is one or less device units when using this style.
PS_DASHDOTDOT	The line or curve drawn with this pen will consist of alternating dashes and double dots. You must specify a pen width that is one or less device units when using this style.
PS_DOT	The line or curve drawn with this pen will be a dotted line. You must specify a pen width that is one or less device units when using this style.
PS_INSIDEFRAME	The line or curve drawn with this pen will be solid. If the GDI function used to draw with this pen uses a bounding rectangle as one of its parameters, the figure will be shrunk so that it fits entirely within the bounding rectangle after taking into account the width of the pen. This behavior applies only to geometric pens.
PS_NULL	The line or curve drawn with this pen will be invisible.
PS_SOLID	The line or curve drawn with this pen will be solid.

Returns	HPEN: If successful, the handle of the pen is returned; otherwise, NULL is returned.
Include File	wingdi.h
See Also	CreatePenIndirect, GetStockObject
Example	See CreatePatternBrush for an example of this function.

CreatePenIndirect　　　■ WINDOWS 95　■ WINDOWS NT

Description	CreatePenIndirect creates a logical pen based on the LOGPEN structure specified.
Syntax	HPEN **CreatePenIndirect**(LOGPEN* *lpLogPen*)
Parameters	
lpLogPen	LOGPEN*: A pointer to a LOGPEN structure that specifies the width and style of the pen. See the definition of the LOGPEN structure below.
Returns	HPEN: If successful, the handle of the pen is returned; otherwise, NULL is returned.
Include File	wingdi.h
See Also	CreatePen, GetStockObject
LOGPEN Definition	

```
typedef struct tagLOGPEN
{
    UINT     lopnStyle;
    POINT    lopnWidth;
```

```
        COLORREF lopnColor;
    } LOGPEN;
```

Members

lopnStyle
: UINT: The style of the pen to create. This must be one of the values listed in Table 15-7.

lopnWidth
: POINT: A POINT structure that specifies the width of the pen in logical units.

lopnColor
: COLORREF: The color of the pen.

Example
: The following code segment creates a red dashed pen identical to the pen created in the CreatePatternBrush example.

```
LOGPEN lp;
HPEN   hPen;

lp.lopnStyle = PS_DASH;
lp.lopnWidth = 1;
lp.lopnColor = RGB(255, 0, 0);

hPen = CreatePenIndirect( &lp );
```

CreatePolygonRgn ■ WINDOWS 95 ■ WINDOWS NT

Description
: CreatePolygonRgn creates a polygon-shaped region based on the set of points specified.

Syntax
: HRGN **CreatePolygonRgn**(CONST POINT* *lpPoints,* int *nPoints,* int *nFillMode*)

Parameters

lpPoints
: CONST POINT*: Points to an array of POINT structures, each of which defines one point in the polygon.

nPoints
: int: Contains the number of points in the *lpPoints* array.

nFillMode
: int: Specifies the method Windows uses to determine which points are included in the interior of the region. Refer to Table 15-8 for details. These are the same modes used when drawing a polygon on a device context.

Table 15-8 Polygon fill mode values

Fill Mode	Description
ALTERNATE	GDI fills the area between odd-numbered and even-numbered polygon sides on each scan line—that is, GDI fills the area between the first and second side, between the third and fourth side, and so on.
WINDING	GDI fills any region that has a nonzero winding value. This value is defined as the number of times a pen used to draw the polygon would go around the region. The direction of each edge of the polygon is important.

Returns	HRGN: If successful, the handle of the region is returned; otherwise, NULL is returned.
Include File	wingdi.h
See Also	CombineRgn, CreateEllipticRgn, CreateEllipticRgnIndirect, CreatePolyPolygonRgn, CreateRectRgn, CreateRectRgnIndirect, CreateRoundRectRgn, ExtCreateRegion, SetPolyFillMode, SetRectRgn
Example	See CombineRgn for an example of this function.

CreatePolyPolygonRgn ■ WINDOWS 95 ■ WINDOWS NT

Description	CreatePolyPolygonRgn creates a region based on a series of polygons defined by the set of points specified.
Syntax	HRGN **CreatePolyPolygonRgn**(CONST POINT* *lpPoints,* int* *lpPolyPoints,* int *nPoints,* int *nFillMode*)
Parameters	
lpPoints	CONST POINT*: Points to an array of POINT structures, each of which defines one point in the polygon.
lpPolyPoints	int*: Points to an array of integers. Each integer in the array defines the number of points in *lpPoints* used for each of the polygons.
nPoints	int: Contains the number of integers in the *lpPolyPoints* array.
nFillMode	int: Specifies the method Windows uses to determine which points are included in the interior of the region. Refer to Table 15-8 for details. These are the same modes used when drawing a polygon on a device context.
Returns	HRGN: If successful, the handle of the region is returned; otherwise, NULL is returned.
Include File	wingdi.h
See Also	CombineRgn, CreateEllipticRgn, CreateEllipticRgnIndirect, CreatePolygonRgn, CreateRectRgn, CreateRectRgnIndirect, CreateRoundRectRgn, ExtCreateRegion, SetPolyFillMode, SetRectRgn
Example	The following example creates a region that consists of two polygons, the first a triangle and the second a square. Figure 15-4 shows how this region appears when the user selects the Test! menu item and the region is filled.

```
LRESULT CALLBACK WndProc( HWND hWnd, UINT uMsg, WPARAM wParam, LPARAM lParam )
{
    switch( uMsg )
    {
        case WM_COMMAND :
                switch( LOWORD( wParam ) )
                {
                    case IDM_TEST :
                        {
```

```
HDC    hDC;
HRGN   hRgn;
POINT  ptList[7];
int    nVertexCount[2];

hDC      = GetDC( hWnd );

// Initialize values.
//..................
ptList[0].x = 60;  ptList[0].y = 10;
ptList[1].x = 10;  ptList[1].y = 60;
ptList[2].x = 110; ptList[2].y = 60;
ptList[3].x = 160; ptList[3].y = 60;
ptList[4].x = 160; ptList[4].y = 160;
ptList[5].x = 60;  ptList[5].y = 160;
ptList[6].x = 60;  ptList[6].y = 60;

nVertexCount[0] = 3;
nVertexCount[1] = 4;

// Create region and fill it.
//...........................
hRgn = CreatePolyPolygonRgn( ptList, nVertexCount, 2, WINDING );
FillRgn( hDC, hRgn, (HBRUSH)GetStockObject(BLACK_BRUSH) );

DeleteObject( hRgn );
ReleaseDC( hWnd, hDC );
}
break;
```

.
.
.

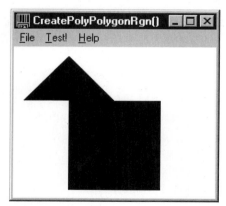

Figure 15-4 CreatePolyPolygonRgn
example

CreateRectRgn ■ WINDOWS 95 ■ WINDOWS NT

Description	`CreateRectRgn` creates a region based on the given rectangle.
Syntax	HRGN **CreateRectRgn**(int *nLeft,* int *nRight,* int *nTop,* int *nBottom*)

Parameters

nLeft
    int: Specifies the x coordinate of the upper-left corner of the bounding rectangle.

nRight
    int: Specifies the x coordinate of the lower-right corner of the bounding rectangle.

nTop
    int: Specifies the y coordinate of the upper-left corner of the bounding rectangle.

nBottom
    int: Specifies the y coordinate of the lower-right corner of the bounding rectangle.

Returns	**HRGN**: If successful, the handle of the created region is returned; otherwise, **NULL** is returned.
Include File	`wingdi.h`
See Also	`CombineRgn`, `CreateEllipticRgn`, `CreateEllipticRgnIndirect`, `CreatePolygonRgn`, `CreatePolyPolygonRgn`, `CreateRectRgnIndirect`, `CreateRoundRectRgn`, `ExtCreateRegion`, `SetRectRgn`
Example	See `CombineRgn` for an example of this function.

CreateRectRgnIndirect ■ WINDOWS 95 ■ WINDOWS NT

Description	`CreateRectRgnIndirect` creates a region based on the given rectangle.
Syntax	HRGN **CreateRectRgnIndirect**(LPRECT *lpRect*)

Parameters

lpRect
    LPRECT: A pointer to a **RECT** structure that defines the bounding rectangle.

Returns	**HRGN**: If successful, the handle of the created region is returned; otherwise, **NULL** is returned.
Include File	`wingdi.h`
See Also	`CombineRgn`, `CreateEllipticRgn`, `CreateEllipticRgnIndirect`, `CreatePolygonRgn`, `CreatePolyPolygonRgn`, `CreateRectRgn`, `CreateRoundRectRgn`, `ExtCreateRegion`, `InvertRgn`, `SetRectRgn`
Example	See `CreateEllipticRgnIndirect` for an example of this function.

CreateRoundRectRgn

■ WINDOWS 95   ■ WINDOWS NT

Description	CreateRoundRectRgn creates a region based on the given rectangle. The corners of the region are rounded.
Syntax	HRGN **CreateRoundRectRgn**(int *nLeft,* int *nRight,* int *nTop,* int *nBottom,* int *nEllipseWidth,* int *nEllipseHeight*)
Parameters	
nLeft	int: Specifies the x coordinate of the upper-left corner of the bounding rectangle.
nRight	int: Specifies the x coordinate of the lower-right corner of the bounding rectangle.
nTop	int: Specifies the y coordinate of the upper-left corner of the bounding rectangle.
nBottom	int: Specifies the y coordinate of the lower-right corner of the bounding rectangle.
nEllipseWidth	int: Defines the width of the ellipse used to create the rounded corners.
nEllipseHeight	int: Defines the height of the ellipse used to create the rounded corners.
Returns	HRGN: If successful, the handle of the created region is returned; otherwise, NULL is returned.
Include File	wingdi.h
See Also	CombineRgn, CreateEllipticRgn, CreateEllipticRgnIndirect, CreatePolygonRgn, CreatePolyPolygonRgn, CreateRectRgn, CreateRectRgnIndirect, ExtCreateRegion, InvertRgn, RoundRect, SetRectRgn
Example	The following example, shown in Figure 15-5, creates a rectangular region with rounded corners and fills the region with a green solid brush when the user selects the Test! menu item.

Figure 15-5 CreateRoundRectRgn example

```
LRESULT CALLBACK WndProc( HWND hWnd, UINT uMsg, WPARAM wParam, LPARAM lParam )
{
   switch( uMsg )
   {
     case WM_COMMAND :
             switch( LOWORD( wParam ) )
             {
               case IDM_TEST :
                   {
                       HDC     hDC;
                       HRGN    hRgn;
                       HBRUSH  hBrush;

                       hDC    = GetDC( hWnd );
                       hBrush = CreateSolidBrush( RGB( 0, 255, 0 ) );
                       hRgn   = CreateRoundRectRgn( 10, 10, 110, 110, 30, 30 );

                       FillRgn( hDC, hRgn, hBrush );

                       DeleteObject( hRgn );
                       DeleteObject( hBrush );
                       ReleaseDC( hWnd, hDC );
                   }
                   break;
                   .
                   .
                   .
```

CreateSolidBrush ■ WINDOWS 95 ■ WINDOWS NT

Description	CreateSolidBrush creates a solid logical brush that has the specified color.
Syntax	HBRUSH **CreateSolidBrush**(COLORREF *crColor*)
Parameters	
crColor	COLORREF: Specifies the RGB values for the brush color.
Returns	HBRUSH: If successful, the handle of the logical brush is returned; otherwise, NULL is returned.
Include File	wingdi.h
See Also	CreateBrushIndirect, CreateHatchBrush, CreatePatternBrush, GetStockObject
Example	See CreateRoundRectRgn for an example of this function.

DeleteObject ■ WINDOWS 95 ■ WINDOWS NT

Description	DeleteObject deletes a logical GDI object. There are many different functions used to create logical GDI objects. All these objects—except those created with GetStockObject—must be deleted using this function. The

objects that should be deleted include pens, bitmaps, brushes, regions, palettes, and fonts. Don't use `DeleteObject` on an object that is currently selected into a device context. Windows 95 will delete an object that is currently selected into a device context, creating a zombie object. Windows NT will fail this call on an object that is currently selected into a device context. If the object being deleted is a pattern brush, the bitmap used to create the brush is not deleted. You must delete the object yourself.

Syntax	BOOL **DeleteObject**(HGDIOBJ *hGdiObject*)
Parameters	
hGdiObject	HGDIOBJ: The handle of a GDI object. This must specify the handle of a pen, bitmap, brush, region, palette, or font. The object must not be currently selected into a device context.
Returns	BOOL: Returns TRUE if successful; otherwise, FALSE is returned.
Include File	wingdi.h
See Also	CreateStockObject
Example	See CombineRgn for an example of this function.

DrawAnimatedRects   ■ WINDOWS 95   ■ WINDOWS NT

Description	DrawAnimatedRects draws a series of rectangles, giving the appearance of a rectangle either opening or closing.
Syntax	BOOL WINAPI **DrawAnimatedRects**(HWND *hWndClip,* int *nAniMode,* LPCRECT *lpRectClosed,* LPCRECT *lpRectOpen*)
Parameters	
hWndClip	HWND: Specifies the handle of a window that will be used to clip the animated rectangles. If this parameter is NULL, then the desktop is used.
nAniMode	int: Specifies the animation mode. The value IDANI_OPEN specifies that the animation moves from closed to open. The value IDANI_CLOSE specifies that the animation moves from open to closed. The value IDANI_CAPTION specifies that the animation rect should include a caption bar.
lpRectClosed	LPCRECT: Points to a rectangle that defines the closed state. This is the starting point when IDANI_OPEN is used and the ending state when IDANI_CLOSE is used.
lpRectOpen	LPCRECT: Points to a rectangle that defines the open state. This is the starting point when IDANI_CLOSE is used, and the ending state when IDANI_OPEN is used.
Returns	BOOL: If successful, returns TRUE. Otherwise, FALSE is returned.
Include File	winuser.h

See Also   DrawCaption

Example   This example animates the closing of a window by drawing successively smaller rectangles and captions, starting with a large rectangle in the upper-left corner of the window, and ending with a rectangle that is the size of the an icon.

```
LRESULT CALLBACK WndProc( HWND hWnd, UINT uMsg, WPARAM wParam, LPARAM lParam )
{
   switch( uMsg )
   {
      case WM_COMMAND :
              switch( LOWORD( wParam ) )
              {
                 case IDM_TEST :
                     {
                         RECT rcStart;
                         RECT rcEnd;

                         GetWindowRect( hWnd, &rcStart );

                         rcEnd.left    = rcStart.right-10;
                         rcEnd.top     = rcStart.bottom-10;
                         rcEnd.right   = rcStart.right;
                         rcEnd.bottom  = rcStart.bottom;

                         DrawAnimatedRects( hWnd, IDANI_CAPTION, &rcStart, &rcEnd );
                     }
                     break;
```

.
.
.

DrawCaption   ■ WINDOWS 95   ■ WINDOWS NT

Description   DrawCaption draws a caption, as is found in the title bar of a normal window.

Syntax   BOOL WINAPI **DrawCaption**(HWND *hWnd,* HDC *hDC,* LPCRECT *lprc,* UINT *uFlags*)

Parameters

hWnd   HWND: The handle to a window that supplies text and an icon for the window caption.

hDC   HDC: The handle of a device context into which the drawing will occur.

lprc   LPRECT: A pointer to a RECT that identifies the bounding rectangle for the caption.

uFlags   UINT: Specifies various drawing flags. This parameter may be set to **0** or a combination of one or more of the values shown in Table 15-9.

Table 15-9 Flag values for `DrawCaption`

Flag Value	Description
DC_ACTIVE	Draws the caption using the colors for an active title bar.
DC_ICON	Draws the icon when drawing the caption text.
DC_INBUTTON	Draws the caption as a button.
DC_SMALLCAP	Draws a small caption.
DC_TEXT	Draws the caption text when drawing the caption.

Returns	BOOL: If successful, TRUE is returned; otherwise, FALSE is returned.
Include File	`winuser.h`
See Also	`DrawEdge`, `DrawAnimatedRects`
Example	This example demonstrates the usage of the **DrawCaption** function to draw a small caption that would be used for tool boxes or other windows with small captions.

```
LRESULT CALLBACK WndProc( HWND hWnd, UINT uMsg, WPARAM wParam, LPARAM lParam )
{
    switch( uMsg )
    {
        case WM_COMMAND :
                switch( LOWORD( wParam ) )
                {
                    case IDM_TEST :
                        {
                            RECT rect;
                            HDC  hDC = GetDC( hWnd );

                            rect.top = 10;
                            rect.left = 10;
                            rect.right = 200;
                            rect.bottom = GetSystemMetrics( SM_CYSMCAPTION )+rect.top;

                            DrawCaption( hWnd, hDC, &rect, DC_ACTIVE | DC_TEXT | DC_SMALLCAP );

                            ReleaseDC( hWnd, hDC );
                        }
                        break;
            .
            .
            .
```

DrawEdge   ■ WINDOWS 95   ■ WINDOWS NT

Description	`DrawEdge` draws one or more edges of a rectangle. The edges are drawn using 3D drawing effects.
Syntax	BOOL **DrawEdge**(HDC *hDC*, LPRECT *lpRect*, UINT *uEdgeType*, UINT *uFlags*)

Parameters

hDC	HDC: Specifies the device context into which the edge is drawn.
lpRect	LPRECT: Specifies the bounding rectangle that defines the edges.
uEdgeType	UINT: Specifies the 3D effect to use on the edge. You must specify either one inner edge flag and one outer edge flag, or one edge type flag. Table 15-10 gives a list of these flags.
uFlags	UINT: Specifies additional drawing flags. Specify one or more of the values in Table 15-11.

Table 15-10 Edge flags used for the *uEdgeType* parameter in DrawEdge

Edge Flag	Description
Inner edge flags	
BDR_RAISEDINNER	Specifies a raised inner edge.
BDR_SUNKENINNER	Specifies a sunken inner edge.
Outer edge flags	
BDR_RAISEDOUTER	Specifies a raised outer edge.
BDR_SUNKENOUTER	Specifies a sunken outer edge.
Edge type flags	
EDGE_BUMP	Equivalent to BDR_RAISEDOUTER and BDR_SUNKENINNER.
EDGE_ETCHED	Equivalent to BDR_SUNKENOUTER and BDR_RAISEDINNER.
EDGE_RAISED	Equivalent to BDR_RAISEDOUTER and BDR_RAISEDINNER.
EDGE_SUNKEN	Equivalent to BDR_SUNKENOUTER and BDR_SUNKENINNER.

Table 15-11 Flag values used for the *uFlags* parameter in DrawEdge

Flag	Description
BF_ADJUST	The rectangle is adjusted to leave room for the client area.
BF_BOTTOM	The bottom edge of the rectangle is drawn.
BF_BOTTOMLEFT	The bottom and left edges of the rectangle are drawn.
BF_BOTTOMRIGHT	The bottom and right edges of the rectangle are drawn.
BF_DIAGONAL	A diagonal edge is drawn.
BF_DIAGONAL_ENDBOTTOMLEFT	A diagonal edge is drawn. The starting point is the top-right corner of the rectangle, and the endpoint is the bottom-left corner of the rectangle.
BF_DIAGONAL_ENDBOTTOMRIGHT	A diagonal edge is drawn. The starting point is the top-left corner of the rectangle, and the endpoint is the bottom-right corner of the rectangle.

Flag	Description
BF_DIAGONAL_ENDTOPLEFT	A diagonal edge is drawn. The starting point is the bottom-right corner of the rectangle, and the endpoint is the top-left corner of the rectangle.
BF_DIAGONAL_ENDTOPRIGHT	A diagonal edge is drawn. The starting point is the bottom-left corner of the rectangle, and the endpoint is the top-right corner of the rectangle.
BF_FLAT	A flat edge is drawn.
BF_LEFT	The left edge of the rectangle is drawn.
BF_MIDDLE	The interior of the rectangle is filled.
BF_MONO	A one-dimensional border is drawn.
BF_RECT	All four edges of the rectangle are drawn.
BF_RIGHT	The right edge of the rectangle is drawn.
BF_SOFT	Soft buttons instead of tiles.
BF_TOP	The top edge of the rectangle is drawn.
BF_TOPLEFT	The top and left edges of the rectangle are drawn.
BF_TOPRIGHT	The top and right edges of the rectangle are drawn.

Returns	BOOL: Returns TRUE if successful; otherwise, FALSE is returned.
Include File	winuser.h
See Also	DrawFocusRect, DrawCaption
Example	The following example draws an edge within the client area of the window. The edge is drawn within a rectangle that is 10 pixels smaller than the client area of the window, and the edge is drawn with an etched appearance.

```
LRESULT CALLBACK WndProc( HWND hWnd, UINT uMsg, WPARAM wParam, LPARAM lParam )
{
    switch( uMsg )
    {
    case WM_PAINT :
            {
                PAINTSTRUCT ps;
                RECT        rcClient;

                BeginPaint( hWnd, &ps );

                // Draw edge
                //..........
                GetClientRect( hWnd, &rcClient );
                InflateRect( &rcClient, -10, -10 );
                DrawEdge( ps.hdc, &rcClient, EDGE_ETCHED, BF_RECT );

                EndPaint( hWnd, &ps );
            }
            break;
            .
            .
            .
```

DrawFocusRect   ■ WINDOWS 95   ■ WINDOWS NT

Description	The rectangle is drawn using an XOR function. To remove the rectangle, simply redraw it in the same position.
Syntax	BOOL **DrawFocusRect**(HDC *hDC,* LPRECT *lpRect*)
Parameters	
hDC	HDC: Specifies the device context into which the rectangle will be drawn.
lpRect	LPRECT: Points to a RECT structure that defines the rectangle to be drawn.
Returns	BOOL: Returns TRUE if successful; otherwise, FALSE is returned.
Include File	winuser.h
See Also	FrameRect
Example	The following example draws a focus rectangle when the user selects the Test! menu item. When the user selects the Test! menu item a second time, the focus rectangle is removed.

```
LRESULT CALLBACK WndProc( HWND hWnd, UINT uMsg, WPARAM wParam, LPARAM lParam )
{
   switch( uMsg )
   {
      case WM_COMMAND :
             switch( LOWORD( wParam ) )
             {
                case IDM_TEST :
                       {
                          RECT rcFocus;
                          HDC  hDC;

                          hDC = GetDC( hWnd );

                          SetRect( &rcFocus, 10, 10, 140, 30 );
                          DrawFocusRect( hDC, &rcFocus );

                          ReleaseDC( hWnd, hDC );
                       }
                       break;
          .
          .
          .
```

DrawFrameControl   ■ WINDOWS 95   ■ WINDOWS NT

Description	DrawFrameControl draws one of several predefined frame controls. You may specify various style flags for the different types of frame controls.
Syntax	BOOL **DrawFrameControl**(HDC *hDC,* LPRECT *lpRect,* UINT *uControlType,* UINT *uControlStyle*)

Parameters

hDC	HDC: Specifies the device context into which the control will be drawn.
lpRect	LPRECT: Points to a RECT structure that defines the bounding rectangle within which the control will be drawn.
uControlType	UINT: Specifies one of the predefined control types described in Table 15-12.
uControlStyle	UINT: Specifies various style flags. The specific style flags depend on the value of *uControlType*. Refer to Table 15-13 for details.

Table 15-12 Control types that may be specified in DrawFrameControl

Control Type	Description
DFC_BUTTON	Draws a button control.
DFC_CAPTION	Draws a window caption.
DFC_MENU	Draws a menu bar.
DFC_SCROLL	Draws a scroll bar.

Table 15-13 Style values for DrawFrameControl

Style Flags	Description
If uControlType is DFC_BUTTON, uControlStyle can be one of the following values:	
DFCS_BUTTON3STATE	Three-state button
DFCS_BUTTONCHECK	Check box
DFCS_BUTTONPUSH	Pushbutton
DFCS_BUTTONRADIO	Radio button
DFCS_BUTTONRADIOIMAGE	Image for radio button (nonsquare needs image)
DFCS_BUTTONRADIOMASK	Mask for radio button (nonsquare needs mask)
If uControlType is DFC_CAPTION, uControlStyle can be one of the following values:	
DFCS_CAPTIONCLOSE	Close button
DFCS_CAPTIONHELP	Help button
DFCS_CAPTIONMAX	Maximize button
DFCS_CAPTIONMIN	Minimize button
DFCS_CAPTIONRESTORE	Restore button
If uControlType is DFC_MENU, uControlStyle can be one of the following values:	
DFCS_MENUARROW	Submenu arrow
DFCS_MENUBULLET	Bullet
DFCS_MENUCHECK	Checkmark

continued on next page

continued from previous page

Style Flags	Description

If uControlType is DFC_SCROLL, uControlStyle can be one of the following values:

DFCS_SCROLLCOMBOBOX	Combo box scroll bar
DFCS_SCROLLDOWN	Down arrow of scroll bar
DFCS_SCROLLLEFT	Left arrow of scroll bar
DFCS_SCROLLRIGHT	Right arrow of scroll bar
DFCS_SCROLLSIZEGRIP	Size grip in bottom-right corner of window
DFCS_SCROLLUP	Up arrow of scroll bar

The following style can be used to adjust the bounding rectangle of the pushbutton:

DFCS_ADJUSTRECT	Bounding rectangle is adjusted to exclude the surrounding edge of the pushbutton.

One or more of the following values can be used to set the state of the control to be drawn:

DFCS_CHECKED	Button is checked.
DFCS_FLAT	Button has a flat border.
DFCS_INACTIVE	Button is inactive (grayed).
DFCS_MONO	Button has a monochrome border.
DFCS_PUSHED	Button is pushed.

Returns	BOOL: Returns TRUE if successful; otherwise, FALSE is returned.
Include File	winuser.h
See Also	FrameRect
Example	The following example draws a frame for a normal pushbutton. Note that only the frame of a pushbutton is drawn; an actual pushbutton window is not created.

```
LRESULT CALLBACK WndProc( HWND hWnd, UINT uMsg, WPARAM wParam, LPARAM lParam )
{
    switch( uMsg )
    {
        case WM_COMMAND :
                switch( LOWORD( wParam ) )
                {
                    case IDM_TEST :
                            {
                                RECT rcButton;
                                HDC  hDC;

                                hDC = GetDC( hWnd );

                                SetRect( &rcButton, 10, 10, 120, 40 );
                                DrawFrameControl( hDC, &rcButton, DFC_BUTTON, DFCS_BUTTONPUSH );

                                ReleaseDC( hWnd, hDC );
                            }
                            break;
```

.
.
.

DrawIcon ■ WINDOWS 95 ■ WINDOWS NT

Description   DrawIcon draws an icon at the specified location within the device context.

Syntax   BOOL **DrawIcon**(HDC *hDC*, int *X*, int *Y*, HICON *hIcon*)

Parameters

hDC   HDC: Specifies the device context into which the control will be drawn.

X   **int**: Specifies the x coordinate in logical units for the upper-left corner of the icon.

Y   **int**: Specifies the y coordinate in logical units for the upper-left corner of the icon.

hIcon   HICON: The handle of the icon to be drawn.

Returns   BOOL: Returns TRUE if successful; otherwise, FALSE is returned.

Include File   winuser.h

See Also   DrawIconEx

Example   The following example loads the application's icon and draws it on the client area when the user selects the Test! menu item. The icon is drawn in its normal size using the **DrawIcon** function and drawn twice its size with the **DrawIconEx** function.

```
LRESULT CALLBACK WndProc( HWND hWnd, UINT uMsg, WPARAM wParam, LPARAM lParam )
{
    switch( uMsg )
    {
    case WM_COMMAND :
            switch( LOWORD( wParam ) )
            {
            case IDM_TEST :
                    {
                        HICON hIcon;
                        HDC   hDC;

                        hDC = GetDC( hWnd );

                        hIcon = LoadIcon( hInst, lpszAppName );
                        DrawIcon( hDC, 10, 10, hIcon );
                        DrawIconEx( hDC, 50, 10, hIcon, 64, 64, 0, NULL, DI_NORMAL );

                        ReleaseDC( hWnd, hDC );
                    }
                    break;
```

.
.

DrawIconEx

Description	DrawIconEx draws an icon at the specified location within the device context. Additionally, the icon may be stretched or compressed, and various raster operations may be applied.
Syntax	BOOL **DrawIconEx**(HDC *hDC,* int *X,* int *Y,* HICON *hIcon,* int *cX,* int *cY,* DWORD *dwRop,* HBRUSH *hBrush,* UINT *uFlags*)
Parameters	
hDC	HDC: Specifies the device context into which the control will be drawn.
X	int: Specifies the x coordinate in logical units for the upper-left corner of the icon.
Y	int: Specifies the y coordinate in logical units for the upper-left corner of the icon.
hIcon	HICON: The handle of the icon to be drawn.
cX	int: Specifies the resulting width of the icon. The icon will be stretched or compressed to this width.
cY	int: Specifies the resulting height of the icon. The icon will be stretched or compressed to this height.
dwRop	DWORD: Specifies the raster operation to perform. The raster operation is used to determine how GDI combines the bitmap of the icon with the colors currently on the device context. If *uFlags* does not include DI_MASK or DI_IMAGE, then this parameter is ignored.
hBrush	HBRUSH: If one of the raster operations specified by *dwRop* requires a brush, the brush identified is used.
uFlags	UINT: Specifies various flags that control the operation of this function. Refer to Table 15-14 for details.

Table 15-14 Flag values for DrawIconEx

Flag	Description
DI_COMPAT	The icon is drawn using the system-defined image, rather than the user-supplied image.
DI_DEFAULTSIZE	The *cX* and *cY* parameters are ignored. The icon is drawn in its original size.
DI_IMAGE	Performs the raster operation defined by *dwRop* on the icon image.
DI_MASK	Performs the raster operation defined by *dwRop* on the icon mask.
DI_NORMAL	This flag is a combination of DI_MASK and DI_IMAGE.

Returns	BOOL: Returns TRUE if successful; otherwise, FALSE is returned.
Include File	winuser.h
See Also	DrawIcon
Example	See the example for the DrawIcon function.

DrawState

Description	DrawState draws an image using various state flags to control the rendering process. In addition, a user-defined callback function can be used to control the drawing of the image.
Syntax	BOOL WINAPI **DrawState**(HDC *hDC,* HBRUSH *hBrush,* DRAWSTATEPROC *fnDrawFunction,* LPARAM *lParam,* WPARAM *wParam,* int *X,* int *Y,* int *cX,* int *cY,* UINT *uFlags*)

Parameters

hDC	HDC: Specifies the device context into which the control will be drawn.
hBrush	HBRUSH: If the *uFlags* parameter includes DSS_MONO, the brush identified by this parameter is used.
fnDrawFunction	DRAWSTATEPROC: Identifies a callback function that may be used to draw the image. If *uFlags* specifies DST_COMPLEX, then this parameter must be specified. If *uFlags* specifies DST_TEXT, then this parameter is optional, and may be NULL. In all other cases this parameter is ignored. See the definition of the callback function below.
lParam	LPARAM: Additional data that depends on the value specified in *uFlags*. Table 15-15 gives details.
wParam	WPARAM: Additional data that depends on the value specified in *uFlags*. Table 15-15 gives details.
X	int: Specifies the x coordinate in logical units for the upper-left corner of the image.
Y	int: Specifies the y coordinate in logical units for the upper-left corner of the image.
cX	int: Specifies the width of the image.
cY	int: Specifies the height of the image.
uFlags	UINT: Specifies various flags that control the operation of this function. Refer to Table 15-15 for details. You must specify one image type flag, and one image state flag.

Table 15-15 Type and state flags for `DrawState`

Flag	Description
Image type flags	
DST_BITMAP	The image to be drawn is a bitmap. The low word of *lParam* contains the bitmap handle.
DST_COMPLEX	This image is a complex image. To render the image, `DrawState` calls the defined callback function. Refer to the example for more details on using this type.
DST_ICON	The image to be drawn is an icon. The low word of *lParam* contains the icon handle.
DST_PREFIXTEXT	Identical to DST_TEXT, except that any ampersand (&) character is interpreted as the standard mnemonic indicator. The character following the ampersand is drawn underlined.
DST_TEXT	The image to be drawn is a text string. *lParam* contains a pointer to the text string, and *wParam* identifies the length of the string. If the length is specified as 0, then the string is assumed to be null terminated.
Image state flags	
DSS_DEFAULT	The image is drawn bold.
DSS_DISABLED	The image is embossed.
DSS_MONO	The image is drawn using the brush identified by the *hBrush* parameter.
DSS_NORMAL	The image is drawn without any modification.
DSS_UNION	The image is dithered.

Returns	BOOL: Returns TRUE if successful; otherwise, FALSE is returned.
Include File	winuser.h
See Also	DrawFrameControl, DrawText
Callback Syntax	BOOL CALLBACK **DrawStateProc**(HDC *hDC*, LPARAM *lData*, WPARAM *wData*, int *cX*, int *cY*)

Callback Parameters

hDC	HDC: The device context in which to draw. This device context is a memory device context with a bitmap selected with dimensions at least as great as those specified by the *cX* and *cY* parameters.
lData	LPARAM: The value passed in the *lParam* parameter of the **DrawState** function.
wData	WPARAM: The value passed in the *wParam* parameter of the **DrawState** function.
cX	int: The *cX* value passed to the **DrawState** function, which specifies the width, in device units, of the image.
cY	int: The *cY* value passed to the **DrawState** function, which specifies the height, in device units, of the image.
Callback Returns	BOOL: Return TRUE if the function succeeds, otherwise, return FALSE.
Example	See the example for the **DrawText** function.

DrawText   ■ Windows 95   ■ Windows NT

Description	DrawText draws the specified text, formatting the output if desired.
Syntax	int **DrawText**(HDC *hDC*, LPSTR *lpTextString,* int *nLength*, LPRECT *lpRect,* UINT *uFlags*)

Parameters

hDC	HDC: Specifies the device context into which the control will be drawn.
lpTextString	LPSTR: A pointer to the string to be drawn.
nLength	int: Specifies the number of characters to draw. If this values is −1, then the string is assumed to be null terminated.
lpRect	LPRECT: Defines the bounding rectangle. The text is formatted within this rectangle.
uFlags	UINT: Specifies various flags that control the formatting process. This parameter may be any combination of the values shown in Table 15-16.

Table 15-16 Flags for DrawText

Flag	Description
DT_BOTTOM	The text is aligned along the bottom of the specified rectangle. DT_SINGLELINE must also be specified.
DT_CALCRECT	The text is not drawn. Instead, DrawText calculates the required size of the rectangle. If the specified text contains multiple lines, then the width of the specified rectangle is used, and the height of the rectangle is increased to accommodate the last line of the text. If there is only one line of text, then the right side of the rectangle is expanded to contain the entire string.
DT_CENTER	Each line of text is centered horizontally within the bounding rectangle.
DT_EDITCONTROL	Duplicates the text-displayed characteristics of a multiline edit control. A partially visible last line is not displayed.
DT_END_ELLIPSIS	
DT_PATH_ELLIPSIS	Replaces part of the given string with ellipses, if necessary, so that the result fits in the specified rectangle. The given string is not modified unless the DT_MODIFYSTRING flag is specified. The DT_END_ELLIPSIS replaces characters at the end of the string, while the DT_PATH_ELLIPSIS replaces characters in the middle of the string, preserving as much as possible of the text after the last backslash (\ ).
DT_EXPANDTABS	Indicates that tab characters within the text string are to be expanded. The default setting for tabs is eight spaces.
DT_EXTERNALLEADING	Includes the font external leading space when calculating line height. Normally, the line height does not include the external leading space.
DT_LEFT	Each line of text is left-justified.
DT_MODIFYSTRING	Modifies the given string to match the displayed text with the DT_END_ELLIPSIS and DT_PATH_ELLIPSIS flags.
DT_NOCLIP	Draws the text without clipping. This allows the operation of DrawText to be somewhat faster.
DT_NOPREFIX	Indicates that ampersand (&) characters within the text are not to be interpreted as prefix characters. Normally, the occurrence of an ampersand causes DrawText to skip the ampersand and underline the character that follows it.
DT_RIGHT	Each line of text is right-justified.

continued on next page

continued from previous page

Flag	Description
DT_RTLREADING	Layout in right-to-left reading order for bidirectional text when the font selected is a Hebrew or Arabic font.
DT_SINGLELINE	Indicates that carriage returns and linefeeds are to be ignored. The text is drawn in a single line.
DT_TABSTOP	Allows changing the default tab setting. Normally, tabs are set at every eight spaces. Using this value, you may change this spacing. The new tab spacing should be placed in the upper eight bits, bits 15–8, of the *uFlags* parameter.
DT_TOP	Indicates that the text is to be aligned along the top edge of the bounding rectangle. DT_SINGLELINE must be specified when using this flag.
DT_VCENTER	Indicates that the text is to be centered vertically within the bounding rectangle. DT_SINGLELINE must be specified when using this flag.
DT_WORDBREAK	Indicates that lines should be broken at the end of the last word that fits horizontally within the rectangle. The text string is continued with the next word on the next line of the rectangle. Carriage returns and linefeeds also break the line.

Returns	**int**: The return value is the height of the formatted text.
Include File	winuser.h
See Also	DrawTextEx, TextOut, ExtTextOut
Example	The following example draws a string of text centered within the window and a disabled text string when the user selects the Test! menu item.

```
LRESULT CALLBACK WndProc( HWND hWnd, UINT uMsg, WPARAM wParam, LPARAM lParam )
{
    switch( uMsg )
    {
      case WM_COMMAND :
            switch( LOWORD( wParam ) )
            {
              case IDM_TEST :
                  {
                     HDC   hDC;
                     RECT  rcClient;

                     hDC = GetDC( hWnd );

                     GetClientRect( hWnd, &rcClient );

                     // Draw Normal Text.
                     //..................
                     DrawText( hDC, "Normal String", 13, &rcClient,
                              DT_SINGLELINE | DT_VCENTER | DT_CENTER );

                     // Draw Disabled Text.
                     //...................
                     DrawState( hDC, NULL, NULL, (LPARAM)"Disabled String", 0,
                              10, 10, 300, 20, DST_TEXT | DSS_DISABLED );

                     ReleaseDC( hWnd, hDC );
                  }
                  break;
```

DrawTextEx ■ WINDOWS 95 ■ WINDOWS NT

Description	DrawTextEx draws the specified text, formatting the output if desired.
Syntax	int **DrawTextEx(** HDC *hDC,* LPSTR *lpTextString,* int *nLength,* LPRECT *lpRect,* UINT *uFlags,* LPDRAWTEXTPARAMS *lpDrawTextParams* **)**
Parameters	
hDC	HDC: Specifies the device context into which the control will be drawn.
lpTextString	LPSTR: A pointer to the string to be drawn.
nLength	int: Specifies the number of characters to draw. If this parameter is −1, then the text string is assumed to be null terminated.
lpRect	LPRECT: Defines the bounding rectangle. The text is formatted within this rectangle.
uFlags	UINT: Specifies various flags that control the formatting process. This parameter may be any combination of the values shown in Table 15-16.
lpDrawTextParams	LPDRAWTEXTPARAMS: A pointer to a **DRAWTEXTPARAMS** structure that contains additional formatting information and return values. This parameter may be **NULL**. See the definition of the **DRAWTEXTPARAMS** structure below.
Returns	int: The return value is the height of the drawn text. Otherwise, **0** is returned.
Include File	winuser.h
See Also	DrawText, TextOut, ExtTextOut

DRAWTEXTPARAMS Definition

```
typedef struct
{
    UINT cbSize;
    int  iTabLength;
    int  iLeftMargin;
    int  iRightMargin;
    UINT uiLengthDrawn;
} DRAWTEXTPARAMS, *LPDRAWTEXTPARAMS;
```

Members	
cbSize	UINT: The size, in bytes, of the structure.
iTabLength	int: The size of each tab stop, in units equal to the average character width.
iLeftMargin	int: The left margin, in units equal to the average character width.
iRightMargin	int: The right margin, in units equal to the average character width.
uiLengthDrawn	UINT: Receives the number of characters processed by **DrawTextEx**, including whitespace characters. The number can be the length of the string or the index of the first line that falls below the drawing area. **DrawTextEx** always processes the entire string if the **DT_NOCLIP** formatting flag is specified.

Example This example demonstrates the **DrawTextEx** function by truncating a long string and placing an ellipsis (…) at the end of the displayable portion of the string. When the user selects the Test! menu item, the long string is displayed on the client area of the window with a bounding rectangle that does not allow the whole string to be displayed.

```
LRESULT CALLBACK WndProc( HWND hWnd, UINT uMsg, WPARAM wParam, LPARAM lParam )
{
   switch( uMsg )
   {
      case WM_COMMAND :
             switch( LOWORD( wParam ) )
             {
                case IDM_TEST :
                       {
                          HDC   hDC;
                          RECT  rcBound;

                          hDC = GetDC( hWnd );

                          SetRect( &rcBound, 10, 10, 100, 30 );
                          DrawTextEx( hDC, "This is a long sample text string.", -1,⇐
&rcBound,
                                    DT_END_ELLIPSIS | DT_SINGLELINE | DT_VCENTER, NULL );

                          ReleaseDC( hWnd, hDC );
                       }
                       break;
                          .
                          .
                          .
```

Ellipse   ■ WINDOWS 95   ■ WINDOWS NT

Description **Ellipse** draws an ellipse that is bounded by the given rectangle. If the rectangle is a perfect square, then the result will be a circle. The ellipse is outlined with the current pen, and filled with the current brush.

Syntax BOOL **Ellipse**(HDC *hDC,* int *nLeft,* int *nTop,* int *nRight,* int *nBottom*)

Parameters

hDC HDC: Specifies the device context that the ellipse is to be drawn in.

nLeft int: Specifies the x coordinate of the upper-left corner of the bounding rectangle.

nTop int: Specifies the y coordinate of the upper-left corner of the bounding rectangle.

nRight int: Specifies the x coordinate of the lower-right corner of the bounding rectangle.

nBottom int: Specifies the y coordinate of the lower-right corner of the bounding rectangle.

Returns	BOOL: Returns TRUE if successful; otherwise, FALSE is returned.
Include File	wingdi.h
See Also	Arc, ArcTo
Example	The following example draws an ellipse that fills the entire client area of the window. Notice that the direction the ellipse is drawn is changed to clockwise from the default with the SetArcDirection function. On Windows 95, this function has no effect.

```
LRESULT CALLBACK WndProc( HWND hWnd, UINT uMsg, WPARAM wParam, LPARAM lParam )
{
   switch( uMsg )
   {
      case WM_PAINT :
              {
                 PAINTSTRUCT ps;
                 RECT        clRect;
                 int         nArcDir;

                 BeginPaint( hWnd, &ps );

                 GetClientRect( hWnd, &clRect );

                 // Get the current arc direction.
                 //................................
                 nArcDir = GetArcDirection( ps.hdc );

                 // Set the arc direction to clockwise.
                 //....................................
                 SetArcDirection( ps.hdc, AD_CLOCKWISE );

                 // Draw the ellipse.
                 //..................
                 Ellipse( ps.hdc, clRect.left, clRect.top,
                                  clRect.right, clRect.bottom );

                 // Restore the arc direction.
                 //...........................
                 SetArcDirection( ps.hdc, nArcDir );

                 EndPaint( hWnd, &ps );
              }
              break;
          .
          .
          .
```

EndPaint ■ WINDOWS 95 ■ WINDOWS NT

Description	EndPaint indicates the end of a painting procedure. It must be used after a BeginPaint, when all painting has been completed. If the caret or cursor was hidden by BeginPaint, then EndPaint will restore it.
Syntax	BOOL **EndPaint**(HWND *hWnd*, LPPAINTSTRUCT *lpPaintStruct*)

Parameters

hWnd	HWND: Window handle of the window to be painted.
lpPaintStruct	LPPAINTSTRUCT: A pointer to a **PAINTSTRUCT** structure. This should be the same structure that was filled in by the call to **BeginPaint**.
Returns	BOOL: This function always returns **TRUE**.
Include File	winuser.h
See Also	BeginPaint
Related Messages	WM_PAINT
Example	See **BeginPaint** or **Ellipse** for an example of this function.

EndPath   ■ WINDOWS 95   ■ WINDOWS NT

Description	EndPath closes the path started with **BeginPath** and selects that path as the current path in a device context.
Syntax	BOOL **EndPath**(HDC *hDC*)
Parameters	
hDC	HDC: Specifies the device context that contains the path to be closed.
Returns	BOOL: Returns **TRUE** if successful; otherwise, **FALSE** is returned.
Include File	wingdi.h
See Also	AbortPath, BeginPath
Example	See **AbortPath** for an example of this function.

EnumObjects   ■ WINDOWS 95   ■ WINDOWS NT

Description	EnumObjects enumerates the pens or brushes available for the given device context. For each pen or brush, the specified user-defined callback routine is called. The callback routine should return **0** to terminate the enumeration and nonzero to continue the enumeration.
Syntax	int **EnumObjects**(HDC *hDC,* int *nObjectType,* GOBJENUMPROC *fnEnumProc,* LPARAM *lParam*)
Parameters	
hDC	HDC: Specifies the device context of the objects to be enumerated.
nObjectType	int: Specifies whether pens or brushes are enumerated. This parameter may be either **OBJ_PEN** or **OBJ_BRUSH**.
fnEnumProc	GOBJENUMPROC: A pointer to a user-defined callback procedure. See the definition of the callback function below.
lParam	LPARAM: This value is an application-defined 32-bit value. It is passed to the procedure defined by *fnEnumProc*.

Returns	**int**: If successful, the last value returned by the callback procedure is returned. Otherwise, −1 is returned.
Include File	`wingdi.h`
See Also	`GetObject`
Callback Syntax	`VOID CALLBACK` **EnumObjectsProc**`( LPVOID` *lpLogObject,* `LPARAM` *lpData* `)`

Callback Parameters

lpLogObject   **LPVOID**: A pointer to a **LOGPEN** or **LOGBRUSH** structure, depending on the value of the *nObjectType* parameter. See the definition of the **LOGBRUSH** structure under the **CreateBrushIndirect** function. See the definition of the **LOGPEN** structure under the **CreatePenIndirect** function.

lpData   **LPARAM**: The application-defined 32-bit value passed to the **EnumObjects** function.

Example   The following example enumerates the logical brushes available in the device context when the user selects the Test! menu item. When the callback is called with a logical brush, it creates a brush of that type and fills a rectangle with the brush.

```
int nHorzPos;

VOID CALLBACK EnumBrushesProc( LPVOID lpObject, LPARAM lParam )
{
    RECT   rcFill;
    HBRUSH hBrush = CreateBrushIndirect( (LPLOGBRUSH)lpObject );

    nHorzPos += 10;

    SetRect( &rcFill, nHorzPos-10, 10, nHorzPos, 50 );
    FillRect( (HDC)lParam, &rcFill, hBrush );

    DeleteObject( hBrush );
}


LRESULT CALLBACK WndProc( HWND hWnd, UINT uMsg, WPARAM wParam, LPARAM lParam )
{
    switch( uMsg )
    {
        case WM_COMMAND :
                switch( LOWORD( wParam ) )
                {
                    case IDM_TEST :
                        {
                            HDC   hDC;

                            hDC = GetDC( hWnd );

                            nHorzPos = 0;
                            EnumObjects( hDC, OBJ_BRUSH,
                                    (GOBJENUMPROC)EnumBrushesProc, hDC );
```

continued on next page

continued from previous page

```
                              ReleaseDC( hWnd, hDC );
                        }
                        break;
```

.
.
.

EqualRect   ■ Windows 95   ■ Windows NT

Description	EqualRect determines if two rectangles are equal by comparing the four coordinates of each rectangle.
Syntax	BOOL **EqualRect**(LPRECT *lpRect1,* LPRECT *lpRect2*)
Parameters	
lpRect1	LPRECT: Specifies a pointer to one of the rectangles.
lpRect2	LPRECT: Specifies a pointer to the other rectangle.
Returns	BOOL: Returns TRUE if the rectangles are equal; otherwise, FALSE is returned.
Include File	winuser.h
See Also	IsRectEmpty, PtInRect
Example	The following code segment checks the two existing rectangles to determine if they are equal and performs different operations, depending on the result.

```
RECT Rect1;
RECT Rect2;

if( !IsRectEmpty(&Rect1) && !IsRectEmpty(&Rect2) )
{
    if(EqualRect(&Rect1, &Rect2))
    {
    //  Rectangles are equal.
    }
    else
    {
    // Rectangles are not equal.
    }
}
else
{
//   One of both of the rectangles is empty.
}
```

EqualRgn   ■ Windows 95   ■ Windows NT

Description	EqualRgn determines if the two given regions are equal. Regions are considered equal if they have the same size and shape.

Syntax	BOOL **EqualRgn**(HRGN *hRegion1*, HRGN *hRegion2*)
Parameters	
hRegion1	HRGN: Specifies the handle of one of the regions to be compared.
hRegion2	HRGN: Specifies the handle of the other region to be compared.
Returns	BOOL: Returns TRUE if the regions are equal; otherwise, FALSE is returned.
Include File	wingdi.h
See Also	CreateRectRgn, CreateRectRgnIndirect
Example	The following code segment checks two existing regions to see if they are equal. Different operations are performed based on the result.

```
HRGN hRegion1;
HRGN hRegion2;

if( EqualRgn(hRegion1, hRegion2) )
{
// Regions are equal
}
else
{
// Regions are not equal
}
```

ExcludeClipRect   ■ WINDOWS 95   ■ WINDOWS NT

Description	**ExcludeClipRect** excludes the specified rectangle from the current clipping region.
Syntax	int **ExcludeClipRect**(HDC *hDC,* int *nLeft,* int *nTop,* int *nRight,* int *nBottom*)
Parameters	
hDC	HDC: Specifies the device context of the clipping region.
nLeft	int: Specifies the x coordinate of the upper-left corner of the bounding rectangle.
nTop	int: Specifies the y coordinate of the upper-left corner of the bounding rectangle.
nRight	int: Specifies the x coordinate of the lower-right corner of the bounding rectangle.
nBottom	int: Specifies the y coordinate of the lower-right corner of the bounding rectangle.
Returns	int: This function returns one of the values specified in Table 15-4.
Include File	wingdi.h

See Also	ExtSelectClipRgn, GetClipBox, GetClipRgn, IntersectClipRect, OffsetClipRgn, SelectClipPath, SelectClipRgn
Example	See the example for the **ExcludeUpdateRgn** function.

ExcludeUpdateRgn   ■ Windows 95   ■ Windows NT

Description	**ExcludeUpdateRgn** removes the current update region from the clipping area of the specified window. This has the effect of preventing future drawing in the invalid area on the device. This function is typically used to exclude the current update region from painting that occurs outside the WM_PAINT message.
Syntax	int **ExcludeUpdateRgn**(HDC *hDC*, HWND *hWindow*)
Parameters	
hDC	HDC: Specifies the device context of the clipping region.
hWindow	HWND: Specifies the window handle of the window to operate on.
Returns	int: This function returns one of the values specified in Table 15-4.
Include File	wingdi.h
See Also	GetUpdateRect, GetUpdateRgn
Example	This example uses the **ExcludeClipRect** function to exclude a portion of the client area during painting. Also, when the user selects the Test! menu item, an area of the client area, which is protected with the **ExcludeUpdateRgn** when an intersecting rectangle is painted, is invalidated.

```
LRESULT CALLBACK WndProc( HWND hWnd, UINT uMsg, WPARAM wParam, LPARAM lParam )
{
   switch( uMsg )
   {
      case WM_PAINT :
              {
                 PAINTSTRUCT ps;
                 RECT         clRect;

                 BeginPaint( hWnd, &ps );

                 GetClientRect( hWnd, &clRect );

                 // Exclude a small rectangle from the paint.
                 //........................................
                 ExcludeClipRect( ps.hdc, 0, 0, 50, 50 );
                 FillRect( ps.hdc, &clRect, GetStockObject( LTGRAY_BRUSH ) );

                 EndPaint( hWnd, &ps );
              }
              break;
```

```
case WM_COMMAND :
    switch( LOWORD( wParam ) )
    {
        case IDM_TEST :
            {
                RECT rect1, rect2;
                HRGN hRgn;
                HDC  hDC;

                // Invalidate a region of the window.
                //.....................................
                SetRect( &rect1, 100, 100, 150, 150 );
                InvalidateRect( hWnd, &rect1, TRUE );

                // Invalidate an intersecting
                // elliptic region of the window.
                //.....................................
                hRgn = CreateEllipticRgn( 80, 80, 130, 130 );
                InvalidateRgn( hWnd, hRgn, TRUE );
                DeleteObject( hRgn );

                hDC = GetDC( hWnd );

                // Exclude the invalidated region of the window.
                //.................................................
                ExcludeUpdateRgn( hDC, hWnd );

                // Draw an intersecting rectangle with
                // the invalid region of the window.
                //.................................
                SetRect( &rect2, 75, 75, 125, 125 );
                FillRect( hDC, &rect2, GetStockObject( GRAY_BRUSH ) );

                ReleaseDC( hWnd, hDC );
            }
            break;
            .
            .
            .
```

ExtCreatePen   ■ WINDOWS 95   ■ WINDOWS NT

Description   ExtCreatePen creates either a cosmetic or geometric logical pen for which
                   you specify the style. With geometric pens, you may specify width, join,
                   and endcap styles. The cosmetic pen is always one device unit wide and
                   does not support endcap and join styles. Drawing with a cosmetic pen is
                   generally faster than using a geometric pen.

Syntax   HPEN **ExtCreatePen**(DWORD *dwPenStyle,* DWORD *dwPenWidth,* CONST
                   LOGBRUSH* *lpLogBrush,* DWORD *dwStyleCount,* DWORD * *lpdwStyleArray*)

Parameters

dwPenStyle	**DWORD**: Specifies various type, style, endcap, and join attributes. Combine one flag from each of the categories using an OR operation. The valid flags are shown in Table 15-17.
dwPenWidth	**DWORD**: Specifies the width of the logical pen. If a geometric pen is used, the width is specified in logical units. If a cosmetic pen is used, the width must be **1**.
lpLogBrush	**CONST LOGBRUSH ***: Points to a **LOGBRUSH** structure. If a geometric pen is used, the attributes from this structure will be used to create the pen. If a cosmetic pen is used, the *lbColor* member specifies the color of the pen, and the *lbStyle* member must be set to **BS_SOLID**. All other members are ignored for cosmetic pens.
dwStyleCount	**DWORD**: If *dwPenStyle* does not include **PS_USERSTYLE**, then this parameter must be **0**. If *dwPenStyle* includes **PS_USERSTYLE**, then this parameter specifies the number of **DWORD** entries that exist in the *lpdwStyleArray* array.
lpdwStyleArray	**DWORD***: A pointer to an array of **DWORD** style values. This parameter must be **NULL** if *dwPenStyle* does not include **PS_USERSTYLE**. Otherwise, the values in the array are interpreted as follows: The first entry is the length of the first dash, the second entry is the length of the first space, the third entry is the length of the second dash, and so on.

Table 15-17 ExtCreatePen *dwPenStyle* values

Flag	Description
The following flags specify the pen type:	
PS_COSMETIC	Creates a cosmetic pen.
PS_GEOMETRIC	Creates a geometric pen.
The following flags specify the pen style:	
PS_ALTERNATE	The line or curve drawn with this pen will have every other pixel set. This style is not supported in Windows 95 and is only valid for cosmetic pens.
PS_DASH	The line or curve drawn with this pen will be a dashed line. You must specify a pen width that is one or less device units when using this style. In Windows 95, this style is not supported for geometric lines.
PS_DASHDOT	The line or curve drawn with this pen will consist of alternating dashes and dots. You must specify a pen width that is one or less device units when using this style. In Windows 95, this style is not supported for geometric lines.
PS_DASHDOTDOT	The line or curve drawn with this pen will consist of alternating dashes and double dots. You must specify a pen width that is one or less device units when using this style. In Windows 95, this style is not supported for geometric lines.
PS_DOT	The line or curve drawn with this pen will be a dotted line. You must specify a pen width that is one or less device units when using this style. In Windows 95, this style is not supported for geometric lines.

Flag	Description

The following flags specify the pen style:

PS_INSIDEFRAME	The line or curve drawn with this pen will be solid. If the GDI function used to draw with this pens uses a bounding rectangle as one of its parameters, the figure will be shrunk so that it fits entirely within the bounding rectangle after taking into account the width of the pen. This behavior applies only to geometric pens.
PS_NULL	The line or curve drawn with this pen will be invisible.
PS_SOLID	The line or curve drawn with this pen will be solid.
PS_USERSTYLE	The line or curve drawn with this pen is based on the values specified in the *lpdwStyleArray* parameter. This style is not supported in Windows 95.

The following flags specify the desired endcap style. These may be used only if PS_GEOMETRIC is also used.

PS_ENDCAP_FLAT	Endcaps are flat.
PS_ENDCAP_ROUND	Endcaps are round.
PS_ENDCAP_SQUARE	Endcaps are square.

The following flags specify the desired join style. These may be used only if PS_GEOMETRIC is also used.

PS_JOIN_BEVEL	Joins are beveled.
PS_JOIN_MITER	Joins are mitered if the miter value falls within the value specified by SetMiterLimit. Otherwise, the joins are beveled.
PS_JOIN_ROUND	Joins are rounded.

Returns   HPEN: If successful, the handle of the logical pen is returned; otherwise, NULL is returned.

Include File   wingdi.h

See Also   CreatePen, CreatePenIndirect, GetStockObject

Example   The following example creates a geometric pen, using rounded endcaps. The pen draws a solid line, using a red solid brush.

```
LRESULT CALLBACK WndProc( HWND hWnd, UINT uMsg, WPARAM wParam, LPARAM lParam )
{
   switch( uMsg )
   {
     case WM_COMMAND :
             switch( LOWORD( wParam ) )
             {
               case IDM_TEST :
                     {
                         HDC      hDC;
                         HPEN     hPen, hOldPen;
                         LOGBRUSH lb;

                         hDC = GetDC( hWnd );

                         // Create a pen.
                         //..............
                         lb.lbStyle = BS_SOLID;
```

continued on next page

continued from previous page

```
        lb.lbColor = RGB( 255, 0, 0 );
        hPen = ExtCreatePen( PS_GEOMETRIC | PS_SOLID |
                             PS_ENDCAP_ROUND,
                             12, &lb, 0, NULL );

        // Select the pen and draw a line.
        //..............................
        hOldPen = SelectObject( hDC, hPen );
        MoveToEx( hDC, 10, 10, NULL );
        LineTo( hDC, 150, 10 );
        SelectObject( hDC, hOldPen );

        DeleteObject( hPen );
        ReleaseDC( hWnd, hDC );
    }
    break;
```

.
.
.

ExtCreateRegion   ■ WINDOWS 95   ■ WINDOWS NT

Description	**ExtCreateRegion** creates a region using the given region data and transformation information.
Syntax	HRGN **ExtCreateRegion**(XFORM* *lpXform,* DWORD *dwRgnCount,* RGNDATA* *lpRgnData*)
Parameters	
lpXform	**XFORM***: A pointer to an **XFORM** structure that defines the desired transformation. If this parameter is **NULL**, then the identity transform is used. See the definition of the **XFORM** structure below.
dwRgnCount	**DWORD**: Specifies the number of bytes pointed to by *lpRgnData*.
lpRgnData	**RGNDATA***: A pointer to a **RGNDATA** structure. This structure contains information that defines how the region is created. See the definition of the **RGNDATA** structure below.
Returns	**HRGN**: Returns the handle to a region if successful; otherwise, **NULL** is returned.
Include File	wingdi.h
See Also	CreateEllipticRgn, CreateEllipticRgnIndirect, CreatePolygonRgn, CreatePolyPolygonRgn, CreateRectRgn, CreateRectRgnIndirect, CreateRoundRectRgn, InvertRgn, SetRectRgn
XFORM Definition	

```
        typedef struct _XFORM
        {
            FLOAT eM11;
            FLOAT eM12;
            FLOAT eM21;
```

```
            FLOAT eM22;
            FLOAT eDx;
            FLOAT eDy;
        } XFORM;
```

Members

eM11   FLOAT: The horizontal scaling component, the cosine rotation angle, or the horizontal component for reflections.

eM12   FLOAT: The sine of the rotation angle or the horizontal proportionality constant for shear operations.

eM21   FLOAT: The negative sine of the rotation angle or the vertical proportionality constant for shear operations.

eM22   FLOAT: The vertical scaling component, the cosine rotation angle, or the vertical reflection component.

eDX   FLOAT: The horizontal translation component.

eDY   FLOAT: The vertical translation component.

RGNDATA Definition

```
typedef struct _RGNDATA
{
    RGNDATAHEADER rdh;
    char          Buffer[1];
} RGNDATA;
```

Members

rdh   RGNDATAHEADER: The members of this structure define the properties of the region. See the definition of the RGNDATAHEADER structure below.

Buffer   char[1]: A buffer that contains the RECT structures that make up region.

RGNDATAHEADER Definition

```
typedef struct _RGNDATAHEADER
{
    DWORD dwSize;
    DWORD iType;
    DWORD nCount;
    DWORD nRgnSize;
    RECT  rcBound;
} RGNDATAHEADER;
```

Members

dwSize   DWORD: The size, in bytes, of the header.

iType   DWORD: The type of region. This must be RDH_RECTANGLES.

nCount   DWORD: The number of rectangles that make up the region.

nRgnSize   DWORD: The size of the buffer required to receive the RECT structures that specify the coordinates of the rectangles that make up the region. If the size is not known, this member can be 0.

rcBound   RECT: The bounding rectangle of the region.

Example   The following example creates a rectangular region and fills it with a black brush. A new region that is 50 percent of the first region is then created with the **ExtCreateRegion** function and filled with a gray brush.

```c
LRESULT CALLBACK WndProc( HWND hWnd, UINT uMsg, WPARAM wParam, LPARAM lParam )
{
    switch( uMsg )
    {
        case WM_COMMAND :
                switch( LOWORD( wParam ) )
                {
                    case IDM_TEST :
                            {
                                LPRGNDATA lpRgn;
                                XFORM     xForm;
                                HDC       hDC;
                                DWORD     dwSize;
                                HRGN      hRgn, hExtRgn;

                                hDC     = GetDC( hWnd );

                                hRgn = CreateRectRgn( 10, 10, 110, 110 );
                                FillRgn( hDC, hRgn, (HBRUSH)GetStockObject(BLACK_BRUSH) );

                                // Get the region data.
                                //....................
                                dwSize = GetRegionData( hRgn, 0, NULL );
                                lpRgn = HeapAlloc( GetProcessHeap(), HEAP_ZERO_MEMORY, dwSize );
                                GetRegionData( hRgn, dwSize, lpRgn );

                                // Scale the region by 50% and fill it with a gray brush.
                                //.......................................................
                                xForm.eM11 = 0.5F;
                                xForm.eM12 = 0.0F;
                                xForm.eM21 = 0.0F;
                                xForm.eM22 = 0.5F;
                                xForm.eDx  = 1.0F;
                                xForm.eDy  = 1.0F;

                                hExtRgn = ExtCreateRegion( &xForm, dwSize, lpRgn );
                                FillRgn( hDC, hExtRgn, (HBRUSH)GetStockObject(GRAY_BRUSH) );

                                DeleteObject( hRgn );
                                DeleteObject( hExtRgn );
                                HeapFree( GetProcessHeap(), 0, lpRgn );

                                ReleaseDC( hWnd, hDC );
                            }
                            break;
```

ExtFloodFill   ■ WINDOWS 95   ■ WINDOWS NT

Description	`ExtFloodFill` fills an area of the given device context using the current brush.
Syntax	BOOL **ExtFloodFill**(HDC *hDC,* int *X,* int *Y,* COLORREF *crColor,* UINT *uFillType*)
Parameters	
hDC	`HDC`: A handle to the device context where the fill is to occur.
X	`int`: Specifies the starting x coordinate, in logical units.
Y	`int`: Specifies the starting y coordinate, in logical units.
crColor	`COLORREF`: Specifies the color that defines the area to be filled. The interpretation of this parameter is dependent on the *uFillType* parameter.
uFillType	`UINT`: This parameter is used to define the area to be filled. Table 15-18 gives the available values for this parameter.

Table 15-18 ExtFloodFill *uFillType* values

Fill Type	Description
FLOODFILLBORDER	The *crColor* parameter specifies a border color. The area within this border is filled. This is identical to the `FloodFill` function.
FLOODFILLSURFACE	The *crColor* parameter specifies a surface color. Filling continues outward in all directions as long as this color is encountered.

Returns	`BOOL`: Returns `TRUE` if successful; otherwise, `FALSE` is returned.
Include File	`wingdi.h`
See Also	`FillRect, FloodFill`
Example	The following example draws a rectangle on the client area. When the user clicks the mouse on the client area, the area is filled with a gray brush. If the area within the rectangle is clicked, only the rectangle is filled.

```
LRESULT CALLBACK WndProc( HWND hWnd, UINT uMsg, WPARAM wParam, LPARAM lParam )
{
   switch( uMsg )
   {
      case WM_PAINT :
            {
                PAINTSTRUCT ps;

                BeginPaint( hWnd, &ps );
                Rectangle( ps.hdc, 10, 10, 110, 110 );
                EndPaint( hWnd, &ps );
            }
            break;
```

continued on next page

continued from previous page

```
case WM_LBUTTONDOWN :
        {
            HBRUSH hOldBrush;
            HDC    hDC = GetDC( hWnd );

            hOldBrush = SelectObject( hDC, GetStockObject(GRAY_BRUSH) );

            ExtFloodFill( hDC, LOWORD(lParam), HIWORD(lParam),
                          RGB(255,255,255), FLOODFILLSURFACE );

            SelectObject( hDC, hOldBrush );

            ReleaseDC( hWnd, hDC );
        }
        break;
            .
            .
            .
```

ExtSelectClipRgn   ■ WINDOWS 95 ■ WINDOWS NT

Description	ExtSelectClipRgn creates a new clipping region by combining the current clipping region with the region specified. In addition, you can control the manner in which GDI combines the two regions.
Syntax	int **ExtSelectClipRgn**(HDC *hDC*, HRGN *hRegion*, int *nCombineMode*)
Parameters	
hDC	HDC: Identifies the device context.
hRegion	HRGN: The handle to a region. This region is combined with the current clipping region using the *nCombineMode* parameter.
nCombineMode	int: Specifies the method that GDI is to use when combining the given region with the current clipping region. You may specify any of the mode values shown in Table 15-3.
Returns	int: The return value is one of the values specified in Table 15-4.
See Also	ExcludeClipRect, GetClipBox, GetClipRgn, IntersectClipRect, OffsetClipRgn, SelectClipPath, SelectClipRgn
Example	The following example creates an elliptic region and rectangular region and sets them as the clipping regions for the device context. The client area of the window is then filled with a gray brush. Only the areas defined by the regions are actually filled.

```
LRESULT CALLBACK WndProc( HWND hWnd, UINT uMsg, WPARAM wParam, LPARAM lParam )
{
    switch( uMsg )
    {
        case WM_COMMAND :
            switch( LOWORD( wParam ) )
            {
```

```
case IDM_TEST :
    {
    HDC  hDC;
    HRGN hRgn1, hRgn2;
    RECT rcClient;

    hDC    = GetDC( hWnd );

    // Create a elliptic and rectangular region and
    // select them as the selected clipping regions.
    //.............................................
    hRgn1 = CreateEllipticRgn( 10, 10, 110, 110 );
    ExtSelectClipRgn( hDC, hRgn1, RGN_COPY );

    hRgn2 = CreateRectRgn( 40, 40, 150, 150 );
    ExtSelectClipRgn( hDC, hRgn2, RGN_OR );

    // Fill the entire client area with gray,
    // only the regions will be filled in.
    //.......................................
    GetClientRect( hWnd, &rcClient );
    FillRect( hDC, &rcClient, GetStockObject(GRAY_BRUSH) );

    DeleteObject( hRgn1 );
    DeleteObject( hRgn2 );
    ReleaseDC( hWnd, hDC );
    }
    break;
```

FillPath ■ WINDOWS 95 ■ WINDOWS NT

Description	FillPath closes any open path, then fills the path using the current brush and polygon fill mode.
Syntax	BOOL **FillPath**(HDC *hDC*)
Parameters	
hDC	HDC: Identifies the device context that contains the desired path.
Returns	BOOL: Returns TRUE if successful; otherwise, FALSE is returned.
Include File	wingdi.h
See Also	BeginPath, EndPath, SetPolyFillMode
Example	The following example fills the current path of the device context using a solid red brush.

```
LRESULT CALLBACK WndProc( HWND hWnd, UINT uMsg, WPARAM wParam, LPARAM lParam )
{
    switch( uMsg )
    {
        case WM_COMMAND :
```

continued on next page

continued from previous page

```
            switch( LOWORD( wParam ) )
            {
                case IDM_TEST :
                    {
                        HBRUSH  hBrush, hOldBrush;
                        HPEN    hPen;
                        int     iROP2;
                        HDC     hDC = GetDC( hWnd );

                        if( BeginPath( hDC ) )
                        {
                            MoveToEx( hDC, 10, 10, NULL );
                            LineTo( hDC, 200, 10 );
                            LineTo( hDC, 200, 200 );

                            // close final figure
                            // and end the path.
                            //...................
                            CloseFigure( hDC );
                            EndPath( hDC );

                            // Fill the path with a red brush.
                            //...............................
                            iROP2 = SetROP2(hDC, R2_MERGEPENNOT);
                            hPen = SelectObject(hDC, GetStockObject(NULL_PEN));
                            hBrush = CreateSolidBrush( RGB(255,0,0) );
                            hOldBrush = SelectObject(hDC, hBrush );

                            FillPath(hDC);

                            // Restore the DC to its previous state
                            //....................................
                            SetROP2(hDC, iROP2);
                            SelectObject(hDC, hPen);
                            SelectObject(hDC, hOldBrush);

                            DeleteObject( hBrush );
                        }

                        ReleaseDC( hWnd, hDC );
                    }
                    break;
```

FillRect ■ WINDOWS 95 ■ WINDOWS NT

Description	FillRect fills the specified rectangle using the given brush.
Syntax	BOOL **FillRect**(HDC *hDC,* LPRECT *lpRect,* HBRUSH *hBrush*)
Parameters	
hDC	HDC: Specifies the device context to fill.
lpRect	LPRECT: A pointer to a **RECT** structure that defines the area to be filled.

hBrush	HBRUSH: The handle of a logical brush that is used to fill the rectangle.
Returns	BOOL: Returns TRUE if successful; otherwise, FALSE is returned.
Include File	wingdi.h
See Also	ExtFloodFill, FloodFill, Rectangle
Example	See ExcludeUpdateRgn for an example of this function.

FillRgn   ■ WINDOWS 95   ■ WINDOWS NT

Description	FillRgn fills the specified region using the given brush.
Syntax	BOOL **FillRgn**(HDC *hDC,* HRGN *hRegion,* HBRUSH *hBrush*)
Parameters	
hDC	HDC: Specifies the device context to fill.
hRegion	HRGN: Specifies the handle to a region to be filled.
hBrush	HBRUSH: The handle of a logical brush that is used to fill the region.
Returns	BOOL: Returns TRUE if successful; otherwise, FALSE is returned.
Include File	wingdi.h
See Also	ExtFloodFill, FloodFill
Example	See ExtCreateRegion for an example of this function.

FlattenPath   ■ WINDOWS 95   ■ WINDOWS NT

Description	FlattenPath flattens the path in the given device context by converting any curves into line sequences.
Syntax	BOOL **FlattenPath**(HDC *hDC*)
Parameters	
hDC	HDC: Identifies the device context that contains the desired path.
Returns	BOOL: Returns TRUE if successful; otherwise, FALSE is returned.
Include File	wingdi.h
See Also	BeginPath, EndPath, WidenPath
Example	The following example converts the curves within a bezier curve to lines with the FlattenPath function when the user selects the Test! menu item.

```
LRESULT CALLBACK WndProc( HWND hWnd, UINT uMsg, WPARAM wParam, LPARAM lParam )
{
   switch( uMsg )
   {
     case WM_COMMAND :
            switch( LOWORD( wParam ) )
            {
```

continued on next page

continued from previous page

```
case IDM_TEST :
    {
        POINT   pts[4];
        int     i;
        HDC     hDC = GetDC( hWnd );

        pts[0].x = 10;   pts[0].y = 50;
        pts[1].x = 30;   pts[1].y = 0;
        pts[2].x = 60;   pts[2].y = 150;
        pts[3].x = 120;  pts[3].y = 50;

        // Draw normal bezier.
        //....................
        if( BeginPath( hDC ) )
        {
            PolyBezier( hDC, pts, 4 );
            EndPath( hDC );
            StrokePath( hDC );
        }

        // Adjust coordinates.
        //....................
        for( i=0; i<4; i++ )
            pts[i].y += 80;

        // Draw bezier converted to lines.
        //................................
        if( BeginPath( hDC ) )
        {
            PolyBezier( hDC, pts, 4 );
            EndPath( hDC );

            FlattenPath( hDC );

            StrokePath( hDC );
        }

        ReleaseDC( hWnd, hDC );
    }
    break;
```

```
.
.
.
```

FrameRect   ■ WINDOWS 95   ■ WINDOWS NT

Description	FrameRect draws the border of the specified rectangle. The interior is not filled. Note that, unlike FrameRgn, this function always assumes that the border has a width and height of one logical unit.
Syntax	BOOL **FrameRect**(HDC *hDC*, LPRECT *lpRect*, HBRUSH *hBrush*)
Parameters	
hDC	HDC: Identifies the device context.
lpRect	LPRECT: A pointer to a RECT structure that defines the rectangle.

hBrush	HBRUSH: The handle of a brush that is used to draw the border of the rectangle. The rectangle is always drawn with a width of one logical unit.
Returns	BOOL: Returns TRUE if successful; otherwise, FALSE is returned.
Include File	winuser.h
See Also	FrameRgn, Rectangle, RoundRect
Example	See InvertRect for an example of this function.

FrameRgn ■ WINDOWS 95 ■ WINDOWS NT

Description	FrameRgn draws the border of the specified region. The interior is not filled.
Syntax	int **FrameRgn**(HDC *hDC,* HRGN *hRegion,* HBRUSH *hBrush,* int *nWidth,* int *nHeight*)
Parameters	
hDC	HDC: Identifies the device context.
hRegion	HRGN: The handle of the region that is to be framed.
hBrush	HBRUSH: The handle of a brush that is used to draw the border of the region.
nWidth	int: Specifies the width of the border, in logical units.
nHeight	int: Specifies the height of the border, in logical units.
Returns	int: Returns TRUE if successful; otherwise, FALSE is returned.
Include File	wingdi.h
See Also	FrameRect, PaintRgn
Example	See InvertRect for an example of this function.

GetArcDirection ■ WINDOWS 95 ■ WINDOWS NT

Description	GetArcDirection returns the direction that GDI draws arcs and rectangles.
Syntax	int **GetArcDirection**(HDC *hDC*)
Parameters	
hDC	HDC: Specifies the desired device context.
Returns	int: The return value is either AD_CLOCKWISE or AD_COUNTERCLOCKWISE if successful. Otherwise, 0 is returned.
Include File	wingdi.h
See Also	SetArcDirection
Example	See the example for the Ellipse function.

GetAspectRatioFilterEx ■ Windows 95 ■ Windows NT

Description	GetAspectRatioFilterEx returns the aspect ratio of the identified device context. The aspect ratio is defined as the ratio between the horizontal and vertical size of a physical pixel on the device.
Syntax	BOOL **GetAspectRatioFilterEx**(HDC *hDC*, LPSIZE *lpAspectRatio*)
Parameters	
hDC	HDC: Identifies the desired device context.
lpAspectRatio	LPSIZE: A pointer to a **SIZE** structure. GDI will fill in this structure with the aspect ratio filter value.
Returns	BOOL: Returns **TRUE** if successful; otherwise, **FALSE** is returned.
Include File	wingdi.h
See Also	SetMapperFlags
Example	The following example retrieves the physical pixel aspect ratio for the specified device and computes a floating-point compensation value that will allow the application to draw perfect circles on the given device.

```
LRESULT CALLBACK WndProc( HWND hWnd, UINT uMsg, WPARAM wParam, LPARAM lParam )
{
    switch( uMsg )
    {
        case WM_COMMAND :
                switch( LOWORD( wParam ) )
                {
                    case IDM_TEST :
                        {
                            SIZE    szAspect;
                            double dRatio = 1.0;
                            HDC     hDC    = GetDC( hWnd );

                            if ( GetAspectRatioFilterEx( hDC, &szAspect ) &&
                                 szAspect.cx != szAspect.cy )
                            {
                                dRatio = (double)szAspect.cx / (double)szAspect.cy;
                            }

                            Ellipse( hDC, 10, (int)(10.0*dRatio), 110, (int)(110.0*dRatio) );

                            ReleaseDC( hWnd, hDC );
                        }
                        break;
                        .
                        .
                        .
```

GetBkColor

Description	GetBkColor returns the background color of the specified device context.
Syntax	COLORREF **GetBkColor**(HDC *hDC*)
Parameters	
hDC	HDC: Identifies the desired device context.
Returns	COLORREF: If successful, the return value is the background color of the specified device context. Otherwise, CLR_INVALID is returned.
Include File	wingdi.h
See Also	SetBkColor, GetBkMode
Example	This example draws a string on the client area of the window with the current background color and mode. The user can change the background color and mode from the Options menu. When the application receives the WM_INITMENU message, the Options menu is initialized with the current background color and mode. Note that this application uses the CS_OWNDC style to create a window with a private device context.

```
LRESULT CALLBACK WndProc( HWND hWnd, UINT uMsg, WPARAM wParam, LPARAM lParam )
{
   switch( uMsg )
   {
      case WM_PAINT :
            {
                PAINTSTRUCT ps;

                BeginPaint( hWnd, &ps );

                TextOut( ps.hdc, 10, 10, "Sample Text", 11 );

                EndPaint( hWnd, &ps );
            }
            break;

      case WM_INITMENU :
            {
                HDC hDC = GetDC( hWnd );

                if ( GetBkColor( hDC ) == RGB( 255, 255, 255 ) )
                   CheckMenuRadioItem( (HMENU)wParam, IDM_WHITE, IDM_BLACK,
                                            IDM_WHITE, MF_BYCOMMAND );
                else if ( GetBkColor( hDC ) == RGB( 192, 192, 192 ) )
                   CheckMenuRadioItem( (HMENU)wParam, IDM_WHITE, IDM_BLACK,
                                            IDM_GRAY, MF_BYCOMMAND );
                else if ( GetBkColor( hDC ) == RGB( 0, 0, 0 ) )
                   CheckMenuRadioItem( (HMENU)wParam, IDM_WHITE, IDM_BLACK,
                                            IDM_BLACK, MF_BYCOMMAND );
```

continued on next page

continued from previous page

```
                    if ( GetBkMode( hDC ) == OPAQUE )
                        CheckMenuRadioItem( (HMENU)wParam, IDM_OPAQUE, IDM_TRANSPARENT,
                                                           IDM_OPAQUE, MF_BYCOMMAND );
                    else
                        CheckMenuRadioItem( (HMENU)wParam, IDM_OPAQUE, IDM_TRANSPARENT,
                                                           IDM_TRANSPARENT, MF_BYCOMMAND );
                    ReleaseDC( hWnd, hDC );
                }
                break;

        case WM_COMMAND :
                switch( LOWORD( wParam ) )
                {
                case IDM_WHITE :
                case IDM_GRAY :
                case IDM_BLACK :
                case IDM_OPAQUE :
                case IDM_TRANSPARENT :
                    {
                        HDC hDC = GetDC( hWnd );

                        switch( LOWORD( wParam ) )
                        {
                            case IDM_WHITE : SetBkColor( hDC, RGB( 255, 255, 255 ) ); break;
                            case IDM_GRAY  : SetBkColor( hDC, RGB( 192, 192, 192 ) ); break;
                            case IDM_BLACK : SetBkColor( hDC, RGB( 0, 0, 0 ) );       break;

                            case IDM_OPAQUE      : SetBkMode( hDC, OPAQUE );      break;
                            case IDM_TRANSPARENT : SetBkMode( hDC, TRANSPARENT ); break;
                        }

                        ReleaseDC( hWnd, hDC );
                        InvalidateRect( hWnd, NULL, TRUE );
                    }
                    break;
                    .
                    .
                    .
```

GetBkMode   ■ WINDOWS 95 ■ WINDOWS NT

Description	GetBkMode returns the current background mode of the specified device context. The background mode determines how the background color is used.
Syntax	int **GetBkMode**(HDC *hDC*)
Parameters	
hDC	HDC: Identifies the desired device context.
Returns	int: If successful, the return value is the background mode of the desired device context. This value will be either OPAQUE or TRANSPARENT. Otherwise, 0 is returned.
Include File	wingdi.h

See Also   SetBkMode

Example   See GetBkColor for an example of this function.

GetBoundsRect   ■ WINDOWS 95   ■ WINDOWS NT

Description   Windows maintains an accumulated bounding rectangle for a device con-
                text. When enabled, this bounding rectangle is enlarged anytime a
                drawing function extends beyond the current bounding rectangle. The
                current bounding rectangle thus defines the smallest rectangle that con-
                tains all drawing within the device context. This routine returns the
                current bounding rectangle.

Syntax   UINT **GetBoundsRect**(HDC *hDC,* LPRECT *lpRect,* UINT *uFlags*)

Parameters

hDC   HDC: Specifies the device context.

lpRect   LPRECT: A pointer to a RECT structure. This structure will be filled in upon
                return from this function.

uFlags   UINT: Specifies various flags that define how **GetBoundsRect** operates. Set
                this parameter to DCB_RESET to clear the current accumulated bounding
                rectangle. If this value is not set, the current accumulated bounding rec-
                tangle is not cleared.

Returns   UINT: The return value specifies various conditions that may have occurred
                during the processing of this function. One of the values in Table 15-19
                may be returned.

Table 15-19 Return values for GetBoundsRect

Return Value	Description
0	The indicated device context is invalid.
DCB_DISABLE	Boundary accumulation has been disabled.
DCB_ENABLE	Boundary accumulation has been enabled.
DCB_RESET	The bounding rectangle is currently empty.
DCB_SET	The bounding rectangle is currently not empty.

Include File   wingdi.h

See Also   SetBoundsRect

Example   This example clears the bounds rectangle and adds two overlapping rec-
                tangles to the bounding rectangle by accumulating them with the
                SetBoundsRect function when the user selects the Test! menu item. The
                resulting bounding rectangle is retrieved with the **GetBoundsRect** function
                and framed.

```
LRESULT CALLBACK WndProc( HWND hWnd, UINT uMsg, WPARAM wParam, LPARAM lParam )
{
    switch( uMsg )
    {
        case WM_COMMAND :
                switch( LOWORD( wParam ) )
                {
                    case IDM_TEST :
                        {
                            RECT rect;
                            HDC  hDC = GetDC( hWnd );

                            // Clear the bounding rectangle.
                            //.............................
                            SetBoundsRect( hDC, NULL, DCB_RESET | DCB_ENABLE );

                            // Add first rectangle to bounds.
                            //.............................
                            SetRect( &rect, 10, 10, 50, 50 );
                            SetBoundsRect( hDC, &rect, DCB_ACCUMULATE );
                            FrameRect( hDC, &rect, GetStockObject( LTGRAY_BRUSH ) );

                            // Add second rectangle to bounds.
                            //.............................
                            SetRect( &rect, 40, 40, 110, 110 );
                            SetBoundsRect( hDC, &rect, DCB_ACCUMULATE );
                            FrameRect( hDC, &rect, GetStockObject( LTGRAY_BRUSH ) );

                            // Retrieve the accumulated bounds rectangle and frame it.
                            //...................................................
                            GetBoundsRect( hDC, &rect, 0 );
                            FrameRect( hDC, &rect, GetStockObject( BLACK_BRUSH ) );

                            ReleaseDC( hWnd, hDC );
                        }
                        break;
                        .
                        .
                        .
```

GetBrushOrgEx

■ WINDOWS 95   ■ WINDOWS NT

Description	GDI maintains a brush origin that defines how a brush is aligned before it is used for painting. The **GetBrushOrgEx** function returns the current setting of the brush origin.
Syntax	BOOL **GetBrushOrgEx**(HDC *hDC*, LPPOINT *lpPoint*)
Parameters	
hDC	HDC: Specifies the desired device context.
lpPoint	LPPOINT: A pointer to a **POINT** structure. This structure will receive the current brush origin.
Returns	BOOL: Returns **TRUE** if successful; otherwise, **FALSE** is returned.

Include File	`wingdi.h`
See Also	`SetBrushOrgEx`
Example	The following code segment retrieves and saves the current brush origin. It then sets the brush origin, performs some drawing function, and resets the brush origin to its original state.

```
POINT ptOldOrigin;
HDC   hDC;

GetBrushOrgEx( hDC, &ptOldOrigin );
SetBrushOrgEx( hDC, 3, 3, NULL );
.
. //Draw with the brush.
.
SetBrushOrgEx( hDC, ptOldOrigin.x, ptOldOrigin.y, NULL );
```

GetClipBox ■ WINDOWS 95 ■ WINDOWS NT

Description	`GetClipBox` returns the smallest rectangle that completely surrounds the currently visible portion of the window. This is based on the current clipping region as well as any overlapping windows. (`GetClipRgn` may be more accurate.)
Syntax	`int GetClipBox( HDC hDC, LPRECT lpRect )`
Parameters	
`hDC`	`HDC`: Specifies the device context.
`lpRect`	`LPRECT`: A pointer to a `RECT` structure. This structure will receive the rectangle coordinates.
Returns	`int`: The return value will be one of the values specified in Table 15-3.
Include File	`wingdi.h`
See Also	`ExcludeClipRect, ExtSelectClipRgn, GetClipRgn, IntersectClipRect, OffsetClipRgn, SelectClipPath, SelectClipRgn`
Example	The following example creates a region and selects it as the clipping region. The clipping box is then retrieved with the `GetClipBox` function and framed to make it visible.

```
LRESULT CALLBACK WndProc( HWND hWnd, UINT uMsg, WPARAM wParam, LPARAM lParam )
{
   switch( uMsg )
   {
      case WM_COMMAND :
            switch( LOWORD( wParam ) )
               {
                  case IDM_TEST :
                        {
                           HRGN hRgn;
                           RECT rect;
                           HDC  hDC = GetDC( hWnd );
```

continued on next page

continued from previous page

```
                    // Create a region and select it as the clipping region.
                    //.................................................
                    hRgn = CreateRectRgn( 10, 10, 110, 110 );
                    SelectClipRgn( hDC, hRgn );

                    // Get the clipping box and frame it.
                    //.................................
                    GetClipBox( hDC, &rect );
                    FrameRect( hDC, &rect, GetStockObject( BLACK_BRUSH ) );

                    DeleteObject( hRgn );
                    ReleaseDC( hWnd, hDC );
                }
                break;
```

.
.
.

GetClipRgn ■ WINDOWS 95 ■ WINDOWS NT

Description	GetClipRgn returns a copy of the current clipping region. This function is similar to the GetClipBox function except that it returns a more accurate bound for the clipping area.
Syntax	int **GetClipRgn**(HDC *hDC,* HRGN *hRegion*)
Parameters	
hDC	HDC: Specifies the device context.
hRegion	HRGN: Specifies a valid handle to an existing region. Upon return from this function, this handle will represent a copy of the clipping region of the specified device context.
Returns	int: This function will return −1 on errors, 1 if successful, and 0 if there is no clipping region for the given device context.
Include File	wingdi.h
See Also	ExcludeClipRect, ExtSelectClipRgn, GetClipBox, IntersectClipRect, OffsetClipRgn, SelectClipPath, SelectClipRgn
Example	This example demonstrates the accuracy of the GetClipRgn function by creating a path and selecting it as the clipping area. Next, the application retrieves the clipping region, which is then filled.

```
LRESULT CALLBACK WndProc( HWND hWnd, UINT uMsg, WPARAM wParam, LPARAM lParam )
{
    switch( uMsg )
    {
        case WM_COMMAND :
                switch( LOWORD( wParam ) )
                {
                    case IDM_TEST :
                        {
```

```
HRGN hRgn;
HDC  hDC = GetDC( hWnd );

// Build triangular path.
//.......................
BeginPath( hDC );
MoveToEx( hDC, 10, 10, NULL );
LineTo( hDC, 110, 10 );
LineTo( hDC, 110, 110 );
CloseFigure( hDC );
EndPath( hDC );

// Select path as clipping area.
//..............................
SelectClipPath( hDC, RGN_COPY );

// Create a dummy region.
//.......................
hRgn = CreateRectRgn( 10, 10, 11, 11 );

// Get the clipping region and fill it.
//.....................................
GetClipRgn( hDC, hRgn );
FillRgn( hDC, hRgn, GetStockObject( BLACK_BRUSH ) );

DeleteObject( hRgn );
ReleaseDC( hWnd, hDC );
}
break;
```

GetCurrentPositionEx ■ Windows 95 ■ Windows NT

Description	GetCurrentPositionEx returns the current position within the device context. The current position can be set with **MoveToEx** and changed, using a variety of drawing functions, such as **LineTo**.
Syntax	BOOL **GetCurrentPositionEx**(HDC *hDC*, LPPOINT *lpPoint*)
Parameters	
hDC	HDC: Specifies the device context.
lpPoint	LPPOINT: A pointer to a **POINT** structure. This structure will receive the coordinates of the current position within the specified device context.
Returns	BOOL: Returns **TRUE** if successful; otherwise, **FALSE** is returned.
Include File	wingdi.h
See Also	MoveToEx
Example	The following code segment retrieves and saves the current position of the specified device context. It then draws a line, which alters the current position. The current position is then set back to its original value.

```
POINT CurrentPoint;
HDC hDC;

if( GetCurrentPositionEx( hDC, &CurrentPoint ) )
{
    LineTo( hDC, 100, 100 );
    MoveToEx( hDC, CurrentPoint.x, CurrentPoint.y, NULL );
}
```

GetMiterLimit ■ Windows 95 ■ Windows NT

Description	GetMiterLimit retrieves the miter limit for the specified device context. GDI will draw miter joins only if they fall within the current miter limit. Joins that are outside the current miter limit are drawn as bevel joins.
Syntax	BOOL **GetMiterLimit**(HDC *hDC*, PFLOAT *pfLimit*)
Parameters	
hDC	HDC: Specifies a device context.
pfLimit	PFLOAT: A pointer to a floating-point value. This value will receive the current miter limit.
Returns	BOOL: Returns TRUE if successful; otherwise, FALSE is returned.
Include File	wingdi.h
See Also	SetMiterLimit
Example	This example demonstrates the miter limit when stroking a path with a mitered pen. Each time the user selects the Test! menu item, the miter limit is increased by one until the miter limit reaches 3, where it is reset. The GetMiterLimit function is used to retrieve the current miter limit so it can be restored after the path is stroked. Another alternative would be to use the third parameter of the SetMiterLimit function to return the current miter limit when the new one is set.

```
LRESULT CALLBACK WndProc( HWND hWnd, UINT uMsg, WPARAM wParam, LPARAM lParam )
{
static FLOAT fMiterLimit = 0.0f;

    switch( uMsg )
    {
        case WM_COMMAND :
                switch( LOWORD( wParam ) )
                {
                    case IDM_TEST :
                            {
                                LOGBRUSH lb;
                                HPEN     hPen, hOldPen;
                                FLOAT    fOldMiter;
                                HDC      hDC = GetDC( hWnd );

                                // Build triangular path.
                                //.....................
```

```
BeginPath( hDC );
MoveToEx( hDC, 20, 20, NULL );
LineTo( hDC, 120, 20 );
LineTo( hDC, 120, 120 );
CloseFigure( hDC );
EndPath( hDC );

// Retrieve the current miter limit.
//...................................
GetMiterLimit( hDC, &fOldMiter );

// Reset the miter limit.
//......................
if ( fMiterLimit == 3.0f )
   fMiterLimit = 0.0f;

fMiterLimit += 1.0f;

lb.lbStyle = BS_SOLID;
lb.lbColor = RGB( 255, 0, 0 );
hPen = ExtCreatePen( PS_GEOMETRIC | PS_SOLID |
                     PS_ENDCAP_ROUND | PS_JOIN_MITER,
                     10, &lb, 0, NULL );

hOldPen = SelectObject( hDC, hPen );

// Set the miter limit, stroke the path,
// and restore the miter limit.
//...................................
SetMiterLimit( hDC, fMiterLimit, NULL );
StrokePath( hDC );
SetMiterLimit( hDC, fOldMiter, NULL );

SelectObject( hDC, hOldPen );

DeleteObject( hPen );
ReleaseDC( hWnd, hDC );
}
break;
```

.
.
.

GetObject ■ WINDOWS 95 ■ WINDOWS NT

Description	GetObject returns information about a bitmap, palette, logical pen, brush, font, or DIB section.
Syntax	int **GetObject**(HGDIOBJ *hGdiObj,* int *nBuffer,* LPVOID *lpBuffer*)
Parameters	
hGdiObj	HGDIOBJ: Specifies the handle of a GDI object. This should be the handle of a logical bitmap, DIB section (created with **CreateDIBSection**), pen, palette, brush, or font.

nBuffer	**int**: The size, in bytes, of the buffer pointed to by *lpBuffer*.
lpBuffer	**LPVOID**: A pointer to a buffer. The data returned is dependent on the value of *hGdiObj*. Refer to Table 15-20 for details. This parameter may be **NULL**.

Table 15-20 Data types for GetObject

Type of Object	Buffer Contents
DIB section	The buffer will contain a DIBSECTION structure.
Logical bitmap	The buffer will contain a BITMAP structure. Only the height, width, and color format information is valid.
Logical brush	The buffer will contain a LOGBRUSH structure.
Logical font	The buffer will contain a LOGFONT structure.
Logical pen	The buffer will contain either an EXTLOGPEN structure or a LOGPEN structure, depending on the type of pen.
Palette	The buffer will contain a WORD structure specifying the number of palette entries that exist within the palette. You can use GetSystemPaletteEntries to retrieve the values.

Returns	**int**: If successful, **GetObject** returns the number of bytes copied into the buffer. If *lpBuffer* is **NULL**, the return value is the required size of the buffer. In the case of an error, the return value is 0.
Include File	wingdi.h
See Also	CreateDIBSection, GetDIBits, GetPaletteEntries, GetRegionData
Example	The following example retrieves the **BITMAP** information for a bitmap and displays the height and width of the bitmap in a message box.

```
LRESULT CALLBACK WndProc( HWND hWnd, UINT uMsg, WPARAM wParam, LPARAM lParam )
{
    switch( uMsg )
    {
    case WM_COMMAND :
            switch( LOWORD( wParam ) )
            {
            case IDM_TEST :
                {
                    TCHAR   szMsg[64];
                    BITMAP  bmp;
                    HBITMAP hBmp = LoadBitmap( hInst, "TestBitmap" );

                    GetObject( hBmp, sizeof( BITMAP ), &bmp );

                    wsprintf( szMsg, "Bitmap Height = %d, Width = %d",
                                    bmp.bmHeight, bmp.bmWidth );

                    MessageBox( hWnd, szMsg, lpszAppName, MB_OK );
                }
                break;
                .
                .
                .
```

GetObjectType

Description	GetObjectType returns the object type of the specified object.
Syntax	DWORD **GetObjectType**(HGDIOBJ *hObject*)
Parameters	
hObject	HGDIOBJ: The handle of the GDI object.
Returns	DWORD: If successful, a value from Table 15-21 is returned that identifies the object type; otherwise, it **0** is returned;

Table 15-21 GetObjectType return values

Value	Meaning
OBJ_BITMAP	Bitmap
OBJ_BRUSH	Brush
OBJ_DC	Device context
OBJ_ENHMETADC	Enhanced metafile device context
OBJ_ENHMETAFILE	Enhanced metafile
OBJ_EXTPEN	Extended pen
OBJ_FONT	Font
OBJ_MEMDC	Memory device context
OBJ_METADC	Metafile device context
OBJ_METAFILE	Metafile
OBJ_PAL	Palette
OBJ_PEN	Pen
OBJ_REGION	Region

Include File	wingdi.h
See Also	GetObject, SelectObject

GetPath

Description	GetPath returns line endpoints and curve control points describing the path currently defined in the specified device context.
Syntax	int **GetPath**(HDC *hDC,* LPPOINT *lpPoints,* LPBYTE *lpTypeArray,* int *nCount*)
Parameters	
hDC	HDC: Specifies the desired device context.

lpPoints	LPPOINT: A pointer to an array of **POINT** structures. This structure will receive the coordinates of points that define the path. Each point in this array is accompanied by one entry in the *lpTypeArray*. The values in the *lpTypeArray* specify how these points should be interpreted.
lpTypeArray	LPBYTE: A pointer to an array of **BYTE** values. Each entry in this array corresponds to one entry in the *lpPoints* array. The values in the *lpPoints* array are interpreted based on the corresponding value in the *lpTypeArray*. Table 15-22 shows these values and their interpretation.
nCount	int: Specifies the number of entries in the *lpPoints* and *lpTypeArray* arrays. These two arrays must be the same size.

Table 15-22 Type values returned by `GetPath`

Type Flag	Description
PT_BEZIERTO	Indicates that the associated point in the *lpPoints* array is part of a bezier curve. PT_BEZIERTO points always occur in groups of three. The point before the PT_BEZIERTO points defines the start of the curve. The first two PT_BEZIERTO points define the control points, and the final PT_BEZIERTO point defines the endpoint.
PT_CLOSEFIGURE	This value, when combined with PT_LINETO or PT_BEZIERTO, indicates that the figure should be closed after drawing the line or curve. The figure is closed by drawing a line from the last point in the figure to the point specified by the most recent PT_MOVETO.
PT_LINETO	Indicates that the associated point in the *lpPoints* array is the second point in a line. The previous point in the *lpPoints* array is the first point in the line.
PT_MOVETO	Indicates that the associated point in the *lpPoints* array is the first point of a line or curve.

Returns	int: If *nCount* is 0, the return value is the number of entries in the arrays that need to be allocated to contain all data. If *nCount* is not 0, then the return value will be the number of items copied into the arrays, if there is sufficient space. If there is not sufficient space, the return value will be −1.
Include File	wingdi.h
See Also	BeginPath, EndPath
Example	The following function determines the amount of data necessary to contain the current path information, allocates the proper space, and then obtains the information for the path.

```
int GetPathInfo( HDC hDC, LPPOINT* plpPointAry, LPBYTE* plpByteAry )
{
    int nPointCount;

    // Retrieve the number of points in path.
    //.....................................
    nPointCount = GetPath( hDC, NULL, NULL, 0 );

    // Allocate memory, the calling application is responsible fore freeing this memory.
    //.............................................................................
```

```
*plpPointAry = HeapAlloc( GetProcessHeap(), HEAP_ZERO_MEMORY, nPointCount*sizeof(POINT) );
*plpByteAry = HeapAlloc( GetProcessHeap(), HEAP_ZERO_MEMORY, nPointCount );

// Retrieve the path information.
//..............................
GetPath( hDC, *plpPointAry, *plpByteAry, nPointCount );

return( nPointCount );
}
```

GetPixel   ■ WINDOWS 95   ■ WINDOWS NT

Description	GetPixel returns the RGB value of the pixel specified. The specified pixel must be within the current clipping region.
Syntax	COLORREF **GetPixel**(HDC *hDC,* int *X,* int *Y*)
Parameters	
hDC	HDC: Specifies the desired device context.
X	int: Identifies the x coordinate of the desired pixel.
Y	int: Identifies the y coordinate of the desired pixel.
Returns	COLORREF: The return value is the RGB value of the specified pixel if successful. Otherwise, the return value is CLR_INVALID.
Include File	wingdi.h
See Also	SetPixelV
Example	See SetPixelV for an example of this function.

GetPolyFillMode   ■ WINDOWS 95   ■ WINDOWS NT

Description	GetPolyFillMode returns the polygon fill mode for the specified device context. The polygon fill mode determines how GDI fills polygons.
Syntax	int **GetPolyFillMode**(HDC *hDC*)
Parameters	
hDC	HDC: Specifies the desired device context.
Returns	int: The return value is one of the valid polygon fill modes. Valid values are defined in Table 15-8.
Include File	wingdi.h
See Also	CreatePolygonRgn, SetPolyFillMode
Example	This example paints a five-pointed star, as shown in Figure 15-6, using the Polygon function and fills the polygon with the current polygon fill mode. The user can change the fill mode with the menu from winding to alternate and back again.

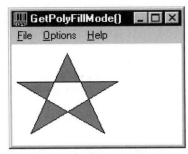

Figure 15-6 GetPolyFillMode
example

```
LRESULT CALLBACK WndProc( HWND hWnd, UINT uMsg, WPARAM wParam, LPARAM lParam )
{
static POINT pt[6];

   switch( uMsg )
   {
      case WM_CREATE :
              pt[0].x = 60;   pt[0].y = 10;
              pt[1].x = 20;   pt[1].y = 100;
              pt[2].x = 115;  pt[2].y = 42;
              pt[3].x = 5;    pt[3].y = 42;
              pt[4].x = 100;  pt[4].y = 100;
              pt[5].x = 60;   pt[5].y = 10;

              SelectObject( GetDC( hWnd ), GetStockObject( GRAY_BRUSH ) );
              break;

      case WM_PAINT :
              {
                 PAINTSTRUCT ps;

                 BeginPaint( hWnd, &ps );
                 Polygon( ps.hdc, pt, 6 );
                 EndPaint( hWnd, &ps );
              }
              break;

      case WM_INITMENU :
              if ( GetPolyFillMode( GetDC( hWnd ) ) == WINDING )
                 CheckMenuRadioItem( (HMENU)wParam, IDM_WINDING, IDM_ALTERNATE,
                                                    IDM_WINDING, MF_BYCOMMAND );
              else
                 CheckMenuRadioItem( (HMENU)wParam, IDM_WINDING, IDM_ALTERNATE,
                                                    IDM_ALTERNATE, MF_BYCOMMAND );
              break;

      case WM_COMMAND :
              switch( LOWORD( wParam ) )
              {
                 case IDM_ALTERNATE :
                 case IDM_WINDING :
```

```
{
    HDC hDC = GetDC( hWnd );
    SetPolyFillMode( GetDC( hWnd ), LOWORD( wParam ) == IDM_WINDING ?
                     WINDING : ALTERNATE );

    // Re-paint window.
    //................
    RedrawWindow( hWnd, NULL, NULL, RDW_ERASE | RDW_INVALIDATE );
}
break;
```

GetRegionData ■ WINDOWS 95 ■ WINDOWS NT

Description	GetRegionData returns information that describes the specified region.
Syntax	DWORD **GetRegionData**(HRGN *hRegion*, DWORD *dwCount*, RGNDATA* *lpRgnData*)
Parameters	
hRegion	HRGN: Specifies the handle to a valid region.
dwCount	DWORD: Specifies the size, in bytes, of the buffer pointed to by *lpRgnData*.
lpRgnData	RGNDATA*: A pointer to a RGNDATA structure. This parameter may be NULL. See the definition of the RGNDATA structure under the ExtCreateRegion function.
Returns	DWORD: If *lpRgnData* is NULL, or if *dwCount* specifies a size that is not sufficient to contain all the data, then the return value is the size, in bytes, of the required buffer. Otherwise, the return value is 1 if the function is successful, and 0 if an error occurs.
Include File	wingdi.h
See Also	ExtCreateRegion, GetRgnBox
Example	See ExtCreateRegion for an example of this function.

GetRgnBox ■ WINDOWS 95 ■ WINDOWS NT

Description	GetRgnBox obtains the smallest rectangle that completely surrounds the given region.
Syntax	int **GetRgnBox**(HRGN *hRegion*, LPRECT *lpRect*)
Parameters	
hRegion	HRGN: Specifies a handle to the desired region.
lpRect	LPRECT: A pointer to a RECT structure. This structure will receive the coordinates of the bounding rectangle.

Returns	int: The return value can be one of the region complexity values specified in Table 15-4.
Include File	wingdi.h
See Also	GetRegionData
Example	The following example creates an elliptic region and retrieves the bounding rectangle. The elliptic region is then filled and the bounding rectangle framed.

```
LRESULT CALLBACK WndProc( HWND hWnd, UINT uMsg, WPARAM wParam, LPARAM lParam )
{
   switch( uMsg )
   {
      case WM_COMMAND :
            switch( LOWORD( wParam ) )
            {
               case IDM_TEST :
                  {
                     HDC   hDC;
                     RECT  rect;
                     HRGN hElRgn;

                     hDC = GetDC( hWnd );

                     hElRgn = CreateEllipticRgn( 10, 10, 110, 110 );
                     GetRgnBox( hElRgn, &rect );

                     FillRgn( hDC, hElRgn, GetStockObject( GRAY_BRUSH ) );
                     FrameRect( hDC, &rect, GetStockObject( BLACK_BRUSH ) );

                     DeleteObject( hElRgn );
                     ReleaseDC( hWnd, hDC );
                  }
                  break;
                  .
                  .
                  .
```

GetROP2   ■ WINDOWS 95   ■ WINDOWS NT

Description	GetROP2 returns the current raster operation that defines how GDI combines foreground colors.
Syntax	int **GetROP2**(HDC *hDC*)
Parameters	
hDC	HDC: Specifies the desired device context.
Returns	int: The return value is one of the raster operation codes listed in Table 15-23.

Table 15-23 Return values for `GetROP2`

Raster Operation Code	Description
R2_BLACK	Pixel is always 0.
R2_COPYPEN	Pixel is the pen color.
R2_MASKNOTPEN	Pixel is a combination of the colors common to both the screen and the inverse of the pen.
R2_MASKPEN	Pixel is a combination of the colors common to both the pen and the screen.
R2_MASKPENNOT	Pixel is a combination of the colors common to both the pen and the inverse of the screen.
R2_MERGENOTPEN	Pixel is a combination of the screen color and the inverse of the pen color.
R2_MERGEPEN	Pixel is a combination of the pen color and the screen color.
R2_MERGEPENNOT	Pixel is a combination of the pen color and the inverse of the screen color.
R2_NOP	Pixel remains unchanged.
R2_NOT	Pixel is the inverse of the screen color.
R2_NOTCOPYPEN	Pixel is the inverse of the pen color.
R2_NOTMASKPEN	Pixel is the inverse of the R2_MASKPEN color.
R2_NOTMERGEPEN	Pixel is the inverse of the R2_MERGEPEN color.
R2_NOTXORPEN	Pixel is the inverse of the R2_XORPEN color.
R2_WHITE	Pixel is always 1.
R2_XORPEN	Pixel is a combination of the colors in the pen and in the screen.

Include File   `wingdi.h`

See Also   `SetROP2`

Example   The following example fills an elliptic region with a gray brush and draws an overlapping rectangle with a hollow brush. The current raster operation setting is saved while it is changed to **R2_NOT** while drawing the rectangle. The raster operation setting is restored after drawing has completed. Note that the current raster operation could be saved using the return value of the **SetROP2** function.

```
LRESULT CALLBACK WndProc( HWND hWnd, UINT uMsg, WPARAM wParam, LPARAM lParam )
{
    switch( uMsg )
    {
        case WM_COMMAND :
                switch( LOWORD( wParam ) )
                {
                    case IDM_TEST :
                            {
                                HBRUSH  hOldBrush;
                                HDC     hDC;
                                HRGN    hElRgn;
                                int     nOldROP;

                                hDC     = GetDC( hWnd );
                                nOldROP = GetROP2( hDC );
                                hElRgn  = CreateEllipticRgn( 10, 10, 110, 110 );
```

continued on next page

continued from previous page

```
                         FillRgn( hDC, hElRgn, GetStockObject( GRAY_BRUSH ) );

                         // Draw hollow rectangle with ROP2 = R2_NOT.
                         //...........................................
                         hOldBrush = SelectObject( hDC, GetStockObject( HOLLOW_BRUSH ) );
                         SetROP2( hDC, R2_NOT );
                         Rectangle( hDC, 30, 30, 130, 130 );

                         // Clean up.
                         //..........
                         SelectObject( hDC, hOldBrush );
                         SetROP2( hDC, nOldROP );
                         DeleteObject( hElRgn );
                         ReleaseDC( hWnd, hDC );
                      }
                      break;
```

GetStockObject   ■ WINDOWS 95   ■ WINDOWS NT

Description	`GetStockObject` returns the handle to one of the predefined system stock objects. These objects exist within the system at all times, and you don't need extra resources to create them. You do not have to delete objects whose handles are obtained using this function.
Syntax	`HGDIOBJ` **`GetStockObject`**`( int `*`nObjectType`*` )`
Parameters	
nObjectType	`int`: Specifies one of the valid stock objects. This parameter can be one of the values listed in Table 15-24.

Table 15-24 Object types specified with `GetStockObject`

Object Type	Description
BLACK_BRUSH	Black brush.
DKGRAY_BRUSH	Dark gray brush. This should be used only in windows that have CS_VREDRAW and CS_HREDRAW class styles.
GRAY_BRUSH	Gray brush. This should be used only in windows that have CS_VREDRAW and CS_HREDRAW class styles.
HOLLOW_BRUSH	Hollow brush (equivalent to NULL_BRUSH).
LTGRAY_BRUSH	Light gray brush. This should be used only in windows that have CS_VREDRAW and CS_HREDRAW class styles.
NULL_BRUSH	Null brush (equivalent to HOLLOW_BRUSH).
WHITE_BRUSH	White brush.
BLACK_PEN	Black pen.
NULL_PEN	Null pen.
WHITE_PEN	White pen.
ANSI_FIXED_FONT	Windows fixed-pitch (monospace) system font.

Object Type	Description
ANSI_VAR_FONT	Windows variable-pitch (proportional space) system font.
DEVICE_DEFAULT_FONT	Device-dependent font. This is only valid for Windows NT.
DEFAULT_GUI_FONT	Default font for user interface objects such as menus and dialog boxes. This object may change at any time due to user preference settings.
OEM_FIXED_FONT	Original equipment manufacturer (OEM) dependent fixed-pitch (monospace) font.
SYSTEM_FONT	System font. By default, Windows uses the system font to draw menus, dialog box controls, and text. In Windows versions 3.0 and later, the system font is a proportionally spaced font; earlier versions of Windows used a monospace system font.
SYSTEM_FIXED_FONT	Fixed-pitch (monospace) system font used in Windows versions earlier than 3.0. This stock object is available for compatibility with earlier versions of Windows.
DEFAULT_PALETTE	Default palette. This palette consists of the static colors in the system palette.

Returns	HGDIOBJ: The return value is a handle to the desired stock object.
Include File	wingdi.h
See Also	CreateBrushIndirect, CreateDIBPatternBrushPt, CreateHatchBrush, CreatePatternBrush, CreatePen, CreatePenIndirect, CreateSolidBrush, ExtCreatePen
Example	See GetRgnBox and GetROP2 for examples of this function.

GetUpdateRect ■ WINDOWS 95 ■ WINDOWS NT

Description	GetUpdateRect retrieves the smallest rectangle that completely contains the current update region of the specified window. The coordinates are returned in client coordinates, unless the window was created with the CS_OWNDC style and the mapping mode is not MM_TEXT.
Syntax	BOOL **GetUpdateRect**(HWND *hWnd,* LPRECT *lpRect,* BOOL *bErase*)
Parameters	
hWnd	HWND: Specifies the window handle of the desired window.
lpRect	LPRECT: A pointer to a RECT structure. This parameter may be NULL.
bErase	BOOL: If this parameter is TRUE and an update region for the window exists, then a WM_ERASEBKGND will be sent to the window.
Returns	BOOL: Returns TRUE if the update region is not empty. Returns FALSE otherwise.
Include File	winuser.h
See Also	ExcludeUpdateRgn, GetUpdateRgn
Example	The following function determines if a given point is within the update rectangle of a window.

```
BOOL IsPointInUpdateRect( HWND hWnd, POINT pt )
{
   RECT   rcUpdate;

   if( GetUpdateRect( hWnd, &rcUpdate, FALSE ) )
      return( PtInRect( &rcUpdate, pt ) );

   return( FALSE );
}
```

GetUpdateRgn ■ Windows 95 ■ Windows NT

Description	GetUpdateRgn retrieves the update region for the specified window. The region is relative to the upper-left corner of the window and is defined in client coordinates.
Syntax	int **GetUpdateRgn**(HWND *hWnd*, HRGN *hRegion*, BOOL *bErase*)
Parameters	
hWnd	HWND: Specifies the window handle of the desired window.
hRegion	HRGN: Specifies the handle of an existing region.
bErase	BOOL: If this parameter is TRUE and an update region for the window exists, then a WM_ERASEBKGND will be sent to the window.
Returns	int: The return value indicates the type of region returned and may be one of the values specified in Table 15-4.
Include File	winuser.h
See Also	ExcludeUpdateRgn, GetUpdateRect
Example	This example is similar to the one for the GetUpdateRect function, with the exception that it works with the update region, which is a more accurate bounds for the update area of a window.

```
BOOL IsPointInUpdateRgn( HWND hWnd, POINT pt )
{
   HRGN hRgnUpdate;
   BOOL bReturn = FALSE;

   // Create a dummy region.
   //....................
   hRgnUpdate = CreateRectRgn( 0, 0, 1, 1 );

   if( GetUpdateRgn( hWnd, hRgnUpdate, FALSE ) )
      bReturn = PtInRgn( hRgnUpdate, pt.x, pt.y ) );

   // Clean up before returning.
   //........................
   DeleteObject( hRgnUpdate );

   return( bReturn );
}
```

InflateRect   ■ WINDOWS 95   ■ WINDOWS NT

Description	InflateRect increases or decreases the height and width of the specified rectangle. Positive values increase the height or width, and negative values decrease the height or width.
Syntax	BOOL **InflateRect**(LPRECT *lpRect,* int *nWidthAmount,* int *nHeightAmount*)
Parameters	
lpRect	LPRECT: A pointer to a RECT structure that contains an existing rectangle.
nWidthAmount	int: Specifies the amount that the width of the rectangle should be increased or decreased.
nHeightAmount	int: Specifies the amount that the height of the rectangle should be increased or decreased.
Returns	BOOL: Returns TRUE if successful; otherwise, FALSE is returned.
Include File	winuser.h
See Also	CopyRect, InvertRect, SetRect, SetRectEmpty, SubtractRect, UnionRect
Example	See CopyRect for an example of this function.

IntersectClipRect   ■ WINDOWS 95   ■ WINDOWS NT

Description	IntersectClipRect modifies the current clipping region. The new clipping region will be the intersection of the existing clipping region and the specified rectangle coordinates.
Syntax	int **IntersectClipRect**(HDC *hDC,* int *nLeft,* int *nTop,* int *nRight,* int *nBottom*)
Parameters	
hDC	HDC: Specifies the device context.
nLeft	int: Specifies the coordinate of the left edge of the rectangle.
nTop	int: Specifies the coordinate of the top edge of the rectangle.
nRight	int: Specifies the coordinate of the right edge of the rectangle.
nBottom	int: Specifies the coordinate of the bottom edge of the rectangle.
Returns	int: The return value identifies the complexity of the resulting clipping region. Refer to Table 15-4 for details.
Include File	wingdi.h
See Also	ExcludeClipRect, ExtSelectClipRgn, GetClipBox, GetClipRgn, OffsetClipRgn, SelectClipPath, SelectClipRgn

Example   The following example demonstrates the use of the `IntersectClipRect` function by creating an elliptic clipping region and intersecting it with a rectangle. The resulting clipping area is painted by filling the entire client area with a gray brush.

```
LRESULT CALLBACK WndProc( HWND hWnd, UINT uMsg, WPARAM wParam, LPARAM lParam )
{
   switch( uMsg )
   {
      case WM_COMMAND :
              switch( LOWORD( wParam ) )
              {
                 case IDM_TEST :
                      {
                         HDC   hDC;
                         HRGN  hElRgn;
                         RECT  rect;

                         hDC    = GetDC( hWnd );
                         hElRgn = CreateEllipticRgn( 10, 10, 110, 110 );

                         // Select a clipping region.
                         //.........................
                         SelectClipRgn( hDC, hElRgn );

                         // Intersect a rectangle with the clipping region.
                         //...............................................
                         IntersectClipRect( hDC, 70, 40, 150, 150 );

                         // Fill the entire client area which will only show
                         // the resulting clipping area.
                         //................................................
                         GetClientRect( hWnd, &rect );
                         FillRect( hDC, &rect, GetStockObject( GRAY_BRUSH ) );

                         DeleteObject( hElRgn );
                         ReleaseDC( hWnd, hDC );
                      }
                      break;
                      .
                      .
                      .
```

IntersectRect   ■ WINDOWS 95   ■ WINDOWS NT

Description   `IntersectRect` computes the intersection rectangle of two source rectangles.

Syntax   BOOL **IntersectRect**(LPRECT *lpDestination*, LPRECT *lpRect1*, LPRECT *lpRect2*)

Parameters

lpDestination   LPRECT: A pointer to the destination rectangle. This rectangle will receive the coordinates of the resulting rectangle.

lpRect1	**LPRECT**: Points to one of the two source rectangles.
lpRect2	**LPRECT**: Points to one of the two source rectangles.
Returns	**BOOL**: Returns **TRUE** if the two rectangles intersect. Otherwise, **FALSE** is returned, and *lpDestination* is set to an empty rectangle.
Include File	winuser.h
See Also	SubtractRect, UnionRect
Example	The following example draws two intersecting rectangles and fills the intersection area of the two rectangles. The intersection is computed with the **IntersectRect** function.

```
LRESULT CALLBACK WndProc( HWND hWnd, UINT uMsg, WPARAM wParam, LPARAM lParam )
{
    switch( uMsg )
    {
        case WM_COMMAND :
                switch( LOWORD( wParam ) )
                {
                    case IDM_TEST :
                        {
                            HDC   hDC;
                            RECT  rect1, rect2, rect3;

                            hDC = GetDC( hWnd );

                            SetRect( &rect1, 10, 10, 80, 80 );
                            SetRect( &rect2, 50, 50, 110, 110 );

                            // Intersect the rectangles.
                            //.....................
                            IntersectRect( &rect3, &rect1, &rect2 );

                            // Draw the rectangles and fill the intersection area.
                            //.....................................................
                            FrameRect( hDC, &rect1, GetStockObject( BLACK_BRUSH ) );
                            FrameRect( hDC, &rect2, GetStockObject( BLACK_BRUSH ) );
                            FillRect( hDC, &rect3, GetStockObject( LTGRAY_BRUSH ) );

                            ReleaseDC( hWnd, hDC );
                        }
                        break;
```

InvalidateRect
■ WINDOWS 95 ■ WINDOWS NT

Description	**InvalidateRect** adds the specified rectangle to the current update region of the given window. The update region defines that portion of the window that must be redrawn.
Syntax	BOOL **InvalidateRect**(HWND *hWnd*, LPRECT *lpRect*, BOOL *bErase*)

Parameters

hWnd	HWND: Specifies the window handle of the desired window.
lpRect	LPRECT: A pointer to a RECT structure.
bErase	BOOL: If this parameter is TRUE and an update region for the window exists, then a WM_ERASEBKGND will be sent to the window.

Returns	BOOL: Returns TRUE if successful; otherwise, FALSE is returned.
Include File	winuser.h
See Also	InvalidateRgn
Example	See GetBkColor for an example of this function.

InvalidateRgn ■ WINDOWS 95 ■ WINDOWS NT

Description	InvalidateRgn adds the specified region to the current update region of the given window. The update region defines that portion of the window that must be redrawn.
Syntax	BOOL **InvalidateRgn**(HWND *hWnd,* HRGN *hRegion,* BOOL *bErase*)

Parameters

hWnd	HWND: Specifies the window handle of the desired window.
hRegion	HRGN: Specifies the handle of an existing region.
bErase	BOOL: If this parameter is TRUE and an update region for the window exists, then a WM_ERASEBKGND will be sent to the window.

Returns	BOOL: Returns TRUE if successful; otherwise, FALSE is returned.
Include File	winuser.h
See Also	InvalidateRect
Example	See ExcludeUpdateRgn for an example of this function.

InvertRect ■ WINDOWS 95 ■ WINDOWS NT

Description	InvertRect inverts all pixels within the specified rectangle. A logical NOT operation is performed on all pixels.
Syntax	BOOL **InvertRect**(HDC *hDC,* LPRECT *lpRect*)

Parameters

hDC	HDC: Specifies the device context.
lpRect	LPRECT: A pointer to a RECT structure that defines the coordinates of the rectangle to be inverted.

Returns	BOOL: Returns TRUE if successful; otherwise, FALSE is returned.
Include File	winuser.h

See Also

`CopyRect, InflateRect, SetRect, SetRectEmpty, SubtractRect,`
`UnionRect`

Example

This example demonstrates two simple pushbuttons. When the example starts, there is a rectangular and an elliptic button drawn on the client area of the window. When the user presses them with the left mouse button, they invert to show a selected state.

```
#define NO_BUTTON        0
#define BUTTON_RECT      1
#define BUTTON_RGN       2

LRESULT CALLBACK WndProc( HWND hWnd, UINT uMsg, WPARAM wParam, LPARAM lParam )
{
static POINT pt;
static RECT  rcButton;
static HRGN  hRgnButton     = NULL;
static BOOL  bHighlite       = FALSE;
static int   nButtonPressed = NO_BUTTON;

    switch( uMsg )
    {
       case WM_CREATE :
               SetRect( &rcButton, 10, 10, 130, 40 );
               hRgnButton = CreateEllipticRgn( 150, 10, 200, 60 );
               break;

       case WM_PAINT : // Draw the buttons.
               {
                   PAINTSTRUCT ps;

                   BeginPaint( hWnd, &ps );

                   FrameRect( ps.hdc, &rcButton, GetStockObject( BLACK_BRUSH ) );
                   FrameRgn( ps.hdc, hRgnButton, GetStockObject( BLACK_BRUSH ), 1, 1 );
                   TextOut( ps.hdc, 20, 16, "Button A", 8 );
                   TextOut( ps.hdc, 170, 27, "B", 1 );

                   EndPaint( hWnd, &ps );
               }
               break;

       case WM_LBUTTONDOWN :
               pt.x = LOWORD( lParam );
               pt.y = HIWORD( lParam );

               // Check if button A was pressed.
               //..............................
               if ( PtInRect( &rcButton, pt ) )
               {
                   HDC hDC = GetDC( hWnd );

                   // Select the button.
                   //....................
                   InvertRect( hDC, &rcButton );
                   ReleaseDC( hWnd, hDC );
```

continued on next page

continued from previous page

```
                    bHighlite = TRUE;
                    nButtonPressed = BUTTON_RECT;
                    SetCapture( hWnd );
                }

                // Check if button B was pressed.
                //..............................
                if ( PtInRegion( hRgnButton, LOWORD( lParam ), HIWORD( lParam ) ) )
                {
                    HDC hDC = GetDC( hWnd );

                    // Select the button.
                    //...................
                    InvertRgn( hDC, hRgnButton );
                    ReleaseDC( hWnd, hDC );

                    bHighlite = TRUE;
                    nButtonPressed = BUTTON_RGN;
                    SetCapture( hWnd );
                }
                break;


            // If the user moves the mouse cursor out of the
            // button, the button is un-highlited, otherwise,
            // the button is highlited.
            //.............................................
        case WM_MOUSEMOVE :
                if ( nButtonPressed != NO_BUTTON )
                {
                    HDC hDC = GetDC( hWnd );

                    pt.x = LOWORD( lParam );
                    pt.y = HIWORD( lParam );

                    switch ( nButtonPressed )
                    {
                        case BUTTON_RECT :
                            if ( PtInRect( &rcButton, pt ) && !bHighlite )
                            {
                                InvertRect( hDC, &rcButton );
                                bHighlite = TRUE;
                            }
                            if ( !PtInRect( &rcButton, pt) && bHighlite )
                            {
                                InvertRect( hDC, &rcButton );
                                bHighlite = FALSE;
                            }
                            break;

                        case BUTTON_RGN :
                            if ( PtInRegion( hRgnButton, pt.x, pt.y ) && !bHighlite )
                            {
                                InvertRgn( hDC, hRgnButton );
                                bHighlite = TRUE;
                            }
                            if ( !PtInRegion( hRgnButton, pt.x, pt.y) && bHighlite )
                            {
```

```
                          InvertRgn( hDC, hRgnButton );
                          bHighlite = FALSE;
                      }
                      break;
              }
              ReleaseDC( hWnd, hDC );
          }
          break;

          // The user let off the mouse button, un-highlite the button.
          //.........................................................
      case WM_LBUTTONUP :
          if ( nButtonPressed != NO_BUTTON )
          {
              if ( bHighlite )
              {
                  HDC hDC = GetDC( hWnd );

                  switch( nButtonPressed )
                  {
                      case BUTTON_RECT : InvertRect( hDC, &rcButton ); break;
                      case BUTTON_RGN  : InvertRgn( hDC, hRgnButton ); break;
                  }
                  ReleaseDC( hWnd, hDC );
                  bHighlite = FALSE;
              }

              nButtonPressed = NO_BUTTON;
              ReleaseCapture();
          }
          break;
          .
          .
          .
```

InvertRgn

Description	InvertRgn inverts all pixels within the specified region. A logical **NOT** operation is performed on all pixels.
Syntax	BOOL **InvertRgn**(HDC *hDC,* HRGN *hRegion*)
Parameters	
hDC	HDC: Specifies the device context.
hRegion	HRGN: The handle of the region to be inverted.
Returns	BOOL: Returns **TRUE** if successful; otherwise, **FALSE** is returned.
Include File	winuser.h
See Also	CombineRgn, CreateEllipticRgn, CreateEllipticRgnIndirect, CreatePolygonRgn, CreatePolyPolygonRgn, CreateRectRgn, CreateRectRgnIndirect, CreateRoundRectRgn, ExtCreateRegion, SetRectRgn
Example	See InvertRect for an example of this function.

IsRectEmpty

Description	IsRectEmpty checks the given rectangle to determine if it is empty. An empty rectangle is defined as one that has no area, for example, a rectangle whose right boundary is one unit to the left of the left boundary.
Syntax	BOOL **IsRectEmpty**(LPRECT *lpRect*)
Parameters	
lpRect	LPRECT: A pointer to a RECT structure that defines the given rectangle.
Returns	BOOL: Returns TRUE if the rectangle is empty; otherwise, FALSE is returned.
Include File	winuser.h
See Also	SetRectEmpty
Example	See EqualRect for an example of this function.

LineDDA

Description	LineDDA is similar to the LineTo function, but instead of drawing pixels into a device context, this function calls a user-supplied function for each pixel. This is useful for drawing lines of a unique style or for animating movement of objects in a straight line.
Syntax	BOOL **LineDDA**(int *nXStart,* int *nYStart,* int nXEnd, int *nYEnd,* LINEDDAPROC *lpLineProc,* LPARAM *lParam*)
Parameters	
nXStart	int: Specifies the x coordinate of the start of the line.
nYStart	int: Specifies the y coordinate of the start of the line.
nXEnd	int: Specifies the x coordinate of the end of the line.
nYEnd	int: Specifies the y coordinate of the end of the line.
lpLineProc	LINEDDAPROC: The address of a callback routine. See the callback syntax below.
lParam	LPARAM: Application-defined data. This parameter is passed to the callback routine and can be used to provide additional information.
Returns	BOOL: Returns TRUE if successful; otherwise, FALSE is returned.
Include File	wingdi.h
See Also	LineTo
Callback Syntax	VOID CALLBACK **LineDDAProc**(int *X,* int *Y,* LPARAM *lpData*)
Callback Parameters	
X	int: The x coordinate of the current point.
Y	int: The y coordinate of the current point.

lpData   LPARAM: The application-defined 32-bit value passed in the *lParam* para-
                meter of the **LineDDA** function.

Example   The following example draws a series of small rectangles along the line
                from (15,15) to (135,300). The points in the line are computed using the
                LineDDA function. In this example, the device context identifier is passed
                to the callback function in the *lParam* parameter. The callback function
                draws rectangles every fifth point.

```
int nPointSkip;

VOID CALLBACK LineDDACallBack( int X, int Y, LPARAM lParam )
{
   HDC hDC = (HDC)lParam;

   nPointSkip++;
   if( nPointSkip < 5 )
      return;

   nPointSkip = 0;
   Rectangle( hDC, X, Y, X+10, Y+10 );
}

LRESULT CALLBACK WndProc( HWND hWnd, UINT uMsg, WPARAM wParam, LPARAM lParam )
{
   switch( uMsg )
   {
      case WM_COMMAND :
              switch( LOWORD( wParam ) )
              {
                 case IDM_TEST :
                      {
                         HDC hDC = GetDC( hWnd );

                         nPointSkip = 0;
                         LineDDA( 15, 15, 135, 300, (LINEDDAPROC)LineDDACallBack,⇐
(LPARAM)hDC );

                         ReleaseDC( hWnd, hDC );
                      }
                      break;
         .
         .
         .
```

LineTo   ■ WINDOWS 95   ■ WINDOWS NT

Description   The **LineTo** function draws a line from the current position to the indicat-
                 ed position. The line is drawn using the current pen. The line is drawn up
                 to, but not including the endpoint.

Syntax   BOOL **LineTo**(HDC *hDC,* int *X,* int *Y*)

Parameters

hDC	HDC: Specifies the desired device context.
X	int: Specifies the x coordinate of the end of the line in logical units.
Y	int: Specifies the y coordinate of the end of the line in logical units.
Returns	BOOL: Returns TRUE if successful; otherwise, FALSE is returned.
Include File	wingdi.h
See Also	LineDDA
Example	See GetMiterLimit for an example of this function.

LockWindowUpdate   ■ WINDOWS 95   ■ WINDOWS NT

Description	LockWindowUpdate temporarily disables updates within the specified window. Only one window can be locked. While a window is locked, Windows discards any drawing done in a device context associated with the window. Windows does accumulate a bounding rectangle of any drawing that is done. Once the window is unlocked, Windows invalidates the accumulated rectangle, which will eventually cause a WM_PAINT message to be sent to the window. To unlock the window, specify a value of NULL for the window handle.
Syntax	BOOL **LockWindowUpdate**(HWND *hWindow*)
Parameters	
hWindow	HWND: The window handle of the window to be locked. NULL unlocks the currently locked window.
Returns	BOOL: Returns TRUE if successful; otherwise, FALSE is returned.
Include File	winuser.h
See Also	RedrawWindow, UpdateWindow
Example	The following example locks the current window, draws a rectangle, and then unlocks the rectangle. Windows will not draw the rectangle but will invalidate that portion of the window and will issue a WM_PAINT message after the window has been unlocked.

```
LRESULT CALLBACK WndProc( HWND hWnd, UINT uMsg, WPARAM wParam, LPARAM lParam )
{
    switch( uMsg )
    {
        case WM_COMMAND :
                switch( LOWORD( wParam ) )
                {
                    case IDM_TEST :
                            {
                                HDC hDC = GetDC( hWnd );

                                LockWindowUpdate( hWnd );
```

```
                Rectangle( hDC, 10, 10, 110, 110 );
                ReleaseDC( hWnd, hDC );

                MessageBox( hWnd, "The rectangle did not paint.",
                            lpszAppName, MB_OK );

                LockWindowUpdate( NULL );

            }
            break;
```

⋮

MoveToEx   ■ WINDOWS 95   ■ WINDOWS NT

Description	MoveToEx moves the current position associated with the specified device context. The current position is used with various drawing functions such as LineTo.
Syntax	BOOL **MoveToEx**(HDC *hDC,* int *X,* int *Y,* LPPOINT *lpPoint*)
Parameters	
hDC	HDC: Specifies the desired device context.
X	int: Specifies the x coordinate of the target point. This is specified in logical units.
Y	int: Specifies the y coordinate of the target point. This is specified in logical units.
lpPoint	LPPOINT: A pointer to a POINT structure. This parameter may be NULL. If specified, MoveToEx places the previous current position in this structure.
Returns	BOOL: Returns TRUE if successful; otherwise, FALSE is returned.
Include File	wingdi.h
See Also	GetCurrentPositionEx
Example	See GetMiterLimit for an example of this function.

OffsetClipRgn   ■ WINDOWS 95   ■ WINDOWS NT

Description	OffsetClipRgn moves the current clipping region of the specified device context.
Syntax	int **OffsetClipRgn**(HDC *hDC,* int *X,* int *Y*)
Parameters	
hDC	HDC: Specifies a device context.
X	int: Specifies the amount that the clipping region should be moved in the x, or horizontal, direction. This value is specified in logical units.

Y	**int**: Specifies the amount that the clipping region should be moved in the y, or vertical, direction. This value is specified in logical units.
Returns	**int**: The complexity of the current clipping region is returned. It may be one of the values shown in Table 15-4.
Include File	`wingdi.h`
See Also	`ExcludeClipRect`, `ExtSelectClipRgn`, `GetClipBox`, `GetClipRgn`, `IntersectClipRect`, `SelectClipPath`, `SelectClipRgn`

OffsetRect ■ WINDOWS 95 ■ WINDOWS NT

Description	`OffsetRect` moves the coordinates of the specified rectangle.
Syntax	BOOL **OffsetRect**(LPRECT *lpRect,* int *X,* int *Y*)
Parameters	
lpRect	**LPRECT**: A pointer to a **RECT** structure that defines the rectangle.
X	**int**: Specifies the amount that the rectangle should be moved in the x, or horizontal, direction. This value is specified in logical units.
Y	**int**: Specifies the amount that the rectangle should be moved in the y, or vertical, direction. This value is specified in logical units.
Returns	**BOOL**: Returns **TRUE** if successful; otherwise, **FALSE** is returned.
Include File	`wingdi.h`
See Also	`Rectangle`, `RoundRect`, `OffsetRgn`
Example	See `CopyRect` for an example of this function.

OffsetRgn ■ WINDOWS 95 ■ WINDOWS NT

Description	`OffsetRgn` moves the coordinates of the specified region.
Syntax	int **OffsetRgn**(HRGN *hRegion,* int *X,* int *Y*)
Parameters	
hRegion	**HRGN**: The handle to an existing region.
X	**int**: Specifies the amount that the region should be moved in the x, or horizontal, direction. This value is specified in logical units.
Y	**int**: Specifies the amount that the region should be moved in the y, or vertical, direction. This value is specified in logical units.
Returns	**int**: The complexity of the current clipping region is returned. It may be one of the values shown in Table 15-4.
Include File	`wingdi.h`
See Also	`OffsetRect`

Example

The following example paints the given region, moves the specified region by 10 logical units in the x direction and 15 logical units in the y direction, and paints it again.

```
LRESULT CALLBACK WndProc( HWND hWnd, UINT uMsg, WPARAM wParam, LPARAM lParam )
{
    switch( uMsg )
    {
        case WM_COMMAND :
                switch( LOWORD( wParam ) )
                {
                    case IDM_TEST :
                        {
                            HRGN hRgn = CreateEllipticRgn( 10, 10, 110, 110 );
                            HDC  hDC  = GetDC( hWnd );

                            // Paint shadow of image.
                            //.....................
                            FillRgn( hDC, hRgn, GetStockObject( GRAY_BRUSH ) );

                            // Move the region to a new location.
                            //...................................
                            OffsetRgn( hRgn, -5, -5 );

                            // Paint the image.
                            //.................
                            PaintRgn( hDC, hRgn );
                            FrameRgn( hDC, hRgn, GetStockObject( BLACK_BRUSH ), 1, 1 );

                            ReleaseDC( hWnd, hDC );
                        }
                        break;
        .
        .
        .
```

PaintRgn   ■ WINDOWS 95   ■ WINDOWS NT

Description	`PaintRgn` draws the specified region into the given device context. The region is drawn using the current brush.
Syntax	BOOL **PaintRgn**(HDC *hDC*, HRGN *hRegion*)
Parameters	
hDC	HDC: Specifies a device context.
hRegion	HRGN: Specifies the region to be drawn.
Returns	BOOL: Returns TRUE if successful; otherwise, FALSE is returned.
Include File	wingdi.h
See Also	FrameRect, FrameRgn
Example	See OffsetRgn for an example of this function.

PathToRegion

Description	PathToRegion converts the current path within the device context into a region, and returns the handle of that region. Once converted, the path is discarded.
Syntax	HRGN **PathToRegion**(HDC *hDC*)
Parameters	
hDC	HDC: Specifies the desired device context.
Returns	HRGN: Returns the handle to a region if successful; otherwise, NULL is returned.
Include File	wingdi.h
See Also	BeginPath, EndPath
Example	The following example creates a path, then converts that path to a region and fills it. Since a device context can contain only one path, this is a good method of creating multiple complex areas.

```
LRESULT CALLBACK WndProc( HWND hWnd, UINT uMsg, WPARAM wParam, LPARAM lParam )
{
   switch( uMsg )
   {
     case WM_COMMAND :
            switch( LOWORD( wParam ) )
            {
               case IDM_TEST :
                   {
                       HDC hDC = GetDC( hWnd );

                       if( BeginPath( hDC ) )
                       {
                          HRGN hRgn;

                          // Build the path.
                          //................
                          MoveToEx( hDC, 10, 10, NULL );
                          LineTo( hDC, 200, 10 );
                          LineTo( hDC, 200, 200 );
                          CloseFigure( hDC );
                          EndPath( hDC );

                          // Convert the path to a region.
                          //..............................
                          hRgn = PathToRegion( hDC );

                          // Fill the region.
                          //................
                          FillRgn( hDC, hRgn, GetStockObject( GRAY_BRUSH ) );

                          DeleteObject( hRgn );
                       }
```

```
        ReleaseDC( hWnd, hDC );
    }
    break;
```

.
.
.

Pie   ■ WINDOWS 95   ■ WINDOWS NT

Description	Pie draws a portion of an ellipse and connects the two endpoints to the center of the ellipse, resulting in a pie-shaped wedge. The figure is drawn with the current pen and filled with the current brush. The endpoints do not have to fall on the circle. Windows will compute the intersection of a line drawn from the center of the circle to the specified endpoint and will use the intersection point.
Syntax	BOOL **Pie**(HDC *hDC,* int *nLeft,* int *nTop,* int *nRight,* int *nBottom,* int *xRadial1,* int *yRadial1,* int *xRadial2,* int *yRadial2*)
Parameters	
hDC	HDC: Specifies the desired device context.
nLeft	int: Specifies the x coordinate of the left edge of the bounding rectangle that defines the ellipse.
nTop	int: Specifies the y coordinate of the top edge of the bounding rectangle that defines the ellipse.
nRight	int: Specifies the x coordinate of the right edge of the bounding rectangle that defines the ellipse.
nBottom	int: Specifies the y coordinate of the bottom edge of the bounding rectangle that defines the ellipse.
xRadial1	int: Specifies the x coordinate of the start point of the partial ellipse.
yRadial1	int: Specifies the y coordinate of the start point of the partial ellipse.
xRadial2	int: Specifies the x coordinate of the endpoint of the partial ellipse.
yRadial2	int: Specifies the y coordinate of the endpoint of the partial ellipse.
Returns	BOOL: Returns TRUE if successful; otherwise, FALSE is returned.
Include File	wingdi.h
See Also	Arc
Example	The following example draws the upper quarter of a circle as a pie wedge when the user selects the Test! menu item. Figure 15-7 shows the result.

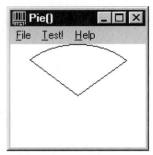

Figure 15-7. Pie example

```
LRESULT CALLBACK WndProc( HWND hWnd, UINT uMsg, WPARAM wParam, LPARAM lParam )
{
    switch( uMsg )
    {
       case WM_COMMAND :
              switch( LOWORD( wParam ) )
              {
                  case IDM_TEST :
                      {
                          RECT rcClient;
                          HDC  hDC = GetDC( hWnd );

                          GetClientRect( hWnd, &rcClient );

                          Pie( hDC, rcClient.left,  rcClient.top,
                                    rcClient.right, rcClient.bottom,
                                    rcClient.right, rcClient.top,
                                    rcClient.left,  rcClient.top );

                          ReleaseDC( hWnd, hDC );
                      }
                      break;
         .
         .
         .
```

PolyBezier   ■ WINDOWS 95   ■ WINDOWS NT

Description	PolyBezier draws one or more bezier curves. A bezier curve is defined by four points: a start point, two control points, and an endpoint. For multiple bezier curves, you must specify four points for the first curve and three additional points for each additional curve, because the endpoint of one curve serves as the start point of the next curve. The device context's current position is not changed.
Syntax	BOOL **PolyBezier**(HDC *hDC*, LPPOINT *lpPoint*, DWORD *dwPoints*)

Parameters

hDC   HDC: Specifies the desired device context.

lpPoint   LPPOINT: A pointer to an array of **POINT** structures. Each point structure
                 defines the coordinates of one point.

dwPoints   DWORD: The number of points in the *lpPoint* array. There must be three
                 points per curve plus the initial start point.

Returns   BOOL: Returns **TRUE** if successful; otherwise, **FALSE** is returned.

Include File wingdi.h

See Also   PolyBezierTo, Polyline, PolylineTo, PolyPolygon, PolyPolyline

Example   See FlattenPath for an example of this function.

PolyBezierTo   ■ WINDOWS 95   ■ WINDOWS NT

Description   PolyBezierTo draws one or more bezier curves. A bezier curve is defined
                 by four points: a start point, two control points, and an endpoint. For
                 multiple bezier curves, you must specify four points for the first curve and
                 three additional points for each additional curve, because the endpoint of
                 one curve serves as the start point of the next curve. Unlike the function
                 PolyBezier, this function sets the device context's current position to the
                 last point in the curve.

Syntax   BOOL **PolyBezierTo**(HDC *hDC,* LPPOINT *lpPoint,* DWORD *dwPoints*)

Parameters

hDC   HDC: Specifies the desired device context.

lpPoint   LPPOINT: A pointer to an array of **POINT** structures. Each point structure
                 defines the coordinates of one point.

dwPoints   DWORD: The number of points in the *lpPoint* array. There must be three
                 points per curve. The current position is used as the starting point.

Returns   BOOL: Returns **TRUE** if successful; otherwise, **FALSE** is returned.

Include File wingdi.h

See Also   PolyBezier, Polyline, PolylineTo, PolyPolygon, PolyPolyline

Example   This example draws a bezier curve, as shown in Figure 15-8, when the
                 user selects the Test! menu item. Unlike the **PolyBezier** function, the
                 starting position of the curve is the current position, which is set with the
                 MoveToEx function. A straight line is painted at the end of the bezier curve
                 to demonstrate how additional painting functions can continue to paint
                 with the updated position.

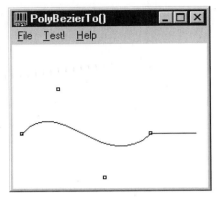

Figure 15-8 PolyBezierTo example

```c
LRESULT CALLBACK WndProc( HWND hWnd, UINT uMsg, WPARAM wParam, LPARAM lParam )
{
    switch( uMsg )
    {
    case WM_COMMAND :
            switch( LOWORD( wParam ) )
            {
                case IDM_TEST :
                    {
                        POINT ptCurve[4];
                        int    i;
                        HDC    hDC = GetDC( hWnd );

                        ptCurve[0].x = 10;  ptCurve[0].y = 100;
                        ptCurve[1].x = 50;  ptCurve[1].y = 50;
                        ptCurve[2].x = 100; ptCurve[2].y = 150;
                        ptCurve[3].x = 150; ptCurve[3].y = 100;

                        // Display point rects.
                        //.....................
                        for( i=0; i < 4; i++ )
                            Rectangle( hDC, ptCurve[i].x-2, ptCurve[i].y-2,
                                            ptCurve[i].x+2, ptCurve[i].y+2 );

                        // Position starting point for the curve.
                        //.......................................
                        MoveToEx( hDC, ptCurve[0].x, ptCurve[0].y, NULL );

                        // Paint the bezier curve.
                        //........................
                        PolyBezierTo( hDC, &ptCurve[1], 3 );

                        // Continue with a line.
                        //......................
                        LineTo( hDC, 200, 100 );

                        ReleaseDC( hWnd, hDC );
                    }
```

```
                break;
        .
        .
        .
```

Polygon

Description	`Polygon` draws a series of lines using the specified points. In addition, a line is drawn from the last point to the first point, closing the figure. The polygon is drawn using the current pen and is filled using the current brush and polygon fill mode.
Syntax	`BOOL Polygon( HDC hDC, LPPOINT lpPoint, int nPoints )`
Parameters	
hDC	`HDC`: Specifies the desired device context.
lpPoint	`LPPOINT`: A pointer to an array of `POINT` structures. Each point structure defines the coordinates of one point. There must be at least two points in the array.
nPoints	`int`: The number of points in the *lpPoint* array. There must be at least two points in the array.
Returns	`BOOL`: Returns `TRUE` if successful; otherwise, `FALSE` is returned.
Include File	`wingdi.h`
See Also	`SetPolyFillMode`
Example	See `GetPolyFillMode` for an example of this function.

Polyline

Description	`Polyline` draws a series of lines using the specified points and the current pen. Unlike `Polygon`, this function does not close or fill the drawn figure.
Syntax	`BOOL Polyline( HDC hDC, LPPOINT lpPoint, int nPoints )`
Parameters	
hDC	`HDC`: Specifies the desired device context.
lpPoint	`LPPOINT`: A pointer to an array of `POINT` structures. Each point structure defines the coordinates of one point. There must be at least two points in the array.
nPoints	`int`: The number of points in the *lpPoint* array. There must be at least two points in the array.
Returns	`BOOL`: Returns `TRUE` if successful; otherwise, `FALSE` is returned.
Include File	`wingdi.h`
See Also	`PolyBezier, PolyBezierTo, PolylineTo, PolyPolygon, PolyPolyline`

Example The following example draws an hourglass-shaped figure. Unlike `Polygon`, the first point must be repeated in order to close the figure.

```
LRESULT CALLBACK WndProc( HWND hWnd, UINT uMsg, WPARAM wParam, LPARAM lParam )
{
   switch( uMsg )
   {
      case WM_COMMAND :
            switch( LOWORD( wParam ) )
            {
               case IDM_TEST :
                  {
                     POINT ptLine[5];
                     HDC   hDC = GetDC( hWnd );

                     ptLine[0].x = 10;  ptLine[0].y = 10;
                     ptLine[1].x = 100; ptLine[1].y = 100;
                     ptLine[2].x = 10;  ptLine[2].y = 100;
                     ptLine[3].x = 100; ptLine[3].y = 10;
                     ptLine[4].x = 10;  ptLine[4].y = 10;

                     Polyline( hDC, ptLine, 5 );

                     ReleaseDC( hWnd, hDC );
                  }
                  break;
```

.
.
.

PolyLineTo   ■ WINDOWS 95 ■ WINDOWS NT

Description `PolyLineTo` draws a series of lines using the specified points and the current pen. Unlike `Polygon`, this function does not close or fill the drawn figure. The current position of the specified device context is set to the last point in the array of points.

Syntax `BOOL PolyLineTo( HDC hDC, LPPOINT lpPoint, DWORD dwPoints )`

Parameters

hDC `HDC`: Specifies the desired device context.

lpPoint `LPPOINT`: A pointer to an array of `POINT` structures. Each point structure defines the coordinates of one point. The first line is drawn between the current position and the first point in the *lpPoint* array.

dwPoints `DWORD`: The number of points in the *lpPoint* array.

Returns `BOOL`: Returns `TRUE` if successful; otherwise, `FALSE` is returned.

Include File `wingdi.h`

See Also `PolyBezier, PolyBezierTo, Polyline, PolyPolygon, PolyPolyline`

Example This example is the same as the example for the `Polyline` function, except that the starting position is set with the `MoveToEx` function. The `Polyline` example uses the first point in the array as the starting point.

```
LRESULT CALLBACK WndProc( HWND hWnd, UINT uMsg, WPARAM wParam, LPARAM lParam )
{
   switch( uMsg )
   {
      case WM_COMMAND :
              switch( LOWORD( wParam ) )
              {
                 case IDM_TEST :
                       {
                         POINT ptLine[4];
                         HDC   hDC = GetDC( hWnd );

                         ptLine[0].x = 100; ptLine[0].y = 100;
                         ptLine[1].x = 10;  ptLine[1].y = 100;
                         ptLine[2].x = 100; ptLine[2].y = 10;
                         ptLine[3].x = 10;  ptLine[3].y = 10;

                         // Set the starting position.
                         //.........................
                         MoveToEx( hDC, 10, 10, NULL );

                         PolyLineTo( hDC, ptLine, 4 );

                         ReleaseDC( hWnd, hDC );
                       }
                       break;
                 .
                 .
                 .
```

PolyPolygon   ■ WINDOWS 95   ■ WINDOWS NT

Description	The **PolyPolygon** function draws a series of polygons, each of which is drawn using the current pen, and filled using the current brush and polygon fill mode. The polygons may overlap.
Syntax	BOOL **PolyPolygon**(HDC *hDC*, LPPOINT *lpPoint*, LPINT *lpVertices*, int *nPolygons*)
Parameters	
hDC	HDC: Specifies a device context.
lpPoint	LPPOINT: A pointer to an array of **POINT** structures. Each entry in this array defines one point.
lpVertices	LPINT: A pointer to an array of integers. Each entry in this array corresponds to one polygon. The value of each entry specifies the number of points in the *lpPoint* array that define the corresponding polygon. This value must be at least two.
nPolygons	int: Specifies the number of entries in the *lpVertices* array.
Returns	BOOL: Returns **TRUE** if successful; otherwise, **FALSE** is returned.
Include File	wingdi.h

See Also   PolyBezier, PolyBezierTo, Polyline, PolylineTo, PolyPolyline

Example   This example is similar to the one for the **CreatePolyPolygonRgn** in that it
               displays the same two polygons. Instead of the polygons being filled, only
               the outline is displayed with the **PolyPolygon** function.

```
LRESULT CALLBACK WndProc( HWND hWnd, UINT uMsg, WPARAM wParam, LPARAM lParam )
{
   switch( uMsg )
   {
     case WM_COMMAND :
             switch( LOWORD( wParam ) )
             {
               case IDM_TEST :
                   {
                       HDC   hDC;
                       POINT ptList[7];
                       int   nVertexCount[2];

                       hDC    = GetDC( hWnd );

                       // Initialize values.
                       //....................
                       ptList[0].x = 60;  ptList[0].y = 10;
                       ptList[1].x = 10;  ptList[1].y = 60;
                       ptList[2].x = 110; ptList[2].y = 60;
                       ptList[3].x = 160; ptList[3].y = 60;
                       ptList[4].x = 160; ptList[4].y = 160;
                       ptList[5].x = 60;  ptList[5].y = 160;
                       ptList[6].x = 60;  ptList[6].y = 60;

                       nVertexCount[0] = 3;
                       nVertexCount[1] = 4;

                       // Draw two polygons
                       //..................
                       PolyPolygon( hDC, ptList, nVertexCount, 2 );

                       ReleaseDC( hWnd, hDC );
                   }
                   break;
         .
         .
         .
```

PolyPolyline   ■ WINDOWS 95   ■ WINDOWS NT

Description   **PolyPolyline** draws a series of line sequences using the current pen. This
               is similar to the **Polyline** function, except that multiple line sequences
               can be drawn in one function call.

Syntax   BOOL **PolyPolyline**(HDC *hDC*, LPPOINT *lpPoint*, LPDWORD
               lpVertices, DWORD *dwPolylines*)

Parameters

hDC   HDC: Specifies a device context.

lpPoint	LPPOINT: A pointer to an array of **POINT** structures. Each entry in this array defines one point.
lpVertices	LPDWORD: A pointer to an array of **DWORD** values. Each entry in this array corresponds to one line sequence. The value of each entry specifies the number of points in the *lpPoint* array that define the corresponding line sequence. This value must be at least two.
dwPolylines	DWORD: Specifies the number of entries in the *lpVertices* array.
Returns	BOOL: Returns **TRUE** if successful; otherwise, **FALSE** is returned.
Include File	wingdi.h
See Also	PolyBezier, PolyBezierTo, Polyline, PolylineTo, PolyPolygon
Example	This example demonstrates the **PolyPolyline** function by drawing a rectangle and a triangle when the user selects the Test! menu item.

```
LRESULT CALLBACK WndProc( HWND hWnd, UINT uMsg, WPARAM wParam, LPARAM lParam )
{
    switch( uMsg )
    {
        case WM_COMMAND :
                switch( LOWORD( wParam ) )
                {
                    case IDM_TEST :
                        {
                            POINT ptLine[9];
                            DWORD dwVert[2];
                            HDC   hDC = GetDC( hWnd );

                            // rectangle.
                            //.................
                            dwVert[0] = 5;
                            ptLine[0].x = 10;  ptLine[0].y = 10;
                            ptLine[1].x = 100; ptLine[1].y = 10;
                            ptLine[2].x = 100; ptLine[2].y = 100;
                            ptLine[3].x = 10;  ptLine[3].y = 100;
                            ptLine[4].x = 10;  ptLine[4].y = 10;

                            // triangle.
                            //..........
                            dwVert[1] = 4;
                            ptLine[5].x = 80;  ptLine[5].y = 50;
                            ptLine[6].x = 140; ptLine[6].y = 110;
                            ptLine[7].x = 20;  ptLine[7].y = 110;
                            ptLine[8].x = 80;  ptLine[8].y = 50;

                            PolyPolyline( hDC, ptLine, dwVert, 2 );

                            ReleaseDC( hWnd, hDC );
                        }
                        break;
```

.
.
.

PolyTextOut

Description	PolyTextOut draws several strings using the font and text colors currently selected in the specified device context.
Syntax	BOOL **PolyTextOut**(HDC *hDC*, CONST POLYTEXT* *pPTxt,* int *nStrings*)
Parameters	
hDC	HDC: The device context to use for drawing.
pPTxt	CONST POLYTEXT*: A pointer to an array of POLYTEXT structures describing the strings to be drawn. The array contains one structure for each string. See the definition of the POLYTEXT structure below.
nStrings	int: The number of POLYTEXT structures in the *pPTxt* array.
Returns	BOOL: If successful, TRUE is returned; otherwise, FALSE is returned.
Include File	wingdi.h
See Also	ExtTextOut, GetTextAlign

POLYTEXT Definition

```
typedef struct _POLYTEXT
{
    int     x;
    int     y;
    UINT    n;
    LPCTSTR lpstr;
    UINT    uiFlags;
    RECT    rcl;
    int     *pdx;
} POLYTEXT;
```

Members	
x	int: The horizontal reference point for the string.
y	int: The vertical reference point for the string.
n	UINT: The number of characters in the string.
lpstr	LPCTSTR: A pointer to a string of text to be drawn.
uiFlags	UINT: Specify ETO_OPAQUE to draw the text opaqued with the current background color. Specify ETO_CLIPPED to clip the string to the given rectangle.
rcl	RECT: Specifies the RECT that defines the opaquing and clipping rectangle.
pdx	int*: An array of values that specify the width value for each character in the string.

PtInRect

Description	PtInRect determines if the specified point lies within the boundaries of the given rectangle. Note that if the point falls on the top or left edge, it is

considered to be inside the rectangle, and if the point falls on the right or bottom edge, it is considered to be outside the rectangle.

Syntax	BOOL **PtInRect**(LPRECT *lpRect,* POINT *ptPoint*)
Parameters	
lpRect	LPRECT: A pointer to a RECT structure that defines the boundaries of the rectangle.
ptPoint	POINT: A POINT structure that defines the point. Note that the actual POINT structure is passed to this function, not a pointer to a POINT structure.
Returns	BOOL: Returns TRUE if the point lies within the rectangle or on the top of left edges. Otherwise, FALSE is returned.
Include File	winuser.h
See Also	PtInRegion, RectInRegion
Example	See InvertRect for an example of this function.

PtInRegion ■ WINDOWS 95   ■ WINDOWS NT

Description	PtInRegion determines if the specified point lies within the indicated region.
Syntax	BOOL **PtInRegion**(HRGN *hRegion,* int *X,* int *Y*)
Parameters	
hRegion	HRGN: The handle of the desired region.
X	int: Specifies the x coordinate of the desired point.
Y	int: Specifies the y coordinate of the desired point.
Returns	BOOL: Returns TRUE if the point lies within the region; otherwise, FALSE is returned.
Include File	winuser.h
See Also	PtInRect, RectInRegion
Example	See InvertRect for an example of this function.

Rectangle ■ WINDOWS 95   ■ WINDOWS NT

Description	Rectangle draws a rectangle defined by the given coordinates. The rectangle is drawn using the current pen and filled using the current brush.
Syntax	BOOL **Rectangle**(HDC *hDC,* int *nLeft,* int *nTop,* int *nRight,* int *nBottom*)
Parameters	
hDC	HDC: Specifies the device context that the arc is to be drawn in.
nLeft	int: Specifies the x coordinate of the upper-left corner of the rectangle.

nTop	**int**: Specifies the y coordinate of the upper-left corner of the rectangle.
nRight	**int**: Specifies the x coordinate of the lower-right corner of the rectangle.
nBottom	**int**: Specifies the y coordinate of the lower-right corner of the rectangle.
Returns	**BOOL**: Returns **TRUE** if successful; otherwise, **FALSE** is returned.
Include File	wingdi.h
See Also	CreateRoundRectRgn, OffsetRect, RoundRect
Example	See **CreatePatternBrush** for an example of this function.

RectInRegion
■ WINDOWS 95   ■ WINDOWS NT

Description	**RectInRegion** determines if any part of the specified rectangle lies within the given region.
Syntax	BOOL **RectInRegion**(HRGN *hRegion,* LPRECT *lpRect*)
Parameters	
hRegion	HRGN: Specifies the handle of a valid region.
lpRect	LPRECT: A pointer to a **RECT** structure.
Returns	**BOOL**: If any portion of the rectangle, except the right and bottom edges, lies within the region, the return value is **TRUE**; otherwise, it is **FALSE**.
Include File	wingdi.h
See Also	PtInRect, PtInRegion
Example	The following code segment determines if any portion of the specified rectangle exists within the given region.

```
RECT rcRectangle;
HRGN hRgn;

if( RectInRgn( hRgn, &rcRectangle))
{
    //  Some portion of the rectangle lies within the region
}
else
{
    //  No portion of the rectangle lies within the region
}
```

RedrawWindow
■ WINDOWS 95   ■ WINDOWS NT

Description	**RedrawWindow** causes the specified rectangle or region of the given window to be updated. Various options allow you to control the update process.
Syntax	BOOL **RedrawWindow**(HWND *hWindow,* LPRECT *lpRect,* HRGN *hRegion,* UINT *uFlags*)

Parameters

hWindow   HWND: Specifies the handle of the window. If this parameter is NULL, the desktop window is updated.

lpRect   LPRECT: A pointer to a RECT structure. This rectangle contains the coordinates of the client area to be updated. This parameter may be NULL. If this parameter and *hRegion* are both NULL, the entire client area is assumed.

hRegion   HRGN: Specifies the handle of the region to be updated. If this parameter is not NULL, then *lpRect* is ignored. If this parameter and *lpRect* are both NULL, the entire client area is assumed.

uFlags   UINT: Specifies various flags that define how the window will be affected, how repainting will occur, and which windows are affected. Refer to Table 15-25 for details.

Table 15-25 RedrawWindow *uFlags* values

Flag	Description
Invalidation flags	
RDW_ERASE	The affected windows will receive a WM_ERASEBKGND message when being redrawn. The RDW_INVALIDATE flag must also be specified.
RDW_FRAME	Causes that section of the nonclient area that intersects the update region to receive a WM_NCPAINT message. The RDW_INVALIDATE flag also must be specified.
RDW_INTERNALPAINT	Forces a WM_PAINT message to be posted to the affected windows regardless of the existence of any invalid region.
RDW_INVALIDATE	Causes the area defined by *hRegion* or *lpRect* to be marked invalid. If both parameters are NULL, the entire client area is invalidated.
Validation flags	
RDW_NOERASE	Causes any pending WM_ERASEBKGND message to be ignored.
RDW_NOFRAME	Causes any pending WM_NCPAINT to be ignored. The RDW_VALIDATE message also must be specified.
RDW_NOINTERNALPAINT	Causes any pending WM_PAINT message to be ignored. WM_PAINT still will be sent if the resulting update area is not NULL.
RDW_VALIDATE	Causes the area defined by *hRegion* or *lpRect* to be marked as valid. Any pending internal WM_PAINT messages are still sent to the window.
Repainting flags	
RDW_ERASENOW	Causes any pending WM_NCPAINT and WM_ERASEBKGND messages to be completed before this function returns. WM_PAINT messages will be handled at the normal time.
RDW_UPDATENOW	Causes any pending WM_NCPAINT, WM_ERASEBKGND, and WM_PAINT messages to be completed before this function returns.

continued on next page

continued from previous page

Flag	Description

Child window control flags. Normally, child windows created without the WS_CLIPCHILDREN flag will be recursively updated. The following flags modify this behavior.

RDW_ALLCHILDREN	Causes all child windows to be affected.
RDW_NOCHILDREN	Causes child windows to remain unaffected.

Returns	BOOL: Returns TRUE if successful; otherwise, FALSE is returned.
Include File	winuser.h
See Also	LockWindowUpdate, UpdateWindow
Example	See GetPolyFillMode for an example of this function.

RoundRect ■ WINDOWS 95 ■ WINDOWS NT

Description	RoundRect draws a rectangle defined by the given coordinates. The rectangle is drawn using the current pen and filled using the current brush. The corners of the rectangle are rounded using the specified ellipse parameters.
Syntax	BOOL **RoundRect**(HDC *hDC,* int *nLeft,* int *nTop,* int *nRight,* int *nBottom,* int *nWidth,* int *nHeight*)
Parameters	
hDC	HDC: Specifies the device context that the arc is to be drawn in.
nLeft	int: Specifies the x coordinate of the upper-left corner of the rectangle.
nTop	int: Specifies the y coordinate of the upper-left corner of the rectangle.
nRight	int: Specifies the x coordinate of the lower-right corner of the rectangle.
nBottom	int: Specifies the y coordinate of the lower-right corner of the rectangle.
nWidth	int: Specifies the width of the ellipse that is used to draw the rounded corners.
nHeight	int: Specifies the height of the ellipse that is used to draw the rounded corners.
Returns	BOOL: Returns TRUE if successful; otherwise, FALSE is returned.
Include File	wingdi.h
See Also	CreateRoundRectRgn, OffsetRect, Rectangle
Example	The following example draws a rectangle with rounded corners. For an example of how this figure would appear, refer to Figure 15-5, and the discussion of CreateRoundRectRgn.

```
LRESULT CALLBACK WndProc( HWND hWnd, UINT uMsg, WPARAM wParam, LPARAM lParam )
{
   switch( uMsg )
   {
      case WM_COMMAND :
```

```
switch( LOWORD( wParam ) )
{
    case IDM_TEST :
            {
                HDC hDC = GetDC( hWnd );
                RoundRect( hDC, 10, 10, 110, 110, 30, 30 );
                ReleaseDC( hWnd, hDC );
            }
            break;
        .
        .
        .
```

SelectClipPath   ■ WINDOWS 95   ■ WINDOWS NT

Description	SelectClipPath combines the current clipping region of the specified device context with the current path.
Syntax	BOOL **SelectClipPath**(HDC *hDC,* int *nCombineMode*)
Parameters	
hDC	HDC: Identifies the desired device context.
nCombineMode	int: Specifies the manner that Windows will use to combine the current clipping region with the current path. This parameter may be one of the values specified in Table 15-3.
Returns	BOOL: Returns TRUE if successful; otherwise, FALSE is returned.
Include File	wingdi.h
See Also	ExcludeClipRect, ExtSelectClipRgn, GetClipBox, GetClipRgn, IntersectClipRect, OffsetClipRgn, SelectClipRgn
Example	See GetClipRgn for an example of this function.

SelectClipRgn   ■ WINDOWS 95   ■ WINDOWS NT

Description	SelectClipRgn sets the specified region as the current clipping region.
Syntax	BOOL **SelectClipRgn**(HDC *hDC,* HRGN *hRegion*)
Parameters	
hDC	HDC: Identifies the desired device context.
hRegion	HRGN: Specifies the handle of a valid region. This region will become the new clipping region for the device context.
Returns	BOOL: Returns TRUE if successful; otherwise, FALSE is returned.
Include File	wingdi.h
See Also	ExcludeClipRect, ExtSelectClipRgn, GetClipBox, GetClipRgn, IntersectClipRect, OffsetClipRgn, SelectClipPath
Example	See GetClipBox for an example of this function.

SetArcDirection

Description	SetArcDirection sets the direction that Windows uses to draw arcs and rectangles.
Syntax	int **SetArcDirection**(HDC *hDC,* int *nDirection*)
Parameters	
hDC	HDC: Specifies the desired device context.
nDirection	int: Specifies the new drawing direction. This parameter may be AD_CLOCKWISE or AD_COUNTERCLOCKWISE.
Returns	int: Returns the old arc direction if successful; otherwise, 0 is returned.
Include File	wingdi.h
See Also	GetArcDirection
Example	See Ellipse for an example of this function.

SetBkColor

Description	SetBkColor sets the background color. The background color is used when drawing text, when converting bitmaps from color to monochrome, and as the gap color with pens.
Syntax	COLORREF **SetBkColor**(HDC *hDC,* COLORREF *crColor*)
Parameters	
hDC	HDC: Specifies the desired device context.
crColor	COLORREF: Specifies the value of the new background color. If the device cannot represent the color directly, then the closest match is used.
Returns	COLORREF: Returns the previous background color.
Include File	wingdi.h
See Also	GetBkColor, SetBkMode, GetBkMode
Example	See GetBkColor for an example of this function.

SetBkMode

Description	SetBkMode sets the current background mode. The background mode specifies the manner that Windows uses to draw the backgrounds of text, the gaps in lines, and to convert color bitmaps to monochrome.
Syntax	int **SetBkMode**(HDC *hDC,* int *nMode*)
Parameters	
hDC	HDC: Specifies the desired device context.

nMode	int: Specifies the background mode, which may be either OPAQUE or TRANSPARENT.
Returns	int: The return value is the previous background mode.
Include File	wingdi.h
See Also	GetBkColor, GetBkMode, SetBkColor
Example	See GetBkColor for an example of this function.

SetBoundsRect   ■ WINDOWS 95   ■ WINDOWS NT

Description	SetBoundsRect allows an application to affect the accumulation rectangle. Windows maintains an accumulation rectangle for all drawing operations.
Syntax	UINT **SetBoundsRect**(HDC *hDC,* LPRECT *lpRect,* UINT *uFlags*)
Parameters	
hDC	HDC: Specifies the device context to be affected.
lpRect	LPRECT: A pointer to a RECT structure. This parameter may be NULL.
uFlags	UINT: Specifies various actions that affect how the accumulation rectangle is modified. This may be a combination of the values shown in Table 15-26.

Table 15-26 SetBoundsRect *uFlags* values

Flag	Description
DCB_ACCUMULATE	Adds the specified rectangle to the accumulation rectangle. If DCB_RESET is also specified, then the accumulation rectangle is set to the specified rectangle.
DCB_DISABLE	Turns off boundary accumulation. This is the default state.
DCB_ENABLE	Turns on boundary accumulation.
DCB_RESET	The current bounding rectangle is cleared. If DCB_ACCUMULATE is also specified, DCB_RESET takes effect before the specified rectangle is added.

Returns	UINT: The return value specifies the previous state of the accumulation rectangle. It may be any of the values specified in Table 15-19.
Include File	wingdi.h
See Also	GetBoundsRect
Example	Refer to GetBoundsRect for an example of this function.

SetBrushOrgEx
■ Windows 95 ■ Windows NT

Description	SetBrushOrgEx sets the brush origin for the specified device context. The next brush that is selected into the device context will be aligned using the brush origin.
Syntax	BOOL **SetBrushOrgEx**(HDC *hDC,* int *X,* int *Y,* LPPOINT *lpPoint*)
Parameters	
hDC	HDC: Specifies the device context.
X	int: Specifies the x coordinate for the new brush origin, in device units. This value must be in the range **0–7**.
Y	int: Specifies the y coordinate for the new brush origin, in device units. This value must be in the range **0–7**.
lpPoint	LPPOINT: A pointer to a **POINT** structure. This parameter may be **NULL**. If specified, the previous brush origin is returned in this structure.
Returns	BOOL: Returns **TRUE** if successful; otherwise, **FALSE** is returned.
Include File	wingdi.h
See Also	GetBrushOrgEx
Example	See **GetBrushOrgEx** for an example of this function.

SetMiterLimit
■ Windows 95 ■ Windows NT

Description	SetMiterLimit sets the miter limit for line joins. If a line join falls within this limit, a miter join will be drawn. Otherwise, a bevel join is drawn.
Syntax	BOOL **SetMiterLimit**(HDC *hDC,* FLOAT *fLimit,* PFLOAT *pfOldLimit*)
Parameters	
hDC	HDC: Specifies a device context.
fLimit	FLOAT: Specifies the new miter limit value. The miter length is defined as the distance from the intersection of the line walls on the inside of the join to the intersection of the line walls on the outside of the join.
pfOldLimit	PFLOAT: A pointer to a **FLOAT**. This parameter may be **NULL**. If specified, the previous miter limit is returned in this parameter.
Returns	BOOL: Returns **TRUE** if successful; otherwise, **FALSE** is returned.
Include File	wingdi.h
See Also	GetMiterLimit
Example	See **GetMiterLimit** for an example of this function.

SetPixel

Description	SetPixel sets the specified pixel to the specified color and returns the old color of the pixel. The function fails if the pixel is outside the current clipping region. Use the GetDeviceCaps function with the RC_BITBLT value to determine if the device supports this function.
Syntax	COLORREF **SetPixelV**(HDC *hDC,* int *X,* int *Y,* COLORREF *crColor*)
Parameters	
hDC	HDC: Specifies a device context.
X	int: The x coordinate, in logical units, of the desired pixel.
Y	int: The y coordinate, in logical units, of the desired pixel.
crColor	COLORREF: The desired color for the pixel.
Returns	COLORREF: Returns the old color of the pixel if successful, otherwise, −1 is returned.
Include File	wingdi.h
See Also	SetPixelV, GetPixel
Example	The usage of this function is similar to that of SetPixelV; see SetPixelV for an example of how that function is used.

SetPixelV

Description	SetPixelV sets the specified pixel to the specified color. If the color cannot be reproduced exactly by the device, then the closest approximation is used. This function fails if the pixel is outside the current clipping region. Use the GetDeviceCaps function with the RC_BITBLT value to determine if the device supports this function. This function is faster than the SetPixel function because it does not need to return the color value of the point actually painted.
Syntax	BOOL **SetPixelV**(HDC *hDC,* int *X,* int *Y,* COLORREF *crColor*)
Parameters	
hDC	HDC: Specifies a device context.
X	int: Specifies the x coordinate of the desired pixel. This is in logical units.
Y	int: Specifies the y coordinate of the desired pixel. This is in logical units.
crColor	COLORREF: Specifies the desired color for the pixel.
Returns	BOOL: Returns TRUE if successful, otherwise, FALSE is returned.
Include File	wingdi.h
See Also	SetPixel, GetPixel

Example   This example displays an image on the client area of the window. When the user selects the Test! menu item, all the black pixels in the image are converted to red with the **GetPixel** and **SetPixelV** functions.

```c
LRESULT CALLBACK WndProc( HWND hWnd, UINT uMsg, WPARAM wParam, LPARAM lParam )
{
    switch( uMsg )
    {
        case WM_PAINT :
            {
                PAINTSTRUCT ps;
                HBITMAP     hBitmap;
                HDC         hDC;

                BeginPaint( hWnd, &ps );

                // Paint the image on the client area.
                //.....................................
                hBitmap = LoadBitmap( hInst, "TESTIMAGE" );
                hDC     = CreateCompatibleDC( ps.hdc );

                SelectObject( hDC, hBitmap );

                BitBlt( ps.hdc, 10, 10, 64, 66, hDC, 0, 0, SRCCOPY );

                DeleteDC( hDC );
                DeleteObject( hBitmap );

                EndPaint( hWnd, &ps );
            }
            break;

        case WM_COMMAND :
            switch( LOWORD( wParam ) )
            {
                case IDM_TEST :
                    {
                        int x, y;
                        HDC hDC = GetDC( hWnd );

                        // Turn all black pixels into red pixels.
                        //.......................................
                        for( y = 0; y < 76; y++ )
                            for( x = 0; x < 74; x++ )
                            {
                                if ( GetPixel( hDC, x, y ) == 0 )
                                    SetPixelV( hDC, x, y, RGB( 255, 0, 0 ) );
                            }

                        ReleaseDC( hWnd, hDC );
                    }
                    break;

                    .
                    .
                    .
```

SetPolyFillMode
■ WINDOWS 95   ■ WINDOWS NT

Description	SetPolyFillMode sets the polygon fill mode for the specified device context. The polygon fill mode determines how Windows fills the interior of polygons.
Syntax	int **SetPolyFillMode**(HDC *hDC,* int *nFillMode*)
Parameters	
hDC	HDC: Specifies the device context.
nFillMode	int: Specifies the desired polygon fill mode. This may be one of the values shown in Table 15-8.
Returns	int: Returns the previous setting of the polygon fill mode.
Include File	wingdi.h
See Also	GetPolyFillMode
Example	See GetPolyFillMode for an example of this function.

SetRect
■ WINDOWS 95   ■ WINDOWS NT

Description	SetRect sets the coordinates of a RECT structure to the given values.
Syntax	BOOL **SetRect**(LPRECT *lpRect,* int *nLeft,* int *nTop,* int *nRight,* int *nBottom*)
Parameters	
lpRect	LPRECT: A pointer to a RECT structure. Windows sets the coordinates of this structure to the specified values.
nLeft	int: Specifies the x coordinate of the upper-left corner of the rectangle.
nTop	int: Specifies the y coordinate of the upper-left corner of the rectangle.
nRight	int: Specifies the x coordinate of the lower-right corner of the rectangle.
nBottom	int: Specifies the y coordinate of the lower-right corner of the rectangle.
Returns	BOOL: Returns TRUE if successful; otherwise, FALSE is returned.
Include File	winuser.h
See Also	SetRectEmpty, SetRectRgn
Example	See CopyRect for an example of this function.

SetRectEmpty
■ WINDOWS 95   ■ WINDOWS NT

Description	SetRectEmpty sets the coordinates of a RECT structure to an empty rectangle.
Syntax	BOOL **SetRectEmpty**(LPRECT *lpRect*)

Parameters

lpRect   **LPRECT**: A pointer to a **RECT** structure. Windows sets the coordinates of this structure to values that specify an empty rectangle.

Returns   **BOOL**: Returns **TRUE** if successful; otherwise, **FALSE** is returned.

Include File   `winuser.h`

See Also   `SetRect, SetRectRgn`

Example   The following code segment initializes a **RECT** structure to an empty rectangle (**0,0,0,0**).

```
RECT rc;

if( SetRectEmpty( &rc ) )
{
    // The rectangle has been set to empty
}
```

SetRectRgn   ■ WINDOWS 95   ■ WINDOWS NT

Description   `SetRectRgn` changes the specified region to a rectangular region with the given coordinates. The region does not contain the bottom or right edges of the rectangle.

Syntax   **BOOL SetRectRgn**(HRGN *hRegion,* int *nLeft,* int *nTop,* int *nRight,* int *nBottom*)

Parameters

hRegion   **HRGN**: The handle of an existing region. The previous region is replaced by the region created with this function.

nLeft   **int**: Specifies the x coordinate of the upper-left corner of the rectangle.

nTop   **int**: Specifies the y coordinate of the upper-left corner of the rectangle.

nRight   **int**: Specifies the x coordinate of the lower-right corner of the rectangle.

nBottom   **int**: Specifies the y coordinate of the lower-right corner of the rectangle.

Returns   **BOOL**: Returns **TRUE** if successful; otherwise, **FALSE** is returned.

Include File   `wingdi.h`

See Also   `SetRect, SetRectEmpty`

Example   This example uses the `SetRectRgn` function to create an increasingly larger rectangle region, which is then framed with the `FrameRgn` function.

```
LRESULT CALLBACK WndProc( HWND hWnd, UINT uMsg, WPARAM wParam, LPARAM lParam )
{
    switch( uMsg )
    {
        case WM_COMMAND :
                switch( LOWORD( wParam ) )
                {
```

```
case IDM_TEST :
    {
        HRGN hRgn = CreateRectRgn( 10, 10, 30, 30 );
        HDC  hDC  = GetDC( hWnd );
        int  i;

        // Draw rectangle regions.
        //......................
        for( i = 0; i < 50; i += 10 )
        {
            SetRectRgn( hRgn, 10, 10, 30+i, 30+i );
            FrameRgn( hDC, hRgn, GetStockObject( BLACK_BRUSH ), 1, 1 );
        }

        DeleteObject( hRgn );

        ReleaseDC( hWnd, hDC );
    }
    break;
```

SetROP2　　　　　　　　　　　　　　■ WINDOWS 95　　■ WINDOWS NT

Description	SetROP2 sets the raster operation code that Windows uses when combining colors with colors that are already present on the device.
Syntax	int **SetROP2**(HDC *hDC,* int *nRasterOp*)
Parameters	
hDC	HDC: Specifies a device context.
nRasterOp	int: Specifies the new raster operation code. Table 15-23 defines several of the more useful ROP codes.
Returns	int: Returns the previous raster operation code.
Include File	wingdi.h
See Also	GetROP2
Example	See FillPath for an example of this function.

StrokeAndFillPath　　　　　　　　　■ WINDOWS 95　　■ WINDOWS NT

Description	StrokeAndFillPath closes any open path in the specified device context. It then draws the outline of the path using the current pen and fills the interior using the current brush.
Syntax	BOOL **StrokeAndFillPath**(HDC *hDC*);
Parameters	
hDC	HDC: Specifies the device context.
Returns	BOOL: Returns TRUE if successful; otherwise, FALSE is returned.

Include File	`wingdi.h`
See Also	`StrokePath`
Example	This example creates a path in the shape of a triangle when the user selects the Test! menu item. The path is widened to the width of a pen that is 8 pixels wide with the **WidenPath** function. The resulting path is then filled with the **StrokeAndFillPath** function. The results are shown in Figure 15-9.

```
LRESULT CALLBACK WndProc( HWND hWnd, UINT uMsg, WPARAM wParam, LPARAM lParam )
{
   switch( uMsg )
   {
      case WM_COMMAND :
            switch( LOWORD( wParam ) )
            {
               case IDM_TEST :
                   {
                      HBRUSH hOldBrush;
                      HPEN   hOldPen, hPen;
                      HDC    hDC = GetDC( hWnd );

                      // Create a wide pen.
                      //..................
                      hPen = CreatePen( PS_SOLID, 8, RGB( 0, 0, 0 ) );

                      hOldPen   = SelectObject( hDC, hPen );
                      hOldBrush = SelectObject( hDC, GetStockObject( LTGRAY_BRUSH ) );

                      // Create a path.
                      //...............
                      BeginPath( hDC );
                      MoveToEx( hDC, 10, 10, NULL );
                      LineTo( hDC, 110, 10 );
                      LineTo( hDC, 110, 110 );
                      CloseFigure( hDC );
                      EndPath( hDC );

                      // Redefine the path as the width of
                      // the pen surrounding the path.
                      //.................................
                      WidenPath( hDC );
                      SelectObject( hDC, hOldPen );

                      // Stroke and fill the path.
                      //..........................
                      StrokeAndFillPath( hDC );

                      DeleteObject( hPen );
                      ReleaseDC( hWnd, hDC );
                   }
                   break;
                   .
                   .
                   .
```

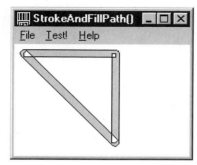

Figure 15-9 StrokeAndFillPath example

StrokePath ■ WINDOWS 95   ■ WINDOWS NT

Description	StrokePath closes any open path in the specified device context. It then draws the outline of the path using the current pen.
Syntax	BOOL **StrokePath**(HDC *hDC*)
Parameters	
hDC	HDC: Specifies the device context.
Returns	BOOL: Returns TRUE if successful; otherwise, FALSE is returned.
Include File	wingdi.h
See Also	StrokeAndFillPath
Example	See GetMiterLimit for an example of this function.

SubtractRect ■ WINDOWS 95   ■ WINDOWS NT

Description	SubtractRect creates a new rectangle by subtracting the two specified rectangles. The two rectangles must overlap.
Syntax	BOOL **SubtractRect**(LPRECT *lpDest,* LPRECT *lpSource1,* LPRECT *lpSource2*)
Parameters	
lpDest	LPRECT: Specifies a pointer to a RECT structure. This structure will receive the results of the subtraction.
lpSource1	LPRECT: Specifies a pointer to a RECT structure. *lpSource2* is subtracted from this rectangle.
lpSource2	LPRECT: Specifies a pointer to a RECT structure. This parameter is subtracted from the rectangle specified by *lpSource1*.
Returns	BOOL: Returns TRUE if successful; otherwise, FALSE is returned.
Include File	winuser.h

See Also	IntersectRect, UnionRect
Example	The following example illustrates the use of **SubtractRect**. Two rectangles are created, and then a third rectangle is created that is the result of a subtraction of the first two rectangles. The first rectangle and the resulting rectangle are framed to show the results.

```
LRESULT CALLBACK WndProc( HWND hWnd, UINT uMsg, WPARAM wParam, LPARAM lParam )
{
   switch( uMsg )
   {
      case WM_COMMAND :
              switch( LOWORD( wParam ) )
              {
                 case IDM_TEST :
                       {
                          RECT rect1, rect2, rect3;
                          HDC   hDC = GetDC( hWnd );

                          SetRect( &rect1, 10, 10, 110, 110 );
                          SetRect( &rect2, 40, 10, 180, 140 );
                          SubtractRect( &rect3, &rect1, &rect2 );

                          FrameRect( hDC, &rect1, GetStockObject( BLACK_BRUSH ) );
                          FrameRect( hDC, &rect3, GetStockObject( BLACK_BRUSH ) );

                          ReleaseDC( hWnd, hDC );
                       }
                       break;
```

.
.
.

UnionRect   ■ Windows 95   ■ Windows NT

Description	UnionRect creates a new rectangle by combining the two specified rectangles. The new rectangle is the smallest rectangle that contains both the specified rectangles.
Syntax	BOOL **UnionRect**(LPRECT *lpDest,* LPRECT *lpSource1,* LPRECT *lpSource2*)
Parameters	
lpDest	LPRECT: Specifies a pointer to a RECT structure. This structure will receive the results of the union.
lpSource1	LPRECT: Specifies a pointer to a RECT structure.
lpSource2	LPRECT: Specifies a pointer to a RECT structure.
Returns	BOOL: Returns TRUE if successful; otherwise, FALSE is returned.
Include File	winuser.h
See Also	IntersectRect, SubtractRect

Example   The following example computes the union of two rectangles when the user selects the Test! menu item. The two source rectangles and the resulting rectangle are then framed.

```
LRESULT CALLBACK WndProc( HWND hWnd, UINT uMsg, WPARAM wParam, LPARAM lParam )
{
   switch( uMsg )
   {
      case WM_COMMAND :
            switch( LOWORD( wParam ) )
            {
               case IDM_TEST :
                  {
                     RECT rect1, rect2, rect3;
                     HDC  hDC = GetDC( hWnd );

                     SetRect( &rect1, 10, 10, 110, 110 );
                     SetRect( &rect2, 40, 10, 180, 140 );
                     UnionRect( &rect3, &rect1, &rect2 );

                     FrameRect( hDC, &rect1, GetStockObject( LTGRAY_BRUSH ) );
                     FrameRect( hDC, &rect2, GetStockObject( LTGRAY_BRUSH ) );
                     FrameRect( hDC, &rect3, GetStockObject( BLACK_BRUSH ) );

                     ReleaseDC( hWnd, hDC );
                  }
                  break;
               .
               .
               .
```

UnrealizeObject   ■ WINDOWS 95   ■ WINDOWS NT

Description   UnrealizeObject unrealizes the logical palette specified. When a logical palette is realized, the colors in the palette are matched against the closest approximations that the device can support. Once this is done, changes to the logical palette are not reflected in the physical palette. In order to update the physical palette, the logical palette must be unrealized and then realized again. This function should not be used on a palette created with GetStockObject.

Syntax   BOOL **UnrealizeObject**(HGDIOBJ *hPalette*)

Parameters

hPalette   HGDIOBJ: Specifies the handle of a logical palette.

Returns   BOOL: Returns TRUE if successful; otherwise, FALSE is returned.

Include File   wingdi.h

See Also   RealizePalette, SelectObject

Example   The following code segment illustrates the use of this function. A logical palette is selected into the device context and realized. It is then unrealized, modified, and realized again. For more information on palettes, see Chapter 16, Palettes and Color Matching.

```
HPALETTE hPalette;
HDC hDC;

HPALETTE OldPalette = (HPALETTE) SelectObject( hDC, hPalette );

// The palette is realized (device palette updated).
//.............................................
RealizePalette( hDC, hPalette );
.
.
.
// The palette is unrealized so it can be modified.
//.............................................
UnrealizeObject( hPalette );
.
. // Modify the palette
.
// The palette is realized again so changes take effect.
//.............................................
RealizePalette( hDC, hPalette );
```

UpdateWindow   ■ WINDOWS 95   ■ WINDOWS NT

Description   UpdateWindow causes Windows to send a **WM_PAINT** message to the specified window. The message is sent directly to the window procedure of the specified window, bypassing the message queue. If the update region is empty, no message is sent.

Syntax   BOOL **UpdateWindow**(HWND *hWindow*)

Parameters

hWindow   HWND: Specifies the window handle of the window to be updated.

Returns   BOOL: Returns **TRUE** if successful; otherwise, **FALSE** is returned.

Include File winuser.h

See Also   LockWindowUpdate, RedrawWindow

Related Messages WM_PAINT

Example   See ValidateRect for an example of this function.

ValidateRect   ■ WINDOWS 95   ■ WINDOWS NT

Description   ValidateRect removes the specified rectangle from the invalid region of the specified window.

Syntax   BOOL **ValidateRect**(HWND *hWindow,* LPRECT *lpRect*)

Parameters

hWindow HWND: Specifies the window handle of the desired window.

lpRect LPRECT: A pointer to a RECT structure. This structure contains the coordinates of the rectangle that is to be removed from the invalid region of the specified window.

Returns BOOL: Returns TRUE if successful; otherwise, FALSE is returned.

Include File winuser.h

See Also ValidateRgn

Example The following example removes a rectangular area and a elliptic region from the invalidation region. It then causes a paint to occur where the rectangle and elliptic region are ignored.

```
LRESULT CALLBACK WndProc( HWND hWnd, UINT uMsg, WPARAM wParam, LPARAM lParam )
{
    switch( uMsg )
    {
        case WM_PAINT :
                {
                    PAINTSTRUCT ps;
                    RECT        rect;

                    BeginPaint( hWnd, &ps );

                    // Fill the entire client area gray.
                    //.................................
                    GetClientRect( hWnd, &rect );
                    FillRect( ps.hdc, &rect, GetStockObject( LTGRAY_BRUSH ) );

                    EndPaint( hWnd, &ps );
                }
                break;

        case WM_COMMAND :
                switch( LOWORD( wParam ) )
                {
                    case IDM_TEST :
                            {
                                RECT rect;
                                HRGN hRgn;
                                HDC  hDC = GetDC( hWnd );

                                SetRect( &rect, 10, 10, 110, 110 );
                                hRgn = CreateEllipticRgn( 120, 10, 220, 110 );

                                // Invalidate the entire client area.
                                //...................................
                                InvalidateRect( hWnd, NULL, FALSE );

                                // Paint and validate the areas
                                // we don't want the default to paint.
                                //.....................................
                                FillRect( hDC, &rect, GetStockObject( WHITE_BRUSH ) );
                                FillRgn( hDC, hRgn, GetStockObject( WHITE_BRUSH ) );
```

continued on next page

continued from previous page

```
                        ValidateRect( hWnd, &rect );
                        ValidateRgn( hWnd, hRgn );

                        DeleteObject( hRgn );

                        // Force the window to paint.
                        //........................
                        UpdateWindow( hWnd );
                    }
                    break;
```

ValidateRgn   ■ WINDOWS 95 ■ WINDOWS NT

Description	ValidateRgn removes the specified region from the invalid region of the specified window.
Syntax	BOOL **ValidateRgn**(HWND *hWindow,* HRGN *hRegion*)
Parameters	
hWindow	HWND: Specifies the window handle of the desired window.
hRegion	HRGN: The handle of a valid region. This region defines the area that is to be removed from the invalid region of the specified window.
Returns	BOOL: Returns TRUE if successful; otherwise, FALSE is returned.
Include File	winuser.h
See Also	ValidateRect
Example	See ValidateRect for an example of this function.

WidenPath   ■ WINDOWS 95 ■ WINDOWS NT

Description	WidenPath redefines the current path of the specified device context. The path is redefined to be the area that would be drawn using the current pen. The pen must be either a geometric pen or a pen with a width of more than one. Any bezier curves within the path are converted into line sequences during the process.
Syntax	BOOL **WidenPath**(HDC *hDC*)
Parameters	
hDC	HDC: Specifies the device context.
Returns	BOOL: Returns TRUE if successful; otherwise, FALSE is returned.
Include File	wingdi.h
See Also	FlattenPath
Example	See StrokeAndFillPath for an example of this function.

16

PALETTES AND COLOR MATCHING

Windows provides palettes to allow applications to display pictures with colors different from the default colors Windows provides. It is common for video cards to have at least 256 simultaneous colors; however, this is not enough colors to display full-color pictures with reasonable accuracy. Full-color pictures can require as many as 16 million colors for an accurate representation. Palettes allow an application to change the default colors to provide the best possible set of colors that will represent the picture most accurately.

Windows 95 also adds image color matching (ICM) capabilities. Image color matching provides accurate and consistent reproductions of color images on all output devices. Applications typically use image color matching to let users create color images on the screen that can then be reproduced exactly on a printer or on other screens. Windows NT 4 has implemented many of the same features and functions as Windows 95; however, ICM is still not implemented.

Hardware Palettes

Most modern computers have video cards that display at least 256 simultaneous colors at 1024×768 resolution. Because a limited number of colors can be shown at one time, video boards must keep track of which colors to use. For example, the 256 colors that can be shown at one time are selected from a range of 256×256×256=16,777,216 possibilities. The range of colors is determined by the video board's use of 3 bytes of information to specify the red, green, and blue (RGB) elements of a color. Most high-end video boards support a video mode, true color, that can display all 16,777,216 possibilities simultaneously.

To show a color on the screen, the video board first sets the RGB values for all the colors that can be shown at one time. These settings are called the hardware color palette. When a pixel is to be displayed, the color of the pixel is set to the RGB value of one of the hardware color palette values. Changing the color of a pixel only requires that a different hardware palette entry be referenced. If the RGB value of a palette entry changes, then every pixel displaying that palette will immediately be changed on the screen.

Hardware palettes are used on video systems for both speed and memory conservation. The ability to specify every pixel's RGB value individually would take about 3 megabytes of memory. Limiting the choices to 256 colors in the palette at one time cuts the memory needed down to 1 megabyte for a resolution of 1024×768. In addition, the color of a pixel can be changed by specifying 1 byte of information, the new palette entry number. This is faster than specifying 3 bytes for the RGB value for each pixel. Speed is a big issue on video equipment, especially with video resolution expanding to 1024×768 and beyond.

Color Palettes in Windows

Windows presents a problem when supporting hardware color palettes. If Windows were to allow any application to change the RGB color settings in the video display hardware palette, every application running on the system would be affected. For example, if the hardware palette color for black were changed to blue, then every black pixel in every visible window would instantly change to blue. This violates the basic principle that Windows applications run as separate windows that do not interfere with each other. Another problem is that Windows applications can run on any system, and various systems have different video capabilities.

Windows gets around these problems with two concepts: the default palette and the logical palette. Both give you ways to deal with the actual display equipment's hardware palette. The system default palette is typically a group of 20 reserved colors that Windows uses to paint menus, buttons, the screen desktop background, and dithered brushes. The actual number of reserved colors can be determined with the **GetDeviceCaps** function and the **NUMRESERVED** index. If the display equipment supports fewer than 20 simultaneous colors, some of the 20 entries will be the same. The system default palette can be reduced to two colors (black and white) with the **SetSystemPaletteUse** function. This is not necessary for most applications, since there are usually enough extra color choices to use without using the 20 reserved colors.

Windows maintains a system palette for each device that uses palettes. The system palette contains the color values for all colors that currently can be displayed by the device. Other than viewing the contents of the system palette, applications cannot access the system palette directly. Windows has complete control of the system palette and permits access only through the use of logical palettes. Applications can view the contents of the system palette by using the **GetSystemPaletteEntries** function.

The Logical Palette

A logical palette is a color palette that an application creates and associates with a device context. Logical palettes let applications define and use colors that meet their specific needs. Applications can create any number of logical palettes, using them for separate device contexts or switching between them for a single device context. An application creates a logical palette by using the **CreatePalette** function.

A logical palette is actually a color table in memory that mimics the hardware palette in the video board. Each entry in the logical palette contains an RGB value that Windows applications can use for creating colored pens, fonts, brushes, and bitmaps. The logical palette can contain more entries than the hardware device actually supports. In this case, the extra logical palette entries are mapped to the closest hardware palette color. If the logical palette contains fewer entries than the hardware palette, some of the hardware colors are not used.

The logical palette gets around the problem of how to deal with systems with small hardware palettes. This still leaves the issue of different applications running at the same time, demanding different colors. There is no escaping the fact that Windows runs on hardware with only one video card and only one hardware palette. If two applications running at the same time both want to use extended color palettes, the programs will interfere with each other.

Windows minimizes the damage caused when several programs use the logical palette by giving the active window priority in specifying colors for the logical palette. Inactive windows make do with whatever colors are left. Inactive windows use any remaining entries in the logical palette, and use the closest matching colors for any remaining requests on the palette. This is not as much of a problem as it might seem, because most applications use only the system colors, which are normally reserved.

The interactions between active and inactive windows using color palettes make communication between applications necessary. Windows sends a **WM_QUERYNEW-PALETTE** message to an application that realizes a logical palette when it is about to get the input focus. This message offers the chance to again realize the palette, regaining colors that may have been lost to other applications while the window was inactive.

The **WM_PALETTECHANGED** message is sent to all windows when any application realizes its logical palette. For inactive windows, this is notification that colors may be lost to the window with the input focus. The **UpdateColors** function lets you efficiently respond to the new palette choices. The example in this chapter with **UpdateColors** shows normal processing logic for handling **WM_PALETTECHANGED** and **WM_QUERYNEW-PALETTE** messages.

Check the capabilities of the physical hardware before using the palette functions. The **GetDeviceCaps** function provides information about what the hardware device can and cannot do. In particular, check the **RASTERCAPS** index value **RC_PALETTE** to see if palette changes are supported. The **NUMCOLORS** index returns the number of colors that can be simultaneously displayed.

Image Color Matching

Windows 95 introduces image color matching to allow applications to consistently reproduce color images on all output devices. Image color matching is disabled by default, to ensure that existing applications continue to display color images as originally intended. An application can enable image color matching for a specific device context by using the **SetICMMode** function.

Image color matching applies to all drawing operations in which colors are given as color values, such as the **FloodFill** function. Image color matching also applies to colors for GDI objects such as pens, brushes, and fonts. It does not apply to device-dependent bitmaps created with the **CreateBitmap** and **CreateCompatibleBitmap** functions.

Image color matching uses logical colors, which are device-independent values that specify a physical color. Logical color values are constant across all devices. Applications and devices, including input devices such as scanners, use logical color values to represent color information. Output devices are responsible for accurately translating a given logical color to a matching physical color. The set of colors that a device can support is known as the gamut. Each device has a different gamut. For example, the screen may be able to display cyans that no printer can produce, and there may be some reds on a printer that never appear on a display. To overcome these differences, Windows uses a process known as gamut matching. This process finds color matches in the gamuts of different devices. Matching is not simply the process of ensuring that each pixel is faithfully reproduced with a given color. Instead, image color matching works within the capabilities of an output device to produce an image in which the colors have the same relation to one another as they do when produced on other devices. Applications can determine if a color is within the gamut of a device by using the **CheckColorsInGamut** function. An application can use the **ColorMatchToTarget** function to preview the colors of a print job on the screen.

Color Spaces

Every device context has an application-definable color space. A color space is a set of colors in which each color is uniquely identified by a set of color coordinates. There are three types of color spaces that image color matching provides: device RGB (red, green, blue), device CMYK (cyan, magenta, yellow, black), and calibrated RGB.

Device RGB and device CMYK are device color spaces that allow applications to use the colors of any arbitrary output device. The device RGB color space is the default color space for all device contexts. The device CMYK color space is typically used with printers that use CMYK color values. The calibrated RGB color space is defined by the 1931 CIE (Commission Internationale de l'Eclairage) XYZ standard. The RGB endpoints are defined by CIE XYZ triplets, three 32-bit values.

Applications can change the color space for a device context from the default by using the **CreateColorSpace** and **SetColorSpace** functions. Setting the color space determines the format of the color information passed by the application to the device and determines how the device should interpret the color information in terms of CIE XYZ.

Color Profiles

Color profiles define the detailed color capabilities of individual devices. For a display device, a color profile defines the chromatics of the phosphors for that device. GDI has limited capabilities in managing profiles on behalf of an application. For this reason applications can enumerate all profiles for a device by using the **EnumICMProfiles** function. The **SetICMProfile** function allows an application to use a specific profile. The **GetICMProfile** function returns the file name of the current profile GDI is using for image color matching for a device context.

Palettes and Color Matching Function Descriptions

Table 16-1 summarizes the palette and color matching functions. Detailed function descriptions follow the table.

Table 16-1 Palettes and color matching function summary

Function	Purpose
AnimatePalette	Rapidly changes the color of objects painted with colors from a logical palette.
CheckColorsInGamut	Determines which colors are within the gamut of the device context.
ColorMatchToTarget	Enables or disables color preview mode for a device context.
CreateColorSpace	Creates a logical color space.
CreateHalftonePalette	Creates a halftone palette.
CreatePalette	Creates a logical palette.
DeleteColorSpace	Deletes a logical color space.
EnumICMProfiles	Enumerates the color profiles supported for a device context.
GetBValue	Retrieves the blue component of an RGB value.
GetGValue	Retrieves the green component of an RGB value.
GetRValue	Retrieves the red component of an RGB value.
GetColorAdjustment	Retrieves the color adjustment values for a device context.
GetColorSpace	Retrieves the handle of the current logical color space for a device context.
GetDeviceGammaRamp	Retrieves the gamma ramp on direct color display boards.
GetICMProfile	Retrieves the name of the color profile for a device context.
GetLogColorSpace	Retrieves information about a logical color space.
GetNearestColor	Retrieves a color value from the system palette that will be used in place of a specified color.
GetNearestPaletteIndex	Finds the palette entry number that most closely matches a given RGB value.
GetPaletteEntries	Determines the color values for a range of entries in a logical palette.
GetSystemPaletteEntries	Determines the colors of each of the system palette items.

continued on next page

continued from previous page

Function	Purpose
GetSystemPaletteUse	Determines if an application can change the system palette.
RealizePalette	Maps the logical palette selected into a device context to the hardware palette.
ResizePalette	Changes the size of the logical palette.
SelectPalette	Selects a color palette into a device context.
SetColorAdjustment	Sets the color adjustment values for a device context.
SetColorSpace	Sets the color space for a device context.
SetDeviceGammaRamp	Sets the gamma ramp on direct color display boards.
SetICMMode	Enables or disables image color matching for a device context.
SetICMProfile	Sets the color profile for a device context.
SetPaletteEntries	Changes the color values in a logical palette.
SetSystemPaletteUse	Allows modifications to the system color palette.
UpdateColors	Redraws the client area when the application does not have the input focus, but has realized a logical palette.
UpdateICMRegKey	Installs, removes, or queries ICM registry entries.

AnimatePalette ■ WINDOWS 95 ■ WINDOWS NT

Description	AnimatePalette replaces entries in a logical palette. This function rapidly changes the colors of objects painted with colors from a logical palette.
Syntax	BOOL **AnimatePalette**(HPALETTE *hPal,* UINT *uStartIndex,* UINT *uEntries,* CONST PALETTEENTRY* *pPE*)
Parameters	
hPal	HPALETTE: The handle of the logical palette.
uStartIndex	UINT: The first logical palette entry to be replaced.
uEntries	UINT: The number of entries to be replaced.
pPE	CONST PALETTEENTRY*: A pointer to the first member of an array of PALETTEENTRY structures used to replace the palette entries. This array must contain at least the number of entries specified by the *uEntries* parameter. See the definition of the PALETTEENTRY structure under the CreatePalette function later in this chapter.
Returns	BOOL: TRUE if successful; otherwise, the return value is FALSE.
Include File	wingdi.h
See Also	CreatePalette
Example	This example creates a rapidly moving red bar. The bar starts at the left side of the client area. When the user selects the Test! menu item, the bar appears to move from the right to the left of the client area. This example will only work on a system that supports more than 128 simultaneous colors. The movement is caused by rapidly changing the color of a series of

128 rectangles placed ahead of time in the client area. To begin, only the leftmost rectangle is colored red. The rest are colored white, so they are not visible. The color of each successive rectangle is changed to red using **AnimatePalette**. This is much faster than painting each rectangle using the **Rectangle** function. The **CS_OWNDC** style must be specified on the window class style of the main window.

```
LRESULT CALLBACK WndProc( HWND hWnd, UINT uMsg, WPARAM wParam, LPARAM lParam )
{
static LPLOGPALETTE pLogPal;
static HPALETTE      hPal;

    switch( uMsg )
    {
      case WM_CREATE :
              {
              int i;

              // Allocate space for the logical palette.
              //.......................................
              pLogPal = HeapAlloc( GetProcessHeap(), HEAP_ZERO_MEMORY,
                             sizeof(LOGPALETTE) +
                             (NUMBERCOLORS * sizeof(PALETTEENTRY)) );

              // Initialize the palette with one red color and make the
              // rest of the colors white.
              //........................................................
              pLogPal->palVersion    = 0x300;
              pLogPal->palNumEntries = NUMBERCOLORS;

              for( i = 0; i < NUMBERCOLORS; i++ )
              {
                  pLogPal->palPalEntry[i].peRed   = 255;
                  pLogPal->palPalEntry[i].peGreen = (i==0 ? 0 : 255 );
                  pLogPal->palPalEntry[i].peBlue  = (i==0 ? 0 : 255 );
                  pLogPal->palPalEntry[i].peFlags = PC_RESERVED;
              }

              // Create the palette.
              //....................
              hPal = CreatePalette( pLogPal );
              }
              break;

      case WM_PAINT :
              {
              PAINTSTRUCT ps;
              HBRUSH      hBrush;
              int         i;

              // Begin painting and select and realize the palette.
              //...................................................
              BeginPaint( hWnd, &ps );
              SelectPalette( ps.hdc, hPal, FALSE );
              RealizePalette( ps.hdc );
```

continued on next page

continued from previous page

```
            // Select a null pen.
            //....................
            SelectObject( ps.hdc, GetStockObject( NULL_PEN ) );

            // Paint a rectangle in each of the
            // colors in our logical palette.
            //..................................
            for ( i = 0; i < NUMBERCOLORS; i++ )
            {
                // Create a brush of the palette color and select it.
                //.................................................
                hBrush = CreateSolidBrush( PALETTEINDEX(i) );
                SelectObject( ps.hdc, hBrush );

                // Paint the rectangle.
                //....................
                Rectangle( ps.hdc, i*4, 0, (i*4)+25, 50 );

                // Select the stock white brush object.
                //....................................
                SelectObject( ps.hdc, GetStockObject( WHITE_BRUSH ) );

                // Delete the brush we created.
                //............................
                DeleteObject( hBrush );
            }

            // End painting.
            EndPaint( hWnd, &ps );
        }
        break;

    case WM_COMMAND :
        switch( LOWORD( wParam ) )
        {
            case IDM_TEST :
                {
                    int i;

                    // Cycle through each of the palette entries
                    // changing one entry at a time to red and then
                    // calling AnimatePalette to show the change.
                    //............................................
                    for ( i = 0; i < NUMBERCOLORS; i++ )
                    {
                        pLogPal->palPalEntry[i].peGreen = 255;
                        pLogPal->palPalEntry[i].peBlue  = 255;
                        if ( i < NUMBERCOLORS-1 )
                        {
                            pLogPal->palPalEntry[i+1].peGreen = 0;
                            pLogPal->palPalEntry[i+1].peBlue  = 0;
                        }
                        else
                        {
                            pLogPal->palPalEntry[0].peGreen = 0;
                            pLogPal->palPalEntry[0].peBlue  = 0;
                        }
```

```
                        AnimatePalette( hPal, 0, NUMBERCOLORS,
                                        pLogPal->palPalEntry );
                    }
                }
                break;

            case IDM_EXIT :
                    DestroyWindow( hWnd );
                    break;
        }
        break;

    case WM_DESTROY :
            // Free the memory for the logical palette
            // and delete the palette object handle.
            //..................................................
            HeapFree( GetProcessHeap(), 0, pLogPal );
            DeleteObject( hPal );

            PostQuitMessage(0);
            break;

    default :
            return( DefWindowProc( hWnd, uMsg, wParam, lParam ) );
    }

    return( OL );
}
```

CheckColorsInGamut   ■ Windows 95 ■ Windows NT

Description	CheckColorsInGamut determines if a set of color values are within the gamut of a device context.
Syntax	BOOL **CheckColorsInGamut**(HDC *hdc*, LPVOID *lpRGBQuad*, LPVOID *lpResult*, DWORD *dwCount*)
Parameters	
hdc	HDC: The device context.
lpRGBQuad	LPVOID: A pointer to an array of RGBQUAD structures that contains the color values to check. See the definition of the RGBQUAD structure below.
lpResult	LPVOID: A pointer to an array of bytes that receives the results of the color checking. This array should have the same number of elements as the array pointed to by *lpRGBQuad*.
dwCount	DWORD: The number of elements in the array pointed to by *lpRGBQuad*.
Returns	BOOL: TRUE if successful; otherwise, the return value is FALSE.
Include File	wingdi.h
See Also	SetICMMode

RGBQUAD **Definition**

```
typedef struct tagRGBQUAD
{
    BYTE rgbBlue;
    BYTE rgbGreen;
    BYTE rgbRed;
    BYTE rgbReserved;
} RGBQUAD;
```

Members

rgbBlue　　　　BYTE: The intensity of blue in the color.

rgbGreen　　　BYTE: The intensity of green in the color.

rgbRed　　　　BYTE: The intensity of red in the color.

rgbReserved　　BYTE: Reserved; must be 0.

Example　　　This example, shown in Figure 16-1, shows how to use the
CheckColorsInGamut function to determine if colors are supported for a
printer device named "HP DeskJet 550C Printer". The results of the test
are displayed when the user selects the Test! menu item.

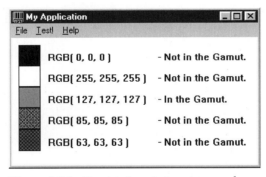

Figure 16-1 CheckColorsInGamut example

```
LRESULT CALLBACK WndProc( HWND hWnd, UINT uMsg, WPARAM wParam, LPARAM lParam )
{
    switch( uMsg )
    {
    case WM_COMMAND :
            switch( LOWORD( wParam ) )
            {
                case IDM_TEST :
                    {
                        LOGCOLORSPACE  ColorSpace;
                        HCOLORSPACE    hColorSpace;
                        RGBQUAD        aRGB[5];
                        BYTE           aResults[5];
                        HBRUSH         hBrush;
                        int            i;
                        HDC            hDC;
```

```
char           szMsg[30];
BOOL           bRet;

// Get a DC for the printer.
//........................
hDC = CreateDC( "WINSPOOL",
                "HP DeskJet 550C Printer",
                NULL, NULL );

// Turn on image color matching.
//..............................
SetICMMode( hDC, ICM_ON );

// Load color array to test.
//.........................
for( i = 0; i < 5; i++ )
{
   aRGB[i].rgbRed   = (i > 0 ? (255 / i) : 0 );
   aRGB[i].rgbGreen = (i > 0 ? (255 / i) : 0 );
   aRGB[i].rgbBlue  = (i > 0 ? (255 / i) : 0 );
   aRGB[i].rgbReserved = 0;
    aResults[i] = 0;
}

// Fill a structure to create a color space.
//..........................................
memset( &ColorSpace, 0, sizeof( ColorSpace ) );
ColorSpace.lcsSignature=(DWORD)0x50534F43;
ColorSpace.lcsVersion=0x00000400;
ColorSpace.lcsSize=sizeof( ColorSpace );
ColorSpace.lcsCSType=LCS_DEVICE_RGB;
ColorSpace.lcsIntent=LCS_GM_BUSINESS;

// Create a color space.
//.....................
hColorSpace = CreateColorSpace( &ColorSpace );
SetColorSpace( hDC, hColorSpace );
GetLastError();

// Check the colors in the gamut.
//..............................
bRet = CheckColorsInGamut( hDC, aRGB, aResults, 5 );

DeleteColorSpace( hColorSpace );
SetICMMode( hDC, ICM_OFF );
DeleteDC( hDC );

// Display the results.
//....................
if ( bRet )
{
   hDC = GetDC( hWnd );

   for( i = 0; i < 5; i++ )
   {
      hBrush = CreateSolidBrush(
                     RGB( aRGB[i].rgbRed,
                          aRGB[i].rgbGreen,
                          aRGB[i].rgbBlue ) );
```

continued on next page

continued from previous page

```
                        SelectObject( hDC, hBrush );

                        Rectangle( hDC, 10, (I*30)+10,
                                        40, (I*30)+40 );

                        wsprintf( szMsg, "RGB( %d, %d, %d )",
                                        aRGB[i].rgbRed,
                                        aRGB[i].rgbGreen,
                                        aRGB[i].rgbBlue );

                        TextOut( hDC, 50, (i*30)+20, szMsg,
                                        strlen( szMsg ) );

                        if ( aResults[i] == CM_OUT_OF_GAMUT )
                            TextOut( hDC, 200, (i*30)+20,
                                        "- Not in the Gamut.", 19 );
                        else
                            TextOut( hDC, 200, (i*30)+20,
                                        "- In the Gamut.", 15 );

                        SelectObject( hDC,
                                        GetStockObject( WHITE_BRUSH ) );
                        DeleteObject( hBrush );
                    }

                    ReleaseDC( hWnd, hDC );
                }
            }
            break;

        case IDM_EXIT :
            DestroyWindow( hWnd );
            break;
        }
        break;

    case WM_DESTROY :
        PostQuitMessage(0);
        break;

    default :
        return( DefWindowProc( hWnd, uMsg, wParam, lParam ) );
    }

    return( OL );
}
```

ColorMatchToTarget   ■ WINDOWS 95   ■ WINDOWS NT

Description   ColorMatchToTarget enables or disables color matching preview for a
device context. When preview is enabled, colors in subsequent output to
the specified device context are displayed as they would appear on the target device context. To enable color matching preview, image color
matching must be enabled for both the target and the preview device context.

Syntax	BOOL **ColorMatchToTarget**(HDC *hdc,* HDC *hdcTarget,* DWORD *dwAction*)
Parameters	
hdc	HDC: The device context to use for preview, typically the display.
hdcTarget	HDC: The target device context, typically a printer.
dwAction	DWORD: One of the values listed in Table 16-2.

Table 16-2 ColorMatchToTarget *dwAction* values

Value	Meaning
CS_ENABLE	Enable color matching preview.
CS_DISABLE	Disable color matching preview.
CS_DELETE_TRANSFORM	Disable preview and delete the color transformation used for previewing.

Returns	BOOL: TRUE if successful; otherwise, the return value is FALSE.
Include File	wingdi.h
See Also	CheckColorsInGamut, SetICMMode
Example	This example shows how to use the **ColorMatchToTarget** function to display a preview of how a color will appear when printed on a printer. When the user selects the Test! menu item, two rectangles are displayed. The first rectangle is blue and the second is displayed in preview mode for the printer "HP DeskJet 550C Printer".

```
LRESULT CALLBACK WndProc( HWND hWnd, UINT uMsg, WPARAM wParam, LPARAM lParam )
{
   switch( uMsg )
   {
      case WM_COMMAND :
            switch( LOWORD( wParam ) )
            {
               case IDM_TEST :
                  {
                     HDC     hPrinterDC, hDC;
                     HBRUSH hBrush;

                     // Get device context for screen and printer.
                     //...........................................
                     hDC        = GetDC( hWnd );
                     hPrinterDC = CreateDC( "WINSPOOL",
                                            "HP DeskJet 550C Printer",
                                            NULL, NULL );

                     // Create a blue brush and select it into the DC.
                     //...............................................
                     hBrush = CreateSolidBrush( RGB( 0, 0, 255 ) );
                     SelectObject( hDC, hBrush );
```

continued on next page

continued from previous page

```
                        // Draw a blue rectangle.
                        //......................
                        Rectangle( hDC, 10, 10, 50, 50 );

                        // Turn on image color matching for both DCs.
                        //...........................................
                        SetICMMode( hDC, ICM_ON );
                        SetICMMode( hPrinterDC, ICM_ON );

                        // Turn on color preview and
                        // draw another rectangle.
                        //..........................
                        ColorMatchToTarget( hDC, hPrinterDC, 1 );
                        Rectangle( hDC, 60, 10, 100, 50 );
                        ColorMatchToTarget( hDC, hPrinterDC, 0 );

                        // Clean up.
                        //..........
                        SelectObject( hDC, GetStockObject( WHITE_BRUSH ) );
                        DeleteObject( hBrush );

                        SetICMMode( hDC, ICM_OFF );
                        SetICMMode( hPrinterDC, ICM_OFF );
                        DeleteDC( hPrinterDC );
                        ReleaseDC( hWnd, hDC );
                }
                break;
```

CreateColorSpace ■ WINDOWS 95 ■ WINDOWS NT

Description	CreateColorSpace creates a logical color space.
Syntax	HCOLORSPACE **CreateColorSpace**(LPLOGCOLORSPACE *lpLogColorSpace*)
Parameters	
lpLogColorSpace	LPLOGCOLORSPACE: A pointer to a **LOGCOLORSPACE** structure, which defines the logical color space to be created. See the definition of the **LOGCOLOR-SPACE** structure below.
Returns	HCOLORSPACE: If successful, a handle that identifies a logical color space; otherwise, **NULL**.
Include File	wingdi.h
See Also	DeleteColorSpace, GetLogColorSpace, SetColorSpace

LOGCOLORSPACE Definition

```
                typedef LONG LCSCSTYPE;
                typedef LONG LCSGAMUTMATCH;

                typedef struct tagLOGCOLORSPACE
                {
```

```
        DWORD          lcsSignature;
        DWORD          lcsVersion;
        DWORD          lcsSize;
        LCSCSTYPE      lcsCSType;
        LCSGAMUTMATCH  lcsIntent;
        CIEXYZTRIPLE   lcsEndpoints;
        DWORD          lcsGammaRed;
        DWORD          lcsGammaGreen;
        DWORD          lcsGammaBlue;
        TCHAR          lcsFilename[MAX_PATH];
    } LOGCOLORSPACE, *LPLOGCOLORSPACE;
```

Members

lcsSignature	DWORD: Color space signature.
lcsVersion	DWORD: Version number; must be **0x00000400**.
lcsSize	DWORD: Size of this structure.
lcsCSType	LCSCSTYPE: Color space type. This can be one of the values listed in Table 16-3.

Table 16-3 LOGCOLORSPACE *lcsCSType* values

Value	Meaning
LCS_DEVICE_RGB	Color values are device RGB values.
LCS_DEVICE_CMYK	Color values are device CMYK values.
LCS_CALIBRATED_RGB	Color values are calibrated RGB values. The values are translated using the endpoints given by the *lcsEndpoints* member before being passed to the device. If this value is not specified, *lcsEndpoints* is ignored.

lcsIntent	LCSGAMUTMATCH: The gamut matching method. This can be one of the values listed in Table 16-4.

Table 16-4 LOGCOLORSPACE *lcsIntent* values

Value	Meaning
LCS_GM_BUSINESS	Maintain saturation. Used for business charts and other situations in which undithered colors are required.
LCS_GM_GRAPHICS	Maintain colormetric match. Used for graphic designs and named colors.
LCS_GM_IMAGES	Maintain contrast. Used for photographs and natural images.

lcsEndpoints	CIEXYZTRIPLE: A **CIEXYZTRIPLE** structure containing the red, green, and blue endpoints. See the definition of the **CIEXYZTRIPLE** structure below.
lcsGammaRed	DWORD: Scale of the red coordinate.
lcsGammaGreen	DWORD: Scale of the green coordinate.
lcsGammaBlue	DWORD: Scale of the blue coordinate.

lcsFilename	**TCHAR[MAX_PATH]**: A character array containing a null-terminated string that names a color profile file. This member is typically set to an empty string but may be used to set the color space to be exactly as specified by a color profile. If a color profile is given, all other members of this structure should be set to reasonable values, even if the values are not 100 percent accurate.

CIEXYZTRIPLE Definition

```
typedef struct tagCIEXYZTRIPLE
{
    CIEXYZ  ciexyzRed;
    CIEXYZ  ciexyzGreen;
    CIEXYZ  ciexyzBlue;
} CIEXYZTRIPLE;
```

Members

ciexyzRed	**CIEXYZ**: The XYZ coordinates of the red endpoint. See the definition of the **CIEXYZ** structure below.
ciexyzGreen	**CIEXYZ**: The XYZ coordinates of the green endpoint.
ciexyzBlue	**CIEXYZ**: The XYZ coordinates of the blue endpoint.

CIEXYZ Definition

```
// Fixed point 2.30.
//................
typedef long FXPT2DOT30, *LPFXPT2DOT30;

typedef struct tagCIEXYZ
{
    FXPT2DOT30 ciexyzX;
    FXPT2DOT30 ciexyzY;
    FXPT2DOT30 ciexyzZ;
} CIEXYZ;
```

Members

ciexyzX	**FXPT2DOT30**: The x coordinate in fix point (2.30).
ciexyzY	**FXPT2DOT30**: The y coordinate in fix point (2.30).
ciexyzZ	**FXPT2DOT30**: The z coordinate in fix point (2.30).
Example	In this example, two rectangles are displayed on the client area, as shown in Figure 16-2, when the user selects the Test! menu item. The color of the first rectangle is blue, which is unmodified. Before the second rectangle is painted, image color matching is turned on and a logical color space is set for the device context. The color of the second rectangle is then red, even though it was painted with the same blue brush as the first rectangle.

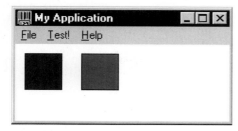

Figure 16-2 `CreateColorSpace` example

```
LRESULT CALLBACK WndProc( HWND hWnd, UINT uMsg, WPARAM wParam, LPARAM lParam )
{
   switch( uMsg )
   {
      case WM_COMMAND :
         switch( LOWORD( wParam ) )
         {
            case IDM_TEST :
               {
                  LOGCOLORSPACE ColorSpace;
                  HCOLORSPACE   hColorSpace;
                  HBRUSH        hBrush, hOldBrush;
                  HDC hDC = GetDC( hWnd );

                  // Fill LOGCOLORSPACE structure with
                  // appropriate values.
                  //..................................
                  ColorSpace.lcsSignature= (DWORD)0x50534F43;
                  ColorSpace.lcsVersion  = 0x00000400;
                  ColorSpace.lcsSize     = sizeof( ColorSpace );
                  ColorSpace.lcsCSType   = LCS_DEVICE_RGB;
                  ColorSpace.lcsIntent   = LCS_GM_BUSINESS;

                  ColorSpace.lcsGammaRed   = 0x00010000;
                  ColorSpace.lcsGammaGreen = 0x00010000;
                  ColorSpace.lcsGammaBlue  = 0x00010000;

                  ColorSpace.lcsEndpoints.ciexyzRed.ciexyzX = 0x000051FB;
                  ColorSpace.lcsEndpoints.ciexyzRed.ciexyzY = 0x000051EB;
                  ColorSpace.lcsEndpoints.ciexyzRed.ciexyzZ = 0x00002B85;

                  ColorSpace.lcsEndpoints.ciexyzGreen.ciexyzX = 0x0000186F;
                  ColorSpace.lcsEndpoints.ciexyzGreen.ciexyzY = 0x0000552D;
                  ColorSpace.lcsEndpoints.ciexyzGreen.ciexyzZ = 0x0000BA23;

                  ColorSpace.lcsEndpoints.ciexyzBlue.ciexyzX = 0x00011693;
                  ColorSpace.lcsEndpoints.ciexyzBlue.ciexyzY = 0x00003D46;
                  ColorSpace.lcsEndpoints.ciexyzBlue.ciexyzZ = 0x00001DED;

                  ColorSpace.lcsFilename[0] = 0;

                  // Create the color space and blue brush.
                  //.......................................
```

continued on next page

continued from previous page

```
hColorSpace = CreateColorSpace( &ColorSpace );
hBrush     = CreateSolidBrush( RGB( 0, 0, 255 ) );

// Select the blue brush into the device context.
//.................................................
hOldBrush = SelectObject( hDC, hBrush );

// Draw a blue rectangle.
//.......................
Rectangle( hDC, 10, 10, 50, 50 );

// Enable image color matching and
// set the color space.
//................................
SetICMMode( hDC, ICM_ON );
SetColorSpace( hDC, hColorSpace );

// Draw another "blue" rectangle that
// shows up as a red rectangle because
// of the color space.
//....................................
Rectangle( hDC, 70, 10, 110, 50 );

// Clean up.
//..........
SetICMMode( hDC, ICM_OFF );

SelectObject( hDC, hOldBrush );

DeleteColorSpace( hColorSpace );
DeleteObject( hBrush );

ReleaseDC( hWnd, hDC );
}
break;
```

CreateHalftonePalette ■ WINDOWS 95 ■ WINDOWS NT

Description	CreateHalftonePalette creates a halftone palette for the specified device context. Use this function to create a halftone palette when the stretching mode of a device context is set to **HALFTONE**. The logical halftone palette returned by CreateHalftonePalette should then be selected and realized into the device context before the **StretchBlt** or **StretchDIBits** function. Use the **DeleteObject** function to delete the palette when it is no longer needed.
Syntax	HPALETTE **CreateHalftonePalette**(HDC *hDC*)
Parameters	
hDC	HDC: The device context for which to create the halftone palette.

Returns	HPALETTE: If successful, the handle of the newly created logical halftone palette; otherwise, **NULL** is returned.
Include File	wingdi.h
See Also	SelectPalette, RealizePalette, GetDeviceCaps, DeleteObject, SetStretchBltMode

CreatePalette   ■ WINDOWS 95 ■ WINDOWS NT

Description	CreatePalette creates a logical palette based on the values specified in a **LOGPALETTE** structure. An application can determine whether a device supports palette operations by calling the **GetDeviceCaps** function with the **RASTERCAPS** value. Use the **SelectPalette** and **RealizePalette** functions to use the newly created palette.
Syntax	HPALETTE **CreatePalette**(CONST LOGPALETTE* *lplgpl*)
Parameters	
lplgpl	CONST LOGPALETTE*: A pointer to a **LOGPALETTE** structure that contains information about the colors in the logical palette to create.
Returns	HPALETTE: If successful, the handle of the newly created logical palette; otherwise, **NULL** is returned.
Include File	wingdi.h
See Also	SelectPalette, RealizePalette, GetDeviceCaps

LOGPALETTE Definition

```
typedef struct tagLOGPALETTE
{
    WORD         palVersion;
    WORD         palNumEntries;
    PALETTEENTRY palPalEntry[1];
} LOGPALETTE;
```

Members

palVersion	WORD: The Windows version number for the structure (currently 0x0300).
palNumEntries	WORD: The number of entries in the array that *palPalEntry* contains.
palPalEntry	PALETTEENTRY[1]: An array of **PALETTEENTRY** structures that define the color and usage of each entry in the logical palette. See the definition of the **PALETTEENTRY** structure below.

PALETTEENTRY Definition

```
typedef struct tagPALETTEENTRY
{
    BYTE peRed;
    BYTE peGreen;
    BYTE peBlue;
    BYTE peFlags;
} PALETTEENTRY;
```

Members

peRed	**BYTE**: The red intensity value.
peGreen	**BYTE**: The green intensity value.
peBlue	**BYTE**: The blue intensity value.
peFlags	**BYTE**: Determines how the palette entry is to be used. This may be set to **NULL** or one of the values listed in Table 16-5.

Table 16-5 PALETTEENTRY *peFlags* values

Flag	Description
PC_EXPLICIT	The low-order word of the logical palette entry designates a hardware palette index.
PC_NOCOLLAPSE	Specifies that the color be placed in an unused entry in the system palette instead of being matched to an existing color in the system palette. If there are no unused entries in the system palette, the color is matched normally.
PC_RESERVED	Specifies that the logical palette entry be used for palette animation; this flag prevents other windows from matching colors to the palette entry, since the color frequently changes. If an unused system palette entry is available, the color is placed in that entry.

Example

This example creates an initial palette with 16 colors of gray (white to black) when it is started. When the user selects the Test! menu item, the palette is expanded by 16 entries, which are filled with shades of blue. A sample of each color in the palette is painted as shown in Figure 16-3.

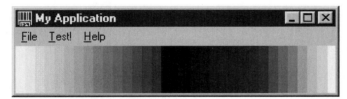

Figure 16-3 `CreatePalette` example

```
#define NUMBERCOLORS 16

LRESULT CALLBACK WndProc( HWND hWnd, UINT uMsg, WPARAM wParam, LPARAM lParam )
{
static LPLOGPALETTE pLogPal;
static HPALETTE      hPal;
static int           nPalSize;

    switch( uMsg )
    {
        case WM_CREATE :
                {
                    int i;

                    nPalSize = NUMBERCOLORS;
```

```
              // Allocate space for palette entries.
              //.................................
              pLogPal = HeapAlloc( GetProcessHeap(), HEAP_ZERO_MEMORY,
                                   sizeof( LOGPALETTE ) +
                                   (NUMBERCOLORS*sizeof( PALETTEENTRY )) );

              // Initialize palette entries with 16 shades of gray.
              //....................................................
              pLogPal->palVersion    = 0x300;
              pLogPal->palNumEntries = NUMBERCOLORS;

              for ( i = 0; i < NUMBERCOLORS-1; i++ )
              {
                  pLogPal->palPalEntry[i].peRed   = 255 - (i*15);
                  pLogPal->palPalEntry[i].peGreen = 255 - (i*15);
                  pLogPal->palPalEntry[i].peBlue  = 255 - (i*15);
                  pLogPal->palPalEntry[i].peFlags = PC_RESERVED;
              }

              // Set black palette entry.
              //.........................
              pLogPal->palPalEntry[i].peRed   = 0;
              pLogPal->palPalEntry[i].peGreen = 0;
              pLogPal->palPalEntry[i].peBlue  = 0;
              pLogPal->palPalEntry[i].peFlags = PC_RESERVED;

              // Create palette.
              //................
              hPal = CreatePalette( pLogPal );
          }
          break;

  case WM_PAINT :
          {
          PAINTSTRUCT ps;
          HBRUSH      hBrush;
          int         i;

          BeginPaint( hWnd, &ps );

          // Select and realize palette.
          //............................
          SelectPalette( ps.hdc, hPal, FALSE );
          RealizePalette( ps.hdc );

          SelectObject( ps.hdc, GetStockObject( NULL_PEN ) );

          // Paint a sample of each color in the palette.
          //.............................................
          for ( i = 0; i < nPalSize; i++ )
          {
              hBrush = CreateSolidBrush( PALETTEINDEX( i ) );
              SelectObject( ps.hdc, hBrush );
              Rectangle( ps.hdc, i*10, 0, (i*10)+11, 50 );
              SelectObject( ps.hdc, GetStockObject( WHITE_BRUSH ) );
              DeleteObject( hBrush );
          }
```

continued on next page

continued from previous page

```
                    EndPaint( hWnd, &ps );
            }
            break;

    case WM_COMMAND:
            switch ( LOWORD( wParam ) )
            {
                case IDM_TEST:
                    {
                        // Add more entries to palette for
                        // 16 shades of blue.
                        //..............................
                        if ( nPalSize == NUMBERCOLORS &&
                             ResizePalette( hPal, NUMBERCOLORS*2 ) )
                        {
                            int           i;
                            PALETTEENTRY pEntry;

                            nPalSize += NUMBERCOLORS;

                            // Initialize each of the new palette entries
                            // with gradient shades of blue.
                            //........................................
                            for( i = 0; i < NUMBERCOLORS/2; i++ )
                            {
                                pEntry.peRed   = 0;
                                pEntry.peGreen = 0;
                                pEntry.peBlue  = i*30;
                                pEntry.peFlags = PC_RESERVED;

                                SetPaletteEntries( hPal, i+NUMBERCOLORS,
                                                   1, &pEntry );
                            }

                            for( ; i < NUMBERCOLORS; i++ )
                            {
                                pEntry.peRed   = (i-(NUMBERCOLORS/2))*30;
                                pEntry.peGreen = (i-(NUMBERCOLORS/2))*30;
                                pEntry.peBlue  = 255;
                                pEntry.peFlags = PC_RESERVED;

                                SetPaletteEntries( hPal, i+NUMBERCOLORS,
                                                   1, &pEntry );
                            }

                            // Force repainting of the window.
                            //................................
                            InvalidateRect( hWnd, NULL, TRUE );
                        }
                    }
                    break;

                case IDM_EXIT:
                    DestroyWindow (hWnd);
                    break;

            }
            break;
```

```
        case WM_DESTROY:
                HeapFree( GetProcessHeap(), 0, pLogPal );
                DeleteObject( hPal );
                PostQuitMessage(0);
                break;

        default:
                return ( DefWindowProc( hWnd, uMsg, wParam, lParam ) );
    }
    return (0);
}
```

DeleteColorSpace   ■ Windows 95   ■ Windows NT

Description	DeleteColorSpace deletes a color space, freeing all internal resources associated with it. This function should be called as soon as a color space is no longer needed.
Syntax	BOOL **DeleteColorSpace**(HCOLORSPACE *hColorSpace*)
Parameters	
hColorSpace	HCOLORSPACE: Handle of the color space to delete, returned from a previous call to the CreateColorSpace function.
Returns	BOOL: TRUE if successful; otherwise, the return value is FALSE.
Include File	wingdi.h
See Also	CreateColorSpace, GetLogColorSpace
Example	See the example for the CreateColorSpace function.

EnumICMProfiles   ■ Windows 95   ■ Windows NT

Description	EnumICMProfiles enumerates the different color profiles that the system supports for a device context by passing the file name of each color profile to an application-defined callback function.
Syntax	int **EnumICMProfiles**(HDC *hdc*, ICMENUMPROC *lpICMEnumFunc*, LPARAM *lParam*)
Parameters	
hdc	HDC: The device context.
lpICMEnumFunc	ICMENUMPROC: The address of the application-defined callback function. See the description of the callback function below.
lParam	LPARAM: Application-supplied data. The data is passed to the callback function for each color profile.
Returns	int: The last value returned by the callback function, which may be 0 if the callback interrupted the enumeration. Otherwise, −1 if there are no color profiles to enumerate or image color matching is not enabled.

Include File	`wingdi.h`
See Also	`GetICMProfile, SetICMProfile`
Callback Syntax	`int CALLBACK` **`EnumICMProfilesProc`**`( LPTSTR` *`lpszFilename,`* `LPARAM` *`lparam`* `)`

Callback Parameters

lpszFilename   **LPTSTR**: A pointer to a null-terminated string specifying the name of the color profile file.

lParam   **LPARAM**: Application-supplied data passed by the **EnumICMProfiles** function.

Callback Returns   **int**: A positive value to continue enumeration, or **0** to stop enumeration. The function must not return a negative value.

Example   This example creates a list box the size of the client area when started. When the user selects the Test! menu item, the **EnumICMProfiles** function adds each of the installed ICM profiles to the list box.

```
LRESULT CALLBACK WndProc( HWND hWnd, UINT uMsg, WPARAM wParam, LPARAM lParam )
{
static HWND hListBox = NULL;

    switch( uMsg )
    {
        case WM_CREATE :
                // Create a listbox to place ICM profile names in.
                //..............................................
                hListBox = CreateWindow( "LISTBOX", "",
                                         WS_CHILD |
                                         WS_VISIBLE |
                                         LBS_STANDARD |
                                         LBS_NOINTEGRALHEIGHT,
                                         0, 0, 10, 10,
                                         hWnd, (HMENU)101,
                                         hInst, NULL );
                break;

        case WM_SIZE :
                // Size listbox to the same size as the
                // client area of the window.
                //..................................
                MoveWindow( hListBox, 0, 0,
                        LOWORD( lParam ), HIWORD( lParam ), FALSE );
                break;

        case WM_COMMAND:
                switch ( LOWORD( wParam ) )
                {
                    case IDM_TEST:
                            {
                            HDC hDC = GetDC( hWnd );

                            // Find all installed ICM profiles and
                            // add them to the list box.
```

```
                    //......................................
                    EnumICMProfiles( hDC, EnumICMProc,
                                     (LPARAM)hListBox );

                    ReleaseDC( hWnd, hDC );
                }
                break;
            .
            .
            .


int CALLBACK EnumICMProc( LPTSTR lpszFilename, LPARAM lParam )
{
    SendMessage( (HWND)lParam, LB_ADDSTRING, O, (LONG)lpszFilename );
    return( 1 );
}
```

GetBValue   ■ WINDOWS 95   ■ WINDOWS NT

Description	GetBValue is a macro that retrieves the intensity value for the blue component of an RGB value.
Syntax	BYTE **GetBValue**(COLORREF *rgb*)
Parameters	
rgb	COLORREF: The RGB color value.
Returns	BYTE: The intensity of the blue component of the specified RGB value.
Include File	wingdi.h
See Also	GetRValue, GetGValue
Example	See the example for the GetNearestColor function.

GetGValue   ■ WINDOWS 95   ■ WINDOWS NT

Description	GetGValue is a macro that retrieves the intensity value for the green component of an RGB value.
Syntax	BYTE **GetGValue**(COLORREF *rgb*)
Parameters	
rgb	COLORREF: The RGB color value.
Returns	BYTE: The intensity of the green component of the specified RGB value.
Include File	wingdi.h
See Also	GetRValue, GetBValue
Example	See the example for the GetNearestColor function.

GetRValue ■ Windows 95 ■ Windows NT

Description	GetRValue is a macro that retrieves the intensity value for the red component of an RGB value.
Syntax	BYTE **GetRValue**(COLORREF *rgb*)
Parameters	
rgb	COLORREF: The RGB color value.
Returns	BYTE: The intensity of the red component of the specified RGB value.
Include File	wingdi.h
See Also	GetGValue, GetBValue
Example	See the example for the GetNearestColor function.

GetColorAdjustment ■ Windows 95 ■ Windows NT

Description	GetColorAdjustment retrieves the color adjustment values for the specified device context. The color adjustment values are used to adjust the input color of the source bitmap for calls to the StretchBlt and StretchDIBits functions when HALFTONE mode is set.
Syntax	BOOL **GetColorAdjustment**(HDC *hDC,* LPCOLORADJUSTMENT *lpca*)
Parameters	
hDC	HDC: The device context for which to retrieve the color adjustment values.
lpca	LPCOLORADJUSTMENT: A pointer to a COLORADJUSTMENT structure that retrieves the color adjustment values. See the definition of the COLORADJUSTMENT structure under the SetColorAdjustment function later in this chapter.
Returns	BOOL: If successful, TRUE is returned; otherwise, FALSE is returned.
Include File	wingdi.h
See Also	SetColorAdjustment, SetStretchBltMode
Example	See the SetColorAdjustment function for an example of this function.

GetColorSpace ■ Windows 95 ■ Windows NT

Description	GetColorSpace retrieves the current handle of the logical color space from a device context.
Syntax	HLOGCOLORSPACE **GetColorSpace**(HDC *hdc*)

Parameters

hdc   HDC: The device context.

Returns   HLOGCOLORSPACE: If successful, the current handle of the logical color space; otherwise, NULL.

Include File   wingdi.h

See Also   GetLogColorSpace, CreateColorSpace, SetColorSpace

Example   This example uses the **GetColorSpace** function to check if a color space is set for the device context of the window's client area when the user selects the Test! menu item. If a color space is set, the color space information is retrieved with the **GetLogColorSpace** function.

```
LRESULT CALLBACK WndProc( HWND hWnd, UINT uMsg, WPARAM wParam, LPARAM lParam )
{
    switch( uMsg )
    {
        case WM_COMMAND:
                switch ( LOWORD( wParam ) )
                {
                    case IDM_TEST:
                        {
                            HLOGCOLORSPACE hCS;
                            HDC hDC = GetDC( hWnd );

                            if ( hCS = GetColorSpace( hDC ) )
                            {
                                LOGCOLORSPACE logCS;

                                // Retrieve the logical
                                // color space information.
                                //........................
                                GetLogColorSpace( hCS, &logCS,
                                                    sizeof(logCS) );

                                // Use the logical color space information.
                                //........................................
                                    .
                                    .
                                    .
                            }
                            else
                                MessageBox( hWnd, "No color space is set.",
                                                    "Message",
                                                    MB_OK | MB_ICONINFORMATION );

                            ReleaseDC( hWnd, hDC );
                        }
                        break;
                .
                .
                .
```

GetDeviceGammaRamp

Description	GetDeviceGammaRamp retrieves the gamma ramp on direct color display boards. Direct color display modes, usually 16-, 24-, or 32-bit color, do not use color lookup tables. Not all direct color video boards support loadable gamma ramps, and this function only succeeds for those that support loadable gamma ramps in hardware.
Syntax	BOOL **GetDeviceGammaRamp**(HDC *hdc,* LPVOID *lpRamp*)
Parameters	
hdc	HDC: The device context.
lpRamp	LPVOID: A pointer to a set of three arrays (red, green, and blue) of 256-byte elements. These arrays are the mapping between color values in the frame buffer and DAC values.
Returns	BOOL: TRUE if successful; otherwise, the return value is FALSE.
Include File	wingdi.h
See Also	SetDeviceGammaRamp
Example	See the example for the SetDeviceGammaRamp function.

GetICMProfile

Description	GetICMProfile retrieves the name of the color profile file for the device associated with a device context. This function fails if image color matching has not been enabled for the device context.
Syntax	BOOL **GetICMProfile**(HDC *hdc,* DWORD *cbName,* LPTSTR *lpszFilename*)
Parameters	
hdc	HDC: The device context.
cbName	DWORD: The size, in bytes, of the buffer that receives the file name.
lpszFilename	LPTSTR: A pointer to a buffer that receives the null-terminated string specifying the full path of the color profile file.
Returns	BOOL: TRUE if successful; otherwise, the return value is FALSE.
Include File	wingdi.h
See Also	SetICMProfile, SetICMMode
Example	See the example for the SetICMProfile function.

GetLogColorSpace ■ Windows 95 ■ Windows NT

Description	GetLogColorSpace retrieves information about the logical color space identified by the given handle. This function copies as much information to the buffer as space allows. To determine the correct size of the buffer to use, applications should check the *lcsSize* member in the LOGCOLORSPACE structure.
Syntax	BOOL **GetLogColorSpace**(HLOGCOLORSPACE *hColorSpace,* LPLOGCOLOR-SPACE *lpbuffer,* DWORD *dwSize*)
Parameters	
hColorSpace	HLOGCOLORSPACE: The handle of the logical color space.
lpBuffer	LPLOGCOLORSPACE: A pointer to a LOGCOLORSPACE structure that receives the logical color space information. See the definition of the LOGCOLOR-SPACE structure under the **CreateColorSpace** function.
dwSize	DWORD: Maximum size, in bytes, of the buffer pointed to by *lpBuffer.*
Returns	BOOL: TRUE if successful; otherwise, the return value is FALSE.
Include File	wingdi.h
See Also	CreateColorSpace, DeleteColorSpace, GetColorSpace
Example	See the example for the GetColorSpace function.

GetNearestColor ■ Windows 95 ■ Windows NT

Description	GetNearestColor returns a color value identifying a color from the system palette that will be displayed when the specified color value is used.
Syntax	COLORREF **GetNearestColor**(HDC *hdc,* COLORREF *crColor*)
Parameters	
hdc	HDC: The device context.
crColor	COLORREF: A color value that identifies a requested color.
Returns	COLORREF: If successful, a color from the system palette that corresponds to the given color value; otherwise, it is CLR_INVALID.
Include File	wingdi.h
See Also	GetNearestPaletteIndex, GetDeviceCaps
Example	This example, shown in Figure 16-4, uses the GetNearestColor function to match the requested color to the available colors in the system palette.

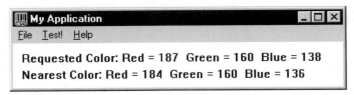

Figure 16-4 GetNearestColor example

```
LRESULT CALLBACK WndProc( HWND hWnd, UINT uMsg, WPARAM wParam, LPARAM lParam )
{
    switch( uMsg )
    {
        case WM_COMMAND:
                switch ( LOWORD( wParam ) )
                {
                    case IDM_TEST:
                        {
                            COLORREF color;
                            char      szMsg[128];
                            HDC hDC = GetDC( hWnd );

                            color = GetNearestColor( hDC,RGB( 187, 160, 138 ) );

                            wsprintf( szMsg,
                                    "Requested Color: Red = %d  Green = %d  Blue = %d",
                                    187, 160, 138 );

                            TextOut( hDC, 10, 10, szMsg, strlen( szMsg ) );

                            wsprintf( szMsg,
                                    "Nearest Color: Red = %d  Green = %d  Blue = %d",
                                    GetRValue( color ),
                                    GetGValue( color ),
                                    GetBValue( color ) );

                            TextOut( hDC, 10, 30, szMsg, strlen( szMsg ) );

                            ReleaseDC( hWnd, hDC );
                        }
                        break;
                    .
                    .
                    .
```

GetNearestPaletteIndex ■ WINDOWS 95 ■ WINDOWS NT

Description	GetNearestPaletteIndex retrieves the index for the entry in a logical palette that most closely matches a specified color value. An application can determine whether a device supports palette operations by calling the GetDeviceCaps function with the RASTERCAPS value.
Syntax	UINT **GetNearestPaletteIndex(** HPALETTE *hPal,* COLORREF *crColor* **)**

Parameters

hPal   HPALETTE: The handle of the logical palette.

crColor   COLORREF: The color to be matched.

Returns   UINT: If successful, the index of the matching entry in the logical palette;
                    otherwise, CLR_INVALID.

Include File   wingdi.h

See Also   GetNearestColor, GetDeviceCaps

Example   This example demonstrates how to use the GetNearestPaletteIndex
                    function to reduce colors to match a grayscale. When the application
                    starts, a 16-color gray color palette is created and displayed along the top
                    of the client area as shown in Figure 16-5. When the user selects the Test!
                    menu item, the GetNearestPaletteIndex function finds a gray color to
                    use for red. A rectangle then appears in the found color.

```
#define NUMBERCOLORS 16

LRESULT CALLBACK WndProc( HWND hWnd, UINT uMsg, WPARAM wParam, LPARAM lParam )
{
static LPLOGPALETTE pLogPal;
static HPALETTE     hPal;

   switch( uMsg )
   {
      case WM_CREATE :
              {
                  int i;

                  // Allocate space for palette entries.
                  //...................................
                  pLogPal = HeapAlloc( GetProcessHeap(), HEAP_ZERO_MEMORY,
                                       sizeof( LOGPALETTE ) +
                                       (NUMBERCOLORS*sizeof( PALETTEENTRY )) );

                  // Initialize palette entries with 16 shades of gray.
                  //..................................................
                  pLogPal->palVersion    = 0x300;
                  pLogPal->palNumEntries = NUMBERCOLORS;

                  for ( i = 0; i < NUMBERCOLORS-1; i++ )
                  {
                      pLogPal->palPalEntry[i].peRed   = 255 - (i*15);
                      pLogPal->palPalEntry[i].peGreen = 255 - (i*15);
                      pLogPal->palPalEntry[i].peBlue  = 255 - (i*15);
                      pLogPal->palPalEntry[i].peFlags = PC_RESERVED;
                  }

                  // Set black palette entry.
                  //........................
                  pLogPal->palPalEntry[i].peRed   = 0;
                  pLogPal->palPalEntry[i].peGreen = 0;
                  pLogPal->palPalEntry[i].peBlue  = 0;
                  pLogPal->palPalEntry[i].peFlags = PC_RESERVED;
```

continued on next page

continued from previous page

```
                    // Create palette.
                    //.................
                    hPal = CreatePalette( pLogPal );
                }
                break;

        case WM_PAINT :
                {
                    PAINTSTRUCT ps;
                    HBRUSH      hBrush;
                    int         i;

                    BeginPaint( hWnd, &ps );

                    // Select and realize palette.
                    //............................
                    SelectPalette( ps.hdc, hPal, FALSE );
                    RealizePalette( ps.hdc );

                    SelectObject( ps.hdc, GetStockObject( NULL_PEN ) );

                    // Paint a sample of each color in the palette.
                    //.............................................
                    for ( i = 0; i < NUMBERCOLORS; i++ )
                    {
                        hBrush = CreateSolidBrush( PALETTEINDEX( i ) );
                        SelectObject( ps.hdc, hBrush );
                        Rectangle( ps.hdc, i*10, 0, (i*10)+11, 50 );
                        SelectObject( ps.hdc, GetStockObject( WHITE_BRUSH ) );
                        DeleteObject( hBrush );
                    }

                    EndPaint( hWnd, &ps );
                }
                break;

        case WM_COMMAND:
                switch ( LOWORD( wParam ) )
                {
                    case IDM_TEST:
                        {
                            COLORREF color;
                            HDC      hDC = GetDC( hWnd );

                            color = GetNearestPaletteIndex( hPal,
                                                     RGB( 255, 0, 0 ) );

                            // Display a rectangle with the color found.
                            //..........................................
                            if ( color != CLR_INVALID )
                            {
                                HBRUSH hBrush;
```

```
                        hBrush = CreateSolidBrush( PALETTEINDEX(color) );

                        SelectObject( hDC, hBrush );
                        Rectangle( hDC, 10, 60, 50, 100 );
                        SelectObject( hDC, GetStockObject(WHITE_BRUSH) );

                        DeleteObject( hBrush );
                    }

                    ReleaseDC( hWnd, hDC );
                }
                break;

            case IDM_EXIT:
                DestroyWindow (hWnd);
                break;
        }
        break;

    case WM_DESTROY:
        HeapFree( GetProcessHeap(), 0, pLogPal );
        DeleteObject( hPal );
        PostQuitMessage(0);
        break;

    default:
        return ( DefWindowProc( hWnd, uMsg, wParam, lParam ) );
    }
    return (0);
}
```

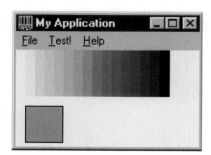

Figure 16-5 `GetNearestPaletteIndex` example

GetPaletteEntries

Description	**GetPaletteEntries** retrieves a specified range of palette entries from a logical palette. An application can determine whether a device supports palette operations by calling the **GetDeviceCaps** function with the **RASTERCAPS** value.
Syntax	UINT **GetPaletteEntries**(HPALETTE *hPal,* UINT *uStartIndex,* UINT *uEntries,* LPPALETTEENTRY *lppe*)
Parameters	
hPal	**HPALETTE**: The handle of the logical palette.
uStartIndex	**UINT**: The first entry in the logical palette to be retrieved.
uEntries	**UINT**: The number of entries in the logical palette to be retrieved.
lppe	**LPPALETTEENTRY**: A pointer to an array of **PALETTEENTRY** structures that receives the palette entries. The array must contain at least as many structures as specified by the *nEntries* parameter. If set to **NULL**, the total number of palette entries in the palette is returned. See the definition of the **PALETTEENTRY** structure under the **CreatePalette** function.
Returns	**UINT**: If successful and *lppe* is not **NULL**, the number of entries retrieved from the logical palette is returned. If *lppe* is **NULL**, the number of entries in the palette is returned. If an error occurs, **0** is returned.
Include File	wingdi.h
See Also	GetSystemPaletteEntries, CreatePalette, GetDeviceCaps
Example	This example shows how to use the **GetPaletteEntries** function to create a new palette that has a subset of the entries that the original palette had. When the user selects the Test! menu item, five entries, beginning with entry **2**, are retrieved from the palette and used to create a new palette.

```
LRESULT CALLBACK WndProc( HWND hWnd, UINT uMsg, WPARAM wParam, LPARAM lParam )
{
static HPALETTE hPal;

    switch( uMsg )
    {
        case WM_CREATE :
                {
                LPLOGPALETTE pLogPal;
                int          i;

                // Allocate space for palette entries.
                //.................................
                pLogPal = HeapAlloc( GetProcessHeap(), HEAP_ZERO_MEMORY,
                                     sizeof( LOGPALETTE ) +
                                     (16*sizeof( PALETTEENTRY )) );

                // Initialize palette entries with 16 shades of gray.
                //.................................................
```

```
                pLogPal->palVersion    = 0x300;
                pLogPal->palNumEntries = 16;

                for ( i = 0; i < 15; i++ )
                {
                    pLogPal->palPalEntry[i].peRed   = 255 - (i*15);
                    pLogPal->palPalEntry[i].peGreen = 255 - (i*15);
                    pLogPal->palPalEntry[i].peBlue  = 255 - (i*15);
                    pLogPal->palPalEntry[i].peFlags = PC_RESERVED;
                }

                // Set black palette entry.
                //........................
                pLogPal->palPalEntry[i].peRed   = 0;
                pLogPal->palPalEntry[i].peGreen = 0;
                pLogPal->palPalEntry[i].peBlue  = 0;
                pLogPal->palPalEntry[i].peFlags = PC_RESERVED;

                // Create palette.
                //...............
                hPal = CreatePalette( pLogPal );
                HeapFree( GetProcessHeap(), 0, pLogPal );
            }
            break;

    case WM_PAINT :
            {
                PAINTSTRUCT ps;
                HBRUSH      hBrush;
                int         i, nNumColors;

                BeginPaint( hWnd, &ps );

                nNumColors = GetPaletteEntries( hPal, 0 , 0, NULL );

                // Select and realize palette.
                //...........................
                SelectPalette( ps.hdc, hPal, FALSE );
                RealizePalette( ps.hdc );

                SelectObject( ps.hdc, GetStockObject( NULL_PEN ) );

                // Paint a sample of each color in the palette.
                //............................................
                for ( i = 0; i < nNumColors; i++ )
                {
                    hBrush = CreateSolidBrush( PALETTEINDEX( i ) );
                    SelectObject( ps.hdc, hBrush );
                    Rectangle( ps.hdc, i*10, 0, (i*10)+11, 50 );
                    SelectObject( ps.hdc, GetStockObject( WHITE_BRUSH ) );
                    DeleteObject( hBrush );
                }

                EndPaint( hWnd, &ps );
            }
            break;
```

continued on next page

continued from previous page

```
        case WM_COMMAND:
                switch ( LOWORD( wParam ) )
                {
                    case IDM_TEST:
                            {
                                LPLOGPALETTE pLogPal;

                                pLogPal = HeapAlloc( GetProcessHeap(),
                                                     HEAP_ZERO_MEMORY,
                                                     sizeof( LOGPALETTE ) +
                                                     (5*sizeof( PALETTEENTRY )) );

                                // Retrieve a subset of the palette entries.
                                //.............................................
                                GetPaletteEntries( hPal, 2, 5,
                                                   pLogPal->palPalEntry );

                                pLogPal->palVersion    = 0x300;
                                pLogPal->palNumEntries = 5;

                                DeleteObject( hPal );

                                // Create a new palette with the
                                // smaller number of entries.
                                //...............................
                                hPal = CreatePalette( pLogPal );
                                HeapFree( GetProcessHeap(), 0, pLogPal );

                                InvalidateRect( hWnd, NULL, TRUE );
                            }
                            break;

                    case IDM_EXIT:
                            DestroyWindow (hWnd);
                            break;
                }
                break;

        case WM_DESTROY:
                DeleteObject( hPal );
                PostQuitMessage(0);
                break;

        default:
                return ( DefWindowProc( hWnd, uMsg, wParam, lParam ) );
    }
    return (0);
}
```

GetSystemPaletteEntries   ■ WINDOWS 95   ■ WINDOWS NT

Description   GetSystemPaletteEntries retrieves a range of palette entries from the system palette that is associated with a context. An application can determine whether a device supports palette operations by calling the GetDeviceCaps function with the RASTERCAPS value.

Syntax	UINT **GetSystemPaletteEntries**(HDC *hdc,* UINT *uStartIndex,* UINT *uEntries,* LPPALETTEENTRY *lppe*)
Parameters	
hdc	**HDC**: The device context.
uStartIndex	**UINT**: The first entry to be retrieved from the system palette.
uEntries	**UINT**: The number of entries to be retrieved from the system palette.
lppe	**LPPALETTEENTRY**: A pointer to an array of **PALETTEENTRY** structures that receives the palette entries. The array must contain at least as many structures as specified by the *uEntries* parameter. If set to **NULL**, it returns the total number of palette entries in the palette. See the definition of the **PALETTEENTRY** structure under the **CreatePalette** function.
Returns	**UINT**: If successful, the number of entries retrieved from the palette; otherwise, the return value is **0**.
Include File	wingdi.h
See Also	GetPaletteEntries, CreatePalette, GetDeviceCaps
Example	This example, shown in Figure 16-6, demonstrates how to dump the RGB content of each color in the system palette. These are the 20 reserved colors that Windows uses to do most drawing.

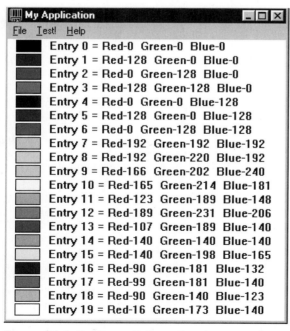

Figure 16-6 GetSystemPaletteEntries example

```
LRESULT CALLBACK WndProc( HWND hWnd, UINT uMsg, WPARAM wParam, LPARAM lParam )
{
static PALETTEENTRY peEntry[20];
static char        szMsg[128];

    switch( uMsg )
    {
        case WM_PAINT :
                {
                    PAINTSTRUCT ps;
                    HBRUSH      hBrush;
                    int         i,nNumEntries;

                    BeginPaint( hWnd, &ps );
                    nNumEntries = GetSystemPaletteEntries( ps.hdc,0,20,peEntry );

                    for( i=0; i < nNumEntries; i++ )
                    {
                        wsprintf( szMsg, "Entry %d = Red-%d  Green-%d  Blue-%d",
                                    i, peEntry[i].peRed,
                                       peEntry[i].peGreen,
                                       peEntry[i].peBlue );

                        hBrush = CreateSolidBrush( PALETTEINDEX( i ) );
                        SelectObject( ps.hdc, hBrush );
                        Rectangle( ps.hdc, 10, (i*17)+1, 40, (i*17)+16 );
                        TextOut( ps.hdc, 50, i*17, szMsg, strlen( szMsg ) );
                        SelectObject( ps.hdc, GetStockObject( WHITE_BRUSH ) );
                        DeleteObject( hBrush );
                    }

                    EndPaint( hWnd, &ps );
                }
                break;
        .
        .
        .
```

GetSystemPaletteUse ■ WINDOWS 95 ■ WINDOWS NT

Description	GetSystemPaletteUse retrieves the current state of the system (physical) palette associated with a device context. By default, the system palette contains 20 static colors that are not changed when an application realizes its logical palette. An application can gain access to most of these colors by calling the SetSystemPaletteUse function.
Syntax	UINT **GetSystemPaletteUse**(HDC *hdc*)
Parameters	
hdc	HDC: The device context.
Returns	UINT: The current state of the system palette associated with the given device context. This can be one of the values listed in Table 16-6.

Table 16-6 `GetSystemPaletteUse` return values

Value	Meaning
SYSPAL_ERROR	The given device context is invalid or does not support a color palette.
SYSPAL_NOSTATIC	The system palette contains no static colors except black and white.
SYSPAL_STATIC	The system palette contains static colors that will not change when an application realizes its logical palette.

Include File	`wingdi.h`
See Also	`GetSystemPaletteEntries`, `SetSystemPaletteUse`, `GetDeviceCaps`
Example	See the example for the `SetSystemPaletteUse` function.

RealizePalette   ■ WINDOWS 95   ■ WINDOWS NT

Description   `RealizePalette` maps palette entries from the currently selected logical palette to the system palette. If the device context (DC) is a memory DC, the color table for the bitmap selected into the DC is modified. If the device context is a display DC, the physical palette for that device is modified.

Syntax   UINT **RealizePalette**(HDC *hdc*)

Parameters

hdc   HDC: The device context into which a logical palette has been selected.

Returns   UINT: If successful, the number of entries in the logical palette mapped to the system palette; otherwise, GDI_ERROR is returned.

Include File   `wingdi.h`

See Also   `SelectPalette`, `CreatePalette`, `GetDeviceCaps`

Example   See the example for the `CreatePalette` function.

ResizePalette   ■ WINDOWS 95   ■ WINDOWS NT

Description   `ResizePalette` increases or decreases the size of a logical palette based on the specified value. If an application calls `ResizePalette` to reduce the size of the palette, the entries remaining in the resized palette are unchanged. If it is called to enlarge the palette, the additional palette entries are set to black and their flags are set to 0.

Syntax   BOOL **ResizePalette**(HPALETTE *hPal,* UINT *uEntries*)

Parameters

hPal   HPALETTE: The handle of the palette to be changed.

uEntries   UINT: The number of entries in the palette after it is resized.

Returns	BOOL: TRUE if successful; otherwise, the return value is FALSE.
Include File	wingdi.h
See Also	CreatePalette
Example	See the example for the CreatePalette function.

SelectPalette ■ Windows 95 ■ Windows NT

Description	SelectPalette selects a logical palette into a device context. An application can select a logical palette into more than one device context. However, changes to a logical palette will affect all device contexts for which it is selected. An application can determine whether a device supports palette operations by calling the GetDeviceCaps function with RASTERCAPS.
Syntax	HPALETTE **SelectPalette**(HDC *hdc,* HPALETTE *hPal,* BOOL *bForceBackground*)
Parameters	
hdc	HDC: The device context.
hPal	HPALETTE: The handle of the logical palette to be selected.
bForceBackground	BOOL: If set to TRUE, RealizePalette causes the logical palette to be mapped in the best possible way to the colors already in the physical palette. If set to FALSE, RealizePalette causes the logical palette to be copied into the device palette when the application is in the foreground. If the *hdc* parameter is a memory device context, this parameter is ignored.
Returns	HPALETTE: If successful, the device context's previous logical palette; otherwise, NULL is returned.
Include File	wingdi.h
See Also	RealizePalette, CreatePalette
Example	See the example for the CreatePalette function.

SetColorAdjustment ■ Windows 95 ■ Windows NT

Description	SetColorAdjustment sets the color adjustment values for a device context using the specified values. The color adjustment values are used to adjust the input color of the source bitmap for calls to the StretchBlt and StretchDIBits functions when HALFTONE mode is set.
Syntax	BOOL **SetColorAdjustment**(HDC *hDC,* CONST COLORADJUSTMENT* *lpca*)
Parameters	
hDC	HDC: The device context for which to set the color adjustment.

lpca	CONST COLORADJUSTMENT*: A pointer to a structure containing the new color adjustment values. See the definition of the COLORADJUSTMENT structure below.
Returns	BOOL: If successful, TRUE is returned; otherwise, FALSE is returned.
Include File	wingdi.h
See Also	GetColorAdjustment, SetStretchBltMode

COLORADJUSTMENT Definition

```
typedef struct   tagCOLORADJUSTMENT
{
    WORD   caSize;
    WORD   caFlags;
    WORD   caIlluminantIndex;
    WORD   caRedGamma;
    WORD   caGreenGamma;
    WORD   caBlueGamma;
    WORD   caReferenceBlack;
    WORD   caReferenceWhite;
    SHORT  caContrast;
    SHORT  caBrightness;
    SHORT  caColorfulness;
    SHORT  caRedGreenTint;
} COLORADJUSTMENT;
```

Members

caSize	WORD: The size, in bytes, of the structure.
caFlags	WORD: Determines how the output image should be prepared. This member may be set to NULL or any combination of the values listed in Table 16-7.

Table 16-7 COLORADJUSTMENT *caFlags* values

Value	Meaning
CA_LOG_FILTER	A logarithmic function should be applied to the final density of the output colors. This will increase the color contrast when the luminance is low.
CA_NEGATIVE	The negative of the original image should be displayed.

caIlluminantIndex	WORD: The type of standard light source under which the image is viewed. This member may be one of the values listed in Table 16-8.

Table 16-8 COLORADJUSTMENT *caIlluminantIndex* values

Value	Meaning
ILLUMINANT_DEVICE_DEFAULT	Device's default.
ILLUMINANT_A	Tungsten lamp.
ILLUMINANT_B	Noon sunlight.

continued on next page

continued from previous page

Value	Meaning
ILLUMINANT_C	NTSC daylight.
ILLUMINANT_D50	Normal print.
ILLUMINANT_D55	Bond paper print.
ILLUMINANT_D65	Standard daylight. Standard for CRTs and pictures.
ILLUMINANT_D75	Northern daylight.
ILLUMINANT_F2	Cool white lamp
ILLUMINANT_TUNGSTEN	Same as ILLUMINANT_A.
ILLUMINANT_DAYLIGHT	Same as ILLUMINANT_C.
ILLUMINANT_FLUORESCENT	Same as ILLUMINANT_F2.
ILLUMINANT_NTSC	Same as ILLUMINANT_C.

caRedGamma WORD: The nth power gamma-correction value for the red primary of the source colors. The value must be in the range from 2500 to 65,000, with **10,000** meaning no gamma correction.

caGreenGamma WORD: The nth power gamma-correction value for the green primary of the source colors. The value must be in the range from 2500 to 65,000, with **10,000** meaning no gamma correction.

caBlueGamma WORD: The nth power gamma-correction value for the blue primary of the source colors. The value must be in the range from 2500 to 65,000, with **10,000** meaning no gamma correction.

caReferenceBlack WORD: The black reference for the source colors. Any colors that are darker than this are treated as black. The value must be in the range from 0 to 4,000.

caReferenceWhite WORD: The white reference for the source colors. Any colors that are lighter than this are treated as white. The value must be in the range from 6,000 to 10,000.

caContrast SHORT: The amount of contrast to be applied to the source object. The value must be in the range from -100 to 100. A value of **0** means no contrast adjustment.

caBrightness SHORT: The amount of brightness to be applied to the source object. The value must be in the range from -100 to 100. A value of **0** means no brightness adjustment.

caColorfulness SHORT: The amount of colorfulness to be applied to the source object. The value must be in the range from -100 to 100. A value of **0** means no colorfulness adjustment.

caRedGreenTint SHORT: The amount of red or green tint adjustment to be applied to the source object. The value must be in the range from -100 to 100. Positive numbers adjust toward red and negative numbers adjust toward green. A value of **0** means no tint adjustment.

Example　　　This example displays a negative of the **"SmileBMP"** when the user selects the Test! menu item. The example uses the **GetColorAdjustment** function to retrieve the current color adjustment values for the device context. The color adjustment values are adjusted to produce a negative image and set with the **SetColorAdjustment** function.

```
LRESULT CALLBACK WndProc( HWND hWnd, UINT uMsg, WPARAM wParam, LPARAM lParam )
{
    switch( uMsg )
    {
        case WM_COMMAND :
                switch( LOWORD( wParam ) )
                {
                    case IDM_TEST :
                        {
                            HBITMAP hBitmap;
                            BITMAP  bm;
                            HDC     hDC;
                            HDC     hMemDC;
                            RECT    rect;
                            COLORADJUSTMENT ca;

                            // Load the bitmap into memory.
                            //...........................
                            hBitmap = LoadBitmap( hInst, "SmileBMP" );

                            // Get the bitmap information.
                            //...........................
                            GetObject( hBitmap, sizeof( BITMAP ), &bm );

                            // Paint the bitmap on the screen.
                            //...............................
                            hDC = GetDC( hWnd );
                            hMemDC = CreateCompatibleDC( hDC );

                            SelectObject( hMemDC, hBitmap );
                            GetClientRect( hWnd, &rect );
                            SetStretchBltMode( hDC, STRETCH_HALFTONE );

                            // Set the color adjustment to produce a
                            // negative image.
                            //.....................................
                            ca.caSize = sizeof( COLORADJUSTMENT );
                            if ( GetColorAdjustment( hDC, &ca ) )
                            {
                                ca.caFlags = CA_NEGATIVE;
                                SetColorAdjustment( hDC, &ca );
                            }

                            // Paint the bitmap the size of the client area.
                            //.............................................
                            StretchBlt( hDC, 0, 0, rect.right, rect.bottom,
                                        hMemDC, 0, 0, bm.bmWidth, bm.bmHeight,
                                        SRCCOPY );
```

continued on next page

continued from previous page

```
                        DeleteDC( hMemDC );
                        ReleaseDC( hWnd, hDC );
                        DeleteObject( hBitmap );
                    }
                    break;
```

SetColorSpace ■ WINDOWS 95 ■ WINDOWS NT

Description	SetColorSpace sets the color space for a device context.
Syntax	BOOL **SetColorSpace**(HDC *hdc,* HCOLORSPACE *hColorSpace*)
Parameters	
hdc	HDC: The device context.
hColorSpace	HCOLORSPACE: The handle of the logical color space.
Returns	BOOL: TRUE if successful; otherwise, the return value is FALSE.
Include File	wingdi.h
See Also	CreateColorSpace
Example	See the example for the **CreateColorSpace** function.

SetDeviceGammaRamp ■ WINDOWS 95 ■ WINDOWS NT

Description	SetDeviceGammaRamp sets the gamma ramp on direct color display boards. Direct color display modes do not use color lookup tables. The direct color modes are usually 16-, 24-, or 32-bit. Not all direct color video boards support loadable gamma ramps.
Syntax	BOOL **SetDeviceGammaRamp**(HDC *hdc,* LPVOID *lpRamp*)
Parameters	
hdc	HDC: The device context.
lpRamp	LPVOID: A pointer to a set of three arrays (red, green, and blue) of 256-byte elements. These arrays are the mapping between color values in the frame buffer and DAC values.
Returns	BOOL: TRUE if successful; otherwise, the return value is FALSE.
Include File	wingdi.h
See Also	GetDeviceGammaRamp
Example	This example shows how the **GetDeviceGammaRamp** and **SetDeviceGammaRamp** functions retrieve and modify the gamma ramp of a

display device. When the user selects the Test! menu item, the example retrieves the gamma ramp for the display and changes the black color to red. The new gamma ramp setting is demonstrated by displaying a red rectangle using a black brush.

```c
typedef struct
{
   BYTE aRed[256];
   BYTE aGreen[256];
   BYTE aBlue[256];
} GAMMASTRUCT;

LRESULT CALLBACK WndProc( HWND hWnd, UINT uMsg, WPARAM wParam, LPARAM lParam )
{
   switch( uMsg )
   {
      case WM_COMMAND:
            switch ( LOWORD( wParam ) )
            {
               case IDM_TEST:
                  {
                     GAMMASTRUCT gs;
                     HDC        hDC = GetDC( hWnd );

                     if( GetDeviceGammaRamp( hDC, &gs ) )
                     {
                        // Change the black entry to red.
                        //...............................
                        gs.aRed[0]   = 255;
                        gs.aGreen[0] = 0;
                        gs.aBlue[0]  = 0;

                        SetDeviceGammaRamp( hDC, &gs );

                        // Display a rectangle; it should be red.
                        //......................................
                        SelectObject( hDC,
                                    GetStockObject( BLACK_BRUSH ) );
                        Rectangle( hDC, 10, 10, 50, 50 );
                     }
                     else
                        MessageBox( hWnd,
                                    "Gamma ramps not supported.",
                                    "Message",
                                    MB_OK | MB_ICONINFORMATION );

                     ReleaseDC( hWnd, hDC );
                  }
                  break;

                     .
                     .
                     .
```

SetICMMode

Description	SetICMMode enables or disables image color matching for a device context.
Syntax	BOOL **SetICMMode**(HDC *hdc,* int *fICM*)
Parameters	
hdc	HDC: The device context.
fICM	int: Set to one of the values listed in Table 16-9.

Table 16-9 SetICMMode *fICM* values

Value	Meaning
ICM_ON	Turn on image color matching.
ICM_OFF	Turn off image color matching.
ICM_QUERY	Return the current mode.

Returns	BOOL: TRUE if successful; otherwise, the return value is FALSE. If *fICM* is set to ICM_QUERY, the function returns ICM_ON or ICM_OFF to indicate the current mode.
Include File	wingdi.h
See Also	SetICMProfile, GetColorSpace
Example	See the example for the CreateColorSpace function.

SetICMProfile

Description	SetICMProfile sets the color profile for a device context.
Syntax	BOOL **SetICMProfile**(HDC *hdc,* LPTSTR *lpFileName*)
Parameters	
hdc	HDC: The device context.
lpFileName	LPTSTR: A pointer to a null-terminated string that contains the name of the color profile file.
Returns	BOOL: TRUE if successful; otherwise, the return value is FALSE.
Include File	wingdi.h
See Also	SetICMMode, EnumICMProfiles
Example	This example displays the current ICM profile when executed. When the user selects the Test! menu item, the "MNP22G21.ICM" profile is set for the device context of the window client area. The window class should specify the CS_OWNDC for this example.

```
LRESULT CALLBACK WndProc( HWND hWnd, UINT uMsg, WPARAM wParam, LPARAM lParam )
{
static char szMsg[256];

   switch( uMsg )
   {
      case WM_CREATE :
            {
                HDC hDC = GetDC( hWnd );
                SetICMMode( hDC, ICM_ON );
                ReleaseDC( hWnd, hDC );
            }
            break;

      case WM_PAINT :
            {
                PAINTSTRUCT ps;
                DWORD       dwSize = sizeof( szMsg )-1;
                BeginPaint( hWnd, &ps );

                TextOut( ps.hdc, 10, 10, "Current ICM Profile: ", 21 );

                if ( GetICMProfile( ps.hdc, &dwSize, szMsg ) )
                   TextOut( ps.hdc, 150, 10, szMsg, strlen( szMsg ) );
                else
                   TextOut( ps.hdc, 150, 10, "None", 4 );

                EndPaint( hWnd, &ps );
            }
            break;


      case WM_COMMAND:
            switch ( LOWORD( wParam ) )
            {
               case IDM_TEST:
                  {
                      HDC hDC = GetDC( hWnd );
                      SetICMProfile( hDC,
                          "c:\\windows\\system\\color\\mnp22g21.icm" );
                      ReleaseDC( hWnd, hDC );
                      InvalidateRect( hWnd, NULL, TRUE );
                  }
                  break;
         .
         .
         .
```

SetPaletteEntries   ■ WINDOWS 95   ■ WINDOWS NT

Description   SetPaletteEntries sets red, green, and blue (RGB) color values and flags
in a range of entries in a logical palette. Even if a logical palette has been
selected and realized, changes to the palette do not affect the system
palette until the application calls RealizePalette again.

Syntax	UINT **SetPaletteEntries**(HPALETTE *hPal,* UINT *uStart,* UINT *uEntries,* CONST PALETTEENTRY* *lppe*)
Parameters	
hPal	HPALETTE: The handle of the logical palette.
uStart	UINT: The first logical palette entry to be set.
uEntries	UINT: The number of logical palette entries to be set.
lppe	CONST PALETTEENTRY*: A pointer to the first member of an array of **PALETTEENTRY** structures containing the color values and flags. See the definition of the **PALETTEENTRY** structure under the **CreatePalette** function.
Returns	UINT: If successful, the number of entries that were set in the logical palette; otherwise, 0 is returned.
Include File	wingdi.h
See Also	CreatePalette, RealizePalette
Example	See the example for the **CreatePalette** function.

SetSystemPaletteUse   ■ Windows 95   ■ Windows NT

Description	**SetSystemPaletteUse** allows an application to specify whether the system palette contains 2 or 20 static colors. The default system palette contains 20 static colors. Static colors cannot be changed when an application realizes a logical palette.
	When an application window moves to the foreground and the **SYSPAL_NOSTATIC** value is specified, the application must use the **GetSysColor** function to save the current system colors. It also must call the **SetSysColors** function to set reasonable values using only black and white. When the application returns to the background or terminates, the previous system colors must be restored.
Syntax	UINT **SetSystemPaletteUse**(HDC *hdc,* UINT *uUsage*)
Parameters	
hdc	HDC: The device context. This device context must refer to a device that supports color palettes. An application can determine whether a device supports palette operations by calling the **GetDeviceCaps** function with **RASTERCAPS**.
uUsage	UINT: The new use of the system palette. This can be one of the values listed in Table 16-10.

able 16-10 `SetSystemPaletteUse` *uUsage* **values**

lue	Meaning
`SPAL_NOSTATIC`	The system palette contains 2 static colors (black and white).
`SPAL_STATIC`	The system palette contains the default 20 static colors that will not change when an application realizes its logical palette.

eturns	`UINT`: If successful, the previous usage of the system palette; otherwise, `SYSPAL_ERROR` is returned.
clude File	`wingdi.h`
ee Also	`GetSystemPaletteUse`, `GetDeviceCaps`, `GetSysColor`, `SetSysColors`
xample	This example displays the current status of the system palette usage. When the user selects the Test! menu item, the example shows how to set up for the usage of the system palette entries by changing the system palette usage to nonstatic. When the application exits, the system palette is restored.

```
RESULT CALLBACK WndProc( HWND hWnd, UINT uMsg, WPARAM wParam, LPARAM lParam )

tatic char szMsg[256];

 switch( uMsg )
 {
     case WM_PAINT :
             {
                 PAINTSTRUCT ps;

                 BeginPaint( hWnd, &ps );

                 TextOut( ps.hdc, 10, 10, "Current Palette Use: ", 21 );

                 if ( GetSystemPaletteUse( ps.hdc ) == SYSPAL_STATIC )
                    TextOut( ps.hdc, 150, 10, "Static", 6 );
                 else
                    TextOut( ps.hdc, 150, 10, "Non-Static", 10 );

                 EndPaint( hWnd, &ps );
             }
             break;


     case WM_COMMAND:
             switch ( LOWORD( wParam ) )
             {
                 case IDM_TEST:
                     {
                         HDC hDC = GetDC( hWnd );
                         SetSystemPaletteUse( hDC, SYSPAL_NOSTATIC );
                         ReleaseDC( hWnd, hDC );
```

continued on next page

continued from previous page

```
                        // Save the system palette colors and
                        // Realize your palette that replaces
                        // the system palette colors...
                                .
                                .
                                .

                        // Notify other applications that the
                        // system colors have changed.
                        //.................................
                        PostMessage( HWND_BROADCAST, WM_SYSCOLORCHANGE,
                                     0, 0L );
                        InvalidateRect( hWnd, NULL, TRUE );
                    }
                    break;

                case IDM_EXIT:
                        DestroyWindow (hWnd);
                        break;
            }
            break;

        case WM_DESTROY:
            {
                HDC hDC = GetDC( hWnd );
                SetSystemPaletteUse( hDC, SYSPAL_STATIC );
                ReleaseDC( hWnd, hDC );

                // Restore system palette colors...
                        .
                        .
                        .

                // Notify other applications that the
                // system colors have changed.
                //.................................
                PostMessage( HWND_BROADCAST, WM_SYSCOLORCHANGE, 0, 0L );
            }
            PostQuitMessage(0);
            break;

        default:
                return ( DefWindowProc( hWnd, uMsg, wParam, lParam ) );
    }
    return (0);
}
```

UpdateColors   ■ WINDOWS 95   ■ WINDOWS NT

Description   UpdateColors updates the client area of a device context by remapping the
                      current colors in the client area to the currently realized logical palette. An
                      inactive window with a realized logical palette may call UpdateColors as
                      an alternative to redrawing its client area soon after a WM_PALETTECHANGED
                      message is received.

UpdateColors typically updates a client area faster than redrawing the area. However, because UpdateColors performs the color translation based on the color of each pixel before the system palette changed, each call to this function results in the loss of some color accuracy.

Syntax	BOOL **UpdateColors**(HDC *hdc*)
Parameters	
hdc	HDC: The device context.
Returns	BOOL: TRUE if successful; otherwise, the return value is FALSE.
Include File	wingdi.h
See Also	RealizePalette
Example	This example shows how an application should react to the WM_QUERYNEW-PALETTE and WM_PALETTECHANGED messages. When a WM_PALETTECHANGED message is received, the program calls the UpdateColors function to make the best use possible of the remaining colors available. The application receives the WM_QUERYNEWPALETTE message right before receiving the input focus, giving the application a chance to realize the logical palette and regain colors lost to other applications when it was inactive.

```
LRESULT CALLBACK WndProc( HWND hWnd, UINT uMsg, WPARAM wParam, LPARAM lParam )
{
static HPALETTE hPal;

   switch( uMsg )
   {

      // Other messages...
            .
            .
            .

      case WM_QUERYNEWPALETTE:
              // About to get focus, so we realize our palette.
              //.........................................
              {
                  HDC hDC = GetDC( hWnd );

                  SelectPalette( hDC, hPal, 0 );
                  if ( RealizePalette( hDC ) )
                     InvalidateRect( hWnd, NULL, TRUE );

                  ReleaseDC( hWnd, hDC );
              }
              break;

      case WM_PALETTECHANGED:
              // Another application changed the palette.
              //.........................................
              if ( (HWND)wParam != hWnd )
              {
                  HDC hDC = GetDC( hWnd );
```

continued on next page

continued from previous page

```
                SelectPalette( hDC, hPal, 0 );
                if ( RealizePalette( hDC ) )
                   UpdateColors( hDC );

                ReleaseDC( hWnd, hDC );
          }
          break;

     default:
             return ( DefWindowProc( hWnd, uMsg, wParam, lParam ) );
   }
   return (0);
```

UpdateICMRegKey   ■ Windows 95   ■ Windows NT

Description	**UpdateICMRegKey** installs, removes, or queries registry entries that identify ICC color profiles or color-matching DLLs. The action carried out is dependent upon the *nCommand* parameter. GDI uses the registry to keep track of ICC profiles installed in the system. Although not required, if ICC profiles are copied to a local directory, they should be placed in the color directory in the Windows system directory.
Syntax	BOOL **UpdateICMRegKey**(DWORD *dwReserved,* DWORD *CMID,* LPTSTR *lpszFileName,* UINT *nCommand*)
Parameters	
dwReserved	DWORD: Reserved; must be 0.
CMID	DWORD: The profile identifier of the color-matching DLL to use with the profile.
lpszFileName	LPTSTR: A pointer to a null-terminated string that specifies the file name of an ICC color profile or a pointer to a **DEVMODE** structure. The meaning of this parameter depends on the value of *nCommand*. See the definition of the **DEVMODE** structure in Chapter 12, The Graphics Device Interface, under the **CreateDC** function.
nCommand	UINT: The action to perform. This can be one of the values listed in Table 16-11.

Table 16-11 UpdateICMRegKey *nCommand* values

Value	Description
ICM_ADDPROFILE	Adds the ICC profile to the ICM branch in the registry.
ICM_DELETEPROFILE	Deletes the ICC profile from the ICM branch in the registry.
ICM_QUERYMATCH	Determines if a profile exists based on the DEVMODE pointed to by *lpszFileName*.
ICM_QUERYPROFILE	Determines if the profile is in the ICM branch of the registry.
ICM_REGISTERICMATCHER	Equates a *CMID* to a color-matching DLL.

Value	Description
ICM_SETDEFAULTPROFILE	Makes the profile first among equals.
ICM_UNREGISTERICMATCHER	Removes the reference between *CMID* and a color-matching DLL.

Returns   BOOL: If successful, TRUE is returned; otherwise, FALSE is returned.

Include File   wingdi.h

17

I/O WITH FILES

The traditional concept of a file is a block of data on a storage device identified by a file name. In the Win32 API, files can be named pipes, communications resources, disk devices, console input or output, or the traditional file. Each of the different file types is the same at the base level, but each has different properties and limitations. The Win32 API file functions enable applications to access files regardless of the underlying file system or device type. However, capabilities vary, depending on the file system or device, and the operating system.

Creating and Opening Files

All types of files are created and opened with one function in the Win32 API, `CreateFile`. An application can specify whether it will read from the file, write to the file, or both. It can also specify whether it wants to share the file for reading, writing, both, or neither. Listing 17-1 shows a code segment that opens an existing file or creates a new file if it does not exist. After opening the file, you can use it to perform read and write operations.

Listing 17-1 Opening and closing a file

```
HANDLE    hFile;

// Open/create the file.
//.....................
hFile = CreateFile( "FILE1.TXT", GENERIC_READ | GENERIC_WRITE,
                    FILE_SHARE_READ, NULL, OPEN_ALWAYS,
                    FILE_ATTRIBUTE_NORMAL, NULL );

if ( hFile != INVALID_HANDLE_VALUE )
{
    // Use the File

    // Close the file.
    //................
    CloseHandle( hFile );
}
```

Windows assigns a file handle to each file that is opened or created. A file handle is a unique identifier that an application uses in functions that access a file. File handles are valid until they are closed with the `CloseHandle` function, which closes the file and flushes the buffers. When an application first starts, it inherits all open file handles that allow inheritance from the process that started it. If the handles do not allow inheritance, the application doesn't inherit them.

An application can open file handles for console input and output. Instead of a file name, the application passes the `"CONIN$"` string as the file name for the console input, and `"CONOUT$"` for the console output. These names will return handles to the console input and output even if the `SetStdHandle` function redirected the standard input handles. Standard input, output, and error handles are retrieved and set with the `GetStdHandle` and `SetStdHandle` functions. These functions allow an application to redirect and use the standard file handles.

Reading and Writing

When a file is first opened, Windows places a file pointer at the beginning of the file. The file pointer marks the current position in the file where the next read or write will take place. As each byte is read or written, Windows advances the file pointer. An application can also move the file pointer position with the `SetFilePointer` function.

An application performs the actual read and write operations with the `ReadFile` and `WriteFile` functions. These functions read and write a specified number of bytes at the location of the file pointer without formatting the data. Listing 17-2 shows a code segment where consecutive calls to `WriteFile` build a string in a file and `ReadFile` reads the string from the file.

Listing 17-2 Reading and writing files

```
HANDLE   hFile;

// Open/create the file.
//.....................
hFile = CreateFile( "FILE1.TXT", GENERIC_READ | GENERIC_WRITE,
                    FILE_SHARE_READ, NULL, OPEN_ALWAYS,
                    FILE_ATTRIBUTE_NORMAL, NULL );

if ( hFile != INVALID_HANDLE_VALUE )
{
    DWORD dwActBytes;
    char  szBuf[128];

    // Write the string "This is a sample." to the file.
    //.................................................
    WriteFile( hFile, "This ", 5, &dwActBytes, NULL );
    WriteFile( hFile, "is ", 3, &dwActBytes, NULL );
    WriteFile( hFile, "a sample.", 9, &dwActBytes, NULL );
```

```
// Set the file pointer back to the beginning of the file.
//..............................................................
SetFilePointer( hFile, 0, 0, FILE_BEGIN );

// Read the string back from the file.
//....................................
ReadFile( hFile, szBuf, 128, &dwActBytes, NULL );

// Null terminate the string.
//...........................
szBuf[dwActBytes] = 0;

// Close the file.
//................
CloseHandle( hFile );
}
```

When the file pointer reaches the end of the file and the application attempts to read from the file, the actual number of bytes read will be **0**, and **ReadFile** will not return an error. The application can change the end-of-file marker, extending or truncating the file, by using the **SetEndOfFile** function. When an application writes past the end of file, the end-of-file marker is moved and the file is extended.

Windows allows more than one application to open a file and write to it. This creates a problem if two applications write to the same location in the file at the same time. To prevent this from happening, applications should lock the area of the file they are going to write to with the **LockFile** function. Locking part of a file prevents all other processes from reading or writing anywhere in the specified area. Attempts to read from or write to a region locked by another process will always fail. When the application is done writing to the file, it unlocks the region of the file using the **UnlockFile** function. All locked regions of a file should be unlocked before closing a file.

Windows allows asynchronous input and output with files, which allows some I/O functions to return immediately before an I/O request has finished. Asynchronous I/O enables an application to continue with other processing and wait for the I/O to be completed at a later time. Another term for asynchronous I/O is overlapped I/O. The **ReadFile** and **WriteFile** functions enable an application to perform overlapped I/O. If an application is going to perform overlapped I/O with a file, the **FILE_FLAG_OVER-LAPPED** flag must be specified when the file is opened. See the **GetOverlappedResult** function later in this chapter for an example.

Sharing Data with File Mapping

File mapping is the copying of a file's contents to a process's virtual address space. When a file is mapped, the copy of the file's contents is called the file view, and the internal structure used to maintain the copy is called the file-mapping object. To share data, another process can create an identical file view in its own virtual address space by using the first process's file-mapping object to create the view.

A common example of processes sharing data is dynamic data exchange (DDE). In Windows 3.x, applications would allocate global memory with the `GMEM_DDESHARE` flag and use the memory handle. In Windows 95 and Windows NT, applications should use file mapping. It is not necessary to actually have a file that is mapped into memory. An application can specify a `0xFFFFFFFF` value for the file handle when calling the `CreateFileMapping` function. This will map a view of the operating system's paging file into memory. See the example under the `MapViewOfFile` function for a detailed example of how file mapping works.

File I/O Function Descriptions

Table 17-1 summarizes the file I/O functions. Detailed function descriptions follow the table.

Table 17-1 File I/O function summary

Function	Purpose
AreFileApisANSI	Determines whether a set of Win32 file functions is using the ANSI or OEM character set code page.
CancelIO	Cancels all pending input and output for the calling thread.
CloseHandle	Closes an open object handle.
CompareFileTime	Compares two 64-bit file times.
CopyFile	Copies an existing file to a new file.
CopyFileEx	Copies an existing file to a new file while preserving extended attributes.
CreateDirectory	Creates a new directory.
CreateDirectoryEx	Creates a new directory with the attributes of a template directory.
CreateFile	Creates, opens, or truncates an object such as a file, pipe, communications resource, disk device, or console.
CreateFileMapping	Creates a named or unnamed file-mapping object for a file.
DeleteFile	Deletes a file.
DosDateTimeToFileTime	Converts MS-DOS date and time values to a 64-bit file time.
FileTimeToDosDateTime	Converts a 64-bit file time to MS-DOS date and time values.
FileTimeToLocalFileTime	Converts a file time based on the Universal Time Coordination (UTC) to a local file time.
FileTimeToSystemTime	Converts a 64-bit file time to system time format.
FindClose	Closes a search handle.
FindCloseChangeNotification	Stops change notification handle monitoring.
FindFirstChangeNotification	Creates a change notification handle.
FindFirstFile	Searches a directory for the first file whose name matches a search name.
FindFirstFileEx	Searches a directory for a file whose name and attributes match a search name.
FindNextChangeNotification	Requests the next change notification handle.
FindNextFile	Finds the next file whose name matches a search name (following a call to FindFirstFile).

Function	Purpose
FlushFileBuffers	Flushes the buffers for a file and writes all buffered data to the file.
FlushViewOfFile	Writes to the disk a byte range within a mapped view of a file.
GetFileAttributes	Returns the attributes of a file.
GetFileAttributesEx	Returns extended attributes of a file.
GetFileInformationByHandle	Retrieves information about a file.
GetFileSize	Retrieves the size, in bytes, of a file.
GetFileTime	Retrieves the date and time that a file was created, last accessed, and last modified.
GetFileType	Returns the type of a file.
GetFullPathName	Retrieves the full path and file name of a file.
GetOverlappedResult	Returns the results of an overlapped operation on an object.
GetStdHandle	Returns a handle for the standard input, standard output, or standard error device.
GetTempFileName	Creates a temporary file name.
GetTempPath	Retrieves the path of the temporary file directory.
LocalFileTimeToFileTime	Converts a local file time to a file time based on Universal Time Coordination (UTC).
LockFile	Locks a region in an open file.
LockFileEx	Locks a byte range of an open file for shared or exclusive access.
MapViewOfFile	Maps a view of a file into the address space of the calling process.
MapViewOfFileEx	Maps a view of a file into a suggested address space of the calling process.
MoveFile	Moves a file or a directory and its children.
MoveFileEx	Moves a file or a directory with extended options.
OpenFileMapping	Opens a named file-mapping object.
ReadFile	Reads data from a file.
ReadFileEx	Reads data from a file asynchronously.
RemoveDirectory	Deletes an empty directory.
SearchPath	Searches for a file.
SetEndOfFile	Moves the end-of-file (EOF) position of a file to the current position of the file pointer.
SetFileApisToANSI	Sets the code page to the ANSI character set code page for Win32 file functions.
SetFileApisToOEM	Sets the code page to the OEM character set code page for Win32 file functions.
SetFileAttributes	Sets a file's attributes.
SetFilePointer	Moves the file pointer of an open file.
SetFileTime	Sets the date and time that a file was created, last accessed, or last modified.
SetStdHandle	Sets the handle for the standard input, standard output, or standard error device.
SystemTimeToFileTime	Converts a system time to a file time.
UnlockFile	Unlocks a region in an open file.
UnlockFileEx	Unlocks a previously locked byte range in an open file.
UnmapViewOfFile	Unmaps a mapped view of a file from the calling process's address space.
WriteFile	Writes data to a file.
WriteFileEx	Writes data to a file asynchronously.

AreFileApisANSI ■ WINDOWS 95 ■ WINDOWS NT

Description AreFileApisANSI determines whether a set of Win32 file functions is using the ANSI or OEM character set code page. This is useful for 8-bit console input and output operations. The functions listed in the See Also are affected by the code page.

Syntax BOOL **AreFileApisANSI**(VOID)

Parameters This function has no parameters.

Returns BOOL: If the set of Win32 file functions is using the ANSI code page, TRUE is returned; otherwise, FALSE is returned if the OEM code page is used.

Include File winbase.h

See Also SetFileApisToANSI, SetFileApisToOEM, CopyFile, CreateDirectory, CreateFile, CreateProcess, DeleteFile, FindFirstFile, FindNextFile, GetCurrentDirectory, GetDiskFreeSpace, GetDriveType, GetFileAttributes, GetFullPathName, GetSystemDirectory, GetTempFileName, GetTempPath, GetVolumeInformation, GetWindowsDirectory, LoadLibrary, LoadLibraryEx, MoveFile, MoveFileEx, RemoveDirectory, SearchPath, SetCurrentDirectory, SetFileAttributes

Example This example shows a function that checks for the file APIs to be set to either ANSI or OEM depending on the value of the parameter passed. If they are not set correctly, they are set to either ANSI or OEM with the SetFileApisToANSI and SetFileApisToOEM functions.

```
VOID CheckFileAPIs( BOOL bANSI )
{
    if ( bANSI && !AreFileApisANSI() )
        SetFileApisToANSI();
    else if ( !bANSI && AreFileApisANSI() )
        SetFileApisToOEM();
}
```

CancelIO ■ WINDOWS 95 ■ WINDOWS NT

Description CancelIO cancels all pending input and output operations that were issued by the calling thread for the given file handle. This function does not cancel I/O operations issued for the file handle by other threads. This only applies to I/O operations that were issued as overlapped I/O. If they were not, the I/O operations would not return in time to allow the thread to call the CancelIO function. All I/O operations that are canceled will complete with the error ERROR_OPERATION_ABORTED.

Syntax BOOL **CancelIO**(HANDLE *hFile*)

Parameters

hFile   `HANDLE`: The handle of the file on which to cancel pending I/O.

Returns   `BOOL`: If successful, `TRUE` is returned; otherwise, `FALSE` is returned.

Include File   `winbase.h`

See Also   `CreateFile, LockFileEx, ReadFile, ReadFileEx, WriteFile, WriteFileEx`

CloseHandle   ■ WINDOWS 95   ■ WINDOWS NT

Description   `CloseHandle` closes an open object handle. This function invalidates the object handle, decrements the object's handle count, and performs object retention checks. Once the last handle of an object is closed, the object is removed from the system. An application can use this function to close the following types of object handles.

- Console input or output
- Event file
- File mapping
- Mutex
- Named pipe
- Process
- Semaphore
- Thread
- Tokens (Windows NT only)

Syntax   `BOOL `**`CloseHandle`**`( HANDLE `*`hObject`*` )`

Parameters

hObject   `HANDLE`: The handle of the object to close.

Returns   `BOOL`: `TRUE` if successful; otherwise, the return value is `FALSE`.

Include File   `winbase.h`

See Also   `CreateFile, DeleteFile`

Example   See the example for the `CompareFileTime` function.

CompareFileTime   ■ WINDOWS 95   ■ WINDOWS NT

Description   `CompareFileTime` compares two 64-bit file times.

Syntax   `LONG `**`CompareFileTime`**`( CONST FILETIME* `*`lpft1,`*` CONST FILETIME* `*`lpft2`*` )`

Parameters

lpft1   CONST FILETIME*: A pointer to a FILETIME structure that specifies the first 64-bit file time. See the definition of the FILETIME structure below.

lpft2   CONST FILETIME*: A pointer to a FILETIME structure that specifies the second 64-bit file time. See the definition of the FILETIME structure below.

Returns

LONG: If successful, the return value is one of the values given in Table 17-2.

Table 17-2 CompareFileTime return values

Value	Meaning
−1	The first file time is less than the second file time.
0	The first file time is equal to the second file time.
+1	The first file time is greater than the second file time.

Include File   winbase.h

See Also   GetFileTime

FILETIME Definition

```
typedef struct _FILETIME
{
    DWORD dwLowDateTime;
    DWORD dwHighDateTime;
} FILETIME;
```

Members

dwLowDateTime   DWORD: The low-order 32 bits of the file time.

dwHighDateTime   DWORD: The high-order 32 bits of the file time.

Example   This example compares the file times of two files, FILE1.TXT and FILE2.TXT, when the user selects the Test! menu item. The results of the CompareFileTime function are checked, and the appropriate message box is displayed with the results of the comparison.

```
LRESULT CALLBACK WndProc( HWND hWnd, UINT uMsg, WPARAM wParam, LPARAM lParam )
{
    switch( uMsg )
    {
        case WM_COMMAND :
            switch( LOWORD( wParam ) )
            {
                case IDM_TEST :
                    {
                        FILETIME ft1, ft2;
                        HANDLE   hFile1, hFile2;
                        int      nResult;
```

```
                hFile1 = CreateFile( "FILE1.TXT", GENERIC_READ,
                                     FILE_SHARE_READ,
                                     NULL, OPEN_ALWAYS,
                                     FILE_ATTRIBUTE_NORMAL, NULL );

                hFile2 = CreateFile( "FILE2.TXT", GENERIC_READ,
                                     FILE_SHARE_READ,
                                     NULL, OPEN_ALWAYS,
                                     FILE_ATTRIBUTE_NORMAL, NULL );

                GetFileTime( hFile1, NULL, NULL, &ft1 );
                GetFileTime( hFile2, NULL, NULL, &ft2 );

                nResult = CompareFileTime( &ft1, &ft2 );

                switch( nResult )
                {
                    case -1 : MessageBox( hWnd,
                                          "FILE2 is newer than FILE1.",
                                          "Message",
                                          MB_OK | MB_ICONINFORMATION );
                              break;

                    case 0  : MessageBox( hWnd,
                                          "FILE1 is the same as FILE2.",
                                          "Message",
                                          MB_OK | MB_ICONINFORMATION );
                              break;

                    case 1  : MessageBox( hWnd,
                                          "FILE1 is newer than FILE2.",
                                          "Message",
                                          MB_OK | MB_ICONINFORMATION );
                              break;
                }

                CloseHandle( hFile1 );
                CloseHanlde( hFile2 );
           }
           break;

           .
           .
           .
```

CopyFile ■ WINDOWS 95 ■ WINDOWS NT

Description	CopyFile copies a file to a new file. The file attributes, such as FILE_ATTRIBUTE_READONLY, are copied to the new file. The security attributes are not copied to the new file.
Syntax	BOOL **CopyFile**(LPCTSTR *lpszExistingFile,* LPCTSTR *lpszNewFile,* BOOL *bFailIfExists*)
Parameters	
lpszExistingFile	LPCTSTR: A pointer to a null-terminated string that contains the name of an existing file to copy.

lpszNewFile	LPCTSTR: A pointer to a null-terminated string that contains the name of the new file.
bFailIfExists	BOOL: Specifies what action to take if a file of the same name as specified by *lpszNewFile* already exists. If set to TRUE and the new file already exists, the function fails. If set to FALSE and the new file already exists, the function overwrites the existing file and succeeds.

Returns   BOOL: TRUE if successful; otherwise, the return value is FALSE.

Include File   winbase.h

See Also   MoveFile, CreateFile, DeleteFile

Example   This example copies the file FILE1.TXT to a file named FILE2.TXT when the user selects the Test! menu item. If FILE2.TXT already exists, the user is prompted before overwriting the existing file.

```
LRESULT CALLBACK WndProc( HWND hWnd, UINT uMsg, WPARAM wParam, LPARAM lParam )
{
   switch( uMsg )
   {
      case WM_COMMAND :
            switch( LOWORD( wParam ) )
            {
               case IDM_TEST :
                  {
                     // Copy the file without overwriting existing files.
                     //..................................................
                     if ( !CopyFile( "FILE1.TXT", "FILE2.TXT", TRUE ) )
                     {
                        if ( GetLastError() == ERROR_FILE_EXISTS &&
                           MessageBox( hWnd,
                              "File already exists.\n" \
                              "Do you want to overwrite?",
                              "Copy",
                              MB_YESNO | MB_ICONQUESTION ) == IDYES )
                        {
                           // Copy the file and overwrite
                           // the existing file.
                           //............................
                           CopyFile( "FILE1.TXT", "FILE2.TXT", FALSE );
                        }
                     }
                  }
                  break;
                  .
                  .
                  .
```

CopyFileEx   ■ WINDOWS 95   ■ WINDOWS NT

Description   CopyFileEx copies an existing file to a new file. This function preserves extended attributes, OLE structured storage, NTFS alternate data streams, and file attributes. Security attributes for the existing file are not copied to the new file. **CopyFileEx** also provides the ability to track the progress of the copy operation.

Syntax	BOOL **CopyFileEx**(LPCTSTR *lpszExistingFile,* LPCTSTR *lpszNewFile,* LPPROGRESS_ROUTINE *lpProgressRoutine,* LPVOID *lpData,* LPBOOL *pbCancel,* DWORD *dwCopyFlags*)

Parameters

lpszExistingFile
LPCTSTR: A pointer to a null-terminated string that specifies the name of the file to copy.

lpszNewFile
LPCTSTR: A pointer to a null-terminated string that specifies the new name of the file.

lpProgressRoutine
LPPROGRESS_ROUTINE: The address of a callback function that is called each time another portion of the file has been copied. This parameter can be **NULL**. See the definition of the callback function below.

lpData
LPVOID: An application-defined value to be passed to the callback function.

pbCancel
LPBOOL: A pointer to a Boolean variable that can be used to cancel the operation. If this flag is set to **TRUE** during the copy operation, the operation is canceled.

dwCopyFlags
DWORD: Determines how the file is to be copied. This parameter can be a combination of the values listed in Table 17-3.

Table 17-3 CopyFileEx *dwCopyFlags* values

Value	Meaning
COPY_FILE_FAIL_IF_EXISTS	The copy operation fails immediately if the target file already exists.
COPY_FILE_RESTARTABLE	Progress of the copy is tracked in the target file in case the copy fails. The failed copy can be restarted at a later time by specifying the same values for the *lpExistingFile* and *lpNewFile* parameters.

Returns	BOOL: If successful, **TRUE** is returned; otherwise, **FALSE** is returned.
Include File	winbase.h
See Also	CreateFile, CopyFile, MoveFile
Callback Syntax	DWORD WINAPI **CopyProgressRoutine**(LARGE_INTEGER *TotalFileSize,* LARGE_INTEGER *TotalBytesTransferred,* LARGE_INTEGER *StreamSize,* LARGE_INTEGER *StreamBytesTransferred,* DWORD *dwStreamNumber,* DWORD *dwCallbackReason,* HANDLE *hSourceFile,* HANDLE, *hDestinationFile,* LPVOID *lpData*)

Callback Parameters

TotalFileSize
LARGE_INTEGER: The size, in bytes, of the file.

TotalBytesTransferred	**LARGE_INTEGER**: The total number of bytes transferred from the source file to the destination file since the copy operation began.
StreamSize	**LARGE_INTEGER**: The total size, in bytes, of the current file stream.
StreamBytesTransferred	**LARGE_INTEGER**: The total number of bytes in the current stream that have been transferred from the source file to the destination file since the copy operation began.
dwStreamNumber	**DWORD**: The current stream. The stream number is **1** the first time the callback function is called.
dwCallbackReason	**DWORD**: The reason the callback function was called. If set to **CALLBACK_CHUNK_FINISHED**, another part of the data file was copied. If set to **CALLBACK_STREAM_SWITCH**, another stream was created and is about to be copied. This is the reason the callback function is called for the first time.
hSourceFile	**HANDLE**: The handle of the source file.
hDestinationFile	**HANDLE**: The handle of the destination file.
lpData	**LPVOID**: The *lpData* parameter passed to the **CopyFileEx** function.
Callback Returns	**DWORD**: The callback function should return **PROGRESS_CONTINUE** to continue the copy operation, **PROGRESS_CANCEL** to cancel the copy operation and delete the destination file, **PROGRESS_STOP** to stop the copy operation, or **PROGRESS_QUIET** to continue the copy operation without further calls to the callback function.

CreateDirectory　　　　■ WINDOWS 95　■ WINDOWS NT

Description	**CreateDirectory** creates a new directory. If the underlying file system is NTFS or another file system that supports security on files and directories, the function applies a specified security descriptor to the new directory. Windows 95 does not use the file and directory security, because it cannot access a drive formatted with the NTFS file system.
Syntax	BOOL **CreateDirectory**(LPCTSTR *lpszPath,* LPSECURITY_ATTRIBUTES *lpSecurityAttributes*)
Parameters	
lpszPath	**LPCTSTR**: A pointer to a null-terminated string that contains the path of the directory to be created. This string must not exceed **MAX_PATH** characters. An application can bypass this limit on Windows NT by calling the wide (**W**) version of **CreateDirectory** and prepending "**\\?**" or "**\\?\UNC**" to turn off path parsing.

lpSecurityAttributes	LPSECURITY_ATTRIBUTES: A pointer to a SECURITY_ATTRIBUTES structure that specifies the security attributes for the directory. The file system must have support for security such as the NTFS file system; otherwise, this parameter has no effect. This parameter does not apply to Windows 95, because Windows 95 does not include a file system that supports security.
Returns	BOOL: TRUE if successful; otherwise, the return value is FALSE.
Include File	winbase.h
See Also	CreateDirectoryEx, RemoveDirectory
Example	This example creates a directory on another computer using CreateDirectory when the user selects the Test menu item. The directory "New Directory" is created on a computer named "Bills-PC" using the share name of "Bills-C".

```
LRESULT CALLBACK WndProc( HWND hWnd, UINT uMsg, WPARAM wParam, LPARAM lParam )
{
   switch( uMsg )
   {
      case WM_COMMAND :
            switch( LOWORD( wParam ) )
            {
               case IDM_TEST :
                  {
                     if ( !CreateDirectory(
                           "\\\\Bills-PC\\Bills-C\\New Directory",
                           NULL ) )
                     {
                        MessageBox( hWnd,
                              "Could not create the directory.",
                              "Error",
                              MB_OK | MB_ICONASTERISK );
                     }
                  }
                  break;
                     .
                     .
                     .
```

CreateDirectoryEx   ■ WINDOWS 95   ■ WINDOWS NT

Description	CreateDirectoryEx is the same as the CreateDirectory function, except that the new directory retains the attributes of a given template directory. If the underlying file system supports security on files and directories, the function applies the given security descriptor to the new directory. The new directory retains the other attributes of the template directory.

Syntax	BOOL **CreateDirectoryEx**(LPCTSTR *lpTemplateDirectory,* LPCTSTR *lpNewDirectory,* LPSECURITY_ATTRIBUTES *lpSecurityAttributes*)

Parameters

lpTemplateDirectory LPCTSTR: A pointer to a null-terminated string that contains the path name of the directory to be used as a template when creating the new directory.

lpNewDirectory LPCTSTR: A pointer to a null-terminated string that contains the path name of the directory to be created.

lpSecurityAttributes LPSECURITY_ATTRIBUTES: A pointer to a SECURITY_ATTRIBUTES structure that specifies the security attributes for the directory. The file system must have support for security such as the NTFS file system; otherwise, this parameter has no effect. This parameter does not apply to Windows 95, because Windows 95 does not include a file system that supports security.

Returns BOOL: TRUE if successful; otherwise, the return value is FALSE.

Include File winbase.h

See Also CreateDirectory, RemoveDirectory

Example This example is the same as the example for the CreateDirectory function, except that the new directory is created with the same attributes as the template directory "Template Directory" using the CreateDirectoryEx function.

```
LRESULT CALLBACK WndProc( HWND hWnd, UINT uMsg, WPARAM wParam, LPARAM lParam )
{
    switch( uMsg )
    {
        case WM_COMMAND :
                switch( LOWORD( wParam ) )
                {
                    case IDM_TEST :
                        {
                            if ( !CreateDirectoryEx(
                                    "\\\\Bills-PC\\Bills-C\\Template Directory"
                                    "\\\\Bills-PC\\Bills-C\\New Directory",
                                    NULL ) )
                            {
                                MessageBox( hWnd,
                                        "Could not create the directory.",
                                        "Error",
                                        MB_OK | MB_ICONASTERISK );
                            }
                        }
                        break;
                        .
                        .
                        .
```

CreateFile   ■ Windows 95 ■ Windows NT

Description	**CreateFile** creates, opens, or truncates a file, pipe, communications resource, disk device, or console. This function also opens a directory for access. **CreateFile** returns a handle that can be used to access the object.
Syntax	HANDLE **CreateFile**(LPCTSTR *lpszName,* DWORD *dwAccess,* DWORD *dwShareMode,* LPSECURITY_ATTRIBUTES *lpSecurityAttributes,* DWORD *dwCreate,* DWORD *dwAttrsAndFlags,* HANDLE *hTemplateFile*)
Parameters	
lpszName	LPCTSTR: A pointer to a null-terminated string that contains the name of the file, pipe, communications resource, disk device, or console to create, open, or truncate. If *lpszName* specifies the path of a directory, this string must not exceed **MAX_PATH** characters. An application can bypass this limit on Windows NT by calling the wide (**W**) version of **CreateFile** and prepending "\\?\" or "\\?\UNC\" to turn off path parsing.
dwAccess	DWORD: The type of access to the file. An application can obtain read access, write access, both read and write access, or device query access. The values listed in Table 17-4 are used for this parameter. Both **GENERIC_READ** and **GENERIC_WRITE** must be set to obtain both read and write access.

Table 17-4 CreateFile *dwAccess* values

Value	Meaning
0	Allows an application to query device attributes without actually accessing the device.
GENERIC_READ	Specifies read access. Data can be read from the file and the file pointer can be moved.
GENERIC_WRITE	Specifies write access. Data can be written to the file and the file pointer can be moved.

dwShareMode	DWORD: Determines how this file is to be shared. This parameter is made up of the values listed in Table 17-5.

Table 17-5 CreateFile *dwShareMode* values

Value	Meaning
0	Prevents the file from being shared.
FILE_SHARE_DELETE	(Windows NT only) Subsequent open operations on the object will succeed only if delete access is requested.

continued on next page

continued from previous page

Value	Meaning
FILE_SHARE_READ	Other open operations can be performed on the file for read access. If opening the client end of a mailslot, this value is specified.
FILE_SHARE_WRITE	Other open operations can be performed on the file for write access.

lpSecurityAttributes   **LPSECURITY_ATTRIBUTES**: A pointer to a **SECURITY_ATTRIBUTES** structure that specifies the security attributes for the directory. The file system must have support for security such as the NTFS file system; otherwise, this parameter has no effect. This parameter does not apply to Windows 95, because Windows 95 does not include a file system that supports security.

dwCreate   **DWORD**: Determines the action to be taken when the file exists or does not exist. This parameter must be one of the values given in Table 17-6.

Table 17-6 CreateFile *dwCreate* values

Value	Meaning
CREATE_ALWAYS	Creates a new file. The function overwrites the file if it exists.
CREATE_NEW	Creates a new file. The function fails if the specified file already exists.
OPEN_ALWAYS	Opens the file, if it exists. If the file does not exist, the function creates the file as if *dwCreate* were CREATE_NEW.
OPEN_EXISTING	Opens the file. The function fails if the file does not exist.
TRUNCATE_EXISTING	Opens the file. Once opened, the file is truncated so that its size is 0 bytes. The calling process must open the file with at least GENERIC_WRITE access. The function fails if the file does not exist.

dwAttrsAndFlags   **DWORD**: Specifies the file attributes and flags for the file. Any combination of the attribute values given in Table 17-7 is acceptable; however, all other file attributes override **FILE_ATTRIBUTE_NORMAL**.

Table 17-7 CreateFile *dwAttrsAndFlags* values

Value	Meaning
FILE_ATTRIBUTE_ARCHIVE	The file is an archive file. This value marks files for backup or removal.
FILE_ATTRIBUTE_ATOMIC_WRITE	Reserved; do not use.
FILE_ATTRIBUTE_COMPRESSED	The file or directory is compressed. For a file, this means that all the data in the file is compressed. If a directory is compressed, newly created files and subdirectories are compressed by default.
FILE_ATTRIBUTE_HIDDEN	The file is hidden.
FILE_ATTRIBUTE_NORMAL	The file has no attributes. This value is valid only if used alone.
FILE_ATTRIBUTE_OFFLINE	The data of the file is not immediately available. Indicates that the file data has been physically moved to offline storage.

Value	Meaning
FILE_ATTRIBUTE_READONLY	The file is read-only.
FILE_ATTRIBUTE_SYSTEM	The file is a system file.
FILE_ATTRIBUTE_TEMPORARY	The file is being used for temporary storage.
FILE_ATTRIBUTE_XACTION_WRITE	Reserved; do not use.
FILE_FLAG_BACKUP_SEMANTICS	(Windows NT only) Opens or creates the file for a backup or restore operation. The operating system ensures that the calling process overrides file security checks, provided it has the necessary permission to do so. The relevant permissions are SE_BACKUP_NAME and SE_RESTORE_NAME. An application can also set this flag to obtain a handle to a directory. A directory handle can be passed to some Win32 functions in place of a file handle.
FILE_FLAG_DELETE_ON_CLOSE	The file will be deleted immediately after all its handles have been closed.
FILE_FLAG_NO_BUFFERING	The file is opened with no intermediate buffering or caching. This can provide performance gains in some situations. An application must meet certain requirements when working with files opened with FILE_FLAG_NO_BUFFERING: ■ File access must begin at offsets within the file that are integer multiples of the volume's sector size. ■ File access must be for numbers of bytes that are integer multiples of the volume's sector size. ■ Buffer addresses for read and write operations must be aligned on addresses in memory that are integer multiples of the volume's sector size. An application can determine a volume's sector size by calling the GetDiskFreeSpace function.
FILE_FLAG_OVERLAPPED	Performs overlapped reading and writing. ReadFile, WriteFile, ConnectNamedPipe, and TransactNamedPipe operations that take a significant amount of time to process return ERROR_IO_PENDING. When the operation is finished, an event is set to the signaled state. When FILE_FLAG_OVERLAPPED is specified, the ReadFile and WriteFile functions must specify an OVERLAPPED structure. When FILE_FLAG_OVERLAPPED is specified, the operating system does not maintain the file pointer. The file position must be passed in the OVERLAPPED structure.
FILE_FLAG_POSIX_SEMANTICS	Indicates that the file is to be accessed according to POSIX rules.
FILE_FLAG_RANDOM_ACCESS	Optimizes file caching for accessing the file randomly.
FILE_FLAG_SEQUENTIAL_SCAN	Optimizes file caching for accessing the file sequentially.
FILE_FLAG_WRITE_THROUGH	Writes will go directly to the file bypassing the cache.

If the CreateFile function opens the client side of a named pipe, the *dwAttrsAndFlags* parameter also can contain Security Quality of Service information. When the calling application specifies the SECURITY_SQOS_PRESENT flag, the *dwAttrsAndFlags* parameter can contain one or more of the values given in Table 17-8.

Table 17-8 CreateFile *dwAttrsAndFlags* security flags

Value	Meaning
SECURITY_ANONYMOUS	Lets you impersonate the client at the Anonymous impersonation level.
SECURITY_CONTEXT_TRACKING	Specifies that the security tracking mode is dynamic. If this flag is not specified, Security Tracking Mode is static.
SECURITY_DELEGATION	Lets you impersonate the client at the Delegation impersonation level.
SECURITY_EFFECTIVE_ONLY	Specifies that only the enabled aspects of the client's security context are available to the server. If this flag is not specified, all aspects of the client's security context are available. This flag allows the client to limit the groups and privileges a server can use while impersonating the client.
SECURITY_IDENTIFICATION	Lets you impersonate the client at the Identification impersonation level.
SECURITY_IMPERSONATION	Lets you impersonate the client at the Impersonation impersonation level.

hTemplateFile	HANDLE: A handle with GENERIC_READ access to a template file. The template file supplies extended attributes for the file being created.
Returns	HANDLE: If successful, the open handle of the file. If the file exists before the function call and *dwCreate* is CREATE_ALWAYS or OPEN_ALWAYS, a call to GetLastError returns ERROR_ALREADY_EXISTS. If the file does not exist before the call, GetLastError returns 0. If the function fails, the return value is INVALID_HANDLE_VALUE.
Include File	winbase.h
See Also	CloseHandle, CreateFile, GetDiskFreeSpace, GetLastError, GetOverlappedResult, GetStdHandle, ReadFile, SetStdHandle, WriteFile
Example	This example opens the file FILE.DAT and writes a string to it when the example starts by processing the WM_CREATE message. The file is opened with read/write access and remains open until the application is closed. When the user selects the Test! menu item, the file pointer is set to the beginning of the file with the SetFilePointer function. The ReadFile function then reads the string from the file. If there were no errors in reading the file, the example displays the string with the MessageBox function.

```
LPCTSTR lpBuffer = "This is the string that will be written to the file.";

LRESULT CALLBACK WndProc( HWND hWnd, UINT uMsg, WPARAM wParam, LPARAM lParam )
{
static HANDLE hFile;

    switch( uMsg )
    {
       case WM_CREATE :
               {
                   DWORD dwWritten;
```

```
                // Open/create a file.
                //....................
                hFile = CreateFile( "FILE.DAT", GENERIC_READ | GENERIC_WRITE,
                                    0, NULL, OPEN_ALWAYS,
                                    FILE_ATTRIBUTE_NORMAL, NULL );

                // Write a string to the file.
                //...........................
                WriteFile( hFile, lpBuffer, strlen( lpBuffer )+1,
                           &dwWritten, NULL );
            }
            break;

    case WM_COMMAND :
            switch( LOWORD( wParam ) )
            {
                case IDM_TEST :
                    {
                        char  szBuf[128];
                        DWORD dwRead;

                        // Make sure the file pointer
                        // is at the beginning of the file.
                        //.................................
                        SetFilePointer( hFile, 0, NULL, FILE_BEGIN );

                        // Read the string from the file and display it.
                        //..............................................
                        if ( ReadFile( hFile, szBuf, strlen( lpBuffer )+1,
                                       &dwRead, NULL ) )
                        {
                            MessageBox( hWnd, szBuf, "Read File", MB_OK );
                        }
                    }
                    break;

                case IDM_EXIT :
                        DestroyWindow( hWnd );
                        break;
            }
            break;

    case WM_DESTROY :
            // Close the file.
            //................
            CloseHandle( hFile );

            PostQuitMessage(0);
            break;

    default :
            return( DefWindowProc( hWnd, uMsg, wParam, lParam ) );
    }

    return( 0L );
}
```

CreateFileMapping
■ WINDOWS 95   ■ WINDOWS NT

Description	`CreateFileMapping` creates a named or unnamed file-mapping object for a file. After an application creates a file-mapping object, the size of the file must not exceed the size of the file-mapping object; if it does, not all of the file's contents will be available for sharing. If an application specifies a size for the file-mapping object that is larger than the size of the named file on disk, the file on disk grows to match the specified size of the file-mapping object.
	In Windows 95, handles that have been used to create file-mapping objects must not be used in subsequent calls to file I/O functions, such as `ReadFile` and `WriteFile`, until the file-mapping is closed.
Syntax	HANDLE **CreateFileMapping**(HANDLE *hFile,* LPSECURITY_ATTRIBUTES *lpSecurityAttributes,* DWORD *dwProtect,* DWORD *dwMaximumSizeHigh,* DWORD *dwMaximumSizeLow,* LPCTSTR *lpszMapName*)
Parameters	
hFile	HANDLE: The handle of the file from which to create a file-mapping object. The file must be opened with an access mode compatible with the protection flags specified by *dwProtect*. It is recommended, though not required, that files and application maps be opened for exclusive access.
	If this parameter is set to 0xFFFFFFFF, the application also must specify a mapping object size in *dwMaximumSizeHigh* and *dwMaximumSizeLow*. The function creates a file-mapping object of the specified size based in the system paging file rather than by a named file. The file-mapping object can be shared by means of inheritance or duplication, or by name.
lpSecurityAttributes	LPSECURITY_ATTRIBUTES: A pointer to a SECURITY_ATTRIBUTES structure that specifies the security attributes for the mapping object. If set to NULL, the file-mapping object is created with a default security descriptor, and the resulting handle is not inherited.
dwProtect	DWORD: The page protection desired for the file view when the file is mapped. This can be one of the values given in Table 17-9.

Table 17-9 `CreateFileMapping` *dwProtect* page protection values

Value	Description
PAGE_READONLY	Gives read-only access to the committed region of pages. The file specified by the *hFile* parameter must have been created with GENERIC_READ access.
PAGE_READWRITE	Gives read-write access to the committed region of pages. The file specified by *hFile* must have been created with GENERIC_READ and GENERIC_WRITE access.

Value	Description
PAGE_WRITECOPY	Gives copy-on-write access to the committed region of pages. The files specified by the *hFile* parameter must have been created with GENERIC_READ and GENERIC_WRITE access.

An application can also specify certain section attributes by combining one or more of the section attribute values given in Table 17-10 with one of the page protection values given in Table 17-9, using the binary OR (|) operator.

Table 17-10 CreateFileMapping *dwProtect* section attributes

Value	Description
SEC_COMMIT	Allocates physical storage in memory or in the paging file on disk for all pages of a section. (This is the default.)
SEC_IMAGE	The file specified by *hFile* is an executable image file. Because the mapping information and file protection are taken from the image file, no other attributes are valid with this value.
SEC_NOCACHE	All pages of a section are to be set as noncacheable. This value requires either the SEC_RESERVE or SEC_COMMIT value to be set also. This attribute is intended for architectures requiring various locking structures to be in memory that is never fetched into the processor's. On 80x86 and MIPS machines, using the cache for these structures only slows down the performance as the hardware keeps the caches coherent. Some device drivers require noncached data so that programs can write through to the physical memory.
SEC_RESERVE	Reserves all pages of a section without allocating physical storage. The reserved range of pages cannot be used by any other allocation operations until it is released. Reserved pages can be committed in subsequent calls to the VirtualAlloc function. This attribute is valid only if the *hFile* parameter is 0xFFFFFFFF.

dwMaximumSizeHigh DWORD: The high-order 32 bits of the maximum size of the file-mapping object. For files of size 4GB or less, this parameter should be 0.

dwMaximumSizeLow DWORD: The low-order 32 bits of the maximum size of the file-mapping object. If this parameter and *dwMaximumSizeHigh* are 0, the maximum size of the file-mapping object is equal to the current size of the file identified by *hFile*.

lpszMapName LPCTSTR: A pointer to a null-terminated string that contains the name of the mapping object. The name can contain any character except the backslash character (\). If set to NULL, the mapping object is created without a name. If this parameter matches the name of an existing named mapping object, the function requests access to the mapping object with the protection specified by *dwProtect*.

Returns HANDLE: If successful, the handle of the file-mapping object; otherwise, NULL is returned. If the object existed before the function call, the GetLastError function returns ERROR_ALREADY_EXISTS, and the return value is a valid handle to the existing file-mapping object.

Include File	winbase.h
See Also	MapViewOfFile, MapViewOfFileEx, OpenFileMapping
Example	See the example for the **MapViewOfFile** function.

DeleteFile ■ WINDOWS 95 ■ WINDOWS NT

Description	**DeleteFile** deletes an existing file. If an application attempts to delete an open file or a file that does not exist, the function fails. On Windows NT, the file cannot be deleted if it is open for I/O or memory-mapped operations. On Windows 95, the file is always deleted.
Syntax	BOOL **DeleteFile**(LPCTSTR *lpszFileName*)
Parameters	
lpszFileName	LPCTSTR: A pointer to a null-terminated string that contains the name of the file to be deleted.
Returns	BOOL: **TRUE** if successful; otherwise, the return value is **FALSE**.
Include File	winbase.h
See Also	CloseHandle, CreateFile
Example	See the example for the **GetTempFileName** function.

DosDateTimeToFileTime ■ WINDOWS 95 ■ WINDOWS NT

Description	**DosDateTimeToFileTime** converts the MS-DOS date and time values to a 64-bit file time.
Syntax	BOOL **DosDateTimeToFileTime**(WORD *wDOSDate,* WORD *wDOSTime,* LPFILETIME *lpft*)
Parameters	
wDOSDate	WORD: The MS-DOS date. The date is a packed 16-bit value in the format outlined in Table 17-11.

Table 17-11 DosDateTimeToFileTime *wDOSDate* values

Bits	Contents
0–4	Day of the month (1–31)
5–8	Month (1=January, 2=February, and so on)
9–15	Year offset from 1980 (add 1980 to get actual year)

wDOSTime	WORD: The MS-DOS time. The time is a packed 16-bit value in the format outlined in Table 17-12.

Table 17-12 DosDateTimeToFileTime *wDOSTime* values

Bits	Contents
0–4	Second divided by 2
5–10	Minute (0–59)
11–15	Hour (0–23 on a 24-hour clock)

lpft	LPFILETIME: A pointer to a **FILETIME** structure that receives the converted 64-bit file time. See the definition of the **FILETIME** structure under the **CompareFileTime** function.
Returns	BOOL: **TRUE** if successful; otherwise, the return value is **FALSE**.
Include File	winbase.h
See Also	FileTimeToDosDateTime, FileTimeToSystemTime, SystemTimeToFileTime, CompareFileTime
Example	This example opens an existing file **FILE.DAT** or creates a new file if it does not exist when the user selects the Test! menu item. The date of the file is then changed to January 1, 1995, and the time is set to 12:00.00 a.m. using the **SetFileTime** function. The application uses the **DosDateTimeToFileTime** function to fill a **FILETIME** structure with the date. Before the date can be set on the file, the application uses the **LocalFileTimeToFileTime** function to convert the time to a UTC time. Note that the two structures used to create the 16-bit packed values for the date and time, **DOSDATE** and **DOSTIME**, are compatible with Visual C++ 2.x. Other compilers may not support the ability to define a bit structure in this manner.

```
typedef struct
{
    WORD Day:5;      // Bits 0-4.
    WORD Month:4;    // Bits 5-8
    WORD Year:7;     // Bits 9-15
} DOSDATE;

typedef struct
{
    WORD Second:5;   // Bits 0-4
    WORD Minute:6;   // Bits 5-10
    WORD Hour:5;     // Bits 11-15
} DOSTIME;

LRESULT CALLBACK WndProc( HWND hWnd, UINT uMsg, WPARAM wParam, LPARAM lParam )
{
    switch( uMsg )
    {
        case WM_COMMAND :
                switch( LOWORD( wParam ) )
                {
```

continued on next page

continued from previous page

```
                case IDM_TEST :
                    {
                        DOSDATE   Date;
                        DOSTIME   Time;
                        FILETIME fTime, fLocTime;
                        HANDLE    hFile;


                        // Open/create a file.
                        //....................
                        hFile = CreateFile( "FILE.DAT",
                                    GENERIC_READ | GENERIC_WRITE,
                                    0, NULL, OPEN_ALWAYS,
                                    FILE_ATTRIBUTE_NORMAL, NULL );

                        // January 1, 1995.
                        //.................
                        Date.Day   = 1;
                        Date.Month = 1;
                        Date.Year  = (1995-1980);

                        // 12:00.00 AM.
                        //.............
                        Time.Second = 0;
                        Time.Minute = 0;
                        Time.Hour   = 0;

                        // Convert DOS date/time to FILETIME structure.
                        //............................................
                        DosDateTimeToFileTime( *(WORD*)&Date,
                                            *(WORD*)&Time, &fLocTime );

                        // Convert the local file time to a UTC file time.
                        //...............................................
                        LocalFileTimeToFileTime( &fLocTime, &fTime );

                        // Set the file time.
                        //...................
                        SetFileTime( hFile, &fTime, &fTime, &fTime );

                        CloseHandle( hFile );
                    }
                    break;
            .
            .
            .
```

FileTimeToDosDateTime   ■ WINDOWS 95   ■ WINDOWS NT

Description	**FileTimeToDosDateTime** converts a 64-bit file time to MS-DOS date and time values.
Syntax	BOOL **FileTimeToDosDateTime**(CONST FILETIME* *lpft,* LPWORD *lpwDOSDate,* LPWORD *lpwDOSTime*)

Parameters

lpft   **CONST FILETIME***: A pointer to a **FILETIME** structure that contains the 64-bit file time to convert to an MS-DOS date and time format. See the definition of the **FILETIME** structure under the **CompareFileTime** function.

lpwDOSDate   **LPWORD**: A pointer to a variable that receives the MS-DOS date. The date is a packed 16-bit value in the format outlined in Table 17-13.

Table 17-13 FileTimeToDosDateTime *lpwDOSDate* values

Bits	Contents
0–4	Day of the month (1–31)
5–8	Month (1=January, 2=February, etc.)
9–15	Year offset from 1980 (add 1980 to get actual year)

lpwDOSTime   **LPWORD**: A pointer to a variable that receives the MS-DOS time. The time is a packed 16-bit value in the format outlined in Table 17-14.

Table 17-14 FileTimeToDosDateTime *lpwDOSTime* values

Bits	Contents
0–4	Second divided by 2
5–10	Minute (0–59)
11–15	Hour (0–23 on a 24-hour clock)

Returns   **BOOL**: **TRUE** if successful; otherwise, the return value is **FALSE**.

Include File   **winbase.h**

See Also   **DosDateTimeToFileTime, FileTimeToSystemTime, SystemTimeToFileTime, CompareFileTime**

Example   See the example for the **FileTimeToLocalFileTime** function.

FileTimeToLocalFileTime ■ Windows 95 ■ Windows NT

Description   **FileTimeToLocalFileTime** converts a file time based on the Universal Time Coordination (referred to as UTC) to a local file time.

Syntax   BOOL **FileTimeToLocalFileTime**(CONST FILETIME* *lpft,* LPFILETIME *lpftLocal*)

Parameters

lpft   **CONST FILETIME***: A pointer to a **FILETIME** structure that contains the UTC-based file time to be converted into a local file time. See the definition of the **FILETIME** structure under the **CompareFileTime** function.

lpftLocal	**LPFILETIME**: A pointer to a **FILETIME** structure that receives the converted local file time. This parameter cannot be the same as the *lpft* parameter. See the definition of the **FILETIME** structure under the **CompareFileTime** function.
Returns	**BOOL**: **TRUE** if successful; otherwise, the return value is **FALSE**.
Include File	**winbase.h**
See Also	**LocalFileTimeToFileTime**, **CompareFileTime**
Example	In this example when the user selects the Test! menu item, the **FILE.DAT** file is opened (or created if it does not exist) and the file date and time is displayed in the client area of the window. The file time is retrieved with the **GetFileTime** function and converted to local time using the **FileTimeToLocalFileTime** function. The local time is broken into a DOS format date and time. The UTC time is broken into a system date and time and displayed. Note that the two structures used to create the 16-bit packed values for the date and time, **DOSDATE** and **DOSTIME**, are compatible with Visual C++. Other compilers may not support the ability to define a bit structure in this manner.

```
typedef struct
{
   WORD Day:5;      // Bits 0-4
   WORD Month:4;    // Bits 5-8
   WORD Year:7;     // Bits 9-15
} DOSDATE;

typedef struct
{
   WORD Second:5;   // Bits 0-4
   WORD Minute:6;   // Bits 5-10
   WORD Hour:5;     // Bits 11-15
} DOSTIME;


LRESULT CALLBACK WndProc( HWND hWnd, UINT uMsg, WPARAM wParam, LPARAM lParam )
{
static HANDLE hFile;

   switch( uMsg )
   {
      case WM_COMMAND :
              switch( LOWORD( wParam ) )
              {
                 case IDM_TEST :
                        {
                            DOSDATE     Date;
                            DOSTIME     Time;
                            FILETIME    fTime, fLocTime;
                            SYSTEMTIME  sysTime;
                            HDC         hDC;
                            HANDLE      hFile;
                            char        szMsg[128];
```

```
            hDC = GetDC( hWnd );

            // Open/create a file.
            //....................
            hFile = CreateFile( "FILE.DAT",
                       GENERIC_READ | GENERIC_WRITE,
                       0, NULL, OPEN_ALWAYS,
                       FILE_ATTRIBUTE_NORMAL, NULL );

            // Retrieve the file time and convert it to
            // local file time.
            //.........................................
            GetFileTime( hFile, NULL, NULL, &fTime );
            FileTimeToLocalFileTime( &fTime, &fLocTime );

            // Convert to DOS date/time.
            //..........................
            FileTimeToDosDateTime( &fLocTime, (WORD*)&Date,
                                   (WORD*)&Time );

            wsprintf( szMsg,
                    "DOS Date/Time: %.2d/%.2d/%d   %d:%.2d:%.2d",
                    Date.Month, Date.Day, Date.Year+1980,
                    Time.Hour, Time.Minute, Time.Second*2 );

            TextOut( hDC, 10, 10, szMsg, strlen( szMsg ) );

            // Convert UTC time to a SYSTEMTIME structure.
            //...........................................
            FileTimeToSystemTime( &fTime, &sysTime );

            wsprintf( szMsg,
                    "System (UTC) Date/Time: %.2d/%.2d/%d " \
                    "%d:%.2d:%.2d.%.4d",
                    sysTime.wMonth, sysTime.wDay,
                    sysTime.wYear, sysTime.wHour,
                    sysTime.wMinute, sysTime.wSecond,
                    sysTime.wMilliseconds );

            TextOut( hDC, 10, 40, szMsg, strlen( szMsg ) );

            CloseHandle( hFile );
            ReleaseDC( hWnd, hDC );
        }
        break;
            .
            .
            .
```

FileTimeToSystemTime   ■ WINDOWS 95   ■ WINDOWS NT

Description   FileTimeToSystemTime converts a 64-bit file time to system time format.

Syntax   BOOL **FileTimeToSystemTime**(CONST FILETIME* *lpft*, LPSYSTEMTIME *lpst*)

Parameters

lpft　　　　CONST FILETIME*: A pointer to a FILETIME structure that contains the file time to convert to a system date and time format. See the description of the FILETIME structure under the CompareFileTime function.

lpst　　　　LPSYSTEMTIME: A pointer to a SYSTEMTIME structure that receives the converted file time. See the definition of the SYSTEMTIME structure below.

Returns　　BOOL: TRUE if successful; otherwise, the return value is FALSE.

Include File　winbase.h

See Also　DosDateTimeToFileTime, FileTimeToDosDateTime, SystemTimeToFileTime, CompareFileTime

SYSTEMTIME Definition

```
typedef struct _SYSTEMTIME
{
    WORD wYear;
    WORD wMonth;
    WORD wDayOfWeek;
    WORD wDay;
    WORD wHour;
    WORD wMinute;
    WORD wSecond;
    WORD wMilliseconds;
} SYSTEMTIME;
```

Members

wYear　　　WORD: The current year.

wMonth　　WORD: The current month; January=1, February=2, and so on.

wDayOfWeek　WORD: The current day of the week; Sunday=0, Monday=1, and so on.

wDay　　　WORD: The current day of the month.

wHour　　　WORD: The current hour.

wMinute　　WORD: The current minute.

wSecond　　WORD: The current second.

wMilliseconds　WORD: The current millisecond.

Example　See the example for the FileTimeToLocalFileTime function.

FindClose　　■ WINDOWS 95　■ WINDOWS NT

Description　FindClose closes a search handle previously created with the FindFirstFile function and used with the FindNextFile function. FindFirstFile and FindNextFile use the search handle to locate files with names that match a search name. After an application calls the FindClose function, the search handle cannot be used in subsequent calls to either the FindNextFile or FindClose function.

Syntax　BOOL **FindClose**(HANDLE *hFindFile*)

Parameters

hFindFile   HANDLE: The search handle to close. This handle must have been previous-
                ly opened by **FindFirstFile**.

Returns   BOOL: **TRUE** if successful; otherwise, the return value is **FALSE**.

Include File winbase.h

See Also   FindFirstFile, FindNextFile

Example   See the example for the **FindFirstChangeNotification** function.

FindCloseChangeNotification   ■ WINDOWS 95 ■ WINDOWS NT

Description   FindCloseChangeNotification stops change notification monitoring for
                 the given handle. After this function is called, the change notification han-
                 dle cannot be used in subsequent calls to either the
                 FindNextChangeNotification or FindCloseChangeNotification func-
                 tion.

Syntax   BOOL **FindCloseChangeNotification**(HANDLE *hChange*)

Parameters

hChange   HANDLE: The change notification handle created by a previous call to the
                 FindFirstChangeNotification function.

Returns   BOOL: **TRUE** if successful; otherwise, the return value is **FALSE**.

Include File winbase.h

See Also   FindFirstChangeNotification, FindNextChangeNotification,
                 WaitForMultipleObjects, WaitForSingleObject

Example   See the example for the FindFirstChangeNotification function.

FindFirstChangeNotification   ■ WINDOWS 95 ■ WINDOWS NT

Description   FindFirstChangeNotification creates a change notification handle and
                 sets up initial change notification filter conditions. A wait on a notification
                 handle succeeds when a change matching the filter conditions occurs in
                 the specified directory or subtree. The WaitForSingleObject and
                 WaitForMultipleObjects functions monitor the specified directory or
                 subtree by using the handle this function returns.

Syntax   HANDLE **FindFirstChangeNotification**(LPCTSTR *lpszPath,* BOOL
                 bWatchSubTree, DWORD *dwFilter*)

Parameters

lpszPath   LPCTSTR: A pointer to a null-terminated string that contains the path of the
                 directory to watch.

bWatchSubTree	**BOOL**: If set to **TRUE**, the function monitors the directory tree rooted at the directory specified by *lpszPath*. If set to **FALSE**, it monitors only the specified directory.
dwFilter	**DWORD**: The filter conditions that satisfy a change notification wait. This parameter can be one or more of the values given in Table 17-15 combined with the binary OR (	) operator.

Table 17-15 FindFirstChangeNotification *dwFilter* values

Value	Meaning
FILE_NOTIFY_CHANGE_ATTRIBUTES	Notify on any attribute change in the watched directory or subtree.
FILE_NOTIFY_CHANGE_DIR_NAME	Notify on any directory name change, creation, or deletion in the watched directory or subtree.
FILE_NOTIFY_CHANGE_FILE_NAME	Notify on any file name change, creation, or deletion in the watched directory or subtree.
FILE_NOTIFY_CHANGE_LAST_WRITE	Notify on any change to the last write-time of files in the watched directory or subtree. The operating system detects a change to the last write-time only when the file is written to the disk. For operating systems that use extensive caching, detection occurs only when the cache is sufficiently flushed.
FILE_NOTIFY_CHANGE_SECURITY	Notify on any security descriptor change in the watched directory or subtree.
FILE_NOTIFY_CHANGE_SIZE	Notify on any file size change in the watched directory or subtree. The operating system detects a change in file size only when the file is written to the disk. For operating systems that use extensive caching, detection occurs only when the cache is sufficiently flushed.

Returns	**HANDLE**: If successful, a handle of a find change notification object; otherwise, **INVALID_HANDLE_VALUE** is returned.
Include File	winbase.h
See Also	FindCloseChangeNotification, FindNextChangeNotification, WaitForMultipleObjects, WaitForSingleObject
Example	In this example, shown in Figure 17-1, the **D:\TEMP** directory is displayed and monitored for any changes. When new files are added, a file size or date changes, or a file is deleted, the window is updated with the new contents of the directory. When the application starts, the **FindFirstChangeNotification** function starts monitoring changes and creates a thread to handle notifications. When a notification is received, the window is updated. The application uses the **FindFirstFile**, **FindNextFile**, and **FindClose** functions to find all the files in the directory.

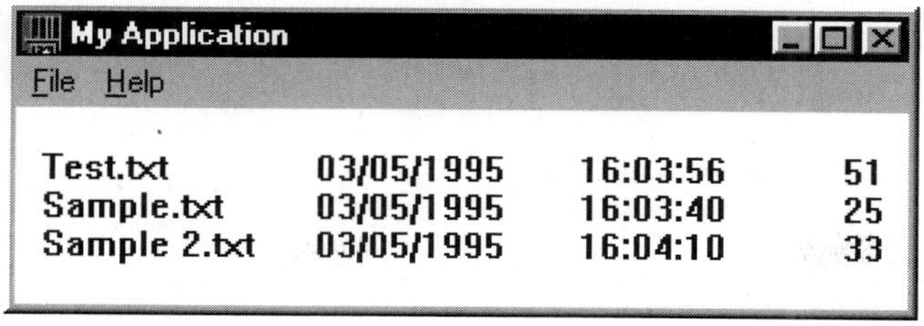

Figure 17-1 FindFirstChangeNotification example

```
static HANDLE hWait = NULL;
static int    nTab  = 50;

DWORD DirChanges( LPDWORD lpdwParam )
{
    HWND    hWnd = (HWND)lpdwParam;

    // Process forever, or until terminated.
    //.....................................
    while( TRUE )
    {
        // Wait for a change notification to happen.
        //..........................................
        if ( WaitForSingleObject( hWait, INFINITE ) == WAIT_OBJECT_0 )
        {
            // Update the window with new information.
            //.......................................
            InvalidateRect( hWnd, NULL, TRUE );
            UpdateWindow( hWnd );
        }

        // Find next change notification.
        //..............................
        FindNextChangeNotification( hWait );
    }

    return( 0 );
}


LRESULT CALLBACK WndProc( HWND hWnd, UINT uMsg, WPARAM wParam, LPARAM lParam )
{
static DWORD  dwID;
static char   szOut[128];
static HANDLE hThread = NULL;

    switch( uMsg )
    {
        case WM_CREATE :
            {
                // Start change notification.
                //..........................
                hWait = FindFirstChangeNotification( "D:\\TEMP", FALSE,
```

continued on next page

continued from previous page

```
                                          FILE_NOTIFY_CHANGE_FILE_NAME |
                                          FILE_NOTIFY_CHANGE_SIZE |
                                          FILE_NOTIFY_CHANGE_LAST_WRITE );

            // Create a thread to monitor changes.
            //...................................
            hThread = CreateThread( NULL, 0,
                                (LPTHREAD_START_ROUTINE)DirChanges,
                                hWnd, 0, &dwID );
        }
        break;

    case WM_PAINT :
            {
            HANDLE           hFind;
            SYSTEMTIME       sysTime;
            FILETIME         fLocTime;
            WIN32_FIND_DATA  fd;
            PAINTSTRUCT      ps;
            int              yPos = 0;
            BOOL             bRet = TRUE;

            BeginPaint( hWnd, &ps );

            // Start listing of files.
            //........................
            hFind = FindFirstFile( "D:\\TEMP\\*.*", &fd );

            // While there are more files, continue processing.
            //.................................................
            while ( hFind != INVALID_HANDLE_VALUE && bRet )
            {
                // Display the file and its information if this is
                // not a directory that we found.
                //................................................
                if ( (fd.dwFileAttributes & FILE_ATTRIBUTE_DIRECTORY) == 0)
                {
                    // Convert the file time to a local time, then to
                    // a SYSTEMTIME structure so we can display it.
                    //...............................................
                    FileTimeToLocalFileTime( &fd.ftLastWriteTime,
                                            &fLocTime );
                    FileTimeToSystemTime( &fLocTime, &sysTime );

                    // Output the file's information.
                    //...............................
                    yPos += 15;
                    wsprintf( szOut,
                        "%s \t %.2d/%.2d/%.4d \t %.2d:%.2d:%.2d \t %d",
                        fd.cFileName,
                        sysTime.wMonth,
                        sysTime.wDay,
                        sysTime.wYear,
                        sysTime.wHour,
                        sysTime.wMinute,
                        sysTime.wSecond,
                        fd.nFileSizeLow );
```

```
                    TabbedTextOut( ps.hdc, 10, yPos, szOut,
                                   strlen( szOut ), 1, &nTab, 10 );
                }

                // Find the next file.
                //..................
                bRet = FindNextFile( hFind, &fd );
            }

            // Close the find.
            //................
            FindClose( hFind );

            EndPaint( hWnd, &ps );
        }
        break;


    case WM_COMMAND :
            switch( LOWORD( wParam ) )
            {
                case IDM_EXIT :
                        DestroyWindow( hWnd );
                        break;
            }
            break;

    case WM_DESTROY :
            // Terminate thread that is waiting for changes.
            //..............................................
            if ( hThread )
                TerminateThread( hThread, 0 );

            // Close the change notification.
            //..............................
            if ( hWait )
                FindCloseChangeNotification( hWait );

            PostQuitMessage(0);
            break;

    default :
            return( DefWindowProc( hWnd, uMsg, wParam, lParam ) );
    }

    return( OL );
}
```

FindFirstFile ■ WINDOWS 95 ■ WINDOWS NT

Description
FindFirstFile searches a directory for the first file whose name matches the specified search file name. FindFirstFile examines subdirectory names as well as file names. An application can subsequently call the FindNextFile function repeatedly to retrieve all files and directories that match the search file name.

Syntax	HANDLE **FindFirstFile**(LPCTSTR *lpszSearchFile,* LPWIN32_FIND_DATA *lpffd*)
Parameters	
lpszSearchFile	LPCTSTR: A pointer to a null-terminated string that contains a valid directory or path and file name, which can contain wildcard characters (***** and **?**). This string must not exceed **MAX_PATH** characters. An application can bypass this limit on Windows NT by calling the wide (**W**) version of **FindFirstFile** and prepending "**\\?**" or "**\\?\UNC**" to turn off path parsing.
lpffd	LPWIN32_FIND_DATA: A pointer to a **WIN32_FIND_DATA** structure that receives information about the found file or subdirectory. The structure can be used in subsequent calls to **FindNextFile** to refer to the found file or directory. See the definition of the **WIN32_FIND_DATA** structure below.
Returns	HANDLE: If successful, a search handle used in subsequent calls to **FindNextFile** or **FindClose**; otherwise, **INVALID_HANDLE_VALUE** is returned.
Include File	winbase.h
See Also	FindFirstFileEx, FindClose, FindNextFile, GetFileAttributes, SetFileAttributes

WIN32_FIND_DATA Definition

```
typedef struct _WIN32_FIND_DATA
{
    DWORD      dwFileAttributes;
    FILETIME   ftCreationTime;
    FILETIME   ftLastAccessTime;
    FILETIME   ftLastWriteTime;
    DWORD      nFileSizeHigh;
    DWORD      nFileSizeLow;
    DWORD      dwReserved0;
    DWORD      dwReserved1;
    TCHAR      cFileName[ MAX_PATH ];
    TCHAR      cAlternateFileName[ 14 ];
} WIN32_FIND_DATA;
```

Members

dwFileAttributes	DWORD: The file attributes of the file found. This member can be one or more of the values listed in Table 17-16.

Table 17-16 WIN32_FIND_DATA *dwFileAttributes* values

Value	Meaning
FILE_ATTRIBUTE_ARCHIVE	The file is an archive file.
FILE_ATTRIBUTE_DIRECTORY	The file is a directory.
FILE_ATTRIBUTE_HIDDEN	The file is hidden.

Value	Meaning
FILE_ATTRIBUTE_NORMAL	The file has no other attributes. (This value is valid only if used alone.)
FILE_ATTRIBUTE_READONLY	The file is read-only.
FILE_ATTRIBUTE_SYSTEM	The file is part of the operating system or is used exclusively by it.
FILE_ATTRIBUTE_TEMPORARY	The file is being used for temporary storage.
FILE_ATTRIBUTE_ATOMIC_WRITE	Reserved; do not use.
FILE_ATTRIBUTE_XACTION_WRITE	Reserved; do not use.

ftCreationTime	FILETIME: The time the file was created. A value of **0,0** indicates that the file system containing the file does not support this time member. See the definition of the FILETIME structure under the CompareFileTime function.
ftLastAccessTime	FILETIME: The time the file was last accessed. A value of **0,0** indicates that the file system containing the file does not support this time member. See the definition of the FILETIME structure under the CompareFileTime function.
ftLastWriteTime	FILETIME: The time the file was last written to. See the definition of the FILETIME structure under the CompareFileTime function.
nFileSizeHigh	DWORD: The high-order word of the file size, in bytes.
nFileSizeLow	DWORD: The low-order word of the file size, in bytes.
dwReserved0	DWORD: Reserved; do not use.
dwReserved1	DWORD: Reserved; do not use.
cFileName	TCHAR[MAX_PATH]: A null-terminated string that is the name of the file.
cAlternateFileName	TCHAR[14]: A null-terminated string that is an alternate name for the file, expressed in 8.3 (*filename.ext*) format.
Example	See the example for the FindFirstChangeNotification function.

FindFirstFileEx ■ WINDOWS 95 ■ WINDOWS NT

Description	FindFirstFileEx searches a directory for a file whose name and attributes match those specified in the function call. If the underlying file system does not support a particular type of filtering, other than directory filtering, FindFirstFileEx fails. Once the first file is found, the application uses FindNextFile to search for other files that match the same pattern with the same filtering being performed. When the search handle is no longer needed, it should be closed using the FindClose function.
Syntax	HANDLE **FindFirstFileEx**(LPCTSTR *lpFileName*, FINDEX_INFO_LEVELS *fInfoLevelId*, LPVOID *lpFindFileData*, FINDEX_SEARCH_OPS *fSearchOp*, LPVOID *lpSearchFilter*, DWORD *dwAdditionalFlags*)

Parameters

lpFileName   LPCTSTR: A pointer to a null-terminated string that specifies a valid directory or path and file name, which can contain wildcard characters (***** and **?**).

fInfoLevelId   FINDEX_INFO_LEVELS: The information level of the returned data. The only value currently defined is **FindExInfoStandard**. If this constant is defined, *lpFindFileData* is a pointer to a **WIN32_FIND_DATA** structure. See the definition of the **WIN32_FIND_DATA** structure under the **FindFirstFile** function.

lpFindFileData   LPVOID: A pointer to the file data. The type of this pointer is determined by the level of information specified in the *fInfoLevelId* parameter.

fSearchOp   FINDEX_SEARCH_OPS: The type of filtering to perform beyond wildcard matching. This can be one of the values listed in Table 17-17.

Table 17-17 FindFirstFileEx *fSearchOp* values

Value	Meaning
FindExSearchNameMatch	Search for a file that matches the specified file name. The *lpSearchFilter* parameter must be NULL when this operation is used.
FindExSearchLimitToDevices	Only device names are returned. Device names are generally accessible through the \\, \\<name> convention. When this search operation is used, the *dwAdditionalFlags* parameter cannot be FIND_FIRST_EX_CASE_SENSITIVE.
FindExSearchLimitToDirectories	This is an advisory flag. If the file system supports directory filtering, the function searches for a file that matches the specified file name that is a directory. If the file system does not support directory filtering, this flag is ignored. The *lpSearchFilter* parameter must be NULL when this search operation is used. If directory filtering is desired, use this flag on all file systems; however, examine the file attribute data stored in *lpFindFileData* to determine whether the function has returned the handle to a directory.

lpSearchFilter   LPVOID: If the search operation requires structured search information, *lpSearchFilter* points to the search criteria. Currently there is no operation that requires extended search information; therefore, set this parameter to **NULL**.

dwAdditionalFlags   DWORD: Additional search flags. Use the **FIND_FIRST_EX_CASE_SENSITIVE** flag for case-sensitive searches.

Returns   HANDLE: If successful, the handle to be used with **FindNextFile** is returned; otherwise, **INVALID_HANDLE_VALUE** is returned.

Include File   winbase.h

See Also   FindFirstFile, FindNextFile, FindClose

Example   This code segment shows the equivalent use of the **FindFirstFileEx** function and **FindFirstFile**.

```
FindFirstFileEx( lpFileName, FindExInfoStandard, lpFindData, FindExSearchNameMatch, NULL, 0 );

FindFirstFile( lpFileName, lpFindData );
```

FindNextChangeNotification ■ WINDOWS 95 ■ WINDOWS NT

Description   FindNextChangeNotification requests that the operating system signal a change notification handle the next time it detects an appropriate change. An application uses this function to wait for another change of the same type as defined by FindFirstChangeNotification.

After the FindNextChangeNotification function returns successfully, the application can wait for notification that a change has occurred by using the WaitForSingleObject or WaitForMultipleObjects function. An application should not call the FindNextChangeNotification function more than once on the same handle without using either WaitForSingleObject or WaitForMultipleObjects.

Syntax   BOOL **FindNextChangeNotification**(HANDLE *hChange*)

Parameters

hChange   HANDLE: The change notification handle created by a previous call to the FindFirstChangeNotification function.

Returns   BOOL: TRUE if successful; otherwise, the return is FALSE.

Include File   winbase.h

See Also   FindCloseChangeNotification, FindFirstChangeNotification, WaitForMultipleObjects, WaitForSingleObject

Example   See the example for the FindFirstChangeNotification function.

FindNextFile ■ WINDOWS 95 ■ WINDOWS NT

Description   FindNextFile finds the next file that matches the search name given to a previous call to FindFirstFile. An application repeatedly calls the FindNextFile function until all files are processed and the function returns FALSE.

Syntax   BOOL **FindNextFile**(HANDLE *hFindFile,* LPWIN32_FIND_DATA *lpffd*)

Parameters

hFindFile   HANDLE: The search handle returned by a previous call to FindFirstFile.

lpffd   LPWIN32_FIND_DATA: A pointer to the WIN32_FIND_DATA structure that receives information about the found file or subdirectory. The structure can be used in subsequent calls to FindNextFile to refer to the found file or directory. See the definition of the WIN32_FIND_DATA structure under the FindFirstFile function.

Returns	BOOL: TRUE if successful; otherwise, the return value is FALSE.
Include File	winbase.h
See Also	FindClose, FindFirstFile, FindFirstFileEx, GetFileAttributes, SetFileAttributes
Example	See the example for the FindFirstChangeNotification function.

FlushFileBuffers █ WINDOWS 95 █ WINDOWS NT

Description	FlushFileBuffers clears the buffers of a file and causes all buffered data to be written to the file.
Syntax	BOOL **FlushFileBuffers**(HANDLE *hFile*)
Parameters	
hFile	HANDLE: The handle of an open file to flush. If this parameter specifies a communications device, the function flushes only the transmit buffer. If this parameter specifies the server end of a named pipe, the function does not return until the client has read all buffered data from the pipe.
Returns	BOOL: TRUE if successful; otherwise, the return value is FALSE.
Include File	winbase.h
See Also	WriteFile, WriteFileEx
Example	See the example for the LockFile function.

FlushViewOfFile █ WINDOWS 95 █ WINDOWS NT

Description	FlushViewOfFile writes a byte range within a mapped view of a file to the disk.
Syntax	BOOL **FlushViewOfFile**(LPCVOID *lpvBase,* DWORD *dwFlush*)
Parameters	
lpvBase	LPCVOID: A pointer to the base address of the byte range to be flushed to the disk representation of the mapped file.
dwFlush	DWORD: The number of bytes to flush. If set to 0, the file is flushed from the base address to the end of the mapping.
Returns	BOOL: TRUE if successful; otherwise, the return value is FALSE.
Include File	winbase.h
See Also	MapViewOfFile, UnmapViewOfFile
Example	See the example for the MapViewOfFile function.

GetFileAttributes ■ WINDOWS 95 ■ WINDOWS NT

Description	`GetFileAttributes` returns the attributes of a file or directory.
Syntax	DWORD **GetFileAttributes**(LPCTSTR *lpszFileName*)
Parameters	
lpszFileName	LPCTSTR: A pointer to a null-terminated string that contains the name of a file or directory. This string must not exceed **MAX_PATH** characters. An application can bypass this limit on Windows NT by calling the wide (**W**) version of **GetFileAttributes** and prepending "\\?\" or "\\?\UNC\" to turn off path parsing.
Returns	DWORD: If successful, the attributes of the specified file; otherwise, **0xFFFFFFFF** is returned. The attributes can be determined by using the binary AND (**&**) operator and the values given in Table 17-16.
Include File	winbase.h
See Also	GetFileAttributesEx, FindFirstFile, FindFirstFileEx, FindNextFile, SetFileAttributes
Example	See the example for the **SetFileAttributes** function.

GetFileAttributesEx ■ WINDOWS 95 ■ WINDOWS NT

Description	`GetFileAttributesEx` returns the attributes of a file or directory. This function is the same as the **GetFileAttributes** function except that it returns additional information about the file or directory.
Syntax	BOOL **GetFileAttributesEx**(LPCTSTR *lpszFileName,* GET_FILEEX_INFO_LEVELS *fInfoLevelId,* LPVOID *lpFileInformation*)
Parameters	
lpszFileName	LPCTSTR: A pointer to a null-terminated string that contains the name of a file or directory. This string must not exceed **MAX_PATH** characters. An application can bypass this limit on Windows NT by calling the wide (**W**) version of **GetFileAttributes** and prepending "\\?\" or "\\?\UNC\" to turn off path parsing.
fInfoLevelId	GET_FILEEX_INFO_LEVELS: An enumeration type value that specifies the set of attribute information to retrieve. Currently the only defined value, **GetFileExInfoStandard**, returns a standard set of attribute information in a **WIN32_FILE_ATTRIBUTE_DATA** structure. Future versions may define other values.
lpFileInformation	LPVOID: A pointer to a buffer that receives the attribute information. Currently, the only structure defined is **WIN32_FILE_ATTRIBUTE_DATA**. See the definition of the **WIN32_FILE_ATTRIBUTE_DATA** below.

Returns	BOOL: If successful, TRUE is returned; otherwise, FALSE is returned.
Include File	winbase.h
See Also	FindFirstFile, FindFirstFileEx, FindNextFile, SetFileAttributes

WIN32_FILE_ATTRIBUTE_DATA Definition

```
typedef struct _WIN32_FILE_ATTRIBUTE_DATA
{
    DWORD    dwFileAttributes;
    FILETIME ftCreationTime;
    FILETIME ftLastAccessTime;
    FILETIME ftLastWriteTime;
    DWORD    nFileSizeHigh;
    DWORD    nFileSizeLow;
} WIN32_FILE_ATTRIBUTE_DATA, *LPWIN32_FILE_ATTRIBUTE_DATA;
```

Members

dwFileAttributes	DWORD: A set of bit flags that specifies FAT-style attribute information for the file or directory. This is the same information returned by the GetFileAttributes function and can be a combination of the values listed in Table 17-16.
ftCreationTime	FILETIME: Specifies when the file or directory was created.
ftLastAccessTime	FILETIME: For a file, the date when the file was last read from or written to. For a directory, the date when the directory was created. The date is always correct; however, the time is set to midnight.
ftLastWriteTime	FILETIME: For a file, the value specifies when the file was last written to. For a directory, the value specifies when the directory was created.
nFileSizeHigh	DWORD: The high-order DWORD of the file size.
nFileSizeLow	DWORD: The low-order DWORD of the file size.

GetFileInformationByHandle ■ WINDOWS 95 ■ WINDOWS NT

Description	GetFileInformationByHandle retrieves information about a file identified by a file handle.
Syntax	BOOL **GetFileInformationByHandle**(HANDLE *hFile*, LPBY_HANDLE_FILE_INFORMATION *lpFileInformation*)
Parameters	
hFile	HANDLE: The handle of the file for which information is returned.
lpFileInformation	LPBY_HANDLE_FILE_INFORMATION: A pointer to a BY_HANDLE_FILE_INFORMATION structure that receives the file information. See the definition of the BY_HANDLE_FILE_INFORMATION structure below.
Returns	BOOL: TRUE if successful; otherwise, the return value is FALSE.
Include File	winbase.h
See Also	GetFileTime, GetFileSize, GetFileType

BY_HANDLE_FILE_INFORMATION Definition

```
typedef struct _BY_HANDLE_FILE_INFORMATION
{
    DWORD    dwFileAttributes;
    FILETIME ftCreationTime;
    FILETIME ftLastAccessTime;
    FILETIME ftLastWriteTime;
    DWORD    dwVolumeSerialNumber;
    DWORD    nFileSizeHigh;
    DWORD    nFileSizeLow;
    DWORD    nNumberOfLinks;
    DWORD    nFileIndexHigh;
    DWORD    nFileIndexLow;
} BY_HANDLE_FILE_INFORMATION;
```

Members

dwFileAttributes
DWORD: The file attributes. This member can be one or more of the values listed in Table 17-16. Use the binary AND (&) operator to determine which attributes are set.

ftCreationTime
FILETIME: The time the file was created. If the underlying file system does not support this time member, *ftCreationTime* is 0. See the definition of the FILETIME structure under the CompareFileTime function.

ftLastAccessTime
FILETIME: The time the file was last accessed. If the underlying file system does not support this time member, *ftLastAccessTime* is 0. See the definition of the FILETIME structure under the CompareFileTime function.

ftLastWriteTime
FILETIME: The last time the file was written to. See the definition of the FILETIME structure under the CompareFileTime function.

dwVolumeSerialNumber
DWORD: The serial number of the volume that contains the file.

nFileSizeHigh
DWORD: The high-order 32 bits of the file size.

nFileSizeLow
DWORD: The low-order 32 bits of the file size.

nNumberOfLinks
DWORD: The number of links to this file. For the FAT file system and HPFS, this is always 1. For NTFS, it may be more than one.

nFileIndexHigh
DWORD: The high-order 32 bits of a unique identifier associated with the file.

nFileIndexLow
DWORD: The low-order 32 bits of a unique identifier associated with the file. This identifier and the volume serial number uniquely identify a file. After a process opens a file, the identifier is constant until the file is closed. An application can use this identifier and the volume serial number to determine whether two handles refer to the same file.

Example

This example, shown in Figure 17-2, shows how to use the GetFileInformationByHandle to retrieve the volume serial number on which the file **FILE.DAT** resides. When the user selects the Test! menu item, the volume serial number is displayed in a message box.

Figure 17-2 GetFileInformationByHandle example

```c
LRESULT CALLBACK WndProc( HWND hWnd, UINT uMsg, WPARAM wParam, LPARAM lParam )
{
    switch( uMsg )
    {
    case WM_COMMAND :
            switch( LOWORD( wParam ) )
            {
                case IDM_TEST :
                    {
                        HANDLE                    hFile;
                        BY_HANDLE_FILE_INFORMATION info;

                        // Open/create file.
                        //..................
                        hFile = CreateFile( "FILE.DAT",
                                    GENERIC_READ | GENERIC_WRITE,
                                    0, NULL, OPEN_ALWAYS,
                                    FILE_ATTRIBUTE_NORMAL, NULL );

                        if ( hFile &&
                            GetFileInformationByHandle( hFile, &info ) )
                        {
                            char szOut[128];

                            wsprintf( szOut,
                                    "'File.dat' is on a disk with a\n" \
                                    "serial number of: %.4X-%.4X",
                                    HIWORD( info.dwVolumeSerialNumber ),
                                    LOWORD( info.dwVolumeSerialNumber ) );

                            MessageBox( hWnd, szOut, "Information",
                                    MB_OK | MB_ICONINFORMATION );
                        }
                        else
                            MessageBox( hWnd, "There was an error!", "Error",
                                    MB_OK | MB_ICONEXCLAMATION );
```

```
        CloseHandle( hFile );
    }
    break;
```

.
.
.

GetFileSize   ■ WINDOWS 95   ■ WINDOWS NT

Description   `GetFileSize` retrieves the size, in bytes, of a file. Using this function with a handle of a nonseeking device, such as a pipe or a communications device, has no meaning. To determine the file type, use the `GetFileType` function.

Syntax   DWORD **GetFileSize**(HANDLE *hFile*, LPDWORD *lpdwFileSizeHigh*)

Parameters

hFile   HANDLE: The handle of an open file whose size is being returned. The handle must have been created with either **GENERIC_READ** or **GENERIC_WRITE** access to the file.

lpdwFileSizeHigh LPDWORD: A pointer to a variable where the high-order 32 bits of the file size are returned. This parameter can be **NULL** if the application does not require the high-order 32 bits.

Returns   DWORD: If successful, the low-order 32 bits of the file size, and, if *lpdwFileSizeHigh* is non-**NULL**, the function puts the high-order 32 bits of the file size into the variable pointed to by that parameter.

If the function fails and if *lpdwFileSizeHigh* is **NULL**, the return value is 0xFFFFFFFF. If *lpdwFileSizeHigh* is non-**NULL** and the function fails, 0xFFFFFFFF is returned and the application must use the **GetLastError** function to determine whether the function succeeded or failed. See the example below for a demonstration of error handling.

Include File   winbase.h

See Also   GetFileType, GetFileTime, GetLastError

Example   In this example, `DisplayFileSize` is defined as a function that checks the type of the file handle. If it is a disk-based file, the file size is retrieved and displayed. If the file is another type of file, a message is displayed indicating that the file is not a disk-based file.

```
VOID DisplayFileSize( HWND hWnd, HANDLE hFile )
{
    char szMsg[128];

    // Check to see if the file is a disk file.
    //.........................................
    if ( GetFileType( hFile ) == FILE_TYPE_DISK )
    {
        DWORD dwSize;
```

continued on next page

continued from previous page

```
      // Get the file size.
      //................
      dwSize = GetFileSize( hFile, NULL );
      wsprintf( szMsg, "File size = %ld", dwSize );
   }
   else
      strcpy( szMsg, "File is not a disk file." );

   MessageBox( hWnd, szMsg, "File size", MB_OK | MB_ICONINFORMATION );
}
```

GetFileTime ■ Windows 95 ■ Windows NT

Description	**GetFileTime** retrieves the date and time that a file was created, last accessed, and last modified. The FAT file system does not record the creation or last access times, but both HPFS and NTFS do record these times.
Syntax	BOOL **GetFileTime**(HANDLE *hFile,* LPFILETIME *lpftCreation,* LPFILETIME *lpftLastAccess,* LPFILETIME *lpftLastWrite*)
Parameters	
hFile	HANDLE: The handle of the file for which to get dates and times. The file handle must have been created with **GENERIC_READ** access to the file.
lpftCreation	LPFILETIME: A pointer to a **FILETIME** structure that receives the date and time the file was created. This parameter can be **NULL** if the application does not require this information. See the definition of the **FILETIME** structure under the **CompareFileTime** function.
lpftLastAccess	LPFILETIME: A pointer to a **FILETIME** structure that receives the date and time the file was last accessed. This parameter can be **NULL** if the application does not require this information.
lpftLastWrite	LPFILETIME: A pointer to a **FILETIME** structure that receives the date and time the file was last written to. This parameter can be **NULL** if the application does not require this information.
Returns	BOOL: **TRUE** if successful; otherwise, the return value is **FALSE**.
Include File	winbase.h
See Also	GetFileSize, GetFileType, SetFileTime
Example	See the example for the **FileTimeToLocalFileTime** function.

GetFileType ■ Windows 95 ■ Windows NT

Description	**GetFileType** returns the type of the file identified by the given file handle.
Syntax	DWORD **GetFileType**(HANDLE *hFile*)

Parameters

hFile   HANDLE: The handle of an open file.

Returns   DWORD: The return value is one of the values listed in Table 17-18.

Table 17-18 GetFileType return values

Value	Meaning
FILE_TYPE_CHAR	The file is a character file, typically an LPT device or a console.
FILE_TYPE_DISK	The file is a disk file.
FILE_TYPE_PIPE	The file is either a named or an anonymous pipe.
FILE_TYPE_UNKNOWN	The type of the file is unknown.

Include File   winbase.h

See Also   GetFileSize, GetFileTime

Example   See the example for the GetFileSize function.

GetFullPathName   ■ WINDOWS 95   ■ WINDOWS NT

Description   GetFullPathName retrieves the full path and file name of a given file. This function merges the name of the current drive and directory with the specified file name to determine the full path and file name of the specified file. It also returns the address of the file name portion of the full path and file name. GetFullPathName does not verify that the resulting path and file name are valid or that they refer to an existing file on the associated volume.

Syntax   DWORD **GetFullPathName**(LPCTSTR *lpszFile,* DWORD *cchPath,* LPTSTR *lpszPath,* LPTSTR* *ppszFilePart*)

Parameters

lpszFile   LPCTSTR: A pointer to a null-terminated string that contains a valid file name.

cchPath   DWORD: The size, in bytes (ANSI) or characters (Unicode), of the buffer for the drive and path.

lpszPath   LPTSTR: A pointer to a buffer that receives a null-terminated string for the name of the drive and path of the file.

ppszFilePart   LPTSTR*: A pointer to a variable that receives the address (in *lpszPath*) of the final file name component in the path.

Returns   DWORD: If successful, the length, in bytes or characters, of the string copied to *lpszPath*. The length does not include the terminating null character. If the *lpszPath* buffer is too small, the return value is the size of the buffer, in bytes or characters, required to hold the path. If the function fails, the return value is **0**.

Include File   `winbase.h`

See Also   `GetTempPath`, `SearchPath`

Example   This example shows how an application uses the `GetFullPathName` function to retrieve the full path of a file. When the user selects the Test! menu item, the full path name of **FILE.DAT** is displayed in a message box.

```
LRESULT CALLBACK WndProc( HWND hWnd, UINT uMsg, WPARAM wParam, LPARAM lParam )
{
    switch( uMsg )
    {
        case WM_COMMAND :
                switch( LOWORD( wParam ) )
                {
                    case IDM_TEST :
                        {
                            LPTSTR lpPart;
                            char   szOut[MAX_PATH+1];

                            if ( GetFullPathName( "FILE.DAT", MAX_PATH,
                                                  szOut, &lpPart ) )
                            {
                                MessageBox( hWnd, szOut,
                                            "Full path for FILE.DAT",
                                            MB_OK | MB_ICONINFORMATION );
                            }
                            else
                                MessageBox( hWnd, "FILE.DAT was not found.",
                                            "File not Found",
                                            MB_OK | MB_ICONEXCLAMATION );
                        }
                        break;
            .
            .
            .
```

GetOverlappedResult ■ WINDOWS 95 ■ WINDOWS NT

Description   `GetOverlappedResult` returns the results of an overlapped operation on the specified file, named pipe, or communications device. On Windows 95, this function only works on serial devices, such as COM ports.

If the *hEvent* member of the **OVERLAPPED** structure is **NULL**, the system uses the state of the *hFile* handle to signal when the operation has been completed. This is discouraged for file, named pipe, or communications-device handles. It is safer to use an event object to avoid confusion when multiple simultaneous overlapped operations are performed on the same handle.

Syntax   `BOOL` **GetOverlappedResult**`( HANDLE hFile, LPOVERLAPPED lpOverlapped, LPDWORD lpcbTransfer, BOOL bWait )`

Parameters

hFile

    HANDLE: The handle of the file, named pipe, or communications device on which the overlapped operation occurred.

lpOverlapped

    LPOVERLAPPED: A pointer to the **OVERLAPPED** structure that was specified when the overlapped operation was started. See the definition of the **OVERLAPPED** structure under the **ReadFile** function later in this chapter.

lpcbTransfer

    LPDWORD: A pointer to a 32-bit variable that receives the number of bytes that were actually transferred by a read or write operation. For a **TransactNamedPipe** operation, this is the number of bytes that were read from the pipe. For a **ConnectNamedPipe** or **WaitCommEvent** operation, this value is undefined.

bWait

    BOOL: If set to **TRUE**, the function does not return until the operation has been completed. If **FALSE** and the operation is still pending, the function returns **FALSE** and the **GetLastError** function returns the value **ERROR_IO_INCOMPLETE**.

Returns

    BOOL: **TRUE** if successful; otherwise, the return value is **FALSE**.

Include File

    winbase.h

See Also

    CreateEvent, GetLastError, ReadFile, WriteFile

Example

    This example writes a string to the **"COM2"** communications port using an overlapped operation. When the user selects the Test! menu item, an event is created and the **"COM2"** port is opened. The string **"ATDT"** is sent to the communications port with the **WriteFile** function as an overlapped operation. The application then uses the **GetOverlappedResult** to wait for the operation to finish.

```
LRESULT CALLBACK WndProc( HWND hWnd, UINT uMsg, WPARAM wParam, LPARAM lParam )
{
    switch( uMsg )
    {
        case WM_COMMAND :
                switch( LOWORD( wParam ) )
                {
                    case IDM_TEST :
                        {
                            HANDLE     hFile, hEvent;
                            DWORD      dwWritten;
                            OVERLAPPED ol;

                            // Create an event object.
                            //........................
                            hEvent = CreateEvent( NULL, FALSE,
                                            FALSE, "WaitCOM2" );

                            // Open COM2 port.
                            //...............
                            hFile = CreateFile( "COM2",
```

continued on next page

continued from previous page

```
                                    GENERIC_READ | GENERIC_WRITE,
                                    0, NULL, OPEN_EXISTING,
                                    FILE_FLAG_OVERLAPPED, NULL );

                    ol.Offset     = 0;
                    ol.OffsetHigh = 0;
                    ol.hEvent     = hEvent;

                    // Send data to COM port.
                    //......................
                    WriteFile( hFile, "ATDT", 4, &dwWritten, &ol );

                    //other program lines...

                    // Wait for result.
                    //.................
                    GetOverlappedResult( hFile, &ol, &dwWritten, TRUE );

                    CloseHandle( hEvent );
                    CloseHandle( hFile );
            }
            break;
```

GetStdHandle ■ WINDOWS 95   ■ WINDOWS NT

Description	GetStdHandle returns a handle for the standard input, standard output, or standard error device. Applications can use handles returned by GetStdHandle to read from and write to the console. These handles can be used by the ReadFile or WriteFile function, or by any of the console functions that access the console input buffer or screen buffer, such as the ReadConsoleInput or WriteConsole function.
Syntax	HANDLE **GetStdHandle**(DWORD *dwDevice*)
Parameters	
dwDevice	DWORD: The device for which to return the handle. This parameter can be one of the values given in Table 17-19.

Table 17-19 GetStdHandle *dwDevice* values

Value	Meaning
STD_INPUT_HANDLE	Standard input handle
STD_OUTPUT_HANDLE	Standard output handle
STD_ERROR_HANDLE	Standard error handle

Returns	**HANDLE**: If successful, the handle of the specified device; otherwise, **INVALID_HANDLE_VALUE** is returned.
Include File	`winbase.h`
See Also	`SetStdHandle`
Example	This example creates a console window, as shown in Figure 17-3, when started with the **AllocConsole** function. When the user selects the Test! menu item, the string **"This string is sent to the console."** is displayed on the console screen.

```c
LRESULT CALLBACK WndProc( HWND hWnd, UINT uMsg, WPARAM wParam, LPARAM lParam )
{
   switch( uMsg )
   {
      case WM_CREATE :
              AllocConsole();
              break;

      case WM_COMMAND :
              switch( LOWORD( wParam ) )
              {
                 case IDM_TEST :
                         {
                            DWORD  dwWritten;
                            HANDLE hOutput = GetStdHandle( STD_OUTPUT_HANDLE );

                            WriteFile( hOutput,
                                    "This string is sent to the console.",
                                    35, &dwWritten, NULL );
                         }
                         break;

                 case IDM_EXIT :
                         DestroyWindow( hWnd );
                         break;
              }
              break;

      case WM_DESTROY :
              FreeConsole();
              PostQuitMessage(0);
              break;

      default :
              return( DefWindowProc( hWnd, uMsg, wParam, lParam ) );
   }

   return( 0L );
}
```

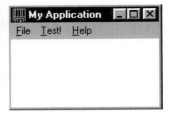

Figure 17-3 GetStdHandle example

GetTempFileName ■ WINDOWS 95 ■ WINDOWS NT

Description GetTempFileName creates a temporary file name of the following form: *path\preuuuu*.tmp. Table 17-20 describes the file name components. When Windows shuts down, temporary files whose names have been created by this function are not automatically deleted.

Table 17-20 GetTempFileName file name components

Component	Meaning
path	Path specified by the *lpszPath* parameter.
pre	First three letters of the *lpszPrefix* string.
uuuu	Hexadecimal value of *uUnique* or a system-generated unique number.

Syntax UINT **GetTempFileName**(LPCTSTR *lpszPath,* LPCTSTR *lpszPrefix,* UINT *uUnique,* LPTSTR *lpszTempFile*)

Parameters

lpszPath LPCTSTR: A pointer to a null-terminated string that contains the path where the function creates the temporary file name. Applications typically specify a period (.) or the result of **GetTempPath** for this parameter. If this parameter is **NULL**, the function fails.

lpszPrefix LPCTSTR: A pointer to a null-terminated string that will be used as the temporary file name prefix.

uUnique UINT: An unsigned integer used in creating the temporary file name. If this parameter is nonzero, it is appended to the temporary file name. If this parameter is **0**, Windows uses the current system time to create a number to append to the file name.

lpszTempFile LPTSTR: A pointer to a buffer that receives the null-terminated temporary file name. This buffer should be at least the length, in bytes, specified by **MAX_PATH** to accommodate the path.

Returns	UINT: If successful, the unique numeric value used in the temporary file name. If the *uUnique* parameter is nonzero, the return value specifies that same number. If the function fails, the return value is 0.
Include File	winbase.h
See Also	CreateFile, GetTempPath
Example	This example shows how to use the GetTempPath and GetTempFileName functions to get a temporary file name. When the application starts, a temporary file is created and opened for usage. When the application ends, the file is closed and deleted.

```c
LRESULT CALLBACK WndProc( HWND hWnd, UINT uMsg, WPARAM wParam, LPARAM lParam )
{
static HANDLE hFile;
static char   szTmpFile[MAX_PATH+1];

   switch( uMsg )
   {
      case WM_CREATE  :
            {
                char szTmpPath[MAX_PATH+1];

                // Get the temporary path and file name.
                //......................................
                GetTempPath( MAX_PATH, szTmpPath );
                GetTempFileName( szTmpPath, "GEN", 0, szTmpFile );

                // Create the new temporary file and open it.
                //......................................
                hFile = CreateFile( szTmpFile, GENERIC_READ | GENERIC_WRITE,
                             0, NULL, OPEN_ALWAYS,
                             FILE_ATTRIBUTE_TEMPORARY, NULL );
            }
            break;


         .
         .
         .


      // Process Messages


         .
         .
         .


      case WM_DESTROY :
            // If the file was created, delete it.
            //......................................
            if ( hFile )
            {
                CloseHandle( hFile );
                DeleteFile( szTmpFile );
            }

            PostQuitMessage(0);
            break;
```

continued on next page

continued from previous page

```
        default :
                return( DefWindowProc( hWnd, uMsg, wParam, lParam ) );
    }

    return( OL );
}
```

GetTempPath   ■ WINDOWS 95   ■ WINDOWS NT

Description	GetTempPath retrieves the path of the directory designated for temporary files. This is the path that should be used for temporary files.
Syntax	DWORD **GetTempPath**(DWORD *dwBuffer,* LPTSTR *lpszTempPath*)
Parameters	
dwBuffer	DWORD: The size, in bytes (ANSI) or characters (Unicode), of the *lpszTempPath* buffer.
lpszTempPath	LPTSTR: A pointer to a string buffer that receives the null-terminated string specifying the temporary file path.
Returns	DWORD: If successful, the length, in bytes (ANSI) or characters (Unicode), of the string copied to *lpszTempPath*. The length does not include the terminating null character. If the function fails, the return value is 0.
	If the return value is greater than *dwBuffer*, the return value is the size, in bytes or characters, of the buffer required to hold the path.
Include File	winbase.h
See Also	GetTempFileName
Example	See the example for the GetTempFileName function.

LocalFileTimeToFileTime   ■ WINDOWS 95   ■ WINDOWS NT

Description	LocalFileTimeToFileTime converts a local file time to a file time based on Universal Time Coordination (UTC).
Syntax	BOOL **LocalFileTimeToFileTime**(CONST FILETIME* *lpftLocal,* LPFILETIME *lpft*)
Parameters	
lpftLocal	CONST FILETIME*: A pointer to a FILETIME structure that contains the local file time to be converted into a UTC-based file time. See the definition of the FILETIME structure under the CompareFileTime function.
lpft	LPFILETIME: A pointer to a FILETIME structure to receive the converted UTC-based file time. This parameter cannot be the same as the *lpftLocal* parameter. See the definition of the FILETIME structure under the CompareFileTime function.

Returns	BOOL: **TRUE** if successful; otherwise, the return value is **FALSE**.
Include File	winbase.h
See Also	FileTimeToLocalFileTime
Example	See the example for the **DosDateTimeToFileTime** function.

LockFile   ■ WINDOWS 95   ■ WINDOWS NT

Description   **LockFile** locks a region in an open file and gives the locking process exclusive access to the specified region while denying all other processes both read and write access to the region. Locks may not overlap an existing locked region of the file. Use the **UnlockFile** function to unlock the region.

Syntax   BOOL **LockFile**(HANDLE *hFile,* DWORD *dwFileOffsetLow,* DWORD *dwFileOffsetHigh,* DWORD *dwLockLow,* DWORD *dwLockHigh*)

Parameters

hFile   HANDLE: The handle of the file with a region to be locked. The file handle must have been created with either **GENERIC_READ** or **GENERIC_WRITE** access to the file (or both).

dwFileOffsetLow   DWORD: The low-order 32 bits of the starting byte offset in the file where the lock should begin.

dwFileOffsetHigh   DWORD: The high-order 32 bits of the starting byte offset in the file where the lock should begin.

dwLockLow   DWORD: The low-order 32 bits of the length of the byte range to be locked.

dwLockHigh   DWORD: The high-order 32 bits of the length of the byte range to be locked.

Returns   BOOL: **TRUE** if successful; otherwise, the return value is **FALSE**.

Include File   winbase.h

See Also   CreateFile, UnlockFile

Example   This example shows a function that performs an update to a record in a file using file locking. A record number is passed in as *dwRecord*, and the offset in the file is calculated based on the size of the **RECORD** structure (this structure is an application-specific structure that represents a record in the file). The section of the file the record will be written to is locked, and the record is updated. If the *bFlush* parameter is set to **TRUE**, the file buffers are flushed with the **FlushFileBuffers** function. The record is then unlocked, and the success of the update is returned.

```
BOOL UpdateRecord( HANDLE hFile, RECORD* lpRecord, DWORD dwRecord, BOOL bFlush )
{
    DWORD  dwWritten;
    BOOL   bRet;
```

continued on next page

continued from previous page

```
    // Lock the region of the file to be updated.
    //................................
    if ( !LockFile( hFile, dwRecord*sizeof( RECORD ), 0, sizeof( RECORD ), 0 ) )
        return( FALSE );

    // Write the record.
    //...................
    SetFilePointer( hFile, dwRecord*sizeof( RECORD ), 0, FILE_BEGIN );
    bRet = WriteFile( hFile, &Record, sizeof( RECORD ), &dwWritten, NULL );

    // Flush the file if necessary.
    //.............................
    if ( bFlush )
        FlushFileBuffers( hFile );

    // Unlock the region of the file to be updated.
    //.............................................
    UnlockFile( hFile, dwRecord*sizeof( RECORD ), 0, sizeof( RECORD ), 0 );

    return( bRet );
}
```

LockFileEx ■ WINDOWS 95 ■ WINDOWS NT

Description	LockFileEx locks a byte range within an open file for shared or exclusive access. Locking a byte range of a file gives an application shared or exclusive access to the range of the file. File locks are not inherited by a new process during process creation. Locking a portion of a file for exclusive access denies all other processes both read and write access to that portion of the file. Locking a portion of a file for shared access denies all processes write access to that portion of the file.
Syntax	BOOL **LockFileEx**(HANDLE *hFile*, DWORD *dwFlags*, DWORD *dwReserved*, DWORD *dwNumberOfBytesToLockLow*, DWORD *dwNumberOfBytesToLockHigh*, LPOVERLAPPED *lpOverlapped*)
Parameters	
hFile	HANDLE: The open handle to the file that is to have a range of bytes locked for shared or exclusive access. The handle must have been created with either GENERIC_READ or GENERIC_WRITE access to the file.
dwFlags	DWORD: Determines how the file is locked. This may be one or more of the values listed in Table 17-21.

Table 17-21 LockFileEx *dwFlags* values

Value	Meaning
LOCKFILE_EXCLUSIVE_LOCK	The function requests an exclusive lock. By default, a shared lock is requested.
LOCKFILE_FAIL_IMMEDIATELY	The function returns immediately if it is unable to acquire the requested lock. By default, it waits.

dwReserved DWORD: Reserved, must be set to 0.

dwNumberOfBytesToLockLow DWORD: The low-order 32 bits of the length of the byte range to lock.

dwNumberOfBytesToLockHigh DWORD: The high-order 32 bits of the length of the byte range to lock.

lpOverlapped LPOVERLAPPED: A pointer to an OVERLAPPED structure that the function uses with the locking request. This required structure contains the file offset of the beginning of the lock range. See the definition of the OVERLAPPED structure under the ReadFile function later in this chapter.

Returns BOOL: If successful, TRUE is returned; otherwise, FALSE is returned.

Include File winbase.h

See Also LockFile, UnlockFileEx

Example This example is identical to the one shown for the LockFile function, except that it uses the LockFileEx function to lock the region of the file and UnlockFileEx to unlock the same region after the update occurs.

```
BOOL UpdateRecord( HANDLE hFile, RECORD* lpRecord, DWORD dwRecord, BOOL bFlush )
{
    DWORD      dwWritten;
    BOOL       bRet;
    OVERLAPPED ol;

    memset( &ol, 0, sizeof( OVERLAPPED ) );
    ol.Offset     = dwRecord*sizeof( RECORD );

    // Lock the region of the file to be updated.
    //..............................................
    if ( !LockFileEx( hFile, 0, 0, sizeof( RECORD ), &ol  ) )
        return( FALSE );

    // Write the record.
    //....................
    SetFilePointer( hFile, dwRecord*sizeof( RECORD ), 0, FILE_BEGIN );
    bRet = WriteFile( hFile, &Record, sizeof( RECORD ), &dwWritten, NULL );

    // Flush the file if necessary.
    //..............................
```

continued on next page

continued from previous page

```
    if ( bFlush )
        FlushFileBuffers( hFile );

    // Unlock the region of the file to be updated.
    //..............................
    UnlockFileEx( hFile, 0, sizeof( RECORD ), 0, &ol );

    return( bRet );
}
```

MapViewOfFile   ■ WINDOWS 95   ■ WINDOWS NT

Description	`MapViewOfFile` maps a view of a file into the address space of the calling process. A process can duplicate a file-mapping object handle into another process by using the `DuplicateHandle` function, or another process can open a file-mapping object by name by using the `OpenFileMapping` function.
Syntax	LPVOID **MapViewOfFile**(HANDLE *hMapObject,* DWORD *dwAccess,* DWORD *dwOffsetHigh,* DWORD *dwOffsetLow,* DWORD *dwMap*)
Parameters	
hMapObject	HANDLE: The open handle of a file-mapping object. `CreateFileMapping` and `OpenFileMapping` return this handle.
dwAccess	DWORD: The type of access to the file view. This parameter can be one of the values given in Table 17-22.

Table 17-22 MapViewOfFile *dwAccess* values

Value	Meaning
FILE_MAP_ALL_ACCESS	Same as FILE_MAP_WRITE.
FILE_MAP_COPY	Copy-on-write access.
FILE_MAP_READ	Read-only access. The *hMapObject* parameter must have been created with PAGE_READWRITE or PAGE_READ protection.
FILE_MAP_WRITE	Read-write access. The *hMapObject* parameter must have been created with PAGE_READWRITE protection.

dwOffsetHigh	DWORD: The high-order 32 bits of the file offset where mapping is to begin.
dwOffsetLow	DWORD: The low-order 32 bits of the file offset where mapping is to begin. The offset must be within the file and be a multiple of the allocation granularity. To obtain the system's memory allocation granularity, use `GetSystemInfo`.
dwMap	DWORD: The number of bytes of the file to map. If set to **0**, the entire file is mapped.

Returns	LPVOID: If successful, the starting address of the mapped view; otherwise, NULL is returned.
Include File	winbase.h
See Also	CreateFileMapping, DuplicateHandle, MapViewOfFileEx, OpenFileMapping, UnMapViewOfFile
Example	This example shows how two processes can share a memory-mapped file. A memory-mapped file is created when the application starts. When the user selects the Test! menu item, a view to the file is mapped, and data is put into the memory. The example then creates a thread and waits on a timer for the data to be modified by the thread. The thread uses the data to display a message box and places the **"Received"** string in the mapped memory when the message box is closed. When the example receives the **WM_TIMER** message, it checks to see if the **"Received"** string has been put in the mapped memory. If it has, the thread and timer are terminated, and the user is notified.

```
DWORD AnotherProcess( LPDWORD lpdwParam )
{
    HANDLE hFileMap;
    LPTSTR lpMapAddress;

    // Open the file mapping.
    //.......................
    hFileMap = OpenFileMapping( FILE_MAP_ALL_ACCESS, FALSE,
                               "MyFileMappingObject" );

    // Map a view to the mapping object.
    //..................................
    lpMapAddress = MapViewOfFile( hFileMap, FILE_MAP_ALL_ACCESS,
                                 0, 0, 0);

    // Display the contents of the memory.
    //....................................
    MessageBox( NULL, lpMapAddress, "Mapped Memory",
               MB_OK | MB_ICONINFORMATION );

    // Set "Received" into the memory.
    //................................
    strcpy( lpMapAddress, "Received" );

    UnmapViewOfFile( lpMapAddress );

    return( 0 );
}


LRESULT CALLBACK WndProc( HWND hWnd, UINT uMsg, WPARAM wParam, LPARAM lParam )
{
static HANDLE hMapFile = NULL;
static HANDLE hThread  = NULL;
static LPTSTR lpMapAddress = NULL;
```

continued on next page

continued from previous page

```
switch( uMsg )
{
    case WM_CREATE :
            // Create a file mapped object.
            //.............................
            hMapFile = CreateFileMapping( (HANDLE)0xFFFFFFFF, NULL,
                                          PAGE_READWRITE,
                                          0,
                                          1024,
                                          "MyFileMappingObject" );

            // Return if the mapping failed.
            //..............................
            if ( !hMapFile )
                return(-1);

            break;


    case WM_TIMER :
            // Check to see if the thread has processed the memory.
            //....................................................
            if ( strcmp( lpMapAddress, "Received" ) == 0 )
            {
                // Kill the timer and thread.
                //...........................
                KillTimer( hWnd, 1 );
                TerminateThread( hThread, 0 );

                // Show the mapped data and unmap the view.
                //.........................................
                MessageBox( hWnd, lpMapAddress, "Done", MB_OK );

                UnmapViewOfFile( lpMapAddress );
            }
            break;

    case WM_COMMAND :
            switch( LOWORD( wParam ) )
            {
                case IDM_TEST :
                    {
                        DWORD   dwID;

                        // Map a view of the file mapped object.
                        //......................................
                        lpMapAddress = MapViewOfFile( hMapFile,
                                                      FILE_MAP_ALL_ACCESS,
                                                      0, 0, 0);

                        // Place data in the view.
                        //........................
                        strcpy( lpMapAddress,
                                "Data passed from main process." );

                        // Make sure the data is flushed to the file.
                        //...........................................
                        FlushViewOfFile( lpMapAddress,
                                         lstrlen( lpMapAddress ) );
```

```
                      // Create a thread to receive the data.
                      //.....................................
                      hThread = CreateThread( NULL, 0,
                              (LPTHREAD_START_ROUTINE)AnotherProcess,
                              NULL, 0, &dwID );

                      // Set a timer to wait for the data to be processed.
                      //.......................................................
                      SetTimer( hWnd, 1, 1000, NULL );
                }
                break;


           case IDM_EXIT :
                  DestroyWindow( hWnd );
                  break;
         }
         break;

    case WM_DESTROY :
           CloseHandle( hMapFile );

           PostQuitMessage(0);
           break;

    default :
           return( DefWindowProc( hWnd, uMsg, wParam, lParam ) );
   }

   return( OL );
}
```

MapViewOfFileEx   ■ WINDOWS 95   ■ WINDOWS NT

Description   MapViewOfFileEx is the same as the MapViewOfFile function, except that the calling process can specify a suggested memory address for the mapped view.

In Windows NT, if the *lpvBase* parameter specifies a base offset, the function succeeds if the given memory region is not already in use by the calling process. In Windows 95, the same memory region has to be available in all other 32-bit processes.

Typically, the suggested address is used to specify that a file should be mapped at the same address in multiple processes. This requires the region of address space to be available in all involved processes. No other memory allocation, including use of the VirtualAlloc function to reserve memory, can take place in the region used for mapping.

Syntax   LPVOID **MapViewOfFileEx**(HANDLE *hMapObject,* DWORD *dwAccess,* DWORD *dwOffsetHigh,* DWORD *dwOffsetLow,* DWORD *dwMap,* LPVOID *lpvBase*)

Parameters

hMapObject	**HANDLE**: The open handle of a file-mapping object. `CreateFileMapping` and `OpenFileMapping` return this handle.
dwAccess	**DWORD**: The type of access to the file view. This parameter can be one of the values given in Table 17-22.
dwOffsetHigh	**DWORD**: The high-order 32 bits of the file offset where mapping is to begin.
dwOffsetLow	**DWORD**: The low-order 32 bits of the file offset where mapping is to begin. The offset must be within the file and be a multiple of the allocation granularity. To obtain the system's memory allocation granularity, use `GetSystemInfo`.
dwMap	**DWORD**: The number of bytes of the file to map. If set to **0**, the entire file is mapped.
lpvBase	**LPVOID**: A pointer to the memory address in the calling process's address space where mapping should begin. This must be a multiple of the system's memory allocation granularity, or the function fails. If there is not enough address space at the specified address, the function fails. If set to **NULL**, the operating system chooses the mapping address, and the function is equivalent to `MapViewOfFile`.
Returns	**LPVOID**: If successful, the starting address of the mapped view; otherwise, **NULL** is returned.
Include File	`winbase.h`
See Also	`CreateFileMapping`, `DuplicateHandle`, `MapViewOfFile`, `OpenFileMapping`, `UnmapViewOfFile`
Example	This example is the same as the one shown for the `MapViewOfFile` function, except that the `MapViewOfFileEx` function is used to make sure that the address used for the mapping object in the thread is the same as the one used in the main process.

```
DWORD AnotherProcess( LPDWORD lpdwParam )
{
   HANDLE hFileMap;
   LPTSTR lpMapAddress;

   // Open the file mapping.
   //....................
   hFileMap = OpenFileMapping( FILE_MAP_ALL_ACCESS, FALSE,
                               "MyFileMappingObject" );

   // Map a view to the mapping object.
   //..................................
   lpMapAddress = MapViewOfFileEx( hFileMap, FILE_MAP_ALL_ACCESS,
                                   0, 0, 0, lpdwParam);

   // Display the contents of the memory.
   //....................................
   MessageBox( NULL, lpMapAddress, "Mapped Memory",
               MB_OK | MB_ICONINFORMATION );
```

```
        // Set "Received" into the memory.
        //.................................
        strcpy( lpMapAddress, "Received" );

        UnmapViewOfFile( lpMapAddress );

        return( 0 );
}


LRESULT CALLBACK WndProc( HWND hWnd, UINT uMsg, WPARAM wParam, LPARAM lParam )
{
static HANDLE hMapFile = NULL;
static HANDLE hThread  = NULL;
static LPTSTR lpMapAddress = NULL;

    switch( uMsg )
    {
        case WM_CREATE :
                // Create a file-mapped object.
                //..............................
                hMapFile = CreateFileMapping( (HANDLE)0xFFFFFFFF, NULL,
                                              PAGE_READWRITE,
                                              0,
                                              1024,
                                              "MyFileMappingObject" );

                // Return if the mapping failed.
                //..............................
                if ( !hMapFile )
                    return(-1);

                break;


        case WM_TIMER :
                // Check to see if the thread has processed the memory.
                //.....................................................
                if ( strcmp( lpMapAddress, "Received" ) == 0 )
                {
                    // Kill the timer and thread.
                    //...........................
                    KillTimer( hWnd, 1 );
                    TerminateThread( hThread, 0 );

                    // Show the mapped data and unmap the view.
                    //.........................................
                    MessageBox( hWnd, lpMapAddress, "Done", MB_OK );

                    UnmapViewOfFile( lpMapAddress );
                }
                break;

        case WM_COMMAND :
                switch( LOWORD( wParam ) )
                {
                    case IDM_TEST :
                            {
                                DWORD   dwID;
```

continued on next page

continued from previous page

```
                             // Map a view of the file mapped object.
                             //....................................
                             lpMapAddress = MapViewOfFile( hMapFile,
                                                           FILE_MAP_ALL_ACCESS,
                                                           0, 0, 0);

                             // Place data in the view.
                             //........................
                             strcpy( lpMapAddress,
                                     "Data passed from main process." );

                             // Make sure the data is flushed to the file.
                             //..........................................
                             FlushViewOfFile( lpMapAddress,
                                              lstrlen( lpMapAddress ) );

                             // Create a thread to receive the data.
                             //....................................
                             hThread = CreateThread( NULL, 0,
                                     (LPTHREAD_START_ROUTINE)AnotherProcess,
                                     lpMapAddress, 0, &dwID );

                             // Set a timer to wait for the data to be processed.
                             //.................................................
                             SetTimer( hWnd, 1, 1000, NULL );
                         }
                         break;

                 case IDM_EXIT :
                         DestroyWindow( hWnd );
                         break;
             }
             break;

    case WM_DESTROY :
             CloseHandle( hMapFile );

             PostQuitMessage(0);
             break;

    default :
             return( DefWindowProc( hWnd, uMsg, wParam, lParam ) );
    }

    return( 0L );
}
```

MoveFile   ■ WINDOWS 95   ■ WINDOWS NT

Description	**MoveFile** moves (renames) an existing file or a directory (including all its children) to a new location on a volume. **MoveFile** will fail on directory moves when the destination is on a different volume. This is because **MoveFile** actually renames the directory and doesn't physically move it.
Syntax	BOOL **MoveFile**(LPCTSTR *lpszExisting*, LPCTSTR *lpszNew*)

Parameters

lpszExisting   LPCTSTR: A pointer to a null-terminated string that contains the name of an existing file or directory.

lpszNew   LPCTSTR: A pointer to a null-terminated string that specifies the new name of the file or directory. The new name must not already exist. A new file may be on a different file system or drive. A new directory must be on the same drive.

Returns   BOOL: TRUE if successful; otherwise the return value is FALSE.

Include File   winbase.h

See Also   CopyFile, GetLastError

Example   This example shows how the MoveFile function is used to move folders (directories). The directory structure is initially set as shown in Figure 17-4(a). When the user selects the Test! menu item, "Folder1" is moved below "Folder2" as shown in Figure 17-4(b).

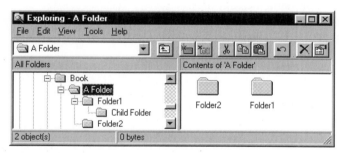

Figure 17-4(a) MoveFile before example

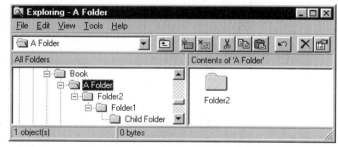

Figure 17-4(b) MoveFile after example

```
LRESULT CALLBACK WndProc( HWND hWnd, UINT uMsg, WPARAM wParam, LPARAM lParam )
{
    switch( uMsg )
    {
        case WM_COMMAND :
                switch( LOWORD( wParam ) )
                {
                    case IDM_TEST :
                            MoveFile("E:\\Book\\A Folder\\Folder1",
                                    "E:\\Book\\A Folder\\Folder2\\Folder1" );
                            break;
        .
        .
        .
```

MoveFileEx   ■ WINDOWS 95   ■ WINDOWS NT

Description	MoveFileEx is the same as the MoveFile function except that it allows extended options for the move operation such as delaying the move until the computer is rebooted. MoveFileEx can also delete files that are in use by the system when the computer is rebooted.
Syntax	BOOL **MoveFileEx**(LPCTSTR *lpExistingFileName,* LPCTSTR *lpNewFileName,* DWORD *dwFlags*)
Parameters	
lpExistingFileName	LPCTSTR: A pointer to a null-terminated string that names the existing file or directory to move or rename.
lpNewFileName	LPCTSTR: A pointer to a null-terminated string that specifies the new name of *lpExistingFileName*. When moving a file, the destination can be on a different file system or drive. When moving a directory, the destination must be on the same drive. On Windows NT, if *dwFlags* specifies MOVEFILE_DELAY_UNTIL_REBOOT, *lpNewFileName* can be NULL. In this case, MoveFileEx registers the *lpExistingFileName* file to be deleted when the system reboots.
dwFlags	DWORD: Specifies how to move the file. This may be a combination of the values listed in Table 17-23.

Table 17-23 MoveFileEx *dwFlags* values

Value	Meaning
MOVEFILE_COPY_ALLOWED	If the file is to be moved to a different volume, the function simulates the move by using the CopyFile and DeleteFile functions. This cannot be combined with the MOVEFILE_DELAY_UNTIL_REBOOT flag.
MOVEFILE_DELAY_UNTIL_REBOOT	(Windows NT) The file is not actually moved until the operating system is restarted. The system moves the file immediately after AUTOCHK is executed, but before creating any paging files.

Value	Meaning
MOVEFILE_REPLACE_EXISTING	If a file of the name specified by *lpNewFileName* already exists, the function replaces its contents with those specified by *lpExistingFileName*.
MOVEFILE_WRITE_THROUGH	(Windows NT) The function does not return until the file has actually been moved on the disk. This guarantees that the move performed as a copy and delete operation is flushed to disk before the function returns.

Returns	BOOL: If successful, TRUE is returned; otherwise, FALSE is returned.
Include File	winbase.h
See Also	MoveFile
Example	This example shows how to use **MoveFileEx** to move a file from one device to another device.

```
LRESULT CALLBACK WndProc( HWND hWnd, UINT uMsg, WPARAM wParam, LPARAM lParam )
{
   switch( uMsg )
   {
      case WM_COMMAND :
            switch( LOWORD( wParam ) )
            {
               case IDM_TEST :
                     MoveFileEx("E:\\Book\\Chapter1.doc",
                              "D:\\Temp\\Chapter1.doc",
                              MOVEFILE_COPY_ALLOWED | MOVEFILE_WRITE_THROUGH );
                     break;
         .
         .
         .
```

OpenFileMapping ■ WINDOWS 95 ■ WINDOWS NT

Description	OpenFileMapping opens a named file-mapping object. An application can use the resulting handle with any function that requires a handle to a file-mapping object.
Syntax	HANDLE **OpenFileMapping**(DWORD *dwDesiredAccess,* BOOL *bInheritHandle,* LPCTSTR *lpName*)
Parameters	
dwDesiredAccess	DWORD: The type of access to the file-mapping object. This parameter can be one of the values given in Table 17-24 and is checked against any security descriptor on the target file-mapping object.

Table 17-24 OpenFileMapping *dwDesiredAccess* values

Value	Meaning
FILE_MAP_WRITE	Read-write access. The target file-mapping object must have been created with PAGE_READWRITE protection.
FILE_MAP_READ	Read-only access. The target file-mapping object must have been created with PAGE_READWRITE or PAGE_READ protection.
FILE_MAP_ALL_ACCESS	Same as FILE_MAP_WRITE.
FILE_MAP_COPY	Copy-on-write access. The target file-mapping object must have been created with PAGE_WRITECOPY protection.

bInheritHandle	**BOOL**: Determines whether the returned handle is to be inherited by a new process during process creation. Set to **TRUE** to indicate that the new process inherits the handle.
lpName	**LPCTSTR**: A pointer to a string that contains the name of the file-mapping object to be opened.
Returns	**HANDLE**: If successful, an open handle to the specified file-mapping object; otherwise, **NULL** is returned.
Include File	winbase.h
See Also	MapViewOfFile
Example	See the example for the **MapViewOfFile** function.

ReadFile   ■ WINDOWS 95   ■ WINDOWS NT

Description	**ReadFile** reads data from a file, starting at the position of the file pointer. After the read operation has been completed, the file pointer is adjusted by the number of bytes actually read, unless the file handle is created with the overlapped attribute. If the file handle is created for overlapped input and output (I/O), the application must adjust the position of the file pointer after the read operation using the **SetFilePointer** function.
Syntax	BOOL **ReadFile**(HANDLE *hFile*, LPVOID *lpBuffer*, DWORD *dwNumberOfBytesToRead*, LPDWORD *lpdwNumberOfBytesRead*, LPOVERLAPPED *lpOverlapped*)
Parameters	
hFile	**HANDLE**: The file to be read. The file handle must have been created with **GENERIC_READ** access to the file.
lpBuffer	**LPVOID**: A pointer to the buffer that receives the data read from the file.
dwNumberOfBytesToRead	**DWORD**: The number of bytes to be read from the file.

lpdwNumberOfBytesRead	LPDWORD: A pointer to a DWORD variable that receives the number of bytes read. ReadFile sets this value to 0 before doing any work or error checking. If this parameter is 0 when ReadFile returns TRUE on a named pipe, the other end of the message-mode pipe called WriteFile with *dwNumberOfBytesToWrite* set to 0.
lpOverlapped	LPOVERLAPPED: A pointer to an OVERLAPPED structure. This structure is required if the file identified by *hFile* was created with FILE_FLAG_OVERLAPPED. See the definition of the OVERLAPPED structure below.

If *hFile* was created with FILE_FLAG_OVERLAPPED and *lpOverlapped* is not NULL, the read operation starts at the offset specified in the OVERLAPPED structure and ReadFile may return before the read operation has been completed. In this case, ReadFile returns FALSE and GetLastError returns the value ERROR_IO_PENDING. The calling process can continue while the read operation finishes. The event specified in the OVERLAPPED structure is set to the signaled state upon completion of the read operation.

If *hFile* is not created with FILE_FLAG_OVERLAPPED and *lpOverlapped* is not NULL, the read operation starts at the offset specified in the OVERLAPPED structure. ReadFile does not return until the read operation has been completed.

Returns	BOOL: TRUE if successful; otherwise, the return value is FALSE.
Include File	winbase.h
See Also	CreateFile, GetLastError, GetOverLappedResult, ReadFileEx, WriteFile

OVERLAPPED Definition

```
typedef struct _OVERLAPPED
{
    DWORD    Internal;
    DWORD    InternalHigh;
    DWORD    Offset;
    DWORD    OffsetHigh;
    HANDLE   hEvent;
} OVERLAPPED;
```

Members

Internal	DWORD: Reserved for operating system use.
InternalHigh	DWORD: Reserved for operating system use.
Offset	DWORD: The low-order 32 bits of the file position at which to start the read. The calling process sets this member before calling the ReadFile or WriteFile function. This member must be set to 0 when reading from or writing to named pipes and communications devices.

OffsetHigh	`DWORD`: The high-order 32 bits of the byte offset at which to start the read. This member must be set to `0` when reading from or writing to named pipes and communications devices.
hEvent	`HANDLE`: The handle of the event to be set to the signaled state when the transfer has been completed. The calling process sets this member before calling the `ReadFile`, `WriteFile`, `ConnectNamedPipe`, or `TransactNamedPipe` function.
Example	See the example for the `WriteFile` function.

ReadFileEx   ■ WINDOWS 95   ■ WINDOWS NT

Description	`ReadFileEx` reads data from a file asynchronously. It is designed exclusively for asynchronous operation. If an application requires synchronous reads, use `ReadFile`, which is designed for both synchronous and asynchronous operation. Asynchronous reads allow the application to perform other processing during a file read operation. When a read operation is complete, the specified callback function is called.
Syntax	BOOL **ReadFileEx**(HANDLE *hFile*, LPVOID *lpBuffer*, DWORD *dwNumberOfBytesToRead*, LPOVERLAPPED *lpOverlapped*, LPOVERLAPPED_COMPLETION_ROUTINE *lpCompletionRoutine*)
Parameters	
hFile	`HANDLE`: A open handle to the file from which the read operation will occur. The file handle must have been created with the `FILE_FLAG_OVERLAPPED` flag and must have `GENERIC_READ` access to the file. In Windows NT this parameter can be any handle opened with the `FILE_FLAG_OVERLAPPED` flag by the `CreateFile` function, or a socket handle returned by the `socket` or `accept` functions. In Windows 95, this parameter can be a communications resource, mailslot, or named pipe handle opened with the `FILE_FLAG_OVERLAPPED` flag by `CreateFile`, or a socket handle. Windows 95 does not support asynchronous operations on disk files.
lpBuffer	`LPVOID`: A pointer to a buffer that receives the data read from the file. This buffer must remain valid for the duration of the read operation and the application should not use it until the read operation is complete.
dwNumberOfBytesToRead	`DWORD`: The number of bytes to read from the file.
lpOverlapped	`LPOVERLAPPED`: A pointer to an `OVERLAPPED` structure that supplies data to be used during the asynchronous file read operation. See the definition of the `OVERLAPPED` structure under the `ReadFile` function.

lpCompletionRoutine	LPOVERLAPPED_COMPLETION_ROUTINE: A pointer to a callback function that is called when the read operation is complete and the calling thread is in an alertable wait state. See the definition of the callback function below.
Returns	BOOL: If successful, TRUE is returned; otherwise, FALSE is returned.
Include File	winbase.h
See Also	WriteFileEx, ReadFile
Callback Syntax	VOID WINAPI **FileIOCompletionRoutine**(DWORD *dwErrorCode,* DWORD *dwNumberOfBytesTransferred,* LPOVERLAPPED *lpOverlapped*)
Callback Parameters	
dwErrorCode	DWORD: The I/O completion status. If set to 0, the I/O was successful. If ERROR_HANDLE_EOF, the operation read past the end of the file.
dwNumberOfBytesTransferred	DWORD: The number of bytes transferred. If an error occurs, this parameter is 0.
lpOverlapped	LPOVERLAPPED: A pointer to the OVERLAPPED structure specified by the asynchronous I/O function. The *hEvent* member is not used by Windows, therefore, the calling application may use this member to pass information to the completion routine. After the callback function is called, the OVERLAPPED structure is not needed. The callback function may deallocate the memory used by the this structure.

RemoveDirectory   ■ WINDOWS 95   ■ WINDOWS NT

Description	RemoveDirectory deletes the specified empty directory.
Syntax	BOOL **RemoveDirectory**(LPCTSTR *lpszDir*)
Parameters	
lpszDir	LPCTSTR: A pointer to a null-terminated string that contains the path of the directory to be removed. The directory must be empty and the calling process must have delete access to the directory.
Returns	BOOL: TRUE if successful; otherwise, the return value is FALSE.
Include File	winbase.h
See Also	CreateDirectory
Example	This example deletes the directory "Child Folder" when the user selects the Test! menu item.

```
LRESULT CALLBACK WndProc( HWND hWnd, UINT uMsg, WPARAM wParam, LPARAM lParam )
{
    switch( uMsg )
    {
        case WM_COMMAND :
                switch( LOWORD( wParam ) )
                {
                    case IDM_TEST :
                        RemoveDirectory(
                          "E:\\Book\\A Folder\\Folder2\\Folder1\\Child Folder");
                        break;
                        .
                        .
                        .
```

SearchPath ■ WINDOWS 95 ■ WINDOWS NT

Description	SearchPath searches for the specified file in a given path or by using the following search order:

- The directory from which the application was loaded
- The current directory
- The Windows system directory
- The Windows directory
- The directories listed in the PATH environment variable

Syntax	DWORD **SearchPath**(LPCTSTR *lpszPath,* LPCTSTR *lpszFile,* LPCTSTR *lpszExtension,* DWORD *dwReturnBuffer,* LPTSTR *lpszReturnBuffer,* LPTSTR* *plpszFilePart*)

Parameters

lpszPath	LPCTSTR: A pointer to a null-terminated string that contains the path to be searched for the file. If set to **NULL**, the function searches the directories as ordered above.
lpszFile	LPCTSTR: A pointer to a null-terminated string that contains the name of the file to search for.
lpszExtension	LPCTSTR: A pointer to a null-terminated string that contains an extension to be added to the file name when searching for the file. The first character of the file name extension must be a period (.). The extension is added only if the specified file name does not end with an extension. If a file name extension is not required or if the file name contains an extension, this parameter can be **NULL**.
dwReturnBuffer	DWORD: The length, in bytes (ANSI) or characters (Unicode), of the buffer that receives the valid path and file name.
lpszReturnBuffer	LPTSTR: A pointer to the buffer for the valid path and file name of the file found.

plpszFilePart	LPTSTR*: A pointer to a variable that receives the address (within *lpszReturnBuffer*) of the last component of the valid path and file name, which is the address of the character immediately following the final back-slash (\) in the path.
Returns	DWORD: If successful, the length, in bytes (ANSI) or characters (Unicode), of the string copied to the buffer. The length does not include the terminating null character. If the return value is greater than *dwReturnBuffer*, the value returned is the size, in bytes or characters, of the buffer required to hold the path. If the function fails, the return value is 0.
Include File	winbase.h
See Also	FindFirstFile, FindNextFile
Example	This example shows how to use the SearchPath function to find the file CALC.EXE. If the file is found, the path is displayed in a message box.

```
LRESULT CALLBACK WndProc( HWND hWnd, UINT uMsg, WPARAM wParam, LPARAM lParam )
{
    switch( uMsg )
    {
        case WM_COMMAND :
                switch( LOWORD( wParam ) )
                {
                    case IDM_TEST :
                        {
                            char    szBuf[MAX_PATH];
                            LPTSTR lpFile;

                            if ( SearchPath( NULL, "CALC.EXE", NULL,
                                            MAX_PATH, szBuf, &lpFile ) )
                            {
                                MessageBox( hWnd, szBuf, "Found", MB_OK );
                            }
                            else
                                MessageBox( hWnd, "Could not find CALC.EXE",
                                            "Not Found", MB_OK );
                        }
                        break;
            .
            .
            .
```

SetEndOfFile   ■ WINDOWS 95   ■ WINDOWS NT

Description	SetEndOfFile moves the end-of-file (EOF) position for the specified file to the current position of the file pointer.
Syntax	BOOL **SetEndOfFile**(HANDLE *hFile*)
Parameters	
hFile	HANDLE: The handle of the file to have its EOF position moved. The file handle must have been created with GENERIC_WRITE access to the file.

Returns	BOOL: TRUE if successful; otherwise, the return value is FALSE.
Include File	winbase.h
See Also	CreateFile
Example	See the example for the WriteFile function.

SetFileApisToANSI   ■ WINDOWS 95   ■ WINDOWS NT

Description	SetFileApisToANSI causes a set of Win32 file functions to use the ANSI character set code page. This function is useful for 8-bit console input and output operations. For a list of functions that are affected by this function, see the AreFileApisANSI function earlier in this chapter.
Syntax	VOID **SetFileApisToANSI**(VOID)
Parameters	This function has no parameters.
Include File	winbase.h
See Also	SetFileApisToOEM, AreFileApisANSI
Example	See the example for the AreFileApisANSI function.

SetFileApisToOEM   ■ WINDOWS 95   ■ WINDOWS NT

Description	SetFileApisToOEM causes a set of Win32 file functions to use the OEM character set code page. This function is useful for 8-bit console input and output operations. For a list of functions that are affected by this function, see the AreFileApisANSI function earlier in this chapter.
Syntax	VOID **SetFileApisToOEM**(VOID)
Parameters	This function has no parameters.
Include File	winbase.h
See Also	SetFileApisToANSI, AreFileApisANSI
Example	See the example for the AreFileApisANSI function.

SetFileAttributes   ■ WINDOWS 95   ■ WINDOWS NT

Description	SetFileAttributes sets a file's attributes.
Syntax	BOOL **SetFileAttributes**(LPCTSTR *lpFileName,* DWORD *dwFileAttributes*)
Parameters	
lpFileName	LPCTSTR: A pointer to a null-terminated string that contains the path of the file whose attributes are to be set. This string must not exceed MAX_PATH characters. An application can bypass this limit on Windows NT by calling

the wide (**W**) version of **SetFileAttributes** and prepending "\\?\" or "\\?\UNC\" to turn off path parsing.

dwFileAttributes   DWORD: The file attributes to set for the file. This parameter can be a combination of the values given in Table 17-25 combined with the binary OR (**|**) operator. However, all other values override **FILE_ATTRIBUTE_NORMAL**.

Table 17-25 SetFileAttributes *dwFileAttributes* values

Value	Meaning
FILE_ATTRIBUTE_ARCHIVE	The file is an archive file.
FILE_ATTRIBUTE_DIRECTORY	The file is a directory.
FILE_ATTRIBUTE_HIDDEN	The file is hidden.
FILE_ATTRIBUTE_NORMAL	The file has no other attributes. This value is valid only if used alone.
FILE_ATTRIBUTE_READONLY	The file is read-only.
FILE_ATTRIBUTE_SYSTEM	The file is part of the operating system or is used exclusively by it.
FILE_ATTRIBUTE_TEMPORARY	The file is being used for temporary storage.
FILE_ATTRIBUTE_ATOMIC_WRITE	Reserved; do not use.
FILE_ATTRIBUTE_XACTION_WRITE	Reserved; do not use.

Returns	BOOL: TRUE if successful; otherwise, the return value is FALSE.
Include File	winbase.h
See Also	GetFileAttributes
Example	This example shows how to check if the FILE_ATTRIBUTE_READONLY attribute is set on the file FILE.DAT. If it is, the attributes are cleared with the SetFileAttributes function before the file is deleted.

```
LRESULT CALLBACK WndProc( HWND hWnd, UINT uMsg, WPARAM wParam, LPARAM lParam )
{
   switch( uMsg )
   {
      case WM_COMMAND :
            switch( LOWORD( wParam ) )
            {
               case IDM_TEST :
                     // Check if the file is read-only.
                     //................................
                     if ( GetFileAttributes("FILE.DAT") |
                          FILE_ATTRIBUTE_READONLY )
                     {
                         // Clear the file attributes.
                         //...........................
                         SetFileAttributes("FILE.DAT",FILE_ATTRIBUTE_NORMAL);
                     }

                     DeleteFile("FILE.DAT");
                     break;
               .
               .
               .
```

SetFilePointer ■ WINDOWS 95 ■ WINDOWS NT

Description   `SetFilePointer` moves the file pointer of an open file. The file pointer indicates where the next read or write will occur in the file. If working on multithreaded applications, be careful when setting the file pointer. If threads share the same file handle and update the file pointer, the sequence must be protected by using a critical section object or mutex object.

Syntax   DWORD **SetFilePointer**(HANDLE *hFile,* LONG *lDistanceToMove,* PLONG *lpDistanceToMoveHigh,* DWORD *dwMoveMethod*)

Parameters

hFile   HANDLE: The handle of the file whose file pointer is to be moved. The file handle must have been created with GENERIC_READ or GENERIC_WRITE access to the file.

lDistanceToMove   LONG: The number of bytes to move the file pointer. A positive value moves the pointer forward in the file, and a negative value moves it backward.

lpDistanceToMoveHigh   PLONG: A pointer to the high-order 32 bits of the 64-bit distance to move. If the value of this parameter is NULL, the function can operate only on files whose maximum size is $(2^{32})-2$. If this parameter is specified, the maximum file size is $(2^{64})-2$. This parameter also receives the high-order word of the new value of the file pointer.

dwMoveMethod   DWORD: The starting point for the file pointer move. This parameter can be one of the values given in Table 17-26.

Table 17-26 SetFilePointer *dwMoveMethod* values

Value	Meaning
FILE_BEGIN	The starting point is 0 or the beginning of the file.
FILE_CURRENT	The current value of the file pointer is the starting point.
FILE_END	The current end-of-file position is the starting point.

Returns   DWORD: If successful, the return value is the low-order 32 bits of the new file pointer, and if *lpDistanceToMoveHigh* is non-NULL, it receives the high-order 32 bits of the new file pointer.

If the function fails and if *lpDistanceToMoveHigh* is NULL, the return value is 0xFFFFFFFF. If the function fails and if *lpDistanceToMoveHigh* is non-NULL, the return value is 0xFFFFFFFF, and GetLastError will return a value other than NO_ERROR.

Include File   winbase.h

See Also	GetLastError, ReadFile, ReadFileEx, WriteFile, WriteFileEx
Example	See the example for the LockFile function.

SetFileTime ■ WINDOWS 95 ■ WINDOWS NT

Description	SetFileTime sets the date and time that a file was created, last accessed, or last modified.
Syntax	BOOL **SetFileTime**(HANDLE *hFile,* CONST FILETIME* *lpftCreation,* CONST FILETIME* *lpftLastAccess,* CONST FILETIME* *lpftLastWrite*)

Parameters

hFile	HANDLE: The handle of the file for which to set the dates and times. The file handle must have been created with GENERIC_WRITE access to the file.
lpftCreation	CONST FILETIME*: A pointer to a FILETIME structure that contains the date and time the file was created. This parameter can be NULL if the application does not need to set this information. See the definition of the FILETIME structure under the CompareFileTime function.
lpftLastAccess	CONST FILETIME*: A pointer to a FILETIME structure that contains the date and time the file was last accessed. This parameter can be NULL if the application does not need to set this information. See the definition of the FILETIME structure under the CompareFileTime function.
lpftLastWrite	CONST FILETIME*: A pointer to a FILETIME structure that contains the date and time the file was last written to. This parameter can be NULL if the application does not want to set this information. See the definition of the FILETIME structure under the CompareFileTime function.
Returns	BOOL: TRUE if successful; otherwise, the return value is FALSE.
Include File	winbase.h
See Also	GetFileSize, GetFileTime, GetFileType
Example	This example shows how to use the SetFileTime function to change the file date and time. The example uses the SystemTimeToFileTime function to convert the SYSTEM date and time structure to a FILETIME date and time. The time is adjusted from local time to UTC time because the SetFileTime function expects a time that is relative to the UTC time.

```
LRESULT CALLBACK WndProc( HWND hWnd, UINT uMsg, WPARAM wParam, LPARAM lParam )
{
    switch( uMsg )
    {
        case WM_COMMAND :
```

continued on next page

continued from previous page

```
            switch( LOWORD( wParam ) )
            {
                case IDM_TEST :
                    {
                        SYSTEMTIME sysTime;
                        FILETIME   fTime, fLocTime;
                        HANDLE     hFile;

                        // Open/create a file.
                        //....................
                        hFile = CreateFile( "File.dat",
                                    GENERIC_READ | GENERIC_WRITE,
                                    0, NULL, OPEN_ALWAYS,
                                    FILE_ATTRIBUTE_NORMAL, NULL );

                        // January 20, 1995
                        //................
                        sysTime.wDay   = 20;
                        sysTime.wMonth = 1;
                        sysTime.wYear  = 1995;

                        // 6:00.00 AM
                        //...........
                        sysTime.wMilliseconds = 0;
                        sysTime.wSecond = 0;
                        sysTime.wMinute = 0;
                        sysTime.wHour   = 6;

                        // Convert SYSTEM date/time to FILETIME structure.
                        //...............................................
                        SystemTimeToFileTime( &sysTime, &fLocTime );

                        // Convert the local file time to a UTC file time.
                        //...............................................
                        LocalFileTimeToFileTime( &fLocTime, &fTime );

                        // Set the file time.
                        //...................
                        SetFileTime( hFile, NULL, NULL, &fTime );

                        CloseHandle( hFile );
                    }
                    break;
```

SetStdHandle ■ WINDOWS 95 ■ WINDOWS NT

Description	SetStdHandle sets the handle for the standard input, standard output, or standard error device.
Syntax	BOOL **SetStdHandle**(DWORD *dwStdHandle*, HANDLE *hHandle*)
Parameters	
dwStdHandle	DWORD: The handle to be set. This parameter can have one of the values listed in Table 17-27.

Table 17-27 SetStdHandle *dwStdHandle* values

Value	Meaning
STD_INPUT_HANDLE	Standard input handle
STD_OUTPUT_HANDLE	Standard output handle
STD_ERROR_HANDLE	Standard error handle

hHandle	HANDLE: The handle to store as the standard input, standard output, or standard error handle.
Returns	BOOL: TRUE if successful; otherwise, the return value is FALSE.
Include File	winbase.h
See Also	GetStdHandle
Example	This example sets the standard error file to a file named ERROR.LOG and then uses the standard error file to output errors when the Test! menu item is selected.

```
LRESULT CALLBACK WndProc( HWND hWnd, UINT uMsg, WPARAM wParam, LPARAM lParam )
{
    switch( uMsg )
    {
        case WM_CREATE :
                {
                    HANDLE hFile;

                    // Create a file for the standard errors.
                    //........................................
                    hFile = CreateFile( "ERROR.LOG",  GENERIC_WRITE,
                                        0, NULL, OPEN_ALWAYS, 0, NULL );

                    // Set the standard error handle to the handle of our file.
                    //..........................................................
                    SetStdHandle( STD_ERROR_HANDLE, hFile );
                }
                break;

        case WM_COMMAND :
                switch( LOWORD( wParam ) )
                {
                    case IDM_TEST :
                            {
                                DWORD  dwWritten;
                                HANDLE hOutput = GetStdHandle( STD_ERROR_HANDLE );

                                // Write an error to the standard error file.
                                //...........................................
                                WriteFile( hOutput,
                                        "Error output: This is a sample error.",
                                        37, &dwWritten, NULL );
                            }
                            break;
```

continued on next page

continued from previous page

```
            case IDM_EXIT :
                    DestroyWindow( hWnd );
                    break;
        }
        break;

    case WM_DESTROY :
            CloseHandle( GetStdHandle( STD_ERROR_HANDLE ) );

            PostQuitMessage(0);
            break;

    default :
            return( DefWindowProc( hWnd, uMsg, wParam, lParam ) );
    }

    return( OL );
}
```

SystemTimeToFileTime   ■ WINDOWS 95   ■ WINDOWS NT

Description	SystemTimeToFileTime converts a system time to a file time.
Syntax	BOOL **SystemTimeToFileTime**(CONST SYSTEMTIME* *lpst,* LPFILETIME *lpft*)
Parameters	
lpst	CONST SYSTEMTIME*: A pointer to a SYSTEMTIME structure that contains the time to be converted. The *wDayOfWeek* member of the SYSTEMTIME structure is ignored. See the definition of the SYSTEMTIME structure under the FileTimeToSystemTime function.
lpft	LPFILETIME: A pointer to a FILETIME structure to receive the converted system time. See the definition of the FILETIME structure under the CompareFileTime function.
Returns	BOOL: TRUE if successful; otherwise, the return value is FALSE.
Include File	winbase.h
See Also	DosDateTimeToFileTime, FileTimeToDosDateTime, FileTimeToSystemTime
Example	See the example for the SetFileTime function.

UnlockFile   ■ WINDOWS 95   ■ WINDOWS NT

Description	UnlockFile unlocks a region in an open file. Unlocking a region enables other processes to access the region.
Syntax	BOOL **UnlockFile**(HANDLE *hFile,* DWORD *dwFileOffsetLow,* DWORD *dwFileOffsetHigh,* DWORD *dwUnlockLow,* DWORD *dwUnlockHigh*)

Parameters

hFile   HANDLE: The handle of the file that contains a region locked with LockFile. The file handle must have been created with either GENERIC_READ or GENERIC_WRITE access to the file.

dwFileOffsetLow   DWORD: The low-order 32 bits of the starting byte offset in the file where the locked region begins.

dwFileOffsetHigh   DWORD: The high-order 32 bits of the starting byte offset in the file where the locked region begins.

dwUnlockLow   DWORD: The low-order 32 bits of the length of the byte range to be unlocked.

dwUnlockHigh   DWORD: The high-order 32 bits of the length of the byte range to be unlocked.

Returns   BOOL: TRUE if successful; otherwise, the return value is FALSE.

Include File   winbase.h

See Also   CreateFile, LockFile

Example   See the example for the LockFile function.

UnlockFileEx   ■ WINDOWS 95   ■ WINDOWS NT

Description   UnlockFileEx unlocks a previously locked byte range that was locked with a call to LockFileEx. The byte range to unlock must correspond exactly to an existing locked byte range. Two adjacent ranges of a file cannot be locked separately and then unlocked using a single range that spans both locked regions.

Syntax   BOOL **UnlockFileEx**(HANDLE *hFile*, DWORD *dwReserved*, DWORD *dwNumberOfBytesToUnlockLow*, DWORD *dwNumberOfBytesToUnlockHigh*, LPOVERLAPPED *lpOverlapped*)

Parameters

hFile   HANDLE: An open handle to the file that is to have an existing locked byte range unlocked. The handle must have been created with either GENERIC_READ or GENERIC_WRITE access to the file.

dwReserved   DWORD: Reserved, must be 0.

dwNumberOfBytesToUnlockLow   DWORD: The low-order 32 bits of the length of the byte range to unlock.

dwNumberOfBytesToUnlockHigh   DWORD: The high-order 32 bits of the length of the byte range to unlock.

lpOverlapped	LPOVERLAPPED: A pointer to an OVERLAPPED structure that the function uses with the unlocking request. This structure contains the file offset of the beginning of the unlock range. See the definition of the OVERLAPPED structure under the ReadFile function.
Returns	BOOL: If successful, TRUE is returned; otherwise, FALSE is returned.
Include File	winbase.h
See Also	LockFileEx, ReadFile
Example	See the example for the LockFileEx function.

UnmapViewOfFile ■ WINDOWS 95 ■ WINDOWS NT

Description	UnmapViewOfFile unmaps a mapped view of a file from the calling process's address space. To commit the data to disk immediately, call FlushViewOfFile before unmapping the view. In Windows 95, files for which the last view has not yet been unmapped are held open with the same sharing restrictions as the original file handle. In Windows NT, files are held open with no sharing restrictions.
Syntax	BOOL **UnmapViewOfFile**(LPVOID *lpBaseAddress*)
Parameters	
lpBaseAddress	LPVOID: A pointer to the base address of the mapped view of a file that is to be unmapped. This parameter must be identical to the value returned by a previous call to MapViewOfFile or MapViewOfFileEx.
Returns	BOOL: If successful, TRUE is returned, and all dirty pages within the specified range are written "lazily" to disk. Otherwise, FALSE is returned.
Include File	winbase.h
See Also	MapViewOfFile, MapViewOfFileEx
Example	See the example for the MapViewOfFile function.

WriteFile ■ WINDOWS 95 ■ WINDOWS NT

Description	WriteFile writes data to a file. The function starts writing data to the file at the position indicated by the file pointer. After the write has been completed, the file pointer is adjusted by the number of bytes actually written, except when the file is opened with FILE_FLAG_OVERLAPPED. If the file handle was created for overlapped input and output (I/O), the application must adjust the position of the file pointer after the write is finished.

Syntax	BOOL **WriteFile**(HANDLE *hFile,* LPCVOID *lpBuffer,* DWORD *dwNumberOfBytesToWrite,* LPDWORD *lpNumberOfBytesWritten,* LPOVERLAPPED *lpOverlapped*)

Parameters

hFile

HANDLE: The handle of the file to be written to. The file handle must have been created with GENERIC_WRITE access to the file.

lpBuffer

LPCVOID: The pointer of the buffer containing the data to be written to the file.

dwNumberOfBytesToWrite

DWORD: The number of bytes to write to the file. Unlike the MS-DOS operating system, Windows NT interprets a value of 0 as specifying a null write operation. A null write operation does not write any bytes but does cause the time stamp to change. Write operations across a network are limited to 65535 bytes.

lpNumberOfBytesWritten

LPDWORD: A pointer to a variable that receives the number of bytes written by this function call. **WriteFile** sets this value to 0 before doing any work or error checking.

lpOverlapped

LPOVERLAPPED: A pointer to an OVERLAPPED structure that is required if *hFile* was opened with FILE_FLAG_OVERLAPPED. This parameter must not be NULL if *hFile* was opened with FILE_FLAG_OVERLAPPED. It must point to a valid OVERLAPPED structure. See the definition of the OVERLAPPED structure under the **ReadFile** function.

If *hFile* was not created with FILE_FLAG_OVERLAPPED and *lpOverlapped* is not NULL, the write operation starts at the offset specified in the OVERLAPPED structure, and **WriteFile** does not return until the write operation has been completed.

Returns

BOOL: TRUE if successful; otherwise, the return value is FALSE.

Include File

winbase.h

See Also

CreateFile, GetOverlappedResult, ReadFile, SetEndOfFile, WriteFileEx

Example

This example opens the file FILE.DAT and writes a string to it when the example starts by processing the WM_CREATE message. The file is opened with read/write access and remains open until the application is closed. When the user selects the Test! menu item, the file pointer is set to the beginning of the file with the SetFilePointer function. The ReadFile function then reads the string from the file. If there were no errors in reading the file, the example displays the string with the MessageBox function and truncates the file with the SetEndOfFile function to 40 characters.

```
LPCTSTR lpBuffer = "This is the string that will be written to the file.";

LRESULT CALLBACK WndProc( HWND hWnd, UINT uMsg, WPARAM wParam, LPARAM lParam )
{
static HANDLE hFile;

    switch( uMsg )
    {
        case WM_CREATE :
                {
                    DWORD dwWritten;

                    // Open/create a file.
                    //.....................
                    hFile = CreateFile( "FILE.DAT", GENERIC_READ | GENERIC_WRITE,
                                        0, NULL, OPEN_ALWAYS,
                                        FILE_ATTRIBUTE_NORMAL, NULL );

                    // Write a string to the file.
                    //............................
                    WriteFile( hFile, lpBuffer, strlen( lpBuffer )+1,
                            &dwWritten, NULL );
                }
                break;

        case WM_COMMAND :
                switch( LOWORD( wParam ) )
                {
                    case IDM_TEST :
                            {
                                char   szBuf[128];
                                DWORD dwRead;

                                // Make sure the file pointer
                                // is at the beginning of the file.
                                //.................................
                                SetFilePointer( hFile, 0, NULL, FILE_BEGIN );

                                // Read the string from the file and display it.
                                //..............................................
                                if ( ReadFile( hFile, szBuf, strlen( lpBuffer )+1,
                                            &dwRead, NULL ) )
                                {
                                    szBuf[dwRead] = 0;

                                    MessageBox( hWnd, szBuf, "Read File", MB_OK );

                                    // Change the end of the file and truncate
                                    // the contents for the next read.
                                    //........................................
                                    SetFilePointer( hFile, 40, NULL, FILE_BEGIN );
                                    SetEndOfFile( hFile );                          }
                            }
                            break;

                    case IDM_EXIT :
                            DestroyWindow( hWnd );
                            break;
```

```
            }
            break;

    case WM_DESTROY :
            // Close the file.
            //.................
            CloseHandle( hFile );

            PostQuitMessage(O);
            break;

    default :
            return( DefWindowProc( hWnd, uMsg, wParam, lParam ) );
    }

    return( OL );
}
```

WriteFileEx   ■ WINDOWS 95   ■ WINDOWS NT

Description   WriteFileEx writes data to a file asynchronously. Unlike the
                    WriteFile function, which is designed for both synchronous and
                    asynchronous operation, WriteFileEx is designed only for asyn-
                    chronous operation. When the write operation is complete, an
                    application-defined callback function is called when the thread is
                    in an alertable wait state.

Syntax   BOOL **WriteFileEx**(HANDLE *hFile*, LPCVOID *lpBuffer*, DWORD
                    dwNumberOfBytesToWrite, LPOVERLAPPED *lpOverlapped*,
                    LPOVERLAPPED_COMPLETION_ROUTINE *lpCompletionRoutine*)

Parameters

hFile   HANDLE: An open file handle for the file to write data. The file
                    handle must be open with the FILE_FLAG_OVERLAPPED flag and
                    the GENERIC_WRITE access. In Windows NT this parameter can be
                    any handle opened with the FILE_FLAG_OVERLAPPED flag by the
                    CreateFile function, or a socket handle returned by the socket
                    or accept functions. In Windows 95, this parameter can be a
                    communications resource, mailslot, or named pipe handle
                    opened with the FILE_FLAG_OVERLAPPED flag by CreateFile, or a
                    socket handle. Windows 95 does not support asynchronous
                    operations on disk files.

lpBuffer   LPCVOID: A pointer to a buffer that contains the data to write to
                    the file. The buffer must remain valid and unused until the write
                    operation completes.

dwNumberOfBytesToWrite   DWORD: The number of bytes to write to the file.

lpOverlapped	**LPOVERLAPPED**: A pointer to an **OVERLAPPED** structure that supplies data to be used during the asynchronous write operation. For files that support byte offsets, you must specify a byte offset at which to start writing to the file. Use the *Offset* and *OffsetHigh* members of the **OVERLAPPED** structure to specify this value. See the definition of the **OVERLAPPED** structure under the **ReadFile** function.
lpCompletionRoutine	**LPOVERLAPPED_COMPLETION_ROUTINE**: A pointer to a callback function that is called when the write operation is completed and the calling thread is in an alertable state. See the definition of the callback function under the **ReadFileEx** function earlier in this chapter.
Returns	**BOOL**: If successful, **TRUE** is returned; otherwise, **FALSE** is returned.
Include File	**winbase.h**
See Also	**ReadFileEx**, **WriteFile**, **SleepEx**

18

THE CLIPBOARD

One goal of the Windows application programmer is to create programs that are so like other Windows programs that the user can easily move back and forth between them without experiencing changes in how the programs look and feel. Ideally, the user should see a homogeneous environment and not notice any separation between programs. In such an environment the user would expect data to be transferable between applications. For example, a calculation produced by one application must be easily imported into a document of another application. The Windows clipboard makes this type of data exchange between applications easy.

The contents of the clipboard at any given moment are a set of memory objects created by the program that has moved data into the clipboard. The API functions and messages that implement the clipboard manage its contents. The clipboard is the sole access protocol to the stored data.

Clipboard Formats

Applications can view the same data differently. Text, for example, may be the unembellished characters of a terminal emulator or the sensational effects of a full-powered modern word processor. Data that is imported by either program from the clipboard should be available in the best format possible. To facilitate this, applications placing data in the clipboard export it in as many ways as possible. This gives the reader of the clipboard an assortment of options from which to choose. The various ways the data is represented in the clipboard are known as *clipboard formats*.

When an application uses the `SetClipboardData` function to place data in the clipboard in a given clipboard format, we say the application *renders* that format. In general, the more clipboard formats your application renders, the more accurately it can exchange data with other Windows applications. For this reason, try to render as many common clipboard formats as possible.

An application that empties the clipboard with the `EmptyClipboard` function and then places data in the clipboard in any format using `SetClipboardData` is called the *clipboard owner*. (This term is somewhat misleading, because once the data is placed into the clipboard, it no longer belongs to the clipboard owner. Instead, the data belongs to Windows.) Other applications that retrieve the data are known as *clipboard readers*. Getting the data from the clipboard does not change clipboard ownership to the reader. A Windows program whose sole purpose is to view the contents of the clipboard is called a *clipboard viewer*. Clipbook, first introduced in Windows for Workgroups, is an example of a clipboard viewer that, via network DDE (dynamic data exchange), allows clipboards of different workstations to be connected like files.

For every clipboard format that is supported by an application, a separate `SetClipboardData` function call must be executed. Data written to the clipboard for each call only replaces the data stored in the clipboard for the specified clipboard format. For this reason, before placing new data in the clipboard, the program must call the `EmptyClipboard` function to purge all stored formats of nonrelevant data that otherwise might be accidentally retained. Calling `EmptyClipboard` also allows the old owner to clean up any memory allocations for specialized formats by processing the `WM_DESTROYCLIPBOARD` message.

Figure 18-1 shows the relationship between the clipboard owner and the clipboard reader. Note that although the clipboard owner renders at least three text formats, including `CF_TEXT`, `CF_OEMTEXT`, and `CF_UNICODETEXT`, the clipboard reader has elected to view the data in the `CF_TEXT` format. The clipboard reader may support other formats as well, but it considers `CF_TEXT` the best of the formats it supports to paste the data.

Table 18-1 lists the predefined clipboard formats and describes the data and the type of handle passed to `SetClipboardData` for each type. The most common type of entry in the clipboard is a global memory block allocated with the `GMEM_DDESHARE` option. This appears in the table as simply `HANDLE`. The constant values for the clipboard formats are defined in the header file `winuser.h`, together with the prototypes for the API functions that define the clipboard interface.

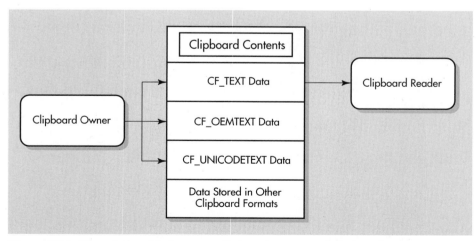

Figure 18-1 The relationship between clipboard owner and clipboard reader

Table 18-1 Predefined clipboard formats

Clipboard Format	Handle Type	Data Description
CF_BITMAP	HBITMAP	The data is a collection of bits.
CF_DIB	HANDLE	A memory object containing a BITMAPINFO structure followed by the bitmap bits.
CF_DIF	HANDLE	Software Arts' Data Interchange Format. This is the native format of VisiCalc and has been adopted as a general data interchange format by other applications.
CF_DSPBITMAP	HBITMAP	A bitmap that is private to an application. This may be used, for example, to pass data between different instances of the same application. Use GetClipboardOwner to determine the clipboard owner.
CF_DSPENHMETAFILE	HENHMETAFILE	An enhanced metafile that is private to an application.
CF_DSPMETAFILEPICT	HANDLE	A memory object containing a METAFILEPICT structure that is private to an application.
CF_DSPTEXT	HANDLE	Text that is private to an application.
CF_ENHMETAFILE	HENHMETAFILE	An enhanced metafile.
CF_GDIOBJFIRST through CF_GDIOBJLAST	HGDIOBJ	Application-defined clipboard formats that are represented by GDI objects. The function DeleteObject is used to destroy the data in this format when the EmptyClipboard function is called.
CF_HDROP	HDROP	A list of files used for drag-and-drop operations. To retrieve file names, use the DragQueryFile function. Use the DragQueryPoint function to retrieve the mouse position for the drop operation.
CF_LOCALE	LCID	The locale used to store text data. Win32 has built-in national language support. Consequently, when data is transferred to the clipboard, the CF_LOCALE is set as well to the locale of the thread that sets the data. An application may change the locale using the SetThreadLocale function.
CF_METAFILEPICT	HANDLE	A memory object containing a METAFILEPICT structure.
CF_OEMTEXT	HANDLE	A memory object containing a null-terminated string of characters in the OEM character set. Lines are separated by the carriage return—line feed (CR/LF) sequence.
CF_OWNERDISPLAY	NULL	Indicates that the clipboard owner will be responsible for displaying the data and updates to the clipboard viewers. The clipboard viewer sends the messages WM_ASKCBFORMATNAME, WM_HPAINTCLIPBOARD, WM_HSCROLLCLIPBOARD, WM_SIZECLIPBOARD, and WM_VSCROLLCLIPBOARD to the clipboard owner.
CF_PALETTE	HPALETTE	A color palette GDI object. This format typically is used when data placed in the clipboard requires a nonstandard palette to display. All viewers should query for this clipboard format before displaying graphical data such as bitmaps.

continued on next page

continued from previous page

Clipboard Format	Handle Type	Data Description
CF_PENDATA	HPENDATA	Data for the pen extensions to the Windows operating system.
CF_PRIVATEFIRST through		
CF_PRIVATELAST		This range denotes private clipboard formats. Windows does not manage these clipboard formats. The clipboard owner must manage resources using the WM_DESTROYCLIPBOARD message.
CF_RIFF	HANDLE	Complex audio support. This is more complex than CF_WAVE support.
CF_SYLK	HANDLE	Microsoft Symbolic Link (SYLK) format. This is found in Multiplan and other applications.
CF_TEXT	HANDLE	A memory object containing a null-terminated string of characters. Lines are separated by the carriage return–line feed (CR/LF) sequence.
CF_TIFF	HANDLE	Tag image file format.
CF_UNICODETEXT	HANDLE	A memory object containing a null-terminated string in the multibyte Unicode global character encoding format.
CF_WAVE	HANDLE	Standard wave file support.

Windows Management of Clipboard Data

Windows manages the contents of the clipboard and the clipboard formats. Not only does Windows keep the data for each format separate so that placing data in one format does not affect data written in another format, but Windows also controls the deletion of the data placed in the clipboard. The data stored in the clipboard for a given format must be deleted when new data is stored in the format or when **EmptyClipboard** is called to delete the entire contents of the clipboard.

Windows deletes clipboard data elements by calling a specific delete function; which function it calls depends on the type of data the clipboard format stores. For Graphics Device Interface (GDI) objects, Windows uses **DeleteObject** to delete the clipboard data. For memory objects, Windows uses **GlobalFree** to free the data. Nested objects with the memory objects (for example, the **HANDLE** to the metafile in the **METAFILEPICT** structure for the **CF_METAFILEPICT** clipboard format) also belong to Windows and are deleted when the associated memory objects are deleted.

Private clipboard formats are an exception to these rules. As you will see, Windows does not manage the data stored in private clipboard formats. In fact, the programs that create the private clipboard formats must manage the data that is stored there. A generalization of the answer to "Who owns the data in the clipboard?" may be "The owners of the clipboard formats where the data is stored." Table 18-1 shows that the owner of most clipboard formats is Windows.

Delayed Rendering of Clipboard Data

There are costs associated with rendering many formats of clipboard data, especially if the application supports graphical formats such as bitmaps or metafiles. Manipulation of GDI objects takes a long time and uses great amounts of memory. It makes no sense to process or store this data if the format is never used.

Fortunately, the Win32 APIs provide an easy method for delaying the placement of the data into the clipboard until a request is made to retrieve the data for a given clipboard format. This practice is known as delayed rendering. To use delayed rendering, simply pass **NULL** as the **HANDLE** of the clipboard data when setting the data using the **SetClipboardData** function. When an application requires rendering of the format, the message **WM_RENDERFORMAT** is sent with the *wParam* variable to indicate which clipboard format is requested.

Delayed rendering saves time and resources. The only drawback is that because of the time required for data to be formatted, the system may appear to be unresponsive immediately after a user requests to paste. In general, however, delayed rendering is considered the best approach when many formats are supported or when you don't have the time to place the data on the clipboard. Remember: Often, data is cut or copied and never pasted.

For an example of delayed rendering, please refer to the examples following the descriptions of the **IsClipboardFormatAvailable** and **GetPriorityClipboardFormat** functions.

CF_OWNERDISPLAY **Format**

A unique clipboard format, **CF_OWNERDISPLAY**, transfers the burden of displaying the clipboard data to the clipboard owner. Under **CF_OWNERDISPLAY**, the clipboard owner receives a set of messages that describe client area changes in the clipboard viewer. Table 18-2 shows these messages.

Table 18-2 Owner display clipboard messages

Message	Meaning
WM_ASKCBFORMATNAME	Sent when the clipboard viewer requests the name of the clipboard format. The clipboard owner must copy *wParam* bytes into the buffer pointed to by *lParam*.
WM_PAINTCLIPBOARD	Sent when the client area of the clipboard viewer needs repainting. The *wParam* parameter is the handle of the window of the clipboard viewer. The *lParam* parameter is a pointer to a PAINTSTRUCT.
WM_SIZECLIPBOARD	Sent when the client area of the clipboard viewer changes size. The *wParam* parameter is the handle of the window of the clipboard viewer. The *lParam* parameter is a pointer to a RECT structure.
WM_HSCROLLCLIPBOARD and WM_VSCROLLCLIPBOARD	Sent when the client area of the clipboard viewer is scrolled. The *wParam* parameter is the handle of the window of the clipboard viewer. The low word of the *lParam* parameter is the type of scroll bar request (the same as the *wParam* parameter in WM_VSCROLL or WM_HSCROLL). The high word of the *lParam* parameter is the thumb position if, and only if, the scroll bar request is SB_THUMBPOSITION.

One highly visible example of `CF_OWNERDISPLAY` is Clipbook, the clipboard viewer of Windows, which seems to know an infinite number of clipboard formats. In reality, the Clipbook leases its client area to the owner of the clipboard data, which, of course, can paint the contents the same way they were displayed in the original document. The only difference to the owner of the clipboard is which window is being painted, but this makes no difference in the logic of the program.

To use the `CF_OWNERDISPLAY` format, pass `NULL` as the data handle in the `SetClipboardData` call, just as in delayed rendering. `WM_RENDERFORMAT`, however, will not be sent to the clipboard owner for this clipboard format. Instead, the Windows message procedure must be modified to treat the messages specific to this clipboard format. Listing 18-1 shows an example `WndProc` that intercepts the clipboard messages.

Listing 18-1 *WndProc* with clipboard messages

```
LRESULT WndProc( HWND hWnd, UINT uMsg, WPARAM wParam, LPARAM lParam )
{
    switch (uMsg)
    {
    case WM_ASKCBFORMATNAME: // Sent when viewer requests name of clipboard format.

        // Copy clipboard format name to request buffer.
        //.................................................
        strncpy((LPSTR)lParam, "OBJFORMAT", wParam);
        break;

    case WM_PAINTCLIPBOARD: // The clipboard viewer needs to paint client area.
        {
            HWND  hWndViewer = (HWND) wParam;
            LPPAINTSTRUCT lpPs = (LPPAINTSTRUCT)  lParam;

            // Paint the clipboard viewer using lpPs->hdc as the display context.
                .
                .
                .

        }
        break;

    case WM_SIZECLIPBOARD: // The clipboard viewer was resized.
        {
            HWND hWndViewer = (HWND) wParam;
            RECT rect = * (RECT *)lParam;

            // Place here any logic for handling changes
            // in the size of the viewer's window.
                .
                .
                .

        }
        break;

    case WM_HSCROLLCLIPBOARD:  // Clipboard is scrolling from left or right.
    case WM_VSCROLLCLIPBOARD:  // Clipboard is scrolling up or down.
        {
```

```
        HWND hWndViewer = (HWND) wParam;
        WORD wScrollRequest = (LOWORD(lParam))
        WORD wThumbPos = 0;

        if (wScrollRequest ==SB_THUMBPOSITION)
        {
            wThumbPos = (HIWORD(lParam));
            // scroll contents of clipboard.
                .
                .
                .

        }
    }
    break;

        .
        .
        .
```

The **CF_OWNERDISPLAY** clipboard format provides the most versatility of all clipboard formats because the originator of the data is responsible for its display. If your application supports an unusual clipboard format (for example, private or registered clipboard formats), you have only two choices for displaying the data outside your application: owner display or writing a clipboard viewer.

Using Private Clipboard Formats

As the name implies, private clipboard formats are restricted to the application in which they are defined. They are not intended for general sharing of the clipboard data; however, private clipboard formats are extremely useful for sharing data across two instances of the same application. If you use private clipboard formats in your application, your system should support at least one standard clipboard format as well.

There are three types of private data formats: the predefined **DSP** clipboard formats, the formats in the **CF_PRIVATEFIRST** through **CF_PRIVATELAST** range, and the clipboard formats that are registered by the application using **RegisterClipboardFormat**. The **DSP** clipboard formats, including **CF_DSPTEXT**, **CF_DSPBITMAP**, **CF_DSPENHMETAFILE**, and **CF_DSPMETAFILEPICT**, are actually a standard clipboard format (respectively, text, bitmap, an enhanced metafile with Win32-specific functions, and a Windows 3.x metafile). Because the formats are known, normal clipboard viewers like Clipbook may be used to display the clipboard contents.

One way this can be used is with a database application. The application may copy the text of a field to the clipboard using the standard **CF_TEXT** clipboard format so that other applications may retrieve the text, but use a private clipboard format to pass such additional data as the name of the database file and the field name to another instance of itself. Pasting from the clipboard into a word processor will copy just the name of an employee, while pasting the clipboard data into another instance of the database application would transfer enough information for the program to perform a relational find on the database.

In order to implement this, you could either attempt to parse any CF_TEXT that the user attempts to paste or use CF_DSPTEXT to weed out the great majority of false attempts to paste a window. Remember, though, that other applications may be using CF_DSPTEXT as well. To be sure that the data obtained is, in fact, data exported by your application, place a signature at the beginning of the memory block; for example, the string "Hello World" may be stored as "MYAPP:Hello World".

Another way the clipboard reader can determine the origin of the data is by using GetClipboardOwner. This function returns the handle of the window of the clipboard owner. Use GetClassName to retrieve the class name of the window to determine if the window belongs to another instance of your application.

The function RegisterClipboardFormat returns a unique integer identifier of a new clipboard format or returns the identifier of the existing format if a clipboard format with the same name is found by Windows. Using registered clipboard formats allows an application to define an application-specific physical storage of the data and guarantees that if clipboard data is stored in this format, its origin is, in fact, an instance of the given application. Because the clipboard format is specific to the application, however, no other application can interpret data stored in this clipboard format.

Windows does not make any attempt to manage data placed into the clipboard with the formats in the range CF_PRIVATEFIRST through CF_PRIVATELAST. Instead, the clipboard owner must delete the data associated with the contents when the clipboard is emptied. Process the message WM_DESTROYCLIPBOARD to do this.

Clipboard Viewers

As stated before, a clipboard viewer is a program whose purpose is to view the contents of the clipboard. Clipboard viewers generally support many formats, but they will not know how to interpret private registered formats correctly. For this reason, you may be required to write a clipboard viewer of your own.

Keep in mind that a clipboard viewer does not own the data that it manipulates. A clipboard viewer must never write to the contents of the clipboard. A clipboard viewer must never leave any element of the clipboard contents locked. Also, because multiple clipboard viewers may be running at any time and messages are relayed from one clipboard viewer to another through a linked list of clipboard viewers, your program must obey these clipboard viewer conventions:

- Save the return value of SetClipboardViewer, which is the next clipboard viewer in the chain. Windows always places new viewers before viewers already installed.

- Pass WM_DRAWCLIPBOARD messages to the next clipboard viewer in the chain, or no other viewer will be updated.

- Pass **WM_CHANGECBCHAIN** messages to the next clipboard viewer in the chain, or the clipboard viewer chain will be broken.

- Monitor **WM_CHANGECBCHAIN** messages for exit of the next viewer in the chain. The *lParam* parameter contains the new next window handle if the next viewer exits.

- When exiting, you must call **ChangeClipboardChain** to remove your viewer from the chain of clipboard viewers using the next viewer value you have saved and maintained.

Clipboard Function Descriptions

Table 18-3 summarizes the clipboard functions. Detailed function descriptions follow the table.

Table 18-3 Clipboard function summary

Function	Purpose
ChangeClipboardChain	Removes a clipboard viewer program from the chain of clipboard viewer programs.
CloseClipboard	Closes the clipboard for reading or writing of its contents.
CountClipboardFormats	Returns the number of clipboard formats rendered by the current clipboard owner.
DragAcceptFiles	Registers a window to accept dropped files.
DragFinish	Releases memory used in transferring file names to the application.
DragQueryFile	Retrieves the file names of the dropped files.
DragQueryPoint	Retrieves the mouse position of the drop operation.
EmptyClipboard	Empties the contents of the clipboard and frees the associated data.
EnumClipboardFormats	Lists all the clipboard formats rendered by the current clipboard owner.
GetClipboardData	Returns a handle to the contents of the clipboard for a given format.
GetClipboardFormatName	Determines the name of a registered clipboard format.
GetClipboardOwner	Returns the window handle of the clipboard owner.
GetClipboardViewer	Returns the window handle of the first viewer in the chain of clipboard viewers.
GetOpenClipboardWindow	Determines the handle of the window that most recently opened the clipboard.
GetPriorityClipboardFormat	Checks the clipboard for availability of desired clipboard formats.
IsClipboardFormatAvailable	Checks the clipboard for availability of a single clipboard format.
OpenClipboard	Opens the clipboard for reading or writing of its contents.
RegisterClipboardFormat	Registers a new clipboard format name with Windows.
SetClipboardData	Sets the contents of the clipboard for a given clipboard format.
SetClipboardViewer	Installs a new viewer at the front of the clipboard viewer chain.

ChangeClipboardChain   ■ WINDOWS 95   ■ WINDOWS NT

Description	ChangeClipboardChain removes a clipboard viewer from the chain of clipboard viewers. ChangeClipboardChain is used typically when the main window of a clipboard viewer is being destroyed.
Syntax	BOOL **ChangeClipboardChain**(HWND *hWnd,* HWND *hWndNext*)
Parameters	
hWnd	HWND: The window handle of the window being removed from the chain of clipboard viewers.
hWndNext	HWND: The window handle of the window that follows *hWnd* in the chain of clipboard viewers. The return value of SetClipboardViewer is the original next viewer. You must monitor WM_CHANGECBCHAIN to determine if the next viewer gets deleted, and update your data accordingly.
Returns	BOOL: TRUE if *hWnd* was removed from the clipboard viewer chain and FALSE on error. To return the error code, use GetLastError.
Include File	winuser.h
See Also	SetClipboardViewer, GetLastError
Related Messages	WM_DRAWCLIPBOARD, WM_CHANGECBCHAIN
Example	This example creates a clipboard viewer. The application will display the current contents of the clipboard if the clipboard contains data in either the CF_TEXT or CF_BITMAP clipboard format. Clicking the Test! menu item empties the clipboard. The viewer installs itself in the clipboard viewer chain when the application starts, and removes itself from the chain on exit. Also, notice that it is a well-behaved clipboard viewer, relaying the WM_DRAWCLIPBOARD and WM_CHANGECBCHAIN messages to the next viewer.

```
VOID SetOwner( HWND hWnd )
{
   TCHAR cName[64];
   TCHAR cTitle[128];
   HWND  hCBOwner = GetClipboardOwner();

   if (hCBOwner == hWnd )
      strcpy( cName, "Local" );
   else
      strcpy( cName, "Another Application" );

   wsprintf( cTitle, "%s - [%s]", lpszAppName, cName );

   SetWindowText( hWnd, cTitle );
}


LRESULT CALLBACK WndProc( HWND hWnd, UINT uMsg, WPARAM wParam, LPARAM lParam )
{
```

```
static HWND hNextViewer ;

   switch( uMsg )
   {
      case WM_CREATE:
              // Make this window a clipboard viewer.
              //........................................
              hNextViewer = SetClipboardViewer( hWnd );
              SetOwner( hWnd );
              break;

      case WM_PAINT:
           {
              PAINTSTRUCT ps;           // Paint params from BeginPaint
              HBITMAP     hBitmap;      // Handle to bitmap on clipboard
              RECT        rClientRect;  // Area to write in
              HANDLE      hMem;         // Handle to text on clipboard

              BeginPaint( hWnd, &ps );
              GetClientRect( hWnd, &rClientRect );

              // Open the clipboard.
              //....................
              OpenClipboard( hWnd );

              // Try to get data as CF_TEXT format first.
              //........................................
              if (hMem = GetClipboardData( CF_TEXT ))
              {
                  LPSTR lpMem  = GlobalLock( hMem );
                  DrawText( ps.hdc, lpMem, -1, &rClientRect, DT_LEFT );
                  GlobalUnlock( hMem );
              }

              // If there is no text, try CF_BITMAP format.
              //..........................................
              else if (hBitmap = GetClipboardData( CF_BITMAP ))
              {
                  BITMAP      bm;
                  HDC hMemDC = CreateCompatibleDC( ps.hdc );

                  SelectObject( hMemDC, hBitmap );
                  GetObject( hBitmap, sizeof (BITMAP), (LPSTR) &bm );
                  BitBlt( ps.hdc, 0, 0, bm.bmWidth, bm.bmHeight, hMemDC, 0, 0, SRCCOPY );

                  DeleteDC( hMemDC );
              }

              CloseClipboard( );
              EndPaint( hWnd, &ps );
           }
           break;

      case WM_DRAWCLIPBOARD:
              if (hNextViewer)
                  // Relay message to next viewer.
                  //.............................
                  SendMessage( hNextViewer, WM_DRAWCLIPBOARD,wParam, lParam );
```

continued on next page

continued from previous page

```
            InvalidateRect( hWnd, NULL, TRUE );
            SetOwner( hWnd );
            break;

    case WM_CHANGECBCHAIN:
            // Process this message to update hNextViewer static
            // if the next clipboard viewer is going away.
            //...................................................
            if ( (HWND)wParam == hNextViewer )
                hNextViewer = (HWND)lParam;
            else if ( hNextViewer )
                // Relay message to next viewer.
                //.............................
                SendMessage( hNextViewer, WM_CHANGECBCHAIN, wParam, lParam );
            break;

    case WM_COMMAND :
            switch( LOWORD( wParam ) )
            {
                case IDM_TEST :
                        // Empty the clipboard.
                        //.....................
                        OpenClipboard( hWnd );
                        EmptyClipboard();
                        CloseClipboard();

                        // Force repaint.
                        //...............
                        InvalidateRect( hWnd, NULL, TRUE );
                        break;

                case IDM_EXIT :
                        DestroyWindow( hWnd );
                        break;
            }
            break;

    case WM_DESTROY :
            // Remove this application from the chain.
            //........................................
            if (hNextViewer && !ChangeClipboardChain( hWnd, hNextViewer ))
            {
                TCHAR szErrMsg[128];
                wsprintf( szErrMsg,
                        "Clipboard chain corrupt. "
                        "Err %d detected. Next viewer: %x",
                        GetLastError(), hNextViewer );

                MessageBox( hWnd, szErrMsg, "System Error", MB_OK );
            }

            PostQuitMessage(0);
            break;

    default :
        return( DefWindowProc( hWnd, uMsg, wParam, lParam ) );
}
```

```
    return( OL );
}
```

CloseClipboard
■ WINDOWS 95 ■ WINDOWS NT

Description	`CloseClipboard` closes the clipboard for reading or writing of its contents. `CloseClipboard` returns control of the clipboard data to Windows. Control should not be passed to Windows while the clipboard is open. Open and close the clipboard while processing a single Windows message.
Syntax	BOOL **CloseClipboard**(VOID)
Parameters	This function has no parameters.
Returns	BOOL: TRUE if the clipboard is successfully closed. FALSE if the clipboard was not open. To get the error code for the error encountered, use `GetLastError`.
Include File	winuser.h
See Also	OpenClipboard, EmptyClipboard, GetLastError
Example	See the examples under `ChangeClipboardChain`.

CountClipboardFormats
■ WINDOWS 95 ■ WINDOWS NT

Description	`CountClipboardFormats` returns the number of clipboard formats rendered by the current owner of the clipboard. Use the `EnumClipboardFormats` function to determine exactly which formats are supported.
Syntax	int **CountClipboardFormats**(VOID)
Parameters	This function has no parameters.
Returns	int: Returns the number of data formats currently in the clipboard. If an error occurs, the return value is 0. Use `GetLastError` to return the error code.
Include File	winuser.h
See Also	EnumClipboardFormats, GetLastError
Example	See the example under `EnumClipboardFormats`.

DragAcceptFiles
■ WINDOWS 95 ■ WINDOWS NT

Description	`DragAcceptFiles` registers the specified window to either accept dropped files or to reject them. If the window accepts dropped files, it will receive the `WM_DROPFILES` message when files are dropped on the window.
Syntax	VOID **DragAcceptFiles**(HWND *hWnd,* BOOL *bAccept*)

Parameters

hWnd	HWND: The window registering whether it accepts dropped files.
bAccept	BOOL: Set to TRUE to accept dropped files. Set to FALSE to discontinue accepting dropped files.

Include File   shellapi.h

See Also   DragQueryFile, DragQueryPoint, DragFinish

Related Messages   WM_DROPFILES

Example   This example accepts dropped files. When one or more files are dropped on the client area, it adds the file names with the drop position to a list view control.

```
HWND hList = NULL;

LRESULT CALLBACK WndProc( HWND hWnd, UINT uMsg, WPARAM wParam, LPARAM lParam )
{
   switch( uMsg )
   {
      case WM_CREATE :
              // Initialize Common Controls.
              //............................
              InitCommonControls();

              hList = CreateWindowEx( WS_EX_CLIENTEDGE, WC_LISTVIEW,
                                "", WS_CHILD | LVS_REPORT | WS_VISIBLE,
                                0, 0, 100, 100, hWnd, (HMENU)101,
                                hInst, NULL );

              // Set up the list view with columns.
              //...................................
              if ( hList )
              {
                  LV_COLUMN col;

                  col.mask     = LVCF_FMT | LVCF_SUBITEM |
                                 LVCF_TEXT | LVCF_WIDTH;
                  col.fmt      = LVCFMT_LEFT;
                  col.cx       = 300;
                  col.pszText  = "Filename";
                  col.iSubItem = 0;
                  ListView_InsertColumn( hList, 0, &col );

                  col.pszText  = "Position";
                  col.iSubItem = 1;
                  col.cx       = 80;
                  ListView_InsertColumn( hList, 1, &col );
              }

              // Start accepting files.
              //......................
              DragAcceptFiles( hWnd, TRUE );
              break;
```

```
case WM_DROPFILES:
        {
            LV_ITEM  item;
            POINT    pt;
            TCHAR    szFilename[MAX_PATH+1];
            UINT     i;
            UINT     nNumFiles = DragQueryFile( (HDROP)wParam, 0xFFFFFFFF, NULL, 0 );

            // Retrieve the position of the drop.
            //...................................
            DragQueryPoint( (HDROP)wParam, &pt );

            item.mask = LVIF_TEXT;
            for ( i=0; i<nNumFiles; i++ )
            {
                DragQueryFile( (HDROP)wParam, i, szFilename, MAX_PATH+1 );

                item.iItem = i;
                item.iSubItem = 0;
                item.pszText = szFilename;
                ListView_InsertItem( hList, &item );

                wsprintf( szFilename, "%d, %d", pt.x, pt.y );
                item.iSubItem = 1;
                ListView_SetItem( hList, &item );

            }

            // Free the memory given to us.
            //............................
            DragFinish( (HDROP)wParam );
        }
        break;
```

.
.
.

DragFinish   ■ WINDOWS 95   ■ WINDOWS NT

Description	DragFinish releases memory that Windows allocated for use in transferring file names to the application.
Syntax	VOID **DragFinish**(HDROP *hDrop*)
Parameters	
hDrop	HDROP: The structure describing dropped files. This handle is retrieved from the *wParam* parameter of the **WM_DROPFILES** message.
Include File	shellapi.h
See Also	DragQueryFile, DragQueryPoint
Related Messages	WM_DROPFILES
Example	See the example for the **DragAcceptFiles** function.

DragQueryFile ■ Windows 95 ■ Windows NT

Description	DragQueryFile retrieves the file names of dropped files during a drag-and-drop operation.
Syntax	UINT **DragQueryFile**(HDROP *hDrop,* UINT *nFile,* LPTSTR *lpszFile,* UINT *cch*)
Parameters	
hDrop	HDROP: Identifies the structure containing the file names of the dropped files. This handle is either retrieved from the clipboard or received with the WM_DROPFILES message.
nFile	UINT: The index of the file to query. If the value is set to 0xFFFFFFFF, a count of files dropped is returned. If the value is between 0 and the total number of files dropped, the file name corresponding to this value is copied to the buffer pointed to by the *lpszFile* parameter.
lpszFile	LPTSTR: A pointer to a buffer that receives the file name of the dropped file. Set to NULL to return the number of characters required to store the file name.
cch	UINT: The size, in characters, of the buffer pointed to by the *lpszFile* parameter.
Returns	UINT: When the function copies a file name to the buffer, the return value is a count of the characters copied, not including the terminating null character. If the index value is 0xFFFFFFFF, the return value is the count of dropped files. If the *lpszFile* parameter is NULL, the return value is the required size, in characters, of the buffer, not including the terminating null character.
Include File	shellapi.h
See Also	DragQueryPoint
Related Messages	WM_DROPFILES
Example	See the example for the **DragAcceptFiles** function.

DragQueryPoint ■ Windows 95 ■ Windows NT

Description	DragQueryPoint retrieves the position of the mouse pointer at the time a file was dropped. The coordinates are relative to the window that received the WM_DROPFILES message.
Syntax	BOOL **DragQueryPoint**(HDROP *hDrop,* LPPOINT *lppt*)
Parameters	
hDrop	HDROP: Identifies the structure containing the file names of the dropped files. This handle is either retrieved from the clipboard or received with the WM_DROPFILES message.

lppt	LPPOINT: A pointer to a **POINT** structure that the function fills with the coordinates of the mouse pointer at the time the file was dropped.
Returns	BOOL: If the drop occurred in the client area of the window, **TRUE** is returned; otherwise, **FALSE** is returned.
Include File	`shellapi.h`
See Also	`DragQueryFile`
Related Messages	`WM_DROPFILES`
Example	See the example for the **DragAcceptFiles** function.

EmptyClipboard ■ WINDOWS 95   ■ WINDOWS NT

Description	**EmptyClipboard** deletes the contents of the clipboard and frees the associated data. This function removes data stored in every clipboard format, guaranteeing that no data is unintentionally left on the clipboard when the owner changes. Calling this function also establishes ownership of the clipboard. The clipboard must be open to use this function. The message `WM_DESTROYCLIPBOARD` is sent to the old owner of the clipboard.
Syntax	BOOL **EmptyClipboard**(VOID)
Parameters	This function has no parameters.
Returns	BOOL: **TRUE** if the clipboard was emptied and **FALSE** on error. Use `GetLastError` to return the error code.
Include File	`winuser.h`
See Also	`OpenClipboard`, `CloseClipboard`, `SetClipboardData`, `GetLastError`
Related Messages	`WM_DRAWCLIPBOARD`, `WM_CHANGECBCHAIN`, `WM_DESTROYCLIPBOARD`
Example	See the example under **ChangeClipboardChain**.

EnumClipboardFormats ■ WINDOWS 95   ■ WINDOWS NT

Description	**EnumClipboardFormats** lists all the clipboard formats rendered by the current clipboard owner. It is used by applications that support more than one means of reading the clipboard. An application may use **EnumClipboardFormats** to select the best format for reading the contents of the clipboard.

EnumClipboardFormats is called repeatedly to determine all of the formats. On the first call, pass **0** to the function, and **EnumClipboardFormats** will return the first format available. On the second and subsequent calls, the last format returned is used as the parameter in the next call. This sequence is repeated until the function returns **0**, which indicates that the last format has been read. **EnumClipboardFormats** returns the clipboard formats in the same order as the **SetClipboardData** calls were made to place the data in the clipboard. An application should always place data in the clipboard starting with the most desirable format (least data lost) and proceed with the next best until there are no more formats that can be rendered.

Syntax	UINT **EnumClipboardFormats**(UINT *uFormat*)
Parameters	

uFormat   UINT: The format number of the last format read. Set to **0** to return the first available clipboard format. Set to any valid clipboard format to return the next available clipboard format.

Returns   UINT: The next rendered clipboard format number. Returns **0** if the last format was read. Also, returns **0** on an error. **GetLastError** may be used to return the error code.

Include File   winuser.h

See Also   CountClipboardFormats, GetClipboardFormatName, SetClipboardData, GetLastError

Example   This example lists all of the clipboard formats available when the user clicks the Test! menu item. For registered clipboard formats (set by applications that call **RegisterClipboardFormat**), the name of the format can be retrieved using **GetClipboardFormatName**. For predefined clipboard formats, the names are not returned by **GetClipboardFormatName**. The listing includes a function called **NameClipFormat** that supplies the names of the predefined formats.

Figure 18-2 shows the list of available clipboard formats after WordPad (shipped with Windows NT 4 and Windows 95) has been used to copy text to the clipboard (Edit/Copy menu item). An application reading or viewing the clipboard could use any of these to obtain the text copied.

EnumClipboardFormats retrieves the formats in the same order that data was added into the clipboard, which should be the priority order. In this case, the most desirable format is a special object format called **"DataObject"**. The next most desirable is **"ObjectDescriptor"**. **"Rich Text Format"**, text with formatting characters, follows. The first predefined format is the **CF_TEXT** format, which includes the text characters but omits formatting characters. The last and least desirable format is **CF_OEMTEXT**, which will have only the OEM character set.

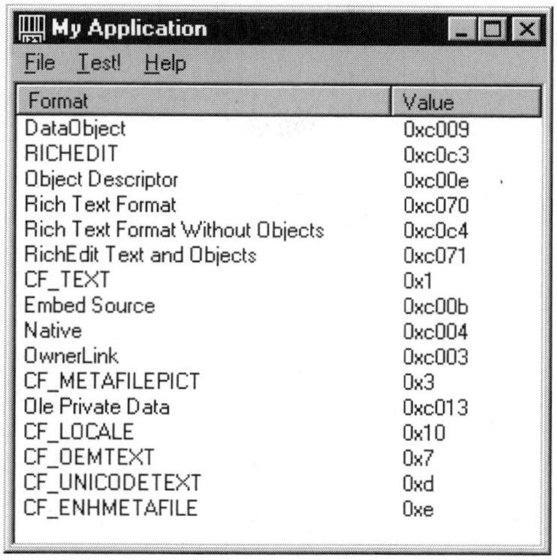

Figure 18-2 `EnumClipboardFormats` example

```c
#define PREDEFINED_CLIPBOARD_FORMAT_COUNT 17

void NameClipFormat( UINT uFormat, TCHAR *cName )
{
    static TCHAR *cClipName[] =
                    {"CF_TEXT", "CF_BITMAP",
                     "CF_METAFILEPICT", "CF_SYLK", "CF_DIF", "CF_TIFF",
                     "CF_OEMTEXT", "CF_DIB", "CF_PALETTE" , "CF_PENDATA", "CF_RIFF",
                     "CF_WAVE", "CF_UNICODETEXT", "CF_ENHMETAFILE"
                    , "CF_HDROP", "CF_LOCALE" };

    static TCHAR *cClipName2[] =
        {"CF_OWNERDISPLAY", "CF_DSPTEXT", "CF_DSPBITMAP", "CF_DSPMETAFILEPICT"};

    int nLengthFormatName = GetClipboardFormatName( uFormat,  cName, 63 );

    if (nLengthFormatName == 0)
    {
        if (uFormat <= PREDEFINED_CLIPBOARD_FORMAT_COUNT)
            strcpy( cName, cClipName[uFormat - CF_TEXT] );
        else if ((uFormat <= CF_DSPMETAFILEPICT) && (uFormat >= CF_OWNERDISPLAY))
            strcpy( cName, cClipName2[uFormat - CF_OWNERDISPLAY] );
        else if (uFormat==0x8e)
            strcpy( cName, "CF_DSPENHMETAFILE" );
        else if (uFormat>=0x300 && uFormat<=0x3ff)
            wsprintf( cName, "CF_GDIOBJFIRST+%d", uFormat-CF_GDIOBJFIRST );
        else
            strcpy( cName, "<Not named>" );
    }
}
```

continued on next page

continued from previous page

```
LRESULT CALLBACK WndProc( HWND hWnd, UINT uMsg, WPARAM wParam, LPARAM lParam )
{
static HWND hList;

    switch( uMsg )
    {
        case WM_COMMAND :
                switch( LOWORD( wParam ) )
                {
                    case IDM_TEST :
                        {
                            int     i;
                            int     nCBFormats;
                            LV_ITEM item;
                            TCHAR   cName[64];
                            unsigned uFormat = 0;

                            //Delete all existing items.
                            //..........................
                            ListView_DeleteAllItems( hList );

                            nCBFormats = CountClipboardFormats();
                            OpenClipboard( hWnd );

                            item.mask = LVIF_TEXT;
                            for (i = 0 ; i < nCBFormats ; i++)
                            {
                                // Enumerate the next format.
                                //..........................
                                uFormat = EnumClipboardFormats( uFormat );

                                NameClipFormat( uFormat, cName );

                                // Add information to list view.
                                //..............................
                                item.iItem = i;
                                item.iSubItem = 0;
                                item.pszText = cName;
                                ListView_InsertItem( hList, &item );

                                wsprintf( cName, "Ox%x", uFormat );
                                item.iSubItem = 1;
                                ListView_SetItem( hList, &item );
                            }
                        }
                        CloseClipboard();
                        break ;
                        .
                        .
                        .
```

GetClipboardData
■ Windows 95   ■ Windows NT

Description   GetClipboardData retrieves a handle to the contents of the clipboard for a given format. If the owner of the clipboard renders the specified data format, a handle to a clipboard memory block is returned of the type listed in Table 18-1. The clipboard must be opened with the OpenClipboard function before GetClipboardData is called. The application should immediately copy the data to a private memory block. Otherwise, another application may empty the clipboard, invalidating the handle. Contents of the clipboard must never remain locked by an application. Unlock the data and close the clipboard with CloseClipboard immediately after retrieving the contents.

Syntax   HANDLE **GetClipboardData**(UINT *uFormat*)

Parameters

uFormat   UINT: Specifies the clipboard format for the data that the application would like to read. The format can be any of the ones listed in Table 18-1 or a registered clipboard format.

Returns   HANDLE: A handle to a shared global memory block. NULL on error. Use GetLastError to return the error code.

Include File   winuser.h

See Also   OpenClipboard, CloseClipboard, SetClipboardData

Related Messages   WM_ASKCBFORMATNAME, WM_HSCROLLCLIPBOARD, WM_PAINTCLIPBOARD, WM_SIZECLIPBOARD, WM_VSCROLLCLIPBOARD

CAUTION

The application calling GetClipboardData should unlock the memory block as soon as it is read. Leaving the clipboard memory block locked while Windows processes messages may cause the system to crash.

Example   See the example under the ChangeClipboardChain function description.

GetClipboardFormatName
■ Windows 95   ■ Windows NT

Description   GetClipboardFormatName returns the name of a registered clipboard format. An application may use GetClipboardFormatName to tell whether a registered format is rendered by the current owner of the clipboard. Only the names of application-registered formats can be found in this way. Predefined Windows formats return NULL.

Syntax	int **GetClipboardFormatName**(UINT *uFormat,* LPTSTR *lpFormatName,* int *nMaxCount*)
Parameters	
uFormat	UINT: The format number. This is a format number returned by **EnumClipboardFormats** or **RegisterClipboardFormat**.
lpFormatName	LPTSTR: A pointer to a memory buffer that will hold the null-terminated name of the clipboard format. The buffer should be at least *nMaxCount* bytes wide.
nMaxCount	int: The maximum string size to be read into the *lpFormatName* buffer. If the clipboard format name is longer, it will be truncated.
Returns	int: The number of characters read is returned, 0 on error. To return the error code, use **GetLastError**.
Include File	winuser.h
See Also	EnumClipboardFormats, RegisterClipboardFormat
Example	See the example in the **NameClipFormat** function under **EnumClipboardFormats**.

GetClipboardOwner ■ Windows 95 ■ Windows NT

Description	**GetClipboardOwner** returns the window handle of the clipboard owner. The clipboard owner is set when an application calls **EmptyClipboard**, which is usually done before setting the data of the clipboard with **SetClipboardData**.
Syntax	HWND **GetClipboardOwner**(VOID)
Parameters	This function has no parameters.
Returns	HWND: The handle of the application that owns the clipboard. NULL if the clipboard is currently unowned. To get extended error information, use **GetLastError**.
Include File	winuser.h
See Also	GetClipboardViewer, GetOpenClipboardWindow
Example	See the example for the **ChangeClipboardChain** function.

GetClipboardViewer ■ Windows 95 ■ Windows NT

Description	**GetClipboardViewer** returns the window handle of the first clipboard viewer in the clipboard viewer chain. An application is added to the clipboard viewer chain using **SetClipboardViewer**. See **ChangeClipboardChain** for an example.
Syntax	HWND **GetClipboardViewer**(VOID)

Parameters	This function has no parameters.
Returns	HWND: The handle of the first window in the clipboard viewer chain. NULL if a clipboard viewer is not running. To get extended error information, use GetLastError.
Include File	winuser.h
See Also	GetClipboardOwner, GetOpenClipboardWindow

GetOpenClipboardWindow   ■ WINDOWS 95   ■ WINDOWS NT

Description	GetOpenClipboardWindow determines the handle of the window that currently has the clipboard open. The clipboard, a shared resource, may be open only for reading and writing of its contents by one application at any given time.
Syntax	HWND **GetOpenClipboardWindow**(VOID)
Parameters	This function has no parameters.
Returns	HWND: The window handle of the window that currently has the clipboard open. If the clipboard is not open (or NULL was used as the window handle in the call to OpenClipboard), the function returns NULL. To get the error code, use GetLastError.
Include File	winuser.h
See Also	GetClipboardOwner, GetClipboardViewer, OpenClipboard

GetPriorityClipboardFormat   ■ WINDOWS 95   ■ WINDOWS NT

Description	GetPriorityClipboardFormat checks the clipboard for the availability of desired data formats. Applications often support more than one clipboard format. Generally, this is done to provide options for clipboard readers that minimize data loss. GetPriorityClipboardFormat allows the clipboard to be scanned using a list of formats provided by a clipboard reader to determine which is the best clipboard format for the reader to use. The first format from the *lpPriorityList* that is available on the clipboard is returned by the function. This will be the best format for the application to read in data from the clipboard using GetClipboardData.
Syntax	int **GetPriorityClipboardFormat**(UINT* *lpPriorityList,* int *nCount*)
Parameters	
lpPriorityList	UINT*: A pointer to an array of UINT values. Each element of the array should contain the number of a desired clipboard format. This is either one of the predefined formats such as CF_TEXT, or a special format returned by either RegisterClipboardFormat or EnumClipboardFormats. The list should be in priority order, with the most desirable formats first.

nCount	**int**: The number of elements in the array pointed to by *lpPriorityList*.
Returns	**int**: The highest priority clipboard format available. If the clipboard is empty, the function returns **NULL**. If the clipboard contains data, but not in any of the desired formats, the function returns **-1**. To get the error code, use **GetLastError**.
Include File	**winuser.h**
See Also	**RegisterClipboardFormat**, **IsClipboardFormatAvailable**, **EnumClipboardFormats**
Example	This example demonstrates several advanced uses of the clipboard. When the example program is started (the **WM_CREATE** message is processed), a clipboard format is registered. In addition, the clipboard is set for delayed rendering of two clipboard formats, **CF_TEXT** and the registered format. With delayed rendering, data is not loaded into the clipboard until it is requested by an application, at which time Windows sends the **WM_RENDERFORMAT** message to the clipboard owner, which responds by loading the data into the clipboard.

Whenever a **WM_PAINT** message is received, the program reads the clipboard. It attempts to read both clipboard formats. The **CF_TEXT** format is read via standard clipboard protocol. Whenever present, its contents will be shown. Before reading the registered clipboard format, the application uses **GetPriorityClipboardFormat** to check which formats are available. In this case, a list of only two desired formats is checked. If the registered format is available, the contents of the clipboard are displayed on the application's client area, as shown in Figure 18-3.

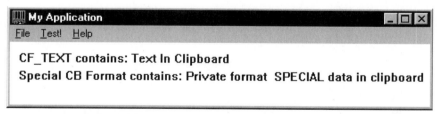

Figure 18-3 Clipboard format preferencing

```
UINT    wClipFormat;

LRESULT CALLBACK WndProc( HWND hWnd, UINT uMsg, WPARAM wParam, LPARAM lParam )
{
    switch( uMsg )
    {
        case WM_CREATE:
                // Register the format "SPECIAL" when the window is created.
                // Multiple instances of the program will only register the format once.
                //.................................................................
                wClipFormat = RegisterClipboardFormat( "SPECIAL" );

                // Set clipboard for delayed rendering.
                //......................................
                OpenClipboard( hWnd );
                EmptyClipboard();
                SetClipboardData( CF_TEXT, 0 );

                if (wClipFormat)
                    SetClipboardData( wClipFormat, 0 );

                CloseClipboard( );
                break ;

        case WM_RENDERALLFORMATS:
        case WM_RENDERFORMAT:
                {
                    HANDLE hMem;
                    LPVOID lpData;

                    OpenClipboard( hWnd );
                    EmptyClipboard( );

                    // Render CF_TEXT format.
                    //.......................
                    hMem = GlobalAlloc( GHND, 64 );
                    lpData = GlobalLock( hMem );
                    lstrcpy( lpData, "Text In Clipboard" );
                    GlobalUnlock( hMem );
                    SetClipboardData( CF_TEXT, hMem );

                    // Render format "SPECIAL".
                    //.........................
                    if (wClipFormat)
                    {
                        hMem = GlobalAlloc( GHND, 64 );
                        lpData = GlobalLock( hMem );
                        lstrcpy( lpData, "Private format SPECIAL data in clipboard" );
                        GlobalUnlock( hMem );
                        SetClipboardData( wClipFormat, hMem );
                    }
                    CloseClipboard( );
                }
                break;
```

continued on next page

continued from previous page

```
case WM_PAINT:
        {
            HANDLE hMem;
            LPVOID lpData;
            PAINTSTRUCT ps;
            char cBuf[128];
            UINT wPriorityList[ 2 ];

            BeginPaint( hWnd, &ps );

            // Check state of CF_TEXT first
            //..............................
            OpenClipboard( hWnd );
            hMem = GetClipboardData( CF_TEXT );
            if ( hMem )
            {
                lpData = GlobalLock( hMem );
                TextOut( ps.hdc, 10, 10, cBuf, wsprintf( cBuf,
                        "CF_TEXT contains: %s", lpData ) ) ;
                GlobalUnlock( hMem );
            }
            CloseClipboard( );

            // Now check state of SPECIAL format
            //..................................
            OpenClipboard( hWnd );
            wPriorityList[ 0 ] = wClipFormat ;
            wPriorityList[ 1 ] = CF_TEXT ;
            if ( IsClipboardFormatAvailable( wClipFormat ) &&
                (wClipFormat = GetPriorityClipboardFormat( wPriorityList, 2 )) )
            {
                hMem = GetClipboardData( wClipFormat );
                lpData = GlobalLock( hMem );
                TextOut( ps.hdc, 10, 30, cBuf, wsprintf( cBuf,
                        "Special CB Format contains: %s", lpData ) );
                GlobalUnlock( hMem );
            }
            else {
                TextOut( ps.hdc, 10, 30, cBuf, wsprintf( cBuf,
                        "Special CB Format not available." ) ) ;
            }
            CloseClipboard( );
            EndPaint( hWnd, &ps );
        }
        break ;

case WM_COMMAND :
        switch( LOWORD( wParam ) )
        {
            case IDM_TEST:
                // Show state of clipboard formats.
                //................................
                InvalidateRect( hWnd, NULL, TRUE );
                break;
    .
    .
    .
```

IsClipboardFormatAvailable ■ WINDOWS 95 ■ WINDOWS NT

Description	`IsClipboardFormatAvailable` tells whether the clipboard contains data in a specific clipboard format. Clipboard readers that only understand one clipboard format should use `IsClipboardFormatAvailable` to determine whether that clipboard format is present. If the reader understands more than one clipboard format, use `GetPriorityClipboardFormat` instead.
Syntax	`BOOL IsClipboardFormatAvailable( UINT wFormat )`
Parameters	
wFormat	`UINT`: The desired clipboard format. This is either one of the predefined formats or a format registered by an application with `RegisterClipboardFormat`.
Returns	`BOOL`: `TRUE` if data of the specified format is available in the clipboard and `FALSE` if not. Use `GetLastError` to return the error code reported by the system.
Include File	`winuser.h`
See Also	`GetPriorityClipboardFormat`, `EnumClipboardFormats`
Example	See the example for the `GetPriorityClipboardFormat` function.

OpenClipboard ■ WINDOWS 95 ■ WINDOWS NT

Description	`OpenClipboard` opens the clipboard for reading and writing of its contents. The clipboard must be open before `GetClipboardData` can read its contents or `SetClipboardData` can set its contents. The clipboard remains open until `CloseClipboard` is called. No application should ever return control to Windows with the clipboard left open. Therefore, the clipboard must be opened and closed during the processing of a single Windows message.
Syntax	`BOOL OpenClipboard( HWND hWnd )`
Parameters	
hWnd	`HWND`: The handle of the window that is opening the clipboard.
Returns	`BOOL`: `TRUE` if the clipboard is opened and `FALSE` on error (for example, if another application has left the clipboard open). `GetLastError` can be used to retrieve the error code.
Include File	`winuser.h`
See Also	`CloseClipboard`, `GetClipboardData`, `SetClipboardData`, `GetOpenClipboardWindow`
Example	See the examples under `ChangeClipboardChain`.

RegisterClipboardFormat ■ WINDOWS 95 ■ WINDOWS NT

Description	`RegisterClipboardFormat` registers a new clipboard format name with Windows. This function is used to add specialized formats to the Windows clipboard that can be used for both interapplication communication (when both applications understand the clipboard format) or as private interinstance communication.
Syntax	UINT **RegisterClipboardFormat**(LPCTSTR *lpFormatName*)
Parameters	
lpFormatName	LPCTSTR: A pointer to a null-terminated character string containing the new format name.
Returns	UINT: The format number used by Windows to index the clipboard format. **NULL** on error. If the format is already registered with Windows, the value returned is consistent with the initial registration.
Include File	`winuser.h`
See Also	`EnumClipboardFormats`, `GetClipboardFormatName`
Example	See the example under `GetPriorityClipboardFormat`.

SetClipboardData ■ WINDOWS 95 ■ WINDOWS NT

Description	`SetClipboardData` places data in the clipboard for a given clipboard format. This is the only way to set the contents of the clipboard. Before an application places any data in the clipboard, the clipboard must be opened with the function `OpenClipboard` and all formats cleared by calling `EmptyClipboard`. After setting the data, immediately call `CloseClipboard`.
Syntax	HANDLE **SetClipboardData**(UINT *wFormat,* HANDLE *hMem*)
Parameters	
wFormat	WORD: Specifies what type of data the memory block referenced by *hMem* contains. The data type can be any of those listed in Table 18-1 or a registered clipboard format.
hMem	HANDLE: A handle to a global memory block that contains the data in the specified format. For delayed rendering of the clipboard, set *hMem* to NULL. This means that the data does not have to be passed to the clipboard until a WM_RENDERFORMAT message is received.
Returns	HANDLE: A handle to the data in the clipboard that this data replaces. This value normally is not used.
Include File	`winuser.h`
See Also	`OpenClipboard`, `GetClipboardData`, `EmptyClipboard`, `CloseClipboard`
Related Messages	WM_RENDERFORMAT, WM_RENDERALLFORMATS

CAUTION

Once the data of the clipboard is set, the memory block belongs to Windows. Applications should not free the data or leave the block locked. Applications using the clipboard should not allow control to pass to Windows while the clipboard is open. In other words, the clipboard should be opened and closed while processing a single Windows message.

Example   See example for the `GetPriorityClipboardFormat` function.

SetClipboardViewer   ■ WINDOWS 95 ■ WINDOWS NT

Description	`SetClipboardViewer` places the given window at the head of the chain of the clipboard viewers. The value returned, the handle of the next clipboard viewer on the chain, must be saved by the caller and kept up-to-date by processing the `WM_CHANGECBCHAIN` message. The handle of the next clipboard viewer is needed to process the `WM_DRAWCLIPBOARD`, `WM_CHANGECBCHAIN`, and `WM_DESTROY` messages.
Syntax	HWND **SetClipboardViewer**(HWND *hWnd*)
Parameters	
hWnd	HWND: The window handle for the window to be added to the clipboard viewer chain.
Returns	HWND: The handle of the next window in the clipboard viewer chain.
Include File	`winuser.h`
See Also	`ChangeClipboardChain`
Related Messages	`WM_DRAWCLIPBOARD`, `WM_CHANGECBCHAIN`
Example	See the example under `ChangeClipboardChain` for a clipboard viewer listing that handles both text and bitmap clipboard data.

19

THE REGISTRY

The registry is the database where configuration information is stored in the Win32 environment. The registry completely replaces the concept of the initialization files of Windows 3.x and is a better solution, because unlike INI files, where information is distributed among many files, the configuration data of the registry is all stored together.

The registry also supports networking and lets individual users store preferences, so applications can customize the user interface for the current user. User registry data can be stored at a central location and imported into the workstation registry when a user logs on. Similarly, a system administrator can remotely access the registries of workstations to resolve conflicts.

Using the registry, shell actions (such as `compile` or `edit`) may be associated with document types. Using the Windows Explorer, when the user clicks the right mouse button on the icon of a document, a contextual menu appears that lists the programmed actions. Other important uses of the registry include OLE registration, internationalization (locale support), network protocols and binding, and (in Windows 95 and to some extent Windows NT 4) plug-and-play support.

The Registry Architecture

One way to explore the registry is to use REGEDIT, the Microsoft utility that allows users and administrators to change the registry and connect with registries on other computers. The display format of the registry in REGEDIT is very similar to how the Windows Explorer displays folders and documents, partly because the structure of the registry is similar to a directory structure. In the terminology of the registry, the equivalent of a folder or directory is a key, and the equivalent of a document or file is a value. A key is a collection of subkeys and values. (Keys that are contained by keys are called subkeys of that key.)

Figure 19-1 shows the relationship between keys and values in the registry. In this example, the root key has one value and two subkeys, Subkey1 and Subkey2. Subkey1 has a single value; Subkey2 has two values and one subkey. The subkey of Subkey2 may have any number of values and subkeys.

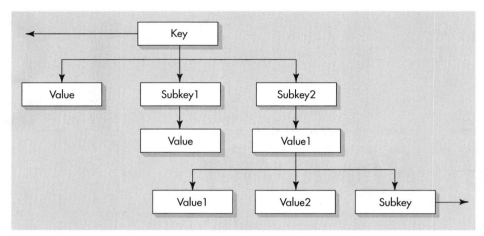

Figure 19-1 Relationships between components of the registry

An application's configuration data is a set of keys and values. For example, many applications store the last documents opened, so that the user can select from a list of the documents most recently used. One way of representing this in the registry is to have a single key named **LastDocuments** and to store the file names of the last few documents opened as values of the key. In this case, **LastDocuments** is very much like an array of file name values. Another way of representing this is to have a key named **LastDocuments** and a subkey for each document stored. In the latter case, each of the subkeys would have one value—the document's file name. The key **LastDocuments** would have no value at all; its only purpose is to group together the other document keys.

Placing Data in the Registry

Use **RegCreateKeyEx** to create keys in the registry. The system will create the necessary structure to add the key, including any intermediate keys not yet present in the registry. The example in Listing 19-1 shows how to create a default icon key in the registry for a new document type with an extension of **.MDC** and an associated document type of **MyDoc**.

Listing 19-1 Creating a registry key

```
HKEY      hKeyExt, hKeyApp;
DWORD     dwDisposition;

// Create the extension key.
//.........................
RegCreateKeyEx( HKEY_CLASSES_ROOT, ".MDC", 0, "",
                REG_OPTION_NON_VOLATILE, KEY_ALL_ACCESS,
                NULL, &hKeyExt, &dwDisposition );
```

```
// Create the application key.
//...........................
RegCreateKeyEx( HKEY_CLASSES_ROOT, "MyDoc\\DefaultIcon",
                0, "", REG_OPTION_NON_VOLATILE, KEY_ALL_ACCESS,
                &hKeyApp, &dwDisposition );
```

To assign values in the registry, use the `RegSetValueEx` function. To finish the registration of the default icon for a new document type, an icon must be set as the value for the key created for the application and the application name must be set as the value for the extension. Listing 19-2 shows how to use the `RegSetValueEx` function to set the values for the keys.

Listing 19-2 Setting a key value

```
RegSetValueEx( hKeyExt,       // Handle of the key.
               NULL,          // Set to NULL for the default value.
               0,
               REG_SZ,
               "MyApplication",
               14 );

RegSetValueEx( hKeyApp, NULL, 0,
               REG_SZ, "MyIcon.ico,0", 13 );
```

The default icon will appear in the Explorer for every document of the type MDC. The example for `RegCreateKeyEx` in the function description section of this chapter shows how the registry may be used to associate a file extension with a document type and how to program shell commands for the document.

The Windows Registry Structure

Windows NT 4 and Windows 95 registries share a common structure and common branches. What this means is that applications written for Windows NT 4 and Windows 95 can expect data to be stored in common locations depending on the type of data it is. Figure 19-2 shows the top level of the Windows registry.

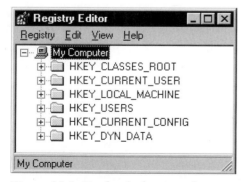

Figure 19-2 Top level of registry for Windows NT 4 and Windows 95

Table 19-1 lists the registry root branches and describes their purpose and relationship with the other branches.

Table 19-1 Common registry branches

Registry Branch	Description
HKEY_CLASSES_ROOT	Part of HKEY_LOCAL_MACHINE, this section contains definitions of document types, file associations, and the shell interface. This key relates to the information stored in the registry for Windows 3.x.
HKEY_CURRENT_USER	Link of HKEY_USERS that corresponds to the settings of the current user. Default users who do not have specific settings use the user settings for .Default.
HKEY_LOCAL_MACHINE	Stores hardware configurations, network protocols, and software classes (HKEY_CLASSES_ROOT).
HKEY_USERS	Used to store user preferences (such as color and sound configurations) and desktop settings. The Software subkey of each user subkey of HKEY_USERS is where applications should store user preferences.
HKEY_CURRENT_CONFIG	This is a link of the display subkey of the selected configuration of the config subkey of the root HKEY_LOCAL_MACHINE. This key will only appear in instances of multiple hardware configurations.
HKEY_DYN_DATA	The Enum subkey records hardware data for each component of the system. The PerfStats subkey measures system performance. This data is generated when the HKEY_PERFORMANCE_DATA key is used in a call to RegQueryKeyEx.

A Windows application should use the registry to store the following class data in the **HKEY_CLASSES_ROOT** section:

- Document types. The various types of documents the application manipulates.

- OLE class ID. The OLE class that an application defines. It must be registered with OLE when that application is installed.

- OLE verbs. The OLE protocol. Each of the verbs describes an action an object can perform; for example, MPLAYER can play a WAV file.

- Shell protocols. The actions that can be invoked by the shell. These choices are displayed in a contextual menu shown when the user right-clicks on the icon of the document.

- Icon shown for document display. Two icons should be provided, a large and a small icon. According to the user preference, the correct one will be used.

Figure 19-3 shows the registry entries for the WordPad document key, a child of the **HKEY_CLASSES_ROOT** key. It has five subkeys: **CLSID**, **DefaultIcon**, **Insertable**, **Protocol**, and **Shell**. The value in the **CLSID** key is an OLE 2.0 class identifier. The value in the **DefaultIcon** key is the name of the icon library and index where the icon is found. The shell will use this information to display WordPad documents. The **Insertable** and **Protocol** subkeys are also OLE specific: **Insertable** is a flag that indicates that an object of this type can appear in the Insert Object dialog of an OLE container, whereas the value in the **Protocol** key defines a tree for **StdFileEditing**, an OLE protocol. Within the **StdFileEditing** key there are subkeys for **Server** (the name of the document server to use when a WordPad document is invoked) and a set of verbs that are named **'0'**, **'1'**, and so on. WordPad only implements one verb: **&edit**.

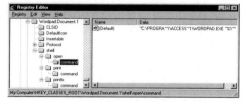

Figure 19-3 Example of keys and subkeys in a WordPad document

Note also the shell key with its three subkeys: **open**, **print**, and **printto**. Each of these keys has a subkey named **command**. The **open** subkey has the same role as the typical file association of Windows 3.x; it is the command used to open (or execute) the document. The **print** option sends the document to the printer. **Printto** is a special interface that allows users to transfer the document to the printer by dragging and dropping it. Any number of verbs can be registered as a shell key. These verbs are displayed in the contextual menu that appears anytime the user right-clicks on the document's icon.

A Windows application should also use the registry to store user preferences in the **Software** key of the individual user's subkey of **HKEY_USERS**. Figure 19-4 shows the **HKEY_USERS** root with two subkeys: **.Default** and **User X**. (Note that under each software subkey is a subkey named **Your App**.) For **.Default** there are two subkeys of **Your App**: **Report Name** and **Data Base**. Under **User X** there is only one: **Data Base**. When **User X** is the current user, the application will find a setting for **Data Base** but not for **Report Name**. The application can enforce this rule by always reading user preferences from the application subkey of the software subkey of the current user, and if they are not found, using the same location for user **.Default**.

Figure 19-4 **User X** and **.Default** application settings

Registry Function Descriptions

Table 19-2 presents a summary of the registry functions. Function descriptions begin immediately after the table.

Table 19-2 Registry function summary

Function	Purpose
RegCloseKey	Closes an open registry key.
RegConnectRegistry	Connects to a predefined registry handle on another computer.
RegCreateKeyEx	Creates a new subkey.
RegDeleteKey	Removes a key from the registry.
RegDeleteValue	Removes a value from a registry key.
RegEnumKeyEx	Enumerates through subkeys of a key.
RegEnumValue	Enumerates through the values of a key.
RegFlushKey	Writes registry changes immediately.
RegLoadKey	Loads a hive into a topmost root key.
RegNotifyChangeKeyValue	Indicates when a registry key or value changes.
RegOpenKeyEx	Opens an existing registry key with Win32 extensions.
RegQueryInfoKey	Returns information about a key.
RegQueryMultipleValues	Retrieves the type and data for a list of value names.
RegQueryValueEx	Returns a value (with Win32 extended data types).
RegReplaceKey	Replaces a key with the contents of a file when the system is restarted.
RegRestoreKey	Reads a hive into a previously stored key.
RegSaveKey	Saves values and subkeys of a subkey to a hive file.
RegSetValueEx	Assigns a value to a key (with new data types).
RegUnLoadKey	Removes a hive from the registry.

RegCloseKey ■ WINDOWS 95 ■ WINDOWS NT

Description RegCloseKey closes the handle of the given open key. Any associated system resources are released. Closing a key does not force waiting writes to immediately occur.

Syntax LONG **RegCloseKey**(HKEY *hKey*)

Parameters

hKey HKEY: The handle of the key to close.

Returns LONG: If the function succeeds, ERROR_SUCCESS is returned; otherwise, an error code is returned to the caller. The function fails if the key is invalid or the key is not open.

Include File	`winreg.h`
See Also	`RegOpenKeyEx`, `RegFlushKey`
Example	See the example for `RegCreateKeyEx`.

RegConnectRegistry ■ WINDOWS 95 ■ WINDOWS NT

Description   `RegConnectRegistry` establishes a connection to a predefined registry handle on another computer. When the handle is no longer needed, the application should close it by calling the `RegCloseKey` function.

Syntax   LONG **RegConnectRegistry**(LPTSTR *lpMachineName,* HKEY *hKey,* PHKEY *phkResult*)

Parameters

lpMachineName   LPTSTR: A pointer to a null-terminated string containing the name of the remote computer. The string should be in the form *computername*. If set to **NULL**, the local computer name is used.

hKey   HKEY: The predefined handle of the registry on the remote computer. Currently the **HKEY_LOCAL_MACHINE** and **HKEY_USERS** are supported. The other keys cannot be remotely accessed.

phkResult   PHKEY: A pointer to an **HKEY** variable that receives a key handle identifying the predefined handle on the remote computer.

Returns   LONG: If successful, **ERROR_SUCCESS** is returned; otherwise, an error value is returned.

Include File   `winreg.h`

See Also   `RegCloseKey`

Example   This code segment shows how to use the `RegConnectRegistry` function to connect to another computer.

```
HKEY ConnectToRemote( LPTSTR lpComputerName, HKEY hKey )
{
    HKEY hRemoteKey;

    if ( RegConnectRegistry( lpComputerName, hKey, &hRemoteKey ) == ERROR_SUCCESS )
        return( hRemoteKey );

    MessageBox( NULL, "Could not connect to remote computer", NULL, MB_OK | MB_ICONSTOP );
    return( NULL );
}
```

RegCreateKeyEx ■ WINDOWS 95 ■ WINDOWS NT

Description   `RegCreateKeyEx` creates or opens a subkey of the specified key.

Syntax   LONG **RegCreateKeyEx**(HKEY *hkey,* LPCTSTR *lpszSubKey,* DWORD *dwReserved,* LPTSTR *lpszClass,* DWORD *dwOptions,* REGSAM

continued on next page

continued from previous page

> samDesired, LPSECURITY_ATTRIBUTES *lpSecurityAttributes,*
> PHKEY *phkResult,* LPDWORD *lpdwDisposition*)

Parameters

hKey HKEY: The key under which the new subkey is to be created. This may be an open key or one of the predefined top-level root keys HKEY_CURRENT_USER, HKEY_USERS, HKEY_LOCAL_MACHINE, or HKEY_CLASSES_ROOT.

lpszSubKey LPCTSTR: Pointer to a null-terminated string containing the name of the new subkey. If the subkey already exists, it is opened.

dwReserved DWORD: Set this value to NULL.

lpszClass LPTSTR: Pointer to a null-terminated string containing the name of the class of the key. If the subkey already exists, this parameter is ignored.

dwOptions DWORD: Special storage options associated with the key. Table 19-3 lists possible values.

Table 19-3 RegCreateKeyEx *dwOptions* values

Registry Key Storage Options	Meaning
REG_OPTION_BACKUP_RESTORE	(Windows NT) The *samDesired* parameter is ignored and the key is opened with the access required to back up or restore the key. If the calling thread has the SE_BACKUP_NAME privilege enabled, the key is opened with ACCESS_SYSTEM_SECURITY and KEY_READ access. If the calling thread has the SE_RESTORE_NAME privilege enabled, the key is opened with ACCESS_SYSTEM_SECURITY and KEY_WRITE access.
REG_OPTION_NON_VOLATILE	The data is not volatile but is saved on disk. When the system is restarted, no keys are lost. RegSaveKey saves keys that are not volatile.
REG_OPTION_VOLATILE	The data is kept in memory and not written to disk. Volatile keys are lost when the system is shut down. Also, RegSaveKey does not save volatile keys. This value is ignored in Windows 95 where a nonvolatile key is created and ERROR_SUCCESS is returned.

samDesired REGSAM: The desired security access for the key. This can be a combination of the values listed in Table 19-4.

Table 19-4 Key access options

Key Access Option	Permissions
KEY_ALL_ACCESS	A combination of KEY_QUERY_VALUE, KEY_ENUMERATE_SUBKEYS, KEY_NOTIFY, KEY_CREATE_SUBKEY, KEY_CREATE_LINK, and KEY_SET_VALUE.
KEY_CREATE_LINK	Allows creation of symbolic links to other subkeys.

Key Access Option	Permissions
KEY_CREATE_SUB_KEY	Allows creation of subkeys.
KEY_ENUMERATE_SUB_KEYS	Allows enumeration of subkeys.
KEY_EXECUTE	Allows reading of the key.
KEY_NOTIFY	Enables change notification (not supported in Windows 95).
KEY_QUERY_VALUE	Allows subkey values to be queried.
KEY_READ	A combination of KEY_QUERY_VALUE, KEY_ENUMERATE_SUB_KEYS, and KEY_NOTIFY.
KEY_SET_VALUE	Allows subkey values to be written.
KEY_WRITE	A combination of KEY_SET_VALUE and KEY_CREATE_SUB_KEY.

lpSecurityAttributes	LPSECURITY_ATTRIBUTES: The security attributes of the key. Specifying **NULL** indicates default security attributes. Default security attributes do not allow handles in one process to be inherited by another process. To allow key handles to be inherited, the *bInheritHandle* member of the structure must be set to **TRUE**. This parameter is ignored in Windows 95.
phkResult	PHKEY: A pointer to an **HKEY** variable that receives the handle to the new subkey.
lpdwDisposition	LPDWORD: A pointer to a **DWORD** variable that receives a disposition value that indicates whether the subkey was created (**REG_CREATED_NEW_KEY**) or an existing subkey was opened (**REG_OPENED_EXISTING_KEY**).
Returns	LONG: If successful, **ERROR_SUCCESS** is returned; otherwise, an error code is returned.
Include File	winreg.h
See Also	RegDeleteKey
Example	When the user selects the Register! menu option, the example creates three entries in the registry, two for a document type **MyDoc** with a shell command and default icon entry, and a third for the extension **.MDC**. The file extension is linked to the document type and the **Test** shell command. After running this example, use the Explorer to right-click on a file with extension **.MDC** to see the contextual menu. Execution of **Test** will load the **MyDoc** file into NotePad. Figure 19-5 shows the registry after running the example. Figure 19-6 shows the new contextual menu for **.MDC** files. When the user selects the Un-Register! menu option, the registry keys are removed.

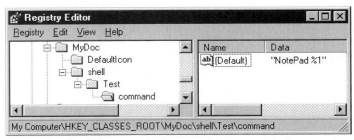

Figure 19-5 `RegCreateKeyEx` example

Figure 19-6 The contextual menu created
by the example

```
LRESULT CALLBACK WndProc( HWND hWnd, UINT uMsg, WPARAM wParam, LPARAM lParam )
{
    switch( uMsg )
    {
      case WM_COMMAND :
            switch( LOWORD( wParam ) )
            {
               case IDM_REGISTER:
                   {
                       LONG  lResult;
                       HKEY  hKeyResult = 0;
                       DWORD dwDisposition = 0;

                       // Create "MyDoc" shell interface.
                       //..................................
                       lResult = RegCreateKeyEx( HKEY_CLASSES_ROOT,
                                     "MyDoc\\shell\\Test\\command", 0,
                                     "", REG_OPTION_VOLATILE, KEY_ALL_ACCESS,
                                     NULL, &hKeyResult, &dwDisposition );

                       // Use Notepad to open the document.
                       //..................................
                       if ( lResult == ERROR_SUCCESS )
                       {
                           lResult = RegSetValueEx( hKeyResult, NULL, 0, REG_SZ,
                                            "NotePad %1", 11 );
```

```
                          RegCloseKey( hKeyResult );
                      }

                      // Create the DefaultIcon for MyDoc
                      //................................
                      lResult = RegCreateKeyEx( HKEY_CLASSES_ROOT,
                                      "MyDoc\\DefaultIcon", 0,
                                      "", REG_OPTION_VOLATILE, KEY_ALL_ACCESS,
                                      NULL, &hKeyResult, &dwDisposition );


                      // Set the default icon.
                      //.....................
                      if ( lResult == ERROR_SUCCESS )
                      {
                          lResult = RegSetValueEx( hKeyResult, NULL, 0, REG_SZ,
                                              "%SystemRoot%\\system32\\shell32.dll,⇐
1", 36 );

                          RegCloseKey( hKeyResult );
                      }

                      // Create .MDC file extension connection.
                      //......................................
                      lResult = RegCreateKeyEx( HKEY_CLASSES_ROOT, ".MDC",
                                          0, "", REG_OPTION_VOLATILE,
                                          KEY_ALL_ACCESS, NULL,
                                          &hKeyResult, &dwDisposition );

                      // Connect .MDC with MyDoc type.
                      //.............................
                      if ( lResult == ERROR_SUCCESS )
                      {
                          lResult = RegSetValueEx( hKeyResult, NULL, 0, REG_SZ,
                                              "MyDoc", 6 );
                          RegCloseKey( hKeyResult );
                      }

                      MessageBox( hWnd, "MyDoc (.MDC) has been registered in the ⇐
registry",
                                      "RegCreateKeyEx()", MB_OK | MB_ICONINFORMATION );
                  }
                  break;

          case IDM_UNREGISTER :
                  {
                  HKEY  hKeyResult = 0;
                  LONG  lResult = RegOpenKeyEx( HKEY_CLASSES_ROOT,
                                          "MyDoc\\shell\\Test\\command",
                                          0, KEY_ALL_ACCESS, &hKeyResult );
                  // Delete default value.
                  //.....................
                  if ( lResult == ERROR_SUCCESS )
                  {
                      lResult = RegDeleteValue( hKeyResult, NULL );
                      RegCloseKey( hKeyResult );
                  }
```

continued on next page

continued from previous page

```
                        lResult = RegOpenKeyEx( HKEY_CLASSES_ROOT,
                                                "MyDoc\\DefaultIcon",
                                                0, KEY_ALL_ACCESS, &hKeyResult );
                        // Delete default value.
                        //......................
                        if ( lResult == ERROR_SUCCESS )
                        {
                            lResult = RegDeleteValue( hKeyResult, NULL );
                            RegCloseKey( hKeyResult );
                        }

                        // Remove the keys.. All subkeys must be removed before
                        // the parent keys can be removed. This is a limitation
                        // of the RegDeleteKey() function.
                        //.......................................................
                        RegDeleteKey( HKEY_CLASSES_ROOT, "MyDoc\\shell\\Test\\command" );
                        RegDeleteKey( HKEY_CLASSES_ROOT, "MyDoc\\shell\\Test" );
                        RegDeleteKey( HKEY_CLASSES_ROOT, "MyDoc\\shell" );
                        RegDeleteKey( HKEY_CLASSES_ROOT, "MyDoc\\DefaultIcon" );
                        RegDeleteKey( HKEY_CLASSES_ROOT, "MyDoc" );
                        RegDeleteKey( HKEY_CLASSES_ROOT, ".MDC" );

                        MessageBox( hWnd, "MyDoc (.MDC) has been removed from the registry",
                                    "RegCreateKeyEx()", MB_OK | MB_ICONINFORMATION );
                    }
                    break;
```

RegDeleteKey ■ WINDOWS 95 ■ WINDOWS NT

Description	**RegDeleteKey** removes a subkey of a given key. On Windows NT, this function will not delete subkeys and will fail if there are subkeys. On Windows 95, the subkeys are deleted.
Syntax	LONG **RegDeleteKey**(HKEY *hKey,* LPCTSTR *lpszSubKey*)
Parameters	
hKey	HKEY: The handle of an open key or any of the predefined key handles HKEY_CLASSES_ROOT, HKEY_CURRENT_USER, HKEY_USERS, or HKEY_LOCAL_MACHINE.
lpszSubKey	LPCTSTR: Pointer to a null-terminated string that contains the name of the subkey to be deleted. The specified key must not have subkeys, although it may have values. The values are deleted when the key is deleted.
Returns	LONG: If successful, ERROR_SUCCESS is returned; otherwise, an error code is returned.
Include File	winreg.h
See Also	RegCreateKeyEx, RegOpenKeyEx
Example	See the example for the **RegCreateKeyEx** function.

RegDeleteValue

Description	RegDeleteValue removes a value from a subkey.
Syntax	LONG **RegDeleteValue**(HKEY *hKey,* LPTSTR *lpszValueName*)
Parameters	
hKey	HKEY: The handle of an open key with **KEY_SET_VALUE** access or one of the predefined keys **HKEY_CLASSES_ROOT**, **HKEY_CURRENT_USER**, **HKEY_USERS**, or **HKEY_LOCAL_MACHINE**.
lpszValueName	LPTSTR: Pointer to a null-terminated string that contains the name of the value to delete. If **NULL**, the default value is removed.
Returns	LONG: **ERROR_SUCCESS** is returned if the function is successful; otherwise, an error code is returned.
Include File	winreg.h
See Also	RegDeleteKey
Example	See the example for **RegCreateKeyEx**.

RegEnumKeyEx

Description	RegEnumKeyEx enumerates the subkeys of the specified open registry key. This function retrieves information about one subkey each time it is called. To enumerate subkeys, an application should initially call the RegEnumKeyEx function with the *dwIndex* parameter set to **0**. The application should then increment the *dwIndex* parameter and call **RegEnumKeyEx** until **ERROR_NO_MORE_ITEMS** is returned. The application can also enumerate the keys from the bottom up by setting *dwIndex* to the index of the last subkey on the first call and decrementing the index until the subkey with the index of **0** is enumerated. Use the **RegQueryInfoKey** function to retrieve the index of the last subkey.
Syntax	LONG **RegEnumKeyEx**(HKEY *hKey,* DWORD *dwIndex,* LPTSTR *lpszName,* LPDWORD *lpcdwName,* LPDWORD *lpdwReserved,* LPTSTR *lpszClassName,* LPDWORD *lpcdwClassName,* PFILETIME *pftLastChanged*)
Parameters	
hKey	HKEY: The open key whose subkeys are to be enumerated. This can be an open key or one of the predefined keys **HKEY_CLASSES_ROOT**, **HKEY_CURRENT_USER**, **HKEY_USERS**, or **HKEY_LOCAL_MACHINE**.
dwIndex	DWORD: The index of the subkey to access. To access the first subkey, set the subkey counter to **0**. To enumerate through the subkey tree, increment the counter before each call until **ERROR_NO_MORE_ITEMS** is returned.
lpszName	LPTSTR: A pointer to a buffer that receives the name of the enumerated subkey. The name of the key is not the fully qualified key, only the name of the subkey itself.

lpcdwName	LPDWORD: A pointer to a DWORD value that contains the size of the buffer *lpszName*. The system attempts to copy the specified number of characters of the subkey name into the buffer. The count must include 1 byte for the null-terminating character. After the call, the content of the address is changed to the number of characters actually copied to the *lpszName* string. Note that this does not count the null-terminating character.
lpdwReserved	LPDWORD: Reserved for future implementation. Set this value to NULL.
lpszClassName	LPTSTR: A pointer to the buffer that receives the class name of the subkey. The number of characters copied into this buffer is supplied by the *lpcdwClassName* parameter. This parameter can be NULL if no class name is being requested.
lpcdwClassName	LPDWORD: A pointer to a DWORD value that contains the length of the class name buffer, *lpszClassName*. The system attempts to copy the specified number of characters of the class name of the subkey into the buffer. This count should include space for the null-terminating character. After the call, the content of the address is changed to the number of characters actually copied to the *lpszClassName* string. Note that this does not count the null-terminating character. This parameter may be NULL if *lpszClassName* is also NULL.
pftLastChanged	PFILETIME: A pointer to a FILETIME variable that receives the time and date of the last write to the subkey. The FILETIME structure is a 64-bit value that represents the number of 100-nanosecond ticks since January 1, 1601.
Returns	LONG: ERROR_SUCCESS if next subkey is found. If the enumeration fails, an error will return. If the code is ERROR_NO_MORE_ITEMS, there are no more subkeys for the given key.
Include File	winreg.h
See Also	RegEnumValue, RegOpenKeyEx
Example	This example creates a window with a tree view control. When the user selects the Test! menu option, the contents of the HKEY_LOCAL_MACHINE registry tree are enumerated and placed into the tree view in the correct hierarchy. The notification thread, which waits for any change to the HKEY_LOCAL_MACHINE key, is also enabled. If a change is detected, the tree view contents are refreshed to reflect the change. To simplify this example, the entire tree is loaded into the tree view control. A more appropriate implementation would only enumerate the top-level keys until the user expands a key, at which time it would load the subkeys for the expanded key. Figure 19-7 shows the results. For more information on the tree view control and other common controls, refer to the *Windows 95 Common Controls & Messages API Bible*.

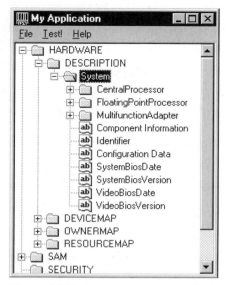

Figure 19-7 RegEnumKeyEx example

```
HWND    hTree  = NULL;
HANDLE hNotify = NULL;

VOID EnumerateRegistry( HKEY hKey, HTREEITEM hParent )
{
    static TV_INSERTSTRUCT tvi;
    static DWORD           dwNameLen;
    static DWORD           dwClassLen;
    static FILETIME        ftime;

    HTREEITEM hNewItem;
    HKEY      hNewKey;
    LPTSTR    lpszName;
    LPTSTR    lpszClass;
    LPTSTR    lpszValueName;
    DWORD     dwMaxNameLen;
    DWORD     dwMaxClassLen;
    DWORD     dwMaxValueNameLen;
    LONG      lReturn;
    DWORD     dwIndex = 0;

    // Retrieve the maximum key name, class name,
    // value name, and value data lengths.
    //........................................
    RegQueryInfoKey( hKey, NULL, NULL, NULL, NULL, &dwMaxNameLen, &dwMaxClassLen,
                    NULL, &dwMaxValueNameLen, NULL, NULL, NULL );

    // Increment by 1 because we need room
    // for the terminating character.
    //............................
```

continued on next page

continued from previous page

```
    dwMaxNameLen++;
    dwMaxClassLen++;
    dwMaxValueNameLen++;

    // Allocate memory to retrieve information into.
    //.............................................
    lpszName      = (LPTSTR)HeapAlloc( GetProcessHeap(), HEAP_ZERO_MEMORY, dwMaxNameLen );
    lpszClass     = (LPTSTR)HeapAlloc( GetProcessHeap(), HEAP_ZERO_MEMORY, dwMaxClassLen );
    lpszValueName = (LPTSTR)HeapAlloc( GetProcessHeap(), HEAP_ZERO_MEMORY, dwMaxValueNameLen );

    tvi.item.mask = TVIF_IMAGE | TVIF_SELECTEDIMAGE | TVIF_TEXT;
    tvi.hInsertAfter = TVI_LAST;

    // Enumerate all the subkeys for the current key.
    //...............................................
    do
    {
        dwNameLen = dwMaxNameLen;
        dwClassLen = dwMaxClassLen;

        lReturn = RegEnumKeyEx( hKey, dwIndex, lpszName, &dwNameLen,
                                NULL, lpszClass, &dwClassLen, &ftime );

        if ( lReturn != ERROR_NO_MORE_ITEMS )
        {
            tvi.item.iImage  = 0;
            tvi.item.iSelectedImage = 1;
            tvi.item.pszText = lpszName;
            tvi.hParent = hParent;

            hNewItem = TreeView_InsertItem( hTree, &tvi );

            if ( RegOpenKeyEx( hKey, lpszName, 0, KEY_ALL_ACCESS,
                               &hNewKey ) == ERROR_SUCCESS )
            {
                EnumerateRegistry( hNewKey, hNewItem );
                RegCloseKey( hNewKey );
            }
        }
        dwIndex++;
    }
    while( lReturn != ERROR_NO_MORE_ITEMS );

    tvi.item.iImage  = 2;
    tvi.item.iSelectedImage = 2;
    dwIndex = 0;

    // Enumerate all the values for the current key.
    //..............................................
    do
    {
        dwNameLen = dwMaxValueNameLen;

        lReturn = RegEnumValue( hKey, dwIndex, lpszValueName,
                                &dwNameLen, 0, NULL, NULL, NULL );

        if ( lReturn != ERROR_NO_MORE_ITEMS )
        {
```

```
                tvi.item.pszText = lpszValueName;
                tvi.hParent = hParent;

                TreeView_InsertItem( hTree, &tvi );
            }

        dwIndex++;
    }
    while( lReturn != ERROR_NO_MORE_ITEMS );

    // Clean up the memory we allocated.
    //.............................
    if ( lpszName )      HeapFree( GetProcessHeap(), 0, lpszName );
    if ( lpszClass )     HeapFree( GetProcessHeap(), 0, lpszClass );
    if ( lpszValueName ) HeapFree( GetProcessHeap(), 0, lpszValueName );
}


VOID FillTreeView()
{
    TreeView_DeleteItem( hTree, TVI_ROOT );
    SendMessage( hTree, WM_SETREDRAW, FALSE, 0 );
    SetCursor( LoadCursor( NULL, IDC_WAIT ) );

    // Fill the TreeView with the contets of HKEY_LOCAL_MACHINE.
    //.........................................................
    EnumerateRegistry( HKEY_LOCAL_MACHINE, TVI_ROOT );

    SendMessage( hTree, WM_SETREDRAW, TRUE, 0 );
    UpdateWindow( hTree );
    SetCursor( LoadCursor( NULL, IDC_ARROW ) );
}


DWORD WINAPI ChangeNotify( LPVOID lpData )
{
    while( TRUE )
    {
        if ( RegNotifyChangeKeyValue( HKEY_LOCAL_MACHINE, TRUE,
                              REG_NOTIFY_CHANGE_NAME, NULL, FALSE ) == ERROR_SUCCESS )
        {
            FillTreeView();
        }
    }

    return( 0 );
}


LRESULT CALLBACK WndProc( HWND hWnd, UINT uMsg, WPARAM wParam, LPARAM lParam )
{
    switch( uMsg )
    {
        case WM_CREATE :
                InitCommonControls();

                // Create a Tree View.
                //....................
```

continued on next page

continued from previous page

```
            hTree = CreateWindowEx( WS_EX_CLIENTEDGE, WC_TREEVIEW,
                                "", WS_CHILD | WS_VISIBLE | TVS_HASLINES
                                | TVS_LINESATROOT | TVS_HASBUTTONS | TVS_DISABLEDRAG-⇐
DROP,
                                0, 0, 100, 100, hWnd, (HMENU)101, hInst, NULL );

            if ( hTree )
            {
                HIMAGELIST hImageList;
                DWORD      dwThreadID;

                // Create an image list for the tree view and assign it.
                //......................................................
                hImageList = ImageList_LoadBitmap( hInst, "TREEIMG", 16,
                                    1, RGB( 0, 255, 0 ) );
                TreeView_SetImageList( hTree, hImageList, TVSIL_NORMAL );

                hNotify = CreateThread( NULL, 0, ChangeNotify, 0,
                                    CREATE_SUSPENDED, &dwThreadID );
            }
            break;

        case WM_SIZE :
            if ( wParam != SIZE_MINIMIZED )
                MoveWindow( hTree, 0, 0, LOWORD( lParam ), HIWORD( lParam ), TRUE );
            break;

        case WM_COMMAND :
            switch( LOWORD( wParam ) )
            {
                case IDM_TEST :
                    FillTreeView();
                    ResumeThread( hNotify );
                    break;
            .
            .
            .
```

RegEnumValue   ■ WINDOWS 95   ■ WINDOWS NT

Description   RegEnumValue enumerates the values of a specified open registry key. It
copies one indexed value name and data block for the key each time it is
called. The application calls **RegEnumValue** with the *dwValueIndex* parameter set to **0** to retrieve the first value. For subsequent calls, the
application increments the *dwValueIndex* parameter by one. When
ERROR_NO_MORE_ITEMS is returned, the enumeration is finished.

Syntax   LONG **RegEnumValue**(HKEY *hKey,* DWORD *dwValueIndex,* LPTSTR
lpszValue, LPDWORD *lpcdwValue,* LPDWORD *lpdwReserved,* LPDWORD
lpdwType, LPBYTE *lpDataBuffer,* LPDWORD *lpcdwDataBuffer*)

Parameters

hKey	HKEY: The open key whose values are to be enumerated. This can be an open key or one of the predefined keys HKEY_CLASSES_ROOT, HKEY_CURRENT_USER, HKEY_USERS, or HKEY_LOCAL_MACHINE.
dwValueIndex	DWORD: The index of the value to be enumerated. To enumerate through all the values, set *dwValueIndex* to 0 before the first call. Then increment the index before each subsequent call.
lpszValue	LPTSTR: A pointer to the buffer that receives the name of the value.
lpcdwValue	LPDWORD: A pointer to a DWORD value that specifies the number of bytes (including the null-termination character) that are requested to be stored in *lpszValue* upon return. After the call this specifies the number of bytes (not counting the null-termination character) that were actually stored.
lpdwReserved	LPDWORD: Reserved; set this parameter to NULL.
lpdwType	LPDWORD: A pointer to a DWORD value that receives the data type of the value. Table 19-5 lists the data types supported in Win32. This field can be NULL if no data type is required.

Table 19-5 Registry data types

Registry Data Type	Description
REG_BINARY	Binary data in any form.
REG_DWORD	A 32-bit number in the native format.
REG_DWORD_BIG_ENDIAN	A 32-bit number in big-endian format. In this format, the most significant byte of a word is the low-order byte.
REG_DWORD_LITTLE_ENDIAN	A 32-bit number in little-endian format (same as REG_DWORD). In this format, the most significant byte of a word is the high-order byte.
REG_EXPAND_SZ	A null-terminated string that contains unexpanded references to environment variables (for example, %PATH%). Windows 95 allows these strings to be stored but not automatically expanded.
REG_LINK	A symbolic link to another subkey.
REG_MULTI_SZ	A list of null-terminated strings, terminated by an additional null character.
REG_NONE	An undefined type.
REG_RESOURCE_LIST	A device-driver resource list.
REG_SZ	A null-terminated string.

lpDataBuffer	LPBYTE: A pointer to a buffer that receives the contents of the value.
lpcdwDataBuffer	LPDWORD: A pointer to a DWORD value that contains the number of bytes in the buffer *lpDataBuffer*. This may be NULL if *lpDataBuffer* is NULL.
Returns	LONG: ERROR_SUCCESS if operation was successful; otherwise, an error code is returned. ERROR_NO_MORE_VALUES is returned when there are no more values for the given subkey.

Include File	winreg.h
See Also	RegEnumKeyEx, RegSetValueEx, RegQueryValueEx
Example	See the example for RegEnumKeyEx.

RegFlushKey   ■ WINDOWS 95   ■ WINDOWS NT

Description	RegFlushKey commands the system to immediately write the specified key and all its subkeys and values to disk. Calling this operation is only necessary if an application requires updates to be written immediately. By default, the system will flush registry changes to the disk after each close of a key and before shutdown, but the registry system uses optimized buffers, so changes may not be written immediately. Extensive use of this function may negatively impact system performance.
Syntax	LONG **RegFlushKey**(HKEY *hKey*)
Parameters	
hKey	HKEY: The key to be flushed to disk. This may be the handle of an open key or one of the predefined keys HKEY_CLASSES_ROOT, HKEY_CURRENT_USER, HKEY_USERS, or HKEY_LOCAL_MACHINE.
Returns	LONG: If successful, ERROR_SUCCESS is returned; otherwise, an error code is returned.
Include File	winreg.h
See Also	RegCloseKey
Example	When the user selects the Test! option, the example creates a key and displays a message box. After the user selects OK on the message box, the new key is flushed to the disk by calling the RegFlushKey function.

```
LRESULT CALLBACK WndProc( HWND hWnd, UINT uMsg, WPARAM wParam, LPARAM lParam )
{
   switch( uMsg )
   {
     case WM_COMMAND :
            switch( LOWORD( wParam ) )
              {
               case IDM_TEST:
                    {
                       DWORD   dwDisposition;
                       HKEY    hKey;

                       // Create a new key.
                       //.................
                       RegCreateKeyEx( HKEY_CLASSES_ROOT, "Flush", 0, "MyClass",
                                  REG_OPTION_NON_VOLATILE, KEY_ALL_ACCESS,
                                  NULL, &hKey, &dwDisposition );

                       MessageBox( hWnd, "After pressing OK, the key is flushed to disk",
                                  "Flush Key", MB_OK | MB_ICONINFORMATION );
```

```
            // Flush the new key.
            //..................
            RegFlushKey( hKey );
        }
        break;
```

.
.
.

RegLoadKey   ■ Windows 95   ■ Windows NT

Description	**RegLoadKey** creates a subkey under **HKEY_USER** or **HKEY_LOCAL_MACHINE** whose contents are loaded from the specified hive file into the subkey. A hive is a collection of keys, subkeys, and values backed by a single file and a **.log** file. To create hives, use **RegSaveKey**.
Syntax	LONG **RegLoadKey**(HKEY *hKey,* LPCTSTR *lpszSubKey,* LPCTSTR *lpszFile*)
Parameters	
hKey	HKEY: The parent key of the hive to be loaded. It may be **HKEY_USER**, **HKEY_LOCAL_MACHINE**, or the return value of **RegConnectRegistry** (a registry node on another computer).
lpszSubKey	LPCTSTR: A pointer to a null-terminated string containing the name of the subkey.
lpszFile	LPCTSTR: A pointer to a null-terminated string containing the name of the hive file that contains the registry data for the new subkey. Note that under FAT file systems the file name may not have an extension.
Returns	LONG: If successful, **ERROR_SUCCESS** is returned; otherwise, an error code is returned.
Include File	winreg.h
See Also	RegSaveKey, RegUnLoadKey, RegRestoreKey, RegDeleteKey
Example	The menu of the example has four options: Save, Load, Unload, and Restore. Choosing Save will create key entries and save them as a hive, Load will load the hive from a file, Unload will remove the key, and Restore will return the key to its previous contents. (Note: **RegRestoreKey** is not supported in Windows 95.)

```
DWORD dwDisp;
HKEY  hKey;

LRESULT CALLBACK WndProc( HWND hWnd, UINT uMsg, WPARAM wParam, LPARAM lParam )
{
    switch( uMsg )
    {
        case WM_COMMAND :
                switch( LOWORD( wParam ) )
                {
```

continued on next page

continued from previous page

```
                case IDM_SAVE:
                    {
                        // Build the contents of the KeyRoot and its subkeys.
                        //.................................................
                        RegCreateKeyEx( HKEY_LOCAL_MACHINE,⇐
"SOFTWARE\\KeyRoot\\Test\\Test1", 0, NULL,
                                        REG_OPTION_NON_VOLATILE, KEY_ALL_ACCESS, NULL,
                                        &hKey, &dwDisp );

                        RegSetValueEx( hKey, "Value1", 0, REG_SZ, "ABC", 14 );
                        RegSetValueEx( hKey, "Value2", 0, REG_SZ, "BCD", 14 );
                        RegCloseKey( hKey );

                        RegCreateKeyEx( HKEY_LOCAL_MACHINE, ⇐
"SOFTWARE\\KeyRoot\\Test\\Test2", 0, NULL,
                                        REG_OPTION_NON_VOLATILE, KEY_ALL_ACCESS, NULL,
                                        &hKey, &dwDisp );
                        RegSetValueEx( hKey, "Value1", 0, REG_SZ, "ZYX", 14 );
                        RegCloseKey( hKey );

                        // Save key, "KeyRoot", in hive, "TheHive".
                        //......................................
                        RegOpenKeyEx( HKEY_LOCAL_MACHINE, "SOFTWARE\\KeyRoot", 0,⇐
KEY_ALL_ACCESS, &hKey );

                        if ( RegSaveKey( hKey, "TheHive.reg", NULL ) == ERROR_SUCCESS )
                        {
                            MessageBox( hWnd, "TheHive was saved", "Save",
                                        MB_OK | MB_ICONINFORMATION );
                        }

                        RegCloseKey( hKey );

                    }
                    break;

                case IDM_LOAD:
                    {
                        if ( RegLoadKey( HKEY_LOCAL_MACHINE, "SOFTWARE\\KeyRoot",
                                        "TheHive.reg" ) == ERROR_SUCCESS )
                        {
                            MessageBox( hWnd, "TheHive was loaded into HKEY_LOCAL_MACHINE",
                                        "Load", MB_OK | MB_ICONINFORMATION );
                        }
                    }
                    break;

                case IDM_UNLOAD:
                    {
                        if ( RegUnLoadKey( HKEY_LOCAL_MACHINE,
                                        "SOFTWARE\\KeyRoot" ) == ERROR_SUCCESS )
                        {
                            MessageBox( hWnd, "TheHive Was Unloaded",
                                        "Unload", MB_OK );
                        }
                    }
                    break;
```

```
        case IDM_RESTORE:
            {
                TCHAR szErrMsg[64];
                LONG  lResult;

                RegCreateKeyEx( HKEY_LOCAL_MACHINE, "SOFTWARE\\KeyRoot", 0, "",
                                REG_OPTION_BACKUP_RESTORE, KEY_ALL_ACCESS,
                                NULL, &hKey, &dwDisp );

                if ( (lResult = RegRestoreKey( hKey, "TheHive.reg", 0 )) !=
ERROR_SUCCESS )
                {
                    wsprintf( szErrMsg, "Error %d occurred", lResult );
                    MessageBox( hWnd, szErrMsg, NULL, MB_OK | MB_ICONSTOP );

                    RegDeleteKey( HKEY_LOCAL_MACHINE, hKey );
                }
                else
                    MessageBox( hWnd, "The Hive was restored", "Restore",
                                MB_OK | MB_ICONINFORMATION );

                RegCloseKey( hKey );
            }
            break;
            .
            .
            .
```

RegNotifyChangeKeyValue   ■ WINDOWS 95   ■ WINDOWS NT

Description	RegNotifyChangeKeyValue indicates when a registry key or any of its subkeys has changed. RegNotifyChangeKeyValue works in either synchronous or asynchronous mode depending on the value of the *bAsynchronous* parameter.
Syntax	LONG **RegNotifyChangeKeyValue**(HKEY *hKey*, BOOL *bWatchSubtree*, DWORD *dwNotifyFilter*, HANDLE *hEvent*, BOOL *bAsynchronous*)
Parameters	
hKey	HKEY: A currently open key or any one of the following predefined handle values: HKEY_CLASSES_ROOT, HKEY_CURRENT_USER, HKEY_LOCAL_MACHINE, or HKEY_USERS.
bWatchSubtree	BOOL: Set to TRUE to watch for changes in the key or any of its subkeys. Set to FALSE to only report changes within the key.
dwNotifyFilter	DWORD: A set of flags that control which changes should be reported. This can be a combination of the values listed in Table 19-6.

Table 19-6 RegNotifyChangeKeyValue *dwNotifyFilter* values

Value	Meaning
REG_NOTIFY_CHANGE_ATTRIBUTES	Any attribute change that occurs in a key or in a key and its subkeys.
REG_NOTIFY_CHANGE_LAST_SET	A change to the last write time within a key or in a key and its subkeys.
REG_NOTIFY_CHANGE_NAME	Any changes to key names that occur; creation or deletion of key names.
REG_NOTIFY_CHANGE_SECURITY	A change to the security-descriptor in a key or in a key and its subkeys.

hEvent	**HANDLE**: The event handle to signal when a change occurs. If the *bAsynchronous* parameter is set to **FALSE**, this parameter is ignored.
bAsynchronous	**BOOL**: Set this parameter to **TRUE** in order to execute this function in asynchronous mode and return immediately. In this mode, when a change occurs, the event handle supplied in the *hEvent* parameter is signaled. If set to **FALSE**, this function executes in synchronous mode and does not return until a change occurs in the registry.
Returns	**LONG**: If successful, **ERROR_SUCCESS** is returned; otherwise, an error value is returned.
Include File	`winreg.h`
See Also	`RegDeleteKey, RegCreateKeyEx`
Example	See the example for the `RegEnumKeyEx` function.

RegOpenKeyEx   ■ WINDOWS 95 ■ WINDOWS NT

Description	RegOpenKeyEx opens a registry subkey with the desired access. Unlike the `RegCreateKeyEx` function, `RegOpenKeyEx` does not create the key if it does not exist. Instead it returns an error code. After the application is finished with the registry key, it should use the `RegCloseKey` function to close it.
Syntax	LONG **RegOpenKeyEx**(HKEY *hKey,* LPCTSTR *lpszSubKey,* DWORD *dwReserved,* REGSAM *samDesired,* PHKEY *phkResult*)
Parameters	
hKey	**HKEY**: The handle of a key that is the parent key of the subkey to be opened. This may be any open key or one of the predefined subkeys **HKEY_CLASSES_ROOT, HKEY_CURRENT_USER, HKEY_USERS,** or **HKEY_LOCAL_MACHINE.**
lpszSubKey	**LPCTSTR**: A pointer to a null-terminated string that contains the name of the subkey to open.
dwReserved	**DWORD**: Reserved. Set to **0**.
samDesired	**REGSAM**: Security access mask. See Table 19-4.
phkResult	**PHKEY**: A pointer to location where the handle to the key is stored.

Returns	LONG: If successful, **ERROR_SUCCESS** is returned; otherwise, an error code is returned.
Include File	winreg.h
See Also	RegCloseKey
Example	See the example for **RegCreateKeyEx**.

RegQueryInfoKey ■ WINDOWS 95 ■ WINDOWS NT

Description	**RegQueryInfoKey** returns information that describes a given registry key. The key handle must have **KEY_QUERY_VALUE** access.
Syntax	LONG **RegQueryInfoKey**(HKEY *hKey,* LPTSTR *lpClass,* LPDWORD *lpdwClass,* LPDWORD *lpdwReserved,* LPDWORD *lpdwSubKeys,* LPDWORD *lpdwMaxSubKey,* LPDWORD *lpdwMaxClass,* LPDWORD *lpdwValues,* LPDWORD *lpdwMaxValueName,* LPDWORD *lpdwMaxValueData,* LPDWORD *lpdwSecurityDesc,* PFILETIME *lpftLastWriteTime*)
Parameters	
hKey	HKEY: The handle of a key that is the parent key of the subkey to be opened. This may be any open key or one of the predefined keys **HKEY_CLASSES_ROOT**, **HKEY_CURRENT_USER**, **HKEY_USERS**, or **HKEY_LOCAL_MACHINE**.
lpClass	LPTSTR: A pointer to a buffer that receives the class name of the key.
lpdwClass	LPDWORD: A pointer to a **DWORD** that specifies the size of the buffer pointed to by the *lpClass* parameter before the call. This size includes the null-terminating character. When the function returns, the value of *lpdwClass* is the number of bytes copied to *lpClass*. The count returned does not include the terminating null character. If there are not enough characters in the buffer, error **ERROR_MORE_DATA** occurs, and the contents of *lpdwClass* indicates how many bytes are needed.
lpdwReserved	LPDWORD: Reserved, set to **NULL**.
lpdwSubKeys	LPDWORD: A pointer to a **DWORD** that receives the number of subkeys for the specified key, *hKey*.
lpdwMaxSubKey	LPDWORD: A pointer to a **DWORD** that receives the length of the longest name of any subkey of the specified key. This length does not include the null-terminating character in its count.
lpdwMaxClass	LPDWORD: A pointer to a **DWORD** that receives the length of the longest name of any class for any subkey of the specified key of this key. This length does not include the null-terminating character in its count.
lpdwValues	LPDWORD: A pointer to a **DWORD** that receives the number of values for the specified key.

lpdwMaxValueName	LPDWORD: A pointer to a DWORD that receives the number of characters in the longest name of any value. This does not include a null-terminating character in its count.
lpdwMaxValueData	LPDWORD: A pointer to a DWORD that receives the number of characters in the longest data component of any value of the key.
lpdwSecurityDesc	LPDWORD: A pointer to a DWORD that receives the number of bytes of the key security descriptor.
lpftLastWriteTime	PFILETIME: A pointer to a FILETIME structure that receives the last time the key or any of its values was modified. A FILETIME structure is a 64-bit quantity that represents the number of 100-nanosecond intervals between the time and January 1, 1601. See the definition of the FILETIME structure under the CompareFileTime function in Chapter 17, I/O with Files.
Returns	LONG: If successful, ERROR_SUCCESS is returned; otherwise, an error code is returned. If ERROR_MORE_DATA is returned, increase the size of the *lpszClassName* buffer.
Include File	winreg.h
See Also	RegEnumKeyEx, RegEnumValue
Example	See the example for the RegEnumKeyEx function.

RegQueryMultipleValues   ■ Windows 95   ■ Windows NT

Description	RegQueryMultipleValues retrieves the type and data for a list of value names associated with an open registry key. This function allows an application to query one or more values of a key with a single function call. If the key is a static key, the system provides all of the values. To prevent excessive serialization, the aggregate data returned by the function cannot exceed 1 megabyte. If the target key is a dynamic key, its provider must provide all the values. This means the provider should fill the results buffer synchronously, providing a consistent view of all the values in the buffer while avoiding excessive serialization. The provider can provide at most 1 megabyte of total output data during a call to this function.

This function is supported remotely; therefore, the key can be that of a remote computer. |
Syntax	LONG **RegQueryMultipleValues**(HKEY *hKey,* PVALENT *val_list,* DWORD *num_vals,* LPTSTR *lpValueBuf,* LPDWORD *lpdwTotSize*)
Parameters	
hKey	HKEY: A currently open key or any of the predefined reserved handle values; HKEY_CLASSES_ROOT, HKEY_CURRENT_USER, HKEY_LOCAL_MACHINE, or HKEY_USERS.

val_list	PVALENT: The address to an array of **VALENT** structures that describe one or more value entries. On input, the **ve_valuename** member of each structure must contain a pointer to the name of the value to retrieve. The function fails if any of the specified values do not exist in the specified key. If the function is successful, each element of the array contains the information for the specified value. See the definition of the **VALENT** structure below.
num_vals	DWORD: The number of elements in the *val_list* array.
lpValueBuf	LPTSTR: A pointer to a buffer that receives the data for each value. If set to **NULL**, the function returns successfully and *lpdwTotSize* returns the required size, in bytes, of the buffer.
lpdwTotSize	LPDWORD: A pointer to a **DWORD** value that specifies the size, in bytes, of the buffer pointed to by the *lpValueBuf* parameter. If *lpValueBuf* is **NULL**, the size, in bytes, of the buffer required to retrieve the data is returned.
Returns	LONG: If successful, **ERROR_SUCCESS** is returned; otherwise, **ERROR_CANTREAD** is returned if the provider of a dynamic key cannot be accessed, **ERROR_MORE_DATA** is returned if the buffer is too small, in which case *lpdwTotSize* receives the size required, or **ERROR_TRANSFER_TOO_LONG** if the total length of the requested data (size of *val_list* + *lpdwTotSize*) is more than the system limit of 1 megabyte.
Include File	winreg.h
See Also	RegQueryValueEx

VALENT Definition

```
typedef struct value_ent
{
    LPTSTR ve_valuename;
    DWORD  ve_valuelen;
    DWORD  ve_valueptr;
    DWORD  ve_type;
}VALENT;
```

Members

ve_valuename	LPTSTR: A pointer to a null-terminated string that contains the name of the value to retrieve.
ve_valuelen	DWORD: The size, in bytes, of the data pointed to by *ve_valueptr*.
ve_valueptr	DWORD: A pointer to the data for the value entry. This is a pointer to the value's data returned in the *lpValueBuf* buffer filled by RegQueryMultipleValues.
ve_type	DWORD: The type of the value entry. This can be one of the values listed in Table 19-5.
Example	This example queries the first 10 Windows Explorer tips from the registry and puts them into a list view control when the user selects the Test! menu item. All the items are queried with a single call to the RegQueryMultipleValues function.

```
HWND hList;

LRESULT CALLBACK WndProc( HWND hWnd, UINT uMsg, WPARAM wParam, LPARAM lParam )
{
    switch( uMsg )
    {
        case WM_COMMAND :
                switch( LOWORD( wParam ) )
                {
                    case IDM_TEST :
                        {
                            int     i;
                            TCHAR   szNames[10][3];
                            VALENT  values[10];
                            HKEY    hKey;
                            DWORD   dwSize;

                            memset( values, 0, sizeof( values ) );
                            ListView_DeleteAllItems( hList );

                            // Fill the names of all the items
                            // we want to retrieve.
                            //.................................
                            for( i = 0; i < 10; i++ )
                            {
                                wsprintf( szNames[i], "%d", i );
                                values[i].ve_valuename = szNames[i];
                            }

                            // Open the registry key where
                            // the values are located.
                            //.............................
                            RegOpenKeyEx( HKEY_LOCAL_MACHINE,
                                "SOFTWARE\\Microsoft\\Windows\\CurrentVersion"
                                "\\Explorer\\Tips", 0, KEY_ALL_ACCESS, &hKey );

                            // Query the size of the buffer required.
                            //.......................................
                            if ( RegQueryMultipleValues( hKey, values, 10,
                                        NULL, &dwSize ) == ERROR_MORE_DATA )
                            {
                                // Allocate the buffer and query the actual values.
                                //.................................................
                                LV_ITEM item;
                                LPTSTR  lpBuf = (LPTSTR)HeapAlloc( GetProcessHeap(),
                                                            HEAP_ZERO_MEMORY, dwSize );

                                RegQueryMultipleValues( hKey, values, 10, lpBuf, &dwSize );

                                // Place the values into the ListView.
                                //....................................
                                item.mask = LVIF_TEXT;
                                for (i = 0 ; i < 10 ; i++)
                                {
                                    item.iItem = i;
                                    item.iSubItem = 0;
                                    item.pszText = values[i].ve_valuename;
                                    ListView_InsertItem( hList, &item );
```

```
            item.pszText = (LPTSTR)values[i].ve_valueptr;
            item.iSubItem = 1;
            ListView_SetItem( hList, &item );
        }
        HeapFree( GetProcessHeap(), 0, lpBuf );
    }
    RegCloseKey( hKey );
}
break;
```

.
.
.

RegQueryValueEx ■ WINDOWS 95 ■ WINDOWS NT

Description	RegQueryValueEx returns the type and data for a specified value name associated with an open registry key.
Syntax	LONG **RegQueryValueEx**(HKEY *hKey,* LPCTSTR *lpszSubKey,* LPTSTR *lpszValueName,* LPDWORD *lpdwReserved,* LPDWORD *lpdwType,* LPBYTE *lpData,* LPDWORD *lpdwData*)
Parameters	
hKey	HKEY: The open registry key that contains the value to query. This may be any open key or one of the predefined keys **HKEY_CLASSES_ROOT**, **HKEY_CURRENT_USER**, **HKEY_USERS**, or **HKEY_LOCAL_MACHINE**.
lpszSubKey	LPCTSTR: A pointer to a null-terminated string that contains the name of the key whose value is to be queried.
lpszValueName	LPTSTR: A pointer to a null-terminated string that contains the name of the value to be read.
lpdwReserved	LPDWORD: Reserved; set to **NULL**.
lpdwType	LPDWORD: The type of data stored in the value. Table 19-5 lists the variable types that can be stored as values.
lpData	LPBYTE: A pointer to the buffer to receive the data stored in the value.
lpdwData	LPDWORD: A pointer to a **DWORD** variable that contains the number of bytes available in the buffer *lpData*. After the call, the system sets the contents to the number of bytes actually copied.
Returns	LONG: If successful, **ERROR_SUCCESS** is returned; otherwise, an error code is returned.
Include File	winreg.h
See Also	RegQueryInfoKey, RegSetValueEx
Example	When the user selects the Test! option in the example, the name of the default icon used by RTF (Rich Text Format) files is queried from the registry and displayed in a message box. Figure 19-8 shows the result.

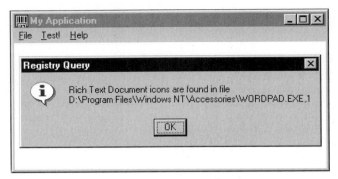

Figure 19-8 `RegQueryValueEx` example

```
LRESULT CALLBACK WndProc( HWND hWnd, UINT uMsg, WPARAM wParam, LPARAM lParam )
{
    switch( uMsg )
    {
        case WM_COMMAND :
                switch( LOWORD( wParam ) )
                {
                    case IDM_TEST:
                        {
                            LONG   lRes1, lRes2;
                            TCHAR  szBuffer[128];
                            TCHAR  szName[64];
                            TCHAR  szIconFile[64];
                            HKEY   hKeyIcons;      // RTF default icon key.
                            HKEY   hKeyFileType;   // RTF file key.

                            // Open a key for rtffile.
                            //........................
                            lRes1 = RegOpenKeyEx( HKEY_CLASSES_ROOT,
                                                  "rtffile\\DefaultIcon",
                                                  0, KEY_ALL_ACCESS, &hKeyIcons );

                            lRes2 = RegOpenKeyEx( HKEY_CLASSES_ROOT,
                                                  "rtffile", 0, KEY_ALL_ACCESS,
                                                  &hKeyFileType );

                            if ( ( lRes1==ERROR_SUCCESS ) && ( lRes2==ERROR_SUCCESS ) )
                            {
                                DWORD dwType;
                                DWORD dwBytes = 64;

                                // Retrieve the document name.
                                //...........................
                                RegQueryValueEx( hKeyFileType, "", 0, &dwType,
                                                 szName, &dwBytes );

                                dwBytes = 64;
                                // Retrieve the icon file name.
                                //............................
                                RegQueryValueEx( hKeyIcons, "", 0, &dwType,
                                                 szIconFile, &dwBytes );
```

```
                    // Make message.
                    //..............
                    wsprintf( szBuffer, "%s icons are found in file\n%s",
                            szName, szIconFile );
            }
            else
                strcpy( szBuffer, "Rich Text File Information Not Found" );

            if ( lRes1 == ERROR_SUCCESS ) RegCloseKey( hKeyIcons );
            if ( lRes2 == ERROR_SUCCESS ) RegCloseKey( hKeyFileType );

            MessageBox( hWnd, szBuffer, "Registry Query",
                    MB_OK | MB_ICONINFORMATION);
        }
        break;
```

.
.
.

RegReplaceKey ■ WINDOWS 95 ■ WINDOWS NT

Description	RegReplaceKey replaces the file backing a key and all its subkeys with another file, so that when the system is next started, the key and subkeys will have the values stored in the new file. On Windows NT, the calling process must have SE_RESTORE_NAME privilege.
Syntax	LONG **RegReplaceKey**(HKEY *hKey,* LPCTSTR *lpSubKey,* LPCTSTR *lpNewFile,* LPCTSTR *lpOldFile*)
Parameters	
hKey	HKEY: Identifies a currently open key. This may be any open key or one of the predefined keys HKEY_CLASSES_ROOT, HKEY_CURRENT_USER, HKEY_USERS, or HKEY_LOCAL_MACHINE.
lpSubKey	LPCTSTR: A pointer to a null-terminated string containing the name of a key whose subkeys and values are replaced by this function. This key must be a subkey of the key identified by the *hKey* parameter. This parameter can be NULL.
lpNewFile	LPCTSTR: A pointer to a null-terminated string containing the name of the file with registration information. This file is typically created by using the RegSaveKey function. When using the FAT file system, the file name cannot have an extension.
lpOldFile	LPCTSTR: A pointer to a null-terminated string containing the name of a file that receives a backup copy of the registry information being replaced. When using the FAT file system, the file name cannot have an extension.
Returns	LONG: If successful, ERROR_SUCCESS is returned; otherwise, a nonzero error code defined in WINERROR.H is returned. Use the FormatMessage function with the FORMAT_MESSAGE_FROM_SYSTEM flag to get a generic description of the error.

Include File	winreg.h
See Also	RegConnectRegistry, RegDeleteKey, RegLoadKey, RegRestoreKey

RegRestoreKey   ■ WINDOWS 95   ■ WINDOWS NT

Description	RegRestoreKey restores the values of a subkey and its subkeys from a file. The restored values completely overwrite the contents of the subkey (including all its subkeys) in memory. This is a destructive replace where the only data about the key that is preserved is the name of the key. Subkeys and values that existed in the node being restored but do not exist in the file copy will be destroyed. This operation will fail if any subkey of the given key is open.
Syntax	LONG **RegRestoreKey**(HKEY *hKey*, LPCTSTR *lpszFile,* DWORD *dwFlags*)
Parameters	
hKey	HKEY: This may be any currently open key or one of the predefined reserved key handles HKEY_CLASSES_ROOT, HKEY_CURRENT_USER, HKEY_LOCAL_MACHINE, or HKEY_USERS.
lpszFile	LPCTSTR: Pointer to a null-terminated string that contains the name of the hive that contains the registry data for the new subkey. This hive file is created using RegSaveKey. Note that under FAT file systems the file name may not have an extension.
dwFlags	DWORD: Set to REG_WHOLE_HIVE_VOLATILE to create a volatile hive that is only stored in memory. This is a new set of registry information that will exist until the system is shut down. If this flag is specified, *hKey* may be only HKEY_USERS or HKEY_LOCAL_MACHINE.
Returns	LONG: ERROR_SUCCESS if function is successful; otherwise, an error code is returned.
Include File	winreg.h
See Also	RegLoadKey, RegUnLoadKey, RegDeleteKey, RegSaveKey
Example	See the example for RegLoadKey.

RegSaveKey   ■ WINDOWS 95   ■ WINDOWS NT

Description	RegSaveKey saves the contents of the registry to a hive, a file that can be reloaded using RegLoadKey or RegRestoreKey.
Syntax	LONG **RegSaveKey**(HKEY *hKey,* LPCTSTR *lpszFile,* LPSECURITY_ATTRIBUTES *lpsaSecurity*)

Parameters

hKey
HKEY: Any currently open key or one of the predefined reserved key handles HKEY_CLASSES_ROOT, HKEY_CURRENT_USER, HKEY_LOCAL_MACHINE, or HKEY_USERS. This handle must have KEY_SET_VALUE access.

lpszFile
LPCTSTR: Pointer to a null-terminated string that contains the name of the file that will contain the registry data for the new subkey. Note that under FAT file systems the file name may not have an extension or it cannot be used by RegLoadKey or RegRestoreKey.

lpsaSecurity
LPSECURITY_ATTRIBUTES: The security attributes of the new file. If this is set to NULL, the file will receive default security attributes and not be inheritable.

Returns
LONG: ERROR_SUCCESS if function is successful; otherwise, an error code is returned.

Include File
winreg.h

See Also
RegLoadKey, RegUnLoadKey, RegRestoreKey, RegDeleteKey

Example
See the example for RegLoadKey.

RegSetValueEx ■ WINDOWS 95 ■ WINDOWS NT

Description
RegSetValueEx sets a named value of any registry subkey. Under Windows NT and Windows 95 there may be multiple named values for any given subkey.

Syntax
LONG **RegSetValueEx**(HKEY *hKey,* LPCTSTR *lpszValueName,* DWORD *dwReserved,* DWORD *dwDataType,* CONST BYTE* *lpData,* DWORD *dwBytes*)

Parameters

hKey
HKEY: The parent key of the subkey whose value is to be set. This may be any open key or one of the predefined keys HKEY_CLASSES_ROOT, HKEY_CURRENT_USER, HKEY_USERS, or HKEY_LOCAL_MACHINE. To open the key, you must use RegOpenKeyEx or RegCreateKeyEx.

lpszValueName
LPCTSTR: Pointer to a null-terminated string that contains the name of the value whose data is to be set. If this is NULL and data type *dwDataType* is REG_SZ, the contents are written to the default value of Windows 3.1x.

dwReserved
DWORD: Reserved; set to 0.

dwDataType
DWORD: The type of data to be stored. See Table 19-5 for data types available.

lpData
CONST BYTE*: Pointer to the data to be stored in the value. Data stored in the registry is limited by memory. Large values should be stored in files, and the file names should be stored in the registry.

dwBytes	DWORD: Length of data to store, not including the null-terminating character.
Returns	LONG: ERROR_SUCCESS if the operation is successful; otherwise, an error code is returned.
Include File	winreg.h
See Also	RegQueryValueEx, RegQueryInfoKey, RegQueryValueEx
Example	See the example for RegCreateKeyEx.

RegUnLoadKey ■ WINDOWS 95 ■ WINDOWS NT

Description	RegUnLoadKey removes a hive key and its subkeys from the registry.
Syntax	LONG **RegUnLoadKey**(HKEY *hKey,* LPCTSTR *lpszSubKey*)
Parameters	
hKey	HKEY: The key to remove; this may be HKEY_USER, HKEY_LOCAL_MACHINE, or the return value of RegConnectRegistry, which is a registry node on another computer.
lpszSubKey	LPCTSTR: Pointer to a null-terminated string that contains the name of the key to remove. All of its subkeys and values will also be removed. The key must be created with RegLoadKey.
Returns	LONG: ERROR_SUCCESS if function is successful; otherwise, an error code is returned.
Include File	winreg.h
See Also	RegSaveKey, RegRestoreKey, RegDeleteKey
Example	See the example for RegLoadKey.

20

INITIALIZATION FILES

Initialization files (often called INI files because their common file extension is `.INI`) are sequential text files that are used for storing system configuration data. Initialization files are the most common method of storing configuration data in Windows 3.x. INI files allow applications to store configuration data separately from that of other applications. Also, using INI files, an application may logically group related settings.

The Win32 API fully supports the initialization file functions for backward compatibility with 16-bit applications. However, it is recommended and even required (for logo compliance) that Win32 applications store their configuration data in the system registry (see Chapter 19, The Registry).

Initialization File Structure

Divisions within the INI file are known as *sections* and are demarcated by bracketed strings called *section names*. Within each section any number of keys can be stored. A key is simply a named configuration setting that can be set or queried programmatically. A key assignment consists of the *key name* (or *tag*), the equal sign, and the *key value*, which is the value returned by the system for the key. You may have only one key assignment per line. Comments are denoted by a semicolon. You may not place comments on section name lines. A sample section of an INI file may look like this:

```
[PREFERENCES]
COLOR = BLUE          ;  This is a comment.
SHAPE = CIRCLE

; A comment may be on a line by itself as well.
LETTERS="a;b;c;d"    ; Semicolons are allowed in a quoted key value.
```

Any number of spaces may be placed between the key name and the equal sign or the key value and the equal sign. Section names and key names in INI files are stored in the same case in which they are first written. Searches for section names and key names are always case insensitive.

Accessing Initialization Files

Most initialization files are also private profile files. This term originated in Windows 3.1 to distinguish application INI files from **WIN.INI** (the only INI file before Windows 3.1). The functions **WritePrivateProfileString** and **WritePrivateProfileInt** store string and integer key values respectively in a private profile file. **GetPrivateProfileString** and **GetPrivateProfileInt** retrieve string and integer key values respectively from a private profile file. The functions **GetPrivateProfileSection** and **WritePrivateProfileSection** read or write entire sections of an INI file. Also, Win32 has added the API function **GetPrivateProfileSectionNames** that returns all the section names defined in a given INI file.

Private profile files are typically stored either in the Windows directory or in the directory where the corresponding application is installed. By default Windows will search for an INI file in the Windows directory. However, a fully qualified path name to the INI file may be specified when calling private profile initialization file functions, so INI files may actually be placed anywhere.

Applications use a parallel set of API functions to access **WIN.INI**. **GetProfileString** and **GetProfileInt** respectively retrieve string key values and integer key values from **WIN.INI**. **WriteProfileString** and **WriteProfileInt** store string key values and integer key values in **WIN.INI**. **GetProfileSection** and **WriteProfileSection** allow entire sections of the **WIN.INI** file to be read or written. There is, however, nothing remarkable about **WIN.INI**, so the private profile file API functions may also be used, if **WIN.INI** is specified as the INI file name.

Mapping Private INI Files

On Windows NT, private profile functions can be mapped to the registry instead of the specified initialization files. This mapping occurs when the initialization file and section are specified in the registry under the **HKEY_LOCAL_MACHINE\Software\Microsoft \Windows NT\CurrentVersion\IniFileMapping** key. This mapping is likely if an application modifies system-component initialization files, such as **CONTROL.INI**, **SYSTEM.INI**, and **WINFILE.INI**. In these cases, the private profile functions act upon the information in the registry, not from the initialization file. The Win32 Profile functions use the following steps to locate initialization information.

1. Look in the registry for the name of the INI file under the **HKEY_LOCAL_MACHINE\ Software\Microsoft\Windows NT\CurrentVersion\IniFileMapping** key.

2. Look for the section name as a value under the INI file key or a subkey of the INI file.

3. If the section name is a named value under the INI file, that value specifies where in the registry to find the keys for the section.

4. If the section name is a subkey under the INI file key, named values under that subkey specify where in the registry to find the keys for the section. If the key

does not exist as a named value, there will be an unnamed value that specifies the default location in the registry where the key is found.

5. If there is no subkey for the INI file, or if there is no entry for the section name, the actual INI file is accessed on the disk.

Once the location in the registry is found, there are several prefixes that change the behavior of the INI file mapping. These prefixes are part of the actual location string. For example, a location string for the color schemes in the `CONTROL.INI` file would be `"#USR:Control Panel\Color Schemes"`. Table 20-1 lists the prefixes and how they change the behavior of the location.

Table 20-1 INI file mapping prefixes

Prefix	Description
!	Forces all writes to go both to the registry and the INI file on disk.
#	Causes the registry value to be set to the value in the Windows 3.x INI file when a new user logs in for the first time after setup.
@	Prevents any reads from going to the INI file on disk if the requested data is not found in the registry.
SYS	The text after the prefix is relative to the `HKEY_LOCAL_MACHINE\SOFTWARE` key.
USR	The text after the prefix is relative to the `HKEY_CURRENT_USER` key.

Initialization File Function Descriptions

Table 20-2 summarizes the initialization file functions. Detailed function descriptions follow the table.

Table 20-2 Initialization file function summary

Function	Purpose
GetPrivateProfileInt	Retrieves an integer value for a key in a private initialization file.
GetPrivateProfileSection	Retrieves all the keys and values of a section of a private INI file.
GetPrivateProfileSectionNames	Retrieves all the section names of a private INI file.
GetPrivateProfileString	Retrieves a string value for a key in a private initialization file.
GetPrivateProfileStruct	Retrieves the data for a key in a private initialization file.
GetProfileInt	Retrieves an integer value from the `WIN.INI` file.
GetProfileSection	Retrieves all the keys and values from a section of `WIN.INI`.
GetProfileString	Retrieves a string value from the `WIN.INI` file.
WritePrivateProfileSection	Stores a section of a private INI file with given keys and values.
WritePrivateProfileString	Stores a string value to a key in a private INI file.
WritePrivateProfileStruct	Copies data into a key for a key in a private initialization file.
WriteProfileSection	Stores an entire section with all keys and values in `WIN.INI`.
WriteProfileString	Stores a string value for a key in `WIN.INI`.

GetPrivateProfileInt

Description   GetPrivateProfileInt returns an integer value associated with a key from a specified section of a private profile file.

Syntax   UINT **GetPrivateProfileInt**(LPCTSTR *lpszSectionName,* LPCTSTR *lpszKeyName,* INT *dwDefault,* LPCTSTR *lpszIniFileName*)

Parameters

lpszSectionName   LPCTSTR: A pointer to a null-terminated string that contains the section name.

lpszKeyName   LPCTSTR: A pointer to a null-terminated string that contains the key name.

dwDefault   INT: The default value to return if the specified key is not found.

lpszIniFileName   LPCTSTR: A null-terminated string that contains the name of the INI file. If *lpszIniFileName* does not contain a fully qualified path name to the INI file, Windows will search for the file in the Windows directory.

Returns   UINT: The integer value of the key if it is found in the specified section of the INI file. If the key is not found, the default value, *dwDefault*, is returned. If the key value is less than zero, **0** is returned instead.

Include File   winbase.h

See Also   GetProfileInt, WritePrivateProfileString, GetPrivateProfileString

Example   The key value for the **Ticks** key in the **TestSection** section of **YOUR.INI** is shown every time the window is painted. Choosing the Test! option writes the current tick count as the key value for **Ticks** and then repaints the window. Figure 20-1 shows the test results.

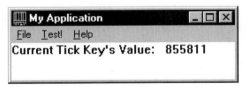

Figure 20-1 GetPrivateProfileInt example

```
LRESULT CALLBACK WndProc( HWND hWnd, UINT uMsg, WPARAM wParam, LPARAM lParam )
{
    switch( uMsg )
    {
        case WM_PAINT:
            {
                // Display contents of Ticks key.
                //............................
                PAINTSTRUCT ps;
                TCHAR szBuffer[128];

                BeginPaint( hWnd, &ps );
```

```
            wsprintf( szBuffer, "Current Tick Key's Value: %8lu",
                    GetPrivateProfileInt( "TestSection",
                                "Ticks", 0, "YOUR.INI" ) );

            TextOut( ps.hdc, 0, 0, szBuffer, strlen( szBuffer ) );
            EndPaint( hWnd, &ps );
        }
        break ;

case WM_COMMAND :
        switch( LOWORD( wParam ) )
        {
          case IDM_TEST:
              {
                  // Write the tick count to the INI file
                  //....................................
                  TCHAR szBuffer[16];
                  wsprintf( szBuffer, "%ld", GetTickCount() );

                  WritePrivateProfileString( "TestSection",
                              "Ticks", szBuffer, "YOUR.INI" );

                  InvalidateRect( hWnd, NULL, TRUE );
                  UpdateWindow( hWnd );
              }
              break;
      .
      .
      .
```

GetPrivateProfileSection   ■ WINDOWS 95   ■ WINDOWS NT

Description   GetPrivateProfileSection fills a supplied buffer with key assignments of a specified section of an INI file. Key assignments are of the form *key=value*. The buffer will consist of a set of sequential null-terminated key assignment strings. The last string in the buffer is terminated by two null characters. In Windows 95, the size of the section being read may not exceed 32K. Windows automatically locks out all updates to the initialization file while the key assignments are being copied into the buffer.

Syntax   DWORD **GetPrivateProfileSection**(LPCTSTR *lpszSectionName*, LPTSTR *lpReturnBuffer*, DWORD *dwcBuffer*, LPCTSTR *lpszIniFileName*)

Parameters

lpszSectionName   LPCTSTR: Pointer to a null-terminated string that contains the section name.

lpReturnBuffer   LPTSTR: Pointer to a buffer that receives the section contents.

dwcBuffer   DWORD: Size of the buffer, *lpReturnBuffer*, that receives the data.

lpszIniFileName   LPCTSTR: Pointer to a null-terminated string that is the name of the private profile file. If *lpszIniFileName* does not contain a fully qualified path name to the file, Windows will search for the INI file in the Windows directory.

Returns	DWORD: The number of characters copied to the buffer, not including the null-terminating character. If not enough space is available to store all the key assignments for the section, the return value is *dwcBuffer*–2.
Include File	winbase.h
See Also	GetProfileSection, WritePrivateProfileSection
Example	The program that produces the output of Figure 20-2 reads the key assignments of the groups section of **PROGMAN.INI** into a list box.

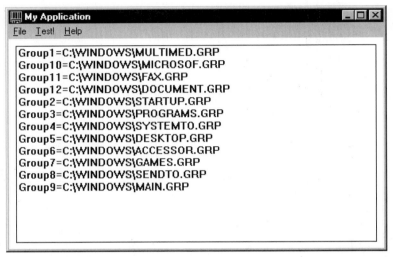

Figure 20-2 GetPrivateProfileSection example

```
HWND hList = NULL;

LRESULT CALLBACK WndProc(HWND hWnd, UINT uMsg, WPARAM wParam, LPARAM lParam)
{
    switch (uMsg)
    {
        case WM_CREATE:
            hList = CreateWindowEx( WS_EX_CLIENTEDGE, "listbox", "",
                                    WS_CHILD | WS_VISIBLE | LBS_STANDARD,
                                    0, 0, 20, 20, hWnd,
                                    (HMENU)101, hInst, NULL );
            break;

        case WM_SIZE :
            if ( wParam != SIZE_MINIMIZED )
                MoveWindow( hList, 0, 0, LOWORD( lParam ), HIWORD( lParam ), TRUE
);
            break;

        case WM_COMMAND:
            switch ( LOWORD( wParam )  )
            {
```

```
case IDM_TEST:
    if ( hList )
    {
        LPTSTR lpTemp;

        // Allocate memory for the data.
        //..............................
        LPTSTR lpBuf = (LPTSTR)HeapAlloc( GetProcessHeap(),
                                 HEAP_ZERO_MEMORY, 0x7FFF );

        SendMessage( hList, LB_RESETCONTENT, 0, 0 );
        GetPrivateProfileSection( "groups",
                    lpBuf, 0x7FFF, "progman.ini");

        // Fill list box until the end of the buffer.
        //............................................
        lpTemp = lpBuf;
        while ( *lpTemp )
        {
            SendMessage( hList, LB_ADDSTRING, 0, (LPARAM)lpTemp );

            // increment past the NULL.
            //.........................
            lpTemp += (strlen(lpTemp) + 1);
        }
        HeapFree( GetProcessHeap(), 0, lpBuf );
    }
    break;
```

.
.
.

GetPrivateProfileSectionNames ■ WINDOWS 95 ■ WINDOWS NT

Description   GetPrivateProfileSectionNames fills a buffer with the names of all the sections of an INI file. The contents of the filled buffer is a list of null-terminated strings. The last section name is followed by an additional null character. While this function is executing, updates to the INI file are blocked by the system.

Syntax   DWORD **GetPrivateProfileSectionNames**(LPTSTR *lpszReturnBuffer*, DWORD *dwBuffer*, LPCTSTR *lpszIniFileName*)

Parameters

lpszReturnBuffer   LPTSTR: Pointer to a buffer to receive the list of section names.

dwBuffer   DWORD: Size of the buffer that receives the list of section names.

lpszIniFileName   LPCTSTR: Pointer to a null-terminated string that is the name of the private profile file. If *lpszIniFileName* does not contain a fully qualified path name to the file, Windows will search for the initialization file in the Windows directory.

Returns   DWORD: The number of bytes that is returned by the system in the *lpszReturnBuffer*. This count does not include the final null-terminating character. If there is not enough room in the buffer to store all the section names, *dwBuffer*–2 is returned and the list of section names will be truncated.

Include File   `winbase.h`

Example   When the user chooses the Test! option from the menu, a list box is filled with the section names of the **WIN.INI** file. Any INI could have been chosen, but the **WIN.INI** file contains more recognizable sections than other INI files—there are sections for fonts, internationalization, and desktop settings, for instance.

```
HWND hList = NULL;

LRESULT CALLBACK WndProc(HWND hWnd, UINT uMsg, WPARAM wParam, LPARAM lParam)
{
    switch (uMsg)
    {
        case WM_CREATE:
                hList = CreateWindowEx( WS_EX_CLIENTEDGE, "listbox", "",
                                        WS_CHILD | WS_VISIBLE | LBS_STANDARD,
                                        0, 0, 20, 20, hWnd,
                                        (HMENU)101, hInst, NULL );
                break;

        case WM_SIZE :
                if ( wParam != SIZE_MINIMIZED )
                    MoveWindow( hList, 0, 0, LOWORD( lParam ), HIWORD( lParam ), TRUE );
                break;

        case WM_COMMAND:
                switch ( LOWORD( wParam )  )
                {
                    case IDM_TEST:
                        if ( hList )
                        {
                            LPTSTR lpTemp;
                            LPTSTR lpBuf = HeapAlloc( GetProcessHeap(),
                                                      HEAP_ZERO_MEMORY,
                                                      0x7FFF );

                            SendMessage( hList, LB_RESETCONTENT, 0, 0 );

                            GetPrivateProfileSectionNames( lpBuf, 0x7FFF, "win.ini");

                            // Fill list box until the end of the buffer.
                            //..............................................
                            lpTemp = lpBuf;
                            while ( *lpTemp )
                            {
                                SendMessage( hList, LB_ADDSTRING, 0, (LPARAM)lpTemp );

                                // jump past null
                                //...............
                                lpTemp += lstrlen(lpTemp) + 1;
                            }
                            HeapFree( GetProcessHeap(), 0, lpBuf );
                        }
```

```
        break;
    .
    .
    .
```

GetPrivateProfileString ■ WINDOWS 95 ■ WINDOWS NT

Description   GetPrivateProfileString returns a string value associated with a key from a specified section of a private profile file.

Syntax   DWORD **GetPrivateProfileString**(LPCTSTR *lpszSectionName,* LPCTSTR *lpszKeyName,* LPCTSTR *lpszDefaultValue,* LPTSTR *lpszReturnBuffer,* DWORD *dwcBuffer,* LPCTSTR *lpszIniFileName*)

Parameters

lpszSectionName   LPCTSTR: A pointer to a null-terminated string that contains the section name. If this parameter is **NULL**, all section names of the INI file are copied into the buffer instead.

lpszKeyName   LPCTSTR: A pointer to a null-terminated string that contains the key name. If this parameter is **NULL**, all key names of the specified section are copied into the buffer instead.

lpszDefaultValue   LPCTSTR: A pointer to a null-terminated string that contains the default value to return if the key is not found in the specified section.

lpszReturnBuffer   LPTSTR: A pointer to the buffer that will be filled by the system. In the typical case of returning a value associated to a key, this buffer will contain a single zero-terminated string. In the case where section names or key names of an INI file are being retrieved (by specifying *lpszSectionName* or *lpszKeyName* respectively to **NULL**), the buffer is filled with a list of zero-terminated strings, and the last string is terminated by two null characters instead of one.

dwcBuffer   DWORD: The size of the buffer, *lpszReturnBuffer*, that receives the data.

lpszIniFileName   LPCTSTR: A pointer to a null-terminated string that is the name of the private profile file. If *lpszIniFileName* does not contain a fully qualified path name to the INI file, Windows will search for the file in the Windows directory.

Returns   DWORD: If the function is successful, the number of characters copied to the buffer, not including the null-terminating character, is returned. If the buffer is too small to query a key value, the return value is *dwcBuffer*−1. If the buffer is too small for all section names or key names to be returned (when *lpszSectionName* or *lpszKeyName* are respectively set to **NULL**), the return value is *dwcBuffer*−2.

Include File   winbase.h

See Also   GetProfileString, WritePrivateProfileString, GetPrivateProfileInt

Example   The key value for the **TickString** key in the **TestSection** section of
YOUR.INI is shown every time the window is painted. Choosing the Test!
option writes the current tick count as the key value for **TickString** and
then repaints the window.

```
TCHAR szBuffer[64];

LRESULT CALLBACK WndProc( HWND hWnd, UINT uMsg, WPARAM wParam, LPARAM lParam )
{
   switch (uMsg)
   {
      case WM_PAINT:
         {
            PAINTSTRUCT ps;

            GetPrivateProfileString( "TestSection", "TickString",
                              "TickString Not Set",  szBuffer, sizeof( szBuffer ),
                              "YOUR.INI" );

            BeginPaint( hWnd, &ps );
            TextOut( ps.hdc, 0, 0, szBuffer, lstrlen( szBuffer ) );
            EndPaint( hWnd, &ps );
         }
         break ;

      case WM_COMMAND:
            switch ( LOWORD( wParam ) )
               {
               case IDM_TEST:
                  wsprintf(szBuffer, "%d Ticks have passed.", GetTickCount());
                  WritePrivateProfileString( "TestSection",
                                 "TickString", szBuffer,
                                 "YOUR.INI" );

                  InvalidateRect( hWnd, NULL, TRUE );
                  UpdateWindow( hWnd );
                  break;
            .
            .
            .
```

GetPrivateProfileStruct   ■ WINDOWS 95   ■ WINDOWS NT

Description   GetPrivateProfileStruct retrieves the data associated with the specified
key in a given section of an initialization file. As the function retrieves the
data, the function calculates a checksum and compares it with the checksum calculated by the **WritePrivateProfileStruct** function when the
data was added to the file.

Syntax   BOOL **GetPrivateProfileStruct**(LPCTSTR *lpszSection*, LPCTSTR
lpszKey, LPVOID *lpStruct*, UINT *uSizeStruct*, LPCTSTR *lpszFile*)

Parameters

lpszSection	LPCTSTR: A pointer to a null-terminated string that contains the section name in the initialization file.
lpszKey	LPCTSTR: A pointer to a null-terminated string that contains the key name whose data is to be retrieved.
lpStruct	LPVOID: A pointer to a buffer that receives the data associated with the file, section, and key names.
uSizeStruct	UINT: The size, in bytes, of the buffer pointed to by the *lpStruct* parameter.
lpszFile	LPCTSTR: A pointer to a null-terminated string that names the initialization file. If this parameter does not contain a full path to the file, Windows searches for the file in the Windows directory.
Returns	BOOL: If successful, TRUE is returned; otherwise, FALSE is returned.
Include File	winbase.h
See Also	WritePrivateProfileStruct

GetProfileInt   ■ WINDOWS 95   ■ WINDOWS NT

Description	GetProfileInt returns an integer value associated with a key from a specified section of the WIN.INI file.
Syntax	UINT **GetProfileInt**(LPCTSTR *lpszSectionName,* LPCTSTR *lpszKeyName,* INT *dwDefault*)

Parameters

lpszSectionName	LPCTSTR: A pointer to a null-terminated string that contains the section name.
lpszKeyName	LPCTSTR: A pointer to a null-terminated string that contains the key name.
dwDefault	INT: The value returned if the key is not found in the specified section of the WIN.INI file.
Returns	UINT: If the key is found in the specified section of the WIN.INI file, the integer value of the key is returned. If the key is not found, the default *dwDefault* is returned. If the key value is less than zero, 0 is returned instead.
Include File	winbase.h
See Also	GetPrivateProfileInt, WriteProfileString
Example	When the user selects the Test! option, the currency number and the number of currency digits is read and displayed.

```
LRESULT CALLBACK WndProc( HWND hWnd, UINT uMsg, WPARAM wParam, LPARAM lParam )
{
    switch (uMsg)    // Process Windows messages.
```

continued on next page

continued from previous page

```
{
    case WM_PAINT:
        {
            PAINTSTRUCT ps;
            TCHAR szBuffer[128];

            UINT uCurrency = GetProfileInt( "Intl", "iCurrency", 0 );
            UINT uCurrencyDigits = GetProfileInt( "Intl", "iCurrDigits", 0 );

            BeginPaint( hWnd, &ps );

            wsprintf( szBuffer, "Currency setting is %d. Number of currency digits is %d.",
                      uCurrency, uCurrencyDigits);
            TextOut( ps.hdc, 0, 0, szBuffer, lstrlen(szBuffer) );
            EndPaint( hWnd, &ps );
        }
        break;
        .
        .
        .
```

GetProfileSection ■ Windows 95 ■ Windows NT

Description	**GetProfileSection** fills a supplied buffer with key assignments of a specified section of the **WIN.INI** file. Key assignments are of the form *key=value*. The buffer will consist of a set of sequential zero-terminated strings of this form. The last string will be terminated by an additional null character. Under Windows 95, the size of the section being read may not exceed 32K.
Syntax	DWORD **GetProfileSection**(LPCTSTR *lpszSectionName,* LPTSTR *lpReturnBuffer,* DWORD *dwBuffer*)
Parameters	
lpszSectionName	LPCTSTR: A pointer to a null-terminated string that contains the section name.
lpReturnBuffer	LPTSTR: A pointer to a buffer that receives the contents of the section.
dwBuffer	DWORD: The size of the buffer.
Returns	DWORD: The number of characters copied to the buffer, not including the null-terminating character. If there is not enough space available to store all the key assignments for the section, the return value is *dwBuffer*–2.
Include File	winbase.h
See Also	GetPrivateProfileSection, WritePrivateProfileSection
Example	Figure 20-3 shows the output of the test program that retrieves the key assignments for the ports section of the **WIN.INI** file.

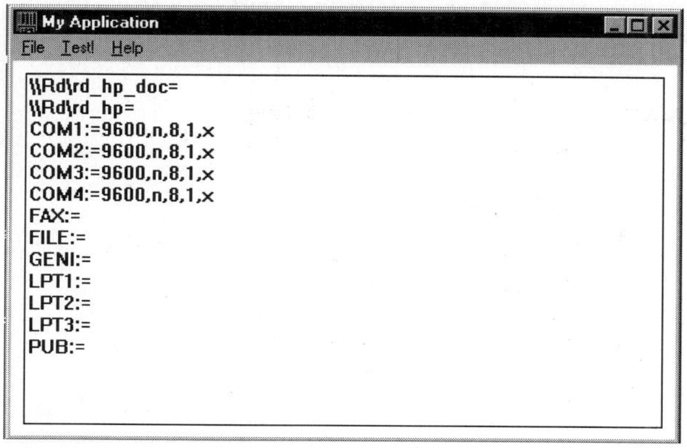

Figure 20-3 GetProfileSection example

```
HWND hList = NULL;

LRESULT CALLBACK WndProc(HWND hWnd, UINT uMsg, WPARAM wParam, LPARAM lParam)
{
    switch (uMsg)
    {
        case WM_CREATE:
                hList = CreateWindowEx( WS_EX_CLIENTEDGE, "listbox", "",
                                        WS_CHILD | WS_VISIBLE | LBS_STANDARD,
                                        0, 0, 20, 20, hWnd,
                                        (HMENU)101, hInst, NULL );
                break;

        case WM_SIZE :
                if ( wParam != SIZE_MINIMIZED )
                    MoveWindow( hList, 0, 0, LOWORD( lParam ), HIWORD( lParam ), TRUE );
                break;

        case WM_COMMAND:
                switch ( LOWORD( wParam )  )
                {
                    case IDM_TEST:
                        if ( hList )
                        {
                            LPTSTR lpTemp;
                            LPTSTR lpBuf = HeapAlloc( GetProcessHeap(),
                                                      HEAP_ZERO_MEMORY,
                                                      0x7FFF );

                            SendMessage( hList, LB_RESETCONTENT, 0, 0 );

                            GetProfileSection( "ports", lpBuf, 0x7fff );

                            // Fill list box until the end of the buffer.
                            //.........................................
                            lpTemp = lpBuf;
                            while ( *lpTemp )
```

continued on next page

continued from previous page

```
                    {
                        SendMessage( hList, LB_ADDSTRING, 0, (LPARAM)lpTemp );

                        // jump past null
                        //..............
                        lpTemp += lstrlen(lpTemp) + 1;
                    }
                    HeapFree( GetProcessHeap(), 0, lpBuf );
                }
                break;
```

.
.
.

GetProfileString   ■ WINDOWS 95   ■ WINDOWS NT

Description	GetProfileString returns a string value associated with a key from a specified section of the **WIN.INI** file.
Syntax	DWORD **GetProfileString**(LPCTSTR *lpszSectionName,* LPCTSTR *lpszKeyName,* LPCTSTR *lpszDefaultValue,* LPTSTR *lpszReturnBuffer,* DWORD *dwBuffer*)
Parameters	
lpszSectionName	LPCTSTR: A pointer to a null-terminated string that contains the section name. If this parameter is **NULL**, all section names of the INI file are copied into the buffer instead.
lpszKeyName	LPCTSTR: A pointer to a null-terminated string that contains the key name. If this value is **NULL**, all key names of the specified section are copied into the buffer instead.
lpszDefaultValue	LPCTSTR: A pointer to a null-terminated string that contains the value returned by the system if no key is found for the specified section.
lpszReturnBuffer	LPTSTR: A pointer to a buffer that will be filled by the system. In the typical case of returning a single key value, this buffer will contain a single zero-terminated string. In the case where section names or key names of the **WIN.INI** file are being queried (by specifying *lpszSectionName* or *lpszKeyName* respectively to **NULL**), the buffer is filled with a list of zero-terminated strings, and the last string is terminated by two null characters instead of one.
dwBuffer	DWORD: The size of the buffer *lpszReturnBuffer* that receives the data.
Returns	DWORD: If the function is successful, the number of characters copied to the buffer, not including the null-terminating character, is returned. If the buffer is too small to query a key value, the return value is *dwBuffer*−1. If the buffer is too small for all section names or key names to be returned (when *lpszSectionName* or *lpszKeyName* are respectively set to **NULL**), the return value is *dwBuffer*−2.

Include File   `winbase.h`

See Also   `WriteProfileString, GetPrivateProfileString, GetProfileInt`

Example   This program changes the settings for the COM1 communication port. When the user selects the Test! option, the settings of the COM1 port are temporarily changed. When the program exits, the settings return to the original values. Figure 20-4 shows the result.

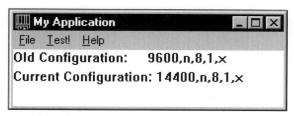

Figure 20-4 `GetProfileString` example

```
LRESULT CALLBACK WndProc( HWND hWnd, UINT uMsg, WPARAM wParam, LPARAM lParam )
{
    static TCHAR szOldConfiguration[64];

    switch( uMsg )
    {
    case WM_CREATE:
            GetProfileString( "Ports",                     // Section Name
                              "COM1:",                     // Key Name
                              "9600,n,8,1,x" ,             // Default COM1 settings
                              szOldConfiguration,          // Old configuration buffer
                              sizeof( szOldConfiguration ) ); // Buffer Size
            break;

    case WM_PAINT:
            {
                PAINTSTRUCT ps;
                TCHAR szBuffer[128];
                TCHAR szCurrentConfiguration[64];

                BeginPaint( hWnd, &ps );

                // Display the old configuration.
                //...............................
                wsprintf( szBuffer, "Old Configuration:    %s", szOldConfiguration );
                TextOut( ps.hdc, 0, 0, szBuffer, strlen( szBuffer ) );


                // Retrieve the new configuration.
                //................................
                GetProfileString( "Ports", "COM1:", "",
                                  szCurrentConfiguration,
                                  sizeof( szCurrentConfiguration ) );
                wsprintf( szBuffer, "Current Configuration: %s",
                          szCurrentConfiguration );
```

continued on next page

continued from previous page

```
                TextOut( ps.hdc, 0, 20, szBuffer, strlen( szBuffer ) );
                EndPaint( hWnd, &ps );
            }
            break;

        case WM_COMMAND:
            switch ( LOWORD( wParam ) )
                {
                case IDM_TEST:
                    // Write the new config to the INI file
                    //.....................................
                    WriteProfileString( "Ports", "COM1:", "14400,n,8,1,x" );

                    InvalidateRect( hWnd, NULL, TRUE );
                    break;
        .
        .
        .
```

WritePrivateProfileSection   ■ WINDOWS 95   ■ WINDOWS NT

Description	**WritePrivateProfileSection** stores a set of key assignments to a specified section of a private profile file. These key assignments replace the contents of the section. Values for keys that exist in a section but not in the list of buffer entries are simply deleted.
Syntax	BOOL **WritePrivateProfileSection**(LPCTSTR *lpszSectionName,* LPCTSTR *lpszSectionData,* LPCTSTR *lpszIniFileName*)
Parameters	
lpszSectionName	LPCTSTR: A pointer to a null-terminated string that contains the section name. If the section name does not exist in the specified INI file, it will be created.
lpszSectionData	LPCTSTR: A pointer to a buffer that contains the keys and values of the section that will be stored. It consists of a list of zero-terminated strings in the form of key assignments: *key=value*. The last string is followed by an extra null character.
lpszIniFileName	LPCTSTR: A pointer to a null-terminated string that contains the name of the private profile file. If *lpszIniFileName* does not contain a fully qualified path name to the file, Windows will search for the file in the Windows directory. If the file does not exist and the fully qualified path name is not specified, Windows will create the profile file in the Windows directory. Windows will not create the profile file if the full path is specified and the file is not found. **WritePrivateProfileString** may be used to create INI files.
Returns	BOOL: **TRUE** if the function is successful. Otherwise, **FALSE** is returned. **GetLastError** returns the error code. Windows 95 keeps **WIN.INI** cached

for performance. If all three parameters are **NULL**, the function flushes the cache to disk.

Include File	`winbase.h`
See Also	`GetPrivateProfileSection`, `WritePrivateProfileString`, `WriteProfileSection`
Example	This example program writes the **TestSection** section of the **YOUR.INI** file when the user chooses the Test! option from the menu.

```
LRESULT CALLBACK WndProc(HWND hWnd, UINT uMsg, WPARAM wParam, LPARAM lParam)
{
    switch (uMsg)
    {
        case WM_COMMAND:
            switch ( LOWORD( wParam ) )
            {
                case IDM_TEST:
                    WritePrivateProfileSection( "TestSection",
                                                "Section Data",
                                                "YOUR.INI" );
                    break;
                .
                .
                .
```

WritePrivateProfileString ■ WINDOWS 95 ■ WINDOWS NT

Description	`WritePrivateProfileString` stores a string value associated with a key from a specified section of a private profile file.
Syntax	BOOL **WritePrivateProfileString**(LPCTSTR *lpszSectionName*, LPCTSTR *lpszKeyName*, LPCTSTR *lpszStringValue*, LPCTSTR *lpszIniFileName*)

Parameters

lpszSectionName LPCTSTR: A pointer to a null-terminated string that contains the name of the section. If *lpszSectionName*, *lpszKeyName*, and *lpszStringValue* are all **NULL**, the system flushes the contents of the INI file to disk.

lpszKeyName LPCTSTR: A pointer to a null-terminated string that contains the name of the key whose value is to be written. If the key does not exist in the section, it is created. If both *lpszKeyName* and *lpszStringValue* are **NULL**, all key names of the specified section are deleted, including the section header itself.

lpszStringValue LPCTSTR: A pointer to a null-terminated string that contains the value to be written for the specified key, *lpszKeyName*, in section *lpszSectionName* of the file *lpszIniFileName*. If this parameter is **NULL**, the key is removed from the section.

lpszIniFileName LPCTSTR: A pointer to a null-terminated string that is the name of the private profile file. If *lpszIniFileName* does not contain a fully qualified path name to the file, Windows will search for the file in the Windows directory. If the file does not exist, it is created in the Windows directory or in the supplied path name.

Returns	**BOOL**: If successful, **TRUE** is returned; otherwise, **FALSE** is returned if the file is being cached or a failure to write a key occurs. **GetLastError** returns the error code.
Include File	winbase.h
See Also	GetProfileString, GetPrivateProfileInt
Example	See the example in GetPrivateProfileString.

WritePrivateProfileStruct ■ WINDOWS 95 ■ WINDOWS NT

Description	**WritePrivateProfileStruct** copies data into the specified key in the given section of an INI file. As it copies the data, the function calculates a checksum and appends it to the end of the data. The checksum is used by the **GetPrivateProfileStruct** function to ensure the integrity of the data.
Syntax	**BOOL WritePrivateProfileStruct(** LPCTSTR *lpszSection,* LPCTSTR *lpszKey,* LPVOID *lpStruct,* UINT *uSizeStruct,* LPCTSTR *lpszFile* **)**

Parameters

lpszSection	**LPCTSTR**: A pointer to a null-terminated string that contains the name of the section to which the structure is stored. If the section does not exist, it is created.
lpszKey	**LPCTSTR**: A pointer to a null-terminated string that contains the name of the key to be associated with the structure. If the key does not exist in the specified section, it is created. If this parameter is **NULL**, the entire section, including all keys and entries within the section, is deleted.
lpStruct	**LPVOID**: A pointer to a buffer that contains the data to copy. If this parameter is **NULL**, the given key is deleted.
uSizeStruct	**UINT**: The size, in bytes, of the buffer pointed to by the *lpStruct* parameter.
lpszFile	**LPCTSTR**: A pointer to a null-terminated string that names the initialization file. If this parameter is **NULL**, the information is copied into the **WIN.INI** file.
Returns	**BOOL**: If the function successfully copies the string to the INI file, the return value is **TRUE**; otherwise, **FALSE** is returned.
Include File	winbase.h
See Also	GetPrivateProfileStruct

WriteProfileSection
■ WINDOWS 95   ■ WINDOWS NT

Description	**WriteProfileSection** stores a set of key assignments to a specified section of the **WIN.INI** file. These key assignments replace the contents of the section. Values for keys that are present in a section but not in the list of buffer entries are simply deleted. While this operation is occurring, no other updates are allowed to the **WIN.INI** file.
Syntax	BOOL **WriteProfileSection**(LPCTSTR *lpszSectionName,* LPCTSTR *lpszSectionData*)

Parameters

lpszSectionName   LPCTSTR: A pointer to a null-terminated string that contains the section name. If the section name does not exist in the specified INI file, it will be created.

lpszSectionData   LPCTSTR: A pointer to a buffer that contains the keys and values of the section that will be stored. It consists of a list of zero-terminated strings in the form of key assignments: *key=value*. The last string is followed by an extra null character.

Returns	BOOL: If successful, **TRUE** is returned; otherwise, **FALSE** is returned. **GetLastError** returns the error code.
Include File	winbase.h
See Also	GetPrivateProfileSection, WritePrivateProfileString
Example	This example program writes a profile section (**MyApp**) with two values to the **WIN.INI** file when the user selects the Test! menu item.

```
LRESULT CALLBACK WndProc(HWND hWnd, UINT uMsg, WPARAM wParam, LPARAM lParam)
{
   switch (uMsg)
   {
      case WM_COMMAND:
            switch ( LOWORD( wParam )  )
            {
               case IDM_TEST:
                  {
                      TCHAR   szBuffer[128];
                      LPTSTR lpCur;

                      memset( szBuffer, 0, sizeof( szBuffer ) );

                      lpCur = szBuffer;
                      strcat( lpCur, "Key1=Value1" );

                      lpCur += strlen( lpCur )+1;
                      strcat( lpCur, "Key2=Value2" );

                      WriteProfileSection( "MyApp", szBuffer );
                  }
                  break;
         .
         .
         .
```

WriteProfileString ■ Windows 95 ■ Windows NT

Description	WriteProfileString stores a string value associated with a key into a specified section of the WIN.INI file.
Syntax	BOOL **WriteProfileString**(LPCTSTR *lpszSectionName,* LPCTSTR *lpszKeyName*, LPCTSTR *lpszStringValue*)

Parameters

lpszSectionName LPCTSTR: A pointer to a null-terminated string that contains the name of the section. On Windows 95, if *lpszSectionName*, *lpszKeyName*, and *lpszStringValue* are all NULL, the system flushes the contents of the INI file to disk.

lpszKeyName LPCTSTR: A pointer to a null-terminated string that contains the name of the key whose value is to be written. If the key does not exist in the section, it is created. If both *lpszKeyName* and *lpszStringValue* are NULL, all key names of the specified section are deleted, including the section header itself.

lpszStringValue LPCTSTR: A pointer to a null-terminated string that contains the value to be written for the specified key, *lpszKeyName*, in section *lpszSectionName* of the WIN.INI file. If this parameter is NULL, the key is removed from the section.

Returns	BOOL: If successful, TRUE is returned; otherwise, FALSE is returned if the file is being cached or a failure to write a key occurs. GetLastError can be used to return the error code.
Include File	winbase.h
See Also	GetProfileInt, GetProfileString, WritePrivateProfileString
Example	See the example for GetProfileString.

21

SYSTEM INFORMATION

The Win32 API provides descriptive system data about the environment under which applications run. This information includes process environment variables, the time, the default locale settings for the system and user, the system color settings, drive information, the system power state, system parameters (including accessibility features), the version (and even build number) of the OS, the type of processor, and the computer name. Using system information, an application can correctly present the resources of the system to the user, respond to changes in the conditions of the system, and operate better within the system limits.

Process Environment Information

An executing process's environment consists of the command line, the process startup parameters, and the environment variables. A process may return this data at any time during its execution by calling the appropriate Win32 API function. This data is first set in the call to `CreateProcess`, which creates the application.

`GetCommandLine` returns the command line. The command line consists of the path name of the process in quotes followed by the arguments. The command line parameters also can be retrieved from the command line string passed to `WinMain` when the process is started, but this command line does not contain the path name of the process.

`GetStartupInfo` returns the `STARTUPINFO` structure of the `CreateProcess` call. Only a few fields of the `STARTUPINFO` structure are relevant to a GUI application, the most important being default size and locations, the show window flag originally passed to the application (also available from the command line), and the startup flags. See the `GetStartupInfo` function description for more information about the `STARTUPINFO` structure.

`CreateProcess` also generates an environment for a process. Each process by default inherits a copy of the environment of its parent process. The `GetEnvironmentStrings` function obtains a pointer to the list of all the environment strings of the current process. `GetEnvironmentVariable` obtains the current value of environment variables, and `SetEnvironmentVariable` allows the value of an environment variable to be changed.

Local Time and System Time

Windows keeps the system time as a UTC (Coordinated Universal Time) value. UTC-based time is Greenwich Mean Time; therefore, applications must make an adjustment to the time in order to derive the local time. The Win32 API provides functions to query and change both the system time and local time. Because local time is merely a derived time, the system time and local time are always kept synchronized.

Dates in the system are stored in the SYSTEMTIME structure, which is defined under the GetSystemTime function later in this chapter. The function GetSystemTime reports the system time (UTC) in a SYSTEMTIME structure. The function SetSystemTime changes the system time to the values specified in a supplied SYSTEMTIME structure. The function GetLocalTime returns the local time as a SYSTEMTIME structure. The function SetLocalTime changes the system time to match the local time set.

Locale and Language Support

A locale is a list of values that describe the regional settings, for example, the language and the currency symbol. In Windows NT 4 and Windows 95, default locales are assigned on a user-by-user basis. The Control Panel's Regional Settings applet allows changes to these settings at any time. Each thread in the system has one associated locale. When a thread is created, the locale of the thread is set to the default locale of the user.

Data stored in a locale includes the country name, the names of the months in the locale language, the abbreviations of all the months in the locale language, code-pages for both OEM and ANSI character sets, the list separator (like the commas in this sentence), the system of measurement, the decimal separator, the thousands separator, the date format, and the currency symbol. Locales (and their effects on character sets) are discussed further in Chapter 22, String Manipulation and Character Sets.

System Information Function Descriptions

Table 21-1 is a summary of the system information functions. Detailed function descriptions follow the table.

Table 21-1 System information function summary

Function	Purpose
ExpandEnvironmentStrings	Expands environment-variable strings and replaces them with defined values.
GetCommandLine	Returns the command line of a process.
GetComputerName	Retrieves the system's computer name.
GetCurrentDirectory	Retrieves the current directory.
GetDiskFreeSpace	Retrieves disk parameters that can be used to calculate the free space remaining.
GetDiskFreeSpaceEx	Retrieves information about the amount of space available on a disk volume.
GetDriveType	Returns the type of physical media associated with a logical path name.

Function	Purpose
GetEnvironmentStrings	Returns a pointer to a list of the environment strings.
GetEnvironmentVariable	Retrieves the value of a given environment variable.
GetLocalTime	Retrieves the local time.
GetLogicalDrives	Returns a bit mask of the currently available drives.
GetLogicalDriveStrings	Returns a buffer with strings that list valid drives in the system.
GetStartupInfo	Retrieves the startup info for a given process.
GetSysColor	Returns the RGB color assigned to a given system color.
GetSystemDefaultLangID	Returns the language ID of the default system locale.
GetSystemDefaultLCID	Returns the locale ID of the default system locale.
GetSystemDirectory	Retrieves the name of the Windows system directory.
GetSystemInfo	Retrieves information about the hardware of the system.
GetSystemPowerStatus	Retrieves information about the current state of the system power.
GetSystemTime	Retrieves the system (UTC) time.
GetTimeZoneInformation	Retrieves information about the time zone.
GetUserDefaultLangID	Returns the language ID of the current user's default locale.
GetUserDefaultLCID	Returns the locale ID of the current user's default locale.
GetUserName	Retrieves the user name of the current thread.
GetVersionEx	Retrieves maximum version information about the system.
GetVolumeInformation	Returns information about the volume and the installed file system.
GetWindowsDirectory	Returns the name of the directory where Windows is installed.
SetComputerName	Changes the name of the system the next time the system is restarted.
SetCurrentDirectory	Changes the current directory.
SetEnvironmentVariable	Changes an environment variable's setting.
SetLocalTime	Changes the time using local time.
SetSysColors	Changes the RGB values assigned to system colors.
SetSystemPowerState	Puts the system in suspended mode.
SetSystemTime	Changes the time using UTC Greenwich Mean Time.
SetTimeZoneInformation	Changes information about the time zone.
SetVolumeLabel	Sets the name of the volume.
SystemParametersInfo	Allows system parameters to be retrieved or set.
VerLanguageName	Returns the name of the language from a language identifier.

ExpandEnvironmentStrings   ■ Windows 95   ■ Windows NT

Description   ExpandEnvironmentStrings expands environment-variable strings and replaces them with their defined values. For each variable reference, the %VariableName% portion is replaced with the current value of that environment variable. The replacement rules are the same as those used by the command interpreter. It is case insensitive, and if the name is not found, the variable is left unchanged.

Syntax	DWORD **ExpandEnvironmentStrings**(LPCTSTR *lpSrc,* LPTSTR *lpDst,* DWORD *nSize*)

Parameters

lpSrc **LPCTSTR**: A pointer to a null-terminated string that contains an environment string that might include environment-variable strings.

lpDst **LPTSTR**: A pointer to a buffer to receive a copy of the source buffer, after all environment-variable name substitutions have been performed.

nSize **DWORD**: The maximum number of characters that can be stored in the buffer pointed to by the *lpDst* parameter. This includes the terminating null character.

Returns **DWORD**: If successful, the number of characters stored in the destination buffer is returned. If this number is greater than the number of characters specified in the *nSize* parameter, the destination buffer was not large enough to hold the expanded strings and the returned value is the required size. If an error occurs, **0** is returned. The application should use the **GetLastError** function for extended error information.

Include File winbase.h

See Also GetEnvironmentStrings, GetEnvironmentVariable

Example This example expands the **%systemroot%** variable within a path to the actual value when the user selects the Test! menu item. The new value is then displayed within a message box.

```
LRESULT CALLBACK WndProc( HWND hWnd, UINT uMsg, WPARAM wParam, LPARAM lParam )
{
    switch( uMsg )
    {
        case WM_COMMAND :
                switch( LOWORD( wParam ) )
                {
                    case IDM_TEST :
                        {
                            TCHAR szNewPath[MAX_PATH+1];

                            // Expand the path to the actual path.
                            //.................................
                            if ( ExpandEnvironmentStrings(
                                        "%systemroot%\\system32\\clock.exe",
                                        szNewPath, sizeof( szNewPath ) ) )
                            {
                                MessageBox( hWnd, szNewPath, "Expanded Path",
                                        MB_OK | MB_ICONINFORMATION );
                            }
                        }
                        break;

                        .
                        .
                        .
```

GetCommandLine

Description   GetCommandLine returns the command line of a process. The command line is a null-terminated string that is one of the parameters specified in the **CreateProcess** call that starts the process.

Syntax   LPTSTR **GetCommandLine**(VOID)

Parameters   This function has no parameters.

Returns   **LPTSTR**: The return value is the address of the command line. Note: The format of the command line is the full path of the program enclosed in quotes followed by unquoted arguments.

Include File   winbase.h

See Also   GetStartupInfo, CreateProcess

Example   See the example under the **GetComputerName** function for an example of this function.

GetComputerName

Description   GetComputerName returns the name of the computer at the time the system was started.

Syntax   BOOL **GetComputerName**(LPTSTR *lpszName,* LPDWORD *lpdwBuffer*)

Parameters

lpszName   LPTSTR: A pointer to a buffer that receives the name of the system. The buffer must be at least **MAX_COMPUTERNAME_LENGTH**+1 bytes.

lpdwBuffer   LPDWORD: A pointer to an address that contains the number of characters in the buffer before the function executes and the number of characters actually copied after the function executes, not including the null-terminating character.

Returns   BOOL: If successful, **TRUE** is returned; otherwise, **FALSE** is returned.

Include File   winbase.h

See Also   SetComputerName

Example   In the example shown below, when the user selects the Test! option of the menu, the name of the computer is first shown and then changed to the first argument on the command line. The command line argument should be in the form */C <name>*. This change only takes effect when the system is restarted. Figure 21-1 shows the result after this program is run for the second time—after the system has been restarted.

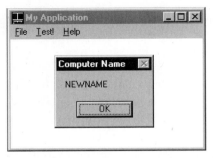

Figure 21-1 `GetComputerName` example

```
LRESULT CALLBACK WndProc(HWND hWnd, UINT uMsg, WPARAM wParam, LPARAM lParam)
{
    switch( uMsg )
    {
        case WM_COMMAND:
              switch ( LOWORD( wParam ) )
              {
                 case IDM_TEST:
                     {
                          LPTSTR lpTemp;
                          char    szCommandLine[MAX_PATH + 1];
                          char    szBuffer[MAX_COMPUTERNAME_LENGTH + 1];
                          DWORD   dwNameSize = MAX_COMPUTERNAME_LENGTH + 1;

                          // Report computer name.
                          //.....................
                          GetComputerName( szBuffer, &dwNameSize );
                          MessageBox( hWnd, szBuffer, "Computer Name", MB_OK );

                          // Parse first token from command line.
                          //......................................
                          strcpy( szCommandLine, GetCommandLine() );
                          lpTemp = strstr( szCommandLine, "/C" );
                          if ( lpTemp )
                          {
                             lpTemp = strtok( lpTemp, "/C" );
                             if  ( lpTemp )
                                SetComputerName( lpTemp );
                          }
                     }
                     break;
                .
                .
                .
```

GetCurrentDirectory   ■ WINDOWS 95   ■ WINDOWS NT

Description   `GetCurrentDirectory` retrieves the current directory of the current
process.

Syntax	DWORD **GetCurrentDirectory**(DWORD *dwCurDir,* LPTSTR *lpszCurDir*)

Parameters

dwCurDir   DWORD: The size of the buffer that is to receive the name of the current directory.

lpszCurDir   LPTSTR: A pointer to a buffer that receives the name of the current directory. The buffer should be long enough to store a directory name (up to **MAX_PATH** characters long) and the null-terminating character.

Returns   DWORD: If the function is successful, the number of characters written to the buffer (not including the null character) is returned; otherwise, **0** is returned. If the function fails because the buffer is not large enough, the return value indicates how many bytes are needed to store the current directory name. This value includes one for the null character that terminates the string. Use **GetLastError** to determine whether the return value indicates that this condition has occurred or whether the function was successful.

Include File   `winbase.h`

See Also   `SetCurrentDirectory`

Example   The example uses **SetCurrentDirectory** to change the directory to whatever is passed on the command line—or the root, if nothing is passed. The command line argument should be in the form /D*<new directory>*. When the user selects the Test! menu item, the current directory is retrieved and displayed in a message box.

```
LRESULT CALLBACK WndProc( HWND hWnd, UINT uMsg, WPARAM wParam, LPARAM lParam )
{
   switch( uMsg )
   {
      case WM_CREATE:
            {
               TCHAR   szCommandLine[MAX_PATH + 1];
               LPTSTR  lpToken = NULL;
               LPTSTR  lpszDirName = NULL;

               strcpy( szCommandLine, GetCommandLine() );

               // Search for extra input after program name.
               //.........................................
               if ( ( lpToken = strstr( szCommandLine, "/D" ) ) )
               {
                  // Get first argument by itself, if there is one.
                  //.........................................
                  lpszDirName = strtok( lpToken, "/D" );
                  if ( lpszDirName )
                  {
                     if ( !SetCurrentDirectory(lpszDirName) )
                        MessageBox( hWnd, "Could not set the current directory",
                                 NULL, MB_OK | MB_ICONASTERISK );
                  }
               }
            }
```

continued on next page

continued from previous page

```
                }
            break;

    case WM_COMMAND :
            switch( LOWORD( wParam ) )
            {
                case IDM_TEST:
                    {
                        TCHAR szBuffer[MAX_PATH + 1];

                        // Query the system for current directory.
                        //.......................................
                        GetCurrentDirectory( sizeof( szBuffer ), szBuffer );
                        MessageBox( hWnd, szBuffer, "Current Directory",
                                    MB_OK | MB_ICONINFORMATION );
                    }
                    break;

                .
                .
                .
```

GetDiskFreeSpace   ■ WINDOWS 95   ■ WINDOWS NT

Description	GetDiskFreeSpace retrieves the format information about a disk, along with the number of free clusters.
Syntax	BOOL **GetDiskFreeSpace**(LPCTSTR *lpszRootPathName,* LPDWORD *lpSectorsPerCluster,* LPDWORD *lpBytesPerSector,* LPDWORD *lpFreeClusters,* LPDWORD *lpClusters*)
Parameters	
lpszRootPathName	LPCTSTR: A pointer to a null-terminated string that contains the path of the root directory for the drive to be queried. For example, to return data about drive C, use the path name **c:**.
lpSectorsPerCluster	LPDWORD: A pointer to a DWORD that receives the number of sectors per cluster. A sector is a contiguous group of bytes stored on disk. A cluster is a block of sectors.
lpBytesPerSector	LPDWORD: A pointer to a DWORD that receives the number of bytes per sector. To determine the number of bytes per cluster, simply multiply the values returned in *lpSectorsPerCluster* by the value in *lpBytesPerSector.*
lpFreeClusters	LPDWORD: A pointer to a DWORD that receives the number of free clusters. Multiply this by the number of sectors per cluster and the number of bytes per sector to determine the free space remaining on disk. Warning: Data compression skews these values significantly.
lpClusters	LPDWORD: A pointer to a DWORD that receives the total number of clusters on the drive.

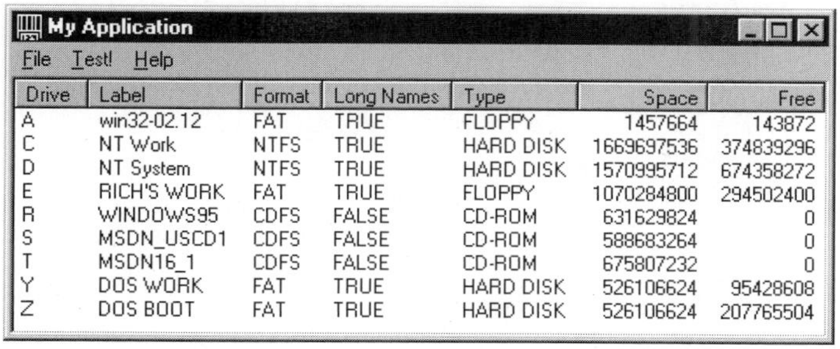

Figure 21-2 `GetDiskFreeSpace` example

Returns
BOOL: If successful, **TRUE** is returned; otherwise, **FALSE** is returned. Use `GetLastError` to return the error code.

Include File
`winbase.h`

See Also
`GetDriveType`

Example
When the user selects the Test! option of this example, volume and disk information is shown for the system drives. `GetLogicalDrives` determines which drives are active in the system. The example uses `GetDriveType` to determine the type of drive and `GetDiskFreeSpace` to determine other disk information. The information is placed in a list view control as shown in Figure 21-2. For more information on the list view control and other common controls, refer to the *Windows 95 Common Controls & Messages API Bible*.

```
HWND hList;

LRESULT CALLBACK WndProc( HWND hWnd, UINT uMsg, WPARAM wParam, LPARAM lParam )
{
   switch( uMsg )
   {
      case WM_COMMAND :
            switch( LOWORD( wParam ) )
            {
               case IDM_TEST:
                     {
                        LV_ITEM item;
                        UINT  uType;
                        DWORD dwBytesPerSector;
                        DWORD dwSectorsPerCluster;
                        DWORD dwTotalClusters;
                        DWORD dwFreeClusters;
                        DWORD dwVolumeSerialNumber;
                        DWORD dwMaxNameLength;
                        DWORD dwFileSystemFlags;
                        DWORD dwFreeSpace;
                        DWORD dwTotalSpace;
                        TCHAR szFileSysName[128];
                        TCHAR szLabel[128];
```

continued on next page

continued from previous page

```
char   szBuffer[MAX_PATH+100];
UINT   nDrive;
UINT   nRow = 0;
DWORD  dwLogicalDrives = GetLogicalDrives();

// Clear all items from the list view.
//...................................
ListView_DeleteAllItems( hList );

for ( nDrive = 0; nDrive < 32; nDrive++ )
{
    // Is drive available?
    //....................
    if ( dwLogicalDrives & (1 << nDrive) )
    {
        // Get disk information.
        //......................
        wsprintf( szBuffer, "%c", nDrive+'A' );

        // Insert new disk into list view.
        //................................
        item.mask = LVIF_TEXT;
        item.iItem = nRow;
        item.iSubItem = 0;
        item.pszText = szBuffer;
        ListView_InsertItem( hList, &item );

        // Retrieve the drive type.
        //.........................
        strcat( szBuffer, ":\\" );
        uType = GetDriveType( szBuffer );

        // Retrieve the free space on the drive.
        //......................................
        GetDiskFreeSpace( szBuffer, &dwBytesPerSector,
                          &dwSectorsPerCluster,
                          &dwFreeClusters,
                          &dwTotalClusters );

        // Retrieve the volume information of the drive.
        //.............................................
        GetVolumeInformation( szBuffer, szLabel,
                          sizeof( szLabel ) - 1,
                          &dwVolumeSerialNumber,
                          &dwMaxNameLength,
                          &dwFileSystemFlags,
                          szFileSysName,
                          sizeof( szFileSysName ) - 1 );

        // Caclulate the drive space.
        //...........................
        dwFreeSpace = dwBytesPerSector *
                      dwSectorsPerCluster * dwFreeClusters;
        dwTotalSpace = dwBytesPerSector *
                       dwSectorsPerCluster * dwTotalClusters;
```

```
                              // Put information into ListView.
                              //...............................
                              item.iSubItem = 1;
                              item.pszText = szLabel;
                              ListView_SetItem( hList, &item );

                              item.iSubItem = 2;
                              item.pszText = szFileSysName;
                              ListView_SetItem( hList, &item );

                              item.iSubItem = 3;
                              item.pszText = (dwMaxNameLength == 255 ? "TRUE" : ⇐
"FALSE");

                              ListView_SetItem( hList, &item );

                              item.iSubItem = 4;
                              item.pszText = (( uType == DRIVE_REMOVABLE ) ? "FLOPPY" :
                                           (( uType == DRIVE_FIXED ) ?  "HARD DISK" :
                                           (( uType == DRIVE_REMOTE ) ? "NETWORK" :
                                           (( uType == DRIVE_CDROM ) ?  "CD-ROM" :
                                           (( uType == DRIVE_RAMDISK ) ? "RAMDISK" :
                                           (( uType == 1 ) ? "DOES NOT EXIST" :
                                           "UNKNOWN DRIVE TYPE" ))))));
                              ListView_SetItem( hList, &item );

                              wsprintf( szBuffer, "%ld", dwTotalSpace );
                              item.iSubItem = 5;
                              item.pszText = szBuffer;
                              ListView_SetItem( hList, &item );

                              wsprintf( szBuffer, "%ld", dwFreeSpace );
                              item.iSubItem = 6;
                              item.pszText = szBuffer;
                              ListView_SetItem( hList, &item );

                              nRow++;
                        }
                  }
            }
            break;
            .
            .
            .
```

GetDiskFreeSpaceEx   WINDOWS 95 ■ WINDOWS NT

Description

GetDiskFreeSpaceEx obtains information about the amount of space available on a disk volume: the total amount of space, the total amount of free space, and the total amount of free space available to the user associated with the calling thread.

Syntax	BOOL **GetDiskFreeSpaceEx**(LPCTSTR *lpDirectoryName,* PULARGE_INTEGER *lpFreeBytesAvailableToCaller,* PULARGE_INTEGER *lpTotalNumberOfBytes,* PULARGE_INTEGER *lpTotalNumberOfFreeBytes*)

Parameters

lpDirectoryName

LPCTSTR: A pointer to a null-terminated string that specifies a directory on the disk of interest. The string can be a UNC name. If set to **NULL**, information about the disk that contains the current directory is obtained.

lpFreeBytesAvailableToCaller

PULARGE_INTEGER: A pointer to a **PULARGE_INTEGER** variable to receive the total number of free bytes on the disk that are available to the user associated with the calling thread. If the operating system implements per-user quotas, this value may be less than the total number of free bytes on the disk.

lpTotalNumberOfBytes

PULARGE_INTEGER: A pointer to a variable to receive the total number of bytes on the disk.

lpTotalNumberOfFreeBytes

PULARGE_INTEGER: A pointer to a variable to receive the total number of free bytes on the disk. This parameter can be **NULL**.

Returns

BOOL: If successful, **TRUE** is returned; otherwise, **FALSE** is returned.

Include File

winbase.h

See Also

GetDiskFreeSpace

GetDriveType   ■ WINDOWS 95   ■ WINDOWS NT

Description

GetDriveType returns the type of drive for a given root path name. A list of drive types is given in Table 21-2.

Syntax

UINT **GetDriveType**(LPCTSTR *lpszRootPathName*)

Parameters

lpszRootPathName

LPCTSTR: A pointer to a null-terminated string that contains the name of the path of the root of the drive being queried. For example, **"C:\\"** may be used to determine the drive type of drive C. If **NULL** is specified, the root of the current directory is used.

Returns

UINT: The drive type. This can be one of the values listed in Table 21-2.

Table 21-2 Types of drives reported by `GetDriveType`

Return Code	Drive Type	Description
0	Unknown	The drive type cannot be determined.
1	Does not exist	The root directory given does not exist.
DRIVE_CDROM	Compact disk	The disk is read by a CD-ROM drive.
DRIVE_FIXED	Hard disk	The disk cannot be removed from the drive.
DRIVE_RAMDISK	Memory	The drive is a RAM disk.
DRIVE_REMOTE	Network drive	The disk is a remote drive.
DRIVE_REMOVABLE	Floppy disk	The disk can be removed from the drive.

Include File	`winbase.h`
See Also	`GetDiskFreeSpace`
Example	See the example under the `GetDiskFreeSpace` function.

GetEnvironmentStrings ■ WINDOWS 95 ■ WINDOWS NT

Description `GetEnvironmentStrings` returns a pointer to the block of environment variables of the process.

Syntax `LPVOID` **`GetEnvironmentStrings( VOID )`**

Parameters This function has no parameters.

Returns `LPVOID`: The return value is a pointer to the list of environment variables. This is a list of null-terminated string equations of the form: *environment-variable=setting*. The last null-terminated string is followed by an additional null character. This data should be treated as read-only. To change an environment variable, use the function `SetEnvironmentVariable`.

Include File `winbase.h`

See Also `GetEnvironmentVariable`, `SetEnvironmentVariable`, `CreateProcess`

Example When the user selects the Test! option, the list of environment strings is placed into a list view control as shown in Figure 21-3.

```
HWND hList;

LRESULT CALLBACK WndProc( HWND hWnd, UINT uMsg, WPARAM wParam, LPARAM lParam )
{
    switch( uMsg )
    {
    case WM_COMMAND :
            switch( LOWORD( wParam ) )
            {
```

continued on next page

continued from previous page

```
case IDM_TEST:
    {
        LV_ITEM item;
        int     nRow = 0;
        LPTSTR  lpValue;
        LPTSTR  lpTemp = GetEnvironmentStrings();

        ListView_DeleteAllItems( hList );

        item.mask = LVIF_TEXT;
        while ( *lpTemp )
        {
            lpValue = strstr( lpTemp+1, "=" );
            if ( lpValue )
            {
                *lpValue = '\0';
                lpValue++;
            }

            item.iItem = nRow;
            item.iSubItem = 0;
            item.pszText = lpTemp;
            ListView_InsertItem( hList, &item );

            item.iSubItem = 1;
            item.pszText = lpValue;
            ListView_SetItem( hList, &item );

            // jump past null.
            //................
            lpTemp += strlen(lpTemp)+1+strlen(lpValue)+1;
        }
    }
    break;
```

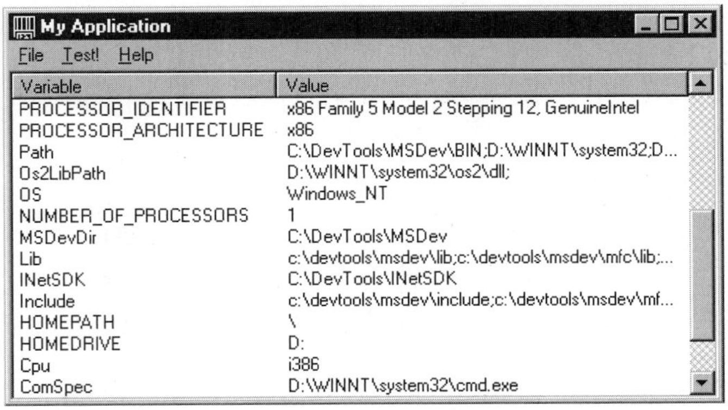

Figure 21-3 `GetEnvironmentStrings` example

GetEnvironmentVariable   ■ WINDOWS 95   ■ WINDOWS NT

Description	GetEnvironmentVariable returns the value associated with an environment variable of the process environment.
Syntax	DWORD **GetEnvironmentVariable**(LPCTSTR *lpszName,* LPTSTR *lpszValue,* DWORD *dwValue*)
Parameters	
lpszName	LPCTSTR: A pointer to a null-terminated string, the environment variable's name.
lpszValue	LPTSTR: A pointer to a buffer to receive the environment variable's value.
dwValue	DWORD: The number of characters in the *lpszValue* buffer.
Returns	DWORD: If the environment variable is not found, 0 is returned; otherwise, the number of characters stored in *lpszValue* is returned. This does not count the terminating null character. If the function fails because the buffer is too small, the return value is the number of characters actually needed to store the value of the variable. Use **GetLastError** to check for this condition or compare the return value of **GetEnvironmentVariable** against the known size of the buffer; if the return value is larger, the buffer can be reallocated to the necessary size, and **GetEnvironmentVariable** may be called again successfully.
Include File	winbase.h
See Also	GetEnvironmentStrings, SetEnvironmentVariable
Example	When the user selects the Test! option from the menu of this example, the value of the environment variable TEST is changed to the value passed on the command line.

```
LRESULT CALLBACK WndProc( HWND hWnd, UINT uMsg, WPARAM wParam, LPARAM lParam )
{
   switch( uMsg )
   {
      case WM_COMMAND :
            switch( LOWORD( wParam ) )
            {
               case IDM_TEST:
                     {
                        TCHAR  szOldValue[256];
                        char   szMessage[2*( MAX_PATH + 1 )];
                        char   szCommandLine[256];
                        LPTSTR lpTemp = NULL;

                        memset( szOldValue, 0, sizeof( szOldValue ) );
                        GetEnvironmentVariable( "Test", szOldValue, sizeof⇐
( szOldValue ) );

                        // Read command line into local buffer.
                        //.....................................
                        strcpy( szCommandLine, GetCommandLine() );
```

continued on next page

continued from previous page

```
                        // Search for extra input after program name.
                        //...............................................
                        lpTemp = strstr( szCommandLine, "/P" );
                        if (lpTemp)
                        {
                            lpTemp = strtok(lpTemp, "/P");
                            if ( lpTemp )
                            {
                                SetEnvironmentVariable( "Test", lpTemp );

                                // Show change in message box.
                                //...........................
                                wsprintf( szMessage, "'Test' was [%s], New Value=[%s]",
                                          szOldValue, lpTemp );

                                MessageBox( hWnd, szMessage,
                                            "Changing Environment Variable", MB_OK );
                            }
                        }
                    }
                    break;
```

.
.
.

GetLocalTime   ■ WINDOWS 95   ■ WINDOWS NT

Description	GetLocalTime retrieves the local time in a **SYSTEMTIME** structure. The time is adjusted for daylight saving time as applicable to the time zone.
Syntax	VOID **GetLocalTime**(LPSYSTEMTIME *lpsi*)
Parameters	
lpsi	LPSYSTEMTIME: A pointer to a **SYSTEMTIME** structure that will be filled with the date and time expressed in local time. See the definition of the **SYSTEMTIME** structure under the **GetSystemTime** function later in this chapter.
Include File	winbase.h
See Also	GetSystemTime, SetSystemTime, SetLocalTime
Example	In the example shown below, the time is adjusted one hour forward each time the user selects the Test! menu item. The system time is restored to its original value upon exit. Note: This example causes the computer to lose the amount of time that it is executing.

```
SYSTEMTIME stSystemTimeEntry;

LRESULT CALLBACK WndProc( HWND hWnd, UINT uMsg, WPARAM wParam, LPARAM lParam )
{
    switch( uMsg )
    {
        case WM_CREATE :
                GetSystemTime( &stSystemTimeEntry );
```

```
                break;

        case WM_DESTROY :
                SetSystemTime( &stSystemTimeEntry );
                PostQuitMessage(0);
                break;

        case WM_COMMAND :
                switch( LOWORD( wParam ) )
                {
                    case IDM_TEST:
                        {
                            SYSTEMTIME st;
                            TCHAR       szBuffer[128];

                            // Get the current time.
                            //......................
                            GetLocalTime( &st );

                            // Add one hour.
                            //..............
                            st.wHour++;
                            if (st.wHour==23)
                                st.wHour = 0;

                            SetLocalTime( &st );

                            // Display new local time.
                            //........................
                            wsprintf(szBuffer, "The new time is %d:%d:%d.%d",
                                    st.wHour, st.wMinute, st.wSecond,
                                    st.wMilliseconds );

                            MessageBox( hWnd, szBuffer, "Added One Hour",
                                    MB_OK | MB_ICONINFORMATION);
                        }
                        break;

        .
        .
        .
```

GetLogicalDrives   ■ WINDOWS 95   ■ WINDOWS NT

Description	GetLogicalDrives returns a bit mask of the logical drives that are currently available. Each bit represents a logical drive. If the bit is set, the logical drive is available; otherwise, it is not set.
Syntax	DWORD **GetLogicalDrives**(VOID)
Parameters	This function has no parameters.
Returns	DWORD: A bit mask of the logical drives. Bits are set if the corresponding drives are available. Bit 0 corresponds to drive A, bit 1 to drive B, bit 2 to drive C, and so forth. If the function fails, **0** is returned.
Include File	winbase.h

See Also	GetLogicalDriveStrings
Example	See the example under the `GetDiskFreeSpace` function.

GetLogicalDriveStrings

Description	`GetLogicalDriveStrings` fills a buffer with strings that specify valid drives in the system.
Syntax	DWORD **GetLogicalDriveStrings**(DWORD *nBufferLength,* LPTSTR *lpBuffer*)
Parameters	
nBufferLength	DWORD: The maximum size, in characters, of the buffer pointed to by *lpBuffer*. The size does not include the terminating null character.
lpBuffer	LPTSTR: A pointer to a buffer that receives a series of null-terminated strings, one for each valid drive in the system, that end with a second null character. The following shows the buffer contents with *<null>* representing the terminating null character: `C:\`*<null>*`D:\`*<null><null>*
Returns	DWORD: If successful, the return value is the length, in characters, of the strings copied to the buffer, not including the terminating null character. If the buffer was not large enough, the return value is the size of the buffer required to hold the drive strings. If the function fails, the return value is `0`.
Include File	`winbase.h`
See Also	GetLogicalDrives

GetStartupInfo ■ WINDOWS 95 ■ WINDOWS NT

Description	`GetStartupInfo` returns information regarding how a process has been set up to appear by its parent process.
Syntax	VOID **GetStartupInfo**(LPSTARTUPINFO *lpsi*)
Parameters	
lpsi	LPSTARTUPINFO: A pointer to a STARTUPINFO structure that was used by the parent process when the calling process was created. The *cb* member of the structure must be initialized to the size of the STARTUPINFO structure before calling `GetStartupInfo`. See the definition of the STARTUPINFO structure below.
Include File	`winbase.h`
See Also	CreateProcess

STARTUPINFO Definition

```
typedef struct _STARTUPINFO
{
```

```
            DWORD   cb;
            LPTSTR  lpReserved;
            LPTSTR  lpDesktop;
            LPTSTR  lpTitle;
            DWORD   dwX;
            DWORD   dwY;
            DWORD   dwXSize;
            DWORD   dwYSize;
            DWORD   dwXCountChars;
            DWORD   dwYCountChars;
            DWORD   dwFillAttribute;
            DWORD   dwFlags;
            WORD    wShowWindow;
            WORD    cbReserved2;
            LPBYTE  lpReserved2;
            HANDLE  hStdInput;
            HANDLE  hStdOutput;
            HANDLE  hStdError;
        } STARTUPINFO, *LPSTARTUPINFO;
```

Members

cb DWORD: The size, in bytes, of the structure.

lpReserved LPTSTR: Reserved; set to **NULL** before passing this structure to **CreateProcess**.

lpDesktop LPTSTR: On Windows NT, this is the pointer to a null-terminated string that specifies either the name of the desktop only or the name of both the window station and desktop for this process. A backslash in the string indicates that the string includes both desktop and window station names. Otherwise, the string is interpreted as a desktop name. If set to **NULL**, the new process inherits the window station and desktop of its parent process.

lpTitle LPTSTR: The title displayed in the title bar if a new console window is created. If **NULL**, the name of the executable file is used as the window title instead. This parameter must be **NULL** for GUI or console processes that do not create a new console window.

dwX DWORD: The x coordinate of the upper-left-hand corner of the window if a new window is created. This member is ignored unless **dwFlags** specifies **STARTF_USESIZE**.

dwY DWORD: The y coordinate of the upper-left-hand corner of the window if a new window is created. This member is ignored unless **dwFlags** specifies **STARTF_USESIZE**.

dwXSize DWORD: The width of the window if a new window is created. This member is ignored unless **dwFlags** specifies **STARTF_USESIZE**.

dwYSize DWORD: The height the window if a new window is created. This member is ignored unless **dwFlags** specifies **STARTF_USESIZE**.

dwXCountChars DWORD: If a new console window is created, this is the screen buffer width in character columns. This member is ignored unless **dwFlags** specifies **STARTF_USECOUNTCHARS**.

dwYCountChars	DWORD: If a new console window is created, this is the screen buffer height in character rows. This member is ignored unless *dwFlags* specifies STARTF_USECOUNTCHARS.
dwFillAttribute	DWORD: The initial text and background colors if a new console window is created in a console application. These values are ignored in GUI applications or unless *dwFlags* specifies STARTF_USEFILLATTRIBUTE. This can be any combination of values FOREGROUND_BLUE, FOREGROUND_GREEN, FOREGROUND_RED, FOREGROUND_INTENSITY, BACKGROUND_BLUE, BACKGROUND_GREEN, BACKGROUND_RED, and BACKGROUND_INTENSITY.
dwFlags	DWORD: Determines whether certain STARTUPINFO members are used when the process creates a window. This can be any combination of the values listed in Table 21-3.

Table 21-3 STARTUPINFO *dwFlags* values

Value	Meaning
STARTF_FORCEOFFFEEDBACK	The feedback cursor is forced off while the process is starting.
STARTF_FORCEONFEEDBACK	The cursor is in feedback mode for two seconds after CreateProcess is called. If during those two seconds the process makes the first GUI call, the system gives five more seconds to the process. If during those five seconds the process shows a window, the system gives five more seconds to the process to finish drawing the window. The system turns the feedback cursor off after the first call to GetMessage, regardless of whether the process is drawing.
STARTF_USECOUNTCHARS	The *dwXCountChars* and *dwYCountChars* members are used.
STARTF_USEFILLATTRIBUTE	The *dwFillAttribute* member is used.
STARTF_USEPOSITION	The *dwX* and *dwY* members are used.
STARTF_USESHOWWINDOW	The *wShowWindow* member is used.
STARTF_USESIZE	The *dwXSize* and *dwYSize* members are used.
STARTF_USESTDHANDLES	Sets the standard input, output, and error of the process to the handles specified in the *hStdInput*, *hStdOutput*, and *hStdError* members of the STARTUPINFO structure. The CreateProcess function's *bInheritHandles* parameter must be set to TRUE for this to work properly.

wShowWindow	WORD: The default value the first time ShowWindow is called. The *nCmdShow* parameter of ShowWindow is ignored. This parameter is ignored unless *dwFlags* specifies STARTF_USESHOWWINDOW. See the ShowWindow function in Chapter 4, Windows Support Functions, for valid values.
cbReserved2	WORD: Reserved; must be 0.
lpReserved2	LPBYTE: Reserved; must be NULL.
hStdInput	HANDLE: The standard input handle of the process if STARTF_USESTDHANDLES is specified.
hStdOutput	HANDLE: The standard output handle of the process if STARTF_USESTDHANDLES is specified.

hStdError	**HANDLE**: The standard error handle of the process if **STARTF_USESTDHAN-DLES** is specified.
Example	When the user selects the Test! option from the menu, the example outputs some of the startup data using a message box.

```
LPTSTR lpszSWNames[11] = { "SW_HIDE",
                    "SW_NORMAL", "SW_SHOWMINIMIZED","SW_MAXIMIZE",
                    "SW_SHOWNOACTIVATE", "SW_SHOW", "SW_MINIMIZE",
                    "SW_SHOWMINNOACTIVE", "SW_SHOWNA", "SW_RESTORE",
                    "SW_SHOWDEFAULT" };


LRESULT CALLBACK WndProc( HWND hWnd, UINT uMsg, WPARAM wParam, LPARAM lParam )
{
   switch( uMsg )
   {
      case WM_COMMAND :
              switch( LOWORD( wParam ) )
              {
                 case IDM_TEST:
                      {
                         STARTUPINFO si;
                         TCHAR szBuffer[255];

                         GetStartupInfo( &si );

                         wsprintf( szBuffer,
                                 "SW: %s, Pos: (%d,%d), Size: (%d,%d) ",
                                 lpszSWNames[si.wShowWindow],
                                 si.dwX, si.dwY, si.dwXSize, si.dwYSize );

                         MessageBox( hWnd, szBuffer, "Startup Info", MB_OK );
                      }
                      break;
                 .
                 .
                 .
```

GetSysColor ■ WINDOWS 95 ■ WINDOWS NT

Description	**GetSysColor** returns the color setting for a specific system color. System colors are set for various display elements of the system. These display elements collectively describe the appearance of all the windows in the environment.
Syntax	DWORD **GetSysColor**(int *nIndex*)
Parameters	
nIndex	**int**: The display element to query. Table 21-8 lists the display elements available.
Returns	**DWORD**: An RGB value that specifies the color contribution of red, green, and blue to the color. Table 21-9 shows representative RGB values for common colors.

Include File	`winbase.h`
See Also	`SetSysColors`
Example	When the user selects the Test! option in the example below, the colors of active and inactive captions are set to red and green, respectively. These changes take place immediately. On exit, the colors are restored to their previous values.

```
COLORREF rgbIniActiveCaption;
COLORREF rgbIniInactiveCaption;

LRESULT CALLBACK WndProc( HWND hWnd, UINT uMsg, WPARAM wParam, LPARAM lParam )
{
    switch( uMsg )
    {
      case WM_CREATE :
            rgbIniActiveCaption = GetSysColor( COLOR_ACTIVECAPTION );
            rgbIniInactiveCaption = GetSysColor( COLOR_INACTIVECAPTION );
            break;

      case WM_DESTROY :
            {
                COLORREF rgbs[2];
                UINT     dispEls[2];

                rgbs[0] = rgbIniActiveCaption;
                dispEls[0] = COLOR_ACTIVECAPTION;

                rgbs[1] = rgbIniInactiveCaption;
                dispEls[1] = COLOR_INACTIVECAPTION;

                SetSysColors( 2, dispEls, rgbs );
            }

            PostQuitMessage(0);
            break;

      case WM_COMMAND :
            switch( LOWORD( wParam ) )
            {
              case IDM_TEST:
                    {
                        COLORREF rgbs[2];    // New color values.
                        int      dispEls[2]; // Elements affected.

                        rgbs[0] = RGB( 255, 0, 0 );
                        dispEls[0] = COLOR_ACTIVECAPTION;

                        rgbs[1] = RGB( 0, 255, 0 );
                        dispEls[1] = COLOR_INACTIVECAPTION;

                        // Set the new colors.
                        //...................
                        SetSysColors( 2, dispEls, rgbs );
                    }
                    break;
```

GetSystemDefaultLangID   ■ WINDOWS 95   ■ WINDOWS NT

Description	GetSystemDefaultLangID returns the default system language identifier (LANGID).
Syntax	LANGID **GetSystemDefaultLangID**(VOID)
Parameters	This function has no parameters.
Returns	**LANGID**: The language identifier of the locale. To get the language name from a **LANGID**, use the **VerLanguageName** function. For more information on the language identifiers, see Table 8-8 under the **MessageBoxEx** function.
Include File	winbase.h
See Also	GetUserDefaultLangID, GetSystemDefaultLCID, VerLanguageName, GetLocaleInfo
Example	In this example, the current values and descriptive data about the locale and language for both the system default and user default are displayed when the user selects the Test! menu item. The results are shown in Figure 21-4.

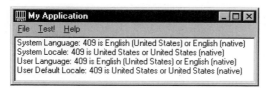

Figure 21-4 GetSystemDefaultLangID example

```
HWND hList;

LRESULT CALLBACK WndProc( HWND hWnd, UINT uMsg, WPARAM wParam, LPARAM lParam )
{
    switch( uMsg )
    {
    case WM_CREATE :
            hList = CreateWindowEx( WS_EX_CLIENTEDGE, "LISTBOX",
                                    "", WS_CHILD | LBS_STANDARD |
                                    LBS_NOINTEGRALHEIGHT | WS_VISIBLE,
                                    0, 0, 10, 10,
                                    hWnd, (HMENU)101, hInst, NULL );

            // Set the font to the correct GUI font.
            //......................................
            SendMessage( hList, WM_SETFONT,
                         (WPARAM)GetStockObject( DEFAULT_GUI_FONT ), 0 );
            break;

    case WM_COMMAND :
            switch( LOWORD( wParam ) )
```

continued on next page

continued from previous page

```
          {
          case IDM_TEST:   // Display system and user defaults.
             {
                LCID    lcidDefault;
                LANGID  langidDefault;
                TCHAR   szMessage[128];
                TCHAR   szDefLang[64];
                TCHAR   szDefNativeLang[64];
                TCHAR   szDefCountry[64];
                TCHAR   szDefNativeCountry[64];

                // Get system default information.
                //...............................
                lcidDefault   = GetSystemDefaultLCID();
                langidDefault = GetSystemDefaultLangID();

                // Determine the string values for the language.
                //...............................................
                VerLanguageName( langidDefault, szDefLang,
                                 sizeof( szDefLang ) );
                GetLocaleInfo( lcidDefault, LOCALE_SNATIVELANGNAME,
                               szDefNativeLang, sizeof( szDefNativeLang ) );
                GetLocaleInfo( lcidDefault, LOCALE_SENGCOUNTRY,
                               szDefCountry, sizeof( szDefCountry ) );
                GetLocaleInfo( lcidDefault, LOCALE_SCOUNTRY,
                               szDefNativeCountry,⇐
sizeof( szDefNativeCountry ) );

                // Add values to list box.
                //........................
                wsprintf( szMessage,
                          "System Language: %X is %s or %s (native) ",
                          langidDefault, szDefLang, szDefNativeLang );
                SendMessage( hList, LB_INSERTSTRING, (WPARAM)-1, ⇐
(LPARAM)szMessage );

                wsprintf( szMessage,
                          "System Locale: %X is %s or %s (native) ",
                          lcidDefault, szDefCountry, szDefNativeCountry );
                SendMessage( hList, LB_INSERTSTRING, (WPARAM)-1, ⇐
(LPARAM)szMessage );

                // Get user default information.
                //.............................
                lcidDefault   = GetUserDefaultLCID();
                langidDefault = GetUserDefaultLangID();

                // Determine the string values for the language.
                //...............................................
                VerLanguageName( langidDefault, szDefLang,
                                 sizeof( szDefLang ) );
                GetLocaleInfo( lcidDefault, LOCALE_SNATIVELANGNAME,
                               szDefNativeLang, sizeof( szDefNativeLang ) );
                GetLocaleInfo( lcidDefault, LOCALE_SENGCOUNTRY,
                               szDefCountry, sizeof( szDefCountry ) );
                GetLocaleInfo( lcidDefault, LOCALE_SCOUNTRY,
                               szDefNativeCountry, ⇐
sizeof( szDefNativeCountry ));
```

```
                        // Add values to the list box.
                        //..........................
                        wsprintf( szMessage,
                                "User Language: %X is %s or %s (native) ",
                                langidDefault, szDefLang, szDefNativeLang );
                        SendMessage( hList, LB_INSERTSTRING, (WPARAM)-1, ⇐
(LPARAM)szMessage );


                        wsprintf( szMessage,
                                "User Default Locale: %X is %s or %s (native) ",
                                lcidDefault, szDefCountry, szDefNativeCountry );
                        SendMessage( hList, LB_INSERTSTRING, (WPARAM)-1, ⇐
(LPARAM)szMessage );
                    }
                    break;
```

GetSystemDefaultLCID ■ WINDOWS 95 ■ WINDOWS NT

Description   GetSystemDefaultLCID returns the locale identifier (LCID) of the default system locale. The current locale is a property of the running thread. It is set to the system default locale unless the user has a different default locale, in which case the user's locale takes precedence. You can change the locale by calling SetThreadLocale.

Syntax   LCID **GetSystemDefaultLCID(VOID)**

Parameters   This function has no parameters.

Returns   LCID: The default system's locale identifier. An LCID is a 32-bit value whose bits are assigned the following meanings:

■ Bits 0–9 are used to denote the primary language.

■ Bits 10–15 are used to distinguish sublanguages (for example American English versus Australian English).

■ Bits 16–19 are used to describe the sort identifier (used to distinguish the use of specialized Japanese, Chinese, and Korean character sets from Unicode).

■ Bits 20–32 are reserved.

Include File   winbase.h

See Also   GetUserDefaultLCID

Example   See the example under the GetSystemDefaultLangID function.

GetSystemDirectory

Description	GetSystemDirectory retrieves the name of the Windows system directory. This is the directory where such things as fonts, icon libraries, and dynamic link libraries are stored.
Syntax	UINT **GetSystemDirectory**(LPTSTR *lpszSysPath,* UINT *uSysPathCount*)
Parameters	
lpszSysPath	LPTSTR: A pointer to a buffer that receives the name of the Windows system directory. Because a directory name may be **MAX_PATH** characters long, a buffer of **MAX_PATH**+1 characters may be required.
uSysPathCount	UINT: The size of the buffer that is to receive the name of the Windows system directory.
Returns	UINT: If the function is successful, the number of characters written to the buffer (not including the null character) is returned; otherwise, **0** is returned. If the function fails because the buffer is not large enough, the return value indicates how many bytes are needed to store the Windows system directory name. This value includes one for the null character that terminates the string. Use **GetLastError** to determine whether the return value indicates that this condition has occurred or whether the function was successful.
Include File	winbase.h
See Also	GetWindowsDirectory
Example	See the example under the **GetWindowsDirectory** function.

GetSystemInfo

Description	GetSystemInfo retrieves information regarding the type of hardware in use by the system.
Syntax	VOID **GetSystemInfo**(LPSYSTEM_INFO *lpSystemInfo*)
Parameters	
lpSystemInfo	LPSYSTEM_INFO: A pointer to a SYSTEM_INFO structure that receives data about the hardware currently running in the system. In multiprocessor environments such as NT, these values may vary depending on the processor that is servicing the application at the time of the call. See the definition of the SYSTEM_INFO structure below.
Include File	winbase.h

SYSTEM_INFO Definition

```
typedef struct _SYSTEM_INFO
{
    WORD    wProcessorArchitecture;
    WORD    wReserved;
    DWORD   dwPageSize;
    LPVOID  lpMinimumApplicationAddress;
    LPVOID  lpMaximumApplicationAddress;
    DWORD   dwActiveProcessorMask;
    DWORD   dwNumberOfProcessors;
    DWORD   dwProcessorType;
    DWORD   dwAllocationGranularity;
    WORD    wProcessorLevel;
    WORD    wProcessorRevision;
} SYSTEM_INFO, *LPSYSTEM_INFO;
```

Members

wProcessorArchitecture	**WORD**: The system processor architecture. On Windows NT and Windows 95, this can be **PROCESSOR_ARCHITEC-TURE_INTEL** for Intel machines. Windows NT can also be **PROCESSOR_ARCHITECTURE_MIPS**, **PROCESSOR_ARCHITEC-TURE_ALPHA**, **PROCESSOR_ARCHITECTURE_PPC**, or **PROCESSOR_ARCHITECTURE_UNKNOWN**.
wReserved	**WORD**: Reserved.
dwPageSize	**DWORD**: The page size and granularity of page protection and commitment. This page size is used by the **VirtualAlloc** function.
lpMinimumApplicationAddress	**LPVOID**: A pointer to the lowest memory address accessible to applications and DLLs.
lpMaximumApplicationAddress	**LPVOID**: A pointer to the highest memory address accessible to applications and DLLs.
dwActiveProcessorMask	**DWORD**: A mask representing the set of processors configured for the system. Bit 0 is the first processor; bit 31 is processor 31.
dwNumberOfProcessors	**DWORD**: The number of processors in the system.
dwProcessorType	**DWORD**: On Windows 95, this member is the type of processor in the system. On Windows NT, this member is not relevant. Use the *wProcessorArchitecture*, *wProcessorLevel*, and *wProcessorRevision* members to determine the type of processor. Windows 95 uses the following values: **PROCES-SOR_INTEL_386**, **PROCESSOR_INTEL_486**, **PROCESSOR_INTEL_PENTIUM**.
dwAllocationGranularity	**DWORD**: The granularity with which virtual memory is allocated. For example, a call to **VirtualAlloc** requests 1 byte, which will actually reserve address space of *dwAllocationGranularity* bytes.

wProcessorLevel	**WORD**: On Windows NT, the system's architecture-dependent processor level. Table 21-4 shows the possible values for each *wProcessorLevel* value.

Table 21-4 SYSTEM_INFO *wProcessorLevel* values

Value	Meaning
PROCESSOR_ARCHITECTURE_INTEL	
3	Intel 80386
4	Intel 80486
5	Pentium
PROCESSOR_ARCHITECTURE_MIPS	**The number is in the form 00xx, where xx is an 8-bit implementation number.**
0004	MIPS R4000
PROCESSOR_ARCHITECTURE_ALPHA	**The number is in the form xxxx, where xxxx is a 16-bit processor version number.**
21064	Alpha 21064
21066	Alpha 21066
21164	Alpha 21164
PROCESSOR_ARCHITECTURE_PPC	**The number is in the form xxxx, where xxxx is a 16-bit processor version number.**
1	PPC 601
3	PPC 603
4	PPC 604
6	PPC 603+
9	PPC 604+
20	PPC 620

wProcessorRevision	**WORD**: On Windows NT, this member specifies an architecture-dependent processor revision. Table 21-5 shows how the revision value is assembled for each type of processor architecture.

Table 21-5 SYSTEM_INFO *wProcessorRevision* values

Processor Architecture	Value
Intel 80386 or 80486	A value of the form *xxyz*. If *xx* is equal to 0xFF, *y*−0xA is the model number, and *z* is the stepping identifier. For example, an Intel 80486-D0 system returns 0xFFD0. If *xx* is not equal to 0xFF, *xx*+'A' is the stepping letter and *yz* is the minor stepping.

Processor Architecture	Value
Intel Pentium, Cyrex, or NextGen 586	A value of the form $xxyy$, where xx is the model number and yy is the stepping.
MIPS	A value of the form $00xx$, where xx is the 8-bit revision number of the processor.
ALPHA	A value of the form $xxyy$, where $xxyy$ is the low-order 16-bits of the processor revision number from the firmware. Display the value in the following form: Model 'A'+xx, Pass yy.
PPC	A value of the form $xxyy$, where $xxyy$ is the low-order 16-bits of the Processor Version Register. Display this value as a fixed-point number ($xx.yy$).

Example

This example displays the system information in a window, shown in Figure 21-5 when the user selects the Test! menu item.

```
HWND hList;

LRESULT CALLBACK WndProc( HWND hWnd, UINT uMsg, WPARAM wParam, LPARAM lParam )
{
   switch( uMsg )
   {
     case WM_COMMAND :
            switch( LOWORD( wParam ) )
            {
               case IDM_TEST:
                  {
                     SYSTEM_INFO si;
                     TCHAR       szBuffer[128];

                     GetSystemInfo( &si );

                     wsprintf( szBuffer, "Architecture: %s, Addr Range %lX-%lX",
                           (si.wProcessorArchitecture == ⇐
PROCESSOR_ARCHITECTURE_INTEL ?
                           "Intel" : "Other"), si.lpMinimumApplicationAddress,
                           si.lpMaximumApplicationAddress);
                     SendMessage( hList, LB_INSERTSTRING,
                           (WPARAM)-1, (LPARAM)szBuffer );

                     wsprintf( szBuffer, "Page Size: %lX, Allocation: %lX",
                           si.dwPageSize, si.dwAllocationGranularity );
                     SendMessage( hList, LB_INSERTSTRING,
                           (WPARAM)-1, (LPARAM)szBuffer );

                     // This only works with Windows NT.
                     //................................
                     wsprintf( szBuffer, "Type of Processor: %s",
                           ( si.wProcessorLevel == 3 ) ? "386" :
                           (( si.wProcessorLevel == 4 ) ? "486" : "PENTIUM" ) );
                     SendMessage( hList, LB_INSERTSTRING,
                           (WPARAM)-1, (LPARAM)szBuffer );
                  }
                  break;
                     .
                     .
                     .
```

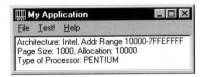

Figure 21-5 `GetSystemInfo`
example

GetSystemPowerStatus

Description	`GetSystemPowerStatus` reports the status of the system's power supply. You can use this function to determine the likelihood of a power outage when the computer is connected to battery power. Power management support must be installed to use `GetSystemPowerStatus`.
Syntax	BOOL **GetSystemPowerStatus**(LPSYSTEM_POWER_STATUS *lpSystemPowerStatus*)
Parameters	
lpSystemPowerStatus	LPSYSTEM_POWER_STATUS: A pointer to a **SYSTEM_POWER_STATUS** structure that receives the power status. See the definition of the **SYSTEM_POWER_STATUS** structure below.
Returns	**BOOL**: If successful, **TRUE** is returned; otherwise, the return value is **FALSE**.
Include File	`winbase.h`, `pbt.h` (for message events)
See Also	SetSystemPowerState
Related Messages	WM_POWERBROADCAST

SYSTEM_POWER_STATUS Definition

```
typedef struct _SYSTEM_POWER_STATUS
{
    BYTE    ACLineStatus;
    BYTE    BatteryFlag;
    BYTE    BatteryLifePercent;
    BYTE    Reserved1;
    DWORD   BatteryLifeTime;
    DWORD   BatteryFullLifeTime;
} SYSTEM_POWER_STATUS, *LPSYSTEM_POWER_STATUS;
```

Members

ACLineStatus	BYTE: AC power status. If set to **0**, it is offline. If set to **1**, it is online; otherwise **255** indicates an unknown status.
BatteryFlag	BYTE: Battery charge status. A value of **1** indicates a high charge status. **2** indicates a low status. **4** means the status is critical. A value of **8** indicates the system is charging. If the system has no battery, a value

of **128** is given; otherwise, a value of **255** indicates the status is unknown.

BatteryLifePercent	BYTE: The percentage of full battery charge remaining. This member can be a value in the range of 0 to 100. If set to **255**, the status is unknown.
Reserved1	BYTE: Reserved; set to **0**.
BatteryLifeTime	DWORD: The number of seconds of battery life remaining, or **0xFFFFFFFF** if remaining seconds are unknown.
BatteryFullLifeTime	DWORD: Number of seconds of battery life when at full charge, or **0xFFFFFFFF** if full lifetime is unknown.

Example
The example shown below uses **GetSystemPowerStatus** to query the system when it is notified that the power is low. When the user selects the Test! menu item, the **SetSystemPowerState** function is used to test the operation.

```
LRESULT CALLBACK WndProc( HWND hWnd, UINT uMsg, WPARAM wParam, LPARAM lParam )
{
    switch( uMsg )
    {
        case WM_POWERBROADCAST:
                if ( wParam == PBT_APMQUERYSUSPEND )
                {
                    SYSTEM_POWER_STATUS sps;

                    GetSystemPowerStatus( &sps );

                    // If not on ACLine & less than 10 percent, let suspend.
                    //...................................................
                    if (!sps.ACLineStatus && sps.BatteryLifePercent<10 )
                    {
                        if ( MessageBox( hWnd, "Do you want to suspend?",
                                "Query Suspend State", MB_YESNO ) == IDYES )
                            return( TRUE );
                        else
                            return( BROADCAST_QUERY_DENY );
                    }
                }
                break;

        case WM_COMMAND :
                switch( LOWORD( wParam ) )
                {
                    case IDM_TEST:
                            // Query suspend power.
                            //....................
                            SetSystemPowerState( FALSE, FALSE );
                            break;
                        .
                        .
                        .
```

GetSystemTime
■ WINDOWS 95   ■ WINDOWS NT

Description	GetSystemTime retrieves a SYSTEMTIME structure that reports the time in Greenwich Mean Time using Coordinated Universal Time (UTC) format.
Syntax	VOID **GetSystemTime**(LPSYSTEMTIME *lpst*)
Parameters	
lpst	LPSYSTEMTIME: A pointer to a SYSTEMTIME structure that receives the current system time. See the definition of the SYSTEMTIME structure below.
Include File	winbase.h
See Also	SetLocalTime, GetLocalTime

SYSTEMTIME Definition

```
typedef struct _SYSTEMTIME
{
    WORD wYear;
    WORD wMonth;
    WORD wDayOfWeek;
    WORD wDay;
    WORD wHour;
    WORD wMinute;
    WORD wSecond;
    WORD wMilliseconds;
} SYSTEMTIME;
```

Members

wYear	WORD: The current year.
wMonth	WORD: The current month; January=1, February=2, etc.
wDayOfWeek	WORD: The current day of week; Sunday=0, Monday=1, etc.
wDay	WORD: The current day of the month.
wHour	WORD: The current hour.
wMinute	WORD: The current minute.
wSecond	WORD: The current second.
wMilliseconds	WORD: The current millisecond.
Example	See the example under the GetLocalTime function.

GetTimeZoneInformation
■ WINDOWS 95   ■ WINDOWS NT

Description	GetTimeZoneInformation retrieves a TIME_ZONE_INFORMATION structure that describes the time zone. This includes two SYSTEMTIME structures that indicate when daylight saving time begins and ends, as well as the various biases to change system time to local time.
	An application can specify daylight saving time and standard time begin dates in absolute or relative dates. With absolute time, the exact day and

month of the year are set. For example, October 28, 1995 at 1:00 a.m. would set the *wMonth* member to **10**, *wDay* member to **28**, *wYear* member to **1995**, and the *wHour* member to **1**. Using a relative date, an application specifies the third Thursday in October by setting the *wDayOfWeek* member to **4** (Thursday), *wMonth* member to **10**, and the *wDay* member to **3** (the third Thursday). Setting the *wDay* member to **5** designates the last occurrence of the *wDayOfWeek* day of the week in a month—for example, the last Thursday in November is specified by setting the *wDayOfWeek* member to **4** (Thursday), the *wMonth* member to **11**, and the *wDay* member to **5**.

Syntax	DWORD **GetTimeZoneInformation**(LPTIME_ZONE_INFORMATION *lptzi*)
Parameters	
lptzi	**LPTIME_ZONE_INFORMATION**: A pointer to a **TIME_ZONE_INFORMATION** structure that receives data about the specified time zone. See the definition of the **TIME_ZONE_INFORMATION** structure below.
Returns	**DWORD**: If the value is **TIME_ZONE_ID_UNKNOWN**, Windows cannot find the current time zone. This can occur if **SetTimeZoneInformation** is called and the **TIME_ZONE_INFORMATION** did not contain transition dates. **TIME_ZONE_ID_STANDARD** means that Windows has found that the time zone is in the range of standard time. **TIME_ZONE_ID_DAYLIGHT** indicates that Windows has detected that the time zone is in its range of daylight saving time. If **0xFFFFFFFF** is returned, use **GetLastError** to determine the cause of the error.
Include File	winbase.h
See Also	SetTimeZoneInformation, GetLocalTime

TIME_ZONE_INFORMATION Definition

```
typedef struct _TIME_ZONE_INFORMATION
{
    LONG        Bias;
    TCHAR       StandardName[32];
    SYSTEMTIME  StandardDate;
    LONG        StandardBias;
    TCHAR       DaylightName[32];
    SYSTEMTIME  DaylightDate;
    LONG        DaylightBias;
} TIME_ZONE_INFORMATION, *TIME_ZONE_INFORMATION;
```

Members

Bias	**LONG**: The current bias, in minutes, for local time translation on this computer. The bias is the difference, in minutes, between Coordinated Universal Time (UTC) and local time. All transformations between UTC and local time are based on the following formula: UTC=local time + *Bias*.
StandardName	**TCHAR[32]**: The null-terminated string associated with the standard time on this operating system. This could contain **"CST"** to indicate Central Standard Time.

StandardDate	SYSTEMTIME: A SYSTEMTIME structure that contains a date and UTC when the transition from daylight time to standard time occurs on this operating system. If this date is not specified, the *wMonth* member in the SYSTEMTIME structure must be 0. If this date is specified, the *DaylightDate* member must also be specified. Local time translations done during the standard-time range are relative to the supplied *StandardBias* value. See the definition of the SYSTEMTIME structure under the GetSystemTime function.
StandardBias	LONG: The bias value to be used during local time translations that occur during standard time. This member is ignored if a value for the *StandardDate* member is not supplied. This value is added to the value of the *Bias* member to form the bias used during standard time. In most time zones, this member is 0.
DaylightName	TCHAR[32]: A null-terminated string associated with daylight saving time on this operating system. This could contain "CDT" for Central Daylight Time.
DaylightDate	SYSTEMTIME: This member is similar to the *StandardDate* member, except that it contains a date and UTC when the transition from standard time to daylight saving time occurs on this operating system.
DaylightBias	LONG: The bias value to be used during local time translations that occur during daylight saving time. This member is ignored if a value for the *DaylightDate* member is not supplied. This value is added to the value of the *Bias* member to form the bias used during daylight saving time. In most time zones, the value of this member is –60.
Example	The example below shows how the time zone information can be changed. When the user selects the Test! option, a message box shows the bias that is added to or subtracted from Greenwich Mean Time to derive the local time, and one hour is then added to the bias. When the program is exited, the time zone information is restored. (Notice that when time zone data is changed, it is the system time that changes, not the local time!)

```
TIME_ZONE_INFORMATION tziInit;

LRESULT CALLBACK WndProc( HWND hWnd, UINT uMsg, WPARAM wParam, LPARAM lParam )
{
    switch( uMsg )
    {
        case WM_CREATE:
                // Save time zone data.
                //....................
                GetTimeZoneInformation( &tziInit );
                break;

        case WM_DESTROY :
                // Restore the time zone.
                //....................
                SetTimeZoneInformation( &tziInit );
                PostQuitMessage(0);
                break;
```

```
case WM_COMMAND :
        switch( LOWORD( wParam ) )
        {
            case IDM_TEST:
                {
                    TIME_ZONE_INFORMATION tziLocal;
                    DWORD                 dwTimeZoneMode;
                    TCHAR                 szBuffer[128];

                    dwTimeZoneMode = GetTimeZoneInformation( &tziLocal );

                    if ( dwTimeZoneMode == TIME_ZONE_ID_STANDARD )
                        wsprintf( szBuffer,
                                  "Time Zone Name: %sST, Bias: %d",
                                  tziLocal.StandardName,
                                  tziLocal.Bias + tziLocal.StandardBias );
                    else
                        wsprintf( szBuffer,
                                  "Time Zone Name: %sDT, Bias: %d",
                                  tziLocal.DaylightName,
                                  tziLocal.Bias + tziLocal.DaylightBias );

                    MessageBox( hWnd, szBuffer, "Time Zone Data", MB_OK );

                    // Change time zone data. Add 60 minutes to Bias.
                    //.............................................
                    tziLocal.Bias += 60;
                    SetTimeZoneInformation( &tziLocal );
                }
                break;
```

.
.
.

GetUserDefaultLangID ■ WINDOWS 95 ■ WINDOWS NT

Description	GetUserDefaultLangID returns the language identifier (LANGID) of the language of the user's default locale.
Syntax	LANGID **GetUserDefaultLangID**(VOID)
Parameters	This function has no parameters.
Returns	LANGID: The language ID of the default user's locale.
Include File	winbase.h
See Also	GetThreadLocale, SetThreadLocale, VerLanguageName, GetUserDefaultLCID
Example	See the example for GetSystemDefaultLangID.

GetUserDefaultLCID ■ WINDOWS 95 ■ WINDOWS NT

Description	GetUserDefaultLCID returns the locale identifier (LCID) of the user's default locale. This is the current locale unless the thread's locale is set by calling SetThreadLocale.

Syntax	`LCID GetUserDefaultLCID( VOID )`
Parameters	This function has no parameters.
Returns	`LCID`: The locale ID of the user's default locale.
Include File	`winbase.h`
See Also	`GetSystemDefaultLCID, SetThreadLocale, GetThreadLocale`
Example	See the example under the `GetSystemDefaultLangID` function.

GetUserName ■ WINDOWS 95 ■ WINDOWS NT

Description	`GetUserName` returns the user name of the current thread. This is the name of the user currently logged onto the system. If the current thread is impersonating another client, the `GetUserName` function returns the user name of the client that the thread is impersonating.
Syntax	`BOOL GetUserName( LPTSTR lpBuffer, LPDWORD lpdwSize )`
Parameters	
lpBuffer	LPTSTR: A pointer to a buffer that receives the null-terminated string containing the user's logon name. If the buffer is not large enough to contain the entire user name, the function fails.
lpdwSize	LPDWORD: A pointer to a `DWORD` variable that, on input, specifies the maximum size, in characters, of the buffer specified by the *lpBuffer* parameter. If this buffer is not large enough to receive the entire user name, the function fails. If the function succeeds, this parameter receives the number of characters copied to the buffer.
Returns	BOOL: If successful, `TRUE` is returned and the variable pointed to by *lpdwSize* contains the number of characters copied to the buffer pointed to by *lpBuffer*. This includes the terminating null character. If the function fails, `FALSE` is returned. Use the `GetLastError` function to retrieve extended error information.
Include File	`winbase.h`
See Also	`GetComputerName`
Example	This example displays the current user name when the user selects the Test! menu item.

```
LRESULT CALLBACK WndProc( HWND hWnd, UINT uMsg, WPARAM wParam, LPARAM lParam )
{
    switch( uMsg )
    {
        case WM_COMMAND :
                switch( LOWORD( wParam ) )
                {
                    case IDM_TEST :
                        {
```

```
            // The current maximum user
            // name in Windows NT 4 is 20 characters.
            TCHAR szUserName[21];
            DWORD dwSize = sizeof( szUserName );

            if ( GetUserName( szUserName, &dwSize ) )
               MessageBox( hWnd, szUserName, "Current User",
                           MB_OK | MB_ICONINFORMATION );
         }
         break;
```

.
.
.

GetVersionEx   ■ WINDOWS 95   ■ WINDOWS NT

Description	**GetVersionEx** retrieves complete version identification information, including the major and minor version of Windows and the build number. This information is returned as an **OSVERSIONINFO** structure.
Syntax	BOOL **GetVersionEx**(LPOSVERSIONINFO *lposvi*)
Parameters	
lposvi	LPOSVERSIONINFO: A pointer to an **OSVERSIONINFO** structure that receives the version information for the operating system. See the definition of the **OSVERSIONINFO** structure below.
Returns	BOOL: If successful, **TRUE** is returned; otherwise, **FALSE** is returned.
Include File	winbase.h

OSVERSIONINFO Definition

```
typedef struct _OSVERSIONINFO
{
    DWORD dwOSVersionInfoSize;
    DWORD dwMajorVersion;
    DWORD dwMinorVersion;
    DWORD dwBuildNumber;
    DWORD dwPlatformId;
    TCHAR szCSDVersion[128];
} OSVERSIONINFO, *LPOSVERSIONINFO;
```

Members

dwOSVersionInfoSize	DWORD: The size, in bytes, of this data structure. This must be initialized before calling the **GetVersionEx** function.
dwMajorVersion	DWORD: The major version number of the operating system. For example, Windows NT 3.51 has a major version of 3; and Windows NT 4.0 has a major version of 4.
dwMinorVersion	DWORD: The minor version number of the operating system. For example, Windows NT 3.51 has a minor version of 51; and Windows NT 4.0 has a minor version of 0.

dwBuildNumber	DWORD: The build number of the operating system. On Windows 95, the build number is in the low-order word. The high-order word contains the major and minor version numbers.
dwPlatformId	DWORD: The operating system platform. This can be one of the values listed in Table 21-6.

Table 21-6 OSVERSIONINFO *dwPlatformId* values

Value	Platform
VER_PLATFORM_WIN32s	Win32s on Windows 3.1
VER_PLATFORM_WIN32_WINDOWS	Win32 on Windows 95
VER_PLATFORM_WIN32_NT	Win32 on Windows NT

szCSDVersion	TCHAR[128]: A null-terminated string that provides arbitrary additional information about the operating system.
Example	When the user selects the Test! option in the example below, a message box appears that shows the version and build number of the Windows system. Figure 21-6 shows the results.

```
LRESULT CALLBACK WndProc( HWND hWnd, UINT uMsg, WPARAM wParam, LPARAM lParam )
{
    switch( uMsg )
    {
    case WM_COMMAND :
            switch( LOWORD( wParam ) )
            {
                case IDM_TEST:
                    {
                        TCHAR          szTitle[128];
                        TCHAR          szBuffer[128];
                        OSVERSIONINFO osvi;

                        osvi.dwOSVersionInfoSize = sizeof(OSVERSIONINFO);
                        GetVersionEx( &osvi );

                        wsprintf( szTitle, "Windows version is %d.%d",
                                osvi.dwMajorVersion, osvi.dwMinorVersion );
                        wsprintf( szBuffer, "Build: %d, Platform ID: %ld",
                                LOWORD(osvi.dwBuildNumber), osvi.dwPlatformId);

                        MessageBox( hWnd, szBuffer, szTitle, MB_OK );
                    }
                    break;
            .
            .
            .
```

Figure 21-6 `GetVersionEx` example

GetVolumeInformation ■ WINDOWS 95 ■ WINDOWS NT

Description `GetVolumeInformation` returns the volume label and data about the volume file system for a given drive.

Syntax BOOL **GetVolumeInformation**(LPCTSTR *lpszRootPathName,* LPTSTR *lpszVolumeName,* DWORD *dwcVolumeNameSize,* LPDWORD *lpdwVolSerialNum,* LPDWORD *lpdwMaxCompLen,* LPDWORD *lpdwFileSysFlags,* LPTSTR *lpszFileSysName,* DWORD *dwcFileSysName*)

Parameters

lpszRootPathName LPCTSTR: Pointer to a string that contains the path name of the root directory of the queried volume. This must be a null-terminated string. If this parameter is **NULL**, the root of the current directory is used.

lpszVolumeName LPTSTR: Pointer to a buffer where the volume name is to be stored as a null-terminated string. A volume name or label is set when the disk is formatted or by using the Properties dialog of the Explorer.

dwcVolumeNameSize DWORD: The number of bytes in the buffer *lpszVolumeName*.

lpdwVolSerialNum LPDWORD: Pointer to a **DWORD** that receives the volume's serial number. This can be **NULL** if no volume serial number is requested.

lpdwMaxCompLen LPDWORD: Pointer to a **DWORD** that is the maximum length of any component in a path name. A file system component is any part of the name found between backslashes. In the VFAT file system (used by Windows 95), High-Performance File System (HPFS—used by OS/2), or NTFS (used by Windows NT), long file names are supported, and **255** will be returned. This is the only information in the system that indicates long file names are supported!

lpdwFileSysFlags LPDWORD: Pointer to a **DWORD** that describes the file system's attributes with the set of flags listed in Table 21-7.

Table 21-7 File system descriptor flags

Flag	Description
FS_CASE_IS_PRESERVED	The case of all alphabetic characters is preserved in the file name stored on disk.
FS_CASE_SENSITIVE	The file system can perform case-sensitive file searches.
FS_FILE_COMPRESSION	The file system supports file-based compression.
FS_PERSISTENT_ACLS	The file system stores access control lists (ACL) for the data stored in the file system and uses them to regulate access to the data. NTFS is an example of a file system that uses ACLs in its access to data stored in the system.
FS_UNICODE_STORED_ON_DISK	File names are stored as Unicode strings.
FS_VOL_IS_COMPRESSED	The specified volume is a compressed volume such as a DoubleSpace volume.

lpszFileSysName	LPTSTR: Pointer to a buffer that receives the name of the file system. A null-terminated string is returned by the system. This may be **NULL** if no file system name is required.
dwcFileSysName	DWORD: The number of characters in the *lpszFileSysName* buffer. This parameter is ignored if *lpszFileSysName* is NULL.
Returns	BOOL: If successful, **TRUE** is returned; otherwise, **FALSE** is returned. Use **GetLastError** to return the error code.
Include File	winbase.h
See Also	SetVolumeLabel, GetDiskFreeSpace, GetDriveType
Example	See the example under the **GetDiskFreeSpace** function.

GetWindowsDirectory   ■ WINDOWS 95   ■ WINDOWS NT

Description	GetWindowsDirectory retrieves the name of the directory where Windows is installed. The Windows directory is the root for the Windows operating system. For example, if the Windows directory is named **WINDOWS** on drive C, the path of the Windows directory retrieved by this function is **C:\WINDOWS**.
Syntax	UINT **GetWindowsDirectory**(LPTSTR *lpszWinPath,* UINT *uWinPathCount*)
Parameters	
lpszWinPath	LPTSTR: A pointer to a buffer that receives the name of the Windows directory. A directory name can be **MAX_PATH** characters long, so a buffer length of **MAX_PATH**+1 is recommended.
uWinPathCount	UINT: The maximum size, in characters, of the buffer pointed to by *lpszWinPath*.
Returns	UINT: If the function is successful, the number of characters written to the buffer (not including the null character) is returned; otherwise, **0** is returned. If the function fails because the buffer is not large enough, the

return value indicates how many bytes are needed to store the Windows directory name. This value includes one for the null character that terminates the string.

Include File   `winbase.h`

See Also   `GetSystemDirectory`

Example   When the user selects Test! menu item in the example below, the Windows directory path and the system directory path are displayed in a message box.

```
LRESULT CALLBACK WndProc( HWND hWnd, UINT uMsg, WPARAM wParam, LPARAM lParam )
{
   switch( uMsg )
   {
     case WM_COMMAND :
            switch( LOWORD( wParam ) )
            {
              case IDM_TEST:
                  {
                     TCHAR szMsg[(MAX_PATH*2) + 40];
                     TCHAR szTmp[MAX_PATH+1];
                     DWORD dwNameSize = MAX_PATH + 1;

                     strcpy( szMsg, "Windows Directory: " );
                     GetWindowsDirectory( szTmp, dwNameSize );
                     strcat( szMsg, szTmp );
                     strcat( szMsg, "\nSystem Directory: " );

                     GetSystemDirectory( szTmp, dwNameSize );
                     strcat( szMsg, szTmp );

                     MessageBox( hWnd, szMsg, "Directory Information",
                                 MB_OK | MB_ICONINFORMATION );
                  }
                  break;
         .
         .
         .
```

SetComputerName   ■ WINDOWS 95   ■ WINDOWS NT

Description   `SetComputerName` changes the name of the computer system. The change will only take place the next time the system is restarted.

Syntax   `BOOL SetComputerName( LPCTSTR lpszComputerName )`

Parameters

lpszComputerName   LPCTSTR: A pointer to a null-terminated string that contains the new name of the computer system. This string may be up to **MAX_COMPUTERNAME** characters in length.

Returns   BOOL: If successful, **TRUE** is returned; otherwise, **FALSE** is returned.

Include File   `winbase.h`

See Also `GetComputerName`

Example See the example under the `GetComputerName` function.

SetCurrentDirectory ■ Windows 95 ■ Windows NT

Description `SetCurrentDirectory` changes the current directory of the running application to the specified path.

Syntax `BOOL SetCurrentDirectory( LPCTSTR lpszCurDir )`

Parameters

lpszCurDir `LPCTSTR`: A pointer to a null-terminated string that specifies the path to be set as the new current directory. This string can be up to `MAX_PATH`+1 characters in length counting the null-terminating character. The path may be a relative path or a fully qualified path. When the path is retrieved, it will always be a fully qualified path.

Returns `BOOL`: If successful, `TRUE` is returned; otherwise, `FALSE` is returned.

Include File `winbase.h`

See Also `GetCurrentDirectory`

Example See the example under the `GetCurrentDirectory` function.

SetEnvironmentVariable ■ Windows 95 ■ Windows NT

Description `SetEnvironmentVariable` changes the value of an existing environment variable or creates a new environment variable with the specified value.

Syntax `BOOL SetEnvironmentVariable( LPCTSTR lpszName, LPCTSTR lpszValue )`

Parameters

lpszName `LPCTSTR`: A pointer to a null-terminated string that specifies the name of the environment variable whose value is to be set.

lpszValue `LPCTSTR`: A pointer to a null-terminated string that contains the new value of the specified environment variable. If this value is `NULL`, the environment variable is deleted.

Returns `BOOL`: If the function succeeds, `TRUE` is returned; otherwise, `FALSE` is returned. To get an error code, use the `GetLastError` function.

Include File `winbase.h`

See Also `GetEnvironmentVariable`, `GetEnvironmentStrings`

Example See the example under the `GetEnvironmentVariable` function.

SetLocalTime
■ Windows 95   ■ Windows NT

Description	SetLocalTime sets the current local time and date. The time is changed to the values supplied in the given SYSTEMTIME structure. This changes both the local time and (by derivation) the system time.
Syntax	BOOL **SetLocalTime**(CONST SYSTEMTIME* *lpsi*)
Parameters	
lpsi	CONST SYSTEMTIME*: A pointer to a SYSTEMTIME structure that contains the date and time to be set. See the definition of the SYSTEMTIME structure under the GetSystemTime function.
Returns	BOOL: If successful, TRUE is returned; otherwise, FALSE is returned. Use GetLastError to return the error code.
Include File	winbase.h
See Also	GetLocalTime, SetSystemTime
Example	See the example under the GetLocalTime function.

SetSysColors
■ Windows 95   ■ Windows NT

Description	SetSysColors changes the RGB values of the specified system colors to the new supplied colors. System colors are set globally for the display elements listed in Table 21-8. The message WM_SYSCOLORCHANGE is sent to all windows to inform them of the change in color. Windows will repaint automatically all the affected components of all visible windows.
Syntax	BOOL **SetSysColors**(int *nDspElements,* CONST INT* *lpnDspElements,* CONST COLORREF* *lpdwRgbValues*)
Parameters	
nDspElements	int: The number of elements in the *lpnDspElements* list of display elements to be modified. This should also be the number of COLORREF elements in the *lpdwRgbValues* list.
lpnDspElements	CONST INT*: A pointer to an array of display element indices. Table 21-8 gives a complete list of display elements from which to select.

Table 21-8 Predefined system color constants

Color Identifier	Description of Display Element
COLOR_3DDKSHADOW	Dark shadow color for 3D effects.
COLOR_3DFACE	Face color for 3D effects.
COLOR_3DHILIGHT	Highlight color for 3D effects (for edges facing the light source).

continued on next page

continued from previous page

Color Identifier	Description of Display Element
COLOR_3DLIGHT	Light color for 3D effects (for edges facing the light source).
COLOR_3DSHADOW	Shadow color for 3D effects (for edges facing away from the light source).
COLOR_ACTIVEBORDER	Color of window border when the window is currently active.
COLOR_ACTIVECAPTION	Color of window caption bar when the window is currently active.
COLOR_APPWORKSPACE	Background color of client area of MDI container.
COLOR_BACKGROUND	Color of Windows desktop.
COLOR_BTNFACE	Face color for pushbuttons.
COLOR_BTNHILIGHT	Color of border highlighting on pushbuttons. (Same as COLOR_3DHILIGHT.)
COLOR_BTNHIGHLIGHT	Same as COLOR_3DHILIGHT.
COLOR_BTNSHADOW	Color of border shading on pushbuttons.
COLOR_BTNTEXT	Color of text on pushbuttons.
COLOR_CAPTIONTEXT	Color of text in caption, size box, and scroll bar arrow box.
COLOR_DESKTOP	Same as COLOR_BACKGROUND.
COLOR_GRAYTEXT	Color of grayed text. Grayed text is used to indicate disabled controls. If the current device driver does not support solid gray color, this value is set to 0.
COLOR_HIGHLIGHT	Background color of selected items (for example in a list).
COLOR_HIGHLIGHTTEXT	Text color of selected items (for example in a list).
COLOR_INACTIVEBORDER	Color of window border when the window is not the active window.
COLOR_INACTIVECAPTION	Color of window caption when the window is not the active window.
COLOR_INACTIVECAPTIONTEXT	Color of text in window caption when the window is not active.
COLOR_INFOBK	Background color for tooltip controls.
COLOR_INFOTEXT	Text color for tooltip controls.
COLOR_MENU	The background color of the menu.
COLOR_MENUTEXT	The color of text in the menu.
COLOR_MSGBOX	The background color of system dialog boxes and message boxes.
COLOR_MSGBOXTEXT	The color of the text of system dialog boxes and message boxes.
COLOR_SCROLLBAR	The background color of the scroll bar control.
COLOR_SHADOW	The color of automatic Windows shadows. This cannot be set in the Control Panel.
COLOR_WINDOW	The background color of a window.
COLOR_WINDOWFRAME	The color of a window frame. This cannot be set in the Control Panel.
COLOR_WINDOWTEXT	The color of the text of a window.

lpdwRgbValues   CONST COLORREF*: A pointer to an array of COLORREF values that correspond to the display elements set in the array pointed to by the *lpnDspElements*. Use the RGB macro to create new colors by specifying the red, green, and blue components. The value of each component varies between 0 and 255, depending on the contribution of the component to the composite color. 0 indicates that the component color is not present, and 255 means that the color is fully present (maximum brightness). Table 21-9 shows a list of common colors and their RGB equivalents.

Table 21-9 Common colors and their RGB equivalents

Color	Red	Green	Blue
Black	0	0	0
Blue	0	0	255
Gray	128	128	128
Green	0	255	0
Magenta	255	0	255
Red	255	0	0
Turquoise	0	255	255
White	255	255	255
Yellow	255	255	0

Returns	BOOL: If successful, TRUE is returned; otherwise, FALSE is returned. Use GetLastError to return the error code.
Include File	winbase.h
See Also	GetSysColor
Related Messages	WM_SYSCOLORCHANGE
Example	See the example under the GetSysColor function.

SetSystemPowerState   ■ Windows 95 ■Windows NT

Description	SetSystemPowerState suspends the system by shutting power down. Depending on the *bForceFlag* parameter, the function either suspends operation immediately or requests permission from all applications and device drivers before doing so. This feature requires Advanced Power Management (APM), which Windows NT 4 does not currently support. Power consumption is minimized during suspension.
Syntax	BOOL **SetSystemPowerState(** BOOL *bSuspendOrHibernate,* BOOL *bForceFlag* **)**
Parameters	
bSuspendOrHibernate	BOOL: Suspension mode. Set to TRUE to suspend using RAM-alive technique. Otherwise, suspends using hibernate technique.
bForceFlag	BOOL: Forced suspension. If set to TRUE, the function sends a PBT_APMSUSPEND message to each application and driver, then immediately suspends operation. If FALSE, the function sends a PBT_APMQUERYSUSPEND message to each application to request permission to suspend operation. These messages are sent via the WM_POWERBROADCAST message.

Returns	**BOOL**: If the power has been suspended and subsequently restored, the return value is **TRUE**; otherwise, **FALSE** is returned. Use the **GetLastError** function to retrieve the extended error code.
Include File	`winbase.h`, `pbt.h`
See Also	`GetSystemPowerStatus`
Related Messages	`WM_POWERBROADCAST`
Example	See the example under the `GetSystemPowerStatus` function.

SetSystemTime ■ WINDOWS 95 ■ WINDOWS NT

Description	`SetSystemTime` changes the time to be the values specified in the supplied **SYSTEMTIME** structure. The values in the structure are absolute; that is, no adjustments are made for local time. Under Windows NT, an application must have the **SE_SYSTEMTIME_NAME** privilege to use this function.
Syntax	`BOOL` **SetSystemTime**`( CONST SYSTEMTIME* `*lpst*` )`
Parameters	
lpst	`CONST SYSTEMTIME*`: A pointer to a **SYSTEMTIME** structure that contains the new system time. See the definition of the **SYSTEMTIME** structure under the `GetSystemTime` function.
Returns	**BOOL**: If successful, **TRUE** is returned; otherwise, **FALSE** is returned.
Include File	`winbase.h`
See Also	`GetSystemTime, SetLocalTime, GetLocalTime`
Example	See the example under the `GetLocalTime` function.

SetTimeZoneInformation ■ WINDOWS 95 ■ WINDOWS NT

Description	`SetTimeZoneInformation` sets the parameters of the current time zone.
Syntax	`BOOL` **SetTimeZoneInformation**`( CONST TIME_ZONE_INFORMATION* `*lptzi*` )`
Parameters	
lptzi	`CONST TIME_ZONE_INFORMATION*`: A pointer to a **TIME_ZONE_INFORMATION** structure that contains the new time zone information. See the definition of the **TIME_ZONE_INFORMATION** structure under the `GetTimeZoneInformation` function.
Returns	**BOOL**: If successful, **TRUE** is returned; otherwise, **FALSE** is returned. Use `GetLastError` to return an error code.
Include File	`winbase.h`
See Also	`GetTimeZoneInformation, GetLastError, GetLocalTime, SetLocalTime`
Example	See the example under the `GetTimeZoneInformation` function.

SetVolumeLabel

Description	SetVolumeLabel changes the label of a given drive to a new specified value. An application can obtain the current volume label with the GetVolumeInformation function.
Syntax	BOOL **SetVolumeLabel**(LPCTSTR *lpszRootPath,* LPCTSTR *lpszVolumeName*)
Parameters	
lpszRootPath	LPCTSTR: A pointer to a null-terminated string that contains the path name of the root directory of the drive of the volume whose label is to be set. If this parameter is **NULL**, the volume of the process's current directory is used.
lpszVolumeName	LPCTSTR: A pointer to a null-terminated string that contains the new volume name. If this value is **NULL**, the current volume name is removed.
Returns	BOOL: If successful, **TRUE** is returned; otherwise, **FALSE** is returned. Use **GetLastError** to return the error code.
Include File	winbase.h
See Also	GetVolumeInformation
Example	The example below displays the volume name, volume serial number, installed file system, and whether there is extended file name support when the user selects the Test! menu item. If an argument is included in the command line, the program will also set the volume label to this value.

```
TCHAR szOriginalLabel[64];

LRESULT CALLBACK WndProc( HWND hWnd, UINT uMsg, WPARAM wParam, LPARAM lParam )
{
    switch( uMsg )
    {
      case WM_CREATE:
              // Store current label for later restore.
              //........................................
              GetVolumeInformation( NULL, szOriginalLabel,
                                    sizeof( szOriginalLabel ),
                                    NULL, NULL, NULL, NULL, 0 );
              break;

      case WM_DESTROY :
              // Restore old label name.
              //.......................
              SetVolumeLabel( NULL, szOriginalLabel );
              PostQuitMessage(0);
              break;

      case WM_COMMAND :
              switch( LOWORD( wParam ) )
              {
                  case IDM_TEST:
```

continued on next page

continued from previous page

```
                        {
                            LPTSTR  lpTemp;
                            TCHAR   szLabel[MAX_PATH + 1];
                            TCHAR   szCommandLine[MAX_PATH+1];
                            TCHAR   szBuffer[2 * MAX_PATH + 32];

                            GetVolumeInformation( NULL, szLabel,
                                                 sizeof( szLabel ),
                                                 NULL, NULL, NULL, NULL, 0 );

                            strcpy( szCommandLine, GetCommandLine() );

                            // Search for extra input after program name.
                            //........................................
                            lpTemp = strstr( szCommandLine, "/V" );
                            if (lpTemp)
                            {
                                lpTemp = strtok(lpTemp, "/V");
                                if (lpTemp)
                                {
                                    wsprintf( szBuffer,
                                            "Orig Label: [%s], Current Label: [%s]",
                                            szOriginalLabel, szLabel );
                                    MessageBox( hWnd, szBuffer, "Changing Volume Label",
                                            MB_OK | MB_ICONINFORMATION );

                                    SetVolumeLabel( NULL, lpTemp );
                                }
                            }
                            else
                                MessageBox( hWnd, szOriginalLabel,
                                            "Volume Label", MB_OK );
                        }
                        break;
```

SystemParametersInfo   ■ WINDOWS 95   ■ WINDOWS NT

Description   SystemParametersInfo queries or sets systemwide parameters. These parameters describe accessibility features, screensaver phases, keyboard and mouse settings, metrics, menu drop alignment, and the current language driver. This function can optionally write updated information to the registry. SystemParametersInfo is primarily intended for use with applications, such as the Control Panel, that allow the user to customize the Windows environment.

Syntax   BOOL **SystemParametersInfo**(UINT *uAction,* UINT *uParam,* PVOID *pvParam,* UINT *fUpdateProfile*)

Parameters

uAction	**UINT**: A command that specifies the system parameter affected and whether it is to be queried or set. This can be one of the values in Table 21-10.
uParam	**UINT**: Generic parameter whose use depends on the action specified in *uAction*. See Table 21-10 for a list of actions and how the parameters are used. If the parameter *uParam* is not specified as used for a given action, set to **0**.
pvParam	**PVOID**: Generic parameter whose use depends on the action specified in *uAction*. See Table 21-10 for a list of actions and how the parameters are used. If the parameter *pvParam* is not specified as used for a given action, set to **NULL**.

Table 21-10 SystemParametersInfo actions and parameters

Action	Description
SPI_GETACCESSTIMEOUT	Retrieves an ACCESSTIMEOUT structure that describes the time-out period of accessibility features such as StickyKeys that allow multiple key sequences to be performed one key at a time. The *pvParam* parameter points to an ACCESSTIMEOUT structure that receives the information. See the definition of the ACCESSTIMEOUT structure below.
SPI_GETANIMATION	Retrieves an ANIMATIONINFO structure that describes the animation effects of the current user. The *pvParam* parameter points to an ANIMATIONINFO structure. See the definition of the ANIMATIONINFO structure below.
SPI_GETBEEP	Indicates whether warning beeper is on. The *pvParam* parameter points to a BOOL value that is set to TRUE if the warning beeper is on; otherwise, it is set to FALSE.
SPI_GETBORDER	Returns border size multiplier that changes the width and height of resizable borders in the system. The *pvParam* parameter points to an integer variable that is set to the border size multiplier.
SPI_GETDEFAULTINPUTLANG	Returns the keyboard layout handle for the system default input language. The *pvParam* parameter points to a 32-bit variable that receives the keyboard layout handle.
SPI_GETDRAGFULLWINDOWS	Determines whether dragging full windows is enabled. The pvParam parameter points to a BOOL value that is set to TRUE if full dragging is enabled; otherwise, it is set to FALSE.
SPI_GETFILTERKEYS	Retrieves a FILTERKEYS structure that describes the FilterKeys accessibility feature. The *pvParam* parameter points to a FILTERKEYS structure. See the definition of the FILTERKEYS structure below.
SPI_GETFONTSMOOTHING	Determines whether the font smoothing feature is enabled. This feature uses font anti-aliasing to make font curves appear smoother by painting pixels at different gray levels. The *pvParam* parameter is a pointer to a BOOL variable that receives TRUE if the feature is enabled; otherwise, it receives FALSE.
SPI_GETGRIDGRANULARITY	Determines the spacing between items placed on the Windows desktop. The *pvParam* parameter points to an integer variable that is set to the desktop grid granularity.

continued on next page

continued from previous page

Action	Description
SPI_GETHIGHCONTRAST	Retrieves a HIGHCONTRAST structure that describes the HighContrast accessibility feature for visually impaired users. The *pvParam* parameter points to a HIGHCONTRAST structure that receives the information. See the definition of the HIGHCONTRAST structure below.
SPI_GETICONMETRICS	Retrieves an ICONMETRICS structure that describes the metrics of icons. The *pvParam* parameter is a pointer to an ICONMETRICS structure that receives the icon metrics. See the definition of the ICONMETRICS structure below.
SPI_GETICONTITLELOGFONT	Retrieves a LOGFONT structure that describes the font that an icon uses to display its title text. The *pvParam* parameter is a pointer to a LOGFONT structure that receives the description of the font. See the definition of the LOGFONT structure under the CreateFontIndirect function in Chapter 12, The Graphics Device Interface.
SPI_GETICONTITLEWRAP	Determines whether icon title wrap is set on or off. The *pvParam* parameter is a pointer to the BOOL variable that receives TRUE if icon title wrap is on, or FALSE if icon title wrap is off.
SPI_GETKEYBOARDDELAY	Retrieves the key repeat-delay setting of the keyboard. The *pvParam* parameter is a pointer to a UINT variable that receives the current repeat-delay setting of the keyboard.
SPI_GETKEYBOARDPREF	Determines whether the user wishes applications to display hidden keyboard interfaces for users that prefer using the keyboard instead of the mouse. The *pvParam* is a pointer to a BOOL variable that is set to TRUE if this condition is in effect; otherwise, it is set to FALSE.
SPI_GETKEYBOARDSPEED	Retrieves the key repeat-speed setting of the keyboard. The *pvParam* parameter is a pointer to a UINT variable that receives the current repeat-speed setting of the keyboard.
SPI_GETLOWPOWERACTIVE	Determines whether the low-power screensaving phase is active or not. This allows screensavers to adjust their behavior to compensate in low-power situations. The BOOL variable pointed to by *pvParam* is set to TRUE if this low-power screensaving phase is active; otherwise, *pvParam* is set to FALSE.
SPI_GETLOWPOWERTIMEOUT	Retrieves the time-out factor for the low-power screensaving phase. Under low-power conditions a screensaver may use a different time-out factor for entering screensaving mode. The *pvParam* parameter is a pointer to an integer variable that receives the current time-out factor for entering the low-power screensaving phase.
SPI_GETMENUDROPALIGNMENT	Determines whether pop-up menus are left-aligned or right-aligned to the menu bar items that activate them. The *pvParam* parameter points to a BOOL variable that is set to TRUE if pop-up menus are right-aligned or to FALSE if pop-up menus are left-aligned.
SPI_GETMINIMIZEDMETRICS	Retrieves a MINIMIZEDMETRICS structure that describes the metrics of minimized windows. The *pvParam* parameter points to a MINIMIZEDMETRICS structure that receives the metrics of minimized windows. See the definition of the MINIMIZEDMETRICS structure below.
SPI_GETMOUSE	Retrieves the mouse threshold and speed. The *pvParam* parameter points to an array of three UINT values. These integers represent the x threshold, y threshold, and mouse speed.
SPI_GETMOUSEKEYS	Retrieves information about the MouseKeys accessibility feature. The *pvParam* parameter points to a MOUSEKEYS structure that receives the MouseKeys accessibility feature. See the definition of the MOUSEKEYS structure below.
SPI_GETMOUSETRAILS	Determines whether the Mouse Trails feature is enabled or disabled. The *pvParam* parameter is a pointer to an INT variable that receives a value of 0 or 1 if the feature is disabled. A value greater than 1 indicates that the feature is enabled; it also indicates the number of cursors drawn in the trail.

Action	Description
SPI_GETNONCLIENTMETRICS	Retrieves the metrics for the nonclient area of nonminimized windows in a NONCLIENTMETRICS structure. The *pvParam* parameter points to a NONCLIENTMETRICS structure that receives the metrics. See the definition of the NONCLIENTMETRICS structure below.
SPI_GETPOWEROFFACTIVE	Determines whether the power-off phase of screensaving is enabled. This mode shuts off power to the screen. The *pvParam* parameter points to a BOOL variable that is set to TRUE if the power-off phase of screensaving is enabled; otherwise, it is set to FALSE.
SPI_GETPOWEROFFTIMEOUT	Retrieves the time-out value for the power-off screensaving phase. The *pvParam* parameter is used as a pointer to an integer variable that receives the current time-out factor for entering the power-off screensaving phase.
SPI_GETSCREENREADER	Determines if a screen reviewer utility that redirects text data to a Braille display or speech synthesizer is present. Querying this setting allows applications to enable the software for visually impaired users by outputting graphical data as speech or Braille code when a screen reviewer is installed. The *pvParam* parameter points to a BOOL variable that is set to TRUE if a screen reviewer utility is installed; otherwise, it is set to FALSE.
SPI_GETSCREENSAVEACTIVE	Determines whether the screensaver is enabled or not. The *pvParam* parameter points to a BOOL variable that is set to TRUE if the screensaver is enabled; otherwise, it is set to FALSE.
SPI_GETSCREENSAVETIMEOUT	Returns the time-out value for screensaving. The *pvParam* parameter points to an integer variable that receives the time-out value in milliseconds.
SPI_GETSERIALKEYS	Retrieves a SERIALKEYS structure that describes the SerialKeys accessibility feature. The *pvParam* parameter is a pointer to a SERIALKEYS structure that receives the information about the SerialKeys accessibility feature. See the definition of the SERIALKEYS structure below.
SPI_GETSHOWSOUNDS	Determines whether a user prefers visual representation of sounds. This allows applications to enable the software for hearing-impaired users by outputting sounds as graphical data. The *pvParam* parameter is a pointer a BOOL variable that is set to TRUE if the ShowSounds feature is enabled.
SPI_GETSOUNDSENTRY	Retrieves a SOUNDSENTRY structure that describes the parameters of the SoundSentry accessibility feature. The *pvParam* parameter is a pointer to a SOUNDSENTRY structure that receives the SoundSentry information. See the definition of the SOUNDSENTRY structure below.
SPI_GETSTICKYKEYS	Retrieves a STICKYKEYS structure that describes the parameters of the StickyKeys accessibility feature. The *pvParam* parameter is a pointer to a STICKYKEYS structure that receives information on the StickyKeys feature. See the definition of the STICKYKEYS structure below.
SPI_GETTOGGLEKEYS	Retrieves a TOGGLEKEYS structure that describes the parameter of the ToggleKeys accessibility feature. The ToggleKeys feature emits a high noise when a modifying key is pressed and a low tone when it is released. The *pvParam* parameter is a pointer to a TOGGLEKEYS structure that receives information about ToggleKeys. See the definition of the TOGGLEKEYS structure below.
SPI_GETWINDOWSEXTENSION	Indicates whether the Windows extension Windows Plus! is installed. Set the uParam parameter to 1. The function returns TRUE if the extension is installed; otherwise, FALSE is returned.
SPI_GETWORKAREA	Gets the size of the desktop's work area. This is the area above the tray. The *pvParam* parameter is a pointer to a RECT structure that receives the metrics of the work area in pixels.
SPI_ICONHORIZONTALSPACING	Changes the horizontal icon spacing. The uParam parameter is set to the number of pixels of horizontal spacing between icons.

continued on next page

continued from previous page

Action	Description
SPI_ICONVERTICALSPACING	Changes the vertical icon spacing. The uParam parameter is set to the number of pixels of vertical spacing between icons.
SPI_SETACCESSTIMEOUT	Changes the time-out period of accessibility features. The pvParam parameter points to an ACCESSTIMEOUT structure that describes the new settings. See the definition of the ACCESSTIMEOUT structure below.
SPI_SETANIMATION	Changes the animation effects of the current use. The pvParam parameter points to an ANIMATIONINFO structure that contains the new settings. See the definition of the ANIMATIONINFO structure below.
SPI_SETBEEP	Turns warning beeper on or off. Set the uParam parameter to TRUE to turn the warning beeper on; otherwise, set it to FALSE.
SPI_SETBORDER	Sets border size multiplier that determines the width of a window's sizing border. The specified language must be displayable using the current system character set. Set the pvParam parameter to point to a 32-bit variable that contains the keyboard layout handle for the default language.
SPI_SETDEFAULTINPUTLANG	Sets the default input language for the system shell and applications. The specified language must be displayable using the current system character set. The pvParam parameter must point to a 32-bit variable that contains the keyboard layout handle for the default language.
SPI_SETDESKPATTERN	Sets the desktop's background pattern to the current value of the pattern key from the registry. This option has no parameters.
SPI_SETDESKWALLPAPER	Sets the desktop's wallpaper. The pvParam parameter points to a null-terminated string containing the name of the bitmap file.
SPI_SETDOUBLECLICKTIME	Sets the interval in milliseconds between two clicks to interpret as one double-click to the value contained in the uParam parameter.
SPI_SETDOUBLECLKHEIGHT	Sets the height of the double-click rectangle that allows interpretation of a second click as a double-click to the value specified in the uParam parameter.
SPI_SETDOUBLECLKWIDTH	Sets the width of the double-click rectangle that allows interpretation of a second click as a double-click to the value specified in the uParam parameter.
SPI_SETDRAGFULLWINDOWS	Turns dragging full windows on or off. If the uParam parameter specifies TRUE, full dragging is turned on; otherwise, it is turned off.
SPI_SETDRAGHEIGHT	Sets the height, in pixels, of the rectangle used to detect the start of a drag operation to the value specified in the uParam parameter.
SPI_SETDRAGWIDTH	Sets the width, in pixels, of the rectangle used to detect the start of a drag operation to the value specified in the uParam parameter.
SPI_SETFILTERKEYS	Sets the parameters of the FilterKeys accessibility feature to the values specified in a FILTERKEYS structure pointed to by the pvParam parameter. See the definition of the FILTERKEYS structure below.
SPI_SETFONTSMOOTHING	Enables or disables the font smoothing feature. To enable the feature, set the uParam parameter to TRUE; otherwise, set to FALSE to disable the feature.
SPI_SETGRIDGRANULARITY	Sets the spacing between items placed to the value of the uParam parameter.
SPI_SETHIGHCONTRAST	Sets the parameters of the HighContrast accessibility feature to the values specified in the HIGHCONTRAST structure pointed to by the pvParam parameter. See the definition of the HIGHCONTRAST structure below.
SPI_SETICONMETRICS	Sets the metrics associated with icons to those specified in the ICONMETRICS structure pointed to by the pvParam parameter. See the definition of the ICONMETRICS structure below.

Action	Description
SPI_SETICONTITLELOGFONT	Sets the font of icon title text to the font described by the LOGFONT structure pointed to by the *pvParam* parameter. See the definition of the LOGFONT structure under the CreateFontIndirect function in Chapter 12, The Graphics Device Interface.
SPI_SETICONTITLEWRAP	Sets icon title wrap on or off. If *uParam* is set to TRUE, wrap is turned on ; otherwise, it is turned off.
SPI_SETKEYBOARDDELAY	Sets key repeat-delay to the value specified in the *uParam* parameter.
SPI_SETKEYBOARDPREF	Sets user preference that reveals hidden keyboard interfaces that replace mouse interfaces. If the *uParam* parameter is set to TRUE, the preference is turned on; otherwise, it is turned off.
SPI_SETKEYBOARDSPEED	Sets key repeat-speed setting of keyboard to the speed, in milliseconds, specified in the *uParam* parameter.
SPI_SETLANGTOGGLE	Sets the hotkey set for switching between input languages. The value sets the shortcut keys in the keyboard property sheets by reading the registry again. The registry must be set before this flag is used. The path in the registry is \HKEY_CURRENT_USER\keyboard layout\toggle. Valid values are 1 for ALT+SHIFT, 2 for CTRL+SHIFT, and 3 for nothing.
SPI_SETLOWPOWERACTIVE	If the *uParam* parameter is set to TRUE, the low-power screensaving phase is activated. If set to FALSE, it is deactivated.
SPI_SETLOWPOWERTIMEOUT	Sets the time-out factor for the low-power screensaver phase to the value, in seconds, specified in the *uParam* parameter.
SPI_SETMENUDROPALIGNMENT	Sets menu drop alignment to left-aligned if the *uParam* parameter is set to TRUE; otherwise, menus are right-aligned.
SPI_SETMINIMIZEDMETRICS	Sets metrics of minimized windows to the values specified in the MINIMIZEDMETRICS structure pointed to by the *pvParam* parameter. See the definition of the MINIMIZEDMETRICS structure below.
SPI_SETMOUSE	Sets mouse parameters to the values specified in the array of three integer values pointed to by the *pvParam* parameter. The three integers represent the x threshold, y threshold, and mouse speed.
SPI_SETMOUSEBUTTONSWAP	Switches meaning of left and right mouse buttons. If the *uParam* is set to TRUE, the meanings are swapped. If set to FALSE, the meanings are restored to original setting.
SPI_SETMOUSEKEYS	Sets MouseKeys accessibility options to the values specified in the MOUSEKEYS structure pointed to by the *pvParam* parameter. See the definition of the MOUSEKEYS structure below.
SPI_SETMOUSETRAILS	Enables or disables the Mouse Trails feature. To disable the feature, set the *uParam* parameter to 0 or 1. To enable the feature, set *uParam* to a value greater than 1 to indicate the number of cursors drawn in the trail.
SPI_SETNONCLIENTMETRICS	Sets metrics for nonclient area of nonminimized windows to the values specified in the NONCLIENTMETRICS structure pointed to by the *pvParam* parameter. See the definition of the NONCLIENTMETRICS structure below.
SPI_SETPENWINDOWS	Specifies that Pen Windows is being loaded or unloaded. If *uParam* is set to TRUE, it is loading; otherwise, it is unloaded.
SPI_SETPOWEROFFACTIVE	Activates or deactivates the power-off phase of screensaving. If *uParam* is set to 1, the power-off phase is activated. Otherwise, setting *uParam* to 0 will deactivate the power-off phase or screensaver.
SPI_SETPOWEROFFTIMEOUT	Sets time-out value for the power-off screensaving phase to the value, in seconds, in *uParam*
SPI_SETSCREENREADER	Indicates that a screen reviewer utility is now running if *uParam* is set to TRUE. If uParam is FALSE, screen reviewing is no longer present.
SPI_SETSCREENSAVEACTIVE	Enables or disables screensaving. If *uParam* is TRUE, the screensaver is enabled; otherwise, it is disabled.

continued on next page

continued from previous page

Action	Description
SPI_SETSCREENSAVETIMEOUT	Sets the time-out value for normal screensave to the number of seconds specified in the *uParam* parameter.
SPI_SETSERIALKEYS	Sets SerialKeys accessibility options to the values specified in the SERIALKEYS structure pointed to by the *pvParam* parameter. See the definition of the SERIALKEYS structure below.
SPI_SETSHOWSOUNDS	Enables or disables the ShowSounds accessibility feature. If *uParam* parameter is set to TRUE, the option is enabled; otherwise, it is disabled.
SPI_SETSOUNDSENTRY	Sets SoundSentry accessibility options to the values specified in the SOUNDSENTRY structure pointed to by the *pvParam* parameter. See the definition of the SOUNDSENTRY structure below. The *uParam* parameter must specify the size of the SOUNDSENTRY structure.
SPI_SETSTICKYKEYS	Sets StickyKeys accessibility options to the values specified in the STICKYKEYS structure pointed to by the *pvParam* parameter. See the definition of the STICKYKEYS structure below. The *uParam* parameter must specify the size of the STICKYKEYS structure.
SPI_SETTOGGLEKEYS	Sets ToggleKeys accessibility options to the values specified in the TOGGLEKEYS structure pointed to by the *pvParam* parameter. See the definition of the TOGGLEKEYS structure below. The *uParam* parameter must specify the size of the TOGGLEKEYS structure.
SPI_SETWORKAREA	Sets the size of the work area to the values specified in the RECT structure pointed to by the *pvParam* parameter.

fUpdateProfile   UINT: Flag that determines whether the user profile in the registry is to be updated. Table 21-11 shows the possible values for *fUpdateProfile*.

Table 21-11 SystemParametersInfo *fUpdateProfile* values

Value	Description
SPIF_SENDCHANGE	Broadcasts WM_WININICHANGE after changing user profile.
SPIF_SENDWININICHANGE	Same as SPIF_SENDCHANGE.
SPIF_UPDATEINIFILE	Writes the changes to the registry.

Returns   BOOL: If successful, **TRUE** is returned; otherwise, **FALSE** is returned. Use GetLastError to return the error code.

Include File   winbase.h

See Also   GetSystemMetrics

Related Messages   WM_WININICHANGE

ACCESSTIMEOUT Definition

```
typedef struct tagACCESSTIMEOUT
{
    UINT  cbSize;
    DWORD dwFlags;
    DWORD iTimeOutMSec;
} ACCESSTIMEOUT;
```

Members

cbSize   UINT: The size, in bytes, of this structure.

dwFlags   DWORD: A set of bit flags that specify properties of the time-out behavior for accessibility features. This can be one or more of the values listed in Table 21-12.

Table 21-12 ACCESSTIMEOUT *dwFlags* values

Value	Meaning
ATF_AVAILABLE	The accessibility time-out period is set.
ATF_ONOFFFEEDBACK	The operating system plays a descending siren sound when the time-out period elapses and the accessibility features are turned off.
ATF_TIMEOUTON	The time-out period has been set for accessibility features. If this flag is not set, the features will not time out even though a time-out period is specified.

iTimeOutMSec   DWORD: The time-out period, in milliseconds.

ANIMATIONINFO Definition

```
typedef struct tagANIMATIONINFO
{
    UINT cbSize;
    int  iMinAnimate;
} ANIMATIONINFO, *LPANIMATIONINFO;
```

Members

cbSize   UINT: The size, in bytes, of the structure.

iMinAnimate   int: The minimize and restore animation is enabled if this member is nonzero. If set to 0, animation is disabled.

FILTERKEYS Definition

```
typedef struct tagFILTERKEYS
{
    UINT  cbSize;
    DWORD dwFlags;
    DWORD iWaitMSec;
    DWORD iDelayMSec;
    DWORD iRepeatMSec;
    DWORD iBounceMSec;
} FILTERKEYS;
```

Members

cbSize   UINT: The size, in bytes, of the structure.

dwFlags   DWORD: A set of bit flags that specify properties of the FilterKeys feature. Table 21-13 lists the defined values.

Table 21-13 FILTERKEYS *dwFlags* values

Value	Meaning
FKF_AVAILABLE	The FilterKeys feature is available.
FKF_CLICKON	The computer makes a click sound when a key is pressed or accepted; that is, if SlowKeys is on, the acceptance is separated from the press and gets a separate click.
FKF_CONFIRMHOTKEY	On Windows 95, a confirmation dialog box appears when the FilterKeys features are activated by using the hotkey.
FKF_FILTERKEYSON	The FilterKeys features are on.
FKF_HOTKEYACTIVE	The user can turn the FilterKeys feature on and off by holding down the SHIFT key for eight seconds.
FKF_HOTKEYSOUND	The computer plays a siren sound when the user turns the FilterKeys feature on or off by using the hotkey.
FKF_INDICATOR	On Windows 95, a visual indicator is displayed when the FilterKeys features are on.

iWaitMSec	DWORD: The length of time, in milliseconds, that the user must hold down a key before it is accepted by the computer.
iDelayMSec	DWORD: The length of time, in milliseconds, that the user must hold down a key before it begins to repeat.
iRepeatMSec	DWORD: The length of time, in milliseconds, between each repetition of the keystroke.
iBounceMSec	DWORD: The amount of time, in milliseconds, that must elapse after releasing a key before the computer will accept a subsequent press of the same key.

HIGHCONTRAST Definition

```
typedef struct tagHIGHCONTRAST
{
    UINT    cbSize;
    DWORD   dwFlags;
    LPTSTR  lpszDefaultScheme;
} HIGHCONTRAST, * LPHIGHCONTRAST;
```

Members

cbSize	UINT: The size, in bytes, of the structure.
dwFlags	DWORD: A combination of the values listed in Table 21-14.

Table 21-14 HIGHCONTRAST *dwFlags* values

Value	Meaning
HCF_AVAILABLE	High Contrast Mode is available.
HCF_CONFIRMHOTKEY	A confirmation dialog appears when the High Contrast Mode is activated by using the hotkey.
HCF_HIGHCONTRASTON	High Contrast Mode is on.
HCF_HOTKEYACTIVE	The user can turn the High Contrast Mode on and off by simultaneously pressing the left ALT, left SHIFT, and PRINT SCREEN keys.

Value	Meaning
HCF_HOTKEYAVAILABLE	The hotkey associated with the High Contrast Mode can be enabled. An application can retrieve this value, but cannot set it.
HCF_HOTKEYSOUND	A siren is played when the user turns the High Contrast Mode on or off by using the hotkey.
HCF_INDICATOR	A visual indicator is displayed when the High Contrast Mode is on. This value is not currently used and is ignored.

lpszDefaultScheme **LPTSTR**: A pointer to a null-terminated string that contains the name of the default color scheme.

ICONMETRICS Definition

```
typedef struct tagICONMETRICS
{
    UINT     cbSize;
    int      iHorzSpacing;
    int      iVertSpacing;
    int      iTitleWrap;
    LOGFONT  lfFont;
} ICONMETRICS, *LPICONMETRICS;
```

Members

cbSize   **UINT**: The size, in bytes, of the structure.

iHorzSpacing **int**: The horizontal spacing, in pixels, for each arranged icon.

iVertSpacing **int**: The vertical spacing, in pixels, for each arranged icon.

iTitleWrap   **int**: If this member is nonzero, icon titles wrap to a new line. If set to **0**, titles do not wrap.

lfFont   **LOGFONT**: The font to use for icon titles. See the definition of the **LOGFONT** structure under the **CreateFontIndirect** function in Chapter 12, The Graphics Device Interface.

MINIMIZEDMETRICS Definition

```
typedef struct tagMINIMIZEDMETRICS
{
    UINT cbSize;
    int  iWidth;
    int  iHorzGap;
    int  iVertGap;
    int  iArrange;
}   MINIMIZEDMETRICS, *LPMINIMIZEDMETRICS;
```

Members

cbSize   **UINT**: The size, in bytes, of the structure.

iWidth   **int**: The width, in pixels, of minimized windows.

iHorzGap **int**: The horizontal gap, in pixels, between arranged minimized windows.

iVertGap **int**: The vertical gap, in pixels, between arranged minimized windows.

iArrange	**int**: The starting position and direction used when arranging minimized windows. The starting position must be one of the values in Table 21-15 and the direction must be one of the values in Table 21-16.

Table 21-15 MINIMIZEDMETRICS *iArrange* starting positions

Value	Meaning
ARW_BOTTOMLEFT	Start at the lower-left corner of the work area.
ARW_BOTTOMRIGHT	Start at the lower-right corner of the work area.
ARW_TOPLEFT	Start at the upper-left corner of the work area.
ARW_TOPRIGHT	Start at the upper-right corner of the work area.

Table 21-16 MINIMIZEDMETRICS *iArrange* directions

Value	Meaning
ARW_LEFT	Arrange left. Use with ARW_BOTTOMRIGHT and ARW_TOPRIGHT.
ARW_RIGHT	Arrange right. Use with ARW_BOTTOMLEFT and ARW_TOPLEFT.
ARW_UP	Arrange up. Use with ARW_BOTTOMLEFT and ARW_BOTTOMRIGHT.
ARW_DOWN	Arrange down. Use with ARW_TOPLEFT and ARW_TOPRIGHT.

MOUSEKEYS Definition

```
typedef struct _MOUSEKEYS
{
    DWORD cbSize;
    DWORD dwFlags;
    DWORD iMaxSpeed;
    DWORD iTimeToMaxSpeed;
    DWORD iCtrlSpeed;
    DWORD dwReserved1;
    DWORD dwReserved2;
} MOUSEKEYS;
```

Members

cbSize	**DWORD**: The size, in bytes, of the structure.
dwFlags	**DWORD**: A set of bit flags that specify MouseKeys properties. The bit-flag values listed in Table 21-17 are defined.

Table 21-17 MOUSEKEYS *dwFlags* values

Value	Meaning
MKF_AVAILABLE	The MouseKeys feature is available.
MKF_CONFIRMHOTKEY	On Windows 95, a confirmation dialog box appears when the MouseKeys feature is activated by using the hotkey.

Value	Meaning
MKF_HOTKEYACTIVE	If this flag is set, the user can turn the MouseKeys feature on and off by using the hotkey, which is left [ALT]+left [SHIFT]+[NUM LOCK].
MKF_HOTKEYSOUND	If this flag is set, the system plays a siren sound when the user turns the MouseKeys feature on or off by using the hotkey.
MKF_INDICATOR	On Windows 95, a visual indicator is displayed when the MouseKeys feature is on.
MKF_MOUSEKEYSON	The MouseKeys feature is on.
MKF_MODIFIERS	On Windows 95, the [CTRL] key increases cursor speed by the value specified by the *iCtrlSpeed* member, and the [SHIFT] key causes the cursor to delay briefly after moving a single pixel, allowing fine positioning of the cursor. If this value is not specified, the [CTRL] and [SHIFT] keys are ignored while the user moves the mouse cursor using the arrow keys.
MKF_REPLACENUMBERS	On Windows 95, the numeric keypad moves the mouse when the [NUM LOCK] key is on. If this flag is not specified, the numeric keypad moves the mouse cursor when the [NUM LOCK] key is off.

iMaxSpeed	DWORD: The maximum speed the mouse cursor attains when an arrow key is held down. On Windows NT the range is 10 to 360. Windows 95 does not perform range checking.
iTimeToMaxSpeed	DWORD: The length of time, in milliseconds, that it takes for the mouse cursor to reach maximum speed when an arrow key is held down. Valid values are from 1000 to 5000.
iCtrlSpeed	DWORD: On Windows 95, the multiplier to apply to the mouse cursor speed when the user holds down the [CTRL] key while using the arrow keys to move the cursor. This value is ignored if **MKF_MODIFIERS** is not set. On Windows NT, this must be set to **0**.
dwReserved1	DWORD: Reserved; set to **0**.
dwReserved2	DWORD: Reserved; set to **0**.

NONCLIENTMETRICS Definition

```
typedef struct tagNONCLIENTMETRICS
{
    UINT    cbSize;
    int     iBorderWidth;
    int     iScrollWidth;
    int     iScrollHeight;
    int     iCaptionWidth;
    int     iCaptionHeight;
    LOGFONT lfCaptionFont;
    int     iSmCaptionWidth;
    int     iSmCaptionHeight;
    LOGFONT lfSmCaptionFont;
    int     iMenuWidth;
    int     iMenuHeight;
    LOGFONT lfMenuFont;
    LOGFONT lfStatusFont;
    LOGFONT lfMessageFont;
} NONCLIENTMETRICS, *LPNONCLIENTMETRICS;
```

Members

cbSize	UINT: The size, in bytes, of the structure.
iBorderWidth	int: The thickness, in pixels, of the sizing border.
iScrollWidth	int: The width, in pixels, of a standard vertical scroll bar.
iScrollHeight	int: The height, in pixels, of a standard horizontal scroll bar.
iCaptionWidth	int: The width, in pixels, of caption buttons.
iCaptionHeight	int: The height, in pixels, of caption buttons.
lfCaptionFont	LOGFONT: A LOGFONT structure that describes the caption font. See the definition of the LOGFONT structure under the CreateFontIndirect function in Chapter 12, The Graphics Device Interface.
iSmCaptionWidth	int: The width, in pixels, of small caption buttons.
iSmCaptionHeight	int: The height, in pixels, of small captions.
lfSmCaptionFont	LOGFONT: A LOGFONT structure that describes the small caption font. See the definition of the LOGFONT structure under the CreateFontIndirect function in Chapter 12, The Graphics Device Interface.
iMenuWidth	int: The width, in pixels, of menu-bar buttons.
iMenuHeight	int: The height, in pixels, of a menu bar.
lfMenuFont	LOGFONT: A LOGFONT structure that describes the font used in menu bars. See the definition of the LOGFONT structure under the CreateFontIndirect function in Chapter 12, The Graphics Device Interface.
lfStatusFont	LOGFONT: A LOGFONT structure that describes the font used in status bars. See the definition of the LOGFONT structure under the CreateFontIndirect function in Chapter 12, The Graphics Device Interface.
lfMessageFont	LOGFONT: A LOGFONT structure that describes the font used in message boxes. See the definition of the LOGFONT structure under the CreateFontIndirect function in Chapter 12, The Graphics Device Interface.

SERIALKEYS Definition

```
typedef struct tagSERIALKEYS
{
    DWORD cbSize;
    DWORD dwFlags;
    LPSTR lpszActivePort;
    LPSTR lpszPort;
    DWORD iBaudRate;
    DWORD iPortState;
} SERIALKEYS, *LPSERIALKEYS;
```

Members

cbSize	DWORD: The size, in bytes, of the structure.
dwFlags	DWORD: A combination of the values listed in Table 21-18.

Table 21-18 SERIALKEYS *dwFlags* values

Value	Meaning
SERKF_ACTIVE	The SerialKeys feature is currently receiving input on the serial port specified by *lpszPort*.
SERKF_AVAILABLE	The SerialKeys feature is available.
SERKF_INDICATOR	A visual indicator is displayed when the SerialKeys feature is on. This value is not currently used and is ignored.
SERKF_SERIALKEYSON	The SerialKeys feature is on.

lpszActivePort	LPSTR: A pointer to a string that contains the name of the serial port that receives input from the communication aid when the SerialKeys feature is on. If no port is being used, this member is NULL. If this member is Auto, the system watches all unused serial ports for input from communication aids.
lpszPort	LPSTR: Reserved; must be NULL.
iBaudRate	DWORD: The baud rate setting for the serial port specified by the *lpszActivePort* member. This member should be set to one of the CBR_ values defined in the Windows header files. If *lpszActivePort* is NULL, this member is 0.
iPortState	DWORD: The state of the port specified by the *lpszActivePort* member. If *lpszActivePort* is NULL, this member is 0; otherwise, it is one of the values listed in Table 21-19.

Table 21-19 SERIALKEYS *iPortState* values

Value	Meaning
0	All input on this port is ignored by the SerialKeys feature.
1	Input on this port is watched for SerialKeys activation sequences when no other application has the port open.
2	All input on this port is treated as SerialKeys commands.

SOUNDSENTRY Definition

```
typedef struct tagSOUNDSENTRY
{
    UINT  cbSize;
    DWORD dwFlags;
    DWORD iFSTextEffect;
    DWORD iFSTextEffectMSec;
    DWORD iFSTextEffectColorBits;
    DWORD iFSGrafEffect;
    DWORD iFSGrafEffectMSec;
    DWORD iFSGrafEffectColor;
    DWORD iWindowsEffect;
    DWORD iWindowsEffectMSec;
    LPTSTR lpszWindowsEffectDLL;
    DWORD iWindowsEffectOrdinal;
} SOUNDSENTRY, *LPSOUNDSENTRY;
```

Members

cbSize	UINT: The size, in bytes, of this structure.
dwFlags	DWORD: A set of flags that specify properties of the SoundSentry feature. The values in Table 21-20 are defined.

Table 21-20 SOUNDSENTRY *dwFlags* values

Value	Meaning
SSF_AVAILABLE	The SoundSentry feature is available.
SSF_SOUNDSENTRYON	The SoundSentry feature is on.

iFSTextEffect	DWORD: The visual signal to present when a text-mode application generates a sound while running in a full-screen virtual machine. This can be one of the values listing in Table 21-21. On Windows NT, set this member to 0.

Table 21-21 SOUNDSENTRY visual signals

Value	Meaning
SSTF_BORDER	Flash the screen border, which is unavailable on some displays.
SSTF_CHARS	Flash characters in the corner of the screen.
SSTF_DISPLAY	Flash the entire display.
SSTF_NONE	No visual signal.

FSTextEffectMSec	DWORD: The duration, in milliseconds, of the visual signal that is displayed when a full-screen, text-mode application generates a sound. On Windows NT, this member must be 0.
iFSTextEffectColorBits	DWORD: The RGB value of the color to be used when displaying the visual signal shown when a full-screen, text-mode application generates a sound. On Windows NT, this member must be 0.
iFSGrafEffect	DWORD: The visual signal to present when a graphics-mode application generates a sound while running in a full-screen virtual machine. This member can be set to SSGF_DISPLAY for no visual signal or SSGF_NONE to flash the entire display. On Windows NT, this member must be 0.
iFSGrafEffectMSec	DWORD: The duration, in milliseconds, of the visual signal that is displayed when a full-screen, graphics-mode application generates a sound. On Windows NT, this member must be 0.
iFSGrafEffectColor	DWORD: The RGB value of the color to be used when displaying the visual signal shown when a full-screen, graphics-mode application generates a sound. On Windows NT, this member must be 0.

iWindowsEffect	DWORD: The visual signal to display when a sound is generated by a Windows-based application or an MS-DOS application running in a window. This can be one of the values listed in Table 21-22.

Table 21-22 SOUNDSENTRY *iWindowsEffect* values

Value	Meaning
SSWF_CUSTOM	Call the SoundSentryProc routine exported by the DLL specified by the *lpszWindowsEffectDLL* member.
SSWF_DISPLAY	Flash the entire display.
SSWF_NONE	No visual signal.
SSWF_TITLE	Flash the title bar of the active window.
SSWF_WINDOW	Flash the active window.

iWindowsEffectMSec	DWORD: The duration, in milliseconds, of the visual signal that is displayed when a Windows-based application or MS-DOS based application running in a window generates a sound. On Windows NT, this member must be 0.
lpszWindowsEffectDLL	LPTSTR: A pointer to a buffer that contains the name of the DLL that contains a **SoundSentryProc** callback function. If this member is **NULL**, no DLL is used. When retrieving information, this member must point to a buffer of length **MAX_PATH**. See the definition of the callback function below.
iWindowsEffectOrdinal	DWORD: This member is reserved for future use on both platforms. It must be set to 0.

STICKYKEYS **Definition**

```
typedef struct tagSTICKYKEYS
{
    DWORD cbSize;
    DWORD dwFlags;
} STICKYKEYS, *LPSTICKYKEYS;
```

Members

cbSize	DWORD: The size, in bytes, of this structure.
dwFlags	DWORD: A combination of the values listed in Table 21-23 that specify the properties of the StickyKeys feature.

Table 21-23 STICKYKEYS *dwFlags* values

Value	Meaning
SKF_AUDIBLEFEEDBACK	The system plays a sound when the user latches, locks, or releases modifier keys using the StickyKeys feature.
SKF_AVAILABLE	The StickyKeys feature is available.

continued on next page

continued from previous page

Value	Meaning
SKF_CONFIRMHOTKEY	On Windows 95, a confirmation dialog appears when the StickyKeys feature is activated by using the hotkey.
SKF_HOTKEYACTIVE	The user can turn the StickyKeys feature on and off by pressing the SHIFT key five times.
SKF_HOTKEYSOUND	The system plays a siren sound when the user turns the StickyKeys feature on or off by using the hotkey.
SKF_INDICATOR	On Windows 95, a visual indicator should be displayed when the StickyKeys feature is on.
SKF_STICKYKEYSON	The StickyKeys feature is on.
SKF_TRISTATE	Pressing a modifier key twice in a row locks down the key until the user presses it a third time.
SKF_TWOKEYSOFF	Releasing a modifier key that has been pressed in combination with any other key turns off the StickyKeys feature.

TOGGLEKEYS Definition

```
typedef struct tagTOGGLEKEYS
{
    DWORD cbSize;
    DWORD dwFlags;
} TOGGLEKEYS, *LPTOGGLEKEYS;
```

Members

cbSize   DWORD: The size, in bytes, of this structure.

dwFlags   DWORD: A combination of the values listed in Table 21-24 that specify the properties of the ToggleKeys feature.

Table 21-24 TOGGLEKEYS *dwFlags* values

Value	Meaning
TKF_AVAILABLE	The ToggleKeys feature is available.
TKD_CONFIRMHOTKEY	On Windows 95, a confirmation dialog box appears when the ToggleKeys feature is activated by using the hotkey.
TKF_HOTKEYACTIVE	The user can turn the ToggleKeys feature on and off by holding down the NUM LOCK key for eight seconds.
TKF_HOTKEYSOUND	The system plays a siren sound when the user turns the ToggleKeys feature on or off by using the hotkey.
TKF_TOGGLEKEYSON	The ToggleKeys feature is on.

Callback Syntax   LRESULT CALLBACK **SoundSentryProc**(DWORD *dwMillisec,* DWORD *fdwEffect*)

Callback Parameters

dwMillisec   DWORD: The duration, in milliseconds, of the visual signal that is displayed when a Windows-based application or MS-DOS based application running in a window generates a sound.

fdwEffect   DWORD: The type of visual signal to display. Currently, this value must always be SSWF_CUSTOM.

Callback Returns   LRESULT: If the visual signal was or will be displayed correctly, the return value is TRUE. If the signal is asynchronous and the status is not available when the function is called, it should also return **TRUE**. If an error prevented the signal from being displayed, the return value is **FALSE**.

Example

When the user selects the Test! option from the menu in this example, message boxes will show the status of two accessibility options: ToggleKeys and MouseKeys. ToggleKeys beep when a (CAPS LOCK), (NUM LOCK), or (SCROLL LOCK) key is pressed. MouseKeys remaps the keys of the numeric pad to move the mouse.

```
LRESULT CALLBACK WndProc( HWND hWnd, UINT uMsg, WPARAM wParam, LPARAM lParam )
{
    switch( uMsg )
    {
    case WM_COMMAND :
            switch( LOWORD( wParam ) )
            {
            case IDM_TEST:
                {
                    TOGGLEKEYS  tk;
                    MOUSEKEYS   mk;
                    BOOL        bRetVal;
                    TCHAR       szBuffer[128];

                    // Get ToggleKeys data.
                    //....................
                    tk.cbSize = sizeof(TOGGLEKEYS);
                    bRetVal = SystemParametersInfo( SPI_GETTOGGLEKEYS,
                                                    tk.cbSize, &tk, 0);
                    if (bRetVal)
                    {
                        if ( tk.dwFlags & tk.dwFlags & TKF_HOTKEYACTIVE )
                            strcpy( szBuffer, "ToggleKeys is in use");
                        else if ( tk.dwFlags & TKF_AVAILABLE )
                            strcpy( szBuffer, "ToggleKeys is off" );
                        else
                            strcpy( szBuffer, "ToggleKeys not available" );

                        MessageBox( hWnd, szBuffer, "ToggleKeys status", MB_OK );
                    }

                    // Get MouseKeys data.
                    //...................
                    mk.cbSize = sizeof(MOUSEKEYS);
                    bRetVal = SystemParametersInfo( SPI_GETMOUSEKEYS,
                                                    mk.cbSize, &mk, 0);
                    if (bRetVal )
                    {
                        if ( mk.dwFlags & MKF_MOUSEKEYSON )
                            lstrcpy( szBuffer, "MouseKey active" );
                        else
                            lstrcpy( szBuffer, "MouseKey not active" );

                        MessageBox( hWnd, szBuffer, "MouseKeys status", MB_OK );
                    }
                }
                break;
```

VerLanguageName

Description	VerLanguageName retrieves the stored name for a given language identifier.
Syntax	DWORD **VerLanguageName**(DWORD *idLanguage,* LPTSTR *lpszLanguageName,* DWORD *dwcLanguageName*)
Parameters	
idLanguage	DWORD: The language identifier whose language name is to be retrieved.
lpszLanguageName	LPTSTR: Pointer to a buffer that receives the stored language name.
dwcLanguageName	DWORD: The number of bytes in the buffer.
Returns	DWORD: The number of bytes copied into the buffer, not including the null character if the function succeeds. If there are not enough bytes in the buffer to get the name, the number of bytes necessary (including the null character) is returned. Attempts to get names for nonexistent languages results in **0**. There are no error codes for this function.
Include File	winbase.h
See Also	GetUserDefaultLangID, GetSystemDefaultLangID
Example	See the example under the **GetSystemDefaultLangID** function.

22

STRING MANIPULATION AND CHARACTER SETS

Character sets are translation tables that give meaning to the strings of bytes in character strings. The interpretation of character data depends not only on its contents, but on the selected character set as well. The Win32 API provides support for the three most important microcomputer character sets: ANSI, OEM, and Unicode. ANSI is the default character set for Windows 95, OEM for MS-DOS, and Unicode for Windows NT. Because data may originate from any of these platforms, an application must be prepared to translate the data from its source representation to the native character set.

The string manipulation functions of the Win32 API are sensitive to the currently selected character set. These functions allow a program to correctly address the string contents, test the type of a given character, and raise or lower its case. The Win32 API also includes the translation functions used to convert a string from one character set representation to another.

Another important element in the Win32 API is locale support. Chapter 21, System Information, discusses the importance of locales for time zone and language support. This chapter fully explores the use of locales in National Language Support (NLS), the name given to the subset of the Win32 API that deals with regional conventions. Applications that exploit the features of NLS will find a much smoother migration path to the international market.

Windows Character Set Translations

The OEM (original equipment manufacturer) character set and ANSI (American National Standards Institute) character set are both derivatives of the ASCII character set. The ASCII (American Standards Committee for Information Interchange) character set is a seven-bit character set that predates microcomputers. The ANSI enhancements include foreign language and mathematical symbols. The OEM character set also adds line-drawing characters that allow character-mode windows to be easily drawn in character-mode MS-DOS programs.

As Figures 22-1 and 22-2 show, there is some difference between foreign language characters in the two character sets. The numeric equivalent of a given character in these figures is calculated by adding the index on the top row to the index on the left side. For example, the code for a capital "A" is 41 hex in both tables. The entry for BE in OEM is an underscore ("_"). For ANSI, the same entry is the symbol for three-quarters ("¾").

In 1989, the ANSI board published a C standard that is sensitive to international requirements. One new concept is support for multibyte character sets (MBCS). In an MBCS, a character may be represented by 1 or 2 bytes. Multibyte character sets are used to represent ideographic characters in Japan, Korea, and China. Multibyte character sets are sometimes called double-byte character sets (DBCS), but this term is misleading, since many characters are actually only 1 byte long. In fact, the single-byte characters of a DBCS largely conform to the same values in the ANSI character set.

In an MBCS, ranges of lead-in characters are declared that designate that the next byte (or trailing byte) also composes the character. This is how single-byte and double-byte characters are distinguished in a character data stream. The function **IsDBCSLeadByte** performs this test on any given byte in the stream. Lead byte ranges are stored in code-page descriptors together with default replacement characters for single-byte to double-byte translations. Because in-stream checks of bytes must be made just to move through the characters of a string, multibyte character sets are not very efficient. Examples of an MBCS are the Japanese Industry Standard (JIS) for Kanji (Japanese code-page 932), the Korean standard (KCS 5601), and the standard in Taiwan (TCA).

Unicode—also referred to as wide character set encoding—is a multibyte character set that is more efficient because every character occupies 2 bytes. With 25,000 characters defined in the 1.1 specification, Unicode has a unique location for nearly every character of every language, including more than 18,000 Han characters. Unicode data

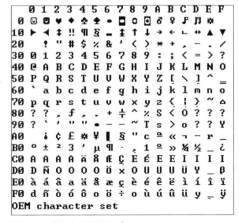

Figure 22-1 OEM character set

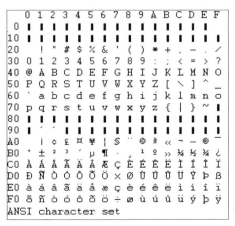

Figure 22-2 ANSI character set

is interchangeable among any systems in the world. Unfortunately, 2 bytes per character adds up to a lot of memory. Increased memory usage is one reason Unicode isn't the native character set of Windows 95.

To translate between ANSI and OEM, use the functions `CharToOem`, `CharToOemBuff`, `OemToChar`, and `OemToCharBuff`. Translations from Unicode to one of the traditional sets is done through `WideCharToMultiByte` and vice versa with `MultiByteToWideChar`.

The function `GetACP` returns the current setting for the ANSI code-page. `GetCPInfo` returns information about the code-page such as how many bytes each character in the page occupies and what the default replacement character is for `WideCharToMultiByte` translations.

Locales

Chapter 21, System Information, discusses locales from the perspective of time zones and language preference. Locales—a concept that also developed from the same 1989 ANSI standard discussed earlier—are also important for specifying code-page preference and time and date format. Other important locale data include the separator character used for displaying large numbers, the decimal character, and the currency symbol. In the function description for `GetLocaleInfo` is a list of locale settings that may be queried. `SetLocaleInfo` modifies the locale settings.

Locales are specific to the thread. The function `SetThreadLocale` changes the locale of a thread. If the locale of the thread is not set, it will use the user default. `EnumSystemLocales` lists the installed locales in the system.

The code-page is another item of data that is stored in the locale. `GetStringTypeA` returns character analysis of a string, specific to the code-page of a locale. `LCMapString` does locale-specific character mapping.

String Manipulation and Character Set Function Descriptions

Table 22-1 lists the Windows API functions that perform string manipulation and character set translation. Complete function descriptions follow the table.

Table 22-1 String manipulation and character set function summary

Function	Purpose
CharLower	Translates a character string to lowercase.
CharLowerBuff	Translates a buffer to lowercase.
CharNext	Positions pointer to next character in a string.
CharNextExA	Positions pointer to next character in a single- or multibyte character string.
CharPrev	Positions pointer to previous character in a string.
CharPrevExA	Positions pointer to previous character in a single- or multibyte character string.
CharToOem	Converts a string from current code-page to OEM character set representation.

continued on next page

continued from previous page

Function	Purpose
CharToOemBuff	Converts a buffer from current code-page to OEM character set representation.
CharUpper	Translates a character string to uppercase.
CharUpperBuff	Translates a character buffer to uppercase.
CompareString	Allows comparison of strings in Latin, Cyrillic, bidirectional, and Far Eastern languages.
ConvertDefaultLocale	Converts a special default locale value to an actual locale identifier.
EnumCalendarInfo	Lists calendar information for a locale.
EnumDateFormats	Lists the long and short date formats that are available for a locale.
EnumSystemCodePages	Lists system code-pages, executing a callback each iteration.
EnumSystemLocales	Lists system locales, executing a callback each iteration.
EnumTimeFormats	Lists the time formats available for a locale.
FoldString	Maps one string to another, performing transformation.
FormatMessage	Provides a way of presenting language-independent messages that are semantically correct.
GetACP	Returns the ANSI code-page.
GetCPInfo	Retrieves code-page information.
GetCurrencyFormat	Formats a number string as a currency string for a locale.
GetDateFormat	Formats a date.
GetLocaleInfo	Returns locale information.
GetNumberFormat	Formats a number string as a number string customized for a locale.
GetOEMCP	Retrieves the identifier of the current OEM code-page of the system.
GetStringTypeEx	Returns character-type information for the characters in either a single- or multibyte string.
GetThreadLocale	Returns the calling thread's current locale.
GetTimeFormat	Formats a time.
IsCharAlpha	Tests if a character is alphabetic.
IsCharAlphaNumeric	Tests if a character is alphanumeric.
IsCharLower	Tests if a character is lowercase.
IsCharUpper	Tests if a character is uppercase.
IsDBCSLeadByte	Tests if a byte is a lead-in byte for a double-byte character in a double-byte character set (DBCS) using the ANSI code-page.
IsDBCSLeadByteEx	Tests if a byte is a lead-in byte for a double-byte character in a double-byte character set (DBCS) using a given code-page.
IsTextUnicode	Determines if a buffer probably contains a form of Unicode text.
IsValidCodePage	Determines if a code-page is valid.
IsValidLocale	Determines if a locale identifier is valid.
LCMapString	Performs locale-dependent mapping of a string.
lstrcat	Concatenates two strings.
lstrcmp	Compares two strings.
lstrcmpi	Performs a case-insensitive comparison of two strings.

Function	Purpose
lstrcpy	Copies a string.
lstrcpyn	Copies a given number of characters from a source string.
lstrlen	Returns the length of a string.
MultiByteToWideChar	Translates character string of given code-page to Unicode character representation.
OemToChar	Translates OEM string to current code-page character set representation.
OemToCharBuff	Translates OEM buffer to current code-page character set representation.
SetLocaleInfo	Allows data regarding a locale to be modified.
SetThreadLocale	Sets the calling thread's current locale.
ToAscii	Translates key pressed to character.
WideCharToMultiByte	Translates Unicode string to character set of specified code-page.
wsprintf	Formats a buffer with a specified list of variables.
wvsprintf	Formats a buffer with an array of data pointers.

CharLower

■ WINDOWS 95   ■ WINDOWS NT

Description

CharLower performs an in-place conversion of a string or returns the conversion of a single character to lowercase based on the current locale.

Syntax

LPTSTR **CharLower**(LPTSTR *lpszString*)

Parameters

lpszString

LPTSTR: A pointer to a zero-terminated string to be converted to lowercase or a single character stored in the low word to be converted.

Returns

LPTSTR: A pointer to the converted data if a string was passed or the single character converted. In the case of conversion of a single character, the high word will be **0**.

Include File

winuser.h

See Also

CharLowerBuff, CharUpper, CharUpperBuff

Example

The example produces the output shown in Figure 22-3, converting the word "aîné"—a word meaning "elder" in French—to uppercase and then to lowercase when the user selects the Test! menu option.

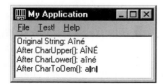

Figure 22-3 CharLower example

```
HWND hList;

LRESULT CALLBACK WndProc( HWND hWnd, UINT uMsg, WPARAM wParam, LPARAM lParam )
{
    switch( uMsg )
    {
    case WM_COMMAND :
            switch( LOWORD( wParam ) )
            {
            case IDM_TEST:
                {
                    TCHAR szBuffer[64];
                    TCHAR szTemp[16];
                    BYTE  szFrench[] = { 0x41, 0xEE, 0x6E, 0xE9, 0 };

                    // Clear the listbox contents.
                    //.........................
                    SendMessage( hList, LB_RESETCONTENT, 0, 0 );

                    // Copy into temporary buffer.
                    //.........................
                    lstrcpy( szTemp, szFrench );

                    // Add results to list box.
                    //.........................
                    wsprintf( szBuffer, "Original String: %s", szTemp );
                    SendMessage( hList, LB_INSERTSTRING, (WPARAM)-1,⇐
(LPARAM)szBuffer );

                    wsprintf( szBuffer, "After CharUpper(): %s", CharUpper(szTemp⇐
);
                    SendMessage( hList, LB_INSERTSTRING, (WPARAM)-1, ⇐
(LPARAM)szBuffer );

                    wsprintf( szBuffer, "After CharLower(): %s", CharLower(szTemp⇐
);
                    SendMessage( hList, LB_INSERTSTRING, (WPARAM)-1,⇐
(LPARAM)szBuffer );

                    CharToOem( szTemp, szTemp );
                    wsprintf( szBuffer, "After CharToOem(): %s", szTemp );
                    SendMessage( hList, LB_INSERTSTRING, (WPARAM)-1,⇐
(LPARAM)szBuffer );
                }
                break;
          .
          .
          .
```

CharLowerBuff ■ Windows 95 ■ Windows NT

Description	**CharLowerBuff** converts a buffer of characters in place to lowercase. The buffer may contain embedded null characters. The current locale language identifier is used.
Syntax	DWORD **CharLowerBuff**(LPTSTR *lpszString*, DWORD *dwBytes*)

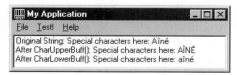

Figure 22-4 `CharLowerBuff` example

Parameters

lpszString   **LPTSTR**: A pointer to a buffer to be lowercased.

dwBytes   **DWORD**: The number of bytes to inspect and convert.

Returns   **DWORD**: The number of bytes in the converted portion of the buffer.

Include File   `winuser.h`

See Also   `CharLower`, `CharUpper`, `CharUpperBuff`

Example   This example shows how the `CharLowerBuff` and `CharUpperBuff` functions work on buffers, performing the same kinds of transformations as `CharUpper` and `CharLower`. What distinguishes `CharLowerBuff` and `CharUpperBuff` is their ability to transform only a certain number of characters and to operate on buffers with embedded null characters. Figure 22-4 shows the results.

```
HWND hList;

LRESULT CALLBACK WndProc( HWND hWnd, UINT uMsg, WPARAM wParam, LPARAM lParam )
{
   switch( uMsg )
   {
      case WM_COMMAND :
              switch( LOWORD( wParam ) )
              {
                 case IDM_TEST:
                      {
                         TCHAR szBuffer[64];
                         TCHAR szTemp[64];
                         static TCHAR szStart[25] = "Special characters here: ";
                         static BYTE  szFrench[] = { 0x41, 0xEE, 0x6E, 0xE9, 0 };

                         // Clear the listbox contents.
                         //............................
                         SendMessage( hList, LB_RESETCONTENT, 0, 0 );

                         // Copy into temporary buffer.
                         //............................
                         lstrcpy( szTemp, szStart );
                         lstrcat( szTemp, szFrench );

                         // Add results to list box.
                         //............................
                         wsprintf( szBuffer, "Original String: %s", szTemp );
                         SendMessage( hList, LB_INSERTSTRING, (WPARAM)-1,⇐
(LPARAM)szBuffer );
```

continued on next page

continued from previous page

```
                        CharUpperBuff( &szTemp[25], lstrlen( szFrench ) );
                        wsprintf( szBuffer, "After CharUpperBuff(): %s", szTemp );
                        SendMessage( hList, LB_INSERTSTRING, (WPARAM)-1,⇐
(LPARAM)szBuffer );

                        CharLowerBuff( &szTemp[25], lstrlen( szFrench ) );
                        wsprintf( szBuffer, "After CharLowerBuff(): %s", szTemp );
                        SendMessage( hList, LB_INSERTSTRING, (WPARAM)-1,⇐
(LPARAM)szBuffer );
                }
                break;
```

CharNext

■ Windows 95   ■ Windows NT

Description	**CharNext** returns a pointer to the next character of the string by adding the width of the current character to the passed address.
Syntax	LPTSTR **CharNext**(LPCTSTR *lpszCurrentChar*)
Parameters	
lpszCurrentChar	LPCTSTR: A pointer to the current character in a string. If the character this points to is the null-termination character, the function returns without incrementing.
Returns	LPTSTR: A pointer to next character or **NULL** if at end of string.
Include File	winuser.h
See Also	CharNextExA, CharPrev
Example	This example demonstrates how strings must be indexed with characters of unknown size. You can't assume that a character is just 1 byte; although all characters in Unicode are 2 bytes, this is not necessarily the case in other multibyte character sets. Figure 22-5 shows the output of an example that advances 28 places down a string and then backtracks two characters. It will work for OEM, ANSI, or Unicode data.

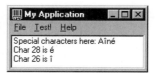

Figure 22-5 CharNext example

```
HWND hList;

LRESULT CALLBACK WndProc( HWND hWnd, UINT uMsg, WPARAM wParam, LPARAM lParam )
{
   switch( uMsg )
   {
     case WM_COMMAND :
             switch( LOWORD( wParam ) )
             {
               case IDM_TEST :
                       {
                         TCHAR  szBuffer[64];
                         TCHAR  szTemp[64];
                         int    i;
                         static TCHAR szStart[25] = "Special characters here: ";
                         static BYTE  szFrench[] = { 0x41, 0xEE, 0x6E, 0xE9, 0 };

                         LPTSTR lpStr = szTemp;

                         lstrcpy( szTemp, szStart );
                         lstrcat( szTemp, szFrench );
                         SendMessage( hList, LB_INSERTSTRING, (WPARAM)-1, (LPARAM)szTemp
);

                         // Advance to the 28th character.
                         //............................
                         for( i=0; i<28; i++ )
                             lpStr = CharNext( lpStr );
                         wsprintf( szBuffer, "Char 28 is %c", *lpStr );
                         SendMessage( hList, LB_INSERTSTRING, (WPARAM)-1,
(LPARAM)szBuffer );

                         // Move back 2 characters.
                         //.......................
                         for( i=0; i<2; i++ )
                             lpStr = CharPrev( szTemp, lpStr );
                         wsprintf( szBuffer, "Char 26 is %c", *lpStr );
                         SendMessage( hList, LB_INSERTSTRING, (WPARAM)-1,
(LPARAM)szBuffer );
                       }
                       break;
       .
       .
       .
```

CharNextExA   ■ WINDOWS 95   ■ WINDOWS NT

Description	CharNextEx positions the pointer at the next character in a single- or multibyte character string.
Syntax	LPSTR **CharNextExA**(WORD *CodePage,* LPCSTR *lpCurrentChar,* DWORD *dwFlags*)
Parameters	
CodePage	WORD: The code-page to use to check lead-byte ranges. This can be one of the code-page values provided in Table 22-2, or set to **0** or **CP_ACP** to use

the system default ANSI code-page. This value can also be set to `CP_OEMCP` to use the default OEM code-page.

Table 22-2 Code-page identifiers

Identifier	Meaning
037	EBCDIC
437	MS-DOS United States
500	EBCDIC "500V1"
708	Arabic (ASMO 708)
709	Arabic (ASMO 449+, BCON V4)
710	Arabic (Transparent Arabic)
720	Arabic (Transparent ASMO)
737	Greek (formerly 437G)
775	Baltic
850	MS-DOS Multilingual (Latin I)
852	MS-DOS Slavic (Latin II)
855	IBM Cyrillic (primarily Russian)
857	IBM Turkish
860	MS-DOS Portuguese
861	MS-DOS Icelandic
862	Hebrew
863	MS-DOS Canadian-French
864	Arabic
865	MS-DOS Nordic
866	MS-DOS Russian
869	IBM Modern Greek
874	Thai
875	EBCDIC
932	Japan
936	Chinese (PRC, Singapore)
949	Korean
950	Chinese (Taiwan, Hong Kong)
1026	EBCDIC
1200	Unicode (BMP of ISO 10646)
1250	Windows 3.1 Eastern European
1251	Windows 3.1 Cyrillic
1252	Windows 3.1 U.S. (ANSI)
1253	Windows 3.1 Greek
1254	Windows 3.1 Turkish
1255	Hebrew

CharToOemBuff

Description

CharToOemBuff translates a specified number of characters in a string from the character set of the current locale to an OEM-defined character set. Characters that do not exist in the OEM character set (the IBM PC's console mode character set) are converted to their nearest equivalent.

Syntax

BOOL **CharToOemBuff**(LPCTSTR *lpszSource,* LPSTR *lpszDest,* DWORD *dwLength*)

Parameters

lpszSource

LPCTSTR: A pointer to a buffer of characters in the current character set. This may be the first character in a string or a pointer to a character within the string.

lpszDest

LPSTR: A pointer to destination buffer to receive OEM-based translation. This buffer may be the same address as *lpszSource*, in which case the translation is performed in place. This cannot be done if using the wide-character version of this function.

dwLength

DWORD: The number of characters to be converted.

Returns

BOOL: Always returns TRUE.

Include File

winuser.h

See Also

CharToOem, OemToCharBuff

Example

This example displays the ANSI and OEM character sets as shown in Figures 22-1 and 22-2 at the beginning of this chapter. Each time the Test! option is selected, the character set display toggles between ANSI and OEM.

```
BOOL  bAnsi = TRUE;
TCHAR szTemp[64];
TCHAR szBuffer[64];

LRESULT CALLBACK WndProc( HWND hWnd, UINT uMsg, WPARAM wParam, LPARAM lParam )
{
   switch( uMsg )
   {
     case WM_PAINT :
              {
                int   i, j;
                HFONT hOldFont;
                PAINTSTRUCT ps;

                BeginPaint( hWnd, &ps );

                if (bAnsi)
                   hOldFont = SelectObject( ps.hdc,
                           GetStockObject( ANSI_FIXED_FONT ) );
                else
                   hOldFont = SelectObject( ps.hdc,
                           GetStockObject( OEM_FIXED_FONT ) );
```

continued on next page

continued from previous page

```
            // Print the column titles.
            //........................
            szTemp[0]=0;
            for ( j=0; j<16; j++ )
            {
                wsprintf( szBuffer, "%X ", j );
                lstrcat( szTemp, szBuffer );
            }
            TextOut( ps.hdc, 22, 0, szTemp, lstrlen( szTemp ) );

            // Print the rows for the character set.
            //.....................................
            for ( i=0; i<16; i++ )
            {
                wsprintf( szTemp, "%2X ", i*16 );
                for ( j=0; j<16; j++ )
                {
                    wsprintf( szBuffer, "%c ", j+i*16 );
                    lstrcat( szTemp, szBuffer );
                }
                if (!bAnsi)
                    CharToOemBuff( szTemp, szTemp, lstrlen( szTemp ) );
                TextOut( ps.hdc, 0, (i + 1)*15, szTemp, lstrlen(szTemp) );
            }

            // Place a title on the character set.
            //...................................
            lstrcpy( szBuffer, bAnsi ? "ANSI character set" :
                    "OEM character set  " );
            TextOut( ps.hdc, 0, 256, szBuffer, lstrlen(szBuffer) );

            SelectObject( ps.hdc, hOldFont );

            EndPaint( hWnd, &ps );
        }
        break;


case WM_COMMAND :
        switch( LOWORD( wParam ) )
        {
            case IDM_TEST:
                    // Toggle the ANSI/OEM character set.
                    //.................................
                    bAnsi = !bAnsi;
                    InvalidateRect( hWnd, NULL, TRUE );
                    break;
        .
        .
        .
```

CharUpper
■ WINDOWS 95   ■ WINDOWS NT

Description   CharUpper performs an in-place conversion of a string or returns the conversion of a single character to uppercase based on the current locale.

Syntax	LPTSTR **CharUpper**(LPTSTR *lpszString*)
Parameters	
lpszString	LPTSTR: A pointer to a null-terminated string or a single character in the low-order word, which is converted to uppercase.
Returns	LPTSTR: A pointer to the converted string or the converted character in the low-order word.
Include File	winuser.h
See Also	CharUpperBuff, CharLower
Example	See the example for the CharLower function.

CharUpperBuff ■ WINDOWS 95 ■ WINDOWS NT

Description	CharUpperBuff converts a buffer of characters in place to uppercase using the current locale language identifier. The buffer may contain embedded null characters.
Syntax	DWORD **CharUpperBuff**(LPTSTR *lpszString*, DWORD *dwBytes*)
Parameters	
lpszString	LPTSTR: A pointer to a buffer that contains one or more characters to process.
dwBytes	DWORD: The number of characters to process in the buffer pointed to by *lpszString*.
Returns	DWORD: If successful, the number of characters processed.
Include File	winuser.h
See Also	CharLower, CharUpper, CharLowerBuff
Example	See the example for the CharLowerBuff function.

CompareString ■ WINDOWS 95 ■ WINDOWS NT

Description	CompareString compares two character strings using the specified locale. Under Windows NT, Unicode is supported for this function, but not for the other platforms.
Syntax	int **CompareString**(LCID *lcidLocale*, DWORD *dwStyle*, LPCTSTR *lpString1*, int *nCnt1*, LPCTSTR *lpString2*, int *nCnt2*)
Parameters	
lcidLocale	LCID: The locale to use for comparing the strings. This can be any locale identifier created with the MAKELCID macro, or one of the predefined locales, LOCALE_SYSTEM_DEFAULT (default system locale) or LOCALE_USER_DEFAULT (default user locale).
dwStyle	DWORD: Comparison modifications. Table 22-3 gives a list of values for *dwStyle*.

Table 22-3 CompareString *dwStyle* values

CompareString **Option**	**Description**
NORM_IGNORECASE	Ignore case.
NORM_IGNOREKANATYPE	Corresponding Hiragana and Katakana compare alike.
NORM_IGNORENONSPACE	Ignore nonspacing characters.
NORM_IGNORESYMBOLS	Ignore symbols.
NORM_IGNOREWIDTH	Ignore differences in character byte width.
NORM_STRINGSORT	Treat punctuation as symbols.

lpString1	LPCTSTR: A pointer to the first string to be compared.
nCnt1	int: The length of the string pointed to by the *lpString1* parameter or −1 if the string is null terminated and the entire string is to be compared.
lpString2	LPCTSTR: A pointer to the second string to be compared.
nCnt2	int: The length of the string pointed to by the *lpString2* parameter or −1 if the string is null terminated and the entire string is to be compared.
Returns	int: If an error occurs, 0 is returned and the application can use the **GetLastError** function to return the error code. A return value of 1 indicates the first string is less than the second string, 2 indicates the strings are equal within the specified length, and 3 indicates the first string is greater than the second string. Subtract two from the return value to create a return value that is like the **lstrcmp** function.
Include File	winnls.h
See Also	lstrcmp, lstrcmpi, GetLocaleInfo
Example	This example shows different levels of accuracy in comparing strings. In the first case, **lstrcmp** is used and of course fails, because it is sensitive to case. In the second case, **lstrcmpi** is used and fails as well—not because it is case sensitive, but because it does not understand locales and accented characters with the same collation code. **CompareString** performs the comparison correctly. Figure 22-6 shows the results.

```
HWND hList;

LRESULT CALLBACK WndProc( HWND hWnd, UINT uMsg, WPARAM wParam, LPARAM lParam )
{
    switch( uMsg )
    {
    case WM_COMMAND :
            switch( LOWORD( wParam ) )
            {
            case IDM_TEST:
                    {
                        int    iResult;
                        TCHAR szBuffer[64];
```

```
                    // ANSI string of accented characters to translate
                    // similar string without accented characters
                    //.............................................
                    static BYTE  szAccentedChars[] =
                                        { 0xE1, 0xE2, 0xE7, 0xE8, 0xED, 0xEC, 0 };
                    static TCHAR szUnaccentedChars[] = "aaCeii";

                    // lstrcmp fails
                    //..............
                    wsprintf( szBuffer, "Result of lstrcmp() (%s = %s): %d",
                                        szAccentedChars, szUnaccentedChars,
                                        lstrcmp( szAccentedChars, szUnaccentedChars⇐
) );
                    SendMessage( hList, LB_INSERTSTRING, (WPARAM)-1,⇐
(LPARAM)szBuffer );


                    // lstrcmpi fails because it only ignores case.
                    //.............................................
                    wsprintf( szBuffer, "Result of lstrcmpi() (%s = %s): %d",
                                        szAccentedChars, szUnaccentedChars,
                                        lstrcmpi( szAccentedChars, szUnaccentedChars⇐
) );
                    SendMessage( hList, LB_INSERTSTRING, (WPARAM)-1,⇐
(LPARAM)szBuffer );


                    // Do CompareStrings in French - it works
                    //......................................
                    iResult = CompareString(
                                        MAKELCID( MAKELANGID( LANG_FRENCH,⇐
SUBLANG_FRENCH ),
                                                    SORT_DEFAULT),
                                        NORM_IGNORECASE | NORM_IGNORENONSPACE |⇐
NORM_IGNOREWIDTH,
                                        szAccentedChars, -1,
                                        szUnaccentedChars, -1 );

                    // We must subtract 2 bias from result to make it
                    // look like strcmp.
                    //...............................................
                    wsprintf( szBuffer, "Result of CompareString() (%s = %s): %d",
                                        szAccentedChars, szUnaccentedChars,
                                        iResult-2 );
                    SendMessage( hList, LB_INSERTSTRING, (WPARAM)-1,⇐
(LPARAM)szBuffer );
                }
                break;

        .
        .
        .
```

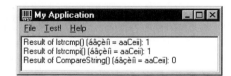

Figure 22-6 CompareString example

ConvertDefaultLocale　　　■ Windows 95　■ Windows NT

Description	ConvertDefaultLocale converts a special default locale value to an actual locale identifier. A call to ConvertDefaultLocale (LOCALE_SYSTEM_DEFAULT) is equivalent to a call to GetSystemDefaultLCID. A similar call with LOCALE_USER_DEFAULT is equivalent to a call to GetUserDefaultLCID.
Syntax	LCID ConvertDefaultLocale(LCID *Locale*)
Parameters	
Locale	LCID: A special default locale value that the function converts to an actual locale identifier. This can be set to LOCALE_SYSTEM_DEFAULT for the system's default locale, LOCALE_USER_DEFAULT for the user's default locale, 0 for the language-neutral default locale, or any sub-language neutral default locale that is created by calling the MAKELCID macro with a primary language value and the SUBLANG_NEUTRAL value.
Returns	LCID: If successful, the appropriate actual locale identifier is returned; otherwise, the value is the *Locale* parameter.
Include File	winnls.h
See Also	GetSystemDefaultLCID, GetUserDefaultLCID

EnumCalendarInfo　　　■ Windows 95　■ Windows NT

Description	EnumCalendarInfo enumerates calendar information for a given locale. The function returns the specified calendar information for all applicable calendars for the locale, or for a single requested calendar, depending on the value of the *Calendar* parameter.
	The calendar information is enumerated by calling an application-defined callback function. It passes the callback function a pointer to a string buffer containing the requested calendar information. This continues until either the last applicable calendar is found or the callback function returns FALSE.
Syntax	BOOL EnumCalendarInfo(CALINFO_ENUMPROC *lpCallInfoEnumProc,* LCID *Locale,* CALID *Calendar,* CALTYPE *CalType*)
Parameters	
lpCallInfoEnumProc	CALINFO_ENUMPROC: A pointer to an application-defined callback function. See the syntax of the callback function below.
Locale	LCID: The locale for which to retrieve calendar information. This parameter can be a locale identifier created with the MAKELCID macro, LOCALE_SYSTEM_DEFAULT for the default system locale, or LOCALE_USER_DEFAULT for the default user locale.

Calendar   **CALID**: The calendar for which information is requested. This can be one of the values listed in Table 22-4.

Table 22-4 EnumCalendarInfo *Calendar* values

Value	Meaning
ENUM_ALL_CALENDARS	Enumerate all applicable calendars for the locale specified by the *Locale* parameter.
1	Gregorian (localized).
2	Gregorian (English strings always).
3	Japanese era.
4	Year of the Republic of China.
5	Tangun era (Korea).

CalType   **CALTYPE**: The type of calendar information to be returned. An application can request only one type at a time. Table 22-5 lists the different available **CALTYPE** constants.

Table 22-5 CALTYPE constants

Constant Name	Meaning
CAL_ICALINTVALUE	An integer value indicating the calendar type of the alternate calendar.
CAL_SCALNAME	The native name of the alternate calendar.
CAL_IYEAROFFSETRANGE	A series of strings separated by null characters that contain the year offsets for each of the era ranges.
CAL_SERASTRING	A series of strings separated by null characters that contain each of the Unicode codepoints specifying the era associated with the particular CAL_IYEAROFFSETRANGE.
CAL_SSHORTDATE	The short date formats applicable to this calendar type.
CAL_SLONGDATE	The long date formats applicable to this calendar type.
CAL_SDAYNAME1–7	The native names of the days of the week. If these values are null, then the day names for this calendar are the same as those contained within the corresponding LCType.
CAL_SABBREVDAYNAME1–7	The native abbreviated names of the days. If these values are null, then the day names for this calendar are the same as those contained within the corresponding LCType.
CAL_SMONTHNAME1–13	The native names of the months. If these values are null, then the month names for this calendar are the same as those contained within the corresponding LCType.
CAL_SABBREVMONTHNAME1–13	The native abbreviated names of the months. If these values are null, then the month names for this calendar are the same as those contained within the corresponding LCType.

Returns   **BOOL**: If successful, **TRUE** is returned; otherwise, **FALSE** is returned. The extended error code is retrieved with a call to the **GetLastError** function, which may return **ERROR_BADDB**, **ERROR_INVALID_FLAGS**, or **ERROR_INVALID_PARAMETER**.

Include File	`winnls.h`
See Also	`EnumDateFormats`
Callback Syntax	`BOOL CALLBACK EnumCalendarInfoProc( LPTSTR lpCalendarInfoString )`

Callback Parameters	
`lpCalendarInfoString`	`LPTSTR`: A pointer to a string buffer containing a null-terminated calendar information string. The string is formatted according to the `CALTYPE` value passed to `EnumCalendarInfo`.
Callback Returns	`BOOL`: To continue enumeration, return `TRUE`; otherwise, return `FALSE` and the enumeration will stop.

EnumDateFormats   ■ WINDOWS 95   ■ WINDOWS NT

Description	`EnumDateFormats` enumerates the long or short date formats that are available for the specified locale, including date formats for any alternate calendars. The function enumerates the date formats by passing date format string pointers, one at a time, to the specified application-defined callback function. This continues until the last date format is found or the callback function returns `FALSE`.
Syntax	`BOOL EnumDateFormats( DATEFMT_ENUMPROC lpDateFmtEnumProc, LCID Locale, DWORD dwFlags )`
Parameters	
`lpDateFmtEnumProc`	`DATEFMT_ENUMPROC`: A pointer to an application-defined callback function. The `EnumDateFormats` function enumerates date formats by making repeated calls to this callback function. See the syntax of the callback function below.
`Locale`	`LCID`: The locale for which to retrieve date format information. This parameter can be a locale identifier created with the `MAKELCID` macro, `LOCALE_SYSTEM_DEFAULT` for the default system locale, or `LOCALE_USER_DEFAULT` for the default user locale.
`dwFlags`	`DWORD`: The date formats that are enumerated. For short date formats, set to `DATE_SHORTDATE`. To return long date formats, set to `DATE_LONGDATE`.
Returns	`BOOL`: If successful, `TRUE` is returned; otherwise, `FALSE` is returned. The extended error code is retrieved with a call to the `GetLastError` function, which may return `ERROR_BADDB`, `ERROR_INVALID_FLAGS`, or `ERROR_INVALID_PARAMETER`.
Include File	`winnls.h`
See Also	`EnumCalendarInfo, EnumTimeFormats`
Callback Syntax	`BOOL CALLBACK EnumDateFormatsProc( LPTSTR lpDateFormatString )`

Callback Parameters

lpDateFormatString   LPTSTR: A pointer to a string buffer containing a null-terminated date format string. This string is a long or short date format depending on the value of the *dwFlags* parameter passed to EnumDateFormats.

Callback Returns   BOOL: To continue enumeration, return TRUE; otherwise, return FALSE to stop the enumeration.

EnumSystemCodePages   ■ WINDOWS 95   ■ WINDOWS NT

Description   EnumSystemCodePages enumerates the code-pages that are either installed on or supported by a system. The function enumerates the code-pages by passing code-page identifiers, one at a time, to the specified application-defined callback function. This continues until all of the installed or supported code-page identifiers have been passed to the callback function, or the callback function returns FALSE.

Syntax   BOOL **EnumSystemCodePages**(CODEPAGE_ENUMPROC *lpCodePageEnumProc,* DWORD *dwFlags*)

Parameters

lpCodePageEnumProc   CODEPAGE_ENUMPROC: A pointer to an application-defined callback function that receives the code-page number as a parameter. See the syntax of the callback function below.

dwFlags   DWORD: CP_INSTALLED enumerates through installed code-pages. CP_SUPPORTED enumerates through all supported code-pages.

Returns   BOOL: TRUE if the function is successful; otherwise, FALSE is returned. The extended error code is retrieved with a call to the GetLastError function, which may return ERROR_BADDB, ERROR_INVALID_FLAGS, or ERROR_INVALID_PARAMETER.

Include File   winnls.h

See Also   EnumSystemLocales, GetCPInfo

Callback Syntax   BOOL CALLBACK **EnumCodePagesProc**(LPTSTR *lpCodePageString*)

Callback Parameters

lpCodePageString   LPTSTR: A pointer to a string buffer containing a null-terminated code-page identifier string.

Callback Returns   BOOL: To continue enumeration, return TRUE; otherwise, return FALSE to stop the enumeration.

Example   This example enumerates the installed code-pages each time the user selects the Test! menu option. For each code-page a descriptive message box is displayed.

```
HWND hList;

// Define code pages typically available.
//.....................................
typedef struct CPListElementtag
{
    UINT uCPId;
    char szCPName[40];
} CPListElement;

CPListElement codepages [50] = {
                          037, "EBCDIC",
                          437, "MS-DOS United States",
                          500, "EBCDIC 500V1",

            .

            .

                        10079, "Macintosh Icelandic",
                        10081, "Macintosh Turkish",
                            0 ,"Undefined"
                    };

BOOL CALLBACK EnumCodePages( LPWSTR lpCPString )
{
    static TCHAR  szBuffer[128];
    static DWORD  wCodePage;
    static CPINFO cpInfo;
    static int i;

    // Get the code page.
    //...................
    sscanf( lpCPString, "%u", &wCodePage );

    i = 0;
    while ( (codepages[i].uCPId != 0) && (codepages[i].uCPId != wCodePage ) )
        i++;

    wsprintf( szBuffer, "Code Page = %d, Name = %s", wCodePage,
              codepages[i].szCPName );

    // Get the character width.
    //.........................
    if ( IsValidCodePage( wCodePage ) )
    {
        char szMore[32];
        GetCPInfo( wCodePage, &cpInfo );
        wsprintf( szMore, " Max Char Width: %d", cpInfo.MaxCharSize );
        lstrcat( szBuffer, szMore );
    }
    else
        lstrcat( szBuffer, " Invalid Code Page" );

    // Add to list box.
    //.................
    SendMessage( hList, LB_INSERTSTRING, (WPARAM)-1, (LPARAM)szBuffer );

    return( TRUE );
}
```

```
LRESULT CALLBACK WndProc( HWND hWnd, UINT uMsg, WPARAM wParam, LPARAM lParam )
{
   switch( uMsg )
   {
      case WM_COMMAND :
             switch( LOWORD( wParam ) )
             {
                case IDM_TEST:
                       // Clear the list box.
                       //...................
                       SendMessage( hList, LB_RESETCONTENT, 0, 0 );

                       EnumSystemCodePages( EnumCodePages, CP_INSTALLED );
                       break;
             .
             .
             .
```

EnumSystemLocales   ■ WINDOWS 95   ■ WINDOWS NT

Description	**EnumSystemLocales** enumerates the locales that are either installed on or supported by a system. The function enumerates locales by passing locale identifiers, one at a time, to the specified application-defined callback function. This continues until all of the installed or supported locale identifiers have been passed to the callback function or the callback function returns **FALSE**.
Syntax	BOOL **EnumSystemLocales**(LOCALE_ENUMPROC *lpLocaleEnumProc,* DWORD *dwFlags*)
Parameters	
lpLocaleEnumProc	LOCALE_ENUMPROC: A pointer to an application-defined callback function that receives the locale number as a parameter. See the callback syntax below.
dwFlags	DWORD: LCID_INSTALLED enumerates the installed locales. LCID_SUPPORTED enumerates all supported locales.
Returns	BOOL: If successful, **TRUE** is returned; otherwise, **FALSE** is returned. The extended error code is retrieved with a call to the **GetLastError** function, which may return **ERROR_BADDB**, **ERROR_INVALID_FLAGS**, or **ERROR_INVALID_PARAMETER**.
Include File	winnls.h
See Also	EnumSystemCodePages, GetLocaleInfo
Callback Syntax	BOOL CALLBACK **EnumLocalesProc**(LPTSTR *lpLocaleString*)
Callback Parameters	
lpLocaleString	LPTSTR: A pointer to a string buffer containing a null-terminated locale identifier string.

Callback Returns BOOL: To continue enumeration, return TRUE; otherwise, return FALSE to stop enumeration.

Example When the user selects the Test! option of the menu in the example, the installed locales of the system are enumerated and added to a list box.

```
HWND hList;

BOOL CALLBACK EnumLocales( LPTSTR lpLocaleString )
{
   static LCID lcid;
   static TCHAR szBuffer[400];
   static TCHAR szCountry[96];
   static TCHAR szLanguage[96];

   // Get the locale ID.
   //...................
   sscanf( (LPSTR) lpLocaleString, "%x", &lcid );

   // Get locale data.
   //.................
   GetLocaleInfo( lcid, LOCALE_SNATIVECTRYNAME, szCountry, 96 );
   GetLocaleInfo( lcid, LOCALE_SNATIVELANGNAME, szLanguage, 96 );

   wsprintf( szBuffer, "Locale: %d, Country: %s, Language: %s",
            lcid, szCountry, szLanguage );

   // Add to list box.
   //.................
   SendMessage( hList, LB_INSERTSTRING, (WPARAM)-1, (LPARAM)szBuffer );

   return( TRUE );
}


LRESULT CALLBACK WndProc( HWND hWnd, UINT uMsg, WPARAM wParam, LPARAM lParam )
{
   switch( uMsg )
   {
      case WM_COMMAND :
            switch( LOWORD( wParam ) )
            {
               case IDM_TEST:
                   SendMessage( hList, LB_RESETCONTENT, 0, 0 );
                   EnumSystemLocales( EnumLocales, LCID_INSTALLED );
                   break;
         .
         .
         .
```

EnumTimeFormats ■ WINDOWS 95 ■ WINDOWS NT

Description EnumTimeFormats enumerates the time formats that are available for a specified locale. The function enumerates the time formats by passing a pointer to a string buffer containing a time format to an application-defined callback function. This continues until the last time format is found or the callback function returns **FALSE**.

Syntax	BOOL **EnumTimeFormats**(TIMEFMT_ENUMPROC *lpTimeFmtEnumProc,* LCID *Locale,* DWORD *dwFlags*)

Parameters

lpTimeFmtEnumProc   TIMEFMT_ENUMPROC: A pointer to an application-defined callback function. See the syntax of the callback function below.

Locale   LCID: The locale for which to retrieve time format information. This can be a locale identifier created with the **MAKELCID** macro, **LOCALE_SYSTEM_DEFAULT** for the default system locale, or **LOCALE_USER_DEFAULT** for the default user locale.

dwFlags   DWORD: Reserved; must be **0**.

Returns   BOOL: If successful, **TRUE** is returned; otherwise, **FALSE** is returned. The extended error code is retrieved with a call to the **GetLastError** function, which may return **ERROR_BADDB**, **ERROR_INVALID_FLAGS**, or **ERROR_INVALID_PARAMETER**.

Include File   winnls.h

See Also   EnumCalendarInfo, EnumDateFormats

Callback Syntax   BOOL CALLBACK **EnumTimeFormatsProc**(LPTSTR *lpTimeFormatString*)

Callback Parameters

lpTimeFormatString   LPTSTR: A pointer to a string buffer containing a null-terminated time format string.

Callback Returns   BOOL: To continue enumeration, return **TRUE**; otherwise, return **FALSE** to stop enumeration.

FoldString   ■ WINDOWS 95   ■ WINDOWS NT

Description   FoldString maps one string to another, performing the specified transformation option.

Syntax   int **FoldString**(DWORD *dwMapFlags,* LPCTSTR *lpSrcStr,* int *cchSrc,* LPTSTR *lpDestStr,* int *cchDest*)

Parameters

dwMapFlags   DWORD: A set of flags that indicate the type of transformation to be used during mapping. This value can be a combination of the values listed in Table 22-6.

Table 22-6 FoldString *dwMapFlags* values

Value	Meaning
MAP_COMPOSITE	Map accented characters to composite characters, in which the accent and base character are represented by two character values. This value cannot be used with MAP_PRECOMPOSED.
MAP_FOLDCZONE	Fold compatibility zone characters into standard Unicode equivalents.
MAP_FOLDDIGITS	Map all digits to Unicode characters 0 through 9.
MAP_PRECOMPOSED	Map accented characters to precomposed characters, in which the accent and base character are combined into a single character value. This value cannot be used with MAP_COMPOSITE.

lpSrcStr	LPCTSTR: A pointer to the string to be mapped.
cchSrc	int: The size, in characters, of the *lpSrcStr* buffer. If set to −1, *lpSrcStr* is assumed to be null terminated and the length is calculated automatically.
lpDestStr	LPTSTR: A pointer to the buffer that receives the mapped string.
cchDest	int: The size, in characters, of the *lpDestStr* buffer. If set to 0, the function returns the number of characters required to hold the mapped string.
Returns	int: If successful, the number of characters written to the destination buffer is returned. If the *cchDest* parameter is 0, the number of characters required to hold the mapped string is returned. If the function failed, 0 is returned and the extended error code is accessible with the GetLastError function.
Include File	winnls.h
See Also	CompareString, LCMapString

FormatMessage   ■ Windows 95   ■ Windows NT

Description	FormatMessage formats a message string using a message definition. The function copies the formatted message text to an output buffer, processing any embedded insert sequences if requested. The function requires a message definition as input. The definition can come from a buffer passed into the function or a message table resource in an already loaded module. The function can also search the system's message table resources for the message definition. A message definition is found based on a message identifier and a language identifier.
Syntax	DWORD **FormatMessage**(DWORD *dwFlags,* LPCVOID *lpSource,* DWORD *dwMessageId,* DWORD *dwLanguageId,* LPTSTR *lpBuffer,* DWORD *nSize,* va_list* *Arguments*)
Parameters	

dwFlags	DWORD: A set of bit flags that specify aspects of the formatting process and how to interpret the *lpSource* parameter. The low-order byte of *dwFlags* specifies how the function handles line breaks in the output buffer. It can also specify the maximum width of a formatted output line. Use the FORMAT_MESSAGE_MAX_WIDTH_MASK constant and bitwise Boolean operations to set and retrieve this maximum width value. If the low-order byte is a nonzero value other than FORMAT_MESSAGE_MAX_WIDTH_MASK, the message is limited to the number of characters and the function ignores regular line breaks in the message. If it is FORMAT_MESSAGE_MAX_WIDTH_MASK, the function ignores regular line breaks in the message definition text. Table 22-7 lists the valid bit flags.

Table 22-7 FormatMessage *dwFlags* values

Value	Meaning
FORMAT_MESSAGE_ALLOCATE_BUFFER	Specifies that the *lpBuffer* parameter is a pointer to a PVOID pointer, and that the *nSize* parameter specifies the minimum number of characters to allocate for an output message buffer. The function allocates a buffer large enough to hold the formatted message, and places a pointer to the allocated buffer at the address specified by *lpBuffer*. The caller should use the GlobalFree function to free the buffer when it is no longer needed.
FORMAT_MESSAGE_ARGUMENT_ARRAY	Specifies that the *Arguments* parameter is not a va_list structure, but instead is just a pointer to an array of 32-bit values that represent the arguments.
FORMAT_MESSAGE_FROM_HMODULE	Specifies that *lpSource* is a module handle containing the message-table resource(s) to search. If the module handle is NULL, the current process's application image file is searched. This flag cannot be used with FORMAT_MESSAGE_FROM_STRING.
FORMAT_MESSAGE_FROM_STRING	Specifies that *lpSource* is a pointer to a null-terminated message definition. The message definition may contain insert sequences, just as the message text in a message table resource may. This flag cannot be used with FORMAT_MESSAGE_FROM_HMODULE or FORMAT_MESSAGE_FROM_SYSTEM.
FORMAT_MESSAGE_FROM_SYSTEM	Specifies that the function should search the system message-table resource(s) for the requested message. If this flag is specified with FORMAT_MESSAGE_FROM_HMODULE, the function searches the system message table if the message is not found in the module specified by *lpSource*. This flag cannot be used with FORMAT_MESSAGE_FROM_STRING. If this flag is specified, an application can pass the result of the GetLastError function to retrieve the message text for a system-defined error.
FORMAT_MESSAGE_IGNORE_INSERTS	Specifies that the insert sequences in the message definition are to be ignored and passed through to the output buffer unchanged. The *Arguments* parameter is ignored.

lpSource	LPCVOID: A pointer to a null-terminated string that contains the message definition when FORMAT_MESSAGE_FROM_STRING is specified. If FORMAT_MESSAGE_FROM_HMODULE is specified, *lpSource* is the module name

	containing the message-table resource to search—or the current process if *lpSource* is **NULL**.
dwMessageId	**DWORD**: The 32-bit message definition ID to search for in the system message resource.
dwLanguageId	**DWORD**: The language ID that specifies the message resource and how replacements occur.
lpBuffer	**LPTSTR**: Output buffer or—in the case of **FORMAT_MESSAGE_ALLOCATE_BUFFER**—a pointer to a location to store a buffer that is allocated by the system using **GlobalAlloc**. The caller must free this buffer after it is finished with the message output.
nSize	**DWORD**: The number of characters to be written to the output buffer or—in the case of **FORMAT_MESSAGE_ALLOCATE_BUFFER**—the minimum buffer size to allocate.
Arguments	**va_list***: Argument list for formatting. This may be a **va_args** pointer or an array of 32-bit values (if **FORMAT_MESSAGE_ARGUMENT_ARRAY** is used). The format codes %1, %2, and so on, refer to the first argument, second argument, and so forth. Table 22-8 shows the available format options that may appear in the format string.

Table 22-8 `FormatMessage` format strings

Format Options	Description
%0	Terminates a message text line without a trailing new line. This is a useful way to append several messages together in long lines that can then be formatted for best appearance by the system's line wrapping.
%1 to %99	Argument insertion strings. Each argument may be followed by a `printf` format string bracketed by exclamation points. The system assumes !s! if no `printf` format is specified. Floating-point formatting with %e, %E, %f, or %g is not supported. If floating data must be formatted, use `sprintf` and copy the string into the message as !s!. You can use an asterisk in place of the precision or width component. In this case, for argument %n, argument %n+1 supplies the precision or `width`, %n+2 supplies the precision, and %n+1 supplies the width, if two asterisks are used.
%%	This is a percent sign.
%n	A hard line break.
`%space character`	A space.
%.	A single period.
%!	An exclamation point.

Returns	**DWORD**: If successful, the total number of characters copied to destination buffer, not including the zero-terminating character, is returned; otherwise, **0** is returned. Use **GetLastError** to return an error code.
Include File	`winbase.h`
See Also	`wsprintf`, `wvsprintf`

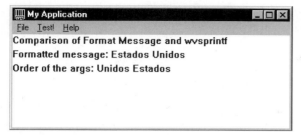

Figure 22-7 `FormatMessage` example

Example   The example shows how semantic meaning can be given to components of a string to resolve the problems with international ordering of messages. Unlike in English, in Portuguese (and most other Romance languages) modifiers follow the noun; for example, disk drive becomes "unidade de disco" (literally, unit of disk). Figure 22-7 shows the results of comparing the `FormatMessage` with `wvsprintf`, another formatting function that takes a list of arguments.

```
BOOL bEnglish = TRUE;
int  iRow     = 0;

LRESULT CALLBACK WndProc( HWND hWnd, UINT uMsg, WPARAM wParam, LPARAM lParam )
{
    switch( uMsg )
    {
        case WM_COMMAND :
                switch( LOWORD( wParam ) )
                {
                    case IDM_TEST:
                        {
                            int     iChars;
                            TCHAR   szNoun[16];
                            TCHAR   szAdjective[16];
                            TCHAR   szMessageFormat[10];
                            LPTSTR  pArgs[16];
                            PVOID   pBuffer = 0;
                            HDC     hDC = GetDC( hWnd );

                            pArgs[0] = szAdjective;    // Argument 1 = adjective
                            pArgs[1] = szNoun;         // Argument 2 = noun
                            pArgs[2] = 0;

                            bEnglish = !bEnglish;
                            if (bEnglish) // If English...
                            {
                                lstrcpy( szMessageFormat, "%1 %2" );
                                lstrcpy( szNoun, "States" );
                                lstrcpy( szAdjective, "United" );
                            }
                            else    // If Spanish...
                            {
```

continued on next page

continued from previous page

```
                        lstrcpy(szMessageFormat, "%2 %1" );
                        lstrcpy( szNoun, "Estados" );
                        lstrcpy( szAdjective, "Unidos" );
                    }

                    // Do smart formatting
                    //....................
                    iChars = FormatMessage( FORMAT_MESSAGE_FROM_STRING |
                                            FORMAT_MESSAGE_ALLOCATE_BUFFER |
                                            FORMAT_MESSAGE_ARGUMENT_ARRAY ,
                                            szMessageFormat, 0, 0, (LPTSTR)&pBuffer,
                                            63, pArgs );

                    // Do output to screen.
                    //.....................
                    if ( iChars > 0 )
                    {
                        TCHAR szOutputBuffer[128];

                        lstrcpy( szOutputBuffer,
                                 "Comparison of Format Message and wvsprintf" );

                        TextOut( hDC, 0, iRow, szOutputBuffer,
                                 lstrlen( szOutputBuffer ) );
                        TextOut( hDC, 0, iRow + 20, szOutputBuffer, wsprintf(
                                 szOutputBuffer, "Formatted message: %s",
                                 (LPTSTR*)pBuffer ) );
                        TextOut( hDC, 0, iRow + 40, szOutputBuffer, wvsprintf(
                                 szOutputBuffer, "Order of the args: %s %s",
                                 (va_list)pArgs ) );
                        iRow += 60;

                        // Free the memory system allocated.
                        //..................................
                        if (pBuffer)
                            GlobalFree( pBuffer );
                    }
                    ReleaseDC( hWnd, hDC );
                }
                break;
```

.
.
.

GetACP   ■ WINDOWS 95   ■ WINDOWS NT

Description	GetACP returns the current ANSI code-page identifier of the system.
Syntax	UINT **GetACP**(VOID)
Parameters	This function has no parameters.
Returns	UINT: If successful, the current ANSI code-page or a default code–page identifier is returned. Table 22-9 lists the ANSI code-page identifiers.

Table 22-9 ANSI code-page identifiers

Identifier	Meaning
874	Thai
932	Japan
936	Chinese (PRC, Singapore)
949	Korean
950	Chinese (Taiwan, Hong Kong)
1200	Unicode (BMP of ISO 10646)
1250	Windows 3.1 Eastern European
1251	Windows 3.1 Cyrillic
1252	Windows 3.1 Latin 1 (U.S., Western Europe)
1253	Windows 3.1 Greek
1254	Windows 3.1 Turkish
1255	Hebrew
1256	Arabic
1257	Baltic

Include File	winnls.h
See Also	GetCPInfo, GetOEMCP

GetCPInfo   ■ WINDOWS 95   ■ WINDOWS NT

Description	GetCPInfo returns information about any valid installed or available code-page.
Syntax	BOOL **GetCPInfo**(UINT *uCodePage,* LPCPINFO *lpCPInfo*)
Parameters	
uCodePage	UINT: The code-page about which information is to be retrieved. This can be one of the code-page values provided in Table 22-2, or set to CP_ACP to use the system default ANSI code-page, CP_MACCP to use the default Macintosh code-page, or CP_OEMCP to use the default OEM code-page.
lpCPInfo	LPCPINFO: A pointer to a CPINFO structure that receives information about the code-page. See the definition of the CPINFO structure below.
Returns	BOOL: If successful, TRUE is returned; otherwise, FALSE is returned and GetLastError will return an error code of ERROR_INVALID_PARAMETER if the code-page is not installed or not available.
Include File	winnls.h
See Also	EnumSystemCodePages, GetACP, GetOEMCP, GetLocaleInfo

CPINFO Definition

```
struct _cpinfo
{
    UINT MaxCharSize;
    BYTE DefaultChar[MAX_DEFAULTCHAR];
    BYTE LeadByte[MAX_LEADBYTES];
} CPINFO, *LPCPINFO;
```

Members

MaxCharSize   UINT: The maximum length, in bytes, of a character in this code-page.

DefaultChar   BYTE[MAX_DEFAULTCHAR]: The default character used in translations into this code-page. This character is used by the **WideCharToMultiByte** function if an explicit default character is not given.

LeadByte   BYTE[MAX_LEADBYTES]: A fixed-length array of lead-byte ranges, where the number of lead-byte ranges is variable. If this code-page has no lead bytes, then every element to the array is **NULL**. The maximum number of lead-byte ranges for any code-page is 5. The array uses 2 bytes to describe each range, with a double-byte null terminator after the last range.

Example   See the example for the **EnumSystemCodePages** function.

GetCurrencyFormat   ■ WINDOWS 95   ■ WINDOWS NT

Description   GetCurrencyFormat formats a number string as a currency string for a specified locale.

Syntax   int **GetCurrencyFormat**(LCID *Locale*, DWORD *dwFlags*, LPCTSTR *lpValue*, CONST CURRENCYFMT* *lpFormat*, LPTSTR *lpCurrencyStr*, int *cchCurrency*)

Parameters

Locale   LCID: The locale for which the currency string is to be formatted. If *lpFormat* is NULL, the function formats the string according to the currency format for this locale; otherwise, the function uses the locale only for formatting information not specified in the **CURRENCYFMT** structure. This parameter can be a locale identifier created by the **MAKELCID** macro, **LOCALE_SYSTEM_DEFAULT** to use the default system locale, or **LOCALE_USER_DEFAULT** to use the default user locale.

dwFlags   DWORD: A bit flag that controls the operation of the function. If *lpFormat* is non-**NULL**, this parameter must be **0**; otherwise, specify the **LOCALE_NOUSEROVERRIDE** flag to format the string using the system default currency format for the specified locale or **0** to format the string using any user overrides to the locale's default currency format.

lpValue   LPCTSTR: A pointer to a null-terminated string containing the number string to format. The string can only contain characters '0' through '9', one decimal point (.) if the number is a floating-point value, and a minus sign in the first character position if the number is a negative value. All other characters are invalid and an error is returned if they are encountered.

lpFormat	**CONST CURRENCYFMT***: A pointer to a **CURRENCYFMT** structure that contains currency formatting information. All members in the structure must contain appropriate values. If set to **NULL**, the function uses the currency format of the specified locale. See the definition of the **CURRENCYFMT** structure below.
lpCurrencyStr	**LPTSTR**: A pointer that points to a buffer to receive the formatted currency string.
cchCurrency	**int**: The size, in characters, of the *lpCurrencyStr* buffer. If *cchCurrency* is **0**, the function returns the number of bytes or characters required to hold the formatted currency string.
Returns	**int**: If successful, the return value is the number of characters written to the buffer pointed to by *lpCurrencyStr*, or if the *cchCurrency* parameter is **0**, the number of characters required to hold the formatted currency string. If the function fails, the return value is **0**. Use the **GetLastError** function to return the error code.
Include File	**winnls.h**
See Also	**GetNumberFormat**

CURRENCYFMT Definition

```
typedef struct _currencyfmt
{
    UINT        NumDigits;
    UINT        LeadingZero;
    UINT        Grouping;
    LPTSTR      lpDecimalSep;
    LPTSTR      lpThousandSep;
    UINT        NegativeOrder;
    UINT        PositiveOrder;
    LPTSTR      lpCurrencySymbol;
} CURRENCYFMT;
```

Members

NumDigits	**UINT**: The number of fractional digits. This is equivalent to the locale information specified by the **LCTYPE** constant value **LOCALE_IDIGITS**.
LeadingZero	**UINT**: Specifies whether to use leading zeros in decimal fields. This is equivalent to the locale information specified by the **LCTYPE** constant value **LOCALE_ILZERO**.
Grouping	**UINT**: The size of each group of digits to the left of the decimal. Values in the range 0–9 are valid.
lpDecimalSep	**LPTSTR**: A pointer to a null-terminated decimal separator string.
lpThousandSep	**LPTSTR**: A pointer to a null-terminated thousands separator string.

NegativeOrder	**UINT**: The negative currency mode. This is equivalent to the locale information specified by the **LCTYPE** constant value **LOCALE_INEGCURR**.
PositiveOrder	**UINT**: The positive currency mode. This is equivalent to the locale information specified by the **LCTYPE** constant value **LOCALE_ICURRENCY**.
lpCurrencySymbol	**LPTSTR**: A pointer to a null-terminated currency symbol string.

GetDateFormat ■ WINDOWS 95   ■ WINDOWS NT

Description	**GetDateFormat** formats a date as a date string for a specified locale. The function formats either a specified date or the local system date using the locale date format or as defined by a given picture.
Syntax	int **GetDateFormat**(LCID *Locale,* DWORD *dwFlags,* CONST SYSTEMTIME* *lpDate,* LPCTSTR *lpDateFormat,* LPTSTR *lpDateStr,* int *nBufferSize*)
Parameters	
Locale	**LCID**: The locale to be used to format the date string. If *lpDateFormat* is **NULL**, the function formats the string according to the date format for this locale. If *lpDateFormat* is not **NULL**, the function uses the locale only for information not specified in the format picture string. This can be a locale created with the **MAKELCID** macro or either **LOCALE_SYSTEM_DEFAULT** or **LOCALE_USER_DEFAULT**, which designate system or user defaults.
dwFlags	**DWORD**: A set of bit flags that specify various function options. If *lpDateFormat* is non-**NULL**, this parameter must be **0**; otherwise, it can be a combination of the values listed in Table 22-10.

Table 22-10 GetDateFormat *dwFlags* values

Value	Meaning
DATE_LONGDATE	Use the long date format. This flag cannot be used with DATE_SHORTDATE.
DATE_SHORTDATE	Use the short date format. This flag is the default and cannot be used with DATE_LONGDATE.
DATE_USE_ALT_CALENDAR	Use the alternate calendar, if one exists, to format the date string. If this flag is set, the function uses the default format for the alternate calendar, rather than using any user overrides. The user overrides will be used only in the event that there is no default format for the specified alternate calendar.
LOCALE_NOUSEROVERRIDE	The function formats the string using the system default date format for the specified locale.

lpDate	**CONST SYSTEMTIME***: A pointer to a **SYSTEMTIME** structure that contains the date information to be formatted. If this pointer is **NULL**, the function uses the current local system date. See the definition of the **SYSTEMTIME** structure under the **GetSystemTime** function in Chapter 21, System Information.

lpDateFormat	LPCTSTR: A pointer to a format picture string to use to form the date string. If set to **NULL**, the function uses the date format of the specified locale. Use the elements in Table 22-11 to construct a format picture string. If spaces are inserted in the format string, they appear in the same location in the output string. The letters must be in uppercase or lowercase as shown in the table. Characters in the format string that are enclosed in single quotation marks will appear in the same location and unchanged in the output string.

Table 22-11 `GetDateFormat` *lpDateFormat* values

Picture	Meaning
d	The day of month as digits with no leading zero for single-digit days.
dd	The day of month as digits with leading zero for single-digit days.
ddd	The day of week as a three-letter abbreviation. The function uses the LOCALE_SABBREVDAYNAME value associated with the specified locale.
dddd	The day of week as its full name. The function uses the LOCALE_SDAYNAME value associated with the specified locale.
M	The month as digits with no leading zero for single-digit months.
MM	The month as digits with leading zero for single-digit months.
MMM	The month as a three-letter abbreviation. The function uses the LOCALE_SABBREVMONTHNAME value associated with the specified locale.
MMMM	The month as its full name. The function uses the LOCALE_SMONTHNAME value associated with the specified locale.
y	The year as last two digits, but with no leading zero for years less than 10.
yy	The year as last two digits, but with leading zero for years less than 10.
yyyy	The year represented by full four digits.
gg	The period/era string. The function uses the CAL_SERASTRING value associated with the specified locale. This element is ignored if the date to be formatted does not have an associated era or period string.

lpDateStr	LPTSTR: A pointer to the buffer that receives the formatted date string.
nBufferSize	int: The size, in characters, of the *lpDateStr* buffer. If set to **0**, the return value is the number of characters needed in a buffer to store the converted date.
Returns	int: If successful, the number of characters written to the *lpDateStr* buffer, or if *nBufferSize* is **0**, the number of characters required to hold the formatted date string. If the function fails, the return value is **0**. Use the **GetLastError** function to retrieve the error code.
Include File	winnls.h
See Also	GetLocaleInfo, SetLocaleInfo, GetTimeFormat
Example	When the user selects Test! from the menu of the example, the system date and time are displayed in a variety of formats, using the locale's configuration. The example also illustrates how **SetLocaleInfo** can be used to change data of a locale and how to use **GetLocaleInfo** for queries.

```
LRESULT CALLBACK WndProc( HWND hWnd, UINT uMsg, WPARAM wParam, LPARAM lParam )
{
    switch( uMsg )
    {
        case WM_COMMAND :
                switch( LOWORD( wParam ) )
                {
                    case IDM_TEST:
                        {
                            TCHAR szBuffer[128];
                            TCHAR szDateBuffer[128];
                            TCHAR sLongDateFormat[65];
                            HDC   hDC = GetDC( hWnd );

                            // Save long date format.
                            GetLocaleInfo( LOCALE_USER_DEFAULT, LOCALE_SLONGDATE,
                                        sLongDateFormat, 64 );

                            // Show date and time.
                            //....................
                            GetDateFormat( LOCALE_USER_DEFAULT, DATE_SHORTDATE,
                                        NULL, NULL, szDateBuffer, 127 );
                            TextOut( hDC, 0, 0, szBuffer, wsprintf( szBuffer,
                                    "The date is %s", szDateBuffer ) );

                            GetDateFormat( LOCALE_USER_DEFAULT, DATE_LONGDATE,
                                        NULL, NULL, szDateBuffer, 127 );
                            TextOut( hDC, 0, 20, szBuffer, wsprintf( szBuffer,
                                    "The long date is %s", szDateBuffer ) );

                            GetTimeFormat( LOCALE_USER_DEFAULT, TIME_FORCE24HOURFORMAT,
                                        NULL, NULL, szDateBuffer, 127 );
                            TextOut( hDC, 0, 40, szBuffer, wsprintf( szBuffer,
                                    "The time is %s", szDateBuffer ) );

                            // Change long date format.
                            //.........................
                            SetLocaleInfo( LOCALE_USER_DEFAULT, LOCALE_SLONGDATE,
                                        "ddth 'day' of MMMM in yyyy" );

                            // Get formatted date in new locale format.
                            //.........................................
                            GetDateFormat( LOCALE_USER_DEFAULT, DATE_LONGDATE,
                                        NULL, NULL, szDateBuffer, 127 );
                            TextOut( hDC, 0, 60, szBuffer, wsprintf( szBuffer,
                                    "The long date is %s", szDateBuffer ));
                            ReleaseDC( hWnd, hDC );

                            // Restore long date format.
                            //.........................
                            SetLocaleInfo( LOCALE_USER_DEFAULT, LOCALE_SLONGDATE,⇐
sLongDateFormat );
                        }
                        break;
            .
            .
            .
```

GetLocaleInfo   ■ WINDOWS 95   ■ WINDOWS NT

Description	**GetLocaleInfo** returns specified information about a given locale. The contents of a locale are described in Tables 22-20 through 22-24 in the description for **SetLocaleInfo**. All of the information stored in a locale is always returned as a string—even data that represents numeric values.
Syntax	int **GetLocaleInfo**(LCID *Locale,* LCTYPE *LCType,* LPTSTR *lpLCDataBuffer,* int *nBufferSize*)
Parameters	
Locale	LCID: The locale identifier of the locale to be queried. This may be any locale created with the **MAKELCID** macro, **LOCALE_SYSTEM_DEFAULT** (system default locale), or **LOCALE_USER_DEFAULT** (user's default locale).
LCType	LCTYPE: Any of the locale identifier constants shown in Tables 22-20 through 22-24. These values are mutually exclusive, with the exception of **LOCALE_NOUSEROVERRIDE**. An application may use the binary OR operator to combine **LOCALE_NOUSEROVERRIDE** with any other value. If used, the function bypasses user overrides, and returns the system default value for the requested **LCID**.
lpLCDataBuffer	LPTSTR: A pointer to the buffer to receive the locale information.
nBufferSize	int: The buffer size, in characters, pointed to by the *lpLCDataBuffer* parameter. If set to **0**, the number of characters needed to store the data is returned and the *lpLCDataBuffer* parameter is ignored.
Returns	int: If successful, the number of characters stored in the buffer is returned. If *nBufferSize* specified a zero value, the number of characters required to store the string is returned. If an error occurs, the function returns **0**. Use **GetLastError** to return an error code. Common errors include **ERROR_INSUFFICIENT_BUFFER**, **ERROR_INVALID_PARAMETER**, or **ERROR_INVALID_FLAGS**.
Include File	winnls.h
See Also	SetLocaleInfo
Example	See the example for the **GetDateFormat** function.

GetNumberFormat   ■ WINDOWS 95   ■ WINDOWS NT

Description	**GetNumberFormat** formats a number string as a number string customized for a locale.
Syntax	int **GetNumberFormat**(LCID *Locale,* DWORD *dwFlags,* LPCTSTR *lpValue,* CONST NUMBERFMT* *lpFormat,* LPTSTR *lpNumberStr,* int *nBufferSize*)

Parameters

Locale **LCID**: The locale for which the number string is to be formatted. If *lpFormat* is **NULL**, the function formats the string according to the number format for this locale; otherwise, the function uses the locale only for formatting information not specified in the **NUMBERFMT**. This parameter can be a locale identifier created by the **MAKELCID** macro, **LOCALE_SYSTEM_DEFAULT** to use the default system locale, or **LOCALE_USER_DEFAULT** to use the default user locale.

dwFlags **DWORD**: Contains a bit flag that controls the operation of the function. If *lpFormat* is non-**NULL**, this parameter must be **0**; otherwise, you can specify the **LOCALE_NOUSEROVERRIDE** flag to format the string using the system default number format for the specified locale or **0** to format the string using any user overrides to the locale's default number format.

lpValue **LPCTSTR**: A pointer to a null-terminated string containing the number string to format. This string can only contain characters '0' through '9', one decimal (.) if the number is a floating-point value, and a minus sign in the first character position if the number is a negative value.

lpFormat **CONST NUMBERFMT***: A pointer to a **NUMBERFMT** structure that contains number formatting information. All members in the structure must contain appropriate values. If set to **NULL**, the function uses the number format of the specified locale. See the definition of the **NUMBERFMT** structure below.

lpNumberStr **LPTSTR**: A pointer to a buffer that receives the formatted number string.

nBufferSize **int**: The size, in characters, of the buffer pointed to by the *lpNumberStr* parameter. If set to **0**, the function returns the number of characters required to hold the formatted number string.

Returns **int**: If successful, the return value is the number of characters written to the buffer pointed to by *lpNumberStr*, or if the *nBufferSize* parameter is **0**, the number of characters required to hold the formatted number string. If the function fails, the return value is **0**. Use the **GetLastError** function to return the error code.

Include File winnls.h

See Also GetCurrencyFormat

NUMBERFMT Definition

```
typedef struct _numberfmt
{
    UINT      NumDigits;
    UINT      LeadingZero;
    UINT      Grouping;
    LPTSTR    lpDecimalSep;
    LPTSTR    lpThousandSep;
    UINT      NegativeOrder;
} NUMBERFMT;
```

Members

NumDigits	**UINT**: The number of fractional digits.
LeadingZero	**UINT**: Specifies whether to use leading zeros in decimal fields.
Grouping	**UINT**: The size of each group of digits to the left of the decimal. Values in the range of 0–9 are valid.
lpDecimalSep	**LPTSTR**: A pointer to a null-terminated string that contains the decimal separator string.
lpThousandSep	**LPTSTR**: A pointer to a null-terminated string that contains the thousands separator.
NegativeOrder	**UINT**: The negative number mode.

GetOEMCP   ■ Windows 95   ■ Windows NT

Description	Retrieves the identifier of the current OEM (original equipment manufacturer) code-page for the system.
Syntax	UINT **GetOEMCP(VOID)**
Parameters	This function has no parameters.
Returns	**UINT**: The OEM code-page identifier or a default identifier if no code-page is current. Table 22-12 lists possible values.

Table 22-12 GetOEMCP return values

Identifier	Meaning
437	MS-DOS United States
708	Arabic (ASMO 708)
709	Arabic (ASMO 449+, BCON V4)
710	Arabic (Transparent Arabic)
720	Arabic (Transparent ASMO)
737	Greek (formerly 437G)
775	Baltic
850	MS-DOS Multilingual (Latin I)
852	MS-DOS Slavic (Latin II)
855	IBM Cyrillic (primarily Russian)
857	IBM Turkish
860	MS-DOS Portuguese
862	Hebrew
861	MS-DOS Icelandic
863	MS-DOS Canadian-French
864	Arabic

continued on next page

continued from previous page

Identifier	Meaning
865	MS-DOS Nordic
866	MS-DOS Russian (former USSR)
869	IBM Modern Greek
874	Thai
932	Japan
936	Chinese (PRC, Singapore)
949	Korean
950	Chinese (Taiwan, Hong Kong)
1361	Korean (Johab)

Include File	`winnls.h`
See Also	`GetACP`, `GetCPInfo`
Example	In this example, the current code-page is displayed in a message box when the user selects the Test! menu item.

```c
static LPCTSTR lpszCPTypes[] =
{
   "MS-DOS United States",
   "MS-DOS Multilingual (Latin I)",
   "MS-DOS Slavic (Latin II)",
   "IBM Cyrillic (primarily Russian)",
   "IBM Turkish",
   "MS-DOS Portuguese",
   "MS-DOS Icelandic",
   "MS-DOS Canadian-French",
   "MS-DOS Nordic",
   "MS-DOS Russian (former USSR)",
   "IBM Modern Greek"
};


LRESULT CALLBACK WndProc( HWND hWnd, UINT uMsg, WPARAM wParam, LPARAM lParam )
{
   switch( uMsg )
   {
      case WM_COMMAND :
            switch( LOWORD( wParam ) )
            {
               case IDM_TEST :
                  {
                     UINT    uCP  = GetOEMCP();
                     LPCTSTR lpCP = "No Code Page.";

                     switch( uCP )
                     {
                        case 437 : lpCP = lpszCPTypes[0]; break;
                        case 850 : lpCP = lpszCPTypes[1]; break;
                        case 852 : lpCP = lpszCPTypes[2]; break;
                        case 855 : lpCP = lpszCPTypes[3]; break;
```

```
                                  case 857 : lpCP = lpszCPTypes[4]; break;
                                  case 860 : lpCP = lpszCPTypes[5]; break;
                                  case 861 : lpCP = lpszCPTypes[6]; break;
                                  case 863 : lpCP = lpszCPTypes[7]; break;
                                  case 865 : lpCP = lpszCPTypes[8]; break;
                                  case 866 : lpCP = lpszCPTypes[9]; break;
                                  case 869 : lpCP = lpszCPTypes[10]; break;
                          }

                          MessageBox( hWnd, lpCP, "Code Page",
                                      MB_OK | MB_ICONINFORMATION );
                  }
                  break;
```

.
.
.

GetStringTypeEx   ■ WINDOWS 95   ■ WINDOWS NT

Description	GetStringTypeEx returns character-type information for the character in either a single- or multibyte string. For each character in the string, the function sets one or more bits in the corresponding 16-bit element of the output array. Each bit identifies a given character type, such as whether the character is a letter, digit, or neither. This function supersedes the GetStringTypeA and GetStringTypeW functions.
Syntax	BOOL **GetStringTypeEx**(LCID *Locale,* DWORD *dwInfoType,* LPCTSTR *lpSrcStr,* int *cchSrc,* LPWORD *lpCharType*)
Parameters	
Locale	LCID: The locale identifier to use for examining the source string. This value uniquely defines the ANSI code-page to use to translate the string pointed by *lpSrcStr* from ANSI to Unicode. The **W** version of this function ignores this parameter. This parameter can be a locale identifier created by the **MAKELCID** macro, **LOCALE_SYSTEM_DEFAULT** to use the default system locale, or **LOCALE_USER_DEFAULT** to use the default user locale.
dwInfoType	DWORD: The type of character information the user wants to retrieve. These types are divided into three different levels. Set this parameter to **CT_CTYPE1** to retrieve character type information, **CT_CTYPE2** to retrieve bidirectional layout information, or **CT_CTYPE3** to retrieve text processing information.
lpSrcStr	LPCTSTR: A pointer to the string for which character types are requested. If *cchSrc* is **−1**, the string is treated as null terminated. This must be a Unicode string for the **W** version and an ANSI string for the **A** version of this function. This string can be a double-byte character set (DBCS) for the **A** version if the locale is appropriate for DBCS.

cchSrc	int: The size, in characters, of the string pointed to by the *lpSrcStr* parameter. If this count includes a null terminator, the function returns character type information for the null terminator. If this value is **−1**, the string is treated as null terminated and the length is calculated automatically.
lpCharType	LPWORD: A pointer to an array of 16-bit values. The length of this array must be large enough to receive one 16-bit value for each character in the source string. The returned values depend on the *dwInfoType* parameter and are listed in Tables 22-13 through 22-15. The values listed in each table are used individually or combined to describe each character, except in the case of **CT_CTYPE2**, where each value is mutually exclusive.

Table 22-13 CT_CTYPE1 values

Name	Meaning
C1_ALPHA	Any linguistic character: alphabetic, syllabary, or ideographic
C1_BLANK	Blank characters
C1_CNTRL	Control characters
C1_DIGIT	Decimal digits
C1_LOWER	Lowercase
C1_PUNCT	Punctuation
C1_SPACE	Space characters
C1_UPPER	Uppercase
C1_XDIGIT	Hexadecimal digits

Table 22-14 CT_CTYPE2 values

Name	Meaning
C2_ARABICNUMBER	Arabic number
C2_BLOCKSEPARATOR	Block separator
C2_COMMONSEPARATOR	Common numeric separator
C2_EUROPENUMBER	European number, digit
C2_EUROPESEPARATOR	European numeric separator
C2_EUROPETERMINATOR	European numeric terminator
C2_LEFTTORIGHT	Left to right
C2_NOTAPPLICABLE	No implicit directionality
C2_OTHERNEUTRAL	Other neutrals
C2_RIGHTTOLEFT	Right to left
C2_SEGMENTSEPARATOR	Segment separator
C2_WHITESPACE	White space

Table 22-15 CT_CTYPE3 values

Name	Meaning
C3_ALPHA	All linguistic characters
C3_DIACRITIC	Diacritic character—accent marks
C3_FULLWIDTH	Full-width (2-byte) character
C3_HALFWIDTH	Half-width (1-byte) character
C3_HIRAGANA	Hiragana character
C3_IDEOGRAPH	Ideographic character
C3_KASHIDA	Arabic Kashida character
C3_KATAKANA	Katakana character
C3_LEXICAL	Lexical character
C3_NONSPACING	Nonspacing character
C3_NOTAPPLICABLE	Not applicable
C3_SYMBOL	Symbol character
C3_VOWELMARK	Vowel

Returns   BOOL: If successful, TRUE is returned; otherwise, FALSE is returned. Use the GetLastError function to retrieve the error code.

Include File   winnls.h

See Also   GetLocaleInfo

Example   This function performs powerful analysis of characters simultaneously. The program example is a modification of the example of **CharToOemBuff** that displays an ANSI table and an OEM table. This example prints the ANSI table and a dump of the flags each character has set (in hex). The graph is a cross-reference that may be used the same way as the original table.

```
#define LEGEND1 "ANSI character set flags. 1=Lower, 2=Upper, 4=Digit, 8=SPACE"
#define LEGEND2 "10=Punctuation, 20=Control, 40=Blank, 80=Hex"

LRESULT CALLBACK WndProc(HWND hWnd, UINT uMsg, WPARAM wParam, LPARAM lParam)
{
   switch (uMsg)
   {
   case WM_COMMAND:
           switch ( LOWORD( wParam ) )
           {
             case IDM_TEST:
                 {
                     int    i, j;
                     HFONT hOldFont;
                     TCHAR szTemp[128];
                     TCHAR szBuffer[128];
                     TCHAR szLittleBuffer[17];
                     WORD  wTypeArray[16];
                     HDC   hDC = GetDC( hWnd );
```

continued on next page

continued from previous page

```
                    hOldFont = SelectObject( hDC, GetStockObject(
                                         ANSI_FIXED_FONT ) );
                    szTemp[0]=0;
                    for ( j=0; j<16; j++ )
                    {
                        wsprintf( szBuffer, "%X ", j );
                        lstrcat( szTemp, szBuffer );
                    }
                    lstrcpy( szBuffer, szTemp );
                    lstrcat( szTemp, " " );

                    for ( j=0; j<16; j++ )
                    {
                        wsprintf( szBuffer, "%X ", j );
                        lstrcat( szTemp, szBuffer );
                    }
                    TextOut(hDC, 22, 0, szTemp, lstrlen(szTemp) );

                    for ( i=0; i<16; i++ )
                    {
                        wsprintf( szTemp, "%2X ", i*16 );
                        szLittleBuffer[0] = 0;
                        for ( j=0; j<16; j++ )
                        {
                            if (i==0 && j==0)
                                lstrcpy( szBuffer, " " );
                            else
                                wsprintf( szBuffer, "%c", j+i*16 );
                            lstrcat( szLittleBuffer, szBuffer );
                            lstrcat( szTemp, szBuffer );
                            lstrcat( szTemp, " " );
                        }
                        GetStringTypeA( LOCALE_USER_DEFAULT,CT_CTYPE1,
                                     szLittleBuffer, 16, &wTypeArray );

                        for ( j=0; j<16; j++ )
                        {
                            wsprintf( szBuffer, "%2X", (BYTE)wTypeArray[j] );
                            lstrcat( szTemp, szBuffer );
                        }

                        TextOut( hDC, 0, (i + 1)*15, szTemp,
                                 lstrlen( szTemp ) );
                    }

                    TextOut( hDC, 60, 256, LEGEND1, lstrlen( LEGEND1 ) );
                    TextOut( hDC, 60, 272, LEGEND2, lstrlen( LEGEND2 ) );
                    TextOut( hDC, 60, 272, szBuffer, lstrlen(szBuffer) );

                    DeleteObject( SelectObject( hDC, hOldFont ) );
                    ReleaseDC( hWnd, hDC );
                }
                break;

        case IDM_EXIT:
                DestroyWindow( hWnd );
                break;
```

```
        }
    break;
.
.
.
```

GetThreadLocale ■ WINDOWS 95 ■ WINDOWS NT

Description GetThreadLocale returns the calling thread's current locale. When a thread is created, it is given the system default thread locale. The system reads the system default thread locale from the registry when the system boots. The system default can be modified for future process and thread creation using Control Panel's Regional Settings application. Under Windows 95, the new settings do not take effect until the system is rebooted.

Syntax LCID **GetThreadLocale**(VOID)

Parameters This function has no parameters.

Returns LCID: The calling thread's 32-bit LCID locale identifier.

Include File winnls.h

See Also SetThreadLocale, GetSystemDefaultLCID, GetUserDefaultLCID

GetTimeFormat ■ WINDOWS 95 ■ WINDOWS NT

Description GetTimeFormat formats the time using the locale time format or the supplied format picture. Use this function to format a provided time or the local system time.

Syntax int **GetTimeFormat**(LCID *Locale,* DWORD *dwFlags,* CONST SYSTEMTIME* *lpTime,* LPCTSTR *lpTimeFormat,* LPTSTR *lpTimeStr,* int *nBufferSize*)

Parameters

Locale LCID: Specifies the locale for which the time string is to be formatted. If *lpTimeFormat* is NULL, the function formats the string according to the time format for this locale; otherwise, the function uses the locale only for information not specified in the format picture string. This parameter can be a locale identifier created by the MAKELCID macro, LOCALE_SYSTEM_DEFAULT to use the default system locale, or LOCALE_USER_DEFAULT to use the default user locale.

dwFlags DWORD: A set of flags that specify various function options. This may be a combination of the flags listed in Table 22-16.

Table 22-16 GetTimeFormat *dwFlags* values

Flag	Meaning
LOCALE_NOUSEROVERRIDE	The string is formatted using the system default time format for the specified locale. This flag cannot be set if *lpTimeFormat* is non-NULL.
TIME_FORCE24HOURFORMAT	Always use a 24-hour time format.
TIME_NOMINUTESORSECONDS	Do not use minutes or seconds.
TIME_NOSECONDS	Do not use seconds.
TIME_NOTIMEMARKER	Do not use a time marker.

lpTime	CONST SYSTEMTIME*: A pointer to the time to format. If NULL, the system time is converted. See the definition of the SYSTEMTIME structure under the GetSystemTime function in Chapter 21, System Information.
lpTimeFormat	LPCTSTR: Format of time to use if locale is not used. This is specified in the same fashion as locale time format pictures.
lpTimeStr	LPTSTR: Buffer to receive the formatted time.
nBufferSize	int: If 0, the return value is the number of characters needed in a buffer to store the formatted time. In this case, *lpTimeStr* is ignored. Otherwise, this specifies the number of bytes in the buffer *lpTimeStr* that receives the formatted time.
Returns	int: The number of characters copied into the buffer, or—if *nBufferSize* is 0—the number of characters required to hold the formatted string.
Include File	winnls.h
See Also	GetLocaleInfo, SetLocaleInfo, GetDateFormat
Example	See the example for the GetDateFormat function.

IsCharAlpha   ■ WINDOWS 95   ■ WINDOWS NT

Description	IsCharAlpha examines a single character and determines whether the character is an alphabetic character. It uses the current language of the locale.
Syntax	BOOL **IsCharAlpha**(TCHAR *ch*)
Parameters	
ch	TCHAR: The character to test.
Returns	BOOL: TRUE if the character is alphabetic; otherwise, FALSE. If an error occurs, you can get the error code using GetLastError.
Include File	winuser.h
See Also	GetStringTypeEx, IsCharAlphaNumeric, IsCharLower, IsCharUpper

Example   This example examines a string and determines the attributes of the various characters: uppercase, lowercase, alphabetic, or alphanumeric.

```c
LRESULT CALLBACK WndProc( HWND hWnd, UINT uMsg, WPARAM wParam, LPARAM lParam )
{
   switch( uMsg )
   {
      case WM_COMMAND :
              switch( LOWORD( wParam ) )
              {
                 case IDM_TEST:
                     {
                         int    i = 0;
                         HDC    hDC = GetDC( hWnd );
                         BYTE   szTemp[]   = { 0, 0 };
                         BYTE   szFrench[] = { 0x37, 0x3E, 0x20, 0x41, 0xEE,
                                               0x6E, 0xE9, 0x20, 0xC1, 0 };
                         LPTSTR p = szFrench;

                         TextOut ( hDC, 10,  0, "String:", 7 );
                         TextOut ( hDC, 10, 15, "Alpha:", 6 );
                         TextOut ( hDC, 10, 30, "AlphaNum:", 9 );
                         TextOut ( hDC, 10, 45, "Lower:", 6 );
                         TextOut ( hDC, 10, 60, "Upper:", 6 );

                         while (*p)
                         {
                             szTemp[0] = *p;

                             TextOut( hDC, 100 + (i*10),  0, szTemp, 1 );
                             TextOut( hDC, 100 + (i*10), 15,
                                     IsCharAlpha(szFrench[i]) ? "1" : "0" , 1);

                             TextOut( hDC, 100 + (i*10), 30,
                                     IsCharAlphaNumeric(szFrench[i]) ?
                                     "1" : "0", 1 );

                             TextOut( hDC, 100 + (i*10), 45,
                                     IsCharLower(szFrench[i]) ? "1" : "0", 1 );

                             TextOut( hDC, 100 + (i*10), 60,
                                     IsCharUpper(szFrench[i]) ? "1" : "0", 1 );

                             p = CharNext( p );

                             // move a column over
                             //..................
                             i++;
                         }
                         ReleaseDC( hWnd, hDC );
                     }
                     break;
```

```
                     .
                     .
                     .
```

IsCharAlphaNumeric　　■ WINDOWS 95　■ WINDOWS NT

Description	IsCharAlphaNumeric examines a single character and determines whether the character is an alphanumeric character. It uses the current language of the locale.
Syntax	BOOL **IsCharAlphaNumeric**(TCHAR *ch*)
Parameters	
ch	TCHAR: The character to test.
Returns	BOOL: TRUE if the character is alphanumeric; otherwise, FALSE. If an error occurs, you can get the error code using GetLastError.
Include File	winuser.h
See Also	GetStringTypeEx, IsCharAlpha, IsCharLower, IsCharUpper
Example	See the example for IsCharAlpha.

IsCharLower　　■ WINDOWS 95　■ WINDOWS NT

Description	IsCharLower examines a single character and determines whether the character is a lowercase alphabetic character. It uses the current language of the locale.
Syntax	BOOL **IsCharLower**(TCHAR *ch*)
Parameters	
ch	TCHAR: The character to test.
Returns	BOOL: TRUE if the character is a lowercase alphabetic character; otherwise, FALSE. If an error occurs, you can get the error code using GetLastError.
Include File	winuser.h
See Also	GetStringTypeEx, IsCharAlphaNumeric, IsCharAlpha, IsCharUpper
Example	See the example for IsCharAlpha.

IsCharUpper　　■ WINDOWS 95　■ WINDOWS NT

Description	IsCharUpper examines a single character and determines whether the character is an uppercase alphabetic character. It uses the current language of the locale.
Syntax	BOOL **IsCharUpper**(TCHAR *ch*)
Parameters	
ch	TCHAR: The character to test.
Returns	BOOL: TRUE if the character is an uppercase alphabetic character; otherwise, FALSE. If an error occurs, you can get the error code using GetLastError.

Include File	winuser.h
See Also	GetStringTypeEx, IsCharAlphaNumeric, IsCharLower, IsCharAlpha
Example	See the example for IsCharAlpha.

IsDBCSLeadByte ■ WINDOWS 95 ■ WINDOWS NT

Description	IsDBCSLeadByte determines whether a given character is the first byte of a double-byte character using the ANSI code-page.
Syntax	BOOL **IsDBCSLeadByte**(BYTE *TestChar*)
Parameters	
TestChar	BYTE: The character to test.
Returns	BOOL: TRUE if the character is a lead-in byte; otherwise, FALSE.
Include File	winnls.h
See Also	IsDBCSLeadByteEx, WideCharToMultiByte

IsDBCSLeadByteEx ■ WINDOWS 95 ■ WINDOWS NT

Description	IsDBCSLeadByteEx determines whether a given character is the first byte of a double-byte character using the specified code-page.
Syntax	BOOL **IsDBCSLeadByteEx**(UINT *uCodePage,* BYTE *TestChar*)
Parameters	
uCodePage	UINT: The code-page to use. This may be any valid code-page, or you may use 0 or the constant CP_ACP to indicate the system default ANSI code-page or CP_OEMCP to indicate the system default OEM code-page.
TestChar	BYTE: The character to test.
Returns	BOOL: TRUE if the character is a lead-in byte; otherwise, FALSE.
Include File	winnls.h
See Also	WideCharToMultiByte

IsTextUnicode ■ WINDOWS 95 ■ WINDOWS NT

Description	IsTextUnicode determines if a buffer possibly contains a form of Unicode text. The function uses various statistical and deterministic methods to make this determination, under the control of flags passed in by the application. When the function returns, the results of such tests are reported.
Syntax	DWORD **IsTextUnicode**(CONST LPVOID *lpBuffer,* int *cb,* LPINT *lpi*)
Parameters	
lpBuffer	CONST LPVOID: A pointer to the input buffer to be examined.

cb	`int`: The size, in bytes, of the input buffer.
lpi	`LPINT`: A pointer to an int that, upon entry to the function, contains a set of flags that specify the tests to be applied to the input buffer text. Upon exit from the function, it contains a set of bit flags indicating the results of the specified tests—**1** if the contents of the buffer pass a test, **0** for failure. Only flags that are set upon entry to the function are significant upon exit. If set to **NULL**, the function uses all available tests to determine if the data in the buffer is probably Unicode text. Valid flags are listed in Table 22-17.

Table 22-17 `IsTextUnicode` flags

Value	Meaning
IS_TEXT_UNICODE_ASCII16	The text is Unicode, and contains nothing but zero-extended ASCII values/characters.
IS_TEXT_UNICODE_BUFFER_TOO_SMALL	There are too few characters in the buffer for meaningful analysis (fewer than 2 bytes).
IS_TEXT_UNICODE_CONTROLS	The text contains Unicode representations of one or more of these nonprinting characters: RETURN, LINEFEED, SPACE, CJK_SPACE, TAB.
IS_TEXT_UNICODE_ILLEGAL_CHARS	The text contains one of these Unicode-illegal characters: embedded Reverse BOM, UNICODE_NUL, CR/LF (packed into one WORD), or 0xFFFF.
IS_TEXT_UNICODE_NOT_ASCII_MASK	This flag constant is a combination of IS_TEXT_UNICODE_NULL_BYTES and three currently unused bit flags.
IS_TEXT_UNICODE_NOT_UNICODE_MASK	This flag constant is a combination of IS_TEXT_UNICODE_ILLEGAL_CHARS, IS_TEXT_UNICODE_ODD_LENGTH, and two currently unused bit flags.
IS_TEXT_UNICODE_NULL_BYTES	The text contains null bytes, which indicate non-ASCII text.
IS_TEXT_UNICODE_ODD_LENGTH	The number of characters in the string is odd. A string of odd length cannot (by definition) be Unicode text.
IS_TEXT_UNICODE_REVERSE_ASCII16	Same as IS_TEXT_UNICODE_ASCII16, except that the Unicode text is byte reversed.
IS_TEXT_UNICODE_REVERSE_CONTROLS	Same as IS_TEXT_UNICODE_CONTROLS, except that the Unicode characters are byte reversed.
IS_TEXT_UNICODE_REVERSE_MASK	This flag constant is a combination of IS_TEXT_UNICODE_REVERSE_ASCII16, IS_TEXT_UNICODE_REVERSE_STATISTICS, IS_TEXT_UNICODE_REVERSE_CONTROLS, IS_TEXT_UNICODE_REVERSE_SIGNATURE.
IS_TEXT_UNICODE_REVERSE_SIGNATURE	The text contains the Unicode byte-reversed byte-order mark (Reverse BOM) 0xFFFE as its first character.
IS_TEXT_UNICODE_REVERSE_STATISTICS	Same as IS_TEXT_UNICODE_STATISTICS, except that the probably-Unicode text is byte reversed.
IS_TEXT_UNICODE_SIGNATURE	The text contains the Unicode byte-order mark (BOM) 0xFEFF as its first character.
IS_TEXT_UNICODE_STATISTICS	The text is probably Unicode, with the determination made by applying statistical analysis. Absolute certainty is not guaranteed.
IS_TEXT_UNICODE_UNICODE_MASK	This flag constant is a combination of IS_TEXT_UNICODE_ASCII16, IS_TEXT_UNICODE_STATISTICS, IS_TEXT_UNICODE_CONTROLS, and IS_TEXT_UNICODE_SIGNATURE.

Returns	DWORD: The function returns nonzero if the data in the buffer passes the specified tests. If the function returns 0, the buffer does not pass all the specified tests. In either case, the int pointed to by *lpi* contains the results of the specific tests the function applied to make its determination.
Include File	winbase.h
See Also	IsDBCSLeadByteEx

IsValidCodePage   ■ Windows 95   ■ Windows NT

Description	IsValidCodePage determines if a code-page is valid.
Syntax	BOOL **IsValidCodePage**(UINT *CodePage*)
Parameters	
CodePage	UINT: The code-page to check. Each code-page is identified by a unique number. See Table 22-2 for a list of code-pages.
Returns	BOOL: If the code-page is valid, TRUE is returned; otherwise, FALSE is returned.
Include File	winnls.h
See Also	GetACP, GetCPInfo, GetOEMCP

IsValidLocale   ■ Windows 95   ■ Windows NT

Description	IsValidLocale determines if a locale identifier is valid. This function currently tests whether a locale identifier is installed or supported on the calling system.
Syntax	BOOL **IsValidLocale**(LCID *Locale,* DWORD *dwFlags*)
Parameters	
Locale	LCID: The locale identifier to be validated. You can use the MAKELCID macro to create a locale identifier.
dwFlags	DWORD: The validity test to apply to the locale identifier. Set to LCID_INSTALLED to test if the locale is both supported and installed. Set to LCID_SUPPORTED to test if the locale is supported.
Returns	BOOL: If the locale passes the specified validity test, the return value is TRUE; otherwise, FALSE is returned.
Include File	winnls.h
See Also	GetLocaleInfo

LCMapString

Description   LCMapString maps a character string to another or creates a sort key for the given string, using locale settings to perform translation. This cannot be an in-place conversion.

Syntax   int **LCMapString**(LCID *lcid,* DWORD *dwMapFlags,* LPCTSTR *lpSource,* int *nSourceSize,* LPTSTR *lpDest,* int *nDestSize*)

Parameters

lcid   LCID: The locale identifier. This may be any valid locale constructed with the MAKELCID macro or one of the two predefined system constants, LOCALE_SYSTEM_DEFAULT or LOCALE_USER_DEFAULT, which designate system or user defaults, respectively.

dwMapFlags   DWORD: Mapping flags that modify the result. Table 22-18 gives a complete list of the LCMapString options.

Table 22-18 LCMapString *dwMapFlags* options

Option	Description
LCMAP_BYTEREVersal	Reverses byte order, exchanging HIBYTES and LOBYTES.
LCMAP_FULLWIDTH	Single-byte characters are mapped to double-byte characters. Cannot be used with LCMAP_HALFWIDTH, which performs the opposite function.
LCMAP_HALFWIDTH	Double-byte characters are mapped to single-byte characters. Cannot be used with LCMAP_FULLWIDTH, which performs the opposite function.
LCMAP_HIRAGANA	Maps Katakana characters to Hiragana. Do not use with LCMAP_KATAKANA.
LCMAP_KATAKANA	Maps Hiragana characters to Katakana. Do not use with LCMAP_HIRAGANA.
LCMAP_LOWERCASE	Maps to lowercase. Can only be used with LCMAP_BYTEREVERSAL.
LCMAP_SORTKEY	Builds a sort key. Use with LCMAP_BYTEREVERSAL, any NORM_ constant, or SORT_STRINGSORT.
LCMAP_UPPERCASE	Maps to uppercase. Can only be used with LCMAP_BYTEREVERSAL.
NORM_IGNORECASE	Establishes case insensitivity.
NORM_IGNOREKANATYPE	Does not distinguish between Hiragana and like Kanatype characters.
NORM_IGNORENOSPACE	Removes nonspacing characters and Japanese accent characters. Nonspacing characters are character modifiers that do not actually occupy space in the string.
NORM_IGNORESYMBOLS	Removes symbols.
NORM_IGNOREWIDTH	Does not distinguish between multibyte and single-byte like characters.
SORT_STRINGSORT	Treats punctuation the same as symbols.

lpSource   LPCTSTR: A pointer to the string to map or to be used to generate a source key.

nSourceSize   int: Size of source string to map.

lpDest	LPTSTR: The destination buffer. This parameter is ignored if *nDestSize* is 0.
nDestSize	int: Number of bytes in the destination buffer, or 0 to determine number of bytes required in the output buffer.
Returns	int: The number of bytes copied to the destination buffer. If *nDestSize* is 0, returns the buffer size needed to receive the mapped string or sort key. If 0 is returned, an error has occurred. Use GetLastError to return the error code.
Include File	winnls.h
See Also	WideCharToMultiByte, MultiByteToWideChar, OemToChar, CharToOem
Example	This example transforms a set of accented characters, first to uppercase and then to lowercase. The function LCMapString performs these transformations.

```
LRESULT CALLBACK WndProc( HWND hWnd, UINT uMsg, WPARAM wParam, LPARAM lParam )
{
    switch( uMsg )
    {
      case WM_COMMAND :
            switch( LOWORD( wParam ) )
            {
              case IDM_TEST:
                    {
                        int   i, iBytesCopied;
                        HFONT hOldFont;
                        TCHAR szBuffer[96];
                        TCHAR szXlatBuffer[33];
                        TCHAR szAccentedChars[33];
                        HDC   hDC = GetDC( hWnd );

                        // Make an ANSI string of characters to translate.
                        //.................................................
                        for (i=0; i<0x10; i++)    szAccentedChars[i] = 0xC0 + i;
                        for (i=0x10; i<0x20; i++) szAccentedChars[i] = 0xd0 + i;
                        szAccentedChars[0x20] = 0;

                        hOldFont = SelectObject( hDC, GetStockObject( ANSI_FIXED_⇐
FONT ) );

                        wsprintf( szBuffer, "Original Buffer: %s", szAccentedChars );
                        TextOut( hDC, 0, 0, szBuffer, lstrlen( szBuffer ) );

                        iBytesCopied = LCMapString( LOCALE_USER_DEFAULT,
                                          LCMAP_UPPERCASE,
                                          szAccentedChars, -1,
                                          szXlatBuffer, 33 );
                        if (iBytesCopied)
                        {
                            wsprintf( szBuffer, "Uppercase Buffer: %s", szXlatBuffer );
                            TextOut( hDC, 0, 20, szBuffer, lstrlen( szBuffer ) );
                        }
```

continued on next page

continued from previous page

```
                    iBytesCopied = LCMapString( LOCALE_USER_DEFAULT,
                                                LCMAP_LOWERCASE,
                                                szAccentedChars, -1,
                                                szXlatBuffer, 33 );
                    if (iBytesCopied)
                    {
                       wsprintf( szBuffer, "Lowercase Buffer: %s", szXlatBuffer );
                       TextOut( hDC, 0, 40, szBuffer, lstrlen( szBuffer ) );
                    }

                    DeleteObject( SelectObject( hDC, hOldFont ) );
                    ReleaseDC( hWnd, hDC );
                 }
                 break;
```

lstrcat   ■ WINDOWS 95 ■ WINDOWS NT

Description	The function **lstrcat** concatenates two strings.
Syntax	LPTSTR **lstrcat**(LPTSTR *lpszString1*, LPCTSTR *lpszString2*)
Parameters	
lpszString1	LPTSTR: A pointer to the first null-terminated string. This must be large enough for the sum of the two strings once they are appended.
lpszString2	LPCTSTR: A pointer to the second null-terminated string. This string will be appended to the end of the first string.
Returns	LPTSTR: If successful, the pointer to the first string is returned. Otherwise, **NULL** is returned and the error flag is set.
Include File	winbase.h
See Also	lstrcpy
Example	The function **lstrcat** is used in most of the examples, including the example for **GetStringTypeEx**.

lstrcmp   ■ WINDOWS 95 ■ WINDOWS NT

Description	The function **lstrcmp** compares two strings using the current language.
Syntax	int **lstrcmp**(LPTSTR *lpszString1*, LPCTSTR *lpszString2*)
Parameters	
lpszString1	LPTSTR: A pointer to the first null-terminated string.
lpszString2	LPCTSTR: A pointer to the second null-terminated string.

Returns	**int**: Negative value if string one is less than string two, a positive value if string one is greater than string two, or **0** if the strings are equal.
Include File	`winbase.h`
See Also	`lstrcmpi`, `CompareString`
Example	See the example for the `CompareString` function.

lstrcmpi ■ Windows 95 ■ Windows NT

Description	The function **lstrcmpi** compares two strings using the current language. This is a case-insensitive comparison.
Syntax	`int lstrcmpi( LPTSTR lpszString1, LPCTSTR lpszString2 )`
Parameters	
lpszString1	**LPTSTR**: A pointer to the first null-terminated string.
lpszString2	**LPCTSTR**: A pointer to the second null-terminated string.
Returns	**int**: Negative value if string one is less than string two, a positive value if string one is greater than string two, or **0** if the strings are equal. The magnitude of the value returned is the difference of the two nonmatching characters.
Include File	`winbase.h`
See Also	`lstrcmp`, `CompareString`
Example	See the example for the `CompareString` function.

lstrcpy ■ Windows 95 ■ Windows NT

Description	The function **lstrcpy** copies a string to another address.
Syntax	`LPTSTR lstrcpy( LPTSTR lpDestBuffer, LPCTSTR lpszSrcString )`
Parameters	
lpDestBuffer	**LPTSTR**: A pointer to a destination buffer to receive the string. The buffer must be large enough to contain the string.
lpszSrcString	**LPCTSTR**: A pointer to the string to be copied. This must be a null-terminated string.
Returns	**LPTSTR**: If successful, the pointer to the destination buffer is returned. Otherwise, **NULL** is returned and the error flag is set.
Include File	`winbase.h`
See Also	`lstrcat`
Example	The function **lstrcpy** is used in most of the examples, including the example for `GetStringTypeEx`.

lstrcpyn
■ WINDOWS 95 ■ WINDOWS NT

Description	**lstrcpyn** copies a specified number of characters for a source string into a buffer.
Syntax	LPTSTR **lstrcpyn**(LPTSTR *lpString1,* LPCTSTR *lpString2,* int *iMaxLength*)
Parameters	
lpString1	LPTSTR: A pointer to a buffer into which the function copies characters. The buffer must be large enough to contain the number of characters specified by *iMaxLength*, including room for a terminating null character.
lpString2	LPCTSTR: A pointer to a null-terminated string from which the function copies characters.
iMaxLength	int: The number of characters to be copied from the string pointed to by *lpString2* into the buffer pointed to by *lpString1*, including a terminating null character.
Returns	LPTSTR: If successful, a pointer to the buffer is returned; otherwise, **NULL** is returned.
Include File	winbase.h
See Also	lstrcat, lstrcmp, lstrcmpi, lstrcpy, lstrlen

lstrlen
■ WINDOWS 95 ■ WINDOWS NT

Description	The **lstrlen** function returns the length of a string.
Syntax	int **lstrlen**(LPTSTR *lpszString*)
Parameters	
lpszString	LPTSTR: A pointer to the a null-terminated string whose length is to be obtained.
Returns	int: The number of characters in the string is returned.
Include File	winbase.h
See Also	wsprintf
Example	The function **lstrlen** is used in many examples in this chapter, including the example for **GetStringTypeEx**.

MultiByteToWideChar
■ WINDOWS 95 ■ WINDOWS NT

Description	**MultiByteToWideChar** translates character strings of the given code-page to a Unicode wide-character string. This cannot be an in-place conversion!

Syntax	int **MultiByteToWideChar**(UINT *uCodePage*, DWORD *dwFlags*, LPCSTR *lpMultiByteStr*, int *nMultiByteSize*, LPWSTR *lpWideCharStr*, int *nWideCharSize*)
Parameters	
uCodePage	UINT: This can be any valid code-page. It also may be **CP_ACP** (default ANSI code-page), **CP_MACCP** (default Macintosh code-page), or **CP_OEMCP** (default IBM code-page).
dwFlags	DWORD: Mapping options as shown in Table 22-19.

Table 22-19 Multibyte translation flags

MultiByteToWideChar **Flag**	**Description**
MB_COMPOSITE	Distinguishes base characters from nonspacing characters. Cannot be used with MB_PRECOMPOSE.
MB_ERR_INVALID_CHARS	Return 0 and set last error if code-page specifies a double-byte character set and any double-byte pair is invalid. ERROR_NO_UNICODE_TRANSLATION is the error code set.
MB_PRECOMPOSED	Always use precomposed characters. Precomposed characters resolve base and nonspacing characters into a single character. This is mutually exclusive with MB_COMPOSITE.
MB_USEGLYPHCHARS	Uses glyph characters instead of control characters.

lpMultiByteStr	LPCSTR: A pointer to the string to convert.
nMultiByteSize	int: The number of bytes to convert. If −1, the string is assumed to be null terminated.
lpWideCharStr	LPWSTR: A pointer to a buffer that receives the Unicode data.
nWideCharSize	int: The number of characters that may be stored in *lpWideCharStr*, or 0 if the size of the converted buffer is being queried. In the latter case, *lpWideCharStr* is not used.
Returns	int: Number of characters copied or—if 0 is specified for *nWideCharSize*—the number of bytes needed to receive the translated string. If 0 is returned, an error has occurred. Use **GetLastError** to return the error code.
Include File	winnls.h
See Also	WideCharToMultiByte
Example	This example shows how wide character strings may be manipulated and transformed. When the user selects the Test! option from the menu of the example, a wide char string is translated into multibyte format and a multibyte format is transformed to wide char.

```
LRESULT CALLBACK WndProc( HWND hWnd, UINT uMsg, WPARAM wParam, LPARAM lParam )
```

```
{
    switch( uMsg )
    {
        case WM_COMMAND :
                switch( LOWORD( wParam ) )
                {
                    case IDM_TEST:
                        {
                            TCHAR szBuffer[128];

                            // Declare a Unicode string.
                            //.........................
                            static WCHAR wc[] = L"This is an example of a wide-char string";

                            // Declare an ANSI string.
                            //......................
                            static TCHAR tc[] = "This is an example of a Mulitple-Bytes⇐
String";

                            WCHAR wb[65];
                            TCHAR tb[65];
                            HDC   hDC = GetDC( hWnd );

                            // Convert wide to multibyte ANSI.
                            //...............................
                            WideCharToMultiByte( CP_ACP, 0, wc, -1, tb, 64, NULL, NULL );
                            TextOut( hDC, 0, 0, szBuffer,
                                    wsprintf( szBuffer, "MultipleByte: %s", tc ) );

                            TextOut( hDC, 0, 20, szBuffer,
                                    wsprintf( szBuffer, "Converted WideChar: %s", tb ) );

                            MultiByteToWideChar( CP_ACP, MB_PRECOMPOSED, tb, -1, wb, 64 );

                            // Wide strings should be the same now.
                            //...................................
                            WideCharToMultiByte( CP_ACP, 0, wb, -1, tb, 64, NULL, NULL );

                            TextOut( hDC, 0, 40, szBuffer,
                                    wsprintf( szBuffer, "Twice-Converted WideChar: %s", ⇐
tb ) );

                            ReleaseDC( hWnd, hDC );
                        }
                        break;
                        .
                        .
                        .
```

OemToChar

Description   OemToChar converts a string from the OEM character set to the character
set of the current locale. If the system cannot find an exact match, the best
alternative is used. This function is important because there is a large
amount of data that originates from the DOS environment. The only way
this OEM data can be displayed using a non-OEM font is to perform an

`OemToChar` translation. Most fonts for Windows are based on Windows ANSI.

Syntax

BOOL **OemToChar**(LPCSTR *lpszSource,* LPTSTR *lpszDest*)

Parameters

lpszSource

LPCSTR: A pointer to a null-terminated string of OEM-based data.

lpszDest

LPTSTR: A pointer to the destination buffer to receive the data of the current character set. This buffer may be the same address as *lpszSource*, in which case the translation is performed in place.

Returns

BOOL: Always returns TRUE.

Include File

winnls.h

See Also

CharToOem, OemToCharBuff

Example

When the user selects the Test! option from the menu of the example, a string is first displayed in OEM and then in ANSI. Notice that the correct font must be selected and the **OemToChar** function must be used to convert the OEM string to an ANSI string.

```
LRESULT CALLBACK WndProc( HWND hWnd, UINT uMsg, WPARAM wParam, LPARAM lParam )
{
   switch( uMsg )
   {
   case WM_COMMAND :
           switch( LOWORD( wParam ) )
           {
           case IDM_TEST:
                   {
                       TCHAR szBuffer[32];
                       HFONT hOldFont;
                       TCHAR szStart[] = "Sword in French: ";
                       BYTE  szFrench[] = { 0x90, 0x70, 0x82, 0x65, 0 };
                       HDC   hDC = GetDC( hWnd );

                       lstrcpy( szBuffer, szStart );
                       lstrcat( szBuffer, szFrench );

                       hOldFont = SelectObject( hDC, GetStockObject(OEM_FIXED_FONT) );
                       TextOut( hDC, 0, 0, szBuffer, lstrlen(szBuffer) );

                       // in-place OEM->char
                       //.................
                       OemToChar( szBuffer, szBuffer );
                       DeleteObject( SelectObject(hDC, GetStockObject(ANSI_FIXED_FONT)⇐
) );

                       TextOut( hDC, 0, 20, szBuffer, lstrlen(szBuffer) );

                       DeleteObject( SelectObject( hDC, hOldFont ) );
                       ReleaseDC( hWnd, hDC );
                   }
                   break;
                   .
                   .
                   .
```

OemToCharBuff

Description	**OemToCharBuff** converts a buffer of data from the OEM character set to the character set of the current locale. If an OEM character does not exist in the current character set—for example line-drawing characters—the nearest equivalent is selected.
Syntax	BOOL **OemToCharBuff**(LPCSTR *lpszSource,* LPTSTR *lpszDest*)
Parameters	
lpszSource	LPCSTR: A pointer to a buffer of OEM character set data to be converted.
lpszDest	LPTSTR: A pointer to destination buffer to receive the converted string. This buffer may be the same address as *lpszSource*, in which case the translation is performed in place. In-place translation cannot be performed with multibyte strings.
Returns	BOOL: Always returns TRUE.
Include File	winnls.h
See Also	CharToOem, OemToChar
Example	This example produces the same output as the example for **OemToChar** using the **OemToCharBuff** function.

```
LRESULT CALLBACK WndProc( HWND hWnd, UINT uMsg, WPARAM wParam, LPARAM lParam )
{
    switch( uMsg )
    {
        case WM_COMMAND :
                switch( LOWORD( wParam ) )
                {
                    case IDM_TEST:
                        {
                            TCHAR szBuffer[32];
                            TCHAR szOemBuffer[32];
                            HFONT hOldFont;
                            TCHAR szStart[] = "Sword in French: ";
                            BYTE  szFrench[] = { 0x90, 0x70, 0x82, 0x65, 0 };
                            HDC   hDC = GetDC( hWnd );

                            lstrcpy( szOemBuffer, szStart );
                            lstrcat( szOemBuffer, szFrench );

                            // Convert the string.
                            //...................
                            OemToCharBuff( szOemBuffer, szBuffer,
                                        lstrlen( szOemBuffer )+1 );

                            hOldFont = SelectObject( hDC, GetStockObject(OEM_FIXED_FONT) );
                            TextOut( hDC, 0, 0, szOemBuffer, lstrlen(szOemBuffer) );

                            DeleteObject( SelectObject( hDC, GetStockObject(ANSI_FIXED_FONT)⇐
) );

                            TextOut( hDC, 0, 20, szBuffer, lstrlen(szBuffer) );
```

```
        DeleteObject( SelectObject( hDC, hOldFont ) );
        ReleaseDC( hWnd, hDC );
    }
    break;
```

.
.
.

SetLocaleInfo   ■ WINDOWS 95   ■ WINDOWS NT

Description   SetLocaleInfo sets specified information about a locale. Locale informa-
                    tion is always returned as a string—even integer values.

Syntax   int **SetLocaleInfo**(LCID *Locale,* LCTYPE *LCType,* LPCTSTR
                    lpszLCDataBuffer)

Parameters

Locale   LCID: The locale identifier of the locale to be set. This may be any locale
                    created with the **MAKELCID** macro, **LOCALE_SYSTEM_DEFAULT** (system default
                    locale), or **LOCALE_USER_DEFAULT** (user's default locale).

LCType   LCTYPE: This may be any of the locale identifier constants shown in Tables
                    22-20 through 22-24.

Table 22-20 Locale language data

Locale Info Constant	Definition
LOCALE_ICOUNTRY	Country code, based on international phone codes. These are also referred to as IBM country codes. (6 bytes)
LOCALE_IDEFAULTANSICODEPAGE	Default ANSI code-page of locale. (6 bytes)
LOCALE_IDEFAULTCOUNTRY	Default country code for new locales. (6 bytes)
LOCALE_IDEFAULTLANGUAGE	Default language identifier for new locales. (5 bytes)
LOCALE_IDEFAULTOEMCODEPAGE	Default OEM code-page of locale. (6 bytes)
LOCALE_ILANGUAGE	The language identifier. For example, Standard French is 0x40c and Canadian French is 0x80c. (4 bytes)
LOCALE_SABBREVCTRYNAME	English abbreviation of country name.
LOCALE_SABBREVLANGNAME	Abbreviation of language name, a three-letter string.
LOCALE_SCOUNTRY	Full localized country name.
LOCALE_SENGCOUNTRY	English name of country.
LOCALE_SENGLANGUAGE	English equivalent language name. This can always be represented in 127-character ANSI subset.
LOCALE_SLANGUAGE	Full localized name of language.
LOCALE_SNATIVECTRYNAME	Native country name in native language.
LOCALE_SNATIVELANGNAME	Language name in native language.

Table 22-21 Locale numeric display format control

Locale Info Constant	Definition
LOCALE_IDIGITS	Number of fractional digits. (3 bytes)
LOCALE_ILZERO	Leading zeros in decimals (1), or none (0). (2 bytes)
LOCALE_INEGNUMBER	How negative numbers are represented: 0 (enclosed parentheses), 1 (leading minus sign), 2 (leading minus sign and space), 3 (trailing minus sign), and 4 (trailing minus sign and space).
LOCALE_SDECIMAL	Decimal separator character(s).
LOCALE_SGROUPING	How digits to left of decimal place are grouped. For example, to group by twos, you may use 2;0. The 0 means that the same grouping is repeated. Thus, the number 1000 would be 10,00 (assuming a comma separator). English uses 3;0, of course.
LOCALE_SLIST	List item separator (for example, comma in English).
LOCALE_SNATIVEDIGITS	Native equivalents of ASCII 0 through 9.
LOCALE_SNEGATIVESIGN	String value for negative sign.
LOCALE_SPOSITIVESIGN	String value for positive sign.
LOCALE_STHOUSAND	Thousands separator for digits left of decimal.

Table 22-22 Locale currency display format information

Locale Currency Information Constant	Definition
LOCALE_ICURRDIGITS	Number of fractional digits for local currency format (3 bytes). For U.S., the value 2 is correct (up to two digits of cents).
LOCALE_ICURRENCY	How currency symbol is displayed: Prefixed=0, suffixed=1, prefixed with separator=2, suffixed with separator=3.
LOCALE_IINTLCURRDIGITS	Number of fractional digits for international currency format. (up to 3 bytes)
LOCALE_INEGCURR	How currency symbol is displayed for negative amounts. Valid values range from 0–15. Also, see LOCALE_INEGSIGNPOSN, LOCALE_INEGSYMPRECEDES, and LOCALE_INEGSEPBYSPACE for a description of the formatting types.
LOCALE_INEGSEPBYSPACE	Specifies whether currency symbol is separated by a space from a negative amount (1) or not (0).
LOCALE_INEGSIGNPOSN	Formatting for negative values. Same parameter values as LOCALE_IPOSSIGNPOSN.
LOCALE_INEGSYMPRECEDES	Specifies whether currency symbol precedes (1) or follows (0) the negative amount.
LOCALE_IPOSSEPBYSPACE	Specifies whether currency symbol is separated by a space from a positive amount (1) or not (0).
LOCALE_IPOSSIGNPOSN	Formatting for positive values. 0: Uses parentheses. 1: Sign comes before the amount and currency symbol. 2: Sign follows the amount and currency symbol. 3: Sign comes immediately before the currency symbol. 4: Sign immediately follows the currency symbol.

Locale Currency Information Constant

Information Constant	Definition
LOCALE_IPOSSYMPRECEDES	Specifies whether currency symbol is a prefix (1) or a suffix (0) for a positive amount.
LOCALE_SCURRENCY	String used as local monetary symbol.
LOCALE_SINTLSYMBOL	A three-character string from ISO 4217 (the internationally recognized currency symbol) followed by a one-character string that separates the currency symbol from the amount.
LOCALE_SMONDECIMALSEP	Character(s) used to separate decimal portion of amount of currency.
LOCALE_SMONGROUPING	Monetary grouping expressed the same as LOCALE_SGROUPING.
LOCALE_SMONTHOUSANDSEP	Character(s) used to separate thousands portion of amount of currency.

Table 22-23 Locale date and time formats

Locale Info Constant	Definition
LOCALE_ICALENDARTYPE	Primary calendar. 1 is U.S. Gregorian, 2 is English Gregorian, 3 is Japan (Year of Emperor), 4 is China (Year of Republic), 5 is Korea (Tangun Era).
LOCALE_ICENTURY	0 (two-digit century), 1 (four-digit century).
LOCALE_IDATE	Month, year, day ordering. 0 is Month-Day-Year, 1 is Day-Month-Year, and 2 is Year-Month-Day. This is for short date format.
LOCALE_IDAYLZERO	Leading zeros in day fields (1) or not (0).
LOCALE_IFIRSTDAYOFWEEK	LOCALE_SDAYNAME1 to LOCALE_SDAYNAME7.
LOCALE_IFIRSTWEEKOFYEAR	If 0, week containing first day of first month is first week. If 1, first full week following 1/1 is the first week. If 2, first week with four days is first week.
LOCALE_ILDATE	Order for long date format.
LOCALE_IMONLZERO	Leading zeros in month fields (1) or not (0).
LOCALE_IOPTIONALCALENDARS	List of other calendars supported. (Zero-separated list of same values as LOCALE_ICALENDARTYPE above.)
LOCALE_ITIME	0 (a.m./p.m. 12-hour clock), 1 (24-hour clock).
LOCALE_ITLZERO	Leading zeros in time fields (1) or not (0).
LOCALE_S1159	String for a.m. designator.
LOCALE_S2359	String for p.m. designator.
LOCALE_SABBREVDAYNAME1 through LOCALE_SABBREVDAYNAME7	Native abbreviated names for days of week.
LOCALE_SABBREVMONTHNAME1 through LOCALE_SABBREVMONTHNAME13	Native abbreviated names for months.
LOCALE_SDATE	Date separator.
LOCALE_SDAYNAME1–LOCALE_SDAYNAME7	Native long names for days of week.
LOCALE_SLONGDATE	Long date format. For example, *dd* " of" *MMMM* "," *yyyy*, for "15 of December, 1994". For format rules, see discussion above.

continued on next page

continued from previous page

Locale Info Constant	Definition
LOCALE_SMONTHNAME1 through	
LOCALE_SMONTHNAME13	Native long names for months.
LOCALE_SSHORTDATE	Short date format. For example, *dd o MM o yy* for 15/12/94.
LOCALE_STIME	Time separator.
LOCALE_STIMEFORMAT	For example, *hh:mm:ss* for 12-hour clock or *HH:mm:ss* for 24-hour clock.

Table 22-24 Miscellaneous locale identifiers

Locale Miscellaneous Identifiers	Definition
LOCALE_IMEASURE	Metric (0) or U.S. (1). (2 bytes)
LOCALE_NOUSEROVERRIDE	Selects system default over user default.

lpszLCDataBuffer	LPCTSTR: A pointer to the null-terminated string that contains the new setting.
Returns	int: The number of characters stored in the buffer or the number required to store the string if *nBufferSize* is 0. If an error occurs, the function returns 0, and GetLastError may be used to return an error code.
Include File	winnls.h
See Also	GetLocaleInfo
Example	See the example for GetDateFormat.

SetThreadLocale ■ WINDOWS 95 ■ WINDOWS NT

Description	SetThreadLocale sets the calling thread's current locale.
Syntax	BOOL **SetThreadLocale**(LCID *Locale*)
Parameters	
Locale	LCID: The new locale for the calling thread. This parameter can be a locale identifier created by the MAKELCID macro, LOCALE_SYSTEM_DEFAULT for the system default, or LOCALE_USER_DEFAULT for the user default.
Returns	BOOL: If successful, TRUE is returned; otherwise, FALSE is returned.
Include File	winnls.h
See Also	GetThreadLocale, GetSystemDefaultLCID, GetUserDefaultLCID

ToAscii

Description	**ToAscii** translates a virtual-key code and keyboard state to the corresponding Windows characters, which are written to a buffer as a list of **WORD** values. This is mainly used with international (non-USA) keyboard translations.
Syntax	int **ToAscii**(UINT *uVirtKey,* UINT *uScanCode,* PBYTE *lpKeyState,* LPWORD *lpwTransKey,* UINT *uState*)
Parameters	
uVirtKey	**UINT**: Virtual-key code to be translated.
uScanCode	**UINT**: The hardware scan code of the key to be translated. The high-order bit is set if the key is up.
lpKeyState	**PBYTE**: An array of bytes for the state of the entire keyboard. Every element of this 256-byte array represents one key. It is indexed by the scan code. If the high-order bit of an array element is set, the key is down. Use **GetKeyboardState** to initialize this array before calling this function.
lpwTransKey	**LPWORD**: A pointer to a buffer that will receive the translated Windows characters.
uState	**UINT**: If **1**, a menu is active; otherwise, **0**.
Returns	**int**: **0** (no translation), **1** (one Windows character was copied), **2** (two characters were copied—the character cannot be represented as a single composite character).
Include File	winuser.h
See Also	GetKeyboardState
Example	This example uses **ToAscii** to convert **WM_KEYDOWN** parameter data into ANSI character equivalents. Every time a key is pressed, the number of translated bytes and the ANSI character is displayed.

```
LRESULT CALLBACK WndProc( HWND hWnd, UINT uMsg, WPARAM wParam, LPARAM lParam )
{
    switch( uMsg )
    {
        case WM_KEYDOWN:
            {
                BYTE   keys[256];
                TCHAR  szBuffer1[32];
                TCHAR  szBuffer2[32];
                WORD   wReturnedValue;

                GetKeyboardState( keys );

                wsprintf( szBuffer1, "ToAscii Returned %d Bytes.",
                          ToAscii( wParam, (lParam >> 16) && 0xFF,
                                   keys, &wReturnedValue, 0 ) );
```

continued on next page

continued from previous page

```
            wsprintf( szBuffer2, "[%c] was the character returned.",
                     (TCHAR)wReturnedValue & 0xFF );

            MessageBox( hWnd, szBuffer2, szBuffer1, MB_OK );
        }
        break;
       .
       .
       .
```

WideCharToMultiByte ■ WINDOWS 95   ■ WINDOWS NT

Description	WideCharToMultiByte translates character strings of the given Unicode wide-character string to characters of a given code-page. This cannot be an in-place conversion!
Syntax	int **WideCharToMultiByte**(UINT *uCodePage,* DWORD *dwFlags,* LPCWSTR *lpWideCharStr,* int *nWideCharLen,* LPSTR *lpMultiByteStr,* int *nMultiByteLength,* LPCSTR *lpDefaultChar,* LPBOOL *lpfUsedDefaultChar*)
Parameters	
uCodePage	UINT: This can be any valid code-page. It also may be **CP_ACP** (default ANSI code-page), **CP_MACCP** (default Macintosh code-page), or **CP_OEMCP** (default IBM code-page).
dwFlags	DWORD: Mapping options—what to do when a precomposed character does not exist for a wide-character translation. Table 22-25 shows these options.

Table 22-25 WideCharToMultiByte *dwFlags* options

WideCharToMultiByte **Flag**	**Description**
WC_COMPOSITECHECK	Translate base/nonspacing character pairs to precomposed characters if they exist.
WC_DEFAULTCHAR	Use the default character specified in the code-page information if no precomposed character is found. Cannot be used with WC_DISCARDNS.
WC_DISCARDNS	Discard nonspacing character if no precomposed character exists. Cannot be used with WC_DEFAULTCHAR.
WC_SEPCHARS	Generate separate chars during conversion.

lpWideCharStr	LPCWSTR: A pointer to the buffer that receives the Unicode data.
nWideCharLen	int: The number of characters that may be stored in *lpWideCharStr* or 0 if the size of the converted buffer is being queried. In the latter case, *lpWideCharStr* is not used.
lpMultiByteStr	LPSTR: A pointer to the buffer that contains the string to be converted.

nMultiByteLength	**int**: The number of bytes to convert. If **–1**, the string is assumed to be null terminated.
lpDefaultChar	**LPCSTR**: Pointer to a multibyte character that will be used if a translation from Unicode to the multibyte character set is not possible. If this parameter is **NULL**, the default character of the code-page is used instead. The default character of the code-page is the *DefaultChar* field of the **CPINFO** structure, which may be obtained using **GetCPInfo**. When **NULL** is used, the function is more efficient.
lpfUsedDefaultChar	**LPBOOL**: Pointer to a Boolean that is set whenever a default translation takes place. If this parameter is **NULL**, default translations will occur but not be reported. The function is more efficient when *lpfUsedDefaultChar* is set to **NULL**.
Returns	**int**: The number of characters copied or—if **0** is specified for *nWideCharLen* —the number of bytes needed to store the translated string. If **0** is returned, an error has occurred. Use **GetLastError** to return the error code.
Include File	winnls.h
See Also	MultiByteToWideChar

wsprintf　　　　　　　　　　　■ Windows 95　■ Windows NT

Description	The function **wsprintf** formats data—using a specified format string—and places the results in a character buffer. Special placeholder characters inside the buffer describe how the other arguments passed to the buffer are interpreted and displayed. For example, a **DWORD** value may be used as an unsigned 32-bit value (its native form) or as a pointer to a string. The function **wsprintf** is declared as **WINAPIV**, which indicates that the C calling convention is used rather than the **WINAPI** standard calling convention. In the C calling convention, arguments are passed from right to left, and the call stack is adjusted by the caller (not by the called code) after the function exits. Standard **WINAPI** calling adjusts the stack in the act of returning from the function. Both **WINAPI** and **WINAPIV** preserve case in the names of functions (unlike Win16's Pascal calling convention).
Syntax	int **wsprintf**(LPTSTR *lpBuffer,* LPCTSTR *lpszFormatString,* *[arguments]*)
Parameters	
lpBuffer	**LPTSTR**: A pointer to a character buffer to hold the output.
lpszFormatString	**LPCTSTR**: A pointer to a null-terminated character string that contains the format of the resulting buffer. Placeholders within the buffer are substituted for the arguments parameters. For example, a typical format string may be: **"A string is %s, and its address is %#X"**. If you call **wsprintf** with this format string and pass the same argument (a string pointer) as the third and fourth parameters in the call, **wsprintf** will substitute the contents of the string for the first

argument and the hex representation of its location (including a leading **0x**) for the second argument. Table 22-26 describes the **wsprintf** data type format options.

Table 22-26 Data type formatting options for wsprintf

Format Options	Description
%c	A TCHAR character—a character of the default character set. That is, if #define UNICODE is specified for the compilation, the type is WCHAR; otherwise, the type is CHAR.
%C	A single character of the nondefault character set. That is, if #define UNICODE is set for the compilation, the type is CHAR; otherwise, the type is WCHAR.
%d, %i	A signed decimal integer value.
%hc, %hC	Always CHAR.
%hs, %hS	Always a string of CHAR or LPSTR.
%lc, %lC	Always WCHAR.
%ld, %li	A long signed decimal integer value.
%ls, %lS	Always LPWSTR, a string of Unicode characters.
%lu	A long unsigned decimal integer value.
%lx, %lX	A long hexadecimal value: %lx uses the letters 'abcdef' to represent digits above 9, %lX uses the letters 'ABCDEF' to represent digits above 9.
%s	An LPTSTR—a string of characters of the default character set. That is, if #define UNICODE is specified, the type is LPWSTR; otherwise, LPSTR.
%S	A string of characters of the nondefault character set. That is, if #define UNICODE is specified, the type is LPSTR; otherwise, the type is LPWSTR.
%u	An unsigned integer value.
%x, %X	A hexadecimal integer value: %lx uses the letters 'abcdef' to represent digits above 9 and %lx uses the letters 'ABCDEF' to represent the digits above 9.

A format string may also have fill modifiers to designate how the fill data will be presented. For example, the '–' prefix changes justification of a field from right-justification to left-justification and the '0' prefix changes the fill character from a blank space to the '0' character. The '#' prefix seen in the first example for the *lpszFormatString* parameter, is another fill modifier that affects only hexadecimal data types (%x, %lx, %X, %lX), placing a leading '0x' before the display of the digits. The fill modifiers, presented in Table 22-27, may be used together.

Table 22-27 Field fill modifier formatting options

Format Options	Description
0	Changes fill character from a space to a '0' character.
#	Prefixes data with the '0x' string, common when displaying hex values.
–	Changes the field justification to pad the output with blanks (or zeros) to the right side rather than the left side (the default).

Finally, a width and precision may be specified for each field. The width specifies the minimum number of characters that are copied to the output buffer. Therefore, if the width is 10 and the contents of the substituted argument is **"Hello"**, the string **"bbbbbHello"** is copied to the buffer ('**b**' in this example represents a fill character). If the string **"HellobWorld"** (11 characters) is passed instead, the entire string is copied into the output buffer. The width specifier never truncates a field.

The precision modifier—a decimal point followed by a number—specifies the minimum number of digits that are copied into the output buffer. The field is zero-filled (by default on the left side) to attain the minimum number of digits. Thus, given a precision of **".10"**, the number 3.14 would be copied to the output buffer as **"00000003.14"**.

The syntax of any format string is

%[–][#][0][<field width>][.<field precision>]<field type>

where **<field width>** and **<field precision>** are numbers that dictate the field's width and precision and **<field type>** determines how the respective argument will be interpreted.

arguments	(variable type): A pointer to a list of data elements that are to be formatted in the text buffer.
Returns	**int**: The number of characters stored in the buffer.
Include File	**winuser.h**
See Also	**wvsprintf**
Example	The function **wsprintf** is used in most of the examples of this chapter, including the example for the function **ToAscii**.

wvsprintf ■ WINDOWS 95 ■ WINDOWS NT

Description The function **wvsprintf** formats data—using a specified format string—and places the results in a character buffer. Like the **wsprintf** function, special placeholder characters inside the buffer describe how data fields are interpreted and displayed, but instead of using a variable number of arguments, **wvsprintf** retrieves its data fields by using a pointer to an array of arguments as its third parameter. This allows **wvsprintf** to use the standard calling convention of Win32.

| Syntax | int **wvsprintf**(LPTSTR *lpBuffer*, LPCTSTR *lpszFormatString*, va_list *argList*) |

Parameters

lpBuffer   LPTSTR: A pointer to a character buffer to hold the output.

lpszFormatString   LPCTSTR: A pointer to a null-terminated character string that contains the format of the resulting buffer. The same rules for format construction of **wsprintf** apply for the function **wvsprintf**.

argList   va_list: A pointer to an array of fields that are substituted in the output buffer for the placeholders of the format string.

Returns   int: The number of characters stored in the buffer.

Include File   winuser.h, stdarg.h

See Also   wsprintf

Example   When the user selects the Test! option the same data is displayed in various formats.

```
LPCTSTR lpTheNumber = "Twenty Seven Hundred Fifty Four";

LRESULT CALLBACK WndProc( HWND hWnd, UINT uMsg, WPARAM wParam, LPARAM lParam )
{
   switch( uMsg )
   {
      case WM_COMMAND :
              switch( LOWORD( wParam ) )
              {
                 case IDM_TEST:
                       {
                           TCHAR szBuffer[128];
                           DWORD dwArgs[3];
                           HDC   hDC = GetDC( hWnd );

                           dwArgs[1] = dwArgs[0] = 2754;
                           dwArgs[2] = (DWORD)lpTheNumber;
                           wvsprintf( szBuffer, "The number %d is hex %x or string %s",
                                 (va_list)dwArgs );
                           TextOut(hDC, 0, 0,  szBuffer, lstrlen(szBuffer));
                           wvsprintf( szBuffer, "The number %d is hex %X or string %s",
                                 (va_list)dwArgs );
                           TextOut(hDC, 0, 20, szBuffer, lstrlen(szBuffer));
                           wvsprintf( szBuffer, "The number %010d is hex %#x = string⇐
%36s",
                                 (va_list)dwArgs );
                           TextOut(hDC, 0, 40, szBuffer, lstrlen(szBuffer));
                           wvsprintf( szBuffer, "The number %-10d is hex %#X = string ⇐
%-36s",
                                 (va_list)dwArgs );
                           TextOut(hDC, 0, 60, szBuffer, lstrlen(szBuffer));

                           ReleaseDC( hWnd, hDC );
                       }
                       break;

                           .
                           .
                           .
```

23

ATOMS

The Win32 API allows applications to store strings in structures known as atom tables. Once a program stores a string in an atom table, the program may reference the string using an atom. An atom is a unique 16-bit value that is associated with a constant string value. Using an atom as a reference to a string is similar to using a memory handle to reference a block of shared global data. Just as an application can pass a memory handle to the Win32 API to obtain a pointer to the contents of a block of data (by using `GlobalLock`), an application can use the Win32 APIs to obtain the value of a string associated with an atom. This string value that an atom represents is known as its atom name.

Atoms may be used by applications to save memory. Storing strings that occur more than once in an application's atom table conserves memory because the string value is stored only once. Other occurrences of the string only occupy the 2 bytes of memory required for the atom, rather than the number of bytes necessary to store a copy of the actual string. Another reason to store strings as atoms is that atom tables speed performance when comparing strings, because instead of comparing each byte of two strings, only the 16-bit atoms of the strings are compared.

Atoms are also important in data exchange between programs. An atom table global to all applications, the global atom table, is used to exchange data between applications. The use of atoms to exchange strings between applications is one of the foundations of dynamic data exchange (DDE). Atoms are also commonly used to store variable-length strings in object linking and embedding (OLE) object descriptors. The use of atoms in OLE data descriptors results in smaller, more easily exchanged, fixed-size structures.

Working with Atom Tables

There are two types of atom tables: local atom tables and the global atom table. Each process has its own local atom table. The value of a local atom is unique to the process in which it is defined. Atoms stored in the global atom table, on the other hand, may be accessed by any application. For any given global atom, the Win32 API will return the same atom to each application for a given atom name.

The **AddAtom** function stores strings in a local atom table. Atom names are stored in exactly the same case in which they are added. Each time **AddAtom** is called for an already existing atom, Windows increments an internal reference count for the atom. **DeleteAtom** is used to decrement this reference count. When the reference count reaches zero, the atom is removed from the atom table.

FindAtom searches the application's local atom table for an atom that matches a given string. The search performed is case insensitive. To return an atom name from the atom table, use **GetAtomName**. The atom name is returned in the same case in which it was first stored.

A parallel set of atom functions allows global atom tables to be managed. **GlobalAddAtom**, for example, adds atoms to a global atom table, just as **AddAtom** adds atoms to a local atom table. The other global atom table functions are **GlobalDeleteAtom**, **GlobalFindAtom**, and **GlobalGetAtomName**.

The last atom function, **InitAtomTable**, sets the number of top-level entries in the local atom table to a given value. By default, the number of top-level entries in both the local atom table and global atom table is 37. This does not mean that only 37 atoms may be placed in the table, but rather that the chance of collision (and therefore slower searches) is more likely with 37 entries in the table than with, for example, 73. **InitAtomTable** must be called before adding atoms to a local atom table. Also, the value passed should always be a prime number. If a prime number is not used, there will likely be more collisions and, therefore, slower searches. There is no corresponding function for setting the global atom table's number of top-level entries.

Using Global Atoms for Data Exchange

While global atoms are used extensively with DDE, you can also use atoms to easily exchange string data between instances of your application. The sender adds a string to the global atom table with the **GlobalAddAtom** function and then sets a message parameter to the value of the atom. The receiver uses the **GlobalFindAtom** function to get the contents of the passed data and deletes the atom using **GlobalDeleteAtom**. It is important to delete the atom; otherwise, the global atom table will become cluttered with unneeded entries.

Listing 23-1 shows how an application can use atoms to perform a simple data exchange. Note that, unlike in DDE, the exact protocol of the communication may be set unilaterally by the application because both sides of the conversation are controlled. This simple case uses **WM_USER** as the message and stores the atom in the low word of the *wParam* parameter.

Listing 23-1 Using global atoms to exchange data

```
// This function is on the sender side of the conversation. It exports the string.

void ExportString( HWND hWnd, LPCTSTR lpszStringToSend )
{
    ATOM aAtom = GlobalAddAtom( lpszStringToSend );
    SendMessage( hWnd, WM_USER, (WPARAM) aAtom, 0 );
}
```

```
LRESULT CALLBACK WndProc( HWND hWnd, UINT uMsg, WPARAM wParam, LPARAM lParam )
{
   switch (uMsg)
   {

      case WM_USER:
        {
            ATOM aAtom = LOWORD( wParam );

            if (aAtom != INVALID_ATOM )
            {
               char szStringReceived[ 65 ];
               GlobalFindAtom( aAtom, szStringReceived, 64 );
               MessageBox( hWnd, szStringReceived, "Received String", MB_OK );
               GlobalDeleteAtom( aAtom );
            }
        }
        break;

        .
        .
        .
```

Refer to the `GlobalAddAtom` function for a working example of this technique.

Integer Atoms

Windows 95 and Windows NT also provide a means of storing strings of decimal numbers into atom tables. These atoms that represent numeric strings are called integer atoms. Only values in the range of 1–49151 (1–BFFF hex) are permitted. An integer's value may be tested against the constant **MAXINTATOM** (defined in `winbase.h`) to determine whether it can be placed in the atom table. Another macro defined in `winbase.h`, **MAKEINTATOM**, converts a number into an integer atom.

Listing 23-2 shows how to use integer atoms. Note that the string stored in the atom table will actually contain the digits of the decimal representation of the integer preceded by a pound sign.

Listing 23-2 *Using integer atoms*

```
char szStoredString[6];
WORD wValue = 1000;
ATOM aValue = AddAtom( MAKEINTATOM( wValue ) );

// The value of the atom is 1000.
// The string will contain "#1000".

GetAtomName( aValue, szStoredString, 6 );
```

Integer atoms are never actually added or deleted from the system. Instead they are synthesized by the atom management functions. In the example just given, the same result would be stored in *szStoredString* if the function **AddAtom** is never called and *wValue* is substituted for *aValue*. It is harmless to call **DeleteAtom** for integer atoms. Because they never exist, they cannot be deleted, yet **DeleteAtom** returns **0** (indicating that the function succeeded) anyway.

Atom Function Descriptions

Table 23-1 summarizes the atom functions. Detailed function descriptions follow the table.

Table 23-1 Atom function summary

Function	Purpose
AddAtom	Stores a string in the application's local atom table or increments the reference count of an existing atom.
DeleteAtom	Decrements the reference count of a local atom and possibly deletes a string from the local atom table.
FindAtom	Determines if a string has been stored in the local atom table.
GetAtomName	Retrieves the stored string associated with a given local atom from the local atom table.
GlobalAddAtom	Stores a string in the system global atom table or increments the reference count of an existing atom.
GlobalDeleteAtom	Decrements the reference count of a global atom and possibly deletes a string from the global atom table.
GlobalFindAtom	Determines if a string is stored in the global atom table.
GlobalGetAtomName	Retrieves a stored string associated with a given global atom from the global atom table.
InitAtomTable	Allows the application to change the number of top-level entries in its local atom table.

AddAtom   ■ WINDOWS 95   ■ WINDOWS NT

Description	**AddAtom** stores a given string in the local atom table of an application. If the string is already stored in the atom table, **AddAtom** increments the reference count of the corresponding atom and returns the same atom as the original string. No duplicate atom names are ever stored in an atom table, including atom names that vary only in case.
Syntax	ATOM **AddAtom**(LPCTSTR *lpszStringToStore*)
Parameters	
lpszStringToStore	LPCTSTR: A pointer to a null-terminated string to store in the atom table. The maximum length of the string is 255 characters. If the first character of the string is # and it is followed by numbers that represent a whole number less than **MAXINTATOM**, an integer atom is returned. Integer atoms do not occupy space in the atom table, yet all atom management functions treat them as legitimate atoms.
Returns	**ATOM**: If successful, the newly added atom is returned. If the string already existed in the atom table, the same atom for the original string is returned. If an error occurs, **0** is returned. The application should use the **GetLastError** function to retrieve the error code.
Include File	winbase.h
See Also	GlobalAddAtom, DeleteAtom, InitAtomTable

Example   This program shows how the atom functions work together. The user can
add or delete an atom by selecting the appropriate menu options.

```c
// Atom Name to store.
//...................
LPCTSTR szAtom = "An atom.";

LRESULT CALLBACK WndProc( HWND hWnd, UINT uMsg, WPARAM wParam, LPARAM lParam )
{
    switch( uMsg )
    {
    case WM_CREATE:
            // Increase number of entries in
            // top area of atom table to 73.
            //.............................
            InitAtomTable( 73 );
            break;

    case WM_PAINT:
        {
            // Show the results of searching for an atom.
            //..........................................
            static PAINTSTRUCT ps;
            static char szWorkArea[33];
            static char szBuffer[128];
            static ATOM aAnAtom;

            aAnAtom = INVALID_ATOM;

            BeginPaint( hWnd, &ps );
            if (aAnAtom = FindAtom( szAtom ))
            {
                GetAtomName( aAnAtom, szWorkArea, 32 );
                wsprintf( szBuffer, "Atom '%s' was found.", szWorkArea );
            }
            else
                lstrcpy( szBuffer, "Atom must be added." );

            TextOut( ps.hdc, 0, 0, szBuffer, lstrlen( szBuffer ) );
            EndPaint( hWnd, &ps );
        }
        break ;

    case WM_COMMAND :
            switch( LOWORD( wParam ) )
            {
            case IDM_ADD:
                    // Adds an atom.
                    //..............
                    AddAtom( szAtom );

                    InvalidateRect( hWnd, NULL, TRUE );
                    break;

            case IDM_DELETE:
                    // Find the atom to delete and delete it.
                    //.......................................
                    if ( FindAtom( szAtom ) )
                        DeleteAtom( FindAtom( szAtom ) );
```

continued on next page

continued from previous page

```
                              InvalidateRect( hWnd, NULL, TRUE );
                              break;
        .
        .
        .
```

DeleteAtom ■ WINDOWS 95 ■ WINDOWS NT

Description	**DeleteAtom** decrements the reference count of a local atom, deleting the atom from the local atom table once the reference count equals zero. Unlike the global atom table, the local atom table is deleted when the program is exited, along with all the stored atoms, so it is not necessary to call **DeleteAtom** for each entry in the atom table. An application can remove an atom no matter how many references there are to the atom by calling **DeleteAtom** in a loop until a non-**NULL** value is returned.
Syntax	ATOM **DeleteAtom**(ATOM *nAtom*)
Parameters	
nAtom	**ATOM**: The atom to delete from the local atom table. This is the value returned by **AddAtom** when the atom is added. Integer atoms cannot be deleted, yet return **NULL** whenever they are used as arguments of **DeleteAtom**.
Returns	**ATOM**: If successful, **NULL** is returned; otherwise, the *nAtom* value is returned if an error occurs. Use **GetLastError** to return the error code.
Include File	**winbase.h**
See Also	AddAtom, FindAtom
Example	For an example of this function, see the example for the **AddAtom** function.

FindAtom ■ WINDOWS 95 ■ WINDOWS NT

Description	**FindAtom** performs a case-insensitive search of the local atom table for an atom name that matches the specified string. If the string is found, the associated atom is returned.
Syntax	ATOM **FindAtom**(LPCTSTR *lpszString*)
Parameters	
lpszString	**LPCTSTR**: A pointer to a null-terminated string to find in the local atom table. If the first character is # and it is followed by digits that represent a number greater than zero and less than **MAXINTATOM**, **FindAtom** returns a synthetic integer atom of the same value to the caller.

Returns	ATOM: If the string is successfully found, a 16-bit atom value for the local atom associated with the string is returned. If no match can be found in the local atom table, **NULL** is returned. Use **GetLastError** to get the error code.
Include File	`winbase.h`
See Also	`AddAtom`, `GlobalFindAtom`
Example	For an example of this function, see the example for the **AddAtom** function.

GetAtomName ■ WINDOWS 95 ■ WINDOWS NT

Description	GetAtomName retrieves the name of an atom that is stored in the local atom table. The name is copied into the supplied buffer.
Syntax	UINT **GetAtomName**(ATOM *nAtom*, LPTSTR *lpBuffer,* int *nSize*)
Parameters	
nAtom	ATOM: The atom value for which to retrieve the name.
lpBuffer	LPTSTR: A pointer to a buffer that will receive the atom name. The buffer must be at least *nSize*+1 bytes long.
nSize	int: The maximum number of characters to copy to *lpBuffer*.
Returns	UINT: If successful, the number of characters copied to the *lpBuffer* memory buffer; otherwise, **0** is returned if an error occurs. Use **GetLastError** to retrieve the error code.
Include File	`winbase.h`
See Also	`AddAtom`, `GlobalGetAtomName`
Example	For an example of this function, see the example for the **AddAtom** function.

GlobalAddAtom ■ WINDOWS 95 ■ WINDOWS NT

Description	GlobalAddAtom stores the specified string in the systemwide global atom table and returns a unique value that identifies that string (an atom). If the string already exists in the global atom table, the same atom is returned that was returned when the string was first added. An atom name stored in the global atom table may be returned by any application using the same atom handle. Thus, an application can pass a string to another application by sending a message and passing the atom as a parameter. The receiving application can retrieve the associated string by calling GlobalGetAtomName.
Syntax	ATOM **GlobalAddAtom**(LPCTSTR *lpszStringToStore*)

Parameters

lpszStringToStore LPCTSTR: A null-terminated string to store in the atom table. The string can be no longer than 255 characters. Although the case of the string is maintained, strings that only differ by case are treated as the same. If the first character of the string is # and it is followed by numbers that represent a whole number less than **MAXINTATOM**, an integer atom is returned. Integer atoms occupy no space in the atom table, yet all the atom management functions treat them as legitimate atoms.

Returns ATOM: If successful, the atom of the stored string. If the string matched one that was already stored, the atom for that string is returned. If the function fails, 0 is returned. The application can retrieve the specific error with the **GetLastError** function.

Include File winbase.h

See Also AddAtom, GlobalDeleteAtom, GlobalGetAtomName

Example This example demonstrates how to use global atoms to exchange string data between running applications. To run this example, start up various instances and arrange them on your desktop so that you can see all of their client areas at once. Now select the Test! menu option in any of the instances. All of the instances should paint the message **Received Transmitted Data** at once.

Global atoms are used to pass the string's value between instances of the application. The program also uses a private message, registered when the application is initialized, to implement the protocol. This message is broadcast to all top-level windows when the Test! menu option is chosen. Only applications that understand the message will attempt to reply. When the message is received, the application uses **GlobalGetAtomName** to retrieve the atom name from the global atom table for the atom passed in *wParam*. Note that the atom is deleted from the global atom table when the program exits. If this is not done, the application will leak memory each time it is run. Figure 23-1 shows the results of running four instances of the application.

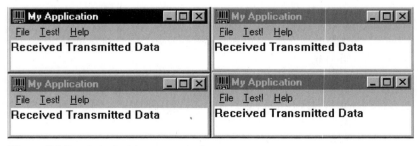

Figure 23-1 GlobalAddAtom example

```
LRESULT CALLBACK WndProc( HWND hWnd, UINT uMsg, WPARAM wParam, LPARAM lParam )
{
static UINT uMessageID = 0;
static ATOM aDataAtom  = INVALID_ATOM;

    switch( uMsg )
    {
    case WM_CREATE :
            // Register a message for private protocol
            // exchange between application instances.
            //.........................................
            uMessageID = RegisterWindowMessage( "MyMessage" );

            // Create atom containing data to exchange.
            //.........................................
            aDataAtom = GlobalAddAtom( "Transmitted Data" );
            break;

        case WM_COMMAND :
            switch( LOWORD( wParam ) )
            {
                case IDM_TEST :
                        PostMessage( HWND_BROADCAST, uMessageID, aDataAtom, 0 );
                        break;

                case IDM_EXIT :
                        DestroyWindow( hWnd );
                        break;
            }
            break;

        case WM_DESTROY :
            // Delete the global atom.
            //........................
            GlobalDeleteAtom( aDataAtom );
            PostQuitMessage(0);
            break;

        default :
            // Check if the message is the registered message.
            //................................................
            if (uMsg == uMessageID)
            {
                TCHAR szBuf[128];
                TCHAR szAtomContent[32];

                HDC hDC = GetDC( hWnd );

                // Get the atom value.
                //....................
                GlobalGetAtomName( (ATOM)wParam, szAtomContent, sizeof(szBuf)-1 );

                // Paint the contents on the window.
                //..................................
                TextOut( hDC, 0, 0, szBuf,
                        wsprintf( szBuf, "Received %s", szAtomContent ) );
```

continued on next page

continued from previous page

```
                    ReleaseDC( hWnd, hDC );
            }
            else
                return( DefWindowProc( hWnd, uMsg, wParam, lParam ) );
    }

    return( OL );
}
```

GlobalDeleteAtom ■ WINDOWS 95 ■ WINDOWS NT

Description GlobalDeleteAtom decreases the reference count of a global atom by one, deleting the atom entry from the global atom table once the reference count equals zero. To avoid memory leaks, GlobalDeleteAtom must be called for every atom created in the global atom table with the GlobalAddAtom function. To avoid causing problems for other applications, call GlobalDeleteAtom only as many times as GlobalAddAtom has been called by the application.

Syntax ATOM GlobalDeleteAtom(ATOM *nAtom*)

Parameters

nAtom ATOM: The atom to delete. This is the value returned by GlobalAddAtom when the atom was added. Integer atoms cannot be deleted, yet the function still returns NULL whenever they are used as arguments.

Returns ATOM: If successful, NULL is returned; otherwise, the *nAtom* value is returned if an error occurs. Use GetLastError to retrieve the error code.

Include File winbase.h

See Also GlobalAddAtom, DeleteAtom

Example See the example for the GlobalAddAtom function.

GlobalFindAtom ■ WINDOWS 95 ■ WINDOWS NT

Description GlobalFindAtom performs a case-insensitive search of the global atom table for a specified string. If the string is found in the global atom table, the associated atom is returned. Because atoms are generally exchanged between applications instead of strings, this function is not often used.

Syntax ATOM GlobalFindAtom(LPCTSTR *lpszString*)

Parameters

lpszString LPCTSTR: A pointer to a null-terminated string to find in the global atom table. If the first character is # and it is followed by digits that represent a number greater than zero and less than MAXINTATOM, GlobalFindAtom will return a synthetic integer atom of the same value to the caller.

Returns	`ATOM`: If successful, the 16-bit atom value for the global atom whose stored string matches *lpszString*. If no match can be found in the global atom table, `NULL` is returned. `GetLastError` may be used to get the error code.
Include File	`winbase.h`
See Also	`FindAtom`, `GlobalGetAtomName`, `GlobalAddAtom`
Example	This example demonstrates the passive exchange of string data between running applications. Run two instances of the application at once. The first time the Test! menu item on any of the applications is selected, the atom containing the string `"Test String"` is not found. This is because it has not been added to the global atom table. After the message `Test String Not Found` is displayed, the atom is added to the global atom table. Choosing the Test! option from any instance will result in the output of `Test String Found`.

```
LPCTSTR szAtom = "Test String";

// Counts times atom is added.
//..........................
int nCount = 0;

LRESULT CALLBACK WndProc( HWND hWnd, UINT uMsg, WPARAM wParam, LPARAM lParam )
{
   switch( uMsg )
   {
      case WM_DESTROY :
            {
               int  i;
               ATOM atom = GlobalFindAtom( szAtom );

               for (i = 0 ; i < nCount ; i++)
                  GlobalDeleteAtom( atom );

               PostQuitMessage(0);
            }
            break;

      case WM_COMMAND :
            switch( LOWORD( wParam ) )
            {
               case IDM_TEST:
                     {
                        HDC hDC = GetDC( hWnd );

                        if ( GlobalFindAtom( szAtom ) )
                           TextOut( hDC, 0, 0, "Test String Found.      ", 18 );
                        else
                        {
                           TextOut( hDC, 0, 0, "Test String Not Found.", 22 );
```

continued on next page

continued from previous page

```
                                // Add the global atom.
                                //....................
                                GlobalAddAtom( szAtom );
                                nCount++;
                        }
                        ReleaseDC( hWnd, hDC );
                }
                break;
```

.
.
.

GlobalGetAtomName ■ WINDOWS 95 ■ WINDOWS NT

Description	GlobalGetAtomName retrieves the atom name that is associated with the given global atom. This function copies the atom name from the global atom table into the provided buffer, *lpBuffer*. Its primary use is for data communication, converting global atoms of other applications to strings.
Syntax	UINT **GlobalGetAtomName**(ATOM *nAtom,* LPTSTR *lpBuffer,* int *nSize*)
Parameters	
nAtom	ATOM: The atom value. This is the value returned by GlobalAddAtom.
lpBuffer	LPTSTR: A pointer to a memory buffer that will contain the character string. The buffer must be at least *nSize* bytes long.
nSize	int: The maximum number of characters to copy to *lpBuffer*.
Returns	UINT: The number of bytes copied to the *lpBuffer* memory buffer is returned. 0 is returned if there is an error. GetLastError may be called to get the error code.
Include File	winuser.h
See Also	GlobalAddAtom, GlobalFindAtom, GetAtomName
Example	See the example for the GlobalAddAtom function.

InitAtomTable ■ WINDOWS 95 ■ WINDOWS NT

Description	InitAtomTable allows the application to set the number of top-level table entries in the local atom table. The default number (if InitAtomTable is not called or NULL is specified in the parameter list) is 37. This is adequate to efficiently store several hundred character strings. Larger values can be set if you plan to store a large number of strings in the local atom table.
Syntax	BOOL **InitAtomTable**(int *nSize*)

Parameters

nSize

  int: The number of top-level entries to set in the local atom table. This value should be a prime number. Set to NULL for the default number of 37 top-level entries. Larger values result in faster retrieval of strings, but require more memory space.

Returns

  BOOL: TRUE if the function was successful, and FALSE on error. Use GetLastError to return the error code.

Include File

  winuser.h

See Also

  AddAtom

Example

  See the example for the AddAtom function.

TIMERS

24

It is often necessary to schedule a periodic event to execute some program code. A word processor may use such an event to trigger file saves; a programming environment, to detect prolonged idle time that can be used for heap garbage collection; and a screen saver, to perform animation on the display. The Win32 API provides timers to achieve this type of operation. Timers are registered events that fire at programmed intervals.

Timers are allocated from a common pool for all processes of the system. Although previous versions of Windows were limited to just a few timers, Windows NT and Windows 95 do not have this constraint. In Windows 95, more than 2,500 system timers may be created. Under NT, it is possible to create more than 10,000 timers.

Using Timers

`SetTimer` creates timers and sets their parameters. A timer is identified by its associated window and an integer value that is unique for the given window. Once a timer is created, it will generate timer events until the timer is destroyed. Timers are automatically freed when the application exits.

The period between timer events of a given timer is known as its firing interval. Although the firing interval is specified in milliseconds, the precision of the timer's firing interval is limited by the precision of the system clock. For more precise resolution, use performance monitor counters (explained later in this chapter) instead.

Listing 24-1 shows the code necessary to create and use a timer. A unique identifier, **MY_TIMER** (value of **1**) is used to distinguish the timer from other timers of the given window. Note that **MY_TIMER** is specified both in the call to set the timer and in the **WM_TIMER** message processing for the given window's class. The window *hWnd* receives a **WM_TIMER** message for the **MY_TIMER** timer every second.

Listing 24-1 Using a timer

```
#define  MY_TIMER  1

int nTimer;

LRESULT CALLBACK WndProc(HWND hWnd, UINT uMsg, WPARAM wParam, LPARAM lParam)
{
    switch (uMsg)
    {
    case WM_CREATE :
            // set a timer with the MY_TIMER ID.
            //..................................
            nTimer = SetTimer( hWnd, MY_TIMER, 1000, NULL );
            break;

    case WM_TIMER:
            switch (wParam)
            {
                case MY_TIMER:
                        // Insert special timer processing code here.
                        break;
            }
            break;
        .
        .
        .
```

Another way of using timers is to supply a **TIMERPROC** callback function as the last parameter of the **SetTimer** function. Instead of creating **WM_TIMER** messages, the system directly calls the application-defined **TIMERPROC** callback function for each timer event.

Listing 24-2 shows how timer callbacks are used. Essentially, the timer-processing code is moved into the **TIMERPROC** function that is specified when **SetTimer** is called.

Listing 24-2 Using timer callbacks

```
#define  MY_TIMER  1

int nTimer;

VOID CALLBACK MyTimerProc( HWND hWnd, UINT uTimerMsg, UINT uTimerID, DWORD dwTime )
{
    // Code for timer MY_TIMER.
}

LRESULT CALLBACK WndProc(HWND hWnd, UINT uMsg, WPARAM wParam, LPARAM lParam)
{
    switch (uMsg)
    {
```

```
case WM_CREATE :
        // set a timer with the MY_TIMER ID.
        //..................................
        nTimer = SetTimer( hWnd, MY_TIMER, 1000, (TIMERPROC)MyTimerProc );
        break;
    .
    .
    .
```

Using callback functions removes some of the complexity from the window class message procedure. Also, using timer callbacks will slightly optimize processing, because the system places control directly in the callback, rather than requiring the application to determine which code to execute for the timer.

SetTimer also allows a timer's parameters to be changed. Both the window handle and the timer identifier must be specified in order to modify an existing timer. Generally this is done to change the interval of a timer; however, **SetTimer** can also change a message-based timer into a callback timer or vice versa.

SetTimer can generate the next unused timer identifier automatically. This value is returned by **SetTimer** when **NULL** is specified as the timer identifier in the call. This feature is especially useful when the number of timers is not known.

An application can create timers without links to a window by specifying **NULL** as the window handle in the **SetTimer** call. When a message-based timer is set up without a link to a window, the application must process **WM_TIMER** messages from the queue in the **PeekMessage-DispatchMessage** loop, because the messages cannot be dispatched without the window handle. Another option is callback timers, which do not require window handles.

KillTimer removes timers from the system. When an application exits, the system automatically releases all of its timers, so there is no need to call **KillTimer** during exit processing.

Windows Time

Timers are implemented using Windows time. In Windows time, time is measured in the number of system timer ticks since Windows started. This value is stored as a 32-bit unsigned integer and wraps back to zero after Windows has been running for just over 49 days. Although improbable, this could occur between two **WM_TIMER** messages, for example. When comparing two times, the wrapping condition must be tested or the code may break.

Functions that use Windows time include **GetTickCount**, and **GetMessageTime**. **GetTickCount** returns the current number of system timer ticks. **GetMessageTime** returns the number of ticks when a given message was created (that is, placed in the message queue).

Performance Monitor Counters

If many timers were created with very short intervals, the system could be completely paralyzed, except for servicing timer events. Windows prevents this by making sure that only one WM_TIMER message will ever exist in a thread's message queue at any given time.

Also, a WM_TIMER message is synthesized by the system only if the queue has no outstanding messages to process. Thus, all other messages are prioritized over WM_TIMER messages. The lone exception is the WM_PAINT message, which even defers to the timer messages.

In most applications the absence of timers firing will not cause a serious problem. If more serious time measurement is called for, however, there is an alternative: performance monitor counters. Performance monitor counters are high-resolution timers that provide the most accurate measurement of time possible in the system. Performance monitor counters are critical for a wide range of applications such as scientific measurements, musical interval timings, game interactions, and (especially) performance monitoring of code execution.

The Win32 API provides two functions for determining performance monitor counter capabilities. QueryPerformanceCounter obtains the current value of the performance monitor counter and QueryPerformanceFrequency returns its number of increments per second.

Timer Function Descriptions

Table 24-1 summarizes the Windows timer functions. Detailed function descriptions follow the table.

Table 24-1 Timer function summary

Function	Purpose
GetTickCount	Returns the number of milliseconds since Windows started.
KillTimer	Destroys a timer event, relinquishing resources to the system.
QueryPerformanceCounter	Returns the current value of the high-resolution performance counter.
QueryPerformanceFrequency	Returns the number of times per second that the high-resolution performance counter is incremented.
SetTimer	Creates a timer event or changes timer event settings.

GetTickCount ■ WINDOWS 95 ■ WINDOWS NT

Description   GetTickCount returns the number of milliseconds elapsed since Windows was started. In general, this function calculates the time elapsed between different calls. The value returned from calls to GetTickCount during message processing will differ from the value returned by GetMessageTime, because **GetTickCount** returns the number of milliseconds from the time Windows started to the time of the call, whereas **GetMessageTime** returns the number of milliseconds from the time Windows started to the time the message was placed on the message queue.

Syntax	DWORD **GetTickCount**(VOID)
Parameters	This function has no parameters.
Returns	DWORD: If successful, the number of milliseconds that have elapsed from system startup is returned.
Include File	winbase.h
See Also	GetMessageTime
Related Messages	WM_TIMER

CAUTION
The value returned is a 32-bit count of milliseconds since system startup. This value wraps after 49.7 days (2^32 milliseconds) of continuous running. Note that when calculating the time difference between two measurements, the second measurement also must be tested to determine if it is less than the first measurement—the case when the clock rolls over between measurements—before taking the difference.

Example   The example shows how **GetTickCount** returns the number of milliseconds since system startup. To display the value, simply click the menu option Test!.

```
LRESULT CALLBACK WndProc( HWND hWnd, UINT uMsg, WPARAM wParam, LPARAM lParam )
{
   switch( uMsg )
   {
     case WM_COMMAND :
            switch( LOWORD( wParam ) )
            {
              case IDM_TEST:
                   {
                      TCHAR szBuffer[65];

                      // Show the results of the GetTickCount()
                      //.......................................
                      wsprintf( szBuffer, "GetTickCount: %lu.", GetTickCount() );
                      MessageBox( hWnd, szBuffer, "GetTickCount() Example", MB_OK );
                   }
                   break;
          .
          .
          .
```

KillTimer

Description	**KillTimer** destroys the specified timer set with the **SetTimer** function. This function does not remove **WM_TIMER** messages already posted to the message queue.
Syntax	BOOL **KillTimer**(HWND *hWnd,* UINT *uTimerID*)
Parameters	
hWnd	**HWND**: The handle of the window associated with the timer. This parameter must be the same as the value passed to the **SetTimer** function. This parameter may be **NULL** in the case of timers not associated with windows.
uTimerID	**UINT**: The timer identifier of the timer to destroy. If the application passed a valid window handle to the **SetTimer** function, this parameter must be the same timer identifier passed to the **SetTimer** function. If the application used a **NULL** window handle with the **SetTimer** function, this parameter must be the timer identifier returned by the **SetTimer** function.
Returns	**BOOL**: If successful, **TRUE** is returned; otherwise, **FALSE** is returned if the timer does not exist. In the event of an error, use **GetLastError** to return the error code.
Include File	winuser.h
See Also	SetTimer
Related Messages	WM_TIMER
Example	This example sets a timer when the user selects the Test! menu item. If the user selects the menu item again within the timer period, a message box with the message **You're fast!** is displayed. If the timer period expires, a message box with the message **You're too slow, you lose!** is displayed. In either condition, the timer is destroyed before the message box is displayed.

```
#define GAME_TIMER 1

BOOL bTimerSet = FALSE;

LRESULT CALLBACK WndProc( HWND hWnd, UINT uMsg, WPARAM wParam, LPARAM lParam )
{
   switch( uMsg )
   {
      case WM_TIMER :
              if ( wParam == GAME_TIMER )
              {
                 KillTimer( hWnd, GAME_TIMER );
                 bTimerSet = FALSE;

                 MessageBox( hWnd, "You're too slow, you lose!", "Lose", MB_OK | MB_⇐
ICONASTERISK );
              }
              break;
```

```
case WM_COMMAND :
     switch( LOWORD( wParam ) )
     {
        case IDM_TEST:
             if ( bTimerSet )
             {
                KillTimer( hWnd, GAME_TIMER );
                bTimerSet = FALSE;

                        MessageBox( hWnd, "You're fast!", "Win", MB_OK | MB_ICON⇐
                                                          EXCLAMATION );
             }
             else
             {
                bTimerSet = TRUE;
                SetTimer( hWnd, GAME_TIMER, 200, NULL );
             }
             break;
```
```
.
.
.
```

QueryPerformanceCounter   ■ WINDOWS 95   ■ WINDOWS NT

Description	QueryPerformanceCounter retrieves the current value of the high-resolution performance counter, if one exists. The frequency of this counter is determined by the value returned from the QueryPerformanceFrequency function. Because this value is 64 bits wide, it can be more precise than the value returned from the GetTickCount function. This greater precision is typically used when determining performance of the system where many transactions can occur within a millisecond.
Syntax	BOOL **QueryPerformanceCounter**(LARGE_INTEGER* pPerformanceCount)
Parameters	
pPerformanceCount	LARGE_INTEGER*: A pointer to a 64-bit value where the contents of the performance counter are stored. If the installed hardware does not support a high-resolution performance counter, **0** can be returned. To determine the frequency of the performance counter, use the QueryPerformance Frequency function.
Returns	BOOL: If the installed hardware supports a high-resolution performance counter, **TRUE** is returned; otherwise, **FALSE** is returned.
Include File	winbase.h
See Also	QueryPerformanceFrequency
Example	When the user selects the Test! option in the example, the current count and frequency of the high-resolution performance counter is displayed in a message box if the hardware supports a high-resolution performance counter; otherwise, an error message box appears.

```
LRESULT CALLBACK WndProc( HWND hWnd, UINT uMsg, WPARAM wParam, LPARAM lParam )
{
    switch( uMsg )
    {
        case WM_COMMAND :
                switch( LOWORD( wParam ) )
                {
                    case IDM_TEST:
                        {
                            // Get Performance Counter Data.
                            // Display data in message box.
                            //.............................
                            TCHAR szBuffer[128];
                            LARGE_INTEGER liPerfFreq = {0, 0};
                            LARGE_INTEGER liPerfCount = {0, 0};

                            if ( QueryPerformanceCounter( &liPerfCount ) )
                            {
                                TCHAR szCounter[64];
                                double dCounter = (double) liPerfCount.LowPart +
                                                  (double) liPerfCount.HighPart *
                                                  (double) 0xFFFFFFFFFFFFFFFF;

                                // Get the frequency.
                                //...................
                                QueryPerformanceFrequency( &liPerfFreq );
                                wsprintf( szBuffer, "Count: %s, Resolution: %lu",
                                        gcvt( dCounter, 40, szCounter ),
                                        liPerfFreq.LowPart );
                            }
                            else
                                lstrcpy( szBuffer, "No high-resolution performance counter." );

                            MessageBox( hWnd, szBuffer, "Performance Counter Report",
                                    MB_OK | MB_ICONINFORMATION );
                        }
                        break;
                        .
                        .
                        .
```

QueryPerformanceFrequency ■ Windows 95 ■ Windows NT

Description	QueryPerformanceFrequency retrieves the resolution of the high-resolution performance counter if the hardware supports such a counter. This frequency is the number of ticks there are per second in the high-resolution performance counter.
Syntax	BOOL **QueryPerformanceFrequency**(LARGE_INTEGER* *pTicksPerSecond*)
Parameters	
pTicksPerSecond	LARGE_INTEGER*: Pointer to a 64-bit value that receives the number of increments made by the performance counter each second.

Returns	BOOL: If the installed hardware supports a high-resolution performance counter, TRUE is returned; otherwise, FALSE is returned. Use the GetLastError function to return the error code.
Include File	winbase.h
See Also	QueryPerformanceCounter
Example	See the example for the QueryPerformanceCounter function.

SetTimer   ■ WINDOWS 95   ■ WINDOWS NT

Description	SetTimer creates or modifies a system timer. A timer is a scheduled event that Windows generates at specified time intervals. Timers can either be used to generate WM_TIMER messages or to set up direct calls to an application-defined callback function.
Syntax	UINT **SetTimer**(HWND *hWnd,* UINT *uTimerID,* UINT *uInterval,* TIMERPROC *fnTimerProc*)
Parameters	
hWnd	HWND: The window associated with the timer. This window must be owned by the calling thread. If this parameter is NULL, the timer is not associated with a window, which means WM_TIMER messages are still generated in the task queue, but they are not processed in the window class message handler and the *uTimerID* parameter is ignored.
uTimerID	UINT: A nonzero numeric value associated with the timer. If a new identifier is specified, a timer is created. If an existing number is supplied, the function will edit the timer information rather than create a new timer. If 0 is specified, the system will generate and return an unused timer identifier. This parameter is ignored if *hWnd* is set to NULL.
uInterval	UINT: The time-out value, in milliseconds.
fnTimerProc	TIMERPROC: A pointer to an application-defined callback function to notify when the time-out value elapses. If set to NULL, WM_TIMER messages are placed in the message queue of the calling thread. If the *hWnd* parameter contains a valid window handle, the window procedure for that window will receive the WM_TIMER message; otherwise, the message must be intercepted in the thread's message loop. See the syntax of the callback function below.
Returns	UINT: If successful, an integer value identifying the new timer is returned. An application can use this value with the KillTimer function to destroy the timer. If the function fails to create a timer, the return value is 0.
Include File	winuser.h
See Also	KillTimer
Related Messages	WM_TIMER

Callback Syntax	`VOID CALLBACK `**`TimerProc`**`( HWND `*`hWnd,`*` UINT `*`uMsg,`*` UINT `*`idEvent,`*`` `*`DWORD `*`dwTime`*`)`

Callback Parameters

hWnd	**HWND**: The window handle associated with the timer.
uMsg	**UINT**: The **WM_TIMER** message.
idEvent	**UINT**: The timer identifier.
dwTime	**DWORD**: The number of milliseconds that have elapsed since Windows was started. This is the value returned by the **GetTickCount** function.
Example	See the example for the **KillTimer** function.

25

PROCESSES, THREADS, AND FIBERS

One of the most significant differences between Windows 3.x and the Win32 platforms (Windows 95 and Windows NT) is the support for multithreaded processes. A *process* is the object that owns all the resources of an application. A *thread* is an independent path of execution within a process that shares its address space, code, and global data. Each thread has its own set of registers, its own stack, and its own input mechanisms, including a private message queue. Windows 95 and Windows NT allocate time slices on a thread-by-thread basis and perform preemptive multitasking based on the priority assigned to each thread. Windows NT also has the ability to use multiple processors to service the threads of a process. More processors means more time slices available for the threads. Because Windows NT has this ability, processes that execute on a machine with two or more processors under Windows NT have the potential of executing much faster than if the same process was executed under Windows 95.

Creating Processes and Threads

The `CreateProcess` function creates both a process object and the main thread object of an application. `CreateProcess` allows the parent process to set the operating environment of the new process, including its working directory, how it should appear by default on the screen, its environment variables, its priority, and the command line it is passed. The new process will execute from the startup address and run until completion. Listing 25-1 shows a fragment of code that invokes Microsoft NotePad as a new process to edit the file named `README.TXT`.

Listing 25-1 Using `CreateProcess` to run a program

```
HANDLE ViewReadMeFile()
{
    STARTUPINFO          siStartInfo;
    PROCESS_INFORMATION  piProcessInfo;
    // initialize with current task's startup info.
    // ..........................................
    GetStartupInfo(&siStartInfo);
    CreateProcess(NULL, "NOTEPAD README.TXT",
                  NULL,          // use default security attributes of process
                  NULL,          // use default security attributes of thread
                  FALSE,         // do not inherit handles from parent process
                  0,             // normal priority (creation flags)
                  NULL,          // use parent environment
                  NULL,          // launch in current directory
                  &siStartInfo,  // startup data
                  &piProcInfo);  // process data returned here

    return( piProcInfo.hProcess );
}
```

The `CreateThread` function creates a new thread within the current process. This function allows a process to divide the work of the application among multiple threads to speed execution time. Common uses for threads are background tasks that in Windows 3.x would have caused the system to wait, such as the pagination that a word processor performs. With a thread, the pagination occurs as the user enters the text of the document, and there is no delay experienced by the user.

Threads share the process's address space and system resources. However, they have their own stack, and in Windows NT, their own security descriptors. The creation of a thread requires the following information:

- The size of the thread's stack.

- The security attributes of the thread. **NULL** may be used for default security or in Windows 95 where security is not supported.

- The address of a procedure at which to begin execution. This must be a function that receives a single 32-bit value as a parameter.

- An optional 32-bit value that is passed to the thread's procedure.

- Flags that allow, among other things, thread priority level to be set.

- An address to store the thread identifier. A thread identifier is a unique systemwide value.

Once an application calls the `CreateThread` function to create the new thread, the function returns a handle to the new thread object. This handle is used to manage the thread and also gives the calling process the ability to kill the thread, if necessary. For an example of how to create threads with the `CreateThread` function, see the `CreateThread` function description later in this chapter.

Fibers

A new addition to the Win32 API introduced with Windows NT 4 is *fibers*. A fiber is a lightweight thread that an application manually schedules. Fibers run in the context of the threads that schedule them and assume the identity of the thread. Each thread can schedule multiple fibers. Fibers do not provide advantages over a well-designed multi-threaded application; however, they do make it easier to port applications that were designed to schedule their own threads.

Since a fiber assumes the identity of the parent thread, it shares the thread's local storage, and if the fiber calls functions that would normally affect the thread, such as **ExitThread**, they are performed for the thread. For example, if a fiber calls the **ExitThread** function, the thread that created the fiber exits. A fiber does not, however, have the same state information associated with it as the associated thread. The only state information maintained for a fiber is its stack, a subset of its registers that are typically preserved across function calls, and the fiber data provided during fiber creation.

A major difference between threads and fibers is that fibers are not preemptively scheduled. The application must schedule a fiber by switching to it from another fiber. However, the system still schedules the threads that create the fibers, so a thread that is currently running a fiber can be preempted. The fiber resumes when its thread resumes running.

Before an application schedules the first fiber, it calls the **ConvertThreadToFiber** function to create an area in which to save fiber state information. The thread becomes the currently executing fiber. The stored state information for this fiber includes the fiber data passed as an argument to **ConvertThreadToFiber**.

The application then uses the **CreateFiber** function to create fibers. This function requires the stack size, starting address, and the fiber data. The starting address is typically a user-supplied function, called the *fiber function*. This function only takes one parameter, which is the fiber data, and does not return a value. If your fiber function returns, the thread running the fiber exits. To execute any fiber created with **CreateFiber**, the application uses the **SwitchToFiber** function. Use the **SwitchToFiber** function with the address of a fiber created by a different thread by using the address returned to the other thread when it called **CreateFiber**. Once the thread is finished with a fiber, it should call the **DeleteFiber** function to clean up the data created for the fiber. Do not delete a fiber created by another thread, because this may cause abnormal termination of the other thread.

Synchronization Objects

Because Windows 95 and Windows NT have preemptive multitasking, the possibility of two threads that access the same memory within a process is a problem. Some threads do not access memory or perform operations that have an impact on other threads within the process. However, if threads do share process resources, system resources, or need to execute in cooperation with each other, some sort of synchronization has to occur. The Win32 API provides *synchronization objects* to allow the threads to work with each other without corrupting memory. Synchronization objects allow access to system resources to be controlled between threads of the same or different processes.

The three basic types of synchronization objects are mutexes, semaphores, and events. What differentiates the various synchronization objects from each other is the condition of setting the signal state. Table 25-1 lists the most common synchronization objects.

Table 25-1 Basic interprocess synchronization objects

Object	Purpose
Mutex	Allows mutually exclusive access.
Semaphore	Allows access to a known number of threads.
Event	Allows access to any number of waiting threads.

A synchronization object has two states: *signaled* and *nonsignaled*. When a synchronization object is in its busy or nonsignaled state, a waiting thread may not proceed. When a synchronization object is signaled, a waiting thread may continue to execute.

Wait functions are a set of API calls that suspend threads until a given set of conditions are true. Wait functions test the signaled state of synchronization objects. If a specified object is signaled, the wait function will terminate and the running thread will continue. Otherwise, the wait function will keep the thread in a highly optimized loop, polling the state of the object until it becomes signaled or a time-out occurs.

The *mutex object* derives its name from the term *mut*ual *ex*clusion. A mutex may only be owned by one thread at a time. Therefore, if a thread owns a mutex and another thread requests ownership, the requesting thread may only acquire the mutex when the owning thread relinquishes its ownership. A famous mutex, the **Win16Lock** or **Win16Mutex**, is used in Windows 95 to protect nonreentrant 16-bit code in GDI and **USER** from the hazards of concurrent execution. The example in the **CreateMutex** function description later in this chapter shows how mutexes are used.

A *semaphore object* starts with an assigned initial count. Every time a thread gets ownership of the object (by using a wait function), the count of the semaphore is reduced by one. Every time a thread releases ownership, the count of the semaphore is increased. If a semaphore's count becomes zero, the semaphore is blocked in the nonsignaled state and no other threads can gain access.

One good use of a semaphore is to control allocation of finite resources. Each request for the resource is controlled by the semaphore, which automatically fails when the programmed limit is reached. Each time the requesting thread no longer needs the resource, the semaphore is released. The count of the semaphore will always parallel the number of resources available. Semaphores are used in the example in the **CreateSemaphore** function description later in this chapter.

Event objects allow any number of threads to have synchronized access to a resource. Access to the resource is granted programmatically. There are two types of event objects: manual-reset event objects and auto-reset event objects.

A *manual-reset* event object is set to the signaled state programmatically by calling the API function `SetEvent`. The event object becomes nonsignaled when the function `ResetEvent` is called. The function `PulseEvent` issues the `SetEvent` and `ResetEvent` in sequence. Manual-reset event objects allow all threads waiting on the event object to proceed. Manual-reset event objects are used in the example for `CreateEvent` later in this chapter.

The *auto-reset* event object resets itself after a single waiting thread is released. All other threads remain waiting until the event becomes nonsignaled again. Auto-reset event objects allow controlled serial access to synchronized code among threads of different processes, just as critical section objects allow serial access to code for threads of the same process. Auto-reset event objects are used in the example for the `OpenEvent` function later in this chapter.

An application can also use the objects listed in Table 25-2 as synchronization objects. They are nonsignaled until the given condition occurs.

Table 25-2 Other synchronization objects

Object	Signal Condition
Change notification	Signaled when a given change occurs in the structure of the file system.
Console input	Signaled when unread console input is ready.
Process	Signaled when a process terminates.
Thread	Signaled when a thread terminates.

Protecting Nonreentrant Code of a Process

Because the global data of a process is shared among all threads, care must be taken to avoid conflicts in data access that could result in program failure. One of the features Win32 provides to protect nonreentrant code is the *critical section object*. A critical section is an object used only for synchronization of the threads of a single process. The `InitializeCriticalSection` function creates a critical section object.

Once the critical section object is constructed, a thread must use the API function `EnterCriticalSection` to gain exclusive access to the protected code. If another thread is executing within the critical section, a thread requesting access to the critical section must wait until the thread that owns the object gives up ownership by calling the function `LeaveCriticalSection`.

Process, Thread, and Fiber Function Descriptions

Table 25-3 lists the process, thread, and fiber functions of the Win32 API. Complete function descriptions follow the table.

Table 25-3 Process, thread, and fiber function summary

Function	Purpose
AttachThreadInput	Redirects input of one thread to another thread.
CancelWaitableTimer	Cancels a waitable timer by setting the timer to the inactive state.
ConvertThreadToFiber	Converts the current thread into a fiber.
CreateEvent	Creates an event object.
CreateFiber	Creates a fiber object.
CreateMutex	Creates a mutex object.
CreateProcess	Creates a process and thread object and starts a process.
CreateProcessAsUser	Creates a process and thread object in the security context of a user.
CreateRemoteThread	Creates a thread that runs in the address space of another process.
CreateSemaphore	Creates a semaphore object.
CreateThread	Creates a thread object and starts a thread.
CreateWaitableTimer	Creates a waitable timer object.
DeleteCriticalSection	Destroys an inactive critical section object.
DeleteFiber	Deletes a fiber object.
DuplicateHandle	Copies the handle of any object so that it can be used by another process.
EnterCriticalSection	Tests a critical section gate, and if unowned, the critical section is entered.
ExitProcess	Ends a process and all the process's threads and returns an exit code.
ExitThread	Ends a single thread of a process.
GetCurrentFiber	Returns the current fiber for the thread.
GetCurrentProcess	Returns the handle of the current process.
GetCurrentProcessId	Returns the ID of the current process.
GetCurrentThread	Returns the handle of the current thread.
GetCurrentThreadId	Returns the ID of the current thread.
GetExitCodeProcess	Returns the exit code of the specified process. Can also be used to determine if the process has completed.
GetExitCodeThread	Returns the exit code of the specified thread. Can also be used to determine if the given thread has completed.
GetFiberData	Returns the data associated with the fiber object.
GetPriorityClass	Determines the priority class of a process.
GetProcessAffinityMask	Returns the affinity mask for a process.
GetProcessHeap	Returns a handle to the calling process's heap.
GetProcessHeaps	Returns an array of handles that contains all the heaps owned by the calling process.
GetProcessPriorityBoost	Returns the priority boost for a process.
GetProcessShutdownParameters	Returns the shutdown parameters for a process.
GetProcessTimes	Returns the times the process has been executing.
GetProcessVersion	Returns the Windows version the process expects.
GetProcessWorkingSetSize	Returns the working set size for a process.
GetQueueStatus	Returns the input state of a thread's queue.

Function	Purpose
GetThreadContext	Used by a debugger to store the machine context of a thread.
GetThreadPriority	Returns the priority class of the given thread.
GetThreadPriorityBoost	Returns the priority boost for a thread.
GetThreadSelectorEntry	Used by debuggers to return the local descriptor table (LDT) entry for a given selector of the specified thread.
GetThreadTimes	Returns the times a thread has been executing.
InitializeCriticalSection	Constructs a critical section object to protect a section of a multithreaded process from execution by more than one thread at a time.
InterlockedCompareExchange	Compares the values of a synchronized long.
InterlockedDecrement	Decrements a synchronized long.
InterlockedExchange	Exchanges a value with the value of a synchronized long.
InterlockedExchangeAdd	Adds a value to a synchronized long.
InterlockedIncrement	Increments a synchronized long.
LeaveCriticalSection	Marks the end of code protected by a critical section object.
MsgWaitForMultipleObjects	Returns when any or all of the given objects become signaled, a given type of input appears in the specified thread's input queue, or a time-out occurs.
MsgWaitForMultipleObjectsEx	Same as MsgWaitForMultipleObjects, except an I/O completion or APC causes the function to also return.
OpenEvent	Returns the handle of a named event object.
OpenMutex	Returns the handle of a named mutex object.
OpenProcess	Returns the handle of a specified process.
OpenSemaphore	Returns the handle of a named semaphore object.
OpenWaitableTimer	Returns the handle of a waitable timer object.
PulseEvent	Changes an event from nonsignaled to signaled and then to nonsignaled again. Used to free waiting threads and then set the event block again.
QueueUserAPC	Queues a user-mode asynchronous procedure call (APC) object to the APC queue of a thread.
RaiseException	Signals a software-generated exception for a thread that can be handled by the application. RaiseException is used also as a communication channel with a debugger.
ReadProcessMemory	Reads memory from a process's address space.
RegisterHotKey	Creates a hotkey for a given thread.
ReleaseMutex	Returns mutex to the signaled state.
ReleaseSemaphore	Increases the count of a semaphore.
ResetEvent	Changes an event to nonsignaled state.
ResumeThread	Resumes execution of a suspended thread.
SetEvent	Changes an event to signaled state.
SetPriorityClass	Sets the priority class of a process.
SetProcessAffinityMask	Sets the affinity mask for a process.
SetProcessPriorityBoost	Sets the priority boost for a process.
SetProcessShutdownParameters	Sets the shutdown parameters for a process.
SetProcessWorkingSetSize	Sets the working set size for a process.

continued on next page

continued from previous page

Function	Purpose
SetThreadAffinityMask	Sets the affinity mask for a thread.
SetThreadContext	Sets the context of a thread.
SetThreadIdealProcessor	Sets the ideal processor for a thread.
SetThreadPriority	Sets the priority class of a thread.
SetThreadPriorityBoost	Sets the priority boost for a thread.
SetUnhandledExceptionFilter	Allows an application to set an exception routine for unhandled exceptions.
SetWaitableTimer	Activates a waitable timer object.
SignalObjectAndWait	Signals an object and waits on another object.
Sleep	Suspends thread execution for a given number of milliseconds. Another thread will be scheduled.
SleepEx	Same as Sleep, except that an I/O completion routine or APC can cause the function to return.
SuspendThread	Suspends a thread's execution.
SwitchToFiber	Schedules a fiber to execute.
TerminateProcess	Terminates the execution of a process.
TerminateThread	Terminates the execution of a thread.
TlsAlloc	Allocates a thread local storage index.
TlsFree	Deallocates a thread local storage index.
TlsGetValue	Returns the memory object assigned to a thread's local storage for a given index.
TlsSetValue	Sets the memory object assigned to a thread's local storage for a given index.
TryEnterCriticalSection	Attempts to enter a critical section and, if successful, takes ownership of the critical section.
UnhandledExceptionFilter	Calls default unhandled exception filter or debugger, if the program is being debugged.
UnregisterHotKey	Deletes a thread's hotkey.
WaitForInputIdle	Waits until there is no input to the thread.
WaitForMultipleObjects	Waits for any one of the specified synchronization objects to be signaled.
WaitForMultipleObjectsEx	Same as WaitForMultipleObjects, except that an I/O completion routine or APC can cause the function to return.
WaitForSingleObject	Waits for a single synchronization object to signal.
WaitForSingleObjectEx	Same as WaitForSingleObject, except that an I/O completion routine or APC can cause the function to return.
WriteProcessMemory	Used mainly by a debugger to write directly into the memory of a process.

AttachThreadInput   ■ Windows 95   ■ Windows NT

Description   **AttachThreadInput** attaches the input mechanisms of one thread to another thread. Input mechanisms include the input focus, keyboard state, mouse capture, queue status, and timer events. Messages are generally sent to the queue of the thread that created the window. With the **AttachThreadInput** function, an application can redirect the messages to another thread's queue. Note: An implicit **AttachThreadInput** occurs when a child window is created in a thread different from that of its parent window.

Syntax	BOOL **AttachThreadInput**(DWORD *idAttachedThread,* DWORD *idAttachingThread,* BOOL *bAttachOrDetach*)

Parameters

idAttachedThread DWORD: The identifier of the thread whose input is to be attached by another thread.

idAttachingThread DWORD: The identifier of the thread that will receive input of the thread specified by *idAttachedThread*.

bAttachOrDetach BOOL: **TRUE** attaches the threads. **FALSE** detaches the threads.

Returns	BOOL: **TRUE** if the function succeeds; otherwise, **FALSE**. Use **GetLastError** to return the error code.
Include File	winuser.h
See Also	GetCurrentThreadId, CreateThread
Example	This example demonstrates how a thread's input mechanisms can be attached by another thread. When the main window is created, a child thread is launched that creates a window and stays in an input loop until the program exits. When the user selects the Test! option from the menu, the program toggles the attached state of the child thread's input and attempts to set the active window to the window of the other thread. This operation succeeds if the input mechanisms are attached, and fails if they are detached.

```
HANDLE hChildThread    = NULL;  // Child thread
DWORD  dwChildThreadId  = 0;     // Child thread ID
DWORD  dwParentThreadId = 0;     // Parent thread ID
HWND   hChildThreadWnd  = NULL;  // Child thread's window
HWND   hParentThreadWnd = NULL;  // Parent thread's window
BOOL   bAttachedInput   = FALSE; // Status of attached input


// Child thread creates a window and loops until program exits.
//.........................................................
DWORD WINAPI ChildThreadProc( LPVOID lpNoData )
{
   MSG msg;
   HWND hWnd = CreateWindow( lpszAppName, "Child Thread's Window",
                             WS_OVERLAPPEDWINDOW, CW_USEDEFAULT, 0,
                             CW_USEDEFAULT, 0, NULL, NULL, hInst, NULL );
   if ( !hWnd )
      return( FALSE );

   ShowWindow( hWnd, SW_SHOW );
   UpdateWindow( hWnd );
```

continued on next page

continued from previous page

```
    while (GetMessage( &msg, NULL, 0, 0 ))
    {
        TranslateMessage( &msg );
        DispatchMessage( &msg );
    }

    return( TRUE );
}



LRESULT CALLBACK WndProc( HWND hWnd, UINT uMsg, WPARAM wParam, LPARAM lParam )
{
    switch( uMsg )
    {
        case WM_CREATE:
                // Set globals and create thread.
                //...............................
                if ( !hChildThread )
                {
                    hParentThreadWnd = hWnd;
                    dwParentThreadId = GetCurrentThreadId();
                    hChildThread = CreateThread( NULL, 0, ChildThreadProc, NULL, 0,⇐
&dwChildThreadId );
                }
                else
                    hChildThreadWnd = hWnd;
                break;

        case WM_COMMAND :
                switch( LOWORD( wParam ) )
                {
                    case IDM_TEST :
                        {
                            HDC hDC = GetDC( hWnd );

                            // Toggle attached thread input.
                            //.............................
                            if ( bAttachedInput )
                                AttachThreadInput( dwChildThreadId,
                                                   dwParentThreadId,
                                                   !bAttachedInput );
                            else
                                AttachThreadInput( dwChildThreadId,
                                                   dwParentThreadId,
                                                   !bAttachedInput );

                            bAttachedInput = !bAttachedInput;

                            // Print Message.
                            //...............
                            TextOut( hDC, 0, 0, bAttachedInput ?
                                    "Input is now Attached   " :
                                    "Input is now Detached   ", 24);
                            ReleaseDC( hWnd, hDC );
```

```
            // Set active window to opposite window.
            // Only succeeds if inputs are attached.
            //......................................
            if ( hWnd == hParentThreadWnd )
                SetActiveWindow( hChildThreadWnd );
            else
                SetActiveWindow( hParentThreadWnd );
        }
        break;
```

.
.
.

CancelWaitableTimer ■ WINDOWS 95 ■ WINDOWS NT

Description	`CancelWaitableTimer` sets the specified waitable timer to the inactive state. The signaled state of the timer is not changed. The function stops the timer before it can be set to the signaled state; therefore, threads performing a wait operation on the timer remain waiting until they time out or the timer is reactivated and its state is set to signaled. Use the `SetWaitableTimer` function to reactivate the timer.
Syntax	BOOL **CancelWaitableTimer**(HANDLE *hTimer*)
Parameters	
hTimer	HANDLE: The timer object. This handle is returned by the `CreateWaitableTimer` or `OpenWaitableTimer` function.
Returns	BOOL: If successful, **TRUE** is returned; otherwise, **FALSE** is returned.
Include File	winbase.h
See Also	SetWaitableTimer, CreateWaitableTimer, OpenWaitableTimer

ConvertThreadToFiber ■ WINDOWS 95 ■ WINDOWS NT

Description	`ConvertThreadToFiber` converts the current thread into a fiber. The application must convert a thread into a fiber before it can schedule other fibers. Applications must use this function because only fibers can execute other fibers. By calling the `ConvertThreadToFiber` function, an area in which to save fiber state information is created and the calling thread becomes the current fiber.
Syntax	LPVOID **ConvertThreadToFiber**(LPVOID *lpParameter*)
Parameters	
lpParameter	LPVOID: A single variable that is passed to the fiber. The fiber retrieves this value by using the `GetFiberData` function.

Returns	**LPVOID**: If successful, the address of the fiber is returned; otherwise, **NULL** is returned. Use the **GetLastError** function to retrieve extended error information.
Include File	`winbase.h`
See Also	`GetFiberData`

CreateEvent ■ WINDOWS 95 ■ WINDOWS NT

Description	**CreateEvent** creates a named or unnamed event object, which can be programmatically set to signaled or nonsignaled with the **SetEvent** function. An application uses events to notify threads of actions and synchronization of threads. For example, one thread creates an event object and sets its state to the nonsignaled state. Another thread uses the event handle with the **WaitForSingleObject** function to wait for the event to be signaled. Once the first thread sets the state of the event object to signaled, the second thread will continue to execute.
Syntax	HANDLE **CreateEvent**(LPSECURITY_ATTRIBUTES *lpSecurityAttribs,* BOOL *bManualReset,* BOOL *bInitialState,* LPCTSTR *lpszEventName*)
Parameters	
lpSecurityAttribs	LPSECURITY_ATTRIBUTES: A pointer to the security attributes structure. The *bInheritHandles* member of this structure must be set to **TRUE** if the event handle can be inherited by child processes. Specifying **NULL** will activate default security, which means the handle cannot be inherited. See the definition of the **SECURITY_ATTRIBUTES** structure below.
bManualReset	BOOL: If **TRUE**, the event created is a manual-reset event. If **FALSE**, the event created is an auto-reset event. A manual-reset event must be programmatically changed to signaled. An auto-reset event is immediately reset when a single waiting thread is released.
bInitialState	BOOL: Determines if the initial state of the event object is signaled (**TRUE**) or nonsignaled (**FALSE**).
lpszEventName	LPCTSTR: A pointer to a null-terminated string of up to **MAX_PATH** characters that contains the event name. The name cannot be the same as any existing mutex, semaphore, or file-mapping object. All objects share the same name space. Object names are case sensitive. An object name may not contain any backslashes. If *lpszEventName* is **NULL**, the object is created without a name.
	If the event object has already been registered with the system, the parameters *bManualReset* and *bInitialState* are ignored. When an event already exists, **CreateEvent** opens the event with an access mode of **EVENT_ALL_ACCESS**. The error **ERROR_ALREADY_EXISTS** will be set. Attempting to create an event with the same name as another nonevent object will fail and set the error **ERROR_INVALID_HANDLE**.

Returns   HANDLE: If successful, the handle of the event object is returned; otherwise, NULL is returned. If the named event object existed before the function call, the GetLastError function returns ERROR_ALREADY_EXISTS; otherwise, it returns 0.

Include File   winbase.h

See Also   CreateProcess, DuplicateHandle, OpenEvent, ResetEvent, SetEvent, WaitForSingleObject, WaitForMultipleObjects

SECURITY_ATTRIBUTES Definition

```
typedef struct _SECURITY_ATTRIBUTES
{
    DWORD   nLength;
    LPVOID  lpSecurityDescriptor;
    BOOL    bInheritHandle;
} SECURITY_ATTRIBUTES;
```

Members

nLength   DWORD: The size, in bytes, of the structure.

lpSecurityDescriptor   LPVOID: A pointer to a security descriptor for the object that controls the sharing of it. If set to NULL, the object may be assigned the default security descriptor of the calling process. In Windows 95, this member is ignored.

bInheritHandle   BOOL: Set to TRUE if the returned handle is inherited by new child processes; otherwise, set to FALSE.

Example   This example demonstrates how to use manual-reset events and semaphores to write synchronized code to control process access to resources. There are four menu options: Read, Write, Quit, and Help. To best see how synchronization works, run three instances and tile them on the desktop. Now in two instances select the read option and in the third select the write option. There is no contention for readers, but the writer must wait for the readers to complete before proceeding. Now select the write operation and two read operations. Read operations must wait for the write operation to complete. The current state of each process is shown in the caption bar. Figure 25-1 shows a session of two waiting reads and one write in progress.

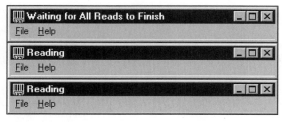

Figure 25-1   CreateEvent example

```
#define SEMAPHORE_MAX_COUNT 10

LPCTSTR lpszReadSem    = "Read Semaphore";
LPCTSTR lpszWriteEvent = "Write Event";

HANDLE  hSemRead    = NULL;
HANDLE  hEventWrite = NULL;

LRESULT CALLBACK WndProc( HWND hWnd, UINT uMsg, WPARAM wParam, LPARAM lParam )
{
   switch( uMsg )
   {
      case WM_CREATE:
              // Make the two synchronization objects.
              //....................................
              hSemRead    = CreateSemaphore( NULL, 10, 10, lpszReadSem );
              hEventWrite = CreateEvent( NULL, TRUE, TRUE, lpszWriteEvent );
              break;

      case WM_COMMAND :
              switch( LOWORD( wParam ) )
              {
                 case IDM_READ:
                     {
                         HANDLE hTmpSemRead;
                         HANDLE hTmpEventWrite;

                         hTmpSemRead= OpenSemaphore( SEMAPHORE_ALL_ACCESS, FALSE,⇐
lpszReadSem );

                         hTmpEventWrite = OpenEvent( SYNCHRONIZE, FALSE, lpszWriteEvent );

                         SetWindowText( hWnd, "Waiting for all Writes to Finish" );

                         // Check that write manual reset event is signaled.
                         //................................................
                         WaitForSingleObject( hEventWrite, INFINITE );

                         // Wait for semaphore.
                         //....................
                         WaitForSingleObject( hSemRead, INFINITE );

                         // Do the simulated read.
                         //.......................
                         SetWindowText( hWnd, "Reading" );
                         Sleep( 5000 );

                         // Release semaphore.
                         //...................
                         ReleaseSemaphore( hSemRead, 1, NULL );
                         SetWindowText( hWnd, "Done Reading" );

                         // Close the temporary handles.
                         //.............................
                         CloseHandle( hTmpSemRead );
                         CloseHandle( hTmpEventWrite );
                     }
                     break;
```

```
            case IDM_WRITE:
                {
                    DWORD   dwSemaphoreCount = 0;
                    HANDLE hTmpSemRead;
                    HANDLE hTmpEventWrite;

                    hTmpSemRead = OpenSemaphore( SEMAPHORE_ALL_ACCESS, FALSE,⇐
lpszReadSem );

                    hTmpEventWrite = OpenEvent( SYNCHRONIZE, FALSE, lpszWriteEvent );

                    // Wait for manual-reset event: it becomes nonsignaled.
                    //.................................................
                    SetWindowText( hWnd, "Waiting for Write Event" );
                    WaitForSingleObject( hEventWrite, INFINITE );
                    ResetEvent( hEventWrite );
                    SetWindowText( hWnd, "Waiting for All Reads to Finish" );

                    // Release semaphore until its count is the maximum allowed.
                    //..............................................................
                    while ( dwSemaphoreCount != SEMAPHORE_MAX_COUNT )
                    {
                        WaitForSingleObject( hSemRead, INFINITE );
                        ReleaseSemaphore( hSemRead, 1, &dwSemaphoreCount );
                        dwSemaphoreCount++;
                    }

                    SetWindowText( hWnd, "Writing" );

                    // Do the simulated write.
                    //........................
                    Sleep( 10000 );
                    SetWindowText( hWnd, "Done Writing" );

                    // SetEvent: event object becomes signaled.
                    //.........................................
                    SetEvent( hEventWrite );

                    // Close the handles.
                    //...................
                    CloseHandle( hTmpSemRead );
                    CloseHandle( hTmpEventWrite );
                }
                break;
            .
            .
            .
```

CreateFiber   ■ WINDOWS 95   ■ WINDOWS NT

Description   **CreateFiber** allocates a fiber object, assigns it a stack, and sets up execution to begin at the application-supplied fiber function. This function does
not schedule the fiber to execute. Use the **SwitchToFiber** function to execute the fiber. Before a thread can call the **SwitchToFiber** function, it must
call the **ConvertThreadToFiber** function so there is a fiber associated with
the thread.

Syntax	LPVOID **CreateFiber**(DWORD *dwStackSize,* LPFIBER_START_ROUTINE *lpStartAddress,* LPVOID *lpParameter*)
Parameters	
dwStackSize	DWORD: The size, in bytes, of the stack for the new fiber. If **0** is specified, the stack size defaults to the same size as that of the main thread. The system increases the stack size dynamically, if necessary. The stack is freed when the thread terminates.
lpStartAddress	LPFIBER_START_ROUTINE: A pointer to the application-defined function to be executed by the fiber and represents the starting address of the fiber. Execution of the newly created fiber does not begin until another fiber calls the **SwitchToFiber** function with this address. See the definition of the **FiberFunc** below.
lpParameter	LPVOID: A single argument that is passed to the fiber. This value can be retrieved by the fiber with the **GetFiberData** function.
Returns	LPVOID: If successful, the address to the fiber is returned; otherwise, **NULL** is returned. Use the **GetLastError** function to retrieve extended error information.
Include File	winbase.h
See Also	ConvertThreadToFiber, SwitchToFiber, GetFiberData
Callback Syntax	VOID WINAPI **FiberFunc**(PVOID *lpParameter*)
Callback Parameters	
lpParameter	PVOID: The value passed as the *lpParameter* parameter to the **CreateFiber** function.

CreateMutex   ■ WINDOWS 95   ■ WINDOWS NT

Description	**CreateMutex** creates a named or unnamed mutex object that is used for process synchronization. A mutex object becomes signaled when it is not owned by any thread. The thread that owns a mutex can specify the same mutex in repeated wait function calls without blocking its execution. This is not normally done for the same mutex; however, this does prevent a thread from deadlocking itself while waiting for a mutex that it already owns. To release its ownership, the thread must call **ReleaseMutex** once for each time that a mutex satisfied a wait. The handle returned has **MUTEX_ALL_ACCESS** access to the new mutex object and can be used in any function that requires a handle to a mutex object. Any thread of the calling process can specify the mutex-object handle in a call to one of the wait functions. Use the **CloseHandle** function to close the mutex object when it is no longer needed. When all the open handles to the mutex are closed, the mutex is destroyed.

Syntax   HANDLE **CreateMutex**(LPSECURITY_ATTRIBUTES *lpSecurityAttribs,*
              BOOL *bInitialOwner,* LPCTSTR *lpszMutexName*)

Parameters

lpSecurityAttribs LPSECURITY_ATTRIBUTES: A pointer to the security attributes structure. The *bInheritHandle* member of this structure must be set to TRUE if the handle is inherited by child processes. Specifying NULL will activate default security, which means the handle cannot be inherited. See the definition of the SECURITY_ATTRIBUTES structure under the CreateEvent function.

bInitialOwner   BOOL: Set to TRUE if the initial owner of the mutex object is the calling thread. Otherwise, the mutex is not owned.

lpszMutexName   LPCTSTR: A pointer to a null-terminated string of up to MAX_PATH characters that contains the mutex name. The name cannot be the same as any existing event, semaphore, or file-mapping object. All objects share the same name space. Object names are case sensitive. An object name may not contain any backslashes. If *lpszMutexName* is NULL, the object is created without a name.

    If the mutex object has already been registered with the system, the parameter *bInitialOwner* is ignored. When a mutex already exists, CreateMutex opens the mutex with an access mode of MUTEX_ALL_ACCESS. The error ERROR_ALREADY_EXISTS will be set. Calling CreateMutex with the same name as an existing nonmutex object will fail and set the error ERROR_INVALID_HANDLE.

Returns   HANDLE: If successful, the handle of the mutex object is returned; otherwise, NULL is returned. If the named mutex object existed before the function call, the GetLastError function returns ERROR_ALREADY_EXISTS; otherwise, it returns 0. To retrieve extended error information, use GetLastError.

Include File   winbase.h

See Also   CreateProcess, DuplicateHandle, OpenMutex, ReleaseMutex, WaitForSingleObject, WaitForMultipleObjects

Example   This example shows a simple demonstration of mutex objects. When Test! is selected, a thread starts that waits for access to a mutex, sleeps, and releases the mutex. Choosing the Test! option multiple times will illustrate mutex contention as shown in Figure 25-2. The threads will be forced into serial execution by the mutex.

Figure 25-2 CreateMutex example

```
LPCTSTR lpszMutex = "Example Mutex";

HANDLE hMutex = NULL;

// Child thread procedure waits until mutex becomes signaled,
// holds the object for five seconds, and then releases it.
//.........................................................
DWORD WINAPI ChildThreadProc( LPDWORD lpData )
{
    TCHAR   szBuffer[128];
    HWND    hWnd       = (HWND)lpData;
    HANDLE hTmpMutex = OpenMutex( MUTEX_ALL_ACCESS, FALSE, lpszMutex );

    wsprintf( szBuffer,"Thread %x waiting for Mutex %x",
            GetCurrentThreadId(), hMutex );

    SendMessage( hWnd, WM_USER, 0, (LPARAM)szBuffer );

    // Wait for signaled mutex.
    //........................
    WaitForSingleObject( hMutex, INFINITE );
    wsprintf( szBuffer,"Thread %x got mutex!", GetCurrentThreadId() );
    SendMessage( hWnd, WM_USER, 0, (LPARAM)szBuffer );

    // Shut out other threads.
    //........................
    Sleep( 5000 );

    // Release mutex.
    //...............
    wsprintf( szBuffer,"Thread %x is done with mutex", GetCurrentThreadId() );
    SendMessage( hWnd, WM_USER, 0, (LPARAM) szBuffer );
    ReleaseMutex( hMutex );

    CloseHandle( hMutex );
    return( 0 );
}
```

```
LRESULT CALLBACK WndProc( HWND hWnd, UINT uMsg, WPARAM wParam, LPARAM lParam )
{
    static HWND hList   = NULL;
    static int  nMsgNum = 0;

    switch( uMsg )
    {
        case WM_CREATE :
                // Create list box.
                //.................
                hList  = CreateWindowEx( WS_EX_CLIENTEDGE, "LISTBOX", "",
                                         LBS_STANDARD | LBS_NOINTEGRALHEIGHT |
                                         WS_CHILD | WS_VISIBLE,
                                         0, 0, 10, 10,
                                         hWnd, (HMENU)101,
                                         hInst, NULL );

                hMutex = CreateMutex( NULL, FALSE, lpszMutex );
                break;

        case WM_USER :
                {
                    TCHAR szBuffer[128];

                    wsprintf( szBuffer, "%3d: %s", ++nMsgNum, (LPTSTR)lParam );
                    SendMessage( hList, LB_INSERTSTRING, (WPARAM)-1, (LPARAM)szBuffer );
                }
                break;

        case WM_COMMAND :
                switch( LOWORD( wParam ) )
                {
                    case IDM_TEST:
                            {
                                DWORD id;

                                // Make a thread.
                                //...............
                                CreateThread( NULL, 0, (LPTHREAD_START_ROUTINE)ChildThreadProc,⇐
hWnd, 0, &id );
                            }
                            break;
            .
            .
            .
```

CreateProcess   ■ Windows 95   ■ Windows NT

Description   CreateProcess creates a new process and its primary thread. The new process executes a specified executable file. A process object and a thread object result from the call. Both the process object and the thread object created can be used as synchronization objects that are nonsignaled until the process or thread is completed. The thread is created with an initial stack whose size is described in the image header of the specified program's executable file. A process only completes if none of its threads are running—thus the primary thread can terminate before the process.

The calling thread can use the **WaitForInputIdle** function to wait until the new process has finished its initialization and is waiting for user input with no input pending. This is useful for synchronization between parent and child processes, because **CreateProcess** returns without waiting for the new process to finish its initialization.

Syntax

BOOL **CreateProcess**(LPCTSTR *lpszModuleName,* LPCTSTR *lpszCommandLine,* LPSECURITY_ATTRIBUTES *lpProcessSecurity,* LPSECURITY_ATTRIBUTES *lpThreadSecurity,* BOOL *bInheritHandles,* DWORD *dwCreateFlags,* LPVOID *lpvEnvironment,* LPCTSTR *lpszCurrentDir,* LPSTARTUPINFO *lpStartInfo,* LPPROCESS_ INFORMATION *lpProcessInfo*)

Parameters

lpszModuleName LPCTSTR: A pointer to a null-terminated string that contains the file name of the module to execute. If a fully qualified path name is supplied, the default current directory is changed to that path. Otherwise, the default behavior is to execute the program in the current directory. If *lpszModuleName* is **NULL**, the name of the program to execute is the first whitespace-delimited token of *lpszCommandLine*. To execute 16-bit applications under Windows NT, set this parameter to **NULL** and specify the executable module in the *lpszCommandLine* parameter. If no extension is supplied with the module name, **.EXE** is assumed and appended to the file name. If the name of the file ends in a period ("."), **EXE** is not appended.

Windows searches for an executable program file in the following order:

1. The directory from which the application is loaded.

2. The current directory.

3. The Windows system directory. Under Windows NT, the 16-bit Windows system directory, **SYSTEM**, is scanned immediately after the 32-bit Windows system directory.

4. The Windows directory returned by **GetWindowsDirectory**.

5. The directories listed in the **PATH** environment variable are then searched in order.

lpszCommandLine LPCTSTR: A null-terminated string that contains the command line for the module to be executed. If *lpszModuleName* is **NULL**, *lpszCommandLine* also must specify the name of the program to run. The command line returned by *GetCommandLine* includes both *lpszModuleName* and *lpszCommandLine*. C runtime processes can use **argc** and **argv** arguments to get parsed whitespace-delimited tokens from the command line. The same search sequence described for the *lpszModuleName* parameter is used.

lpProcessSecurity LPSECURITY_ATTRIBUTES: A pointer to the security attributes structure. The *bInheritHandle* element of this structure must be set to **TRUE** if the handle is inherited by other processes. Specifying **NULL** will activate default security, which means the handle cannot be inherited. See the definition of the **SECURITY_ATTRIBUTES** structure under the **CreateEvent** function.

lpThreadSecurity   **LPSECURITY_ATTRIBUTES**: A pointer to the security attributes structure. The *bInheritHandle* element of this structure must be set to **TRUE** if the handle is inherited by other processes. Specifying **NULL** will activate default security, which means the handle cannot be inherited. See the definition of the **SECURITY_ATTRIBUTES** structure under the **CreateEvent** function.

bInheritHandles   **BOOL**: Set to **TRUE** if the new process inherits handles from the calling process. The new process inherits each inheritable open handle in the calling process. Inherited handles have the same value and access privileges as the original handles.

dwCreateFlags   **DWORD**: A set of flags that control the priority and the creation of the process. This field allows the priority class of the process object to be set along with execution modes. There are two types of flags: create flags and priority setting flags. Create flags are shown in Table 25-4.

Priority class flags describe the priority class of the process. Priority class is also set using the *dwCreateFlags* parameter of **CreateProcess**. Priority settings are mutually exclusive. If no priority class is set, the flag **NORMAL_PRIORITY_CLASS** is used. Table 25-5 presents priority classes in order from lowest priority to highest.

Table 25-4 `CreateProcess` create flags

Create Flag	Meaning
CREATE_DEFAULT_ERROR_MODE	The process does not inherit the error mode of the parent process as is the norm for child processes. The process uses the default error mode set using `SetErrorMode`.
CREATE_NEW_CONSOLE	The new console-mode process gets its own console. This option is incompatible with `DETACHED_PROCESS`.
CREATE_NEW_PROCESS_GROUP	The new process is the root process of a new process group, a process, and its descendants.
CREATE_SEPARATE_WOW_VDM	(Windows NT only) Executes a 16-bit Windows-based program in a separate virtual DOS machine (VDM).
CREATE_SHARED_WOW_VDM	(Windows NT only) Executes a 16-bit Windows-based program in the shared virtual DOS machine (VDM).
CREATE_SUSPENDED	Creates the process with the primary thread suspended. The thread does not run until the `ResumeThread` function is called.
CREATE_UNICODE_ENVIRONMENT	(Windows NT only) The environment variables of `lpvEnvironment` use Unicode characters.
DEBUG_ONLY_THIS_PROCESS	Indicates that the debugger of the current process is not attached to the child process.
DEBUG_PROCESS	The new process is being debugged by the calling process. The system will generate debug events in the calling process when they occur in the new process.
DETACHED_PROCESS	The new console process has no console, but does not use the console of the current process. Use AllocConsole to create a console.

Table 25-5 CreateProcess priority class flags

Priority Class Flag	Meaning
HIGH_PRIORITY_CLASS	Higher priority task. This highly responsive setting can affect the multitasking nature of the system by not letting other tasks run. An example of this priority would be the Windows Task List, which must respond quickly and interrupt the normal priority processes.
IDLE_PRIORITY_CLASS	Lowest priority task. This runs only when system is idle. An example of a process where this priority is used is a screen saver.
NORMAL_PRIORITY_CLASS	Basic priority for a process.
REALTIME_PRIORITY_CLASS	The highest possible priority. This priority preempts the threads of all other processes, including operating system processes performing important tasks. A real-time process should not execute for more than a very brief interval.

lpvEnvironment	LPVOID: A pointer to the environment settings for the new process. This is a list of null-terminated equations of the form *variable=value*. The last setting is terminated by an extra null character.
lpszCurrentDir	LPCTSTR: A pointer to a null-terminated string that contains the directory path to use as the current directory of the new process.
lpStartInfo	LPSTARTUPINFO: A pointer to a STARTUPINFO structure that describes how the main application window is to appear (minimized, maximized, or normal), its size and location, and window caption (if these arguments are not set by the called process). See the definition of the STARTUPINFO structure below.
lpProcessInfo	LPPROCESS_INFORMATION: A pointer to a PROCESS_INFORMATION structure for the new process. CreateProcess fills this structure if the call is successful. See the definition of the PROCESS_INFORMATION structure below.
Returns	BOOL: If successful, TRUE is returned; otherwise, FALSE. Use GetLastError to return the error code.
Include File	winbase.h
See Also	CloseHandle, CreateRemoteThread, CreateThread, ExitProcess, GetExitCodeProcess, GetLastError, GetStartupInfo, OpenProcess, SetErrorMode, TerminateProcess

STARTUPINFO Definition

```
typedef struct _STARTUPINFO
{
DWORD    cb;
LPTSTR   lpReserved;
LPTSTR   lpDesktop;
LPTSTR   lpTitle;
DWORD    dwX;
DWORD    dwY;
DWORD    dwXSize;
```

```
    DWORD    dwYSize;
    DWORD    dwXCountChars;
    DWORD    dwYCountChars;
    DWORD    dwFillAttribute;
    DWORD    dwFlags;
    WORD     wShowWindow;
    WORD     cbReserved2;
    LPBYTE   lpReserved2;
    HANDLE   hStdInput;
    HANDLE   hStdOutput;
    HANDLE   hStdError;
} STARTUPINFO, *LPSTARTUPINFO;
```

Members

cb

DWORD: The size, in bytes, of the structure.

lpReserved

LPTSTR: Reserved. Set this member to **NULL** before using this structure with the **CreateProcess**.

lpDesktop

LPTSTR: (Windows NT) A pointer to a zero-terminated string that specifies either the name of the desktop only or the name of both the desktop and window station for this process. A backslash in the string indicates that it includes both desktop and window station names. If set to **NULL**, the new process inherits the desktop and window station of its parent process. If set to an empty string, the system determines if a new desktop and window station need to be created.

lpTitle

LPTSTR: Used for console processes. This is the title displayed in the title bar if a new console window is created. If set to **NULL**, the name of the executable file is used as the window title. This member must be set to **NULL** for GUI or console processes that do not create a new console window.

dwX

DWORD: The x offset, in pixels, of the upper-left corner of the window, in screen coordinates, if a new window is crated. This member is ignored unless *dwFlags* specifies **STARTF_USEPOSITION**.

dwY

DWORD: The y offset, in pixels, of the upper-left corner of the window, in screen coordinates, if a new window is crated. This member is ignored unless *dwFlags* specifies **STARTF_USEPOSITION**.

dwXSize

DWORD: The width, in pixels, of the window if a new window is created. This member is ignored unless *dwFlags* specifies **STARTF_USESIZE**.

dwYSize

DWORD: The height, in pixels, of the window if a new window is created. This member is ignored unless *dwFlags* specifies **STARTF_USESIZE**.

dwXCountChars

DWORD: If a new console window is created, this member specifies the screen buffer width in character columns. This member is ignored unless *dwFlags* specifies **STARTF_USECOUNTCHARS**.

dwYCountChars

DWORD: If a new console window is created, this member specifies the screen buffer height in character rows. This member is ignored unless *dwFlags* specifies **STARTF_USECOUNTCHARS**.

dwFillAttribute	**DWORD**: The initial text and background colors if a new console window is created. This value can be any combination of the following values. For example, **FOREGROUND_RED	BACKGROUND_RED	BACKGROUND_GREEN	BACKROUND_BLUE** produces red text on a white background.

          FOREGROUND_BLUE
          FOREGROUND_GREEN
          FOREGROUND_RED
          FOREGROUND_INTENSITY
          BACKGROUND_BLUE
          BACKGROUND_GREEN
          BACKGROUND_RED
          BACKGROUND_INTENSITY

dwFlags	**DWORD**: A set of flags that determine which members of the **STARTUPINFO** structure are used when the process creates a window. Any combination of the flags listed in Table 25-6.

Table 25-6 STARTUPINFO *dwFlags* values

Value	Meaning
STARTF_FORCEOFFFEEDBACK	Forces the feedback cursor off while the process is starting.
STARTF_FORCEONFEEDBACK	Forces the feedback cursor on for two seconds after CreateProcess is called. If during those two seconds the process makes the first GUI call, the system gives five more seconds to the process. If during those five seconds the process shows a window, the system gives five more seconds to the process to finish drawing the window. The system turns the feedback cursor off after the first call to GetMessage, regardless of whether the process is drawing.
STARTF_USECOUNTCHARS	Uses the *dwXCountChars* and *dwYCountChars* members.
STARTF_USEFILLATTRIBUTE	Uses the *dwFillAttribute* members.
STARTF_USEPOSITION	Uses the *dwX* and *dwY* members.
STARTF_USESHOWWINDOW	Uses the *wShowWindow* member.
STARTF_USESIZE	Uses the *dwXSize* and *dwYSize* members.
STARTF_USESTDHANDLES	Sets the standard input of the process, standard output, and standard error handles to the handles specified in the *hStdInput*, *hStdOutput*, and *hStdError* members. The bInheritHandles parameter of the CreateProcess function.

wShowWindow	**WORD**: The default value the first time **ShowWindow** is called when the process is created. This can be any of the **SW_** values listed for the **ShowWindow** function. This member is ignored unless *dwFlags* specifies **STARTF_USESHOWWINDOW**.
cbReserved2	**WORD**: Reserved; must be **0**.
lpReserved2	**LPBYTE**: Reserved; must be **NULL**.

hStdInput	HANDLE: The standard input handle of the process if the value STARTF_USESTDHANDLES is specified in the *dwFlags* member.
hStdOutput	HANDLE: The standard output handle of the process if the value STARTF_USESTDHANDLES is specified in the *dwFlags* member.
hStdError	HANDLE: The standard error handle of the process if the value STARTF_USESTDHANDLES is specified in the *dwFlags* member.

PROCESS_INFORMATION Definition

```
typedef struct _PROCESS_INFORMATION
{
HANDLE hProcess;
HANDLE hThread;
DWORD  dwProcessId;
DWORD  dwThreadId;
} PROCESS_INFORMATION;
```

Members

hProcess	HANDLE: A handle to the newly created process. This handle is used to specify the process in all functions that perform operations on the process object.
hThread	HANDLE: A handle to the primary thread of the newly created process. The handle is used to specify the thread in all functions that perform operations on the thread object.
dwProcessId	DWORD: The global process identifier used to identify a process.
dwThreadId	DWORD: The global thread identifier used to identify the primary thread of the new process.
Example	This example executes the calculator program, CALC, as a child process. When the menu option Test! is selected, CALC is executed and the parent process loops until CALC is terminated, printing an occasional message while it waits for the user to exit. Figure 25-3 shows the results.

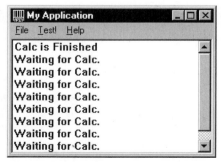

Figure 25-3 CreateProcess example

```
HWND hList = NULL;

LRESULT CALLBACK WndProc( HWND hWnd, UINT uMsg, WPARAM wParam, LPARAM lParam )
{
    switch( uMsg )
    {
    case WM_CREATE :
            // Create list box.
            //.................
            hList  = CreateWindowEx( WS_EX_CLIENTEDGE, "LISTBOX", "",
                                     LBS_STANDARD | LBS_NOINTEGRALHEIGHT |
                                     WS_CHILD | WS_VISIBLE,
                                     0, 0, 10, 10,
                                     hWnd, (HMENU)101,
                                     hInst, NULL );
            break;

    case WM_COMMAND :
            switch( LOWORD( wParam ) )
            {
                case IDM_TEST:
                    {
                        STARTUPINFO         si;
                        PROCESS_INFORMATION pi;

                        // Initialize structures.
                        //.......................
                        ZeroMemory( &si, sizeof(STARTUPINFO) );
                        ZeroMemory( &pi, sizeof(PROCESS_INFORMATION) );

                        si.cb         = sizeof( STARTUPINFO );
                        si.dwFlags    = STARTF_USESHOWWINDOW;
                        si.wShowWindow = SW_SHOWNORMAL;

                        CreateProcess( NULL, "CALC", NULL, NULL, FALSE,
                                       0, NULL, NULL, &si, &pi );

                        WaitForInputIdle( GetCurrentProcess(), INFINITE );

                        // Loop until process terminates.
                        //..............................
                        if ( pi.hProcess )
                        {
                            DWORD dwExitCode = STILL_ACTIVE;
                            while ( dwExitCode == STILL_ACTIVE )
                            {
                                WaitForSingleObject( pi.hProcess, 1000 );
                                GetExitCodeProcess( pi.hProcess, &dwExitCode );
                                SendMessage( hList, LB_INSERTSTRING, 0, (LPARAM)"Waiting for⇐
Calc." );

                                UpdateWindow( hWnd );
                            }
                            SendMessage( hList, LB_INSERTSTRING, 0, (LPARAM)"Calc is⇐
Finished" );
                        }
                    }
                    break;
            .
            .
            .
```

CreateProcessAsUser ■ WINDOWS 95 ■ WINDOWS NT

Description CreateProcessAsUser is similar to the **CreateProcess** function, except that the new process runs in the security context of the user represented by the *hToken* parameter. By default, the new process is noninteractive; that is, it runs on a desktop that is not visible and cannot receive user input. The new process inherits the environment of the calling process by default. All the parameters, except for *hToken*, are the same as those of the **CreateProcess** function.

Syntax BOOL **CreateProcessAsUser**(HANDLE *hToken,* LPCTSTR *lpszModuleName,* LPTSTR *lpszCommandLine,* LPSECURITY_ATTRIBUTES *lpProcessSecurity,* LPSECURITY_ATTRIBUTES *lpThreadSecurity,* BOOL *bInheritHandles,* DWORD *dwCreateFlags,* LPVOID *lpvEnvironment,* LPCTSTR *lpszCurrentDir,* LPSTARTUPINFO *lpStartInfo,* LPPROCESS_INFORMATION *lpProcessInfo*)

Parameters

hToken HANDLE: A handle to a primary token that represents a user. The user represented by the token must have read and execute access to the application. The application can use the security function **LogonUser** to get a primary token that represents a specified user. Alternatively, the application can use the security function **DuplicatetokenEx** to convert an impersonation token into a primary token. This allows a server application that is impersonating a client to create a process that has the security context of the client.

lpszModuleName LPCTSTR: See the **CreateProcess** function for a description of this parameter.

lpszCommandLine LPTSTR: See the **CreateProcess** function for a description of this parameter.

lpProcessSecurity LPSECURITY_ATTRIBUTES: See the **CreateProcess** function for a description of this parameter.

lpThreadSecurity LPSECURITY_ATTRIBUTES: See the **CreateProcess** function for a description of this parameter.

bInheritHandles BOOL: See the **CreateProcess** function for a description of this parameter.

dwCreateFlags DWORD: See the **CreateProcess** function for a description of this parameter.

lpvEnvironment LPVOID: See the **CreateProcess** function for a description of this parameter.

lpszCurrentDir LPCTSTR: See the **CreateProcess** function for a description of this parameter.

lpStartInfo LPSTARTUPINFO: See the **CreateProcess** function for a description of this parameter.

lpProcessInfo	LPPROCESS_INFORMATION: See the **CreateProcess** function for a description of this parameter.
Returns	BOOL: If successful, TRUE is returned; otherwise, FALSE is returned. Use the **GetLastError** function to retrieve extended error information.
Include File	winbase.h
See Also	CreateProcess
Example	See the example for the **CreateProcess** function. Although the example does not use this function directly, it is similar to the **CreateProcess** function.

CreateRemoteThread   ■ WINDOWS 95   ■ WINDOWS NT

Description	**CreateRemoteThread** creates a thread that runs in the address space of another process. The new thread has access to all objects opened by the process. The returned thread handle is created with full access to the new thread. If a security descriptor is not provided, the handle may be used in any function that requires a thread object handle. When a security descriptor is provided, an access check is performed on all subsequent uses of the handle before access is granted. If the access check denies access, the calling process cannot use the handle to gain access to the thread.
Syntax	HANDLE **CreateRemoteThread**(HANDLE *hProcess,* LPSECURITY_ ATTRIBUTES *lpThreadAttributes,* DWORD *dwStackSize,* LPTHREAD_START_ROUTINE *lpStartAddress,* LPVOID *lpParameter,* DWORD *dwCreationFlags,* LPDWORD *lpThreadId*)
Parameters	
hProcess	HANDLE: The handle of the process in which the thread is to be created. The handle must have PROCESS_CREATE_THREAD access.
lpThreadAttributes	LPSECURITY_ATTRIBUTES: A pointer to a SECURITY_ATTRIBUTES structure that specifies a security descriptor for the new thread and determines whether child processes can inherit the returned handle. If set to NULL, the thread receives a default security descriptor and the handle cannot be inherited. See the definition of the SECURITY_ ATTRIBUTES structure under the **CreateEvent** function.
dwStackSize	DWORD: The size, in bytes, of the stack for the new thread. If set to 0, the stack size defaults to the same size as that of the primary thread of the process. The stack is allocated automatically in the memory space of the process and is freed when the thread terminates. The stack size grows as necessary.

lpStartAddress	LPTHREAD_START_ROUTINE: A pointer to an application-defined function that is the starting address of the new thread. This function is declared with the WINAPI calling convention and takes a 32-bit pointer as an argument and returns a 32-bit value. Once the function returns, the thread is terminated.
lpParameter	LPVOID: A pointer to a single 32-bit value passed to the thread.
dwCreationFlags	DWORD: Flags that control the creation of the thread. If the CREATE_SUSPENDED flag is specified, the thread is created in a suspended state and will not run until the ResumeThread function is called. If set to 0, the thread runs immediately after creation.
lpThreadId	LPDWORD: A pointer to a 32-bit variable that receives the thread identifier.
Returns	HANDLE: If successful, the handle to the new thread is returned; otherwise, NULL is returned. Use the GetLastError function to retrieve extended error information.
Include File	winbase.h
See Also	CloseHandle, CreateProcess, CreateThread, ResumeThread

CreateSemaphore   ■ WINDOWS 95   ■ WINDOWS NT

Description	CreateSemaphore creates a named or unnamed semaphore object. A semaphore, which uses a counter for synchronization, is signaled when its counter's value is greater than zero and nonsignaled when its counter is zero. Each time the semaphore is taken (for example with a WaitForSingleObject function), the semaphore counter is decremented. Each time the semaphore is released with ReleaseSemaphore, the semaphore counter is incremented. The count can never be less than zero or greater than the value specified in the *lSemMaxCount* parameter.
Syntax	HANDLE **CreateSemaphore**(LPSECURITY_ATTRIBUTES *lpSecurity,* LONG *lSemInitialCount,* LONG *lSemMaxCount,* LPCTSTR *lpszSemName*)
Parameters	
lpSecurity	LPSECURITY_ATTRIBUTES: A pointer to a SECURITY_ATTRIBUTES structure that determines whether the returned handle can be inherited by child processes. If set to NULL, the handle cannot be inherited. The *bInheritHandle* member of this structure must be set to TRUE if the handle can be inherited by other processes. See the definition of the SECURITY_ATTRIBUTES structure under the CreateEvent function.
lSemInitialCount	LONG: The initial value of the semaphore counter. This value must be greater than or equal to zero and less than or equal to *lSemMaxCount*.
lSemMaxCount	LONG: The maximum value of the semaphore counter. This value must be greater than zero.

lpszSemName	LPCTSTR: A pointer to a null-terminated string of up to **MAX_PATH** characters that contains the semaphore name. The name cannot be the same as any existing event, mutex, or file-mapping object. All objects share the same name space. Object names are case sensitive. An object name may not contain any backslashes. If *lpszSemName* is **NULL**, the object is created without a name.
	If the semaphore object has already been registered with the system, the parameters *lSemMaxCount* and *lSemInitialCount* are ignored. When a semaphore already exists, **CreateSemaphore** opens the object with an access mode of **SEMAPHORE_ALL_ACCESS** and the error **ERROR_ALREADY_EXISTS** is set. Calling **CreateSemaphore** with the same name as an existing nonsemaphore object will fail and set the error **ERROR_INVALID_HANDLE**.
Returns	HANDLE: If successful, a handle to the semaphore object is returned; otherwise, **NULL** is returned. Use **GetLastError** to return the extended error information.
Include File	winbase.h
See Also	CloseHandle, DuplicateHandle, OpenSemaphore, ReleaseSemaphore, WaitForSingleObject, WaitForMultipleObjects
Example	This example uses semaphores to allow only four threads to execute the child thread procedure. When the user selects the Test! option, a new thread is started. The thread procedure first attempts to get a semaphore with a maximum count of four, looping until it is successful. No matter how many times Test! is chosen, the protected code will only allow four threads at a time.

```
LPCTSTR lpszSemaphore = "Test Semaphore";

// This is a child thread procedure that waits for a semaphore,
// holds the semaphore for five seconds, and releases the semaphore.
// Threads that cannot get semaphores will wait until other threads exit.
//.................................................................

DWORD WINAPI ChildThreadProc( LPDWORD lpData )
{
    TCHAR szBuffer[256];
    DWORD dwSemCount  = 0;
    HWND  hList       = (HWND)lpData;
    HANDLE hSemaphore = OpenSemaphore( SYNCHRONIZE | SEMAPHORE_MODIFY_STATE, FALSE,⇐
lpszSemaphore );

    wsprintf( szBuffer,"Thread %x waiting for semaphore %x",
            GetCurrentThreadId(), hSemaphore );

    SendMessage( hList, LB_INSERTSTRING, (WPARAM)-1, (LPARAM)szBuffer );
```

```
    // Check for signaled semaphore.
    //.............................
    WaitForSingleObject( hSemaphore, INFINITE );
    wsprintf( szBuffer,"Thread %x got semaphore", GetCurrentThreadId() );
    SendMessage( hList, LB_INSERTSTRING, (WPARAM)-1, (LPARAM)szBuffer );
    Sleep( 5000 );

    // Release semaphore.
    //...................
    ReleaseSemaphore( hSemaphore, 1, &dwSemCount );

    wsprintf( szBuffer,"Thread %x is done with semaphore. Its count was %ld.",
              GetCurrentThreadId(), dwSemCount );

    SendMessage( hList, LB_INSERTSTRING, (WPARAM)-1, (LPARAM)szBuffer );

    CloseHandle( hSemaphore );

    return( 0 );
}


LRESULT CALLBACK WndProc( HWND hWnd, UINT uMsg, WPARAM wParam, LPARAM lParam )
{
static HWND    hList = NULL;
static HANDLE hSemaphore = NULL;

    switch( uMsg )
    {
        case WM_CREATE:
                // Create list box.
                //.................
                hList  = CreateWindowEx( WS_EX_CLIENTEDGE, "LISTBOX", "",
                                         LBS_STANDARD | LBS_NOINTEGRALHEIGHT |
                                         WS_CHILD | WS_VISIBLE,
                                         0, 0, 10, 10,
                                         hWnd, (HMENU)101,
                                         hInst, NULL );

                hSemaphore = CreateSemaphore( NULL, 4, 4, lpszSemaphore );
                break;

        case WM_SIZE :
                if ( wParam != SIZE_MINIMIZED )
                    MoveWindow( hList, 0, 0, LOWORD( lParam ), HIWORD( lParam ), TRUE );
                break;

        case WM_COMMAND :
                switch( LOWORD( wParam ) )
                {
                    case IDM_TEST:
                        {
                            DWORD dwChildId;

                            CreateThread( NULL, 0, ChildThreadProc, hList, 0, &dwChildId );
                        }
                        break;
            .
            .
            .
```

CreateThread ■ WINDOWS 95 ■ WINDOWS NT

Description	**CreateThread** creates a thread that will execute within the address space of the calling process. The thread object can be used as a synchronization object. It is created in the nonsignaled state and becomes signaled when the thread is completed. The thread execution begins at the function specified by the *lpStartAddr* parameter. If this function returns, the **DWORD** return value is used to terminate the thread with an implicit call to the **ExitThread** function. Use the **GetExitCodeThread** function to get the thread's return value. The thread is created with a thread priority of **THREAD_PRIORITY_NORMAL**. Use the **GetThreadPriority** and **SetThreadPriority** functions to get and set the priority value of the thread. The thread object remains in the system until the thread has terminated and all handles to it have been closed through a call to **CloseHandle**.
Syntax	HANDLE **CreateThread**(LPSECURITY_ATTRIBUTES *lpSecurity*, DWORD *cbStack*, LPTHREAD_START_ROUTINE *lpStartAddr*, LPVOID *lpvThreadParam*, DWORD *dwCreateFlags*, LPDWOR *lpdwThreadId*)

Parameters

lpSecurity	**LPSECURITY_ATTRIBUTES**: A pointer to a **SECURITY_ATTRIBUTES** structure that defines the security attributes of the new thread. If the *bInheritHandle* member of this structure is set to **TRUE**, the handle can be inherited by child processes; otherwise, the handle cannot be inherited. Specifying **NULL** will activate default security, which means the handle cannot be inherited.
cbStack	**DWORD**: The size, in bytes, allocated for the thread's stack. If **0** is specified, the stack size defaults to the same size as the stack size of the primary thread. The stack is allocated in the memory space of the process and is freed when the thread terminates. The stack dynamically grows, when necessary.
lpStartAddr	**LPTHREAD_START_ROUTINE**: A pointer to the starting address of the thread. This is typically the address of a function declared with the syntax shown below. A thread function takes a pointer to a **DWORD** as a parameter and returns a **DWORD**.

```
DWORD WINAPI ThreadProc( LPDWORD lpData )
```

lpvThreadParam	**LPVOID**: Specifies a single 32-bit value passed to the thread.
dwCreateFlags	**DWORD**: Allows **CREATE_SUSPENDED** to be set, which will start the thread in suspended mode. The thread will execute only when it receives a **ResumeThread** call. If *dwCreateFlags* is **0**, the thread starts immediately after the **CreateThread** function is called.
lpdwThreadId	**LPDWORD**: A pointer to a **DWORD** variable that receives the new thread ID.

Returns	**HANDLE**: If the function succeeds, a handle to the new thread object is returned; otherwise, **NULL** is returned. Use the **GetLastError** function to retrieve extended error information.
Include File	`winbase.h`
See Also	`CloseHandle`, `CreateProcess`, `CreateRemoteThread`, `ExitThread`, `GetExitCodeThread`, `GetLastError`, `OpenThreadToken`, `SetErrorMode`, `TerminateProcess`, `TerminateThread`

> **NOTE**
> If C runtime library functions, such as `_getch` and `srand`, are used in the thread, `_beginthread` or `_beginthreadex` should be used instead of `CreateThread`. This allows initialization of the runtime library to occur. Likewise, use `_endthread` and `_endthreadex`, respectively, rather than `ExitThread`, or memory leakage will occur. Note that `_endthread` and `_endthreadex` close the handle of the thread, making it invalid, so if they are used, the thread object cannot be used for synchronization.

Example	See the example for the **CreateSemaphore** function.

CreateWaitableTimer ■ WINDOWS 95 ■ WINDOWS NT

Description	**CreateWaitableTimer** creates a named or unnamed waitable timer object. The returned handle is created with the **TIMER_ALL_ACCESS** access right. This handle can be used in any function that requires a handle to a timer object. Use the **CloseHandle** function to close the handle when it is no longer needed. The system closes the handle automatically when the process terminates. The timer object is destroyed when its last handle has been closed.
Syntax	HANDLE **CreateWaitableTimer(** LPSECURITY_ATTRIBUTES *lpTimerAttributes,* BOOL *bManualReset,* LPCTSTR *lpTimerName* **)**
Parameters	
lpTimerAttributes	**LPSECURITY_ATTRIBUTES**: A pointer to a **SECURITY_ATTRIBUTES** structure that specifies a security descriptor for the new timer object and determines whether child processes can inherit the returned handle. If set to **NULL**, the timer object gets a default security descriptor and the handle cannot be inherited. See the definition of the **SECURITY_ATTRIBUTES** structure under the **CreateEvent** function.
bManualReset	**BOOL**: Set to **TRUE** if the timer is a manual-reset notification timer; otherwise, the timer is a synchronization timer.
lpTimerName	**LPCTSTR**: A pointer to a null-terminated string specifying the name of the timer object. The name is limited to **MAX_PATH** characters and can contain any character except the backslash path-separator character (\).

Name comparison is case sensitive. If the name matches the name of an already existing named timer object, the call returns successfully and the **GetLastError** function returns **ERROR_ALREADY_EXISTS**. If set to **NULL**, the timer object is created without a name. The name must not be in use for any event, semaphore, mutex, or file-mapping object.

Returns **HANDLE**: If successful, a handle to the new timer object is returned; otherwise, **NULL** is returned. Use the **GetLastError** function to retrieve extended error information.

Include File `winbase.h`

See Also `CancelWaitableTimer, CloseHandle, OpenWaitableTimer`

DeleteCriticalSection ■ Windows 95 ■ Windows NT

Description **DeleteCriticalSection** releases all resources associated with an unowned critical section object. Once the critical section object is deleted, **EnterCriticalSection**, **TryEnterCriticalSection**, and **LeaveCriticalSection** will fail for the deleted object.

Syntax VOID **DeleteCriticalSection**(LPCRITICAL_SECTION *lpcsCriticalSection*)

Parameters

lpcsCriticalSection LPCRITICAL_SECTION: A pointer to critical section object to delete.

Include File `winbase.h`

See Also `EnterCriticalSection, LeaveCriticalSection, InitializeCriticalSection, TryEnterCriticalSection`

Example See the example for **EnterCriticalSection**.

DeleteFiber ■ Windows 95 ■ Windows NT

Description **DeleteFiber** deletes an existing fiber and all data associated with the fiber. This data includes the stack, a subset of the registers, and the fiber data. If the currently running fiber calls **DeleteFiber**, the **ExitThread** function is called and the thread terminates. If the currently running fiber is deleted by another thread, the thread associated with the fiber is likely to terminate abnormally because the fiber stack has been freed.

Syntax VOID **DeleteFiber**(LPVOID *lpFiber*)

Parameters

lpFiber LPVOID: The address of the fiber to delete.

Include File `winbase.h`

See Also `ExitThread`

DuplicateHandle   ■ WINDOWS 95   ■ WINDOWS NT

Description	DuplicateHandle creates a copy of a specified handle to an object. This allows a process to access an object created in another process.
Syntax	BOOL **DuplicateHandle**(HANDLE *hSourceProcess,* HANDLE *hSourceObject,* HANDLE *hTargetProcess,* LPHANDLE *lphTarget,* DWORD *dwAccessFlags,* BOOL *bInherit,* DWORD *dwOptions*)
Parameters	
hSourceProcess	HANDLE: The process owning the handle to be duplicated. PROCESS_DUP_HANDLE process access is required to duplicate the object handle. The process object of the source process must be open.
hSourceObject	HANDLE: The object handle to duplicate. This is an open object handle that is valid in the context of the source process. Table 25-7 lists objects whose handles may be duplicated by this function.

Table 25-7 Object types for DuplicateHandle

Object	Description
Communication port	Returned by the CreateFile function.
Console input	Returned by the CreateFile function when CONIN$ is specified, or by the GetStdHandle function when STD_INPUT_HANDLE is specified. These handles can only be duplicated for use in the same process.
Console output	Returned by the CreateFile function when CONOUT$ is specified, or by the GetStdHandle function when STD_OUTPUT_HANDLE is specified. These handles can only be duplicated for use in the same process.
Event	Returned by the CreateEvent or OpenEvent function.
File	Returned by the CreateFile function.
File mapping	Returned by the CreateFileMapping function.
Mutex	Returned by the CreateMutex or OpenMutex function.
Pipe	Returned by the CreateNamedPipe or CreateFile function. An anonymous pipe handle is returned by the CreatePipe function.
Process	Returned by the CreateProcess, GetCurrentProcess, or OpenProcess function.
Registry key	Returned by the RegCreateKeyEx or RegOpenKeyEx function. Keys returned by the RegConnectRegistry function cannot be used with the DuplicateHandle function.
Semaphore	Returned by the CreateSemaphore or OpenSemaphore function.
Thread	Returned by the CreateProcess, CreateThread, CreateRemoteThread, or GetCurrentThread function.

hTargetProcess	HANDLE: An open process for which the duplicate handle is being created. The process object must have PROCESS_DUP_HANDLE process access.
lphTarget	LPHANDLE: A pointer to a variable that receives the duplicate handle. If set to NULL, the function duplicates the handle, but does not return the duplicate handle value to the caller.

dwAccessFlags	DWORD: Access flag settings for the new handle to the object. This parameter is ignored if DUPLICATE_SAME_ACCESS is set in *dwOptions*; otherwise, the flags that can be specified depend on the type of object whose handle is being duplicated. The new handle can have more access than the original handle. See the functions for each object type for more information on the valid flags.
bInherit	BOOL: Indicates whether the new handle can be inherited by children of the target process. If TRUE, the duplicate handle can be inherited. If FALSE, the new handle cannot be inherited.
dwOptions	DWORD: Allows specification of additional options. This parameter can be 0, or one or more of defined flags. The DUPLICATE_CLOSE_SOURCE flag closes the source handle, even if DuplicateHandle results in an error. The DUPLICATE_SAME_ACCESS flag causes the DuplicateHandle function to ignore the *dwAccessFlags* parameter, and the target handle has the same access as the source handle.
Returns	BOOL: If successful, TRUE is returned; otherwise, FALSE is returned. Use GetLastError to return the error code. The new handle is stored at the address passed in *lphTarget*.
Include File	winbase.h
See Also	CloseHandle, OpenEvent, OpenMutex, OpenProcess, OpenSemaphore, WaitForSingleObject, WaitForMultipleObjects
Example	This example uses the DuplicateHandle function to create a duplicate mutex for a new process. When the user chooses Test! from the menu of the window, the program creates a mutex and starts a new process of the example program. DuplicateHandle creates a handle of the mutex for the new process's context. A WM_USER message is posted with the duplicated handle in the *wParam* argument. The process receives the message and locks the mutex.

```
LRESULT CALLBACK WndProc( HWND hWnd, UINT uMsg, WPARAM wParam, LPARAM lParam )
{
    switch( uMsg )
    {
    case WM_CREATE:
            // If child set child name.
            //........................
            if ( strstr( GetCommandLine(), "CHILD" ) )
                SetWindowText( hWnd, lpszChildTitle );
            else
                // position parent to left of child
                //.................................
                MoveWindow( hWnd, 0, 0, 200, 200, TRUE );
            break;

    case WM_USER:
            {
                HDC hDC = GetDC( hWnd );
                TextOut( hDC, 0, 0, "Waiting for mutex", 17);
```

```
            // Get mutex.
            //...........
            WaitForSingleObject( ( HANDLE )wParam, INFINITE );
            TextOut( hDC, 0, 20, "Got mutex", 9);

            // Wait for a while.
            //..................
            Sleep( 3000 );

            TextOut( hDC, 0, 40, "Released mutex", 14);
            ReleaseMutex( ( HANDLE )wParam );
        }
        break;

    case WM_COMMAND :
        switch( LOWORD( wParam ) )
        {
            case IDM_TEST:
                {
                    HANDLE hAlias;
                    STARTUPINFO si;
                    PROCESS_INFORMATION pi;

                    // Create a process and export mutex handle.
                    //..........................................
                    ZeroMemory( &si, sizeof( STARTUPINFO ) );
                    ZeroMemory( &pi, sizeof( PROCESS_INFORMATION ) );

                    si.cb          = sizeof( STARTUPINFO );
                    si.dwFlags     = STARTF_USESHOWWINDOW;
                    si.wShowWindow = SW_HIDE;

                    CreateProcess( NULL, "DUPHANDL.EXE CHILD",
                                   NULL, NULL, FALSE,
                                   0, NULL, NULL, &si, &pi );

                    // If process is created.
                    //.......................
                    if ( pi.hProcess )
                    {
                        HWND hWndChild;
                        HANDLE hMutex = CreateMutex( NULL, FALSE, "TEST_MUTEX" );

                        DuplicateHandle( GetCurrentProcess(), hMutex,
                                         pi.hProcess, &hAlias,
                                         SYNCHRONIZE, FALSE, 0 );

                        // Let initialization of new process occur.
                        //.........................................
                        WaitForInputIdle( GetCurrentProcess(), INFINITE );

                        // Get external window address.
                        //.............................
                        while ( (hWndChild = FindWindow( lpszAppName, lpszChildTitle ))⇐
== NULL);
```

continued on next page

continued from previous page

```
                        // Move it over to left.
                        //....................
                        MoveWindow( hWndChild, 200, 0, 200, 200, TRUE );
                        ShowWindow( hWndChild, SW_SHOWNORMAL );

                        PostMessage( hWndChild, WM_USER, ( WPARAM )hAlias, 0 );
                        CloseHandle( hMutex );

                        // Wait for a while.
                        //...................
                        Sleep( 5000 );

                        // Terminate the child process.
                        //............................
                        TerminateProcess( pi.hProcess, 0 );
                    }
                }
                break;
```

EnterCriticalSection ■ WINDOWS 95 ■ WINDOWS NT

Description   EnterCriticalSection waits for ownership of the specified critical section object. The function returns once the calling thread is granted ownership. Critical section objects enforce mutual-exclusion synchronization among the threads of a single process. Once a thread owns the critical section object, it can call EnterCriticalSection for the same critical section object without causing deadlock against itself. LeaveCriticalSection must be called as many times as the thread has entered the critical section before other threads can gain ownership of the object. To enable mutually exclusive access to a shared resource, each thread calls EnterCriticalSection or TryEnterCriticalSection to request owner-ship of the critical section before executing any section of code that accesses the protected resource.

Syntax   VOID **EnterCriticalSection**(LPCRITICAL_SECTION *lpcs*)

Parameters

lpcs   LPCRITICAL_SECTION: A pointer to a critical section object.

Include File   winbase.h

See Also   CreateMutex, DeleteCriticalSection, InitializeCriticalSection, LeaveCriticalSection

Example   This example allows only one thread to execute the critical code (a five-second sleep) in the middle of the child thread procedure. Every time the user selects Test!, a new thread is created. The critical section object in the thread procedure serializes execution.

```
CRITICAL_SECTION cs;

DWORD WINAPI ChildThreadProc( LPDWORD lpdwData )
{
    TCHAR szBuffer[256];
    HWND  hWnd  = (HWND)lpdwData;

    wsprintf( szBuffer, "Thread %x waiting for critical section", GetCurrentThreadId() );
    SendMessage( hWnd, WM_USER, 0, (LPARAM)szBuffer );

    // Enter protected code.
    //......................
    EnterCriticalSection( &cs );
    wsprintf( szBuffer,"Thread %x in critical section", GetCurrentThreadId() );
    SendMessage( hWnd, WM_USER, 0, (LPARAM)szBuffer );

    // Where critical code would go if we had some.
    //.............................................
    Sleep( 5000 );

    // All done now, let someone else in.
    //...................................
    LeaveCriticalSection( &cs );
    wsprintf( szBuffer,"Thread %x has exited critical section", GetCurrentThreadId() );
    SendMessage( hWnd, WM_USER, 0, (LPARAM)szBuffer );

    return( 0 );
}


LRESULT CALLBACK WndProc( HWND hWnd, UINT uMsg, WPARAM wParam, LPARAM lParam )
{
    static HWND hList = NULL;

    switch( uMsg )
    {
    case WM_CREATE:
            // A critical section must be
            // initialized before it is used.
            //................................
            InitializeCriticalSection(&cs);

            // Create list box.
            //.................
            hList  = CreateWindowEx( WS_EX_CLIENTEDGE, "LISTBOX", "",
                                     LBS_STANDARD | LBS_NOINTEGRALHEIGHT |
                                     WS_CHILD | WS_VISIBLE,
                                     0, 0, 10, 10,
                                     hWnd, (HMENU)101,
                                     hInst, NULL );
            break;

    case WM_USER:
            {
                // Show synchronization activity.
                //...............................
                TCHAR szBuffer[128];
                static int msg_num = 0;
```

continued on next page

continued from previous page

```
                wsprintf( szBuffer, "%3d: %s", ++msg_num, (LPTSTR)lParam );
                SendMessage( hList, LB_INSERTSTRING,
                             (WPARAM)-1, (LPARAM)szBuffer );
            }
            break;

    case WM_DESTROY :
            DeleteCriticalSection( &cs );
            PostQuitMessage(0);
            break;

    case WM_COMMAND :
            switch( LOWORD( wParam ) )
            {
                case IDM_TEST:
                    {
                        DWORD dwChildID;
                        CreateThread( NULL, 0, ChildThreadProc, hWnd, 0, &dwChildID );
                    }
                    break;
        .
        .
        .
```

ExitProcess ■ WINDOWS 95 ■ WINDOWS NT

Description   **ExitProcess** ends a process and all its threads and returns a common exit code. This allows a clean process shutdown, including execution of process detach code for all linked DLLs. Once a process is exited, the states of its process object and all of its thread objects become signaled. The termination status (returned by **GetExitCodeProcess**) is changed from **STILL_ACTIVE** to the exit code specified in the parameter *uExitCode*. Terminating a process does not affect child processes that it starts or remove it from the system. Only when the last handle to the process is closed is the process object removed from the operating system.

Syntax   VOID **ExitProcess**(UINT *uExitCode*)

Parameters

uExitCode   UINT: The exit code for the process and all threads that are terminated as a result of this call. Use the **GetExitCodeProcess** function to retrieve the process's exit code.

Include File   winbase.h

See Also   GetExitCodeThread, GetExitCodeProcess, ExitThread, CloseHandle

---

NOTE

The ExitProcess, ExitThread, CreateThread, CreateRemoteThread functions, and a process that is starting as a result of a call by CreateProcess are serialized between each other within a process. Only one of these events can occur in an address space at a time.

ExitThread   ■ Windows 95   ■ Windows NT

Description	**ExitThread** ends a thread. This is the preferred method of exiting a thread. When this function is called explicitly or by returning from a thread procedure, the current thread's stack is deallocated and the thread terminates. Once a thread is exited, the state of its thread object becomes signaled. Also, the termination status returned by **GetExitCodeThread** is changed from **STILL_ACTIVE** to the exit code specified in the parameter *uExitCode*. Terminating a thread does not affect any child processes that it starts. The thread is not removed from the system until all handles to the thread are closed.
Syntax	VOID **ExitThread**(UINT *uExitCode*)
Parameters	
uExitCode	UINT: The exit code for the calling thread. Use the **GetExitCodeThread** function to retrieve a thread's exit code.
Include File	winbase.h
See Also	GetExitCodeThread, GetExitCodeProcess, ExitProcess, CloseHandle
Example	See the example for the **GetExitCodeThread** function.

GetCurrentFiber   ■ Windows 95   ■ Windows NT

Description	**GetCurrentFiber** returns the address of the current fiber. This function allows the application to retrieve the address of the current fiber at any time.
Syntax	PVOID **GetCurrentFiber**(VOID)
Parameters	This function has no parameters.
Returns	PVOID: The address of the currently running fiber.
Include File	winnt.h
See Also	CreateFiber, ConvertThreadToFiber

GetCurrentProcess   ■ Windows 95   ■ Windows NT

Description	**GetCurrentProcess** returns a pseudohandle for the current process. This handle is a special constant that is interpreted as the current process handle. The calling process can use this handle to specify its own process whenever a process handle is required. This handle is not inherited by child processes. The handle has the maximum possible access to the process object.

A process can create a real handle to itself that is valid in the context of other processes and can be inherited by other processes by specifying the pseudohandle as the source handle in a call to the **DuplicateHandle** function. Alternatively, a process can also use the **OpenProcess** function to open a real handle to itself.

Syntax	HANDLE **GetCurrentProcess**(VOID)
Parameters	This function has no parameters.
Returns	HANDLE: The pseudohandle to the current process.
Include File	winbase.h
See Also	GetCurrentProcessId, GetCurrentThread, DuplicateHandle, OpenProcess
Example	This example creates a thread and displays the pseudohandles and IDs of the current process and the new thread when the user selects the Test! menu item.

```
DWORD WINAPI ChildThreadProc( LPDWORD lpdwData )
{
   TCHAR szBuffer[256];
   HWND  hWnd = (HWND)lpdwData;

   wsprintf(szBuffer,
            "Process Handle = %x, ID = %x, Thread: Handle = %x, ID = %x",
            GetCurrentProcess(), GetCurrentProcessId(),
            GetCurrentThread(), GetCurrentThreadId());
   MessageBox( hWnd, szBuffer, "Process/Thread Report", MB_OK );

   return( 0 );
}



LRESULT CALLBACK WndProc( HWND hWnd, UINT uMsg, WPARAM wParam, LPARAM lParam )
{
   switch( uMsg )
   {
      case WM_COMMAND :
             switch( LOWORD( wParam ) )
             {
                case IDM_TEST:
                      {
                          DWORD dwChildId;

                          CreateThread( NULL, 0, ChildThreadProc, hWnd, 0, &dwChildId );
                      }
                      break;
                .
                .
                .
```

GetCurrentProcessId ■ WINDOWS 95 ■ WINDOWS NT

Description	`GetCurrentProcessId` returns the process ID of the currently executing process.
Syntax	DWORD **GetCurrentProcessId(VOID)**
Parameters	This function has no parameters.
Returns	`DWORD`: The process ID of the current process. This is a unique identifier throughout the system until the process has been closed.
Include File	`winbase.h`
See Also	`GetCurrentProcess, GetCurrentThreadId`
Example	See the example for the `GetCurrentProcess` function.

GetCurrentThread ■ WINDOWS 95 ■ WINDOWS NT

Description	`GetCurrentThread` returns a pseudohandle of the currently executing thread within the current process. This handle is a special constant that is interpreted as the current thread handle. The calling thread can use this handle to specify itself whenever a thread handle is required. This handle is not inherited by child processes. The handle has the maximum possible access to the thread object. The thread can create a real handle of itself by using the pseudohandle as the source handle in a call to the `DuplicateHandle` function.
Syntax	HANDLE **GetCurrentThread(VOID)**
Parameters	This function has no parameters.
Returns	`HANDLE`: The pseudohandle of the current thread.
Include File	`winbase.h`
See Also	`GetCurrentProcess, GetCurrentThreadId, DuplicateHandle, CloseHandle`
Example	See the example for the `GetCurrentProcess` function.

GetCurrentThreadId ■ WINDOWS 95 ■ WINDOWS NT

Description	`GetCurrentThreadId` returns the thread ID of the calling thread. This is a unique identifier for the thread that may be used systemwide until the thread is closed.
Syntax	DWORD **GetCurrentThreadId(VOID)**
Parameters	This function has no parameters.
Returns	`DWORD`: The thread ID of the calling thread.

Include File	winbase.h
See Also	GetCurrentProcessId, GetCurrentThread
Example	See the example for the GetCurrentProcess function.

GetExitCodeProcess ■ WINDOWS 95 ■ WINDOWS NT

Description	GetExitCodeProcess returns the termination status of the specified process. An application can use this function to determine whether a specific process is still running. If the process has not terminated, the termination status is STILL_ACTIVE.
Syntax	BOOL GetExitCodeProcess(HANDLE *hProcess,* LPDWORD *lpdwExitCode*)
Parameters	
hProcess	HANDLE: Identifies a process object. Under Windows NT, this process object must have PROCESS_QUERY_INFORMATION access to return the termination status.
lpdwExitCode	LPDWORD: A pointer to a 32-bit variable that receives the process termination status. If the process is not yet terminated, STILL_ACTIVE is received. The process termination status is the value passed in TerminateProcess or ExitProcess, the value returned from main or WinMain, or it is an exception value set by an unhandled exception that causes the process to terminate.
Returns	BOOL: If successful, TRUE is returned; otherwise FALSE is returned. Use the GetLastError function to retrieve extended error information.
Include File	winbase.h
See Also	GetExitCodeThread, TerminateProcess, ExitProcess, WinMain
Example	See the example for the CreateProcess function.

GetExitCodeThread ■ WINDOWS 95 ■ WINDOWS NT

Description	GetExitCodeThread returns the termination status of the specified thread. Use this function to determine whether a specific thread is still running. If the thread is still executing, the status is STILL_ACTIVE.
Syntax	BOOL GetExitCodeThread(HANDLE *hThread,* LPDWORD *lpdwExitCode*)
Parameters	
hThread	HANDLE: Identifies a thread object. This handle must have THREAD_QUERY_INFORMATION access to return the termination status.
lpdwExitCode	LPDWORD: A pointer to a 32-bit variable that receives the thread termination status. If the thread has not yet terminated, STILL_ACTIVE is received; otherwise, the thread's termination status is the value passed in

TerminateThread or ExitThread, the return value of the thread function, or the return value from the process if it terminates before the thread is received.

Returns

BOOL: If successful, TRUE is returned; otherwise, FALSE is returned. Use GetLastError to return extended error information.

Include File

winbase.h

See Also

ExitThread, TerminateThread, GetExitCodeProcess

Example

This example starts a thread that loops forever, displaying message boxes when the user selects the Test! menu item. The main thread waits for the child thread to finish by checking the status with the GetExitCodeThread function. The thread exits with the ExitThread function when the user answers YES to the message box question.

```
VOID ThreadProcess()
{
   if ( MessageBox( NULL, "Do you want to exit the thread?",
                    "Exit Thread", MB_YESNO | MB_ICONQUESTION ) == IDYES )
   {
      // Exit the thread.
      //..................
      ExitThread( IDYES );
   }
}


DWORD WINAPI ThreadProc( LPDWORD lpdwData )
{
   // Loop forever..
   //...............
   while( TRUE )
   {
      ThreadProcess();
   }

   return( 0 );
}


LRESULT CALLBACK WndProc( HWND hWnd, UINT uMsg, WPARAM wParam, LPARAM lParam )
{
   switch( uMsg )
   {
      case WM_COMMAND :
              switch( LOWORD( wParam ) )
              {
                 case IDM_TEST:
                         {
                            DWORD dwId;
                            TCHAR szBuffer[128];
                            DWORD dwExitCode = 0;
                            HANDLE hThread = CreateThread( NULL, 0, ThreadProc, NULL, 0, ⇐
&dwId );
```

continued on next page

continued from previous page

```
                        // Wait for thread to exit.
                        //.......................
                        while ( dwExitCode != IDYES )
                        {
                            WaitForSingleObject( hThread, 1000 );
                            GetExitCodeThread( hThread, &dwExitCode );
                        }

                        wsprintf( szBuffer, "Exit code of thread: %lX", dwExitCode );
                        MessageBox( hWnd, szBuffer, "Exit Code", MB_OK |⇐
MB_ICONINFORMATION );
                    }
                    break;
        .
        .
        .
```

GetFiberData   ■ WINDOWS 95 ■ WINDOWS NT

Description	**GetFiberData** returns the fiber data associated with the current fiber. This is the value passed to the **CreateFiber** or **ConvertThreadToFiber** function in the *lpParameter* parameter. This value is also received as the parameter to the fiber function.
Syntax	PVOID **GetFiberData**(VOID)
Parameters	This function has no parameters.
Returns	PVOID: The fiber data for the current fiber.
Include File	winnt.h
See Also	CreateFiber, ConvertThreadToFiber

GetPriorityClass   ■ WINDOWS 95 ■ WINDOWS NT

Description	**GetPriorityClass** returns the priority class of the specified process. The priority of each thread is calculated using the priority class of the process and the priority value of each thread of the process, which is set by calling **SetThreadPriority**. Threads are scheduled round-robin for each priority level. Priority levels are exclusive. Only when all executable threads at all higher levels are satisfied will threads at lower levels be scheduled.
Syntax	DWORD **GetPriorityClass**(HANDLE *hProcess*)
Parameters	
hProcess	HANDLE: Identifies a process object. Under Windows NT, this handle must have PROCESS_QUERY_INFORMATION access.
Returns	DWORD: If successful, the priority class is returned. The valid priority classes are listed in Table 25-8.

Table 25-8 Process priority classes

Priority Class Flag	Meaning
IDLE_PRIORITY_CLASS	Lowest priority task. This runs only when system is idle.
NORMAL_PRIORITY_CLASS	Basic priority for a process.
HIGH_PRIORITY_CLASS	Higher priority task. This highly responsive setting can affect the multitasking nature of the system by not letting other tasks run.
REALTIME_PRIORITY_CLASS	Preempts even operating system actions. Avoid using this priority setting unless the situation is absolutely time-critical.

Include File	`winbase.h`
See Also	`CreateProcess`, `SetThreadPriority`, `GetThreadPriority`, `SetPriorityClass`
Example	This example allows the user to select the priority class of the process. After each selection, the process performs a CPU-intensive function and displays the results, together with the priority class returned from the OS. Figure 25-4 shows some sample results.

```
// Function that wastes CPU time.
//............................
DWORD GoWasteSomeCPU()
{
   long i, j;
   DWORD dwTicksNow = GetTickCount();

   for ( i = 0; i < 100000; i ++ )
      for ( j = 0; j < 1000; j ++ );

   return( GetTickCount() - dwTicksNow );
}


VOID TestResults( HWND hList )
{
   TCHAR szBuffer[128];
   DWORD dwPrCls = GetPriorityClass( GetCurrentProcess() );

   wsprintf( szBuffer, "Priority Class is %s, Time spent: %ld",
                       (dwPrCls == NORMAL_PRIORITY_CLASS ? "NORMAL" :
                       (dwPrCls == REALTIME_PRIORITY_CLASS ? "REALTIME" :
                       (dwPrCls == HIGH_PRIORITY_CLASS ? "HIGH" : "IDLE" ))),
                       GoWasteSomeCPU() );

   SendMessage( hList, LB_INSERTSTRING, (WPARAM)-1, (LPARAM)szBuffer );
}


LRESULT CALLBACK WndProc( HWND hWnd, UINT uMsg, WPARAM wParam, LPARAM lParam )
{
   static HWND hList = NULL;
   static UINT uPriorityClass = 0;
```

continued on next page

continued from previous page

```
    switch( uMsg )
    {
    case WM_CREATE :
            // Create list box.
            //.................
            hList = CreateWindowEx( WS_EX_CLIENTEDGE, "LISTBOX", "",
                                    LBS_STANDARD | LBS_NOINTEGRALHEIGHT |
                                    WS_CHILD | WS_VISIBLE,
                                    0, 0, 10, 10,
                                    hWnd, (HMENU)101,
                                    hInst, NULL );
            break;

    case WM_SIZE :
            if ( wParam != SIZE_MINIMIZED )
                MoveWindow( hList, 0, 0, LOWORD( lParam ), HIWORD( lParam ), TRUE );
            break;

    case WM_INITMENU:
            CheckMenuRadioItem( (HMENU)wParam, IDM_IDLE, IDM_REALTIME,
                                uPriorityClass, MF_BYCOMMAND );
            break;

    case WM_COMMAND :
            switch( LOWORD( wParam ) )
            {
                case IDM_IDLE:
                case IDM_NORMAL:
                case IDM_HIGH:
                case IDM_REALTIME:
                        uPriorityClass = LOWORD( wParam );
                        SetPriorityClass( GetCurrentProcess(),
                                (uPriorityClass == IDM_IDLE ? IDLE_PRIORITY_CLASS :
                                (uPriorityClass == IDM_NORMAL ? NORMAL_PRIORITY_CLASS :
                                (uPriorityClass == IDM_HIGH ? HIGH_PRIORITY_CLASS :
                                                    REALTIME_PRIORITY_CLASS))) );

                        TestResults( hList );
                        break;
                .
                .
                .
```

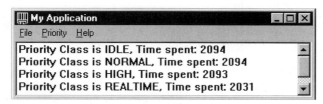

Figure 25-4   GetPriorityClass example

GetProcessAffinityMask ■ Windows 95 ■ Windows NT

Description GetProcessAffinityMask retrieves the process affinity mask for the specified process and the system affinity mask for the system. A process affinity mask is a bit vector in which each bit represents the processors that a process is allowed to run on. A system affinity mask is a bit vector in which each bit represents the processors that are configured on the system. A process is only allowed to run on the processors configured on the system.

Syntax BOOL **GetProcessAffinityMask**(HANDLE *hProcess,* LPDWORD *lpProcessAffinityMask,* LPDWORD *lpSystemAffinityMask*)

Parameters

hProcess HANDLE: An open handle to the process whose affinity mask is to be retrieved. This handle must have the PROCESS_QUERY_INFORMATION access on Windows NT.

lpProcessAffinityMask LPDWORD: A pointer to a DWORD that receives the process affinity mask.

lpSystemAffinityMask LPDWORD: A pointer to a DWORD that receives the system affinity mask.

Returns BOOL: If successful, TRUE is returned; otherwise FALSE is returned. On Windows 95, both affinity masks are set to a value of 1.

Include File winbase.h

See Also SetProcessAffinityMask, SetThreadAffinityMask

GetProcessHeap ■ Windows 95 ■ Windows NT

Description GetProcessHeap returns a handle to the default process heap. This handle can be used to allocate memory from the process heap using HeapAlloc.

Syntax HANDLE **GetProcessHeap**(VOID)

Parameters This function has no parameters.

Returns HANDLE: If successful, the handle of the process's default heap is returned; otherwise, NULL is returned.

Include File winbase.h

See Also HeapAlloc, GetProcessHeaps

Example This example allocates a string to receive a greeting message, which is then output to the screen in a message box when the user selects the Test! menu item.

```
LRESULT CALLBACK WndProc( HWND hWnd, UINT uMsg, WPARAM wParam, LPARAM lParam )
{
   switch( uMsg )
   {
```

continued on next page

continued from previous page

```
      case WM_COMMAND :
            switch( LOWORD( wParam ) )
            {
                case IDM_TEST:
                    {
                        // Allocate space for message.
                        //............................
                        LPVOID lpText = HeapAlloc( GetProcessHeap(), 0, 32 );

                        wsprintf( lpText, "The Heap Address is %lX", lpText );
                        MessageBox( hWnd, lpText, "GetProcessHeap()", MB_OK );

                        HeapFree( GetProcessHeap(), 0, lpText );
                    }
                    break;
```

```
                .
                .
                .
```

GetProcessHeaps   ■ Windows 95 ■ Windows NT

Description	GetProcessHeaps returns the handle to the default process heap and all other heaps owned by the calling process.
Syntax	DWORD **GetProcessHeaps**(DWORD *dwNumberOfHeaps,* PHANDLE *pProcessHeaps*)
Parameters	
dwNumberOfHeaps	DWORD: The maximum number of heap handles that can be returned in the array of handles pointed to by the *pProcessHeaps* parameter.
pProcessHeaps	PHANDLE: A pointer to a buffer that receives an array of heap handles.
Returns	DWORD: The number of valid heap handles returned in the buffer pointed to by *pProcessHeaps* is returned. If the return value is greater than *dwNumberOfHeaps*, no handles are returned and the return value indicates the number of valid heap handles of the calling process. Zero is returned if an error occurs.
Include File	winbase.h
See Also	GetProcessHeap, HeapAlloc

GetProcessPriorityBoost   ■ Windows 95 ■ Windows NT

Description	GetProcessPriorityBoost retrieves the priority boost control state of the specified process.
Syntax	BOOL **GetProcessPriorityBoost**(HANDLE *hProcess,* PBOOL *pDisablePriorityBoost*)

Parameters

hProcess	**HANDLE**: A handle to the process. The handle must have **PROCESS_QUERY_INFORMATION** access right under Windows NT.
pDisablePriorityBoost	**PBOOL**: A pointer to a Boolean variable that receives the priority boost control state. A value of **TRUE** indicates that dynamic boosting is disabled. A value of **FALSE** indicates normal behavior.
Returns	**BOOL**: If successful, **TRUE** is returned; otherwise, **FALSE** is returned. Use the **GetLastError** function to retrieve extended error information.
Include File	winbase.h
See Also	SetProcessPriorityBoost

GetProcessShutdownParameters ■ WINDOWS 95 ■ WINDOWS NT

Description	**GetProcessShutdownParameters** retrieves shutdown parameters for the calling process.
Syntax	BOOL **GetProcessShutdownParameters**(LPDWORD *lpdwLevel,* LPDWORD *lpdwFlags*)

Parameters

lpdwLevel	**LPDWORD**: A pointer to a variable that receives the shutdown priority level. Higher levels shut down first. System level shutdown orders are reserved for system components. Table 25-9 lists the level conventions. All processes start at shutdown level 0x280.

Table 25-9 GetProcessShutdownParameters *lpdwLevel* values

Value	Meaning
000–0FF	System-reserved last shutdown range.
100–1FF	Application-reserved last shutdown range.
200–2FF	Application-reserved "in between" shutdown range.
300–3FF	Application-reserved first shutdown range.
400–4FF	System-reserved first shutdown range.

lpdwFlags	**LPDWORD**: A pointer to a variable that receives the shutdown flags. It can be set to **SHUTDOWN_NORETRY**, which indicates that the system will not show a retry dialog box for the user if this process takes longer than the specified time-out to shut down. Instead the process is directly exited.
Returns	**BOOL**: If successful, **TRUE** is returned; otherwise, **FALSE** is returned.
Include File	winbase.h
See Also	SetProcessShutdownParameters

GetProcessTimes   ■ Windows 95   ■ Windows NT

Description	`GetProcessTimes` retrieves timing information about a specified process. All times are expressed using **FILETIME** data structures. For a definition of this structure, see the **CompareFileTime** function in Chapter 17, I/O with Files. Process creation and exit times are points in time expressed as the amount of time that has elapsed since midnight on January 1, 1601, GMT. Use the Win32 API functions to convert such values to more useful forms. Process kernel mode and user mode times are amounts of time elapsed.
Syntax	BOOL **GetProcessTimes**(HANDLE *hProcess,* LPFILETIME *lpCreationTime,* LPFILETIME *lpExitTime,* LPFILETIME *lpKernelTime,* LPFILETIME *lpUserTime*)
Parameters	
hProcess	HANDLE: An open handle that specifies the process whose timing information is retrieved. This handle must be created with PROCESS_QUERY_INFORMATION access.
lpCreationTime	LPFILETIME: A pointer to a **FILETIME** structure that receives the creation time of the process.
lpExitTime	LPFILETIME: A pointer to a **FILETIME** structure that receives the exit time of the process. If the process has not exited, the content of this structure is undefined.
lpKernelTime	LPFILETIME: A pointer to a **FILETIME** structure that receives the amount of time that the process has executed in kernel mode. This is the sum of the time that each thread owned by the process has spent in kernel mode.
lpUserTime	LPFILETIME: A pointer to a **FILETIME** structure that receives the amount of time that the process has executed in user mode. This is the sum of the time that each thread owned by the process has spent in user mode.
Returns	BOOL: If successful, **TRUE** is returned; otherwise, **FALSE** is returned. Use the **GetLastError** function to retrieve extended error information.
Include File	`winbase.h`
See Also	`FileTimeToDosDateTime`, `FileTimeToLocalFileTime`, `FileTimeToSystemTime`

GetProcessVersion   ■ Windows 95   ■ Windows NT

Description	`GetProcessVersion` retrieves the major and minor version numbers of the Windows version on which a specified process expects to run. The version number returned by this function is the version number stamped in the image header of the EXE file the process is running.
Syntax	DWORD **GetProcessVersion**(DWORD *ProcessId*)

Parameters

ProcessId   `DWORD`: The process identifier of the process for which to retrieve the version information. If set to `0`, the calling process is used.

Returns   `DWORD`: If successful, the version of Windows on which the process expects to run is returned. The high word of the return value contains the major version number. The low word of the return value contains the minor version number. If an error occurs, `0` is returned. Use the `GetLastError` to retrieve extended error information.

Include File   `winbase.h`

See Also   `GetProcessWorkingSetSize`

GetProcessWorkingSetSize ■ WINDOWS 95 ■ WINDOWS NT

Description   `GetProcessWorkingSetSize` retrieves the minimum and maximum *working set* sizes, in bytes, of a specified process. The working set of a process is the set of memory pages currently visible to the process in physical RAM memory. These sizes affect the virtual memory paging behavior of a process.

Syntax   `BOOL` **GetProcessWorkingSetSize(** `HANDLE` *hProcess,* `LPDWORD` *lpMinWorkingSetSize,* `LPDWORD` *lpMaxWorkingSetSize* **)**

Parameters

hProcess   `HANDLE`: An open handle to the process for which to retrieve the working set sizes. The handle must have the `PROCESS_QUERY_INFORMATION` access rights.

lpMinWorkingSetSize   `LPDWORD`: A pointer to a variable that receives the minimum working set size, in bytes, of the specified process. The virtual memory manager attempts to keep at least this much memory resident in the process whenever the process is active.

lpMaxWorkingSetSize   `LPDWORD`: A pointer to a variable that receives the maximum working set size, in bytes, of the specified process. The virtual memory manager attempts to keep no more than this much memory resident in the process whenever the process is active when memory is in short supply.

Returns   `BOOL`: If successful, `TRUE` is returned; otherwise, `FALSE` is returned. Use the `GetLastError` function to retrieve extended error information.

Include File   `winbase.h`

See Also   `SetProcessWorkingSetSize`

GetQueueStatus

Description	GetQueueStatus returns the status of the calling thread's message queue. The status indicates the type of messages found in the queue. The presence of a QS_ flag in the return value does not guarantee that a subsequent call to the PeekMessage or GetMessage function will return a message. These functions perform some internal filtering that may cause the message to be processed internally.
Syntax	DWORD **GetQueueStatus**(UINT *uFlags*)
Parameters	
uFlags	UINT: Indicates the type of messages to check for. This can be one or more of the values listed in Table 25-10.

Table 25-10 Queue status types

Value	Meaning
QS_ALLEVENTS	An input message, WM_TIMER, WM_PAINT, WM_HOTKEY, or posted message is in the queue.
QS_ALLINPUT	Any message is in the queue.
QS_HOTKEY	A WM_HOTKEY message is in the queue.
QS_INPUT	An input message is in the queue. QS_KEY or QS_MOUSE.
QS_KEY	A WM_KEYUP, WM_KEYDOWN, WM_SYSKEYUP, or WM_SYSKEYDOWN message is in the queue.
QS_MOUSE	A WM_MOUSEMOVE or mouse-button message, QS_MOUSEBUTTON.
QS_MOUSEBUTTON	A mouse-button message (WM_LBUTTONUP, WM_RBUTTONDOWN, WM_LBUTTONDBLCLK).
QS_MOUSEMOVE	A WM_MOUSEMOVE message is in the queue.
QS_PAINT	A WM_PAINT message is in the queue.
QS_POSTMESSAGE	A posted message (other than an input message) is in the queue.
QS_SENDMESSAGE	A message sent by another thread or application is in the queue.
QS_TIMER	A WM_TIMER message is in the queue.

Returns	DWORD: The high word indicates the types of messages currently in the queue. The low-order word indicates the types of messages that have been added to the queue and that are still in the queue since the last call to the GetQueueStatus, GetMessage, or PeekMessage function.
Include File	winbase.h
See Also	GetMessage, PeekMessage, SendMessage, PostMessage
Example	This example sleeps for five seconds when the user selects the Test! menu item. This allows the user to generate events that are posted to the message queue. The status of the queue is displayed for the user to view.

```
LRESULT CALLBACK WndProc( HWND hWnd, UINT uMsg, WPARAM wParam, LPARAM lParam )
{
   switch( uMsg )
   {
      case WM_COMMAND :
              switch( LOWORD( wParam ) )
              {
                 case IDM_TEST:
                        {
                           TCHAR szBuffer[128];
                           HDC hDC = GetDC( hWnd );

                           // Pause five seconds to fill queue.
                           //................................
                           TextOut( hDC, 0, 0, szBuffer, wsprintf(szBuffer, "%s", "DO INPUT"⇐
));

                           Sleep( 5000 );

                           // check queue for keyboard input.
                           //................................
                           wsprintf( szBuffer, "Queue Status - QS KEY - %x ",
                                   HIWORD( GetQueueStatus( QS_KEY ) ) );
                           TextOut( hDC, 0, 20, szBuffer, lstrlen( szBuffer ) );

                           // check queue for any mouse input.
                           //................................
                           wsprintf( szBuffer, "Queue Status - QS MOUSE - %x ",
                                   HIWORD( GetQueueStatus( QS_MOUSE ) ) );
                           TextOut( hDC, 0, 40, szBuffer, lstrlen( szBuffer ) );

                           ReleaseDC( hWnd, hDC );
                        }
                        break;
                 .
                 .
                 .
```

GetThreadContext   ■ WINDOWS 95   ■ WINDOWS NT

Description   GetThreadContext returns the execution context of the specified thread.
                    This function allows a selective context to be retrieved based on the value
                    of the *ContextFlags* member of the **CONTEXT** structure. Use the
                    SuspendThread function to suspend the thread before calling the
                    GetThreadContext function for running threads.

Syntax   BOOL **GetThreadContext**(HANDLE *hThread,* LPCONTEXT *lpContext*)

Parameters

hThread   HANDLE: The thread object whose context is to be returned. On Windows
                    NT, this handle must have **THREAD_GET_CONTEXT** access.

lpContext	LPCONTEXT: A pointer to address of a CONTEXT structure that receives the appropriate context of the specified thread. The CONTEXT structure is highly computer specific. Currently, there are CONTEXT structures defined for Intel, MIPS, Alpha, and PowerPC processors. Refer to the WINNT.H header file for definitions of these structures.
Returns	BOOL: If successful, TRUE is returned; otherwise, FALSE is returned. Use GetLastError to return extended error information.
Include File	winbase.h
See Also	SetThreadContext, SuspendThread, CreateThread
Example	This example shows the thread context at the time the user chooses the Test! menu item.

```
LRESULT CALLBACK WndProc( HWND hWnd, UINT uMsg, WPARAM wParam, LPARAM lParam )
{
   switch( uMsg )
   {
     case WM_COMMAND :
            switch( LOWORD( wParam ) )
            {
               case IDM_TEST:
                   {
                       CONTEXT context;
                       TCHAR szBuffer[128];

                       context.ContextFlags = CONTEXT_FULL | CONTEXT_DEBUG_REGISTERS;
                       GetThreadContext( GetCurrentThread(), &context );

                       wsprintf( szBuffer, "CS=%X, EIP=%X, FLAGS=%X, DR1=%X",
                               context.SegCs, context.Eip, context.EFlags, context.Dr1⇐
);
                       MessageBox( hWnd, szBuffer, "Selected Values of Thread Context",⇐
MB_OK );
                   }
                   break;

                   .
                   .
                   .
```

GetThreadPriority ■ WINDOWS 95 ■ WINDOWS NT

Description	GetThreadPriority returns the assigned thread priority level for the specified thread. The priority value of the thread and the process priority class determine the thread's base priority level.
Syntax	int **GetThreadPriority**(HANDLE *hThread*)
Parameters	
hThread	HANDLE: Identifies the thread object whose priority is being queried. On Windows NT, the thread object must have THREAD_QUERY_INFORMATION access.

Returns	`int`: If the function succeeds, the thread's priority level, listed in Table 25-11, is returned; otherwise, it returns `THREAD_PRIORITY_ERROR_RETURN`. Use `GetLastError` to return extended error information.

Table 25-11 Thread base priority levels

Priority	Meaning
THREAD_PRIORITY_ABOVE_NORMAL	Indicates one point greater than normal for priority class.
THREAD_PRIORITY_BELOW_NORMAL	Indicates one point less than normal for priority class.
THREAD_PRIORITY_HIGHEST	Indicates two points greater than normal for priority class.
THREAD_PRIORITY_IDLE	For REALTIME_PRIORITY_CLASS: base priority of 16. All other priority classes: base priority is 1.
THREAD_PRIORITY_LOWEST	Indicates two points less than normal for priority class.
THREAD_PRIORITY_NORMAL	Indicates normal priority for the priority class.
THREAD_PRIORITY_TIME_CRITICAL	For REALTIME_PRIORITY_CLASS: base priority of 31. All other priority classes: base priority is 15.

Include File	`winbase.h`
See Also	`CreateThread`, `GetPriorityClass`, `SetPriorityClass`, `SetThreadPriority`
Example	This example shows how thread priority affects the processing of the system. Choosing one of the five priority options changes the priority and executes a test. When the test completes, the priority and results are displayed to the screen.

```
// Function that wastes CPU time.
//.............................
DWORD GoWasteSomeCPU()
{
    long i, j;
    DWORD dwTicksNow = GetTickCount();

    for ( i = 0; i < 100000; i ++ )
       for ( j = 0; j < 1000; j ++ );

    return( GetTickCount() - dwTicksNow );
}


VOID TestResults( HWND hList )
{
    TCHAR szBuffer[128];
    int   nThrPri = GetThreadPriority( GetCurrentThread() );

    wsprintf( szBuffer, "Priority for Thread %lX is %s, Test Speed: %ld",
                     GetCurrentThreadId(),
                     (nThrPri == THREAD_PRIORITY_LOWEST ? "LOWEST" :
```

continued on next page

continued from previous page

```
                              (nThrPri == THREAD_PRIORITY_BELOW_NORMAL ? "LOW" :
                              (nThrPri == THREAD_PRIORITY_NORMAL ? "NORMAL" :
                              (nThrPri == THREAD_PRIORITY_ABOVE_NORMAL ? "HIGH" :
                                                                        "BEST" )))),
                          GoWasteSomeCPU() );

    SendMessage( hList, LB_INSERTSTRING, (WPARAM)-1, (LPARAM)szBuffer );
}


LRESULT CALLBACK WndProc( HWND hWnd, UINT uMsg, WPARAM wParam, LPARAM lParam )
{
    static HWND hList = NULL;
    static UINT uPriority = 0;

    switch( uMsg )
    {
    case WM_COMMAND :
            switch( LOWORD( wParam ) )
            {
                case IDM_WORST:
                case IDM_LOW:
                case IDM_NORMAL:
                case IDM_HIGH:
                case IDM_BEST:
                        uPriority = LOWORD( wParam );
                        SetThreadPriority( GetCurrentThread(),
                                (uPriority == IDM_WORST ?   THREAD_PRIORITY_LOWEST :
                                (uPriority == IDM_LOW ?     THREAD_PRIORITY_BELOW_NORMAL  :
                                (uPriority == IDM_NORMAL ? THREAD_PRIORITY_NORMAL   :
                                (uPriority == IDM_HIGH ?    THREAD_PRIORITY_ABOVE_NORMAL :
                                                            THREAD_PRIORITY_HIGHEST)))) );

                        TestResults( hList );
                        break;
                  .
                  .
                  .
```

GetThreadPriorityBoost ■ Windows 95 ■ Windows NT

Description	GetThreadPriorityBoost retrieves the priority boost control state of the specified thread.
Syntax	BOOL **GetThreadPriorityBoost**(HANDLE *hThread,* PBOOL *pDisablePriorityBoost*)
Parameters	
hThread	HANDLE: A handle to the thread. The thread handle must have THREAD_QUERY_INFORMATION access.
pDisablePriorityBoost	PBOOL: A pointer to a Boolean variable that receives the priority boost control state. A value of TRUE indicates that dynamic boosting is disabled.

Returns	BOOL: If successful, **TRUE** is returned; otherwise, **FALSE** is returned. Use the **GetLastError** function to retrieve extended error information.
Include File	winbase.h
See Also	SetThreadPriorityBoost

GetThreadSelectorEntry   ■ WINDOWS 95   ■ WINDOWS NT

Description	**GetThreadSelectorEntry** returns an LDT (local descriptor table) for the specified selector and thread. The LDT entry converts a segment-relative address to a linear address: a combination of the page table (10 high bits), the page (10 middle bits), and offset within the 4K page (12 low bits). This function only works on x86-based systems. Debuggers use this function to convert segment-relative addresses to linear virtual addresses.
Syntax	BOOL **GetThreadSelectorEntry**(HANDLE *hThread,* DWORD *dwSelector,* LPLDT_ENTRY *lpLDTEntry*)
Parameters	
hThread	HANDLE: The handle of the thread object containing the specified selector. The handle must have **THREAD_QUERY_INFORMATION** access.
dwSelector	DWORD: The global or local selector value to look up in the thread's descriptor table.
lpLDTEntry	LPLDT_ENTRY: A pointer to an **LDT_ENTRY** structure that receives the local descriptor table entry for the selector. See the definition of the **LDT_ENTRY** structure below.
Returns	BOOL: For Windows 95, **TRUE** if the selector is valid, **FALSE** if the selector is invalid. Use **GetLastError** to return the error code.
Include File	winbase.h
See Also	ReadProcessMemory, WriteProcessMemory

LDT_ENTRY Definition

```
typedef struct _LDT_ENTRY
{
    WORD LimitLow;
    WORD BaseLow;
    union
    {
        struct
        {
            BYTE BaseMid;
            BYTE Flags1;
            BYTE Flags2;
            BYTE BaseHi;
        } Bytes;
        struct
        {
```

continued on next page

1315

continued from previous page

```
                         DWORD BaseMid : 8;
                         DWORD Type : 5;
                         DWORD Dpl : 2;
                         DWORD Pres : 1;
                         DWORD LimitHi : 4;
                         DWORD Sys : 1;
                         DWORD Reserved_0 : 1;
                         DWORD Default_Big : 1;
                         DWORD Granularity : 1;
                         DWORD BaseHi : 8;
                     } Bits;
                 } HighWord;
             } LDT_ENTRY, *PLDT_ENTRY;
```

Members

LimitLow   WORD: The low 16 bits of the address of the last byte in the segment.

BaseLow   WORD: The low 16 bits of the base address of the segment.

BaseMid   BYTE: Middle bits (16–23) of the base address of the segment.

Flags1   BYTE: Values from the *Type*, *Dpl*, and *Pres* members in the **Bits** structure.

Flags2   BYTE: Values of the *LimitHi*, *Sys*, *Reserved_0*, *Default_Big*, and *Granularity* members in the **Bits** structure.

Type   DWORD:5: A bit mask that indicates the type of segment. This can be one of the values listed in Table 25-12.

Table 25-12 Segment types

Value	Meaning
0	Read-only data segment
1	Read-write data segment
2	Unused segment
3	Read-write expand-down data segment
4	Execute-only code segment
5	Executable-readable code segment
6	Execute-only "conforming" code segment
7	Executable-readable "conforming" code segment

Dpl   DWORD:2: The privilege level of the descriptor. This member is an integer value in the range 0 (most privileged) through 3 (least privileged).

Pres   DWORD:1: Present flag. This member is set to 1 if the segment is present in physical memory or 0 if it is not.

LimitHi   DWORD:4: The high bits (16–19) of the address of the last byte in the segment.

Sys	**DWORD:1**: The space that is available to system programmers. This member might be used for marking segments in some system-specific way.
Reserved_0	**DWORD:1**: Reserved.
Default_Big	**DWORD:1**: The size of segment. If the segment is a data segment, this member contains **1** if the segment is larger than 64KB or **0** if the segment is smaller than or equal to 64KB. If the segment is a code segment, this member is set to **1** if the segment is a code segment and runs with the default (native mode) instruction set. This member contains **0** if the code segment is an 80286 code segment and runs with 16-bit offsets and the 80286-compatible instruction set.
Granularity	**DWORD:1**: The granularity. This member contains **0** if the segment is byte granular, **1** if the segment is page granular.
BaseHi	**BYTE**: High bits (24–31) of the base address of the segment.
Example	This example returns a thread selector entry for the default data selector DS when the user selects the Test! menu item. The results are displayed to the user.

```
LRESULT CALLBACK WndProc( HWND hWnd, UINT uMsg, WPARAM wParam, LPARAM lParam )
{
   switch( uMsg )
   {
      case WM_COMMAND :
             switch( LOWORD( wParam ) )
             {
                case IDM_TEST:
                     {
                        TCHAR     szBuffer[128];
                        DWORD     dwBaseAddr;
                        LDT_ENTRY ldtEntry;
                        CONTEXT   context;

                        context.ContextFlags = CONTEXT_FULL;

                        GetThreadContext( GetCurrentThread(), &context );
                        GetThreadSelectorEntry( GetCurrentThread(),
                                     context.SegDs,
                                     &ldtEntry );

                        dwBaseAddr = ldtEntry.BaseLow +
                              (DWORD) ldtEntry.HighWord.Bits.BaseMid << 8 +
                              (DWORD) ldtEntry.HighWord.Bits.BaseHi << 16;

                        wsprintf( szBuffer,
                              "LDT entry for %lX. Base = %lX, Type = %X, Priv = %X ",
                              context.SegDs, dwBaseAddr, ldtEntry.HighWord.Bits.Type,
                              ldtEntry.HighWord.Bits.Dpl );

                        MessageBox( hWnd, szBuffer, "Thread Selector Entry", MB_OK );
                     }
                     break;
```

.
.
.

GetThreadTimes ■ WINDOWS 95 ■ WINDOWS NT

Description	GetThreadTimes retrieves timing information about a specified thread. All times are returned in FILETIME data structures. For a definition of this structure, see the CompareFileTime function in Chapter 17, I/O with Files. Thread creation and exit times are points in time expressed as the amount of time that has elapsed since midnight on January 1, 1601, GMT. Use the Win32 API functions to convert such values to more generally useful forms. The thread kernel mode and user mode times are amounts of time.
Syntax	BOOL **GetThreadTimes**(HANDLE *hThread,* LPFILETIME *lpCreationTime,* LPFILETIME *lpExitTime,* LPFILETIME *lpKernelTime,* LPFILETIME *lpUserTime*)
Parameters	
hThread	HANDLE: An open handle to the thread for which to retrieve timing information. This handle must have THREAD_QUERY_INFORMATION access.
lpCreationTime	LPFILETIME: A pointer to a FILETIME structure that receives the creation time of the thread.
lpExitTime	LPFILETIME: A pointer to a FILETIME structure that receives the exit time of the thread.
lpKernelTime	LPFILETIME: A pointer to a FILETIME structure that receives the amount of time the thread has executed in kernel mode.
lpUserTime	LPFILETIME: A pointer to a FILETIME structure that receives the amount of time the thread has executed in user mode.
Returns	BOOL: If successful, TRUE is returned; otherwise, FALSE is returned. Use the GetLastError function to retrieve extended error information.
Include File	winbase.h
See Also	GetProcessTimes, FileTimeToDosDateTime, FileTimeToLocalFileTime, FileTimeToSystemTime

InitializeCriticalSection ■ WINDOWS 95 ■ WINDOWS NT

Description	InitializeCriticalSection sets up a critical section object. This function must be called before EnterCriticalSection is executed. The threads of a single process can use a critical section object for mutual-exclusion synchronization. The process is responsible for allocating the memory used by a critical section object, which it can do by declaring a variable of type CRITICAL_SECTION. Once a critical section is initialized, use the EnterCriticalSection, TryEnterCriticalSection, and LeaveCriticalSection functions.
Syntax	VOID **InitializeCriticalSection**(LPCRITICAL_SECTION *lpCriticalSection*)

Parameters

lpCriticalSection LPCRITICAL_SECTION: A pointer to a critical section object to be initialized.

Include File `winbase.h`

See Also `EnterCriticalSection`, `LeaveCriticalSection`, `TryEnterCriticalSection`, `DeleteCriticalSection`

Example See the example for `EnterCriticalSection`.

InterlockedCompareExchange ■ WINDOWS 95 ■ WINDOWS NT

Description `InterlockedCompareExchange` prevents more than one thread from using the same variable simultaneously. It performs an atomic comparison of the values specified in the *pDestination* and *pComperand* parameters and exchange of the values, based on the outcome of the comparison. If the *pDestination* value is equal to the *pComperand* value, the *pExchange* value is stored in the address specified by *pDestination*; otherwise, no operation is performed.

The `InterlockedCompareExchange`, `InterlockedDecrement`, `InterlockedExhange`, `InterlockedExchangeAdd`, and `InterlockedIncrement` functions provide a simple mechanism for synchronizing access to a variable that is shared by multiple threads.

Syntax PVOID **InterlockedCompareExchange**(PVOID* *pDestination,* PVOID *pExchange,* PVOID *pComperand*)

Parameters

pDestination PVOID*: The address of the destination value.

pExchange PVOID: The exchange value.

pComperand PVOID: The value to compare to *pDestination*.

Returns PVOID: If successful, the initial value of the destination is returned.

Include File `winbase.h`

See Also `InterlockedDecrement`, `InterlockedExchange`, `InterlockedExchangeAdd`, `InterlockedIncrement`

InterlockedDecrement ■ WINDOWS 95 ■ WINDOWS NT

Description `InterlockedDecrement` decrements the interlocked 32-bit long variable and checks the resulting value. An interlocked variable is kept synchronized by the system.

Syntax LONG **InterlockedDecrement**(LPLONG *lpLongVal*)

Parameters

lpLongVal LPLONG: A pointer to the interlocked variable to decrement.

Returns	LONG: If the result of the operation is **0**, the return value is **0**. If the result is less than zero, the value returned will be less than zero, but not necessarily the value of the interlocked long. If the result is greater than zero, the value returned will be greater than zero, but not necessarily the value of the interlocked long.
Include File	`winbase.h`
See Also	`CreateFileMapping`, `InterlockedExchange`, `InterlockedIncrement`
Example	This example uses shared memory and a simple interlocked long. Run multiple instances of the example and choose to increment, decrement, or exchange with the value for each process. The exchanged value is the handle of the main window of each process.

```
LRESULT CALLBACK WndProc( HWND hWnd, UINT uMsg, WPARAM wParam, LPARAM lParam )
{
    static HANDLE   hMap = 0;
    static LONG*    lpData = NULL;
    static TCHAR    szOperation[128];

    switch( uMsg )
    {
    case WM_CREATE:
            // Create file-mapping object.
            hMap = CreateFileMapping( (HANDLE) 0xFFFFFFFF, NULL,
                                PAGE_READWRITE, 0, 4096,
                                "SHARED_VALUE");

            lpData = (LONG*) MapViewOfFile( hMap, FILE_MAP_ALL_ACCESS,
                                0, 0, 4 );
            break;

    case WM_COMMAND :
            szOperation[0] = 0;

            switch( LOWORD( wParam ) )
            {
                case IDM_INC:
                        InterlockedIncrement( lpData );
                        lstrcpy( szOperation, "Increment" );
                        break;

                case IDM_DEC:
                        InterlockedDecrement( lpData );
                        lstrcpy( szOperation, "Decrement" );
                        break;

                case IDM_EXC:
                        InterlockedExchange( lpData, (LONG)hWnd );
                        lstrcpy( szOperation, "Exchange" );
                        break;

                case IDM_EXIT :
                        DestroyWindow( hWnd );
                        break;
            }
```

```
if ( szOperation[0] )
{
    TCHAR szBuffer[128];

    wsprintf( szBuffer, "Interlocked Value: %ld", *lpData );
    MessageBox( hWnd, szBuffer, szOperation, MB_OK );
}
break;
```

.
.
.

InterlockedExchange ■ WINDOWS 95 ■ WINDOWS NT

Description	InterLockedExchange swaps the interlocked 32-bit variable for another long value and checks the resulting value. An interlocked variable is kept synchronized by the system.
Syntax	LONG **InterlockedExchange**(LPLONG *lpLongVal,* LONG *lNewVal*)
Parameters	
lpLongVal	LPLONG: A pointer to the interlocked variable to exchange.
lNewVal	LONG: The value to be stored in the interlocked variable.
Returns	LONG: The prior value pointed to by *lpLongVal* is returned.
Include File	winbase.h
See Also	CreateFileMapping, InterlockedDecrement, InterlockedIncrement
Example	See the example for the InterlockedDecrement function.

InterlockedExchangeAdd ■ WINDOWS 95 ■ WINDOWS NT

Description	InterlockedExchangeAdd performs an atomic addition of an increment value to a specified variable.
Syntax	LONG **InterlockedExchangeAdd**(PLONG *pAddend,* LONG *lIncrement*)
Parameters	
pAddend	PLONG: The address of the number that will have the *lIncrement* number added to it.
lIncrement	LONG: The number to be added to the variable pointed to by the *pAddend* parameter.
Returns	LONG: The initial value of the *pAddend* parameter is returned.
Include File	winbase.h
See Also	InterlockedCompareExchange, InterlockedDecrement, InterlockedExchange, InterlockedIncrement

InterlockedIncrement ■ Windows 95 ■ Windows NT

Description	**InterlockedIncrement** adds one to the interlocked 32-bit long variable and checks the resulting value.
Syntax	LONG **InterlockedIncrement**(LPLONG *lpLongValue*)
Parameters	
lpLongValue	LPLONG: A pointer to the interlocked variable to increment.
Returns	LONG: If the result of the operation is **0**, the return value is **0**. If the result is less than zero, the value returned will be less than zero, but not necessarily the value of the interlocked long. If the result is greater than zero, the value returned will be greater than zero, but not necessarily the value of the interlocked long.
Include File	winbase.h
See Also	CreateFileMapping, InterlockedDecrement, InterlockedExchange
Example	See the example for the **InterlockedDecrement** function.

LeaveCriticalSection ■ Windows 95 ■ Windows NT

Description	**LeaveCriticalSection** relinquishes ownership of a critical section object. Ownership must be released by calling the **LeaveCriticalSection** function as many times as the owning thread executes **EnterCriticalSection** for the same object.
Syntax	VOID **LeaveCriticalSection**(LPCRITICAL_SECTION *lpcsCriticalSection*)
Parameters	
lpcsCriticalSection	LPCRITICAL_SECTION: A pointer to the critical section object used with the corresponding call to **EnterCriticalSection** or **TryEnterCriticalSection**.
Include File	winbase.h
See Also	CreateMutex, DeleteCriticalSection, InitializeCritical Section, EnterCriticalSection, TryEnterCriticalSection
Example	See the example for the **EnterCriticalSection** function.

MsgWaitForMultipleObjects ■ Windows 95 ■ Windows NT

Description	**MsgWaitForMultipleObjects** suspends a thread until any or all of the specified objects become signaled, a specified input type appears in the thread's input queue, or a time-out occurs. Preexisting input on the input queue does not make the function return immediately. The function waits for new input.

Syntax	DWORD **MsgWaitForMultipleObjects**(DWORD *dwObjectCount,* LPHANDLE *lpObjectHandles,* BOOL *bWaitAll,* DWORD *dwTimeout,* DWORD *dwInputWakeMask*)
Parameters	
dwObjectCount	DWORD: The number of objects specified in the *lpObjectHandles* array. The maximum number of object handles is **MAXIMUM_WAIT_OBJECTS**−1.
lpObjectHandles	LPHANDLE: A pointer to a list of object handles with **SYNCHRONIZE** access for which this function will wait to become signaled.
bWaitAll	BOOL: If **TRUE**, all objects in the list *lpObjectHandles* must become signaled for the function to exit. If **FALSE**, the function is satisfied if only one of the objects reaches the signaled state.
dwTimeout	DWORD: The time-out interval, in milliseconds. If *dwTimeout* is **0**, the function tests the states of the objects and returns immediately. If *dwTimeout* is **INFINITE**, the function will wait forever or until the condition is satisfied.
dwInputWakeMask	DWORD: Input queue status that will satisfy the wait function. This can be any combination of the flags described in Table 25-10 under the **GetQueueStatus** function description.
Returns	DWORD: If successful, the return value is the event that caused the function to return. For a wait object that satisfies the condition, the system returns **WAIT_OBJECT_0** plus the index into the array *lpObjectHandles* to the member that satisfies the condition. If the function fails, **0xFFFFFFFF** is returned and **GetLastError** will return the error code. **WAIT_TIMEOUT** indicates that the function timed out before returning.
Include File	winbase.h

> **NOTE**
> The ownership of the objects does not change until the thread owns all the objects in the list if *bWaitAll* is TRUE. A mutex that was available may not become owned, because another thread may gain ownership while the waiting thread waits for all the objects in the list.

See Also	WaitForSingleObject, WaitForMultipleObjects
Example	This example creates a thread that prints a message and waits for a signaled event or a mouse button message when the user selects the Test! menu item. The **"Pulse Event"** option uses the **PulseEvent** API call to quickly signal the event to release all waiting threads and then sets it to the nonsignaled state again. Figure 25-5 shows output of the example.

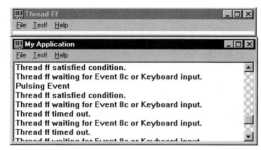

Figure 25-5 `MsgWaitForMultipleObjects` example

```
LPCTSTR lpszPulseEvent = "PULSE_EVENT";

DWORD WINAPI ChildThreadProc( LPDWORD lpdwData )
{
    HWND    hThreadWnd;     // Handle of window for this thread.
    HANDLE  hEvent;         // Handle to event.
    TCHAR   szBuffer[128];  // General work area for string formatting.
    HWND    hList = (HWND)lpdwData;

    wsprintf( szBuffer, "Thread %lX", GetCurrentThreadId() );
    hThreadWnd = CreateWindow( lpszAppName, szBuffer, WS_OVERLAPPEDWINDOW, 0, 0,
                               100, 100, (HWND)NULL, NULL, hInst, (LPTSTR)NULL );
    if (!hThreadWnd)
        return( 1 );

    // Display the window and open the pulse event.
    //..............................................
    ShowWindow( hThreadWnd, SW_SHOWNORMAL );
    UpdateWindow( hThreadWnd );

    hEvent = OpenEvent( SYNCHRONIZE, FALSE, lpszPulseEvent );

    // Loop forever going into and out of wait state.
    //..............................................
    while( TRUE )
    {
        MSG    msg;
        DWORD  dwTest;

        // Use a PeekMessage() loop so it will NOT wait for
        // the next message to be placed in the queue.
        //..............................................
        while( PeekMessage( &msg, 0, 0, 0, PM_REMOVE )  )
        {
            TranslateMessage( &msg );
            DispatchMessage( &msg );
        }

        wsprintf( szBuffer, "Thread %x waiting for Event %x or Keyboard input.",
                  GetCurrentThreadId(), hEvent );
```

```
        SendMessage( hList, LB_INSERTSTRING, (WPARAM)-1, (LPARAM)szBuffer );

        // Check for manual event or keyboard input.
        //.............................................
        dwTest = MsgWaitForMultipleObjects( 1, &hEvent, FALSE, 10000, QS_KEY );
        if (dwTest != WAIT_TIMEOUT)
            wsprintf( szBuffer,"Thread %x satisfied condition.", GetCurrentThreadId() );
        else
            wsprintf( szBuffer,"Thread %x timed out.", GetCurrentThreadId() );

        SendMessage( hList, LB_INSERTSTRING, (WPARAM)-1, (LPARAM)szBuffer );
    }

    CloseHandle( hEvent );

    return( 0 );
}


LRESULT CALLBACK WndProc( HWND hWnd, UINT uMsg, WPARAM wParam, LPARAM lParam )
{
static HWND    hList = NULL;
static HANDLE hEvent = NULL;

    switch( uMsg )
    {
    case WM_CREATE:
            // Create list box.
            //.................
            if ( !hList )
                hList = CreateWindowEx( WS_EX_CLIENTEDGE, "LISTBOX", "",
                                        LBS_STANDARD | LBS_NOINTEGRALHEIGHT |
                                        WS_CHILD | WS_VISIBLE,
                                        0, 0, 10, 10,
                                        hWnd, (HMENU)101,
                                        hInst, NULL );

            if ( !hEvent )
            {
                SECURITY_ATTRIBUTES sa;

                sa.nLength              = sizeof( SECURITY_ATTRIBUTES );
                sa.lpSecurityDescriptor = NULL;
                sa.bInheritHandle       = TRUE;
                hEvent = CreateEvent( &sa, TRUE, FALSE, lpszPulseEvent );
            }
            break;

    case WM_SIZE :
            if ( wParam != SIZE_MINIMIZED && hWnd == GetParent( hList ) )
                MoveWindow( hList, 0, 0, LOWORD( lParam ), HIWORD( lParam ), TRUE );
            break;

    case WM_COMMAND :
            switch( LOWORD( wParam ) )
            {
            case IDM_TEST:
                    {
                        DWORD dwChildId;
```

continued on next page

continued from previous page

```
                      CreateThread( NULL, 0, ChildThreadProc, hList, 0, &dwChildId );
                }
                break;

        case IDM_PULSE:
                SendMessage( hList, LB_INSERTSTRING, (WPARAM)-1, (LPARAM)"Pulsing
Event" );

                PulseEvent( hEvent );
                break;

                .
                .
                .
```

MsgWaitForMultipleObjectsEx ■ Windows 95 ■ Windows NT

Description MsgWaitForMultipleObjectsEx is the same as the MsgWaitForMultipleObjects function, except that it has more control over what events will cause the function to return.

MsgWaitForMultipleObjectsEx returns when either any one or all of the specified objects are in the signaled state, an I/O completion routine or asynchronous procedure call (APC) is queued to the thread, or the time-out interval elapses.

Syntax DWORD **MsgWaitForMultipleObjectsEx**(DWORD *dwCount,* LPHANDLE *pHandles,* DWORD *dwMilliseconds,* DWORD *dwWakeMask,* DWORD *dwFlags*)

Parameters

dwCount DWORD: The number of objects specified in the *pHandles* array. The maximum number of object handles is **MAXIMUM_WAIT_OBJECTS**−1.

pHandles LPHANDLE: A pointer to an array of object handles. The array can contain handles to multiple types of objects. The handles must have the **SYNCHRONIZE** access.

dwMilliseconds DWORD: The time-out interval, in milliseconds. The function returns if the interval elapses, even if the conditions specified are not met. If set to **0**, the function tests the states of the specified objects and returns immediately. If set to **INFINITE**, the function's time-out interval never elapses.

dwWakeMask DWORD: The input types for which an input event object handle will be added to the array of object handles. This can be any combination of the values listed in Table 25-10 under the **GetQueueStatus** function description.

dwFlags DWORD: The wait type. This can be any combination of **MWMO_WAITALL** and **MWMO_ALERTABLE**, or set to **0**. If set to **0**, the function returns when any one of the objects is signaled. The return value indicates the object whose state caused the function to return. If **MWMO_WAITALL** is specified, the function returns when all objects in the array are signaled at the same time. If

MWMO_ALERTABLE is specified, the function also returns if an APC has been queued to the thread with **QueueUserAPC**.

Returns   **DWORD**: If successful, the return value indicates the event that caused the function to return. For a wait object that satisfies the condition, the system returns **WAIT_OBJECT_0** plus the index into the array *lpObjectHandles* to the member that satisfies the condition. If the function fails, 0xFFFFFFFF is returned and **GetLastError** will return the error code. **WAIT_TIMEOUT** indicates that the function timed out before returning. **WAIT_IO_COMPLETION** is returned if the wait was ended by a user-mode asynchronous procedure call (APC) queued to the thread.

Include File   winuser.h

See Also   MsgWaitForMultipleObjects

OpenEvent   ■ WINDOWS 95   ■ WINDOWS NT

Description   OpenEvent obtains the handle of a named event object. This function enables multiple processes to open handles for the same event object. The function succeeds only if some process has already created the event by using the **CreateEvent** function. Use the **CloseHandle** function when the handle is no longer needed.

Syntax   HANDLE **OpenEvent**(DWORD *dwAccessFlag,* BOOL *bInherit,* LPCTSTR *lpszEventName*)

Parameters

dwAccessFlag   **DWORD**: The desired access to the event object. This can be a combination of the values listed in Table 25-13.

Table 25-13 OpenEvent *dwAccessFlag* options

Access	Description
EVENT_ALL_ACCESS	Specifies all possible access flags for the event object.
EVENT_MODIFY_STATE	Enables use of the event handle in the SetEvent and ResetEvent functions to modify the event's state.
SYNCHRONIZE	(Windows NT) Enables use of the event handle in any of the wait functions to wait for the event's state to be signaled.

bInherit   **BOOL**: Set to **TRUE** if the handle can be inherited by child processes, otherwise, set to **FALSE**.

lpszEventName   **LPCTSTR**: A pointer to a null-terminated string of up to **MAX_PATH** characters that contains the case-sensitive event name.

Returns   **HANDLE**: If successful, the handle of the event object is returned; otherwise, **FALSE** is returned. Use **GetLastError** to return the extended error code.

Include File   winbase.h

| See Also | `DuplicateHandle`, `OpenMutex`, `OpenSemaphore`, `CreateEvent`, `CloseHandle` |
| Example | See the example for the `MsgWaitForMultipleObjects` function. |

OpenMutex ■ WINDOWS 95 ■ WINDOWS NT

Description	`OpenMutex` returns the handle of an existing named mutex object. This function allows multiple processes to open handles to the same mutex object. The function succeeds only if some process has already created the mutex by using the `CreateMutex` function. Use the `CloseHandle` function when the handle is no longer needed.
Syntax	HANDLE **OpenMutex**(DWORD *dwAccessFlag,* BOOL *bInherit,* LPCTSTR *lpszMutexName*)
Parameters	
dwAccessFlag	DWORD: The desired access to the mutex object. The possible values are listed Table 25-14.

Table 25-14 OpenMutex *dwAccessFlag* options

Access	Description
MUTEX_ALL_ACCESS	Specifies all possible access flags for the mutex object.
SYNCHRONIZE	(Windows NT) Enables use of the event handle in any of the wait functions.

bInherit	BOOL: Set to **TRUE** if the handle can be inherited by child processes; otherwise, set to **FALSE**.
lpszMutexName	LPCTSTR: A pointer to a null-terminated string of up to **MAX_PATH** characters that contains the case-sensitive mutex name.
Returns	HANDLE: If successful, the handle of the mutex object is returned; otherwise, **FALSE** is returned. Use `GetLastError` to return the extended error code.
Include File	`winbase.h`
See Also	`DuplicateHandle`, `CreateMutex`, `ReleaseMutex`, `WaitForSingleObject`, `WaitForMultipleObjects`, `CloseHandle`
Example	See the example for the `CreateMutex` function.

OpenProcess
■ WINDOWS 95   ■ WINDOWS NT

Description   OpenProcess obtains a handle for an existing process object.

Syntax   HANDLE **OpenProcess**(DWORD *dwAccess*, BOOL *bInherit,* DWORD *dwProcessId*)

Parameters

dwAccess   DWORD: Access rights to process object. This can be one or more of the values listed in Table 25-15.

Table 25-15 OpenProcess *dwAccess* options

Access	Description
PROCESS_ALL_ACCESS	Specifies unlimited access to process object.
PROCESS_CREATE_PROCESS	Used internally.
PROCESS_CREATE_THREAD	Enables using the handle in CreateRemoteThread to create a thread in the process.
PROCESS_DUP_HANDLE	Lets the process object be used in DuplicateHandle.
PROCESS_QUERY_INFORMATION	Allows information regarding the process object to be obtained by such functions as GetPriorityClass.
PROCESS_SET_INFORMATION	Allows information regarding the process object to be modified by such functions as SetPriorityClass.
PROCESS_TERMINATE	Enables using the process handle in the TerminateProcess function to terminate the process.
PROCESS_VM_OPERATION	Enables using the process handle in the VirtualProtectEx and WriteProcessMemory functions to modify the virtual memory of the process.
PROCESS_VM_READ	Enables using the handle in ReadProcessMemory to read from the virtual memory of the process.
PROCESS_VM_WRITE	Enables using the handle in WriteProcessMemory to write to the virtual memory of the process.
SYNCHRONIZE	Enables using the process handle in any of the wait functions to wait for the process to terminate.

bInherit   BOOL: If TRUE, child processes inherit access rights to this object. If FALSE, no access rights are shared.

dwProcessId   DWORD: The systemwide process identifier.

Returns   HANDLE: The handle of the process object if the function succeeds; otherwise, FALSE. Use GetLastError to return the error code.

Include File   winbase.h

See Also   DuplicateHandle, GetCurrentProcessId, WaitForSingleObject, WaitForMultipleObjects

Example   This example demonstrates direct data exchange between processes. OpenProcess opens a handle to the process. ReadProcessMemory and WriteProcessMemory move data between the address spaces of the two processes.

```
LPVOID  lpHeapData          = NULL;
LPVOID  lpExtData           = NULL;
DWORD   dwDebuggeeProcessID = 0;
TCHAR   szBuffer[256];

LRESULT CALLBACK WndProc( HWND hWnd, UINT uMsg, WPARAM wParam, LPARAM lParam )
{
    switch( uMsg )
    {
        case WM_CREATE:
            {
                // Allocate some heap data for exchange.
                //.......................................
                lpHeapData = HeapAlloc( GetProcessHeap(), 0, 256 );

                // If child set child name.
                //.........................
                if ( strstr( GetCommandLine(), "DEBUGGEE" ) )
                {
                    SetWindowText( hWnd, "DEBUGGEE" );
                    dwDebuggeeProcessID = GetCurrentProcessId();
                    lstrcpy( lpHeapData, "@@@ Debuggee Data @@@");
                    SetMenu( hWnd, 0 );
                }
                else
                {
                    // Position parent above child.
                    //.............................
                    SetWindowText( hWnd, "DEBUGGER" );
                    lstrcpy(lpHeapData, "<<<< Debugger Data >>>>");
                }
            }
            break;

        case WM_USER:
                // Used to return value of the heap data.
                //.......................................
                return( (LRESULT)lpHeapData );

        case WM_COMMAND :
                switch( LOWORD( wParam ) )
                {
                    case IDM_LAUNCH:
                        {
                            STARTUPINFO si;
                            PROCESS_INFORMATION pi;
                            HWND hWndEx;

                            // Only one can be debugged at a time.
                            //....................................
                            if (FindWindow(lpszAppName, "DEBUGGEE")!=0)
                                break;

                            ZeroMemory(&si, sizeof(STARTUPINFO));
                            ZeroMemory(&pi, sizeof(PROCESS_INFORMATION));
                            si.cb=sizeof(STARTUPINFO);
                            CreateProcess( NULL, "OPENPROC.EXE DEBUGGEE",
                                        NULL, NULL, FALSE, 0, NULL,
                                        NULL, &si, &pi );
                            dwDebuggeeProcessID = pi.dwProcessId;
```

```
            // Let initialization of new process occur.
            //....................................
            if ( pi.dwProcessId )
            {
                WaitForInputIdle( GetCurrentProcess(), INFINITE );
                while ((hWndEx = FindWindow(lpszAppName, "DEBUGGEE"))==0);
                lpExtData = (LPVOID) SendMessage(hWndEx, WM_USER, 0, 0);
            }
        }
        break;

    case IDM_READ:
        {
            TCHAR szData[256];
            DWORD dwBytesRead = 0;
            HANDLE hDebuggee = OpenProcess( PROCESS_VM_READ, FALSE,
                                            dwDebuggeeProcessID );

            ReadProcessMemory( hDebuggee, lpExtData,
                               szData, 255, &dwBytesRead );
            wsprintf( szBuffer, "%ld Bytes Read. Data=%s",
                      dwBytesRead, szData );
            MessageBox( hWnd, szBuffer, "Reading Process", MB_OK );

            CloseHandle( hDebuggee );
        }
        break;

    case IDM_WRITE:
        {
            DWORD dwBytesWritten = 0;
            HANDLE hDebuggee = OpenProcess( PROCESS_VM_WRITE, FALSE,
                                            dwDebuggeeProcessID );

            WriteProcessMemory( hDebuggee, lpExtData,
                                lpHeapData, 255, &dwBytesWritten );
            wsprintf(szBuffer, "%ld Bytes Written", dwBytesWritten);
            MessageBox( hWnd, lpExtData, "Writing Process", MB_OK );

            CloseHandle( hDebuggee );
        }
        break;
```

```
  .
  .
  .
```

OpenSemaphore   ■ WINDOWS 95   ■ WINDOWS NT

Description   OpenSemaphore opens an existing named semaphore object. The semaphore must have been previously created with the **CreateSemaphore** function. Use the **CloseHandle** function to close the returned handle when it is no longer needed.

Syntax   HANDLE **OpenSemaphore**(DWORD *dwAccessFlag*, BOOL *bInherit*,
LPCTSTR *lpszSemName*)

Parameters

dwAccessFlag	DWORD: The desired access of the semaphore object. This can be a combination of the values listed in Table 25-16.

Table 25-16 OpenSemaphore *dwAccessFlag* options

Access	Description
SEMAPHORE_ALL_ACCESS	Specifies all possible access flags for the semaphore.
SEMAPHORE_MODIFY_STATE	Enables use of the handle in ReleaseSemaphore.
SYNCHRONIZE	(Windows NT) Enables use of the handle in any of the wait functions.

bInherit	BOOL: Set to TRUE if the handle can be inherited by child processes; otherwise, set to FALSE.
lpszSemName	LPCTSTR: A pointer to a null-terminated string that contains the case-sensitive name of the semaphore.
Returns	HANDLE: The handle of the semaphore if the function succeeds; otherwise, FALSE. Use GetLastError to return the error code.
Include File	winbase.h
See Also	DuplicateHandle, OpenEvent, OpenMutex, CreateSemaphore, CloseHandle
Example	See the example for the CreateSemaphore function.

OpenWaitableTimer   ■ WINDOWS 95   ■ WINDOWS NT

Description	OpenWaitableTimer returns a handle to an existing named waitable timer object. This function allows multiple processes to open handles to the same timer object. OpenWaitableTimer succeeds only if some process has already created the timer using the CreateWaitableTimer function.
Syntax	HANDLE **OpenWaitableTimer**(DWORD *dwDesiredAccess,* BOOL *bInheritHandle,* LPCTSTR *lpTimerName*)
Parameters	
dwDesiredAccess	DWORD: The requested access to the timer object. This can be one or more of the values listing in Table 25-17.

Table 25-17 Waitable timer access

Value	Meaning
TIMER_ALL_ACCESS	All possible access rights for the timer object.
TIMER_MODIFY_STATE	Enables use of the timer handle in the SetWaitableTimer and CancelWaitableTimer functions to modify the timer's state.
SYNCHRONIZE	Enables use of the timer handle in any of the wait functions to wait for the timer's state to be signaled.

bInheritHandle	**BOOL**: Set to **TRUE** if the handle is inheritable by child processes; otherwise, the handle cannot be inherited.
lpTimerName	**LPCTSTR**: A pointer to a null-terminated string specifying the name of the timer object. The name is limited to **MAX_PATH** characters and can any character except the backslash (\).
Returns	**HANDLE**: If successful, the handle to the timer object is returned; otherwise, **NULL** is returned. Use the **GetLastError** function to retrieve extended error information.
Include File	winbase.h
See Also	CancelWaitableTimer, CloseHandle, CreateWaitableTimer, SetWaitableTimer

PulseEvent ■ WINDOWS 95 ■ WINDOWS NT

Description	**PulseEvent** performs a single operation that sets the state of an event object to signaled and then nonsignaled. For a manual-reset event object, all waiting threads that can be released immediately are released. For an auto-reset event object, the function resets the state to nonsignaled and returns after releasing a single waiting thread, even if multiple threads are waiting. If no threads are waiting, or if no thread can be released immediately, **PulseEvent** sets the event object's state to nonsignaled and returns.
Syntax	**BOOL PulseEvent(HANDLE** *hEvent* **)**
Parameters	
hEvent	**HANDLE**: The event object to be pulsed. The event must have **EVENT_MODIFY_STATE** access.
Returns	**BOOL**: **TRUE** if the function succeeds; otherwise, **FALSE**. Use **GetLastError** to return the error code.
Include File	winbase.h
See Also	OpenEvent, CreateEvent, MsgWaitForMultipleObjects, WaitForSingleObject, WaitForMultipleObjects
Example	See the example for the **MsgWaitForMultipleObjects** function.

QueueUserAPC ■ WINDOWS 95 ■ WINDOWS NT

Description	**QueueUserAPC** adds a user-mode asynchronous procedure call (APC) object to the APC queue of the specified thread. The APC support in the operating system allows an application to queue an APC object. Each thread has its own APC queue. The queuing of an APC is a request for the thread to call the APC function. Windows issues a software interrupt to direct the thread to call the APC function.

Syntax	DWORD **QueueUserAPC**(PAPCFUNC *pfnAPC,* HANDLE *hThread,* DWORD *dwData*)
Parameters	
pfnAPC	PAPCFUNC: A pointer to an application-defined APC function to be called when the specified thread performs an alertable wait operation. This function accepts a single 32-bit parameter.
hThread	HANDLE: The handle of the thread. This handle must have THREAD_SET_CONTEXT access.
dwData	DWORD: A single DWORD argument that is passed to the APC function pointed to by the *pfnAPC* parameter.
Returns	DWORD: If successful, a nonzero value is returned; otherwise, 0 is returned.
Include File	winbase.h
See Also	MsgWaitForMultipleObjectsEx

RaiseException   ■ WINDOWS 95   ■ WINDOWS NT

Description	RaiseException raises an exception in the calling thread. This function enables a process to use structured exception handling to handle private, software-generated, application-defined exceptions.
Syntax	VOID **RaiseException**(DWORD *dwExceptionCode,* DWORD *dwExceptionFlags,* DWORD *dwArgCount,* CONST DWORD* *lpdwArgs*)
Parameters	
dwExceptionCode	DWORD: Exception code of exception being raised. Windows will clear bit 28 of this code. Thus, 0xFFFFFFFF will become 0xEFFFFFFF. To retrieve this code from the exception handler, use the function GetExceptionCode.
dwExceptionFlags	DWORD: Specifies whether execution can continue after exception is handled. If 0, processing continues. If set to EXCEPTION_NONCONTINUABLE and the process continues, EXCEPTION_NONCONTINUABLE_EXCEPTION occurs.
dwArgCount	DWORD: The number of arguments in *lpdwArgs* array. This value cannot exceed EXCEPTION_MAXIMUM_PARAMETERS. If *lpdwArgs* is NULL, this parameter is ignored.
lpdwArgs	CONST DWORD*: Arguments to the filter expression of the exception handler.
Include File	winbase.h
See Also	GetThreadContext, UnhandledExceptionFilter, SetUnhandledExceptionFilter
Example	See the example for the SetUnhandledExceptionFilter function.

ReadProcessMemory   ■ Windows 95   ■ Windows NT

Description	ReadProcessMemory reads data from a specified process. The entire area to be read must be accessible, or the function fails.
Syntax	BOOL **ReadProcessMemory**(HANDLE *hProcess,* LPVOID *lpSource,* LPVOID *lpDest,* DWORD *dwByteCount,* LPDWORD *lpdwBytesRead*)
Parameters	
hProcess	HANDLE: Process whose memory is to be read.
lpSource	LPVOID: A pointer to bytes to be read. The process object must have **PROCESS_VM_READ** and **PROCESS_VM_OPERATION** access and all bytes in the range must be accessible.
lpDest	LPVOID: A pointer containing the destination of the read operation.
dwByteCount	DWORD: The number of bytes to read.
lpdwBytesRead	LPDWORD: A pointer to where number of bytes read is stored. If **NULL**, this parameter is ignored.
Returns	BOOL: **TRUE** if the function succeeds; otherwise, **FALSE**. Use **GetLastError** to return the error code.
Include File	winbase.h
See Also	WriteProcessMemory
Example	See the example for the **OpenProcess** function.

RegisterHotKey   ■ Windows 95   ■ Windows NT

Description	RegisterHotKey defines a systemwide hotkey for the current thread. When a key is pressed, the system looks for a match against all hotkeys. Upon finding a match, the system posts the **WM_HOTKEY** message to the message queue of the thread that registered the hotkey. This message is posted to the beginning of the queue, so it is removed by the next iteration of the message loop.
Syntax	BOOL **RegisterHotKey**(HWND *hWnd,* int *idHotKey,* UINT *uModifiers,* UINT *uVirtualKeyCode*)
Parameters	
hWnd	HWND: The window notified when the hotkey is pressed. If **NULL**, the **WM_HOTKEY** messages are posted to the message queue of the thread and must be processed in the message loop.
idHotKey	int: The identifier of the hotkey. Identifiers cannot be duplicated in the same application. For hotkeys defined in an application, the application must specify a value between 0x0000 and 0xBFFF. For hotkeys defined in a dynamic link library (DLL), specify a value in the range 0xC000 through 0xFFFF by using **GlobalAddAtom** to return a unique identifier.

uModifiers	UINT: Specifies keys that must be pressed in combination with the key specified by the *uVirtualKeyCode* parameter. This can be set to one of the values listed in Table 25-18.

Table 25-18 Hotkey modifiers

Value	Meaning
0	No modifier key.
MOD_ALT	Either ALT key must be pressed.
MOD_CONTROL	Either CTRL key must be pressed.
MOD_SHIFT	Either SHIFT key must be pressed.

uVirtualKeyCode	UINT: Specifies the virtual-key code of the hotkey. If a hotkey with this virtual-key code has already been defined, and the identifier supplied is not the same as the previous definition, the hotkey definition is changed to use the new identifier.
Returns	BOOL: If successful, TRUE is returned; otherwise, FALSE is returned. Use GetLastError to return the error code.
Include File	winbase.h
See Also	GlobalAddAtom, UnregisterHotKey
Related Messages	WM_HOTKEY
Example	This example uses hotkeys to suspend, resume, and terminate threads. Choosing Test! from the menu will create a thread. ALT-S suspends threads, ALT-R resumes threads, and ALT-K terminates a thread. The affected thread is always the last thread launched.

```
#define RESUME_KEY      101
#define SUSPEND_KEY     102
#define TERMINATE_KEY 103

DWORD WINAPI ThreadProc( LPDWORD lpdwData)
{
   TCHAR szBuffer[128];
   HWND  hWnd = (HWND)lpdwData;

   wsprintf( szBuffer, "Starting Thread ID = %lX", GetCurrentThreadId() );
   SetWindowText( hWnd, szBuffer );
   Sleep( 10000 );

   wsprintf( szBuffer, "Thread %lX finished execution", GetCurrentThreadId() );
   SetWindowText( hWnd, szBuffer );

   return( 0 );
}
```

```
LRESULT CALLBACK WndProc( HWND hWnd, UINT uMsg, WPARAM wParam, LPARAM lParam )
{
    static HANDLE hChild = NULL;

    switch( uMsg )
    {
    case WM_CREATE:
            RegisterHotKey( hWnd, RESUME_KEY, MOD_ALT, 'R' );
            RegisterHotKey( hWnd, SUSPEND_KEY, MOD_ALT, 'S' );
            RegisterHotKey( hWnd, TERMINATE_KEY, MOD_ALT, 'K' );
            break;

    case WM_DESTROY :
            UnregisterHotKey( hWnd, RESUME_KEY );
            UnregisterHotKey( hWnd, SUSPEND_KEY );
            UnregisterHotKey( hWnd, TERMINATE_KEY );
            PostQuitMessage(0);
            break;

    case WM_HOTKEY:
            {
                TCHAR szBuffer[128];
                DWORD dwExitCodeThread = STILL_ACTIVE;

                lstrcpy( szBuffer, "No Child Thread Running" );
                if (hChild)
                    GetExitCodeThread(hChild, &dwExitCodeThread);

                if (dwExitCodeThread==STILL_ACTIVE)
                    switch (wParam)
                    {
                    case SUSPEND_KEY:
                        wsprintf( szBuffer, "Suspending thread %lX", hChild );
                        SuspendThread( hChild );
                        break;

                    case RESUME_KEY:
                        wsprintf( szBuffer, "Resuming thread %lX", hChild );
                        ResumeThread( hChild );
                        break;

                    case TERMINATE_KEY:
                        wsprintf( szBuffer, "Terminating thread %lX", hChild );
                        TerminateThread( hChild, FALSE );
                        hChild = NULL;
                        break;
                    }

                SetWindowText( hWnd, szBuffer );
            }
            break;

    case WM_COMMAND :
            switch( LOWORD( wParam ) )
            {
                case IDM_TEST:
                    {
```

continued on next page

continued from previous page

```
                              // Start a thread. Only one thread at at time.
                              //.........................................
                              DWORD dwExitCodeThread;
                              DWORD dwChild;

                              if (hChild)
                                 GetExitCodeThread( hChild, &dwExitCodeThread );

                              if (dwExitCodeThread!=STILL_ACTIVE)
                                 hChild = CreateThread( NULL, 0, ThreadProc, hWnd, 0, &dwChild );
                           }
                           break;
```

.
.
.

ReleaseMutex   ■ WINDOWS 95   ■ WINDOWS NT

Description	**ReleaseMutex** releases a mutex object. The mutex object becomes signaled if the function succeeds.
Syntax	BOOL **ReleaseMutex**(HANDLE *hMutex*)
Parameters	
hMutex	HANDLE: The handle of mutex object to be released. It must be owned by the thread.
Returns	BOOL: TRUE if the function succeeds; otherwise, FALSE. Use GetLastError to return the error code.
Include File	winbase.h
See Also	DuplicateHandle, OpenMutex, CreateMutex, WaitForSingleObject, WaitForMultipleObjects
Example	See the example for the CreateMutex function.

ReleaseSemaphore   ■ WINDOWS 95   ■ WINDOWS NT

Description	**ReleaseSemaphore** increases the count of a semaphore object. The count may increase to the maximum count set for the object in the CreateSemaphore call.
Syntax	BOOL **ReleaseSemaphore**(HANDLE *hSemaphore,* LONG *lReleaseCount,* LPLONG *lplPreviousCount*)
Parameters	
hSemaphore	HANDLE: The handle of the semaphore object to be released.
lReleaseCount	LONG: The number to add to the semaphore count.
lplPreviousCount	LPLONG: A pointer to location to store previous count. If NULL, this parameter is ignored.

Returns	BOOL: TRUE if the function succeeds; otherwise, FALSE. Use GetLastError to return the error code.
Include File	winbase.h
See Also	DuplicateHandle, OpenSemaphore, CreateSemaphore, WaitForSingleObject, WaitForMultipleObjects
Example	See the example for the CreateSemaphore function.

ResetEvent ■ WINDOWS 95 ■ WINDOWS NT

Description	ResetEvent sets the state of the event object to nonsignaled. A nonsignaled event blocks waiting threads.
Syntax	BOOL **ResetEvent**(HANDLE *hEvent*)
Parameters	
hEvent	HANDLE: The event object to change to nonsignaled state.
Returns	BOOL: TRUE if the function succeeds; otherwise, FALSE. Use GetLastError to return the error code.
Include File	winbase.h
See Also	SetEvent, DuplicateHandle, OpenEvent, CreateEvent, WaitForSingleObject, WaitForMultipleObjects
Example	See the example for the CreateEvent function.

ResumeThread ■ WINDOWS 95 ■ WINDOWS NT

Description	ResumeThread resumes execution of a suspended thread. A suspend count is kept for each thread. When SuspendThread is called, the count is incremented. When ResumeThread is called, the count is decremented. When the suspend count of a suspended thread reaches zero, execution resumes.
Syntax	DWORD **ResumeThread**(HANDLE *hThread*)
Parameters	
hThread	HANDLE: The handle to the object of the suspended thread.
Returns	DWORD: If the function succeeds, the previous suspend count is returned. Otherwise, 0xFFFFFFFF is returned. Use GetLastError to return the error code.
Include File	winbase.h
See Also	SuspendThread, Sleep
Example	See the example for the RegisterHotKey function.

SetEvent
■ Windows 95   ■ Windows NT

Description	**SetEvent** changes the state of the event object to signaled. A signaled event will allow a thread waiting for the event to continue execution.
Syntax	BOOL **SetEvent**(HANDLE *hEvent*)
Parameters	
hEvent	HANDLE: The event object whose state is to be changed to signaled.
Returns	BOOL: TRUE if the function succeeds; otherwise, FALSE. Use GetLastError to return the error code.
Include File	winbase.h
See Also	ResetEvent, DuplicateHandle, OpenEvent, CreateEvent, WaitForSingleObject, WaitForMultipleObjects
Example	See the example for the **CreateEvent** function.

SetPriorityClass
■ Windows 95   ■ Windows NT

Description	**SetPriorityClass** adjusts the priority class of a given process. The priority of each thread is calculated using the priority class of the process and the priority value of each thread of the process that is set using the function **SetThreadPriority**. Threads are scheduled in a round-robin fashion at each priority level. Priority levels are exclusive. Only when all executable threads at all higher levels are satisfied will threads at lower levels be scheduled.
Syntax	BOOL **SetPriorityClass**(HANDLE *hProcess,* DWORD *dwPriorityClass*)
Parameters	
hProcess	HANDLE: Identifies a process object. This process object must have PROCESS_SET_INFORMATION access to return the termination status.
dwPriorityClass	DWORD: The new priority class of the object. This can be one of the values listed in Table 25-19.

Table 25-19 SetPriorityClass *dwPriorityClass* **options**

Priority Class Flag	Meaning
IDLE_PRIORITY_CLASS	Lowest priority task. This runs only when system is idle.
NORMAL_PRIORITY_CLASS	Basic priority for a process.
HIGH_PRIORITY_CLASS	Higher priority task. This highly responsive setting can affect the system multitasking, not letting other tasks run.
REALTIME_PRIORITY_CLASS	Preempts even operating system actions. Do not use this setting unless the situation is absolutely time-critical.

Returns	**BOOL**: If the function succeeds, **TRUE** is returned; otherwise, **FALSE** is returned. Use **GetLastError** to return the error code.
Include File	**winbase.h**
See Also	**CreateProcess**, **SetThreadPriority**, **GetThreadPriority**, **GetPriorityClass**
Example	See the example for the **GetPriorityClass** function.

SetProcessAffinityMask ■ WINDOWS 95 ■ WINDOWS NT

Description	**SetProcessAffinityMask** sets a processor affinity mask for the threads of a specified process. A process affinity mask is a bit vector in which each bit represents the processor on which the threads of the process are allowed to run. The value of the process affinity mask must be a subset of the mask values returned from the **GetProcessAffinityMask** function.
Syntax	**BOOL SetProcessAffinityMask**(HANDLE *hProcess,* DWORD *dwProcessAffinityMask*)
Parameters	
hProcess	**HANDLE**: A handle, with the **PROCESS_SET_INFORMATION** access, to the process for which to set the affinity mask.
dwProcessAffinityMask	**DWORD**: The affinity mask for the threads of the process.
Returns	**BOOL**: If successful, **TRUE** is returned; otherwise, **FALSE** is returned. Use the **GetLastError** function to retrieve extended error information.
Include File	**winbase.h**
See Also	**GetProcessAffinityMask**, **CreateProcess**

SetProcessPriorityBoost ■ WINDOWS 95 ■ WINDOWS NT

Description	**SetProcessPriorityBoost** disables the ability of Windows NT to temporarily boost the priority of the threads of the specified process. When a thread is executing in one of the dynamic priority classes, Windows NT temporarily boosts the thread's priority when it is taken out of a wait state. **SetProcessPriorityBoost** can disable this feature for the threads belonging to the specified process.
Syntax	**BOOL SetProcessPriorityBoost**(HANDLE *hProcess,* BOOL *bDisablePriorityBoost*)
Parameters	
hProcess	**HANDLE**: A handle, with **PROCESS_SET_INFORMATION** access, to the process for which to change the priority boost.
bDisablePriorityBoost	**BOOL**: Set to **TRUE** to disable the priority boost for the specified process. **FALSE** restores normal behavior.

Returns	**BOOL**: If successful, **TRUE** is returned; otherwise, **FALSE** is returned. Use the **GetLastError** function to retrieve extended error information.
Include File	**winbase.h**
See Also	**GetProcessPriorityBoost**

SetProcessShutdownParameters   ■ Windows 95   ■ Windows NT

Description	**SetProcessShutdownParameters** sets the shutdown parameters for the calling process. A process can change the shutdown order relative to the other processes in the system.
Syntax	**BOOL SetProcessShutdownParameters**(DWORD *dwLevel,* DWORD *dwFlags*)
Parameters	
dwLevel	**DWORD**: The shutdown priority for the calling process relative to other processes in the system. The system shuts down processes from high values to low. The highest and lowest shutdown priorities are reserved for system components. This parameter must be in the ranges listed in Table 25-9 under the **GetProcessShutdownParameters** function.
dwFlags	**DWORD**: Specifies the shutdown flags. Currently the only value this can be is **SHUTDOWN_NORETRY**, which indicates that the system will not show a retry dialog box for the user if this process takes longer than the specified time-out to shut down. Instead, the process is directly exited.
Returns	**BOOL**: If successful; **TRUE** is returned; otherwise, **FALSE** is returned.
Include File	**winbase.h**
See Also	**GetProcessShutdownParameters**

SetProcessWorkingSetSize   ■ Windows 95   ■ Windows NT

Description	**SetProcessWorkingSetSize** sets the minimum and maximum working set sizes for the specified process. The working set size of a process controls the memory pages currently visible to the process in physical RAM memory. These pages are resident and available for an application to use without triggering a page fault. If both the minimum and maximum values are set to **0xFFFFFFFF**, the function temporarily trims the working set of the process to zero, which causes the process to be swapped out of physical RAM memory.
Syntax	**BOOL SetProcessWorkingSetSize**(HANDLE *hProcess,* DWORD *dwMinWorkingSetSize,* DWORD *dwMaxWorkingSetSize*)
Parameters	
hProcess	**HANDLE**: An open handle, with **PROCESS_SET_QUOTA** access, to the process for which to set the working set sizes.

dwMinWorkingSetSize	**DWORD**: The minimum working set size, in bytes, for the process. The virtual memory manager attempts to keep at least this much memory resident in the process whenever the process is active.
dwMaxWorkingSetSize	**DWORD**: The maximum working set size, in bytes, for the process. The virtual memory manager attempts to keep no more than this much memory resident in the process whenever the process is active and memory is in short supply.
Returns	**BOOL**: If successful, **TRUE** is returned; otherwise, **FALSE** is returned. Use the **GetLastError** function to retrieve extended error information.
Include File	`winbase.h`
See Also	`GetProcessWorkingSetSize`

SetThreadAffinityMask   ■ Windows 95   ■ Windows NT

Description	**SetThreadAffinityMask** sets the processor affinity mask for a specified thread. The thread affinity mask is a bit vector in which each bit represents the processors that a thread is allowed to run on. This must be a subset of the process affinity mask for the parent process.
Syntax	DWORD **SetThreadAffinityMask**(HANDLE *hThread,* DWORD *dwThreadAffinityMask*)
Parameters	
hThread	**HANDLE**: A handle, with **THREAD_SET_INFORMATION** access, to the thread for which to set the affinity mask.
dwThreadAffinityMask	**DWORD**: The affinity mask for the thread. On Windows 95, this value must be **1**.
Returns	**DWORD**: If successful, the previous affinity mask is returned; otherwise, **0** is returned. Use the **GetLastError** function to retrieve extended error information.
Include File	`winbase.h`
See Also	`SetThreadIdealProcessor`, `GetProcessAffinityMask`

SetThreadContext   ■ Windows 95   ■ Windows NT

Description	**SetThreadContext** sets the context in the specified thread. This allows the selective context to be set based on the value of the *ContextFlags* member of the **CONTEXT** structure. This function is usually used on threads that are being debugged. Do not try to set the context for a running thread; the results are unpredictable. Use the **SuspendThread** function to suspend the thread before calling **SetThreadContext**.

Syntax	BOOL **SetThreadContext**(HANDLE *hThread,* CONST LPCONTEXT *lpContext*)
Parameters	
hThread	HANDLE: The thread object whose context is to be set. On Windows NT, this handle must have **THREAD_SET_CONTEXT** access.
lpContext	CONST LPCONTEXT: A pointer to address of a **CONTEXT** structure that contains the context to be set in the specified thread. The value of the *ContextFlags* member of this structure specifies which portions of a thread's context is set. The **CONTEXT** structure is highly computer specific. Currently, there are **CONTEXT** structures defined for Intel, MIPS, Alpha, and PowerPC processors. Refer to the **WINNT.H** header file for definitions of these structures.
Returns	BOOL: If successful, **TRUE** is returned; otherwise, **FALSE** is returned. Use **GetLastError** to return extended error information.
Include File	winbase.h
See Also	GetThreadContext, SuspendThread, CreateThread

SetThreadIdealProcessor ■ WINDOWS 95 ■ WINDOWS NT

Description	SetThreadIdealProcessor specifies the preferred processor for a thread. The system schedules threads on their preferred processors whenever possible. Use the **GetSystemInfo** function to determine the number of processors on the computer. Also use the **GetProcessAffinityMask** function to check the processors on which the thread is allowed to run.
Syntax	DWORD **SetThreadIdealProcessor**(HANDLE *hThread,* DWORD *dwIdealProcessor*)
Parameters	
hThread	HANDLE: A handle, with **THREAD_SET_INFORMATION** access, to the thread for which to set the preferred processor.
dwIdealProcessor	DWORD: The number of the preferred processor for the thread. A value of **MAXIMUM_PROCESSORS** tells the system that the thread has no preferred processor.
Returns	DWORD: If successful, the previous preferred processor of the thread is returned; otherwise, −1 is returned. Use the **GetLastError** function to retrieve extended error information.
Include File	winbase.h
See Also	SetThreadAffinityMask, GetSystemInfo, GetProcessAffinityMask

SetThreadPriority ■ WINDOWS 95 ■ WINDOWS NT

Description	SetThreadPriority changes the priority level for a given thread. The priority value of the thread and the process priority class determine the thread's base priority level.
Syntax	BOOL **SetThreadPriority**(HANDLE *hThread,* int *iPriority*)
Parameters	
hThread	HANDLE: The handle to the thread object whose priority is being set. The thread object must have **THREAD_SET_INFORMATION** access.
iPriority	int: The new priority of the thread. Table 25-20 shows possible settings.

Table 25-20 Priority levels of threads

Priority	Meaning
THREAD_PRIORITY_TIME_CRITICAL	A base priority level of 15 for IDLE_PRIORITY_CLASS, NORMAL_PRIORITY_CLASS, or HIGH_PRIORITY_CLASS processes, and a base priority level of 31 for REALTIME_PRIORITY_CLASS processes.
THREAD_PRIORITY_HIGHEST	Two levels above normal priority for this class.
THREAD_PRIORITY_ABOVE_NORMAL	One level above normal priority for this class.
THREAD_PRIORITY_NORMAL	Normal priority for this class.
THREAD_PRIORITY_BELOW_NORMAL	One level below normal priority for this class.
THREAD_PRIORITY_LOWEST	Two levels below normal priority for this class.
THREAD_PRIORITY_IDLE	A base priority level of 1 for IDLE_PRIORITY_CLASS, NORMAL_PRIORITY_CLASS, or HIGH_PRIORITY_CLASS processes, and a base priority level of 16 for REALTIME_PRIORITY_CLASS processes.

Returns	BOOL: If the function succeeds, **TRUE** is returned; otherwise **FALSE** is returned. Use **GetLastError** to return the error code.
Include File	winbase.h
See Also	CreateThread, CreateProcess, SetPriorityClass, GetThreadPriority
Example	See the example for the GetThreadPriority function.

SetThreadPriorityBoost ■ WINDOWS 95 ■ WINDOWS NT

Description	SetThreadPriorityBoost disables the ability of Windows NT to temporarily boost the priority of the specified thread.
Syntax	BOOL **SetThreadPriorityBoost**(HANDLE *hThread,* BOOL *bDisablePriorityBoost*)

Parameters

hThread HANDLE: A handle, with **THREAD_SET_INFORMATION** access, for which priority boost is changed.

bDisablePriorityBoost BOOL: Set to **TRUE** to disable the dynamic boosting of the priority. **FALSE** restores the normal behavior.

Returns BOOL: If successful; **TRUE** is returned; otherwise, **FALSE** is returned. Use the **GetLastError** function to retrieve extended error information.

Include File winbase.h

See Also GetThreadPriorityBoost

SetUnhandledExceptionFilter ■ WINDOWS 95 ■ WINDOWS NT

Description SetUnhandledExceptionFilter allows an application to place an exception filter that will be called if an unhandled exception occurs. Exceptions are generally trapped by local exception handlers, but when they are not, the unhandled exception filter of the thread is executed. This function allows the application to intervene with its own filter at the topmost level of exception processing.

Syntax LPTOP_LEVEL_EXCEPTION_FILTER **SetUnhandledExceptionFilter** (LPTOP_LEVEL_EXCEPTION_FILTER *lpTopLevelFilter*)

Parameters

lpTopLevelFilter LPTOP_LEVEL_EXCEPTION_FILTER: The filter to be called if an unhandled exception occurs. The default handler **UnhandledException Filter** will be set if **NULL** is passed, thus removing any exception filter previously set at this level. See the definition of the exception filter function below.

Returns LPTOP_LEVEL_EXCEPTION_FILTER: The previous exception filter is returned.

Include File winbase.h

See Also UnhandledExceptionFilter, GetThreadContext, RaiseException

Callback Syntax LONG **ExceptionFilterProc**(LPEXCEPTION_POINTERS *lpExceptionPointers*)

Callback Parameters

lpExceptionPointers LPEXCEPTION_POINTERS: A pointer to an **EXCEPTION_POINTERS** structure that contains information about the exception that occurred. See the definition of the **EXCEPTION_POINTERS** structure below.

Callback Returns LONG: The filter function should return one of the values listed in Table 25-21.

Table 25-21 Exception filter return values

Return Value	Meaning
EXCEPTION_EXECUTE_HANDLER	Commands the system to execute the associated exception handler upon return. If there is no exception handler, the process will terminate.
EXCEPTION_CONTINUE_EXECUTION	Returns from exception filter and continues execution from the point of the exception. The filter may modify the data to fix the problem that produced the exception. The data provided through LPEXCEPTION_POINTERS includes a description of the context of the thread at the time of the exception and a description of the exception itself.
EXCEPTION_CONTINUE_SEARCH	Calls UnhandledExceptionFilter, which, depending on the current error mode, may invoke the application error message box or return to a debugger if the application is being debugged.

EXCEPTION_POINTERS Definition

```
typedef struct _EXCEPTION_POINTERS
{
    PEXCEPTION_RECORD ExceptionRecord;
    PCONTEXT ContextRecord;
} EXCEPTION_POINTERS;
```

Members

ExceptionRecord PEXCEPTION_RECORD: A pointer to an **EXCEPTION_RECORD** structure that contains a machine-independent description of the exception. See the definition of the **EXCEPTION_RECORD** structure below.

ContextRecord PCONTEXT: A pointer to a context record that contains the state of the processor. Currently, there are **CONTEXT** structures defined for Intel, MIPS, Alpha, and PowerPC processors. Refer to the **WINNT.H** header file for definitions of these structures.

EXCEPTION_RECORD Definition

```
typedef struct _EXCEPTION_RECORD
{
    DWORD ExceptionCode;
    DWORD ExceptionFlags;
    struct _EXCEPTION_RECORD *ExceptionRecord;
    PVOID ExceptionAddress;
    DWORD NumberParameters;
    DWORD ExceptionInformation[EXCEPTION_MAXIMUM_PARAMETERS];
} EXCEPTION_RECORD;
```

Members

ExceptionCode DWORD: The reason the exception occurred. This is the code generated by a hardware exception, or the code specified in the **RaiseException** function for a software-generated exception. Table 25-22 lists common exceptions likely to occur due to common programming errors.

Table 25-22 Common software exceptions

Value	Meaning
EXCEPTION_ACCESS_VIOLATION	The thread tried to read from or write to a virtual address for which it does not have the appropriate access.
EXCEPTION_ARRAY_BOUNDS_EXCEEDED	The thread tried to access an array element that is out of bounds and the underlying hardware supports bounds checking.
EXCEPTION_BREAKPOINT	A breakpoint was encountered.
EXCEPTION_DATATYPE_MISALIGNMENT	The thread tried to read or write data that is misaligned on hardware that does not provide alignment. For example, 16-bit values must be aligned on 2-byte boundaries, 32-bit values on 4-byte boundaries, and so on.
EXCEPTION_FLT_DENORMAL_OPERAND	One of the operands in a floating-point operation is denormal. A denormal value is one that is too small to represent as a standard floating-point value.
EXCEPTION_FLT_DIVIDE_BY_ZERO	The thread tried to divide a floating-point value by a floating-point divisor of zero.
EXCEPTION_FLT_INEXACT_RESULT	The result of a floating-point operation cannot be represented exactly as a decimal fraction.
EXCEPTION_FLT_INVALID_OPERATION	This exception represents any floating-point exception not included in this list.
EXCEPTION_FLT_OVERFLOW	The exponent of a floating-point operation is greater than the magnitude allowed by the corresponding type.
EXCEPTION_FLT_STACK_CHECK	The stack overflowed or underflowed as the result of a floating-point operation.
EXCEPTION_FLT_UNDERFLOW	The exponent of a floating-point operation is less than the magnitude allowed by the corresponding type.
EXCEPTION_ILLEGAL_INSTRUCTION	The thread tried to execute an invalid instruction.
EXCEPTION_IN_PAGE_ERROR	The thread tried to access a page that was not present, and the system was unable to load the page. For example, this exception might occur if a network connection is lost while running a program over the network.
EXCEPTION_INT_DIVIDE_BY_ZERO	The thread tried to divide an integer value by an integer divisor of zero.
EXCEPTION_INT_OVERFLOW	The result of an integer operation caused a carry out of the most significant bit of the result.
EXCEPTION_INVALID_DISPOSITION	An exception handler returned an invalid disposition to the exception dispatcher. Programmers using a high-level language such as C should never encounter this exception.
EXCEPTION_NONCONTINUABLE_EXCEPTION	The thread tried to continue execution after a noncontinuable exception occurred.
EXCEPTION_PRIV_INSTRUCTION	The thread tried to execute an instruction whose operation is not allowed in the current machine mode.
EXCEPTION_SINGLE_STEP	A trace trap or other single-instruction mechanism signaled that one instruction has been executed.
EXCEPTION_STACK_OVERFLOW	The thread used up its stack.

ExceptionFlags	`DWORD`: Exception flags for the exception. This member can be either set to `0`, indicating a continuable exception, or `EXCEPTION_NONCONTINUABLE`, indicating a noncontinuable exception. Any attempt to continue execution after a noncontinuable exception causes the `EXCEPTION_NONCONTINUABLE_EXCEPTION`.
ExceptionRecord	`EXCEPTION_RECORD*`: A pointer to an associated `EXCEPTION_RECORD` structure. Exception records can be chained together to provide additional information when nested exceptions occur.
ExceptionAddress	`PVOID`: The address where the exception occurred.
NumberParameters	`DWORD`: The number of parameters associated with the exception. This is the number of defined elements in the *ExceptionInformation* array.
ExceptionInformation	`DWORD[EXCEPTION_MAXIMUM_PARAMETERS]`: An array of additional 32-bit arguments that describe the exception. The `RaiseException` function can specify this array of arguments. For most exception codes, the array elements are undefined. `EXCEPTION_ACCESS_VIOLATION` does define array elements. The first element of the array contains a read-write flag that indicates the type of operation that caused the access violation. If this value is `0`, the thread attempted to read the inaccessible data. If this value is `1`, the thread attempted to write to an inaccessible address. The second array element specifies the virtual address of the inaccessible data.

Example

This example sets up an unhandled exception filter and shows how handled exceptions are trapped in exception handlers and unhandled exceptions are trapped in the unhandled exception filter.

```
#define OUR_EXCEPTION   0xE0000001

LONG WINAPI OurUnhandledExceptionFilter(LPEXCEPTION_POINTERS lpExceptionData)
{
    EXCEPTION_RECORD *ExceptionRecord = lpExceptionData->ExceptionRecord;
    CONTEXT *ContextRecord = lpExceptionData->ContextRecord;

    if (ExceptionRecord->ExceptionCode==OUR_EXCEPTION)
    {
        MessageBox( NULL, "Trapped raised exception", "Unhandled Exception Filter", MB_OK );
        return EXCEPTION_EXECUTE_HANDLER;
    }
    else
        return EXCEPTION_CONTINUE_SEARCH;
}


LRESULT CALLBACK WndProc( HWND hWnd, UINT uMsg, WPARAM wParam, LPARAM lParam )
{
    switch( uMsg )
    {
    case WM_COMMAND :
```

continued on next page

continued from previous page

```
            switch( LOWORD( wParam ) )
            {
                case IDM_TEST:
                    {
                        TCHAR szBuffer[128];
                        HDC hDC = GetDC( hWnd );

                        // Set unhandled exception handler.
                        //................................
                        SetUnhandledExceptionFilter(OurUnhandledExceptionFilter);

                        // Raise exception try block.
                        //..........................
                        try
                        {
                            wsprintf( szBuffer, "Raising OUR_EXCEPTION first time" );
                            MessageBox( hWnd, szBuffer, "Try Block", MB_OK );
                            RaiseException(OUR_EXCEPTION, 0, 0, NULL);
                        }
                        except( GetExceptionCode() == OUR_EXCEPTION )
                        {
                            wsprintf( szBuffer, "Trapped OUR_EXCEPTION in normal filter" );
                            MessageBox( hWnd, szBuffer, "Except Block", MB_OK );
                        }

                        // Raise exception again using unhandled exception filter.
                        //.......................................................
                        try
                        {
                            wsprintf( szBuffer, "Raising OUR_EXCEPTION second time" );
                            MessageBox( hWnd, szBuffer, "Try Block", MB_OK );
                            RaiseException(OUR_EXCEPTION, 0, 0, NULL);
                        }
                        except ( UnhandledExceptionFilter(GetExceptionInformation()) )
                        {
                            wsprintf( szBuffer, "Execution of except block for ⇐
OUR_EXCEPTION." );

                            MessageBox( hWnd, szBuffer, "Except Block", MB_OK );
                        }

                        ReleaseDC(hWnd, hDC);
                    }
                    break;
                        .
                        .
                        .
```

SetWaitableTimer

Description   SetWaitableTimer activates the specified waitable timer. When the time occurs, the timer is signaled and the thread that set the timer calls the optional completion routine. Timers are initially created as inactive. Once the SetWaitableTimer function is called, the timer is activated. If the timer is already active when SetWaitableTimer is called, the timer is stopped, then it is reactivated.

Syntax	BOOL **SetWaitableTimer**(HANDLE *hTimer*, const LARGE_ INTEGER* *pDueTime*, LONG *lPeriod*, PTIMERAPCROUTINE *pfnCompletionRoutine*, LPVOID *lpArgToCompletionRoutine*, BOOL *bResume*)
Parameters	
hTimer	HANDLE: The timer object to activate. This is returned from the CreateWaitableTimer or OpenWaitableTimer functions.
pDueTime	const LARGE_INTEGER*: The time delay, in 100-nanosecond intervals, before the timer is set to signaled. Use the format described by the FILETIME structure. (See the definition of the FILETIME structure under the CompareFileTime function in Chapter 17, I/O with Files.) Positive values indicate absolute time. Negative values indicate relative time. The actual timer accuracy depends on the capability of the hardware.
lPeriod	LONG: The period, in milliseconds, of the timer. If set to 0, the timer is signaled once. If greater than zero, the timer is periodic. A periodic timer automatically reactivates each time the period elapses, until the timer is canceled using the CancelWaitableTimer function or reset with the SetWaitableTimer function. If less than zero, the function fails.
pfnCompletionRoutine	PTIMERAPCROUTINE: An optional completion routine. This function is called when the timer is signaled. See the syntax of this callback function below.
lpArgToCompletionRoutine	LPVOID: A pointer to the structure that is passed to the completion routine when the timer is signaled.
bResume	BOOL: Specifies whether to restore a system in suspended power conservation mode when the timer state is set to signaled. If set to TRUE on a platform that does not support a restore, the call will succeed, but GetLastError returns ERROR_NOT_SUPPORTED.
Returns	BOOL: If successful, TRUE is returned; otherwise, FALSE is returned. Use the GetLastError function to retrieve extended error information.
Include File	winbase.h
See Also	CancelWaitableTimer, CreateWaitableTimer, OpenWaitableTimer
Callback Syntax	VOID **CompletionProc**(LPVOID *lpArgToCompletionRoutine*, DWORD *dwTimerLowValue*, DWORD *dwTimerHighValue*)
Callback Parameters	
lpArgToCompletionRoutine	LPVOID: The argument for the completion routine specified with the SetWaitableTimer function.
dwTimerLowValue	DWORD: The low value of the time at which the timer was signaled using the FILETIME format.

dwTimerHighValue	**DWORD**: The high value of the time at which the timer was signaled using the **FILETIME** format.

SignalObjectAndWait ■ Windows 95 ■ Windows NT

Description	**SignalObjectAndWait** allows the caller to atomically signal an object and wait on another object.
Syntax	DWORD **SignalObjectAndWait**(HANDLE *hObjectToSignal,* HANDLE *hObjectToWaitOn,* DWORD *dwMilliseconds,* BOOL *bAlertable*)
Parameters	
hObjectToSignal	**HANDLE**: A handle to the object to signal. This object can be a semaphore, mutex, or an event. If the handle is a semaphore, **SEMAPHORE_MODIFY_STATE** access is required. If it is an event, **EVENT_MODIFY_STATE** access is required. If it is a mutex, **SYNCHRONIZE** access is required.
hObjectToWaitOn	**HANDLE**: The handle of the object to wait for.
dwMilliseconds	**DWORD**: The time-out interval, in milliseconds. The function returns if the interval elapses, even if the object's state is nonsignaled and no completion or asynchronous procedure call (APC) objects are queued. If set to **0**, the function tests the object's state, checks for queued completion routines or APCs, and returns immediately. If set to **INFINITE**, the interval never expires.
bAlertable	**BOOL**: Specifies whether the function returns when the system queues an I/O completion routine or an APC for the calling thread. Set to **TRUE** to return on one of these; otherwise, set to **FALSE**.
Returns	**DWORD**: If successful, a value that indicates the event that caused the function to return is returned; otherwise, the return value is **0xFFFFFFFF**. Use the **GetLastError** function to retrieve extended error information. If successful, one of the values listed in Table 25-23 is returned.

Table 25-23 SignalObjectAndWait return values

Value	Meaning
WAIT_ABANDONED	The specified object is a mutex object that was not released by the thread that owned the mutex object before the owning thread terminated. Ownership of the mutex object is granted to the calling thread, and the mutex is set to nonsignaled.
WAIT_IO_COMPLETION	One or more I/O completion routines or user-mode APCs are queued for execution.
WAIT_OBJECT_0	The state of the specified object is signaled.
WAIT_TIMEOUT	The time-out interval elapsed, and the object's state is nonsignaled.

Include File	`winbase.h`
Callback Syntax	`VOID APIENTRY` **`SignalProc`**`( LPVOID` *`lpArgToCompletionRoutine,`* `DWORD` *`dwTimerLowValue,`* `DWORD` *`dwTimerHighValue`* `)`

Callback Parameters

`lpArgToCompletionRoutine`	`LPVOID`: The argument passed to the `SetWaitableTimer` function.
`dwTimerLowValue`	`DWORD`: The low-order 32 bits of the timer interval.
`dwTimerHighValue`	`DWORD`: The high-order 32 bits of the timer interval.
See Also	`MsgWaitForMultipleObjects`

Sleep ■ WINDOWS 95 ■ WINDOWS NT

Description	`Sleep` suspends execution of the current thread for a specified interval.
Syntax	`VOID` **`Sleep`**`( DWORD` *`dwMilliseconds`* `)`

Parameters

`dwMilliseconds`	`DWORD`: The number of milliseconds to suspend execution. A value of `0` causes the running thread to give up the remainder of its time slice to any other thread of equal priority that is ready to run. If no other thread of the same or higher priority is ready, the function returns immediately. If *`dwMilliseconds`* is set to `INFINITE`, the thread is suspended indefinitely.
Include File	`winbase.h`
See Also	`SuspendThread`
Example	See the example for the `RegisterHotKey` function.

SleepEx ■ WINDOWS 95 ■ WINDOWS NT

Description	`SleepEx` causes the current thread to enter a wait state until either an I/O completion callback function is called, an asynchronous procedure call (APC) is queued to the thread, or the time-out interval elapses.
Syntax	`DWORD` **`SleepEx`**`( DWORD` *`dwMilliseconds,`* `BOOL` *`bAlertable`* `)`

Parameters

`dwMilliseconds`	`DWORD`: The duration, in milliseconds, of the delay. A value of `0` causes the function to return immediately. A value of `INFINITE` cause an infinite delay.
`bAlertable`	`BOOL`: Set to `TRUE` if the function may terminate early due to an I/O completion callback function or an APC. Set to `FALSE` if the time-out period must elapse before the function returns.

Returns	DWORD: Zero is returned if the time-out interval elapsed. The return value is WAIT_IO_COMPLETION if the function returned due to one or more I/O completion callback functions.
Include File	winbase.h
See Also	Sleep, QueueUserAPC, ReadFileEx, WriteFileEx

SuspendThread ■ WINDOWS 95 ■ WINDOWS NT

Description	SuspendThread adds one to the suspend count. Whenever the suspend count of a thread is greater than zero, the thread is suspended. ResumeThread decrements the suspend count.
Syntax	DWORD **SuspendThread**(HANDLE *hThread*)
Parameters	
hThread	HANDLE: The handle to the object of the thread to be suspended.
Returns	DWORD: The previous suspend count is returned if the function succeeds; otherwise, 0xFFFFFFFF is returned. Use GetLastError to return the error code.
Include File	winbase.h
See Also	ResumeThread, Sleep
Example	See the example for the **RegisterHotKey** function.

SwitchToFiber ■ WINDOWS 95 ■ WINDOWS NT

Description	SwitchToFiber schedules a fiber to execute.
Syntax	VOID **SwitchToFiber**(LPVOID *lpFiber*)
Parameters	
lpFiber	LPVOID: The address of the fiber to execute.
Include File	winbase.h
See Also	CreateFiber, ConvertThreadToFiber

TerminateProcess ■ WINDOWS 95 ■ WINDOWS NT

Description	TerminateProcess ends a process and all of its threads. TerminateProcess is usually called by a parent process to terminate one of the processes it creates.
Syntax	BOOL **TerminateProcess**(HANDLE *hProcess*, UINT *uExitCode*)
Parameters	
hProcess	HANDLE: The process object to terminate. The handle must have PROCESS_TERMINATE access.

uExitCode	**UINT**: The process exit code to set.
Returns	**BOOL**: **TRUE** if process is terminated. Otherwise, **FALSE** is returned. Use **GetLastError** to get the error code.
Include File	**winbase.h**

> **NOTE**
> Termination of a process with **TerminateProcess** does not perform any DLL unlink code. Memory leaks may occur if DLLs are not properly exited.

See Also	**TerminateThread, ExitThread, ExitProcess, GetExitCodeProcess, GetExitCodeThread**
Example	See the example for the **DuplicateHandle** function.

TerminateThread ■ WINDOWS 95 ■ WINDOWS NT

Description	**TerminateThread**, which ends a thread, is usually called by a parent thread to terminate a thread that fails to complete normally.
Syntax	**BOOL TerminateThread(HANDLE** *hThread,* **UINT** *uExitCode* **)**
Parameters	
hThread	**HANDLE**: The thread object to be terminated. The handle must have **THREAD_TERMINATE** access.
uExitCode	**UINT**: The thread exit code to set.
Returns	**BOOL**: **TRUE** if thread is terminated. Otherwise, **FALSE** is returned. Use **GetLastError** to return the error code.
Include File	**winbase.h**

> **NOTE**
> Termination of a thread with **TerminateThread** does not perform any DLL unlink code. Memory leaks may occur if DLLs are not properly deinitialized. Also, the initial stack is not deallocated.

See Also	**TerminateProcess, ExitThread, ExitProcess, GetExitCodeProcess, GetExitCodeThread**
Example	See the example for **RegisterHotKey**.

TlsAlloc ■ WINDOWS 95 ■ WINDOWS NT

Description	**TlsAlloc** allocates a thread local storage (TLS) index. Any thread of the process can use a TLS index to store and retrieve values that are local to

the thread. The constant **TLS_MINIMUM_AVAILABLE** defines the minimum number of TLS indices available to each process.

Syntax	DWORD **TlsAlloc**(VOID)
Parameters	This function has no parameters.
Returns	**DWORD**: If the function succeeds, a TLS index is returned; otherwise, **0xFFFFFFFF** is returned. Use **GetLastError** to return the error code.
Include File	**winbase.h**
See Also	**TlsSetValue, TlsGetValue, TlsFree**
Example	This example shows a process that allocates a TLS index and starts different threads. Each thread allocates a block of data and uses **TlsSetValue** to store the block to the allocated TLS slot. When the user selects the Test! option, the threads all execute and show their locally stored data using **TlsGetValue** to resolve the pointer. **TlsFree** is used when the program exits.

```
DWORD TLSIndex = 0;
BOOL  fAbort;

VOID ShowRunningThread( HWND hWnd )
{
   HDC hDC = GetDC( hWnd );
   TextOut(hDC, 0, 0, TlsGetValue( TLSIndex ), lstrlen( TlsGetValue( TLSIndex ) ) );
   ReleaseDC( hWnd, hDC );
}


DWORD WINAPI ThreadProc( LPDWORD lpdwData )
{
   HWND hWnd = (HWND)lpdwData;
   LPVOID lpVoid = HeapAlloc( GetProcessHeap(), 0, 128 );

   wsprintf( lpVoid, "Instance %8lx is now running.   ", GetCurrentThreadId() );
   TlsSetValue( TLSIndex, lpVoid );

   while ( !fAbort )
   {
      Sleep( 500 );
      ShowRunningThread( hWnd );
      Sleep( 0 );
   }
   HeapFree( GetProcessHeap(), 0, lpVoid );

   return( 0 );
}


LRESULT CALLBACK WndProc( HWND hWnd, UINT uMsg, WPARAM wParam, LPARAM lParam )
{
   switch( uMsg )
   {
   case WM_CREATE:
           TLSIndex = TlsAlloc();
           break;
```

```
    case WM_DESTROY:
            TlsFree( TLSIndex );
            PostQuitMessage( 0 );
            break;

    case WM_COMMAND :
            switch( LOWORD( wParam ) )
            {
                case IDM_TEST:
                    {
                        int i;
                        HANDLE hThreads[4];   // Array of threads to wait for.
                        DWORD dwChildID;      // Child ID - discarded.

                        fAbort = FALSE;

                        for (i=0; i<4; i++)
                            hThreads[i] = CreateThread( NULL, 0, ThreadProc,
                                                        hWnd, 0, &dwChildID );
                        // Wait half a minute.
                        //....................
                        WaitForMultipleObjects( 4, hThreads, TRUE, 28000 );
                        fAbort = TRUE;
                        WaitForMultipleObjects( 4, hThreads, TRUE, 2000 );

                        // Clean screen.
                        //..............
                        InvalidateRect( hWnd, NULL, TRUE );
                        UpdateWindow( hWnd );
                    }
                    break;
```

TlsFree ■ WINDOWS 95 ■ WINDOWS NT

Description	**TlsFree** releases a thread local storage (TLS) index. This does not release any data that was allocated and set to the TLS index slot. It is the responsibility of each thread to manage its TLS.
Syntax	BOOL **TlsFree**(DWORD *dwTlsIndex*)
Parameters	
dwTlsIndex	**DWORD**: Specifies an allocated TLS index to be freed.
Returns	**BOOL**: **TRUE** if the function succeeds; otherwise, **FALSE**. Use **GetLastError** to return the error code.
Include File	winbase.h
See Also	TlsAlloc, TlsGetValue, TlsSetValue
Example	See the example for the **TlsAlloc** function.

TlsGetValue
■ WINDOWS 95 ■ WINDOWS NT

Description	**TlsGetValue** returns a memory element stored in a thread local storage (TLS) index that is specified.
Syntax	LPVOID **TlsGetValue**(DWORD *dwTlsIndex*)
Parameters	
dwTlsIndex	DWORD: Specifies an allocated TLS index that will be used to retrieve a thread-relative pointer to memory.
Returns	LPVOID: A pointer to allocated data-if successful; otherwise, **FALSE**. Use **GetLastError** to return the error code.
Include File	winbase.h
See Also	TlsAlloc, TlsFree, TlsSetValue
Example	See the example for the **TlsAlloc** function.

TlsSetValue
■ WINDOWS 95 ■ WINDOWS NT

Description	**TlsSetValue** stores memory in a thread local storage (TLS) index that is specified.
Syntax	BOOL **TlsSetValue**(DWORD *dwTlsIndex,* LPVOID *lpvData*)
Parameters	
dwTlsIndex	DWORD: The TLS index that is used to store a thread-relative data pointer.
lpvData	LPVOID: A pointer to the memory to store in the TLS slot.
Returns	BOOL: **TRUE** if successful; otherwise, **FALSE**. Use **GetLastError** to return the error code.
Include File	winbase.h
See Also	TlsAlloc, TlsFree, TlsGetValue
Example	See the example for the **TlsAlloc** function.

TryEnterCriticalSection
■ WINDOWS 95 ■ WINDOWS NT

Description	**TryEnterCriticalSection** attempts to enter a critical section without blocking. If the call is successful, the calling thread takes ownership of the critical section; otherwise, it returns immediately.
Syntax	DWORD **TryEnterCriticalSection**(LPCRITICAL_SECTION *lpCriticalSection*)
Parameters	
lpCriticalSection	LPCRITICAL_SECTION: The critical section object.

Returns	DWORD: If the critical section is successfully entered or the current thread already owns the critical section, the return value is nonzero. If another thread already owns the critical section, the return value is 0.
Include File	winbase.h
See Also	DeleteCriticalSection, EnterCriticalSection, InitializeCriticalSection, LeaveCriticalSection

UnhandledExceptionFilter ■ WINDOWS 95 ■ WINDOWS NT

Description	UnhandledExceptionFilter passes an exception to the debugger if the process is being debugged. If not, it activates the Application Error message box and causes the exception handler to execute. This function can be called only from within the filter expression of a **try-except** exception handler.
Syntax	LONG **UnhandledExceptionFilter**(LPEXCEPTION_POINTERS *lpExceptionInfo*)
Parameters	
lpExceptionInfo	LPEXCEPTION_POINTERS: A structure describing the exception and the context at the time of the exception.
Returns	LONG: See Table 25-21 under the function SetUnhandledExceptionFilter for a list of the return values of this function.
Include File	winbase.h
See Also	SetUnhandledExceptionFilter, SetErrorMode
Example	See the example for the SetUnhandledExceptionFilter function.

UnregisterHotKey ■ WINDOWS 95 ■ WINDOWS NT

Description	UnregisterHotKey removes the definition of a hotkey from the system.
Syntax	BOOL **UnregisterHotKey**(HWND *hWnd,* int *idHotKey*)
Parameters	
hWnd	HWND: The window notified when hotkey is pressed. This may be NULL.
idHotKey	int: The identifier of the hotkey to be deleted.
Returns	BOOL: TRUE if the function succeeds; otherwise, FALSE. Use GetLastError to return the error code.
Include File	winbase.h

NOTE
If, in a DLL, an atom was allocated to generate a unique value for the key ID, then the atom must be deleted.

See Also   GlobalDeleteAtom, RegisterHotKey

Related Messages   WM_HOTKEY

Example   See the example for the RegisterHotKey function.

WaitForInputIdle   ■ WINDOWS 95   ■ WINDOWS NT

Description   WaitForInputIdle suspends execution until a given process has input pending or a given time-out occurs. This allows a launched process to initialize itself before attempting interprocess communication.

Syntax   DWORD **WaitForInputIdle**(HANDLE *hProcess,* DWORD *dwTimeout*)

Parameters

hProcess   HANDLE: The process object that is being tested for no input pending condition.

dwTimeout   DWORD: The number of milliseconds to elapse before time-out occurs.

Returns   DWORD: The return value is 0 if wait was satisfied, WAIT_TIMEOUT if time-out elapses, or 0xFFFFFFFF if an error occurs. Use GetLastError to get the error code.

Include File   winbase.h

See Also   WaitForSingleObject, WaitForMultipleObjects

Example   See the example for the CreateProcess function.

WaitForMultipleObjects   ■ WINDOWS 95   ■ WINDOWS NT

Description   WaitForMultipleObjects is a wait function that returns only when any or all of the objects listed in a list become signaled or the specified time-out interval elapses.

Syntax   DWORD **WaitForMultipleObjects**(DWORD *dwObjectCount,* CONST HANDLE* *lphObjectList,* BOOL *bWaitAll,* DWORD *dwTimeoutInterval*)

Parameters

dwObjectCount   DWORD: The number of the object handle in the array *lphObjectList*. The maximum number of object handles allowed is MAXIMUM_WAIT_OBJECTS.

lphObjectList   CONST HANDLE*: Points to an array of object handles. The array can contain handles of the various types outlined in Table 25-24. All handles must have SYNCHRONIZE access.

Table 25-24 Object types for `WaitForMultipleObjects`

Object	Description
Change notification	The `FindFirstChangeNotification` function returns this handle.
Console input	Returned by the `CreateFile` function or by the `GetStdHandle` function.
Event	The `CreateEvent` or `OpenEvent` function returns this handle.
Mutex	The `CreateMutex` or `OpenMutex` function returns this handle.
Process	The `CreateProcess` or `OpenProcess` function returns this handle.
Semaphore	The `CreateSemaphore` or `OpenSemaphore` function returns this handle.
Thread	The `CreateProcess`, `CreateThread`, or `CreateRemoteThread` function returns this handle.
Timer	The `CreateWaitableTimer` or `OpenWaitableTimer` function returns this handle.

[handwritten note in margin: note: You can only wait for 64 process handles at one time (per process).]

bWaitAll	BOOL: Wait for any (**FALSE**) or all (**TRUE**) of the objects to become signaled.
dwTimeoutInterval	DWORD: If **0**, the states of the objects are tested and the function returns immediately. If **INFINITE**, there is no time-out. Otherwise, this parameter specifies the number of milliseconds to wait.
Returns	DWORD: If successful, the return value specifies which object caused the wait function to return. Otherwise, **WAIT_FAILED** is returned. Use `GetLastError` to retrieve the error code. Table 25-25 summarizes the return values.

Table 25-25 Return values of `WaitForMultipleObjects`

Return Value	Meaning
TRUE	All objects signaled, *bWaitAll* is TRUE.
WAIT_OBJECT_0 to	
WAIT_OBJECT_0 + *dwObjectCount*–1	First object signaled, *bWaitAll* is FALSE.
WAIT_ABANDONED_0 to	
WAIT_ABANDONED_0 + *dwObjectCount*–1	First mutex abandoned, *bWaitAll* is FALSE.
WAIT_TIMEOUT	Time-out occurred before objects satisfied wait condition.

Include File	`winbase.h`
See Also	`WaitForSingleObject`
Example	See the example for `TlsAlloc`.

WaitForMultipleObjectsEx ■ WINDOWS 95 ■ WINDOWS NT

Description	`WaitForMultipleObjectsEx` returns when either any one or all of the specified objects are in the signaled state, an I/O completion routine or

asynchronous procedure call (APC) is queued to the thread, or the time-out interval occurs.

Syntax	DWORD **WaitForMultipleObjectsEx**(DWORD *nCount,* CONST HANDLE* *lpHandles,* BOOL *bWaitAll,* DWORD *dwMilliseconds,* BOOL *bAlertable*)
Parameters	
nCount	DWORD: The number of object handles to wait for in the array pointed to by the *lpHandles* parameter. The maximum number of object handles is **MAXIMUM_WAIT_OBJECTS**.
lpHandles	CONST HANDLE*: A pointer to an array of handles to objects to wait for. On Windows NT, the handles must have the **SYNCHRONIZE** access.
bWaitAll	BOOL: Set to **TRUE** if all objects must be in the signaled state before the function returns; otherwise, **FALSE** allows the function to return once one object is in the signaled state.
dwMilliseconds	DWORD: The time-out period, in milliseconds. If this period elapses without the objects being signaled or an I/O completion routine or APC being queued, the function returns.
bAlertable	BOOL: Set to **TRUE** to allow an I/O completion routine or an APC to cause this function to return.
Returns	DWORD: If successful, the return value indicates the event that caused the function to return. If the function fails, the return value is **0xFFFFFFFF**. Use the **GetLastError** function to retrieve extended error information. Table 25-25 lists the possible return values if successful. Additionally, the **WAIT_IO_COMPLETION** value is returned if one or more I/O completion routines are queued for execution.
Include File	winbase.h
See Also	WaitForMultipleObjects

WaitForSingleObject ■ WINDOWS 95 ■ WINDOWS NT

Description	**WaitForSingleObject** returns only when the object specified in the parameter list becomes signaled or a time-out interval elapses.
Syntax	DWORD **WaitForSingleObject**(HANDLE *hObject,* DWORD *dwTimeoutInterval*)
Parameters	
hObject	HANDLE: Object to wait for. Object must have **SYNCHRONIZE** access.
dwTimeoutInterval	DWORD: If **0**, the object is tested and the function returns immediately. If **INFINITE**, there is no time-out. Otherwise, this parameter specifies the number of milliseconds to wait.
Returns	DWORD: If successful, the return value is **WAIT_OBJECT_0**, **WAIT_ABANDONED**, or **WAIT_TIMEOUT**. **WAIT_OBJECT_0** indicates that the specified object

became signaled. If the object is a mutex, **WAIT_ABANDONED** indicates that the thread owning the mutex terminated without relinquishing ownership (so ownership transfers to the caller). **WAIT_TIMEOUT** indicates that no satisfactory event took place in the allotted time. If an error occurs, **WAIT_FAILED** will be returned and **GetLastError** can be used to retrieve the error code.

Include File   winbase.h

See Also   WaitForMultipleObjects

Example   When the user selects the Test! menu option , a thread starts that waits for an event, sleeps, and releases the event. Auto-reset events enforce a serial implementation, because the event is automatically set to nonsignaled when the first waiting thread acquires the object.

```
DWORD WINAPI ChildThreadProc( LPDWORD lpdwData )
{
    TCHAR szBuffer[256];
    HWND  hWnd          = (HWND)lpdwData;
    HANDLE hAutoEvent = OpenEvent( SYNCHRONIZE, FALSE, "EXAMPLE-AUTOEVENT");

    wsprintf( szBuffer, "Thread %x waiting for Event %x",
              GetCurrentThreadId(), hAutoEvent );
    SendMessage( hWnd, WM_USER, 0, (LPARAM)szBuffer );

    // Check that write auto reset is signaled.
    //..........................................
    WaitForSingleObject( hAutoEvent, INFINITE );
    wsprintf( szBuffer,"Thread %x got event", GetCurrentThreadId() );
    SendMessage( hWnd, WM_USER, 0, (LPARAM)szBuffer );
    Sleep( 5000 );

    // Release event.
    //...............
    wsprintf( szBuffer,"Thread %x is done with event", GetCurrentThreadId() );
    SendMessage( hWnd, WM_USER, 0, (LPARAM)szBuffer );
    SetEvent( hAutoEvent );
    CloseHandle( hAutoEvent );

    return( 0 );
}


LRESULT CALLBACK WndProc( HWND hWnd, UINT uMsg, WPARAM wParam, LPARAM lParam )
{
    static HANDLE hAutoEvent = NULL;

    switch( uMsg )
    {
        case WM_CREATE :
                hAutoEvent = CreateEvent( NULL, FALSE, TRUE, "EXAMPLE-AUTOEVENT");
                break;

        case WM_DESTROY :
                if ( hAutoEvent )
```

continued on next page

continued from previous page

```
                CloseHandle( hAutoEvent );

            PostQuitMessage(0);
            break;

    case WM_USER:
            {
                // Message to show synchronization actions.
                TCHAR szBuffer[101];
                static int row = 0;
                static int msg_num = 1;
                HDC hDC = GetDC( hWnd );

                FillMemory( szBuffer, 100, 32 );
                TextOut( hDC, 0, row, szBuffer, 100 );
                wsprintf( szBuffer, "%3d: %s", msg_num++, (LPTSTR)lParam );
                TextOut( hDC, 0, row, szBuffer, lstrlen( szBuffer ) );

                row = ( row > 200 ) ? 0 : (row += 20);
                ReleaseDC( hWnd, hDC );
            }
            break;

    case WM_COMMAND :
            switch( LOWORD( wParam ) )
            {
                case IDM_TEST:
                    {
                        DWORD id = 0;
                        CreateThread( NULL, 0, ChildThreadProc, hWnd, 0, &id );
                    }
                    break;
        .
        .
        .
```

WaitForSingleObjectEx ■ WINDOWS 95 ■ WINDOWS NT

Description	WaitForSingleObjectEx returns when the specified object is in the signaled state, an I/O completion routine or asynchronous procedure call (APC) is queued to the thread, or the time-out interval occurs.
Syntax	DWORD **WaitForSingleObjectEx**(HANDLE *hHandle,* DWORD *dwMilliseconds,* BOOL *bAlertable*)
Parameters	
hHandle	HANDLE: A handle to the object for which to wait. On Windows NT, this handle must have **SYNCHRONIZE** access.
dwMilliseconds	DWORD: The time-out interval, in milliseconds. The function returns if the interval elapses, even if the object's state is nonsignaled.
bAlertable	BOOL: Set to **TRUE** to allow an I/O completion routine or an APC to cause this function to return.

Returns   DWORD: If successful, a value that indicates the event that caused the function to return is returned; otherwise, the return value is 0xFFFFFFFF. Use the GetLastError function to retrieve extended error information. If successful, one of the values listed in Table 25-26 is returned.

Table 25-26 WaitForSingleObjectEx **return values**

Value	Meaning
WAIT_ABANDONED	The specified object is a mutex object that was not released by the thread that owned the mutex object before the owning thread terminated. Ownership of the mutex object is granted to the calling thread, and the mutex is set to nonsignaled.
WAIT_IO_COMPLETION	One or more I/O completion routines or user-mode APCs are queued for execution.
WAIT_OBJECT_0	The state of the specified object is signaled.
WAIT_TIMEOUT	The time-out interval elapsed, and the object's state is nonsignaled.

Include File   winbase.h

See Also   WaitForSingleObject

WriteProcessMemory   ■ WINDOWS 95   ■ WINDOWS NT

Description   WriteProcessMemory writes data into the memory in a specified process.

Syntax   BOOL **WriteProcessMemory**(HANDLE *hProcess,* LPVOID *lpBaseAddress,* LPVOID *lpBuffer,* DWORD *dwByteCount,* LPDWORD *lpdwBytesWritten*)

Parameters

hProcess   HANDLE: The process whose memory is to be written.

lpBaseAddress   LPVOID: A pointer to address to be written. The entire area must be accessible. The process must have PROCESS_VM_WRITE and PROCESS_VM_OPERATION access.

lpBuffer   LPVOID: A pointer to the source data to be copied into *lpBaseAddress*.

dwByteCount   DWORD: The number of bytes to write.

lpdwBytesWritten   LPDWORD: A pointer to the address where number of bytes written will be stored. If NULL, this parameter is ignored.

Returns   BOOL: TRUE if the function succeeds; otherwise, FALSE. Use GetLastError to return the error code.

Include File   winbase.h

See Also   ReadProcessMemory, OpenProcess

Example   See the example for the OpenProcess function.

ERROR AND EXCEPTION PROCESSING

The Win32 API provides full support for error and exception processing. This feature is extremely important to developers, because the dynamic nature of Windows increases the chances that operations that usually succeed may fail under unforeseen circumstances. The use of error and exception processing provides for robust applications that are less vulnerable to the ever-changing conditions of the system. Furthermore, in the event of a system failure, the application can exit gracefully.

Writing Exception Handlers and Filters

Listing 26-1 is an example of code that attempts to protect itself from errors in the traditional way, by performing operations and then testing their outcomes. The code tests for both violation of the routine's protocol contract (invalid passed parameters) and system errors, such as when the system has run out of resources. Most of the time such errors will not happen, although the time spent validating the parameters may be lost thousands of times in the life of the program.

Listing 26-1 Traditional use of the Windows API

```
BOOL PaintTheBitmap ( HWND hWnd, HBITMAP hBitmap)
{
   BOOL bReturnCode = FALSE;

   // Check passed parameters.
   //........................
   if ( hWnd && hBitmap)
   {
      HDC hDC = GetDC( hWnd );
```

continued on next page

continued from previous page

```
        // Check the DC - a limited GDI resource.
        //........................................
        if ( hDC )
        {
            HDC hDcMem = CreateCompatibleDC ( hDC );

            // Check the memory DC - a limited GDI resource.
            //.............................................
            if ( hDcMem )
            {
                BITMAP bmInfo;
                HBITMAP hOneBitBitMap = SelectObject( hDcMem, hBitmap );

                // Was object selected?
                //.....................
                if ( hOneBitBitMap )
                {
                    GetObject( hBitmap, (LPTSTR) &bmInfo );
                    BitBlt(hDC, 0, 0, bm.bmWidth, bm.bmHeight, hDcMem, 0, 0, SRCCPY);
                    SelectObject ( hDcMem, hOneBitBitMap );
                    bReturnCode = TRUE;
                }
                DeleteDC(hDcMem);
            }
            ReleaseDC (hWnd, hDC );
        }
    }
    return bReturnCode;
}
```

Every time this code executes, the parameter validation occurs before you ever attempt to execute the code that does the real work. This degradation adds up, because these types of checks must be done any time you interface with the API. Not a single test in this code can be eliminated.

The workaround is to code with **try** blocks. A **try** block is a compiler-supplied mechanism that allows a block of code to be attempted, and if something goes wrong in the course of executing that section, it allows the program to attempt to recover. This leads to a clearer program and more efficient execution as well. Listing 26-2 shows the same operation as above. Notice that if no exceptions occur, the logic is very straightforward.

Listing 26-2 Using exception handlers

```
BOOL PaintTheBitmap ( HWND hWnd, HBITMAP hBitmap )
{
    try
    {
        BITMAP bmInfo;
        HDC hDCMem = NULL;
        HANDLE hOneBitBitMap = NULL;
        HDC hDC = GetDC ( hWnd );
```

```
    // Raise exception if the DC is invalid.
    //.........................................
    if ( !hDC ) RaiseException( 1, EXCEPTION_NONCONTINUABLE_EXCEPTION, 0, NULL );

    hDCMem = CreateCompatibleDC( hDC );

    // Raise exception if the hDcMem is invalid.
    //.............................................
    if ( !hDCMem ) RaiseException( 1, EXCEPTION_NONCONTINUABLE_EXCEPTION, 0, NULL );

    hOneBitBitMap = SelectObject( hDCMem, hBitmap );

    // Raise exception if the bitmap was not selected.
    //...................................................
    if ( !hOneBitBitMap ) RaiseException( 1, EXCEPTION_NONCONTINUABLE_EXCEPTION, 0, NULL );

    GetObject( hBitmap, (LPTSTR) &bmInfo );
      BitBlt ( hDC, 0, 0, bm.bmWidth, bm.bmHeight, hDcMem, 0, 0, SRCCPY );
    SelectObject( hDCMem, hOneBitBitMap );

    DeleteDC( hDCMem );
    ReleaseDC( hDC );
}
except( EXCEPTION_EXECUTE_HANDLER )
{
    if ( hDCMem ) DeleteDC( hDCMem );
    if ( hDC ) ReleaseDC( hDC );

    return( FALSE );
}

return( TRUE );
}
```

Notice that there are three components to each **try-except** clause. The first is the **try** clause itself, which contains the keyword **try** and a block of code to execute. Then there is the exception filter clause, which is the keyword **except** and the parameter enclosed in parentheses. The exception filter determines the action of the system at this level of the exception cascade. The value **EXCEPTION_EXECUTE_HANDLER** (see Table 25-17 in the function description for **SetUnhandledExceptionFilter**) indicates that the block after the exception filter is to be executed for any exception. The exception filter can also be used to select exceptions that are to be processed in the exception handler.

Another useful exception construct is the **try-finally** statement. Like the **try-except** statement, **try-finally** begins with a **try** clause. Instead of using exception filters and exception handlers, however, **try-finally** uses termination handlers. A termination handler is a block of code that follows the keyword **finally**. When an exception occurs—or, in fact, when any condition causes the **try** block to exit—the code in the termination handler is executed. Like **try-except** statements, **try-finally** statements also can be nested. See the example under the **AbnormalTermination** function later in this chapter for an example of the **try-finally** statement.

Win32 API for Exception Handling

The Win32 API includes a set of error-related functions that provide more information about the error. **GetExceptionCode** returns the exception code of the current exception. It may be called only from within an exception filter. Use **GetExceptionCode** to test both hardware and software exceptions (software exceptions may be set by using **RaiseException** as discussed in Chapter 25, Processes, Threads, and Fibers).

Within an exception handler, the function **GetExceptionInformation** returns the full context of the system, including the exception code. Within a termination block—the code that follows the **finally** keyword—call **AbnormalTermination** to determine whether the **try** block executed completely. **AbnormalTermination** does not test whether an exception occurred, because there are other ways to abort a **try** block—**goto**, **return**, **leave**, and so on.

SetErrorMode allows the system error mode to be changed. The system error mode controls how certain critical errors are handled by the system. This can be used, for example, to display an application-specific debugging interface instead of the typical Unhandled Exception box when an exception occurs. Another reason to change the system mode is to avoid the message box that appears when the system fails to find a component file, for example if a DLL is conditionally included in an application. Immediately after the dependent module is loaded, the error mode should be restored to its default value.

Error and Exception Processing Function Descriptions

Table 26-1 lists the Windows API functions that relate to error and exception processing. Complete function descriptions follow the table.

Table 26-1 Error and exception processing function summary

Function	Description
AbnormalTermination	Determines whether the previous try block ran to completion.
Beep	Produces the default beep sound.
GetExceptionCode	Determines exception code in a filter function.
GetExceptionInformation	Obtains information about the context of the processor and memory when an exception occurs.
GetLastError	Returns the error code from a thread's local storage.
SetErrorMode	Changes the system error trapping.
SetLastError	Sets the error code of a thread's local storage.
SetLastErrorEx	Sets the error code and importance in a thread's local storage.

AbnormalTermination

Description AbnormalTermination indicates whether the **try** block of a **try-finally** statement terminated normally. The function can be called only from within the **finally** block of a **try-finally** statement. The **try** block terminates normally only if execution leaves the block sequentially after executing the last statement in the block. Statements such as **return**, **goto**, **continue**, or **break**, which cause execution to leave the **try** block, result in abnormal termination of the block. Abnormal termination of a **try** block can cause the system to search backward through all stack frames to determine whether any termination handlers must be called. This can cause efficiency problems. Therefore, you should avoid abnormal terminations within **try** blocks.

Syntax BOOL **AbnormalTermination**(VOID)

Parameters This function has no parameters.

Returns BOOL: If the **try** block terminated abnormally, the return value is **TRUE**; otherwise, it is **FALSE**.

Include File excpt.h

See Also GetExceptionCode, GetExceptionInformation

Example This example shows how exceptions can be trapped in the system and how information about the state of the system is obtained. When the user selects the Test! option from the menu of the example, a software exception and then a hardware exception are raised. The exceptions are trapped in an exception handler and a termination handler respectively. AbnormalTermination is used in the termination handler to alert the user that the proceeding operation failed to complete. Figure 26-1 shows the results.

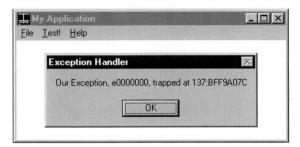

Figure 26-1 AbnormalTermination example

```
#define OUR_EXCEPTION   0xE0000000

DWORD TestException(DWORD dwExceptionCodeReceived,
                    LPEXCEPTION_POINTERS lpExceptionInfo, LPCONTEXT lpContext,
                    LPEXCEPTION_RECORD lpExceptionRecord, DWORD dwTestException )
{
    *lpContext = *lpExceptionInfo->ContextRecord;
    *lpExceptionRecord = *lpExceptionInfo->ExceptionRecord;

    if ( dwExceptionCodeReceived == dwTestException )
        return( EXCEPTION_EXECUTE_HANDLER );
    else
        return( EXCEPTION_CONTINUE_SEARCH );
}


LRESULT CALLBACK WndProc( HWND hWnd, UINT uMsg, WPARAM wParam, LPARAM lParam )
{
    switch( uMsg )
    {
    case WM_COMMAND :
            switch( LOWORD( wParam ) )
            {
                case IDM_TEST:
                    {
                        char szBuffer[128];

                        LPCONTEXT lpContext = (LPCONTEXT)
                                HeapAlloc(GetProcessHeap(), 0, sizeof(CONTEXT));

                        LPEXCEPTION_RECORD lpExcptRec = (LPEXCEPTION_RECORD)
                                HeapAlloc(GetProcessHeap(), 0, sizeof(EXCEPTION_RECORD));

                        // Raise exception try block.
                        //.........................
                        try
                        {
                            RaiseException( OUR_EXCEPTION, 0, 0, NULL );
                        }
                        except( TestException(GetExceptionCode(),⇐
GetExceptionInformation(),
                                    lpContext, lpExcptRec, OUR_EXCEPTION ) )
                        {
                            wsprintf( szBuffer, "Our Exception, %x, trapped at %X:%X",
                                    lpExcptRec->ExceptionCode,
                                    lpContext->SegCs,
                                    lpContext->Eip );
                            MessageBox( hWnd, szBuffer, "Exception Handler", MB_OK );
                        }

                        try
                        {
                            int i = 1;

                            // This will cause a divide by zero exception.
                            // After the user selects the OK, the finally
                            // handler is called and a message box displayed.
                            //...........................................
                            i = i / 0;
```

```
    }
    finally
    {
        wsprintf( szBuffer, "Abnormal Termination: %d", ⇐
AbnormalTermination() );

        Beep( 1000, 1000 );
        MessageBox( hWnd, szBuffer, "Finally Handler", MB_OK );
    }

    HeapFree( GetProcessHeap(), 0, lpExcptRec );
    HeapFree( GetProcessHeap(), 0, lpContext );
}
break;
```

.
.
.

Beep   ■ WINDOWS 95   ■ WINDOWS NT

Description	The `Beep` function is defined in the Win32 API to produce tones on the speaker of a specified frequency and duration. Under Windows 95, `Beep` will only produce the default system beep.
Syntax	`BOOL Beep( DWORD dwFreq, DWORD dwDuration )`
Parameters	
dwFreq	`DWORD`: The frequency of the sound, expressed in hertz, or cycles per second. The allowed range is 37 through 32,767 (0x25 to 0x7fff hex). This parameter is ignored in Windows 95.
dwDuration	`DWORD`: Time in milliseconds. If *dwDuration* is –1, the operation produces a sound until the speaker is programmed again. This parameter is ignored in Windows 95.
Returns	`BOOL`: `TRUE` if the function succeeds; otherwise, it is `FALSE`. Use `GetLastError` to return the error code.
Include File	`winbase.h`
See Also	`GetLastError`
Example	See the example for the `AbnormalTermination` function.

GetExceptionCode   ■ WINDOWS 95   ■ WINDOWS NT

Description	`GetExceptionCode` retrieves a code that identifies the type of exception that occurred. An application can only call this function from within the filter expression or exception-handler block of a **try-except** exception handler.
Syntax	`DWORD GetExceptionCode( VOID )`
Parameters	This function has no parameters.

Returns	DWORD: The type of exception is returned. Table 26-2 lists common hardware exceptions. GetExceptionCode also traps software exceptions produced by RaiseException, which is covered in Chapter 25, Processes, Threads, and Fibers.

Table 26-2 Standard hardware exceptions

Exception Code Constant	Description
STATUS_ACCESS_VIOLATION	This is a read or write to an inaccessible memory location. This also may be an attempt to execute data or write into a code page with an invalid selector.
STATUS_BREAKPOINT	A hardware-defined breakpoint (for debuggers only).
STATUS_FLOATING_DIVIDE_BY_ZERO	Occurs when a float is divided by 0.0.
STATUS_FLOATING_OVERFLOW	Occurs when a float's exponent overflows positively.
STATUS_FLOATING_UNDERFLOW	Occurs when a float's exponent overflows negatively.
STATUS_ILLEGAL_INSTRUCTION	Execution of an invalid instruction.
STATUS_INTEGER_DIVIDE_BY_ZERO	Integer division by zero.
STATUS_INTEGER_OVERFLOW	Occurs when an integer's range is exceeded.
STATUS_PRIVILEGED_INSTRUCTION	Execution of a privileged instruction outside of Ring-0 code.
STATUS_SINGLE_STEP	Execution of a single step (for debuggers only).

Include File	excpt.h
See Also	RaiseException, GetExceptionInformation, UnhandledExceptionFilter, SetUnhandledExceptionFilter
Example	See the example for the AbnormalTermination function.

GetExceptionInformation   ■ WINDOWS 95   ■ WINDOWS NT

Description	GetExceptionInformation returns pointers to structures that describe the state of the machine and the executing thread at the time of an exception. An application can only call this function from within the filter expression of a try-except exception handler.
Syntax	LPEXCEPTION_POINTERS GetExceptionInformation(VOID)
Parameters	This function has no parameters.
Returns	LPEXCEPTION_POINTERS: A pointer to an EXCEPTION_POINTERS structure that contains a pointer to a CONTEXT structure that describes the machine at the time of the exception and a pointer to an EXCEPTION_RECORD structure that describes the conditions of the exception. See the definition of the EXCEPTION_RECORD and EXCEPTION_POINTERS structures below. The CONTEXT structure is processor-specific register data. See the definition of this structure in the WINNT.H header file.

Include File	`excpt.h`
See Also	`GetExceptionCode, UnhandledExceptionFilter,` `SetUnhandledExceptionFilter`

EXCEPTION_POINTERS Definition

```
typedef struct _EXCEPTION_POINTERS
{
    PEXCEPTION_RECORD ExceptionRecord;
    PCONTEXT ContextRecord;
} EXCEPTION_POINTERS, *LPEXCEPTION_POINTERS;
```

Members

ExceptionRecord	PEXCEPTION_RECORD: A pointer to an **EXCEPTION_RECORD** structure. See the definition of the **EXCEPTION_RECORD** structure below.
ContextRecord	PCONTEXT: A pointer to a **CONTEXT** structure. See the definition of the **CONTEXT** structure in the **WINNT.H** header file.

EXCEPTION_RECORD Definition

```
typedef struct _EXCEPTION_RECORD
{
    DWORD ExceptionCode;
    DWORD ExceptionFlags;
    struct _EXCEPTION_RECORD *ExceptionRecord;
    PVOID ExceptionAddress;
    DWORD NumberParameters;
    DWORD ExceptionInformation[EXCEPTION_MAXIMUM_PARAMETERS];
} EXCEPTION_RECORD, *PEXCEPTION_RECORD;
```

Members

ExceptionCode	DWORD: The reason the exception occurred. This is the code generated by a hardware exception, or the code specified in the **RaiseException** function for a software-generated exception.
ExceptionFlags	DWORD: The exception flags. This member can be either **0**, indicating a continuable exception, or **EXCEPTION_NONCONTINUABLE**, indicating a noncontinuable exception.
ExceptionRecord	EXCEPTION_RECORD*: A pointer to an associated **EXCEPTION_RECORD** structure. Exception records can be chained together to provide additional information when nested exceptions occur.
ExceptionAddress	PVOID: The address where the exception occurred.
NumberParameters	DWORD: The number of parameters associated with the exception. This is the number of defined elements in the *ExceptionInformation* array.
ExceptionInformation	DWORD[EXCEPTION_MAXIMUM_PARAMETERS]: An array of additional 32-bit arguments that describe the exception. The **RaiseException** function can specify this array of arguments.
Example	See the example for the **AbnormalTermination** function.

GetLastError

Description	GetLastError returns the last error set by the system in the thread's local storage area. GetLastError is thread dependent, which means errors will not be shared among threads of a process. You should call the GetLastError function immediately when a function's return value indicates that such a call will return useful data. That is because some functions call SetLastError(0) when they succeed, wiping out the error code set by the most recently failed function. Most functions in the Win32 API that set the thread's last error code value set it when they fail. See the documentation for the individual function to determine the return code that indicates the function fails.
Syntax	DWORD **GetLastError**(VOID)
Parameters	This function has no parameters.
Returns	DWORD: The last error code set by SetLastError for the calling thread.
Include File	winbase.h
See Also	SetLastError, SetLastErrorEx
Example	This example shows how to create a function that sets its own error with the SetLastError function and retrieves the error code after the function returns with the GetLastError function.

```
#define USRERROR_NUMBER_NEGATIVE 0x10000000

BOOL RangeFunction( int a, int b )
{
   if ( a < 0 || b < 0 )
   {
      SetLastError( USRERROR_NUMBER_NEGATIVE );
      return( FALSE );
   }

   // Other code here.
   //................

   return( TRUE );
}


LRESULT CALLBACK WndProc( HWND hWnd, UINT uMsg, WPARAM wParam, LPARAM lParam )
{
   switch( uMsg )
   {
      case WM_COMMAND :
              switch( LOWORD( wParam ) )
              {
                 case IDM_TEST :
                     if ( !RangeFunction( 10, -1 ) )
                     {
                        if ( GetLastError() == USRERROR_NUMBER_NEGATIVE )
                           MessageBox( hWnd, "The range includes a negative number",
                                     "Error", MB_OK | MB_ICONEXCLAMATION );
```

```
        else
            MessageBox( hWnd, "General Error", "Error",
                        MB_OK | MB_ICONEXCLAMATION );
    }
    break;
        .
        .
        .
```

SetErrorMode

Description	**SetErrorMode** changes the way the system behaves when processing certain error conditions. This is set on a process-by-process basis, and child processes inherit the mode of the parent process.
Syntax	UINT **SetErrorMode**(UINT *uNewErrorMode*)
Parameters	
uNewErrorMode	UINT: The new error mode to be assigned. Table 26-3 gives a list of the values.

Table 26-3 SetErrorMode *uNewErrorMode* values

Error Mode	Description
SEM_FAILCRITICALERRORS	This turns off critical errors, such as drive not ready. The errors are sent to the calling process.
SEM_NOALIGNMENTFAULTEXCEPT	Indicates that for certain CPUs, Windows will automatically fix memory alignment faults and make them invisible.
SEM_NOGPFAULTERRORBOX	Disables the display of the general protection fault box that allows specifics about the condition of an exception to be seen. This should be set only if the application can provide more information than the standard GPF message box interface.
SEM_NOOPENFILEERRORBOX	Turns off the message box displayed when a file is not found. The error is returned to the calling process.

Returns	UINT: The previous mode.
Include File	winbase.h
See Also	SetUnhandledExceptionFilter, UnhandledExceptionFilter

SetLastError

Description	**SetLastError** sets the last-error code for the calling thread. The application can then use the **GetLastError** function to retrieve the error code.
Syntax	VOID **SetLastError**(DWORD *dwErrorCode*)

Parameters

dwErrorCode   DWORD: The error code to be set. Bit 29 is reserved for application-defined error codes that will not conflict with the system's error codes.

Include File   `winbase.h`

See Also   `SetLastErrorEx`

Example   See the example for the `GetLastError` function.

SetLastErrorEx   ■ Windows 95   ■ Windows NT

Description   `SetLastErrorEx` sets the last-error code. This function is identical to the `SetLastError` function; the second parameter is not currently implemented.

Syntax   `VOID` **`SetLastErrorEx`**`( DWORD dwErrorCode, DWORD dwErrorType )`

Parameters

dwErrorCode   DWORD: The error code to be set. Bit 29 is reserved for application-defined error codes that will not conflict with the system's error codes.

dwErrorType   DWORD: The error type. If the process is being debugged, the debugger may take certain actions based on the error type. If not set to **0**, *dwErrorType* may have any of the values listed in Table 26-4.

Table 26-4 `SetLastErrorEx` *dwErrorType* values

Error Type	Description
SLE_ERROR	The function received invalid data and failed completely.
SLE_MINORERROR	The function received invalid data and recovered.
SLE_WARNING	The function received potentially bad data but recovered.

Include File   `winbase.h`

See Also   `GetLastError, SetLastError`

27

MULTIPLE-DOCUMENT INTERFACE (MDI)

Many programs deal with only one file or document at a time. These applications are classified as *single-document interface,* or SDI, applications. An example of an SDI application is the Windows Notepad applet. However, users often need to see multiple documents at a time, or be able to present multiple views into the same document. Applications that let the user do this are called *multiple-document interface,* or MDI, applications.

An MDI application consists of three types of windows. The main window of the application is known as the MDI frame window. It consists of the title bar, sizing border, system menu, minimize button, and other system-defined features. An MDI application registers a window class and provides a window procedure for the MDI frame window, just as it would for a normal application window. An MDI application does not display output in its MDI frame window's client area, however. Instead, it creates an MDI client window that occupies the client area of the MDI frame window. The MDI client window belongs to the preregistered window class MDICLIENT. The MDI client window supports the creation and management of individual MDI child windows within which the document information is displayed. An MDI application may wish to display different types of document information, and therefore may contain different types of MDI child windows. Figure 27-1 shows a simple MDI application, and identifies the MDI frame window, client window, and child window.

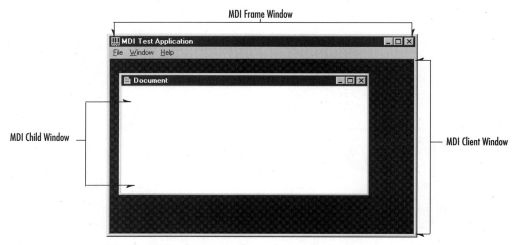

Figure 27-1 Anatomy of an MDI application

Creating an MDI Application

The first step in creating an MDI application is to register your window classes. You will need a window class for the MDI frame window, and a window class for each different type of MDI child window that your application supports. The class structure for an MDI frame window is filled in like the class structure for an SDI application's main window. The class structure for an MDI child window is filled in like the class structure for child windows in SDI applications, with two exceptions. First, the class structure for an MDI child window should specify an **ICON**, since the user can minimize MDI child windows within the MDI frame window. Second, the menu name should be **NULL**, since an MDI child window does not have its own menu. The example in Listing 27-1 illustrates the registration of two window classes. **MyMDIApp** is the class name of an MDI frame window class, and **MDIChild** is the class name of an MDI child window class.

Listing 27-1 Registration of MDI window classes

```
LPCTSTR lpszAppName = "MyMDIApp";
LPCTSTR lpszChild   = "MDIChild";
LPCTSTR lpszTitle   = "MDI Test Application";

int APIENTRY WinMain( HINSTANCE hInstance, HINSTANCE hPrevInstance, LPTSTR lpCmdLine, ⇐
int nCmdShow )
{
    MSG        msg;
    HWND       hWnd;
    WNDCLASSEX wc;
```

```
    // Register the main application window class.
    //.........................................
    wc.style          = CS_HREDRAW | CS_VREDRAW;
    wc.lpfnWndProc    = (WNDPROC)WndProc;
    wc.cbClsExtra     = 0;
    wc.cbWndExtra     = 0;
    wc.hInstance      = hInstance;
    wc.hIcon          = LoadIcon( hInstance, lpszAppName );
    wc.hCursor        = LoadCursor(NULL, IDC_ARROW);
    wc.hbrBackground  = (HBRUSH)(COLOR_APPWORKSPACE+1);
    wc.lpszMenuName   = lpszAppName;
    wc.lpszClassName  = lpszAppName;
    wc.cbSize         = sizeof(WNDCLASSEX);
    wc.hIconSm        = LoadImage( hInstance, lpszAppName,
                                   IMAGE_ICON, 16, 16,
                                   LR_DEFAULTCOLOR );
    if ( !RegisterClassEx( &wc ) )
        return( FALSE );

    // Register the window class for the MDI child windows.
    //....................................................
    wc.lpfnWndProc    = (WNDPROC)ChildWndProc;
    wc.hIcon          = LoadIcon( hInstance, lpszChild );
    wc.hCursor        = LoadCursor( NULL, IDC_ARROW );
    wc.hbrBackground  = (HBRUSH)(COLOR_WINDOW+1);
    wc.lpszMenuName   = NULL;
    wc.lpszClassName  = lpszChild;
    wc.hIconSm        = LoadImage( hInstance, lpszChild,
                                   IMAGE_ICON, 16, 16,
                                   LR_DEFAULTCOLOR );
    if ( !RegisterClassEx( &wc ) )
        return( FALSE );
}
```

After you register the window classes, create the MDI frame window just as you would in an SDI application, which is shown in Listing 27-2.

Listing 27-2 Creating an MDI frame window

```
        .
        .
        .
// Create the main application window.
//..................................
hWnd = CreateWindow( lpszAppName, lpszTitle, WS_OVERLAPPEDWINDOW,
                     CW_USEDEFAULT, 0, CW_USEDEFAULT, 0,
                     NULL, NULL, hInstance, NULL );

if ( !hWnd )
    return( FALSE );

ShowWindow( hWnd, nCmdShow );
UpdateWindow( hWnd );
        .
        .
        .
```

MDI applications must call the `TranslateMDISysAccel` function in the main message loop to process the predefined MDI specific accelerator keys. For MDI applications that have an accelerator table, you must call the `TranslateMDISysAccel` function before the call to `TranslateAccelerator` in order to allow Windows to handle any predefined MDI accelerators before the application-specific accelerators. Since this test application does not have an accelerator table, only the `TranslateMDISysAccel` function is called, as shown in the following code segment:

```
        .
        .
        .
while( GetMessage( &msg, NULL, 0, 0) )
{
    if ( hWndClient && TranslateMDISysAccel( hWndClient, &msg ) )
        continue;

    TranslateMessage( &msg );
    DispatchMessage( &msg );
}
        .
        .
        .
```

Once the main message loop for your application is running, it becomes the responsibility of the MDI frame window's window procedure to coordinate the creation and management of the individual MDI child windows.

The MDI Frame Window

The MDI frame window is responsible for creating the MDI client window, usually during processing of the **WM_CREATE** message. You create the MDI client window using the preregistered window class MDICLIENT as shown in Listing 27-3. The MDI client window will dynamically alter one of the pop-up menu items in the frame window's menu bar, so you must pass the menu handle for the pop-up menu that the MDI client window is to alter as the final parameter to the **CreateWindowEx** function. For more detailed information on how the MDI client window alters this pop-up menu, refer to Menus in MDI Applications later in this chapter.

Listing 27-3 Creating the MDI frame window

```
HWND hWndClient = NULL;

// An ID that is different than all menu ids.
//...........................................
#define ID_CHILDWINDOW 1000

LRESULT CALLBACK WndProc( HWND hWnd, UINT uMsg, WPARAM wParam, LPARAM lParam )
{
    switch( uMsg )
    {
```

```
case WM_CREATE :
    {
        CLIENTCREATESTRUCT ccs;

        // Assign the 'Window' menu.
        //.........................
        ccs.hWindowMenu = GetSubMenu( GetMenu( hWnd ), 1 );
        ccs.idFirstChild = ID_CHILDWINDOW;

        // Create the client window.
        //.........................
        hWndClient = CreateWindowEx( WS_EX_CLIENTEDGE, "MDICLIENT",
                                     NULL,
                                     WS_CHILD | WS_CLIPCHILDREN,
                                     0, 0, 0, 0,
                                     hWnd, (HMENU)0xCA0, hInst, &ccs);

        ShowWindow( hWndClient, SW_SHOW );
    }
    break;
    .
    .
    .
```

One additional style bit is available when creating the MDI client window. If you create the MDI client with the **MDIS_ALLCHILDSTYLES** style bit, Windows will not limit the valid style bits for MDI child windows. If the MDI client window is created without the **MDIS_ALLCHILDSTYLES** style bit set, then only those values listed in Table 27-1 may be specified. Use of the **MDIS_ALLCHILDSTYLES** style bit allows an application to create MDI child windows with nonstandard MDI child behaviors.

Table 27-1 CreateMDIWindow *dwStyle* values

Value	Description
WS_HSCROLL	Window has a horizontal scroll bar.
WS_MAXIMIZE	Window is created maximized.
WS_MINIMIZE	Window is created minimized.
WS_VSCROLL	Window has a vertical scroll bar.

The MDI frame window is also responsible for creating and destroying the individual MDI child windows. You create MDI child windows using either the **CreateMDIWindow** function or the **WM_MDICREATE** window message. This is typically done in response to menu items such as File Open, File New, File Save, and File Close. The example in Listing 27-4, taken from the window procedure of the MDI frame window, illustrates the creation of an MDI child window in response to the menu item **IDM_NEW**.

Listing 27-4 Creating a new MDI child window

```
LRESULT CALLBACK WndProc( HWND hWnd, UINT uMsg, WPARAM wParam, LPARAM lParam )
{
    switch( uMsg )
    {
    case WM_COMMAND :
            switch( LOWORD( wParam ) )
            {
            case IDM_NEW :
                {
                    HWND hWndChild;

                    // Create a new child window.
                    //...........................
                    hWndChild = CreateMDIWindow( (LPTSTR)lpszChild, "Document", 0L,
                                            CW_USEDEFAULT, CW_USEDEFAULT,
                                            CW_USEDEFAULT, CW_USEDEFAULT,
                                            hWndClient, hInst, 0L);

                    ShowWindow( hWndChild, SW_SHOW );
                }
                break;
                 .
                 .
                 .
```

In all cases where the MDI frame window procedure does not explicitly handle a particular message, that message must be passed to the **DefFrameProc** function, as opposed to the **DefWindowProc** function in a normal window procedure. This allows Windows to provide default MDI behavior.

The MDI Child Window

The work that would normally be done in an SDI application's main window is carried out in MDI applications by the MDI child window. The window procedure for an MDI child window is identical to its SDI counterpart, with the exception of default message processing. An MDI child window uses the function **DefMDIChildProc** to handle unprocessed window messages.

The major difference between an SDI application window and an MDI child window is that the SDI application contains only one instance of the application window, which is used to manipulate one set of data. An MDI application will usually have several instances of the MDI child window, all acting on different sets of data. Note, however, that there is only one window procedure specified for all instances of a given MDI child window. This means that the code in the window procedure for an MDI child window must be able to determine which instance of the data the current message is for.

The window procedure is passed the window handle of the MDI child window as its first parameter. You can use one of several techniques to associate a particular set of data with this window handle.

The **CreateMDIWindow** function and the **WM_MDICREATE** message allow the creating procedure, typically an MDI frame window, to pass a 32-bit value to the MDI child window during the processing of its **WM_CREATE** message. This 32-bit value could contain a pointer to the data structure that this MDI child window is to access. The MDI child window could then store this pointer in one of the window's extra bytes. Allocate space for the data by specifying a value that is the number of bytes required to contain a pointer to your data structure for the *cbWndExtra* member of the **WNDCLASS** structure when registering the window class. The MDI child window then can use **GetWindowLong**, casting as appropriate, to retrieve this pointer. The example in Listing 27-5 illustrates how an MDI child window would retrieve this 32-bit value during processing of its **WM_CREATE** message.

Listing 27-5 Retrieving 32-bit value in **WM_CREATE**

```
LRESULT ChildWndProc( HWND hWndChild, UINT uMsg, WPARAM wParam, LPARAM lParam )
{
    static LPARAM FrameParam;

    switch( uMsg )
    {
        case WM_CREATE :
                {
                    LPCREATESTRUCT lpCreateStruct = (LPCREATESTRUCT)lParam;
                    LPMDICREATESTRUCT lpMDICreateStruct =
                                (LPMDICREATESTRUCT)lpCreateStruct->lpCreateParams;

                    FrameParam = lpMDICreateStruct->lParam;
                }
                break;
            .
            .
            .
```

An application can use window properties instead of using the window's extra bytes. The advantage to window properties is that you do not need to allocate extra space for the data when registering the window class. In addition, window properties are accessed using strings, which can be self-documenting. In this case, the value of the window property would be a pointer to the data structure associated with the given window.

Finally, some applications may find it more appropriate to keep individual data structures in a linked list, and to include the window handle of the window associated with a given data structure as part of the structure itself. It is then necessary only to traverse the linked list, matching window handles in the data structure against the window handle given to the window procedure to determine for which data structure a given message is intended.

Menus in MDI Applications

The MDI frame window menu should include a window pop-up menu item. This pop-up menu item is typically defined just before the Help pop-up menu item, and contains the submenu items Tile, Cascade, Arrange Icons, and Close All Child Windows. These are implemented using the window messages defined later in this chapter. In addition, the MDI client window will add the names of newly created MDI child windows to the bottom of the pop-up menu item you specify when creating the MDI client window.

Figure 27-2 shows a simple MDI application. There are currently four MDI child windows open, one of which has been minimized to the bottom of the MDI client window. Notice the Window menu. The MDI client window has dynamically placed the names of the four MDI child windows at the bottom of the pop-up menu, and has placed a checkmark next to the currently active MDI child window.

Windows provides several accelerator keys for MDI applications. It requires no extra code to implement these accelerators. These functions are provided simply by using the MDI versions of the default message-processing functions in the MDI frame and MDI child windows, using the MDI accelerator translation function in your main message loop, and having an MDI client window of the MDICLIENT class. Table 27-2 defines these new accelerator keys.

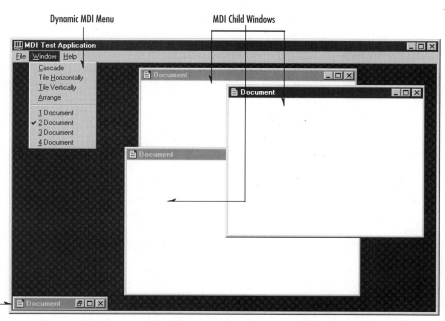

Figure 27-2   A simple MDI application

Table 27-2 Accelerator keys for MDI applications

Accelerator Key	Purpose
`ALT`-`-`	Opens the MDI child windows system menu.
`F4`	Closes the active MDI child window.
`F6`	Activates the next MDI child window.
`SHIFT`-`F6`	Activates the previous MDI child window.

MDI Function and Message Descriptions

Table 27-3 specifies the Windows functions and messages used to implement the MDI application interface. Detailed descriptions of each function and message follow the table.

Table 27-3 MDI function and message summary

Function	Purpose
ArrangeIconicWindows	Arranges minimized MDI child windows at the bottom of the MDI client window.
CascadeWindows	Arranges nonminimized MDI child windows in a cascade (overlapped) arrangement.
CreateMDIWindow	Creates a new MDI child window and returns its window handle.
DefFrameProc	Used in the window procedure of an MDI frame window to process any unhandled window messages.
DefMDIChildProc	Used in the window procedure of an MDI child window to process any unhandled window messages.
TileWindows	Arranges nonminimized MDI child windows in a tiled (nonoverlapped) arrangement.
TranslateMDISysAccel	Used in the main message loop of an MDI application to handle any predefined window accelerators specific to MDI windows.

Message	Purpose
WM_MDIACTIVATE	When sent to an MDI client window, causes a new MDI child window to be activated. When received by an MDI child window, indicates that the window is being either activated or deactivated.
WM_MDICASCADE	When sent to an MDI client window, causes all of the MDI child windows to be cascaded.
WM_MDICREATE	When sent to an MDI client window, creates a new MDI child window.
WM_MDIDESTROY	Indicates to an MDI child window that it is being destroyed.
WM_MDIGETACTIVE	When sent to an MDI client window, returns the window handle of the currently active MDI child window.
WM_MDIICONARRANGE	When sent to an MDI client window, causes all of the minimized MDI child windows icons to be arranged along the bottom of the MDI client window.
WM_MDIMAXIMIZE	When sent to an MDI client window, causes the specified MDI child window to be maximized.
WM_MDINEXT	When sent to an MDI client window, causes the MDI child window after (or before) the specified MDI child window to become active.

continued on next page

continued from previous page

Message	Purpose
WM_MDIREFRESHMENU	When sent to an MDI client window, causes the MDI client to update the state of the menu after changes have been made.
WM_MDIRESTORE	When sent to an MDI client window, causes the indicated MDI child window to be restored from either a maximized or minimized state.
WM_MDISETMENU	When sent to an MDI client window, sets the MDI frame menu to the indicated menu. This allows MDI child windows to implement individual menus.
WM_MDITILE	When sent to an MDI client window, causes all MDI child windows to be tiled.

ArrangeIconicWindows ■ WINDOWS 95 ■ WINDOWS NT

Description   **ArrangeIconicWindows** arranges all minimized MDI child windows. An application also can use the **WM_MDIICONARRANGE** message as an alternative. Windows will arrange the minimized MDI child windows along the bottom of the MDI client window.

Syntax   UINT **ArrangeIconicWindows**(HWND *hWndClient*)

Parameters

hWndClient   HWND: Specifies the window handle of the MDI client window that manages this MDI child window.

Returns   UINT: If successful, the height of one row of icons is returned; otherwise, **0** is returned.

Include File   winuser.h

Related Messages   WM_MDIICONARRANGE

Example   The following code segment would appear as part of the window procedure for the MDI frame window, responding to a menu item with the identifier **IDM_ARRANGE**.

```
HWND hWndClient;

LRESULT CALLBACK WndProc( HWND hWnd, UINT uMsg, WPARAM wParam, LPARAM lParam )
{
    switch( uMsg )
    {
        case WM_COMMAND :
            switch( LOWORD( wParam ) )
            {
                case IDM_ARRANGE :
                    ArrangeIconicWindows( hWndClient );
                    break;
                .
                .
                .
```

CascadeWindows
■ WINDOWS 95 ■ WINDOWS NT

Description	`CascadeWindows` arranges all nonminimized MDI child windows in a cascaded (overlapped) manner. `CascadeWindows` is similar to the `WM_MDICASCADE` message and identical to the `CascadeChildWindows` function, except that the user can specify the window handles of the windows to be affected, and can limit the area of the MDI client window that is used.
Syntax	WORD WINAPI **CascadeWindows**(HWND *hWndParent,* WORD *wFlags,* LPCRECT *lpWindowRect,* WORD *nWindowCount,* CONST HWND* *lpWndArray*)
Parameters	
hWndParent	HWND: Specifies the window handle of the parent window. Child windows of the parent window will be arranged. This parameter typically specifies the MDI client window handle. If this parameter is **NULL**, the desktop window is assumed.
wFlags	WORD: Specifies various arrangement flags. Table 27-4 gives a list of valid values, which is currently only a single value.

Table 27-4 `CascadeWindows` *wFlags* values

Value	Meaning
`MDITILE_SKIPDISABLED`	Prevents disabled MDI child windows from being cascaded.

lpWindowRect	LPCRECT: Points to a **RECT** structure that defines the boundaries within which the child windows are arranged. If this parameter is **NULL**, the entire client area of the parent window is assumed.
nWindowCount	WORD: Specifies the number of window handles included in the *lpWndArray* array. This value is ignored if *lpWndArray* is **NULL**.
lpWndArray	CONST HWND*: Specifies an array of child window handles. If this parameter is **NULL**, then all child windows of the parent window are subject to being arranged.
Returns	WORD: If successful, the number of windows arranged is returned; otherwise, **0** is returned.
Include File	`winuser.h`
See Also	`CascadeChildWindows, TileChildWindows, TileWindows`
Related Messages	`WM_MDICASCADE`
Example	The following code segment responds to the Cascade menu item.

```
HWND hWndClient;

LRESULT CALLBACK WndProc( HWND hWnd, UINT uMsg, WPARAM wParam, LPARAM lParam )
{
    switch( uMsg )
    {
    case WM_COMMAND :
            switch( LOWORD( wParam ) )
            {
            case IDM_CASCADE :
                    CascadeWindows( hWndClient, MDITILE_SKIPDISABLED, NULL, O, NULL );
                    break;
        .
        .
        .
```

CreateMDIWindow   ■ WINDOWS 95   ■ WINDOWS NT

Description	**CreateMDIWindow** creates an MDI child window. An application must use this function to create MDI child windows, rather than using the **CreateWindow** or **CreateWindowEx** functions. An application also can use the **WM_MDICREATE** message as an alternative.
Syntax	HWND **CreateMDIWindow**(LPCTSTR *lpszClassName*, LPCTSTR *lpszWindowName*, DWORD *dwStyle*, int *x*, int *y*, int *nWidth*, int *nHeight*, HWND *hWndClient*, HINSTANCE *hInstance*, LPARAM *lParam*)
Parameters	
lpszClassName	LPCTSTR: Points to a null-terminated string specifying the class name of the MDI child window. The class name must have been registered by a call to **RegisterClass**.
lpszWindowName	LPCTSTR: Points to a null-terminated string that specifying the window name.
dwStyle	DWORD: Specifies the window styles of the MDI child window. If the MDI client was created specifying the style **MDIS_ALLCHILDSTYLES**, then any window styles listed in the discussion of **CreateWindow** can be specified. Otherwise, only the styles shown in Table 27-1 may be specified.
x	**int**: Specifies the initial horizontal position, in client coordinates, of the MDI child window. Use the value **CW_USEDEFAULT** to allow Windows to assign a default value to this parameter.
y	**int**: Specifies the initial vertical position, in client coordinates, of the MDI child window. Use the value **CW_USEDEFAULT** to allow Windows to assign a default value to this parameter.
nWidth	**int**: Specifies the initial width, in client coordinates, of the MDI child window. Use the value **CW_USEDEFAULT** to allow Windows to assign a default value to this parameter.

nHeight	**int**: Specifies the initial height, in client coordinates, of the MDI child window. Use the value **CW_USEDEFAULT** to allow Windows to assign a default value to this parameter.
hWndClient	**HWND**: Specifies the window handle of the MDI client window that is to manage this MDI child window.
hInstance	**HINSTANCE**: Identifies the instance of the application that is creating the MDI child window.
lParam	**LPARAM**: An application-defined value. This value is passed to the MDI child window during the processing of the **WM_CREATE** message. When the MDI child window receives a **WM_CREATE** message, the *lParam* of this message contains a pointer to a **CREATESTRUCT** structure. The first member of this structure, *lpCreateParams*, contains a pointer to an **MDICREATESTRUCT** structure. The *lParam* member of this structure contains the 32-bit value of *lParam* from the **CreateMDIWindow** function. See the definition of the **CREATESTRUCT** structure below. See the definition of the **MDICREATESTRUCT** structure under the **WM_MDICREATE** message.
Returns	**HWND**: If successful, this function returns the window handle of the new MDI child window; otherwise, it returns **NULL**.
Include File	winuser.h
Related Messages	WM_MDICREATE

CREATESTRUCT Definition

```
typedef struct tagCREATESTRUCT
{
    LPVOID      lpCreateParams;
    HINSTANCE   hInstance;
    HMENU       hMenu;
    HWND        hwndParent;
    int         cy;
    int         cx;
    int         y;
    int         x;
    LONG        style;
    LPCTSTR     lpszName;
    LPCTSTR     lpszClass;
    DWORD       dwExStyle;
} CREATESTRUCT;
```

Members

lpCreateParams	**LPVOID**: A pointer to data to be used for creating the window. In Windows NT, this member is the address of a **SHORT** (16-bit) value that specifies the size, in bytes, of the window creation data. This value is followed by the creation data. When referring to the data pointed to by this parameter, because the pointer may not be **DWORD** aligned, the application should use a pointer declared as **UNALIGNED**.
hInstance	**HINSTANCE**: The instance handle of the module that owns the new window.
hMenu	**HMENU**: The menu to be used by the new window.

hwndParent	**HWND**: The parent window handle, if the window is a child window. If the window is owned, this member identifies the owner window. If the window is not a child or owned window, this member is **NULL**.
cy	**int**: The height, in pixels, of the new window.
cx	**int**: The width, in pixels, of the new window.
y	**int**: The y coordinate of the upper left corner of the new window. If the new window is a child window, coordinates are relative to the parent window. Otherwise, the coordinates are relative to the screen origin.
x	**int**: The x coordinate of the upper left corner of the new window. If the new window is a child window, coordinates are relative to the parent window. Otherwise, the coordinates are relative to the screen origin.
style	**LONG**: The style for the new window. This is a combination of the window styles valid for use with the **CreateWindow** function.
lpszName	**LPCTSTR**: A pointer to a null-terminated string that specifies the name of the new window.
lpszClass	**LPCTSTR**: A pointer to a null-terminated string that specifies the class name of the new window.
dwExStyle	**DWORD**: The extended style for the new window. This is a combination of the extended window styles valid for use with the **CreateWindowEx** function.
Example	This example creates a new MDI child window when the user selects the New menu item. The currently active MDI child window is closed when the user selects the Close menu item.

```
HWND hWndClient;

LRESULT CALLBACK WndProc( HWND hWnd, UINT uMsg, WPARAM wParam, LPARAM lParam )
{
   switch( uMsg )
   {
      case WM_COMMAND :
            switch( LOWORD( wParam ) )
            {
               case IDM_NEW :
                     {
                        HWND hWndChild;

                        // Create a new child window.
                        //.........................
                        hWndChild = CreateMDIWindow( (LPTSTR)lpszChild, "Document", 0L,
                                                CW_USEDEFAULT, CW_USEDEFAULT,
                                                CW_USEDEFAULT, CW_USEDEFAULT,
                                                hWndClient, hInst, 0L);

                        ShowWindow( hWndChild, SW_SHOW );
                     }
                     break;
```

```
        case IDM_CLOSE :
            {
                HWND hActiveWnd;

                // Close the active child window.
                //..............................
                hActiveWnd = (HWND)SendMessage( hWndClient, WM_MDIGETACTIVE, 0, 0 );

                if ( hActiveWnd )
                    SendMessage( hWndClient, WM_MDIDESTROY, (WPARAM)hActiveWnd, 0 );
            }
            break;

        default :
                return( DefFrameProc( hWnd, hWndClient, uMsg, wParam, lParam ) );
        }
        break;

    case WM_DESTROY :
        PostQuitMessage(0);
        break;
        .
        .
        .

    default :
            return( DefFrameProc( hWnd, hWndClient, uMsg, wParam, lParam ) );
    }
    return( 0L );
}
```

DefFrameProc ■ Windows 95 ■ Windows NT

Description	The window procedure of an MDI frame window passes all unprocessed messages to **DefFrameProc**. **DefFrameProc** allows Windows to provide default MDI application behavior.
Syntax	LRESULT **DefFrameProc**(HWND *hWndFrame*, HWND *hWndClient,* UINT *uMsg,* WPARAM *wParam,* LPARAM: *lParam*)
Parameters	
hWndFrame	HWND: Specifies the window handle of the MDI frame window.
hWndClient	HWND: Specifies the window handle of the MDI client window.
uMsg	UINT: Specifies the message to be processed.
wParam	WPARAM: Specifies additional data, specific to this message.
lParam	LPARAM: Specifies additional data, specific to this message.
Returns	LRESULT: The return value is specific to the message being processed. The MDI frame windows window procedure should simply return **DefFrameProc**'s return value.
Include File	winuser.h
See Also	DefMDIChildProc, DefWindowProc
Example	See the example for the **CreateMDIWindow** function.

DefMDIChildProc   ■ WINDOWS 95   ■ WINDOWS NT

Description	The window procedure of an MDI child window passes all unprocessed messages to this function. `DefMDIChildProc` allows Windows to provide default MDI application behavior.
Syntax	LRESULT **DefMDIChildProc**(HWND *hWndChild,* UINT *uMsg,* WPARAM *wParam,* LPARAM *lParam*)
Parameters	
hWndChild	HWND: Specifies the window handle of the MDI child window.
uMsg	UINT: Specifies the message to be processed.
wParam	WPARAM: Specifies additional data, specific to this message.
lParam	LPARAM: Specifies additional data, specific to this message.
Returns	LRESULT: The return value is specific to the message being processed. The MDI child window's window procedure should simply return `DefMDIChildProc`'s return value.
Include File	`winuser.h`
See Also	`DefFrameProc, DefWindowProc`
Example	The following code segment shows the implementation of a minimal window procedure for an MDI child window.

```
LRESULT CALLBACK ChildWndProc( HWND hWnd, UINT uMsg, WPARAM wParam, LPARAM lParam )
{
   switch( uMsg )
   {
     default :
         return( DefMDIChildProc( hWnd, uMsg, wParam, lParam ) );
   }
   return( OL );
}
```

TileWindows   ■ WINDOWS 95   ■ WINDOWS NT

Description	`TileWindows` arranges all nonminimized MDI child windows in a tiled (nonoverlapped) manner. This function is similar to the **WM_MDITILE** message and identical to the `TileChildWindows` function, except that the user can specify the window handles of the windows to be affected, and can limit the area of the MDI client window that is used.
Syntax	WORD WINAPI **TileWindows**(HWND *hWndParent,* WORD *wFlags,* LPCRECT *lpWindowRect,* WORD *nWindowCount,* CONST HWND* *lpWndArray*)
Parameters	

hWndParent	**HWND**: Specifies the window handle of the parent window. Child windows of the parent window will be arranged. This parameter typically specifies the MDI client window handle. If this parameter is **NULL**, the desktop window is assumed.
wFlags	**WORD**: Specifies various arrangement flags. Table 27-4 gives a list of valid values. In addition, the **MDITILE_VERTICAL** and **MDITILE_HORIZONTAL** flags from Table 27-5 may be specified.
lpWindowRect	**LPCRECT**: Points to a **RECT** structure that defines the boundaries within which the child windows are arranged. If this parameter is **NULL**, the entire client area of the parent window is assumed.
nWindowCount	**WORD**: Specifies the number of window handles included in the *lpWndArray* array. This value is ignored if *lpWndArray* is **NULL**.
lpWndArray	**CONST HWND***: Specifies an array of child window handles. If this parameter is **NULL**, then all child windows of the parent window are subject to being arranged.
Returns	**WORD**: If successful, the number of windows arranged is returned; otherwise, **0** is returned.
Include File	`winuser.h`
See Also	`CascadeChildWindows`, `CascadeWindows`, `TileChildWindows`
Related Messages	`WM_MDITILE`
Example	This code segment responds to the user's selecting the Tile Horizontally and Tile Vertically menu items.

```
HWND hWndClient;

LRESULT CALLBACK WndProc( HWND hWnd, UINT uMsg, WPARAM wParam, LPARAM lParam )
{
   switch( uMsg )
   {
      case WM_COMMAND :
             switch( LOWORD( wParam ) )
             {
                case IDM_TILEHORZ :
                       TileWindows( hWndClient, MDITILE_HORIZONTAL, NULL, 0, NULL );
                       break;

                case IDM_TILEVERT :
                       TileWindows( hWndClient, MDITILE_VERTICAL, NULL, 0, NULL );
                       break;

                .
                .
                .
```

TranslateMDISysAccel　　　■ WINDOWS 95　■ WINDOWS NT

Description　　An MDI application must call **TranslateMDISysAccel** in its main message loop before calling the normal **TranslateAccelerator** function. This gives the system a chance to interpret standard MDI accelerator keys before the message is processed by the application.

Syntax　　BOOL **TranslateMDISysAccel**(HWND *hWndClient,* LPMSG *lpMsg*)

Parameters

hWndClient　　HWND: The window handle of the MDI client window.

lpMsg　　LPMSG: Pointer to the MSG structure containing the current message.

Returns　　BOOL: If the message was handled by this function, the return value is **TRUE**, and no further message processing is required. If this message returns **FALSE**, the message was not processed, and normal message processing should continue.

Include File　　winuser.h

See Also　　TranslateAccelerator

Example　　The following sequence of code shows the main message loop for a typical MDI application.

```
        .
        .
        .
while( GetMessage( &msg, NULL, 0, 0) )
{
    if ( hWndClient && TranslateMDISysAccel( hWndClient, &msg ) )
        continue;
    TranslateMessage( &msg );
    DispatchMessage( &msg );
}
        .
        .
        .
```

WM_MDIACTIVATE　　　■ WINDOWS 95　■ WINDOWS NT

Description　　**WM_MDIACTIVATE** is a message sent to the MDI client window to force one of the MDI child windows to become the active window. This is usually done by the default window procedure handler in response to predefined accelerator keys. If an MDI child window receives this message, it indicates that the MDI child window is either becoming the active window, or is no longer the active window.

Parameters

wParam　　HWND: The window handle of the MDI child window to be activated.

lParam	**HWND**: When this message is sent, this parameter is unused and should be set to **0**. When this message is received by an MDI child window, this parameter is the window handle of the MDI child window that is being deactivated.
Returns	**LRESULT**: If this message is processed by an MDI child window, the return value should be set to **0**.
Include File	**winuser.h**
Related Messages	**WM_MDIGETACTIVE, WM_MDINEXT, WM_NCACTIVATE**

WM_MDICASCADE   ■ Windows 95   ■ Windows NT

Description	**WM_MDICASCADE** is a message sent to the MDI client window to cause all nonminimized MDI child windows to be rearranged in a cascaded (overlapped) arrangement.
Parameters	
wParam	**UINT**: The only value currently supported for this parameter is **MDITILE_SKIPDISABLED**, which prevents disabled MDI child windows from being moved.
lParam	**LPARAM**: Not used; set to **0**.
Returns	**BOOL**: If successful, the return value is **TRUE**; otherwise, it is **FALSE**.
Include File	**winuser.h**
See Also	**CascadeWindows**
Related Messages	**WM_MDIICONARRANGE, WM_MDITILE**

WM_MDICREATE   ■ Windows 95   ■ Windows NT

Description	**WM_MDICREATE** is a message sent to the MDI client window to create a new MDI child window.
Parameters	
wParam	**WPARAM**: Not used; set to **0**.
lParam	**LPMDICREATESTRUCT**: A pointer to an **MDICREATESTRUCT** structure. This structure is used by the MDI client window in the creation of the new MDI child window. See the definition of the **MDICREATESTRUCT** structure below.
Returns	**HWND**: If this message is successful, it returns the window handle of the new MDI child window; otherwise, it returns **NULL**.
Include File	**winuser.h**
See Also	**CreateMDIWindow**

Related Messages   WM_CREATE, WM_MDIDESTROY

MDICREATESTRUCT Definition

```
typedef struct tagMDICREATESTRUCT
{
    LPCTSTR szClass;
    LPCTSTR szTitle;
    HANDLE  hOwner;
    int     x;
    int     y;
    int     cx;
    int     cy;
    DWORD   style;
    LPARAM  lParam;
} MDICREATESTRUCT, *LPMDICREATESTRUCT;
```

Members

szClass   LPCTSTR: A pointer to a null-terminated string specifying the name of the window class of the MDI child window. The class name must have been registered by a previous call to the **RegisterClass** or **RegisterClassEx** function.

szTitle   LPCTSTR: A pointer to a null-terminated string that represents the title of the MDI child window. Windows displays the title in the child window's title bar.

hOwner   HANDLE: The instance handle of the application creating the MDI client window.

x   int: The initial horizontal position, in client coordinates, of the MDI child window. If this member is **CW_USEDEFAULT**, the MDI child window is assigned the default horizontal position.

y   int: The initial vertical position, in client coordinates, of the MDI child window. If this member is **CW_USEDEFAULT**, the MDI child window is assigned the default vertical position.

cx   int: The initial width, in device units, of the MDI child window. If this member is **CW_USEDEFAULT**, the MDI child window is assigned the default width.

cy   int: The initial height, in device units, of the MDI child window. If this member is set to **CW_USEDEFAULT**, the MDI child window is assigned the default height.

style   DWORD: The style of the MDI child window. If the MDI client window was created with the **MDIS_ALLCHILDSTYLES** window style, this member can be any combination of the window styles listed in the description of the **CreateWindow** function. Otherwise, this member can be one or more of the values listed in Table 27-1.

lParam   LPARAM: An application-defined 32-bit value.

WM_MDIDESTROY ■ WINDOWS 95 ■ WINDOWS NT

Description	**WM_MDIDESTROY** is a message sent to an MDI client window to cause the indicated MDI child window to be closed.
Parameters	
wParam	**HWND**: Indicates which MDI child window is to be closed.
lParam	**LPARAM**: Not used; set to **0**.
Returns	**LRESULT**: This message always returns **0**.
Include File	winuser.h
Related Messages	WM_MDICREATE

WM_MDIGETACTIVE ■ WINDOWS 95 ■ WINDOWS NT

Description	**WM_MDIGETACTIVE** is a message sent to the MDI client window to determine which MDI child window is currently the active window.
Parameters	
wParam	**WPARAM**: Not used; set to **0**.
lParam	**LPBOOL**: An optional pointer to a Boolean variable that receives a value that indicates the maximized state of the MDI child window. A **TRUE** value indicates the MDI child window is maximized. Set to **NULL** if this value is not required.
Returns	**HWND**: If successful, this returns the window handle of the MDI child window that is currently active. Otherwise, it returns **NULL**.
Include File	winuser.h
See Also	GetWindowLong
Related Messages	WM_MDIACTIVATE

WM_MDIICONARRANGE ■ WINDOWS 95 ■ WINDOWS NT

Description	**WM_MDIICONARRANGE** is a message sent to the MDI client window to rearrange all minimized MDI child windows. Icons representing the minimized child windows are arranged along the bottom of the MDI client window.
Parameters	This message has no parameters.
Returns	This message does not return a value.
Include File	winuser.h
See Also	ArrangeIconicWindows
Related Messages	WM_MDICASCADE, WM_MDITILE, WM_MDIRESTORE

WM_MDIMAXIMIZE   ■ Windows 95   ■ Windows NT

Description	WM_MDIMAXIMIZE is a message sent to the MDI client window to maximize an MDI child window. A maximized MDI child window occupies the entire MDI client window, appends its caption text to the MDI frame window's caption, places a RESTORE button on the far right of the MDI frame window's menu bar, and places its SYSTEM menu button on the far left of the MDI frame window's menu bar.
Parameters	
wParam	HWND: The window handle of the MDI child window to be maximized.
lParam	LPARAM: Not used; set to 0.
Returns	LRESULT: The return value is always 0.
Include File	winuser.h
Related Messages	WM_MDIRESTORE

WM_MDINEXT   ■ Windows 95   ■ Windows NT

Description	WM_MDINEXT is a message sent to the MDI client window that will activate either the next MDI child window or the previous MDI child window.
Parameters	
wParam	HWND: The window handle of an MDI child window. The MDI child window to be activated is either the next or the previous MDI child window, with relation to this window.
lParam	UINT: If this parameter is 0, the next MDI child window is activated; otherwise, the previous MDI child window is activated.
Returns	The return value is always 0.
Include File	winuser.h
Related Messages	WM_MDIACTIVATE, WM_MDIGETACTIVE

WM_MDIREFRESHMENU   ■ Windows 95   ■ Windows NT

Description	WM_MDIREFRESHMENU is a message sent to the MDI client window to refresh the MDI frame window's menu bar. This is usually done after the application has made some modifications to the menu. After sending this message, the application must call DrawMenuBar to redraw the menu.
Parameters	This message has no parameters.
Returns	HMENU: If successful, the return value is the handle of the MDI frame windows menu; otherwise, it is NULL.

Include File	winuser.h
See Also	DrawMenuBar
Related Messages	WM_MDISETMENU

WM_MDIRESTORE ■ WINDOWS 95   ■ WINDOWS NT

Description	**WM_MDIRESTORE** is a message sent to the MDI client window to restore a minimized or maximized MDI child window to its original size before being minimized or maximized.
Parameters	
wParam	**HWND**: Indicates the MDI child window to be restored.
lParam	**LPARAM**: Not used; set to **0**.
Returns	**LRESULT**: The return value is always **0**.
Include File	winuser.h
Related Messages	WM_MDIMAXIMIZE

WM_MDISETMENU ■ WINDOWS 95   ■ WINDOWS NT

Description	**WM_MDISETMENU** is a message sent to the MDI client window to associate a different menu with the application window. You can replace either the entire menu bar or just the pop-up menu item being dynamically altered by the MDI client window.
Parameters	
wParam	**HMENU**: The menu handle of the menu that is to replace the MDI frame window's menu bar. If you're not replacing the entire menu bar, set this parameter to **NULL**.
lParam	**HMENU**: The menu handle of the menu that is to replace the MDI frame window's pop-up menu that is being dynamically altered by the MDI client window. If you're not replacing the pop-up menu, this parameter should be **NULL**.
Returns	**HMENU**: If successful, the return value is the menu handle of the MDI frame window's menu bar; otherwise, it is **NULL**.
Include File	winuser.h
See Also	DrawMenuBar
Related Messages	WM_MDIREFRESHMENU

WM_MDITILE ■ WINDOWS 95   ■ WINDOWS NT

Description WM_MDITILE is a message sent to the MDI client window to cause all non-minimized MDI child windows to be rearranged in a tiled (nonoverlapped) arrangement.

Parameters

wParam UINT: Specifies a tile flag. This parameter may be one of the values shown in Table 27-5.

Table 27-5 WM_MDITILE parameter values

Value	Description
MDITILE_HORIZONTAL	Tiles the windows so that they extend the width of the MDI client window.
MDITILE_SKIPDISABLED	Prevents disabled MDI child windows from being affected.
MDITILE_VERTICAL	Tiles the windows so that they extend the height of the MDI client window.

lParam LPARAM: Not used; must be 0.

Returns BOOL: If successful, the return value is TRUE; otherwise, it is FALSE.

Include File winuser.h

See Also TileWindows

Related Messages WM_MDICASCADE, WM_MDIICONARRANGE

28

INTERFACING WITH HELP FILES

Because Windows provides standard functionality for many common application tasks, application designers can concentrate on providing extra features. As a result, applications have become extremely powerful. Unfortunately, as applications become more powerful, they also become more complicated. Providing written documentation rarely solves this problem, because typical users are not inclined to read a manual until they have reached a fairly high level of frustration.

The obvious solution to this problem is to provide your documentation in an online format. Windows provides an application called Windows Help (`WINHLP32.EXE`) that allows the user to easily browse through online documentation that is in the standard help file (`.HLP`) format. In addition, Windows provides functions and messages that an application can use to interact with Windows Help. This interaction allows an application to provide context-sensitive help, tips, training cards, and other features not available in written documentation.

When creating the help file, you specify the help text, bitmaps, sounds, and other resources that will be used by Windows Help. The help text consists of the actual documentation, as well as the specification of keywords, titles, browsing order, and other information. These are all combined by the Windows Help Compiler into the help (HLP) file that your application will reference.

Providing User Access to the Help File

Your application can use several methods to present your help file to the user. At a minimum, your application should provide a Help menu item as the rightmost item on the menu bar. This pop-up menu should have at a minimum the submenu items listed in Table 28-1. Figure 28-1 shows an example of a common help menu.

Figure 28-1   Common Help menu

Table 28-1 Items to include in the Help menu item in Windows 95 applications	
Menu Item	**Description**
Help Topics	Brings up the Windows help index (the Help Finder).
About <*application*>	Displays a dialog box identifying the application, version, etc. This menu item should be separated from the others by a menu separator.

Your application should define these menu items in its resource file, and process the associated **WM_COMMAND** messages in its window procedure. To process the About menu item, the application typically displays a dialog box that contains the application's icon, version number, copyright information, and any other identification information. Figure 28-2 shows an example of the dialog box displayed by the Windows **NOTEPAD.EXE** application in response to the About menu item. The other menu items are processed by using the **WinHelp** function, which provides interaction between the application and the Windows help system. Refer to the description of the **WinHelp** function later in this chapter for more information.

The example in Listing 28-1 shows how to handle the Help Topics and About menu items.

Listing 28-1 Help menu options example

```
LRESULT CALLBACK WndProc( HWND hWnd, UINT uMsg, WPARAM wParam, LPARAM lParam )
{
    switch( uMsg )
    {
    case WM_COMMAND :
            switch( LOWORD( wParam ) )
            {
                case IDM_HELP_TOPICS :
                        WinHelp( hWnd, "HELPTEST.HLP", HELP_FINDER, 0 );
                        break;

                case IDM_ABOUT :
                        DialogBox( hInst, "AboutBox", hWnd, (DLGPROC)About );
                        break;

                case IDM_EXIT :
                        DestroyWindow( hWnd );
                        break;
            }
            break;
```

```
    case WM_DESTROY :
            // Close Help file if it is displayed.
            //.......................................
            WinHelp( hWnd, "HELPTEST.HLP", HELP_QUIT, 0 );
            PostQuitMessage(0);
            break;

    default :
            return( DefWindowProc( hWnd, uMsg, wParam, lParam ) );
    }
    return( 0L );
}
```

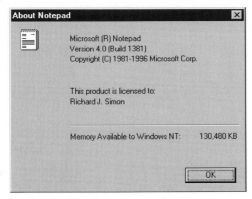

Figure 28-2   The About dialog box

Providing Context-Sensitive Help

In addition to providing a Help menu item, whenever possible your application should provide *context-sensitive help*. Context-sensitive help uses the **WinHelp** function to display a topic that is determined based on the current state of the application. When a user requests context-sensitive help, Windows sends your application a **WM_HELP** message. The user requests context-sensitive help by pressing F1, or clicking on the Help icon (if available) in the application's title bar, and then clicking on a menu, control, or window in your application for which to receive help. This results in a different form of the **WM_HELP** message being sent to your application. In either case, the *lParam* parameter of the **WM_HELP** message points to a **HELPINFO** structure that your application can use to determine which help topic to display. The application should process the **WM_HELP** message by calling **WinHelp** with the **HELP_WM_HELP** flag and an array of control IDs and context help IDs.

If possible, applications should also provide a pop-up menu with a What's This? menu item that displays context-sensitive help for the item on which the right mouse button was clicked. This is done by processing the **WM_CONTEXTMENU** message and calling the `WinHelp` function with `HELP_CONTEXTMENU` and the same array of control IDs and context help IDs as used with the `WM_HELP` message.

The example in Listing 28-2 illustrates the handling of the `WM_HELP` and `WM_CONTEXTMENU` messages in a dialog procedure to provide context-sensitive help.

Listing 28-2 Context-sensitive help in a dialog box

```
LRESULT CALLBACK HlpDialog( HWND hDlg, UINT message, WPARAM wParam, LPARAM lParam )
{
    static DWORD nIDs[] = { IDC_RADIO1, HELP_BASE+IDC_RADIO1,
                            IDC_RADIO2, HELP_BASE+IDC_RADIO2,
                            IDC_RADIO3, HELP_BASE+IDC_RADIO3,
                            IDOK,       HELP_BASE+IDOK,
                            IDCANCEL,   HELP_BASE+IDCANCEL,
                            IDHELP,     HELP_BASE+IDHELP,
                            0, 0 };

    switch (message)
    {
        case WM_HELP :
            {
                int       i = 0;
                LPHELPINFO lpInfo = (LPHELPINFO)lParam;

                // Make sure that the window is within our help IDs.
                // This eliminates the "No help..." message.
                //.................................................
                while( nIDs[i] )
                {
                    if ( nIDs[i] == (DWORD)GetWindowLong( lpInfo->hItemHandle, GWL_ID ) )
                    {
                        WinHelp( lpInfo->hItemHandle, "HELPTEST.HLP",
                                 HELP_WM_HELP, (DWORD)(LPVOID)nIDs );
                        break;
                    }
                    i += 2;
                }
            }
            break;

        case WM_CONTEXTMENU :
            {
                int i = 0;

                // Make sure that the window is within our help IDs.
                // This eliminates the "No help..." message.
                //.................................................
                while( nIDs[i] )
                {
                    if ( nIDs[i] == (DWORD)GetWindowLong( (HWND)wParam, GWL_ID ) )
                    {
                        WinHelp( (HWND)wParam, "HELPTEST.HLP",
                                 HELP_CONTEXTMENU, (DWORD)(LPVOID)nIDs );
                        break;
                    }
                    i += 2;
                }
```

```
        }
        break;
    .
    .
    .
```

Applications can use the **SetMenuContextHelpID** and **SetWindowContextHelpID** functions to set the context ID values for their menus, windows, and controls. These values are then passed to your application in the *dwContextID* member of the **HELPIN-FO** structure with the **WM_HELP** message. You can query the context ID values of menus, windows, and controls by using the **GetMenuContextHelpID** and **GetWindowContextHelpID** functions.

Using Training Card Help

Training cards provide a more interactive approach to the Windows help system and help the user perform complex tasks by leading them through the process. An application initiates training card help by combining the **HELP_TCARD** flag with another command in a call to **WinHelp**. Windows Help will display the requested topic, which normally will contain one or more authorable buttons that the user can select. When the user selects one of these buttons, or carries out some other action, Windows help sends a **WM_TCARD** message to the application, indicating the user's action. See the example under the **WM_TCARD** message later in this chapter for an example of an application using training card help.

Help Files Function and Message Descriptions

Table 28-2 summarizes the functions and messages used to interface with help files. A detailed description of each function and message follows the table.

Table 28-2 Help files function and message summary

Function	Purpose
GetMenuContextHelpId	Retrieves the help context ID of the specified menu.
GetWindowContextHelpId	Retrieves the help context ID of the specified window or control.
SetMenuContextHelpId	Sets the help context ID of the specified menu.
SetWindowContextHelpId	Sets the help context ID of the specified window or control.
WinHelp	Executes the Windows help engine.

Message	Purpose
WM_HELP	Sent to an application when the user presses the F1 key or clicks on the question mark icon in the application's title bar.
WM_TCARD	Allows interaction between an application and the Windows help engine during a training card session.

GetMenuContextHelpId   ■ Windows 95   ■ Windows NT

Description	GetMenuContextHelpId retrieves the help context ID of the specified menu. This ID value is set using the SetMenuContextHelpId function.
Syntax	DWORD **GetMenuContextHelpId**(HMENU *hMenu*)
Parameters	
hMenu	HMENU: Specifies the menu handle of the menu whose context ID is to be returned.
Returns	DWORD: The context ID of the specified menu, if successful. Otherwise, the value 0 is returned.
Include File	winuser.h
See Also	SetMenuContextHelpId

GetWindowContextHelpId   ■ Windows 95   ■ Windows NT

Description	GetWindowContextHelpId retrieves the help context ID of the specified window or control. This ID value is set using the SetWindowContextHelpId function. A window or control that has not had its help context ID set inherits the ID of its parent.
Syntax	DWORD **GetWindowContextHelpId**(HWND *hWindow*)
Parameters	
hWindow	HWND: Specifies the window or control handle of the window whose context ID is to be returned.
Returns	DWORD: The context ID of the specified window, if successful. Otherwise, the value 0 is returned.
Include File	winuser.h
See Also	SetWindowContextHelpId

SetMenuContextHelpId   ■ Windows 95   ■ Windows NT

Description	SetMenuContextHelpId sets the help context ID of the specified menu. This ID value is retrieved using the GetMenuContextHelpId function. The menu context ID is available through the HELPINFO structure during processing of the WM_HELP message.
Syntax	BOOL **SetMenuContextHelpId**(HMENU *hMenu*, DWORD *dwContextHelpID*)
Parameters	
hMenu	HMENU: Specifies the menu handle of the menu whose context ID is to be set.
dwContextHelpID	DWORD: Specifies the help context ID. The menu item's help context ID is set to this value.

Returns	BOOL: If successful, **TRUE** is returned; otherwise, **FALSE** is returned.
Include File	`winuser.h`
See Also	`GetMenuContextHelpId`

SetWindowContextHelpId   ■ WINDOWS 95   ■ WINDOWS NT

Description	**SetWindowContextHelpId** sets the help context ID of the specified window or control. Retrieve this ID value using the **GetWindowContextHelpId** function. A window or control that has not had its help context ID set inherits the ID of its parent. The window or control context ID is available through the **HELPINFO** structure during processing of the **WM_HELP** message.
Syntax	BOOL **SetWindowContextHelpId**(HWND *hWindow,* DWORD *dwContextHelpID*)
Parameters	
hWindow	HWND: Specifies the window or control handle of the window whose context ID is to be returned.
dwContextHelpID	DWORD: Specifies the help context ID. The window or control item's help context ID is set to this value.
Returns	BOOL: If successful, **TRUE** is returned; otherwise, **FALSE** is returned.
Include File	`winuser.h`
See Also	`GetWindowContextHelpId`

WinHelp   ■ WINDOWS 95   ■ WINDOWS NT

Description	**WinHelp** provides interaction between the Windows help system and the application. This function starts Windows Help (**WINHLP32.EXE**) and passes additional data indicating the nature of the help requested by the application. The application specifies the name and, where required, the directory path of the help file to display. Before closing the window that requested the help, the application must call **WinHelp** with the *uCommand* parameter set to **HELP_QUIT**. Until all applications have done this, Windows Help will not terminate. If **WinHelp** was called with the **HELP_CONTEXTPOPUP** command, this is not necessary.
Syntax	BOOL **WinHelp**(HWND *hWnd,* LPCTSTR *lpszHelpFile,* UINT *uCommand,* DWORD *dwData*)
Parameters	
hWnd	HWND: The window handle of the window requesting help. This is normally the application's main window, except when *uCommand* is **HELP_CONTEXTMENU** or **HELP_WM_HELP**, in which case it is the ID of the control or window about which help is requested.

lpszHelpFile	**LPCTSTR**: The name of the application's HLP file. The file name may have a greater-than sign (>) and window name specified after it, in which case the help is displayed in a secondary window of the type specified by the window name. This secondary window name must have been specified in the **WINDOWS** section of the HPJ file.
uCommand	**UINT**: The command for the Windows help system. This command may be any of the values listed in Table 28-3.
dwData	**DWORD**: Provides additional data as required by the *uCommand* parameter.

Table 28-3 `WinHelp` *uCommand* values

Value	Description
HELP_COMMAND	Executes the identified help macros. The *dwData* parameter points to a string of help macros, separated by semicolons. If a macro has both a short name and a long name, use the short name.
HELP_CONTENTS	Causes Windows Help to display the topic that is identified as the contents topic in the HPJ file. This is typically used by Windows 3.x applications when the user clicks on the Help Contents menu item. Windows 95 and Windows NT 4.x applications should use the HELP_FINDER command instead of HELP_CONTENTS.
HELP_CONTEXT	Causes Windows Help to display the topic that is associated with the 32-bit context ID specified by the *dwData* parameter.
HELP_CONTEXTMENU	Causes Windows Help to display the help menu for the selected window, and then display the associated help topic in a pop-up window. The *dwData* parameter points to an array of DWORD pairs. The first DWORD in each pair is the identifier of a window or control, and the second DWORD is the context ID of the associated topic.
HELP_CONTEXTPOPUP	Causes Windows Help to display the topic that is associated with the 32-bit context ID specified by the *dwData* parameter. The topic is displayed in a pop-up window.
HELP_FINDER	Displays the help file topic list.
HELP_FORCEFILE	Ensures that Windows Help is displaying the proper HLP file. If the specified HLP file is not being displayed, Windows Help opens it. Otherwise, no action is performed.
HELP_HELPONHELP	Displays the WINHELP.HLP help file, providing help on using the Windows help system. This is typically used by Windows 3.x applications when the user clicks on the Help On Using Help menu item. Windows 95 and Windows NT 4.x applications should use the HELP_FINDER command instead of HELP_HELPONHELP.
HELP_INDEX	Displays the help file index. This is typically used by Windows 3.x applications when the user clicks on the Help Index menu item. Windows 95 and Windows NT 4.x applications should use the HELP_FINDER command instead of HELP_INDEX.
HELP_KEY	Searches the HLP file for topics that specify a keyword matching the keyword pointed to by the *dwData* parameter. If more than one topic matches the keyword, the matching topics are listed in a dialog box.
HELP_MULTIKEY	Searches the HLP file for topics that specify a keyword matching the given keyword. The *dwData* parameter points to a MULTIKEYHELP structure that identifies the keyword table to search and the keyword string.
HELP_PARTIALKEY	Searches the HLP file for topics that specify a keyword matching the keyword pointed to by the *dwData* parameter. If more than one topic matches the keyword, the index tab is displayed. You can force Windows Help to display the index tab by specifying an empty string as the keyword.

Value	Description
HELP_QUIT	Informs the Windows help system that the application has finished using help. The HLP file will be closed, and the help window will be removed.
HELP_SETCONTENTS	Sets the context identifier for the contents topic. Windows Help will display this topic in response to a HELP_CONTENTS command or when the user clicks the Contents button in the help window. The *dwData* parameter specifies a 32-bit context ID for the topic that is to become the contents topic.
HELP_SETINDEX	Specifies which keyword table is to be displayed in the Help Topics dialog box.
HELP_SETWINPOS	Sets the size and position of the main help window, or a secondary window. The *dwData* parameter points to a HELPWININFO structure, defined below.
HELP_TCARD	Initiates training card help. This command cannot be used alone, but must be combined with one of the other help commands using the bitwise OR operation.
HELP_WM_HELP	An application can use this command in response to a WM_HELP message. In this case, the hWnd parameter should be the handle of the control as passed in the HELPINFO structure. The *dwData* parameter points to an array of DWORD pairs. The first DWORD of each pair specifies a control identifier, and the second DWORD specifies the context ID of a help topic to be displayed for that control identifier.

Returns	BOOL: If successful, TRUE is returned; otherwise, FALSE is returned.
Include File	winuser.h
See Also	GetMenuContextHelpID, GetWindowContextHelpID, SetMenuContextHelpID, SetWindowContextHelpID
Related Messages	WM_HELP, WM_TCARD

HELPWININFO Definition

```
typedef struct
{
    int    wStructSize;
    int    x;
    int    y;
    int    dx;
    int    dy;
    int    wMax;
    TCHAR rgchMember[2];
} HELPWININFO;
```

Members

wStructSize   int: The size, in bytes, of the structure.

x   int: The x coordinate, in screen coordinates, of the upper-left corner of the window.

y   int: The y coordinate, in screen coordinates, of the upper-left corner of the window.

dx   int: The width, in pixels, of the window.

dy   int: The height, in pixels, of the window.

wMax   int: Specifies how to show the window. This member can be any of the show states available with the **ShowWindow** function.

rgchMember	TCHAR[2]: The name of the window.
Example	See Listing 28-1 at the beginning of this chapter for an example of this function.

WM_HELP ■ Windows 95 ■ Windows NT

Description	**WM_HELP** is a message sent to an application when the user requests context-sensitive help. This can happen when the user presses the F1 key or clicks on the Help icon (if available) on the application's title bar, and then clicks on a control, window, or menu item.
	Normally, an application responds to this message by issuing the **HELP_WM_HELP** command with the **WinHelp** function, using information in the **HELPINFO** structure.
Parameters	
wParam	WPARAM: Not used.
lParam	LPHELPINFO: Points to a **HELPINFO** structure identifying the help request. See the definition of the **HELPINFO** structure below.
Returns	BOOL: An application should return **TRUE** if it processes this message.
See Also	WinHelp
Related Messages	WM_TCARD
HELPINFO Definition	

```
typedef  struct  tagHELPINFO
{
    UINT     cbSize;
    int      iContextType;
    int      iCtrlId;
    HANDLE   hItemHandle;
    DWORD    dwContextId;
    POINT    MousePos;
} HELPINFO, *LPHELPINFO;
```

Members	
cbSize	UINT: The size, in bytes, of the structure.
iContextType	int: The type of context for which help is requested. Set to **HELPINFO_MENUITEM** if help is requested for a menu item; otherwise, set to **HELPINFO_WINDOW** if help is requested for a control or window.
iCtrlId	int: The identifier of the window or control if *iContextType* is **HELPINFO_WINDOW**; otherwise, it is the identifier of the menu item.
hItemHandle	HANDLE: The handle of the child window or control if *iContextType* is **HELPINFO_WINDOW**; otherwise, it is the handle of the associated menu.
dwContextId	DWORD: The help context identifier of the window or control.
MousePos	POINT: The screen coordinates of the mouse cursor.

Example	See Listing 28-2 at the beginning of this chapter for an example of this message.

WM_TCARD ■ Windows 95 ■ Windows NT

Description	The Windows help system sends **WM_TCARD** to the application when the user clicks on an authorable button that is associated with the **Tcard** help macro or performs some other action within a training card session of Windows Help.
Parameters	
wParam	**WPARAM**: Identifies the action that the user has taken. This may be any of the values listed in Table 28-4.
lParam	**LPARAM**: Specifies additional data depending on the value of *wParam*.

Table 28-4 WM_TCARD *wParam* values

Value	Description
HELP_TCARD_DATA	The user has clicked an authorable button. The *dwData* parameter contains a 32-bit value specified by the help author.
HELP_TCARD_NEXT	The user has clicked an authorable Next button.
HELP_TCARD_OTHER_CALLER	A different application has requested training card help.
IDABORT	The user has clicked an authorable Abort button.
IDCANCEL	The user has clicked an authorable Cancel button.
IDCLOSE	The user has closed the training card help session.
IDHELP	The user has clicked an authorable Help button.
IDIGNORE	The user has clicked an authorable Ignore button.
IDNO	The user has clicked an authorable No button.
IDOK	The user has clicked an authorable OK button.
IDRETRY	The user has clicked an authorable Retry button.
IDYES	The user has clicked an authorable Yes button.

Returns	**LRESULT**: An application should return **0**.
See Also	WinHelp
Related Messages	WM_HELP
Example	The following example initiates a training card help session and responds to the **WM_TCARD** messages **IDOK**, **IDCANCEL**, and **IDABORT**. The example also processes the **HELP_TCARD_DATA** message by checking the appropriate radio button based on the user's selection in the training session.

```
LRESULT CALLBACK HlpDialog( HWND hDlg, UINT message, WPARAM wParam, LPARAM lParam )
{
    switch( message )
    {
        case WM_TCARD :
                switch( wParam )
                {
                    case IDOK :
                            EndDialog( hDlg, IDOK );
                            break;

                    case IDCANCEL :
                            EndDialog( hDlg, IDCANCEL );
                            break;

                    case IDABORT :
                            EnableWindow( hDlg, TRUE );
                            break;

                    case HELP_TCARD_DATA :
                            CheckRadioButton( hDlg, IDC_RADIO1, IDC_RADIO3, lParam );
                            break;
                }
                break;

        case WM_COMMAND:
                switch( LOWORD( wParam ) )
                {
                    case IDOK :
                            EndDialog( hDlg, IDOK );
                            break;

                    case IDCANCEL :
                            EndDialog( hDlg, IDCANCEL );
                            break;

                    case IDHELP :
                            WinHelp( hDlg, "HELPTEST.HLP", HELP_TCARD | HELP_CONTEXT,⇐
IDH_TRAINING );
                            EnableWindow( hDlg, FALSE );
                            break;
                }
                break;
    }
    return (FALSE);
}
```

29

FILE DECOMPRESSION AND INSTALLATION

When operating systems were simpler, and the typical user was interested in computers as a hobby, file installation was fairly easy. Most applications simply came with a document that told users to copy all the necessary files to their hard disk, and that was all there was to it.

Today's Windows NT and Windows 95 environment is considerably more complicated, and the typical user is more interested in accomplishing tasks than in understanding how the computer works. Satisfying these users made application installation programs significantly more difficult to develop. An installation program now must deal with such things as compressed installation files and multiple versions of system libraries. The Win32 API contains functions that allow your application to deal with these situations. In addition, it also contains many functions that help your application work with compressed files. You can use these functions in any situation, but they are used most often in conjunction with application installation packages.

File Installation Overview

Consider, as an example, the problem posed by the existence of multiple versions of the common dialog library `COMMDLG.DLL`. This library provides common dialog boxes for applications. Imagine that a computer user has installed a new application package that uses the latest version of this library. Everything is working well. The user then purchases a copy of your application that the local software store has had on its shelf for several months. Your application also uses the `COMMDLG.DLL` library, but since it was packaged some months ago, it includes a rather old copy of this library. If your installation program simply copies the `COMMDLG.DLL` library to the user's system, your application will work fine, but the original application that required the newer version of the library will no longer function correctly. Your installation program has caused a problem for the user by unintentionally replacing a newer version of the `COMMDLG.DLL` library with an older version.

This is just one example of where your installation program must be smart enough to realize that some files are shared by multiple programs and that it should never overwrite a newer version with an older one. On the reverse side, it is good practice to ask the user before overwriting an older version with a newer version. This is because some newer versions of common files can also cause problems for older programs, and the user should have the choice.

Many of these problems are covered when using one of the third-party installation packages that are available. These programs generally deal with a script that is interpreted, and the third-party software actually performs the installation. This chapter covers the Win32 APIs that are available to help you write your own installation program.

Installing the Proper Version

Because of the problem outlined in the previous section, application installation programs should not blindly copy files to the user's system. Instead, an application should determine if a version of the file already exists, and whether or not the existing file is newer than the file about to be installed. Windows provides the `VerFindFile` and `VerInstallFile` functions just for this purpose. `VerFindFile` determines where an application should install a given file. It checks the system for existing copies of the file, and returns information that is then used by `VerInstallFile`. Listing 29-1 shows a function that uses the `VerFindFile` and `VerInstallFile` functions to determine where to install a shared file and to install it.

Listing 29-1 Installing with version checking

```
        .
        .
        .
// Install a shared file with version checking.
//..............................................
InstallSharedFile( "COMMDLG.DLL", "C:\\MYAPP" );

        .
        .
        .

DWORD InstallSharedFile( LPCTSTR szFileToInstall, LPCTSTR szDirectory )
{
    TCHAR szWinDir[_MAX_PATH];    // Holds the windows directory.
    TCHAR szCurDir[_MAX_PATH];    // Returns path to preexisting file.
    TCHAR szDestDir[_MAX_PATH];   // Returns recommended path for file.
    TCHAR szTmpFile[_MAX_PATH];   // Buffer for temporary file name.
    UINT uCurLen = MAX_PATH;      // Holds the length of szCurDir.
    UINT uDestLen = MAX_PATH;     // Holds the length of szDestDir.
```

```
UINT uTmpLen = MAX_PATH;        // Holds the length of szTmpFile.
DWORD dwStatus;                 // Return value from function.

// Get the windows directory.
//........................
GetWindowsDirectory( szWinDir, sizeof(szWinDir) );

// Find out if this file exists on the system already and where.
//.............................................................
dwStatus = VerFindFile( VFFF_ISSHAREDFILE, szFileToInstall, szWinDir, szDirectory,
                        szCurDir, &uCurLen, szDestDir, &uDestLen );

if ( dwStatus == VFF_FILEINUSE )
    MessageBox( "This file is in use, close all applications and try again.",
                "Install", MB_OK | MB_ICONSTOP );
else
    dwStatus = VerInstallFile( O, szFileToInstall, szFileToInstall,
                               "A:\\", szDestDir, szCurDir, szTmpFile, &uTmpLen );

return( dwStatus );
}
```

The first parameter to **VerFindFile** indicates whether or not the file is private to this application. In the example above, **VFF_ISSHAREDFILE** indicates that the given file is shared among different Windows applications. After the call to **VerFindFile**, the buffer *szDestDir* will contain the location for the new file that Windows recommends. The buffer *szCurDir* will contain the location of any preexisting version of the file. The return value from **VerFindFile** can be one of the values shown in Table 29-5 in the description of this function.

After having called **VerFindFile**, and assuming that no errors were encountered, the application can use **VerInstallFile** to actually install the file. **VerInstallFile** copies the new file into a temporary file, decompressing it, if necessary. It then checks the version information of any preexisting file. If **VerInstallFile** finds no problems, the new file is installed in place of the original file. **VerInstallFile** returns a bit mask containing one or more of the values shown in Table 29-7 indicating the success or failure of the installation. Refer to the description of **VerInstallFile** later in this chapter for more information.

The Version Resource

You should include a *version information resource* within executable files, libraries, and controls. Create this resource just as you do other Windows resources, such as bitmaps and menus—with a resource editor. If an error occurs while installing files, the application can retrieve the version information resource to display useful error messages to the user. An application can retrieve the version information resource for any file with the **GetFileVersionInfoSize**, **GetFileVersionInfo**, and **VerQueryValue** functions. Listing 29-2 shows an example of a version resource.

Listing 29-2 Version resource

```
1 VERSIONINFO
    FILEVERSION 1,0,0,1
    PRODUCTVERSION 1,0,0,1
    FILEFLAGSMASK 0x3fL
#ifdef _DEBUG
    FILEFLAGS 0x1L
#else
    FILEFLAGS 0x0L
#endif
    FILEOS 0x4L
    FILETYPE 0x1L
    FILESUBTYPE 0x0L
    BEGIN
        BLOCK "StringFileInfo"
        BEGIN
            BLOCK "040904b0"
            BEGIN
                VALUE "Comments", "This is a sample version information header.\0"
                VALUE "CompanyName", "Waite Group Press\0"
                VALUE "FileDescription", "Sample Application\0"
                VALUE "FileVersion", "1.01\0"
                VALUE "InternalName", "VerQuery\0"
                VALUE "LegalCopyright", "Copyright \251 1996\0"
                VALUE "OriginalFilename", "VerQuery.RC\0"
                VALUE "ProductName", "Version Query Example\0"
                VALUE "ProductVersion", "1.0\0"
            END
        END
        BLOCK "VarFileInfo"
        BEGIN
            VALUE "Translation", 0x409, 1200
        END
    END
```

Once you have retrieved the version information resource, you can use **VerQueryInfo** to obtain specific values. Refer to the description of **VerQueryValue** for details on retrieving information from the version information resource.

File Decompression

The version support functions already discussed can automatically handle compressed files. Sometimes it is useful for an application to be able to decompress files independently of the version control functions. Windows provides a number of functions for this purpose.

If an application is decompressing a file, it can use the **LZCopy** function to accomplish this. Before using the **LZCopy** function, the application must open the source and destination files with the **LZOpenFile** function. This function is similar to the **CreateFile** function, and returns file handles that are used by **LZCopy**, **LZRead**, and **LZSeek**. If a file is already opened with the **CreateFile** function, use that file handle with the **LZInit** function to obtain an equivalent handle as returned by the **LZOpenFile** function. Finally, after the files have been copied, the application uses the

LZClose function to close the file handles. A compressed file may have embedded within it the name of the uncompressed file.

An application can use the **GetExpandedName** function to retrieve this name. If the compressed file does not have the original file name embedded within it, then this function simply returns the name of the compressed file.

If your application requires a large read-only file, you can save space on the user's system by keeping the file compressed. The Win32 API provides the **LZRead** and **LZSeek** functions to allow you to read data from a compressed file as if it were uncompressed. The **LZRead** and **LZSeek** are functionally similar to the **ReadFile** and **SetFilePointer** functions. However, the Win32 API does not provide functions to compress files. Compressing files is done with the **COMPRESS.EXE** utility, a console application that compresses files using a scheme that is compatible with the functions shown in this chapter.

File Decompression and Installation Function Descriptions

Table 29-1 summarizes the file decompression and installation functions. A detailed description of each function follows the table.

Table 29-1 File decompression and installation function summary

Function	Purpose
GetExpandedName	Retrieves the original file name of a compressed file. The file must have been compressed using the /r switch.
GetFileVersionInfo	Obtains the version information resource from a Win32 executable file.
GetFileVersionInfoSize	Returns the size of the version information resource in a Win32 executable file.
LZClose	Closes the file opened with LZOpenFile.
LZCopy	Copies a file with decompression.
LZInit	Initializes the decompression library for multiple file operations.
LZOpenFile	Opens a file for use with other decompression functions.
LZRead	Reads from a file that was opened with LZOpenFile with decompression.
LZSeek	Moves the read pointer for a file opened with LZOpenFile with decompression.
VerFindFile	Determines where a file should be installed, searching for existing versions of the file.
VerInstallFile	Installs a file, decompressing as needed.
VerQueryValue	Obtains specific version information from the buffer returned by GetFileVersionInfo.

GetExpandedName   ■ Windows 95   ■ Windows NT

Description   **GetExpandedName** retrieves the original name of a compressed file, if the file was compressed using the Microsoft compression program **COMPRESS.EXE** and the **/r** switch was specified.

Syntax	INT **GetExpandedName**(LPTSTR *lpszSourceFile,* LPTSTR *lpszOriginalName*)
Parameters	
lpszSourceFile	LPTSTR: A pointer to a null-terminated string that contains the file name of the compressed file.
lpszOriginalName	LPTSTR: A pointer to a buffer that receives the original name of the uncompressed file. If the compressed file was not compressed with the /r switch, then the source file name will be copied to this buffer.
Returns	INT: If successful, a value of 1. Otherwise, LZERROR_BADVALUE.
Include File	lzexpand.h
Example	The following example retrieves the original file name of the compressed file COMP.DO_.

```
LRESULT CALLBACK WndProc( HWND hWnd, UINT uMsg, WPARAM wParam, LPARAM lParam )
{
   switch( uMsg )
   {
      case WM_COMMAND :
            switch( LOWORD( wParam ) )
            {
               case IDM_TEST :
                     {
                         TCHAR szLongName[MAX_PATH];

                         if ( GetExpandedName( "COMP.DO_", szLongName ) != ⇐
LZERROR_BADVALUE )
                             MessageBox( hWnd, "Expanded File name.", szLongName, MB_OK );
                     }
                     break;
                 .
                 .
                 .
```

GetFileVersionInfo   ■ WINDOWS 95   ■ WINDOWS NT

Description	GetFileVersionInfo retrieves the version information resource from a Win32 executable file, library, or control. An application must include VERSION.LIB to reference this function. GetFileVersionInfoSize obtains the size of the buffer needed to hold the version information resource for any given file. After allocating an appropriate buffer, the application can use GetFileVersionInfo to retrieve the version information resource.
Syntax	BOOL **GetFileVersionInfo**(LPTSTR *lpszFileName,* DWORD *dwReserved,* DWORD *dwBufferSize,* LPVOID *lpBuffer*)
Parameters	
lpszFileName	LPTSTR: A pointer to a buffer containing the name of the file from which the version information is to be retrieved.

dwReserved	DWORD: This parameter is ignored.
dwBufferSize	DWORD: On entry, contains the size of the buffer pointed to by *lpBuffer*. On return, this parameter contains the actual size of the buffer required to contain the version resource. If the buffer is not large enough to contain the version resource, the resource is truncated to fit.
lpBuffer	LPVOID: A pointer to a buffer that will contain the version resource.
Returns	BOOL: If successful, TRUE is returned; otherwise, the return value is FALSE.
Include File	winver.h
See Also	GetFileVersionInfoSize, VerQueryValue
Example	The following example uses GetFileVersionInfoSize to retrieve the size of the version resource, then uses GetFileVersionInfo to retrieve the version information. The "CompanyName", "FileVersion", and "ProductName" strings are then retrieved from the StringFileInfo section of the version information. Refer to Listing 29-2 at the beginning of this chapter for the version information in the resource file used with this example.

```
LRESULT CALLBACK WndProc( HWND hWnd, UINT uMsg, WPARAM wParam, LPARAM lParam )
{
    static HWND hList;

    switch( uMsg )
    {
        case WM_CREATE :
                hList = CreateWindowEx( WS_EX_CLIENTEDGE, "LISTBOX", "",
                                        LBS_STANDARD | WS_CHILD | WS_VISIBLE,
                                        0, 0, 10, 10,
                                        hWnd, (HMENU)101, hInst, NULL );
                break;

        case WM_SIZE :
                MoveWindow( hList, 0, 0, LOWORD( lParam ), HIWORD( lParam ), TRUE );
                break;

        case WM_COMMAND :
                switch( LOWORD( wParam ) )
                {
                    case IDM_TEST :
                            {
                                DWORD  dwSize;
                                DWORD  dwReserved;
                                LPVOID lpBuffer;

                                dwSize   = GetFileVersionInfoSize( "GETVERIN.EXE", &dwReserved );
                                lpBuffer = HeapAlloc( GetProcessHeap(), HEAP_ZERO_MEMORY, ⇐
dwSize );

                                if ( lpBuffer && GetFileVersionInfo( "GETVERIN.EXE", 0, dwSize,⇐
lpBuffer ) )
                                {
                                    LPTSTR lpStr;
                                    DWORD  dwLength;
```

continued on next page

continued from previous page

```
                          // Retrieve version information.
                          //..............................
                          VerQueryValue( lpBuffer, ⇐
"\\StringFileInfo\\040904b0\\CompanyName",
                                         &lpStr, &dwLength );
                          SendMessage( hList, LB_INSERTSTRING, (WPARAM)-1, ⇐
(LPARAM)lpStr );

                          VerQueryValue( lpBuffer, ⇐
"\\StringFileInfo\\040904b0\\FileVersion",
                                         &lpStr, &dwLength );
                          SendMessage( hList, LB_INSERTSTRING, (WPARAM)-1, ⇐
(LPARAM)lpStr );

                          VerQueryValue( lpBuffer, ⇐
"\\StringFileInfo\\040904b0\\ProductName",
                                         &lpStr, &dwLength );
                          SendMessage( hList, LB_INSERTSTRING, (WPARAM)-1, ⇐
(LPARAM)lpStr );
                     }
                     if ( lpBuffer )
                         HeapFree( GetProcessHeap(), 0, lpBuffer );
                 }
                 break;
        .
        .
        .
```

GetFileVersionInfoSize ■ WINDOWS 95 ■ WINDOWS NT

Description	`GetFileVersionInfoSize` retrieves the size of the version information resource of the specified file. This information allows an application to allocate a buffer of the appropriate size for use with the `GetFileVersionInfo` function. An application must include `VERSION.LIB` to reference this function.
Syntax	DWORD **GetFileVersionInfoSize**(LPTSTR *lpszFileName,* LPDWORD *lpdwReserved*)
Parameters	
lpszFileName	LPTSTR: A pointer to a buffer containing the name of a file. The size of the version information resource within this file is returned.
lpdwReserved	LPDWORD: A pointer to a DWORD value. This function sets the value of this DWORD to 0.
Returns	DWORD: The size, in bytes, of the version information resource contained within the specified file.
Include File	`winver.h`
See Also	`GetFileVersionInfo`, `VerQueryValue`
Example	See `GetFileVersionInfo` for an example of this function.

LZClose
■ Windows 95 ■ Windows NT

Description	LZClose closes the file handle that was obtained by using the LZOpenFile function.
Syntax	VOID **LZClose**(INT *hFile*)
Parameters	
hFile	INT: Identifies the file to be closed. This value was returned by a previous call to LZOpenFile.
Include File	lzexpand.h
See Also	LZOpenFile
Example	See LZCopy for an example of this function.

LZCopy
■ Windows 95 ■ Windows NT

Description	LZCopy copies a source file to a destination file. If the source file is compressed, the destination file will be decompressed.
Syntax	LONG **LZCopy**(INT *hSourceFile,* INT *hDestFile*)
Parameters	
hSourceFile	INT: The handle identifying a file opened with the LZOpenFile function. This file may be compressed.
hDestFile	INT: The handle identifying a file opened with the LZOpenFile function. If the source file is a compressed file, the destination file will be decompressed.
Returns	LONG: If successful, the size, in bytes, of the destination file; otherwise, a value less than zero is returned, which specifies an error condition. Table 29-2 gives specific error values.

Table 29-2 LZ function error codes

Return Value	Description
LZERROR_BADINHANDLE	The parameter specified for *hSourceFile* was not valid.
LZERROR_BADOUTHANDLE	The parameter specified for *hDestFile* was not valid.
LZERROR_BADVALUE	One of the input parameters is not valid.
LZERROR_GLOBALLOC	The maximum number of open compressed files has been exceeded or an error occurred allocating memory for the decompression process.
LZERROR_GLOBLOCK	An error occurred locking the memory used for the decompression buffer.
LZERROR_READ	The source file could not be read. This could be due to specifying a corrupt compressed file.
LZERROR_WRITE	There is insufficient space for the output file.

Include File	lzexpand.h
See Also	LZClose, LZInit, LZOpenFile
Example	This example copies the compressed file **COMP.DO_** to an uncompressed file, **Sample Document.DOC**, when the user presses the Test! menu item.

```
LRESULT CALLBACK WndProc( HWND hWnd, UINT uMsg, WPARAM wParam, LPARAM lParam )
{
   switch( uMsg )
   {
      case WM_COMMAND :
              switch( LOWORD( wParam ) )
              {
                 case IDM_TEST :
                     {
                         INT      hSource;
                         INT      hDestination;
                         LONG     lRet;
                         OFSTRUCT OfStruct;

                         // Open the source and destination.
                         //.................................
                         hSource = LZOpenFile( "COMP.DO_", &OfStruct, OF_READ );
                         hDestination = LZOpenFile( "Sample Document.DOC", &OfStruct, ⇐
OF_CREATE );

                         // Decompress the document.
                         //.........................
                         lRet = LZCopy( hSource, hDestination );

                         // Close the files.
                         //.................
                         LZClose( hSource );
                         LZClose( hDestination );

                         if ( lRet > 0 )
                             MessageBox( hWnd, "File copied.", lpszTitle,
                                         MB_OK | MB_ICONINFORMATION );
                         else
                             MessageBox( hWnd, "File NOT copied!", lpszTitle,
                                         MB_OK | MB_ICONASTERISK );
                     }
                     break;
                 .
                 .
                 .
```

LZInit   ■ WINDOWS 95   ■ WINDOWS NT

Description	LZInit converts a file handle obtained by the **CreateFile** function into a file handle that can be used with the various decompression functions. If the file is compressed, then **LZInit** allocates the appropriate buffers to allow decompression.
Syntax	INT **LZInit**(INT *hFile*)

Parameters

hFile   INT: The file handle of a file opened with `CreateFile`.

Returns   INT: A new file handle that can be used with the file decompression library.

Include File   `lzexpand.h`

See Also   `LZRead`, `LZSeek`, `LZOpenFile`, `CreateFile`

Example   The following code segment opens a file using the normal `CreateFile` function. It then uses `LZInit` to convert the file handle into one usable by the decompression library, and performs a read and a seek on the file with the `LZSeek` and `LZRead` functions.

```
HFILE       hNormalFile;
LONG        SeekLocation;
INT         hCompressedFile;

// First, open the file as a normal file.
//.....................................
hNormalFile = CreateFile( lpszFileName, GENERIC_READ, 0,
                    NULL, OPEN_EXISTING, 0, NULL );

       .
       .
       .

// We have determined that this is a compressed file. Switch to the
// file decompression library routines.

// Convert handle to LZ handle and read data.
//.....................................
hCompressedFile = LZInit( hNormalFile );
LZRead( hCompressedFile, &SeekLocation, sizeof(SeekLocation) );
LZSeek( hCompressedFile, SeekLocation, 0 );

       .
       .
       .
```

LZOpenFile   ■ WINDOWS 95   ■ WINDOWS NT

Description   `LZOpenFile` prepares files for use by other decompression functions, deletes files, and creates new uncompressed files.

Syntax   INT **LZOpenFile**(LPTSTR *lpFileName*, LPOFSTRUCT *lpOpenStruct*, WORD *wStyle*)

Parameters

lpFileName   LPTSTR: A pointer to a buffer containing the name of the file to open.

lpOpenStruct   LPOFSTRUCT: A pointer to an **OFSTRUCT** structure. This function will fill the values of the **OFSTRUCT** structure the first time the file is opened. This structure then can be used by subsequent calls to `LZOpenFile`. See the definition of the **OFSTRUCT** structure below.

wStyle	WORD: Specifies a bit mask of various actions. This can be one or more of the values listed in Table 29-3.

Table 29-3 LZOpenFile *wStyle* values

Value	Meaning
OF_CREATE	Directs LZOpenFile to create a new file. If the file already exists, it is truncated to zero length.
OF_DELETE	Deletes the file.
OF_EXIST	Opens the file and then closes it to test for a file's existence.
OF_PARSE	Fills the OFSTRUCT structure but carries out no other action.
OF_PROMPT	Displays a dialog box if the requested file does not exist. The dialog box informs the user that Windows cannot find the file, and it contains Retry and Cancel buttons. Choosing the Cancel button directs LZOpenFile to return a "file not found" error message.
OF_READ	Opens the file for reading only.
OF_READWRITE	Opens the file for reading and writing.
OF_REOPEN	Opens the file using information in the reopen buffer.
OF_SHARE_DENY_NONE	Opens the file without denying other processes read or write access to the file. LZOpenFile fails if the file has been opened in compatibility mode by any other process.
OF_SHARE_DENY_READ	Opens the file and denies other processes read access to the file. LZOpenFile fails if the file has been opened in compatibility mode or has been opened for read access by any other process.
OF_SHARE_DENY_WRITE	Opens the file and denies other processes write access to the file. LZOpenFile fails if the file has been opened in compatibility mode or has been opened for write access by any other process.
OF_SHARE_EXCLUSIVE	Opens the file in exclusive mode, denying other processes both read and write access to the file. LZOpenFile fails if the file has been opened in any other mode for read or write access, even by the current process.
OF_WRITE	Opens the file for writing only.

Returns	INT: An integer value identifying the open file if successful. Otherwise, it returns a value less than zero, specifying an error condition. Refer to Table 29-2 for possible return values.
Include File	lzexpand.h
See Also	LZClose, LZCopyFile
OFSTRUCT Definition	

```
typedef struct _OFSTRUCT
            {
    BYTE cBytes;
    BYTE fFixedDisk;
    WORD nErrCode;
    WORD Reserved1;
    WORD Reserved2;
    CHAR szPathName[OFS_MAXPATHNAME];
} OFSTRUCT;
```

Members

cBytes	BYTE: The size, in bytes, of the structure.
fFixedDisk	BYTE: Specifies whether the file is on a hard disk. Set to a non-zero value if the file is on a hard disk.
nErrCode	WORD: The MS-DOS error code.
Reserved1	WORD: Reserved; do not use.
Reserved2	WORD: Reserved; do not use.
szPathName	CHAR[OFS_MAXPATHNAME]: The path and file name of the file.
Example	See the example for the LZCopy function.

LZRead ■ WINDOWS 95 ■ WINDOWS NT

Description	LZRead reads data from a file opened with LZOpenFile or LZInit. From the point of view of the application, this function is identical to a normal file read. LZRead handles all required decompression.
Syntax	INT **LZRead**(INT *hFile,* LPTSTR *lpBuffer,* INT *nByteCount*)
Parameters	
hFile	INT: A file handle retrieved by using LZOpenFile or LZInit.
lpBuffer	LPTSTR: A pointer to the buffer where the data is to be placed.
nByteCount	INT: Specifies the number of bytes to read. This value is in reference to uncompressed data.
Returns	INT: If successful, the number of bytes actually read; otherwise, the return value is an error code. Refer to Table 29-2 for possible error codes.
Include File	lzexpand.h
See Also	LZInit, LZSeek
Example	See the example for the LZInit function.

LZSeek ■ WINDOWS 95 ■ WINDOWS NT

Description	LZSeek moves the read pointer of the specified file.
Syntax	LONG **LZSeek**(INT *hFile,* LONG *lOffset,* INT *iFrom*)
Parameters	
hFile	INT: A file handle retrieved by using LZOpenFile or LZInit.
lOffset	LONG: Specifies the distance, in bytes, that the read pointer is to be moved. This value is in reference to uncompressed data. This value may be negative to move backward in the file.
iFrom	INT: A flag specifying how the read pointer is to be moved. Refer to Table 29-4 for specific values for this parameter.

Table 29-4 LZSeek iFrom values

Value	Meaning
0	Moves the read pointer to the position indicated, starting at the beginning of the file.
1	Moves the read pointer the specified number of bytes from the current position.
2	Moves the read pointer the specified number of bytes from the end of the file.

Returns	LONG: If successful, the new absolute position of the read pointer; otherwise, the return value is an error code. Refer to Table 29-2 for possible error codes.
Include File	lzexpand.h
See Also	LZInit, LZRead
Example	LZInit gives an example of this function.

VerFindFile   ■ Windows 95   ■ Windows NT

Description	VerFindFile recommends the proper location that an application should use when installing a specific file. This recommendation is based on whether a version of the file already exists on the user's system. The values returned by this function should be used in a subsequent call to VerInstallFile to actually install the file. An application must include VERSION.LIB to reference this function.
Syntax	DWORD **VerFindFile**(DWORD *dwFlags*, LPTSTR *szFileName*, LPTSTR *szWindowsDirectory*, LPTSTR *szApplicationDirectory*, LPTSTR *szCurrentDirectory*, LPDWORD *lpdwCurrentLength*, LPTSTR *szDestinationDirectory*, LPDWORD *lpdwDestinationLength*)
Parameters	
dwFlags	DWORD: If this parameter is **VFFF_ISSHAREDFILE**, then the file is considered to be a shared file, that is, used by multiple applications. If this parameter is **0**, then the file is considered to be private to this application.
szFileName	LPTSTR: A pointer to the name of the file. This should include only a file name and extension. It should not include a drive letter or path.
szWindowsDirectory	LPTSTR: A pointer to the name of the directory where Windows is running or will be run. You can use the **GetWindowsDirectory** function to obtain this value.

szApplicationDirectory	**LPTSTR**: A pointer to the name of the directory where the application is being installed.
szCurrentDirectory	**LPTSTR**: A pointer to a buffer where this function returns the directory if any existing version of the file is located. If there is no existing version of the file, this buffer will contain a zero-length string.
lpdwCurrentLength	**LPDWORD**: A pointer to a **DWORD** value. On entry to this function, this **DWORD** should be set to the length of the *szCurrentDirectory* buffer. On return from this function, this **DWORD** will be set to the length of the string returned. If *szCurrentDirectory* is too small to contain the entire path, then this parameter is set to the number of bytes required to hold the path name.
szDestinationDirectory	**LPTSTR**: A pointer to a buffer where Windows will place the directory name of the location that it recommends be used to install the file.
lpdwDestinationLength	**LPDWORD**: A pointer to a **DWORD** value. On entry to this function, this value should be set to the length of the *szDestinationDirectory* buffer. On return from this function, this value will be set to the length of the string returned. If *szDestinationDirectory* is too small to contain the entire path, then this parameter is set to the number of bytes required to hold the path name.
Returns	**DWORD**: The return value is a bit mask indicating various results. It can be one or more of the values shown in Table 29-5.

Table 29-5 `VerFindFile` return flags

Bit Value	Description
VFF_BUFFTOOSMALL	Either *lpdwCurrentLength* or *lpdwDestinationLength* specified that the respective buffer was too small to contain the entire path name.
VFF_CURNEDEST	A previous version of the file exists, but is not in the recommended location.
VFF_FILEINUSE	A previous version of the file exists, and is currently being used by Windows or another application. The file may not be deleted or replaced.

Include File	`winver.h`
See Also	`VerInstallFile`
Example	Refer to Listing 29-1 at the beginning of this chapter for an example of this function.

VerInstallFile

Description

VerInstallFile installs a specific file. The file is decompressed, if necessary, and version information is checked against any preexisting file. An application must include **VERSION.LIB** to reference this function.

Syntax

DWORD **VerInstallFile**(DWORD *dwFlags,* LPTSTR *szSrcFileName,* LPTSTR *szDestFileName,* LPTSTR *szSrcDirectory,* LPTSTR *szDestDirectory,* LPTSTR *szExistingDirectory,* LPTSTR *szTempName,* LPDWORD *lpdwTempLength*)

Parameters

dwFlags

DWORD: Various flags that may be used to alter the operation of this function. Table 29-6 gives valid values for this parameter.

Table 29-6 VerInstallFile *dwFlags* values

Bit Mask	Meaning
VIFF_DONTDELETEOLD	If a previous version of the file exists in a directory other than the recommended destination directory, using this flag will keep VerInstallFile from removing the old file.
VIFF_FORCEINSTALL	Forces VerInstallFile to install the new file regardless of any version or type mismatch with an existing file. If VIFF_DONTDELETEOLD is not specified, and the previous version of the file exists in a different directory, it will be deleted. If the previous version of the file exists in the destination directory specified, it will be overwritten regardless of the setting of VIFF_DONTDELETEOLD.

szSrcFileName

LPTSTR: The name of the file to be installed. This can only include the file name and extension. No path or drive information should be included.

szDestFileName

LPTSTR: The name this file should be given once installed. This can include only the file name and extension. No path or drive information should be included. This parameter allows the file to be renamed during the installation process.

szSrcDirectory

LPTSTR: The drive and directory where the source file exists.

szDestDirectory

LPTSTR: The drive and directory where the file is to be installed. This is usually the *szDestinationDirectory* parameter of **VerFindFile**.

szExistingDirectory

LPTSTR: The location where a preexisting version of the file can be found. This is usually the *szCurrentDirectory* parameter of **VerFindFile**.

szTempName

LPTSTR: A buffer where this function will store the temporary name used during the file-installation process.

lpdwTempLength

LPDWORD: The size of the *szTempName* buffer. On return, this parameter will indicate the actual size of the *szTempName* string.

Returns	DWORD: A bit mask that indicates various exception conditions during the installation process. One or more of the values defined in Table 29-7 may be included.

Table 29-7 `VerInstallFile` return codes

Bit Mask	Meaning
VIF_ACCESSVIOLATION	Installation of the new file failed due to an access violation.
VIF_BUFFTOOSMALL	The temporary file name buffer is too small to contain the name of the temporary file.
VIF_CANNOTCREATE	The temporary file could not be created.
VIF_CANNOTDELETE	The destination file could not be deleted.
VIF_CANNOTDELETECUR	The destination file exists in a different directory, VIFF_DONTDELETEOLD was not specified, and the existing version of the file could not be deleted.
VIF_CANNOTREADDST	The preexisting file could not be read; therefore, no version information could be obtained.
VIF_CANNOTREADSRC	The new file could not be read.
VIF_CANNOTRENAME	The preexisting file was deleted, but the temporary file could not be renamed.
VIF_DIFFCODEPG	The new file and the preexisting file specify different code page values.
VIF_DIFFLANG	The new file and the preexisting file specify different language or code page values.
VIF_DIFFTYPE	The new file has a different type, subtype, or operating system identifier than the preexisting file.
VIF_FILEINUSE	The preexisting file is currently in use by Windows.
VIF_MISMATCH	The new file and the preexisting file differ in some manner.
VIF_OUTOFMEMORY	There is not enough memory to complete the installation. This is generally caused by running out of memory while trying to decompress a file.
VIF_OUTOFSPACE	Insufficient disk space on the destination drive for the new file.
VIF_SHARINGVIOLATION	Installation of the new file failed due to a sharing violation.
VIF_SRCOLD	The new file is older than the preexisting file.
VIF_TEMPFILE	Indicates that a temporary file has been left in the destination directory due to some installation error. Other bits will be set indicating the specific error. An application should remove the temporary file when it is no longer needed.
VIF_WRITEPROT	The preexisting file has been write-protected.

Include File	`winver.h`
See Also	`VerFindFile`
Example	Refer to Listing 29-1 at the beginning of this chapter for an example of this function.

VerQueryValue   ■ WINDOWS 95   ■ WINDOWS NT

Description	`VerQueryValue` retrieves specific information from the version information resource that was obtained using `GetFileVersionInfo`. An application must include **VERSION.LIB** to reference this function.

Syntax	BOOL **VerQueryValue**(LPVOID *lpVerInfo,* LPTSTR *lpszKey,* LPVOID *lpvPointerToData,* LPUINT *lpdwDataLength*)

Parameters

lpVerInfo	**LPVOID**: A pointer to the version information resource. This data is typically obtained by a call to **GetFileVersionInfo**.
lpszKey	**LPTSTR**: Identifies which version information value to return. Table 29-8 gives details.
lpvPointerToData	**LPVOID**: A pointer to a buffer where this function will place a pointer to the requested version information.
lpdwDataLength	**LPUINT**: A pointer to a **UINT** that this function will set to the length of the data pointed to by *lpvPointerToData*.

Table 29-8 Rules for the *lpszKey* parameter of VerQueryValue

String Form	Description
\	Specifies the fixed version information. Using this key returns a pointer to a VS_FIXEDFILEINFO structure within the version information resource. See the definition of the VS_FIXEDFILEINFO structure below.
\VarFileInfo*Translation*	Specifies the language/character set translation table. A pointer to the translation table is returned. An application will use the information in this table to build the strings needed to access the language-specific information in the version information resource. The translation table consists of an array of two WORD entries. The first word in each entry is the language ID, and the second word in each entry is the character set.
\StringFileInfo*<LanguageAndCharacterSet>**<String>*	Specifies an entry in the language-specific section of the version information resource. The *<LanguageAndCharacterSet>* string should be an ASCII string specifying the language ID and character set ID obtained from the language/character set translation table. This must be specified as a hexadecimal string. The *<String>* string specifies which string to retrieve. The following predefined strings may be used:"CompanyName", "FileDescription", "FileVersion", "InternalName", "LegalCopyright", "OriginalFilename", "ProductName", "ProductVersion". As an example, the following string would retrieve the company name from language ID 1033, character set 1252: "\\StringFileInfo\\040904E4\\CompanyName".

Returns	**BOOL**: If successful, **TRUE** is returned; otherwise **FALSE** is returned.
Include File	winver.h

See Also   `GetFileVersionInfo`

VS_FIXEDFILEINFO Definition

```
typedef struct _VS_FIXEDFILEINFO
{
    DWORD dwSignature;
    DWORD dwStrucVersion;
    DWORD dwFileVersionMS;
    DWORD dwFileVersionLS;
    DWORD dwProductVersionMS;
    DWORD dwProductVersionLS;
    DWORD dwFileFlagsMask;
    DWORD dwFileFlags;
    DWORD dwFileOS;
    DWORD dwFileType;
    DWORD dwFileSubtype;
    DWORD dwFileDateMS;
    DWORD dwFileDateLS;
} VS_FIXEDFILEINFO;
```

Members

dwSignature **DWORD**: This member contains the value **0xFEEF04BD**. This is used searching a file for the **VS_FIXEDFILEINFO** structure.

dwStrucVersion **DWORD**: The binary version number of this structure. The high-order word of this member contains the major version number, and the low-order word contains the minor version number. This value must be greater than 0x00000029.

dwFileVersionMS **DWORD**: The most significant 32 bits of the file's binary version number. This member is used with *dwFileVersionLS* to form a 64-bit value used for numeric comparisons.

dwFileVersionLS **DWORD**: The least significant 32 bits of the file's binary version number. This member is used with *dwFileVersionMS* to form a 64-bit value used for numeric comparisons.

dwProductVersionMS **DWORD**: The most significant 32 bits of the binary version number of the product with which this file was distributed. This member is used with *dwProductVersionLS* to form a 64-bit value used for numeric comparisons.

dwProductVersionLS **DWORD**: The least significant 32 bits of the binary version number of the product with which this file was distributed. This member is used with *dwProductVersionMS* to form a 64-bit value used for numeric comparisons.

dwFileFlagsMask **DWORD**: A bit mask that specifies the valid bits in *dwFileFlags* member. A bit is set only if its corresponding value was defined when the file was created.

dwFileFlags **DWORD**: A bit mask that specifies the Boolean attributes of the file. This member can include one or more of the values listed in Table 29-9.

Table 29-9 VS_FIXEDFILEINFO *dwFileFlags* values

Flag	Description
VS_FF_DEBUG	The file contains debugging information or is compiled with debugging features enabled.
VS_FF_INFOINFERRED	The file's version structure was created dynamically. Some of the members in this structure may be empty or incorrect. This flag should never be set in a file's VS_VERSION_INFO data.
VS_FF_PATCHED	The file has been modified and is not identical to the original shipping file of the same version number.
VS_FF_PRERELEASE	The file is a development version, not a commercially released product.
VS_FF_PRIVATEBUILD	The file was not built using standard release procedures. If this flag is set, StringFileInfo should contain a PrivateBuild entry.
VS_FF_SPECIALBUILD	The file was built by the original company using standard release procedures but is a variation of the normal file of the same version number. If this flag is set, StringFileInfo should contain a SpecialBuild entry.

dwFileOS   DWORD: The operating system for which this file was designed. This member can be one of the values listed in Table 29-10.

Table 29-10 VS_FIXEDFILEINFO *dwFileOS* values

Value	Description
VOS_DOS	The file was designed for MS-DOS.
VOS_DOS_WINDOWS16	The file was designed for 16-bit Windows running on MS-DOS.
VOS_DOS_WINDOWS32	The file was designed for the Win32 API running on MS-DOS.
VOS_OS216	The file was designed for 16-bit OS/2.
VOS_OS216_PM16	The file was designed for 16-bit Presentation Manager running on 16-bit OS/2.
VOS_OS232	The file was designed for 32-bit OS/2.
VOS_OS232_PM32	The file was designed for 32-bit Presentation Manager running on 32-bit OS/2.
VOS_PM16	The file was designed for 16-bit Presentation Manager.
VOS_PM32	The file was designed for 32-bit Presentation Manager.
VOS_NT	The file was designed for Windows NT.
VOS_NT_WINDOWS32	The file was designed for the Win32 API running on Windows NT.
VOS_UNKNOWN	The operating system for which the file was designed is unknown to Windows.
VOS_WINDOWS16	The file was designed for 16-bit Windows.
VOS_WINDOWS32	The file was designed for the Win32 API.

dwFileType   DWORD: The general type of file. This member can be one of the values listed in Table 29-11. Other values may be defined and not listed in this table because they are reserved for future use by Microsoft.

Table 29-11 VS_FIXEDFILEINFO *dwFileType* values

Value	Description
VFT_APP	The file contains an application.
VFT_DLL	The file contains a dynamic link library (DLL).
VFT_DRV	The file contains a device driver. If *dwFileType* is VFT_DRV, *dwFileSubtype* contains a more specific description of the driver.
VFT_FONT	The file contains a font. If *dwFileType* is VFT_FONT, *dwFileSubtype* contains a more specific description of the font file.
VFT_STATIC_LIB	The file contains a static-link library.
VFT_UNKNOWN	The file type is unknown to Windows.
VFT_VXD	The file contains a virtual device.

dwFileSubtype   DWORD: The specific function of the file. Normally this member is set to 0, except for values of *dwFileType* VFT_DRV, VFT_FONT, and VFT_VXD. If *dwFileType* is VFT_DRV, *dwFileSubtype* can be one of the values listed in Table 29-12. If *dwFileType* is VFT_FONT, *dwFileSubtype* can be one of the values listed in Table 29-13. If *dwFileType* is VFT_VXD, *dwFileSubtype* contains the virtual device identifier included in the virtual device control block. All *dwFileSubtype* values not listed here are reserved for future use by Microsoft.

Table 29-12 VS_FIXEDFILEINFO *dwFileSubtype* values for VFT_DRV types

Value	Description
VFT2_DRV_DISPLAY	The file contains a display driver.
VFT2_DRV_INSTALLABLE	The file contains an installable driver.
VFT2_DRV_KEYBOARD	The file contains a keyboard driver.
VFT2_DRV_LANGUAGE	The file contains a language driver.
VFT2_DRV_MOUSE	The file contains a mouse driver.
VFT2_DRV_NETWORK	The file contains a network driver.
VFT2_DRV_PRINTER	The file contains a printer driver.
VFT2_DRV_SOUND	The file contains a sound driver.
VFT2_DRV_SYSTEM	The file contains a system driver.
VFT2_UNKNOWN	The driver type is unknown by Windows.

Table 29-13 VS_FIXEDFILEINFO *dwFileSubtype* values for VFT_FONT types

Value	Description
VFT2_FONT_RASTER	The file contains a raster font.
VFT2_FONT_TRUETYPE	The file contains a TrueType font.
VFT2_FONT_VECTOR	The file contains a vector font.
VFT2_UNKNOWN	The font type is unknown by Windows.

dwFileDateMS	DWORD: The most significant 32 bits of the file's creation date and time stamp. This member is used with the *dwFileDateLS* member to form a 64-bit binary value.
dwFileDateLS	DWORD: The least significant 32 bits of the file's creation date and time stamp. This member is used with *dwFileDateMS* member to form a 64-bit binary value.
Example	See **GetFileVersionInfo** for an example of this function.

30

DYNAMIC LINK LIBRARIES

Dynamic link libraries (DLLs) provide an important facility within the Windows operating system. DLLs provide the ability to plug prewritten modules into the operating system, allowing applications to share common code, modularize commonly used functions, and provide extendibility. The Windows operating system itself is comprised mostly of DLLs, and any application that makes use of the Win32 API is making use of the DLL facility. An application can gain the use of procedures located within a DLL by two methods: loadtime dynamic linking and runtime dynamic linking.

Loadtime Dynamic Linking

An application employs loadtime dynamic linking by specifying the names of the DLL procedures directly in the source code. The linker inserts references to these procedures when it locates them in an import library linked with the application or by using the `IMPORTS` section of the module definition file for the application. When the application is executed, the Windows loader loads the DLLs into memory and resolves these references.

This is the easiest form of dynamic linking, but it can cause problems under special circumstances. For example, if an application references a DLL procedure in this manner, the DLL must exist when the application is executed, even if the application never actually calls that procedure. Also, the application must know at compile time the names of all procedures that will be loadtime linked.

Runtime Dynamic Linking

Although runtime dynamic linking overcomes the limitations of loadtime dynamic linking, it does requires more work on the part of the application. Rather than specify at compile time the DLL procedures that an application wishes to use, the application uses the `LoadLibrary`, `LoadLibraryEx`, `GetProcAddress`, and `FreeLibrary` functions to specify at runtime the names of the DLLs and procedures that it wishes to reference.

Runtime dynamic linking also allows an application to provide support for functionality that is not available when the application is created. For example, a word processing application can provide conversion routines inside DLLs that convert between different file formats. If runtime dynamic linking is used, new conversion DLLs can be added that contain conversion routines for new file formats that did not exist when the application was written. Since the application determines what conversion DLLs exist at runtime, installing the new DLLs allows the application to make use of the new conversion procedures. The application would use the `FindFirstFile` and `FindNextFile` functions to retrieve the names of the DLLs that are present. It could then load each DLL, obtain the address of the conversion procedure, and place these addresses in a structure that it would later use during the file conversion process. For an example of this, see the example under the `LoadLibrary` function later in this chapter.

When using `GetProcAddress`, you must specify the routine whose address you wish to obtain. You can specify the name of the routine as an ASCII string or you may specify the ordinal number of the routine. See the description of `GetProcAddress` later in this chapter. Although using ordinal numbers is more efficient than using procedure names when calling `GetProcAddress`, you should be aware of potential problems.

Routines in the DLL are kept in a name table. Windows uses the ordinal number as an index to this table when resolving references to the routines. The only check that is made by Windows is to ensure that the ordinal number is within the range of the name table. If DLL routines are assigned ordinal numbers that are not contiguous (that is, there are gaps in the numbering), it is possible to specify a number that is within the range of the name table but references an unused entry. `GetProcAddress` will blindly return the invalid entry in the name table for this ordinal. The result most likely will be a general protection fault when the application attempts to make use of the returned address. In addition, if the developer of the DLL allows the linker to assign default ordinal numbers to the routines in the DLL, it is possible that a new version of the DLL will have a different ordinal number assignment scheme. This would obviously cause `GetProcAddress` to return the address of the wrong routine.

Creating Dynamic Link Libraries

The steps involved in creating a DLL are very similar to those for creating standard Windows executable programs. The source code for a DLL is identical to the source code for any executable module. The following code segment shows the source code for a very simple DLL.

```
#include <windows.h>

// AddNumbers - This is a routine in a DLL that an application may call.

int AddNumbers( int n1, int n2 )
{
    return( n1 + n2 );
}
```

This is the same as any subroutine you might code for an ordinary application. The differences occur in the module definition file (`.DEF`). The linker uses the module definition file to provide information specific to the creation of DLLs. The following code segment illustrates a minimal module definition file for the example given above.

```
LIBRARY MyDll

EXPORTS
    AddNumbers @1
```

The function **AddNumbers** is defined as being exported (from the perspective of the DLL) and is assigned the ordinal value of **1**. The ordinal value is optional and, if omitted, is assigned by the linker automatically. When the object file created from the source code example above is linked with the example module definition file, the result is the dynamic link library.

If your application will be using runtime dynamic linking to access this DLL, then you've completed the creation process. If you plan to use loadtime dynamic linking to access this DLL, then you must complete a few more tasks first.

Since loadtime dynamic linking requires resolution of all references at compile/link time, you must first provide a header file (`.H`) that defines the routines in your DLL. The header file typically contains prototype definitions for all public entry points in the DLL, as well as any structures or definitions. For the above code segments, the header file would be defined as follows:

```
// Header file for MYDLL.DLL - Defines entry points

int AddNumbers(int n1, int n2);
```

Applications employing loadtime dynamic linking with your DLL will include this file to gain the definition of the **AddNumbers** routine. This will satisfy the compiler. The linker, however, needs to know where to find the routine **AddNumbers**. This is typically done by linking the application with an import library that is created from your module definition file. This import library will tell the linker that the routine **AddNumbers** exists within the file **MYDLL.DLL**. Many development platforms create the import library for you. However, if you must create the import library yourself, you can use the **LIB.EXE** utility with a command line similar to the following:

```
lib /machine:IX86 /OUT:mydll.lib /DEF:mydll.def
```

This example creates an import library suitable for use on x86-based platforms. The application would include the library **MYDLL.LIB** as input to the linker, allowing the references to the DLL to be properly resolved.

If an import library is not provided with the DLL, then an application using loadtime dynamic linking must employ the module definition file to inform the linker of the locations of the DLL routines. This is done using the **IMPORTS** section of the module definition file. An application using the DLL shown in these examples would include the following lines in its module definition file:

```
IMPORTS
    MyDll.MyDllFunc
```

Accessing Data Within a DLL

When a DLL dynamically allocates memory, that memory is allocated on behalf of the process that is calling the DLL. This memory is accessible only to threads belonging to this process. This would include memory allocated using `GlobalAlloc`, `LocalAlloc`, `HeapAlloc`, `VirtualAlloc`, or any of the standard C library routines, such as `malloc` and `new`.

If a DLL dynamically allocates memory, so that it can be shared among all of the processes currently using the DLL, it should use the file-mapping functions to create named shared memory. For more details on file mapping, see Chapter 17, I/O with Files.

Global and static variables declared in the DLL's source code exist within the data segment of the DLL. Each process attached to the DLL is provided with its own copy of this data segment.

It is possible for the module definition file to change the default attributes of global and static data, allowing the data to be shared among all processes using the DLL. For example, including the following line in the module definition file will cause the DLL's initialized data to be shared among all processes, while uninitialized data will remain private to each process. This statement requires the DLL source file to indicate which data to place within the `.GLOBALS` data segment. For an example, refer to the `DLLEntryPoint` description later in this chapter.

```
SECTIONS
    .GLOBALS READ WRITE SHARED
```

Finally, a DLL can make use of the thread local storage functions to provide a table of values that are unique to each thread accessing the DLL. For more information on thread local storage, refer to Chapter 25, Processes, Threads, and Fibers. In addition, use of thread local storage typically requires implementation of a notification entry point within the DLL.

Using the DLL Notification Entry Point

The DLL notification entry point allows a DLL to be informed every time a process attaches to, or detaches from, the DLL, or a process attached to the DLL creates or destroys a thread. To implement a DLL notification entry point, you must code a function in your DLL, based on the `DLLEntryPoint` prototype function.

```
BOOL DLLEntryPoint(HINSTANCE hInstDLL, DWORD dwNotification, LPVOID lpReserved);
```

The function name `DLLEntryPoint` is simply a placeholder. By default the linker looks for a function with the name `DLLMain`. You may name the function anything you wish if you specify the DLL entry point. This is typically done by using an `/entry` switch on the linker command line, as shown in the following code segment:

```
link /entry:MyEntry /machine:IX86 mydll.obj
```

Refer to the detailed description of this function for more information.

Dynamic Link Libraries Function Descriptions

Table 30-1 summarizes the functions used to work with dynamic link libraries. A detailed description of each of these functions follows the table.

Table 30-1 Dynamic link library function summary

Function	Purpose
DisableThreadLibraryCalls	Prevents Windows from sending notifications to the specified library during thread creation and termination.
DLLEntryPoint	Optional notification entry point for dynamic link libraries.
FreeLibrary	Decrements the usage count of a loaded DLL and releases the DLL from memory when the usage count reaches zero.
FreeLibraryAndExitThread	Decrements the usage count of a loaded DLL and releases the DLL from memory when the usage count reaches zero. Terminates the calling thread.
GetProcAddress	Returns the address of a routine located in a DLL.
LoadLibrary	If necessary, loads a DLL into memory. Increments the DLL's usage count and returns a handle to the DLL.
LoadLibraryEx	If necessary, loads a DLL into memory. Increments the DLL's usage count and returns a handle to the DLL. Allows the calling application to disable notifications to the DLL during process and thread creation and termination.

DisableThreadLibraryCalls ■ WINDOWS 95 ■ WINDOWS NT

Description   DisableThreadLibraryCalls informs Windows that it should no longer notify the specified DLL whenever the application creates or terminates threads. You must be careful when using this function because DLLs may need to provide per-thread structures or resources. If you are certain that no DLLs require the thread notification messages, and your application creates and destroys many threads, using DisableThreadLibraryCalls can improve performance. This function will fail if the DLL has active static thread local storage.

Syntax   BOOL DisableThreadLibraryCalls(HMODULE *hDLLibrary*)

Parameters

hDLLibrary   HMODULE: A handle to the DLL. This handle is returned by the LoadLibrary function.

Returns   BOOL: If the function is successful, it returns TRUE. Otherwise, it returns FALSE. The application can obtain further information by calling GetLastError.

Include File   winbase.h

See Also   LoadLibrary, LoadLibraryEx

DLLEntryPoint

Description	Windows will call a DLL's **DLLEntryPoint** function to notify the DLL of certain important events. Use of this routine is optional; however, for a DLL to implement it, the name of the function must be provided to the linker as the library's execution entry point. The name **DLLEntryPoint** is simply a placeholder. **DLLMain** is the default entry point name. If the DLL includes a **DLLMain** function, there is no need for specifying the entry point at link time. However, Windows will call whatever function is specified as the library's entry point at link time if the name is other than **DLLMain**.

Syntax

BOOL DLLEntryPoint(HINSTANCE *hInstDLL,* DWORD *dwNotification,* LPVOID *lpReserved*)

Parameters

hInstDLL	**HINSTANCE**: The instance handle of the DLL itself.
dwNotification	**DWORD**: Notification code. See Table 30-2 for a list of valid notification codes that may be sent by Windows.
lpReserved	**LPVOID**: Reserved; set to **NULL**.

Table 30-2 Dynamic link library notification codes

Notification Code	Description
DLL_PROCESS_ATTACH	Informs the DLL that a new process is attaching. A DLL_THREAD_ATTACH notification is not generated for any threads that currently exist within the process, including the initial thread.
DLL_PROCESS_DETACH	Informs the DLL that the executing process is finished with the DLL, either because the process has terminated or it has freed the library.
DLL_THREAD_ATTACH	Informs the DLL that a new thread has been created by a process that is attached to the DLL.
DLL_THREAD_DETACH	Informs the DLL that the executing thread is terminating.

Returns	**BOOL**: The return value is ignored for all notification codes except **DLL_PROCESS_ATTACH**. When **DLL_PROCESS_ATTACH** is used, the DLL should return **TRUE** if initialization was successful and the application may continue. If the DLL returns **FALSE**, then the application will be terminated if it is using loadtime dynamic linking or will receive an error code from **LoadLibrary** or **LoadLibraryEx** if it is using runtime dynamic linking.
Example	The following example illustrates the **DLLMain** notification entry point. This example simply keeps track of the number of processes and threads currently attached.

```
// Make this data shared among all
// all applications that use this DLL.
//................................
```

```
#pragma data_seg( ".GLOBALS" )
int nProcessCount = 0;
int nThreadCount = 0;
#pragma data_seg()

BOOL WINAPI DLLMain( HINSTANCE hInstDLL, DWORD dwNotification, LPVOID lpReserved )
{
   switch(dwNotification)
   {
      case DLL_PROCESS_ATTACH :
              // DLL initialization code goes here. Formerly this
              // would be in the LibMain function of a 16-bit DLL.
              //.................................................
              nProcessCount++;
              return( TRUE );

      case DLL_PROCESS_DETACH :
              // DLL cleanup code goes here. Formerly this would
              // be in the WEP function of a 16-bit DLL.
              //.................................................
              nProcessCount--;
              break;

      case DLL_THREAD_ATTACH :
              // Special initialization code for new threads goes here.
              // This is so the DLL can "Thread Protect" itself.
              //.................................................
              nThreadCount++;
              break;

      case DLL_THREAD_DETACH :
              // Special cleanup code for threads goes here.
              //.................................................
              nThreadCount--;
              break;
   }
   return( FALSE );
}
```

FreeLibrary

■ WINDOWS 95 ■ WINDOWS NT

Description	An application uses the **FreeLibrary** function to inform Windows that it no longer needs the indicated DLL. Windows will decrement the usage count for the DLL; if the usage count reaches zero, Windows will release the DLL from memory.
Syntax	BOOL FreeLibrary(HMODULE *hDLLibrary*)
Parameters	
hDLLibrary	HMODULE: A handle to the DLL. This handle is returned by the LoadLibrary function.
Returns	BOOL: If the function is successful, it returns **TRUE**; otherwise, it returns **FALSE**. The application can obtain further information by calling GetLastError.

Include File	winbase.h
See Also	LoadLibrary, LoadLibraryEx
Example	See LoadLibrary for an example of this function.

FreeLibraryAndExitThread ■ WINDOWS 95 ■ WINDOWS NT

Description	An application uses the FreeLibraryAndExitThread function to inform Windows that it no longer needs the indicated DLL and that the calling thread should terminate. Windows will decrement the usage count for the DLL, and if the usage count reaches zero, Windows will release the DLL from memory. Finally, Windows will terminate the calling thread.
	This function is an atomic combination of FreeLibrary and ExitThread. It is useful in situations where the calling thread is created and executes within a DLL. The thread cannot simply call FreeLibrary, because Windows may unload the DLL, causing the thread's code to become invalid before the thread has had a chance to regain control and call ExitThread.
Syntax	BOOL FreeLibraryAndExitThread(HMODULE *hDLLibrary*)
Parameters	
hDLLibrary	HMODULE: A handle to the DLL. This handle is returned by the LoadLibrary function.
Returns	BOOL: If this function is successful, it does not return. After freeing the indicated library, the calling thread is terminated and does not regain control. Otherwise, FALSE is returned.
Include File	winbase.h
See Also	ExitThread, FreeLibrary, LoadLibrary, LoadLibraryEx
Example	The following example illustrates the use of this function. It is assumed that the following code exists within a loaded DLL and is making use of another DLL. When this function is called, the indicated library will be freed, and the calling thread will exit. If the function returns, the application issues a fatal error.

```
HMODULE hModule;

hModule = LoadLibrary("MYDLLLIB.DLL");
        .
        .
        .
FreeLibraryAndExit(hModule);
FatalError("Current thread is unable to terminate.");
```

GetProcAddress ■ WINDOWS 95 ■ WINDOWS NT

Description Use **GetProcAddress** to obtain the address of a function that resides within a DLL. The application can then use this address to invoke the function.

Syntax FARPROC **GetProcAddress**(HMODULE *hDLLibrary,* LPCSTR *lpszProcName*)

Parameters

hDLLibrary HMODULE: A handle to the DLL. This handle is returned by the **LoadLibrary** function.

lpszProcName LPCSTR: This parameter can be either a pointer to a null-terminated string identifying the procedure or the ordinal number of a procedure. If an ordinal number is used, the ordinal must be in the low word, and the high word must be **0**.

Returns FARPROC: If the function is successful, it returns the address of the requested procedure's entry point. Otherwise, the return value is **NULL**. The application can obtain further information by calling **GetLastError**.

Include File winbase.h

See Also FreeLibrary, LoadLibrary, LoadLibraryEx

Example See **LoadLibrary** for an example of this function.

LoadLibrary ■ WINDOWS 95 ■ WINDOWS NT

Description **LoadLibrary** obtains the module handle of a DLL. If the DLL is not resident in memory, Windows will load it. Windows then increments the usage count for the library and returns a module handle that identifies the library.

Syntax HANDLE **LoadLibrary**(LPCSTR *lpszLibraryName*)

Parameters

lpszLibraryName LPCSTR: Points to a null-terminated string that specifies the file name of the module to load. This module may be a DLL or an executable module. If no file extension is specified, **.DLL** is assumed. If no path name is specified, Windows searches for the DLL first in the directory from which the calling application was loaded, then in the current directory, the Windows system directory, the Windows directory, and finally, through all directories referenced in the **PATH** environment string.

Returns HANDLE: If this function is successful, it returns the module handle of the loaded library. Otherwise, it returns **NULL**. The application can obtain further information by calling **GetLastError**.

Include File winbase.h

See Also FreeLibrary, FindResource, GetProcAddress, LoadLibraryEx, LoadResource

Example   The following example loads the library **GDI32.DLL** and uses **GetProcAddress** to obtain the address of the routines **BeginPath**, **EndPath**, and **StrokePath**. These routines do not exist in older versions of Windows NT. If the routines were simply referenced using loadtime dynamic linking, the application would not load under versions of Windows NT where these functions are not available. Using runtime dynamic linking, the application is able to continue with conventional drawing, even though the path functions do not exist.

```
LRESULT CALLBACK WndProc( HWND hWnd, UINT uMsg, WPARAM wParam, LPARAM lParam )
{
    switch( uMsg )
    {
    case WM_COMMAND :
            switch( LOWORD( wParam ) )
            {
                case IDM_TEST :
                    {
                        // Get the instance handle of the GDI DLL.
                        //......................................
                        HINSTANCE hLib = LoadLibrary( "GDI32.DLL" );

                        if ( hLib )
                        {
                            // Get the function pointers to the path functions needed.
                            //............................................................
                            FARPROC fpBeginPath  = GetProcAddress( hLib, "BeginPath" );
                            FARPROC fpEndPath    = GetProcAddress( hLib, "EndPath" );
                            FARPROC fpStrokePath = GetProcAddress( hLib, "StrokePath" );
                            HDC hDC = GetDC( hWnd );

                            // If paths are supported, draw with them.
                            // Otherwise, use standard drawing.
                            //......................................
                            if ( fpBeginPath && fpEndPath && fpStrokePath )
                            {
                                (*fpBeginPath)( hDC );
                                LineTo( hDC, 200, 100 );
                                (*fpEndPath)( hDC );
                                (*fpStrokePath)( hDC );
                            }
                            else
                                LineTo( hDC, 200, 100 );

                            ReleaseDC( hWnd, hDC );
                            FreeLibrary( hLib );
                        }
                        else
                            MessageBox( hWnd, "DLL could not be loaded",
                                        NULL, MB_OK | MB_ICONASTERISK );
                    }
                    break;
                    .
                    .
                    .
```

LoadLibraryEx

Description
LoadLibraryEx obtains the module handle of a DLL with the option of not notifying the **DLLEntryPoint**. If the DLL is not resident in memory, Windows will load it. Windows then increments the usage count for the library and returns a module handle that identifies the library.

Syntax
HANDLE **LoadLibraryEx**(LPCSTR *lpszLibraryName,* HANDLE *hReserved,* DWORD *dwFlags*)

Parameters

lpszLibraryName
LPCSTR: Points to a null-terminated string that specifies the file name of the module to load. This module may be a DLL or an executable module. If no file extension is specified, **.DLL** is assumed. If no path name is specified, Windows searches for the DLL first in the directory from which the calling application was loaded, then in the current directory, the Windows system directory, the Windows directory, and finally, through all directories referenced in the **PATH** environment string.

hReserved
HANDLE: Reserved; must be **NULL**.

dwFlags
DWORD: If this value is **DONT_RESOLVE_DLL_REFERENCES**, calls to the **DLLEntryPoint** function will not be generated for process and thread creation and termination. If this value is **0**, then this function is identical to **LoadLibrary**.

Returns
HANDLE: If this function is successful, it returns the module handle of the loaded library. Otherwise, it returns **NULL**. The application can obtain further information by calling **GetLastError**.

Include File
winbase.h

See Also
FreeLibrary, FindResource, GetProcAddress, LoadResource

Example
The following example loads a DLL into memory, obtains the address of a procedure within the library, calls the library function, and finally frees the library. Note that Windows will not generate calls to the DLL's **DLLMain** routine during this code.

```
typedef int (*ADDNUMBERS)(int, int);

LRESULT CALLBACK WndProc( HWND hWnd, UINT uMsg, WPARAM wParam, LPARAM lParam )
{
    switch( uMsg )
    {
        case WM_COMMAND :
            switch( LOWORD( wParam ) )
            {
                case IDM_TEST :
                    {
                        // Get the instance handle of the MyDLL.DLL.
                        //.........................................
                        HINSTANCE hLib = LoadLibraryEx( "MyDLL.DLL", 0,
                                               DONT_RESOLVE_DLL_REFERENCES );
```

continued on next page

continued from previous page

```
            if ( hLib )
            {
                // Get the function pointers to the function needed.
                //.................................................
                ADDNUMBERS fpAddNumbers = (ADDNUMBERS)GetProcAddress( hLib, ⇐
"AddNumbers" );

                if ( fpAddNumbers )
                {
                    TCHAR szMsg[32];
                    int   nAnswer = (*fpAddNumbers)( 10, 20 );

                    wsprintf( szMsg, "10 + 20 = %d", nAnswer );
                    MessageBox( hWnd, szMsg, lpszTitle,
                                MB_OK | MB_ICONINFORMATION );
                }
                else
                    MessageBox( hWnd, "Cannot find function!", NULL,
                                MB_OK | MB_ICONASTERISK );

                FreeLibrary( hLib );
            }
            else
                MessageBox( hWnd, "DLL could not be loaded",
                            NULL, MB_OK | MB_ICONASTERISK );
        }
        break;
            .
            .
            .
```

INDEX

Symbols

&, 234
.DEF file extension, 1439
0xFFFFFFFF, 379
6 HeapAlloc dwFlags value, 483
16-bit Windows Applications, converting, 54-66

A

AbnormalTermination code listing, 1372-1373
AbnormalTermination exception processing function, 1371-1373
AbortDoc code listing, 673-675
AbortDoc printing function, 673-675
AbortPath code listing, 749-750
AbortPath drawing functions, 749-750
ACCEL fVirt values, 243
Accelerator keys, MDI applications, 1386-1387
Accessibility applications, 49
Accessing INI files, 1078
AccessResource function, 55
ACCESSTIMEOUT dwFlags values, 1151
ActivateKeyboardLayout hKL values, 397
ActivateKeyboardLayout uFlags values, 397
ActivateKeyboardLayout user input functions, 396-397
Activating windows, 7, 9
AddAtom atom function, 1234, 1236-1238
AddAtom code listing, 1237-1238
AddFontResource code listing, 509-510
AddFontResource function, 296
AddFontResource GDI function, 509-510
AdjustWindowRect windows support functions, 95, 98
AdjustWindowRect code listing, 97-98
AllocDStoCSAlias function, 55
AllocResource function, 55
AllocSelector function, 55
American Standards Committee for Information Interchange (ASCII), 1163
AngleArc code listing, 750-751
AngleArc drawing functions, 750-751
AnimatePalette code listing, 880-883

AnimatePalette color functions, 880-883
ANOSE bXHeight values, 717
ANSI (American National Standards Institute), 1163
    code page identifiers, 1193
    character set, translating, 1163-1164
ANSI character set, translating, 1165
AnsiLower function, 55
AnsiLowerBuff function, 55
AnsiNext function, 56
AnsiPrev function, 56
AnsiToOem function, 56
AnsiUpper function, 56
AnsiUpperBuff function, 56
Appearances, 40
    flat controls, 41-42
    windows, changing, 93
AppendMenu code listing, 237-238
AppendMenu function, 236-238
AppendMenu uFlags values, 237
Applications
    accessibility, 49
    atoms, accessing, 1233-1234
    clipboard, 1041
    dynamic linking, 1437-1438
    installation programs, 1416-1417
    installing, 47-51
    MDI, 1379
        accelerator keys, 1386-1387
        creating, 1380-1381
    memory, saving, 1233
    menus, MDI, 1386
    SDI, 1379
    supporting on networks, 50
    uninstalling, 49
    windows SDI, 1384-1385
Applications windows, 234
Arc code listing, 751-752
Arc control, 751
Arc drawing functions, 752
Architectures, registry, 1043-1044
ArcTo drawing functions, 752-753

D

H

J-K

M

U

Books have a substantial influence on the destruction of the forests of the Earth. For example, it takes 17 trees to produce one ton of paper. A first printing of 30,000 copies of a typical 480-page book consumes 108,000 pounds of paper, which will require 918 trees!

Waite Group Press™ is against the clear-cutting of forests and supports reforestation of the Pacific Northwest of the United States and Canada, where most of this paper comes from. As a publisher with several hundred thousand books sold each year, we feel an obligation to give back to the planet. We will therefore support organizations that seek to preserve the forests of planet Earth.

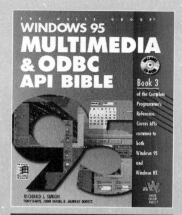
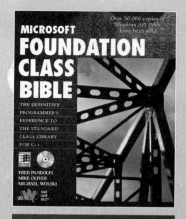

Message from the
Publisher

WELCOME TO OUR NERVOUS SYSTEM

Some people say that the World Wide Web is a graphical extension of the information superhighway, just a network of humans and machines sending each other long lists of the equivalent of digital junk mail.

I think it is much more than that. To me, the Web is nothing less than the nervous system of the entire planet—not just a collection of computer brains connected together, but more like a billion silicon neurons entangled and recirculating electro-chemical signals of information and data, each contributing to the birth of another CPU and another Web site.

Think of each person's hard disk connected at once to every other hard disk on earth, driven by human navigators searching like Columbus for the New World. Seen this way the Web is more of a super entity, a growing, living thing, controlled by the universal human will to expand, to be more. Yet, unlike a purposeful business plan with rigid rules, the Web expands in a nonlinear, unpredictable, creative way that echoes natural evolution.

We created our Web site not just to extend the reach of our computer book products but to be part of this synaptic neural network, to experience, like a nerve in the body, the flow of ideas and then to pass those ideas up the food chain of the mind. Your mind. Even more, we wanted to pump some of our own creative juices into this rich wine of technology.

TASTE OUR DIGITAL WINE

And so we ask you to taste our wine by visiting the body of our business. Begin by understanding the metaphor we have created for our Web site—a universal learning center, situated in outer space in the form of a space station. A place where you can journey to study any topic from the convenience of your own screen. Right now we are focusing on computer topics, but the stars are the limit on the Web.

If you are interested in discussing this Web site or finding out more about the Waite Group, please send me email with your comments, and I will be happy to respond. Being a programmer myself, I love to talk about technology and find out what our readers are looking for.

Sincerely,

Mitchell Waite

Mitchell Waite, C.E.O. and Publisher

200 Tamal Plaza
Corte Madera, CA 94925
415-924-2575
415-924-2576 fax

Website:
http://www.waite.com/waite

CREATING THE HIGHEST QUALITY COMPUTER BOOKS IN THE INDUSTRY

Waite Group Press

Come Visit

WAITE.COM

Waite Group Press
World Wide Web Site

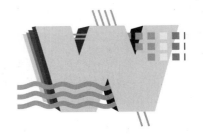

Now find all the latest information on Waite Group books at our new Web site, **http://www.waite.com/waite.** You'll find an online catalog where you can examine and order any title, review upcoming books, and send email to our authors and editors. Our FTP site has all you need to update your book: the latest program listings, errata sheets, most recent versions of Fractint, POV Ray, Polyray, DMorph, and all the programs featured in our books. So download, talk to us, ask questions, on **http://www.waite.com/waite.**

The New Arrivals Room has all our new books listed by month. Just click for a description, Index, Table of Contents, and links to authors.

The Backlist Room has all our books listed alphabetically.

The People Room is where you'll interact with Waite Group employees.

Links to Cyberspace get you in touch with other computer book publishers and other interesting Web sites.

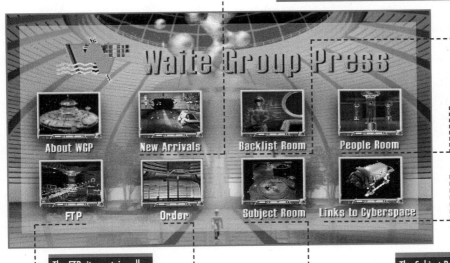

The FTP site contains all program listings, errata sheets, etc.

The Order Room is where you can order any of our books online.

The Subject Room contains typical book pages that show description, Index, Table of Contents, and links to authors.

World Wide Web:

COME SURF OUR TURF—THE WAITE GROUP WEB

http://www.waite.com/waite
Gopher: gopher.waite.com
FTP: ftp.waite.com

This is a legal agreement between you, the end user and purchaser, and The Waite Group®, Inc., and the authors of the programs contained in the disk. By opening the sealed disk package, you are agreeing to be bound by the terms of this Agreement. If you do not agree with the terms of this Agreement, promptly return the unopened disk package and the accompanying items (including the related book and other written material) to the place you obtained them for a refund.

SOFTWARE LICENSE

1. The Waite Group, Inc. grants you the right to use one copy of the enclosed software programs (the programs) on a single computer system (whether a single CPU, part of a licensed network, or a terminal connected to a single CPU). Each concurrent user of the program must have exclusive use of the related Waite Group, Inc. written materials.

2. The program, including the copyrights in each program, is owned by the respective author and the copyright in the entire work is owned by The Waite Group, Inc. and they are therefore protected under the copyright laws of the United States and other nations, under international treaties. You may make only one copy of the disk containing the programs exclusively for backup or archival purposes, or you may transfer the programs to one hard disk drive, using the original for backup or archival purposes. You may make no other copies of the programs, and you may make no copies of all or any part of the related Waite Group, Inc. written materials.

3. You may not rent or lease the programs, but you may transfer ownership of the programs and related written materials (including any and all updates and earlier versions) if you keep no copies of either, and if you make sure the transferee agrees to the terms of this license.

4. You may not decompile, reverse engineer, disassemble, copy, create a derivative work, or otherwise use the programs except as stated in this Agreement.

GOVERNING LAW

This Agreement is governed by the laws of the State of California.

LIMITED WARRANTY

The following warranties shall be effective for 90 days from the date of purchase: (i) The Waite Group, Inc. warrants the enclosed disk to be free of defects in materials and workmanship under normal use; and (ii) The Waite Group, Inc. warrants that the programs, unless modified by the purchaser, will substantially perform the functions described in the documentation provided by The Waite Group, Inc. when operated on the designated hardware and operating system. The Waite Group, Inc. does not warrant that the programs will meet purchaser's requirements or that operation of a program will be uninterrupted or error-free. The program warranty does not cover any program that has been altered or changed in any way by anyone other than The Waite Group, Inc. The Waite Group, Inc. is not responsible for problems caused by changes in the operating characteristics of computer hardware or computer operating systems that are made after the release of the programs, nor for problems in the interaction of the programs with each other or other software.

THESE WARRANTIES ARE EXCLUSIVE AND IN LIEU OF ALL OTHER WARRANTIES OF MERCHANTABILITY OR FITNESS FOR A PARTICULAR PURPOSE OR OF ANY OTHER WARRANTY, WHETHER EXPRESS OR IMPLIED.

EXCLUSIVE REMEDY

The Waite Group, Inc. will replace any defective disk without charge if the defective disk is returned to The Waite Group, Inc. within 90 days from date of purchase.

This is Purchaser's sole and exclusive remedy for any breach of warranty or claim for contract, tort, or damages.

LIMITATION OF LIABILITY

THE WAITE GROUP, INC. AND THE AUTHORS OF THE PROGRAMS SHALL NOT IN ANY CASE BE LIABLE FOR SPECIAL, INCIDENTAL, CONSEQUENTIAL, INDIRECT, OR OTHER SIMILAR DAMAGES ARISING FROM ANY BREACH OF THESE WARRANTIES EVEN IF THE WAITE GROUP, INC. OR ITS AGENT HAS BEEN ADVISED OF THE POSSIBILITY OF SUCH DAMAGES.

THE LIABILITY FOR DAMAGES OF THE WAITE GROUP, INC. AND THE AUTHORS OF THE PROGRAMS UNDER THIS AGREEMENT SHALL IN NO EVENT EXCEED THE PURCHASE PRICE PAID.

COMPLETE AGREEMENT

This Agreement constitutes the complete agreement between The Waite Group, Inc. and the authors of the programs, and you, the purchaser.

Some states do not allow the exclusion or limitation of implied warranties or liability for incidental or consequential damages, so the above exclusions or limitations may not apply to you. This limited warranty gives you specific legal rights; you may have others, which vary from state to state.

MACMILLAN COMPUTER PUBLISHING USA

A VIACOM COMPANY

Technical ---- Support:

If you cannot get the CD/Disk to install properly, or you need assistance with a particular situation in the book, please feel free to check out the Knowledge Base on our Web site at **http://www.superlibrary.com/general/support**. We have answers to our most Frequently Asked Questions listed there. If you do not find your specific question answered, please contact Macmillan Technical Support at **(317) 581-3833**. We can also be reached by email at **support@mcp.com**.

SATISFACTION REPORT CARD

Please fill out this card if you wish to know of future updates to *Windows NT Win32 API SuperBible,* or to receive our catalog.

SATISFACTION CARD

First Name: _____ Last Name: _____

Street Address: _____

City: _____ State: _____ Zip: _____

Email Address _____

Daytime Telephone: (_____) _____

Date product was acquired: Month _____ Day _____ Year _____ Your Occupation: _____

Overall, how would you rate *Windows NT Win32 API SuperBible?*

☐ Excellent   ☐ Very Good   ☐ Good
☐ Fair   ☐ Below Average   ☐ Poor

What did you like MOST about this book? _____
_____
_____

What did you like LEAST about this book? _____
_____
_____

Please describe any problems you may have encountered with installing or using the disk: _____
_____

How did you use this book (problem-solver, tutorial, reference...)?
_____

What is your level of computer expertise?
☐ New   ☐ Dabbler   ☐ Hacker
☐ Power User   ☐ Programmer   ☐ Experienced Professional

What computer languages are you familiar with? _____
_____

Please describe your computer hardware:

Computer _____ Hard disk _____
5.25" disk drives _____ 3.5" disk drives _____
Video card _____ Monitor _____
Printer _____ Peripherals _____
Sound Board _____ CD-ROM _____

Where did you buy this book?

☐ Bookstore (name): _____
☐ Discount store (name): _____
☐ Computer store (name): _____
☐ Catalog (name): _____
☐ Direct from WGP   ☐ Other _____

What price did you pay for this book? _____

What influenced your purchase of this book?

☐ Recommendation   ☐ Advertisement
☐ Magazine review   ☐ Store display
☐ Mailing   ☐ Book's format
☐ Reputation of Waite Group Press ☐ Other

How many computer books do you buy each year? _____

How many other Waite Group books do you own? _____

What is your favorite Waite Group book? _____
_____

Is there any program or subject you would like to see Waite Group Press cover in a similar approach? _____
_____

Additional comments? _____
_____
_____

Please send to: **Waite Group Press**
                      200 Tamal Plaza
                      Corte Madera, CA 94925

☐ **Check here for a free Waite Group catalog**